THE RANGE OF LITERATURE
Third Edition

The Range of Literature

THIRD EDITION

edited by

Elisabeth W. Schneider,
The University of California at Santa Barbara

Albert L. Walker
Iowa State University

and ## Herbert E. Chidls
Oregon State University

D. VAN NOSTRAND COMPANY
New York Cincinnati Toronto London Melbourne

D. Van Nostrand Company Regional Offices:
New York Cincinnati Millbrae

D. Van Nostrand Company International Offices:
London Toronto Melbourne

Copyright © 1973 by Litton Educational Publishing, Inc.

Library of Congress Catalog Card Number 70-186727

ISBN 0-442-27439-4

Published by D. Van Nostrand Company
450 West 33rd Street, New York, N. Y. 10001

10 9 8 7 6 5 4 3 2 1

Cover design by Jack Messerole

Grateful acknowledgment is made to the following publishers and individuals for permission to reprint material which is in copyright by them or of which they are the authorized publishers:

THE AMERICAN MUSEUM OF NATURAL HISTORY: For "Song of the Black Bear" (Navajo) from Pliny Earle Goddard's *Navajo Texts, Anthropological Papers of the American Museum of Natural History,* Vol. 34, pp. 176, 178 (1933).

MISS OONE AULT: For "Who Would Have Thought" by Thomas Howell; "Brown Is My Love," Anonymous; "Thou Sleepest Fast," Anonymous; "To a Lady to Answer Directly With Yea or Nay" by Sir Thomas Wyatt; "The Lover Showeth How He Is Forsaken of Such as He Sometime Enjoyed" by Sir Thomas Wyatt; and "Song" by George Peele— all from *Elizabethan Lyrics,* 3rd ed., 1949, edited by Norman Ault.

THE BELKNAP PRESS OF HARVARD UNIVERSITY: For "What shall I do when the Summer troubles," "The Soul selects," "A loss of something ever felt I," and "Finding is the first Act" from *The Poems of Emily Dickinson,* edited by Thomas H. Johnson, copyright 1955 by The President and Fellows of Harvard College.

STERLING A. BROWN: For "Slim in Hell" from *Black Voices,* edited by Abraham Chapman, published by New American Library, Inc.; and "Mose" from *Southern Road,* published by Harcourt Brace Jovanovich.

JONATHAN CAPE AND HARRISON SMITH, INC.: For "The Hermit" from *Collected Poems* by W. H. Davies.

CITY LIGHTS BOOKS: For "A Supermarket in California" from *Howl and Other Poems* by Allen Ginsberg, copyright © 1956, 1959 by Allen Ginsberg.

THE CLARENDON PRESS, OXFORD: For "Triolet," "Nightingales," and "November" from *The Shorter Poems of Robert Bridges,* published by The Clarendon Press, Oxford.

COWARD-MC CANN, INC.: For "The Cherry Orchard" by Anton Chekhov, translated by Jennie Covan, copyright 1922 by Morris Gest, copyright renewed 1950 by Coward-McCann, Inc.

CROWN PUBLISHERS, INC.: For "Hodel" from *The Old Country* by Sholom Aleichem, translated by Julius and Frances Butwin, copyright © 1946 by Crown Publishers, Inc.

DELACORTE PRESS: For "Harrison Bergeron," copyright © 1961 by Kurt Vonnegut, Jr., from the book *Welcome to the Monkey House* by Kurt Vonnegut, Jr. A Seymour Lawrence Book/Delacorte Press. Originally appeared in *Fantasy and Science Fiction*.

J. M. DENT & SONS LTD: For "Heart of Darkness" from *Youth* by Joseph Conrad, © 1903. Reprinted by permission of the Trustees of the Joseph Conrad Estate and J. M. Dent & Sons.

DIAL PRESS: For "Tell Me How Long the Train's Been Gone," copyright © 1967 by James Baldwin (this material appears, in slightly altered form, in *Tell Me How Long the Train's Been Gone* by James Baldwin); and "This Morning, This Evening, So Soon," copyright © 1960 by James Baldwin, from *Going to Meet the Man* by James Baldwin, originally from *Atlantic Monthly.*

DOUBLEDAY & COMPANY: For "Epidermal Macabre," copyright 1932 by Theodore Roethke; "Elegy," © 1955 by New Republic, Inc.; "The Happy Three" and "Geranium," 1963 by Beatrice Roethke as Administratrix of the Estate of Theodore Roethke—all from the book *Collected Poems of Theodore Roethke;* and "A Doll's House" from *Ghosts and Three Other Plays* by Henrik Ibsen, translated by Michael Meyer, copyright © 1966 by Michael Meyer.

FABER & FABER: For "On the Move" and "The Wheel of Fortune" from *The Sense of Movement* by Thom Gunn; and "To My Mother" from *Selected Poems* by George Barker.

FARRAR, STRAUS & GIROUX: For "The Magic Barrel" from *The Magic Barrel* by Bernard Malamud, copyright © 1954, 1958 by Bernard Malamud; and "Everything That Rises Must Converge" from *Everything That Rises Must Converge* by Flannery O'Connor, copyright © 1961, 1965 by The Estate of Mary Flannery O'Connor.

GROVE PRESS, INC.: For "The Police" by Slawomir Mrozek, from *Six Plays,* copyright © 1967 (English version) by Nicholas Bethell.

HARCOURT BRACE JOVANOVICH: For "Rebellion," "As a Plane Tree by the Water," and "Mr. Edwards and the Spider" from *Lord Weary's Castle* by Robert Lowell, copyright © 1944, 1946 by Robert Lowell; "The Love Song of J. Alfred Prufrock," "Journey of the Magi," and "Rhapsody on a Windy Night" from *Collected Poems 1909–1962* by T. S. Eliot, copyright 1936 by Harcourt Brace Jovanovich, Inc., copyright © 1963, 1964 by T. S. Eliot; "Autumn" and "Embankment" from *Speculations* by T. E. Hulme; "a pretty a day," copyright 1940 by E. E. Cummings, copyright 1968 by Marion Morehouse Cummings and "nobody loses all the time," copyright 1926 by Horace Liveright, renewed 1954 by E. E. Cummings—both from *Poems 1923–1954* by E. E. Cummings; "Flowering Judas" from *Flowering Judas and Other Stories* by Katherine Anne Porter, copyright 1930, 1958 by Katherine Anne Porter; "Fog" and "Limited" from *Chicago Poems* by Carl Sandburg, copyright 1916 by Holt, Rinehart and Winston, Inc., copyright renewed 1944 by Carl Sandburg, reprinted by permission of Harcourt Brace Jovanovich, Inc.; "Boy at the Window," copyright 1952 by The New Yorker Magazine, Inc., reprinted from *Things of This World* by Richard Wilbur; "Still, Citizen Sparrow" from *Ceremony and Other Poems* by Richard Wilbur, copyright 1948, 1949, 1950 by Richard Wilbur; "Antigone": an English Version by Dudley Fitts and Robert Fitzgerald, copyright 1939 by Harcourt Brace Jovanovich, Inc., copyright 1967 by Dudley Fitts and Robert Fitzgerald. *Caution!* This version of *Antigone* is the sole property of the authors and is fully protected by copyright. All rights, including professional, amateur, motion picture, recitation, lecturing, public reading, radio broadcasting, and television, are strictly reserved. Inquiries on all rights should be addressed to Harcourt Brace Jovanovich, Inc., 757 Third Ave., New York, N.Y. 10017.

HARPER & ROW, PUBLISHERS, INC.: For "Under Cover" from *Outcrop* by Abbie Huston Evans, copyright 1928 by Harper & Brothers, renewed 1956 by Abbie Huston Evans; "The Lovepet" from *Crow* by Ted Hughes, copyright © 1971 by Ted Hughes, originally appeared in *The New Yorker;* "The Ballad of Late Annie" from *Selected Poems* by Gwendolyn Brooks, copyright 1949 by Gwendolyn Brooks Blakely; "The Old-Marrieds" from *A Street in Bronzeville* by Gwendolyn Brooks, copyright 1944, 1945 by Gwendolyn Brooks Blakely; and "The Eagles of the Valle Grande" from pp. 14–22 of *House Made of Dawn* by N. Scott Momaday: copyright © 1967 by N. Scott Momaday, reprinted by permission of Harper & Row, Publishers, Inc., and of the author.

HOLT, RINEHART AND WINSTON, INC.: For "The Death of the Hired Man," "The Runaway," "Nothing Gold Can Stay," "Desert Places," "After Apple-Picking," "Dust of

Snow," and "Fire and Ice" from *The Poetry of Robert Frost,* edited by Edward Connery Lathem, copyright 1923, 1930, 1939, © 1969 by Holt, Rinehart and Winston, Inc., copyright 1936, 1951, © 1958 by Robert Frost, copyright © 1964, 1967 by Lesley Frost Ballantine; "The rain, it streams on stone and hillock" and "Easter Hymn" from *The Collected Poems of A. E. Housman,* copyright 1922 by Holt, Rinehart and Winston, Inc., copyright 1936, 1950 by Barclays Bank Ltd., copyright © 1964 by Robert E. Symons.

HOUGHTON MIFFLIN COMPANY: For "You, Andrew Marvell" from *Poems* by Archibald MacLeish, copyright 1952 by Archibald MacLeish, by permission and arrangement with Houghton Mifflin Company, the authorized publishers; and "J.B." by Archibald MacLeish, copyright © 1958 by Archibald MacLeish.
Caution! Professionals and amateurs are hereby warned that *J.B.,* being fully protected under the Copyright Laws of the United States of America, the British Commonwealth, including the Dominion of Canada, and all other countries of the Copyright Union, the Berne Convention, the Pan-American Copyright Convention, and the Universal Copyright Convention, is subject to license and royalty. All rights including, but not limited to, reproduction in whole or in part by any process or method, professional use, amateur use, film, recitation, lecturing, public reading, recording, taping, radio casting, and the rights of translation into foreign languages, are strictly reserved.

INDIANA UNIVERSITY PRESS: For "The Treehouse" by James A. Emanuel and "If the Stars Should Fall" by Samuel Allen—both from *New Negro Poets: USA,* edited by Langston Hughes, copyright © 1964 by Langston Hughes.

INTERNATIONAL FAMOUS AGENCY, INC.: For "To Hell With Dying" by Alice Walker, from *Best Short Stories by Negro Writers* (published by Little, Brown, Inc.), copyright © 1967 by Alice Walker. Reprinted by permission of Monica McCall, International Famous Agency.

LIVERIGHT PUBLISHING CORPORATION: For "Becky" from *Cane* by Jean Toomer, copyright renewed 1951 by Jean Toomer.

THE MACMILLAN COMPANY: For "No Second Troy," "That the Night Come," and "The Cold Heaven," copyright 1912 by The Macmillan Company, renewed 1940 by Bertha Georgie Yeats; "The Three Beggars" and "The Magi," copyright 1916 by The Macmillan Company, renewed 1944 by Bertha Georgie Yeats; "Her Praise" and "The Balloon of the Mind," copyright 1919 by The Macmillan Company, renewed 1947 by Bertha Georgie Yeats; "The Second Coming," copyright 1924 by The Macmillan Company, renewed 1952 by Bertha Georgie Yeats; "Among School Children," copyright 1928 by The Macmillan Company, renewed 1956 by Bertha Georgie Yeats; "Meru," copyright 1934 by The Macmillan Company, renewed 1952 by Bertha Georgie Yeats; "Lapis Lazuli," copyright 1940 by Bertha Georgie Yeats, renewed 1968 by Bertha Georgie Yeats, Michael Butler Yeats, and Anne Yeats—all from *Collected Poems* by William Butler Yeats; "The Oxen," copyright 1925 by The Macmillan Company; "Waiting Both," copyright 1925 by The Macmillan Company, renewed 1953 by Lloyds Bank, Ltd.; "He Abjures Love" and "Channel Firing"—all from *Collected Poems* by Thomas Hardy; "Mr. Flood's Party" from *Collected Poems* by Edwin Arlington Robinson, copyright 1921 by Edwin Arlington Robinson, renewed 1949 by Ruth Nivison; "No Swan So Fine," "To a Steam Roller," and "Sojourn in the Whale" from *Collected Poems* by Marianne Moore, copyright 1935 by Marianne Moore, renewed 1963 by Marianne Moore and T. S. Eliot; "On the Suicide of a Friend" and "The Party" from *The Self-Made Man* by Reed Whittemore, copyright © 1959 by Reed Whittemore; and "The New Villa" from *The Witch and Other Stories* by Anton Chekhov, translated from the Russian by Constance Garnett: copyright 1918 by The Macmillan Company, renewed 1946 by Constance Garnett.

THE MARVELL PRESS: For "Reasons for Attendance" and "Next, Please" from *The Less Deceived* by Philip Larkin.

MRS. ELLEN C. MASTERS: For "Lucinda Matlock" from *Spoon River Anthology* by Edgar Lee Masters, published by The Macmillan Company.

HAROLD MATSON COMPANY, INC.: For "A Sick Call" by Morley Callaghan, copyright 1932, 1959 by Morley Callaghan. Originally appeared in *The Atlantic Monthly,* September, 1932.

MOORE PUBLISHING COMPANY: For "Samantha Is My Negro Cat," "You Tell Me," and

"Persecuted, Betrayal, Volkswagen Blues" by William J. Harris, from the book *Nine Black Poets.*

WILLIAM MORRIS AGENCY, INC.: For "Flying Home" by Ralph Ellison, copyright © 1944 and renewed 1972 by Ralph Ellison, reprinted by permission of William Morris Agency, Inc., on behalf of the author. Originally appeared in *Cross-Section,* May 29, 1944.

THE NATION: For "Euroclydon" by Abbie Huston Evans, printed in *The Nation* for December 27, 1952, and appearing in *Fact of Crystal* by Abbie Huston Evans (published by Harcourt Brace Jovanovich, 1961).

NEW DIRECTIONS: For "Jean Beicke" from *The Farmers' Daughters* by William Carlos Williams, copyright 1938 by William Carlos Williams, renewed 1957 by Florence Williams, © by New Directions; "Lament of the Frontier Guard," "The River-Merchant's Wife: a Letter," and "Ancient Music" from *Personae* by Ezra Pound, copyright 1926 by Ezra Pound; "The Yachts" and "Spring and All" from *Collected Earlier Poems* by William Carlos Williams, copyright 1938 by William Carlos Williams; "Fern Hill," "After the Funeral," and "The force that through the green fuse drives the flower" from *The Poems of Dylan Thomas,* copyright 1938, 1939, 1946 by New Directions Publishing Corporation; "A Race of Sound" and "A City Child's Day" from *Long Live Man* by Gregory Corso, copyright © 1961 by New Directions Publishing Corporation; and "Don't let that horse," "Constantly risking absurdity," and "The Pennycandystore beyond the El" from *A Coney Island of the Mind,* copyright © 1958 by Lawrence Ferlinghetti.

W.W. NORTON & COMPANY: For "Guitar Recitativos" from *Uplands, New Poems* by A. R. Ammons, copyright © 1970 by A. R. Ammons.

HAROLD OBER ASSOCIATES: For "Close Your Eyes!" and "Idolatry" by Arna Bontemps, from *Personals,* copyright © 1963 by Arna Bontemps.

OCTOBER HOUSE, INC.: For "Middle Passage" and "Frederick Douglass" by Robert Hayden from *Selected Poems,* copyright © 1966 by Robert Hayden; and "Unidentified Flying Object," "Voice in the Wilderness," and "A Plague of Starlings" by Robert Hayden from *Words in the Mourning Time,* copyright © 1970 by Robert Hayden.

OXFORD UNIVERSITY PRESS: For "Spring and Fall," "Thou art indeed just, Lord," "No worst, there is none," "Pied Beauty," and "The Windhover" from *Poems of Gerard Manley Hopkins;* and "Museums," "Bagpipe Music," and "Sunday Morning" from *The Collected Poems of Louis MacNeice,* edited by E. R. Dodds, copyright © The Estate of Louis MacNeice 1966.

NORMAN HOLMES PEARSON: For "Lethe" from *Collected Poems* by H.D.

RANDOM HOUSE—ALFRED A. KNOPF: For "A Raisin in the Sun" by Lorraine Hansberry, copyright © 1958, 1959, 1966 by Robert Nemiroff as Executor of the Estate of Lorraine Hansberry; "The Guest" from *Exile and the Kingdom* by Albert Camus, translated by Justin O'Brien, copyright © 1957, 1958 by Alfred A. Knopf, Inc.; "The Blue Hotel" from *Stephen Crane: An Omnibus,* edited by Robert Wooster Stallman, copyright 1952 by Alfred A. Knopf, Inc.; "Two Soldiers" from *Collected Stories of William Faulkner,* copyright 1942 by William Faulkner, renewed 1970 by Estelle Faulkner and Jill Faulkner Summers, by permission of Random House, Inc.; "Guests of the Nation" from *More Stories of Frank O'Connor,* copyright 1954 by Frank O'Connor, published 1954 by Alfred A. Knopf; "Delta Autumn" from *Go Down Moses and Other Stories* by William Faulkner, copyright 1942 by William Faulkner, renewed 1970 by Estelle Faulkner and Jill Faulkner Summers, reprinted by permission of Random House, Inc.; "The Lift That Went Down into Hell" from *The Eternal Smile and Other Stories* by Pär Lagerkvist, copyright 1954 by Random House, Inc.; "The Colossus," copyright © 1961 by Sylvia Plath, and "Frog Autumn," copyright © 1959 by Sylvia Plath—both from *The Colossus and Other Poems* by Sylvia Plath, by permission of Alfred A. Knopf, Inc.; "I, Too" from *Selected Poems* by Langston Hughes, copyright 1926 by Alfred A. Knopf, Inc. and renewed 1954 by Langston Hughes; "O What is that Sound Which So Thrills" from *Collected Shorter Poems 1927–1957* by W. H. Auden, copyright 1937 and renewed 1965 by W. H. Auden, reprinted by permission of Random House, Inc.; "Without Benefit of Declaration" from *The Panther and the Lash* by Langston Hughes, copyright © 1967 by Arna Bontemps and George Huston Bass, reprinted by permission of Alfred A. Knopf, Inc.; "Desert" from *The Selected Poems of Langston Hughes,* copyright 1947 by Langston Hughes, reprinted by permission of Alfred A. Knopf, Inc.; "The Unknown Citizen,"

"Musée des Beaux Arts," and "In Memory of W. B. Yeats" from *Collected Shorter Poems 1927–1957* by W. H. Auden, copyright 1940 and renewed 1951 by W. H. Auden, reprinted by permission of Alfred A. Knopf, Inc.; "The Inquisitors" from *Selected Poems* by Robinson Jeffers, copyright 1948 by Robinson Jeffers, reprinted by permission of Random House, Inc.; "Cries of Evening" from *Collected Poems 1928–1953* by Stephen Spender, copyright 1934 by The Modern Library, Inc., reprinted by permission of Random House, Inc.; "Blue Girls," copyright 1927 by Alfred A. Knopf, Inc. and renewed 1955 by John Crowe Ransom, and "Bells for John Whiteside's Daughter," copyright 1924 by Alfred A. Knopf, Inc. and renewed 1952 by John Crowe Ransom—both from *Selected Poems, Rev. Ed.* by John Crowe Ransom; "The Death of a Soldier," "Peter Quince at the Clavier," "Domination of Black," "The Snow Man," and "Sunday Morning," copyright 1923 and renewed 1951 by Wallace Stevens; "A Rabbit as King of the Ghosts," copyright 1942 by Wallace Stevens and renewed 1970 by Holly Stevens Stephenson; and "The idea of Order at Key West," copyright 1936 by Wallace Stevens and renewed 1964 by Holly Stevens Stephenson—all from *The Collected Poems of Wallace Stevens* by permission of Alfred A. Knopf, Inc.

VIRGINIA RICE: For "Relatives Out West" by Paul Horgan from *Figures in a Landscape* (published by Harper & Row, 1940), copyright © 1938 by Paul Horgan and renewed © 1966 by Paul Horgan.

SCHOCKEN BOOKS INC.: For "A Country Doctor" from *The Penal Colony* of Franz Kafka, copyright © 1948 by Schocken Books Inc.

CHARLES SCRIBNER'S SONS: For "In Another Country" (Copyright 1927 by Charles Scribner's Sons, renewal copyright 1955) from *Men Without Women* by Ernest Hemingway; "Debbie Go Home" from *Tales from a Troubled Land* by Alan Paton, copyright © 1961 Alan Paton; "Miniver Cheevy" (Copyright 1907 Charles Scribner's Sons; renewal copyright 1935) from *The Town Down the River* by Edwin Arlington Robinson; and "Question" from *Another Animal: Poems, Poets of Today 1* by May Swenson, copyright 1954 by May Swenson.

THE SOCIETY OF AUTHORS: For "The House" from *Collected Poems, 1919–1934* by Walter de la Mare, copyright 1941; "The Ghost," "The Old Men," and "The Listeners," Book 1 from *Collected Poems, 1901–1918* by Walter de la Mare. All the above reprinted by permission of the Literary Trustees of Walter de la Mare and The Society of Authors as their representative.

THE SWALLOW PRESS: For "A Side-Gallery for Some Insects" and "Socrates Entranced" from *Between Matter and Principle* by Alan Stephens, copyright 1963 by Alan Stephens; and "What I will think of as the white dog truth" from *Tree Meditation and Others* by Alan Stephens, copyright © 1970 by Alan Stephens.

MRS. HELEN THOMAS: For "Gallows" from *Poems* by Edward Thomas; "Out in the Dark" and "The New House" from *Collected Poems* by Edward Thomas.

MRS. JAMES THURBER: For "File and Forget" by James Thurber, copyright © 1953 James Thurber, from *Thurber Country,* published by Simon and Schuster. Originally printed in *The New Yorker.*

UNIVERSITY OF DETROIT PRESS: For "The Flight in the Desert" by Brother Antoninus, from *The Crooked Lines of God* (1960).

UNIVERSITY OF NEW MEXICO PRESS: For "The Bear" by N. Scott Momaday from *New Mexico Quarterly,* Vol. XXXI:1, Spring 1961, p. 46, copyright 1961 by The University of New Mexico Press.

UNIVERSITY OF OKLAHOMA PRESS: For "Going Away" from *The Ten Grandmothers* by Alice Marriott, copyright 1945 by the University of Oklahoma Press.

THE VANGUARD PRESS: For "Colonel Fantock" from *The Collected Poems of Edith Sitwell,* copyright 1954 by Edith Sitwell.

THE VIKING PRESS: For "The Boarding House" from *Dubliners* by James Joyce, originally published by B. W. Huebsch, Inc. in 1916, copyright © 1967 by the Estate of James Joyce (all rights reserved); "Please Don't Kill Anything" from *I Don't Need You Any More* by Arthur Miller, copyright © 1960 by Arthur Miller (all rights reserved); and "Pot-Luck Among the Casuals" from *Selected Poems* by Marsden Hartley, copyright 1945 by Norma Berger.

The aid of two persons so far exceeded the
call of duty or affection as to be intelligently marvelous:

Jauvanta Maurine Walker

Elizabeth Richardson Childs

Contents

FICTION

*Page numbers in lightface italic denote the location of editorial apparatus. Page numbers in boldface denote the first page of a selection or section.

A Range of Human Experience / *193*

Twentieth Century Causes: Betrayals and Loyalties / *297*

POETRY

Themes / 440

Forms / 517

Eleven Representative Poets / 551

Recent Modes / 613

DRAMA

The Art of Reading Plays / 675

Thematic Potentials in Fiction, Poetry, and Drama / *xxv*

Index of Literary Terms / *xxxv*

Index of Titles and Authors / *xxxviii*

Preface

In presenting this Third Edition of *The Range of Literature,* we have continued to emphasize the act, or art, of reading, for it has been our experience that perceptive reading enlarges what we know of the world and of ourselves. Such reading touches images, memories, choices, things we feel, fear, or deeply care about. Perceptive reading helps us define our humanity. This is one compelling reason for courses in literature.

Yet, in practice, young men and women having a first college experience with imaginative literature do not always receive the full rewards of reading. Such rewards are most likely to occur, we have found, when some knowledge of the elements of literature is fostered, with some grasp of the wide range of purposes and effects among authors, and some awareness of the many modes of writing. Therefore we shall try to show, through brief editorial analysis and comment at appropriate points in the text, the many ways in which a reader can enter into the experience offered by a story, a poem, a play. And we shall try to show how the structure and style of a story, poem, or play can affect and guide the reader's experience. Though our editorial comments bear directly on the act of reading, we attempt to avoid standing between student and instructor or between the reader and the literature. The comments merely open doors.

As in earlier editions, we shall attempt to illuminate both the power and the varied uses of literary forms. We retain in this edition a smaller proportion of earlier writing while increasing the proportion of twentieth century writing, with a resulting stronger emphasis on contemporary issues and concerns. Yet we hope the reader will soon discover connections between older and newer, to the point of realizing that a very small effort at "translation" will merge writings of different dates or genres under one label: human significance.

An example of this fusing of earlier and contemporary human concerns is the section of fiction entitled "What We Were and What We Are: The Present As the Past Unfinished." Readings there are intended to show that first-rate imaginative literature does not allow us to feel or live as if we came from nowhere, were caused by nothing, or as if our human actions, impulses, or beliefs are of today only. Sections in the poetry and drama parts of the book continue that thesis. The poetry section contains an expanded series of poets to be read in depth, and the drama section adds fresh contemporary plays to its presentation of classic dramatic literature.

Throughout this edition, editorial apparatus has been condensed and reorganized so that it is most extensive toward the beginning of each section, tapers off as the section proceeds, and culminates in notes, comments, and questions at the end. This is in keeping with our assumption that, given some useful guidance at the outset and at certain appropriate points along the way, the reader will begin to move under his or her own power. And that, of course, is precisely how the study of literature ought to work.

We shall be pleased if the Third Edition of *The Range of Literature* continues to aid students in becoming perceptive readers—with all that perceptive reading can be taken to mean.

EWS
ALW
HEC

FICTION

The Art of Reading Fiction

The reading of fiction can be an almost passive occurrence or it can be active—an art, a skill used with purpose and based on knowledge.

Any college student knows that reading is a psychological transaction between a reader and the material he or she is reading. Purely passive reading often results in the unnoticed transfer into the reader's mind of beliefs or attitudes which the author has expressed. This is a fairly dangerous process, for who wants to be limited to superficial acceptance of another's attitudes or guided by unexamined ideas? Active reading cannot be so innocent or unaware. It requires more energy, yet it will yield rewards we cannot obtain in any other way.

In this first section, we shall concentrate primarily on one topic: What are the things that can happen, and do happen, when people read good fiction skillfully, with full awareness? The same topic can be phrased in another way: How can a reader make sure that the important things happen? What should he look for, notice, or realize, as he reads? And what should he know about the techniques, or methods, that writers of fiction use? Without such knowledge, he cannot properly look, notice, realize.

We shall explore in this section, as examples, five quite different stories that show a wide range of values and techniques, and we shall indicate, as appropriate, a range of tactics that readers can use to obtain the most from each story. We believe these examples will provide an orderly and clear development, from the relatively simple to the more complex.

A further comment concerning the scope, variety, and significance of fiction seems desirable before you begin considering the five stories. We refer to a wider perspective that should never be forgotten: our modern, familiar world of print and reading has evolved from quite another, that of storytellers and storyhearers. Just consider the number of human communications you yourself have heard that included some variant of "Once upon a time . . . !" Personal everyday talk contains this storytelling quality: Did you hear? Do you know? What happened next? What do you suppose "they" will say, think, do?

Here is the heart of an incalculable amount of communication. The urges of storyteller and listener meet, even combine. From fictional or storytelling elements, individuals both create and define, inevitably, a part of their private "worlds" or "visions." The fact of print—and a reader receiving meaning from it, or a writer sending meaning through it—changes in no way the essential functions that storytelling and storyhearing have always served.

Long before the days of print, some stories conveyed instruction, and wisdom; others were primarily for delight; still others served to capture and preserve, through oral repetition, a truth as the storyteller perceived it, lest it vanish from memory. Other stories used words as a means of influence or power, to bring about changes in attitudes or expectations in teller or listener—to describe and avert evil, or to strengthen, create purpose, bring joy. Has anything really changed? We suggest that stories, whether written or spoken, modern or ancient, long or short, serve primordial needs that center in the sending and receiving of a wide range of meanings. The same kinds of purposes and results continue in any contemporary fiction that is likely to endure.

Some older examples suggest themselves: the Fables of Aesop; the Trotting Coyote Stories of the native American Navahos; and, quite different, Homer's epic which transmits the marvelous legend of Troy.

The oral quality of ancient storytelling comes through to us today in print, especially through dialogue. The storytelling tradition strongly colors Sholom Aleichem's "Hodel," for example, which you will read later (page 195). And then there is Ralph Ellison's story "Flying Home" (page 244), in which one fictional character asks another, "You boys ever sit around and swap lies?" This gambit lets the speaker, an old hand at storytelling, display his talents. But he qualifies what he is about to say by indicating that it isn't always lies.

There are other stories in our heritage which refer to real or mythical beings, natural or supernatural forces, even floods and other geological events important in mankind's history. The same basic human urges and needs, involving codes of behavior and attitudes and values, exist in the printed stories we read today— stated or implied.

You should not let the term "fiction" mislead you. Fiction has too often mirrored fact, too often conveyed meanings sought out of human need, as people faced the complexity of themselves and their times.

We do not wish to get between you, as reader, and your own fresh and clear perceptions. In a quick foreword to each story we will therefore limit ourselves to remarks that may help you to get at the story itself. After each story, we will make comments about the materials and techniques used in it. We hope you will read each story before you use our comments. Then you may wish to use the comments as a way of checking up on us—or of checking your own awareness. From time to time, as the examples permit, we shall discuss various aspects of *fiction and fictional techniques, all aimed at the original topic: What happens when we read, and how can the act of reading be improved?*

Note *An asterisk (*) before a title signifies that notes, problems, or questions on that story can be found in the supplementary material beginning on page 374.*

SOME CHARACTERISTICS OF FICTION

As a first example, we present the story "Two Soldiers," by William Faulkner, a winner of the Nobel Prize for Literature. We suggest that you begin your practice in active, effective reading by taking time to sense the flavor and meaning of small details in this story, which a hurried reading could obscure. Reading for action alone, or merely for "what happens," is a mistaken tactic guaranteed to cost you both pleasure and understanding. You could just as well read a synopsis. So—take your time with this story.

*Two Soldiers

WILLIAM FAULKNER

Me and Pete would go down to Old Man Killegrew's and listen to his radio. We would wait until after supper, after dark, and we would stand outside Old Man Killegrew's parlor window, and we could hear it because Old Man Killegrew's wife was deaf, and so he run the radio as loud as it would run, and so me and Pete could hear it plain as Old Man Killegrew's wife could, I reckon, even standing outside with the window closed.

And that night I said, "What? Japanese? What's a pearl harbor?" and Pete said, "Hush."

And so we stood there, it was cold, listening to the fellow in the radio talking, only I couldn't make no heads nor tails neither out of it. Then the fellow said that would be all for a while, and me and Pete walked back up the road to home, and Pete told me what it was. Because he was nigh twenty and he had done finished the Consolidated last June and he knowed a heap: about them Japanese dropping bombs on Pearl Harbor and that Pearl Harbor was across the water.

"Across what water?" I said. "Across that Government reservoy up at Oxford?"

"Naw," Pete said. "Across the big water. The Pacific Ocean."

We went home. Maw and pap was already asleep, and me and Pete laid in the bed, and I still couldn't understand where it was, and Pete told me again—the Pacific Ocean.

"What's the matter with you?" Pete said. "You're going on nine years old. You been in school now ever since September. Ain't you learned nothing yet?"

"I reckon we ain't got as fer as the Pacific Ocean yet," I said.

We was still sowing the vetch then that ought to been all finished by the fifteenth of November, because pap was still behind, just like he had been ever since me and Pete had knowed him. And we had firewood to git in, too, but every night me and Pete would go down to Old Man Killegrew's and stand outside his parlor window in the cold and listen to his radio; then we would come back home and lay in the bed and Pete would tell me what it was. That is, he would tell me for a while. Then he wouldn't tell me. It was like he didn't want to talk about it no more. He would tell me to shut up because he wanted to go to sleep, but he never wanted to go to sleep.

He would lay there, a heap stiller than if he was asleep, and it would be something, I could feel it coming out of him, like he was mad at me even, only I knowed he wasn't thinking about me, or like he was worried about something, and it wasn't that neither, because he never had nothing to worry about. He never got behind like pap, let alone stayed behind. Pap give him ten acres when he graduated from the Consolidated, and me and Pete both reckoned pap was durn glad to get shut of at least ten acres, less to have to worry with himself; and Pete had them ten acres all sowed to vetch and busted out and bedded for the winter, and so it wasn't that. But it was something. And still we would go down to Old Man Killegrew's every night and listen to his radio, and they was at it in the Philippines now, but General MacArthur was holding um. Then we would come back home and lay in the bed, and Pete wouldn't tell me nothing or talk at all. He would just lay there still as a ambush and when I would touch him, his side or his leg would feel hard and still as iron, until after a while I would go to sleep.

Then one night—it was the first time he had said nothing to me except to jump on me about not chopping enough wood at the wood tree where we was cutting—he said, "I got to go."

"Go where?" I said.

"To that war," Pete said.

"Before we even finish gittin' in the firewood?"

"Firewood, hell," Pete said.

"All right," I said. "When we going to start?"

But he wasn't even listening. He laid there, hard and still as iron in the dark. "I got to go," he said. "I jest ain't going to put up with no folks treating the Unity States that way."

"Yes," I said. "Firewood or no firewood, I reckon we got to go."

This time he heard me. He laid still again, but it was a different kind of still.

"You?" he said. "To a war?"

"You'll whup the big uns and I'll whup the little uns," I said.

Then he told me I couldn't go. At first I thought he just never wanted me tagging after him, like he wouldn't leave me go with him when he went sparking them girls of Tull's. Then he told me the Army wouldn't leave me go because I was too little, and then I knowed he really meant it and that I couldn't go nohow noways. And somehow I hadn't believed until then that he was going himself, but now I knowed he was and that he wasn't going to leave me go with him a-tall.

"I'll chop the wood and tote the water for you-all then!" I said. "You got to have wood and water!"

Anyway, he was listening to me now. He wasn't like iron now.

He turned onto his side and put his hand on my chest because it was me that was laying straight and hard on my back now.

"No," he said. "You got to stay here and help pap."

"Help him what?" I said. "He ain't never caught up nohow. He can't get no further behind. He can sholy take care of this little shirttail of a farm while me and you are whupping them Japanese. I got to go too. If you got to go, then so have I."

"No," Pete said. "Hush now. Hush." And he meant it, and I knowed he did. Only I made sho from his own mouth. I quit.

"So I just can't go then," I said.

"No," Pete said. "You just can't go. You're too little, in the first place, and in the second place ——"

"All right," I said. "Then shut up and leave me go to sleep."

So he hushed then and laid back. And I laid there like I was already asleep, and pretty soon he was asleep and I knowed it was the wanting to go to the war that had worried him and kept him awake, and now that he had decided to go, he wasn't worried any more.

The next morning he told maw and pap. Maw was all right. She cried.

"No," she said, crying, "I don't want him to go. I would rather go myself in his place, if I could. I don't want to save the country. Them Japanese could take it and keep it, so long as they left me and my family and my children alone. But I remember my brother Marsh in that other war. He had to go to that one when he wasn't but nineteen, and our mother couldn't understand it then any more than I can now. But she told Marsh if he had to go, he had to go. And so, if Pete's got to go to this one, he's got to go to it. Jest don't ask me to understand why."

But pap was the one. He was the feller. "To the war?" he said. "Why, I just don't see a bit of use in that. You ain't old enough for the draft, and the country ain't being invaded. Our President in Washington, D.C., is watching the conditions and he will notify us. Besides, in that other war your ma just mentioned, I was drafted and sent clean to Texas and was held there nigh eight months until they finally quit fighting. It seems to me that that, along with your Uncle Marsh who received a actual wound on the battlefields of France, is enough for me and mine to have to do to protect the country, at least in my lifetime. Besides, what'll I do for help on the farm with you gone? It seems to me I'll get mighty far behind."

"You been behind as long as I can remember," Pete said. "Anyway, I'm going. I got to."

"Of course he's got to go," I said. "Them Japanese ——"

"You hush your mouth!" maw said, crying. "Nobody's talking to you! Go and get me a armful of wood! That's what you can do!"

So I got the wood. And all the next day, while me and Pete and pap was getting in as much wood as we could in that time because Pete said how pap's idea of plenty of wood was one more stick laying against the wall that maw ain't put on the fire yet. Maw was getting Pete ready to go. She washed and mended his clothes and cooked him a shoe box of vittles. And that night me and Pete laid in the bed and listened to her packing his grip and crying, until after a while Pete got up in his nightshirt and went back there, and I could hear them talking, until at last maw said, "You got to go, and so I want you to go. But I don't understand it, and I won't never, and so don't expect me to." And Pete come back and got into the bed again and laid again still and hard as iron on his back, and then he said, and he wasn't talking to me, he wasn't talking to nobody: "I got to go. I just got to."

"Sho you got to," I said. "Them Japanese ——" He turned over hard, he kind of surged over onto his side, looking at me in the dark.

"Anyway, you're all right," he said. "I expected to have more trouble with you than with all the rest of them put together."

"I reckon I can't help it neither," I said. "But maybe it will run a few years longer and I can get there. Maybe someday I will jest walk in on you."

"I hope not," Pete said. "Folks don't go to wars for fun. A man don't leave his maw crying just for fun."

"Then why are you going?" I said.

"I got to," he said. "I just go to. Now you go on to sleep. I got to ketch that early bus in the morning."

"All right," I said. "I hear tell Memphis is a big place. How will you find where the Army's at?"

"I'll ask somebody where to go to join it," Pete said. "Go on to sleep now."

"Is that what you'll ask for? Where to join the Army?" I said.

"Yes," Pete said. He turned onto his back again. "Shut up and go to sleep."

We went to sleep. The next morning we et breakfast by lamplight because the bus would pass at six o'clock. Maw wasn't crying now. She jest looked grim and busy, putting breakfast on the table while we et it. Then she finished packing Pete's grip, except he never wanted to take no grip to the war, but maw said decent folks never went nowhere, not even to a war, without a change of clothes and something to tote them in. She put in the shoe box of fried chicken and biscuits and she put the Bible in, too, and then it was time to go. We didn't know until then that maw wasn't going to the bus. She jest brought Pete's cap and overcoat, and still she didn't cry no more, she jest stood with her hands on Pete's shoulders and she didn't move, but somehow, and just holding Pete's shoulders, she looked as hard and fierce as when Pete had turned toward me in the bed last night and tole me that anyway I was all right.

"They could take the country and keep the country, so long as they never bothered me and mine," she said. Then she said, "Don't never forget who you are. You ain't rich and the rest of the world outside of Frenchman's Bend never heard of you. But your blood is good as any blood anywhere, and don't you never forget it."

Then she kissed him, and then we was out of the house, with pap toting Pete's grip whether Pete wanted him to or not. There wasn't no dawn even yet, not even after we had stood on the highway by the mailbox, a while. Then we seen the lights of the bus coming and I was watching the bus until it come up and Pete flagged it, and then, sho enough, there was daylight—it had started while I wasn't watching. And now me and Pete expected pap to say something else foolish, like he done before, about how Uncle Marsh getting wounded in France and that trip to Texas pap taken in 1918 ought to be enough to save the Unity States in 1942, but he never. He done all right too. He jest said, "Good-by, son. Always remember what your ma told you and write her whenever you find the time." Then he shaken Pete's hand, and Pete looked at me a minute and put his hand on my head and rubbed my head durn nigh hard enough to wring my neck off and jumped into the bus, and the feller wound the door shut and the bus begun to hum; then it was moving, humming and grinding and whining louder and louder; it was going fast, with two little red lights behind it that never seemed to get no littler, but jest seemed to be running together until pretty soon they would touch and jest be one light. But they never did, and then the bus was gone, and even like it was, I could have pretty nigh busted out crying, nigh to nine years old and all.

Me and pap went back to the house. All that day we worked at the wood tree, and so I never had no good chance until about middle of the afternoon. Then I taken my slingshot and I would have liked to took all my bird eggs, too, because Pete had give me his collection and he holp me with mine, and he would like to git the box and look at them as good as I would, even if he was nigh twenty years old. But the box was too big to tote a long ways and have to worry with, so I just taken the shikepoke egg, because it was the best un, and wropped it up good into a matchbox and hid it and the slingshot under the corner of the barn. Then we et supper and went to bed, and I thought then how if I would 'a' had to stayed in that room and that bed like that even for one more night, I jest couldn't 'a' stood it. Then I could hear pap snoring, but I never heard no sound from maw, whether she was asleep or not, and I don't reckon she was. So I taken my shoes and drapped them out the window, and then I clumb out like I used to watch Pete do when he was still jest seventeen and pap held that he was too young yet to be tomcatting around at night, and wouldn't leave him out, and I put on my shoes and went to the barn and got the slingshot and the shikepoke egg and went to the highway.

It wasn't cold, it was jest durn confounded dark, and that highway stretched on in front of me like, without nobody using it, it had stretched out half again as fer just like a man does when he lays down, so that for a time it looked like full sun was going to ketch me before I had finished them twenty-two miles to Jefferson. But it didn't. Daybreak was jest starting when I walked up the hill into town. I could smell breakfast cooking in the cabins and I wished I had thought to brought me a cold biscuit, but that was too late now. And Pete had told me Memphis was a piece beyond Jefferson, but I never knowed it was no eighty miles. So I stood there on that empty square, with daylight coming and coming and the street lights still burning and that Law looking down at me, and me still eighty miles from Memphis, and it had took me all night to walk jest twenty-two miles, and so, by the time I got to Memphis at that rate, Pete would 'a' done already started for Pearl Harbor.

"Where do you come from?" the Law said.

And I told him again. "I got to get to Memphis. My brother's there."

"You mean you ain't got any folks around here?" the Law said. "Nobody but that brother? What are you doing way off down here and your brother in Memphis?"

And I told him again, "I got to get to Memphis. I ain't got no time to waste talking about it and I ain't got time to walk it. I got to git there today."

"Come on here," the Law said.

We went down another street. And there was the bus, jest like when Pete got into it yestiddy morning, except there wasn't no lights on it now and it was empty. There was a regular bus dee-po like a railroad dee-po, with a ticket counter and a feller behind it, and the Law said, "Set down over there," and I set down on the bench, and the Law said, "I want to use your telephone," and he talked in the telephone a minute and put it down and said to the feller behind the ticket counter, "Keep your eye on him. I'll be back as soon as Mrs. Habersham can arrange to get herself up and dressed." He went out. I got up and went to the ticket counter.

"I want to go to Memphis," I said.

"You bet," the feller said. "You set down on the bench now. Mr. Foote will be back in a minute."

"I don't know no Mr. Foote," I said. "I want to ride that bus to Memphis."

"You got some money?" he said. "I'll cost you seventy-two cents."

I taken out the matchbox and unwrapped the shikepoke egg. "I'll swap you this for a ticket to Memphis," I said.

"What's that?" he said.

"It's a shikepoke egg," I said. "You never seen one before. It's worth a dollar. I'll take seventy-two cents fer it."

"No," he said, "the fellers that own that bus insist on a cash basis. If I started swapping tickets for bird eggs and livestock and such, they would fire me. You go and set down on the bench now, like Mr. Foote ——"

I started for the door, but he caught me, he put one hand on the ticket counter and jumped over it and caught up with me and reached his hand out to ketch my shirt. I whupped out my pocketknife and snapped it open.

"You put a hand on me and I'll cut it off," I said.

I tried to dodge him and run at the door, but he could move quicker than any grown man I ever see, quick as Pete almost. He cut me off and stood with his back against the door and one foot raised a little, and there wasn't no other way to get out. "Get back on that bench and stay there," he said.

And there wasn't no other way out. And he stood there with his back against the door. So I went back to the bench. And then it seemed like to me that dee-po was full of folks. There was that Law again, and there was two ladies in fur coats and their faces already painted. But they still looked like they had got up in a hurry and they still never liked it, a old one and a young one, looking down at me.

"He hasn't got a overcoat!" the old one said. "How in the world did he ever get down here by himself?"

'I ask you," the Law said. "I couldn't get nothing out of him except his brother is in Memphis and he wants to get back up there."

"That's right," I said. "I got to git to Memphis today."

"Of course you must," the old one said. "Are you sure you can find your brother when you get to Memphis?"

"I reckon I can," I said. "I ain't got but one and I have knowed him all my life. I reckon I will know him again when I see him."

The old one looked at me. "Somehow he doesn't look like he lives in Memphis," she said.

"He probably don't," the Law said. "You can't tell though. He might live anywhere, overhalls or not. This day and time they get scattered overnight from he—— hope to breakfast; boys and girls, too, almost before they can walk good. He might have been in Missouri or Texas either yestiddy, for all we know. But he don't seem to have any doubt his brother is in Memphis. All I know to do is send him up there and leave him look."

"Yes," the old one said.

The young one set down on the bench by me and opened a hand satchel and taken out a artermatic writing pen and some papers.

"Now, honey," the old one said, "we're going to see that you find your brother, but we must have a case history for our files first. We want to know your name and your brother's name and where you were born and when your parents died."

"I don't need no case history neither," I said. "All I want is to get to Memphis. I got to get there today."

"You see?" the Law said. He said it almost like he enjoyed it. "That's what I told you."

"You're lucky, at that, Mrs. Habersham," the bus feller said. "I don't think he's got a gun on him, but he can open that knife da—— I mean, fast enough to suit any man."

But the old one just stood there looking at me.

"Well," she said. "Well. I really don't know what to do."

"I do," the bus feller said. "I'm going to give him a ticket out of my own pocket, as a measure of protecting the company against riot and bloodshed. And when Mr. Foote tells the city board about it, it will be a civic matter and they will not only reimburse me, they will give me a medal too. Hey, Mr. Foote?"

But never nobody paid him no mind. The old one still stood looking down at me. She said "Well," again. Then she taken a dollar from her purse and give it to the bus feller. "I suppose he will travel on a child's ticket, won't he?"

"Wellum," the bus feller said, "I just don't know what the regulations would be. Likely I will be fired for not crating him and marking the crate Poison. But I'll risk it."

Then they were gone. Then the Law come back with a sandwich and give it to me.

"You're sure you can find that brother?" he said.

"I ain't yet convinced why not," I said. "If I don't see Pete first, he'll see me. He knows me too."

Then the Law went out for good, too, and I et the sandwich. Then more folks come in and bought tickets, and then the bus feller said it was time to go, and I got into the bus just like Pete done, and we was gone.

I seen all the towns. I seen all of them. When the bus got to going good, I found out I was jest about wore out for sleep. But there was too much I hadn't never saw before. We run out of Jefferson and run past fields and woods, then we would run into another town and out of that un and past fields and woods again, and then into another town with stores and gins and water tanks, and we run along by the railroad for a spell and I seen the signal arm move, and then I seen the train and then some more towns, and I was jest about plumb wore out for sleep, but I couldn't resk it. Then Memphis begun. It seemed like, to me, it went on for miles. We would pass a patch of stores and I would think that was sholy it and the bus would even stop. But it wouldn't be Memphis yet and we would go on again past water tanks and smokestacks on top of the mills, and if they was gins and sawmills, I never knowed there was that many and I never seen any that big, and where they got enough cotton and logs to run um I don't know.

Then I seen Memphis. I knowed I was right this time. It was standing up into the air. It looked like about a dozen whole towns bigger than Jefferson was set up on one edge in a field, standing up into the air higher than ara hill in all Yoknapatawpha County. Then we was in it, with the bus stopping ever' few feet, it seemed like to me, and cars rushing past on both sides of it and the street crowded with folks from ever'where in town that day, until I didn't see how there could 'a' been nobody left in Mis'sippi a-tall to even sell me a bus ticket, let alone write out no case histories. Then the bus stopped. It was another bus dee-po, a heap bigger than the one in Jefferson. And I said, "All right. Where do folks join the Army?"

"What?" the bus feller said.

And I said it again, "Where do folks join the Army?"

"Oh," he said. Then he told me how to get there. I was afraid at first I wouldn't ketch on how to do in a town big as Memphis. But I caught on all right. I never had to ask but twice more. Then I was there, and I was durn glad to git out of all them rushing cars and shoving folks and all that racket fer a spell, and I thought, It won't be long now, and I thought how if there was any kind of a crowd there that had done already joined the Army, too, Pete would likely see me before I seen him. And so I walked into the room. And Pete wasn't there.

He wasn't even there. There was a soldier with a big arrerhead on his sleeve, writing, and two fellers standing in front of him, and there was some more folks there, I reckon. It seems to me I remember some more folks there.

I went to the table where the soldier was writing, and I said, "Where's Pete?" and he looked up and I said, "My brother. Pete Grier. Where is he?"

"What?" the soldier said. "Who?"

And I told him again. "He joined the Army yestiddy. He's going to Pearl Harbor. So am I. I want to ketch him. Where you all got him?" Now they were all looking at me, but I never paid them no mind. "Come on," I said. "Where is he?"

The soldier had quit writing. He had both hands spraddled out on the table. "Oh," he said. "You're going, too, hah?"

"Yes," I said. "They got to have wood and water. I can chop it and tote it. Come on. Where's Pete?"

The soldier stood up. "Who let you in here?" he said. "Go on. Beat it."

"Durn that," I said. "You tell me where Pete ——"

I be dog if he couldn't move faster than the bus feller even. He never come over the table, he come around it, he was on me almost before I knowed it, so that I jest had time to jump back and whup out my pocketknife and snap it open and hit one lick, and he hollered and jumped back and grabbed one hand with the other and stood there cussing and hollering.

One of the other fellers grabbed me from behind, and I hit at him with the knife, but I couldn't reach him.

Then both of the fellers had me from behind, and then another soldier come out of a door at the back. He had on a belt with a britching strop over one shoulder.

"What the hell is this?" he said.

"That little son cut me with a knife!" the first soldier hollered. When he said that I tried to git at him again, but both them fellers was holding me, two against one, and the soldier with the backing strop said, "Here, here. Put your knife up, feller. None of us are armed. A man don't knife-fight folks that are barehanded." I could begin to hear him then. He sounded jest like Pete talked to me. "Let him go," he said. They let me go. "Now what's all the trouble about?" And I told him. "I see," he said. "And you come up to see if he was all right before he left."

"No," I said. "I came to ——"

But he had already turned to where the first soldier was wropping a hand-kerchief around his hand.

"Have you got him?" he said. The first soldier went back to the table and looked at some papers.

"Here he is," he said. "He enlisted yestiddy. He's in a detachment leaving this morning for Little Rock." He had a watch stropped on his arm. He looked at it. "The train leaves in about fifty minutes. If I know country boys, they're probably all down there at the station right now."

"Get him up here," the one with the backing strop said. "Phone the station. Tell the porter to get him a cab. And you come with me," he said.

It was another office behind that un, with jest a table and some chairs. We sat there while the soldier smoked, and it wasn't long; I knowed Pete's feet soon as I heard them. Then the first soldier opened the door and Pete come in. He never had no soldier clothes on. He looked jest like he did when he got on the bus yestiddy morning, except it seemed to me like it was at least a week, so much had happened, and I had done had to do so much traveling. He come in and there he was, looking at me like he hadn't never left home, except that here we was in Memphis, on the way to Pearl Harbor.

"What in durnation are you doing here?" he said.

And I told him, "You got to have wood and water to cook with. I can chop it and tote it for you-all."

"No," Pete said. "You're going back home."

"No, Pete," I said. "I got to go too. I got to. It hurts my heart, Pete."

"No," Pete said. He looked at the soldier. "I jest don't know what could have happened to him, lootenant," he said. "He never drawed a knife on anybody before in his life." He looked at me. "What did you do it for?"

"I don't know," I said. "I jest had to. I jest had to git here. I jest had to find you."

"Well, don't you never do it again, you hear?" Pete said. "You put that knife in your pocket and you keep it there. If I ever again hear of you drawing it on anybody, I'm coming back from wherever I am at and whup the fire out of you. You hear me?"

"I would pure cut a throat if it would bring you back to stay," I said. "Pete," I said. "Pete."

"No," Pete said. Now his voice wasn't hard and quick no more, it was almost quiet, and I knowed now I wouldn't never change him. "You must go home. You must look after maw, and I am depending on you to look after my ten acres. I want you to go back home. Today. Do you hear?"

"I hear," I said.

"Can he get back home by himself?" the soldier said.

"He come up here by himself," Pete said.

"I can get back, I reckon," I said. "I don't live in but one place. I don't reckon it's moved."

Pete taken a dollar out of his pocket and give it to me. "That'll buy your bus ticket right to our mailbox," he said. "I want you to mind the lootenant. He'll send you to the bus. And you go back home and you take care of maw and look after my ten acres and keep that durn knife in your pocket. You hear me?"

"Yes, Pete," I said.

"All right," Pete said. "Now I got to go." He put his hand on my head again. But this time he never wrung my neck. He just laid his hand on my head a minute. And then I be dog if he didn't lean down and kiss me, and I heard his feet and then the door, and I never looked up and that was all, me setting there, rubbing the place where Pete kissed me and the soldier throwed back in his chair, looking out the window and coughing. He reached into his pocket and handed something to me without looking around. It was a piece of chewing gum.

"Much obliged," I said. "Well, I reckon I might as well start back. I got a right fer piece to go."

"Wait," the soldier said. Then he telephoned again and I said again I better start back, and he said again, "Wait. Remember what Pete told you."

So we waited, and then another lady come in, old, too, in a fur coat, too, but she smelled all right, she never had no artermatic writing pen nor no case history neither. She come in and the soldier got up, and she looked around quick until she saw me, and come and put her hand on my shoulder light and quick and easy as maw herself might 'a' done it.

"Come on," she said. "Let's go home to dinner."

"Nome," I said. "I got to ketch the bus to Jefferson."

"I know. There's plenty of time. We'll go home and eat dinner first."

She had a car. And now we was right down in the middle of all them other cars. We was almost under the busses, and all them crowds of people on the street close enough to where I could have talked to them if I had knowed who they was. After a while she stopped the car. "Here we are," she said, and I looked at it, and if all that was her house, she sho had a big family. But all of it wasn't. We crossed a hall with trees growing in it and went into a little room without nothing in it but a nigger dressed up in a uniform a heap shinier than them soldiers had, and the nigger shut the door, and then I hollered, "Look out!" and grabbed, but it was all right; that whole little room jest went right on up and stopped and the door opened and we was in another hall, and the lady unlocked a door and we went in, and there was another soldier, a old feller, with a britching strop, too, and a silver-colored bird on each shoulder.

"Here we are," the lady said. "This is Colonel McKellogg. Now, what would you like for dinner?"

"I reckon I'll jest have some ham and eggs and coffee," I said.

She had done started to pick up the telephone. She stopped. "Coffee?" she said. "When did you start drinking coffee?"

"I don't know," I said. "I reckon it was before I could remember."

"You're about eight, aren't you?" she said.

"Nome," I said. "I'm eight and ten months. Going on eleven months."

She telephoned then. Then we set there and I told them how Pete had jest left that morning for Pearl Harbor and I had aimed to go with him, but I would have to go back home to take care of maw and look after Pete's ten acres, and she said how they had a little boy about my size, too, in a school in the East. Then a nigger, another one, in a short kind of shirttail coat, rolled a kind of wheelbarrer in. It had my ham and eggs and a glass of milk and a piece of pie, too, and I thought I was hungry. But when I taken the first bite I found out I couldn't swallow it, and I got up quick.

"I got to go," I said.

"Wait," she said.

"I got to go," I said.

"Just a minute," she said. "I've already telephoned for the car. It won't be but a minute now. Can't you drink the milk even? Or maybe some of your coffee?"

"Nome," I said. "I ain't hungry. I'll eat when I git home." Then the telephone rung. She never even answered it.

"There," she said. "There's the car." And we went back down in that 'ere little moving room with the dressed-up nigger. This time it was a big car with a soldier driving it. I got into the front with him. She give the soldier a dollar. "He might get hungry," she said. "Try to find a decent place for him."

"O.K., Mrs. McKellogg," the soldier said.

Then we was gone again. And now I could see Memphis good, bright in the sunshine, while we was swinging around it. And first thing I knowed, we was back on the same highway the bus run on this morning—the patches of stores and them big gins and sawmills, and Memphis running on for miles, it seemed like to me, before it begun to give out. Then we was running again between the fields and woods, running fast now, and except for that soldier, it was like I hadn't never been to Memphis a-tall. We was going fast now. At this rate, before I knowed it we would be home again, and I thought about me riding up to Frenchman's Bend in this big car with a soldier running it, and all of a sudden I begun to cry. I never knowed I was fixing to, and I couldn't stop it. I set there by that soldier, crying. We was going fast.

PUBLIC AND PRIVATE FACT

You will have noticed that "Two Soldiers" is easy to read, as much other good fiction is. Quality does not necessarily mean difficulty! The story obviously deals with war, especially the effects of war on a little family. It hardly matters whether the particular war is in Viet Nam or elsewhere, at the present time or earlier. Now a war is a large, disagreeable, public fact, and all sorts of people can and do take all sorts of attitudes toward this fact. Some see a chance to make money, some a problem of getting into the right branch of the service, some a problem of living or dying, some a problem of morality or of ethics. Such human reactions are as "real" as the fact of war itself. In "Two Soldiers" Faulkner represents still other

FORCE OF THE PRIVATE SUBJECTIVE WORLD

reactions and attitudes. To understand what fiction does, we need to realize that an author deals with both public, objective fact and inner, subjective fact—and that the second is as real a force in life as the first. It is the force inside us which leads to decisions and sets directions. It is the part of our human nature which sets a value on things and people and events, with consequent results in the way we think, feel, and act.

What happens when we read fiction is about as follows: The work of fiction sets before us various situations and people, with their thoughts, feelings and actions. We like and dislike, we approve or disapprove, we discover ideas and attitudes. We stretch our minds and feelings. We begin to realize the variety, complexity and mystery of human beings. All this includes us.

How does the process work in "Two Soldiers"? The two brothers in the story are not confused, or cynical, or self-seeking, or doubtful about personal values. They are not ashamed of affection, or afraid of the big world, or afraid of being laughed at. They know nothing about cities, or colleges, or the Reserve Officer's Training Corps. Faulkner presents them with respect and affection. They can be unhappy or have misfortune (in the sequel to this story, the older brother is killed); but they are whole, secure in their values.

WHY AUTHORS SOMETIMES WRITE ABOUT HUMAN TROUBLE

Readers have remarked that "Two Soldiers" is a strangely "comforting" story, in spite of the fact that it deals with human trouble. The reason is easy to see, and the "comfort" does not lie in the humor of the story. The two brothers are images of human soundness. They represent a kind of balance and surety which every living person would like to possess, which war and misfortune cannot destroy. This story is a clear example of why good authors will often write about trouble, for trouble can reveal human quality. The "comfort" or "consolation" which some readers receive from such an account of human quality is different from the fake reassurance about life which the usual "happy ending" of the commercial story provides. The problem here is real. There is no false "solution."

FUNCTIONS OF HUMOR

The humor in "Two Soldiers" is enjoyable itself, and it relieves the more serious emotion from time to time, allowing the author to build the emotion still higher. This is a classic function of humor. If you will notice the points at which humor occurs, in relation to the serious emotional climaxes, you will begin to appreciate the skill, the art, with which the story is written. There are three or four kinds or causes of humor in "Two Soldiers." We leave discovery of these to the reader, with the assurance that the story is worth re-reading for that purpose alone. Since humor, like other effects, depends on the reader as well as on the story, it is profitable to ask whether this story would seem humorous to two real persons like the two brothers, and to think over the meaning of the answer. Something about the nature of humor will be discovered.

CONTRAST AND COMPARISON

"Tell Me How Long the Train's Been Gone," by James Baldwin, is the second example of fiction in this first section. This story, like "Two Soldiers," involves two brothers and a small family; yet it is so strikingly different that it provides opportunities for a reader to extend his or her awareness and skill in basic ways. A younger brother again is the narrator. Like the younger brother in Faulkner's story, this brother has his own kind of "innocence," though it is much more troubled and complex. There is even a war on, in a *sense: the daily warfare in the streets of Harlem. The family in "Tell Me How Long the Train's Been Gone" is threatened in definite ways, yet it retains a warmth of affection and a hard-won unity. "Tell Me How Long the Train's Been Gone" presents an environment unfamiliar to many who live elsewhere in the United States, though the urban setting it evokes may be familiar to more of us. Good fiction, of course, widens our awareness and shapes our imaginings in exactly this way.*

*tell me how long the train's been gone

JAMES BALDWIN

My brother, Caleb, was seventeen when I was ten. We were very good friends. In fact, he was my best friend and, for a very long time, my only friend.

I do not mean to say that he was always nice to me. I got on his nerves a lot, and he resented having to take me around with him and be responsible for me when there were so many other things he wanted to be doing. Therefore, his hand was often up against the side of my head, and my tears caused him to be punished many times. But I knew, somehow, anyway, that when he was being punished for my tears, he was not being punished for anything he had done to me; he was being punished because that was the way we lived; and his punishment, oddly, helped unite us. More oddly still, even as his great hand caused my head to stammer and dropped a flame-colored curtain before my eyes, I understood that he was not striking *me.* His hand leapt out because he could not help it, and I received the blow because I was there. And it happened, sometimes, before I could even catch my breath to howl, that the hand that had struck me grabbed me and held me, and it was difficult indeed to know which of us was weeping. He was striking, striking out, striking out, striking out; the hand asked me to forgive him. I felt his bewilderment through the membrane of my own. I also felt that he was trying to teach me something. And I had, God knows, no other teachers.

For our father—how shall I describe our father?—was a ruined Barbados peasant, exiled in a Harlem which he loathed, where he never saw the sun or sky he remembered, where life took place neither indoors nor without, and where there was no joy. By which I mean no joy that he remembered. Had he been able to bring with him any of the joy he had felt on that far-off island, then the air of the sea and the impulse to dancing would sometimes have transfigured our dreadful rooms. Our lives might have been very different.

But no, he brought with him from Barbados only black rum and blacker pride and magic incantations, which neither healed nor saved.

He did not understand the people among whom he found himself; they had no coherence, no stature and no pride. He came from a race which had been flourishing at the very dawn of the world—a race greater and nobler than Rome or Judea, mightier than Egypt—he came from a race of kings, kings who had never been taken in battle, kings who had never been slaves. He spoke to us of tribes and empires, battles, victories and monarchs of whom we had never heard—they were not mentioned in our textbooks—and invested us with glories in which we felt more awkward than in the secondhand shoes we wore. In the stifling room of his pretensions and expectations, we stumbled wretchedly about, stubbing our toes, as it were, on rubies, scraping our shins on golden caskets, bringing down, with a childish cry, the splendid purple tapestry on which, in pounding gold and scarlet, our destinies and our inheritance were figured. It could scarcely have been otherwise, since a child's major attention has to be concentrated on how to fit into a world which, with every passing hour, reveals itself as merciless.

If our father was of royal blood and we were royal children, our father was certainly the only person in the world who knew it. The landlord did not know it; our father never mentioned royal blood to *him*. When we were late with our rent, which was often, the landlord threatened, in terms no commoner had ever used before a king, to put us in the streets. He complained that our shiftlessness, which he did not hesitate to consider an attribute of the race, had forced him, an old man with a weak heart, to climb all these stairs to plead with us to give him the money we owed him. And this was the last time; he wanted to make sure we understood that this was the last time.

Our father was younger than the landlord, leaner, stronger and bigger. With one blow, he could have brought the landlord to his knees. And we knew how much he hated the man. For days on end, in the wintertime, we huddled around the gas stove in the kitchen, because the landlord gave us no heat. When windows were broken, the landlord took his time about fixing them; the wind made the cardboard we stuffed in the windows rattle all night long; and when snow came, the weight of the snow forced the cardboard inward and onto the floor. Whenever the apartment received a fresh coat of paint, we bought the paint and did the painting ourselves; we killed the rats. A great chunk of the kitchen ceiling fell one winter, narrowly missing our mother.

We all hated the landlord with a perfectly exquisite hatred, and we would have been happy to see our proud father kill him. We would have been glad to help. But our father did nothing of the sort. He stood before the landlord, looking unutterably weary. He made excuses. He apologized. He swore that it would never happen again. (We knew that it *would* happen again.) He begged for time. The landlord would finally go down the stairs, letting us and all the neighbors know how good-hearted he was, and our father would walk into the kitchen and pour himself a glass of rum.

But we knew that our father would never have allowed any black man to speak to him as the landlord did, as policemen did, as storekeepers and welfare workers and pawnbrokers did. No, not for a moment. He would have thrown him out of the house. He would certainly have made a black man know that he was not the descendant of slaves! He had made them know it so often that he had almost no friends among them, and if we had followed his impossible lead, we would have had no friends, either. It was scarcely worthwhile being the descendant of kings if the kings were black and no one had ever heard of them.

And it was bcause of our father, perhaps, that Caleb and I clung to each other, in spite of the great difference in our ages; or, in another way, it may have been precisely the difference in our ages that made the clinging possible. I don't know. It is really not the kind of thing anyone can ever know. I think it may be easier to love the really helpless younger brother, because he cannot enter into competition with one on one's own ground, or on any ground at all, and can never question one's role or jeopardize one's authority. In my own case, certainly, it did not occur to me to compete with Caleb, and I could not have questioned his role or his authority, because I needed both. He was my touchstone, my model and my only guide.

Anyway, our father, dreaming bitterly of Barbados, despised and mocked by his neighbors and all but ignored by his sons, held down his unspeakable factory job, spread his black gospel in bars on the weekends, and drank his rum. I do not know if he loved our mother. I think he did.

They had had five children—only Caleb and I, the first and the last, were left. We were both dark, like our father; but two of the three dead girls had been fair, like our mother.

She came from New Orleans. Her hair was not like ours. It was black, but softer and finer. The color of her skin reminded me of the color of bananas. Her skin was as bright as that, and contained that kind of promise, and she had tiny freckles around her nose and a small black mole just above her upper lip. It was the mole, I don't know why, which made her beautiful. Without it, her face might have been merely sweet, merely pretty. But the mole was funny. It had the effect of making one realize that our mother liked funny things, liked to laugh. The mole made one look at her eyes—large, extraordinary dark eyes, eyes which seemed always to be amused by something, eyes which looked straight out, seeming to see everything, seeming to be afraid of nothing. She was a soft, round, plump woman. She liked nice clothes and dangling jewelry, which she mostly didn't have, and she liked to cook for large numbers of people, and she loved our father.

She knew him—knew him through and through. I am not being coy or colloquial but bluntly and sadly matter-of-fact when I say that I will now never know what she saw in him. What she saw was certainly not for many eyes; what she saw got him through his working week and his Sunday rest; what she saw saved him. She saw that he was a man. For her, perhaps, he was a great man. I think, though, that, for our mother, any man was great who aspired to become a man: this meant that our father was very rare and precious. I used to wonder how she took it, how she bore it—his rages, his tears, his cowardice.

On Saturday nights, he was almost always evil, drunk and maudlin. He came home from work in the early afternoon and gave our mother some money. It was never enough, of course, but he always kept enough to go out and get drunk. She never protested, at least not as far as I know. Then she would go out shopping. I would usually go with her, for Caleb would almost always be out somewhere, and our mother didn't like the idea of leaving me alone in the house. And this was probably, after all, the best possible arrangement. People who disliked our father were sure (for that very reason) to like our mother; and people who felt that Caleb was growing to be too much like his father could feel that I, after all, might turn out like my mother. Besides, it is not, as a general rule, easy to hate a small child. One runs the risk of looking ridiculous, especially if the child is with his mother.

And especially if that mother is Mrs. Proudhammer. Mrs. Proudhammer knew very well what people thought of Mr. Proudhammer. She knew, too, exactly how much she owed in each store she entered, how much she was going to be able to pay, and what she had to buy. She entered with a smile, ready.

"Evening. Let me have some of them red beans there."

"Evening. You know, you folks been running up quite a little bill here."

"I'm going to give you something on it right now. I need some cornmeal and flour and some rice."

"You know, I got my bills to meet, too, Mrs. Proudhammer."

"Didn't I just tell you I was going to pay? I want some cornflakes too, and some milk." Such merchandise as she could reach, she had already placed on the counter.

"When do you think you're going to be able to pay this bill? All of it, I mean."

"You know I'm going to pay it just as soon as I can. How much does it all come to? Give me that end you got there of that chocolate cake." The chocolate cake was for Caleb and me. "Well, now you put this against the bill." Imperiously, as though it were the most natural thing in the world, she put two or three dollars on the counter.

"You lucky I'm softhearted, Mrs. Proudhammer."

"Things sure don't cost this much downtown—you think I don't know it? Here." And she paid him for what she had bought. "Thank you. You been mighty kind."

And we left the store. I often felt that in order to help her, I should have filled my pockets with merchandise while she was talking. But I never did, not only because the store was often crowded or because I was afraid of being caught by the storekeeper, but because I was afraid of humiliating her. When I began to steal, not very much later, I stole in stores that were not in our neighborhood, where we were not known.

When we had to do "heavy" shopping, we went marketing under the bridge at Park Avenue—Caleb, our mother and I; and sometimes, but rarely, our father came with us. The most usual reason for heavy shopping was that some

3d ed.
c.1

relatives of our mother's, or old friends of both our mother's and our father's, were coming to visit. We were certainly not going to let them go away hungry —not even if it meant, as it often did mean, spending more than we had. In spite of what I have been suggesting about our father's temperament, and no matter how difficult he may sometimes have been with us, he was much too proud to offend any guest of his; on the contrary, his impulse was to make them feel that his home was theirs; and besides, he was lonely, lonely for his past, lonely for those faces which had borne witness to that past. Therefore, he would sometimes pretend that our mother did not know how to shop, and our father would come with us, under the bridge, in order to teach her.

There he would be, then, uncharacteristically, in shirt-sleeves, which made him look rather boyish; and as our mother showed no desire to take shopping lessons from him, he turned his attention to Caleb and me. He would pick up a fish, opening the gills and holding it close to his nose. "You see that? That fish looks fresh, don't it? Well, that fish ain't as fresh as I am, and I *been* out of the water. They done doctored that fish. Come on." And we would walk away, a little embarrassed but, on the whole, rather pleased that our father was so smart.

Meantime, our mother was getting the marketing done. She was very happy on days like this, because our father was happy. He was happy, odd as his expression of it may sound, to be out with his wife and his two sons. If we had been on the island that had been witness to his birth, instead of the un-speakable island of Manhattan, he felt that it would not have been so hard for us all to trust and love each other. He sensed, and I think he was right, that on that other, never to be recovered island, his sons would have looked on him very differently, and he would have looked very differently on his sons. Life would have been hard there, too; we would have fought there, too, and more or less blindly suffered and more or less blindly died. But we would not have been (or so it was to seem to all of us forever) so wickedly menaced by the mere fact of our relationship, would not have been so frightened of enter-ing into the central, most beautiful and valuable facts of our lives. We would have been laughing and cursing and tussling in the water, instead of stammer-ing under the bridge; we would have known less about vanished African king-doms and more about each other. Or, not at all impossibly, more about both.

If it was summer, we bought a watermelon, which either Caleb or our father carried home, fighting with each other for this privilege. They looked very like each other on those days—both big, both black, both laughing.

Caleb always looked absolutely helpless when he laughed. He laughed with all his body, perhaps touching his shoulder against yours, or putting his head on your chest for a moment, and then careering off you, halfway across the room or down the block. I will always hear his laughter. He was always happy on such days, too. If our father needed his son, Caleb certainly needed his father. Such days, however, were rare—one of the reasons, probably, that I remember them now.

Eventually, we all climbed the stairs into that hovel which, at such moments, was our castle. One very nearly felt the drawbridge rising behind us as our father locked the door.

The bathtub could not yet be filled with cold water and the melon placed in the tub, because this was Saturday, and, come evening, we all had to bathe. The melon was covered with a blanket and placed on the fire escape. Then we unloaded what we had bought, rather impressed by our opulence, though our father was always, by this time, appalled by the money we had spent. I was always sadly aware that there would be nothing left of all this once tomorrow had come and gone and that most of it, after all, was not for us, but for others.

Our mother was calculating the pennies she would need all week—carfare for our father and for Caleb, who went to a high school out of our neighborhood; money for the life insurance; money for milk for me at school; money for light and gas; money put away, if possible, toward the rent. She knew just about what our father had left in *his* pockets and was counting on him to give me the money I would shortly be demanding to go to the movies. Caleb had a part-time job after school and already had his movie money. Anyway, unless he was in a very good mood or needed me for something, he would not be anxious to go to the movies with me.

Our mother never insisted that Caleb tell her where he was going, nor did she question him as to how he spent the money he made. She was afraid of hearing him lie, and she did not want to risk forcing him to lie. She was operating on the assumption that he was sensible and had been raised to be honorable and that he, now more than ever, needed his privacy.

But she was very firm with him, nevertheless. "I do not want to see you rolling in here at three in the morning, Caleb. I want you here in time to eat, and you know you got to take your bath."

"Yes, indeed, ma'am. Why can't I take my bath in the morning?"

"Don't you start being funny. You know you ain't going to get up in time to take no bath in the morning."

"Don't nobody want you messing around in that bathroom all morning long, man," said our father. "You just git back in the house like your ma's telling you."

"Besides," I said, "you never wash out the tub."

Caleb looked at me in mock surprise and from a great height, allowing his chin and his lids simultaneously to drop and swiveling his head away from me.

"I see," he said, "that everyone in this family is ganging up on me. All right, Leo. I was planning to take you to the show with me, but now I've changed my mind."

"I'm sorry," I said quickly. "I take it back."

"You take *what* back?"

"What I said—about you not washing out the tub."

"Ain't no need to take it back," our father said stubbornly. "It's true. A man don't take back nothing that's true."

"So *you* say," Caleb said, with a hint of a sneer. But before anyone could possibly react to this, he picked me up, scowling into my face, which he held just above his own. "You take it back?"

"Leo ain't going to take it back," our father said.

Now I was in trouble. Caleb watched me, a small grin on his face. "You take it back?"

"Stop teasing that child, and put him down," our mother said. "The trouble ain't that Caleb don't wash out the tub—he just don't wash it out very clean."

"I never knew him to wash it out," our father said, "unless I was standing behind him."

"Well, ain't neither one of you much good around the house," our mother said.

Caleb laughed and set me down. "You didn't take it back," he said.

I said nothing.

"I guess I'm just going to have to go on without you."

Still, I said nothing.

"You going to have that child to crying in a minute," our mother said. "If you going to take him go on and take him. Don't do him like that."

Caleb laughed again. "I'm going to take him. The way he got them eyes all ready to water, I'd better take him somewhere." We walked toward the door. "But you got to make up *your* mind," he said to me, "to say what *you* think is right."

I grabbed Caleb's hand, the signal for the descent of the drawbridge. Our mother watched us cheerfully as we walked out; our father watched us balefully. Yet there was a certain humor in his face, too, and a kind of pride.

"Dig you later," Caleb said, and the door closed behind us.

The hall was dark, smelling of cooking, of stale wine, of rotting garbage. We dropped down the stairs, Caleb going two at a time, pausing at each landing, briefly, to glance back up at me. I dropped down behind him as fast as I could. When I reached the street level, Caleb was already on the stoop, joking with some of his friends, who were standing in the doorway—who seemed always to be in the doorway.

I didn't like Caleb's friends, because I was afraid of them. I knew the only reason they didn't try to make life hell for me, the way they made life hell for a lot of the other kids, was because they were afraid of Caleb. I went through the door, passing between my brother and his friends, down to the sidewalk, feeling, as they looked briefly at me and then continued joking with Caleb, what they felt—that here was Caleb's round-eyed, frail and useless sissy of a little brother. They pitied Caleb for having to take me out. On the other hand, they also wanted to go to the show, but didn't have the money. Therefore, in silence, I could crow over them even as they despised me. But this was always a terribly risky, touch-and-go business, for Caleb might, at any moment, change his mind and drive me away.

I always stood, those Saturday afternoons, in fear and trembling, holding on to the small shield of my bravado, while waiting for Caleb to come down the steps of the stoop, away from his friends, to me. I braced myself, always, for the moment when he would turn to me, saying, "Okay, kid. You run along. I'll see you later."

This meant that I would have to go the movies by myself and hang around in front of the box office waiting for some grown-up to take me in. I could not go back upstairs, for this would be informing my mother and father that Caleb had gone off somewhere after promising to take me to the movies.

Neither could I simply hang around, playing with the kids on the block. For one thing, my demeanor, as I came out of the house, very clearly indicated that I had better things to do than play with *them;* for another, they were not terribly anxious to play with *me;* and, finally, my remaining on the block would have had exactly the same effect as my going upstairs. To remain on the block after Caleb's dismissal was to put myself at the mercy of the block and to put Caleb at the mercy of our parents.

So I prepared myself, those Saturdays, to respond with a cool "Okay. See you later," and then to turn indifferently away, and walk. This was surely the most terrible moment. The moment I turned away, I was committed, I was trapped, and I then had miles to walk, so it seemed to me, before I would be out of sight, before the block ended and I could turn onto the avenue. I wanted to run out of that block, but I never did. I never looked back. I forced myself to walk very slowly, looking neither right nor left, striving to seem at once distracted and offhand; concentrating on the cracks in the sidewalk and stumbling over them; trying to whistle, feeling every muscle in my body, feeling that all the block was watching me, and feeling, which was odd, that I deserved it.

And then I reached the avenue, and turned, still not looking back, and was released from those eyes at least; but now I faced other eyes, eyes coming toward me. These eyes were the eyes of children stronger than me, who would steal my movie money; these eyes were the eyes of white cops, whom I feared, whom I hated with a literally murderous hatred; these eyes were the eyes of old folks, who might wonder what I was doing on this avenue by myself.

And then I got to the show. Sometimes someone would take me in right away, and sometimes I would have to stand there and wait, watching the faces coming to the box office. And this was not easy, since I didn't, after all, want everyone in the neighborhood to know I was loitering outside the movie house waiting for someone to take me in. If it came to our father's attention, he would kill both Caleb and me.

Eventually, I would see a face which looked susceptible. I would rush up to him—it was usually a man, for men were less likely to be disapproving—and whisper, "Take me in," and give him my dime. Sometimes the man simply took the dime and disappeared inside; sometimes he gave my dime back to me and took me in anyway. Sometimes I ended up wandering around the streets—but I couldn't wander into a strange neighborhood, because I would be beaten up if I did—until I figured the show was out. It was dangerous to get home too early, and, of course, it was practically lethal to arrive too late. If all went well, I could cover for Caleb, saying that I had left him with some boys on the stoop. Then, if *he* came in too late, it could not be considered my fault.

But if wandering around this way was not without its dangers, neither was it without its discoveries and delights. I discovered subways. I discovered, that is, that I could ride on subways by myself and, furthermore, that I could usually ride for nothing. Sometimes, when I ducked under the turnstile, I was caught, and sometimes great black ladies seized on me as a pretext for long, very loud, ineffably moral lectures about wayward children breaking their parents' hearts. Sometimes, doing everything in my power not to attract their attention, I endeavored to took as though I were in the charge of a respectable-looking man or woman, entering the subway in their shadow and sitting very still beside them. It was best to try to sit *between* two such people, for each would automatically assume that I was with the other. There I would sit, then, in a precarious anonymity, watching the people, listening to the roar, watching the lights of stations flash by. It seemed to me that nothing was faster than a subway train, and I loved the speed, because the speed was dangerous.

For a time, during these expeditions, I simply sat and watched the people. Lots of people would be dressed up, for this was Saturday night. The women's hair would be all curled and straightened, and the lipstick on their full lips looked purple and make-believe against the dark skins of their faces. They wore very fancy capes or coats, in wonderful colors, and long dresses, and sometimes they had jewels in their hair, and sometimes they wore flowers on their dresses. They were almost as beautiful as movie stars. And so the men with them seemed to think.

The hair of the men was slick and wavy, brushed up into pompadours; or they wore very sharp hats, brim flicked down dangerously over one eye, with perhaps one flower in the lapel of their many-colored suits. They laughed and talked with their girls, but quietly, for there were white people in the car. The white people would scarcely ever be dressed up and did not speak to each other at all—only read their papers and stared at the advertisements. But they fascinated me more than the colored people did, because I knew nothing at all about them and could not imagine what they were like.

Underground, I received my first apprehension of New York neighborhoods and, underground, first felt what may be called a civic terror. I very soon realized that after the train had passed a certain point, going uptown or downtown, all the colored people disappeared. The first time I realized this, I panicked and got lost. I rushed off the train, terrified of what these white people might do to me, with no colored person around to protect me—even to scold me, even to beat me; at least, their touch was familiar, and I knew that they did not, after all, intend to kill me—and got on another train only because I saw a black man on it. But almost everyone else was white.

The train did not stop at any of the stops I remembered. I became more and more frightened, frightened of getting off the train and frightened of staying on it, frightened of saying anything to the man and frightened that he would get off the train before I could say anything to him. He was my salvation, and he stood there in the unapproachable and frightening form that salvation so often takes. At each stop, I watched him with despair.

To make matters worse, I suddenly realized that I had to pee. Once I realized it, this need became a torment; the horror of wetting my pants in front of all these people made the torment greater. Finally, I tugged at the man's sleeve. He looked down at me with a gruff, amused concern; then, reacting, no doubt to the desperation in my face, he bent closer.

I asked him if there was a bathroom on the train.

He laughed. "No," he said, "but there's a bathroom in the station." He looked at me again. "Where're you going?"

I told him that I was going home.

"And where's home?"

I told him.

This time he did not laugh. "Do you know where you are?" he said.

I shook my head. At that moment, the train came into a station, and after several hours, it rolled to a stop. The doors opened, and the man led me to the bathroom. I ran in, and I hurried, because I was afraid he would disappear. But I was glad he had not come in with me.

When I came out, he stood waiting for me. "Now," he said, "you in Brooklyn. You ever hear of Brooklyn? What you doing out here by yourself?"

"I got lost," I said.

"I *know* you got lost. What I want to know is how *come* you got lost? Where's your mama? Where's your daddy?"

I almost said that I didn't have any, because I liked his face and his voice and was half hoping to hear him say that *he* didn't have any little boy and would just as soon take a chance on me. But I told him that my mama and daddy were at home.

"And do they know where *you* are?"

I said, "No." There was a pause.

"Well, I know they going to make your tail hot when they see you." He took my hand. "Come on."

And he led me along the platform and then down some steps and along a narrow passage and then up some steps onto the opposite platform. I was very impressed by this maneuver; in order to accomplish the same purpose, I had always left the subway station and gone up into the street. Now that the emergency was over, I was in no great hurry to leave my savior. I asked him if he had a little boy.

"Yes," he said, "and if *you* was my little boy, I'd paddle your behind so you couldn't sit down for a week."

I asked him how old was his little boy, what was his name and if his little boy was at home.

"He *better* be at home!" He looked at me and laughed. "His name is Jonathan. He ain't but five years old." His gaze refocused, sharpened. "How old are you?"

I told him that I was ten, going on eleven.

"You a pretty bad little fellow," he said then.

I tried to look repentant, but I would not have dreamed of denying it.

"Now, look here," he said, "this here's the uptown side. Can you read, or don't you never go to school?" I assured him that I could read. "Now, to get where you going, you got to change trains." He told me where. "Here, I'll write it down for you." He found some paper in his pocket but no pencil. We heard the train coming. He looked about him in helpless annoyance, looked at his watch, looked at me. "It's all right. I'll tell the conductor."

But the conductor, standing between two cars, had rather a mean pink face.

My savior looked at him dubiously. "He *might* be all right. But we better not take no chances." He pushed me ahead of him into the train. "You know you right lucky that I got a little boy? If I didn't, I swear I'd just let you go on and *be* lost. You don't know the kind of trouble you going to get me in at home. My wife ain't *never* going to believe *this* story."

I told him to give me his name and address and I would write a letter to his wife and to his little boy, too.

This caused him to laugh harder than ever. "You only say that because you know I ain't got no pencil. You are, one *hell* of a shrewd little boy."

I told him that then maybe we should get off the train and that I would go back home with him.

This made him grave. "What does your father do?"

This question made me uneasy. I stared at him for a long time before I answered. "He works in a —" I could not pronounce the word— "he has a job."

He nodded. "I see. Is he home now?"

I really did not know, and I said I did not know.

"And what does your mother do?"

"She stays home."

Again he nodded. "You got any brothers or sisters?"

I told him no.

"I see. What's your name?"

"Leo."

"Leo what?"

"Leo Proudhammer."

He saw something in my face. "What do you want to be when you grow up, Leo?"

"I want to be—" and I had never said this before—"I want to be a—a movie actor. I want to be a—actor."

"You pretty skinny for that," he said.

"That's all right," I told him. "Caleb's going to teach me to swim. That's how you get big."

"Who's Caleb?"

I opened my mouth, I started to speak. I checked myself as the train roared into a station. He glanced out the window, but did not move. "He swims," I said.

"Oh," he said after a very long pause, during which the doors slammed and the train began to move. "Is he a good swimmer?"

I said that Caleb was the best swimmer in the world.

"Okay," my savior said, "okay," and put his hand on my head again and smiled at me.

I asked him what his name was.

"Charles," he said, "Charles Williams. But you better call me *Uncle* Charles, you little devil, because you have certainly ruined my Saturday night." The train came into a station. "Here's where we change," he said.

We got out of the train and crossed the platform and waited.

"Now," he said, "this train stops exactly where you going. Tell me where you going."

I stared at him.

"I want you," he said, "to tell me exactly where you *going.* I can't be fooling with you all night."

I told him.

"You sure that's right?"

I told him I was sure.

"I got a very good memory," he said. "Give me your address. Just say it, I'll remember it."

So I said it, staring into his face as the train came roaring in.

"If you don't go straight home," he said, "I'm going to come see your daddy, and when we find you, you'll be mighty sorry." He pushed me into the train and put one shoulder against the door. "Go on, now," he said, loud enough for all the car to hear. "Your mama'll meet you at the station where I told you to get off." He repeated my subway stop, pushed the angry door with his shoulder, and then said gently, "Sit down, Leo." He remained in the door until I sat down. "So long, Leo," he said then, and stepped backward out. The doors closed. He grinned at me and waved, and the train began to move.

I waved back. Then he was gone, the station was gone, and I was on my way back home.

I never saw that man again, but I made up stories about him, I dreamed about him, I even wrote a letter to him and his wife and his little boy, but I never mailed it.

I never told Caleb anything about my solitary expeditions. I don't know why. I think that he might have liked to know about them. I suppose, finally, at bottom, I said nothing because my expeditions belonged to me.

Another time, it was raining, and it was still too early for me to go home. I felt very, very low that day. It was one of the times that my tongue and my body refused to obey me, and I had not been able to work up the courage to ask anyone to take me in to the show. The ticket taker was watching me, or so I thought, with a hostile suspicion. Actually, it's very unlikely he was thinking at all, and certainly not of me. But I walked away from the show, because I could no longer bear his eyes, or anybody's eyes.

I walked the long block east from the movie house. The street was empty, black and glittering. The water soaked through my coat at the shoulders, and water dripped down my neck from my cap. I began to be afraid. I could not stay out in the rain, because then my father and mother would know I had been wandering the streets. I would get a beating, and, though Caleb was too old to get a beating, he and my father would have a terrible fight, and Caleb would blame it all on me and would not speak to me for days.

I began to hate Caleb. I wondered where he was. I started in the direction of our house, only because I did not know what else to do. Perhaps Caleb would be waiting for me on the stoop.

The avenue, too, was very long and silent. Somehow, it seemed old, like a picture in a book. It stretched straight before me, endless, and the street-lights did not so much illuminate it as prove how dark it was. The rain was falling harder. Cars sloshed by, sending up sheets of water. From the bars, I heard music, faintly, and many voices. Straight ahead of me a woman walked, very fast, head down, carrying a shopping bag. I reached my corner and crossed the wide avenue. There was no one on my stoop.

Now I was not even certain what time it was; but I knew it wasn't time yet for the show to be over. I walked into my hallway and wrung out my cap. I was sorry that I had not made someone take me in to the show, because now I did not know what to do. I *could* go upstairs and say that we had not liked the movie and had left early and that Caleb was with some boys on the stoop. But this would sound strange, and Caleb, who would not know what story I had told, would, therefore, be greatly handicapped when he came home.

I could not stay in my hallway, because my father might not be at home and might come in. I could not go into the hallway of another building, because if any of the kids who lived in the building found me, they would have the right to beat me up. I could not go back out into the rain. I stood next to the big, cold radiator, and I began to cry. But crying wasn't going to do me any good, either, especially as there was no one to hear me.

So I stepped out on my stoop again and stood there for a long time, wondering what to do. Then I thought of a condemned house, around the corner from us. We played there sometimes, though it was very dangerous and we were not supposed to. What possessed me to go there now, I don't know, except that I could not think of another dry place in the whole world. I started running east, down our block. I turned two corners and came to the house, with its black window sockets. The house was completely dark. I had forgotten how afraid I was of the dark, but the rain was drenching me. I ran down the cellar steps and clambered into the house through one of the broken windows. I squatted there in a still, dry dread, not daring to look into the house but staring outward. I was holding my breath. I heard an endless scurrying in the darkness, a perpetual busyness, and I thought of rats, of their teeth and ferocity and fearful size, and I began to cry again.

I don't know how long I squatted there this way or what was in my mind. I listened to the rain and the rats. Then I was aware of another sound—I had been hearing it for a while without realizing it. This was a moaning sound, a sighing sound, a sound of strangling, which mingled with the sound of the rain and with a muttering, cursing human voice. The sounds came from the door that led to the backyard.

I wanted to stand, but I crouched lower; wanted to run, but could not move. Sometimes the sounds seemed to come closer, and I knew that this meant my death; sometimes they diminished or ceased altogether, and then I knew that my assailant was looking for me. I looked toward the backyard door, and I seemed to see, silhouetted against the driving rain, a figure, half bent, moaning, leaning against the wall, in indescribable torment; then there seemed to be two figures, sighing and grappling, moving so quickly that it was impossible to tell which was which, two creatures, each in a dreadful, absolute, silent single-mindedness attempting to strangle the other!

I watched, crouching low. A very powerful and curious excitement mingled itself with my terror and made the terror greater. I could not move. I did not dare move. The figures were quieter now. It seemed to me that one of them was a woman, and she seemed to be crying, pleading for her life. But her sobbing was answered only by a growling sound. The muttered, joyous curses began again; the murderous ferocity began again, more bitterly than ever. The sobbing began to rise in pitch, like a song.

Then everything was still, all movement ceased. Then I heard only the rain and the scurrying of the rats. It was over; one of them, or both of them, lay stretched out, dead or dying in this filthy place. It happened in Harlem every Saturday night. I could not catch my breath to scream. Then I heard a laugh, a low, happy, wicked laugh, and the figure turned in my direction and seemed to start toward me.

Then I screamed and stood straight up, bumping my head on the window frame and losing my cap, and scrambled up the cellar steps. I ran head down, like a bull, away from that house and out of that block. I ran up the steps of my stoop and bumped into Caleb.

"Where the hell have you been? Hey! What's the matter with you?"

I had jumped up on him, almost knocking him down, trembling and sobbing.

"You're *soaked.* Leo, what's the matter? Where's your cap?"

But I could not say anything. I held him around the neck with all my might, and I could not stop shaking.

"Come on, Leo," Caleb said, in a different tone, "tell me what's the matter." He pried my arms loose and held me away from him, so that he could look into my face. "Oh, little Leo. Little Leo. What's the matter, baby?" He looked as though he were about to cry himself, and this made me cry harder than ever. He took out his handkerchief and wiped my face and made me blow my nose. My sobs began to lessen, but I could not stop trembling. He thought that I was trembling from cold, and he rubbed his hands roughly up and down my back and rubbed my hands between his. "What's the matter?"

I did not know how to tell him.

"Somebody try to beat you up?"

I shook my head. "No."

"What movie did you see?"

"I didn't go. I couldn't find nobody to take me in."

"And you just been wandering around in the rain all night?"

"Yes."

He sat down on the hallway steps. "Oh, Leo." Then, "You mad at me?"

I said, "No. I was scared."

He nodded. "I reckon you were, man." He wiped my face again. "You ready to go upstairs? It's getting late."

"Okay."

"How'd you lose your cap?"

"I went in a hallway to wring it out—and—I put it on the radiator, and I heard some people coming—and—I ran away, and I forgot it."

"We'll say you forgot it in the movies."

"Okay."

We started up the stairs.

"Leo," he said, "I'm sorry about tonight. I'm really sorry. I won't let it happen again. You believe me?"

"Sure. I believe you." I smiled up at him.

He squatted down. "Give us a kiss."

I kissed him.

"Okay. Climb up. I'll give you a ride. Hold on, now."

He carried me piggyback up the stairs.

Thereafter, we evolved a system, which did not, in fact, work too badly. When things went wrong and he could not be found, I was to leave a message for him at a certain store on the avenue. This store had a bad reputation—more than candy and hot dogs and soda pop were sold there; Caleb himself had told me this and told me not to hang out there. But he said he would see to it that they treated me all right.

I went in the store one Saturday night, and one of the boys who was always there, a boy about Caleb's age, looked up and smiled and said, "You looking for your brother? Come on, I'll take you to him."

This was not the agreed-on formula. I was to be *taken* to Caleb only in cases of real emergency, which wasn't the case this time. I was there because the show was over a little earlier than usual, and since it was only about a quarter past eleven, I figured I had about half an hour to wait for Caleb.

When the boy made his invitation, I assumed it was because of some prearrangement with the owner of the store, a very dour, silent black man, who looked at me from behind his counter and said nothing.

I said, "Okay," and the boy, whose name was Arthur, said, "Come on, Sonny. I'm going to take you to a party." He took my hand and led me across the avenue and into a long, dark block.

We walked the length of the block in silence, crossed another avenue and went into a big house in the middle of the block. We were in a big vestibule, with four locked apartment doors staring away from each other. It was not really clean, but it was fairly clean. We climbed three flights of stairs. Arthur knocked on the door, a very funny knock, not loud. After a moment, I heard a scraping sound, then the sound of a chain rattling and a bolt being pulled back. The door opened.

A lady, very black and rather fat, wearing a blue dress, held the door for us. She said, "Come on in. Now, what you doing here with this child?"

"Had to do it. It's all right. It's Caleb's brother."

We started down a long, dark hall, with closed rooms on either side of it, toward the living room. One of the rooms was the kitchen. A smell of barbecue made me realize that I was hungry. The living room was really two living rooms. The far one looked out on the street. There were six or seven people in the room, women and men. They looked exactly like the men and women who frightened me when I saw them standing on the corners, laughing and joking in front of the bars. But they did not seem frightening here. A record player was going, not very loud. They had drinks in their hands, and there were half-empty plates of food around the room. Caleb was sitting on the sofa, with his arm around a girl in a yellow dress.

"Here's your little brother," said the fat black lady in blue.

Arthur said to Caleb, "It was just better for him not to have to wait there tonight."

Caleb smiled at me. I was tremendously relieved that he was not angry. I was delighted by this party, even though it made me shy. "Come on over here," Caleb said. I went to the sofa. "This is my kid brother. His name is Leo. Leo, this is Dolores. Say hello to Dolores."

•Dolores smiled at me—I thought she was very pretty—and said, "I'm very happy to meet you, Leo. How've you been?"

"Just fine," I said.

"Don't you want to know how *she's* been?" Caleb grinned.

"No," said the fat black lady, and laughed. "I'm sure he don't want to know that. I bet he's hungry. You been stuffing yourself all night, Caleb. Let me give him a little bit of my barbecue and a glass of ginger ale." She already was beginning to propel me out of the room.

I looked at Caleb. Caleb said, "Just remember we ain't got all night. Leo, this is Miss Mildred. She cooked everything, and she's a might good friend of mine. What do you say to Miss Mildred, Leo?"

"Dig Caleb being the big brother," Arthur muttered, and laughed.

"Thank you, Miss Mildred," I said.

"Come on in the kitchen," she said, "and let me try to put some flesh on them bones." She walked me into the kitchen. "Now, you sit right over there," she said. "Won't take me but a minute to warm this up." She sat me at the kitchen table and gave me a napkin and poured the ginger ale. "What grade you in at school, Leo?" I told her. "You must be a right smart boy, then," she said, with a pleased smile. "Do you like school, Leo?"

I told her what I liked best was Spanish and history and English composition.

This caused her to look more pleased than ever. "What do you want to be when you grow up?"

Somehow, I could not tell her what I had told the man, my friend, on the train. I said I wasn't sure, that maybe I would be a schoolteacher.

"That's just what I wanted to be," she said proudly, "and I studied right hard for it, too, and I believe I would have made it, but then I had to go and get myself mixed up with some no-count nigger. I didn't have no sense. I didn't have no better sense but to marry him. Can you beat that?" And she laughed and set my plate in front of me. "Go on, now, eat. Foolish me. Now, your brother," she said suddenly, "he's a right fine boy. He wants to make something of himself. He's got ambition. That's what I like — *ambition.* Don't you let him be foolish. Like me. You like my barbecue?"

"Yes, ma'am," I said. "It's good."

"Let me give you some more ginger ale," she said, and poured it.

I was beginning to be full. But I didn't want to go, although I knew that, now, it was really beginning to be late. While Miss Mildred talked and moved about the kitchen, I listened to the voices coming from the other room, the voices and the music. They were playing a kind of purple, lazy dance music, a music that was already in my bones, along with the wilder music from which the purple music sprang. The voices were not like the music, though they corroborated it. I listened to a girl's voice, gravelly and low, indignant and full of laughter. The room was full of laughter. It exploded, at intervals, and rolled through the living room and hammered at the walls of the kitchen.

Every once in a while, I heard Caleb, booming like a trumpet, drowning out the music. I wondered how often Caleb came here and how he had met these people, who were so different, at least as it seemed to me, from any of the people who ever came to our house.

Then Caleb's hand was on my neck. Dolores stood in the doorway, smiling. "You stuffed yourself enough, little brother?" Caleb said. "Because we got to get out of here now."

We walked slowly down the hall, Miss Mildred, Dolores and Caleb and me. We reached the door, which had a metal pole built into it in such a way as to prevent its being opened from the outside, and a heavy piece of chain around the top of the three locks.

Miss Mildred began, patiently, to open the door. "Leo," she said, "don't you be no stranger. You make your brother bring you back to see me, you hear?" She got the pole out of the way and then undid the chain. To Caleb, she said, "Bring him by some afternoon. I ain't got nothing to do. I'll be glad to look after him." The last lock yielded, and Miss Mildred opened the door. We were facing the bright hall lights: no, the building was not very clean. "Good night, Leo," Miss Mildred said, and then she said good night to Dolores and Caleb. She closed the door.

I heard the scraping sound again, and we walked down the stairs.

"She's nice," I said.

Caleb said, yawning, "Yeah, she's a very nice lady." Then he said, "Now, I don't want you telling nobody at home about this, you hear?" I swore I wouldn't tell. "It's our secret," Caleb said.

It was colder in the streets than it had been before.

Caleb took Dolores' arm. "Let's get you to your subway," he said.

We started walking up the wide, dark avenue. We reached the brightly lit kiosk, which came up out of the sidewalk like some unbelievably malevolent awning or the suction apparatus of a monstrous vacuum cleaner.

"By-by," Caleb said, and kissed Dolores on the nose. "I got to run. See you Monday after school."

"By-by," Dolores said. She bent down and kissed me quickly on the cheek. "By-by, Leo. Be good." She hurried down the steps.

Caleb and I began walking very fast, down the avenue, toward our block. The subway station was near the movie house, and the movie house was dark. We knew we were late; we did not think we were *that* late.

"It was a *very* long show, wasn't it?" Caleb said.

"Yes." I said.

"What did we see? Better tell me about *both* pictures. Just in case."

I told him as well as I could as we hurried down the avenue. Caleb had great powers of concentration and could figure out enough from what I said to know what to say if the necessity arose.

But our troubles, that night, came from a very different source than our parents. I had just reached the point in my breathless narration where the good girl is murdered by the Indians and the hero vows revenge. We were hurrying down the long block that led east to our house when we heard a car braking and were blinded by bright lights and were pushed up against a wall.

"Turn around," a voice said. "And keep your hands in the air."

It may seem funny, but I felt as though Caleb and I had conjured up a movie —that if I had not been describing a movie to him, we would not have suddenly found ourselves in the middle of one. Or was it the end? I had never been so frightened in my life.

We did as we were told. I felt the grainy brick beneath my fingers. A hand patted me all over my body, every touch humiliating. Beside me, I heard Caleb catch his breath.

"Turn around," the voice said.

The great lights of the police car had gone out; I could see the car at the curb, the doors open. I did not dare look at Caleb, for I felt that this would, somehow, be used against us. I stared at the two policemen, young, white, tight-lipped and self-important.

They turned a flashlight first on Caleb, then on me. "Where you boys going?"

"Home," Caleb said. I could hear his breathing. "We live in the next block." And he gave the address.

"Where've you been?"

Now I heard the effort Caleb was making not to surrender either to rage or panic. "We just took my girl to the subway station. We were at the movies." And then, forced out of him, weary, dry and bitter, "This here's my brother. I got to get him home. He ain't but ten years old."

"What movie did you see?"

And Caleb told them. I marveled at his memory. But I also knew that the show had let out about an hour or so before. I feared that the policemen might also know this. But they didn't.

"You got any identification?"

"My brother doesn't. I do."

"Let's see it."

Caleb took out his wallet and handed it over.

They looked at his wallet, looked at us, handed it back. "Get on home," one of them said. They got into their car and drove off.

"Thanks," Caleb said. "Thanks, all you scum-bag Christians." His accent was now as irredeemably of the islands as was the accent of our father. I had never heard this sound in his voice before. And then, suddenly, he looked down at me and laughed and hugged me. "Come on, let's get home. Little Leo. Were you scared?"

"Yes," I said. "Were you?"

"Damn right, I was scared. But—damn!—they must have seen that you weren't but ten years old."

"You didn't *act* scared," I said.

We were in our own block, approaching our stoop. "Well. We certainly have a good excuse for being late," he said. He grinned. Then he said, "Leo, I'll tell you something. I'm glad this happened. It had to happen one day, and I'm glad it happened while I was with you—of course, I'm glad you were with *me,* too, because if it hadn't been for you, they'd have pulled me."

"What for?"

"Because I'm black," Caleb said. "That's what for."

I said nothing. I said nothing, because what he said was true, and I knew it. It seemed, now, that I had always known it, though I had never been able to say it. But I did not understand it. I was filled with an awful wonder; it hurt my chest and paralyzed my tongue. *Because you're black.* I tried to think, but I couldn't. I only saw the policemen, those murderous eyes again, those hands. Were they people?

"Caleb," I asked, "are white people people?"

"What are you talking about, Leo?"

"I mean, are white people—*people?* People like us?"

He looked down at me. His face was very strange and sad. It was a face I had never seen before. We were in the house now, and we climbed a few more stairs, very slowly. Then, "All I can tell you, Leo, is—well, *they* don't think they are."

I thought of the landlord. Then I thought of my schoolteacher, a lady named Mrs. Nelson. I liked her very much. I thought she was very pretty. She had long yellow hair, like someone I had seen in the movies, and a nice laugh, and we all liked her, all the kids I knew. The kids who were not in her class wished they were. I liked to write compositions for her, because she seemed really interested. But she was white. Would she hate me all my life because I was black? It didn't seem possible. She didn't hate me now; I was pretty sure of that. And yet, what Caleb had said was true.

"Caleb," I asked, "are all white people the same?"

"I never met a good one."

I asked, "Not even when you were little? In school?"

Caleb said, "Maybe. I don't remember." He smiled at me. "I never met a good one, Leo. But that's not saying that *you* won't. Don't look so frightened."

We were in front of our door. Caleb raised his hand to knock.

I held his hand. "Caleb," I whispered, "what about Mama?"

"Well, Mama." I stared at him; he watched me very gravely. "Mama—Mama's almost white."

"But that don't make her white. You got to be *all* white to be white." He laughed. "Poor Leo. Don't feel bad. I know you don't understand it now. I'll try to explain it to you, little by little." He paused. "But our mama is a colored woman. You can tell she's a colored woman because she's married to a colored *man,* and she's got two colored *children.* Now, you know ain't no white lady going to do a thing like that." He watched me, smiling. "You understand that?" I nodded. "Well, you going to keep me here all night with your questions, or can we go on in now?"

He knocked, and our mother opened the door. "About time," she said drily. She had her hair piled in a knot on the top of her head. I liked her hair that way. "You must have sat through that movie four or five times. You're going to ruin your eyes, and that'll just be too bad for you, because you know we ain't got no money to be buying you no glasses. Leo, you go on inside and get ready to take your bath."

"Let him come over here a minute," our father said. He was sitting in the one easy chair, near the window. He was drunk, but not as drunk as I had seen him, and this was a good-mood drunk. In this mood, he talked about the islands his mother and father and kinfolk and friends, the feast days, the singing, the dancing and the sea.

I approached him, and he pulled me to him, smiling, and held me between his thighs. "How's my big man?" he asked, smiling and rubbing his hand, gently, over my hair. "Did you have a good time tonight?"

Caleb sat on a straight chair near him, leaning forward. "Let Leo tell you why we so late. Tell them what happened, Leo."

"We were coming down the block," I began—and I watched my father's face. Suddenly, I did not want to tell him. Something in Caleb's tone had alerted him, and he watched me with a stern and frightened apprehension. My mother came and stood beside him, one hand on his shoulder. I looked at Caleb. "Maybe you could tell it better," I said.

"Go on, start. I'll fill in."

"We were coming down the block," I said, "coming from the movies." I looked at Caleb.

"It's not the way we usually come," Caleb said.

My father and I stared at each other. There was, suddenly, between us, an overwhelming sorrow. It had come from nowhere. "We got stopped by the cops," I said. Then I could not continue. I looked helplessly at Caleb, and Caleb told the story.

As Caleb spoke, I watched my father's face. I don't know how to describe what I saw. I felt his arm tighten, tighten; his lips became bitter, and his eyes grew dull. It was as though—after indescribable, nearly mortal effort, after grim years of fasting and prayer, after the loss of all he had, and after having been promised by the Almighty that he had paid the price and no more would be demanded of his soul, which was harbored now—it was as though in the midst of his joyful feasting and dancing, crowned and robed, a messenger arrived to tell him that a great error had been made, and that it was all to be done again. Before his eyes, then, the banquet and the banquet wines and the banquet guests departed, the robe and crown were lifted, and he was alone, frozen out of his dream, with all that before him which he had thought was behind him.

My father looked as stunned and still and as close to madness as that, and his encircling arm began to hurt me, but I did not complain. I put my hand on his face, and he turned to me; he smiled—he was very beautiful then!—and he put his great hand on top of mine. He turned to Caleb. "That's all that happened? You didn't say nothing?"

"What could I say? It might have been different if I'd been by myself. But I had Leo with me, and I was afraid of what they might do to Leo."

"No, you did right, man. I got no fault to find. You didn't take their badge number?"

Caleb snickered. "What for? You know a friendly judge? We got money for a lawyer? Somebody they going to *listen* to? They get us in that precinct house and make us confess to all kinds of things and sometimes even kill us, and don't nobody give a damn. Don't nobody care what happens to a black man. If they didn't need us for work, they'd have killed us all off a long time ago. They did it to the Indians."

"That's the truth," our mother said. "I wish I could say different, but it's the truth." She stroked our father's shoulder. "We just thank the Lord it wasn't no worse. We just got to say: Well, the boys got home safe tonight."

I asked, "Daddy, how come they do us like they do?"

My father looked at us for a long time. Finally, he said, "Leo, if I could tell you that, maybe I'd be able to make them stop. But don't let them make you afraid. You hear?"

I said, "Yes, sir." But I knew that I was already afraid.

"Let's not talk about it no more," our mother said. "If you two is hungry, I got some pork chops back there."

Caleb grinned at me. "Little Leo might be hungry. He stuffs himself like a pig. But I ain't hungry. Hey, old man—" he nudged my father's shoulder; nothing would be refused us tonight— "why don't we have a taste of your rum? All right?"

Our mother laughed. "I'll go get it," she said. She started out of the room.

"Reckon we can give Leo a little bit, too?" our father asked. He pulled me onto his lap.

"In a big glass of water," our mother said, laughing. She took one last look at us before she went into the kitchen. "My," she said, "I sure am surrounded by some pretty men! My, my, my!"

Tactics for Readers

We can look now at the way "Two Soldiers" and "Tell Me How Long the Train's Been Gone" begin. This is a tactic always useful but particularly so just now, for it will clarify basic points about how to read and what to notice or look for.

HOW A STORY BEGINS

To get started, you should reread the first several paragraphs in each of the two stories. By doing so, you will observe that each story is told from the point of view of one of the characters, a general technique called first-person narrative. Each is a narrator's story of events as he remembers, sees, or feels them; the author, of course, has invented this narrator as a way of getting the story told.

USES OF SUMMARY NARRATIVE

In addition, you will notice that each author uses a second fictional technique called summary narrative; this is a way of reporting what generally or typically happens, as summarized in this instance by the narrator. For example:

■ *in the Faulkner:*
    We would wait until after supper, after dark, and we would

stand outside Old Man Killegrew's parlor window, and we could hear it . . . , even standing outside with the windows closed.

- *in the Baldwin:*

  But I knew, somehow, anyway, that when he was being punished for my tears, he was not being punished for anything he had done to me; he was being punished because that was the way we lived; and his punishment, oddly, helped unite us.

In each instance the narrator is reporting something that happened many times, so often as to be typical. This is the basic use of summary narrative; it allows an author to show what was true in general, or what happened over a period of time. You will notice, however, that Faulkner has managed at the same time to convey the "reality" of a particular situation: "dark . . . standing outside with the windows closed." This is a kind of double use, or effect, of summary narrative. Baldwin, on the other hand, does not use summary narrative to suggest the sensory reality of a particular situation as early in his story, though he does so later.

DRAMATIC NARRATIVE Both authors soon turn away from summary narrative and introduce immediate, second-by-second accounts of what the narrator does, says, sees, hears—in specific situations. If you were to write a story tomorrow, you might find it necessary to emphasize some situations through dramatic second-by-second treatment, whereas other materials of the story might be summarized in a narrative fashion. For the second-by-second technique, we shall use here the term dramatic narrative, or one-time/one-place narrative.

DICTION AND SENTENCE STRUCTURE Now, in spite of the general similarity of technique, do the two stories really seem to be alike? We know already that Faulkner's use of summary narrative thus far is slightly different from Baldwin's. If we look more closely and examine the diction, the words, the vocabulary in these two stories, what do we find? A first impression is that both authors use fairly simple diction: short and ordinary words. Yet looking further into the Baldwin story we come across words such as the following: responsible, bewilderment, membrane, impulse, transfigured, incantations, coherence, stature, and many others. It is impossible to imagine such language in the mouth of the younger brother in "Two Soldiers." It wouldn't sound right. We thus discover that the stories are different in another way, for the Faulkner is truly colloquial in tone; it has the sound of speech, and we can believe that the words are exactly the kind the younger brother in "Two Soldiers" would use. His language, indeed, becomes a main attraction, a source of reality and humor. The Baldwin has much less of the colloquial tone and much more a tone of reflection, of "remembering." Even the sentence structure shows this more "mental" quality: "But I knew, somehow, anyway, . . . and his punishment, oddly, helped unite us." Though diction and sentence structure in the Baldwin story are to some degree "simple," they are also more complex, not in the same tone at all as in "Two Soldiers." The Baldwin narrator is older and is telling the story much later in his life than at the time of the action. The narrator in the Faulkner is closer in time to the events he reports, and his style fits this fact, just as the Baldwin style fits his narrator. Both word repetition and sentence structure in the Faulkner contribute to the humor; a like effect is not sought in the Baldwin. It is beside the point to ask which story, or technique, is "better." Each author has used a style suitable to his purposes and to the effects he wants to achieve.

GENERAL STATEMENTS

We have observed a meditative quality in "Tell Me How Long," a "distance" between the narrator and the events he reports. This facet of style makes it possible for Baldwin, as author, to put into the narrator's mouth general ideas that would surprise us if found in the Faulkner story. We have already seen one example: "his punishment, oddly, helped unite us." Among Baldwin's major powers as a writer is his ability to notice and convey important and subtle human truth, often a generalization arising from events, and his technique in "Tell Me How Long" allows him to do just this. If you wish to, you can go through the Baldwin story and find dozens of examples of this quality—that is, insight into realities of feeling, often expressed in general terms.

TECHNIQUE AND MEANING

To summarize: A reader can learn a great deal by examining in detail the way a story is told, and useful clues can be found from the way a story begins. A competent reader will be able to compare and contrast the unique effects two authors gain, even though the two may be using the same general techniques of writing. We cannot attempt here a full discussion of the meanings in "Tell Me How Long." We should leave much of this, indeed, for the reader to do. One major point, however, can be stressed: The Baldwin story conveys a complexity, variety, and force in personal feelings that are not attempted in the Faulkner. Attempts to handle strong emotions such as anger, hate, and fierce loyalty are problems for Baldwin's characters, and one of the most difficult tasks for any author is to represent strong emotion convincingly. It isn't that the emotions in "Two Soldiers" are not "strong"; it is simply that more is attempted in "Tell Me How Long." The attempt succeeds because Baldwin's technique provides opportunities for general, insightful remarks. We thus reach a point at which the thing we call "technique," including "style," is almost inseparable from the author's purposes and meanings. But we would not grasp these purposes and meanings so clearly if we did not, in a sense, "see" them developing, and this "seeing" on our part is made possible by a perception of the way the story is told.

The two stories discussed so far are thus different in what they attempt and achieve, and the question, "Which is the better story?" is still beside the point. The Faulkner is probably more unified in tone, through its colloquial style. Baldwin "shifts gears" more often, in a technical and stylistic sense, to fit his very different story.

BASIC STRATEGIES IN READING

Some characteristics of fiction, including definitions of three fictional techniques, have now been discussed. By means of a third example, we come to materials of a somewhat different kind. The strategies to be described are really important understandings about reading, without which misunderstandings are likely. These matters will be covered in comments that follow the next story. The discussion of fictional techniques, already begun, will continue.

The next piece of fiction will allow us to raise another basic question, that of an author's major emphasis in a story. "A Sick Call" is in some ways more difficult to read than were "Two Soldiers" and "Tell Me How Long," for reasons that will be explained. One source of difficulty is the fact that the story touches emotional allegiances among readers. This in itself can cause misreading. Yet this story has never, to our knowledge, left a reader indifferent.

A Sick Call

MORLEY CALLAGHAN

1

Sometimes Father Macdowell mumbled out loud and took a deep wheezy breath as he walked up and down the room and read his office. He was a huge old priest, white-headed except for a shiny baby-pink bald spot on the top of his head, and he was a bit deaf in one ear. His florid face had many fine red interlacing vein lines. For hours he had been hearing confessions and he was tired, for he always had to hear more confessions than any other priest at the cathedral; young girls who were in trouble, and wild but at times repentant young men, always wanted to tell their confessions to Father Macdowell, because nothing seemed to shock or excite him, or make him really angry, and he was even tender with those who thought they were most guilty.

While he was mumbling and reading and trying to keep his glasses on his nose, the house girl knocked on the door and said, "There's a young lady here to see you, Father. I think it's about a sick call."

"Did she ask for me especially?" he said in a deep but slightly cracked voice.

"Indeed she did, Father. She wanted Father Macdowell and nobody else."

So he went out to the waiting room, where a girl about thirty years of age, with fine brown eyes, fine cheek bones, and rather square shoulders, was sitting daubing her eyes with a handkerchief. She was wearing a dark coat with a gray wolf collar. "Good evening, Father," she said. "My sister is sick. I wanted you to come and see her. We think she's dying."

"Be easy, child; what's the matter with her? Speak louder. I can hardly hear you."

"My sister's had pneumonia. The doctor's coming back to see her in an hour. I wanted you to anoint her, Father."

"I see, I see. But she's not lost yet. I'll not give her extreme unction now. That may not be necessary. I'll go with you and hear her confession."

"Father, I ought to let you know, maybe. Her husband won't want to let you see her. He's not a Catholic, and my sister hasn't been to church in a long time."

"Oh, don't mind that. He'll let me see her," Father Macdowell said, and he left the room to put on his hat and coat.

2

When he returned, the girl explained that her name was Jane Stanhope, and her sister lived only a few blocks away. "We'll walk and you tell me about your sister," he said. He put his black hat square on the top of his head, and pieces of white hair stuck out awkwardly at the sides. They went to the avenue together.

The night was mild and clear. Miss Stanhope began to walk slowly, because Father Macdowell's rolling gait didn't get him along the street very quickly. He walked as if his feet hurt him, though he wore a pair of large, soft, specially constructed shapeless shoes. "Now, my child, you go ahead and tell me about your sister," he said, breathing with difficulty, yet giving the impression that nothing could have happened to the sister which would make him feel indignant.

There wasn't much to say, Miss Stanhope replied. Her sister had married John Williams two years ago, and he was a good, hard-working fellow, only he was very bigoted and hated all church people. "My family wouldn't have anything to do with Elsa after she married him, though I kept going to see her," she said. She was talking in a loud voice to Father Macdowell so he could hear her.

"Is she happy with her husband?"

"She's been very happy, Father. I must say that."

"Where is he now?"

"He was sitting beside her bed. I ran out because I thought he was going to cry. He said if I brought a priest near the place he'd break the priest's head."

"My goodness. Never mind, though. Does your sister want to see me?"

"She asked me to go and get a priest, but she doesn't want John to know she did it."

3

Turning into a side street, they stopped at the first apartment house, and the old priest followed Miss Stanhope up the stairs. His breath came with great difficulty. "Oh dear, I'm not getting any younger, not one day younger. It's a caution how a man's legs go back on him," he said. As Miss Stanhope rapped on the door, she looked pleadingly at the old priest, trying to ask him not to be offended at anything that might happen, but he was smiling and looking huge in the narrow hallway. He wiped his head with his handkerchief.

The door was opened by a young man in a white shirt with no collar, with a head of thick black wavy hair. At first he looked dazed, then his eyes got bright with excitement when he saw the priest, as though he were glad to see someone he could destroy with pent-up energy. "What do you mean, Jane?" he said. "I told you not to bring a priest around here. My wife doesn't want to see a priest."

"What's that you're saying, young man?"

"No one wants you here."

"Speak up. Don't be afraid. I'm a bit hard of hearing." Father Macdowell smiled rosily. John Williams was confused by the unexpected deafness in the priest, but he stood there, blocking the door with sullen resolution as if waiting for the priest to try to launch a curse at him.

"Speak to him, Father," Miss Stanhope said, but the priest didn't seem to hear her; he was still smiling as he pushed past the young man, saying, "I'll go in and sit down, if you don't mind, son. I'm here on God's errand, but I don't mind saying I'm all out of breath from climbing those stairs."

John was dreadfully uneasy to see he had been brushed aside, and he followed the priest into the apartment and said loudly, "I don't want you here."

Father Macdowell said, "Eh, eh?" Then he smiled sadly. "Don't be angry with me, son," he said. "I'm too old to try and be fierce and threatening." Looking around, he said, "Where's your wife?" and he started to walk along the hall, looking for the bedroom.

John followed him and took hold of his arm. "There's no sense in your wasting your time talking to my wife, do you hear?" he said angrily.

Miss Stanhope called out suddenly, "Don't be rude, John."

"It's he that's being rude. You mind your business," John said.

"For the love of God let me sit down a moment with her, anyway. I'm tired," the priest said.

"What do you want to say to her? Say it to me, why don't you?"

4

Then they both heard someone moan softly in the adjoining room, as if the sick woman had heard them. Father Macdowell, forgetting that the young man had hold of his arm, said, "I'll go in and see her for a moment, if you don't mind," and he began to open the door.

"You're not going to be alone with her, that's all," John said, following him into the bedroom.

Lying on the bed was a white-faced, fair girl, whose skin was so delicate that her cheek bones stood out sharply. She was feverish, but her eyes rolled toward the door, and she watched them coming in. Father Macdowell took off his coat, and as he mumbled to himself he looked around the room at the mauve-silk bed light and the light wallpaper with the tiny birds in flight. It looked like a little girl's room. "Good evening, Father," Mrs. Williams whispered. She looked scared. She didn't glance at her husband. The notion of dying had made her afraid. She loved her husband and wanted to die loving him, but she was afraid, and she looked up at the priest.

"You're going to get well, child," Father Macdowell said, smiling and patting her hand gently.

John, who was standing stiffly by the door, suddenly moved around the big priest, and he bent down over the bed and took his wife's hand and began to caress her forehead.

"Now if you don't mind, my son, I'll hear your wife's confession," the priest said.

"No, you won't, John said abruptly. "Her people didn't want her, and they left us together, and they're not going to separate us now. She's satisfied with me." He kept looking down at her face as if he could not bear to turn away.

Father Macdowell nodded his head up and down and sighed. "Poor boy," he said. "God bless you." Then he looked at Mrs. Williams, who had closed her eyes, and he saw a faint tear on her cheek. "Be sensible, my boy," he said. "You'll have to let me hear your wife's confession. Leave us alone awhile."

"I'm going to stay right here," John said, and he sat down on the end of the bed. He was working himself up and staring savagely at the priest. All of a sudden he noticed the tears on his wife's cheeks, and he muttered as though bewildered, "What's the matter, Elsa? What's the matter, darling? Are we bothering you? Just open your eyes and we'll go out of the room and leave you alone till the doctor comes." Then he turned and said to the priest, "I'm not going to leave you here with her, can't you see that? Why don't you go?"

"I could revile you, my son. I could threaten you; but I ask you, for the peace of your wife's soul, leave us alone." Father Macdowell spoke with patient tenderness. He looked very big and solid and immovable as he stood by the bed. "I liked your face as soon as I saw you," he said to John. "You're a good fellow."

John still held his wife's wrist, but he rubbed one hand through his thick hair and said angrily, "You don't get the point, sir. My wife and I were always left alone, and we merely want to be left alone now. Nothing is going to separate us. She's been content with me. I'm sorry, sir; you'll have to speak to her with me here, or you'll have to go."

"No, you'll have to go for a while," the priest said patiently.

5

Then Mrs. Williams moved her head on the pillow and said jerkily, "Pray for me, Father."

So the old priest knelt down by the bed, and with a sweet unruffled expression on his florid face he began to pray. At times his breath came with a whistling noise as though a rumbling were inside him, and at other times he sighed and was full of sorrow. He was praying that young Mrs. Williams might get better, and while he prayed he knew that her husband was more afraid of losing her to the Church than losing her to death.

All the time Father Macdowell was on his knees, with his heavy prayer book in his two hands, John kept staring at him. John couldn't understand the old priest's patience and tolerance. He wanted to quarrel with him, but he kept on watching the light from overhead shining on the one baby-pink bald spot on the smooth white head, and at last he burst out, "You don't understand, sir! We've been very happy together. Neither you nor her people came near her when she was in good health, so why should you bother her now? I don't want anything to separate us now; neither does she. She came with me. You see you'd be separating us, don't you?" He was trying to talk like a reasonable man who had no prejudices.

Father Macdowell got up clumsily. His knees hurt him, for the floor was hard. He said to Mrs. Williams in quite a loud voice, "Did you really intend to give up everything for this young fellow?" and he bent down close to her so he could hear.

"Yes, Father," she whispered.

"In Heaven's name, child, you couldn't have known what you were doing."

"We loved each other, Father. We've been very happy."

"All right. Supposing you were. What now? What about all eternity, child?"

"Oh, Father, I'm very sick and I'm afraid." She looked up to try to show him how scared she was, and how much she wanted him to give her peace.

He sighed and seemed distressed, and at last he said to John, "Were you married in the church?"

"No, we weren't. Look here, we're talking pretty loud and it upsets her."

"Ah, it's a crime that I'm hard of hearing, I know. Never mind, I'll go." Picking up his coat, he put it over his arm; then he sighed as if he were very tired, and he said, "I wonder if you'd just fetch me a glass of water. I'd thank you for it."

John hesitated, glancing at the tired old priest, who looked so pink and white and almost cherubic in his utter lack of guile.

"What's the matter?" Father Macdowell said.

John was ashamed of himself for appearing so sullen, so he said hastily, "Nothing's the matter. Just a moment. I won't be a moment." He hurried out of the room.

6

The old priest looked down at the floor and shook his head; and then, sighing and feeling uneasy, he bent over Mrs. Williams, with his good ear down to her, and he said, "I'll just ask you a few questions in a hurry, my child. You answer them quickly and I'll give you absolution." He made the sign of the cross over her and asked if she repented for having strayed from the Church, and if she had often been angry, and whether she had always been faithful, and if she had ever lied or stolen—all so casually and quickly as if it hadn't occurred to him that such a young woman could have serious sins. In the same breath he muttered, "Say a good act of contrition to yourself and that will be all, my dear." He had hardly taken a minute.

When John returned to the room with the glass of water in his hand, he saw the old priest making the sign of the cross. Father Macdowell went on praying without even looking up at John. When he had finished, he turned and said, "Oh, there you are. Thanks for the water. I needed it. Well, my boy, I'm sorry if I worried you."

John hardly said anything. He looked at his wife, who had closed her eyes, and he sat down on the end of the bed. He was too disappointed to speak.

Father Macdowell, who was expecting trouble said, "Don't be harsh, lad."

"I'm not harsh," he said mildly, looking up at the priest. "But you weren't quite fair. And it's as though she turned away from me at the last moment. I didn't think she needed you."

"God bless you, bless the both of you. She'll get better," Father Macdowell said. But he felt ill at ease as he put on his coat, and he couldn't look directly at John.

7

Going along the hall, he spoke to Miss Stanhope, who wanted to apologize for her brother-in-law's attitude. "I'm sorry if it was unpleasant for you, Father," she said.

"It wasn't unpleasant," he said. "I was glad to meet John. He's a fine fellow. It's a great pity he isn't a Catholic. I don't know as I played fair with him."

As he went down the stairs, puffing and sighing, he pondered the question of whether he had played fair with the young man. But by the time he reached the street he was rejoicing amiably to think he had so successfully ministered to one who had strayed from the faith and had called out to him at the last moment. Walking along with the rolling motion as if his feet hurt him, he muttered, "Of course they were happy as they were . . . in a worldly way. I wonder if I did come between them?"

He shuffled along, feeling very tired, but he couldn't help thinking, "What beauty there was to his staunch love for her!" Then he added quickly, "But it was just a pagan beauty, of course."

As he began to wonder about the nature of this beauty, for some reason he felt inexpressibly sad.

FINDING A STORY'S CENTER OF EMPHASIS

On one campus, written comments on "A Sick Call" were made by more than three hundred college students, both men and women, immediately after reading. These first quick responses were obviously influenced by beliefs about religion. Some Protestants, and a few readers who described themselves as skeptics, resented Father Macdowell and said that he was "dishonest" or "hypocritical." One self-styled agnostic said, "It is a pity that unhappiness has to be caused by mere matters of belief." Other readers, Protestant, Catholic, and Jewish, said that Father Macdowell was doing his duty as he saw it, and that the young husband would "get over" his disappointment.

The remarks quoted above show what can happen first when people read fiction which touches emotion or belief. These first quick responses, which might be called Phase 1 in the reading of some stories, may or may not be appropriate to the total content of a story or to the author's apparent intentions, just as first impressions of real people or problems may be accurate or inaccurate. One of the convenient things about reading is that we can respond freely and then think it over. All-out reactions to people and problems in real life can cause trouble, and they are sometimes hard to modify because of pride. Reading is safer than life, yet it too provides material for reflection, for seeing what is marginal and what is central in a human problem or human character.

IMMEDIATE AND DELAYED RESPONSES

Phase 2 in skilled reading may therefore include reflection, which often involves rereading. A good way to begin this process of reflection is to ask what the author emphasizes, what seem to be his attitudes toward the fictional persons and situations he presents as "real." Or we can ask the same question in another way: What does the author do with each of the story elements—action (including conflict and plot), characters, setting, words? It is apparent immediately that action and character will provide the main clues in "A Sick Call," since little depends on setting or environment in this story and since the "wording" reveals the author's attitudes only slightly.

Why should we indulge in deliberate reflection about a piece of reading? Simply because meanings will be missed if we don't. Why do we reflect about anything, rethink anything? To improve our grasp of ideas or problems, to refine our powers of observation and judgment. Therefore, some reflection about "A Sick Call" is in order.

First of all, the author gives most of his attention to Father Macdowell. The very title of the story names a duty of clergymen: to make emergency calls on the dangerously ill. The story begins with Father Macdowell and ends with him. At the beginning, in addition to details of a favorable kind, there is emphasis on Father Macdowell's reputation for tolerance. At the end, he even admits a doubt about his own action: "I don't know as I played fair with him." This is favorable characterization again: we find it more attractive in a person to admit a doubt or a fault than to brazen it out or conceal it. At the end, Father Macdowell recognizes the young man's integrity and love and indulges in a piece of self-reassurance that doesn't work very well: "But it was just a pagan beauty, of course. . . . As he began to wonder about the nature of this beauty, for some reason he felt inexpressibly sad."

So we have part of the answer to the question "What is emphasized?" It is Father Macdowell's story. Since he cannot be characterized in a vacuum, his character appears in action as he deals with a real and important problem. John's attitude is a reality, a determined purpose arising from a time when the young couple were all-sufficient for each other. The characterization of John is thus a means to an end. The end is (1) clear characterization of Father Macdowell, and (2) a quick but not superficial view of the ethical problem created by John's attitude and action.

As to the author's attitude, it is easy to recognize that this is not the kind of story in which an author takes sides, in the sense of approving one character to the limit and disapproving another. He presents Father Macdowell as sincere in his vocation, to the point of using an undeniable trick as a means to an end. (Who would respect a clergyman who would fail to help the sick and thus abandon a duty at a moment's notice?) The author further portrays Father Macdowell as honest with himself—up to that familiar human point at which most people will resist anything that seems to challenge a belief or a way of life. At this point Father Macdowell experiences a sadness he doesn't wholly understand. He has glimpsed, in John and the marriage, an apparently true value, the "nature" of which saddens him. This value seems independent of religion and apparently is not caused by religion. No wonder he feels sad, without quite understanding the reason. Like many another human being, he wants to believe that his action is "right." Thus the author respects Father Macdowell but nevertheless shows him as vulnerable, human.

The young man is presented with equal respect. Much of this favorable characterization is achieved through the mind of the priest. The suggestion is made, however, that John's admirable desire to be everything to his wife carries with it a preoccupation with self, an unwillingness to believe that his wife can possibly need anything he cannot offer. The wife's need to see a priest—whether John thinks it sensible or not—is presented as a reality which John is about to ignore. John and Father Macdowell are thus more alike than may at first appear. Each has a direction in life. Each is capable of overriding other values or principles as he persists in the direction chosen—Father Macdowell consciously, John unknowingly. Each will work hard to believe what he wants to believe. Each is capable of honesty when the facts have to be faced.

So the author presents both characters with respect. The moment we realize this fact, we see that it is a means to still another end: the author is dramatizing a truth of human experience—that any all-out devotion to a cause or a settled objective may finally force an individual to give up the objective or take some other action that in itself is far from desirable or admirable. This, in capsule form, is part of the history of most all-out causes and programs of action. If the author had tried to present one character as wholly "right" and the other as wholly "wrong," he would not have been able to emphasize this important fact of experience with the same effect, for the story would then present a battle between causes, with one cause "winning." To get the effect he wants, he presents both characters as persons whose steadiness of purpose forces them into awkward choices. The story is thus a far cry from inferior fiction with its wholly "right" and "wrong" characters and its problems that are "solved" so much more easily than are the genuine dilemmas of life. (The author is—deliberately?—vague about the degree of the wife's danger, and the priest makes no preparation to give the regular service for the dying. These may be signs of a careless "tolerance" or optimism, a note which is struck at the beginning of the story. Father Macdowell is a vulnerable human being who comforts a sick woman.)

GETTING OFF THE TRACK It was apparent, in the study of readers' responses we referred to earlier, that many readers did not see the central meanings of the story under discussion because emotions got in the way. Those who said that John would eventually get over his disappointment were not even talking about the story before them; they were writing one of their own, in their own minds, with a happier ending. Those who used the story as "proof" of fixed personal ideas about religion were not reading what is there either, for the author of this story could hold any religious point of view we might care to name and still say exactly what he says—if he were sufficiently observant. The story is not an argument about religion. It is a representation of a common and important human problem—or, rather, of several problems. The story happens to deal with religion, but the same major ethical problems—ends-means, self-absorption, possessiveness—occur in many other situations, with similar human reactions. These problems, these human dilemmas, are the center of emphasis.

It seems desirable to make an effort to see what an author is trying to do. Otherwise, we use a story merely as a stimulus to call up our own familiar ideas, and we never meet a new idea.

Implied Meanings in Fiction It is relatively easy to read and enjoy a story like "Two Soldiers," where action and humor carry the reader along while other effects are achieved in the realm of characterization and deeper feeling. Much good fiction is fully as easy.

"A Sick Call" is slightly more difficult, for reasons other than the fact, already shown, that readers can be deceived by their emotions into misinterpretation. The reader of "A Sick Call" is in the position of receiving various bits of information which finally form a conclusion. We read such a story for implied meanings rather than for meanings stated directly and literally. This problem nearly always puzzles the reader meeting it for the first time, though a sensitive reader would notice that the author's attitude toward Father Mac-

dowell is suggested within fifty to a hundred words of the opening of the story. The following questions occur to many readers.

1. *Why don't authors come right out and say what they mean? Why convey meaning in such an indirect way?*

These are natural questions. They express genuine puzzlement and perhaps a certain amount of resentment of the author's method. But both questions rest on a misunderstanding of human communication, a failure to realize that we all pick implied meanings out of experience every day of our lives. Real people seldom describe themselves as honest or dishonest, as saints, sinners, or hypocrites. They reveal such things by what they say and do, indirectly. Some authors want as much "reality" as they can get and so do not want to insert morals or state meanings in literal terms. When we read such authors, we interpret what their characters say and do, just as we interpret real events. There is nothing unnatural about the process.

The indirect, dramatic method of writing a story is actually a compliment to the reader, who is assumed to be as good an observer when he reads as when he notes the behavior of people he knows. One reader remarked that he liked Hemingway's fiction because "he isn't always telling me what to think; he presents the characters and lets me draw my own conclusions." Strictly speaking, authors who use the indirect, dramatic method only seem not to guide the reader, while actually employing many techniques to convey attitude and emphasis. Authors will always want to communicate their judgments, but outright moralizing in the manner of the nineteenth century is out of fashion today and is thus relatively ineffective with many readers.

Finally, there are some meanings which cannot be stated directly, and certain other meanings lose force when stated directly. If the author of "Two Soldiers" had said, at every opportunity, "These are fine boys; I admire these boys," he would have insulted the reader, lessened the force of the story, and not really conveyed his attitudes. The experience of reading fiction is not that of reading generalizations or lectures or sermons. It is, rather, an experience during which a good reader will feel the impact of characters, action, setting, and words, and will grasp essential meanings. (See the comments on symbolism, pp. 79-84).

2. *Do I have to make a time-consuming analysis every time I read good fiction?*

The answer is No, but the inexperienced reader may easily believe it is surely Yes.

First, much good fiction is not as difficult as the question assumes.

Second, the problem is simply that of developing a new reading habit—the habit, or skill, of noticing implied meanings, including the implications of action and event. This skill develops quickly once the problem is recognized. A reader who will give sharp attention to detail in just a few stories will soon find that he begins to notice much more with little or no special effort. It is mainly a matter of realizing that the author is using details of speech, description, or action to suggest *meanings*.

The person who learns to be more aware of implied meanings will develop a power that is useful quite apart from reading. The ability to understand implications is valuable in all verbal communication except at the simplest and most literal level. This ability is used in all first-class observation of human character and action, for actions have meanings and implications, whether reported in fiction or observed in life. The person who is steadily unaware of the implications of what he sees, hears, says, and does is the person who "can't take a hint," the person who lives in a naïve, over-simple world of literal meaning. We can of course observe people and events in a crude manner, without reflection or insight, as the history of human error proves. But we cannot read first-class literature skillfully without using our full human powers.

"EASY" AND "DIFFICULT" READING

There is still another interference with effective reading which you may want to consider. It is caused by wishes that lie deep in human nature and affect our choice of what we read. These well-concealed wishes often stem from erroneous ideas familiar to everyone. Here is one such idea:

■ *All pleasure must be easy; if it isn't easy, it can't be pleasure.*

This is well-loved and cherished nonsense. All major forms of personal achievement are difficult in some way (self-knowledge, for example), but they produce special satisfactions or "pleasures" as a result, often as a by-product. "Pleasure" in reading some fiction can obviously mean pure escape from thought or knowledge of any kind. But it can also mean a sounder view of experience, a cure for provinciality or stereotyped thought. This second kind of "pleasure" isn't always "easy," but it is infinitely more valuable.

A second idea, equally inaccurate, is urged sometimes by those who like to regard themselves as "practical" people with no time for nonsense:

■ *The purpose of literature is to provide pleasure for the lighter hours. It is one of life's decorations or frills, with no practical value.*

Entertainment and easy pleasure are indeed obtained from some very good literature, with such definite effects on the way we feel that these effects are valuable in a real sense. But to classify literature as "mere" entertainment is to reveal something like an absolute lack of knowledge—if the idea is stated seriously. The idea is not often meant seriously. It is just one of those notions we wouldn't think of trying to defend, because we know it can't be done. We are determined nevertheless to use the idea, for the "mere entertainment, no practical value" line of thought conceals something—a personal unwillingness to use mind or emotion for exploration and discovery, especially self-discovery. The results might be disturbing.

The fear of being disturbed is revealed in a third idea, also taking the form of a judgment about "practicality":

■ Serious literature is too serious! Problems are always being presented that stir people up. Authors are always writing about trouble, and we have enough trouble anyway.

This judgment is a far cry from the notion that literature is "merely" a decoration or a frill of living. But the three ideas taken together make a convenient excuse for avoiding any reading more meaningful than the latest commercial story. It is tempting and natural to use one or more of these excuses when we think about reading. If there is one desire common to people in their reflective moments, it is the desire for a simple, neat view of life. We like to believe that existence is simple rather than complex, and that "answers" are easy. Good literature, taken as a whole, will not support so naïve a view and is bound to disturb the reader who insists on simple views as his equipment for living.

But in avoiding serious literature, we overlook the fact that it offers its own kind of reassurance, as was indicated in the discussion of "Two Soldiers." It doesn't always stir people up; frequently it consoles without falsifying problems. Frequently it increases our respect for the potential of other men and women, and thus our respect for ourselves. Equally important, good literature presents attitudes, choices, and decisions that men have found useful in their efforts to live happily—or with courage and dignity—in the real world.

Everyone's life contains problems, of course. But the "practical" man overlooks the other fact that pretending a problem doesn't exist is not a solution. Good authors do not all have ready-made philosophies to offer, yet they can provide the reader with just the insight he may need into causes, just the attitude he may need as a source of balance, a preparation against surprise, a cure for over-simple views. Inferior literature is the only place in the world where problems are "solved" quickly, easily, and forever. In a sense, the reading we do is somewhat like fishing. Why fish in poor water?

It is true that an individual can stand only so much "reality," only so much thought about problems. Everyone has his own private stopping point. Our purpose in talking about the desire not to know, not to look, and the wishful logic that results, is to describe the nature of the choice every person makes when he decides what to read or not read, and to suggest that good literature is neither so difficult nor so impractical as wishful thinking may say it is. The choice usually lies not between easy pleasure and no pleasure at all but between dreaming and thinking, between a dangerously unreal view of human affairs and a beginning of knowledge.

Third-Person Narrative   Stories told from a third-person point of view, such as "A Sick Call," may include several technical variations, each of which has its own advantages: third-person narrative with unity of focus, third-person *narrative with* shifting focus, *third-person narrative with* author's comment, *third-person narrative with "objective" view of persons and events, and combinations of these variations.*

UNITY OF FOCUS Unity of focus *means that everything in the story is viewed through the senses, mind, and emotion of one character, who is spoken of by the author in the third person (He or she saw, did, said, thought, felt, remembered, and so on). This rather strict method is close in some of its effects to the second-by-second narration in the first person which we mentioned on page 39, for events reported in this way seem real and immediate. But there are some things a first-person narrator probably would not talk about which seem quite natural if reported as occurring in the mind of a character presented in the third person. Some detail of sensation and thought appears natural in the third person which would not be natural in conversation. Much detail presented in the third person would seem labored or dull in the first person, especially stream-of-consciousness detail. Thus the third-person point of view, with unity of focus, is a major tool for presenting the reality of thought, observation, feeling—man's inner life.*

SHIFT OF FOCUS Shift of focus *means that events are reported as if seen first by one character and then by another. Here the author assumes omniscience—that is, full knowledge of what goes on in the mind and experience of each character. This method is useful for showing the grounds of human difference—the dramatic fact that events may not be understood or valued in the same way by different persons. Differences between people can be presented in other ways, of course, but a shift of focus often has special power in causing the reader to share the inner experiences of contrasting characters. Though the focus in "A Sick Call" is mainly that of the mind of Father Macdowell, it does shift briefly to the mind of the young husband.*

AUTHOR'S COMMENT Author's comment, *often used in third-person stories, is used in two forms in "A Sick Call." Early in the story we are told:*

> He was a huge old priest, white-headed except for a shiny baby-pink bald spot on the top of his head . . . nothing seemed to shock or excite him or make him really angry, and he was even tender with those who thought they were most guilty.

This is the author speaking—describing, giving information directly. If he describes things which can be known or seen by some character in the story as well as by the author, we get a sort of borderline point of view which could be the author's or the character's, or both. The final part of the author's comment just cited has another characteristic. It is summary narrative, summarizing the priest's nature and actions over a period of time, months or years ("nothing seemed to shock or excite him . . .").

Author's comment of a third kind—more overt and noticeable—occurs when the author, in his own person, takes time out from the story to reflect, philosophize, or moralize. This device was much more popular in the nineteenth century—in the novels of Charles Dickens, for example—than it is now, and it does not occur in "A Sick Call."

OBJECTIVE POINT OF VIEW
The so-called objective point of view in fiction means that actions, events, speech, and so forth are reported as if seen not by any character in the story but by an unnamed observer outside the story. Nothing is said of what goes on in the mind or feeling of any character. The unnamed observer is of course the author, who reports events much as he might see them acted out on a stage, or in the street. The author who uses this technique in its strictest form must rely on the behavior of the characters to suggest his central meanings, must never report their inner thoughts or feelings, and must avoid author's comment. If he uses the technique strictly, he must be especially careful with description—careful, that is, not to use "loaded" or connotative words. A pure and consistent objective technique, however, is probably nonexistent in fiction.

It is important to realize that the term "objective point of view" as applied to fiction refers only to a particular way of telling a story. It does not mean that the author is trying to conceal his attitudes or be truly dispassionate, for value judgments are a major ingredient in fiction. Some authors—James Joyce, for example—have tried on occasion to be objective in attitude as well as in technique and have found it impossible, for judgments are revealed by the very materials selected for a story, if in no other way. The important point for the reader is that a relatively objective story, in the technical sense, is often a tool for conveying a sense of implacable, relentless process, as in many stories by Hemingway.

Obviously, the major points of view in story-telling mentioned here are subject to adaptations and combinations by individual authors. What we have been saying about point of view means simply that an author can communicate his meanings or attitudes in several ways, at several levels, ranging from the dramatic to the deliberately expository. The experienced reader notices the way a story is told and makes the most of it, realizing that each method has its own limitations and advantages.

MAJOR EFFECTS OF READING FICTION

In discussing strategies for readers, above, we emphasized some psychological barriers to effective reading, particularly certain assumptions and misunderstandings that can interfere. Now we turn directly to major effects that occur as people read fiction.

READING AS AN EXPERIENCE INVOLVING EMOTION

The reading of fiction is, first of all, an experience which involves the reader's capacities in several ways. A frequent part of this experience is a degree of emotional involvement. The reaction to "A Sick Call" is, as we have shown, partly an emotional response to labels ("priest," "young husband," "young wife") and to a problem which stirs religious allegiances in some readers. Emotional involvement in "Two Soldiers" and "Tell Me How Long the Train's Been Gone" includes a degree of sympathy and respect for the two brothers—indeed, for the family.

But merely classifying these emotional results as either "identification" or "empathy" helps little, for those terms conceal subtleties: the causes and nature of the emotional results vary widely. Often the most accurate way of describing what happens when we read certain stories is to say that, at certain levels, we "take sides" in a conflict, as many readers of "A Sick Call" did. In that story the author did not take sides but regarded both main characters with sympathy. The reader had to discover that for himself, and such a discovery is often an element in the art of reading. In some other stories, the author does take sides, in the sense of disposing his respect or sympathy in one direction rather than another. But the fundamental fact is that reading is an experience which often involves the reader's emotions and that readers frequently describe such an experience as pleasurable.

PSYCHOLOGY OF ART

Emotion aroused directly in a life situation is not always pleasurable —fear, for example. Emotion aroused by a work of art usually is pleasurable. Why this should be so is a question which theorists from the ancient Greeks forward have tried to answer—but there is no doubt whatever that it is so. A reader is partly an observer and partly—at a safe distance—a participant, vicariously. A story itself is not, of course, the events it represents. As Kenneth Burke has said, it is symbolic action, but it can stir emotion. (Some theorists have said that the pleasure arises from the fact of imitation, the medium of art being used to imitate human experience.)

SENTIMENTALITY AND STEREOTYPING

Occasionally a writer tries to make his story carry more emotion than we feel is appropriate. We call his story a "tear-jerker" and accuse the writer of sentimentality. We mean that he asks for a stronger response than the story, as presented, seems to justify. This may mean that he lacks art—skill in handling his materials, in conveying what they mean to him. It may be that he is confused, or doesn't know his subject intimately, or is insincere. Any one of these causes can produce writing which we call "unconvincing," and this leads to the charge of sentimentality, for we cannot take the emotion seriously if the story as a whole is unconvincing.

The emotion evoked by the younger brother in "Two Soldiers" is an example. As a character with courage and purpose who is young and naïve, he could have been presented in a general, stereotyped manner—and failed to move the experienced reader. The treatment he is given, on the other hand, is specific—in the detail of the familiar environment, in the attitudes of all the characters, in the impact of the city, and especially in the thoughts, feelings, actions, and language of the boy. No character in "A Sick Call" is presented in as complete or individual a way, and the feeling aroused is of a different kind, somewhat closer to one's reaction to a stereotyped presentation. (And yet "A Sick Call" is so condensed, so economicai in its use of detail, that it is a distinct achievement, and Father Macdowell is almost an individual.)

Inferior fiction does not differ from better fiction in the general subjects or situations presented. Some of the worst stories and novels ever written deal with "universal" subjects like father-love, mother-love, and just plain "love," as we all know. Inexperienced readers will respond to stereotyped fiction that leaves other readers cold, just as the inexperienced are less acute in sizing up people and events in real life. Our response to anything outside us—a book, another person, a problem, an idea—depends on the nature of that thing and, also, on our own experience and maturity. Probably the best way for a reader to learn the differences between first-rate and mediocre fiction is to refine his judgments through wide reading and specific comparisons of the effects achieved and the way they are achieved. If we know what effects are typical, such as the effects being described here, we read more alertly.

To summarize: The reading of fiction is an experience that can involve emotion, and we read for this effect among others. When emotion is touched, a skillful reader can keep an eye on himself. He can learn the nature of his own reactions, his emotional allegiances, his judgments. Emotional self-knowledge is gained only through experiences which do involve emotion. Reading is one such experience.

CURIOSITY AND "CARING" IN READING

Curiosity about "what will happen next" in a story or novel is probably the commonest effect of reading fiction—at the time of reading. Even the thinnest story makes this appeal in some degree. We may think we know how a story will end, yet we read on to make sure. We may be sure that a character will solve his problem, but we read on to find out how. We know in advance, for example, that the younger boy in "Two Soldiers" will not be permitted to join the Army. But curiosity remains as to how he will be persuaded to go home, and there is additional curiosity as to how he will feel, how he will take the final No, the realized separation from his brother. This kind of interest on the reader's part approaches a "caring" about the fictional character. It arises usually when the story has led us to know the character as an individual in the same second-by-second way we know ourselves and other real people. Such an interest, once aroused, causes us to make demands on the story and on the author. The author of "Two Soldiers" must do something to satisfy our interest in the younger brother's final state of mind and feeling, or the story will lack an element which belongs in it organically, functionally, a lack which would make the reader feel cheated.

When we say that a story is, as the phrase goes, "a work of art," we mean partly this functional, organic completeness, for a genuine work of art—by the commonest definition—contains everything it needs to be complete, with nothing extra, nothing unrelated or out of proportion. A good writer provides, in a way, a complete mental and emotional journey for the reader. As T. S. Eliot has said, we go "into and out of" the situation or problem raised in a story or through its characters. If "Two Soldiers" had ended when the older brother said, "You must go home. . . . I am depending on you to look after my ten acres," it would have been incomplete functionally and therefore artistically.

A skilled reader will notice his own curiosity and the forms it takes, especially when some degree of "caring" is attached to action or characters. He knows that the arousal of curiosity about what will happen next is the author's bait to keep the reader's attention while deeper understandings of human character or ideas or problems begin to take shape. A deliberate comparison of the function of curiosity and "caring" in two or more stories will increase your alertness and enjoyment, through increasing your knowledge of what is possible and valuable in fiction.

FICTION AS A SOURCE OF IDEAS AND BELIEFS

A reader of fiction receives an as if picture of "reality," especially in fiction written in the so-called realistic mode. For example, from "Two Soldiers" we receive a picture of the external environment in which the boys have grown up, and of the mental environment—attitudes of father and mother, their views of past history as it has touched them, attitudes toward work, toward the new war, toward the land. We receive also a picture of the inner working of the younger brother's mind, and we learn what the older brother feels through what he says and does. All such elements constitute the basic "reality" in a work of fiction. This reality is "given," assumed for the purposes of the story. We read as if all the details are real and correct, ranging all the way from the fact that the family burns wood to major events in the younger brother's mind.

On the basis of the "reality" in a story we form general beliefs, justified or not: there are patriotic people in the Deep South; mothers can teach their children self-respect ("your blood is good as any blood anywhere, and don't you never forget it"); Hitler, who thought us decadent in 1943, could have learned something to his profit from this story; and so on. Social-problem novels often convey general beliefs about fact, such as the idea that bad conditions in one segment of society will cause eventual harm to people living in "better" segments of society. Such beliefs about fact arise from the highly detailed "reality" in some novels.

FICTION AS A SOURCE OF VALUE JUDGMENTS

In addition to the as if or symbolic picture of "reality" in fiction, we also receive a view of human values. These values are "realities" too, in fiction and in life, in the sense that people believe in them and live by them. In addition to showing the reader of "Two Soldiers" that the older brother is patriotic ("I jest ain't going to put up with no folks treating the Unity States that way") or that the brothers both have courage, the story clearly implies value judgments: patriotism is a good and admirable thing; courage is to be respected. These are judgments as to what should be, what is good or bad, desirable or undesirable. The value picture grows when the father states his characteristic view of military service, and the mother hers ("They could take the country and keep the country, so long as they never bothered me and mine").

To understand fiction—or indeed much human communication—it is essential to recognize the dual "content" which has just been described:

- There is in every story an as if picture of environment, characters, and events—suited to the purposes of the story. There is also an indication of what the fictional characters desire or value, together with the qualities of character and the attitudes that underlie their efforts. An attitude or a trait of character is as clearly a "fact," a force, as is any purely external detail.

- A corresponding double effect occurs as we read. We may form beliefs or develop feelings on the basis of the as if "reality" presented in the story. We react to signs of the author's valuations—approvals and disapprovals. Such elements come close to being what the author wants to "say," if we wish to think in such terms.

Any fragment of daily experience shows us that events or "facts" are uninteresting and neutral, just as in fiction, except as human beings attach value to them. A human being is a valuing being, with capacity for infinite variety in judgment. Good literature is the most complete and forceful record of this human capacity. Though the report of external "fact" which appears in fiction is often important and influential, the record it provides of man's values—with his conflicts and choices—is more important and more abiding.

This basic duality of fiction—that it presents both events and a valuing of events—bears on what has been called the reader's "emotional involvement." If we admire or dislike a fictional character, it is largely because he represents values of which we approve or disapprove; we may even disapprove of his actions but value him, a reaction which occurs often enough in daily life. Thus the values emphasized in a story through its characters are often the basic and strongest source of emotional appeal. Responses at this level are much more lasting than are the momentary stirrings of curiosity.

Values do not affect us much, however, when they are merely stated in abstract language. They have to be presented in dramatic, concrete form to be moving—and this is precisely what the detailed "reality" in fiction does. A word like "justice" is relatively uninteresting and unexciting in the abstract. But in the context of a historical situation like the American Revolution, or the human action in a novel, such an idea can be felt so powerfully as to change the lives or purposes of real people. The philosopher Plato knew this. He so feared the influence of "wrong" ideas powerfully presented, especially ideas of value, that he would have outlawed poetry in his ideal Republic.

QUALITIES OF BETTER FICTION *The fact that fiction is written at many levels of quality and for purposes ranging from mere entertainment to an attempt to present deeply held values places a genuine burden on the reader who wishes to develop his powers of discrimination. It has already been suggested that one difference between inferior and better fiction may lie in the degree to which the characters are individualized, or in the avoidance of stereotypes which represent experience crudely. It has also been suggested that the same general problems or types of character may appear in fiction at any level. The differences, then, in addition to those already mentioned, might best be understood in three ways:*

1. *What seem to be the writer's general motives—that is, the reasons why he writes at all? Is he a commercialist, or is he trying seriously to "say something"? A writer can have both motives—Shakespeare did, for example—and our judgment then must rest on further questions.*

2. *How specific and complex are the handling of detail and the dramatization of ideas, problems, attitudes, values?*

3. *What degree of skill, of artistry, is attained—including power or subtlety in the use of language?*

WRITERS' PURPOSES *These questions are related. A high degree of artistry is frequently evidence that the writer is serious in what he attempts and is not merely a commercialist; but artistry in itself is no guarantee that the writer will have important meanings to convey. Nor does relative lack of attention to art necessarily indicate absence of serious purpose. Some of the greatest writers, Tolstoy for example, have not been heavily occupied with the art of what they produced. Too, it is impossible in many instances to distinguish between what is said (the content) and the way it is said (the form). General, abstract ideas may indeed be picked out of most stories, but the author's full grasp of an idea—and thus the reader's—is inseparable from the form in which the idea is conveyed: the total story or novel with all its detail. For one thing, the form controls the order in which a reader will experience and understand what the author is presenting.*

As to the writer's motives, we must understand that the general reason why a man writes at all is not the same as his purpose or intention in a particular piece of writing, which we infer mainly from the writing itself. Most writers, of course, need to make enough money, in some way, for food and shelter. But motives other than the commercial are always involved in the best writing. There is, for example, the desire for achievement. There is the desire to convey with force that which the writer holds to be true or valuable. There is the desire to use a talent, to do perfectly the thing one's powers enable him to try. A person with unusual ability is almost compelled to use it in order to complete himself, to be a whole person. That a purely commercial motive is insufficient for production of the finest art or the best scientific research any reader can prove for himself by observing people of genuine achievement, whether in the arts or in the sciences.

Fiction supplies, then, a vast array of pictures of "reality" and of ideas and beliefs on which we use our minds and emotions. Some of these pictures are so incomplete, so hastily contrived, as to be useless or even dangerous. Others constitute the most accurate and subtle art that serious and gifted men and women can produce. We cannot prevent or stop the influence of the arts—popular or otherwise—unless we live in caves and agree not to draw on the walls or tell each other stories. What we can do is develop awareness as we read, including awareness of what it means to say, "This is a work of art." A wise man once said that a major result of education is the ability to recognize excellence when we see it.

FICTION AS ART

The art, the skill, of a story is not the first thing most people think of as a source of pleasure in fiction, yet the art is what causes the more obvious effects, such as interest in action, suspense, characters, humor, even ideas and problems. When a reader says that a story or novel has power, he is usually making an indirect comment on the art or skill of the author. Such a reader, quite soundly, views the art of the thing as a means to various ends. He does not regard art as a special source of pleasure, and yet it is, or can be. As experience grows, most readers begin to see that major effects in the realm of emotion or idea or "reality" are indeed inseparable from the writer's powers as an artist, and they begin to develop this final form of appreciation and knowledge.

STORY ELEMENTS AND THEIR INTERRELA- TIONSHIPS

A writer of fiction has a limited number of devices or story elements to work with:

- *The action, including what are called "plot" and "conflict."*

- *One or more fictional characters—with all that any one of them is represented as thinking, saying, feeling, doing, which returns us to the idea of action.*

- *The setting, or environment.*

- *Words—the language, through which all the foregoing is presented; or the language used directly for remarks or comments by the author, speaking in his own person and not through the dramatic action. Words are the basic medium.*

The writer uses these story elements, and only these, including what he can manage to suggest through them, to produce such effects as the following, singly and in combination:

- *The reader sees an as if picture of "reality" at some level of detail—and on this picture a number of other effects depend.*

- *The reader is curious—mainly about what will happen, and why and how; sometimes about the nature of a problem, a phase of experience, the meaning of an idea.*

- *He or she is moved emotionally, from causes which have been indicated, especially by the values dramatized.*

- *The reader is at times amused.*

- *He understands—and often shares—a belief about fact or a value judgment (including moral and ethical judgments).*

- *He is informed, especially as to the potentialities of human behavior, choices, values.*

- *He receives aesthetic satisfaction.*

The art of fiction, like the other arts, is complex. Complexity can arise from the fact that the author may intend only one major effect but achieve it through other effects which serve as means to the main end. The humor in "Two Soldiers" is not the main effect in that story, but it is nevertheless an effect, which the author achieves deliberately as an aid in producing still other effects. A specific problem of reading is therefore to discover what the various effects of a story or novel are and to see clearly their relationship. The act of noticing the various effects intended or attempted leads to criticism of a practical kind. "Two Soldiers," for example, carries a stronger appeal to both humor and curiosity in the last half or two-thirds. This raises the question of whether the first third is needed, and this in turn raises the further question of what is achieved in the early pages of the story. As soon as we ask this question, we become aware of certain facts: (1) The two brothers and their relationship are made very real in the quiet opening of the story. (2) The mother's attitude is made real and believable, with the result that we can believe in the older brother's decision as both difficult and serious. (3) The customary way of life is made clear. (4) The main narrative question is stated. Without these elements, the remainder of the story would lose much of the force it finally develops. Thinking into a story in this manner brings a clearer appreciation of the interrelationships the author has achieved, the structure.

The elements in a story—action or plot, character, setting, words—are related and interdependent just as the effects are, for these elements are the tools the author uses in producing the various related effects. For example, even a bare outline of action can convey meaning. A man from a "poor" area kills a man from a "good" area while robbing a house. This action in itself conveys the idea that bad conditions in one segment of society may harm the rest of society. But the bare record of action does little to create understanding or arouse feeling and judgment. The moment we add the "reality" of the characters involved, in such a way that the reader begins to "know" them as human beings, as individuals, in that moment other effects are achieved. It is much like the difference between hearing that an unidentified person has been hurt in an accident and hearing that someone we know has been hurt. The second report has an extra dimension, which involves "caring."

Each story element, therefore, has its own work to do, and each adds meaning to the others. Characterization amounts to little without action, and action is made more meaningful by characterization. Setting, or environment, is slightly different. It may be used heavily for special purposes, or lightly as minimum information, minimum "reality."

CONFLICT AND PLOT
In thinking about "action," however, it is necessary to realize that overt or external action is only one kind; subjective action—events in the mind—often has vital importance. As parts of the larger concept "action," the words "conflict" and "plot" now deserve brief attention.

We can identify the "conflict" in a story by asking one question: What is opposed to what in this story? Two characters may be in opposition, as in "A Sick Call." There may be conflict in a character's mind, or he may be in conflict with something outside himself, such as the social judgment that very young boys are not permitted to join the Army. There may be conflict with some phase of external nature, or a conflict of ideas. Perhaps the most functional way of thinking about conflct is to ask what values are in opposition. If a reader thinks that he can represent a story fairly by naming the subject of the conflict, or by stating an especially prominent idea, he will probably state what is often called the "theme" of the story. For example, we may say that the theme of "A Sick Call" is the problem of ethical judgment, or of ends and means, or of human unawareness of motives. The trouble with stating the so-called theme of a story is that what we finally get is often rather barren, an oversimplification which is usually abstract and uninteresting compared with the much richer experience of the story itself.

In the modern period many "slice-of-life" stories have been written which seem to contain no very definite conflict; they seem to be just series of incidents, like sequences of events in daily life. These stories are written in such a way because the authors believe that the result is more like life, more "real." If we search a "slice-of-life" story carefully enough, however, we will usually find that values of some kind are in conflict.

"Plot" is different from "conflict." The plot of a story is its plan, which includes the development of the conflict or the development of any series of events supposed to carry meaning. We may know that the major conflict in "Two Soldiers" is that of the younger brother's desire versus a social rule, but the plot consists of all the steps, small and large, which are needed to show the reality and meaning of the major conflict. Plot thus includes all the separate events of the story, arranged in order. Choice of events for major and minor emphasis is an element in the art the writer employs.

(Some events in certain stories or plays are merely summarized; others are developed in detail.)

What has been said about story elements and the various effects they produce has important applications to skillful reading. Skillful reading of a story can be approached in at least two ways:

1. *Knowing already what the major effects can be, a reader can watch for these effects and try to be more and more aware of their relationships. Increased satisfaction in reading is usually the result.*

2. *Knowing what the essential story elements are, he can ask what elements the author depends on in a story, including a possible dependence on the suggestive power of words. He can ask what the implications of characters and action are. Increased accuracy in seeing meanings is usually the result. A good way to begin is to try to retell a story by relating the action alone. It will usually become apparent that this is not the "whole" story, or even the real story. Attention is thus drawn to other meanings.*

ART AS AN ORDERING OF EXPERIENCE

Enjoyment of the art of a story is partly a pleasure in the fine and effective working together of all elements, from language to action. It is the same pleasure we receive from an expert, near-perfect performance of any kind. It is partly an appreciation of technique, as we slowly learn more about technique. Finally, this enjoyment arises because experience viewed through a work of literary art is ordered experience. Everything in the story can be seen in relation to everything else, and it all makes its own kind of sense. Life itself, the daily drag of people and events, does not seem as orderly, for it contains distractions, puzzles, elements that seem not to fit, connections and causalities that are obscure. The artist imposes his own kind of order on the raw materials of experience. He shows parts of experience in relation to one another, and reveals all sorts of connections and meanings. By so doing, he deeply influences our views of life. A work of art is thus an image or symbol of completeness, with no loose ends, no functionless parts or details, with things of importance highlighted. We like this effect, sometimes without quite knowing why, for we deeply prefer order to disorder, "point" to pointlessness. Science provides a somewhat similar satisfaction by reporting the regular, orderly causalties in nature, in its own way and for its own purposes. The great world religions assert pattern and purpose in life, thus ordering experience in their own way. These three—art, science, religion—are indeed major sources of order and purpose in man's life and thought.

The literary artist, however, is not the representative of any fixed system. He speaks as an individual, ordering experience in his own way, coming to terms with phases of experience that are important to him. If he does this with sufficient insight and skill, other people find his report valuable. The thing he does with special power is to dramatize those human values which are forces in all our lives, sources of purpose and order and continuity.

FURTHER STRATEGIES
IN READING

Some of the major techniques of fiction and elements in fiction have now been defined through examples. It has become clear that identifying a general technique, although necessary, is only a beginning in seeing the precise ways in which a given author achieves his results—or in seeing what the results are in terms of meanings, feelings, ideas, and reader involvements of many kinds. A closer look is necessary. It has become clear also that techniques and meanings are at times difficult to separate, for good fiction is an art in which various ingredients work together and are separable mainly for purposes of discussion. In addition to all the foregoing, certain general misunderstandings have now been described that can hamper any reader and cause loss of meaning.

SATIRIC HUMOR *The next story, "File and Forget" by James Thurber, reveals an attitude of mind profoundly different from the author-attitudes we observed earlier. For one thing—a big thing—there is in "File and Forget" a satiric humor. This humor arises partly from the absurdities reported in the story, but it issues in a more profound way from certain assumptions the author of "File and Forget" makes— or pretends to make—about himself. This author feels himself under attack by forces he can identify but not control. He can do nothing about it except write this story. He sees himself as bedeviled by the routines and errors of clerks, correspondents, subauthorities and top authorities, who apparently cannot read. He has written clear requests to them, but he can only conclude, desperately, that he has somehow lost communication with the human race, or that part of it which inhabits the publishing business. In order to express his despair, this author prints a series of letters that report a condition of uncaring illiteracy among his correspondents. This is a humor of helplessness. Who has not felt helpless in a similar way when he has tried to explain his reasonable desires to a remote and brief authority?*

*FILE AND FORGET

JAMES THURBER

I want to thank my secretary, Miss Ellen Bagley, for putting the following letters in order. I was not up to the task myself, for reasons that will, I think, become clear to the reader.

J. T.

WEST CORNWALL, CONN.
NOVEMBER 2, 1949

Miss Alma Winege,
The Charteriss Publishing Co.,
132 East What Street,
New York, N.Y.

DEAR MISS WINEGE:

Your letter of October 25th, which you sent to me in care of The Homestead, Hot Springs, Ark., has been forwarded to my home in West Cornwall, Conn., by The Homestead, Hot Springs, Va. As you know, Mrs. Thurber and I sometimes visit this Virginia resort, but we haven't been there for more than a year. Your company, in the great tradition of publishers, has sent so many letters to me at Hot Springs, Ark., that the postmaster there has simply taken to sending them on to the right address, or what would be the right address if I were there. I explained to Mr. Cluffman, and also to Miss Lexy, when I last called at your offices, that all mail was to be sent to me at West Cornwall until further notice. If and when I go to The Homestead, I will let you know in advance. Meanwhile, I suggest that you remove from your files all addresses of mine except the West Cornwall one. Another publishing firm recently sent a letter to me at 65 West 11th Street, an address I vacated in the summer of 1930. It would not come as a surprise to me if your firm, or some other publishers, wrote me in care of my mother at 568 Oak Street, Columbus, Ohio. I was thirteen years old when we lived there, back in 1908.

As for the contents of your letter of the 25th, I did not order thirty-six copies of Peggy Peckham's book, "Grandma Was a Nudist." I trust that you have not shipped these books to me in care of The Homestead, Hot Springs, Ark., or anywhere else.

Sincerely yours,
J. THURBER

P.S. Margaret Peckham, by the way, is not the author of this book. She is the distinguished New York psychiatrist whose "The Implications of Nudism" was published a couple of years ago. She never calls herself Peggy.

J. T.

WEST CORNWALL, CONN.
NOVEMBER 3, 1949

Miss Alma Winege,
The Charteriss Publishing Co.,
132 East What Street,
New York, N.Y.
DEAR MISS WINEGE:

In this morning's mail I received a card from the Grand Central branch of the New York Post Office informing me that a package of books had been delivered to me at 410 East 57th Street. The branch office is holding the package for further postage, which runs to a considerable amount. I am enclosing the notification card, since these must be the thirty-six copies of "Grandma Was a Nudist." I have not lived at 410 East 57th Street since the fall of 1944. Please see to it that this address is removed from your files, along with The Homestead address.

Whoever ordered those books, if anyone actually did, probably wonders where they are.

Sincerely yours,
J. THURBER

THE CHARTERISS PUBLISHING COMPANY
NEW YORK, N.Y.

NOVEMBER 5, 1949

Mr. James M. Thurber,
West Cornwall, Conn.
DEAR MR. THURBER:

I am dreadfully sorry about the mixup over Miss Peckham's book. We have been pretty much upset around here since the departure of Mr. Peterson and Mr. West, and several new girls came to us with the advent of Mr. Jordan. They have not yet got their "sea legs," I am afraid, but I still cannot understand from what file our shipping department got your address as 165 West 11th Street. I have removed the 57th Street address from the files and also the Arkansas address and I trust that we will not disturb your tranquillity further up there in Cornwall. It must be lovely this time of year in Virginia and I envy you and Mrs. Thurber. Have a lovely time at The Homestead.

Sincerely yours,
ALMA WINEGE

P.S. What you had to say about "Grandma" amused us all.

A. W.

COLUMBUS, OHIO
NOVEMBER 16, 1949

DEAR MR. THURBER:

I have decided to come right out with the little problem that was accidentally dumped in my lap yesterday. I hope you will forgive me for what happened, and perhaps you can suggest what I should do with the books. There are three dozen of them and, unfortunately, they arrived when my little son Donald was alone downstairs. By the time I found out about the books, he had torn off the wrappings and had built a cute little house out of them. I have placed them all on a shelf out of his reach while awaiting word as to where to send them. I presume I could ship them to you C.O.D. if I can get somebody to wrap them properly.

I heard from old Mrs. Winston next door that you and your family once lived here at 568 Oak Street. She remembers you and your brothers as cute little tykes who were very noisy and raised rabbits and guinea pigs. She says your mother was a wonderful cook. I am sorry about Donald opening the books and I hope you will forgive him.

Sincerely yours,
CLARA EDWARDS
(Mrs. J. C.)

WEST CORNWALL, CONN.
Mr. Leon Charteriss.   NOVEMBER 19, 1949
The Charteriss Publishing Co.,
132 East What Street,
New York, N.Y.
DEAR MR. CHARTERISS,

I am enclosing a letter from a Mrs. J. C. Edwards, of Columbus, Ohio, in the fervent hope that you will do something to stop this insane flux of books. I never ordered these books. I have not read "Grandma Was a Nudist." I do not intend to read it. I want something done to get these volumes off my trail and cut out of my consciousness.

I have written Miss Winege about the situation, but I am afraid to take it up with her again, because she might send them to me in care of the Department of Journalism at Ohio State University, where I was a student more than thirty years ago.

Sincerely yours,
J. THURBER

P.S. I never use my middle initial, but your firm seems to think it is "M." It is not.

J. T.

THE CHARTERISS PUBLISHING COMPANY
NEW YORK, N.Y.
Mr. James M. Thurber,   NOVEMBER 23, 1949
West Cornwall, Conn.
DEAR MR. THURBER:

Mr. Charteriss has flown to California on a business trip and will be gone for several weeks. His secretary has turned your letter of the 19th over to me. I have asked Mr. Cluffman to write to Miss Clara Edwards in Columbus and arrange for the reshipment of the thirty-six copies of "Grandma Was a Nudist."

I find, in consulting the records, that you have three times ordered copies of your own book, "Thurber's Ark," to be shipped to you at West Cornwall, at the usual discount rate of forty er cent. I take it that hat you really wanted was thirty-six copies of your own book and they are being sent out to you today with our regrets for the discomfort we have caused you. I hope you will be a little patient with us during this so trying period of reorganization.

Cordially yours,

JEANNETTE GAINES

Stock Order Dept.

P.S. You will be happy to know that we have traced down the gentleman who ordered those copies of "Grandma."

WEST CORNWALL, CONN.

NOVEMBER 25, 1949

Mr. Henry Johnson,
The Charteriss Pub. Co.,
New York, N.Y.

DEAR HARRY:

Since the reorganization at Charteriss, I have the forlorn and depressing feeling that I no longer know anybody down there except you. I know that this immediate problem of mine is not in your field, but I turn to you as a last resource. What I want, or rather what I don't want, is simple enough, Harry. God knows it is simple.

I don't want any more copies of my book. I don't want any more copies of my book. I don't want any more copies of my book.

As ever,

JIM

P.S. It has just occurred to me that I haven't seen you for more than two years. Let's have a drink one of these days. I'll give you a ring the next time I'm in the city.

J. T.

THE CHARTERISS PUBLISHING COMPANY

NEW YORK, N.Y.

Mr. James Grover Thurber,   NOVEMBER 26, 1949
Cornwall, Conn.

DEAR JIM THURBER:

I haven't had the pleasure of meeting you since I had the great good luck to join forces with Charteriss, but I look forward to our meeting with a high heart. Please let me know the next time you are in the city, as I should like to wine and dine you and perhaps discuss the new book that I feel confident you have in you. If you don't want to talk shop, we can discuss the record of our mutual football team. You were at Northwestern some years ahead of my time, I believe, but I want you to know that they still talk about Jimmy Thurber out there.

Your letter to Harry Johnson has just come to my attention, and I regret to say that Harry is no longer with us. He went to Simon and Schuster in the summer of 1948. I want you to feel, however, that every single one of us here is your friend, willing and eager to drop everything to do your slightest bidding. All of us feel very deeply about your having turned against your book "Thurber's Ark." I note that in your present mood you have the feeling that you never want to see it again. Well, Jim, let me assure you that this is just a passing fancy, derived from a moment of depression. When you put in your last order for thirty-six copies, you must surely have had some definite use in mind for them, and I am banking on twenty years' experience in the book-publishing game when I take the liberty of sending these twenty books off to you today. There is one thing I am something of an expert at, if I do say so myself, and that is the understanding of the "creative spirit."

We have a new system here, which is to send our authors not ten free copies, as of old, but fifteen. Therefore, five of the thirty-six copies will reach you with our compliments. The proper deductions will be made on the record.

Don't forget our dinner date.

Cordially,
CLINT JORDAN

P.S. I approve of your decision to resume the use of your middle name. It gives a book dignity and flavor to use all three names. I think it was old Willa Cather who started the new trend, when she dropped the Seibert.

C. J.

THE CHARTERISS PUBLISHING COMPANY
NEW YORK, N.Y.

DEAR THURBER: DECEMBER 13, 1949

Just back at the old desk after a trip to California and a visit with my mother, who is eighty-nine now but as chipper as ever. She would make a swell Pro-file. Ask me about her someday.

Need I say I was delighted to hear from the staff when I got back about your keen interest in "Grandma Was a Nudist"? The book has been moving beautifully, and its ceiling has gone sky-high. We're planning a brief new advertising campaign and I'd be tickled pink if you would be good enough to bat out a blurb for us.

Yours,
LEON

THE CHARTERISS PUBLISHING COMPANY
NEW YORK, N.Y.

Mr. James M. Thurber,   DECEMBER 15, 1949
West Cornwall, Conn.
DEAR MR. THURBER:

I hope you will forgive me—indeed, all of us—for having inexcusably mis-laid the address of the lady to whom the thirty-six copies of "Grandma Was a Nudist" were sent by mistake. I understand that we have already dispatched to you at your home another thirty-six volumes of that book.

My apologies again.

Sincerely yours,
H. F. CLUFFMAN

WEST CORNWALL, CONN.
DECEMBER 19, 1949

Mr. H. F. Cluffman,
The Charteriss Publishing Co.,
132 East What Street,
New York, N.Y.

DEAR MR. CLUFFMAN:

The lady's name is Mrs. J. C. Edwards, and she lives at 568 Oak Street, Columbus, Ohio.

I have explained as clearly as I could in previous letters that I did not order thirty-six copies of "Grandma Was a Nudist." If you have actually shipped to me another thirty-six copies of this book, it will make a total of seventy-two copies, none of which I will pay for. The thirty-six copies of "Thurber's Ark" that Mr. Jordan has written me he intends to send to West Cornwall would bring up to one hundred and eight the total number of books that your firm, by a conspiracy of confusion unique even in the case of publishers, has mistakenly charged to my account. You may advise Mr. Jordan that I do not wish to receive the five free copies he mentioned in his letter.

If your entire staff of employees went back to *Leslie's Weekly,* where they belong, it would set my mind at rest.

Sincerely yours,
J. THURBER

P.S. I notice that you use only my middle initial, "M." Mr. Jordan and I —or was it Mr. Charteriss?—have decided to resume the use of the full name, which is Murfreesboro.

J. T.

WEST CORNWALL, CONN.
DECEMBER 27, 1949

Mr. Leon Charteriss,
The Charteriss Publishing Co.,
132 East What Street,
New York, N.Y.

DEAR MR. CHARTERISS:

I am sure you will be sorry to learn that Mr. Thurber has had one of his spells as a result of the multiplication of books and misunderstanding that began with Miss Alma Winege's letter of October 25, 1949. Those of us around Mr. Thurber are greatly disturbed by the unfortunate circumstances that have caused him to give up writing, at least temporarily, just after he had resumed work following a long fallow period.

Thirty-six copies of Mr. Thurber's book and thirty-six copies of "Grandma

Was a Nudist" have arrived at his home here, and he has asked me to advise you that he intends to burn all seventy-two. West Cornwall is scarcely the community for such a demonstration—he proposes to burn them in the middle of U.S. Highway No. 7—since the town regards with a certain suspicion any writer who has not won a Pulitzer Prize. I am enclosing copies of all the correspondence between your company and Mr. Thurber, in the hope that someone connected with your firm will read it with proper care and intelligence and straighten out this deplorable and inexcusable situation.

Mr. Thurber wishes me to tell you that he does not want to hear from any of you again.

Sincerely yours,
ELLEN BAGLEY
Secretary to Mr. Thurber

THE CHARTERISS PUBLISHING COMPANY
NEW YORK, N.Y.

Mr. James Murfreesboro Thurber,   DECEMBER 28, 1949
72 West,
Cornwall, Conn.
DEAR MR. THURBER:

I have at hand your letter of December 19th, the opening paragraph of which puzzles me. You send me the following name and address—Mrs. J. C. Edwards, 568 Oak Street, Columbus, Ohio—but it is not clear what use you wish me to make of this. I would greatly appreciate it if you would clear up this small matter for me.

Sincerely yours,
H. F. CLUFFMAN

P.S. *Leslie's Weekly* ceased publication many years ago. I could obtain the exact date if you so desire.

H. F. C.

THE CHARTERISS PUBLISHING COMPANY
NEW YORK, N.Y.

Mr. James M. Thurber,   DECEMBER 29, 1949
West Cornwall, Conn.
DEAR MR. THURBER:

You will be sorry to hear that Mr. Charteriss was taken suddenly ill with a virus infection. His doctor believes that he lost his immunity during his visit to the West Coast. He is now in the hospital, but his condition is not serious.

Since the departure of Miss Gaines, who was married last week, I have taken over the Stock Order Department for the time being. I did not take the liberty of reading your enclosures in the letter to Mr. Charteriss, but sent them directly to him at the hospital. I am sure that he will be greatly cheered up by them when he is well enough to read. Meanwhile, I want you to know that you can repose all confidence in the Stock Order Department to look after your needs, whatever they may be.

Sincerely yours,
GLADYS MACLEAN

P.S. I learned from Mr. Jordan that you were a friend of Willa Cather's. Exciting!

COLUMBUS, OHIO
JANUARY 3, 1950

DEAR JAMIE:

I don't understand the clipping from the Lakeville *Journal* Helen's mother sent me, about someone burning all those books of yours in the street. I never heard of such a thing, and don't understand how they could have taken the books without your knowing it, or what you were doing with so many copies of the novel about the naked grandmother. Imagine, at her age! She couldn't carry on like that in Columbus, let me tell you. Why, when I was a girl, you didn't dare walk with a man after sunset, unless he was your husband, and even then there was talk.

It's a good thing that state policeman came along in time to save most of the books from being completely ruined, and you must be thankful for the note Mr. Jordan put in one of the books, for the policeman would never have known who they belonged to if he hadn't found it.

A Mrs. Edwards phoned this morning and said that her son Donald collects your books and wants to send them to you—to be autographed, I suppose. Her son has dozens of your books and I told her you simply wouldn't have time to sign all of them, and she said she didn't care what you did with them. And then she said they weren't your books at all, and so I just hung up on her.

Be sure to bundle up when you go out.

With love,
MOTHER

P.S. This Mrs. Edwards says she lives at 568 Oak Street. I told her we used to live there and she said God knows she was aware of that. I don't know what she meant. I was afraid this little boy would send you all those books to sign and so I told his mother that you and Helen were at The Homestead, in Hot Springs. You don't suppose she would send them there, do you?

And here, gentle reader, I know you will be glad to leave all of us.

SERIOUS ASPECTS OF SATIRE *If we now do a bit of transfer or extrapolation from the story, we can see that the helplessness in "File and Forget" is not just that of an author driven to despair by his publishers and their representatives. The story could be a report from any man or woman who encounters a phrase-crazy, fashionably trite, and essentially dishonest or thoughtless habit of mind in those who receive inquiries* and give answers, in any context. If we happen to know more about Thurber's writing, we know he was acutely aware of man's status in the face of disease, death, or ignorance—and that he placed particular emphasis on ignorance, unawareness and uncaring irresponsibility. To call all this "the absurd" in human life, as some have done, is to simplify it and excuse it—by inventing a new category that will allow us to forget it. In this story Thurber is much more than a humorist or satirist. He uses the weapon of humor in what he knows may be a losing battle, but he does not intend to forget. He thus antedates much of the talk about "the absurd" which has become fashionable today. He even antedates complaints about computers, for no computer can do anything it is not programmed to do by a human being, where responsibility continues to rest. A fair summary of "File and Forget" might be: Many do not care, or care to think, but Thurber does!

As to technique in "File and Forget," it is easy to assume that all we have here is a series of letters that tell a story. This assumption overlooks Thurber's precise knowledge of business style, including the words and false phrases of respect, concern, and caring that appear in such endeavors. It also overlooks Thurber's precise knowledge of the way in which organizations change and yet remain the same. Most of all, it overlooks the neat satiric barbs everywhere in this series of letters, for the letter writers reveal themselves, as in much first-person communication.

We have emphasized the serious meanings of "File and Forget" and have suggested in a general way the range of inspired absurdities built into the story by the author. It would appear that the readers of Thurber's letters either could not see or could not remember or did not wish either to see or to remember. We have the impression that a numbered list of separate errors recorded in these letters would run to several dozen, though we have never tried to assemble a total. We suggest that a reader could experience both fun and despair by assembling such a list. If one further step were taken, namely, to classify the separate kinds of human error there displayed, despair would increase—together with admiration for Thurber's power of mordant satire!

SATIRIC NONREALISM

Pär Lagerkvist, author of the next story, is another winner of the Nobel Prize for Literature. Lift is the common word in England for elevator. Since elevators do not actually go down into Hell, the story is understood at once to be an example of nonrealistic fiction, at least in part. Two central facts to hold in mind about a story that contains nonrealistic elements are these: (1) the author is probably trying to represent problems or ideas or attitudes that are real; and (2) the nonrealistic machinery is a means to that end. The reader himself must decide what the strange or unusual elements in the story do.

*The Lift That Went Down into Hell

PÄR LAGERKVIST

Translated by Alan Blair

Mr. Smith, a prosperous businessman, opened the elegant hotel lift and amorously handed in a gracile creature smelling of furs and powder. They nestled together on the soft seat and the lift started downward. The little lady extended her half-open mouth, which was moist with wine, and they kissed. They had dined up on the terrace, under the stars; now they were going out to amuse themselves.

"Darling, how divine it was up there," she whispered. "So poetic sitting there with you, like being up among the stars. That's when you really know what love is. You do love me, don't you?"

Mr. Smith answered with a kiss that lasted still longer; the lift went down.

"A good thing you came, my darling," he said; "otherwise I'd have been in an awful state."

"Yes, but you can just imagine how insufferable he was. The second I started getting ready he asked where I was going. 'I'll go where I please,' I said. 'I'm no prisoner.' Then he deliberately sat and stared at me the whole time I was changing, putting on my new beige—do you think it's becoming? What do you think looks best, by the way, perhaps pink after all?"

"Everything becomes you, darling," the man said, "but I've never seen you so lovely as this evening."

She opened her fur coat with a gratified smile, they kissed for a long time, the lift went down.

"Then when I was ready to go he took my hand and squeezed it so that it still hurts, and didn't say a word. He's so brutal, you've no idea! 'Well, good-bye,' I said. But not a word from him. He's so unreasonable, so frightfully, I can't stand it."

"Poor little thing," said Mr. Smith.

"As though I can't go out for a bit and enjoy myself. But then he's so deadly serious, you've no idea. He can't take anything simply and naturally. It's as though it were a matter of life and death the whole time."

"Poor pet, what you must have gone through."

"Oh, I've suffered terribly. Terribly. No one has suffered as I have. Not until I met you did I know what love is."

"Sweetheart," Smith said, hugging her; the lift went down.

"Fancy," she said, when she had got her breath after the embrace, "sitting with you up there gazing at the stars and dreaming—oh, I'll never forget it. You see, the thing is—Arvid is impossible, he's so everlastingly solemn, he hasn't a scrap of poetry in him, he has no feeling for it."

"Darling, it's intolerable."

"Yes, isn't it—intolerable. But," she went on, giving him her hand with a smile, "let's not sit thinking of all that. We're out to enjoy ourselves. You do really love me?"

"Do I!" he said, bending her back so that she gasped; the lift went down. Leaning over her he fondled her; she blushed.

"Let us make love tonight—as never before. Hm?" he whispered.

She pressed him to her and closed her eyes; the lift went down.

Down and down it went.

At last Smith got to his feet, his face flushed.

"But what's the matter with the lift?" he exclaimed. "Why doesn't it stop? We've been sitting here for ever so long talking, haven't we?"

"Yes, darling, I suppose we have, time goes so quickly."

"Good Heavens, we've been sitting here for ages! What's the idea?"

He glanced out through the grill. Nothing but pitch darkness. And the lift went on and on at a good, even pace, deeper and deeper down.

"Heavens alive, what's the idea? It's like dropping down into an empty pit. And we've been doing this for God knows how long."

They tried to peep down into the abyss. It was pitch dark. They just sank and sank down into it.

"This is all going to hell," Smith said.

"Oh dear," the woman wailed, clinging to his arm, "I'm so nervous. You'll have to pull the emergency brake."

Smith pulled for all he was worth. It was no good. The lift merely plunged down and down interminably.

"It's frightful," she cried. "What are we going to do!"

"Yes, what the devil is one to do?" Smith said. "This is crazy."

The little lady was in despair and burst into tears.

"There, there, my sweet, don't cry, we must be sensible. There's nothing we can do. There now, sit down. That's right, now we'll sit here quietly both of us, close together, and see what happens. It must stop some time or there'll be the devil to pay."

They sat and waited.

"Just think of something like this happening," the woman said. "And we were going out to have fun."

"Yes, it's the very devil," Smith said.

"You do love me, don't you?"

"Darling," Smith said, putting his arms around her; the lift went down.

At last it stopped abruptly. There was such a bright light all around that it hurt the eyes. They were in hell. The Devil slid the grill aside politely.

"Good evening," he said with a deep bow. He was stylishly dressed in tails that hung on the hairy top vertebra as on a rusty nail.

Smith and the woman tottered out in a daze. "Where in God's name are we?" they exclaimed, terrified by the weird apparition. The Devil, a shade embarrassed, enlightened them.

"But it's not as bad as it sounds," he hastened to add. "I hope you will have quite a pleasant time. I gather it's just for the night?"

"Yes, yes!" Smith assented eagerly, "it's just for the night. We're not going to stay, oh no!"

The little lady clung tremblingly to his arm. The light was so corrosive and yellow green that they could hardly see, and there was a hot smell, they thought. When they had grown a little more used to it they discovered they were standing as it were in a square, around which houses with glowing doorways towered up in the darkness; the curtains were drawn but they could see through the chinks that something was burning inside.

"You are the two who love each other?" the Devil inquired.

"Yes, madly," the lady answered, giving him a look with her lovely eyes.

"Then this is the way," he said, and asked them to follow please. They slunk into a murky side street leading out of the square. An old cracked lantern was hanging outside a filthy, grease-stained doorway.

"Here it is." He opened the door and retired discreetly.

They went in. A new devil, fat, fawning, with large breasts and purple powder caked on the moustache around her mouth, received them. She smiled wheezily, a good-natured, knowing look in her beady eyes; around the horns in her forehead she had twined tufts of hair and fastened them with small blue silk ribbons.

"Oh, is it Mr. Smith and the little lady?" she said. "It's in number eight then." And she gave them a large key.

They climbed the dim, greasy staircase. The stairs were slippery with fat; it was two flights up. Smith found number eight and went in. It was a fairly large, musty room. In the middle was a table with a grubby cloth; by the wall a bed with smoothed-down sheets. They thought it all very nice. They took off their coats and kissed for a long time.

A man came in unobtrusively from another door. He was dressed like a waiter but his dinner jacket was well cut and his shirtfront so clean that it gleamed ghostlike in the semidarkness. He walked silently, his feet making no sound, and his movements were mechanical, unconscious almost. His features were stern, the eyes looking fixedly straight ahead. He was deathly pale; in one temple he had a bullet wound. He got the room ready, wiped the dressing table, brought in a chamberpot and a slop pail.

They didn't take much notice of him, but as he was about to go Smith said, "I think we'll have some wine. Bring us half a bottle of Madeira." The man bowed and disappeared.

Smith started getting undressed. The woman hesitated.

"He's coming back," she said.

"Pshaw, in a place like this you needn't mind. Just take your things off." She got out of her dress, pulled up her panties coquettishly and sat on his knee. It was lovely.

"Just think," she answered, "sitting here together, you and I, alone, in such a queer, romantic place. So poetic, I'll never forget it."

"Sweetheart," he said. They kissed for a long time.

The man came in again, soundlessly. Softly, mechanically, he put down the glasses, poured out the wine. The light from the table lamp fell on his face. There was nothing special about him except that he was deathly pale and had a bullet wound in his temple.

The woman leaped up with a scream.

"Oh my God! Arvid! Is it you? Is it you? Oh God in Heaven, he's dead! He's shot himself!"

The man stood motionless, just staring in front of him. His face showed no suffering; it was merely stern, very grave.

"But Arvid, what have you done, what have you done! How could you! My dear, if I'd suspected anything like that, you know I'd have stayed at home. But you never tell me anything. You never said anything about it, not a word! How was I to know when you never told me! Oh my God . . ."

Her whole body was shaking. The man looked at her as at a stranger; his gaze was icy and gray, just went straight through everything. The sallow face gleamed, no blood came from the wound, there was just a hole there.

"Oh, it's ghastly, ghastly!" she cried. "I won't stay here! Let's go at once. I can't stand it."

She grabbed her dress, hat and fur coat and rushed out, followed by Smith. They slipped going down the stairs, she sat down, got spittle and cigarette ash on her behind. Downstairs the woman with the moustache was standing, smiling good-naturedly and knowingly and nodding her horns.

Out in the street they calmed down a little. The woman put on her clothes, straightened herself, powdered her nose. Smith put his arm protectingly round her waist, kissed away the tears that were on the point of falling—he was so good. They walked up into the square.

The head devil was walking about there, they ran into him again. "You *have* been quick," he said. "I hope you've been comfortable."

"Oh, it was dreadful," the lady said.

"No, don't say that, you can't think that. You should have been here in the old days, it was different then. Hell is nothing to complain of now. We do all we can not to make it too obvious, on the contrary to make it enjoyable."

"Yes," Mr. Smith said, "I must say it's a little more humane anyway, that's true."

"Oh," the Devil said, "we've had everything modernized, completely re-arranged, as it should be."

"Yes, of course, you must keep up with the times."

"Yes, it's only the soul that suffers nowadays."

"Thank God for that," said the lady.

The Devil conducted them politely to the lift. "Good evening," he said with a deep bow, "welcome back." He shut the grill after them, the lift went up.

"Thank God that's over," they both said, relieved, and nestled up to one another on the seat.

"I should never have got through it without you," she whispered. He drew her to him, they kissed for a long time. "Fancy," she said, when she had got her breath after the embrace, "his doing such a thing! But he's always had such queer notions. He's never been able to take things simply and naturally, as they are. It's as though it were a matter of life and death the whole time."

"It's absurd," Smith said.

"He might have *told* me! Then I'd have stayed. We could have gone out another evening instead."

"Yes, of course," Smith said, "of course we could."

"But, darling, let's not sit thinking of that," she whispered, putting her arms around his neck. "It's over now."

"Yes, little darling, it's over now." He clasped her in his arms; the lift went up.

USE OF NONREALISTIC ELEMENTS *Why would a serious writer include in a story such an element as the Hell-destined elevator in "Lift"?*

■ *To attract attention? Possibly, for it does so.*

■ *To help convey briefly, intensely, an aspect of life that otherwise would have to be spelled out at length and with less interest? Very probably, for an artist wants economy of method with maximum effect. As we shall see, the elevator makes it possible to express important meanings with great brevity.*

■ *To suggest a reality of experience for which the author cannot find a better expression? Very probably. Many things cannot be said directly, literally. Many more cannot be said as well directly as indirectly. It is a reality, in "Lift," that the man and woman are "going down," morally. Their first trip in the elevator is a symbol of this and a basic aid in conveying still other meanings, as analysis of the story will show.*

The use of any nonrealistic device is almost a promise to the reader that special meanings will arise from it. The reader may have to work harder at interpretation of nonrealism than at a wholly realistic story. But he will find the going easier if he remembers the basic notion that nonrealistic symbolism has exactly the same functions as the more familiar symbolism of a story in the realistic mode: to help the writer with the effective expression or communication of meaning.

In discussing what we have called "emotional involvement" we suggested that a concrete presentation of "reality" often sharpens the reader's emotional response, whereas abstractions alone are not very moving. It is easy to see that "Lift" retains the advantage of concreteness, even in its nonrealistic material. An elevator is real enough; it is the journey of this particular elevator which takes us away from ordinary "reality."

SYMBOLISM *We hear much today about "symbolism" in fiction and about something called "nonrepresentational" or "abstract" art. This is not the place to discuss the latter, except to say that a good work of art will satisfy basic human needs, however strange the artistic method may seem to be. But a brief comment on symbolism is necessary before we proceed with discussion of "The Lift That Went Down into Hell."*

The number 3 is a symbol, used to represent three objects, ideas, parts, functions, and so forth. The number is not the things it represents. In the same way, the word tree or house is a symbol, not the real thing. Language itself is symbolic. Characters in a story, thus, are not real people but collections of detail reported by means of words. Even the most "realistic" story is symbolic, in the sense that any story is a representation, an image, of people and places and events. A story exists in the mind of the author and reaches the mind of the reader through the medium of words, which in turn may refer to things we know in the world of actuality or even the world of dreams.

We do most of our thinking with symbols—mathematical, verbal, rhythmic, pictorial, and so on. These symbols have various relations to so-called "real" events. They refer also to such things as the motions of our minds, or the causalities in test tubes and nuclear reactors. We represent all things, from the most objective to the most subjective, by means of symbols. We must do this in order to talk or think about our experience. If the experience is complex, then the symbols we use are likely to have complex interrelationships.

The people and events and settings in a story are likely to be interesting in themselves. They are likely also to suggest still other people, events, places, or problems which we often know about or can imagine. "Two Soldiers," for example, is interesting just as a story, but it is also a symbol of possible reactions to war, and of a way of life in a specific environment. "A Sick Call," too, is interesting just as a story, but it symbolizes certain realities in human wishing and thinking and loving; further, it is a symbol of the universal and never-ceasing problem of ends and means. The reader might note that such a story, involving characters in action, is itself rather concrete, but that a concrete symbol, through its power of suggestion, can represent abstract matters, such as love, or loyalty, or "the problem of ends and means." The symbolism mentioned thus far is in general "realistic"—that is, the symbols refer to people and events and problems that we can recognize easily as probable elements in human experience.

A second way in which symbols are used is to represent traditional meanings. For example, the number 3 has been used throughout much of history, in particular contexts, to represent the Trinity, or combinations of gods in the Hindu religion, or broad divisions of nature, or cardinal colors. If a young woman should be named Athene, in life or in fiction, the very name would symbolize wisdom or mental brilliance to anyone who knew the traditional, abstract qualities associated with the goddess Athene. We will return later to this question of traditional symbols.

Some writers of fiction pose unnecessary problems for the reader by what amounts to a pointless and cluttered multiplication of symbols. But the present author, Lagerkvist, does not belong in the class of writers who play with symbols as substitutes for meaning. Instead, he uses symbolism—in both a traditional and a special way—to communicate meaning.

CONCRETE SYMBOLISM

We have emphasized that all language is symbolic and that the most interesting symbols are likely to be concrete—that is, things as definite and as available to our senses as a flag, or the sensory reality of a man, a woman, a field in sunlight, all represented by means of words. But there is more to the use of concrete symbolism than interest. There is the fact that some ideas and feelings cannot be conveyed directly, literally, but must be conveyed by means of concrete symbols suggesting realities of a more abstract nature.

As an approach to the discussion of "Lift," consider for a moment what happens when people read or see such a drama as Shakespeare's Othello. *The person seeing or reading this play about a famous general who comes to believe certain lies about the behavior of his wife finds himself in a special position, for he knows that the lies are lies, though Othello (the fictional character) does not. Othello sees motives and meanings in his wife's behavior that are not really there at all, and a complex of misunderstanding and jealousy develops in a seemingly uncheckable manner. The reader or viewer is slowly impressed with a fatality in the whole sequence of events, for the motives of the characters are as real as anything in the world and apparently will not change. This special, ironic knowledge begins to arouse definite feelings in the reader or viewer. There is the sense of fatality, already mentioned, somewhat like the feeling we have when we see an accident about to happen that we cannot prevent. There is also fear, because the uncheckable forces in this play are human passions, motives and beliefs. Men and women are supposed to be in command of themselves—that is, we like to think we are. Yet in this play a terrible action (murder and suicide) is prepared and committed simply because one man believes what a "friend" tells him. It does little good to ask why Othello was so foolish as to believe the lies he was told, for we know in our hearts that we do believe those we love and trust. Therefore we pity him, a victim of trust and of his passion.*

The play is thus a symbol of wholly possible human behavior, which results for the reader or viewer in ironic knowledge, pity, fear. The moment we dare to think of human life as containing motives and misunderstandings that grow in force until they cannot be stopped or changed, in that moment we fear. No amount of abstract talk will produce this effect, but a story will—through the power of concrete symbolism. The story is of course interesting in itself, but a further level of interest and feeling lies in the fact that the concrete symbol—the story with all its elements—causes us to recognize the deeper meanings, the universal application and truth.

So with "The Lift That Went Down into Hell." In trying to read "A Sick Call" carefully, we began by asking what the author seemed to be emphasizing, and we found the answer in a combination of characters and action, plus a small amount of descriptive language that suggested the author's attitudes. "Lift" contains characters (the man, the woman—unnamed, we observe—and the denizens of Hell). The action of the man and woman is pointed in the direction of a "good time." But something unexpected happens (the elevator) and because of this still other things happen which the man and woman must adjust to. If we look for signs of the author's attitude toward the man and woman, it begins to seem that the elevator, with the action and characterization it makes possible, is one sign: the man and woman do not know where they are going; unexpected events have taken them in charge. Thus, the elevator begins to convey meaning—the proper function of any symbol, realistic or unrealistic. At first, physically, the man and woman are going down, and later we find that they are going down, in a moral sense. Later, they think they are going up, and physically they are, but we know better, for the trips down and back, with the events in Hell and the Devil's comments, have thrown an ironic light on everything the man and woman say and do and think.

DRAMATIC IRONY *In other words, we receive a view of the characters that the characters themselves do not have, and this view—the author's attitude—arises from special ironic knowledge which comes from (1) the elevator, (2) the comments made by the Devil, (3) the events in Hell, including the description, and (4) what the man and woman say and do in the context of the other elements of the story. When the Devil shows that he knows he will see the man and woman again, for example, we realize it is only a matter of time until "soul torture" occurs. From many other signs, we know what is fated to happen. The husband, whether "really" shot in the head or not, might just as well be as far as his marriage is concerned: he is married to a woman who can say that he is too "serious" about marriage. In not replying, the husband shows his knowledge that the marriage is "dead," that no message from him can now reach his wife, that she is bound on her course. The Devil's early reference to the man and woman, "You are the two who love each other?" is an ironic comment which keys everything else he says. Once we see the communicative purpose of the trip to Hell, including the Devil and the "apartment" (Number 8) and its caretaker and the action there, the various details of the story fall into place, and there is no lost motion, no meaningless act or word. The basic characteristic of the wife—and of her escort—is unawareness. She is unaware of the nature of the journey—a symbol of life—which starts as the elevator goes down; she learns nothing from the incidents of the journey itself; she has a blind and selfish expectation that life will continue to be pleasant and amusing, in spite of the* terrible symbolic meanings the journey assumes for the observer—the reader of the story.

"Lift" can thus be read as a plain moral story, for it is certainly that—at a minimum level. But the story is also much more. The reader who sees the elevator and the trip to Hell as a source of ironic knowledge—knowledge that the man and woman are fatally unable to share—will receive a twist of feeling somewhat similar to that delivered by the play Othello. But sympathy and respect are not developed for the man and woman in "Lift" as they are for the main characters in Othello; therefore, the elements of "caring" and of pity and fear cannot be as strong. The attitude is one of sardonic amusement rather than sympathy and respect, and it is revealed strongly through the comments of the Devil, who is a major device by means of which the author's attitudes enter the story. (Other means, of course, include the descriptive details and the action in Hell.) The Devil knows what sin is, and by the same token knows what good is, which the man and woman are destroying. The Devil is amused. So is the author, in a grim kind of way.

"Lift" can be read, too, as a realistic statement—through the power of symbol—that a special trip to Hell, with reservations in advance, would not deter some of us from our usual course of action. It is also a symbol of the ingenuity and determination a human being can exert in fooling himself, the excuses he can invent, his human capacity to forget or refuse to see the sure consequences of action and attitude. So the whole is a moral story on several levels. Though it contains nonrealistic elements, it is a symbol of various possible realities in human life.

SPECIAL USES OF SYMBOLS Throughout the discussion of "Lift" an obvious point was omitted deliberately—that the meaning of the story, the fact that it works at all as a story, depends on use of the familiar Christian symbols of Hell and the Devil. These symbols work so well that we are hardly aware of this as we read, yet they are, of course, another example of what was referred to earlier as traditional symbolism. Such symbols work because their connotations are widely understood. In a culture unfamiliar with Christianity, these symbols might not be effective at all.

Symbols can be used, however, in a third way, as something more than well-established representations whose meanings can be translated directly and easily. There are authors who develop through repeated use their own private sets of symbols, which can be recognized and interpreted correctly only if their repeated uses are studied. An example is a rather special use the writer Ralph Ellison makes of the symbol of flying in his story "Flying Home" (pp. 244-258). Obviously, no author is likely to write a story involving an airplane pilot without some allusion to the idea of flying, but we notice quickly that Ellison builds on this symbol in such special ways as to create a pattern of meanings. The idea of flying suggests immediately such opposites as crashing, falling, or being grounded—

negative poles of the positive idea. Man's long-held desire to fly, like any ideal, carries with it implications of possible failure as well as success. The central symbol thus begins to take on a fuller range of meanings.

The general meanings noted above translate, as the story develops, into a diversity of interrelated elements such as the following: (1) a young pilot and a plane crash, (2) a piece of ground (compare "grounded") owned by a man who resents the pilot, (3) a boy whose desire to fly brought a crash (the pilot when younger), (4) images of buzzards and eagles, with a range of positive to negative connotations, and (5) a man who believes he was once "dead" and given angel wings in Heaven, but was kicked out of Heaven and grounded in the State of Alabama.

Meanings accumulate further as we learn that flying for the young pilot has overtones touching his educational and social status and the proving of his individual ability in the face of odds. The process continues as he learns that an older, uneducated Southern black has had similar aspirations and longings, expressed through an imaginative experience of angel wings and unequal treatment in Heaven.

Already, one finds it impossible to reread either the story's title or the story itself without experiencing these growths in meaning, all achieved through special uses of a symbol. But the process includes still more: the positive-negative polarity reaches a climax in the buzzard-and-gold image at the story's close, prepared for by the experience of a watcher of flying objects. This watcher of the skies can gaze at the sun, but the experience makes it impossible for him to distinguish between one color and another—for sure. Thus the final use of a special symbol draws attention to the essentials of man's quest for significance, self-respect, achievement in life, and to the ambivalent mystery of personal identity.

SUMMARY: SYMBOLISM From this brief analysis, it is apparent that symbols have a wide range of functions in fiction, which can be summarized as follows:

1. Every word is a symbol, and language itself is symbolic. Thus, any story is symbolic in that the characters and events symbolize human experience at some level of complexity. It is important to remember that an author can attach added significance to any word, detail, image, or idea he wishes to repeat, or to any set of such elements he may wish to arrange in a pattern. Whether the details, images, words or ideas are realistic or nonrealistic hardly matters. The clue is this repetition of elements or the arrangement of elements in a meaningful pattern, or both.

2. Traditional symbols, well-known within a given culture, such as the symbols of a widely known religion or profession or way of life, can have the effect of adding a universal significance to an otherwise plain story, as we have seen.

3. Some symbols are so treated as to be almost private, esoteric. New symbols can be invented. Storytellers who have

built their own special meanings into symbols of a more general, or even traditional, nature have perhaps been better communicators of meaning than have those who have tried to create entirely new symbol systems. There is nothing new about the idea of flying, but Ralph Ellison, as we have indicated, built new meanings into it. If we should examine various fictional presentations of Hell and Satan, we would find that Lagerkvist has used the traditional meanings in part but has also built special meanings of his own into the character of Satan and the geography and mechanism of Hell. Every new interpretation Lagerkvist has added would be called a special use of these symbols. Every established meaning he has used would be called traditional.

We have come a long way from relatively simple though effective stories such as "Two Soldiers." The approach to questions concerning symbols and to the interrelationships among elements in a work of art has been deliberately slow. But the reader who reflects on these matters will begin to develop a more complex understanding of the ways in which imaginative art works, and he will be less concerned about exact correspondences between the symbols in a work of art and what may be thought of as "the facts" of either life or history.

FICTIONAL MODES
Most fiction is written in the realistic mode—as if the persons and events represent probable or possible "realities." We have seen that some fiction is based on particular social or historical events, with an almost perfect relationship between fiction and certain kinds of factual detail. But we have also observed that much fiction does not concern itself with "reality" of this type at all, and aims at a more universal significance. Some, as we have seen, employs nonrealistic elements in order to communicate meanings which apply to the real world. Such fiction, by its very tone and method, often seems close to the outright fable. So-called "science" fiction, an example of which we shall read later, ordinarily uses strange settings or strange gadgets, genuine scientific information at some level— and human beings superficially portrayed. Science fiction, as a form, is today beginning to achieve the depth and complexity which are characteristic of more traditional forms. We have seen also that commercial fiction, such as the Western or the detective story, has its own characteristics, and there is no trouble in realizing that its main business is entertainment.

The broad categories or kinds of fiction just named are quite easy to recognize. The most important distinction is probably that between the author who is frankly trying to entertain and the one who is using fictional methods seriously as a means of communicating matters that seem important to him. The serious writer can usually be recognized by his artistry: wording, sentence structure, interdependence of elements, clarity of emphasis, economy of means.

Knowing that a story is, in general, "realistic" or "nonrealistic," or that it is "commercial" or relatively "serious" in its intent is often useful in helping the reader to a correct set of expectations. But suppose the author is writing realistic satire—a story with seemingly "real" characters whom the author intends to laugh at, good-humoredly or bitterly? True, he may use exaggeration to the point that we cannot miss his intention, or he may use overt author-comment with the same result. Many a satirist, however, in speaking or in writing, uses a deadpan manner. His attitude and intention may dawn on us slowly, but without this knowledge we cannot read him correctly.

What to do? A reader can usually secure one anchor, one fundamental clue by noting every sign of the author's attitude toward events and especially toward characters, as we have emphasized throughout the present discussion. The signs of an author's attitude, though often small, are cumulative. Once a general direction is apparent, it is possible to read with pleasure and understanding.

What We Were and What We Are

THE PRESENT AS THE PAST UNFINISHED

*When the chips are down in any crisis, what you have to draw on finally
is not what happened in the time that you yourself have been on earth,
but what came before you. This is what gets you through your crisis
finally. And somewhere in yourself you carry all of that. You have to be
in great trouble to turn to it and use it, or to suspect that you have to;
but when you are in trouble, that's what you turn to, which means it must
be there.*

—James Baldwin[1]

*These words about the human past as a source of help in a deeply
troubled present are worth thinking about. They indicate in context that James Baldwin was aware of forces of several kinds in past
American life, forces still operative among us in many ways. He may
have been suggesting that one gets outside his own immediate and
present experience, if only briefly, by realizing and admitting that
certain events have in fact occurred and are now having their
results. He may be suggesting that wisdom, even sanity, at times
requires recognition of past events and actions as related to
continuing realities, causalities, and relationships in our present
human behavior.*

The fiction presented here under the heading What We Were and
What We Are *reports aspects of human behavior before our time.
The first four pieces reflect parts of the American past—from about*

---

[1] From an interview conducted by Eve Auchincloss and Nancy Lynch, *The Black
American Writer, I: Fiction* (Pelican Book), edited by C.W.E. Bigsby and first
published by Everett/Edwards, Inc., 1969. Penguin Books, Inc., Baltimore, Maryland: 1971, page 207.

1880 to 1920. The last represents the European and colonial past, which has also helped shape us into what we are.

In this second major section of our book we shall continue to introduce and follow each piece of fiction with commentary—but the trend will be toward brevity, so that the reader can take over. In later sections, there will be no editorial comments on individual pieces of fiction.

The author of "Going Away," the story which follows, spent years in learning from Kiowa Indians about their history and legends. Alice Marriott's story is thus based on materials reported by the Kiowas, but it is presented in fictional form—a good example of the close relation that can exist between humanly felt truth and a fictional treatment. The author herself has said of this work, "where the feelings of a person are described, it is only because he himself said that he felt that way. . . ." The time of the action is 1883. The place is the American Southwest, before a State such as Oklahoma ever existed. The reader of this apparently simple story may be surprised at the weight of meaning it carries, as well as its applicability to more recent times.

Going Away

ALICE MARRIOTT[1]

Spear Woman could never have told which of her children she loved the best. Some mothers could, but having a preference always sounded silly to her. Her children and Bow Woman's were all mixed up in her mind, so that sometimes she wasn't sure of which ones she was the mother. They all lived and grew and played together, and she loved them all.

Hunting Horse felt a little bit different. Two of the children he would always remember by their mothers. He would remember his youngest son, who was Spear Woman's child, and he would remember the daughter who had been

[1] From *The Ten Grandmothers,* by Alice Marriott. Copyright 1945 by the University of Oklahoma Press.

born during the horse corral winter. Those two he could never be mistaken about.

If they had been rich, it was likely that Hunting Horse would have made a favorite son of this youngest. He would have gotten him the best of everything. That boy would have had the finest clothes, the very best horse there was, if his father could have had his way.

As it was, they had no way of making a favorite son of him. Fewer and fewer families could have favorites and those who had enough horses and other things to have one didn't always take the trouble. Things weren't the way they had been, when to have a favorite was to give honor and credit to the whole family. Now it was different. People used to say they made a big fuss over their favorite because the young men might go off on a raid and get killed. Now there was no more raiding, and no more danger on that account.

Hunting Horse was a man who could surprise you with what he would say. Even when you knew him as well as Spear Woman did, he could be surprising. She was surprised now, because Hunting Horse had taken a streak of not talking. He was a man who liked to talk and who talked a lot. Then, a while back, he had just stopped. He was not gloomy or unhappy, and he always answered when you spoke to him, but he just didn't start saying things for himself.

Spear Woman let him alone for seven days, and then she became tired of the way he was acting and spoke to him about it.

"What's the matter with you, going around here with your mouth shut tight like an old terrapin?"

"I've been thinking," answered Hunting Horse. "I've been thinking a lot."

"You've been thinking off and on all your life," Spear Woman told him. "I don't see why you have to act as if it hurt you now."

"I never thought things before that did hurt me," he said. "It all seems hard. I guess you better get Bow Woman. Maybe, if we all talk it over, it will help."

Bow Woman was in her own tipi, sewing moccasins. It was late summer, and she was trying to get enough ahead to take the children through the winter. She brought the moccasins and her awl and sinew with her and came and sat in Spear Woman's tipi.

"I've been thinking," said Hunting Horse again. "I've been thinking a whole lot. Some of the things I've been thinking about you know. You know how the buffalo have gone. Buffalo Coming Out tried to bring them back, and it killed him. He died, and his mother died within a year."

"That's true," said Spear Woman. "They just died. The power was too strong for him to live with after it failed. So it killed them."

Hunting Horse didn't seem to pay much attention to her. "That's not what I'm thinking about," he went on. "It's more than that. Buffalo were what we had to live on, and they're gone. Now we live any way we can. Deer meat, jackrabbit meat, rations, just about anything we can get."

"I don't know that anybody ever thinks about anything but food any more," put in Bow Woman. "That's not such new, important thinking."

"I'm coming to the new thinking," said Hunting Horse. "You be quiet. I have to explain what made me think it. Well! All this means that old thinking and old ways have got to change. People are going to have to live differently. They're living differently right now, but they won't give up and admit it. They keep on saying they're living the old life, when anybody can see the way the're living is nothing like it."

"That's true," said Spear Woman. She hated it, but ever since the buffalo-coming-out ceremony had failed, she had felt more strongly how different everything was always going to be from what they had known.

"It means living in a new world—new things and new rules for doing them by," Hunting Horse was going on. "That's going to be hard for us older ones. Some of those things we won't be able to learn. Other things we can pick up easy. But some of our children are young enough. They can learn everything, all about the new living."

Spear Woman spoke before she knew. "But that means our children will think differently and live differently from us."

Hunting Horse nodded his head. "That's what it means, all right."

Bow Woman spoke up. "I don't like that. I don't like that way of doing things. I want my children to live like me and think like me."

"Listen," said Hunting Horse. "This is what I've been thinking. I think this is the way it is. If our children stay here and live with us and don't see any-body else, then they'll grow up living and thinking like us all right. But that will make it harder for them. Sooner or later they'll have to get away from us and be around other people. The more they're like those other people, the easier it'll be for them to get along."

"That's true," said Spear Woman. "It's the men like Eagle Plume, that just look like everybody else and don't show much in crowds, that live the longest and seem to get along the best."

"That's it," said Hunting Horse. "I don't think our children are just like everybody else. I think they would show up in crowds. But I want to give them a chance to learn how other people are thinking and doing, and then they can be leaders and show other people what to do."

"That's a good plan," said Bow Woman. "How are you going to work it?"

"This way," Hunting Horse told her. "I'm going to take my youngest son and send him to Fort Sill. The officers have a school for Indian children there. They'll teach him what he ought to know."

It seemed to Spear Woman that things were turning over and over inside her. She would never have thought that Hunting Horse could think these things. It was as if he had picked up a big stick of firewood and hit her on the head with it. She put her hand over her heart, that was jumping up and down, and tried to hold it steady. "When do you want him to go?" she asked.

"Right away," said Hunting Horse, "as soon as you can get him ready. I've thought and thought about this, and it seems that it's what we'll have to do."

Spear Woman looked through the tipi flaps and watched the children tumbling in the sun like puppies. They were rolling over and over.

"He's such a little boy," she said. "Let him stay home another year. He's learning by playing. Children learn a lot from each other. That's the way we learned all we know."

"He's got to go while he's still little," Hunting Horse told her, "or he won't have time to learn all the things he needs. He's got to learn English and reading and writing. The way he is now, he isn't learning about anything but living."

Spear Woman stopped pleading then. She knew what that son meant to Hunting Horse. If he was hitting her with a stick she couldn't see, he was hitting himself, too. After that they didn't talk about it at all. She and Bow Woman just started to get things ready. They did the best they could, because they wanted their boy to look right beside the other children.

It took them four days. They cleaned all his clothes. Bow Woman finished the moccasins for him. They dressed him in the best they had, with paint on his face and along the parting of his hair. Hunting Horse got the old, rawhide cradle they had made in the horse corral and took his own old, long, crawdad earrings from it. He fastened them in the boy's ears. "These are kind of family earrings," he said. "It looks like your turn to inherit."

The little boy was pleased with himself, you could tell. When they had him all dressed, he went around, stepping carefully like a wild turkey so as to show off his good clothes without getting his new moccasins dirty. While he was parading, Spear Woman got a pony for him and Hunting Horse's blue roan, and brought them up.

"Now," she said, "you two men are ready. You can ride." She was surprised at the easy way her own voice came out of her mouth.

Hunting Horse had got down and was fussing with his headstall. It reminded her of the time he asked her to ride in the Sun Dance parade with him. "You get your horse, too," he told her. "We'll all three ride out on this raid."

Spear Woman pulled a deep breath for the first time in the four days. She would get to go along. That way she would be with her boy a little while longer. It meant that Hunting Horse wouldn't have to ride back alone, either. She'd been dreading that for him.

When she was ready, they started. They went down past Cutthroat Gap and along the creek, going south and east, to get to the fort. The fall coolness was all around them, turning to heat at midday. They stopped and rested until the noon had cooled off and then went on again. Their stopping-place was beside a little, clear spring, coming out on the east side of the hill below the gap. There was water cress in the pool it made, and they pulled up handfuls and ate it with their dried meat for lunch.

It was mid-afternoon when they reached the school. Children were playing in front of the square, stone building. They surprised Spear Woman, because they all looked alike. She could not understand how twenty children, each with his own face and his own voice, could manage to look all like one child. It was a good thing her boy was coming. He would be one that would stand out and look different.

The man who was in charge of the school came over and shook hands. He called one of the bigger boys, and sent him off somewhere. When the boy came back, he had Wood Fire with him, as interpreter.

"Do you want this boy to go to school here?" he asked. Wood Fire's Kiowa seemed to get worse every time you saw him. It was all getting mixed up with the way he talked English.

"That's what we brought him for," was what Hunting Horse said in his good, clear Kiowa. You knew when he talked that he used all the right parts of his throat, the way he ought to.

"What's his name?" asked Wood Fire. That surprised Spear Woman. You didn't usually come right out and ask what somebody's name was. If you didn't know it already, you hinted around until somebody else told you.

"Grass Stem," she said. Hunting Horse just stood there. He was the one who had made the plan, and they were working it out, but he seemed to be more surprised by what was happening than she was.

"The boy's name is Grass Stem, and the father's name is Hunting Horse," said Wood Fire in English to the school teacher. He had known what the next question would be.

"Grass Stem Hunting Horse," said the school teacher. "That's a long name. We'll have to shorten it. Bring the boy along."

Wood Fire held out his hand, and the little boy took it. He looked littler that moment than he had in his cradle. Spear Woman kept her face stiff and rigid so that her tears wouldn't melt it. "Can we stay a few minutes with him?" she asked. "Do we have to leave him right now?"

Wood Fire shook his head. "You can stay awhile," he told her. "You can stay until he gets on his school clothes and comes out. That way you'll know everything is all right for him; and you can take home those things he has on."

"Can't he keep on those clothes?" asked Spear Woman. "Those are his good clothes. It makes him happy to have them on. He's going to be lonesome when we're gone. He's just a little boy."

The child stood next to Wood Fire and watched the other boys play. His long braids hung down his back, and the silver earrings swung beside his face. He shook his head, and they swung hard.

"None of the other boys has on clothes like these," he said. "They all look alike, and I look different. If I stay here, I want to look like them." He took Wood Fire's hand and went off with him towards the school building.

Now it was beginning. Spear Woman sat down on the grass beside Hunting Horse and thought. All of these changes she had felt were coming, all of these changes they had all known were coming, began here in her own child. It had hurt her when the child pulled itself out of her body, but nothing like the way it hurt her now he was pulling himself out of her heart. He wouldn't want to hurt her or to leave her, and already she was hurt clear through and he had gone farther than he could ever go again. So she sat and pulled up grass stems one at a time and saw them in her hand and threw them away.

Hunting Horse was still. He was being hurt, but not in the same way, and he could keep it from showing better. He had wanted this hurt and had looked for it, and pain that you expected was not so bad as that which came to you unaware. His hands were still, and he watched the schoolhouse door.

It was only because Wood Fire was walking beside him that they knew Grass Stem when he came out. He looked taller, as if the stiff blue trousers and stiff white shirt had grown him up into a man. He was picking his feet up and putting them down carefully. This time it was so he wouldn't spoil the big new shoes that went all around his feet. But the thing that surprised Spear Woman was that they had cut off his hair and had taken off the long, silver earrings. He came beside Wood Fire towards them, not holding to the man's hand any more, but walking alone. He was holding a little bundle under his arm.

He stood in front of them, a long, little way off. His face was steady, without any jerking like getting ready to cry. In some ways, he seemed to understand what was happening better than they did. He held out the bundle to Spear Woman.

"You'd better take these back," he said. "I'm not going to need them."

Hunting Horse took the bundle and stood there over his child. "Are you going to be all right, son?" he asked.

The little boy looked back at him for a moment. "Yes, father."

"Can he come home sometime?" Hunting Horse asked Wood Fire. "He might get homesick."

"He can come home at Christmas," Wood Fire answered. "That's in the middle of winter. And then he can come home again for all next summer. That way you can see him."

"Not in between times?" asked Spear Woman. "Just those two times and not in between?"

"Schoolmaster likes it better if he doesn't," Wood Fire answered. "It makes it easier for the child. But you can send him things, and if you can get the trader to help you, you can write him letters. All those things you'll have to send to him by his school name."

"He gets a new name now?"

"He gets a new name, like when a young man kills an enemy in battle and they change his name to do him honor. This is the same thing." He turned to the child. "Tell your mother your new name."

"Stanley Hunt," said the child in his strong little voice.

"That's a good name," said Wood Fire. "Stanley is the name of one of the officers, and *Hunt* is for his father. It's like *Hunting Horse,* only shorter. That's the name he'll go by here. Can you remember it?"

They practiced it a few times, and then they must leave. Even if it meant riding all night when the owls were flying, they had to go back. It hurt them too much to stay here.

Hunting Horse shook hands with his son. "Good-bye, Stanley Hunt," was all he said. Spear Woman didn't say even that much. She just gathered the little boy to her and held him close for a minute, and then she turned and got on her horse. They rode off together, while Stanley went across the yard to play with the other boys.

As was suggested, "Going Away" carries a weight of meanings. Easily identified are realities such as family feelings and the emotions that appear in a child and his parents when he goes away from home for the first time. Other elements, not so directly stated but surely present, are the mixtures of idealism and blindness sometimes found in those who conduct schools, including the hurts that can be delivered, perhaps unconsciously, by those who try to "teach" the young, especially those from an unfamiliar social group or culture. One might suspect, more broadly, that hurts are delivered by any human change of any kind at any age. A good story throws out broadening meanings in exactly this way.

The reader who admits to himself that actions such as those in "Going Away" are not only part of the American past but also existent in the human condition at any time, may come to see that anger or indignation, or approval, can be beside the point: These things occurred, they still occur, and they must be understood as factors in human behavior. If we concentrate only on the "hurt," which should not at all be taken lightly, we may fail to recognize other elements. To focus exclusively on the evils presented in "Going Away," for example, is to miss the fact that the boy begins immediately and directly his own process of dealing with his new environment. By making this clear, the author avoids a one-sided or sentimental reaction.

The reader who looks closely at "Going Away" will observe that some of its technical features aid in the balanced effect suggested above:

- The language and sentence structure are relatively simple; the sentences are short, mainly declarative and factual in tone.

- A third-person point of view is used, with a shifting focus that allows the author to represent inner feelings, as well as to describe details of action, dress, setting, and to report things said.

- The author makes occasional use of summary narrative: "Now there was no more raiding, and no more danger on that account." Author's comment is slight in this story if, indeed, it appears at all except through descriptive detail.

- Concrete detail is used strongly, purposefully, as a means of achieving reality and stirring emotion: "His long braids hung down his back, and the silver earrings swung beside his face." This detail, in its context, plants a question in a reader's mind: How long will these braids last in the new environment?

- The author moves skillfully and easily between past and present time, and between specific and general remarks, all within a technique that contains considerable subtlety though it may appear to be "simple."

The second story in this section, "Relatives Out West," has a time of action almost exactly that of "Going Away," the early 1880's. The place is another part of the American Southwest. The author, Paul Horgan, is not only a perceptive creative writer but also one of our most knowledgeable authorities on the Southwest, its history, and its people—a Pulitzer Prize winner. He writes from his own knowledge, as important authors so often do.

In "Relatives Out West" we encounter psychological and ethical-religious experiences. We are invited to share, first of all, the force and impact of the land itself: "furies . . . somehow dwell plausibly in this Western land." The narrator, an Anglo-American rancher, thinking of solitary riders sometimes seen, remarks that "human beings cross and vanish in this terrain like any other beings proper to it," and that passing riders are "humanity," "man upon his earth." Such observations and feelings about people and the land take us further than we at first suspect: the rancher, ironically, is beginning to adopt attitudes toward the land similar to those held by its earlier inhabitants—the Apache Indians. Such remarks take us almost to a point of forgetting issues like race—to a point, indeed, at which the earth itself may become a source of belief and attitude, a central human reality. The phrase, "other beings proper to it," brings man and other living creatures on the earth close together, as in the American Indian religions. Thus the setting of this story is both realistic, in the usual sense-impression way, and symbolic of human religions that center on the earth, its "beings," and the natural forces that play upon it and in it.

A reader, then, can follow Horgan's treatment of the Western land as a kind of accompaniment or counterpoint to the dramatic action, and can notice that "Relatives Out West" contains in fact not one, but several stories: There is a story about the land and its influences, as we have indicated. There is a story of the desire to kill, with forces that limit this desire. There is a story of human dignity—in the rancher himself and, very clearly, in the Apache leader and holy man who possesses "that measured confidence of behavior which all personages have." There is a story of anger, "which was just the other side of my fear." These words are spoken, admitted, realized by the rancher himself. There is a realization shared by two men of two races that "I am concerned with what I am and believe, just as you are for yourself."

Here then, from our past, are images of self-knowledge and dignity under pressure.

RELATIVES OUT WEST

PAUL HORGAN

The letter was still a living thing, long after its writer had vanished. Something of his nature arose and moved off the stiff pages, where the writing was formal even when the words were passionate. The ink was by now pale sepia. The pages whispered and cracked delicately when they were handled, however carefully. This is what they said:

from Dark Spring Ranch
New Mexico, Bonito Valley,
August 1, 1881.

My Dear Brother,

Now I will write to accept your offer of the cherrywood piano, which stands in the Rogers Street house. It seemed for a little while that we would have no place to put the piano; but now that we are truly settled here in the West, it will seem so strange and so fine to have it. This letter will not reach you in time to get the piano started off to us before the winter freight; but we shall hopefully regard the spring, and by early summer Susan and the children and I may be able to gather in the evening and sing a little hymn of praise for your generosity. Leonora is now five years old and could start playing soon. As for Martin, who is twelve, he stirs with adventure and his imagination shows him furies which somehow dwell plausibly in this Western land.

Yes, I have much to tell you that will make my boy Martin seem a realist.

We live in a beautiful valley of New Mexico which has the character of foothills, and beyond which in every direction save one the great tempers of mountains hover in the sky. We are isolated, though a few hundred yards from our front door occasional travelers ride by in the sunny dust that smells hot, if you will permit me this locution. What I notice most is that life here dwells in a timeless absolute, compound of white sunlight, spotted hills, the waft of

PAUL HORGAN / Relatives Out West **95**

great cloudy domes from the mountains to the plains, and the rising and falling humors of the little river of our valley, which at home would be styled a creek. Human beings cross and vanish in this terrain like any other beings proper to it; without the important sense which was our common way at home, in the East, where our values made life. Here, when I see riders pass, I think, "They might be of any historical age; they are humanity; so man upon his earth must always have looked." Yes, if my health had not decided my emigration, I would never have learned this much history, however hard I worked at my teaching in the college at home.

My health, by the way, is good. Praise God, so is that of my dear ones. We have all worked so hard for over a year that lately when the fruits of our work were threatened in a strange and terrifying fashion it was for each other that we suffered, and I do believe that this open life of making new places frees people to one another perhaps more really as the Scriptures intended than any other life I know of.

A word of the property: we call it Dark Spring Ranch because there is a heavy grove of cottonwood trees airily domed with shadow, below which our land falls away to the valley floor, and the rude highway. Behind our house rises a faulted cliff of diversely banded rock casting a grave shadow down its own face even at noon. And at the base of this cliff, running from the darkness of a low, deep cave, is a spring, yielding us our water. We have cleared much land about the spring and the house, and the soil is gravelly, so that it presents an ordered and civilized appearance. The house is of adobe clay, with three bedrooms, a study for me, and a common room, one end of which has the kitchen. We built it beneath the trees. Thus when indoors you can almost believe that the green hills of the East surround you outside. Below, in the valley, and above, on the hills, our cattle are pastured. And for the children, there is the indescribable fascination of archaeology; for formerly, and quite recently, Apache Indians lived on the property, and little remnants of this occupancy are always turning up—broken arrows, etc.—to delight them. The chance to buy the place fell my way simply because a certain Captain Hughes, who lives up the valley near Lincoln, had tried for years to possess it from the Indians, who refused to move, a filthy and capricious tribe. But suddenly one day they were gone, and Captain Hughes drove to Santa Fe in his waggon and cleared the title to the place and bought it. Shortly afterward I ventured up that valley, and managed to persuade him to sell it to me, which he did, he declared, only because he needed money to send to creditors in Hellespont, Ohio. We became friendly over the affair, and he lent much aid in our early struggles. He is middle-aged, a physical and reckless man, generous I am sure, something of a fool in his view of the world, yet valiant in our terms out here. He has a red face and white hair and droll blue eyes. Susan likes him, and will feed him lavishly whenever he comes. He is gallant with her, and she is always looking at me to see how I regard his flirtings. But she is so plucky, in this spiny land, and so pretty, so truly a good wife in what many women would regard as a vast whim on the part of their husbands, that I am delighted when we have Captain Hughes, to remind her of the life she left behind, and will help to create anew here.

We truly have a sense of community in the family, and it was not long before we were settled and every day looking forward to the evening, when I would write, Susan would sew, or the children would read to us by turn. There was a surprise one evening when Susan hung up a red curtain across the window and in the lamplight it had a very rich look, with our white marble-topped table before it. It was in Susan's style, for she has a genius at concocting a triumph with practically nothing to go on. If she has ever regretted joining her fortunes with mine, and sinking her legacy from her father, Doctor Martin, into our new property, I have never seen sign of it.

Not even lately, after a hazardous and woeful experience we have all had—a sort of reminder that however exalted I may become in my philosophical view of history in this land, the point of view may be rudely jarred by events.

One day in July it became necessary for Martin and me to ride up the valley to Captain Hughes's place on an errand. It was a sweet, hot day; and as we rode, we thought of the cool cavernous dark spring at home. I asked Martin what the broken rock terraces of the cliff above the spring reminded him of; and he said they reminded him of ruined cities, looked at from a great distance. This was so striking and so suggestive, that we fell into a long discussion (which means that I did the talking). My boy is only twelve, but now and then strikes us all with some imaginative charm like that until we marvel all over again at the quality of mind in growth, which none can see, or touch, but which yields seeable and touchable things. Miniature slabs of archaeology, those faulted and shattered rock terraces, Aztec cities, blocked with shadow on the hillside above our spring! As we rode, I pointed out to Martin the river and the broad hills on both sides of it, and the rain canyons that gashed their faces with earth that sometimes looked almost vermilion. These places were alive with legends and secrecies of both outlaw and myth. When cattle were stolen, these rusty canyons hid them; they were dry almost all year—until a cloud-burst, when they would run with violence, tearing away rock and root as if some malevolent god were coursing his anger there. We talked about myths and their source in the acts of nature, and of gods that grew from symbols of elements into symbols of action, for all peoples, in their own terms. (Martin listens well, with his yellow head and his sunburned face. My theory is that one notion in twenty may lodge itself within. This will be a satisfactory average, I feel.)

Before we knew it, we were at Captain Hughes's house, which is a Mexican style house containing almost no furniture. Mostly, he had large chests heavily padlocked containing firearms, the instrument of security in these times and places, he really believes. Thus something boyish about him, but efficacious, too. He greeted us warmly, and fed us, and we did our business. Then he entertained us with a tale of an Indian—Moojo, he called him—who was a member of the Apaches formerly living at Dark Spring.

He said he'd always remembered this particular Indian as the perfect museum type, with hook nose, sharp cheekbones, tall, and in his eyes the eagle's incommunicable resentments. He said Moojo once happened to arrive at his house one day while a missionary priest from Santa Fe was pausing for lunch and rest. He said the priest and the Indian presented a wonderful picture. He said the priest was sharp and amiable, a skeptic and still a friend. And the Indian, by ironic little suggestions, gave the impression that he, too, was a holy man and that the two of them supported a very good and necessary thing in life; but just the same, brothers in the same profession did not need to put on airs with each other, etc. As Captain Hughes told it, it made a very droll story, for he is something of a raconteur, especially after a few whiskies.

Now, today, who should turn up in the vicinity but this same Moojo, the Indian. He had left that morning, before we got there. He came and sat and stared at Hughes, and said nothing, but had the air of someone with work to do. He was leaner, said Hughes, and dirty, and older; but the same Indian who had vanished inexplicably from the Dark Spring place years before. "A very suggestible man," said Hughes of the Indian. "You can't lay eyes on him without thinking he is somebody. He has that measured confidence of behavior which all personages have."

We rode back later in the afternoon. It was still hot, but the dust was low in the valley, and filtered with sunlight.

It was evening before we reached home. Glad for the cooler air, and the sight of our great groves of trees, we hurried a little. Around a bend we saw a fire burning on the hillside above Dark Spring, amazing and beautiful in the shadow-filling twilight. At first we did not understand it, but then suddenly I thought it might be a signal. I spurred my horse, and Martin hurried too. We flung down the road. Such a clear evening, I shall never forget how it looked and how we felt. The fire burned like a bush in the green-blue dusk. The nearer we came, the surer I was of something fearful.

Susan was by the roadside waiting under the big cottonwood that hoods across it. We could just see her face in the twilight. I jumped down, and she said, "Oh, Eben, have you seen Leonora?" And I replied, "No, is she gone," and then Susan cried bitterly and fell against me as if she might let her weakness flow off her. I raised her up to my saddle and we stood looking up at her in the early darkness, while she explained what had happened.

In the afternoon Leonora went to the spring to play, as the children did every day, building rock castles, &c. There was much work to do in the house, and Susan was busy at it. Presently she noticed that our little girl did not run in and out as she so often did; and Susan went to the open and called, but there was no answer; and she strolled toward the spring, but she was not there. There was a little cairn of rocks, and that was all. She called. Her voice sang ghostly back at her from the echo of the spring. No, at first she could not believe that the child was gone. My wife walked back to the house and looked there. Then she was overwhelmed by the land, I could see how. A little girl suited to sweet homely cares lost on those hills where the heat lived, and snakes, and the savage cactus! Susan called and searched all afternoon; and when the dusk approached, she built a fire on the rocky shelves above the spring, thinking the child would see it and come home. Where could she be? How far could she have strayed? So I asked myself; and then I became enraged, which was just the other face of my fear.

Once in the house, Susan was busy and desperately brisk about feeding us. We fed Martin, and then I said to him that he must get on his horse and go back to Captain Hughes, who would bring his men for a search. He set off. His heart was in his mouth. He adored his sister. It was a knightly mission, and tried him surely. I took a lantern, to see with my own eyes, and went to the spring and all about, and up the scaly hill; and the rock shards slid and crashed, but I found nothing. The spring was black and clear. Susan would not speak or face me. Her grief was full of shame; and it is curious but we were almost estranged for that night, each begging silently for some strength in the other, and getting none.

After midnight came Hughes and several men from his place. With lanterns again, we climbed and called in the hills. The stars were out and presently we could see by starlight. The vast mountain-held calm of that night humbled our lives and rebuked our human terror. Shortly before dawn we went to the house to drink coffee. Captain Hughes had his whisky. He was red and menacing against whatever fate had our child. He muttered and swore from time to time, and half the time made Susan turn her head away in a rush of tears, and again, made her smile gratefully at him. He was baffled, the man of action yet knowing no act to do.

Dawn presently; the lifting of a great cup of darkness off the horizons, and the lateral planes of light assuring the eye. Then in comes Martin, white and pleading with me to come and be quiet but to come and see.

Susan heard him and nodded now, with passionate resignation in her little haggard face.

So I went with him, not knowing what he had found, but I was ready for anything but what I saw. On the miniature city ruins of the rocks above the spring sat a Toltec image, completely implausible in the widening dawn, yet in another way, a figure quite proper to the place. It is an Indian, whispered Martin to me, and we were a hundred feet away; and as if he heard, the Indian turned his head mildly and gazed upon us. I told Martin to fetch Captain Hughes, alone, without the others; and then I strode to the spring and called up to the figure. What was he doing here? To which he answered in a rusty voice, "My home." Hughes was there right then, and he took out his pistol, and said, Moojo, come down here or I shall blow your filthy face off, but the Indian simply sat there, and we could see him better, for it was now white in the sky, and daylight. Hughes scrambled up the rocks and grasped the Indian and sent him falling like a cat down the slippery place to the spring level. "What have you done with that child?" demanded Hughes. And the Indian said nothing, and Hughes probed his gun into the Indian's middle; but he still said nothing. Then Hughes said, why did you come here? and then the Indian answered, as before, "My home." "Yes, he once lived here," said Hughes, and then said we must lock him up, "give me a room, and I will get the word out of him." Hughes called his men; they came, with Susan. They took Moojo to the house and placed him in our bedroom and stood guard. The men were now drunk on fury and fatigue, were ready to hang him and shoot him; the impetus of tragedy was speeding all of us in our desires. Susan had seen the Indian sharply as he went by her, and she smelled him, and the alien mystery of his kind when she thought of her child too; this caused her nearly to cry out, but she did not, but hurried to Martin, to smooth his hair, and see if his hands were dirty, and to pull down his jacket, and smile at him as if to say, "Come, darling, don't worry; we must keep our heads."

In the bedroom Hughes managed to get nothing from the Indian. He came out presently and said that there was surely something very odd here, killing him would do no good, yet he could not say how to make him tell whether or no Leonora was hidden somewhere by him. He would say only that this was his home, as if that explained whatever we might want to know. So they kept him in the bedroom; and we set out to search again, leaving a guard at the window and one at the door of the Indian's prison.

We rode on horseback this time.

High on the hill rims above the ranch we looked back frequently to see if there was any smoke standing in the gold blasting heat, for that was a signal to tell if she was recovered. We saw none, and went to ride on the white-speckled hills under the white sun baking the straw-colored earth. There were great wafting caverns of shade let into the airy domes of the cottonwoods far below us. When we went back late in the afternoon, it was silent and deserted-appearing; we stopped to listen, hearing only doves in the alamosa trees. How dark our spring looked to us indeed! that we had always blessed as such a pure source of life out of the secret rock! It had had a power almost prayer-like for us, and rather than lose our pure water, in this land where water is more priceless than gold, we would have sacrificed almost everything else to God.

We prayed much in the following days.

I need not describe to you, the sufferings that made Susan so worn and pitiful, nor Martin's angry blusterings against the cage of his unknown bafflement. The Indian was kept prisoner, and Hughes tried him with all threats and rewards! but he would not speak. He would eat. But even as four days went by, he refused to drink. A mug of water was passed to him fresh from the spring every day. He never touched it. Nor did he drink from the spring when he was let out under guard at intervals. He had a moribund and ironic dignity. He coughed much. His eyes were sunken and his skin gray-brown. His presence stank with some morbid emanation. I decided he was dying of tuberculosis. When he coughed, he was like a lice-wracked eagle that opens its roman beak and almost soundlessly passes out air and whitely blinks its mad eyes. Try as we would we could not but think he must have some connection with our darling little child's loss. If she had simply wandered, and been lost, then now, five days later, what of her poor little life was left in the arid world?

We tried again and again, but every physical trial at finding her was turned back. I came home one day to find that two of Hughes's men had hurt and tortured the Indian with a hot iron; but he would not speak. I went and spoke to him, in pantomime as much as anything, begging him for the sake of whatever he believed in to yield us up news or denial, but he would not say. He was feverish, reeking, and his tongue hung from being parched. I brought him water, but he cawed silently at me like the furious captive bird. What could so perversely strengthen him but some terrible faith?

That fifth night, sleeping as we must, we were awakened by the shambling tread of thunder on the mountains, and then a fury of wind passing with a cry down the valley, and then rain, such torrents that in the summer night all

Nature seemed to be drinking of it and breathing anew and knowing succor in the dark. My wife and I lay in the dark, and all our courage of the past days seemed like too dry a burden to carry longer; and we wept. It was a poor kind of peace to find, but it came before we slept again; for we had submitted in our hearts to whatever it might be that we must suffer the rest of our lives, which had to be carried ahead no matter what.

The next morning the Indian was taken outdoors for his guarded interval; and the first thing he did was fall down on the earth, which was left puddled and pungent by the furious rainstorm, and at a puddle of rain water he drank and drank, sighing like an animal. The guards gazed at each other, and at me, and they were primitive men, red-faced and bearded and young, and they thought slowly; but what struck them at once was how for days Moojo had refused water from the spring, only to fall on the ground and drink muddy rain water.

They took him back soon.

It at once occurred to me that the Indian regarded the spring as somehow taboo. How very easily water could be held as something sacred in this country, water which sprang alive from the mysterious interior of the earth. I went to the room where the Indian was, and went in, and he lay on his back on the floor. He was sweating and looked gray; he kept his eyes closed, and I spoke to him with a word or two. But he paid no attention. There was a kind of mortal resignation to him, and he lay like a man expecting to die. He wore a flannel shirt and blue cotton pants. His bones stuck them out and made slack between. He lay there like a manifestation of evil; and I flew into a passion and kicked him, out of the most shameful motive in the world, my powerlessness. He opened his eyes and gave me an occult glare, and slowly wracked himself to crouching, once more the hot-eyed stinking eagle, and the red furnace that burned in his head showed light and color in his eyes; and somehow I translated from him a sense of another man suffering, doomed even, and miserably awaiting a solution beyond his own making. It was as if his presence said to mine, "I am concerned with what I am and believe, just as you are for yourself. Men have many ways. When they are in conflict, one way dies." I turned around and left him. He coughed horribly.

Hughes came and I told him of the curious water preference. Now Hughes was in his way, too, a primitive man and often had only contributions of a lusty nature to make to our scattered society. Today he declared, with the air of a man of academic fame, that it meant only one thing, and that was the d——ned silly Indian business of making a god out of something perfectly natural; and if Moojo would not drink from the spring but would drink from the earth, then he was frightened of the spring, and it seemed to him the first clue of any kind to come to us in the whole sad affair. He marched into the bedroom, and took the Indian up by his hair and clattered him along, walking in front of him, making brutal remarks the while, which the Indian suffered with barely the resistance of his weakened steps. The guards came too, and in their young faces was the open, boyish delight in violence that had so long been denied them. Their eyes kindled. Once out of doors, a kind of Western joy seemed to appear, man acting the law as it occurred to him.

They brought Moojo toward the spring; and when he saw whither they dragged him, he shrieked and fell limp and as if boneless in their hold.

Hughes swore and looked at me, and dragged the Indian closer to the gray rocky pool under the ledges. The day glistened with light after rain, and we were blinded by the brilliance of it. My family stood with me, and we were all sure and awfully imaginative, at this collapse of the Indian's, that he knew the answer we hardly could ask. Hughes bent the man's neck down so that his face was above the water, and the man gasped and beat the rocks with his palms and choked on his running breath. Hughes splashed the spring water on him, and he hissed like a nest of snakes. He winced in their hold, and turned; and his face was up to the sky, and we could only pity him for the picture it made of a man's unholy fear of whatever in life was his master. There certainly lay revealed the Indian's real life, something that ruled his spirit and made his virtue or his sin; his life, or demanded his death. He coughed and doubled himself against Captain Hughes's boots, and then crawled a few feet from the spring and bent his forehead to the dirt and rubbed dirt into his hair. We were all silent at this, under the hardly stirring cottonwoods. Then the most extraordinary experience of my life: I saw the unfolding of a mythology, and perceived the power of its terms.

By pantomime and his few English words, and by surprisingly stimulating questions from Captain Hughes, the Indian conveyed the following to us:

That he had long been a holy man of his tribe; that he had gained a knowledge of all the gods of the earth and the heaven from those who had talked to gods; that a god lived in the earth who was the father and the spirit of all the springs, the underground water; this god could appear in spirit in any spring all over the world; that it appeared very frequently, asking plaintively (Moojo enacted this in his rusty voice) that sacrifice and appeasement be made for the wrong done so long ago; that this wrong committed against the god who gave life from the caverns of the world consisted in the theft of his two children, the spring god's children, who vanished when earth was young, and moon not yet old, and this father the god sang to them through all the springs of the earth, but they never answered him, or came back, though all the fishes in the rivers knew and all the ferns of the forest. The bounty of a spring makes life sweet. The god may ask what he will. Every priest has at one time or another heard the god speak in his soul, and tell him what he wants. This god said he wanted his son and his daughter back; and if that was not in the priest's power, then a boy and a girl of the earth must be sent, their sweet lives given to the mystery of the earth source. It was often done. The springs lived on.

This was the mythology.

You can imagine its effect upon us.

Then the Indian said that, some time before, God had spoken to him. But he was the priest of a degenerate people, none of whom would agree to the sacrifice. In shame he had fled the spring, accompanied by his sacrilegious followers. They had crawled westward and destiny caused them nearly to die several times by the parching of their bodies; three times crossing the plains toward Arizona they had come upon springs only to find them dry. No peace dwelt with them. Presently Moojo himself fell ill, and coughed, and burned, and the air of heaven smelled foul to himself, and he inquired of himself if he would die now, and the answer came to him that he would die. He would be a spirit without a face or a name if he died unfaithful to God. He came back with three women to the ritual at Dark Spring, to offer his love to God and earn peace for himself before and after he should die. That was all he needed to explain. He fell exhausted and doomed on the ground, and Hughes let him be for a moment. Hughes was moved and sickened and in a sense chastened by the intensity of this confession of a creature's spirit. Heaven only knows how a belief gets lodged; but once it is, then man is mighty in its terms.

A breath from poor Susan awoke us all again from that mysterious moment.

Hughes took up his victim again, and shook him and demanded now to know what of our little Leonora. This story came forth as sadly and as freely as the first part. He had come to the spring to make peace, to promise that he would find a son and a daughter for the god, when he saw Nora playing among the little rocks. He took her, and held her, and ran across the hill and out of sight to his pony; then they ran to the valley, and up a rain canyon, and there the child was in the care of three women who came with him, and who waited until a son should be granted to him. He had come back, and there was my son Martin, who became frightened and ran in at dawn to tell me; and we came out, and the whole household astir at dawn set upon the Indian, and he was captured before he could make off with Martin. He would die now. He rubbed more earth on his head as if to woo gentleness of that element too.

Of course we were mounted in a very few minutes and, with Moojo tied to a saddle and his hands roped behind him, we set off to find the poor little girl. He led us mournfully, now appearing to have no resentment. God had abandoned him, for some reason which he could only rue bitterly and bow his neck to. My own emotions interested me when I thought about it later. Have you ever wanted to kill someone? My impulse was to kill the Indian; and at the time I believed myself to have every right to do it, though ordinarily I am the mildest of men, as you know, far more interested in motives than in acts, as I suppose the speculative intellect is inclined to be.

Everywhere we rode we saw evidences of the violent rain; there were fresh wounds in the face of the earth, and the sandy ground was twinkling and sucking at the air through its moisture.

My reason said to me that I must not kill Moojo in revenge, once he had restored our child to us. It is said that Apaches are very capricious people, and might return to do damage to anyone that disfavored them.

I considered that we might move away; might go to Arizona; even go back to the East, and take up our old life there again, and my mind raced with the images of that time and place, the life you live, brother, and surely this was mildly hysterical in me. I said to myself deliberately that moving away to any place was not possible. Every cent we had is in the Dark Spring Ranch, and I knew Hughes could not buy it back, for the money I paid him he paid to his bank in Hellespont, Ohio. How, too, risk my health which the West gave back to me?

But when we found Leonora, and the three Indian women up a scraggly arroyo where the rain had driven them for shelter to a kind of alcove in the red earth cut by some storm long past, I thought of one more thing, and I held her tightly and said that the poor little thing must go back to our home at Dark Spring and there be restored to a life without fear in the very place where fear had been born to her. She was hungry and dirty, and thin. She cried and cried when she saw me, and shut her eyes as if never to look again upon anything in the outside world. I kissed her and petted her, but she could not stop, and the most dreadful imaginings occurred to me as to whether she had been hurt or beaten or mistreated; but I could find no marks of that, and I wished for Susan to calm her. I took her to a little turn in the canyon and called Martin to follow, and gave her to him to hug and hold, and his clumsy pattings reminded her of play, perhaps, where my anguished caresses had deepened her sense of woe; and soon she was smiling and sighing, and regarding us with a bewildered and peaceful stare, like a very little baby.

I went back to see about the Indians. The three women were positively mellow with dirt and its smells. One of them was sullen, a young woman who was pregnant. The other two were ancients, and they ingratiated themselves with cordial gibberish delivered through toothless lips, and bowed and ducked, indicating their camp remains with signals of hospitality. Moojo seemed unrelated to them. He sat on his horse, still tied.

Captain Hughes took charge presently, and sent his men up the valley with all the Indians, to deliver them to the commandant at Fort Banning, in the mountains. He said he would follow with a statement of the case. I heard him caution the men severely against lynching the Indian, explaining with much gravity that anything might start up a dangerous thing among all the Apaches in this part of the plains. They went off; and we started back to Dark Spring, with little Nora riding before on my saddle.

We had got barely three miles on our way when we heard fast riding overtaking us; and it was one of Hughes's young men, who came red and breathless with amazement to report that on their way to Fort Banning, Moojo, the Indian, had appeared docile enough, until they came to a place where the road lifted over a hill that had a ridge of whitish rocks along the rim, a place I knew well. From the road it looked like a rolling hill, but at the crest one saw that a sharp cliff fell away down the other side. Well, up this hill dashed Moojo, on his pony, and the men dared not shoot; and at the top they saw him hurry and the horse stumble on some loose stones, and then how quickly they vanished! over the other side of what seemed to be a hill. They followed, of course, and below the cliff found him dead and the horse badly hurt, so they shot it. Captain Hughes asked, "What about the women?" and the young cowboy replied, oddly mistaking his meaning in the excitement of the news, that the women seemed not at all surprised at what their man had done, just as if they knew he meant to do it, and as if they knew, with him, that the cliff was there all the time. With that, Hughes said to let the women go on to Fort Banning, where they would probably be provisioned and sent to the nearest Apaches. The young man looked at each of us in the fullness of his tale, and then went riding off to overtake the escort party on the road to Fort Banning, where they waited by the hill and its cliff and its dead.

And now it was easy to be compassionate over the Indian. We rode on home; and my darling Susan had her little girl back, hugging and kissing her, and then saying nothing about the fearful six days but exclaiming how much she needed to wash and put on a clean dress and have her hair brushed out. Martin was oddly shy with his little sister, as if danger had matured them both. But later in the day they were together by the spring and it no longer seemed a place of mystery and lifelong aptness to fright.

There are dangers greater than those I have described to you, and fear itself is one; and of the truth of this, the wretched Moojo himself was proof. With this reflection I will end the history of our adventure, and ask you to give to everyone the news of their relatives out West.

Your aff. brother,
EBEN

The long letter made a packet, thick and well established in its creases. On the back of the last page, the handwriting changed, and was slender and threadlike, difficult to read. But the interest of a postscript is usually that of an afterthought off its guard; and when the pale exquisite writing became familiar and so decipherable, this is what it said:

P.S. Of what Eben has told you I will say nothing, my dear Seth, for such things were better to be forgotten, and displaced by happier things. Send word, then, soon, about the piano, for I do really think that our life here will no longer be isolated if we can make our own music.

Devotedly yours,
SUSAN.

You will probably have seen that this story permits extrapolations bearing on such basic questions as these: "Who am I? What am I? Who is this other person?" It asks us about ourselves.

A quick point of fact may help with the process of realizing how much "Relatives Out West" contains. As far as is known, it is a fact that the earlier inhabitants of this country, the native Americans, had religions in which all facets of external nature—all animals, plants, men and earth, all skies and weathers—shared a "cosmos," a common world. The land itself, and everything that grew or moved upon it, was part of this religious view. The Anglo-American rancher is subject to at least two strands of influence—his new environment and his older religion, to which he refers often. His ultimate decency arises from—where?

The third piece of fiction exploring the topic What We Were and What We Are *is "Becky," by Jean Toomer. The place is the State of Georgia. The time of action, the early years of the present century: last of the horse-and-buggy days, the beginning of the T-Model Ford era. The action is separated by only thirty to forty years from such events as those in "Going Away" or "Relatives Out West," and like the actions in these stories, it may seem far behind us, until we reflect. "Becky" is then as close to us as that odd person we knew about who lived somewhere on the outskirts of town or behaved strangely on our block, a shadowing of our consciousness and our conscience. Readers may be puzzled more than a little at first by "Becky," but it rewards a thoughtful reading.*

BECKY

JEAN TOOMER

Becky was the white woman who had two Negro sons. She's dead; they've gone away. The pines whisper to Jesus. The Bible flaps its leaves with an aimless rustle on her mound.

Becky had one Negro son. Who gave it to her? Damn buck nigger, said the white folks' mouths. She wouldnt tell. Common, God-forsaken, insane white shameless wench, said the white folks' mouths. Her eyes were sunken, her neck stringy, her breasts fallen, till then. Taking their words, they filled her, like a bubble rising—then she broke. Mouth setting in a twist that held her eyes, harsh, vacant, staring . . . Who gave it to her? Low-down nigger with no self-respect, said the black folks' mouths. She wouldnt tell. Poor Catholic poor-white crazy woman, said the black folks' mouths. White folks and black folks built her cabin, fed her and her growing baby, prayed secretly to God who'd put His cross upon her and cast her out.

When the first was born, the white folks said they'd have no more to do with her. And black folks, they too joined hands to cast her out . . . The pines whispered to Jesus . . . The railroad boss said not to say he said it, but she could live, if she wanted to, on the narrow strip of land between the railroad and the road. John Stone, who owned the lumber and the bricks, would have shot the man who told he gave the stuff to Lonnie Deacon, who stole out there at night and built the cabin. A single room held down to earth . . . O fly away to Jesus . . . by a leaning chimney . . .

Six trains each day rumbled past and shook the ground under her cabin. Fords, and horse- and mule-drawn buggies went back and forth along the road. No one ever saw her. Trainmen, and passengers who'd heard about her, threw out papers and food. Threw out little crumpled slips of paper scribbled with prayers, as they passed her eye-shaped piece of sandy ground. Ground island-ized between the road and railroad track. Pushed up where a blue-sheen God with listless eyes could look at it. Folks from the town took turns, unknown, of course, to each other, in bringing corn and meat and sweet potatoes. Even sometimes snuff . . . O thank y Jesus . . . Old David Georgia, grinding cane and boiling syrup, never went her way without some sugar sap. No one ever saw her. The boy grew up and ran around. When he was five years old as folks reckoned it, Hugh Jourdon saw him carrying a baby. "Becky has another son," was what the whole town knew. But nothing was said, for the part of man that says things to the likes of that had told itself that if there was a Becky, that Becky now was dead.

The two boys grew. Sullen and cunning . . . O pines, whisper to Jesus; tell Him to come and press sweet Jesus-lips against their lips and eyes . . . It seemed as though with those two big fellows there, there could be no room for Becky. The part that prayed wondered if perhaps she'd really died, and they had buried her. No one dared ask. They'd beat and cut a man who meant nothing at all in mentioning that they lived along the road. White or colored? No one knew, and least of all themselves. They drifted around from job to job. We, who had cast out their mother because of them, could we take them in? They answered black and white folks by shooting up two men and leaving town. "Godam the white folks; godam the niggers," they shouted as they left town. Becky? Smoke curled up from her chimney; she must be there. Trains passing shook the ground. The ground shook the leaning chimney. Nobody noticed it. A creepy feeling came over all who saw that thin wraith of smoke and felt the trembling of the ground. Folks began to take her food again. They quit it soon because they had a fear. Becky if dead might be a hant, and if alive—it took some nerve even to mention it . . . O pines, whisper to Jesus . . .

It was Sunday. Our congregation had been visiting at Pulverton, and were coming home. There was no wind. The autumn sun, the bell from Ebenezer Church, listless and heavy. Even the pines were stale, sticky, like the smell of food that makes you sick. Before we turned the bend of the road that would show us the Becky cabin, the horses stopped stock-still, pushed back their ears, and nervously whinnied. We urged, then whipped them on. Quarter of a mile away thin smoke curled up from the leaning chimney . . . O pines, whisper to Jesus . . . Goose-flesh came on my skin though there still was neither chill nor wind. Eyes left their sockets for the cabin. Ears burned and throbbed. Uncanny eclipse! fear closed my mind. We were just about to pass . . . Pines shout to Jesus! . . the ground trembled as a ghost train rumbled by. The chimney fell into the cabin. Its thud was like a hollow report, ages having passed since it went off. Barlo and I were pulled out of our seats. Dragged to the door that had swung open. Through the dust we saw the bricks in a mound upon the floor. Becky, if she was there, lay under them. I thought I heard a groan. Barlo, mumbling something, threw his Bible on the pile. (No one has ever touched it.) Somehow we got away. My buggy was still on the road. The last thing that I remember was whipping old Dan like fury; I remember nothing after that—that is, until I reached town and folks crowded round to get the true word of it.

Becky was the white woman who had two Negro sons. She's dead; they've gone away. The pines whisper to Jesus. The Bible flaps its leaves with an aimless rustle on her mound.

"Becky" is the story of a life, or part of a life. It is closer to poetry in technique than most stories, for it employs rhythmic drive and flow and many of the devices of poetry to heighten mood and build tension—and it achieves its multiple effects in fewer than a thousand words. Jean Toomer, we should note, was a poet, as well as a story-writer. The major technique in "Becky" is summary narrative interspersed with brief references to particular incidents or details, plus some use of direct author's comment. The prefatory and final refrains, together with interspersed repetition of words and phrases carrying emotion, have the effect of a kind of brooding comment. The last long paragraph, however, immediately before the final refrain, comes as a shock. Suddenly the author switches to first-person narrative: "It was Sunday . . . I remember nothing after that—that is, until I reached town and folks crowded round to get the true word of it." This abrupt effective change in focus is reminiscent of Faulkner, but Jean Toomer wrote "Becky" before Faulkner had developed his impressive techniques.

This story is like some new kind of movie or television camera, yet to be invented, making one long slow pass over Becky, a removed woman whose life holds symbolic importance for so many in a small community. This new and strange camera does not focus for long on any particular detail or dramatic action, for the author-as-cameraman selects events to be quickly seen, heard, and obscured without much explanation. The camera does pick up a few significant actions of human beings: the "railroad boss" who finds the land on which Becky could live; John Stone, who supplies lumber and bricks for the cabin where Becky lives, though he "would have shot the man who told he gave the stuff to Lonnie Deacon, who stole out there at night and built the cabin."

So Becky, outcast from two races, serves the author as a focus for a complex of attitudes and actions combining various degrees of ethical-moral weight, positive to negative. (Certainly the painfully familiar human mixture in someone who performs kind acts in secret, or out of "guilt," is present.) Becky herself is hardly seen in the story, if at all, but she is reported on one significant point: "She wouldn't tell."

We may conclude that many people in the community suggested in this story are reacting to a symbol, and in a confusion of ways. Is it possible, then, to believe that much human behavior is textured like this, composed of open or secret reactions to situations that disturb? In this context of moral or ethical contradiction or confusion, we should consider the probable meanings of the repeated references to Jesus.

The main story in "Becky" is clear enough in its general outline; a woman lived and died. But over the whole the author meditates, and so do we. In a powerful way the story raises questions concerning the scope of our awareness. But the questions are asked with admirable reserve.

Stephen Crane, author of "The Blue Hotel," actually saw the Western plains country in snow and blizzard at about the time of his story, the early 1880's. But he was not describing that more northern area in the manner of Paul Horgan, or with Horgan's range of purposes. Although Crane does emphasize the weather and the inhabitants of a remote place he uses these elements in order to drive home an idea. "The Blue Hotel" presents a stranger ("the Swede") walking into a plains town, already convinced of what he will find there. He has been reading "dime novel" accounts of the dangerous West. The inhabitants of the place react in their own way, and this becomes a central fact of the story. What would your reaction be to a stranger who already "knows" all about you, on the basis of stereotypes, and therefore feels no need really to look at you or to listen? Do young people, or old, today have to endure ready-made conclusions about themselves?

*THE BLUE HOTEL

STEPHEN CRANE

1

The Palace Hotel at Fort Romper was painted a light blue, a shade that is on the legs of a kind of heron, causing the bird to declare its position against any background. The Palace Hotel, then, was always screaming and howling in a way that made the dazzling winter landscape of Nebraska seem only a gray swampish hush. It stood alone on the prairie, and when the snow was falling the town two hundred yards away was not visible. But when the traveller alighted at the railway station he was obliged to pass the Palace Hotel before he could come upon the company of low clapboard houses which composed Fort Romper, and it was not to be thought that any traveller could pass the Palace Hotel without looking at it. Pat Scully, the proprietor, had proved himself a master of strategy when he chose his paints. It is true that on clear days, when the great transcontinental expresses, long lines of swaying Pullmans, swept through Fort Romper, passengers were overcome at the sight, and the cult that knows the brown-reds and the subdivisions of the dark greens of the East expressed shame, pity, horror, in a laugh. But to the citizens of this prairie town and to the people who would naturally stop there, Pat Scully had performed a feat. With this opulence and splendor, these creeds, classes, egotisms, that streamed through Romper on the rails day after day, they had no color in common.

As if the displayed delights of such a blue hotel were not sufficiently enticing, it was Scully's habit to go every morning and evening to meet the leisurely trains that stopped at Romper and work his seductions upon any man that he might see wavering, gripsack in hand.

One morning, when a snow-crusted engine dragged its long string of freight cars and its one passenger coach to the station, Scully performed the marvel of catching three men. One was a shaky and quick-eyed Swede, with a great shining cheap valise; one was a tall bronzed cowboy, who was on his way to a ranch near the Dakota line; one was a little silent man from the East, who didn't look it, and didn't announce it. Scully practically made them prisoners.

He was so nimble and merry and kindly that each probably felt it would be the height of brutality to try to escape. They trudged off over the creaking board sidewalks in the wake of the eager little Irishman. He wore a heavy fur cap squeezed tightly down on his head. It caused his two red ears to stick out stiffly, as if they were made of tin.

At last, Scully, elaborately,, with boisterous hospitality, conducted them through the portals of the blue hotel. The room which they entered was small. It seemed to be merely a proper temple for an enormous stove, which, in the center, was humming with godlike violence. At various points on its surface the iron had become luminous and glowed yellow from the heat. Beside the stove Scully's son Johnnie was playing High-Five with an old farmer who had whiskers both gray and sandy. They were quarrelling. Frequently the old farmer turned his face toward a box of sawdust—colored brown from tobacco juice —that was behind the stove, and spat with an air of great impatience and irritation. With a loud flourish of words Scully destroyed the game of cards, and bustled his son upstairs with part of the baggage of the new guests. He himself conducted them to three basins of the coldest water in the world. The cowboy and the Easterner burnished themselves fiery red with this water, until it seemed to be some kind of metal-polish. The Swede, however, merely dipped his fingers gingerly and with trepidation. It was notable that throughout this series of small ceremonies the three travellers were made to feel that Scully was very benevolent. He was conferring great favors upon them. He handed the towel from one to another with an air of philanthropic impulse.

Afterward they went to the first room, and, sitting about the stove, listened to Scully's officious clamor at his daughters,, who were preparing the midday meal. They reflected in the silence of experienced men who tread carefully amid new people. Nevertheless, the old farmer, stationary, invincible in his chair near the warmest part of the stove, turned his face from the sawdust-box frequently and addressed a glowing commonplace to the strangers. Usually he was answered in short but adequate sentences by either the cowboy or the Easterner. The Swede said nothing. He seemed to be occupied in making furtive estimates of each man in the room. One might have thought that he had the sense of silly suspicion which comes to guilt. He resembled a badly frightened man.

Later, at dinner, he spoke a little, addressing his conversation entirely to Scully. He volunteered that he had come from New York, where for ten years he had worked as a tailor. These facts seemed to strike Scully as fascinating, and afterward he volunteered that he had lived at Romper for fourteen years. The Swede asked about the crops and the price of labor. He seemed barely to listen to Scully's extended replies. His eyes continued to rove from man to man.

Finally, with a laugh and a wink, he said that some of these Western communities were very dangerous; and after his statement he straightened his legs under the table, tilted his head, and laughed again, loudly. It was plain that the demonstration had no meaning to the others. They looked at him wondering and in silence.

As the men trooped heavily back into the front room, the two little windows presented views of a turmoiling sea of snow. The huge arms of the wind were making attempts—mighty, circular, futile—to embrace the flakes as they sped. A gate-post like a still man with a blanched face stood aghast amid this profligate fury. In a hearty voice Scully announced the presence of a blizzard. The guests of the blue hotel, lighting their pipes, assented with grunts of lazy masculine contentment. No island of the sea could be exempt in the degree of this little room with its humming stove. Johnnie, son of Scully, in a tone which defined his opinion of his ability as a card-player, challenged the old farmer of both gray and sandy whiskers to a game of High-Five. The farmer agreed with a contemptuous and bitter scoff. They sat close to the stove, and squared their knees under a wide board. The cowboy and the Easterner watched the game with interest. The Swede remained near the window, aloof, but with a countenance that showed signs of an inexplicable excitement.

The play of Johnnie and the gray-beard was suddenly ended by another quarrel. The old man arose while casting a look of heated scorn at his adversary. He slowly buttoned his coat, and then stalked with fabulous dignity from the room. In the discreet silence of all the other men the Swede laughed. His laughter rang somehow childish. Men by this time had begun to look at him askance, as if they wished to inquire what ailed him.

A new game was formed jocosely. The cowboy volunteered to become the partner of Johnnie, and they all then turned to ask the Swede to throw in his lot with the little Easterner. He asked some questions about the game, and, learning that it wore many names, and that he had played it when it was under an alias, he accepted the invitation. He strode toward the men nervously, as if he expected to be assaulted. Finally, seated, he gazed from face to face and laughed shrilly. This laugh was so strange that the Easterner looked up quickly, the cowboy sat intent and with his mouth open, and Johnnie paused, holding the cards with still fingers.

Afterward there was a short silence. Then Johnnie said, "Well, let's get at it. Come on now!" They pulled their chairs forward until their knees were bunched under the board. They began to play, and their interest in the game caused the others to forget the manner of the Swede.

The cowboy was a board-whacker. Each time that he held superior cards he whanged them, one by one, with exceeding force, down upon the improvised table, and took the tricks with a glowing air of prowess and pride that sent thrills of indignation into the hearts of his opponents. A game with a board-whacker in it is sure to become intense. The countenances of the Easterner and the Swede were miserable whenever the cowboy thundered down his aces and kings, while Johnnie, his eyes gleaming with joy, chuckled and chuckled.

Because of the absorbing play none considered the strange ways of the Swede. They paid strict heed to the game. Finally, during a lull caused by a new deal, the Swede suddenly addressed Johnnie: "I suppose there have been a good many men killed in this room." The jaws of the others dropped and they looked at him.

"What in hell are you talking about?" said Johnnie.

The Swede laughed again his blatant laugh, full of a kind of false courage and defiance. "Oh, you know what I mean all right," he answered.

"I'm a liar if I do!" Johnnie protested. The card was halted, and the men stared at the Swede. Johnnie evidently felt that as the son of the proprietor he should make a direct inquiry. "Now, what might you be drivin' at, mister?" he asked. The Swede winked at him. It was a wink full of cunning. His fingers shook on the edge of the board. "Oh, maybe you think I have been to nowheres. Maybe you think I'm a tenderfoot?"

"I don't know nothin' about you," answered Johnnie, "and I don't give a damn where you've been. All I got to say is that I don't know what you're driving at. There hain't never been nobody killed in this room."

The cowboy, who had been steadily gazing at the Swede, then spoke: "What's wrong with you, mister?"

Apparently it seemed to the Swede that he was formidably menaced. He shivered and turned white near the corners of his mouth. He sent an appealing glance in the direction of the little Easterner. During these moments he did not forget to wear his air of advanced pot-valor. "They say they don't know what I mean," he remarked mockingly to the Easterner.

The latter answered after prolonged and cautious reflection. "I don't understand you," he said, impassively.

The Swede made a movement then which announced that he thought he had encountered treachery from the only quarter where he had expected sympathy, if not help. "Oh, I see you are all against me. I see—"

The cowboy was in a state of deep stupefaction. "Say," he cried, as he tumbled the deck violently down upon the board, "say, what are you gittin' at, hey?"

The Swede sprang up with the celerity of a man escaping from a snake on the floor. "I don't want to fight!" he shouted. "I don't want to fight!"

The cowboy stretched his long legs indolently and deliberately. His hands were in his pockets. He spat into the sawdust-box. "Well, who the hell thought you did?" he inquired.

The Swede backed rapidly toward a corner of the room. His hands were out protectingly in front of his chest, but he was making an obvious struggle to control his fright. "Gentlemen," he quavered, "I suppose I am going to be killed before I can leave this house! I suppose I am going to be killed before I can leave this house!" In his eyes was the dying-swan look. Through the windows could be seen the snow turning blue in the shadow of dusk. The wind tore at the house, and some loose thing beat regularly against the clapboards like a spirit tapping.

A door opened, and Scully himself entered. He paused in surprise as he noted the tragic attitude of the Swede. Then he said, "What's the matter here?"

The Swede answered him swiftly and eagerly: "These men are going to kill me."

"Kill you!" ejaculated Scully. "Kill you! What are you talkin'?"

The Swede made the gesture of a martyr.

Scully wheeled sternly upon his son. "What is this, Johnnie?"

The lad had grown sullen. "Damned if I know," he answered. "I can't make no sense to it." He began to shuffle the cards, fluttering them together with an angry snap. "He says a good many men have been killed in this room, or something like that. And he says he's goin' to be killed here too. I don't know what ails him. He's crazy, I shouldn't wonder."

Scully then looked for explanation to the cowboy, but the cowboy simply shrugged his shoulders.

"Kill you?" said Scully again to the Swede. "Kill you? Man, you're off your nut."

"Oh, I know," burst out the Swede. "I know what will happen. Yes, I'm crazy—yes. Yes, of course, I'm crazy—yes. But I know one thing—" There was a sort of sweat of misery and terror upon his face. "I know I won't get out of here alive."

The cowboy drew a deep breath, as if his mind was passing into the last stages of dissolution. "Well, I'm doggoned," he whispered to himself.

Scully wheeled suddenly and faced his son. "You've been troublin' this man!"

Johnnie's voice was loud with its burden of grievance. "Why, good Gawd, I ain't done nothin' to 'im."

The Swede broke in. "Gentlemen, do not disturb yourselves. I will leave this house. I will go away, because"—he accused them dramatically with his glance—"because I do not want to be killed."

Scully was furious with his son. "Will you tell me what is the matter, you young divil? What's the matter, anyhow? Speak out!"

"Blame it!" cried Johnnie in despair, "don't I tell you I don't know? He—he says we want to kill him, and that's all I know. I can't tell what ails him."

The Swede continued to repeat: "Never mind, Mr. Scully; never mind. I will leave this house. I will go away, because I do not wish to be killed. Yes, of course, I am crazy—yes. But I know one thing! I will go away. I will leave this house. Never mind, Mr. Scully; never mind. I will go away."

"You will not go 'way," said Scully. "You will not go 'way until I hear the reason of this business. If anybody has troubled you I will take care of him. This is my house. You are under my roof, and I will not allow any peaceable man to be troubled here." He cast a terrible eye upon Johnnie, the cowboy, and the Easterner.

"Never mind, Mr. Scully; never mind. I will go away. I do not wish to be killed." The Swede moved toward the door which opened upon the stairs. It was evidently his intention to go at once for his baggage.

"No, no," shouted Scully peremptorily; but the white-faced man slid by him and disappeared. "Now," said Scully severely, "what does this mane?"

Johnnie and the cowboy cried together: "Why, we didn't do nothin' to 'im!"

Scully's eyes were cold. "No," he said, "you didn't?"

Johnnie swore a deep oath. "Why, this is the wildest loon I ever see. We didn't do nothin' at all. We were jest sittin' here playin' cards, and he—"

The father suddenly spoke to the Easterner. "Mr. Blanc," he asked, "what has these boys been doin'?"

The Easterner reflected again. "I didn't see anything wrong at all," he said at last, slowly.

Scully began to howl. "But what does it mane?" He stared ferociously at his son. "I have a mind to lather you for this, my boy."

Johnnie was frantic. "Well, what have I done?" he bawled at his father.

3

"I think you are tongue-tied," said Scully finally to his son, the cowboy, and the Easterner; and at the end of this scornful sentence he left the room.

Upstairs the Swede was swiftly fastening the straps of his great valise. Once his back happened to be half turned toward the door, and, hearing a noise there, he wheeled and sprang up, uttering a loud cry. Scully's wrinkled visage showed grimly in the light of the small lamp he carried. This yellow effulgence, streaming upward, colored only his prominent features, and left his eyes, for instance, in mysterious shadow. He resembled a murderer.

"Man! man!" he exclaimed, "have you gone daffy?"

"Oh, no! Oh, no!" rejoined the other. "There are people in this world who know pretty nearly as much as you do—understand?"

For a moment they stood gazing at each other. Upon the Swede's deathly pale cheeks were two spots brightly crimson and sharply edged, as if they had been carefully painted. Scully placed the light on the table and sat himself on the edge of the bed. He spoke ruminatively. "By cracky, I never heard of such a thing in my life. It's a complete muddle. I can't, for the soul of me, think how you ever got this idea into your head." Presently he lifted his eyes and asked: "And did you sure think they were going to kill you?"

The Swede scanned the old man as if he wished to see into his mind. "I did," he said at last. He obviously suspected that this answer might precipitate an outbreak. As he pulled on a strap his whole arm shook, the elbow wavering like a bit of paper.

Scully banged his hand impressively on the footboard of the bed. "Why, man, we're goin' to have a line of ilictric street-cars in this town next spring."

" 'A line of electric street-cars,' " repeated the Swede, stupidly.

"And," said Scully, "there's a new railroad goin' to be built down from Broken Arm to here. Not to mintion the four churches and the smashin' big brick schoolhouse. Then there's the big factory, too. Why, in two years Romper'll be a met-tro-*pol*-is."

Having finished the preparation of his baggage, the Swede straightened himself. "Mr. Scully," he said, with sudden hardihood, "how much do I owe you?"

"You don't owe me anythin'," said the old man, angrily.

"Yes, I do," retorted the Swede. He took seventy-five cents from his pocket and tendered it to Scully; but the latter snapped his fingers in disdainful refusal. However, it happened that they both stood gazing in a strange fashion at three silver pieces on the Swede's open palm.

"I'll not take your money," said Scully at last. "Not after what's been goin' on here." Then a plan seemed to strike him. "Here," he cried, picking up his lamp and moving toward the door. "Here! Come with me a minute."

"No," said the Swede, in overwhelming alarm.

"Yes," urged the old man. "Come on! I want you to come and see a picter—just across the hall—in my room."

The Swede must have concluded that his hour was come. His jaw dropped and his teeth showed like a dead man's. He ultimately followed Scully across the corridor, but he had the step of one hung in chains.

Scully flashed the light high on the wall of his own chamber. There was revealed a ridiculous photograph of a little girl. She was leaning against a balustrade of gorgeous decoration, and the formidable bang to her hair was prominent. The figure was as graceful as an upright sled-stake, and, withal, it was of the hue of lead. "There," said Scully, tenderly, "that's the picter of my little girl that died. Her name was Carrie. She had the purtiest hair you ever saw! I was that fond of her, she—"

Turning then, he saw that the Swede was not contemplating the picture at all, but, instead, was keeping keen watch on the gloom in the rear.

"Look, man!" cried Scully, heartily. "That's the picter of my little gal that died. Her name was Carrie. And then here's the picter of my oldest boy, Michael. He's a lawyer in Lincoln, an' doin' well. I gave that boy a grand eddication, and I'm glad for it now. He's a fine boy. Look at 'im now. Ain't he bold as blazes, him there in Lincoln, an honored an' respicted gintleman! An honored and respicted gintleman," concluded Scully with a flourish. And, so saying, he smote the Swede jovially on the back.

The Swede faintly smiled.

"Now," said the old man, "there's only one more thing." He dropped suddenly to the floor and thrust his head beneath the bed. The Swede could hear his muffled voice. "I'd keep it under my piller if it wasn't for that boy Johnnie. Then there's the old woman— Where is it now? I never put it twice in the same place. Ah, now come out with you!"

Presently he backed clumsily from under the bed, dragging with him an old coat rolled into a bundle. "I've fetched him," he muttered. Kneeling on the floor, he unrolled the coat and extracted from its heart a large yellow-brown whisky-bottle.

His first maneuver was to hold the bottle up to the light. Reassured, apparently, that nobody had been tampering with it, he thrust it with a generous movement toward the Swede.

The weak-kneed Swede was about to eagerly clutch this element of strength, but he suddenly jerked his hand away and cast a look of horror upon Scully.

"Drink," said the old man affectionately. He had risen to his feet, and now stood facing the Swede.

There was a silence. Then again Scully said: "Drink!"

The Swede laughed wildly. He grabbed the bottle, put it to his mouth; and as his lips curled absurdly around the opening and his throat worked, he kept his glance, burning with hatred, upon the old man's face.

After the departure of Scully the three men, with the cardboard still upon their knees, preserved for a long time an astounded silence. Then Johnnie said: "That's the dod-dangedest Swede I ever see."

"He ain't no Swede," said the cowboy, scornfully.

"Well, what is he then?" cried Johnnie. "What is he then?"

"It's my opinion," replied the cowboy deliberately, "he's some kind of a Dutchman." It was a venerable custom of the country to entitle as Swedes all light-haired men who spoke with a heavy tongue. In consequence the idea of the cowboy was not without its daring. "Yes, sir," he repeated. "It's my opinion this feller is some kind of a Dutchman."

"Well, he says he's a Swede, anyhow," muttered Johnnie, sulkily. He turned to the Easterner: "What do you think, Mr. Blanc?"

"Oh, I don't know," replied the Easterner.

"Well, what do you think makes him act that way?" asked the cowboy.

"Why, he's frightened." The Easterner knocked his pipe against a rim of the stove. "He's clear frightened out of his boots."

"What at?" cried Johnnie and the cowboy together.

The Easterner reflected over his answer.

"What at?" cried the others again.

"Oh, I don't know, but it seems to me this man has been reading dime novels, and he thinks he's right out in the middle of it—the shootin' and stabbin' and all."

"But," said the cowboy, deeply scandalized, "this ain't Wyoming, ner none of them places. This is Nebrasker."

"Yes," added Johnnie, "an' why don't he wait till he gits *out West?*"

The travelled Easterner laughed. "It isn't different there even—not in these days. But he thinks he's right in the middle of hell."

Johnnie and the cowboy mused long.

"It's awful funny," remarked Johnnie at last.

"Yes," said the cowboy. "This is a queer game. I hope we don't git snowed in, because then we'd have to stand this here man bein' around with us all the time. That wouldn't be no good."

"I wish pop would throw him out," said Johnnie.

Presently they heard a loud stamping on the stairs, accompanied by ringing jokes in the voice of old Scully, and laughter, evidently from the Swede. The men around the stove stared vacantly at each other. "Gosh!" said the cowboy. The door flew open, and old Scully, flushed and anecdotal, came into the room. He was jabbering at the Swede, who followed him, laughing bravely. It was the entry of two roisterers from a banquet hall.

"Come now," said Scully sharply to the three seated men, "move up and give us a chance at the stove." The cowboy and the Easterner obediently sidled their chairs to make room for the new-comers. Johnnie, however, simply arranged himself in a more indolent attitude, and then remained motionless.

"Come! Git over, there," said Scully.

"Plenty of room on the other side of the stove," said Johnnie.

"Do you think we want to sit in the draught?" roared the father.

But the Swede here interposed with a grandeur of confidence. "No, no. Let the boy sit where he likes," he cried in a bullying voice to the father.

"All right! All right!" said Scully, deferentially. The cowboy and the Easterner exchanged glances of wonder.

The five chairs were formed in a crescent about one side of the stove. The Swede began to talk; he talked arrogantly, profanely, angrily. Johnnie, the cowboy, and the Easterner maintained a morose silence, while old Scully appeared to be receptive and eager, breaking in constantly with sympathetic ejaculations.

Finally the Swede announced that he was thirsty. He moved in his chair, and said that he would go for a drink of water.

"I'll git it for you," cried Scully at once.

"No," said the Swede, contemptuously. "I'll get it for myself." He arose and stalked with the air of an owner off into the executive parts of the hotel.

As soon as the Swede was out of hearing Scully sprang to his feet and whispered intensely to the others: "Upstairs he thought I was tryin' to poison 'im."

"Say," said Johnnie, "this makes me sick. Why don't you throw 'im out in the snow?"

"Why, he's all right now," declared Scully. "It was only that he was from the East, and he thought this was a tough place. That's all. He's all right now."

The cowboy looked with admiration upon the Easterner. "You were straight," he said. "You were on to that there Dutchman."

"Well," said Johnnie to his father, "he may be all right now, but I don't see it. Other time he was scared, but now he's too fresh."

Scully's speech was always a combination of Irish brogue and idiom, Western twang and idiom, and scraps of curiously formal diction taken from the storybooks and newspapers. He now hurled a strange mass of language at the head of his son. "What do I keep? What do I keep? What do I keep?" he demanded, in a voice of thunder. He slapped his knee impressively, to indicate that he himself was going to make reply, and that all should heed. "I keep a hotel," he shouted. "A hotel, do you mind? A guest under my roof has sacred privileges. He is to be intimidated by none. Not one word shall he hear that would prijudice him in favor of goin' away. I'll not have it. There's no place in this here town where they can say they iver took in a guest of mine because he was afraid to stay here." He wheeled suddenly upon the cowboy and the Easterner. "Am I right?"

"Yes, Mr. Scully," said the cowboy, "I think you're right."

"Yes, Mr. Scully," said the Easterner, "I think you're right."

5

At six-o'clock supper, the Swede fizzed like a fire-wheel. He sometimes seemed on the point of bursting into riotous song, and in all his madness he was encouraged by old Scully. The Easterner was encased in reserve; the cowboy sat in wide-mouthed amazement, forgetting to eat, while Johnnie wrathily demolished great plates of food. The daughters of the house, when they were obliged to replenish the biscuits, approached as warily as Indians, and, having succeeded in their purpose, fled with ill-concealed trepidation. The Swede domineered the whole feast, and he gave it the appearance of a cruel bacchanal. He seemed to have grown suddenly taller; he gazed, brutally disdainful, into every face. His voice rang through the room. Once when he jabbed out harpoon-fashion with his fork to pinion a biscuit, the weapon nearly impaled the hand of the Easterner, which had been stretched quietly out for the same biscuit.

After supper, as the men filed toward the other room, the Swede smote Scully ruthlessly on the shoulder. "Well, old boy, that was a good, square meal." Johnnie looked hopefully at his father; he knew that shoulder was tender from an old fall; and, indeed, it appeared for a moment as if Scully was going to flame out over the matter, but in the end he smiled a sickly smile and remained silent. The others understood from his manner that he was admitting his responsibility for the Swede's new view-point.

Johnnie, however, addressed his parent in an aside. "Why don't you license somebody to kick you downstairs?" Scully scowled darkly by way of reply.

When they were gathered about the stove, the Swede insisted on another game of High-Five. Scully gently deprecated the plan at first, but the Swede turned a wolfish glare upon him. The old man subsided, and the Swede canvassed the others. In his tone there was always a great threat. The cowboy and the Easterner both remarked indifferently that they would play. Scully said that he would presently have to go to meet the 6.58 train, and so the Swede turned menacingly upon Johnnie. For a moment their glances crossed like blades, and then Johnnie smiled and said, "Yes, I'll play."

They formed a square, with the little board on their knees. The Easterner and the Swede were again partners. As the play went on, it was noticeable that the cowboy was not board-whacking as usual. Meanwhile, Scully, near the lamp, had put on his spectacles and, with an appearance curiously like an old priest, was reading a newspaper. In time he went out to meet the 6.58 train, and, despite his precautions, a gust of polar wind whirled into the room as he opened the door. Besides scattering the cards, it chilled the players to the marrow. The Swede cursed frightfully. When Scully returned, his entrance disturbed a cosy and friendly scene. The Swede again cursed. But presently they were once more intent, their heads bent forward and their hands moving swiftly. The Swede had adopted the fashion of board-whacking.

Scully took up his paper and for a long time remained immersed in matters which were extraordinarily remote from him. The lamp burned badly, and once he stopped to adjust the wick. The newspaper, as he turned from page to page, rustled with a slow and comfortable sound. Then suddenly he heard three terrible words: "You are cheatin'!"

Such scenes often prove that there can be little of dramatic import in environment. Any room can present a tragic front; any room can be comic. This little den was now hideous as a torture-chamber. The new faces of the men themselves had changed it upon the instant. The Swede held a huge fist in front of Johnnie's face, while the latter looked steadily over it into the blazing orbs of his accuser. The Easterner had grown pallid; the cowboy's jaw had dropped in that expression of bovine amazement which was one of his important mannerisms. After the three words, the first sound in the room was made by Scully's paper as it floated forgotten to his feet. His spectacles had also fallen from his nose, but by a clutch he had saved them in air. His hand, grasping the spectacles, now remained poised awkwardly and near his shoulder. He stared at the card-players.

Probably the silence was while a second elapsed. Then, if the floor had been suddenly twitched out from under the men they could not have moved quicker. The five had projected themselves headlong toward a common point. It happened that Johnnie, in rising to hurl himself upon the Swede, had stumbled slightly because of his curiously instinctive care for the cards and the board. The loss of the moment allowed time for the arrival of Scully, and also allowed the cowboy time to give the Swede a great push which sent him staggering back. The men found tongue together, and hoarse shouts of rage, appeal, or fear burst from every throat. The cowboy pushed and jostled feverishly at the Swede, and the Easterner and Scully clung wildly to Johnnie; but through the smoky air, above the swaying bodies of the peace-compellers, the eyes of the two warriors ever sought each other in glances of challenge that were at once hot and steely.

Of course the board had been overturned, and now the whole company of cards was scattered over the floor, where the boots of the men trampled the fat and painted kings and queens as they gazed with their silly eyes at the war that was waging above them.

Scully's voice was dominating the yells. "Stop now! Stop, I say! Stop, now—"

Johnnie, as he struggled to burst through the rank formed by Scully and the Easterner, was crying, "Well, he says I cheated! He says I cheated! I won't allow no man to say I cheated! If he says I cheated, he's a —— ——!"

The cowboy was telling the Swede, "Quit, now! Quit, d'ye hear—"

The screams of the Swede never ceased: "He did cheat! I saw him! I saw him—"

As for the Easterner, he was importuning in a voice that was not heeded: "Wait a moment, can't you? Oh, wait a moment. What's the good of a fight over a game of cards? Wait a moment—".

In this tumult no complete sentences were clear. "Cheat"—"Quit"—"He says"—these fragments pierced the uproar and rang out sharply. It was remarkable that, whereas Scully undoubtedly made the most noise, he was the least heard of any of the riotous band.

Then suddenly there was a great cessation. It was as if each man had paused for breath; and although the room was still lighted with the anger of men, it could be seen that there was no danger of immediate conflict, and at once Johnnie, shouldering his way forward, almost succeeded in confronting the Swede. "What did you say I cheated for? What did you say I cheated for? I don't cheat, and I won't let no man say I do!"

The Swede said, "I saw you! I saw you!"

"Well," cried Johnnie, "I'll fight any man what says I cheat!"

"No, you won't," said the cowboy. "Not here."

"Ah, be still, can't you?" said Scully, coming between them.

The quiet was sufficient to allow the Easterner's voice to be heard. He was repeating, "Oh, wait a moment, can't you? What's the good of a fight over a game of cards? Wait a moment!"

Johnnie, his red face appearing above his father's shoulder, hailed the Swede again. "Did you say I cheated?"

The Swede showed his teeth. "Yes."

"Then," said Johnnie, "we must fight."

"Yes, fight," roared the Swede. He was like a demoniac. "Yes, fight! I'll show you what kind of a man I am! I'll show you who you want to fight! Maybe you think I can't fight! Maybe you think I can't! I'll show you, you skin, you card-sharp! Yes, you cheated! You cheated! You cheated!"

"Well, let's go at it, then, mister," said Johnnie, coolly.

The cowboy's brow was beaded with sweat from his efforts in intercepting all sorts of raids. He turned in despair to Scully. "What are you goin' to do now?"

A change had come over the Celtic visage of the old man. He now seemed all eagerness; his eyes glowed.

"We'll let them fight," he answered, stalwartly. "I can't put up with it any longer. I've stood this damned Swede till I'm sick. We'll let them fight."

6

The men prepared to go out of doors. The Easterner was so nervous that he had great difficulty in getting his arms into the sleeves of his new leather coat. As the cowboy drew his fur cap down over his ears his hands trembled. In fact, Johnnie and old Scully were the only ones who displayed no agitation. These preliminaries were conducted without words.

Scully threw open the door. "Well, come on," he said. Instantly a terrific wind caused the flame of the lamp to struggle at its wick, while a puff of black smoke sprang from the chimney-top. The stove was in mid-current of the blast, and its voice swelled to equal the roar of the storm. Some of the scarred and bedabbled cards were caught up from the floor and dashed helplessly against the farther wall. The men lowered their heads and plunged into the tempest as into a sea.

No snow was falling, but great whirls and clouds of flakes, swept up from the ground by the frantic winds, were streaming southward with the speed of bullets. The covered land was blue with the sheen of an unearthly satin, and there was no other hue save where, at the low, black railway station—which seemed incredibly distant—one light gleamed like a tiny jewel. As the men floundered into a thigh-deep drift, it was known that the Swede was bawling out something. Scully went to him, put a hand on his shoulder, and projected an ear. "What's that you say?" he shouted.

"I say," bawled the Swede again, "I won't stand much show against this gang. I know you'll all pitch on me."

Scully smote him reproachfully on the arm. "Tut, man!" he yelled. The wind tore the words from Scully's lips and scattered them far alee.

"You are all a gang of—" boomed the Swede, but the storm also seized the remainder of this sentence.

Immediately turning their backs upon the wind, the men had swung around a corner to the sheltered side of the hotel. It was the function of the little house to preserve here, amid this great devastation of snow, an irregular V-shape of heavily encrusted grass, which crackled beneath the feet. One could imagine the great drifts piled against the windward side. When the party reached the comparative peace of this spot it was found that the Swede was still bellowing.

"Oh, I know what kind of a thing this is! I know you'll all pitch on me. I can't lick you all!"

Scully turned upon him panther-fashion. "You'll not have to whip all of us. You'll have to whip my son Johnnie. An' the man what troubles you durin' that time will have me to dale with."

The arrangements were swiftly made. The two men faced each other, obedient to the harsh commands of Scully, whose face, in the subtly luminous gloom, could be seen set in the austere impersonal lines that are pictured on the countenances of the Roman veterans. The Easterner's teeth were chattering, and he was hopping up and down like a mechanical toy. The cowboy stood rock-like.

The contestants had not stripped off any clothing. Each was in his ordinary attire. Their fists were up, and they eyed each other in a calm that had the elements of leonine cruelty in it.

During this pause, the Easterner's mind, like a film, took lasting impressions of three men—the iron-nerved master of the ceremony; the Swede, pale, motionless, terrible; and Johnnie, serene yet ferocious, brutish yet heroic. The entire prelude had in it a tragedy greater than the tragedy of action, and this aspect was accentuated by the long, mellow cry of the blizzard, as it sped the tumbling and wailing flakes into the black abyss of the south.

"Now!" said Scully.

The two combatants leaped forward and crashed together like bullocks. There was heard the cushioned sound of blows, and of a curse squeezing out from between the tight teeth of one.

As for the spectators, the Easterner's pent-up breath exploded from him with a pop of relief, absolute relief from the tension of the preliminaries. The cowboy bounded into the air with a yowl. Scully was immovable as from supreme amazement and fear at the fury of the fight which he himself had permitted and arranged.

For a time the encounter in the darkness was such a perplexity of flying arms that it presented no more detail than would a swiftly revolving wheel. Occasionally a face, as if illumined by a flash of light, would shine out, ghastly and marked with pink spots. A moment later, the men might have been known as shadows, if it were not for the involuntary utterance of oaths that came from them in whispers.

Suddenly a holocaust of warlike desire caught the cowboy, and he bolted forward with the speed of a broncho. "Go it, Johnnie! Go it! Kill him! Kill him!"

Scully confronted him. "Kape back," he said; and by his glance the cowboy could tell that this man was Johnnie's father.

To the Easterner there was a monotony of unchangeable fighting that was an abomination. This confused mingling was eternal to his sense, which was concentrated in a longing for the end, the priceless end. Once the fighters lurched near him, and as he scrambled hastily backward he heard them breathe like men on the rack.

"Kill him, Johnnie! Kill him! Kill him! Kill him!" The cowboy's face was contorted like one of those agony masks in museums.

"Keep still," said Scully, icily.

Then there was a sudden loud grunt, incomplete, cut short, and Johnnie's body swung away from the Swede and fell with sickening heaviness to the grass. The cowboy was barely in time to prevent the mad Swede from flinging himself upon the prone adversary. "No, you don't," said the cowboy, interposing an arm. "Wait a second."

Scully was at his son's side. "Johnnie! Johnnie, me boy!" His voice had a quality of melancholy tenderness. "Johnnie! Can you go on with it?" He looked anxiously down into the bloody, pulpy face of his son.

There was a moment of silence, and then Johnnie answered in his ordinary voice, "Yes, I—it—yes."

Assisted by his father he struggled to his feet. "Wait a bit now till you git your wind," said the old man.

A few paces away the cowboy was lecturing the Swede. "No, you don't! Wait a second!"

The Easterner was plucking at Scully's sleeve. "Oh, this is enough," he pleaded. "This is enough! Let it go as it stands. This is enough!"

"Bill," said Scully, "git out of the road." The cowboy stepped aside. "Now." The combatants were actuated by a new caution as they advanced toward collision. They glared at each other, and then the Swede aimed a lightning blow that carried with it his entire weight. Johnnie was evidently half stupid from weakness, but he miraculously dodged, and his fist sent the overbalanced Swede sprawling.

The cowboy, Scully, and the Easterner burst into a cheer that was like a chorus of triumphant soldiery, but before its conclusion the Swede had scuffled agilely to his feet and come in berserk abandon at his foe. There was another perplexity of flying arms, and Johnnie's body again swung away and fell, even as a bundle might fall from a roof. The Swede instantly staggered to a little wind-waved tree and leaned upon it, breathing like an engine, while his savage and flame-lit eyes roamed from face to face as the men bent over Johnnie. There was a splendor of isolation in his situation at this time which the Easterner felt once when, lifting his eyes from the man on the ground, he beheld that mysterious and lonely figure, waiting.

"Are you any good yet, Johnnie?" asked Scully in a broken voice.

The son gasped and opened his eyes languidly. After a moment he answered, "No—I ain't—any good—any—more." Then, from shame and bodily ill, he began to weep, the tears furrowing down through the blood-stains on his face. "He was too—too—too heavy for me."

Scully straightened and addressed the waiting figure. "Stranger," he said, evenly, "it's all up with our side." Then his voice changed into that vibrant huskiness which is commonly the tone of the most simple and deadly announcements. "Johnnie is whipped."

Without replying, the victor moved off on the route to the front door of the hotel.

The cowboy was formulating new and unspellable blasphemies. The Easterner was startled to find that they were out in a wind that seemed to come direct from the shadowed arctic floes. He heard again the wail of the snow as it was flung to its grave in the south. He knew now that all this time the cold had been sinking into him deeper and deeper, and he wondered that he had not perished. He felt indifferent to the condition of the vanquished man.

"Johnnie, can you walk?" asked Scully.

"Did I hurt—hurt him any?" asked the son.

"Can you walk, boy? Can you walk?"

Johnnie's voice was suddenly strong. There was a robust impatience in it. "I asked you whether I hurt him any!"

"Yes, yes, Johnnie," answered the cowboy, consolingly; "he's hurt a good deal."

They raised him from the ground, and as soon as he was on his feet he went tottering off, rebuffing all attempts at assistance. When the party rounded the corner they were fairly blinded by the pelting of the snow. It burned their faces like fire. The cowboy carried Johnnie through the drift to the door. As they entered, some cards again rose from the floor and beat against the wall.

The Easterner rushed to the stove. He was so profoundly chilled that he almost dared to embrace the glowing iron. The Swede was not in the room. Johnnie sank into a chair and, folding his arms on his knees, buried his face in them. Scully, warming one foot and then the other at a rim of the stove, muttered to himself with Celtic mournfulness. The cowboy had removed his fur cap, and with a dazed and rueful air he was running one hand through his tousled locks. From overhead they could hear the creaking of boards, as the Swede tramped here and there in his room.

The sad quiet was broken by the sudden flinging open of a door that led toward the kitchen. It was instantly followed by an inrush of women. They precipitated themselves upon Johnnie amid a chorus of lamentation. Before they carried their prey off to the kitchen, there to be bathed and harangued with that mixture of sympathy and abuse which is a feat of their sex, the mother straightened herself and fixed old Scully with an eye of stern reproach. "Shame be upon you, Patrick Scully!" she cried. "Your own son, too. Shame be upon you!"

"There, now! Be quiet, now!" said the old man, weakly.

"Shame be upon you, Patrick Scully!" The girls, rallying to this slogan, sniffed disdainfully in the direction of those trembling accomplices, the cowboy and the Easterner. Presently they bore Johnnie away, and left the three men to dismal reflection.

"I'd like to fight this here Dutchman myself," said the cowboy, breaking a long silence.

Scully wagged his head sadly. "No, that wouldn't do. It wouldn't be right. It wouldn't be right."

"Well, why wouldn't it?" argued the cowboy. "I don't see no harm in it."

"No," answered Scully, with mournful heroism. "It wouldn't be right. It was Johnnie's fight, and now we mustn't whip the man just because he whipped Johnnie."

"Yes, that's true enough," said the cowboy; "but—he better not get fresh with me, because I couldn't stand no more of it."

"You'll not say a word to him," commanded Scully, and even then they heard the tread of the Swede on the stairs. His entrance was made theatric. He swept the door back with a bang and swaggered to the middle of the room. No one looked at him. "Well," he cried, insolently, at Scully, "I s'pose you'll tell me now how much I owe you?"

The old man remained stolid. "You don't owe me nothin'."

"Huh!" said the Swede, "huh! Don't owe 'im nothin'."

The cowboy addressed the Swede. "Stranger, I don't see how you come to be so gay around here."

Old Scully was instantly alert. "Stop!" he shouted, holding his hand forth, fingers upward. "Bill, you shut up!"

The cowboy spat carelessly into the sawdust-box. "I didn't say a word, did I?" he asked.

"Mr. Scully," called the Swede, "how much do I owe you?" It was seen that he was attired for departure, and that he had his valise in his hand.

"You don't owe me nothin'," repeated Scully in the same imperturbable way.

"Huh!" said the Swede. "I guess you're right. I guess if it was any way at all, you'd owe me somethin'. That's what I guess." He turned to the cowboy. " 'Kill him! Kill him! Kill him!' " he mimicked, and then guffawed victoriously. " 'Kill him!' " He was convulsed with ironical humor.

But he might have been jeering the dead. The three men were immovable and silent, staring with glassy eyes at the stove.

The Swede opened the door and passed into the storm, giving one derisive glance backward at the still group.

As soon as the door was closed, Scully and the cowboy leaped to their feet and began to curse. They trampled to and fro, waving their arms and smashing into the air with their fists. "Oh, but that was a hard minute!" wailed Scully. "That was a hard minute! Him there leerin' and scoffin'! One bang at his nose was worth forty dollars to me that minute! How did you stand it, Bill?"

"How did I stand it?" cried the cowboy in a quivering voice. "How did I stand it? Oh!"

The old man burst into sudden brogue. "I'd loike to take that Swade," he wailed, "and hould 'im down on a shtone flure and bate 'im to a jelly wid a shtick!"

The cowboy groaned in sympathy. "I'd like to git him by the neck and ha-ammer him"— he brought his hand down on a chair with a noise like a pistol-shot—"hammer that there Dutchman until he couldn't tell himself from a dead coyote!"

"I'd bate 'im until he—"

"I'd show *him* some things—"

And then together they raised a yearning, fanatic cry—"Oh-o-oh! if we only could—"

"Yes!"

"Yes!"

"And then I'd—"

"O-o-oh!"

8

The Swede, tightly gripping his valise, tacked across the face of the storm as if he carried sails. He was following a line of little naked, grasping trees which, he knew, must mark the way of the road. His face, fresh from the pounding of Johnnie's fists, felt more pleasure than pain in the wind and the driving snow. A number of square shapes loomed upon him finally, and he knew them as the houses of the main body of the town. He found a street and made travel along it, leaning heavily upon the wind whenever, at a corner, a terrific blast caught him.

He might have been in a deserted village. We picture the world as thick with conquering and elate humanity, but here, with the bugles of the tempest pealing, it was hard to imagine a peopled earth. One viewed the existence of man then as a marvel, and conceded a glamor of wonder to these lice which were caused to cling to a whirling, fire-smitten, ice-locked, disease-stricken, space-lost bulb. The conceit of man was explained by this storm to be the very engine of life. One was a coxcomb not to die in it. However, the Swede found a saloon.

In front of it an indomitable red light was burning, and the snowflakes were made blood-color as they flew through the circumscribed territory of the lamp's shining. The Swede pushed open the door of the saloon and entered. A sanded expanse was before him, and at the end of it four men sat about a table drinking. Down one side of the room extended a radiant bar, and its guardian was leaning upon his elbows listening to the talk of the men at the table. The Swede dropped his valise upon the floor and, smiling fraternally upon the barkeeper, said, "Gimme some whisky, will you?" The man placed a bottle, a whisky-glass, and a glass of ice-thick water upon the bar. The Swede poured himself an abnormal portion of whisky and drank it in three gulps. "Pretty bad night," remarked the bartender, indifferently. He was making the pretension of blindness which is usually a distinction of his class; but it could have been seen that he was furtively studying the half-erased blood-stains on the face of the Swede. "Bad night," he said again.

"Oh, it's good enough for me," replied the Swede, hardily, as he poured himself some more whisky. The barkeeper took his coin and maneuvered it through its reception by the highly nickelled cash-machine. A bell rang; a card labelled "20 cts." had appeared.

"No," continued the Swede, "this isn't too bad weather. It's good enough for me."

"So?" murmured the barkeeper, languidly.

The copious drams made the Swede's eyes swim, and he breathed a trifle heavier. "Yes, I like this weather. I like it. It suits me." It was apparently his design to impart a deep significance to these words.

"So?" murmured the bartender again. He turned to gaze dreamily at the scroll-like birds and bird-like scrolls which had been drawn with soap upon the mirrors in back of the bar.

"Well, I guess I'll take another drink," said the Swede, presently. "Have something?"

"No, thanks; I'm not drinkin'," answered the bartender. Afterward he asked, "How did you hurt your face?"

The Swede immediately began to boast loudly. "Why, in a fight. I thumped the soul out of a man down here at Scully's hotel."

The interest of the four men at the table was at last aroused.

"Who was it?" said one.

"Johnnie Scully," blustered the Swede. "Son of the man what runs it. He will be pretty near dead for some weeks, I can tell you. I made a nice thing of him, I did. He couldn't get up. They carried him in the house. Have a drink?"

Instantly the men in some subtle way encased themselves in reserve. "No, thanks," said one. The group was of curious formation. Two were prominent local business men; one was the district attorney; and one was a professional gambler of the kind known as "square." But a scrutiny of the group would not have enabled an observer to pick the gambler from the men of more reputable pursuits. He was, in fact, a man so delicate in manner, when among people of fair class, and so judicious in his choice of victims, that in the strictly masculine part of the town's life he had come to be explicitly trusted and admired. People called him a thoroughbred. The fear and contempt with which his craft was regarded were undoubtedly the reason why his quiet dignity shone conspicuous above the quiet dignity of men who might be merely hatters, billiard-markers, or grocery-clerks. Beyond an occasional unwary traveller who came by rail, this gambler was supposed to prey solely upon reckless and senile farmers, who, when flush with good crops, drove into town in all the pride and confidence of an absolutely invulnerable stupidity. Hearing at times in circuitous fashion of the despoilment of such a farmer, the important men of Romper invariably laughed in contempt of the victim, and if they thought of the wolf at all, it was with a kind of pride at the knowledge that he would never dare think of attacking their wisdom and courage. Besides, it was popular that this gambler had a real wife and two real children in a neat cottage in a suburb, where he led an exemplary home life; and when any one even suggested a discrepancy in his character, the crowd immediately vociferated descriptions of this virtuous family circle. Then men who led exemplary home lives, and men who did not lead exemplary home lives, all subsided in a bunch, remarking that there was nothing more to be said.

However, when a restriction was placed upon him—as, for instance, when a strong clique of members of the new Pollywog Club refused to permit him, even as a spectator, to appear in the rooms of the organization—the candor and gentleness with which he accepted the judgment disarmed many of his foes and made his friends more desperately partisan. He invariably distinguished between himself and a respectable Romper man so quickly and frankly that his manner actually appeared to be a continual broadcast compliment.

And one must not forget to declare the fundamental fact of his entire position in Romper. It is irrefutable that in all affairs outside his business, in all matters that occur eternally and commonly between man and man, this thieving card-player was so generous, so just, so moral, that, in a contest, he could have put to flight the consciences of nine tenths of the citizens of Romper.

And so it happened that he was seated in this saloon with the two prominent local merchants and the district attorney.

The Swede continued to drink raw whisky, meanwhile babbling at the barkeeper and trying to induce him to indulge in potations. "Come on. Have a drink. Come on. What—no? Well, have a little one, then. By gawd, I've whipped a man to-night, and I want to celebrate. I whipped him good, too. Gentlemen," the Swede cried to the men at the table, "have a drink?"

"Ssh!" said the barkeeper.

The group at the table, although furtively attentive, had been pretending to be deep in talk, but now a man lifted his eyes toward the Swede and said, shortly, "Thanks. We don't want any more."

At this reply the Swede ruffled out his chest like a rooster. "Well," he exploded, "it seems I can't get anybody to drink with me in this town. Seems so, don't it? Well!"

"Ssh!" said the barkeeper.

"Say," snarled the Swede, "don't you try to shut me up. I won't have it. I'm a gentleman, and I want people to drink with me. And I want 'em to drink with me now. *Now*—do you understand?" He rapped the bar with his knuckles.

Years of experience had calloused the bartender. He merely grew sulky. "I hear you," he answered.

"Well," cried the Swede, "listen hard then. See those men over there? Well, they're going to drink with me, and don't you forget it. Now you watch."

"Hi!" yelled the barkeeper, "this won't do!"

"Why won't it?" demanded the Swede. He stalked over to the table, and by chance laid his hand upon the shoulder of the gambler. "How about this?" he asked wrathfully. "I asked you to drink with me."

The gambler simply twisted his head and spoke over his shoulder. "My friend, I don't know you."

"Oh, hell!" answered the Swede, "come and have a drink."

"Now, my boy," advised the gambler, kindly, "take your hand off my shoulder and go 'way and mind your own business." He was a little, slim man, and it seemed strange to hear him use this tone of heroic patronage to the burly Swede. The other men at the table said nothing.

"What! You won't drink with me, you little dude? I'll make you, then! I'll make you!" The Swede had grasped the gambler frenziedly at the throat, and was dragging him from his chair. The other men sprang up. The barkeeper dashed around the corner of his bar. There was a great tumult, and then was seen a long blade in the hand of the gambler. It shot forward, and a human body, this citadel of virtue, wisdom, power, was pierced as easily as if it had been a melon. The Swede fell with a cry of supreme astonishment.

The prominent merchants and the district attorney must have at once tumbled out of the place backward. The bartender found himself hanging limply to the arm of a chair and gazing into the eyes of a murderer.

"Henry," said the latter, as he wiped his knife on one of the towels that hung beneath the bar rail, "you tell 'em where to find me. I'll be home, waiting for 'em." Then he vanished. A moment afterward the barkeeper was in the street dinning through the storm for help and, moreover, companionship.

The corpse of the Swede, alone in the saloon, had its eyes fixed upon a dreadful legend that dwelt atop of the cash-machine: "This registers the amount of your purchase."

9

Months later, the cowboy was frying pork over the stove of a little ranch near the Dakota line, when there was a quick thud of hoofs outside, and presently the Easterner entered with the letters and the papers.

"Well," said the Easterner at once, "the chap that killed the Swede has got three years. Wasn't much, was it?"

"He has? Three years?" The cowboy poised his pan of pork, while he ruminated upon the news. "Three years. That ain't much."

"No. It was a light sentence," replied the Easterner as he unbuckled his spurs. "Seems there was a good deal of sympathy for him in Romper."

"If the bartender had been any good," observed the cowboy, thoughtfully, "he would have gone in and cracked that there Dutchman on the head with a bottle in the beginnin' of it and stopped all this here murderin'."

"Yes, a thousand things might have happened," said the Easterner, tartly.

The cowboy returned his pan of pork to the fire, but his philosophy continued. "It's funny, ain't it? If he hadn't said Johnnie was cheatin' he'd be alive this minute. He was an awful fool. Game played for fun, too. Not for money. I believe he was crazy."

"I feel sorry for that gambler," said the Easterner.

"Oh, so do I," said the cowboy. "He don't deserve none of it for killin' who he did."

"The Swede might not have been killed if everything had been square."

"Might not have been killed?" exclaimed the cowboy. "Everythin' square? Why, when he said that Johnnie was cheatin' and acted like such a jackass? And then in the saloon he fairly walked up to git hurt?" With these arguments the cowboy browbeat the Easterner and reduced him to rage.

"You're a fool!" cried the Easterner, viciously. "You're a bigger jackass than the Swede by a million majority. Now let me tell you one thing. Let me tell you something. Listen! Johnnie *was* cheating!"

" 'Johnnie,' " said the cowboy, blankly. There was a minute of silence, and then he said, robustly, "Why, no. The game was only for fun."

"Fun or not," said the Easterner, "Johnnie was cheating. I saw him. I know it. I saw him. And I refused to stand up and be a man. I let the Swede fight it out alone. And you—you were simply puffing around the place and wanting to fight. And then old Scully himself! We are all in it! This poor gambler isn't even a noun. He is kind of an adverb. Every sin is the result of collaboration. We, five of us, have collaborated in the murder of this Swede. Usually there are from a dozen to forty women really involved in every murder, but in this case it seems to be only five men—you, I, Johnnie, old Scully; and that fool of an unfortunate gambler came merely as a culmination, the apex of a human movement, and gets all the punishment."

The cowboy, injured and rebellious, cried out blindly into this fog of mysterious theory: "Well, I didn't do anythin', did I?"

As readers, we sit comfortably outside the storm and the violence of events in "The Blue Hotel." Amusement is one possible effect of this story—if we stick to the first seven parts: amusement of that safe and superior variety that occurs when we see other people driven to rage, bordering on despair, by behavior that seems past any commonsense understanding. Yet our amusement acquires an increasingly somber tone; the stranger's behavior seems as extreme as the uncontrollable and real storm outside that remote hotel. All in the hotel experience increasing strain, and even this may be amusing up to a point. But it is a nervous amusement.

Interestingly, after we read "The Blue Hotel," we can see that it may be related, in a serious way, to the story "Becky." In "Becky," individuals react in various but secret ways to all that Becky's life symbolizes for them, basically unaware of the springs of their own behavior, for which they take no responsibility. The individuals in "The Blue Hotel" are also up against a phenomenon they do not understand but nevertheless see as threatening. They too are unaware except in retrospect. In Part 9 of the story, one individual, the Easterner, reveals his awareness of a responsibility that should have been assumed earlier. It is now too late, and all he can feel is guilt and self-blame. The author makes it clear that the Easterner is alone in this, for the cowboy is caused to say, "Well, I didn't do anythin', did I?" Which is exactly the point! We can summarize by saying that both "Becky" and "The Blue Hotel" raise behavioral issues and questions that are every bit as alive today as in the past.

Technically, "The Blue Hotel" is a complex of various ways of getting a story told. The basic technique is third-person narrative that shades off at times into summary narrative or author's comment and then back again. Though the general tone is that of objective reporting, the objectivity is not "pure," for the author feeds precise images into his account so often that we feel a flavor of rather brilliant author-comment and description which cannot pass as objective. When you have read the story by Ernest Hemingway later in this book, it will be easy for you to see why Hemingway praised this story. It is written crisply enough, and sufficiently from the outside of people and events, to be a forerunner of Hemingway's style, including his sardonic humor.

With "Heart of Darkness" we turn from the American to the European past of the late nineteenth century, in order to secure a larger picture of what was going on in the world at that time.

In this short novel, Joseph Conrad does exactly what important authors so often do: he qualifies as a first-rate and sensitive reporter of big forces operating in his own time, partly because of his wide travel and experience as a sea captain. Conrad saw European exploitative colonialism for what it was. He traces its course from head offices in Belgium and across the seas to its mad functioning in the pursuit of gain in Africa. Here is a bureaucracy indeed, at all its levels, well before our own time, with petty authorities, supersalesmen, a suspicion of influence peddling, an inevitable though unconscious self-poisoning. The story reads like a frightening preview of our century and of causalities that will not be denied. It is a still unfinished part of our past.

As you begin reading "Heart of Darkness," take time, once more, to recognize the way the story is told. You will notice that the first nine paragraphs are in the voice of the author himself. After that, the tale is taken up mainly by a narrator named Marlow, a seafaring man like Conrad; this is the main device by means of which Conrad will tell his story. Marlow, the narrator, like Conrad in the opening paragraphs of the story, speaks in a meditative tone, musing on the fact that England itself, and its River Thames, was once a savage place that was entered by outsiders called Romans. Marlow will proceed to tell a story from his own life, in which he and others entered a continent, one of the dark places on the earth, by means of a river. He will speak in a thoughtful way that carries irony upon irony, as he meditates on the course of history and the fortunes of man on this planet. Once you become aware that Marlow is indulging a talent for ironic description, and even for humor, you can begin to savor multiple pleasures from the very words and descriptions in this story. Though the story could not be more "serious" in its meanings, that is no reason why a reader should not enjoy its accuracy concerning people and its frequently satiric humor. "Heart of Darkness," in a way, is a test of one's readership. It lacks the simplicity and the pace of a shorter story. But it offers richer rewards. A reader should savor this story, word by word, issue by issue, until he can grasp the huge complexity being presented.

*HEART OF DARKNESS

JOSEPH CONRAD

1

The *Nellie,* a cruising yawl, swung to her anchor without a flutter of the sails, and was at rest. The flood had made, the wind was nearly calm, and being bound down the river, the only thing for it was to come to and wait for the turn of the tide.

The sea-reach of the Thames stretched before us like the beginning of an interminable waterway. In the offing the sea and the sky were welded together without a joint, and in the luminous space the tanned sails of the barges drifting up with the tide seemed to stand still in red clusters of canvas sharply peaked, with gleams of varnished sprits. A haze rested on the low shores that ran out to sea in vanishing flatness. The air was dark above Gravesend, and farther back still seemed condensed into a mournful gloom, brooding motionless over the biggest, and the greatest, town on earth.

The Director of Companies was our captain and our host. We four affectionately watched his back as he stood in the bows looking to seaward. On the whole river there was nothing that looked half so nautical. He resembled a pilot, which to a seaman is trustworthiness personified. It was difficult to realize his work was not out there in the luminous estuary, but behind him, within the brooding gloom.

Between us there was, as I have already said somewhere, the bond of the sea. Besides holding our hearts together through long periods of separation, it had the effect of making us tolerant of each other's yarns—and even convictions. The Lawyer—the best of old fellows—had, because of his many years and many virtues, the only cushion on deck, and was lying on the only rug. The Accountant had brought out already a box of dominoes, and was toying architecturally with the bones. Marlow sat cross-legged right aft, leaning against the mizzen-mast. He had sunken cheeks, a yellow complexion, a straight back, an ascetic aspect, and, with his arms dropped, the palms of hands outwards, resembled an idol. The director, satisfied the anchor had good hold, made his way aft and sat down amongst us. We exchanged a few words lazily. Afterwards there was silence on board the yacht. For some reason or other we did not begin that game of dominoes. We felt meditative, and fit for nothing but placid staring. The day was ending in a serenity of still and exquisite brilliance. The water shone pacifically; the sky, without a speck, was a benign immensity of unstained light; the very mist on the Essex marshes was like a gauzy and radiant fabric, hung from the wooded rises inland, and draping the low shores in diaphanous folds. Only the gloom to the west, brooding over the upper reaches, became more somber every minute, as if angered by the approach of the sun.

And at last, in its curved and imperceptible fall, the sun sank low, and from glowing white changed to a dull red without rays and without heat, as if about to go out suddenly, stricken to death by the touch of that gloom brooding over a crowd of men.

Forthwith a change came over the waters, and the serenity became less brilliant but more profound. The old river in its broad reach rested unruffled at the decline of day, after ages of good service done to the race that peopled its banks, spread out in the tranquil dignity of a waterway leading to the uttermost ends of the earth. We looked at the venerable stream not in the vivid flush of a short day that comes and departs forever, but in the august light of abiding memories. And indeed nothing is easier for a man who has, as the phrase goes, "followed the sea" with reverence and affection, than to evoke the great spirit of the past upon the lower reaches of the Thames. The tidal current runs to and fro in its unceasing service, crowded with memories of men and ships it had borne to the rest of home or to the battles of the sea. It had known and served all the men of whom the nation is proud, from Sir Francis Drake to Sir John Franklin, knights all, titled and untitled—the great knights-errant of the sea. It had borne all the ships whose names are like jewels flashing in the night of time, from the *Golden Hind* returning with her round flanks full of treasure, to be visited by the Queen's Highness and thus pass out of the gigantic tale, to the *Erebus* and *Terror,* bound on other conquests—and that never returned. It had known the ships and the men. They had sailed from Deptford, from Greenwich, from Erith—the adventurers and the settlers; kings' ships and the ships of men on 'Change; captains, admirals, the dark "interlopers" of the Eastern trade, and the commissioned "generals" of East India fleets. Hunters for gold or pursuers of fame, they all had gone out on that stream, bearing the sword, and often the torch, messengers of the might within the land, bearers of a spark from the sacred fire. What greatness had not floated on the ebb of that river into the mystery of an unknown earth! . . . The dreams of men, the seed of commonwealths, the germs of empires.

The sun set; the dusk fell on the stream, and lights began to appear along the shore. The Chapman lighthouse, a three-legged thing erect on a mud-flat, shone strongly. Lights of ships moved in the fairway—a great stir of lights going up and going down. And farther west on the upper reaches the place of the monstrous town was still marked ominously on the sky, a brooding gloom in sunshine, a lurid glare under the stars.

"And this also," said Marlow suddenly, "has been one of the dark places on the earth."

He was the only man of us who still "followed the sea." The worst that could be said of him was that he did not represent his class. He was a seaman, but he was a wanderer, too, while most seamen lead, if one may so express it, a sedentary life. Their minds are of the stay-at-home order, and their home is always with them—the ship; and so is their country—the sea. One ship is very much like another, and the sea is always the same. In the immutability of their surroundings the foreign shores, the foreign faces, the changing immensity of life, glide past, veiled not by a sense of mystery but by a slightly disdainful ignorance; for there is nothing mysterious to a seaman unless it be the sea itself, which is the mistress of his existence and as inscrutable as Destiny. For the rest, after his hours of work, a casual stroll or a casual spree on shore suffices to unfold for him the secret of a whole continent, and generally he finds the secret not worth knowing. The yarns of seamen have a direct simplicity, the whole meaning of which lies within the shell of a cracked nut. But Marlow was not typical (if his propensity to spin yarns be excepted), and to him the meaning of an episode was not inside like a kernel but outside, enveloping the tale which brought it out only as a glow brings out a haze, in the likeness of one of these misty halos that sometimes are made visible by the spectral illumination of moonshine.

His remark did not seem at all surprising. It was just like Marlow. It was accepted in silence. No one took the trouble to grunt even; and presently he said, very slow—

"I was thinking of very old times, when the Romans first came here, nineteen hundred years ago—the other day. . . . Light came out of this river since —you say Knights? Yes; but it is like a running blaze on a plain, like a flash of lightning in the clouds. We live in the flicker—may it last as long as the old earth keeps rolling! But darkness was here yesterday. Imagine the feelings of a commander of a fine—what d'ye call 'em?—trireme in the Mediterranean, ordered suddenly to the north; run overland across the Gauls in a hurry; put in charge of one of these craft the legionaries—a wonderful lot of handy men they must have been, too—used to build, apparently by the hundred, in a month or two, if we may believe what we read. Imagine him here—the very end of the world, a sea the color of lead, a sky the color of smoke, a kind of ship about as rigid as a concertina—and going up this river with stores, or orders, or what you like. Sand-banks, marshes, forests, savages,—precious little to eat fit for a civilized man, nothing but Thames water to drink. No Falernian wine here, no going ashore. Here and there a military camp lost in a wilderness, like a needle in a bundle of hay—cold, fog, tempests, disease, exile, and death,— death skulking in the air, in the water, in the bush. They must have been dying like flies here. Oh, yes—he did it. Did it very well, too, no doubt, and without thinking much about it either, except afterwards to brag of what he had gone through in his time, perhaps. They were men enough to face the darkness. And perhaps he was cheered by keeping his eye on a chance of promotion to the fleet at Ravenna by and by, if he had good friends in Rome and survived the awful climate. Or think of a decent young citizen in a toga—perhaps too much dice, you know—coming out here in the train of some prefect, or tax-gatherer, or trader even, to mend his fortunes. Land in a swamp, march through the woods, and in some inland post feel the savagery, the utter savagery, had closed round him,—all that mysterious life of the wilderness that stirs in the forest, in the jungles, in the hearts of wild men. There's no initiation either into such mysteries. He has to live in the midst of the incomprehensible, which is also detestable. And it has a fascination, too, that goes to work upon him. The fascination of the abomination—you know, imagine the growing regrets, the longing to escape, the powerless disgust, the surrender, the hate."

He paused.

"Mind," he began again, lifting one arm from the elbow, the palm of the hand outwards, so that, with his legs folded before him, he had the pose of a Buddha preaching in European clothes and without a lotus-flower—"Mind, none of us would feel exactly like this. What saves us is efficiency—the devotion to efficiency. But these chaps were not much account, really. They were no colonists; their administration was merely a squeeze, and nothing more, I suspect. They were conquerors, and for that you want only brute force—nothing to boast of, when you have it, since your strength is just an accident arising from the weakness of others. They grabbed what they could get for the sake of what was to be got. It was just robbery with violence, aggravated murder on a great scale, and men going at it blind—as is very proper for those who tackle a darkness. The conquest of the earth, which mostly means the taking it away from those who have a different complexion or slightly flatter noses than ourselves, is not a pretty thing when you look into it too much. What redeems it is the idea only. An idea at the back of it; not a sentimental pretense but an idea; and an unselfish belief in the idea—something you can set up, and bow down before, and offer a sacrifice to. . . ."

He broke off. Flames glided in the river, small green flames, red flames, white flames, pursuing, overtaking, joining, crossing each other—then separating slowly or hastily. The traffic of the great city went on in the deepening night upon the sleepless river. We looked on, waiting patiently—there was nothing else to do till the end of the flood; but it was only after a long silence, when he said, in a hesitating voice, "I suppose you fellows remember I did once turn fresh-water sailor for a bit," that we knew we were fated, before the ebb began to run, to hear about one of Marlow's inconclusive experiences.

"I don't want to bother you much with what happened to me personally," he began, showing in this remark the weakness of many tellers of tales who seem so often unaware of what their audiences would best like to hear; "yet to understand the effect of it on me you ought to know how I got out there, what I saw, how I went up that river to the place where I first met the poor chap. It was the farthest point of navigation and the culminating point of my experience. It seemed somehow to throw a kind of light on everything about me—and into my thoughts. It was somber enough, too—and pitiful—not extraordinary in any way—not very clear either. No, not very clear. And yet it seemed to throw a kind of light.

"I had then, as you remember, just returned to London after a lot of Indian Ocean, Pacific, China Seas—a regular dose of the East—six years or so, and I was loafing about, hindering you fellows in your work and invading your homes, just as though I had got a heavenly mission to civilize you. It was very fine for a time, but after a bit I did get tired of resting. Then I began to look for a ship—I should think the hardest work on earth. But the ships wouldn't even look at me. And I got tired of that game, too.

"Now when I was a little chap I had a passion for maps. I would look for hours at South America, or Africa, or Australia, and lose myself in all the glories of exploration. At that time there were many blank spaces on the earth, and when I saw one that looked particularly inviting on a map (but they all look that) I would put my finger on it and say, When I grow up I will go there. The North Pole was one of these places, I remember. Well, I haven't been there yet, and shall not try now. The glamour's off. Other places were scattered about the Equator, and in every sort of latitude all over the two hemispheres. I have been in some of them, and . . . well, we won't talk about that. But there was one yet—the biggest, the most blank, so to speak—that I had a hankering after.

"True, by this time it was not a blank space any more. It had got filled since my boyhood with rivers and lakes and names. It had ceased to be a blank space of delightful mystery—a white patch for a boy to dream gloriously over. It had become a place of darkness. But there was in it one river especially, a mighty big river, that you could see on the map, resembling an immense snake uncoiled, with its head in the sea, its body at rest curving afar over a vast country, and its tail lost in the depths of the land. And as I looked at the map of it in a shop-window, it fascinated me as a snake would a bird—a silly little bird. Then I remembered there was a big concern, a Company for trade on that river. Dash it all! I thought to myself, they can't trade without using some kind of craft on that lot of fresh water—steamboats! Why shouldn't I try to get charge of one? I went on along Fleet Street, but could not shake off the idea. The snake had charmed me.

"You understand it was a Continental concern, that Trading society; but I have a lot of relations living on the Continent, because it's cheap and not so nasty as it looks, they say.

"I am sorry to own I began to worry them. This was already a fresh departure for me. I was not used to getting things that way, you know. I always went my own road and on my own legs where I had a mind to go. I wouldn't have believed it of myself; but, then—you see—I felt somehow I must get there by hook or by crook. So I worried them. The men said 'My dear fellow,' and did nothing. Then—would you believe it?—I tried the women. I, Charlie Marlow, set the women to work—to get a job. Heavens! Well, you see, the notion drove me. I had an aunt, a dear enthusiastic soul. She wrote: 'It will be delightful. I am ready to do anything, anything for you. It is a glorious idea. I know the wife of a very high personage in the Administration, and also a man who has lots of influence with,' etc., etc. She was determined to make no end of fuss to get me appointed skipper of a river steamboat, if such was my fancy.

"I got my appointment—of course; and I got it very quick. It appears the Company had received news that one of their captains had been killed in a scuffle with the natives. This was my chance, and it made me the more anxious to go. It was only months and months afterwards, when I made the attempt to recover what was left of the body, that I heard the original quarrel arose from a misunderstanding about some hens. Yes, two black hens. Fresleven—

that was the fellow's name, a Dane—thought himself wronged somehow in the bargain, so he went ashore and started to hammer the chief of the village with a stick. Oh, it didn't surprise me in the least to hear this, and at the same time to be told that Fresleven was the gentlest, quietest creature that ever walked on two legs. No doubt he was; but he had been a couple of years already out there engaged in the noble cause, you know, and he probably felt the need at last of asserting his self-respect in some way. Therefore he whacked the old nigger mercilessly, while a big crowd of his people watched him, thunderstruck, till some man—I was told the chief's son—in desperation at hearing the old chap yell, made a tentative jab with a spear at the white man—and of course it went quite easy between the shoulder-blades. Then the whole population cleared into the forest, expecting all kinds of calamities to happen, while, on the other hand, the steamer Fresleven commanded left also in a bad panic, in charge of the engineer, I believe. Afterwards nobody seemed to trouble much about Fresleven's remains, till I got out and stepped into his shoes. I couldn't let it rest, though; but when an opportunity offered at last to meet my predecessor, the grass growing through his ribs was tall enough to hide his bones. They were all there. The supernatural being had not been touched after he fell. And the village was deserted, the huts gaped black, rotting, all askew within the fallen enclosures. A calamity had come to it, sure enough. The people had vanished. Mad terror had scattered them, men, women, and children, through the bush, and they had never returned. What became of the hens I don't know either. I should think the cause of progress got them, anyhow. However, through this glorious affair I got my appointment, before I had fairly begun to hope for it.

"I flew around like mad to get ready, and before forty-eight hours I was crossing the Channel to show myself to my employers, and sign the contract. In a very few hours I arrived in a city that always makes me think of a whited sepulcher. Prejudice no doubt. I had no difficulty in finding the Company's offices. It was the biggest thing in the town, and everybody I met was full of it. They were going to run an over-sea empire, and make no end of coin by trade.

"A narrow and deserted street in deep shadow, high houses, innumerable windows with venetian blinds, a dead silence, grass sprouting between the stones, imposing carriage archways right and left, immense double doors standing ponderously ajar. I slipped through one of these cracks, went up a swept and ungarnished staircase, as arid as a desert, and opened the first door I came to. Two women, one fat and the other slim, sat on strawbottomed chairs, knitting black wool. The slim one got up and walked straight at me— still knitting with down-cast eyes—and only just as I began to think of getting out of her way, as you would for a somnambulist, stood still, and looked up. Her dress was as plain as an umbrella-cover, and she turned round without a word and preceded me into a waiting-room. I gave my name, and looked about. Deal table in the middle, plain chairs all round the walls, on one end a large shining map, marked with all the colors of a rainbow. There was a vast amount of red—good to see at any time, because one knows that some real work is done in there, a deuce of a lot of blue, a little green, smears of orange, and, on the East Coast, a purple patch, to show where the jolly pioneers of progress drink the jolly lager-beer. However, I wasn't going into any of these. I was going into the yellow. Dead in the center. And the river was there—fascinating —deadly—like a snake. Ough! A door opened, a white-haired secretarial head, but wearing a compassionate expression, appeared, and a skinny forefinger beckoned me into the sanctuary. Its light was dim, and a heavy writing-desk squatted in the middle. From behind that structure came out an impression of pale plumpness in a frock-coat. The great man himself. He was five feet six, I should judge, and had his grip on the handle-end of ever so many millions. He shook hands, I fancy, murmured vaguely, was satisfied with my French. *Bon voyage.*

"In about forty-five seconds I found myself again in the waiting-room with the compassionate secretary, who, full of desolation and sympathy, made me sign some document. I believe I undertook amongst other things not to disclose any trade secrets. Well, I am not going to.

"I began to feel slightly uneasy. You know I am not used to such cere-monies, and there was something ominous in the atmosphere. It was just as though I had been let into some conspiracy—I don't know—something not quite right; and I was glad to get out. In the outer room the two women knitted black wool feverishly. People were arriving, and the younger one was walking back and forth introducing them. The old one sat on her chair. Her flat cloth slippers were propped up on a foot-warmer, and a cat reposed on her lap. She wore a starched white affair on her head, had a wart on one cheek, and silver-rimmed spectacles hung on the tip of her nose. She glanced at me above the glasses. The swift and indifferent placidity of that look troubled me. Two youths with foolish and cheery countenances were being piloted over, and she threw at them the same quick glance of unconcerned wisdom. She seemed to know all about them and about me, too. An eerie feeling came over me. She seemed uncanny and fateful. Often far away there I thought of these two, guarding the door of Darkness, knitting black wool as for a warm pall, one introducing, introducing continuously to the unknown, the other scrutinizing the cheery and foolish faces with unconcerned old eyes. *Ave!* Old knitter of black wool. *Morituri te salutant.* Not many of those she looked at ever saw her again—not half, by a long way.

"There was yet a visit to the doctor. 'A simple formality,' assured me the secretary, with an air of taking an immense part in all my sorrows. Accordingly a young chap wearing his hat over the left eyebrow, some clerk I suppose,— there must have been clerks in the business, though the house was as still as a house in a city of the dead—came from somewhere up-stairs, and led me forth. He was shabby and careless, with ink-stains on the sleeves of his jacket, and his cravat was large and billowy, under a chin shaped like the toe of an old boot. It was a little too early for the doctor, so I proposed a drink, and thereupon he developed a vein of joviality. As we sat over our vermouths he glorified the Company's business, and by and by I expressed casually my sur-prise at him not going out there. He became very cool and collected all at once. 'I am not such a fool as I look, quoth Plato to his disciples,' he said sententiously, emptied his glass with great resolution, and we rose.

"The old doctor felt my pulse, evidently thinking of something else the while. 'Good, good for there,' he mumbled, and then with a certain eagerness asked me whether I would let him measure my head. Rather surprised, I said Yes, when he produced a thing like calipers and got the dimensions back and front and every way, taking notes carefully. He was an unshaven little man in a threadbare coat like a gaberdine, with his feet in slippers, and I thought him a harmless fool. 'I always ask leave, in the interests of science, to measure the crania of those going out there,' he said. 'And when they come back, too?' I asked. 'Oh, I never see them,' he remarked; 'and, moreover, the changes take place inside, you know.' He smiled, as if at some quiet joke. 'So you are going out there. Famous. Interesting, too.' He gave me a searching glance, and made another note. 'Ever any madness in your family?' he asked, in a matter-of-fact tone. I felt very annoyed. 'Is that question in the interests of science, too?' 'It would be,' he said, without taking notice of my irritation, 'interesting for science to watch the mental changes of individuals, on the spot, but . . .' 'Are you an alienist?' I interrupted. 'Every doctor should be—a little,' answered that original, imperturbably. 'I have a little theory which you Messieurs who go out there must help me to prove. This is my share in the advantages my country shall reap from the possession of such a magnificent dependency. The mere wealth I leave to others. Pardon my questions, but you are the first Englishman coming under my observation . . .' I hastened to assure him I was not in the least typical. 'If I were,' said I, 'I wouldn't be talking like this with you.' 'What you say is rather profound, and probably erroneous,' he said, with a laugh. 'Avoid irritation more than exposure to the sun. Adieu. How do you English say, eh? Good-by. Ah! Good-by. Adieu. In the tropics one must before everything keep calm.' . . . He lifted a warning forefinger. . . . *'Du calme, du calme. Adieu.'*

"One thing more remained to do—say good-by to my excellent aunt. I found her triumphant. I had a cup of tea—the last decent cup of tea for many days— and in a room that most soothingly looked just as you would expect a lady's drawing-room to look, we had a long quiet chat by the fireside. In the course of these confidences it became quite plain to me I had been represented to the wife of the high dignitary, and goodness knows to how many more people besides, as an exceptional and gifted creature—a piece of good fortune for the Company—a man you don't get hold of every day. Good heavens! and I was going to take charge of a two-penny-half-penny river-steamboat with a penny whistle attached! It appeared, however, I was also one of the Workers, with a capital—you know. Something like an emissary of light, something like a lower sort of apostle. There had been a lot of such rot let loose in print and talk just about that time, and the excellent woman, living right in the rush of all that humbug, got carried off her feet. She talked about 'weaning those ignorant millions from their horrid ways,' till, upon my word, she made me quite uncomfortable. I ventured to hint that the Company was run for profit.

" 'You forget, dear Charlie, that the laborer is worthy of his hire,' she said, brightly. It's queer how out of touch with truth women are. They live in a world of their own, and there has never been anything like it, and never can be. It is too beautiful altogether, and if they were to set it up it would go to pieces before the first sunset. Some confounded fact we men have been living contentedly with ever since the day of creation would start up and knock the whole thing over.

"After this I got embraced, told to wear flannel, be sure to write often, and so on—and I left. In the street—I don't know why—a queer feeling came to me that I was an impostor. Odd thing that I, who used to clear out for any part of the world at twenty-four hours' notice, with less thought than most men give to the crossing of a street, had a moment—I won't say of hesitation, but of startled pause, before this commonplace affair. The best way I can explain it to you is by saying that, for a second or two, I felt as though, instead of going to the center of a continent, I were about to set off for the center of the earth.

'I left in a French steamer, and she called in every blamed port they have out there, for, as far as I could see, the sole purpose of landing soldiers and custom-house officers. I watched the coast. Watching a coast as it slips by the ship is like thinking about an enigma. There it is before you—smiling, frowning, inviting, grand, mean, insipid, or savage, and always mute with an air of whispering, Come and find out. This one was almost featureless, as if still in the making, with an aspect of monotonous grimness. The edge of a colossal jungle, so dark-green as to be almost black, fringed with white surf, ran straight, like a ruled line, far, far away along a blue sea whose glitter was blurred by a creeping mist. The sun was fierce, the land seemed to glisten and drip with steam. Here and there grayish-whitish specks showed up clustered inside the white surf, with a flag flying above them perhaps. Settlements some centuries old, and still no bigger than pinheads on the untouched expanse of their background. We pounded along, stopped, landed soldiers; went on, landed custom-house clerks to levy toll in what looked like a God-forsaken wilderness, with a tin shed and a flag-pole lost in it; landed more soldiers—to take care of the custom-house clerks, presumably. Some, I heard, got drowned in the surf; but whether they did or not, nobody seemed particularly to care. They were just flung out there, and on we went. Every day the coast looked the same, as though we had not moved; but we passed various places—trading places—with names like Gran' Bassam, Little Popo; names that seemed to belong to some sordid farce acted in front of a sinister back-cloth. The idleness of a passenger, my isolation amongst all these men with whom I had no point of contact, the oily and languid sea, the uniform somberness of the coast, seemed to keep me away from the truth of things, within the toil of a mournful and senseless delusion. The voice of the surf heard now and then was a positive pleasure, like the speech of a brother. It was something natural, that had its reason, that had a meaning. Now and then a boat from the shore gave one a momentary contact with reality. It was paddled by black fellows. You could see from afar the white of their eyeballs glistening. They shouted, sang; their bodies streamed with perspiration; they had faces like grotesque masks—these chaps; but they had bone, muscle, a wild vitality, an intense energy of movement, that was as natural and true as the surf along their coast. They wanted no excuse for being there. They were a great comfort to look at. For a time I would feel I belonged still to a world of straightforward facts; but the feeling would not last long. Something would turn up to scare it away. Once, I remember, we came upon a man-of-war anchored off the coast. There wasn't even a shed there, and she was shelling the bush. It appears the French had one of their wars going on thereabouts. Her ensign dropped limp like a rag; the muzzles of the long six-inch guns stuck out all over the low hull; the greasy, slimy swell swung her up lazily and let her down, swaying her thin masts. In the empty immensity of earth, sky, and water, there she was, incomprehensible, firing into a continent. Pop, would go one of the six-inch guns; a small flame would dart and vanish, a little white smoke would disappear, a tiny projectile would give a feeble screech—and nothing happened. Nothing could happen. There was a touch of insanity in the proceeding, a sense of lugubrious drollery in the sight; and it was not dissipated by somebody on board assuring me earnestly there was a camp of natives—he called them enemies!—hidden out of sight somewhere.

"We gave her her letters (I heard the men in that lonely ship were dying of fever at the rate of three a day) and went on. We called at some more places with farcical names, where the merry dance of death and trade goes on in a still and earthy atmosphere as of an overheated catacomb; all along the formless coast bordered by dangerous surf, as if Nature herself had tried to ward off intruders; in and out of rivers, streams of death in life, whose banks were rotting into mud, whose waters, thickened into slime, invaded the contorted mangroves, that seemed to writhe at us in the extremity of an impotent despair. Nowhere did we stop long enough to get a particularized impression, but the general sense of vague and oppressive wonder grew upon me. It was like a weary pilgrimage amongst hints for nightmares.

"It was upward of thirty days before I saw the mouth of the big river. We anchored off the seat of the government. But my work would not begin till some two hundred miles farther on. So as soon as I could I made a start for a place thirty miles higher up.

"I had my passage on a little sea-going steamer. Her captain was a Swede, and knowing me for a seaman, invited me on the bridge. He was a young man, lean, fair, and morose, with lanky hair and a shuffling gait. As we left the miserable little wharf, he tossed his head contemptuously at the shore. 'Been living there?' he asked. I said, 'Yes.' 'Fine lot these government chaps—are they not?' he went on, speaking English with great precision and considerable bitterness. 'It is funny what some people will do for a few francs a month. I wonder what becomes of that kind when it goes up-country?' I said to him I expected to see that soon. 'So-o-o!' he exclaimed. He shuffled athwart, keeping one eye ahead vigilantly. 'Don't be too sure,' he continued. 'The other day I took up a man who hanged himself on the road. He was a Swede, too.' 'Hanged himself! Why, in God's name?' I cried. He kept on looking out watchfully. 'Who knows? The sun too much for him, or the country perhaps.'

"At last we opened a reach. A rocky cliff appeared, mounds of turned-up earth by the shore, houses on a hill, others with iron roofs, amongst a waste of excavations, or hanging to the declivity. A continuous noise of the rapids above hovered over this scene of inhabited devastation. A lot of people, mostly black and naked, moved about like ants. A jetty projected into the river. A blinding sunlight drowned all this at times in a sudden recrudescence of glare.

'There's your Company's station,' said the Swede, pointing to three wooden barrack-like structures on the rocky slope. 'I will send your things up. Four boxes did you say? So. Farewell.'

"I came upon a boiler wallowing in the grass, then found a path leading up the hill. It turned aside for the bowlders, and also for an undersized railway-truck lying there on its back with its wheels in the air. One was off. The thing looked as dead as the carcass of some animal. I came upon more pieces of decaying machinery, a stack of rusty rails. To the left a clump of trees made a shady spot, where dark things seemed to stir feebly. I blinked, the path was steep. A horn tooted to the right, and I saw the black people run. A heavy and dull detonation shook the ground, a puff of smoke came out of the cliff, and that was all. No change appeared on the face of the rock. They were building a railway. The cliff was not in the way or anything; but this objectless blasting was all the work going on.

"A slight clinking behind me made me turn my head. Six black men advanced in a file, toiling up the path. They walked erect and slow, balancing small baskets full of earth on their heads, and the clink kept time with their footsteps. Black rags were wound round their loins, and the short ends behind waggled to and fro like tails. I could see every rib, the joints of their limbs were like knots in a rope; each had an iron collar on his neck, and all were connected together with a chain whose bights swung between them, rhythmically clinking. Another report from the cliff made me think suddenly of that ship of war I had seen firing into a continent. It was the same kind of ominous voice; but these men could by no stretch of imagination be called enemies. They were called criminals, and the outraged law, like the bursting shells, had come to them, an insoluble mystery from the sea. All their meager breasts panted together, the violently dilated nostrils quivered, the eyes stared stonily up-hill. They passed me within six inches, without a glance, with that complete, death-like indifference of unhappy savages. Behind this raw matter one of the reclaimed, the product of the new forces at work, strolled despondently, carrying a rifle by its middle. He had a uniform jacket with one button off, and seeing a white man on the path, hoisted his weapon to his shoulder with alacrity. This was simple prudence, white men being so much alike at a distance that he could not tell who I might be. He was speedily reassured, and with a large, white, rascally grin, and a glance at his charge, seemed to take me into partnership in his exalted trust. After all, I also was a part of the great cause of these high and just proceedings.

"Instead of going up, I turned and descended to the left. My idea was to let that chain-gang get out of sight before I climbed the hill. You know I am not particularly tender; I've had to strike and to fend off. I've had to resist and to attack sometimes—that's only one way of resisting—without counting the exact cost, according to the demands of such sort of life as I had blundered into. I've seen the devil of violence, and the devil of greed, and the devil of hot desire; but, by all the stars! these were strong, lusty, red-eyed devils, that swayed and drove men—men, I tell you. But as I stood on this hillside, I foresaw that in the blinding sunshine of that land I would become acquainted with a flabby, pretending, weak-eyed devil of a rapacious and pitiless folly. How insidious he could be, too, I was only to find out several months later and a thousand miles farther. For a moment I stood appalled, as though by a warning. Finally I descended the hill, obliquely, towards the trees I had seen.

"I avoided a vast artificial hole somebody had been digging on the slope, the purpose of which I found it impossible to divine. It wasn't a quarry or a sandpit, anyhow. It was just a hole. It might have been connected with the philanthropic desire of giving the criminals something to do. I don't know. Then I nearly fell into a very narrow ravine, almost no more than a scar in the hillside. I discovered that a lot of imported drainage-pipes for the settlement had been tumbled in there. There wasn't one that was not broken. It was a wanton smash-up. At last I got under the trees. My purpose was to stroll into the shade for a moment; but no sooner within than it seemed to me I had stepped into the gloomy circle of some Inferno. The rapids were near, and an uninterrupted, uniform, headlong, rushing noise filled the mournful stillness of the grove, where not a breath stirred, not a leaf moved, with a mysterious sound—as though the tearing pace of the launched earth had suddenly become audible.

"Black shapes crouched, lay, sat between the trees leaning against the trunks, clinging to the earth, half coming out, half effaced within the dim light, in all the attitudes of pain, abandonment, and despair. Another mine on the cliff went off, followed by a slight shudder of the soil under my feet. The work was going on. The work! And this was the place where some of the helpers had withdrawn to die.

"They were dying slowly—it was very clear. They were not enemies, they were not criminals, they were nothing earthly now,—nothing but black shadows of disease and starvation, lying confusedly in the greenish gloom. Brought from all the recesses of the coast in all the legality of time contracts, lost in uncongenial surroundings, fed on unfamiliar food, they sickened, became inefficient, and were then allowed to crawl away and rest. These moribund shapes were free as air—and nearly as thin. I began to distinguish the gleam of the eyes under the trees. Then, glancing down, I saw a face near my hand. The black bones reclined at full length with one shoulder against the tree, and slowly the eyelids rose and the sunken eyes looked up at me, enormous and vacant, a kind of blind, white flicker in the depths of the orbs, which died out slowly. The man seemed young—almost a boy—but you know with them it's hard to tell. I found nothing else to do but to offer him one of my good Swede's ship's biscuits I had in my pocket. The fingers closed slowly on it and held —there was no other movement and no other glance. He had tied a bit of white worsted round his neck—Why? Where did he get it? Was it a badge—an ornament—a charm—a propitiatory act? Was there any idea at all connected with it? It looked startling round his black neck, this bit of white thread from beyond the seas.

"Near the same tree two more bundles of acute angles sat with their legs drawn up. One, with his chin propped on his knees, stared at nothing, in an intolerable and appalling manner: his brother phantom rested its forehead, as if overcome with a great weariness; and all about others were scattered in every pose of contorted collapse, as in some picture of a massacre or a pestilence. While I stood horror-struck, one of these creatures rose to his hands and knees, and went off on all-fours towards the river to drink. He lapped out of his hand, then sat up in the sunlight, crossing his shins in front of him, and after a time let his woolly head fall on his breastbone.

"I didn't want any more loitering in the shade, and I made haste towards the station. When near the buildings I met a white man, in such an unexpected elegance of get-up that in the first moment I took him for a sort of vision. I saw a high starched collar, white cuffs, a light alpaca jacket, snowy trousers, a clean necktie, and varnished boots. No hat. Hair parted, brushed, oiled, under a green-lined parasol held in a big white hand. He was amazing, and had a penholder behind his ear.

"I shook hands with this miracle, and I learned he was the Company's chief accountant, and that all the book-keeping was done at this station. He had come out for a moment, he said, 'to get a breath of fresh air.' The expression sounded wonderfully odd, with its suggestion of sedentary desk-life. I wouldn't have mentioned the fellow to you at all, only it was from his lips that I first heard the name of the man who is so indissolubly connected with the memories of that time. Moreover, I respected the fellow. Yes; I respected his collars, his vast cuffs, his brushed hair. His appearance was certainly that of a hairdresser's dummy; but in the great demoralization of the land he kept up his appearance. That's backbone. His starched collars and got-up shirt-fronts were achievements of character. He had been out nearly three years; and, later, I could not help asking him how he managed to sport such linen. He had just the faintest blush, and said modestly, 'I've been teaching one of the native women about the station. It was difficult. She had a distaste for the work.' Thus this man had verily accomplished something. And he was devoted to his books, which were in apple-pie order.

"Everything else in the station was in a muddle,—heads, things, buildings. Strings of dusty niggers with splay feet arrived and departed; a stream of manufactured goods, rubbishy cottons, beads, and brass-wire set into the depths of darkness, and in return came a precious trickle of ivory.

"I had to wait in the station for ten days—an eternity. I lived in a hut in the yard, but to be out of the chaos I would sometimes get into the accountant's office. It was built of horizontal planks, and so badly put together that, as he bent over his high desk, he was barred from neck to heels with narrow strips of sunlight. There was no need to open the big shutter to see. It was hot there, too; big flies buzzed fiendishly, and did not sting, but stabbed. I sat generally on the floor, while, of faultless appearance (and even slightly scented), perching on a high stool, he wrote, he wrote. Sometimes he stood up for exercise. When a truckle-bed with a sick man (some invalid agent from up-country) was put in there, he exhibited a gentle annoyance. 'The groans of this sick person,' he said, 'distract my attention. And without that it is extremely difficult to guard against clerical errors in this climate.'

"One day he remarked, without lifting his head, 'In the interior you will no doubt meet Mr. Kurtz.' On my asking who Mr. Kurtz was, he said he was a first-class agent; and seeing my disappointment at this information, he added slowly, laying down his pen, 'He is a very remarkable person.' Further questions elicited from him that Mr. Kurtz was at present in charge of a trading post, a very important one, in the true ivory-country, at 'the very bottom of there. Sends in as much ivory as all the others put together. . . .' He began to write again. The sick man was too ill to groan. The flies buzzed in a great peace.

"Suddenly there was a growing murmur of voices and a great tramping of feet. A caravan had come in. A violent babble of uncouth sounds burst out on the other side of the planks. All the carriers were speaking together, and in the midst of the uproar the lamentable voice of the chief agent was heard 'giving it up' tearfully for the twentieth time that day. . . . He rose slowly. 'What a frightful row,' he said. He crossed the room gently to look at the sick man, and returning, said to me, 'He does not hear.' 'What! Dead?' I asked, startled. 'No, not yet,' he answered, with great composure. Then, alluding with a toss of the head to the tumult in the station-yard, 'When one has got to make correct entries, one comes to hate those savages—hate them to the death.' He remained thoughtful for a moment. 'When you see Mr. Kurtz,' he went on, 'tell him for me that everything here'—he glanced at the desk—'is very satisfactory. I don't like to write to him—with those messengers of ours you never know who may get hold of your letter—at that Central Station.' He stared at me for a moment with his mild, bulging eyes. 'Oh, he will go far, very far,' he began again. 'He will be a somebody in the Administration before long. They, above —the Council in Europe, you know—mean him to be.'

"He returned to his work. The noise outside had ceased, and presently in going out I stopped at the door. In the steady buzz of flies the homeward-bound agent was lying flushed and insensible; the other, bent over his books, was making correct entries of perfectly correct transactions; and fifty feet below the doorstep I could see the still tree-tops of the grove of death.

"Next day I left that station at last, with a caravan of sixty men, for a two-hundred-mile tramp.

"No use telling you much about that. Paths, paths, everywhere; a stamped-in network of paths spreading over the empty land, through long grass, through burnt grass, through thickets, down and up chilly ravines, up and down stony hills ablaze with heat; and a solitude, a solitude, nobody, not a hut. The population had cleared out a long time ago. Well, if a lot of mysterious niggers armed with all kinds of fearful weapons suddenly took to traveling on the road between Deal and Gravesend, catching the yokels right and left to carry heavy loads for them, I fancy every farm and cottage thereabouts would get empty very soon. Only here the dwellings were gone, too. Still I passed through several abandoned villages. There's something pathetically childish in the ruins of grass walls. Day after day, with the stamp and shuffle of sixty pair of bare feet behind me, each pair under a 60-lb. load. Camp, cook, sleep, strike camp, march. Now and then a carrier dead in harness, at rest in the long grass near the path, with an empty water-gourd and his long staff lying by his side. A great silence around and above. Perhaps on some quiet night the tremor of far-off drums, sinking, swelling, a tremor vast, faint; a sound weird, appealing, suggestive, and wild—and perhaps with as profound a meaning as the sound of bells in a Christian country. Once a white man in an unbuttoned uniform, camping on the path with an armed escort of lank Zanzibaris, very hospitable and festive—not to say drunk. Was looking after the upkeep of the road, he declared. Can't say I saw any road or any upkeep, unless the body of a middle-aged negro, with a bullet-hole in the forehead, upon which I absolutely stumbled three miles farther on, may be considered as a permanent improvement. I had a white companion, too, not a bad chap, but rather too fleshy and with the exasperating habit of fainting on the hot hillsides, miles away from the least bit of shade and water. Annoying, you know, to hold your own coat like a parasol over a man's head while he is coming-to. I couldn't help asking him once what he meant by coming there at all. 'To make money, of course. What do you think?' he said, scornfully. Then he got fever, and had to be carried in a hammock slung under a pole. As he weighed sixteen stone I had no end of rows with the carriers. They jibbed, ran away, sneaked off with their loads in the night—quite a mutiny. So, one evening, I made a speech in English with gestures, not one of which was lost to the sixty pairs of eyes before me, and the next morning I started the hammock off in front all right. An hour afterwards I came upon the whole concern wrecked in a bush—man, hammock, groans, blankets, horrors. The heavy pole had skinned his poor nose. He was very anxious for me to kill somebody, but there wasn't the shadow of a carrier near. I remembered the old doctor—'It would be interesting for science to watch the mental changes of individuals, on the spot.' I felt I was becoming scientifically interesting. However, all that is to no purpose. On the fifteenth day I came in sight of the big river again, and hobbled into the Central Station. It was on a back water surrounded by scrub and forest, with a pretty border of smelly mud on one side, and on the three others enclosed by a crazy fence of rushes. A neglected gap was all the gate it had, and the first glance at the place was enough to let you see the flabby devil was running that show. White men with long staves in their hands appeared languidly from amongst the buildings, strolling up to take a look at me, and then retired out of sight somewhere. One of them, a stout, excitable chap with black mustaches, informed me with great volubility and many digressions, as soon as I told him who I was, that my steamer was at the bottom of the river. I was thunderstruck. What, how, why? Oh, it was 'all right.' The 'manager himself' was there. All quite correct. 'Everybody had behaved splendidly! splendidly!'—'you must,' he said in agitation, 'go and see the general manager at once. He is waiting!'

"I did not see the real significance of that wreck at once. I fancy I see it now, but I am not sure—not at all. Certainly the affair was too stupid—when I think of it—to be altogether natural. Still. . . . But at the moment it presented itself simply as a confounded nuisance. The steamer was sunk. They had started two days before in a sudden hurry up the river with the manager on board, in charge of some volunteer skipper, and before they had been out three hours they tore the bottom out of her on stones, and she sank near the south bank. I asked myself what I was to do there, now my boat was lost. As a matter of fact, I had plenty to do in fishing my command out of the river. I had to set about it the very next day. That, and the repairs when I brought the pieces to the station, took some months.

"My first interview with the manager was curious. He did not ask me to sit down after my twenty-mile walk that morning. He was commonplace in complexion, in feature, in manners, and in voice. He was of middle size and of ordinary build. His eyes, of the usual blue, were perhaps remarkably cold, and he certainly could make his glance fall on one as trenchant and heavy as an ax. But even at these times the rest of his person seemed to disclaim the intention. Otherwise there was only an indefinable, faint expression of his lips, something stealthy—a smile—not a smile—I remember it, but I can't explain. It was unconscious, this smile was, though just after he had said something it got intensified for an instant. It came at the end of his speeches like a seal applied on the words to make the meaning of the commonest phrase appear absolutely inscrutable. He was a common trader, from his youth up employed in these parts—nothing more. He was obeyed, yet he inspired neither love nor fear, nor even respect. He inspired uneasiness. That was it! Uneasiness. Not a definite mistrust—just uneasiness—nothing more. You have no idea how effective such a . . . a . . . faculty can be. He had no genius for organizing, for initiative, or for order even. That was evident in such things as the deplorable state of the station. He had no learning, and no intelligence. His position had come to him—why? Perhaps because he was never ill. . . He had served three terms of three years out there. . . . Because triumphant health in the general rout of constitutions is a kind of power in itself. When he went home on leave he rioted on a large scale—pompously. Jack ashore—with a difference—in externals only. This one could gather from his casual talk. He originated nothing, he could keep the routine going—that's all. But he was great. He was great by this little thing that it was impossible to tell what could control such a man. He never gave that secret away. Perhaps there was nothing within him. Such a suspicion made one pause—for out there there were no external checks. Once when various tropical diseases had laid low almost every 'agent' in the station, he was heard to say, 'Men who come out here should have no entrails.' He sealed the utterance with that smile of his, as though it had been a door opening into a darkness he had in his keeping. You fancied you had seen things—but the seal was on. When annoyed at meal-times by the constant quarrels of the white men about precedence, he ordered an immense round table to be made, for which a special house had to be built. This was the station's mess-room. Where he sat was the first place —the rest were nowhere. One felt this to be his unalterable conviction. He was neither civil nor uncivil. He was quiet. He allowed his 'boy'—an overfed young negro from the coast—to treat the white men, under his very eyes, with provoking insolence.

"He began to speak as soon as he saw me. I had been very long on the road. He could not wait. Had to start without me. The up-river stations had to be relieved. There had been so many delays already that he did not know who was dead and who was alive, and how they got on—and so on, and so on. He paid no attention to my explanations, and, playing with a stick of sealing-wax, repeated several times that the situation was 'very grave, very grave.' There were rumors that a very important station was in jeopardy, and its chief, Mr. Kurtz, was ill. Hoped it was not true. Mr. Kurtz was . . . I felt weary and irritable. Hang Kurtz, I thought. I interrupted him by saying I had heard of Mr. Kurtz on the coast. 'Ah! So they talk of him down there,' he murmured to himself. Then he began again, assuring me Mr. Kurtz was the best agent he had, an exceptional man, of the greatest importance to the Company; therefore

I could understand his anxiety. He was, he said, 'very, very uneasy.' Certainly he fidgeted on his chair a good deal, exclaimed, 'Ah, Mr. Kurtz!' broke the stick of sealing-wax and seemed dumfounded by the accident. Next thing he wanted to know 'how long it would take to' . . . I interrupted him again. Being hungry, you know, and kept on my feet too, I was getting savage. 'How can I tell?' I said. 'I haven't even seen the wreck yet—some months, no doubt.' All this talk seemed to me so futile. 'Some months,' he said. 'Well, let us say three months before we can make a start. Yes. That ought to do the affair.' I flung out of his hut (he lived all alone in a clay hut with a sort of veranda) muttering to myself my opinion of him. He was a chattering idiot. Afterwards I took it back when it was borne in upon me startlingly with what extreme nicety he had estimated the time requisite for the 'affair.'

"I went to work the next day, turning, so to speak, my back on that station. In that way only it seemed to me I could keep my hold on the redeeming facts of life. Still, one must look about sometimes; and then I saw this station, these men strolling aimlessly about in the sunshine of the yard. I asked myself sometimes what it all meant. They wandered here and there with their absurd long staves in their hands, like a lot of faithless pilgrims bewitched inside a rotten fence. The word 'ivory' rang in the air, was whispered, was sighed. You would think they were praying to it. A taint of imbecile rapacity blew through it all, like a whiff from some corpse. By Jove! I've never seen anything so unreal in my life. And outside, the silent wilderness surrounding this cleared speck on the earth struck me as something great and invincible, like evil or truth, waiting patiently for the passing away of this fantastic invasion.

"Oh, these months! Well, never mind. Various things happened. One evening a grass shed full of calico, cotton prints, beads, and I don't know what else, burst into a blaze so suddenly that you would have thought the earth had opened to let an avenging fire consume all that trash. I was smoking my pipe quietly by my dismantled steamer, and saw them all cutting capers in the light, with their arms lifted high, when the stout man with mustaches came tearing down to the river, a tin pail in his hand, assured me that everybody was 'behaving splendidly, splendidly,' dipped about a quart of water and tore back again. I noticed there was a hole in the bottom of his pail.

"I strolled up. There was no hurry. You see the thing had gone off like a box of matches. It had been hopeless from the very first. The flame had leaped high, driven everybody back, lighted up everything—and collapsed. The shed was already a heap of embers glowing fiercely. A nigger was being beaten near by. They said he had caused the fire in some way; be that as it may, he was screeching most horribly. I saw him, later, for several days, sitting in a bit of shade looking very sick and trying to recover himself: afterwards he arose and went out—and the wilderness without a sound took him into its bosom again. As I approached the glow from the dark I found myself at the back of two men, talking. I heard the name of Kurtz pronounced, then the words, 'take advantage of this unfortunate accident.' One of the men was the manager. I wished him a good evening. 'Did you ever see anything like it—eh? it is incredible,' he said, and walked off. The other man remained. He was a first-class agent, young, gentlemanly, a bit reserved, with a forked little beard and a hooked nose. He was stand-offish with the other agents, and they on their side said he was the manager's spy upon them. As to me, I had hardly ever spoken to him before. We got into talk, and by and by we strolled away from the hissing ruins. Then he asked me to his room, which was in the main building of the station. He struck a match, and I perceived that this young aristocrat had not only a silver-mounted dressing-case but also a whole candle all to himself. Just at that time the manager was the only man supposed to have any right to candles. Native mats covered the clay walls; a collection of spears, assegais, shields, knives was hung up in trophies. The business intrusted to this fellow was the making of bricks—so I had been informed; but there wasn't a fragment of a brick anywhere in the station, and he had been there more than a year—waiting. It seems he could not make bricks without something, I don't know what—straw maybe. Anyway, it could not be found there, and as it was not likely to be sent from Europe, it did not appear clear to me what he was waiting for. An act of special creation perhaps. However, they were all waiting —all the sixteen or twenty pilgrims of them—for something; and upon my word it did not seem an uncongenial occupation, from the way they took it, though the only thing that ever came to them was disease—as far as I could see. They beguiled the time by backbiting and intriguing against each other in a foolish kind of way. There was an air of plotting about that station, but nothing came of it, of course. It was as unreal as everything else—as the philanthropic pretense of the whole concern, as their talk, as their government, as their show of work. The only real feeling was a desire to get appointed to a trading-post where ivory was to be had, so that they could earn percentages. They intrigued and slandered and hated each other only on that account,—but as to effectually lifting a little finger—oh, no. By heavens! there is something after all in the world allowing one man to steal a horse while another must not look at a halter. Steal a horse straight out. Very well. He has done it. Perhaps he can ride. But there is a way of looking at a halter that would provoke the most charitable of saints into a kick.

"I had no idea why he wanted to be sociable, but as we chatted in there it suddenly occurred to me the fellow was trying to get at something—in fact, pumping me. He alluded constantly to Europe, to the people I was supposed to know there—putting leading questions as to my acquaintances in the sepulchral city, and so on. His little eyes glittered like mica discs—with curiosity—though he tried to keep up a bit of superciliousness. At first I was astonished, but very soon I became awfully curious to see what he would find out from me. I couldn't possibly imagine what I had in me to make it worth his while. It was very pretty to see how he baffled himself, for in truth my body was full only of chills, and my head had nothing in it but that wretched steamboat business. It was evident he took me for a perfectly shameless prevaricator. At last he got angry, and, to conceal a movement of furious annoyance, he yawned. I rose. Then I noticed a small sketch in oils, on a panel, representing a woman, draped and blindfolded, carrying a lighted torch. The background was somber—almost black. The movement of the woman was stately, and the effect of the torch-light on the face was sinister.

"It arrested me, and he stood by civilly, holding an empty half-pint champagne bottle (medical comforts) with the candle stuck in it. To my question he said Mr. Kurtz had painted this—in this very station more than a year ago—while waiting for means to go to his trading-post. 'Tell me, pray,' said I, 'who is this Mr. Kurtz?'

" 'The chief of the Inner Station,' he answered in a short tone, looking away. 'Much obliged,' I said, laughing. 'And you are the brickmaker of the Central Station. Every one knows that.' He was silent for a while. 'He is a prodigy,' he said at last. 'He is an emissary of pity, and science, and progress, and devil knows what else. We want,' he began to declaim suddenly, 'for the guidance of the cause intrusted to us by Europe, so to speak, higher intelligence, wide sympathies, a singleness of purpose.' 'Who says that?' I asked. 'Lots of them,' he replied. 'Some even write that; and so *he* comes here, a special being, as you ought to know.' 'Why ought I to know?' I interrupted, really surprised. He paid no attention. 'Yes. To-day he is chief of the best station, next year he will be assistant-manager, two years more and . . . but I daresay you know what he will be in two years' time. You are of the new gang—the gang of virtue. The same people who sent him specially also recommended you. Oh, don't say no. I've my own eyes to trust.' Light dawned upon me. My dear aunt's influential acquaintances were producing an unexpected effect upon that young man. I nearly burst into a laugh. 'Do you read the Company's confidential correspondence?' I asked. He hadn't a word to say. It was great fun. 'When Mr. Kurtz,' I continued, severely, 'is General Manager, you won't have the opportunity.'

"He blew the candle out suddenly, and we went outside. The moon had risen. Black figures strolled about listlessly, pouring water on the glow, whence proceeded a sound of hissing; steam ascended in the moonlight, the beaten nigger groaned somewhere. 'What a row the brute makes!' said the indefatigable man with the mustaches, appearing near us. 'Serve him right. Transgression—punishment—bang! Pitiless, pitiless. That's the only way. This will prevent all conflagrations for the future. I was just telling the manager. . . .' He noticed my companion, and became crestfallen all at once. 'Not in bed yet,' he said, with a kind of servile heartiness; 'it's so natural. Ha! Danger—agitation.' He vanished. I went on to the river-side, and the other followed me. I heard a scathing murmur at my ear, 'Heap of muffs—go to.' The pilgrims could be seen in knots gesticulating, discussing. Several had still their staves in their hands. I verily believe they took these sticks to bed with them. Beyond the fence the forest stood up spectrally in the moonlight, and through the dim stir, through the faint sounds of that lamentable courtyard, the silence of the land went home to one's very heart—its mystery, its greatness, the amazing reality of its concealed life. The hurt nigger moaned feebly somewhere near by, and then fetched a deep sigh that made me mend my pace away from there. I felt a hand introducing itself under my arm. 'My dear sir,' said the fellow, 'I don't want to be misunderstood, and especially by you, who will see Mr. Kurtz long before I can have that pleasure. I wouldn't like him to get a false idea of my disposition. . . .'

"I let him run on, this papier-mâché Mephistopheles, and it seemed to me that if I tried I could poke my forefinger through him, and would find nothing inside but a little loose dirt, maybe. He, don't you see, had been planning to be assistant-manager by and by under the present man, and I could see that the coming of that Kurtz had upset them both not a little. He talked precipitately, and I did not try to stop him. I had my shoulders against the wreck of my steamer, hauled up on the slope like a carcass of some big river animal. The smell of mud, of primeval mud, by Jove! was in my nostrils, the high stillness of primeval forests was before my eyes; there were shiny patches on the black creek. The moon had spread over everything a thin layer of silver—over the rank grass, over the mud, upon the wall of matted vegetation standing higher than the wall of a temple, over the great river I could see through a somber gap glittering, glittering, as it flowed broadly by without a murmur. All this was great, expectant, mute, while the man jabbered about himself. I wondered whether the stillness on the face of the immensity looking at us two were meant as an appeal or as a menace. What were we who had strayed in here? Could we handle that dumb thing, or would it handle us? I felt how big, how confoundedly big, was that thing that couldn't talk, and perhaps was deaf as well. What was in there? I could see a little ivory coming out from there, and I had heard Mr. Kurtz was in there. I had heard enough about it, too—God knows! Yet somehow it didn't bring any image with it—no more than if I had been told an angel or a fiend was in there. I believed it in the same way one of you might believe there are inhabitants in the planet Mars. I knew once a Scotch sailmaker who was certain, dead sure, there were people in Mars. If you asked him for some idea how they looked and behaved, he would get shy and mutter something about 'walking on all-fours.' If you as much as smiled, he would—though a man of sixty-four—offer to fight you. I would not have gone so far as to fight for Kurtz, but I went for him near enough to a lie. You know I hate, detest, and can't bear a lie, not because I am straighter than the rest of us, but simply because it appalls me. There is a taint of death, a flavor of mortality in lies—which is exactly what I hate and detest in the world—what I want to forget. It makes me miserable and sick, like biting something rotten would do. Temperament, I suppose. Well, I went near enough to it by letting the young fool there believe anything he liked to imagine as to my influence in Europe. I became in an instant as much of a pretense as the rest of the bewitched pilgrims. This simply because I had a notion it somehow would be of help to that Kurtz whom at the time I did not see—you understand. He was just a word for me. I did not see the man in the name any more than you do. Do you see him? Do you see the story? Do you see anything? It seems to me I am trying to tell you a dream—making a vain attempt, because no relation of a dream can convey the dream-sensation, that commingling of absurdity, surprise, and bewilderment in a tremor of struggling revolt, that notion of being captured by the incredible which is of the very essence of dreams. . . ."

He was silent for a while.

". . . No, it is impossible; it is impossible to convey the life-sensation of any given epoch of one's existence—that which makes its truth, its meaning—its subtle and penetrating essence. It is impossible. We live, as we dream—alone. . . ."

He paused again as if reflecting, then added—

"Of course in this you fellows see more than I could then. You see me, whom you know. . . ."

It had become so pitch dark that we listeners could hardly see one another. For a long time already he, sitting apart, had been no more to us than a voice. There was not a word from anybody. The others might have been asleep, but I was awake. I listened, I listened on the watch for the sentence, for the word, that would give me the clew to the faint uneasiness inspired by this narrative that seemed to shape itself without human lips in the heavy night-air of the river.

". . . Yes—I let him run on," Marlow began again, "and think what he pleased about the powers that were behind me. I did! And there was nothing behind me! There was nothing but that wretched, old, mangled steamboat I was leaning against, while he talked fluently about 'the necessity for every man to get on.' 'And when one comes out here, you conceive, it is not to gaze at the moon.' Mr. Kurtz was a 'universal genius,' but even a genius would find it easier to work with 'adequate tools—intelligent men.' He did not make bricks—why, there was a physical impossibility in the way—as I was well aware; and if he did secretarial work for the manager, it was because 'no sensible man rejects wantonly the confidence of his superiors.' Did I see it? I saw it. What more did I want? What I really wanted was rivets, by heavens! Rivets. To get on with the work—to stop the hole. Rivets I wanted. There were cases of them down at the coast—cases—piled up—burst—split! You kicked a loose rivet at every second step in that station yard on the hillside. Rivets had rolled into the grove of death. You could fill your pockets with rivets for the trouble of stooping down—and there wasn't one rivet to be found where it was wanted. We had plates that would do, but nothing to fasten them with. And every week the messenger, a lone negro, letter-bag on shoulder and staff in hand, left our station for the coast. And several times a week a coast caravan came in with trade goods—ghastly glazed calico that made you shudder only to look at it; glass beads, valued about a penny a quart, confounded spotted cotton handkerchiefs. And no rivets. Three carriers could have brought all that was wanted to set that steamboat afloat.

"He was becoming confidential now, but I fancy my unresponsive attitude must have exasperated him at last, for he judged it necessary to inform me he feared neither God nor devil, let alone any mere man. I said I could see that very well, but what I wanted was a certain quantity of rivets—and rivets were what really Mr. Kurtz wanted, if he had only known it. Now letters went to the coast every week. . . . 'My dear sir,' he cried, 'I write from dictation.' I demanded rivets. There was a way—for an intelligent man. He changed his manner; became very cold, and suddenly began to talk about a hippopotamus; wondered whether sleeping on board the steamer (I stuck to my salvage night and day) I wasn't disturbed. There was an old hippo that had the bad habit of getting out on the bank and roaming at night over the station grounds. The pilgrims used to turn out in a body and empty every rifle they could lay hands on at him. Some even had sat up o' nights for him. All this energy was wasted, though. 'That animal has a charmed life,' he said; 'but you can say this only of brutes in this country. No man—you apprehend me?—no man here bears a charmed life.' He stood there for a moment in the moonlight with his delicate hooked nose set a little askew, and his mica eyes glittering without a wink, then, with a curt Good night, he strode off. I could see he was disturbed and considerably puzzled, which made me feel more hopeful than I had been for days. It was a great comfort to turn from that chap to my influential friend, the battered, twisted, ruined, tin-pot steamboat. I clambered on board. She rang under my feet like an empty Huntley & Palmer biscuit-tin kicked along a gutter; she was nothing so solid in make, and rather less pretty in shape, but I had expended enough hard work on her to make me love her. No influential friend would have served me better. She had given me a chance to come out a bit—to find out what I could do. No, I don't like work. I had rather laze about and think of all the fine things that can be done. I don't like work—no man does—but I like what is in the work,—the chance to find yourself. Your own reality—for yourself, not for others—what no other man can ever know. They can only see the mere show, and never can tell what it really means.

"I was not surprised to see somebody sitting aft, on the deck, with his legs dangling over the mud. You see I rather chummed with the few mechanics there were in that station, whom the other pilgrims naturally despised—on account of their imperfect manners, I supose. This was the foreman—a boilermaker by trade—a good worker. He was a lank, bony, yellow-faced man, with big intense eyes. His aspect was worried, and his head was as bald as the palm of my hand; but his hair in falling seemed to have stuck to his chin, and had prospered in the new locality, for his beard hung down to his waist. He was a widower with six young children (he had left them in charge of a sister of his to come out there), and the passion of his life was pigeon-flying. He was an enthusiast and a connoisseur. He would rave about pigeons. After work hours he used sometimes to come over from his hut for a talk about his children and his pigeons; at work, when he had to crawl in the mud under the bottom of the steamboat, he would tie up that beard of his in a kind of white serviette he brought for the purpose. It had loops to go over his ears. In the evening he could be seen squatted on the bank rinsing that wrapper in the creek with great care, then spreading it solemnly on a bush to dry.

"I slapped him on the back and shouted, 'We shall have rivets!' He scrambled to his feet exclaiming, "No! Rivets!" as though he couldn't believe his ears. Then in a low voice, 'You . . . eh?' I don't know why we behaved like lunatics. I put my finger to the side of my nose and nodded mysteriously. 'Good for you!' he cried, snapped his fingers above his head, lifting one foot. I tried a jig. We capered on the iron deck. A frightful clatter came out of that hulk, and the virgin forest on the other bank of the creek sent it back in a thundering roll upon the sleeping station. It must have made some of the pilgrims sit up in their hovels. A dark figure obscured the lighted doorway of the manager's hut, vanished, then, a second or so after, the doorway itself vanished, too. We stopped, and the silence driven away by the stamping of our feet flowed back again from the recesses of the land. The great wall of vegetation, an exuberant and entangled mass of trunks, branches, leaves, boughs, festoons, motionless in the moonlight, was like a rioting invasion of soundless life, a rolling wave of plants, piled up, crested, ready to topple over the creek, to sweep every little man of us out of his little existence. And it moved not. A deadened burst of mighty splashes and snorts reached us from afar, as though an ichthyosaurus had been taking a bath of glitter in the great river. 'After all,' said the boiler-maker in a reasonable tone, 'why shouldn't we get the rivets?' Why not, indeed! I did not know of any reason why we shouldn't. 'They'll come in three weeks,' I said, confidently.

"But they didn't. Instead of rivets there came an invasion, an infliction, a visitation. It came in sections during the next three weeks, each section headed by a donkey carrying a white man in new clothes and tan shoes, bowing from that elevation right and left to the impressed pilgrims. A quarrelsome band of footsore sulky niggers trod on the heels of the donkeys; a lot of tents, camp-stools, tin boxes, white cases, brown bales would be shot down in the courtyard, and the air of mystery would deepen a little over the muddle of the station. Five such installments came, with their absurd air of disorderly flight with the loot of innumerable outfit shops and provision stores, that, one would think, they were lugging, after a raid, into the wilderness for equitable division. It was an inextricable mess of things decent in themselves but that human folly made look like the spoils of thieving.

"This devoted band called itself the Eldorado Exploring Expedition, and I believe they were sworn to secrecy. Their talk, however, was the talk of sordid buccaneers: it was reckless without hardihood, greedy without audacity, and cruel without courage; there was not an atom of foresight or of serious intention in the whole batch of them, and they did not seem aware these things are wanted for the work of the world. To tear treasure out of the bowels of the land was their desire, with no more moral purpose at the back of it than there is in burglars breaking into a safe. Who paid the expenses of the noble enterprise I don't know; but the uncle of our manager was leader of that lot.

"In exterior he resembled a butcher in a poor neighborhood, and his eyes had a look of sleepy cunning. He carried his fat paunch with ostentation on his short legs, and during the time his gang infested the station spoke to no one but his nephew. You could see these two roaming about all day long with their heads close together in an everlasting confab.

"I had given up worrying myself about the rivets. One's capacity for that kind of folly is more limited than you would suppose. I said Hang!—and let things slide. I had plenty of time for meditation, and now and then I would give some thought to Kurtz. I wasn't very interested in him. No. Still, I was curious to see whether this man, who had come out equipped with moral ideas of some sort, would climb to the top after all and how he would set about his work when there."

2

"One evening as I was lying flat on the deck of my steamboat, I heard voices approaching—and there were the nephew and the uncle strolling along the bank. I laid my head on my arm again, and had nearly lost myself in a doze, when somebody said in my ear, as it were: 'I am as harmless as a little child, but I don't like to be dictated to. Am I the manager—or am I not? I was ordered to send him there. It's incredible.' . . . I became aware that the two were standing on the shore alongside the forepart of the steamboat, just below my head. I did not move; it did not occur to me to move: I was sleepy. 'It *is* unpleasant,' grunted the uncle. 'He has asked the Administration to be sent there,' said the other, 'with the idea of showing what he could do; and I was instructed accordingly. Look at the influence that man must have. Is it not frightful?' They both agreed it was frightful, then made several bizarre remarks: 'Make rain and fine weather—one man—the Council—by the nose'—bits of absurd sentences that got the better of my drowsiness, so that I had pretty near the whole of my wits about me when the uncle said, 'The climate may do away with this difficulty for you. Is he alone there?' 'Yes,' answered the manager; 'he sent his assistant down the river with a note to me in these terms: "Clear this poor devil out of the country, and don't bother sending more of that sort. I had rather be alone than have the kind of men you can dispose of with me." It was more than a year ago. Can you imagine such impudence!' 'Anything since then?' asked the other, hoarsely. 'Ivory,' jerked the nephew; 'lots of it— prime sort—lots—most annoying, from him.' 'And with that?' questioned the heavy rumble, 'Invoice,' was the reply fired out, so to speak. Then silence. They had been talking about Kurtz.

"I was broad awake by this time, but, lying perfectly at ease, remained still, having no inducement to change my position. 'How did that ivory come all this way?' growled the elder man, who seemed very vexed. The other explained that it had come with a fleet of canoes in charge of an English half-caste clerk Kurtz had with him; that Kurtz had apparently intended to return himself, the station being by that time bare of goods and stores, but after coming three hundred miles, had suddenly decided to go back, which he started to do alone in a small dugout with four paddlers, leaving the half-caste to continue down the river with the ivory. The two fellows there seemed astounded at anybody attempting such a thing. They were at a loss for an adequate motive. As to me, I seemed to see Kurtz for the first time. It was a distinct glimpse: the dugout, four paddling savages, and the lone white man turning his back suddenly on the headquarters, on relief, on thoughts of home—perhaps; setting his face towards the depths of the wilderness, towards his empty and desolate station. I did not know the motive. Perhaps he was just simply a fine fellow who stuck to his work for its own sake. His name, you understand, had not been pronounced once. He was 'that man.' The half-caste, who, as far as I could see, had conducted a difficult trip with great prudence and pluck, was invariably alluded to as 'that scoundrel.' The 'scoundrel' had reported that the 'man' had been very ill—had recovered imperfectly. . . . The two below me moved away then a few paces, and strolled back and forth at some little distance. I heard: 'Military post—doctor—two hundred miles— quite alone now—unavoidable delays—nine months—no news—strange rumors.' They approached again, just as the manager was saying, 'No one, as far as I know, unless a species of wandering trader—a pestilential fellow, snapping ivory from the natives.' Who was it they were talking about now? I gathered in snatches that this was some man supposed to be in Kurtz's district, and of whom the manager did not approve. 'We will not be free from unfair competition till one of these fellows is hanged for an example,' he said. 'Certainly,' grunted the other; 'get him hanged! Why not? Anything—anything can be done in this country. That's what I say; nobody here, you understand, *here,* can endanger your position. And why? You stand the climate—you outlast them all. The danger is in Europe; but there before I left I took care to————' They moved off and whispered, then their voices rose again. 'The extraordinary series of delays is not my fault. I did my best.' The fat man sighed. 'Very sad.' 'And the pestiferous absurdity of his talk,' continued the other; 'he bothered me enough when he was here. "Each station should be like a beacon on the road towards better things, a center for trade of course, but also for humanizing, improving, instructing." Conceive you—that ass! And he wants to be manager! No, it's————' Here he got choked by excessive indignation, and I lifted my head the least bit. I was surprised to see how near they were—right under me. I could have spat upon their hats. They were looking on the ground, absorbed in thought. The manager was switching his leg with a slender twig: his sagacious relative lifted his head. 'You have been well since you came out this time?' he asked. The other gave a start. 'Who? I? Oh! Like a charm—like a charm. But the rest—oh, my goodness! All sick. They die so quick, too, that I haven't the time to send them out of the country—it's incredible!' 'H'm. Just so,' grunted the uncle. 'Ah! my boy, trust to this—I say, trust to this.' I saw him extend his short flipper of an arm for a gesture that took in the forest, the creek, the mud, the river,—seemed to beckon with a dishonoring flourish before the sunlit face of the land a treacherous appeal to the lurking death, to the hidden evil, to the profound darkness of its heart. It was so startling that I leaped to my feet and looked back at the edge of the forest, as though I had expected an answer of some sort to that black display of confidence. You know the foolish notions that come to one sometimes. The high stillness confronted these two figures with its ominous patience, waiting for the passing away of a fantastic invasion.

"They swore aloud together—out of sheer fright, I believe—then pretending not to know anything of my existence, turned back to the station. The sun was low; and leaning forward side by side, they seemed to be tugging painfully uphill their two ridiculous shadows of unequal length, that trailed behind them slowly over the tall grass without bending a single blade.

"In a few days the Eldorado Expedition went into the patient wilderness, that closed upon it as the sea closes over a diver. Long afterwards the news came that all the donkeys were dead. I know nothing as to the fate of the less valuable animals. They, no doubt, like the rest of us, found what they deserved. I did not inquire. I was then rather excited at the prospect of meeting Kurtz very soon. When I say very soon I mean it comparatively. It was just two months from the day we left the creek when we came to the bank below Kurtz's station.

"Going up that river was like traveling back to the earliest beginnings of the world, when vegetation rioted on the earth and the big trees were kings. An empty stream, a great silence, an impenetrable forest. The air was warm, thick, heavy, sluggish. There was no joy in the brilliance of sunshine. The long stretches of the waterway ran on, deserted, into the gloom of over-shadowed distances. On silvery sandbanks hippos and alligators sunned themselves side by side. The broadening waters flowed through a mob of wooded islands; you lost your way on that river as you would in a desert, and butted all day long against shoals, trying to find the channel, till you thought yourself bewitched and cut off for ever from everything you had known once—somewhere—far away—in another existence perhaps. There were moments when one's past came back to one, as it will sometimes when you have not a moment to spare to yourself; but it came in the shape of an unrestful and noisy dream, remembered with wonder amongst the overwhelming realities of this strange world of plants, and water, and silence. And this stillness of life did not in the least resemble a peace. It was the stillness of an implacable force brooding over an inscrutable intention. It looked at you with a vengeful aspect. I got used to it afterwards; I did not see it any more; I had no time. I had to keep guessing at the channel; I had to discern, mostly by inspiration, the signs of hidden banks; I watched for sunken stones; I was learning to clap my teeth smartly before my heart flew out, when I shaved by a fluke some infernal sly old snag that would have ripped the life out of the tin-pot steam-boat and drowned all the pilgrims; I had to keep a look-out for the signs of dead wood we could cut up in the night for next day's steaming. When you have to attend to things of that sort, to the mere incidents of the surface, the reality—the reality, I tell you—fades. The inner truth is hidden—luckily, luckily. But I felt it all the same; I felt often its mysterious stillness watching me at my monkey tricks, just as it watches you fellows performing on your respective tight-ropes for—what is it? half-a-crown a tumble———"

"Try to be civil, Marlow," growled a voice, and I knew there was at least one listener awake besides myself.

"I beg your pardon. I forgot the heartache which makes up the rest of the price. And indeed what does the price matter, if the trick be well done? You do your tricks very well. And I didn't do badly either, since I managed not to sink that steamboat on my first trip. It's a wonder to me yet. Imagine a blind-folded man set to drive a van over a bad road. I sweated and shivered over that business considerably, I can tell you. After all, for a seaman, to scrape the bottom of the thing that's supposed to float all the time under his care is the unpardonable sin. No one may know of it, but you never forget the thump—eh? A blow on the very heart. You remember it, you dream of it, you wake up at night and think of it—years after—and go hot and cold all over. I don't pre-tend to say that steamboat floated all the time. More than once she had to wade for a bit, with twenty cannibals splashing around and pushing. We had enlisted some of these chaps on the way for a crew. Fine fellows—cannibals—in their place. They were men one could work with, and I am grateful to them. And, after all, they did not eat each other before my face: they had brought along a provision of hippo-meat which went rotten, and made the mystery of the wilderness stink in my nostrils. Phoo! I can sniff it now. I had the manager on board and three or four pilgrims with their staves—all complete. Sometimes we came upon a station close by the bank, clinging to the skirts of the unknown, and the white men rushing out of a tumble-down hovel, with great gestures of joy and surprise and welcome, seemed very strange—had the appearance of being held there captive by a spell. The word ivory would ring in the air for a while—and on we went again into the silence, along empty reaches, round the still bends, between the high walls of our winding way, reverberating in hollow claps the ponderous beat of the stern-wheel. Trees, trees, millions of trees, massive, immense, running up high; and at their foot, hugging the bank against the stream, crept the little begrimed steamboat, like a sluggish beetle crawling on the floor of a lofty portico. It made you feel very small, very lost, and yet it was not altogether depressing, that feeling. After all, if you were small, the grimy beetle crawled on—which was just what you wanted it to do. Where the pilgrims imagined it crawled to I don't know. To some place where they expected to get something, I bet! For me it crawled towards Kurtz—exclusively; but when the steam-pipes started leaking we crawled very slow. The reaches opened before us and closed behind, as if the forest had stepped leisurely across the water to bar the way for our return. We penetrated deeper and deeper into the heart of darkness. It was very quiet there. At night sometimes the roll of drums behind the curtain of trees would run up the river and remain sustained faintly, as if hovering in the air high over our heads, till the first break of day. Whether it meant war, peace, or prayer we could not tell. The dawns were heralded by the descent of a chill stillness; the wood-cutters slept, their fires burned low; the snapping of a twig would make you start. We were wanderers on a prehistoric earth, on an earth that wore the aspect of an unknown planet. We could have fancied ourselves the first of men taking possession of an accursed inheritance, to be subdued at the cost of profound anguish and of excessive toil. But suddenly, as we struggled round a bend, there would be a glimpse of rush walls, of peaked grass-roofs, a burst of yells, a whirl of black limbs, a mass of hands clapping, of feet stamping, of bodies swaying, of eyes rolling, under the droop of heavy and motionless foliage. The steamer toiled along slowly on the edge of a black and incomprehensible frenzy. The prehistoric man was cursing us, praying to us, welcoming us—who could tell? We were cut off from the comprehension of our surroundings; we glided past like phantoms, wondering and secretly appalled, as sane men would be before an enthusiastic outbreak in a madhouse. We could not understand because we were too far and could not remember, because we were traveling in the night of first ages, of those ages that are gone, leaving hardly a sign—and no memories.

"The earth seemed unearthly. We are accustomed to look upon the shackled form of a conquered monster, but there—there you could look at a thing monstrous and free. It was unearthly, and the men were———— No. they were not inhuman. Well, you know, that was the worst of it—this suspicion of their not being inhuman. It would come slowly to one. They howled and leaped, and spun, and made horrid faces; but what thrilled you was just the thought of their humanity—like yours—the thought of your remote kinship with this wild and passionate uproar. Ugly. Yes, it was ugly enough; but if you were man enough you would admit to yourself that there was in you just the faintest trace of a response to the terrible frankness of that noise, a dim suspicion of there being a meaning in it which you—you so remote from the night of first ages—could comprehend. And why not? The mind of man is capable of anything—because everything is in it, all the past as well as all the future. What was there after all? Joy, fear, sorrow, devotion, valor, rage—who can tell?—but truth—truth stripped of its cloak of time. Let the fool gape and shudder—the man knows, and can look on without a wink. But he must at least be as much of a man as these on the shore. He must meet that truth with his own true stuff—with his own inborn strength. Principles won't do. Acquisitions, clothes, pretty rags—rags that would fly off at the first good shake. No; you want a deliberate belief. An appeal to me in this fiendish row—is there? Very well; I hear; I admit, but I have a voice, too, and for good or evil mine is the speech that cannot be silenced. Of course, a fool, what with sheer fright and fine sentiments, is always safe. Who's that grunting? You wonder I didn't go ashore for a howl and a dance? Well, no—I didn't. Fine sentiments, you say? Fine sentiments, be hanged! I had no time. I had to mess about with white-lead and strips of woolen blanket helping to put bandages on those leaky steam-pipes—I tell you. I had to watch the steering, and circumvent those snags, and get the tinpot along by hook or by crook. There was surface-truth enough in these things to save a wiser man. And between whiles I had to look after the savage who was fireman. He was an improved specimen; he could fire up a vertical boiler. He was there below me, and, upon my word, to look at him was as edifying as seeing a dog in a parody of breeches and a feather hat, walking on his hind-legs. A few months of training had done for that really fine chap. He squinted at the steam-gauge and at the water-gauge with an evident effort of intrepidity—and he had filed teeth, too, the poor devil, and the wool of his pate shaved into queer patterns, and three ornamental scars on each of his cheeks. He ought to have been clapping his hands and stamping his feet on the bank, instead of which he was hard at work, a thrall to strange witchcraft, full of improving knowledge. He was useful because he had been instructed; and what he knew was this—that should the water in that transparent thing disappear, the evil spirit inside the boiler would get angry through the greatness of his thirst, and take a terrible vengeance. So he sweated and fired up and watched the glass fearfully (with an impromptu charm, made of rags, tied to his arm, and a piece of polished bone, as big as a watch, stuck flatways through his lower lip), while the wooded banks slipped past us slowly, the short noise was left behind, the interminable miles of silence —and we crept on, towards Kurtz. But the snags were thick, the water was treacherous and shallow, the boiler seemed indeed to have a sulky devil in it, and thus neither that fireman nor I had any time to peer into our creepy thoughts.

"Some fifty miles below the Inner Station we came upon a hut of reeds, an inclined and melancholy pole, with the unrecognizable tatters of what had been a flag of some sort flying from it, and a neatly stacked wood-pile. This was unexpected. We came to the bank, and on the stack of firewood found a flat piece of board with some faded pencil-writing on it. When deciphered it said: 'Wood for you. Hurry up. Approach cautiously.' There was a signature, but it was illegible—not Kurtz—a much longer word. 'Hurry up.' Where? Up the river? 'Approach cautiously.' We had not done so. But the warning could not have been meant for the place where it could be only found after approach. Something was wrong above. But what—and how much? That was the question. We commented adversely upon the imbecility of that telegraphic style. The bush around said nothing, and would not let us look very far, either. A torn curtain of red twill hung in the doorway of the hut, and flapped sadly in our faces. The dwelling was dismantled; but we could see a white man had lived there not very long ago. There remained a rude table—a plank on two posts; a heap of rubbish reposed in a dark corner, and by the door I picked up a book. It had lost its covers, and the pages had been thumbed into a state of extremely dirty softness; but the back had been lovingly stitched afresh with white cotton thread, which looked clean yet. It was an extraordinary find. Its title was, *An Inquiry into some Points of Seamanship,* by a man Towser, Towson—some such name —Master in his Majesty's Navy. The matter looked dreary reading enough, with illustrative diagrams and repulsive tables of figures, and the copy was sixty years old. I handled this amazing antiquity with the greatest possible tenderness, lest it should dissolve in my hands. Within, Towson or Towser was inquiring earnestly into the breaking strain of ships' chains and tackle, and other such matters. Not a very enthralling book; but at the first glance you could see there a singleness of intention, an honest concern for the right way of going to work, which made these humble pages, thought out so many years ago, luminous with another than a professional light. The simple old sailor, with his talk of chains and purchases, made me forget the jungle and the pilgrims in a delicious sensation of having come upon something unmistakably real. Such a book being there was wonderful enough; but still more astounding were the notes penciled in the margin, and plainly referring to the text. I couldn't believe my eyes! They were in cipher! Yes, it looked like cipher. Fancy a man lugging with him a book of that description into this nowhere and studying it—and making notes—in cipher at that! It was an extravagant mystery.

"I had been dimly aware for some time of a worrying noise, and when I lifted my eyes I saw the wood-pile was gone, and the manager, aided by all the pilgrims, was shouting at me from the river-side. I slipped the book into my pocket. I assure you to leave off reading was like tearing myself away from the shelter of an old and solid friendship.

"I started the lame engine ahead. 'It must be this miserable trader—this intruder,' exclaimed the manager, looking back malevolently at the place we had left. 'He must be English,' I said. 'It will not save him from getting into trouble if he is not careful,' muttered the manager darkly. I observed with assumed innocence that no man was safe from trouble in this world.

"The current was more rapid now, the steamer seemed at her last gasp, the stern-wheel flopped languidly, and I caught myself listening on tiptoe for the next beat of the boat, for in sober truth I expected the wretched thing to give up every moment. It was like watching the last flickers of a life. But still we crawled. Sometimes I would pick out a tree a little way ahead to measure our progress towards Kutz by, but I lost it invariably before we got abreast. To keep the eyes so long on one thing was too much for human patience. The manager displayed a beautiful resignation. I fretted and fumed and took to arguing with myself whether or no I would talk openly with Kurtz; but before I could come to any conclusion it occurred to me that my speech or my silence, indeed any action of mine, would be a mere futility. What did it matter what any one knew or ignored? What did it matter who was manager? One gets sometimes such a flash of insight. The essentials of this affair lay deep under the surface, beyond my reach, and beyond my power of meddling.

"Towards the evening of the second day we judged ourselves about eight miles from Kurtz's station. I wanted to push on; but the manager looked grave, and told me the navigation up there was so dangerous that it would be advisable, the sun being very low already, to wait where we were till next morning. Moreover, he pointed out that if the warning to approach cautiously were to be followed, we must approach in daylight—not at dusk, or in the dark. This was sensible enough. Eight miles meant nearly three hours' steaming for us, and I could also see suspicious ripples at the upper end of the reach. Nevertheless, I was annoyed beyond expression at the delay, and most unreasonably, too, since one night more could not matter much after so many months. As we had plenty of wood, and caution was the word, I brought up in the middle of the stream. The reach was narrow, straight, with high sides like a railway cutting. The dusk came gliding into it long before the sun had set. The current ran smooth and swift, but a dumb immobility sat on the banks. The living trees, lashed together by the creepers and every living bush of the undergrowth, might have been changed into stone, even to the slenderest twig, to the lightest leaf. It was not sleep—it seemed unnatural, like a state of trance. Not the faintest sound of any kind could be heard. You looked on amazed, and began to suspect yourself of being deaf—then the night came suddenly, and struck you blind as well. About three in the morning some large fish leaped, and the loud splash made me jump as though a gun had been fired. When the sun rose there was a white fog, very warm and clammy, and more blinding than the night. It did not shift or drive; it was just there, standing all round you like something solid. At eight or nine, perhaps, it lifted as a shutter lifts. We had a glimpse of the towering multitude of trees, of the immense matted jungle, with the blazing little ball of the sun hanging over it—all perfectly still—and then the white shutter came down again, smoothly, as if sliding in greased grooves. I ordered the chain, which we had begun to heave in, to be paid out again. Before it stopped running with a muffled rattle, a cry, a very loud cry, as of infinite desolation, soared slowly in the opaque air. It ceased. A complaining clamor, modulated in savage discords, filled our ears. The sheer unexpectedness of it made my hair stir under my cap. I don't know how it struck the others: to me it seemed as though the mist itself had screamed, so suddenly, and apparently from all sides at once, did this tumultuous and mournful uproar arise. It culminated in a hurried outbreak of almost intolerably excessive shrieking, which stopped short, leaving us stiffened in a variety of silly attitudes, and obstinately listening to the nearly as appalling and excessive silence. 'Good God! What is the meaning——' stammered at my elbow one of the pilgrims,—a little fat man, with sandy hair and red whiskers, who wore side-spring boots, and pink pyjamas tucked into his socks. Two others remained open-mouthed a whole minute, then dashed into the little cabin, to rush out incontinently and stand darting scared glances, with Winchesters at 'ready' in their hands. What we could see was just the steamer we were on, her outlines blurred as though she had been on the point of dissolving, and a misty strip of water, perhaps two feet broad, around her—and that was all. The rest of the world was nowhere, as far as our eyes and ears were concerned. Just nowhere. Gone, disappeared; swept off without leaving a whisper or a shadow behind.

"I went forward, and ordered the chain to be hauled in short, so as to be ready to trip the anchor and move the steamboat at once if necessary. 'Will they attack?' whispered an awed voice. 'We will be all butchered in this fog,' murmured another. The faces twitched with the strain, the hands trembled slightly, the eyes forgot to wink. It was very curious to see the contrast of expressions of the white men and of the black fellows of our crew, who were as much strangers to that part of the river as we, though their homes were only eight hundred miles away. The whites, of course, greatly discomposed, had besides a curious look of being painfully shocked by such an outrageous row. The others had an alert, naturally interested expression; but their faces were essentially quiet, even those of the one or two who grinned as they hauled at the chain. Several exchanged short, grunting phrases, which seemed to settle the matter to their satisfaction. Their headman, a young, broad-chested black, severely draped in dark-blue fringed cloths, with fierce nostrils and his hair all done up artfully in oily ringlets, stood near me. 'Aha!' I said, just for good fellowship's sake. 'Catch 'im,' he snapped, with a bloodshot widening of his eyes and a flash of sharp teeth—'catch 'im. Give 'im to us.' 'To you, eh?' I asked; 'what would you do with them?' 'Eat 'im!' he said, curtly, and, leaning his elbow on the rail, looked out into the fog in a dignified and profoundly pensive attitude. I would no doubt have been properly horrified, had it not occurred to me that he and his chaps must be very hungry: that they must have been growing increasingly hungry for at least this month past. They had been engaged for six months (I don't think a single one of them had any clear idea of time, as we at the end of countless ages have. They still belonged to the beginnings of time—had no inherited experience to teach them as it were), and of course, as long as there was a piece of paper written over in accordance with some farcical law or other made down the river, it didn't enter anybody's head to trouble how they would live. Certainly they had brought with them some rotten hippo-meat, which couldn't have lasted very long, anyway, even if the pilgrims hadn't, in the midst of a shocking hullabaloo, thrown a considerable quantity of it overboard. It looked like a high-handed proceeding; but it was really a case of legitimate self-defense. You can't breathe dead hippo waking, sleeping, and eating, and at the same time keep your precarious grip on existence. Besides that, they had given them every week three pieces of brass wire, each about nine inches long; and the theory was they were to buy their provisions with that currency in river-side villages. You can see how *that* worked. There were either no villages, or the people were hostile, or the director, who like the rest of us fed out of tins, with an occasional old he-goat thrown in, didn't want to stop the steamer for some more or less recondite reason. So, unless they swallowed the wire itself, or made loops of it to snare the fishes with, I don't see what good their extravagant salary could be to them. I must say it was paid with a regularity worthy of a large and honorable trading company. For the rest, the only thing to eat—though it didn't look eatable in the least—I saw in their possession was a few lumps of some stuff like half-cooked dough, of a dirty lavender color, they kept wrapped in leaves, and now and then swallowed a piece of, but so small that it seemed done more for the looks of the thing than for any serious purpose of sustenance. Why in the name of all the gnawing devils of hunger they didn't go for us—they were thirty to five—and have a good tuck-in for once, amazes me now when I think of it. They were big powerful men, with not much capacity to weigh the consequences, with courage, with strength, even yet, though their skins were no longer glossy and their muscles no longer hard. And I saw that something restraining, one of those human secrets that baffle probability, had come into play there. I looked at them with a swift quickening of interest—not because it occurred to me I might be eaten by them before very long, though I own to you that just then I perceived—in a new light, as it were—how unwholesome the pilgrims looked, and I hoped, yes, I positively hoped, that my aspect was not so—what shall I say?—so—unappetizing: a touch of fantastic vanity which fitted well with the dream-sensation that pervaded all my days at that time. Perhaps I had a little fever, too. One can't live with one's finger everlastingly on one's pulse. I had often 'a little fever,' or a little touch of other things—the playful paw-strokes of the wilderness, the preliminary trifling before the more serious onslaught which came in due course. Yes; I looked at them as you would on any human being, with a curiosity of their impulses, motives, capacities, weaknesses, when brought to the test of an inexorable physical necessity. Restraint! What possible restraint? Was it superstition, disgust, patience, fear—or some kind of primitive honor? No fear can stand up to hunger, no patience can wear it out, disgust simply does not exist where hunger is; and as to superstition, beliefs, and what you may call principles, they are less than chaff in a breeze. Don't you know the devilry of lingering starvation, its exasperating torment, its black thoughts, its somber and brooding ferocity? Well, I do. It takes a man all his inborn strength to fight hunger properly. It's really easier to face bereavement, dishonor, and the perdition of one's soul—than this kind of prolonged hunger. Sad, but true. And these chaps, too, had no earthly reason for any kind of scruple. Restraint! I would just as soon have expected restraint from a hyena prowling amongst the corpses of a battlefield. But there was the fact facing me—the fact dazzling, to be seen, like the foam on the depths of the sea, like a ripple on an unfathomable enigma, a mystery greater —when I thought of it—than the curious, inexplicable note of desperate grief in this savage clamor that had swept by us on the river-bank, behind the blind whiteness of the fog.

"Two pilgrims were quarreling in hurried whispers as to which bank. 'Left.' 'No, no; how can you? Right, right, of course.' 'It is very serious,' said the manager's voice behind me; 'I would be desolated if anything should happen to Mr. Kurtz before we came up.' I looked at him, and had not the slightest doubt he was sincere. He was just the kind of man who would wish to preserve appearances. That was his restraint. But when he muttered something about going on at once, I did not even take the trouble to answer him. I knew, and he knew, that it was impossible. Were we to let go our hold of the bottom, we would be absolutely in the air—in space. We wouldn't be able to tell where we were going to—whether up or down stream, or across—till we fetched against one bank or the other,—and then we wouldn't know at first which it was. Of course I made no move. I had no mind for a smash-up. You couldn't imagine a more deadly place for a shipwreck. Whether drowned at once or not, we were sure to perish speedily in one way or another. 'I authorize you to take all the risks,' he said, after a short silence. 'I refuse to take any,' I said, shortly; which was just the answer he expected, though its tone might have surprised him. 'Well, I must defer to your judgment. You are captain,' he said, with marked civility. I turned my shoulder to him in sign of my appreciation, and looked into the fog. How long would it last? It was the most hopeless look-out. The approach to this Kurtz grubbing for ivory in the wretched bush was beset by as many dangers as though he had been an enchanted princess sleeping in a fabulous castle. 'Will they attack, do you think?' asked the manager, in a confidential tone.

"I did not think they would attack, for several obvious reasons. The thick fog was one. If they left the bank in their canoes they would get lost in it, as we would be if we attempted to move. Still, I had also judged the jungle of both banks quite impenetrable—and yet eyes were in it, eyes that had seen us. The river-side bushes were certainly very thick; but the undergrowth behind was evidently penetrable. However, during the short lift I had seen no canoes anywhere in the reach—certainly not abreast of the steamer. But what made the idea of attack inconceivable to me was the nature of the noise—of the cries we had heard. They had not the fierce character boding immediate hostile intention. Unexpected, wild, and violent as they had been, they had given me an irresistible impression of sorrow. The glimpse of the steamboat had for some reason filled those savages with unrestrained grief. The danger, if any, I expounded, was from our proximity to a great human passion let loose. Even extreme grief may ultimately vent itself in violence—but more generally takes the form of apathy. . . .

"You should have seen the pilgrims stare! They had no heart to grin, or even to revile me: but I believe they thought me gone mad—with fright, maybe. I delivered a regular lecture. My dear boys, it was no good bothering. Keep a look-out? Well, you may guess I watched the fog for the signs of lifting as a cat watches a mouse; but for anything else our eyes were of no more use to us than if we had been buried miles deep in a heap of cotton-wool. It felt like it, too—choking, warm, stifling. Besides, all I said, though it sounded extravagant, was absolutely true to fact. What we afterwards alluded to as an attack was really an attempt at repulse. The action was very far from being aggressive—it was not even defensive, in the usual sense: it was undertaken under the stress of desperation, and in its essence was purely protective.

"It developed itself, I should say, two hours after the fog lifted, and its commencement was at a spot, roughly speaking, about a mile and a half below Kurtz's station. We had just floundered and flopped round a bend, when I saw an islet, a mere grassy hummock of bright green, in the middle of the stream.

It was the only thing of the kind; but as we opened the reach more, I perceived it was the head of a long sandbank, or rather of a chain of shallow patches stretching down the middle of the river. They were discolored, just awash, and the whole lot was seen just under the water, exactly as a man's backbone is seen running down the middle of his back under the skin. Now, as far as I did see, I could go to the right or to the left of this. I didn't know either channel, of course. The banks looked pretty well alike, the depth appeared the same; but as I had been informed the station was on the west side, I naturally headed for the western passage.

"No sooner had we fairly entered it than I became aware it was much narrower than I had supposed. To the left of us there was the long uninterrupted shoal, and to the right a high, steep bank heavily overgrown with bushes. Above the bush the trees stood in serried ranks. The twigs overhung the current thickly, and from distance to distance a large limb of some tree projected rigidly over the stream. It was then well on in the afternoon, the face of the forest was gloomy, and a broad strip of shadow had already fallen on the water. In this shadow we steamed up—very slowly, as you may imagine. I sheered her well inshore—the water being deepest near the bank, as the sounding-pole informed me.

"One of my hungry and forbearing friends was sounding in the bows just below me. This steamboat was exactly like a decked scow. On the deck, there were two little teak-wood houses, with doors and windows. The boiler was in the fore-end, and the machinery right astern. Over the whole there was a light roof, supported on stanchions. The funnel projected through that roof, and in front of the funnel a small cabin built of light planks served for a pilot-house. It contained a couch, two camp-stools, a loaded Martini-Henry leaning in one corner, a tiny table, and the steering-wheel. It had a wide door in front and a broad shutter at each side. All these were always thrown open, of course. I spent my days perched up there on the extreme fore-end of that roof, before the door. At night I slept, or tried to, on the couch. An athletic black belonging to some coast tribe, and educated by my poor predecessor, was the helmsman. He sported a pair of brass earrings, wore a blue cloth wrapper from the waist to the ankles, and thought all the world of himself. He was the most unstable kind of fool I had ever seen. He steered with no end of a swagger while you were by; but if he lost sight of you, he became instantly the prey of an abject funk, and would let that cripple of a steamboat get the upper hand of him in a minute.

"I was looking down at the sounding-pole, and feeling much annoyed to see at each try a little more of it stick out of that river, when I saw my poleman give up the business suddenly, and stretch himself flat on the deck, without even taking the trouble to haul his pole in. He kept hold on it though, and it trailed in the water. At the same time the fireman, whom I could also see below me, sat down abruptly before his furnace and ducked his head. I was amazed. Then I had to look at the river mighty quick, because there was a snag in the fairway. Sticks, little sticks, were flying about—thick: they were whizzing before my nose, dropping below me, striking behind me against my pilot-house. All this time the river, the shore, the woods, were very quiet—perfectly quiet. I could only hear the heavy splashing thump of the stern-wheel and the patter of these things. We cleared the snag clumsily. Arrows, by Jove! We were being shot at! I stepped in quickly to close the shutter on the land-side. That fool-helmsman, his hands on the spokes, was lifting his knees high, stamping his feet, champing his mouth, like a reined-in horse. Confound him! And we were staggering within ten feet of the bank. I had to lean right out to swing the heavy shutter, and I saw a face amongst the leaves on the level with my own, looking at me very fierce and steady; and then suddenly, as though a veil had been removed from my eyes, I made out, deep in the tangled gloom, naked breasts, arms, legs, glaring eyes,—the bush was swarming with human limbs in movement, glistening, of bronze color. The twigs shook, swayed, and rustled, the arrows flew out of them, and then the shutter came to. 'Steer her straight,' I said to the helmsman. He held his head rigid, face forward; but his eyes rolled, he kept on lifting and setting down his feet gently, his mouth foamed a little. 'Keep quiet!' I said in a fury. I might just as well have ordered a tree not to sway in the wind. I darted out. Below me there was a great scuffle of feet on the iron deck; confused exclamations; a voice screamed, 'Can you turn back?' I caught sight of a V-shaped ripple on the water ahead. What? Another snag! A fusillade burst out under my feet. The pilgrims had opened with their Winchesters, and were simply squirting lead into that bush. A deuce of a lot of smoke came up and drove slowly forward. I swore at it. Now I couldn't see the ripple or the snag either. I stood in the doorway, peering, and the arrows came in swarms. They might have been poisoned, but they looked as though they wouldn't kill a cat. The bush began to howl. Our wood-cutters raised a warlike whoop; the report of a rifle just at my back deafened me. I glanced over my shoulder, and the pilot-house was yet full of noise and smoke when I made a dash at the wheel. The fool-nigger had dropped everything, to throw the shutter open and let off that Martini-Henry. He stood before the wide opening, glaring, and I yelled at him to come back, while I straightened the sudden twist out of that steamboat. There was no room to turn even if I had wanted to, the snag was somewhere very near ahead in that confounded smoke, there was no time to lose, so I just crowded her into the bank—right into the bank, where I knew the water was deep.

"We tore slowly along the overhanging bushes in a whirl of broken twigs and flying leaves. The fusillade below stopped short, as I had foreseen it would when the squirts got empty. I threw my head back to a glinting whizz that traversed the pilot-house, in at one shutter-hole and out at the other. Looking past that mad helmsman, who was shaking the empty rifle and yelling at the shore, I saw vague forms of men running bent double, leaping, gliding, distinct, incomplete, evanescent. Something big appeared in the air before the shutter, the rifle went overboard, and the man stepped back swiftly, looked at me over his shoulder in an extraordinary, profound, familiar manner, and fell upon my feet. The side of his head hit the wheel twice, and the end of what appeared a long cane clattered round and knocked over a little camp-stool. It looked as though after wrenching that thing from somebody ashore he had lost his balance in the effort. The thin smoke had blown away, we were clear of the snag, and looking ahead I could see that in another hundred yards or so I would be free to sheer off, away from the bank; but my feet felt so very warm and wet that I had to look down. The man had rolled on his back and stared straight up at me; both his hands clutched that cane. It was the shaft of a spear that, either thrown or lunged through the opening, had caught him in the side just below the ribs; the blade had gone in out of sight, after making a frightful gash; my shoes were full; a pool of blood lay very still, gleaming dark-red under the wheel; his eyes shone with an amazing luster. The fusillade burst out again. He looked at me anxiously, gripping the spear like something precious, with an air of being afraid I would try to take it away from him. I had to make an effort to free my eyes from his gaze and attend to the steering. With one hand I felt above my head for the line of the steam whistle, and jerked out screech after screech hurriedly. The tumult of angry and warlike yells was checked instantly, and then from the depths of the woods went out such a tremulous and prolonged wail of mournful fear and utter despair as may be imagined to follow the flight of the last hope from the earth. There was a great commotion in the bush; the shower of arrows stopped, a few dropping shots rang out sharply—then silence, in which the languid beat of the stern-wheel came plainly to my ears. I put the helm hard a-starboard at the moment when the pilgrim in pink pyjamas, very hot and agitated, appeared in the doorway. 'The manager sends me——' he began in an official tone, and stopped short. 'Good God!' he said, glaring at the wounded man.

"We two whites stood over him, and his lustrous and inquiring glance enveloped us both. I declare it looked as though he would presently put to us some question in an understandable language; but he died without uttering a sound, without moving a limb, without twitching a muscle. Only in the very last moment, as though in response to some sign we could not see, to some whisper we could not hear, he frowned heavily, and that frown gave to his black death-mask an inconceivably somber, brooding, and menacing expression. The luster of inquiring glance faded swiftly into vacant glassiness. 'Can you steer?' I asked the agent eagerly. He looked very dubious; but I made a grab at his arm, and he understood at once I meant him to steer whether or no. To tell you the truth, I was morbidly anxious to change my shoes and socks. 'He is dead,' murmured the fellow, immensely impressed. 'No doubt about it,' said I, tugging like mad at the shoe-laces. 'And by the way, I suppose Mr. Kurtz is dead as well by this time.'

"For the moment that was the dominant thought. There was a sense of extreme disappointment, as though I had found out I had been striving after something altogether without a substance. I couldn't have been more disgusted if I had traveled all this way for the sole purpose of talking with Mr. Kurtz. Talking with . . . I flung one shoe overboard, and became aware that that was exactly what I had been looking forward to—a talk with Kurtz. I made the strange discovery that I had never imagined him as doing, you know, but as discoursing. I didn't say to myself, 'Now I will never see him,' or 'Now I will never shake him by the hand,' but, 'Now I will never hear him.' The man presented himself as a voice. Not of course that I did not connect him with some sort of action. Hadn't I been told in all the tones of jealousy and admiration that he had collected, bartered, swindled, or stolen more ivory than all the other agents together? That was not the point. The point was in his being a gifted creature, and that of all his gifts the one that stood out preëminently, that carried with it a sense of real presence, was his ability to talk, his words—the gift of expression, the bewildering, the illuminating, the most exalted and the most contemptible, the pulsating stream of light, or the deceitful flow from the heart of an impenetrable darkness.

"The other shoe went flying unto the devil-god of that river. I thought, by Jove! it's all over. We are too late; he has vanished—the gift has vanished, by means of some spear, arrow, or club. I will never hear that chap speak after all,—and my sorrow had a startling extravagance of emotion, even such as I had noticed in the howling sorrow of these savages in the bush. I couldn't have felt more of lonely desolation somehow, had I been robbed of a belief or had missed my destiny in life. . . . Why do you sigh in this beastly way, somebody? Absurd? Well, absurd. Good Lord! mustn't a man ever—Here, give me some tobacco." . . .

There was a pause of profound stillness, then a match flared, and Marlow's lean face appeared, worn, hollow, with downward folds and dropped eyelids, with an aspect of concentrated attention; and as he took vigorous draws at his pipe, it seemed to retreat and advance out of the night in the regular flicker of the tiny flame. The match went out.

"Absurd!" he cried. "This is the worst of trying to tell. . . . Here you all are, each moored with two good addresses, like a hulk with two anchors, a butcher round one corner, a policeman round another, excellent appetites, and temperature normal—you hear—normal from year's end to year's end. And you say, Absurd! Absurd be—exploded! Absurd! My dear boys, what can you expect from a man who out of sheer nervousness had just flung overboard a pair of new shoes! Now I think of it, it is amazing I did not shed tears. I am, upon the whole, proud of my fortitude. I was cut to the quick at the idea of having lost the inestimable privilege of listening to the gifted Kurtz. Of course I was wrong. The privilege was waiting for me. Oh, yes, I heard more than enough. And I was right, too. A voice. He was very little more than a voice. And I heard—him—it—this voice—other voices—all of them were so little more than voices—and the memory of that time itself lingers around me, impalpable, like a dying vibration of one immense jabber, silly, atrocious, sordid, savage, or simply mean, without any kind of sense. Voices, voices—even the girl herself—now——"

He was silent for a long time.

"I laid the ghost of his gifts at last with a lie," he began, suddenly. "Girl! What? Did I mention a girl? Oh, she is out of it—completely. They—the women I mean—are out of it—should be out of it. We must help them to stay in that beautiful world of their own, lest ours gets worse. Oh, she had to be out of it. You should have heard the disinterred body of Mr. Kurtz saying, 'My Intended.' You would have perceived directly then how completely she was out of it. And the lofty frontal bone of Mr. Kurtz! They say the hair goes on growing sometimes, but this—ah—specimen, was impressively bald. The wilderness had patted him on the head, and, behold, it was like a ball—an ivory ball; it had caressed him, and—lo!—he had withered; it had taken him, loved him, embraced him, got into his veins, consumed his flesh, and sealed his soul to its own by the inconceivable ceremonies of some devilish initiation. He was its spoiled and pampered favorite. Ivory? I should think so. Heaps of it, stacks of it. The old mud shanty was bursting with it. You would think there was not a single tusk left either above or below the ground in the whole country. 'Mostly fossil,' the manager had remarked, disparagingly. It was no more fossil than I am; but they call it fossil when it is dug up. It appears these niggers do bury the tusks sometimes—but evidently they couldn't bury this parcel deep enough to save the gifted Mr. Kurtz from his fate. We filled the steamboat with it, and had to pile a lot on the deck. Thus he could see and enjoy as long as he could see, because the appreciation of this favor had remained with him to the last. You should have heard him say, 'My ivory.' Oh, yes, I heard him. 'My intended, my ivory, my station, my river, my——' everything belonged to him. It made me hold my breath in expectation of hearing the wilderness burst into a prodigious peal of laughter that would shake the fixed stars in their places. Everything belonged to him—but that was a trifle. The thing was to know what he belonged to, how many powers of darkness claimed him for their own. That was the reflection that made you creepy all over. It was impossible—it was not good for one either—trying to imagine. He had taken a high seat amongst the devils of the land—I mean literally. You can't understand. How could you?—with solid pavement under your feet, surrounded by kind neighbors ready to cheer you or to fall on you, stepping delicately between the butcher and the policeman, in the holy terror of scandal and gallows and lunatic asylums—how can you imagine what particular region of the first ages a man's untrammeled feet may take him into by the way of solitude—utter solitude without a policeman—by the way of silence—utter silence, where no warning voice of a kind neighbor can be heard whispering of public opinion? These little things make all the great difference. When they are gone you must fall back upon your own innate strength, upon your own capacity for faithfulness. Of course you may be too much of a fool to go wrong—too dull even to know you are being assaulted by the powers of darkness. I take it, no fool ever made a bargain for his soul with the devil: the fool is too much of a fool, or the devil too much of a devil—I don't know which. Or you may be such a thunderingly exalted creature as to be altogether deaf and blind to anything but heavenly sights and sounds. Then the earth for you is only a standing place—and whether to be like this is your loss or your gain I won't pretend to say. But most of us are neither one nor the other. The earth for us is a place to live in, where we must put up with sights, with sounds, with smells, too, by Jove!—breathe dead hippo, so to speak, and not be contaminated. And there, don't you see? your strength comes in, the faith in your ability for the digging of unostentatious holes to bury the stuff in—your power of devotion, not to yourself, but to an obscure, back-breaking business. And that's difficult enough. Mind, I am not trying to excuse or even explain—I am trying to account to myself for—for—Mr. Kurtz—for the shade of Mr. Kurtz. This initiated wraith from the back of Nowhere honored me with its amazing confidence before it vanished altogether. This was because it could speak English to me. The original Kurtz had been educated partly in England, and —as he was good enough to say himself—his sympathies were in the right place. His mother was half-English, his father was half-French. All Europe contributed to the making of Kurtz; and by and by I learned that, most appropriately, the International Society for the Suppression of Savage Customs had intrusted him with the making of a report, for its future guidance. And he had written it, too. I've seen it, I've read it. It was eloquent, vibrating with eloquence, but too high-strung, I think. Seventeen pages of close writing he had found time for! But this must have been before his—let us say—nerves, went wrong, and caused him to preside at certain midnight dances ending with unspeakable rites, which—as far as I reluctantly gathered from what I heard at various times —were offered up to him—do you understand?—to Mr. Kurtz himself. But it was a beautiful piece of writing. The opening paragraph, however, in the light of later information, strikes me now as ominous. He began with the argument that we whites, from the point of development we had arrived at, 'must necessarily appear to them [savages] in the nature of supernatural beings—we approach them with the might as of a deity,' and so on, and so on. 'By the simple exercise of our will we can exert a power for good practically unbounded,' etc. etc. From that point he soared and took me with him. The peroration was magnificent, though difficult to remember, you know. It gave me the notion of an exotic Immensity ruled by an august Benevolence. It made me tingle with enthusiasm. This was the unbounded power of eloquence—of words—of burning noble words. There were no practical hints to interrupt the magic current of phrases, unless a kind of note at the foot of the last page, scrawled evidently much later, in an unsteady hand, may be regarded as the exposition of a method. It was very simple, and at the end of that moving appeal to every altruistic sentiment it blazed at you, luminous and terrifying, like a flash of lightning in a serene sky: 'Exterminate all the brutes!' The curious part was that he had apparently forgotten all about that valuable postscriptum, because, later on, when he in a sense came to himself, he repeatedly entreated me to take good care of 'my pamphlet' (he called it), as it was sure to have in the future a good influence upon his career. I had full information about all these things, and, besides, as it turned out, I was to have the care of his memory. I've done enough for it to give me the indisputable right to lay it, if I choose, for an everlasting rest in the dust-bin of progress, amongst all the sweepings and, figuratively speaking, all the dead cats of civilization. But then, you see, I can't choose. He won't be forgotten. Whatever he was, he was not common. He had the power to charm or frighten rudimentary souls into an aggravated witch-dance in his honor; he could also fill the small souls of the pilgrims with bitter misgivings: he had one devoted friend at least, and he had conquered one soul in the world that was neither rudimentary nor tainted with self-seeking. No; I can't forget him, though I am not prepared to affirm the fellow was exactly worth the life we lost in getting to him. I missed my late helmsman awfully,— I missed him even while his body was still lying in the pilot-house. Perhaps you will think it passing strange this regret for a savage who was no more account than a grain of sand in a black Sahara. Well, don't you see, he had done something, he had steered; for months I had him at my back—a help—an instrument. It was a kind of partnership. He steered for me—I had to look after him, I worried about his deficiencies, and thus a subtle bond had been created, of which I only became aware when it was suddenly broken. And the intimate profundity of that look he gave me when he received his hurt remains to this day in my memory—like a claim of distant kinship affirmed in a supreme moment.

"Poor fool! If he had only left that shutter alone. He had no restraint, no restraint—just like Kurtz—a tree swayed by the wind. As soon as I had put on a dry pair of slippers, I dragged him out, after first jerking the spear out of his side, which operation I confess I performed with my eyes shut tight. His heels leaped together over the little door-step; his shoulders were pressed to my breast; I hugged him from behind desperately. Oh! he was heavy, heavy; heavier than any man on earth, I should imagine. Then without more ado I tipped him overboard. The current snatched him as though he had been a wisp of grass, and I saw the body roll over twice before I lost sight of it for ever. All the pilgrims and the manager were then congregated on the awning-deck about the pilot-house, chattering at each other like a flock of excited magpies, and there was a scandalized murmur at my heartless promptitude. What they wanted to keep that body hanging about for I can't guess. Embalm it, maybe. But I had also heard another, and a very ominous, murmur on the deck below. My friends the wood-cutters were likewise scandalized, and with a better show of reason—though I admit that the reason itself was quite inadmissible. Oh, quite! I had made up my mind that if my late helmsman was to be eaten, the fishes alone should have him. He had been a very second-rate helmsman while alive, but now he was dead he might have become a first-class temptation, and possibly cause some startling trouble. Besides, I was anxious to take the wheel, the man in pink pyjamas showing himself a hopeless duffer at the business.

"This I did directly the simple funeral was over. We were going half-speed, keeping right in the middle of the stream, and I listened to the talk about me. They had given up Kurtz, they had given up the station; Kurtz was dead, and the station had been burnt—and so on—and so on. The red-haired pilgrim was beside himself with the thought that at least this poor Kurtz had been properly avenged. 'Say! We must have made a glorious slaughter of them in the bush. Eh? What do you think? Say?' He positively danced, the bloodthirsty little gingery beggar. And he had nearly fainted when he saw the wounded man! I could not help saying, 'You made a glorious lot of smoke, anyhow.' I had seen, from the way the tops of the bushes rustled and flew, that almost all the shots had gone too high. You can't hit anything unless you take aim and fire from the shoulder; but these chaps fired from the hip with their eyes shut. The retreat, I maintained—and I was right—was caused by the screeching of the steam-whistle. Upon this they forgot Kurtz, and began to howl at me with indignant protests.

"The manager stood by the wheel murmuring confidentially about the necessity of getting well away down the river before dark at all events, when I saw in the distance a clearing on the river-side and the outlines of some sort of building. 'What's this?' I asked. He clapped his hands in wonder. 'The station!' he cried. I edged in at once, still going half-speed.

"Through my glasses I saw the slope of a hill interspersed with rare trees and perfectly free from undergrowth. A long decaying building on the summit was half buried in the high grass; the large holes in the peaked roof gaped black from afar; the jungle and the woods made a background. There was no enclosure or fence of any kind; but there had been one apparently, for near the house half-a-dozen slim posts remained in a row, roughly trimmed, and with their upper ends ornamented with round carved balls. The rails, or whatever there had been between, had disappeared. Of course the forest surrounded all that. The river-bank was clear, and on the water-side I saw a white man under a hat like a cart-wheel beckoning persistently with his whole arm. Examining the edge of the forest above and below, I was almost certain I could see movements—human forms gliding here and there. I steamed past prudently, then stopped the engines and let her drift down. The man on the shore began to shout, urging us to land. 'We have been attacked,' screamed the manager. 'I know—I know. It's all right,' yelled back the other, as cheerful as you please. 'Come along. It's all right. I am glad.'

"His aspect reminded me of something I had seen—something funny I had seen somewhere. As I maneuvered to get alongside, I was asking myself, 'What does this fellow look like?' Suddenly I got it. He looked like a harlequin. His clothes had been made of some stuff that was brown holland probably, but it was covered with patches all over, with bright patches, blue, red, and yellow, —patches on the back, patches on the front, patches on elbows, on knees; colored binding around his jacket, scarlet edging at the bottom of his trousers; and the sunshine made him look extremely gay and wonderfully neat withal, because you could see how beautifully all this patching had been done. A beardless, boyish face, very fair, no features to speak of, nose peeling, little blue eyes, smiles and frowns chasing each other over that open countenance like sunshine and shadow on a wind-swept plain. 'Look out, captain!' he cried; 'there's a snag lodged in here last night.' 'What! Another snag?' I confess I swore shamefully. I had nearly holed my cripple, to finish off that charming trip. The harlequin on the bank turned his little pug-nose up to me. 'You English?' he asked, all smiles. 'Are you?' I shouted from the wheel. The smiles vanished, and he shook his head as if sorry for my disappointment. Then he brightened up. 'Never mind!' he cried, encouragingly. 'Are we in time?' I asked. 'He is up there,' he replied, with a toss of the head up the hill, and becoming gloomy all of a sudden. His face was like the autumn sky, overcast one moment and bright the next.

"When the manager, escorted by the pilgrims, all of them armed to the teeth, had gone to the house this chap came on board. 'I say, I don't like this. These natives are in the bush,' I said. He assured me earnestly it was all right. 'They are simple people,' he added; 'well, I am glad you came. It took me all my time to keep them off.' 'But you said it was all right,' I cried. 'Oh, they meant no harm,' he said; and as I stared he corrected himself, 'Not exactly.' Then vivaciously, 'My faith, your pilot-house wants a clean-up!' In the next breath he advised me to keep enough steam on the boiler to blow the whistle in case of any trouble. 'One good screech will do more for you than all your rifles. They are simple people,' he repeated. He rattled away at such a rate he quite overwhelmed me. He seemed to be trying to make up for lots of silence, and actually hinted, laughing, that such was the case. 'Don't you talk with Mr. Kurtz?' I said. 'You don't talk with that man—you listen to him,' he exclaimed with severe exaltation. 'But now——' He waved his arm, and in the twinkling of an eye was in the uttermost depths of despondency. In a moment he came up again with a jump, possessed himself of both my hands, shook them continuously, while he gabbled: 'Brother sailor . . . honor . . . pleasure . . . delight . . . introduce myself . . . Russian . . . son of an arch-priest . . . Government of Tambov. . . . What? Tobacco! English tobacco; the excellent English tobacco! Now, that's brotherly. Smoke? Where's a sailor that does not smoke?'

"The pipe soothed him, and gradually I made out he had run away from school, had gone to sea in a Russian ship; ran away again; served some time in English ships; was now reconciled with the arch-priest. He made a point of that. 'But when one is young one must see things, gather experience, ideas; enlarge the mind.' 'Here!' I interrupted. 'You can never tell! Here I met Mr. Kurtz,' he said, youthfully solemn and reproachful. I held my tongue after that. It appears he had persuaded a Dutch trading-house on the coast to fit him out with stores and goods, and had started for the interior with a light heart, and no more idea of what would happen to him than a baby. He had been wandering about that river for nearly two years alone, cut off from everybody and everything. 'I am not so young as I look. I am twenty-five,' he said. 'At first old Van Shuyten would tell me to go to the devil,' he narrated with keen enjoyment; 'but I stuck to him, and talked and talked, till at last he got afraid I would talk the hind-leg off his favorite dog, so he gave me some cheap things and a few guns, and told me he hoped he would never see my face again. Good old Dutchman, Van Shuyten. I've sent him one small lot of ivory a year ago, so that he can't call me a little thief when I get back. I hope he got it. And for the rest I don't care. I had some wood stacked for you. That was my old house. Did you see?'

"I gave him Towson's book. He made as though he would kiss me, but restrained himself. 'The only book I had left, and I thought I had lost it,' he said, looking at it ecstatically. 'So many accidents happen to a man going about alone, you know. Canoes get upset sometimes—and sometimes you've got to clear out so quick when the people get angry.' He thumbed the pages. 'You made notes in Russian?' I asked. He nodded. 'I thought they were written in cipher,' I said. He laughed, then became serious. 'I had lots of trouble to keep these people off,' he said. 'Did they want to kill you?' I asked. 'Oh, no!' he cried, and checked himself. 'Why did they attack us?' I pursued. He hesitated, then said shamefacedly, "They don't want him to go.' 'Don't they?' I said curiously. He nodded a nod full of mystery and wisdom. 'I tell you,' he cried, 'this man has enlarged my mind.' He opened his arms wide, staring at me with his little blue eyes that were perfectly round."

3

"I looked at him, lost in astonishment. There he was before me, in motley, as though he had absconded from a troupe of mimes, enthusiastic, fabulous. His very existence was improbable, inexplicable, and altogether bewildering.

He was an insoluble problem. It was inconceivable how he had existed, how he had succeeded in getting so far, how he had managed to remain—why he did not instantly disappear. 'I went a little farther,' he said, 'then still a little farther—till I had gone so far that I don't know how I'll ever get back. Never mind. Plenty time. I can manage. You take Kurtz away quick—quick—I tell you.' The glamour of youth enveloped his parti-colored rags, his destitution, his loneliness, the essential desolation of his futile wanderings. For months—for years—his life hadn't been worth a day's purchase; and there he was gallantly, thoughtlessly alive, to all appearance indestructible solely by the virtue of his few years and of his unreflecting audacity. I was seduced into something like admiration—like envy. Glamour urged him on, glamour kept him unscathed. He surely wanted nothing from the wilderness but space to breathe in and to push on through. His need was to exist, and to move onwards at the greatest possible risk, and with a maximum of privation. If the absolutely pure, uncalculating, unpractical spirit of adventure had ever ruled a human being, it ruled this be-patched youth. I almost envied him the possession of this modest and clear flame. It seemed to have consumed all thought of self so completely, that even while he was talking to you, you forgot that it was he—the man before your eyes—who had gone through these things. I did not envy him his devotion to Kurtz, though. He had not meditated over it. It came to him and he accepted it with a sort of eager fatalism. I must say that to me it appeared about the most dangerous thing in every way he had come upon so far.

"They had come together unavoidably, like two ships becalmed near each other, and lay rubbing sides at last. I suppose Kurtz wanted an audience, because on a certain occasion, when encamped in the forest, they had talked all night, or more probably Kurtz had talked. 'We talked of everything,' he said, quite transported at the recollection. 'I forgot there was such a thing as sleep. The night did not seem to last an hour. Everything! Everything! . . . Of love, too.' 'Ah, he talked to you of love!' I said, much amused. 'It isn't what you think,' he cried, almost passionately. 'It was in general. He made me see things —things.'

"He threw his arms up. We were on deck at the time, and the headman of my wood-cutters, lounging near by, turned upon him his heavy and glittering eyes. I looked around, and I don't know why, but I assure you that never, never before, did this land, this river, this jungle, the very arch of this blazing sky, appear to me so hopeless and so dark, so impenetrable to human thought, so pitiless to human weakness. 'And, ever since, you have been with him, of course?' I said.

"On the contrary. It appears their intercourse had been very much broken by various causes. He had, as he informed me proudly, managed to nurse Kurtz through two illnesses (he alluded to it as you would to some risky feat), but as a rule Kurtz wandered alone, far in the depths of the forest. 'Very often coming to this station, I had to wait days and days before he would turn up,' he said. 'Ah, it was worth waiting for!—sometimes.' 'What was he doing? exploring or what?' I asked. 'Oh, yes, of course;' he had discovered lots of villages, a lake, too—he did not know exactly in what direction; it was dangerous to inquire too much—but mostly his expeditions had been for ivory. 'But he had no goods to trade with by that time,' I objected. 'There's a good lot of cartridges left even yet,' he answered, looking away. 'To speak plainly, he raided the country,' I said. He nodded. 'Not alone, surely!' He muttered something about the villages round that lake. 'Kurtz got the tribe to follow him, did he?' I suggested. He fidgeted a little. 'They adored him,' he said. The tone of these words was so extraordinary that I looked at him searchingly. It was curious to see his mingled eagerness and reluctance to speak of Kurtz. The man filled his life, occupied his thoughts, swayed his emotions. 'What can you expect?' he burst out; 'he came to them with thunder and lightning, you know —and they had never seen anything like it—and very terrible. He could be very terrible. You can't judge Mr. Kurtz as you would an ordinary man. No, no, no! Now—just to give you an idea—I don't mind telling you, he wanted to shoot me, too, one day—but I don't judge him.' 'Shoot you!' I cried. 'What for?' 'Well, I had a small lot of ivory the chief of that village near my house gave me. You see I used to shoot game for them. Well, he wanted it, and wouldn't hear reason. He declared he would shoot me unless I gave him the ivory and then cleared out of the country, because he could do so, and had a fancy for it, and there was nothing on earth to prevent him killing whom he jolly well pleased. And it was true, too. I gave him the ivory. What did I care! But I didn't clear out. No, no. I couldn't leave him. I had to be careful, of course, till we got friendly again for a time. He had his second illness then. Afterwards I had to keep out of the way; but I didn't mind. He was living for the most part in those villages on the lake. When he came down to the river, sometimes he would take to me, and sometimes it was better for me to be careful. This man suffered too much. He hated all this, and somehow he couldn't get away. When I had a chance I begged him to try and leave while there was time; I offered to go back with him. And he would say yes, and then he would remain; go off on another ivory hunt; disappear for weeks; forget himself amongst these people —forget himself—you know.' 'Why! he's mad,' I said. He protested indignantly. Mr. Kurtz couldn't be mad. If I had heard him talk, only two days ago, I wouldn't dare hint at such a thing. . . . I had taken up my binoculars while we talked, and was looking at the shore, sweeping the limit of the forest at each side and at the back of the house. The consciousness of there being people in that bush, so silent, so quiet—as silent and quiet as the ruined house on the hill—made me uneasy. There was no sign on the face of nature of this amazing tale that was not so much told as suggested to me in desolate exclamations, completed by shrugs, in interrupted phrases, in hints ending in deep sighs. The woods were unmoved, like a mask—heavy, like the closed door of a prison —they looked with their air of hidden knowledge, of patient expectation, of unapproachable silence. The Russian was explaining to me that it was only lately that Mr. Kurtz had come down to the river, bringing along with him all the fighting men of that lake tribe. He had been absent for several months— getting himself adored, I suppose—and had come down unexpectedly, with the intention to all appearance of making a raid either across the river or down stream. Evidently the appetite for more ivory had got the better of the—what shall I say?—less material aspirations. However he had got much worse sud- denly. 'I heard he was lying helpless, and so I came up—took my chance,' said the Russian. 'Oh, he is bad, very bad.' I directed my glass to the house. There were no signs of life, but there was the ruined roof, the long mud wall peeping above the grass, with three little square window-holes, no two of the same size; all this brought within reach of my hand, as it were. And then I made a brusque movement, and one of the remaining posts of that vanished fence leaped up in the field of my glass. You remember I told you I had been struck at the distance by certain attempts at ornamentation, rather remarkable in the ruinous aspect of the place. Now I had suddenly a nearer view, and its first result was to make me throw my head back as if before a blow. Then I went carefully from post to post with my glass, and I saw my mistake. These round knobs were not ornamental but symbolic; they were expressive and puzzling, striking and disturbing—food for thought and also for vultures if there had been any looking down from the sky; but at all events for such ants as were industrious enough to ascend the pole. They would have been even more impressive, those heads on the stakes, if their faces had not been turned to the house. Only one, the first I had made out, was facing my way. I was not so shocked as you may think. The start back I had given was really nothing but a movement of surprise. I had expected to see a knob of wood there, you know. I returned deliberately to the first I had seen—and there it was, black, dried, sunken, with closed eyelids,—a head that seemed to sleep at the top of that pole, and with the shrunken dry lips showing a narrow white line of the teeth, was smiling, too, smiling continuously at some endless and jocose dream of that eternal slumber.

"I am not disclosing any trade secrets. In fact, the manager said afterwards that Mr. Kurtz's methods had ruined the district. I have no opinion on that point, but I want you clearly to understand that there was nothing exactly profitable in these heads being there. They only showed that Mr. Kurtz lacked restraint in the gratification of his various lusts, that there was something wanting in him—some small matter which, when the pressing need arose, could not be found under his magnificent eloquence. Whether he knew of this deficiency himself I can't say. I think the knowledge came to him at last—only at the very last. But the wilderness had found him out early, and had taken on him a terrible vengeance for the fantastic invasion. I think it had whispered to him things about himself which he did not know, things of which he had no conception till he took counsel with this great solitude—and the whisper had proved irresistibly fascinating. It echoed loudly within him because he was hollow at the core. . . . I put down the glass, and the head that had appeared near enough to be spoken to seemed at once to have leaped away from me into inaccessible distance.

"The admirer of Mr. Kurtz was a bit crestfallen. In a hurried, indistinct voice he began to assure me he had not dared to take these—say, symbols—down. He was not afraid of the natives; they would not stir till Mr. Kurtz gave the word. His ascendancy was extraordinary. The camps of these people surrounded the place, and the chiefs came every day to see him. They would crawl. . . . 'I don't want to know anything of the ceremonies used when approaching Mr. Kurtz,' I shouted. Curious, this feeling that came over me that such details would be more intolerable than those heads drying on the stakes under Mr. Kurtz's windows. After all, that was only a savage sight, while I seemed at one bound to have been transported into some lightless region of subtle horrors, where pure, uncomplicated savagery was a positive relief, being something that had a right to exist—obviously—in the sunshine. The young man looked at me with surprise. I suppose it did not occur to him that Mr. Kurtz was no idol of mine. He forgot I hadn't heard any of these splendid monologues on, what was it? on love, justice, conduct of life—or what not. If it had come to crawling before Mr. Kurtz, he crawled as much as the veriest savage of them all. I had no idea of the conditions, he said: these heads were the heads of rebels. I shocked him excessively by laughing. Rebels! What would be the next definition I was to hear? There had been enemies, criminals, workers—and these were rebels. Those rebellious heads looked very subdued to me on their sticks. 'You don't know how such a life tries a man like Kurtz,' cried Kurtz's last disciple. 'Well, and you?' I said. 'I! I! I am a simple man. I have no great thoughts. I want nothing from anybody. How can you compare me to . . . ?' His feelings were too much for speech, and suddenly he broke down. 'I don't understand,' he groaned. 'I've been doing my best to keep him alive, and that's enough. I had no hand in all this. I have no abilities. There hasn't been a drop of medicine or a mouthful of invalid food for months here. He was shamefully abandoned. A man like this, with such ideas. Shamefully! Shamefully! I—I—haven't slept for the last ten nights. . . .'

"His voice lost itself in the calm of the evening. The long shadows of the forest had slipped downhill while we talked, had gone far beyond the ruined hovel, beyond the symbolic row of stakes. All this was in the gloom, while we down there were yet in the sunshine, and the stretch of the river abreast of the clearing glittered in a still and dazzling splendor, with a murky and overshadowed bend above and below. Not a living soul was seen on the shore. The bushes did not rustle.

"Suddenly round the corner of the house a group of men appeared, as though they had come up from the ground. They waded waist-deep in the grass, in a compact body, bearing an improvised stretcher in their midst. Instantly, in the emptiness of the landscape, a cry arose whose shrillness pierced the still air like a sharp arrow flying straight to the very heart of the land; and, as if by enchantment, streams of human beings—of naked human beings —with spears in their hands, with bows, with shields, with wild glances and savage movements, were poured into the clearing by the dark-faced and pensive forest. The bushes shook, the grass swayed for a time, and then everything stood still in attentive immobility.

" 'Now, if he does not say the right thing to them we are all done for,' said the Russian at my elbow. The knot of men with the stretcher had stopped, too, halfway to the steamer, as if petrified. I saw the man on the stretcher sit up, lank and with an uplifted arm, above the shoulders of the bearers. 'Let us hope that the man who can talk so well of love in general will find some particular reason to spare us this time,' I said. I resented bitterly the absurd danger of our situation, as if to be at the mercy of that atrocious phantom had been a dishonoring necessity. I could not hear a sound, but through my glasses I saw the thin arm extended commandingly, the lower jaw moving, the eyes of that apparition shining darkly far in its bony head that nodded with grotesque jerks. Kurtz—Kurtz—that means short in German—don't it? Well, the name was as true as everything else in his life—and death. He looked at least seven feet long. His covering had fallen off, and his body emerged from it pitiful and appalling as from a winding-sheet. I could see the cage of his ribs all astir, the bones of his arm waving. It was as though an animated image of death carved out of old ivory had been shaking its hand with menaces at a motionless crowd of men made of dark and glittering bronze. I saw him open his mouth wide—it gave him a weirdly voracious aspect, as though he had wanted to swallow all the air, all the earth, all the men before him. A deep voice reached me faintly. He must have been shouting. He fell back suddenly. The stretcher shook as the bearers staggered forward again, and almost at the same time I noticed that the crowd of savages was vanishing without any perceptible movement of retreat, as if the forest that had ejected these beings so suddenly had drawn them in again as the breath is drawn in a long aspiration.

"Some of the pilgrims behind the stretcher carried his arms—two shot-guns, a heavy rifle, and a light revolver-carbine—the thunderbolts of that pitiful Jupiter. The manager bent over him murmuring as he walked beside his head. They laid him down in one of the little cabins—just a room for a bedplace and a camp-stool or two, you know. We had brought his belated correspondence, and a lot of torn envelopes and open letters littered his bed. His hand roamed feebly amongst these papers. I was struck by the fire of his eyes and the composed languor of his expression. It was not so much the exhaustion of disease. He did not seem in pain. This shadow looked satiated and calm, as though for the moment it had had its fill of all the emotions.

"He rustled one of the letters, and looking straight in my face said, 'I am glad.' Somebody had been writing to him about me. These special recommendations were turning up again. The volume of tone he emitted without effort, almost without the trouble of moving his lips, amazed me. A voice! a voice! It was grave, profound, vibrating, while the man did not seem capable of a whisper. However, he had enough strength in him—factitious no doubt—to very nearly make an end of us, as you shall hear directly.

"The manager appeared silently in the doorway; I stepped out at once and he drew the curtain after me. The Russian, eyed curiously by the pilgrims, was staring at the shore. I followed the direction of his glance.

"Dark human shapes could be made out in the distance, flitting indistinctly against the gloomy border of the forest, and near the river two bronze figures, leaning on tall spears, stood in the sunlight under fantastic head-dresses of spotted skins, warlike and still in statuesque repose. And from right to left along the lighted shore moved a wild and gorgeous apparition of a woman.

"She walked with measured steps, draped in striped and fringed cloths, treading the earth proudly, with a slight jingle and flash of barbarous ornaments. She carried her head high; her hair was done in the shape of a helmet; she had brass leggings to the knee, brass wire gauntlets to the elbow, a crimson spot on her tawny cheek, innumerable necklaces of glass beads on her neck; bizarre things, charms, gifts of witch-men, that hung about her, glittered and trembled at every step. She must have had the value of several elephant tusks upon her. She was savage and superb, wild-eyed and magnificent; there was something ominous and stately in her deliberate progress. And in the hush that had fallen suddenly upon the whole sorrowful land, the immense wilderness, the colossal body of the fecund and mysterious life seemed to look at her, pensive, as though it had been looking at the image of its own tenebrous and passionate soul.

"She came abreast of the steamer, stood still, and faced us. Her long shadow fell to the water's edge. Her face had a tragic and fierce aspect of wild sorrow and of dumb pain mingled with the fear of some struggling, half-shaped resolve. She stood looking at us without a stir, and like the wilderness itself, with an air of brooding over an inscrutable purpose. A whole minute passed, and then she made a step forward. There was a low jingle, a glint of yellow metal, a sway of fringed draperies, and she stopped as if her heart had failed her. The young fellow by my side growled. The pilgrims murmured at my back. She looked at us all as if her life had depended upon the unswerving steadiness of her glance. Suddenly she opened her bared arms and threw them up rigid above her head, as though in an uncontrollable desire to touch the sky, and at the same time the swift shadows darted out on the earth, swept around on the river, gathering the steamer into a shadowy embrace. A formidable silence hung over the scene.

"She turned away slowly, walked on, following the bank, and passed into the bushes to the left. Once only her eyes gleamed back at us in the dusk of the thickets before she disappeared.

" 'If she had offered to come aboard I really think I would have tried to shoot her,' said the man of patches, nervously. 'I have been risking my life every day for the last fortnight to keep her out of the house. She got in one day and kicked up a row about those miserable rags I picked up in the store-room to mend my clothes with. I wasn't decent. At least it must have been that, for she talked like a fury to Kurtz for an hour, pointing at me now and then. I don't understand the dialect of this tribe. Luckily for me, I fancy Kurtz felt too ill that day to care, or there would have been mischief. I don't understand. . . . No—it's too much for me. Ah, well, it's all over now.'

"At this moment I heard Kurtz's deep voice behind the curtain: 'Save me! —save the ivory, you mean. Don't tell me. Save *me!* Why, I've had to save you. You are interrupting my plans now. Sick! Sick! Not so sick as you would like to believe. Never mind. I'll carry my ideas out yet—I will return. I'll show you what can be done. You with your little peddling notions—you are interfering with me. I will return. I. . . .'

"The manager came out. He did me the honor to take me under the arm and lead me aside. 'He is very low, very low,' he said. He considered it necessary to sigh, but neglected to be consistently sorrowful. 'We have done all we could for him—haven't we? But there is no disguising the fact, Mr. Kurtz has done more harm than good to the Company. He did not see the time was not ripe for vigorous action. Cautiously, cautiously—that's my principle. We must be cautious yet. The district is closed to us for a time. Deplorable! Upon the whole, the trade will suffer. I don't deny there is a remarkable quantity of ivory—mostly fossil. We must save it, at all events—but look how precarious the position is—and why? Because the method is unsound.' 'Do you,' said I, looking at the shore, 'call it "unsound method?"' 'Without doubt', he exclaimed, hotly. 'Don't you?' . . . 'No method at all,' I murmured after a while. 'Exactly,' he exulted. 'I anticipated this. Shows a complete want of judgment. It is my duty to point it out in the proper quarter.' 'Oh,' said I, 'that fellow—what's his name?—the brickmaker, will make a readable report for you.' He appeared confounded for a moment. It seemed to me I had never breathed an atmosphere so vile, and I turned mentally to Kurtz for relief—positively for relief. 'Nevertheless I think Mr. Kurtz is a remarkable man,' I said with emphasis. He started, dropped on me a cold heavy glance, said very quietly, 'he *was*,' and turned his back on me. My hour of favor was over; I found myself lumped along with Kurtz as a partisan of methods for which the time was not ripe: I was unsound! Ah! but it was something to have at least a choice of nightmares.

"I had turned to the wilderness really, not to Mr. Kurtz, who, I was ready to admit, was as good as buried. And for a moment it seemed to me as if I also were buried in a vast grave full of unspeakable secrets. I felt an intolerable weight oppressing my breast, the smell of the damp earth, the unseen presence of victorious corruption, the darkness of an impenetrable night. . . . The Russian tapped me on the shoulder. I heard him mumbling and stammering something about 'brother seaman—couldn't conceal—knowledge of matters that would affect Mr. Kurtz's reputation.' I waited. For him evidently Mr. Kurtz was not in his grave; I suspect that for him Mr. Kurtz was one of the immortals. 'Well!' said I at last, 'speak out. As it happens, I am Mr. Kurtz's friend—in a way.'

"He stated with a good deal of formality that had we not been 'of the same profession,' he would have kept the matter to himself without regard to consequences. 'He suspected there was an active ill will towards him on the part of these white men that———' 'You are right,' I said, remembering a certain conversation I had overheard. 'The manager thinks you ought to be hanged.' He showed a concern at this intelligence which amused me at first. 'I had better get out of the way quietly,' he said, earnestly. 'I can do no more for Kurtz now, and they would soon find some excuse. What's to stop them? There's a military post three hundred miles from here.' 'Well, upon my word,' said I, 'perhaps you had better go if you have any friends amongst the savages near by.' 'Plenty,' he said. 'They are simple people—and I want nothing, you know.' He stood biting his lip, then: 'I don't want any harm to happen to these whites here, but of course I was thinking of Mr. Kurtz's reputation—but you are a brother seaman and———' 'All right,' said I, after a time. 'Mr. Kurtz's reputation is safe with me.' I did not know how truly I spoke.

"He informed me, lowering his voice, that it was Kurtz who had ordered the attack to be made on the steamer. 'He hated sometimes the idea of being taken away—and then again. . . . But I don't understand these matters. I am a simple man. He thought it would scare you away—that you would give it up, thinking him dead. I could not stop him. Oh, I had an awful time of it this last month.' 'Very well,' I said. 'He is all right now.' 'Ye-e-es,' he muttered, not very convinced apparently. 'Thanks,' said I; 'I shall keep my eyes open.' 'But quiet—eh?' he urged, anxiously. 'It would be awful for his reputation if anybody here————' I promised a complete discretion with great gravity. 'I have a canoe and three black fellows waiting not very far. I am off. Could you give me a few Martini-Henry cartridges?' I could, and did, with proper secrecy. He helped himself, with a wink at me, to a handful of my tobacco. 'Between sailors —you know—good English tobacco.' At the door of the pilot-house he turned round—'I say, haven't you a pair of shoes you could spare?' He raised one leg. 'Look.' The soles were tied with knotted strings sandal-wise under his bare feet. I rooted out an old pair, at which he looked with admiration before tucking them under his left arm. One of his pockets (bright red) was bulging with cartridges, from the other (dark blue) peeped 'Towson's Inquiry,' etc., etc. He seemed to think himself excellently well equipped for a renewed encounter with the wilderness. 'Ah! I'll never, never meet such a man again. You ought to have heard him recite poetry—his own, too, it was, he told me. Poetry!' He rolled his eyes at the recollection of these delights. 'Oh, he enlarged my mind!' 'Good-by,' said I. He shook hands and vanished in the night. Sometimes I ask myself whether I had ever really seen him—whether it was possible to meet such a phenomenon! . . .

"When I woke up shortly after midnight his warning came to my mind with its hint of danger that seemed, in the starred darkness, real enough to make me get up for the purpose of having a look round. On the hill a big fire burned, illuminating fitfully a crooked corner of the station-house. One of the agents with a picket of a few of our blacks, armed for the purpose, was keeping guard over the ivory; but deep within the forest, red gleams that wavered, that seemed to sink and rise from the ground amongst confused columnar shapes of intense blackness, showed the exact position of the camp where Mr. Kurtz's adorers were keeping their uneasy vigil. The monotonous beating of a big drum filled the air with muffled shocks and a lingering vibration. A steady droning sound of many men chanting each to himself some weird incantation came out from the black, flat wall of the woods as the humming of bees comes out of a hive, and had a strange narcotic effect upon my half-awake senses. I believe I dozed off leaning over the rail, till an abrupt burst of yells, an overwhelming outbreak of a pent-up and mysterious frenzy, woke me up in a bewildered wonder. It was cut short all at once, and the low droning went on with an effect of audible and soothing silence. I glanced casually into the little cabin. A light was burning within, but Mr. Kurtz was not there.

"I think I would have raised an outcry if I had believed my eyes. But I didn't believe them at first—the thing seemed so impossible. The fact is I was completely unnerved by a sheer blank fright, pure abstract terror, unconnected with any distinct shape of physical danger. What made this emotion so overpowering was—how shall I define it?—the moral shock I received, as if something altogether monstrous, intolerable to thought and odious to the soul, had been thrust upon me unexpectedly. This lasted of course the merest fraction of a second, and then the usual sense of commonplace, deadly danger, the possibility of a sudden onslaught and massacre, or something of the kind, which I saw impending, was positively welcome and composing. It pacified me, in fact, so much, that I did not raise an alarm.

"There was an agent buttoned up inside an ulster and sleeping on a chair on deck within three feet of me. The yells had not awakened him; he snored very slightly; I left him to his slumbers and leaped ashore. I did not betray Mr. Kurtz—it was ordered I should never betray him—it was written I should be loyal to the nightmare of my choice. I was anxious to deal with this shadow by myself alone,—and to this day I don't know why I was so jealous of sharing with any one the peculiar blackness of that experience.

"As soon as I got on the bank I saw a trail—a broad trail through the grass. I remember the exultation with which I said to myself, 'He can't walk—he is crawling on all-fours—I've got him.' The grass was wet with dew. I strode rapidly with clenched fists. I fancy I had some vague notion of falling upon him and giving him a drubbing. I don't know. I had some imbecile thoughts. The knitting old woman with the cat obtruded herself upon my memory as a most improper person to be sitting at the other end of such an affair. I saw a row of pilgrims squirting lead in the air out of Winchesters held to the hip. I thought I would never get back to the steamer, and imagined myself living alone and unarmed in the woods to an advanced age. Such silly things—you know. And I remember I confounded the beat of the drum with the beating of my heart, and was pleased at its calm regularity.

"I kept to the track though—then stopped to listen. The night was very clear; a dark blue space, sparkling with dew and starlight, in which black things stood very still. I thought I could see a kind of motion ahead of me. I was strangely cocksure of everything that night. I actually left the track and ran in a wide semicircle (I verily believe chuckling to myself) so as to get in front of that stir, of that motion I had seen—if indeed I had seen anything. I was circumventing Kurtz as though it had been a boyish game.

"I came upon him, and, if he had not heard me coming, I would have fallen over him, too, but he got up in time. He rose, unsteady, long, pale, indistinct, like a vapor exhaled by the earth, and swayed slightly, misty and silent before me; while at my back the fires loomed between the trees, and the murmur of many voices issued from the forest. I had cut him off cleverly; but when actually confronting him I seemed to come to my senses, I saw the danger in its right proportion. It was by no means over yet. Suppose he began to shout? Though he could hardly stand, there was still plenty of vigor in his voice. 'Go away— hide yourself,' he said, in that profound tone. It was very awful. I glanced back. We were within thirty yards from the nearest fire. A black figure stood up, strode on long black legs, waving long black arms, across the glow. It had horns—antelope horns, I think—on its head. Some sorcerer, some witch-man, no doubt: it looked fiend-like enough. 'Do you know what you are doing?' I whispered. 'Perfectly,' he answered, raising his voice for that single word: it sounded to me far off and yet loud, like a hail through a speaking-trumpet. If he makes a row we are lost, I thought to myself. This clearly was not a case for fisticuffs, even apart from the very natural aversion I had to beat that Shadow—this wandering and tormented thing. 'You will be lost,' I said—'utterly lost.' One gets sometimes such a flash of inspiration, you know. I did say the right thing, though indeed he could not have been more irretrievably lost than he was at this very moment, when the foundations of our intimacy were being laid—to endure—to endure—even to the end—even beyond.

" 'I had immense plans,' he muttered irresolutely. 'Yes,' said I; 'but if you try to shout I'll smash your head with————' There was not a stick or a stone near. 'I will throttle you for good,' I corrected myself. 'I was on the threshold of great things,' he pleaded, in a voice of longing, with a wistfulness of tone that made my blood run cold. 'And now for this stupid scoundrel————' 'Your success in Europe is assured in any case,' I affirmed, steadily. I did not want to have the throttling of him, you understand—and indeed it would have been very little use for any practical purpose. I tried to break the spell—the heavy, mute spell of the wilderness—that seemed to draw him to its pitiless breast by the awakening of forgotten and brutal instincts, by the memory of gratified and monstrous passions. This alone, I was convinced, had driven him out to the edge of the forest, to the bush, towards the gleam of fires, the throb of drums, the drone of weird incantations; this alone had beguiled his unlawful soul beyond the bounds of permitted aspirations. And, don't you see, the terror of the position was not in being knocked on the head—though I had a very lively sense of that danger, too—but in this, that I had to deal with a being to whom I could not appeal in the name of anything high or low. I had, even like the niggers, to invoke him—himself—his own exalted and incredible degradation. There was nothing either above or below him, and I knew it. He had kicked himself loose of the earth. Confound the man! he had kicked the very earth to pieces. He was alone, and I before him did not know whether I stood on the ground or floated in the air. I've been telling you what we said—repeating the phrases we pronounced—but what's the good? They were common everyday words—the familiar, vague sounds exchanged on every waking day of life. But what of that? They had between them, to my mind, the terrific suggestiveness of words heard in dreams, of phrases spoken in nightmares. Soul! If anybody had ever struggled with a soul, I am the man. And I wasn't arguing with a lunatic either. Believe me or not, his intelligence was perfectly clear—concentrated, it is true, upon himself with horrible intensity, yet clear; and therein was my only chance—barring, of course, the killing him there and then, which wasn't so good, on account of unavoidable noise. But his soul was mad. Being alone in the wilderness, it had looked within itself, and, by heavens! I tell you, it had gone mad. I had—for my sins, I suppose—to go through the ordeal of looking into it myself. No eloquence could have been so withering to one's belief in mankind as his final burst of sincerity. He struggled with himself, too. I saw it,—I heard it. I saw the inconceivable mystery of a soul that knew no restraint, no faith, and no fear, yet struggling blindly with itself. I kept my head pretty well; but when I had him at last stretched on the couch, I wiped my forehead, while my legs shook under me as though I had carried half a ton on my back down that hill. And yet I had only supported him, his bony arm clasped round my neck—and he was not much heavier than a child.

"When next day we left at noon, the crowd, of whose presence behind the curtain of trees I had been acutely conscious all the time, flowed out of the woods again, filled the clearing, covered the slope with a mass of naked, breathing, quivering, bronze bodies. I steamed up a bit, then swung downstream, and two thousand eyes followed the evolutions of the splashing, thumping, fierce river-demon beating the water with its terrible tail and breathing black smoke into the air. In front of the first rank, along the river, three men, plastered with bright red earth from head to foot, strutted to and fro restlessly. When we came abreast again, they faced the river, stamped their feet, nodded their horned heads, swayed their scarlet bodies; they shook towards the fierce river-demon a bunch of black feathers, a mangy skin with a pendent tail— something that looked like a dried gourd; they shouted periodically together strings of amazing words that resembled no sounds of human language; and the deep murmurs of the crowd, interrupted suddenly, were like the responses of some satanic litany.

"We had carried Kurtz into the pilot-house: there was more air there. Lying on the couch, he stared through the open shutter. There was an eddy in the mass of human bodies, and the woman with helmeted head and tawny cheeks rushed out to the very brink of the stream. She put out her hands, shouted something, and all that wild mob took up the shout in a roaring chorus of articulated, rapid, breathless utterance.

" 'Do you understand this?' I asked.

"He kept on looking out past me with fiery, longing eyes, with a mingled expression of wistfulness and hate. He made no answer, but I saw a smile, a smile of indefinable meaning, appear on his colorless lips that a moment after twitched convulsively. 'Do I not?' he said slowly, gasping, as if the words had been torn out of him by a supernatural power.

"I pulled the string of the whistle, and I did this because I saw the pilgrims on deck getting out their rifles with an air of anticipating a jolly lark. At the sudden screech there was a movement of abject terror through that wedged mass of bodies. 'Don't! don't you frighten them away,' cried some one on deck disconsolately. I pulled the string time after time. They broke and ran, they leaped, they crouched, they swerved, they dodged the flying terror of the sound. The three red chaps had fallen flat, face down on the shore, as though they had been shot dead. Only the barbarous and superb woman did not so much as flinch, and stretched tragically her bare arms after us over the somber and glittering river.

"And then that imbecile crowd down on the deck started their little fun, and I could see nothing more for smoke.

"The brown current ran swiftly out of the heart of darkness, bearing us down towards the sea with twice the speed of our upward progress; and Kurtz's life was running swiftly, too, ebbing, ebbing out of his heart into the sea of in- exorable time. The manager was very placid, he had no vital anxieties now, he took us both in with a comprehensive and satisfied glance: the 'affair' had come off as well as could be wished. I saw the time approaching when I would be left alone of the party of 'unsound method.' The pilgrims looked upon me with disfavor. I was, so to speak, numbered with the dead. It is strange how I accepted this unforeseen partnership, this choice of nightmares forced upon me in the tenebrous land invaded by these mean and greedy phantoms.

"Kurtz discoursed. A voice! a voice! It rang deep to the very last. It survived his strength to hide in the magnificent folds of eloquence the barren darkness of his heart. Oh, he struggled! he struggled! The wastes of his weary brain were haunted by shadowy images now—images of wealth and fame revolving obsequiously round his unextinguishable gift of noble and lofty expression. My Intended, my station, my career, my ideas—these were the subjects for the occasional utterances of elevated sentiments. The shade of the original Kurtz frequented the bedside of the hollow sham, whose fate it was to be buried presently in the mold of primeval earth. But both the diabolic love and the unearthly hate of the mysteries it had penetrated fought for the possession of that soul satiated with primitive emotions, avid of lying fame, of sham distinction, of all the appearances of success and power.

"Sometimes he was contemptibly childish. He desired to have kings meet him at railway-stations on his return from some ghastly Nowhere, where he intended to accomplish great things. 'You show them you have in you something that is really profitable, and then there will be no limits to the recognition of your ability,' he would say. 'Of course you must take care of the motives—right motives—always.' The long reaches that were like one and the same reach, monotonous bends that were exactly alike, slipped past the steamer with their multitude of secular trees looking patiently after this grimy fragment of another world, the forerunner of change, of conquest, of trade, of massacres, of blessings. I looked ahead—piloting. 'Close the shutter,' said Kurtz suddenly one day; 'I can't bear to look at this.' I did so. There was a silence. 'Oh, but I will wring your heart yet!' he cried at the invisible wilderness.

"We broke down—as I had expected—and had to lie up for repairs at the head of an island. This delay was the first thing that shook Kurtz's confidence. One morning he gave me a packet of papers and a photograph—the lot tied together with a shoe-string. 'Keep this for me,' he said. 'This noxious fool' (meaning the manager) 'is capable of prying into my boxes when I am not looking.' In the afternoon I saw him. He was lying on his back with closed eyes, and I withdrew quietly, but I heard him mutter, 'Live rightly, die, die. . . .' I listened. There was nothing more. Was he rehearsing some speech in his sleep, or was it a fragment of a phrase from some newspaper article? He had been writing for the papers and meant to do so again, 'for the furthering of my ideas. It's a duty.'

"His was an impenetrable darkness. I looked at him as you peer down at a man who is lying at the bottom of a precipice where the sun never shines. But I had not much time to give him, because I was helping the engine-driver to take to pieces the leaky cylinders, to straighten a bent connecting-rod, and in other such matters. I lived in an infernal mess of rust, filings, nuts, bolts, spanners, hammers, ratchet-drills—things I abominate, because I don't get on with them. I tended the little forge we fortunately had aboard; I toiled wearily in a wretched scrap-heap—unless I had the shakes too bad to stand.

"One evening coming in with a candle I was startled to hear him say a little tremulously, 'I am lying here in the dark waiting for death.' The light was within a foot of his eyes. I forced myself to murmur, 'Oh, nonsense!' and stood over him as if transfixed.

"Anything approaching the change that came over his features I have never seen before, and hope never to see again. Oh, I wasn't touched. I was fascinated. It was as though a veil had been rent. I saw on that ivory face the expression of somber pride, of ruthless power, of craven terror—of an intense and hopeless despair. Did he live his life again in every detail of desire, temptation, and surrender during that supreme moment of complete knowledge? He cried in a whisper at some image, at some vision—he cried out twice, a cry that was no more than a breath—

" 'The horror! The horror!'

"I blew the candle out and left the cabin. The pilgrims were dining in the mess-room, and I took my place opposite the manager, who lifted his eyes to give me a questioning glance, which I successfully ignored. He leaned back, serene, with that peculiar smile of his sealing the unexpressed depths of his meanness. A continuous shower of small flies streamed upon the lamp, upon the cloth, upon our hands and faces. Suddenly the manager's boy put his insolent black head in the doorway, and said in a tone of scathing contempt—

" 'Mistah Kurtz—he dead.'

"All the pilgrims rushed out to see. I remained, and went on with my dinner. I believe I was considered brutally callous. However, I did not eat much. There was a lamp in there—light, don't you know—and outside it was so beastly, beastly dark. I went no more near the remarkable man who had pronounced a judgment upon the adventures of his soul on this earth. The voice was gone. What else had been there? But I am of course aware that next day the pilgrims buried something in a muddy hole.

"And then they very nearly buried me.

"However, as you see I did not go to join Kurtz there and then. I did not. I remained to dream the nightmare out to the end, and to show my loyalty to Kurtz once more. Destiny. My destiny! Droll thing life is—that mysterious arrangement of merciless logic for a futile purpose. The most you can hope from it is some knowledge of yourself—that comes too late—a crop of unextinguishable regrets. I have wrestled with death. It is the most exciting contest you can imagine. It takes place in an impalpable grayness, with nothing underfoot, with nothing around, without spectators, without clamor, without glory, without the great desire of victory, without the great fear of defeat, in a sickly atmosphere of tepid skepticism, without much belief in your own right, and still less in that of your adversary. If such is the form of ultimate wisdom, then life is a greater riddle than some of us think it to be. I was within a hair's breadth of the last opportunity for pronouncement, and I found with humiliation that probably I would have nothing to say. This is the reason why I affirm that Kurtz was a remarkable man. He had something to say. He said it. Since I had peeped over the edge myself, I understand better the meaning of his stare, that could not see the flame of the candle, but was wide enough to embrace the whole universe, piercing enough to penetrate all the hearts that beat in the darkness. He had summed up—he had judged. 'The horror!' He was a remarkable man. After all, this was the expression of some sort of belief; it had candor, it had conviction, it had a vibrating note of revolt in its whisper, it had the appalling face of a glimpsed truth—the strange commingling of desire and hate. And it is not my own extremity I remember best—

a vision of grayness without form filled with physical pain, and a careless contempt for the evanescence of all things—even of this pain itself. No! It is his extremity that I seem to have lived through. True, he had made that last stride, he had stepped over the edge, while I had been permitted to draw back my hesitating foot. And perhaps in this is the whole difference; perhaps all the wisdom, and all truth, and all sincerity, are just compressed into that inappreciable moment of time in which we step over the threshold of the invisible. Perhaps! I like to think my summing-up would not have been a word of careless contempt. Better his cry—much better. It was an affirmation, a moral victory paid for by innumerable defeats, by abominable terrors, by abominable satisfactions. But it was a victory! That is why I have remained loyal to Kurtz to the last, and even beyond, when a long time after I heard once more, not his own voice, but the echo of his magnificent eloquence thrown to me from a soul as translucently pure as a cliff of crystal.

"No, they did not bury me, though there is a period of time which I remember mistily, with a shuddering wonder, like a passage through some inconceivable world that had no hope in it and no desire. I found myself back in the sepulchral city resenting the sight of people hurrying through the streets to filch a little money from each other, to devour their infamous cookery, to gulp their unwholesome beer, to dream their insignificant and silly dreams. They trespassed upon my thoughts. They were intruders whose knowledge of life was to me an irritating pretense, because I felt so sure they could not possibly know the things I knew. Their bearing, which was simply the bearing of commonplace individuals going about their business in the assurance of perfect safety, was offensive to me like the outrageous flauntings of folly in the face of a danger it is unable to comprehend. I had no particular desire to enlighten them, but I had some difficulty in restraining myself from laughing in their faces, so full of stupid importance. I daresay I was not very well at that time. I tottered about the streets—there were various affairs to settle—grinning bitterly at perfectly respectable persons. I admit my behavior was inexcusable, but then my temperature was seldom normal in these days. My dear aunt's endeavors to 'nurse up my strength' seemed altogether beside the mark. It was not my strength that wanted nursing, it was my imagination that wanted soothing. I kept the bundle of papers given me by Kurtz, not knowing exactly what to do with it. His mother had died lately, watched over, as I was told, by his Intended. A clean-shaved man, with an official manner and wearing gold-rimmed spectacles, called on me one day and made inquiries, at first circuitous, afterwards suavely pressing, about what he was pleased to denominate certain 'documents.' I was not surprised, because I had had two rows with the manager on the subject out there. I had refused to give up the smallest scrap out of that package, and I took the same attitude with the spectacled man. He became darkly menacing at last, and with much heat argued that the Company had the right to every bit of information about its 'territories.' And said he, 'Mr. Kurtz's knowledge of unexplored regions must have been necessarily extensive and peculiar—owing to his great abilities and to the deplorable circumstances in which he had been placed: therefore———' I assured him Mr. Kurtz's knowledge, however extensive, did not bear upon the problems of commerce or administration. He invoked then the name of science. 'It would be an incalculable loss if,' etc., etc. I offered him the report on the 'Suppression of Savage Customs,' with the postscriptum torn off. He took it up eagerly, but ended by sniffing at it with an air of contempt. 'This is not what we had a right to expect,' he remarked. 'Expect nothing else,' I said. 'There are only private letters.' He withdrew upon some threat of legal proceedings, and I saw him no more; but another fellow, calling himself Kurtz's cousin, appeared two days later, and was anxious to hear all the details about his dear relative's last moments. Incidentally he gave me to understand that Kurtz had been essentially a great musician. 'There was the making of an immense success,' said the man, who was an organist, I believe, with lank gray hair flowing over a greasy coat-collar. I had no reason to doubt his statement; and to this day I am unable to say what was Kurtz's profession, whether he ever had any—which was the greatest of his talents. I had taken him for a painter who wrote for the papers, or else for a journalist who could paint—but even the cousin (who took snuff during the interview) could not tell me what he had been—exactly. He was a universal genius—on that point I agreed with the old chap, who thereupon blew his nose noisily into a large cotton handkerchief and withdrew in senile agitation, bearing off some family letters and memoranda without importance. Ultimately a journalist anxious to know something of the fate of his 'dear colleague' turned up. This visitor informed me Kurtz's proper sphere ought to have been politics 'on the popular side.' He had furry straight eyebrows, bristly hair cropped short, an eye-glass on a broad ribbon, and, becoming expansive, confessed his opinion that Kurtz really couldn't write a bit—'but heavens! how that man could talk. He electrified large meetings. He had faith—don't you see?—he had the faith. He could get himself to believe anything—anything. He would have been a splendid leader of an extreme party.' 'What party?' I asked. 'Any party,' answered the other. 'He was an—an—extremist.' Did I not think so? I assented. Did I know, he asked, with a sudden flash of curiosity, 'what it was that had induced him to go out there?' 'Yes,' said I, and forthwith handed him the famous Report for publication, if he thought fit. He glanced through it hurriedly, mumbling all the time, judged 'it would do,' and took himself off with this plunder.

"Thus I was left at last with a slim packet of letters and the girl's portrait. She struck me as beautiful—I mean she had a beautiful expression. I know that the sunlight can be made to lie, too, yet one felt that no manipulation of light and pose could have conveyed the delicate shade of truthfulness upon those features. She seemed ready to listen without mental reservation, without suspicion, without a thought for herself. I concluded I would go and give her back her portrait and those letters myself. Curiosity? Yes; and also some other feeling perhaps. All that had been Kurtz's had passed out of my hands: his soul, his body, his station, his plans, his ivory, his career. There remained only his memory and his Intended—and I wanted to give that up, too, to the past, in a way—to surrender personally all that remained of him with me to that oblivion which is the last word of our common fate. I don't defend myself. I had no clear perception of what it was I really wanted. Perhaps it was an impulse of unconscious loyalty, or the fulfillment of one of those ironic necessities that lurk in the facts of human existence. I don't know. I can't tell. But I went.

"I thought his memory was like the other memories of the dead that accumulate in every man's life—a vague impress on the brain of shadows that had fallen on it in their swift and final passage; but before the high and ponderous door, between the tall houses of a street as still and decorous as a well-kept alley in a cemetery, I had a vision of him on the stretcher, opening his mouth voraciously, as if to devour all the earth with all its mankind. He lived then before me; he lived as much as he had ever lived—a shadow insatiable of splendid appearances, of frightful realities; a shadow darker than the shadow of the night, and draped nobly in the folds of a gorgeous eloquence. The vision seemed to enter the house with me—the stretcher, the phantom-bearers, the wild crowd of obedient worshippers, the gloom of the forest, the glitter of the reach between the murky bends, the beat of the drum, regular and muffled like the beating of a heart—the heart of a conquering darkness. It was a moment of triumph for the wilderness, an invading and vengeful rush which, it seemed to me, I would have to keep back alone for the salvation of another soul. And the memory of what I had heard him say afar there, with the horned shapes stirring at my back, in the glow of fires, within the patient woods, those broken phrases came back to me, were heard again in their ominous and terrifying simplicity. I remembered his abject pleading, his abject threats, the colossal scale of his vile desires, the meanness, the torment, the tempestuous anguish of his soul. And later on I seemed to see his collected languid manner, when he said one day, 'This lot of ivory now is really mine. The Company did not pay for it. I collected it myself at a very great personal risk. I am afraid they will try to claim it as theirs though. H'm. It is a difficult case. What do you think I ought to do—resist? Eh? I want no more than justice.' . . . He wanted no more than justice—no more than justice. I rang the bell before a mahogany door on the first floor, and while I waited he seemed to stare at me out of the glassy panel—stare with that wide and immense stare embracing, condemning, loathing all the universe. I seemed to hear the whispered cry, 'The horror! The horror!'

"The dusk was falling. I had to wait in a lofty drawing-room with three long windows from floor to ceiling that were like three luminous and bedraped columns. The bent gilt legs and backs of the furniture shone in indistinct curves. The tall marble fireplace had a cold and monumental whiteness. A grand piano stood massively in a corner; with dark gleams on the flat surfaces like a somber and polished sarcophagus. A high door opened—closed. I rose.

"She came forward, all in black, with a pale head, floating towards me in the dusk. She was in mourning. It was more than a year since his death, more than a year since the news came; she seemed as though she would remember and mourn for ever. She took both my hands in hers and murmured, 'I had heard you were coming.' I noticed she was not very young—I mean not girlish. She had a mature capacity for fidelity, for belief, for suffering. The room seemed to have grown darker, as if all the sad light of the cloudy evening had taken refuge on her forehead. This fair hair, this pale visage, this pure brow, seemed surrounded by an ashy halo from which the dark eyes looked out at me. Their glance was guileless, profound, confident, and trustful. She carried her sorrowful head as though she were proud of that sorrow, as though she would say, I—I alone know how to mourn for him as he deserves. But while we were still shaking hands, such a look of awful desolation came upon her face that I perceived she was one of those creatures that are not the play-things of Time. For her he had died only yesterday. And, by Jove! the impression was so powerful that for me, too, he seemed to have died only yesterday—nay, this very minute. I saw her and him in the same instant of time—his death and her sorrow—I saw her sorrow in the very moment of his death. Do you understand? I saw them together—I heard them together. She had said, with a deep catch of the breath, 'I have survived' while my strained ears seemed to hear distinctly, mingled with her tone of despairing regret, the summing up whisper of his eternal condemnation. I asked myself what I was doing there, with a sensation of panic in my heart as though I had blundered into a place of cruel and absurd mysteries not fit for a human being to behold. She motioned me to a chair. We sat down. I laid the packet gently on the little table, and she put her hand over it. . . .'You knew him well,' she murmured, after a moment of mourning silence.

" 'Intimacy grows quickly out there,' I said. 'I knew him as well as it is possible for one man to know another.'

" 'And you admired him,' she said. 'It was impossible to know him and not to admire him. Was it?'

" 'He was a remarkable man,' I said, unsteadily. Then before the appealing fixity of her gaze, that seemed to watch for more words on my lips, I went on, 'It was impossible not to——'

" 'Love him,' she finished eagerly, silencing me into an appalled dumbness. 'How true! how true! But when you think that no one knew him so well as I! I had all his noble confidence. I knew him best.'

" 'You knew him best,' I repeated. And perhaps she did. But with every word spoken the room was growing darker, and only her forehead, smooth and white, remained illumined by the unextinguishable light of belief and love.

" 'You were his friend,' she went on. 'His friend,' she repeated, a little louder. 'You must have been, if he had given you this, and sent you to me. I feel I can speak to you—and oh! I must speak. I want you—you who have heard his last words—to know I have been worthy of him. . . . It is not pride. . . . Yes! I am proud to know I understood him better than any one on earth—he told me so himself. And since his mother died I have had no one—no one—to—to——'

"I listened. The darkness deepened. I was not even sure he had given me the right bundle. I rather suspect he wanted me to take care of another batch of his papers which, after his death, I saw the manager examining under the lamp. And the girl talked, easing her pain in the certitude of my sympathy; she talked as thirsty men drink. I had heard that her engagement with Kurtz had been disapproved by her people. He wasn't rich enough or something. And indeed I don't know whether he had not been a pauper all his life. He had given me some reason to infer that it was his impatience of comparative poverty that drove him out there.

" '. . . Who was not his friend who had heard him speak once?' she was saying. 'He drew men towards him by what was best in them.' She looked at me with intensity. "It is the gift of the great,' she went on, and the sound of her low voice seemed to have the accompaniment of all the other sounds, full of mystery, desolation, and sorrow, I had ever heard—the ripple of the river, the soughing of the trees swayed by the wind, the murmurs of the crowds, the faint ring of incomprehensible words cried from afar, the whisper of a voice speaking from beyond the threshold of an eternal darkness. 'But you have heard him! You know!' she cried.

" 'Yes, I know,' I said with something like despair in my heart, but bowing my head before the faith that was in her, before that great and saving illusion that shone with an unearthly glow in the darkness, in the triumphant darkness from which I could not have defended her—from which I could not even defend myself.

" 'What a loss to me—to us!'—she corrected herself with beautiful generosity; then added in a murmur, 'To the world.' By the last gleams of twilight I could see the glitter of her eyes, full of tears—of tears that would not fall.

" 'I have been very happy—very fortunate—very proud,' she went on. 'Too fortunate. Too happy for a little while. And now I am unhappy for—for life.'

"She stood up; her fair hair seemed to catch all the remaining light in a glimmer of gold. I rose, too.

" 'And of all this,' she went on, mournfully, 'of all his promise, and of all his greatness, of his generous mind, of his noble heart, nothing remains—nothing but a memory. You and I——'

" 'We shall always remember him,' I said, hastily.

" 'No!' she cried. 'It is impossible that all this should be lost—that such a life should be sacrificed to leave nothing—but sorrow. You know what vast plans he had. I knew of them, too—I could not perhaps understand—but others knew of them. Something must remain. His words, at least, have not died.'

" 'His words will remain,' I said.

" 'And his example,' she whispered to herself. 'Men looked up to him—his goodness shone in every act. His example——'

" 'True,' I said; 'his example too. Yes, his example. I forgot that.'

" 'But I do not. I cannot—I cannot believe—not yet. I cannot believe that I shall never see him again, that nobody will see him again, never, never, never.'

"She put out her arms as if after a retreating figure, stretching them black and with clasped pale hands across the fading and narrow sheen of the window. Never see him! I saw him clearly enough then. I shall see this eloquent phantom as long as I live, and I shall see her, too, a tragic and familiar Shade, resembling in this gesture another one, tragic also, and bedecked with powerless charms, stretching bare brown arms over the glitter of the internal stream, the stream of darkness. She said suddenly very low, 'He died as he lived.'

" 'His end,' said I, with dull anger stirring in me, 'was in every way worthy of his life.'

" 'And I was not with him,' she murmured. My anger subsided before a feeling of infinite pity.

" 'Everything that could be done——' I mumbled.

" 'Ah, but I believed in him more than any one on earth—more than his own mother, more than—himself. He needed me! Me! I would have treasured every sigh, every word, every sign, every glance.'

"I felt like a chill grip on my chest. 'Don't,' I said, in a muffled voice.

" 'Forgive me. I—I—have mourned so long in silence—in silence. . . . You were with him—to the last? I think of his loneliness. Nobody near to understand him as I would have understood. Perhaps no one to hear. . . .'

" 'To the very end,' I said, shakily. 'I heard his very last words. . . .' I stopped in a fright.

" 'Repeat them,' she murmured in a heartbroken tone. 'I want—I want—something—something—to—to live with.'

"I was on the point of crying at her, 'Don't you hear them?' The dusk was repeating them in a persistent whisper all around us, in a whisper that seemed to swell menacingly like the first whisper of a rising wind. 'The horror! the horror!'

" 'His last word—to live with,' she insisted. 'Don't you understand I loved him—I loved him—I loved him!'

"I pulled myself together and spoke slowly.

" 'The last word he pronounced was—your name.'

"I heard a light sigh and then my heart stood still, stopped dead short by an exulting and terrible cry, by the cry of inconceivable triumph and of unspeakable pain. 'I knew it—I was sure!' . . . She knew. She was sure. I heard her weeping; she had hidden her face in her hands. It seemed to me that the house would collapse before I could escape, that the heavens would fall upon my head. But nothing happened. The heavens do not fall for such a trifle. Would they have fallen, I wonder, if I had rendered Kurtz that justice which was his due? Hadn't he said he wanted only justice? But I couldn't. I could not tell her. It would have been too dark—too dark altogether. . . ."

Marlow ceased, and sat apart, indistinct and silent, in the pose of a meditating Buddha. Nobody moved for a time. "We have lost the first of the ebb," said the Director, suddenly. I raised my head. The offing was barred by a black bank of clouds, and the tranquil waterway leading to the uttermost ends of the earth flowed somber under an overcast sky—seemed to lead into the heart of an immense darkness.

"Heart of Darkness" is both symbolic and representational in a realistic way. It represents and symbolically repeats and reinforces the aggressive history of man on this earth, the overrunning of one culture by another, the "ideals" of a dominant culture that can [may? . . . do?] in their turn, slide into falsity and self-deception. It is an old story, brilliantly presented. There may arise from this record a residue of human worth and decency. The reader should try to decide whether this residual quality attaches finally to "Mr. Kurtz" or to Marlow-Conrad, who perceives and meditates.

A Range of Human Experience

The selections in this section confront the reader with a range of fictional techniques and with revelations of human potential in widely separated environments and times of action. The stories are arranged in small groups, as shown below, because those in each group bear on one another in some important way.

Though the first three stories, for example, could hardly be more unlike, each draws the reader into a cultural reality, an ambience unmistakably its own. "Hodel" conveys the flavor of a speaker and a cultural heritage; yet the speaker is not only a wise but a truly individual person. "The Magic Barrel" functions similarly, in a sense, but the story assumes the form of a question that any young person can encounter: "If I try to use my cultural-religious heritage in order to solve a particular problem in my life, will it work? Will I get help?" The story answers the question, and in the process two or three individual characters are created (something the so-called "short story," incidentally, is not supposed to be able to accomplish). The third piece is a rarity indeed: it conveys an immediacy of thought, feeling, and action experienced by a young man about to be caught between two cultures. He acts out his older culture in order to feel, sense, test its values and meanings. Thus "The Eagles of the Valle Grande," among other things, reports an act of piety. Perhaps we have said enough to indicate one way in which the first three stories relate to one another. There are others. Stories in this group include:

- *"Hodel," by Sholom Aleichem*
- *"The Magic Barrel," by Bernard Malamud*
- *"The Eagles of the Valle Grande," by N. Scott Momaday*

The second small group of stories displays some shared implications more readily. But we would call special attention to the possible bearing that "Harrison Bergeron" may have on "Flying Home" for the reader who wishes to use fiction to think with. We might add that "Flying Home" contains at least two qualities that lift it far above "problem" fiction of usual kinds: (1) There is rare and imaginative humor, despite the serious burden of the story, and (2) The author uses connotative images and symbols with accumulative force. Stories in this group include:

- "Everything That Rises Must Converge," by Flannery O'Connor
- "Debbie Go Home," by Alan Paton
- "Flying Home," by Ralph Ellison
- "Harrison Bergeron," by Kurt Vonnegut, Jr.

That the third group deals with the subject of death is true enough. But the several emphases in this group are not those that our dominant culture in the United States so stresses: "Let's don't mention it or refer to it," "Let's pretend it doesn't exist," or "I'd as soon be dead as be forty." As good literature should do, the stories in this group reveal nonsimplistic attitudes, the center of which is not the pronoun I. Stories in this group include:

- "In Another Country," by Ernest Hemingway
- "Jean Beicke," by William Carlos Williams
- "To Hell With Dying," by Alice Walker

The fourth group presents individual people who are victims of traditional-conventional attitudes in others. "The New Villa" is a particularly acute report of the force of practically atavistic group attitudes brought against a family, and brought long ago before the invention of what we call sociology. Stories here include:

- "The Boarding House," by James Joyce
- "The New Villa," by Anton Chekhov

The final story is an excursion into that mixture of thought-feeling-symbol-action which may curse or color any life:

- "A Country Doctor," by Franz Kafka

*Hodel

SHOLOM ALEICHEM

You look, Mr. Sholom Aleichem, as though you were surprised that you hadn't seen me for such a long time . . . You're thinking that Tevye has aged all at once, his hair has turned gray . . .

Ah, well, if you only knew the troubles and heartaches he has endured of late! How is it written in our Holy Books? "Man comes from dust, and to dust he returns." Man is weaker than a fly, and stronger than iron. Whatever plague there is, whatever trouble, whatever misfortune—it never misses me. Why does it happen that way? Maybe because I am a simple soul who believes everything that everyone says. Tevye forgets that our wise men have told us a thousand times: "Beware of dogs . . ."

But I ask you, what can I do if that's my nature? I am, as you know, a trusting person, and I never question God's ways. Whatever He ordains is good. Besides, if you do complain, will it do you any good? That's what I always tell my wife. "Golde," I say, "you're sinning. We have a *Medresh*[1] . . ."

"What do I care about a *Medresh?*" she says. "We have a daughter to marry off. And after her are two more almost ready. And after these two—three more —may the Evil Eye spare them!"

"Tut," I say. "What's that? Don't you know, Golde, that our sages have thought of that also? There is a *Medresh* for that, too . . ."

But she doesn't let me finish. "Daughters to be married off," she says, "are a stiff *Medresh* in themselves."

So try to explain something to a woman!

Where does that leave us? Oh, yes, with a houseful of daughters, bless the Lord. Each one prettier than the next. It may not be proper for me to praise my own children, but I can't help hearing what the whole world calls them, can I? Beauties, every one of them! And especially Hodel, the one that comes after Tzeitl, who, you remember, fell in love with the tailor. And is this Hodel beautiful . . . How can I describe her to you? Like Esther in the Bible, "of beautiful form and fair to look upon." And as if that weren't bad enough, she has to have brains, too. She can write and she can read—Yiddish and Russian both. And books—she swallows like dumplings. You may be wondering how a daughter of Tevye happens to be reading books, when her father deals in butter and cheese? That's what I'd like to know myself . . .

But that's the way it is these days. Look at these lads who haven't got a pair

---

[1] See pp. 376-377 for glossary of Hebrew words.

of pants to their name, and still they want to study! Ask them, "What are you studying? Why are you studying?" They can't tell you. It's their nature, just as it's a goat's nature to jump into gardens. Especially since they aren't even allowed in the schools. "Keep off the grass!" read all the signs as far as they're concerned. And yet you ought to see how they go after it! And who are they? Workers' children. Tailors' and cobblers', so help me God! They go away to Yehupetz or to Odessa, sleep in garrets, eat what Pharaoh ate during the plagues—frogs and vermin—and for months on end do not see a piece of meat before their eyes. Six of them can make a banquet on a loaf of bread and a herring. Eat, drink and be merry! That's the life!

Well, so one of that band had to lose himself in our corner of the world. I used to know his father—he was a cigarette-maker, and as poor as a man could be. But that is nothing against the young fellow. For if Rabbi Jochanan wasn't too proud to mend boots, what is wrong with having a father who makes cigarettes? There is only one thing I can't understand: why should a pauper like that be so anxious to study? True, to give the devil his due, the boy has a good head on his shoulders, an excellent head. Pertschik, his name was, but we called him "Feferel"—"Peppercorn." And he looked like a peppercorn, little, dark, dried up and homely, but full of confidence and with a quick, sharp tongue.

Well, one day I was driving home from Boiberik where I had got rid of my load of milk and butter and cheese, and as usual I sat lost in thought, dreaming of many things, of this and that, and of the rich people of Yehupetz who had everything their own way while Tevye, the *shlimazl,* and his wretched little horse slaved and hungered all their days. It was summer, the sun was hot, the flies were biting, on all sides the world stretched endlessly. I felt like spreading out my arms and flying!

I lift up my eyes, and there on the road ahead of me I see a young man trudging along with a package under his arm, sweating and panting. "Rise, O Yokel the son of Flekel, as we say in the synagogue;" I called out to him. "Climb into my wagon and I'll give you a ride. I have plenty of room. How is it written? 'If you see the ass of him that hateth thee lying under its burden, thou shalt forebear to pass it by.' Then how about a human being?"

At this the *shlimazl* laughs, and climbs into the wagon.

"Where might the young gentleman be coming from?" I ask.

"From Yehupetz."

"And what might a young gentleman like you be doing in Yehupetz?" I ask.

"A young gentleman like me is getting ready for his examinations."

"And what might a young gentleman like you be studying?"

"I only wish I knew!"

"Then why does a young gentleman like you bother his head for nothing?"

"Don't worry, Reb Tevye. A young gentleman like me knows what he's doing."

"So—if you know who *I* am, tell me who *you* are!"

"Who am I? I'm a man."

"I can see that you're not a horse. I mean, as we Jews say, *whose* are you?"

"Whose should I be but God's?"

"I know that you're God's. It is written, 'All living things are His.' I mean, whom are you descended from? Are you from around here, or from Lithuania?"

"I am *descended*," he says, "from Adam, our father. I *come* from right around here. You know who we are."

"Well then, who is your father? Come, tell me."

"My father," he says, "was called Pertschik."

I spat with disgust. "Did you have to torture me like this all that time? Then you must be Pertschik the cigarette-maker's son!"

"Yes, that's who I am. Pertschik the cigarette-maker's son."

"And you go to the university?"

"Yes—the university."

"Well," I said, "I'm glad to hear it. Man and fish and fowl—you're all trying to better yourselves! But tell me, my lad, what do you live on, for instance?"

"I live on what I eat."

"That's good," I say. "And what do you eat?"

"I eat anything I can get."

"I understand," I say. "You're not particular. If there is something to eat, you eat. If not, you bite your lip and go to bed hungry. But it's all worthwhile as long as you can attend the university. You're comparing yourself to those rich people of Yehupetz . . ."

At these words Pertschik bursts out, "Don't you dare compare me to them! They can go to hell as far as I care!"

"You seem to be somewhat prejudiced against the rich," I say. "Did they divide your father's inheritance among themselves?"

"Let me tell you," says he, "it may well be that you and I and all the rest of us have no small share in *their* inheritance."

"Listen to me," I answer. "Let your enemies talk like that. But one thing I can see: you're not a bashful lad. You know what a tongue is for. If you have the time, stop at my house tonight and we'll talk a little more. And if you come early, you can have supper with us, too."

Our young friend didn't have to be asked twice. He arrived at the right moment—when the borsht was on the table and the *knishes* were baking in the oven. "Just in time!" I said. "Sit down. You can say grace or not, just as you please. I'm not God's watchman; I won't be punished for your sins." And as I talk to him I feel myself drawn to the fellow somehow; I don't know why. Maybe it's because I like a person one can talk to, a person who can understand a quotation and follow an argument about philosophy or this or that or something else . . . That's the kind of person I am.

And from that evening on our young friend began coming to our house almost every day. He had a few private students and when he was through giving his lessons he'd come to our house to rest up and visit for a while. What the poor fellow got for his lessons you can imagine for yourself, if I tell you that the very richest people used to pay their tutors three *rubles* a month; and besides their regular duties they were expected to read telegrams for them, write out addresses, and even run errands at times. Why not? As the passage says, "If you eat bread you have to earn it." It was lucky for him that most of the time he used to eat with us. For this he used to give my daughters lessons, too. One good turn deserves another. And in this way he became almost a member of the family. The girls saw to it that he had enough to eat and my wife kept his shirts clean and his socks mended. And it was at this time that we changed his Russian name of Pertschik to Feferel. And it can truthfully be said that we all came to love him as though he were one of us, for by nature he was a likable young man, simple, straightforward, generous. Whatever he had he shared with us.

There was only one thing I didn't like about him, and that was the way he had of suddenly disappearing. Without warning he would get up and go off; we looked around, and there was no Feferel. When he came back I would ask, "Where were you, my fine-feathered friend?" And he wouldn't say a word. I don't know how you are, but as for me, I dislike a person with secrets. I like a person to be willing to tell what he's been up to. But you can say this for him: when he did start talking, you couldn't stop him. He poured out everything. What a tongue he had! "Against the Lord and against His anointed; let us break their bands asunder." And the main thing was to break the bands . . . He had the wildest notions, the most peculiar ideas. Everything was upside down, topsy-turvy. For instance, according to his way of thinking, a poor man was far more important than a rich one, and if he happened to be a worker too, then he was really the brightest jewel in the diadem! He who toiled with his hands stood first in his estimation.

"That's good," I say, "but will that get you any money?"

At this he becomes very angry and tries to tell me that money is the root of all evil. Money, he says, is the source of all falsehood, and as long as money amounts to something nothing will ever be done in this world in the spirit of justice. And he gives me thousands of examples and illustrations that make no sense whatever.

"According to your crazy notions," I tell him, "there is no justice in the fact that my cow gives milk and my horse draws a load." I didn't let him get away with anything. That's the kind of man Tevye is . . .

But my Feferel can argue too. And how he can argue! If there is something on his mind, he comes right out with it. One evening we were sitting on my stoop talking things over—discussing philosophic matters—when he suddenly said, "Do you know, Reb Tevye, you have very fine daughters."

"Is that so?" said I. "Thanks for telling me. After all, they have someone to take after."

"The oldest one especially is a very bright girl," said he. "She's all there!"

"I know without your telling me," said I. "The apple never falls very far from the tree."

And I glowed with pride. What father isn't happy when his children are praised? How should I have known that from such an innocent remark would grow such fiery love?

Well, one summer twilight I was driving through Boiberik, going from *datcha* to *datcha* with my goods, when someone stopped me. I looked up and saw that it was Ephraim the matchmaker. And Ephraim, like all matchmakers, was concerned with only one thing—arranging marriages. So when he sees me here in Boiberik he stops me and says, "Excuse me, Reb Tevye, I'd like to tell you something."

"Go ahead," I say, stopping my horse, "as long as it's good news."

"You have," says he, "a daughter."

"I have," I answer, "seven daughters."

"I know," says he. "I have seven, too."

"Then together," I tell him, "we have fourteen."

"But joking aside," he says, "here is what I have to tell you. As you know, I am a matchmaker; and I have a young man for you to consider, the very best there is, a regular prince. There's not another like him anywhere."

"Well," I say, "that sounds good enough to me. But what do you consider a prince? If he's a tailor or a shoemaker or a teacher, you can keep him. I'll find my equal or I won't have anything. As the *Medresh* says . . ."

"Ah, Reb Tevye," says he, "you're beginning with your quotations already! If a person wants to talk to you he has to study up first . . . But better listen to the sort of match Ephraim has to offer you. Just listen and be quiet."

And then he begins to rattle off all his client's virtues. And it really sounds like something . . . First of all, he comes from a very fine family. And that is very important to me, for I am not just a nobody either. In our family you will find all sorts of people—spotted, striped and speckled, as the Bible says. There are plain, ordinary people, there are workers, and there are property owners . . . Secondly, he is a learned man who can read small print as well as large; he knows all the Commentaries by heart. And that is certainly not a small thing, either, for an ignorant man I hate even worse than pork itself. To me an un-lettered man is worse—a thousand times worse—than a hoodlum. You can go around bareheaded, you can even walk on your head if you like, but if you know what Rashi and the others have said, you are a man after my own heart . . . And on top of everything, Ephraim tells me, this man of his is rich as can be. He has his own carriage drawn by two horses so spirited that you can see a vapor rising from them. And that I don't object to, either. Better a rich man than a poor one! God Himself must hate a poor man, for if He did not, would He have made him poor?

"Well," I ask, "what more do you have to say?"

"What more can I say? He wants me to arrange a match with you. He is dying, he's so eager. Not for you, naturally, but for your daughter. He wants a pretty girl."

"He is dying?" I say. "Then let him keep dying . . . And who is this treasure of yours? What is he? A bachelor? A widower? Is he divorced? What's wrong with him?"

"He is a bachelor," says Ephraim. "Not so young any more, but he's never been married."

"And what is his name, may I ask?"

But this he wouldn't tell me. "Bring the girl to Boiberik," he says, "and then I'll tell you."

"Bring her?" says I. "That's the way one talks about a horse or a cow that's being brought to market. Not a girl!"

Well, you know what these matchmakers are. They can talk a stone wall into moving. So we agreed that early next week I would bring my daughter to Boiberik. And driving home, all sorts of wonderful thoughts came to me, and

I imagined my Hodel riding in a carriage drawn by spirited horses. The whole world envied me, not so much for the carriage and horses as for the good deeds I accomplished through my wealthy daughter. I helped the needy with money—let this one have twenty-five *rubles*, that one fifty, another a hundred. How do we say it? "Other people have to live too . . ." That's what I think to myself as I ride home in the evening, and I whip my horse and talk to him in his own language.

"Hurry, my little horse," I say, "move your legs a little faster and you'll get your oats that much sooner. As the Bible says, 'If you don't work, you don't eat' . . ."

Suddenly I see two people coming out of the woods—a man and a woman. Their heads are close together and they are whispering to each other. Who could they be, I wonder, and I look at them through the dazzling rays of the setting sun. I could swear the man was Feferel. But whom was he walking with so late in the day? I put my hand up and shield my eyes and look closely. Who was the damsel? Could it be Hodel? Yes, that's who it was! Hodel! So? So that's how they'd been studying their grammar and reading their books together? Oh, Tevye, what a fool you are . . .

I stop the horse and call out:

"Good evening! And what's the latest news of the war? How do you happen to be out here this time of the day? What are you looking for—the day before yesterday?"

At this the couple stops, not knowing what to do or say. They stand there, awkward and blushing, with their eyes lowered. Then they look up at me, I look at them, and they look at each other . . .

"Well," I say, "you look as if you hadn't seen me in a long time. I am the same Tevye as ever, I haven't changed by a hair."

I speak to them half angrily, half jokingly. Then my daughter, blushing harder than ever, speaks up:

"Father, you can congratulate us."

"Congratulate you?" I say. "What's happened? Did you find a treasure buried in the woods? Or were you just saved from some terrible danger?"

"Congratulate us," says Feferel this time. "We're engaged."

"What do you mean—engaged?"

"Don't you know what engaged means?" says Feferel, looking me straight in the eye. "It means that I'm going to marry her and she's going to marry me."

I look him back in the eye and say, "When was the contract signed? And why didn't you invite me to the ceremony? Don't you think I have a slight interest in the matter?" I joke with them and yet my heart is breaking. But Tevye is not a weakling. He wants to hear everything out. "Getting married," I say, "without matchmakers, without an engagement feast?"

"What do we need matchmakers for?" says Feferel. "We arranged it between ourselves."

"So?" I say. "That's one of God's wonders! But why were you so silent about it?"

"What was there to shout about?" says he. "We wouldn't have told you now, either, but since we have to part soon, we decided to have the wedding first."

This really hurt. How do they say it? It hurt to the quick. Becoming engaged without my knowledge—that was bad enough, but I could stand it. He loves her; she loves him—that I'm glad to hear. But getting married? That was too much for me . . .

The young man seemed to realize that I wasn't too well pleased with the news. "You see, Reb Tevye," he offered, "this is the reason: I am about to go away."

"When are you going?"

"Very soon."

"And where are you going?"

"That I can't tell you. It's a secret."

What do you think of that? A secret! A young man named Feferel comes into our lives—small, dark, homely, disguises himself as a bridegroom, wants to marry my daughter and then leave her—and he won't even say where he's going! Isn't that enough to drive you crazy?

"All right," I say. "A secret is a secret. Everything you do seems to be a secret. But explain this to me, my friend. You are a man of such—what do you call it?—integrity; you wallow in justice. So tell me, how does it happen that you suddenly marry Tevye's daughter and then leave her? Is that integrity? Is that justice? It's lucky that you didn't decide to rob me or burn my house down!"

"Father," says Hodel, "you don't know how happy we are now that we've told you our secret. It's like a weight off our chests. Come, father, kiss me."

And they both grab hold of me, she on one side, he on the other, and they begin to kiss and embrace me, and I to kiss them in return. And in their great excitement they begin to kiss each other. It was like going to a play. "Well," I say at last, "maybe you've done enough kissing already? It's time to talk about practical things."

"What, for instance?" they ask.

"For instance," I say, "the dowry, clothes, wedding expenses, this, that and the other . . ."

"We don't need a thing," they tell me. "We don't need anything. No this, no that, no other."

"Well then, what do you need?" I ask.

"Only the wedding ceremony," they tell me.

What do you think of that! . . . Well, to make a long story short, nothing I said did any good. They went ahead and had their wedding, if you want to call it a wedding. Naturally it wasn't the sort that I would have liked. A quiet little wedding—no fun at all. And besides there was a wife I had to do something about. She kept plaguing me: what were they in such a hurry about? Go try to explain their haste to a woman. But don't worry. I invented a story—"great, powerful and marvelous," as the Bible says, about a rich aunt in Yehupetz, an inheritance, all sorts of foolishness.

And a couple of hours after this wonderful wedding I hitched up my horse and wagon and the three of us got in, that is, my daughter, my son-in-law and I, and off we went to the station at Boiberik. Sitting in the wagon, I steal a look at the young couple, and I think to myself: what a great and powerful Lord we have and how cleverly He rules the world. What strange and fantastic beings He has created. Here you have a new young couple, just hatched; he is going off, the Good Lord alone knows where, and is leaving her behind—and do you see either one of them shed a tear, even for appearance's sake? But never mind; Tevye is not a curious old woman. He can wait. He can watch and see . . .

At the station I see a couple of young fellows, shabbily dressed, down-at-the-heels, coming to see my happy bridegroom off. One of them is dressed like a peasant with his blouse worn like a smock over his trousers. The two whisper together mysteriously for several minutes. Look out, Teyve, I say to myself. You have fallen among a band of horse thieves, pickpockets, housebreakers or counterfeiters.

Coming home from Boiberik I can't keep still any longer and tell Hodel what I suspect. She bursts out laughing and tries to assure me that they were very honest young men, honorable men, whose whole life was devoted to the welfare of humanity; their own private welfare meant nothing to them. For instance, the one with his blouse over his trousers was a rich man's son. He had left his parents in Yehupetz and wouldn't take a penny from them.

"Oh," said I, "that's just wonderful. An excellent young man! All he needs, now that he has his blouse over his trousers and wears his hair long, is a harmonica, or a dog to follow him, and then he would really be a beautiful sight!" I thought I was getting even with her for the pain she and this new husband of hers had caused me; but did she care? Not at all! She pretended not to understand what I was saying. I talked to her about Feferel and she answered me with "the cause of humanity" and "workers" and other such talk.

"What good is your humanity and your workers," I say, "if it's all a secret? There is a proverb: 'Where there are secrets, there is knavery.' But tell me the truth now. Where did he go, and why?"

"I'll tell you anything," she says, "but not that. Better don't ask. Believe me, you'll find out yourself in good time. You'll hear the news—and maybe very soon—and good news at that."

"Amen," I say. "From your mouth into God's ears! But may our enemies understand as little about it as I do."

"That," says she, "is the whole trouble. You'll never understand."

"Why not?" say I. "Is it so complicated? It seems to me that I can understand even more difficult things."

"These things you can't understand with your brain alone," she says. "You have to feel them, you have to feel them in your heart."

And when she said this to me, you should have seen how her face shone and her eyes burned. Ah, those daughters of mine! They don't do anything halfway. When they become involved in anything it's with their hearts and minds, their bodies and souls.

Well, a week passed, then two weeks—five—six—seven . . . and we heard nothing. There was no letter, no news of any kind. "Feferel is gone for good," I said, and glanced over at Hodel. There wasn't a trace of color in her face. And at the same time she didn't rest at all; she found something to do every minute of the day, as though trying to forget her troubles. And she never once mentioned his name, as if there never had been a Feferel in the world!

But one day when I came home from work I found Hodel going about with her eyes swollen from weeping. I made a few inquiries and found out that someone had been to see her, a long-haired young man who had taken her aside and talked to her for some time. Ah! That must have been the young fellow who had disowned his rich parents and pulled his blouse down over his trousers. Without further delay I called Hodel out into the yard and bluntly asked her:

"Tell me, daughter, have you heard from him?"

"Yes."

"Where is he—your predestined one?"

"He is far away."

"What is he doing there?"

"He is serving time."

"Serving time?"

"Yes."

"Why? What did he do?"

She doesn't answer me. She looks me straight in the eyes and doesn't say a word.

"Tell me, my dear daughter," I say, "according to what I can understand, he is not serving for a theft. So if he is neither a thief nor a swindler, why is he serving? For what good deeds?"

She doesn't answer. So I think to myself, "If you don't want to, you don't have to. He is your headache, not mine." But my heart aches for her. No matter what you say, I'm still her father . . .

Well, it was the evening of *Hashono Rabo.* On a holiday I'm in the habit of resting and my horse rests too. As it is written in the Bible: "Thou shalt rest from thy labors and so shall thy wife and thine ass . . ." Besides, by that time of the year there is very little for me to do in Boiberik. As soon as the holidays come and the *shofar* sounds, all the summer *datchas* close down and Boiberik becomes a desert. At that season I like to sit at home on my own stoop. To me it is the finest time of the year. Each day is a gift from heaven. The sun no longer bakes like an oven, but caresses with a heavenly softness. The woods are still green, the pines give out a pungent smell. In my yard stands the *succah*—the booth I have built for the holiday, covered with branches, and around me the forest looks like a huge *succah* designed for God Himself. Here, I think, God celebrates His *Succos,* here and not in town, in the noise and tumult where people run this way and that panting for breath as they chase after a small crust of bread and all you hear is money, money, money . . .

As I said, it is the evening of *Hashono Rabo.* The sky is a deep blue and myriads of stars twinkle and shine and blink. From time to time a star falls through the sky, leaving behind it a long green band of light. This means that someone's luck has fallen . . . I hope it isn't my star that is falling, and somehow Hodel comes to mind. She has changed in the last few days, has come to life again. Someone, it seems, has brought her a letter from him, from over there. I wish I knew what he had written, but I won't ask. If she won't speak, I won't either. Tevye is not a curious old woman. Tevye can wait.

And as I sit thinking of Hodel, she comes out of the house and sits down near me on the stoop. She looks cautiously around and then whispers, "I have something to tell you, father. I have to say goodbye to you, and I think it's for always."

She spoke so softly that I could barely hear her, and she looked at me in a way that I shall never forget.

"What do you mean—goodbye for always?" I say to her, and turn my face aside.

"I mean I am going away early tomorrow morning, and we shall possibly never see each other again."

"Where are you going, if I may be so bold as to ask?"

"I am going to him."

"To him? And where is he?"

"He is still serving, but soon they'll be sending him away."

"And you're going there to say goodbye to him?" I ask, pretending not to understand.

"No. I am going to follow him," she says. "Over there."

"There? Where is that? What do they call the place?"

"We don't know the exact name of the place, but we know that it's far—terribly, terribly far."

And she speaks, it seems to me, with great joy and pride, as though he had done something for which he deserved a medal. What can I say to her? Most fathers would scold a child for such talk, punish her, even beat her maybe. But Tevye is not a fool. To my way of thinking anger doesn't get you anywhere. So I tell her a story.

"I see, my daughter, as the Bible says, 'Therefore shalt thou leave thy father and mother'—for a Feferel you are ready to forsake your parents and go off to a strange land, to some desert across the frozen wastes, where Alexander of Macedon, as I once read in a story book, once found himself stranded among savages . . ."

I speak to her half in fun and half in anger, and all the time my heart weeps. But Tevye is no weakling; I control myself. And Hodel doesn't lose her dignity either; she answers me word for word, speaking quietly and thoughtfully. And Tevye's daughters can talk.

And though my head is lowered and my eyes are shut, still I seem to see her —her face is pale and lifeless like the moon, but her voice trembles . . . Shall I fall on her neck and plead with her not to go? I know it won't help. Those daughters of mine—when they fall in love with somebody, it is with their heads and hearts, their bodies and souls.

Well, we sat on the doorstep a long time—maybe all night. Most of the time we were silent, and when we did speak it was in snatches, a word here, a word there. I said to her, "I want to ask you only one thing: did you ever hear of a girl marrying a man so that she could follow him to the ends of the earth?" And she answered, "With him I'd go anywhere." I pointed out how foolish that was. And she said, "Father, you will never understand." So I told her a little fable—about a hen that hatched some ducklings. As soon as the ducklings could move they took to the water and swam, and the poor hen stood on shore, clucking and clucking.

"What do you say to that, my daughter?"

"What can I say?" she answered. "I am sorry for the poor hen; but just because she stood there clucking, should the ducklings have stopped swimming?"

There is an answer for you. She's not stupid, that daughter of mine.

But time does not stand still. It was beginning to get light already, and from within the house my old woman was muttering. More than once she had called out that it was time to go to bed, but seeing that it didn't help she stuck her head out of the window and said to me—with her usual benediction, "Tevye, what's keeping you?"

"Be quiet, Golde," I answered. "Remember what the Psalm says, "Why are the nations in an uproar, and why do the peoples mutter in vain?' Have you forgotten that it's *Hashono Rabo* tonight? Tonight all our fates are decided and the verdict is sealed. We stay up tonight . . . Listen to me, Golde, you light the samovar and make some tea while I go to get the horse and wagon ready. I am taking Hodel to the station in the morning." And once more I make up a story about how she has to go to Yehupetz, and from there farther on, because of that same old inheritance. It is possible, I say, that she may have to stay there through the winter and maybe the summer too, and maybe even another winter; and so we ought to give her something to take along—some linen, a dress, a couple of pillows, some pillow slips, and things like that.

And as I give these orders I tell her not to cry. "It's *Hashono Rabo* and on *Hashono Rabo* one mustn't weep. It's a law." But naturally they don't pay any attention to me, and when the time comes to say goodbye they all start weeping—their mother, the children and even Hodel herself. And when she came to say goodbye to her older sister Tzeitl (Tzeitl and her husband spend their holidays with us) they fell on each other's necks and you could hardly tear them apart.

I was the only one who did not break down. I was firm as steel—though inside I was more like a boiling samovar. All the way to Boiberik we were silent, and when we came near the station I asked her for the last time to tell me what it was that Feferel had really done. If they were sending him away, there must have been a reason. At this she became angry and swore by all that was holy that he was innocent. He was a man, she insisted, who cared nothing about himself. Everything he did was for humanity at large, especially for those who toiled with their hands—that is, the workers. That made no sense to me. "So he worries about the world" I told her. "Why doesn't the world worry a little about him? Nevertheless, give him my regards, that Alexander of Macedon of yours, and tell him I rely on his honor (For he is a man of honor, isn't he?) to treat my daughter well. And write to your old father some times."

When I finish talking she falls on my neck and begins to weep. "Goodbye, father," she cries. "Goodbye! God alone knows when we shall see each other again."

Well, that was too much for me. I remembered this Hodel when she was still a baby and I carried her in my arms, I carried her in my arms . . . Forgive me, Mr. Sholom Aleichem, for acting like an old woman. If you only knew what a daughter she is. If you could only see the letters she writes. Oh, what a daughter . . .

And now, let's talk about more cheerful things. Tell me, what news is there about the cholera in Odessa?

THE MAGIC BARREL

BERNARD MALAMUD

Not long ago there lived in uptown New York, in a small, almost meager room, though crowded with books, Leo Finkle, a rabbinical student in the Yeshivah University. Finkle, after six years of study, was to be ordained in June and had been advised by an acquaintance that he might find it easier to win himself a congregation if he were married. Since he had no present prospects of marriage, after two tormented days of turning it over in his mind, he called in Pinye Salzman, a marriage broker whose two-line advertisement he had read in the *Forward.*

The matchmaker appeared one night out of the dark fourth-floor hallway of the graystone rooming house where Finkle lived, grasping a black, strapped portfolio that had been worn thin with use. Salzman, who had been long in the business, was of slight but dignified build, wearing an old hat, and an over-coat too short and tight for him. He smelled frankly of fish, which he loved to eat, and although he was missing a few teeth, his presence was not displeas-ing, because of an amiable manner curiously contrasted with mournful eyes. His voice, his lips, his wisp of beard, his bony fingers were animated, but give him a moment of repose and his mild blue eyes revealed a depth of sadness, a characteristic that put Leo a little at ease although the situation, for him, was inherently tense.

He at once informed Salzman why he had asked him to come, explaining that his home was in Cleveland, and that but for his parents, who had married comparatively late in life, he was alone in the world. He had for six years devoted himself almost entirely to his studies, as a result of which, understandably, he had found himself without time for a social life and the company of young women. Therefore he thought it the better part of trial and error—of embarrassing fumbling—to call in an experienced person to advise him on these matters. He remarked in passing that the function of the marriage broker was ancient and honorable, highly approved in the Jewish community, because it made practical the necessary without hindering joy. Moreover, his own parents had been brought together by a matchmaker. They had made, if not a financially profitable marriage—since neither had possessed any worldly goods to speak of—at least a successful one in the sense of their everlasting devotion to each other. Salzman listened in embarrassed surprise, sensing a sort of apology. Later, however, he experienced a glow of pride in his work, an emotion that had left him years ago, and he heartily approved of Finkle.

The two went to their business. Leo had led Salzman to the only clear place in the room, a table near a window that overlooked the lamp-lit city. He seated himself at the matchmaker's side but facing him, attempting by an act of will to suppress the unpleasant tickle in his throat. Salzman eagerly unstrapped his portfolio and removed a loose rubber band from a thin packet of much-handled cards. As he flipped through them, a gesture and sound that physically hurt Leo, the student pretended not to see and gazed steadfastly out the window. Although it was still February, winter was on its last legs, signs of which he had for the first time in years begun to notice. He now observed the round white moon, moving high in the sky through a cloud menagerie, and watched with half-open mouth as it penetrated a huge hen, and dropped out of her like an egg laying itself. Salzman, though pretending through eyeglasses he had just slipped on, to be engaged in scanning the writing on the cards, stole occasional glances at the young man's distinguished face, noting with pleasure the long, severe scholar's nose, brown eyes heavy with learning, sensitive yet ascetic lips, and a certain, almost hollow quality of the dark cheeks. He gazed around at shelves upon shelves of books and let out a soft, contented sigh.

When Leo's eyes fell upon the cards, he counted six spread out in Salzman's hand.

"So few?" he asked in disappointment.

"You wouldn't believe me how much cards I got in my office," Salzman replied. "The drawers are already filled to the top, so I keep them now in a barrel, but is every girl good for a new rabbi?"

Leo blushed at this, regretting all he had revealed of himself in a curriculum vitae he had sent to Salzman. He had thought it best to acquaint him with his strict standards and specifications, but in having done so, felt he had told the marriage broker more than was absolutely necessary.

He hesitantly inquired, "Do you keep photographs of your clients on file?"

"First comes family, amount of dowry, also what kind promises," Salzman replied, unbuttoning his tight coat and settling himself in the chair. "After comes pictures, rabbi."

"Call me Mr. Finkle. I'm not yet a rabbi."

Salzman said he would, but instead called him doctor, which he changed to rabbi when Leo was not listening too attentively.

Salzman adjusted his horn-rimmed spectacles, gently cleared his throat and read in an eager voice the contents of the top card:

"Sophie P. Twenty four years. Widow one year. No children. Educated high school and two years college. Father promises eight thousand dollars. Has wonderful wholesale business. Also real estate. On the mother's side comes teachers, also one actor. Well known on Second Avenue."

Leo gazed up in surprise. "Did you say a widow?"

"A widow don't mean spoiled, rabbi. She lived with her husband maybe four months. He was a sick boy she made a mistake to marry him."

"Marrying a widow has never entered my mind."

"This is because you have no experience. A widow, especially if she is young and healthy like this girl, is a wonderful person to marry. She will be thankful to you the rest of her life. Believe me, if I was looking now for a bride, I would marry a widow."

Leo reflected, then shook his head.

Salzman hunched his shoulders in an almost imperceptible gesture of disappointment. He placed the card down on the wooden table and began to read another:

"Lily H. High school teacher. Regular. Not a substitute. Has savings and new Dodge car. Lived in Paris one year. Father is successful dentist thirty-five years. Interested in professional man. Well Americanized family. Wonderful opportunity."

"I knew her personally," said Salzman. "I wish you could see this girl. She is a doll. Also very intelligent. All day you could talk to her about books and theyater and what not. She also knows current events."

"I don't believe you mentioned her age?"

"Her age?" Salzman said, raising his brows. "Her age is thirty-two years."

Leo said after a while, "I'm afraid that seems a little too old."

Salzman let out a laugh. "So how old are you, rabbi?"

"Twenty-seven."

"So what is the difference, tell me, between twenty-seven and thirty-two? My own wife is seven years older than me. So what did I suffer?—Nothing. If Rothschild's a daughter wants to marry you, would you say on account her age, no?"

"Yes," Leo said dryly.

Salzman shook off the no in the yes. "Five years don't mean a thing. I give you my word that when you will live with her for one week you will forget her age. What does it mean five years—that she lived more and knows more than somebody who is younger? On this girl, God bless her, years are not wasted. Each one that it comes makes better the bargain."

"What subject does she teach in high school?"

"Languages. If you heard the way she speaks French, you will think it is music. I am in the business twenty-five years, and I recommend her with my whole heart. Believe me, I know what I'm talking, rabbi."

"What's on the next card?" Leo said abruptly.

Salzman reluctantly turned up the third card:

"Ruth K. Nineteen years. Honor student. Father offers thirteen thousand cash to the right bridegroom. He is a medical doctor. Stomach specialist with marvelous practice. Brother in law owns own garment business. Particular people."

Salzman looked as if he had read his trump card.

"Did you say nineteen?" Leo asked with interest.

"On the dot."

"Is she attractive?" He blushed. "Pretty?"

Salzman kissed his finger tips. "A little doll. On this I give you my word. Let me call the father tonight and you will see what means pretty."

But Leo was troubled. "You're sure she's that young?"

"This I am positive. The father will show you the birth certificate."

"Are you positive there isn't something wrong with her?" Leo insisted.

"Who says there is wrong?"

"I don't understand why an American girl her age should go to a marriage broker."

A smile spread over Salzman's face.

"So for the same reason you went, she comes."

Leo flushed. "I am pressed for time."

Salzman, realizing he had been tactless, quickly explained. "The father came, not her. He wants she should have the best, so he looks around himself. When we will locate the right boy he will introduce him and encourage. This makes a better marriage than if a young girl without experience takes for herself. I don't have to tell you this."

"But don't you think this young girl believes in love?" Leo spoke uneasily.

Salzman was about to guffaw but caught himself and said soberly, "Love comes with the right person, not before."

Leo parted dry lips but did not speak. Noticing that Salzman had snatched a glance at the next card, he cleverly asked, "How is her health?"

"Perfect," Salzman said, breathing with difficulty. "Of course, she is a little lame on her right foot from an auto accident that it happened to her when she was twelve years, but nobody notices on account she is so brilliant and also beautiful."

Leo got up heavily and went to the window. He felt curiously bitter and upbraided himself for having called in the marriage broker. Finally, he shook his head.

"Why not?" Salzman persisted, the pitch of his voice rising.

"Because I detest stomach specialists."

"So what do you care what is his business? After you marry her do you need him? Who says he must come every Friday night in your house?"

Ashamed of the way the talk was going, Leo dismissed Salzman, who went home with heavy, melancholy eyes.

Though he had felt only relief at the marriage broker's departure, Leo was in low spirits the next day. He explained it as arising from Salzman's failure to produce a suitable bride for him. He did not care for his type of clientele. But when Leo found himself hesitating whether to seek out another matchmaker, one more polished than Pinye, he wondered if it could be—his protestations to the contrary, and although he honored his father and mother—that he did not, in essence, care for the matchmaking institution? This thought he quickly put out of his mind yet found himself still upset. All day he ran around in the woods—missed an important appointment, forgot to give out his laundry, walked out of a Broadway cafeteria without paying and had to run back with the ticket in his hand; had even not recognized his landlady in the street when she passed with a friend and courteously called out, "A good evening to you, Doctor Finkle." By nightfall, however, he had regained sufficient calm to sink his nose into a book and there found peace from his thoughts.

Almost at once there came a knock on the door. Before Leo could say enter, Salzman, commercial cupid, was standing in the room. His face was gray and meager, his expression hungry, and he looked as if he would expire on his feet. Yet the marriage broker managed, by some trick of the muscles, to display a broad smile.

"So good evening. I am invited?"

Leo nodded, disturbed to see him again, yet unwilling to ask the man to leave.

Beaming still, Salzman laid his portfolio on the table. "Rabbi, I got for you tonight good news."

"I've asked you not to call me rabbi. I'm still a student."

"Your worries are finished. I have for you a first-class bride."

"Leave me in peace concerning this subject." Leo pretended lack of interest.

"The world will dance at your wedding."

"Please, Mr. Salzman, no more."

"But first must come back my strength," Salzman said weakly. He fumbled with the portfolio straps and took out of the leather case an oily paper bag, from which he extracted a hard, seeded roll and a small, smoked white fish. With a quick motion of his hand he stripped the fish out of its skin and began ravenously to chew. "All day in a rush," he muttered.

Leo watched him eat.

"A sliced tomato you have maybe?" Salzman hesitantly inquired.

"No."

The marriage broker shut his eyes and ate. When he had finished he carefully cleaned up the crumbs and rolled up the remains of the fish, in the paper bag. His spectacled eyes roamed the room until he discovered, amid some piles of books, a one-burner gas stove. Lifting his hat he humbly asked, "A glass tea you got, rabbi?"

Conscience-stricken, Leo rose and brewed the tea. He served it with a chunk of lemon and two cubes of lump sugar, delighting Salzman.

After he had drunk his tea, Salzman's strength and good spirits were restored.

"So tell me, rabbi," he said amiably, "you considered some more the three clients I mentioned yesterday?"

"There was no need to consider."

"Why not?"

"None of them suits me."

"What then suits you?"

Leo let it pass because he could give only a confused answer.

Without waiting for a reply, Salzman asked, "You remember this girl I talked to you—the high school teacher?"

"Age thirty-two?"

But, surprisingly, Salzman's face lit in a smile. "Age twenty-nine."

Leo shot him a look. "Reduced from thirty-two?"

"A mistake," Salzman avowed. "I talked today with the dentist. He took me to his safety deposit box and showed me the birth certificate. She was twenty-nine years last August. They made her a party in the mountains where she went for her vacation. When her father spoke to me the first time I forgot to write the age and I told you thirty-two, but now I remember this was a different client, a widow."

"The same one you told me about? I thought she was twenty-four?"

"A different. Am I responsible that the world is filled with widows?"

"No, but I'm not interested in them, nor for that matter, in school teachers."

Salzman pulled his clasped hands to his breast. Looking at the ceiling he devoutly exclaimed. "Yiddishe kinder, what can I say to somebody that he is not interested in high school teachers? So what then you are interested?"

Leo flushed but controlled himself.

"In what else will you be interested," Salzman went on, "if you not interested in this fine girl that she speaks four languages and has personally in the bank ten thousand dollars? Also her father guarantees further twelve thousand. Also she has a new car, wonderful clothes, talks on all subjects, and she will give you a first-class home and children. How near do we come in our life to paradise?"

"If she's so wonderful, why wasn't she married ten years ago?"

"Why?" said Salzman with a heavy laugh. "—Why? Because she is *partikiler*. This is why. She wants the *best*."

Leo was silent, amused at how he had entangled himself. But Salzman had aroused his interest in Lily H., and he began seriously to consider calling on her. When the marriage broker observed how intently Leo's mind was at work on the facts he had supplied, he felt certain they would soon come to an agreement.

Late Saturday afternoon, conscious of Salzman, Leo Finkle walked with Lily Hirschorn along Riverside Drive. He walked briskly and erectly, wearing with distinction the black fedora he had that morning taken with trepidation out of the dusty hat box on his closet shelf, and the heavy black Saturday coat he had thoroughly whisked clean. Leo also owned a walking stick, a present from a distant relative, but quickly put temptation aside and did not use it. Lily, petite and not unpretty, had on something signifying the approach of spring. She was au courant, animatedly, with all sorts of subjects, and he weighed her words and found her suprisingly sound—score another for Salzman, whom he uneasily sensed to be somewhere around hiding perhaps high in a tree along the street, flashing the lady signals with a pocket mirror; or perhaps a cloven-hoofed Pan, piping nuptial ditties as he danced his invisible way before them, strewing wild buds on the walk and purple grapes in their paths, symbolizing fruit of a union, though there was of course still none.

Lily startled Leo by remarking, "I was thinking of Mr. Salzman, a curious figure, wouldn't you say?"

Not certain what to answer, he nodded.

She bravely went on, blushing, "I for one am grateful for his introducing us. Aren't you?"

He courteously replied, "I am."

"I mean," she said with a little laugh—and it was all in good taste, or at least gave the effect of being not in bad—"do you mind that we came together so?"

He was not displeased with her honesty, recognizing that she meant to set the relationship aright, and understanding that it took a certain amount of experience in life, and courage, to want to do it quite that way. One had to have some sort of past to make that kind of beginning.

He said that he did not mind. Salzman's function was traditional and honorable—valuable for what it might achieve, which, he pointed out, was frequently nothing.

Lily agreed with a sigh. They walked on for a while and she said after a long silence, again with a nervous laugh, "Would you mind if I asked you something a little bit personal? Frankly, I find the subject fascinating." Although Leo shrugged, she went on half embarrassedly, "How was it that you came to your calling? I mean was it a sudden passionate inspiration?"

Leo, after a time, slowly replied, "I was always interested in the Law."

"You saw revealed in it the presence of the Highest?"

He nodded and changed the subject. "I understand that you spent a little time in Paris, Miss Hirschorn?"

"Oh, did Mr. Salzman tell you, Rabbi Finkle?" Leo winced but she went on, "It was ages ago and almost forgotten. I remember I had to return for my sister's wedding."

And Lily would not be put off. "When," she asked in a trembly voice, "did you become enamored of God?"

He stared at her. Then it came to him that she was talking not about Leo Finkle, but of a total stranger, some mystical figure, perhaps even passionate prophet that Salzman had dreamed up for her—no relation to the living or dead. Leo trembled with rage and weakness. The trickster had obviously sold her a bill of goods, just as he had him, who'd expected to become acqainted with a young lady of twenty-nine, only to behold, the moment he laid eyes upon her strained and anxious face, a woman past thirty-five and aging rapidly. Only his self control had kept him this long in her presence.

"I am not," he said gravely, "a talented religious person," and in seeking words to go on, found himself possessed by shame and fear. "I think," he said in a strained manner, "that I came to God not because I loved Him, but because I did not."

This confession he spoke harshly because its unexpectedness shook him.

Lily wilted. Leo saw a profusion of loaves of bread go flying like ducks high over his head, not unlike the winged loaves by which he had counted himself to sleep last night. Mercifully, then, it snowed, which he would not put past Salzman's machinations.

He was infuriated with the marriage broker and swore he would throw him out of the room the minute he reappeared. But Salzman did not come that night, and when Leo's anger had subsided, an unaccountable despair grew in its place. At first he thought this was caused by his disappointment in Lily, but before long it became evident that he had involved himself with Salzman without a true knowledge of his own intent. He gradually realized—with an emptiness that seized him with six hands—that he had called in the broker to find him a bride because he was incapable of doing it himself. This terrifying insight he had derived as a result of his meeting and conversation with Lily Hirschorn. Her probing questions had somehow irritated him into revealing—to himself more than her—the true nature of his relationship to God, and from that it had come upon him, with shocking force, that apart from his parents, he had never loved anyone. Or perhaps it went the other way, that he did not love God so well as he might, because he had not loved man. It seemed to Leo that his whole life stood starkly revealed and he saw himself for the first time as he truly was—unloved and loveless. This bitter but somehow not fully unexpected revelation brought him to a point of panic, controlled only by extraordinary effort. He covered his face with his hands and cried.

The week that followed was the worst of his life. He did not eat and lost weight. His beard darkened and grew ragged. He stopped attending seminars and almost never opened a book. He seriously considered leaving the Yeshivah, although he was deeply troubled at the thought of the loss of all his years of study—saw them like pages torn from a book, strewn over the city—and at the devastating effect of this decision upon his parents. But he had lived without knowledge of himself, and never in the Five Books and all the Commentaries—mea culpa—had the truth been revealed to him. He did not know where to turn, and in all this desolating loneliness there was no *to whom,* although he often thought of Lily but not once could bring himself to go downstairs and make the call. He became touchy and irritable, especially with his landlady, who asked him all manner of personal questions; on the other hand, sensing his own disagreeableness, he waylaid her on the stairs and apologized abjectly, until mortified, she ran from him. Out of this, however, he drew the consolation that he was a Jew and that a Jew suffered. But gradually, as the long and terrible week drew to a close, he regained his composure and some idea of purpose in life: to go on as planned. Although he was imperfect, the ideal was not. As for his quest of a bride, the thought of continuing afflicted him with anxiety and heartburn, yet perhaps with this new knowledge of himself he would be more successful than in the past. Perhaps love would now come to him and a bride to that love. And for this sanctified seeking who needed a Salzman?

The marriage broker, a skeleton with haunted eyes, returned that very night. He looked, withal, the picture of frustrated expectancy—as if he had steadfastly waited the week at Miss Lily Hirschorn's side for a telephone call that never came.

Casually coughing, Salzman came immediately to the point: "So how did you like her?"

Leo's anger rose and he could not refrain from chiding the matchmaker: "Why did you lie to me, Salzman?"

Salzman's pale face went dead white, the world had snowed on him.

"Did you not state that she was twenty-nine?" Leo insisted.

"I give you my word—"

"She was thirty-five, if a day. *At least* thirty-five."

"Of this don't be too sure. Her father told me—"

"Never mind. The worst of it was that you lied to her."

"How did I lie to her, tell me?"

"You told her things about me that weren't true. You made me out to be more, consequently less than I am. She had in mind a totally different person, a sort of semi-mystical Wonder Rabbi."

"All I said, you was a religious man."

"I can imagine."

Salzman sighed. "This is my weakness that I have," he confessed. "My wife says to me I shouldn't be a salesman, but when I have two fine people that they would be wonderful to be married, I am so happy that I talk too much." He smiled wanly. "This is why Salzman is a poor man."

Leo's anger left him. "Well, Salzman, I'm afraid that's all."

The marriage broker fastened hungry eyes on him.

"You don't want any more a bride?"

"I do," said Leo, "but I have decided to seek her in a different way. I am no longer interested in an arranged marriage. To be frank, I now admit the necessity of premarital love. That is, I want to be in love with the one I marry."

"Love?" said Salzman, astounded. After a moment he remarked, "For us, our love is our life, not for the ladies. In the ghetto they—"

"I know, I know," said Leo. "I've thought of it often. Love, I have said to myself, should be a by-product of living and worship rather than its own end. Yet for myself I find it necessary to establish the level of my need and fulfill it."

Salzman shrugged but answered, "Listen, rabbi, if you want love, this I can find for you also. I have such beautiful clients that you will love them the minute your eyes will see them."

Leo smiled unhappily. "I'm afraid you don't understand."

But Salzman hastily unstrapped his portfolio and withdrew a manila packet from it.

"Pictures," he said, quickly laying the envelope on the table.

Leo called after him to take the pictures away, but as if on wings of the wind, Salzman had disappeared.

March came. Leo had returned to his regular routine. Although he felt not quite himself yet—lacked energy—he was making plans for a more active social life. Of course it would cost something, but he was an expert in cutting corners; and when there were no corners left he would make circles rounder. All the while Salzman's pictures had lain on the table, gathering dust. Occasionally as Leo sat studying, or enjoying a cup of tea, his eyes fell on the manila envelope, but he never opened it.

The days went by and no social life to speak of developed with a member of the opposite sex—it was difficult, given the circumstances of his situation. One morning Leo toiled up the stairs to his room and stared out the window at the city. Although the day was bright his view of it was dark. For some time he watched the people in the street below hurrying along and then turned with a heavy heart to his little room. On the table was the packet. With a sudden relentless gesture he tore it open. For a half-hour he stood by the table in a state of excitement, examining the photographs of the ladies Salzman had included. Finally, with a deep sigh he put them down. There were six, of varying degrees of attractiveness, but look at them long enough and they all became Lily Hirschorn: all past their prime, all starved behind bright smiles, not a true personality in the lot. Life, despite their frantic yoohooings, had passed them by; they were pictures in a brief case that stank of fish. After a while, however, as Leo attempted to return the photographs into the envelope, he found in it another, a snapshot of the type taken by a machine for a quarter. He gazed at it a moment and let out a cry.

Her face deeply moved him. Why, he could at first not say. It gave him the impression of youth—spring flowers, yet age—a sense of having been used to the bone, wasted; this came from the eyes, which were hauntingly familiar, yet absolutely strange. He had a vivid impression that he had met her before, but try as he might he could not place her although he could almost recall her name, as if he had read it in her own handwriting. No, this couldn't be; he would have remembered her. It was not, he affirmed, that she had an extraordinary beauty—no, though her face was attractive enough; it was that *something* about her moved him. Feature for feature, even some of the ladies of the photographs could do better; but she leaped forth to his heart—had *lived,* or wanted to—more than just wanted, perhaps regretted how she had lived—had somehow deeply suffered: it could be seen in the depths of those reluctant eyes, and from the way the light enclosed and shone from her, and within her, opening realms of possibility: this was her own. Her he desired. His head ached and eyes narrowed with the intensity of his gazing, then as if an obscure fog had blown up in the mind, he experienced fear of her and was aware that he had received an impression, somehow, of evil. He shuddered, saying softly, it is thus with us all. Leo brewed some tea in a small pot and sat sipping it without sugar, to calm himself. But before he had finished drinking, again with excitement he examined the face and found it good: good for Leo Finkle. Only such a one could understand him and help him seek whatever he was seeking. She might, perhaps, love him. How she had happened to be among the discards in Salzman's barrel he could never guess, but he knew he must urgently go find her.

Leo rushed downstairs, grabbed up the Bronx telephone book, and searched for Salzman's home address. He was not listed, nor was his office. Neither was he in the Manhattan book. But Leo remembered having written down the address on a slip of paper after he had read Salzman's advertisement in the "personals" column of the *Forward*. He ran up to his room and tore through his papers, without luck. It was exasperating. Just when he needed the matchmaker he was nowhere to be found. Fortunately Leo remembered to look in his wallet. There on a card he found his name written and a Bronx address. No phone number was listed, the reason—Leo now recalled—he had originally communicated with Salzman by letter. He got on his coat, put a hat on over his skull cap and hurried to the subway station. All the way to the far end of the Bronx he sat on the edge of his seat. He was more than once tempted to take out the picture and see if the girl's face was as he remembered it, but he refrained, allowing the snapshot to remain in his inside coat pocket, content to have her so close. When the train pulled into the station he was waiting at the door and bolted out. He quickly located the street Salzman had advertised.

The building he sought was less than a block from the subway, but it was not an office building, nor even a loft, nor a store in which one could rent office space. It was a very old tenement house. Leo found Salzman's name in pencil on a soiled tag under the bell and climbed three dark flights to his apartment. When he knocked, the door was opened by a thin, asthmatic, gray-haired woman, in felt slippers.

"Yes?" she said, expecting nothing. She listened without listening. He could have sworn he had seen her, too, before but knew it was an illusion.

"Salzman—does he live here? Pinye Salzman," he said, "the matchmaker?"

She stared at him a long minute. "Of course."

He felt embarrassed. "Is he in?"

"No." Her mouth, though left open, offered nothing more.

"The matter is urgent. Can you tell me where his office is?"

"In the air." She pointed upward.

"You mean he has no office?" Leo asked.

"In his socks."

He peered into the apartment. It was sunless and dingy, one large room divided by a half-open curtain, beyond which he could see a sagging metal bed. The near side of the room was crowded with rickety chairs, old bureaus, a three-legged table, racks of cooking utensils, and all the apparatus of a kitchen. But there was no sign of Salzman or his magic barrel, probably also a figment of the imagination. An odor of frying fish made Leo weak to the knees.

"Where is he?" he insisted. "I've got to see your husband."

At length she answered, "So who knows where he is? Every time he thinks a new thought he runs to a different place. Go home, he will find you."

"Tell him Leo Finkle."

She gave no sign she had heard.

He walked downstairs, depressed.

But Salzman, breathless, stood waiting at his door.

Leo was astounded and overjoyed. "How did you get here before me?"

"I rushed."

"Come inside."

They entered. Leo fixed tea, and a sardine sandwich for Salzman. As they were drinking he reached behind him for the packet of pictures and handed them to the marriage broker.

Salzman put down his glass and said expectantly, "You found somebody you like?"

"Not among these."

The marriage broker turned away.

"Here is the one I want." Leo held forth the snapshot.

Salzman slipped on his glasses and took the picture into his trembling hand. He turned ghastly and let out a groan.

"What's the matter?" cried Leo.

"Excuse me. Was an accident this picture. She isn't for you."

Salzman frantically shoved the manila packet into his portfolio. He thrust the snapshot into his pocket and fled down the stairs.

Leo, after momentary paralysis, gave chase and cornered the marriage broker in the vestibule. The landlady made hysterical outcries but neither of them listened.

"Give me back the picture, Salzman."

"No." The pain in his eyes was terrible.

"Tell me who she is then."

"This I can't tell you. Excuse me."

He made to depart, but Leo, forgetting himself, seized the matchmaker by his tight coat and shook him frenziedly.

"Please," sighed Salzman. *"Please."*

Leo ashamedly let him go. "Tell me who she is," he begged. "It's very important for me to know."

"She is not for you. She is a wild one—wild, without shame. This is not a bride for a rabbi."

"What do you mean wild?"

"Like an animal. Like a dog. For her to be poor was a sin. This is why to me she is dead now."

"In God's name, what do you mean?"

"Her I can't introduce to you," Salzman cried.

"Why are you so excited?"

"Why, he asks," Salzman said, bursting into tears. "This is my baby, my Stella, she should burn in hell."

Leo hurried up to bed and hid under the covers. Under the covers he thought his life through. Although he soon fell asleep he could not sleep her out of his mind. He woke, beating his breast. Though he prayed to be rid of her, his prayers went unanswered. Through days of torment he endlessly struggled not to love her; fearing success, he escaped it. He then concluded to convert her to goodness, himself to God. The idea alternately nauseated and exalted him.

He perhaps did not know he had come to a final decision until he encountered Salzman in a Broadway cafeteria. He was sitting alone at a rear table, sucking the bony remains of a fish. The marriage broker appeared haggard, and transparent to the point of vanishing.

Salzman looked up at first without recognizing him. Leo had grown a pointed beard and his eyes were weighted with wisdom.

"Salzman," he said, "love has at last come to my heart."

"Who can love from a picture?" mocked the marriage broker.

"It is not impossible."

"If you can love her, then you can love anybody. Let me show you some new clients that they just sent me their photographs. One is a little doll."

"Just her I want," Leo murmured.

"Don't be a fool, doctor. Don't bother with her."

"Put me in touch with her, Salzman," Leo said humbly. "Perhaps I can be of service."

Salzman had stopped eating and Leo understood with emotion that it was now arranged.

Leaving the cafeteria, he was, however, afflicted by a tormenting suspicion that Salzman had planned it all to happen this way.

Leo was informed by letter that she would meet him on a certain corner, and she was there one spring night, waiting under a street lamp. He appeared, carrying a small bouquet of violets and rosebuds. Stella stood by the lamp post, smoking. She wore white with red shoes, which fitted his expectations, although in a troubled moment he had imagined the dress red, and only the shoes white. She waited uneasily and shyly. From afar he saw that her eyes— clearly her father's—were filled with desperate innocence. He pictured, in her, his own redemption. Violins and lit candles revolved in the sky. Leo ran forward with flowers outthrust.

Around the corner, Salzman, leaning against a wall, chanted prayers for the dead.

The Eagles of the Valle Grande

N. SCOTT MOMADAY[1]

He had seen a strange thing, an eagle overhead with its talons closed upon a snake. It was an awful, holy sight, full of magic and meaning.

The Eagle Watchers Society was the sixth to go into the kiva at the summer and autumn rain retreats. It was an important society, and it stood apart from the others in a certain way. This difference—this superiority—had come about a long time ago. Before the middle of the last century, there was received into the population of the town a small group of immigrants from the Tanoan city of Bahkyula, a distance of seventy or eighty miles to the east. These immigrants were a wretched people, for they had experienced great suffering. Their land bordered upon the Southern Plains, and for many years they had been an easy mark for marauding bands of buffalo hunters and thieves. They had endured every kind of persecution until one day they could stand no more and their spirit broke. They gave themselves up to despair and were then at the mercy of the first alien wind. But it was not a human enemy that overcame them at last; it was a plague. They were struck down by so deadly a disease that when the epidemic abated, there were fewer than twenty survivors in all. And this remainder, too, should surely have perished among the ruins of

[1] This is a sketch from *House Made of Dawn,* for which Momaday was awarded the Pulitzer Prize for Fiction. Under its present title, the story had appeared in slightly different form in *New Mexico Quarterly,* Summer 1967. The Valle Grande lies in the Jémez Mountains of New Mexico, northeast of the Pueblo of Jémez and west of the atomic energy research center of Los Alamos. Abel, the main character of the novel, has grown up in the pueblo and returned to it disturbed by his experiences in World War II. When this story begins, he has been remembering how things were for him before he went away.

Bahkyula had it not been for these *patrones,* these distant relatives who took them in at the certain risk of their own lives and the lives of their children and grandchildren. It is said that the cacique himself went out to welcome and escort the visitors in. The people of the town must have looked narrowly at those stricken souls who walked slowly toward them, wild in their eyes with grief and desperation. The Bahkyush immigrants brought with them little more than the clothes on their backs, but even in this moment of deep hurt and humiliation they thought of themselves as a people. They carried four things that should serve thereafter to signal who they were: a sacred flute; the bull and horse masks of Pecos; and the little wooden statue of their patroness María de los Angeles, whom they called Porcingula. Now, after the intervening years and generations, the ancient blood of this forgotten tribe still ran in the veins of men.

The Eagle Watchers Society was the principal ceremonial organization of the Bahkyush. Its chief, Patiestewa, and all its members were direct descendants of those old men and women who had made that journey along the edge of oblivion. There was a look about these men, even now. It was as if, conscious of having come so close to extinction, they had got a keener sense of humility than their benefactors, and paradoxically a greater sense of pride. Both attributes could be seen in such a man as old Patiestewa. He was hard, and he appeared to have seen more of life than had other men. In their uttermost peril long ago, the Bahkyush had been fashioned into seers and soothsayers. They had acquired a tragic sense, which gave to them as a race so much dignity and bearing. They were medicine men; they were rainmakers and eagle hunters.

He was not thinking of the eagles. He had been walking since daybreak down from the mountain where that year he had broken a horse for the rancher John Raymond. By the middle of the morning he was on the rim of the Valle Grande, a great volcanic crater that lay high up on the western slope of the range. It was the right eye of the earth, held open to the sun. Of all places that he knew, this valley alone could reflect the great spatial majesty of the sky. It was scooped out of the dark peaks like the well of a great, gathering storm, deep umber and blue and smoke-colored. The view across the diameter was magnificent; it was an unbelievably great expanse. As many times as he had been there in the past, each new sight of it always brought him up short, and he had to catch his breath. Just there, it seemed, a strange and brilliant light lay upon the world, and all the objects in the landscape were washed clean and set away in the distance. In the morning sunlight the Valle Grande was dappled with the shadows of clouds and vibrant with rolling winter grass. The clouds were always there, huge, sharply described, and shining in the pure air. But the great feature of the valley was its size. It was almost too great for the eye to hold, strangely beautiful and full of distance. Such vastness makes for illusion, a kind of illusion that comprehends reality, and where it exists there is always wonder and exhilaration. He looked at the facets of a boulder that lay balanced on the edge of the land, and the first thing beyond, the vague misty field out of which it stood, was the floor of the valley itself, pale and blue-green, miles away. He shifted the focus of his gaze, and he could just make out the clusters of dots that were cattle grazing along the river in the faraway plain.

Then he saw the eagles across the distance, two of them, riding low in the depths and rising diagonally toward him. He did not know what they were at first, and he stood watching them, their far, silent flight erratic and wild in the bright morning. They rose and swung across the skyline, veering close at last, and he knelt down behind the rock, dumb with pleasure and excitement, holding on to them with his eyes.

They were golden eagles, a male and a female, in their mating flight. They were cavorting, spinning and spiraling on the cold, clear columns of air, and they were beautiful. They swooped and hovered, leaning on the air, and swung close together, feinting and screaming with delight. The female was full-grown, and the span of her broad wings was greater than any man's height. There was a fine flourish to her motion; she was deceptively, incredibly fast, and her pivots and wheels were wide and full-blown. But her great weight was streamlined and perfectly controlled. She carried a rattlesnake; it hung shining from her feet, limp and curving out in the trail of her flight. Suddenly her wings and tail fanned, catching full on the wind, and for an instant she was still, widespread and spectral in the blue, while her mate flared past and away, turning around in the distance to look for her. Then she began to beat upward at an angle from the rim until she was small in the sky, and she let go of the snake. It fell slowly, writhing and rolling, floating out like a bit of silver thread against the wide backdrop of the land. She held still above, buoyed up on the cold current, her crop and hackles gleaming like copper in the sun. The male swerved and sailed. He was younger than she and a little more than half as large. He was quicker, tighter in his moves. He let the carrion drift by; then suddenly he gathered himself and stooped, sliding down in a blur of motion to the strike. He hit the snake in the head, with not the slightest deflection of his course or speed, cracking its long body like a whip. Then he rolled and swung upward in a great pendulum arc, riding out his momentum. At the top of his glide he let go of the snake in turn, but the female did not go for it. Instead she soared out over the plain, nearly out of sight, like a mote receding into the haze of the far mountain. The male followed, and Abel watched them go, straining to see, saw them veer once, dip and disappear.

Now there was the business of the society. It was getting on toward the end of November, and the eagle hunters were getting ready to set forth to the mountains. He brooded for a time, full of a strange longing; then one day he went to old Patiestewa and told him of what he had seen. "I think you had better let me go," he said. The old chief closed his eyes and thought about it for a long time. Then he answered: "Yes, I had better let you go."

The next day the Bahkyush eagle watchers started out on foot, he among them, northward through the canyon and into the high timber beyond. They were gone for days, holding up here and there at the holy places where they must pray and make their offerings. Early in the morning they came out of the trees on the edge of the Valle Grande. The land fell and reached away in the early light as far as the eye could see, the hills folding together and the gray grass rolling in the plain, and they began the descent. At midmorning they came to the lower meadows in the basin. It was clear and cold, and the air was thin and sharp like a shard of glass. They needed bait, and they circled out and apart, forming a ring. When the circle was formed, they converged slowly toward the center, clapping and calling out in a high, flat voice that carried only a little way. And as they closed, rabbits began to jump up from the grass and bound. They got away at first, many of them, while the men were still a distance apart, but gradually the ring grew small and the rabbits crept to the center and hid away in the brush. Now and then one of them tried to break away, and the nearest man threw his stick after it. These weapons were small curved clubs, and they were thrown with deadly accuracy by the eagle hunters, so that when the ring was of a certain size and the men only a few feet apart, very few of the animals got away.

He bent close to the ground, his arm cocked and shaking with tension. A great jack-rabbit buck bounded from the grass, straight past him. It struck the ground beyond and sprang again, nearly thirty feet through the air. He spun around and hurled the stick. It struck the jack rabbit a glancing blow just as it bounded again, and the animal slumped in the air and fell heavily to the ground.

The clapping and calling had stopped. He could feel his heart beating and the sweat growing cold on his skin. There was something like remorse or disappointment now that the rabbits were still and strewn about on the ground. He picked one of the dead animals from the brush—it was warm and soft, its eyes shining like porcelain, full of the luster of death—then the great buck, which was not dead but only stunned and frozen with fear. He felt the warm living weight of it in his hands; it was brittle with life, taut with hard, sinewy strength.

When he had bound the bait together and placed it in the sack, he gathered bunches of tall grass and cut a number of evergreen boughs from a thicket in the plain; these he tied in a bundle and carried in a sling on his back. He went to the river and washed his head in order to purify himself. When all was ready, he waved to the others and started off alone to the cliffs. When he came to the first plateau, he rested and looked out across the valley. The sun was high, and all around there was a pale, dry uniformity of light, a winter glare on the clouds and peaks. He could see a crow circling low in the distance. Higher on the land, where a great slab of white rock protruded from the mountain, he saw the eagle-hunt house; he headed for it. The house was a small tower of stone, built around a pit, hollow and open at the top. Near it was a shrine, a stone shelf in which there was a slight depression. There he placed a prayer offering. He got into the house, and with boughs he made a latticework of beams across the top and covered it with grass. When it was finished, there was a small opening at the center. Through it he raised the rabbits and laid them down on the boughs. He could see here and there through the screen, but his line of vision was vertical, or nearly so, and his quarry would come from the sun. He began to sing, now and then calling out, low in his throat.

The eagles soared southward, high above the Valle Grande. They were almost too high to be seen. From their vantage point the land below reached away on either side to the long, crooked tributaries of the range; down the great open corridor to the south were the wooded slopes and the canyon, the desert and the far end of the earth bending on the sky. They caught sight of the rabbits and were deflected. They veered and banked, lowering themselves into the crater, gathering speed. By the time he knew of their presence, they were low and coming fast on either side of the pit, swooping with blinding speed. The male caught hold of the air and fell off, touching upon the face of the cliff in order to flush the rabbits, while the female hurtled in to take her prey on the run. Nothing happened; the rabbits did not move. She overshot the trap and screamed. She was enraged and she hurled herself around in the air. She swung back with a great clamor of her wings and fell with fury on the bait. He saw her in the instant she struck. Her foot flashed out and one of her talons laid the jack rabbit open the length of its body. It stiffened and jerked, and her other foot took hold of its skull and crushed it. In that split second, when the center of her weight touched down upon the trap, he reached for her. His hands closed upon her legs and he drew her down with all his strength. For one instant only did she recoil, splashing her great wings down upon the beams and boughs—and she very nearly broke from his grasp; but then she was down in the darkness of the well, hooded, and she was still.

At dusk he met with the other hunters in the plain. San Juanito, too, had got an eagle, but it was an aged male and poor by comparison. They gathered around the old eagle and spoke to it, bidding it return with their good will and sorrow to the eagles of the crags. They fixed a prayer plume to its leg and let it go. He watched it back away and stoop, flaring its wings on the ground, glowering, full of fear and suspicion. Then it took leave of the ground and beat upward, clattering through the still shadows of the valley. It gathered speed, driving higher and higher until it reached the shafts of reddish-gold final light that lay like bars across the crater. The light caught it up and set a dark blaze upon it. It leveled off and sailed. Then it was gone from sight, but he looked after it for a time. He could see it still in the mind's eye and hear in his memory the awful whisper of its flight on the wind. It filled him with longing. He felt the great weight of the bird which he held in the sack. The dusk was fading quickly into night, and the others could not see that his eyes were filled with tears.

That night, while the others ate by the fire, he stole away to look at the great bird. He drew the sack open; the bird shivered, he thought, and drew itself up. Bound and helpless, his eagle seemed drab and shapeless in the moonlight, too large and ungainly for flight. The sight of it filled him with shame and disgust. He took hold of its throat in the darkness and cut off its breath.

everything that rises must converge

FLANNERY O'CONNOR

Her doctor had told Julian's mother that she must lose twenty pounds on account of her blood pressure, so on Wednesday nights Julian had to take her downtown on the bus for a reducing class at the Y. The reducing class was designed for working girls over fifty, who weighed from 165 to 200 pounds. His mother was one of the slimmer ones, but she said ladies did not tell their age or weight. She would not ride the buses by herself at night since they had been integrated, and because the reducing class was one of her few pleasures, necessary for her health, and *free*, she said Julian could at least put himself out to take her, considering all she did for him. Julian did not like to consider all she did for him, but every Wednesday night he braced himself and took her.

She was almost ready to go, standing before the hall mirror, putting on her hat, while he, his hands behind him, appeared pinned to the door frame, waiting like Saint Sebastian for the arrows to begin piercing him. The hat was new and had cost her seven dollars and a half. She kept saying, "Maybe I shouldn't have paid that for it. No, I shoudn't have. I'll take it off and return it tomorrow. I shouldn't have bought it."

Julian raised his eyes to heaven. "Yes, you should have bought it," he said. "Put it on and let's go." It was a hideous hat. A purple velvet flap came down on one side of it and stood up on the other; the rest of it was green and looked like a cushion with the stuffing out. He decided it was less comical than jaunty and pathetic. Everything that gave her pleasure was small and depressed him.

She lifted the hat one more time and set it down slowly on top of her head. Two wings of gray hair protruded on either side of her florid face, but her eyes, sky-blue, were as innocent and untouched by experience as they must have been when she was ten. Were it not that she was a widow who had struggled fiercely to feed and clothe and put him through school and who was supporting him still, "until he got on his feet," she might have been a little girl that he had to take to town.

"It's all right, it's all right," he said. "Let's go." He opened the door himself and started down the walk to get her going. The sky was a dying violet and the houses stood out darkly against it, bulbous liver-colored monstrosities of a uniform ugliness though no two were alike. Since this had been a fashionable neighborhood forty years ago, his mother persisted in thinking they did well to have an apartment in it. Each house had a narrow collar of dirt around it in which sat, usually, a grubby child. Julian walked with his hands in his pockets, his head down and thrust forward and his eyes glazed with the determination to make himself completely numb during the time he would be sacrificed to her pleasure.

The door closed and he turned to find the dumpy figure, surmounted by the atrocious hat, coming toward him. "Well," she said, "you only live once and paying a little more for it, I at least won't meet myself coming and going."

"Some day I'll start making money," Julian said gloomily—he knew he never would—"and you can have one of those jokes whenever you take the fit." But first they would move. He visualized a place where the nearest neighbors would be three miles away on either side.

"I think you're doing fine," she said, drawing on her gloves. "You've only been out of school a year. Rome wasn't built in a day."

She was one of the few members of the Y reducing class who arrived in hat and gloves and who had a son who had been to college. "It takes time," she said, "and the world is in such a mess. This hat looked better on me than any of the others, though when she brought it out I said, 'Take that thing back. I wouldn't have it on my head,' and she said, 'Now wait till you see it on,' and when she put it on me, I said, 'We-ull,' and she said, 'If you ask me, that hat does something for you and you do something for the hat, and besides,' she said, 'with that hat, you won't meet yourself coming and going.' "

Julian thought he could have stood his lot better if she had been selfish, if she had been an old hag who drank and screamed at him. He walked along, saturated in depression, as if in the midst of his martyrdom he had lost his faith. Catching sight of his long, hopeless, irritated face, she stopped suddenly with a grief-stricken look, and pulled back on his arm. "Wait on me," she said. "I'm going back to the house and take this thing off and tomorrow I'm going to return it. I was out of my head. I can pay the gas bill with that seven-fifty."

He caught her arm in a vicious grip. "You are not going to take it back," he said. "I like it."

"Well," she said, "I don't think I ought . . ."

"Shut up and enjoy it," he muttered, more depressed than ever.

"With the world in the mess it's in," she said, "it's a wonder we can enjoy anything. I tell you, the bottom rail is on the top."

Julian sighed.

"Of course," she said, "if you know who you are, you can go anywhere." She said this every time he took her to the reducing class. "Most of them in it are not our kind of people," she said, "but I can be gracious to anybody. I know who I am."

"They don't give a damn for your graciousness," Julian said savagely. "Knowing who you are is good for one generation only. You haven't the foggiest idea where you stand now or who you are."

She stopped and allowed her eyes to flash at him. I most certainly do know who I am," she said, "and if you don't know who you are, I'm ashamed of you."

"Oh hell," Julian said.

"Your great-grandfather was a former governor of this state," she said.

"Your grandfather was a prosperous landowner. Your grandmother was a Godhigh."

"Will you look around you," he said tensely, "and see where you are now?" and he swept his arm jerkily out to indicate the neighborhood, which the growing darkness at least made less dingy.

"You remain what you are," she said. "Your great-grandfather had a plantation and two hundred slaves."

"There are no more slaves," he said irritably.

"They were better off when they were," she said. He groaned to see that she was off on that topic. She rolled onto it every few days like a train on an open track. He knew every stop, every junction, every swamp along the way, and knew the exact point at which her conclusion would roll magestically into the station: "It's ridiculous. It's simply not realistic. They should rise, yes, but on their own side of the fence."

"Let's skip it," Julian said.

"The ones I feel sorry for," she said, "are the ones that are half white. They're tragic."

"Will you skip it?"

"Suppose we were half white. We would certainly have mixed feelings."

"I have mixed feelings now," he groaned.

"Well let's talk about something pleasant," she said. "I remember going to Grandpa's when I was a little girl. Then the house had double stairways that went up to what was really the second floor—all the cooking was done on the first. I used to like to stay down in the kitchen on account of the way the walls smelled. I would sit with my nose pressed against the plaster and take deep breaths. Actually the place belonged to the Godhighs but your grandfather Chestny paid the mortgage and saved it for them. They were in reduced circumstances," she said, "but reduced or not, they never forgot who they were."

"Doubtless that decayed mansion reminded them," Julian muttered. He never spoke of it without contempt or thought of it without longing. He had seen it once when he was a child before it had been sold. The double stairways had rotted and been torn down. Negroes were living in it. But it remained in his mind as his mother had known it. It appeared in his dreams regularly. He would stand on the wide porch, listening to the rustle of oak leaves, then wander through the high-ceilinged hall into the parlor that opened onto it and gaze at the worn rugs and faded draperies. It occurred to him that it was he, not she, who could have appreciated it. He preferred its threadbare elegance to anything he could name and it was because of it that all the neighborhoods they had lived in had been a torment to him—whereas she had hardly known the difference. She called her insensitivity "being adjustable."

"And I remember the old darky who was my nurse, Caroline. There was no better person in the world. I've always had a great respect for my colored friends," she said. "I'd do anything in the world for them and they'd . . . ."

"Will you for God's sake get off that subject?" Julian said. When he got on a bus by himself, he made it a point to sit down beside a Negro, in reparation as it were for his mother's sins.

"You're mighty touchy tonight," she said. "Do you feel all right?"

"Yes I feel all right," he said. "Now lay off."

She pursed her lips. "Well, you certainly are in a vile humor," she observed. "I just won't speak to you at all."

They had reached the bus stop. There was no bus in sight and Julian, his hands still jammed in his pockets and his head thrust forward, scowled down the empty street. The frustration of having to wait on the bus as well as ride on it began to creep up his neck like a hot hand. The presence of his mother was borne in upon him as she gave a pained sigh. He looked at her bleakly. She was holding herself very erect under the preposterous hat, wearing it like a banner of her imaginary dignity. There was in him an evil urge to break her spirit. He suddenly unloosened his tie and pulled it off and put it in his pocket.

She stiffened. "Why must you look like *that* when you take me to town?" she said. "Why must you deliberately embarrass me?"

"If you'll never learn where you are," he said, "you can at least learn where I am."

"You look like a—thug," she said.

"Then I must be one," he murmured.

"I'll just go home," she said. "I will not bother you. If you can't do a little thing like that for me . . . "

Rolling his eyes upward, he put his tie on. "Restored to my class," he muttered. He thrust his face toward her and hissed, "True culture is in the mind, the *mind*," he said, and tapped his head, "the mind."

"It's in the heart," she said, "and in how you do things and how you do things is because of who you *are*."

"Nobody in the damn bus cares who you are."

"I care who I am," she said icily.

The lighted bus appeared on top of the next hill and as it approached, they moved out into the street to meet it. He put his hand under her elbow and hoisted her up on the creaking step. She entered with a little smile, as if she were going into a drawing room where everyone had been waiting for her. While he put in the tokens, she sat down on one of the broad front seats for three which faced the aisle. A thin woman with protruding teeth and long yellow hair was sitting on the end of it. His mother moved up beside her and left room for Julian beside herself. He sat down and looked at the floor across the aisle where a pair of thin feet in red and white canvas sandals were planted.

His mother immediately began a general conversation meant to attract anyone who felt like talking. "Can it get any hotter?" she said and removed from her purse a folding fan, black with a Japanese scene on it, which she began to flutter before her.

"I reckon it might could," the woman with the protruding teeth said, "but I know for a fact my apartment couldn't get no hotter."

"It must get the afternoon sun," his mother said. She sat forward and looked up and down the bus. It was half filled. Everybody was white. "I see we have the bus to ourselves," she said. Julian cringed.

"For a change," said the woman across the aisle, the owner of the red and white canvas sandals. "I come on one the other day and they were thick as fleas—up front and all through."

"The world is in a mess everywhere," his mother said. "I don't know how we've let it get in this fix."

"What gets my goat is all those boys from good families stealing automobile tires," the woman with the protruding teeth said. "I told my boy, I said you may not be rich but you been raised right and if I ever catch you in any such mess, they can send you on to the reformatory. Be exactly where you belong."

"Training tells," his mother said. "Is your boy in high school?"

"Ninth grade," the woman said.

"My son just finished college last year. He wants to write but he's selling typewriters until he gets started," his mother said.

The woman leaned forward and peered at Julian. He threw her such a malevolent look that she subsided against the seat. On the floor across the aisle there was an abandoned newspaper. He got up and got it and opened it out in front of him. His mother discreetly continued the conversation in a lower tone but the woman across the aisle said in a loud voice, "Well that's nice. Selling typewriters is close to writing. He can go right from one to the other."

"I tell him," his mother said, "that Rome wasn't built in a day."

Behind the newspaper Julian was withdrawing into the inner compartment of his mind where he spent most of his time. This was a kind of mental bubble in which he established himself when he could not bear to be a part of what was going on around him. From it he could see out and judge but in it he was safe from any kind of penetration from without. It was the only place where he felt free of the general idiocy of his fellows. His mother had never entered it but from it he could see her with absolute clarity.

The old lady was clever enough and he thought that if she had started from any of the right premises, more might have been expected of her. She lived according to the laws of her own fantasy world, outside of which he had never seen her set foot. The law of it was to sacrifice herself for him after she had first created the necessity to do so by making a mess of things. If he had permitted her sacrifices, it was only because her lack of foresight had made them necessary. All of her life had been a struggle to act like a Chestny without the Chestny goods, and to give him everything she thought a Chestny ought to have; but since, said she, it was fun to struggle, why complain? And when you had won, as she had won, what fun to look back on the hard times! He could not forgive her that she had enjoyed the struggle and that she thought *she* had won.

What she meant when she said she had won was that she had brought him up successfully and had sent him to college and that he had turned out so well—good looking (her teeth had gone unfilled so that his could be straightened), intelligent (he realized he was too intelligent to be a success), and with a future ahead of him (there was of course no future ahead of him). She excused his gloominess on the grounds that he was still growing up and his radical ideas on his lack of practical experience. She said he didn't yet know a thing about "life," that he hadn't even entered the real world—when already he was as disenchanted with it as a man of fifty.

The further irony of all this was that in spite of her, he had turned out so well. In spite of going to only a third-rate college, he had, on his own initiative, come out with a first-rate education; in spite of growing up dominated by a small mind, he had ended up with a large one; in spite of all her foolish views, he was free of prejudice and unafraid to face facts. Most miraculous of all, instead of being blinded by love for her as she was for him, he had cut himself emotionally free of her and could see her with complete objectivity. He was not dominated by his mother.

The bus stopped with a sudden jerk and shook him from his meditation. A woman from the back lurched forward with little steps and barely escaped falling in his newspaper as she righted herself. She got off and a large Negro got on. Julian kept his paper lowered to watch. It gave him a certain satisfaction to see injustice in daily operation. It confirmed his view that with a few exceptions there was no one worth knowing within a radius of three hundred miles. The Negro was well dressed and carried a briefcase. He looked around and then sat down on the other end of the seat where the woman with the red and white canvas sandals was sitting. He immediately unfolded a newspaper and obscured himself behind it. Julian's mother's elbow at once prodded insistently into his ribs. "Now you see why I won't ride on these buses by myself," she whispered.

The woman with the red and white canvas sandals had risen at the same time the Negro sat down and had gone further back in the bus and taken the seat of the woman who had got off. His mother leaned forward and cast her an approving look.

Julian rose, crossed the aisle, and sat down in the place of the woman with the canvas sandals. From this position, he looked serenely across at his mother. Her face had turned an angry red. He stared at her, making his eyes the eyes of a stranger. He felt his tension suddenly lift as if he had openly declared war on her.

He would have liked to get in conversation with the Negro and to talk with him about art or politics or any subject that would be above the comprehension of those around them, but the man remained entrenched behind his paper. He was either ignoring the change of seating or had never noticed it. There was no way for Julian to convey his sympathy.

His mother kept her eyes fixed reproachfully on his face. The woman with the protruding teeth was looking at him avidly as if he were a type of monster new to her.

"Do you have a light?" he asked the Negro.

Without looking away from his paper, the man reached in his pocket and handed him a packet of matches.

"Thanks," Julian said. For a moment he held the matches foolishly. A NO SMOKING sign looked down upon him from over the door. This alone would not have deterred him; he had no cigarettes. He had quit smoking some months before because he could not afford it. "Sorry," he muttered and handed back the matches. The Negro lowered the paper and gave him an annoyed look. He took the matches and raised the paper again.

His mother continued to gaze at him but she did not take advantage of his momentary discomfort. Her eyes retained their battered look. Her face seemed to be unnaturally red, as if her blood pressure had risen. Julian allowed no glimmer of sympathy to show on his face. Having got the advantage, he wanted desperately to keep it and carry it through. He would have liked to teach her a lesson that would last her a while, but there seemed no way to continue the point. The Negro refused to come out from behind his paper.

Julian folded his arms and looked stolidly before him, facing her but as if he did not see her, as if he had ceased to recognize her existence. He visualized a scene in which, the bus having reached their stop, he would remain in his seat and when she said, "Aren't you going to get off?" he would look at her as at a stranger who had rashly addressed him. The corner they got off on was usually deserted, but it was well lighted and it would not hurt her to walk by herself the four blocks to the Y. He decided to wait until the time came and then decide whether or not he would let her get off by herself. He would have to be at the Y at ten to bring her back, but he could leave her wondering if he was going to show up. There was no reason for her to think she could always depend on him.

He retired again into the high-ceilinged room sparsely settled with large pieces of antique furniture. His soul expanded momentarily but then he became aware of his mother across from him and the vision shriveled. He studied her coldly. Her feet in little pumps dangled like a child's and did not quite reach the floor. She was training on him an exaggerated look of reproach. He felt completely detached from her. At that moment he could with pleasure have slapped her as he would have slapped a particularly obnoxious child in his charge.

He began to imagine various unlikely ways by which he could teach her a lesson. He might make friends with some distinguished Negro professor or lawyer and bring him home to spend the evening. He would be entirely justified but her blood pressure would rise to 300. He could not push her to the extent of making her have a stroke, and moreover, he had never been successful at making any Negro friends. He had tried to strike up an acquaintance on the bus with some of the better types, with ones that looked like professors or ministers or lawyers. One morning he had sat down next to a distinguished-looking dark brown man who had answered his questions with a sonorous solemnity but who had turned out to be an undertaker. Another day he had sat down beside a cigar-smoking Negro with a diamond ring on his finger, but after a few stilted pleasantries, the Negro had rung the buzzer and risen, slipping two lottery tickets into Julian's hand as he climbed over him to leave.

He imagined his mother lying desperately ill and his being able to secure only a Negro doctor for her. He toyed with that idea for a few minutes and then dropped it for a momentary vision of himself participating as a sympathizer in a sit-in demonstration. This was possible but he did not linger with it. Instead, he approached the ultimate horror. He brought home a beautiful suspiciously Negroid woman. Prepare yourself, he said. There is nothing you can do about it. This is the woman I've chosen. She's intelligent, dignified, even good, and she's suffered and she hasn't thought it *fun*. Now persecute us, go ahead and persecute us. Drive her out of here, but remember, you're driving me too. His eyes were narrowed and through the indignation he had generated, he saw his mother across the aisle, purple-faced, shrunken to the dwarf-like proportions of her moral nature, sitting like a mummy beneath the ridiculous banner of her hat.

He was tilted out of his fantasy again as the bus stopped. The door opened with a sucking hiss and out of the dark a large, gaily dressed, sullen-looking colored woman got on with a little boy. The child, who might have been four, had on a short plaid suit and a Tyrolean hat with a blue feather in it. Julian hoped that he would sit down beside him and that the woman would push in beside his mother. He could think of no better arrangement.

As she waited for her tokens, the woman was surveying the seating possibilities—he hoped with the idea of sitting where she was least wanted. There was something familiar-looking about her but Julian could not place what it was. She was a giant of a woman. Her face was set not only to meet opposition but to seek it out. The downward tilt of her large lower lip was like a warning sign: DON'T TAMPER WITH ME. Her bulging figure was encased in a green crepe dress and her feet overflowed in red shoes. She had on a hideous hat. A purple velvet flap came down on one side of it and stood up on the other; the rest of it was green and looked like a cushion with the stuffing out. She carried a mammoth red pocketbook that bulged throughout as if it were stuffed with rocks.

To Julian's disappointment, the little boy climbed up on the empty seat beside his mother. His mother lumped all children, black and white, into the common category, "cute," and she thought little Negroes were on the whole cuter than little white children. She smiled at the little boy as he climbed on the seat.

Meanwhile the woman was bearing down upon the empty seat beside Julian. To his annoyance, she squeezed herself into it. He saw his mother's face change as the woman settled herself next to him and he realized with satisfaction that this was more objectionable to her than it was to him. Her face seemed almost gray and there was a look of dull recognition in her eyes, as if suddenly she had sickened at some awful confrontation. Julian saw that it was because she and the woman had, in a sense, swapped sons. Though his mother would not realize the symbolic significance of this, she would feel it. His amusement showed plainly on his face.

The woman next to him muttered something unintelligible to herself. He was conscious of a kind of bristling next to him, a muted growling like that of an angry cat. He could not see anything but the red pocketbook upright on the bulging green thighs. He visualized the woman as she had stood waiting for her tokens—the ponderous figure, rising from the red shoes upward over the solid hips, the mammoth bosom, the haughty face, to the green and purple hat.

His eyes widened.

The vision of the two hats, identical, broke upon him with the radiance of a brilliant sunrise. His face was suddenly lit with joy. He could not believe that Fate had thrust upon his mother such a lesson. He gave a loud chuckle so that she would look at him and see that he saw. She turned her eyes on him slowly. The blue in them seemed to have turned a bruised purple. For a moment he had an uncomfortable sense of her innocence, but it lasted only a second before principle rescued him. Justice entitled him to laugh. His grin hardened until it said to her as plainly as if he were saying aloud: Your punishment exactly fits your pettiness. This should teach you a permanent lesson.

Her eyes shifted to the woman. She seemed unable to bear looking at him and to find the woman preferable. He became conscious again of the bristling presence at his side. The woman was rumbling like a volcano about to become active. His mother's mouth began to twitch slightly at one corner. With a sinking heart, he saw incipient signs of recovery on her face and realized that this was going to strike her suddenly as funny and was going to be no lesson at all. She kept her eyes on the woman and an amused smile came over her face as if the woman were a monkey that had stolen her hat. The little Negro was looking up at her with large fascinated eyes. He had been trying to attract her attention for some time.

"Carver!" the woman said suddenly. "Come heah!"

When he saw that the spotlight was on him at last, Carver drew his feet up and turned himself toward Julian's mother and giggled.

"Carver!" the woman said. "You heah me? Come heah!"

Carver slid down from the seat but remained squatting with his back against the base of it, his head turned slyly around toward Julian's mother, who was smiling at him. The woman reached a hand across the aisle and snatched him to her. He righted himself and hung backwards on her knees, grinning at Julian's mother. "Isn't he cute?" Julian's mother said to the woman with the protruding teeth.

"I reckon he is," the woman said without conviction.

The Negress yanked him upright but he eased out of her grip and shot across the aisle and scrambled, giggling wildly, onto the seat beside his love.

"I think he likes me," Julian's mother said, and smiled at the woman. It was the smile she used when she was being particularly gracious to an inferior. Julian saw everything lost. The lesson had rolled off her like rain on a roof.

The woman stood up and yanked the little boy off the seat as if she were snatching him from contagion. Julian could feel the rage in her at having no weapon like his mother's smile. She gave the child a sharp slap across his leg. He howled once and then thrust his head into her stomach and kicked his feet against her shins. "Be-have," she said vehemently.

The bus stopped and the Negro who had been reading the newspaper got off. The woman moved over and set the little boy down with a thump between herself and Julian. She held him firmly by the knee. In a moment he put his hands in front of his face and peeped at Julian's mother through his fingers.

"I see yoooooooo!" she said and put her hand in front of her face and peeped at him.

The woman slapped his hand down. "Quit yo' foolishness," she said, "before I knock the living Jesus out of you!"

Julian was thankful that the next stop was theirs. He reached up and pulled the cord. The woman reached up and pulled it at the same time. Oh my God, he thought. He had the terrible intuition that when they got off the bus together, his mother would open her purse and give the little boy a nickel. The gesture would be as natural to her as breathing. The bus stopped and the woman got up and lunged to the front, dragging the child, who wished to stay on, after her. Julian and his mother got up and followed. As they neared the door, Julian tried to relieve her of her pocketbook.

"No," she murmured, "I want to give the little boy a nickel."

"No!" Julian hissed. "No!"

She smiled down at the child and opened her bag. The bus door opened and the woman picked him up by the arm and descended with him, hanging at her hip. Once in the street she set him down and shook him.

Julian's mother had to close her purse while she got down the bus step but as soon as her feet were on the ground, she opened it again and began to rummage inside. "I can't find but a penny," she whispered, "but it looks like a new one."

"Don't do it!" Julian said fiercely between his teeth. There was a streetlight on the corner and she hurried to get under it so that she could better see into her pocketbook. The woman was heading off rapidly down the street with the child still hanging backward on her hand.

"Oh little boy!" Julian's mother called and took a few quick steps and caught up with them just beyond the lamppost. "Here's a bright new penny for you," and she held out the coin, which shone bronze in the dim light.

The huge woman turned and for a moment stood, her shoulders lifted and her face frozen with frustrated rage, and stared at Julian's mother. Then all at once she seemed to explode like a piece of machinery that had been given one ounce of pressure too much. Julian saw the black fist swing out with the red pocketbook. He shut his eyes and cringed as he heard the woman shout, "He don't take nobody's pennies!" When he opened his eyes, the woman was disappearing down the street with the little boy staring wide-eyed over her shoulder. Julian's mother was sitting on the sidewalk.

"I told you not to do that," Julian said angrily. "I told you not to do that!"

He stood over her for a minute, gritting his teeth. Her legs were stretched out in front of her and her hat was on her lap. He squatted down and looked her in the face. It was totally expressionless. "You got exactly what you deserved," he said. "Now get up."

He picked up her pocketbook and put what had fallen out back in it. He picked the hat up off her lap. The penny caught his eye on the sidewalk and he picked that up and let it drop before her eyes into the purse. Then he stood up and leaned over and held his hands out to pull her up. She remained immobile. He sighed. Rising above them on either side were black apartment buildings, marked with irregular retangles of light. At the end of the block a man came out of a door and walked off in the opposite direction. "All right," he said, "suppose somebody happens by and wants to know why you're sitting on the sidewalk?"

She took the hand and, breathing hard, pulled heavily up on it and then stood for a moment, swaying slightly as if the spots of light in the darkness were circling around her. Her eyes, shadowed and confused, finally settled on his face. He did not try to conceal his irritation. "I hope this teaches you a lesson," he said. She leaned forward and her eyes raked his face. She seemed trying to determine his identity. Then, as if she found nothing familiar about him, she started off with a headlong movement in the wrong direction.

"Aren't you going on to the Y?" he asked.

"Home," she muttered.

"Well, are we walking?"

For answer she kept going. Julian followed along, his hands behind him. He saw no reason to let the lesson she had had go without backing it up with an explanation of its meaning. She might as well be made to understand what had happened to her. "Don't think that was just an uppity Negro woman," he said. "That was the whole colored race which will no longer take your condescending pennies. That was your black double. She can wear the same hat as you, and to be sure," he added gratuitously (because he thought it was funny), "it looked better on her than it did on you. What all this means," he said, "is that the old world is gone. The old manners are obsolete and your graciousness is not worth a damn." He thought bitterly of the house that had been lost for him. "You aren't who you think you are," he said.

She continued to plow ahead, paying no attention to him. Her hair had come undone on one side. She dropped her pocketbook and took no notice. He stooped and picked it up and handed it to her but she did not take it.

"You needn't act as if the world had come to an end," he said, "because it hasn't. From now on you've got to live in a new world and face a few realities for a change. Buck up," he said, "it won't kill you."

She was breathing fast.

"Let's wait on the bus," he said.

"Home," she said thickly.

"I hate to see you behave like this," he said. "Just like a child. I should be able to expect more of you." He decided to stop where he was and make her stop and wait for a bus. "I'm not going any farther," he said, stopping. "We're going on the bus."

She continued to go on as if she had not heard him. He took a few steps and caught her arm and stopped her. He looked into her face and caught his breath. He was looking into a face he had never seen before. "Tell Grandpa to come get me," she said.

He stared, stricken.

"Tell Caroline to come get me," she said.

Stunned, he let her go and she lurched forward again, walking as if one leg were shorter than the other. A tide of darkness seemed to be sweeping her from him. "Mother!" he cried. "Darling, sweetheart, wait!" Crumpling, she fell to the pavement. He dashed forward and fell at her side, crying, "Mamma, Mamma!" He turned her over. Her face was fiercely distorted. One eye, large and staring, moved slightly to the left as if it had become unmoored. The other remained fixed on him, raked his face again, found nothing and closed.

"Wait here, wait here!" he cried and jumped up and began to run for help toward a cluster of lights he saw in the distance ahead of him. "Help, help!" he shouted, but his voice was thin, scarcely a thread of sound. The lights drifted farther away the faster he ran and his feet moved numbly as if they carried him nowhere. The tide of darkness seemed to sweep him back to her, postponing from moment to moment his entry into the world of guilt and sorrow.

DEBBIE GO HOME

ALAN PATON

It was too late to do anything or hide anything. There was the front gate clicking and Jim de Villiers walking up the path, one hour before his time. The room was strewn with paper and pins, and there was Janie in the new white dress, that cost more than any dress had ever cost in that house, or in most other houses that they knew.

Janie was in a panic because she saw her father walking up the front path, an hour before his time. She was a docile child, and obeyed her father in almost everything. Now she and her mother were deceiving him, and they were going to be caught in the act. She wanted to run, hide, cry, anything but stand there and wait.

Mrs. de Villiers saw that her daughter was in a panic, wringing her hands and wanting to run and hide. "Stand still," she said sharply. "It was my doing, and I'll take the medicine. And don't talk unless your father orders you to."

Then Jim de Villiers opened the front door that led him immediately into the combined living, dining, sitting room of the small house. He was angry at once. It didn't look good to see your daughter in a panic because you got home unexpectedly. It didn't look good to see your wife standing on guard, assuming already that you were going to attack her and her daughter. It didn't look good anyhow to see that you had stumbled on a secret that wasn't meant for you. What if one of his friends had been with him! That would have been a fine thing to see.

He put down his hat and his lunch tin, and then he looked at the scene, daughter being fitted by mother into a dress of some stuff all shining and silver. Then because no one would speak, he had to say, "What's all this about?"

"It's a dress, Jim," said his wife. Some other time he could have laughed, not now, with the whole thing hanging over him. But she didn't wait for him to laugh or not to laugh. She went on as though she had learned a speech in the minute that it took him from the gate to the door.

"It's the first Debutantes' Ball," she said, "and it's going to be next month in the City Hall. Our girls are going to be received by the Administrator and his wife. I didn't think you'd like it, Jim, so I thought we wouldn't tell you."

"Why didn't you think I wouldn't like it?" he asked, purposely obtuse, "I've nothing against a ball."

She didn't answer him, so he said, "who's organising it?"

"The Parkside Mothers' Club, Jim."

De Villiers sat down. "The Parkside Mothers' Club, eh? But what about the Parkside fathers? Are you making fools of them all?"

"They don't hold your views, Jim."

"They don't," he agreed. "If they did, we shouldn't be outcasts in the country where we were born."

He returned to his attack. "Why did you think I'd be against the ball?" he asked.

He watched her stonily, and he looked at his daughter too, but she didn't look at him.

"Shall I tell you why?" he said, and when she didn't answer, he said again, "shall I tell you why?" So that she replied unwillingly "yes, you tell me why."

He went to the job with satisfaction.

"You've got some high white folks to receive our girls," he said. "They'll smile at them and shake their hands, and the Administrator will talk a lot of shit about the brotherhood of man and the sisterhood of women. But if one of our girls went to his house next week, it would be to the back door."

He looked at his daughter and said to her angrily, "haven't you got any pride? Why can't you be what you are, instead of what the white people think you ought to be? They don't think you're good enough to shake hands with them, but for the sake of this brotherhood shit you're allowed to shake hands with the Administrator. I suppose you're proud of that."

He continued to look at Janie, but she would not look at him.

"Talk to me, Jim," said his wife pleadingly, "I got her into this."

The girl came to life.

"You didn't," she said. "I wanted to be presented from the time I first heard."

"Shut your bloody mouth," her father shouted at her. "You don't belong to the Parkside Mothers' Club, do you?"

He turned to his wife. "I'll talk to you," he said. "You want our girls to be received by the Administrator, do you? Received into what? Into a world where they take away your vote and your house. Do you need a white Administrator to do that? How can a white man receive you into our kind of world? And why the hell should he?"

His anger was overpowering him and he stood up.

"Who made him Administrator?" he shouted. "The Government, the same

bloody Government that took away our votes and our houses, and can make me a black man tomorrow if they feel like it. So you get their man to come and receive our daughters at a ball?"

He rounded on his daughter.

"Wait till your brother gets back from the university," he said. "Tell him you're going to a Debutantes' Ball, and a white man is going to welcome you into the shitting world that he and his friends have made for you. What do you think he'll have to say?"

He put his head in his hands in such a way that his wife called out "Jim, Jim," and took a step towards him.

"Don't touch me," he said. "It's you who's driving me mad, licking the hand that whips us. Making me ashamed of all coloured people."

Mother and daughter watched him anxiously, but he suddenly pulled himself together.

"Where did you get the money for the dress?" he asked. "From what I give you?"

"No, Jim. I sewed for it."

"How much was it?"

"Four pounds."

He spoke to his daughter. "Take it off," he said, "and never put it on again." He sat down again, trembling a little.

Janie looked at her mother.

"Go to your room and take it off," said her mother, "and stay there till you're called."

When her daughter had gone she said, "Jim, go and lie down."

"Lie down? What for?"

"You're sick."

"Yes, I'm sick all right, of all this belly-creeping to the same people that take away our rights."

She shook her head at him.

"Why are you home early?" she asked.

She knew him well. He could never hide anything, it all showed in his face. Something was badly wrong. When something was wrong, all the heart went out of him.

"There's trouble at the factory," she said.

He put his head in his hands again, this time covering his face. She went and stood by him, and said to him, "have they put you off?"

He shook his head. "Not yet," he said.

"When will they put you off?"

"We don't know. It's not certain yet."

"What's the matter? Is the market bad?"

"No."

"Jim, I can't hear you, speaking through your hands like that." She took his hands away from his face, and knelt down by him, holding them.

"Are they dissatisfied, Jim?"

"No."

"Do they say you're too old?"

"No."

Baffled, she searched his face. He had brought bad news, but he couldn't tell.

"Jim, you must tell me. I *must* know."

Then it came, seeming to tear at him as it came out.

"It's a new law," he said hoarsely. "A new law. The Industrial Conciliation Act."

"What does it say, Jim?"

"It says the Minister can reserve any occupation. So we may have to go. We, we. The Coloured men."

She jumped to her feet. "The wickedness," she said. "O the wickedness!"

She had no more to say, nor he, until she asked him again, "Why did you come home early, Jim?"

"I was sick," he said. "Just plain sick. I seemed to bring up all the food I ever ate. The boss said, what's the matter, Jim? I said it just made me sick to hear there was such a law."

"The wickedness," she said. "O the wickedness!"

"The boss said, Jim, it's not my fault. I said to him, you're white, aren't you? So he went away."

Suddenly he shouted at her.

"I suppose you think I did wrong. I suppose you think I should of got down on my belly and licked his hand."

"No, Jim, I would never have wanted that."

"But you want your daughter to shake their hands, and curtsy to them, and be received into their bloody world!"

"That's why!" she said. "There's many a hard thing coming to her as well. I'd like her to have one night, in a nice dress and the coloured lights, dancing before the Administrator in the City Hall. We get kicks aplenty. I wanted her to have a boost. And for one night the young men will be wearing gloves, and bowing to her as gentlemanly as you like, not pawing at her in some dark yard."

"It was good enough for us," he said.

"You never pawed at me," she said. "But don't you want it to be better for her? Don't you want her to begin where you left off?"

"Where I left off?" he asked. "Where did I leave off? With a law that took away my job, and a law that took away my vote, and a law that's going to take away my house, all because I've a coloured skin? Can't you see it's going to be worse for her?"

"That may be," she said. "That's more reason I want her to have just this one night. Jim, go and lie down. I'll bring you a cup of tea."

He got to his feet.

"All right, I'll go," he said. Then perhaps he thought he was being too obedient. He said, "you go and comfort the debutante."

He went into their bedroom and shut the door, and she sat down and put her head in her hands too, not so much hopelessly because she was never hopeless, but because she couldn't see a way out of this hopeless mess. She sat there thinking for a long time, till a voice said to her, "what's got you down, ma?"

"Nothing's got me down," she said, "not yet. Johnny, how long have you been home?"

"Quite a time," said Johnny, "quite a time."

He was a gum-chewing nonchalant, and one of the militant students at the university.

"How many things have you heard?" she asked, "One or two?"

"Two."

"What are they?"

"The lost job," he said. "And the lost ball."

"And the lost mother," she said, "who doesn't know what to do. But it's your father I worry about."

"He hopes too much," said Johnny. "He knows what the world is like, yet he goes on hoping. And when the blow comes, it knocks him down."

"Don't you hope?" she asked.

"I hope?" he said. He laughed with worldly wisdom. "I hope for nothing," he said fiercely, "nothing, nothing, nothing. I hope for nothing that I won't get my own way." He laughed again. "You ought to be pleased that I'm that way," he said. "What does the Bible say? Blessed is he who hopes for nothing for he shall not be disappointed."

"The Bible doesn't say that," she said.

He shrugged his shoulders.

"How would I know? But even if the Bible doesn't say it, it's God's own truth."

"Johnny, you've got to help. You can think what you like, believe what you like. But you've got to help me to get Janie to that Ball."

His face turned ugly.

"To be received by the Administrator," he said. "Not me."

"I know what you say," she said. "That he's white. I know he's white too. But the night of the Ball he's the Administrator, he's not white any more, he's got no colour."

"He's always got colour for me," said Johnny, "a dirty stinking white. And I'll help no sister of mine to shake his hand. Can you see the sense of it? It's not the ordinary people we're allowed to shake hands with, only the big shots. How does that make sense to you?"

"It makes sense to me," she said pleadingly. "He's the Administrator, he belongs to us all." She waved him quiet, "Give me a chance to speak," she said, "I know we didn't elect him or appoint him," she said, "but in a way he's above all colour. But that's not my argument, Johnny. . . ."

"I know your argument," he said. "You want her to have one night, one night of magic and romance. You want her to go in a shining silver dress, like the Duchess of Musgrave Road." He parodied her argument without pity. *"She'll get kicks, poor little girl, and they'll take something more away from her when she grows up, and they'll call her a tottie and think that she'd sell herself for a bottle of gin, but this one night—just this one night—let them treat her like a queen."*

The boy was pouring it out hot and strong, till he looked at his mother, and saw that she had put her head in her hands again. He lost his enthusiasm at once, and said to her "Why should I help you for that?"

She didn't lift her head, but she said to him, "because I'm your mother, because it's your mother wants this one thing, this one harmless thing."

There was a knock at the door, and she said to him in a whisper, "I can't face a visitor, make some excuse." Then he saw that she was afraid of weeping. He opened the door, and went out quickly, but in a minute he was back. His mother was wiping her eyes, and she said to him, "who was it?"

"Someone wanting the Tomlinsons," he said.

He stood and looked at her, and remembered a thousand acts of love. He went to her and said "don't cry, ma, I'll do it for you. This once, and never again."

"I shan't want it again," she said. "Only this once."

He threw up his eyes to heaven piously. *"Only this once," he said in a false high voice, "let her be treated like a queen."*

She blew her nose and laughed.

"Tell your father, I'm making the tea," she said. "I hope this won't get you into trouble with the Unity Movement, Johnny."

"That would no doubt cause you grief and pain," he said.

"I can't say that," she said, "but I don't want trouble for you."

"I'll look after myself," he said, chewing his gum.

He went to his parents' bedroom and knocked on the door. His father said "come in," and there he was lying on the bed.

"Have a cigarette, dad."

"Thanks, Johnny, don't mind if I do."

"Smoke while you can," advised his son cynically. "Ma's told me about the job. Has it got you down?"

"Yes, son," said his father apologetically. "For the time it's got me down."

"It's because you hope for the best and fear for the worst," said his son. "I expect the worst, so when it comes, I don't take it hard."

"You were lucky," said his father defensively. "I was brought up in a world where we always hoped for the best. But you live in a time when no false hopes are left. I was a Smuts man, don't forget."

"Smuts," said Johnny contemptuously. "Who was Smuts?"

"Johnny," said his father, "you see me down now, but I want to be up tomorrow. I want to speak at the union meeting. Will you help me with a speech?"

"A hard speech?"

Jim de Villiers considered it.

"I want a fighting speech," he said. "I want to stand up for our rights, but I don't want to blackguard the whites. I don't want trouble, Johnny."

"You don't, eh? Then why don't you let Janie go to the Ball?"

Jim looked at his son. "I don't get you," he said. "Are you wanting Janie to go to the Ball?"

Johnny chewed his gum. "I don't want her to go to the Ball," he said carelessly. "But her going to the Ball is the price of a speech."

His father sat up on the bed. "Do I hear you right?" he asked.

"You hear me right," said Johnny. "It's the price for a fighting speech, free of all hatred, bitterness, resentment, full of shit about freedom and the rights of man. No one will give you a better."

"Why are you doing this, Johnny?"

Johnny chewed his gum. "Because Ma said to me, I'm your mother," he said. "And your mother wants your sister to have a night as a queen."

He looked at his father with expressionless eyes.

His father said, "I don't understand you, Johnny."

"You don't have to understand me," said Johnny. "You just have to tell me, is she going to the Ball?"

"I don't understand you, Johnny. It was mainly because of you that I said she couldn't go."

"Now it'll be mainly because of me that you'll say she can go," said Johnny.

Jim de Villiers lay down again. "You beat me," he said.

"I beat lots of people," said his son. "Just tell me, can she go, so I can get on with the speech."

"All right, she can go," he said, "on one condition. Tell me how you justify it."

"Rock-bottom necessity," said Johnny. "If I boycott American food, and I'm dying of hunger, and everywhere round me is American food, then I eat American food."

"You eat American food so you can go on boycotting it," said de Villiers.

Johnny smiled against his will. "You're getting better," he said. "Listen, Dad, I can't study in a house of weeping women."

"Was your mother weeping?"

"As near as she gets."

"Son, don't tell her we bargained for it."

"O.K. I won't. See you again."

He went to his room which was no more than a bit of enclosed verandah, and sat down at his small table to think about the speech on freedom and the rights of man. Then on second thoughts he got up, and hauled some posters out from under his bed and put them against the wall where they could be seen. They were all headed DEBUTANTES BALL. One said, DEBBIE GO HOME, and another, ornamented with a bar of music, asked WHO STOLE MY VOTE AWAY? The third one was his own, but his friends thought it was too learned, for it said: WELCOME, SPICK LITTLE LICKSPITTLE. When he had put them up, he sat down at the table, but his thoughts were not on the speech, they were on his mother's entrance.

Then she burst in, with her eyes shining, and she would have embraced him if she had not suddenly seen the new decorations.

"I suppose you came to thank me," he said.

"I did."

She sat down in the other chair, and looked at the posters.

"You can't do that now," she said.

"Why not?"

"You can't," she said. *"You can't give with one hand and take away with the other."*

"I gave you your share," he said hotly. *"That's my share there."*

"You can't do it," she said. *"If you take your share, mine's worth nothing. Do you think that's fair?"*

"I can't help it," he said. *"We fixed this up long before I knew you wanted Janie to go."* When she said nothing, he went on, *"what we're doing is an important thing. You can't just stop because your sister's going to a ball."*

"I understand what you're doing," she said. *"I understand what you want, you and your friends. But don't you ever let up? Don't you ever have mercy on anyone?"*

"Mercy," he said, with a sudden flight of fancy, *"it's like a door of a cage. Open it once, and everything's gone."*

"Do you know Hazel's going to the Ball?" she asked.

"Yes," he said defiantly.

"What about Fred?" she asked. *"Is he acting the same way as you?"*

"Yes."

"The world's mad," she said. She stood up and rubbed her brow with the back of her hand. *"Brother against sister, husband against wife. You know what Christ said?"*

He looked at her with annoyance. She took an unfair advantage of him by talking religion. He could sneer at white people's religion, but not at hers.

"Go your own way," she said. *"But let me teach you one thing about giving. When you give, give with your whole heart. Don't keep half of it back."*

She went out and closed his door. As all his attention had been on her entrance, now it was on her exit. He heard no doors opening, no voices speaking. The house was quite silent. When he could stand it no more, he followed her, and found her sitting in the livingroom, in the evening dark.

"What are you doing?" he asked.

She answered him in a matter-of-fact voice. That was her way, that was why you had to live your life with her to know what she was.

"I'm thinking it out," she said.

She didn't ask for help, he knew she wouldn't ask any. A spiritless husband, a day-dreaming daughter, a tough son, they weren't much use to her.

"If it'll help you," he said, "I won't let Janie see me."

She considered his proposition. "How will you do that?" she asked. "You know where the cars will stop, outside the main foyer. Where will you be, inside or out?"

"Wouldn't you like to know?" he asked. "All I'm saying is, I won't let Janie see me."

"Is Fred doing the same for Hazel?" she asked.

He could not help admiring her cleverness.

"That's Fred's business," he said.

She got up and he saw that she was intending to kiss him, so he waved her away.

"Don't thank me too much," he said harshly.

"She'll see all the others."

But she kissed him all the same.

"Give the kiss to Fred," she said. "Now I'll go and tell Janie the news."

At Janie's door she turned and gave him a smile.

"You'd better get on with your father's speech," she said.

FLYING HOME

RALPH ELLISON

When Todd came to, he saw two faces suspended above him in a sun so hot and blinding that he could not tell if they were black or white. He stirred, feeling a pain that burned as though his whole body had been laid open to the sun which glared into his eyes. For a moment an old fear of being touched by white hands seized him. Then the very sharpness of the pain began slowly to clear his head. Sounds came to him dimly. He done come to. Who are they? he thought. Naw he ain't, I coulda sworn he was white. Then he heard clearly:

"You hurt bad?"

Something within him uncoiled. It was a Negro sound.

"He's still out," he heard.

"Give 'im time. . . . Say, son, you hurt bad?"

Was he? There was that awful pain. He lay rigid, hearing their breathing and trying to weave a meaning between them and his being stretched painfully upon the ground. He watched them warily, his mind traveling back over a painful distance. Jagged scenes, swiftly unfolding as in a movie trailer, reeled through his mind, and he saw himself piloting a tailspinning plane and landing and landing and falling from the cockpit and trying to stand. Then, as in a great silence, he remembered the sound of crunching bone, and now, looking up into the anxious faces of an old Negro man and a boy from where he lay in the same field, the memory sickened him and he wanted to remember no more.

"How you feel, son?"

Todd hesitated, as though to answer would be to admit an inacceptable weakness. Then, "It's my ankle," he said.

"Which one?"

"The left."

With a sense of remoteness he watched the old man bend and remove his boot, feeling the pressure ease.

"That any better?"

"A lot. Thank you."

He had the sensation of discussing someone else, that his concern was with some far more important thing, which for some reason escaped him.

"You done broke it bad," the old man said. "We have to get you to a doctor."

He felt that he had been thrown into a tailspin. He looked at his watch; how long had he been here? He knew there was but one important thing in the world, to get the plane back to the field before his officers were displeased.

"Help me up," he said. "Into the ship."

"But it's broke too bad. . . ."

"Give me your arm!"

"But, son . . ."

Clutching the old man's arm he pulled himself up, keeping his left leg clear, thinking, "I'd never make him understand," as the leather-smooth face came parallel with his own.

"Now, let's see."

He pushed the old man back, hearing a bird's insistent shrill. He swayed giddily. Blackness washed over him, like infiinity.

"You best sit down."

"No, I'm O.K."

"But, son. You jus' gonna make it worse. . . ."

It was a fact that everything in him cried out to deny, even against the flaming pain in his ankle. He would have to try again.

"You mess with that ankle they have to cut your foot off," he heard.

Holding his breath, he started up again. It pained so badly that he had to bite his lips to keep from crying out and he allowed them to help him down with a pang of despair.

"It's best you take it easy. We gon' git you a doctor."

Of all the luck, he thought. Of all the rotten luck, now I have done it. The fumes of high-octane gasoline clung in the heat, taunting him.

"We kin ride him into town on old Ned," the boy said.

Ned? He turned, seeing the boy point toward an ox team browsing where the buried blade of a plow marked the end of a furrow. Thoughts of himself riding an ox through the town, past streets full of white faces, down the concrete runways of the airfield made swift images of humiliation in his mind. With a pang he remembered his girl's last letter. "Todd," she had written, "I don't need the papers to tell me you had the intelligence to fly. And I have always known you to be as brave as anyone else. The papers annoy me. Don't you be contented to prove over and over again that you're brave or skillful just because you're black, Todd. I think they keep beating that dead horse because they don't want to say why you boys are not yet fighting. I'm really disappointed, Todd. Anyone with brains can learn to fly, but then what? What about using it, and who will you use it for? I wish, dear, you'd write about this. I sometimes think they're playing a trick on us. It's very humiliating. . . ." He wiped cold sweat from his face, thinking, What does she know of humiliation? She's never been down South. Now the humiliation would come. When you must have them judge you, knowing that they never accept your mistakes as your own, but hold it against your whole race—that was humiliation. Yes, and humiliation was when you could never be simply yourself, when you were always a part of this old black ignorant man. Sure, he's all right. Nice and kind and helpful. But he's not you. Well, there's one humiliation I can spare myself.

"No," he said, "I have orders not to leave the ship. . . ."

"Aw," the old man said. Then turning to the boy, "Teddy, then you better hustle down to Mister Graves and get him to come. . . ."

"No, wait!" he protested before he was fully aware. Graves might be white. "Just have him get word to the field, please. They'll take care of the rest."

He saw the boy leave, running.

"How far does he have to go?"

"Might' nigh a mile."

He rested back, looking at the dusty face of his watch. But now they know something has happened, he thought. In the ship there was a perfectly good radio, but it was useless. The old fellow would never operate it. That buzzard knocked me back a hundred years, he thought. Irony danced within him like the gnats circling the old man's head. With all I've learned I'm dependent upon this "peasant's" sense of time and space. His leg throbbed. In the plane, instead of time being measured by the rhythms of pain and a kid's legs, the instruments would have told him at a glance. Twisting upon his elbows he saw where dust had powdered the plane's fuselage, feeling the lump form in his throat that was always there when he thought of flight. It's crouched there, he thought, like the abandoned shell of a locust. I'm naked without it. Not a machine, a suit of clothes you wear. And with a sudden embarrassment and wonder he whispered, "It's the only dignity I have. . . ."

He saw the old man watching, his torn overalls clinging limply to him in the heat. He felt a sharp need to tell the old man what he felt. But that would be meaningless. If I tried to explain why I need to fly back, he'd think I was simply afraid of white officers. But it's more than fear . . . a sense of anguish clung to him like the veil of sweat that hugged his face. He watched the old man, hearing him humming snatches of a tune as he admired the plane. He felt a furtive sense of resentment. Such old men often came to the field to watch the pilots with childish eyes. At first it had made him proud; they had been a meaningful part of a new experience. But soon he realized they did not understand his accomplishments and they came to shame and embarrass him, like the distasteful praise of an idiot. A part of the meaning of flying had gone then, and he had not been able to regain it. If I were a prizefighter I would be more human, he thought. Not a monkey doing tricks, but a man. They were pleased simply that he was a Negro who could fly, and that was not enough. He felt cut off from them by age, by understanding, by sensibility, by technology and by his need to measure himself against the mirror of other men's appreciation. Somehow he felt betrayed, as he had when as a child he grew to discover that his father was dead. Now for him any real appreciation lay with his white officers; and with them he could never be sure. Between ignorant black men and condescending whites, his course of flight seemed mapped by the nature of things away from all needed and natural landmarks. Under some sealed orders, couched in ever more technical and mysterious terms, his path curved swiftly away from both the shame the old man symbolized and the cloudy terrain of white men's regard. Flying blind, he knew but one point of landing and there he would receive his wings. After that the enemy would appreciate his skill and he would assume his deepest meaning, he thought sadly, neither from those who condescended nor from those who praised without understanding, but from the enemy who would recognize his manhood and skill in terms of hate. . . .

He sighed, seeing the oxen making queer, prehistoric shadows against the dry brown earth.

"You just take it easy, son," the old man soothed. "That boy won't take long. Crazy as he is about airplanes."

"I can wait," he said.

"What kinda airplane you call this here'n?"

"An Advanced Trainer," he said, seeing the old man smile. His fingers were like gnarled dark wood against the metal as he touched the low-slung wing.

" 'Bout how fast can she fly?"

"Over two hundred an hour."

"Lawd! That's so fast I bet it don't seem like you moving!"

"Holding himself rigid, Todd opened his flying suit. The shade had gone and he lay in a ball of fire.

"You mind if I take a look inside? I was always curious to see. . . ."

"Help yourself. Just don't touch anything."

He heard him climb upon the metal wing, grunting. Now the questions would start. Well, so you don't have to think to answer. . . .

He saw the old man looking over into the cockpit, his eyes bright as a child's.

"You must have to know a lot to work all these here things."

He was silent, seeing him step down and kneel beside him.

"Son, how come you want to fly way up there in the air?"

Because it's the most meaningful act in the world . . . because it makes me less like you, he thought.

But he said: "Because I like it, I guess. It's as good a way to fight and die as I know."

"Yeah? I guess you right," the old man said. "But how long you think before they gonna let you all fight?"

He tensed. This was the question all Negroes asked, put with the same timid hopefulness and longing that always opened a greater void within him than that he had felt beneath the plane the first time he had flown. He felt light-headed. It came to him suddenly that there was something sinister about the conversation, that he was flying unwillingly into unsafe and uncharted regions. If he could only be insulting and tell this old man who was trying to help him to shut up!

"I bet you one thing . . ."

"Yes?"

"That you was plenty scared coming down."

He did not answer. Like a dog on a trail the old man seemed to smell out his fears and he felt anger bubble within him.

"You sho' scared me. When I seen you coming down in that thing with it a-rollin' and a-jumpin' like a pitchin' hoss, I thought sho' you was a goner. I almost had me a stroke!"

He saw the old man grinning, "Ever'thin's been happening round here this morning, come to think of it.

"Like what?" he asked.

"Well, first thing I know, here come two white fellers looking for Mister Rudolph, that's Mister Graves's cousin. That got me worked up right away...."

"Why?"

"Why? 'Cause he done broke outta the crazy house, that's why. He liable to kill somebody," he said. "They oughta have him by now though. Then here you come. First I think it's one of them white boys. Then doggone if you don't fall outta there. Lawd, I'd done heard about you boys but I haven't never seen one o' you-all. Cain't tell you how it felt to see somebody what look like me in a airplane!"

The old man talked on, the sound streaming around Todd's thoughts like air flowing over the fuselage of a flying plane. You were a fool, he thought, remembering how before the spin the sun had blazed bright against the billboard signs beyond the town, and how a boy's blue kite had bloomed beneath him, tugging gently in the wind like a strange, odd-shaped flower. He had once flown such kites himself and tried to find the boy at the end of the invisible cord. But he had been flying too high and too fast. He had climbed steeply away in exultation. Too steeply, he thought. And one of the first rules you learn is that if the angle of thrust is too steep the plane goes into a spin. And then, instead of pulling out of it and going into a dive you let a buzzard panic you. A lousy buzzard!

"Son, what made all that blood on the glass?"

"A buzzard," he said, remembering how the blood and feathers had sprayed back against the hatch. It had been as though he had flown into a storm of blood and blackness.

"Well, I declare! They's lots of 'em around here. They after dead things. Don't eat nothing what's alive."

"A little bit more and he would have made a meal out of me," Todd said grimly.

"They bad luck all right. Teddy's got a name for 'em, calls 'em jimcrows," the old man laughed.

"It's a damned good name."

"They the damnedest birds. Once I seen a hoss all stretched out like he was sick, you know. So I hollers, 'Gid up from there, suh!' Just to make sho! An' doggone, son, if I don't see two ole jimcrows come flying right up outa that hoss's insides! Yessuh! The sun was shinin' on 'em and they couldn't a been no greasier if they'd been eating barbecue."

Todd thought he would vomit, his stomach quivered.

"You made that up," he said.

"Nawsuh! Saw him just like I see you."

"Well, I'm glad it was you."

"You see lots a funny things down here, son."

"No, I'll let you see them," he said.

"By the way, the white folks round here don't like to see you boys up there in the sky. They ever bother you?"

"No."

"Well, they'd like to."

"Someone always wants to bother someone else," Todd said. "How do you know?"

"I just know."

"Well," he said defensively, "no one has bothered us."

Blood pounded in his ears as he looked away into space. He tensed, seeing a black spot in the sky, and strained to confirm what he could not clearly see.

"What does that look like to you?" he asked excitedly.

"Just another bad luck, son."

Then he saw the movement of wings with disappointment. It was gliding smoothly down, wings outspread, tail feathers gripping the air, down swiftly— gone behind the green screen of trees. It was like a bird he had imagined there, only the sloping branches of the pines remained, sharp against the pale stretch of sky. He lay barely breathing and stared at the point where it had disappeared, caught in a spell of loathing and admiration. Why did they make them so disgusting and yet teach them to fly so well? It's like when I was up in heaven, he heard, starting.

The old man was chuckling, rubbing his stubbled chin.

"What did you say?"

"Sho', I died and went to heaven . . . maybe by time I tell you about it they be done come after you."

"I hope so," he said wearily.

"You boys ever sit around and swap lies?"

"Not often. Is this going to be one?"

"Well, I ain't so sho', on account of it took place when I was dead."

The old man paused, "That wasn't no lie 'bout the buzzards, though."

"All right," he said.

"Sho' you want to hear 'bout heaven?"

"Please," he answered, resting his head upon his arm.

"Well, I went to heaven and right away started to sproutin' me some wings. Six good ones, they was. Just like them the white angels had. I couldn't hardly believe it. I was so glad that I went off on some clouds by myself and tried 'em out. You know, 'cause I didn't want to make a fool outta myself the first thing. . . ."

It's an old tale, Todd thought. Told me years ago. Had forgotten. But at least it will keep him from talking about buzzards.

He closed his eyes, listening.

". . . First thing I done was to git up on a low cloud and jump off. And dog- gone, boy, if them wings didn't work! First I tried the right; then I tried the left; then I tried 'em both together. Then Lawd, I started to move on out among the folks. I let 'em see me. . . ."

He saw the old man gesturing flight with his arms, his face full of mock pride as he indicated an imaginary crowd, thinking, It'll be in the newspapers, as he heard, ". . . so I went and found me some colored angels—somehow I didn't believe I was an angel till I seen a real black one, ha, yes! Then I was sho'—but they tole me I better come down 'cause us colored folks had to wear a special kin' a harness when we flew. That was how come they wasn't flyin'. Oh yes, an' you had to be extra strong for a black man even, to fly with one of them harnesses. . . ."

This is a new turn, Todd thought, what's he driving at?

"So I said to myself, I ain't gonna be bothered with no harness! Oh naw! 'Cause if God let you sprout wings you oughta have sense enough not to let nobody make you wear something what gits in the way of flyin'. So I starts to flyin'. Heck, son," he chuckled, his eyes twinkling, "you know I had to let eve'ybody know that old Jefferson could fly good as anybody else. And I could too, fly smooth as a bird! I could even loop-the-loop—only I had to make sho' to keep my long white robe down roun' my ankles. . . ."

Todd felt uneasy. He wanted to laugh at the joke, but his body refused, as of an independent will. He felt as he had as a child when after he had chewed a sugar-coated pill which his mother had given him, she had laughed at his efforts to remove the terrible taste.

". . . Well," he heard, "I was doing all right 'til I got to speeding. Found out I could fan up a right strong breeze, I could fly so fast. I could do all kin'sa stunts too. I started flying up to the stars and divin' down and zooming roun' the moon. Man, I like to scare the devil outa some ole white angels. I was raisin' hell. Not that I meant any harm, son. But I was just feeling good. It was so good to know I was free at last. I accidentally knocked the tips offa some stars and they tell me I caused a storm and a coupla lynchings down here in Macon County—though I swear I believe them boys what said that was making up lies on me. . . ."

He's mocking me, Todd thought angrily. He thinks it's a joke. Grinning down at me . . . His throat was dry. He looked at his watch; why the hell didn't they come? Since they had to, why? One day I was flying down one of them heavenly streets. You got yourself into it, Todd thought. Like Jonah in the whale.

"Justa throwin' feathers in everybody's face. An' ole Saint Peter called me in. Said, 'Jefferson, tell me two things, what you doin' flyin' without a harness; an' how come you flyin' so fast?' So I tole him I was flyin' without a harness 'cause it got in my way, but I couldn'ta been flyin' so fast, 'cause I wasn't usin' but one wing. Saint Peter said, 'You wasn't flyin' with but one wing?' 'Yessuh,' I says, scared-like. So he says, 'Well, since you got sucha extra fine pair of wings you can leave off yo' harness awhile. But from now on none of that there one-wing flyin', 'cause you gittin' up too damn much speed!' "

And with one mouth full of bad teeth you're making too damned much talk, thought Todd. Why don't I send him after the boy? His body ached from the hard ground and seeking to shift his position he twisted his ankle and hated himself for crying out.

"It gittin' worse?"

"I . . . I twisted it," he groaned.

"Try not to think about it, son. That's what I do."

He bit his lips, fighting pain with counter-pain as the voice resumed its rhythmical droning. Jefferson seemed caught in his own creation.

" . . . After all that trouble I just floated roun' heaven in slow motion. But I forgot, like colored folks will do, and got to flyin' with one wing again. This time I was restin' my old broken arm and got to flyin' fast enough to shame the devil. I was comin' so fast, Lawd, I got myself called befo' ole Saint Peter again. He said, 'Jeff, didn't I warn you 'bout that speedin'?' 'Yessuh,' I says, 'but it was an accident.' He looked at me sad-like and shook his head and I knowed I was gone. He said, 'Jeff, you and that speedin' is a danger to the heavenly community. If I was to let you keep on flyin', heaven wouldn't be nothin' but uproar. Jeff, you got to go!' Son, I argued and pleaded with that old white man, but it didn't do a bit of good. They rushed me straight to them pearly gates and gimme a parachute and a map of the state of Alabama . . .''

Todd heard him laughing so that he could hardly speak, making a screen between them upon which his humiliation glowed like fire.

"Maybe you'd better stop awhile," he said, his voice unreal.

"Ain't much more," Jefferson laughed. "When they gimme the parachute ole Saint Peter ask me if I wanted to say a few words before I went. I felt so bad I couldn't hardly look at him, specially with all them white angels standin' around. Then somebody laughed and made me mad. So I tole him, 'Well, you done took my wings. And you puttin' me out. You got charge of things so's I can't do nothin' about it. But you got to admit just this: While I was up here I was the flyinest sonofabitch what ever hit heaven!"

At the burst of laughter Todd felt such an intense humiliation that only great violence would wash it away. The laughter which shook the old man like a boiling purge set up vibrations of guilt within him which not even the intricate machinery of the plane would have been adequate to transform and he heard himself screaming, "Why do you laugh at me this way?"

He hated himself at that moment, but he had lost control. He saw Jefferson's mouth fall open, "What—?"

"Answer me!"

His blood pounded as though it would surely burst his temples and he tried to reach the old man and fell, screaming, "Can I help it because they won't let us actually fly? Maybe we are a bunch of buzzards feeding on a dead horse, but we can hope to be eagles, can't we? Can't we?"

He fell back, exhausted, his ankle pounding. The saliva was like straw in his mouth. If he had the strength he would strangle this old man. This grinning, gray-headed clown who made him feel as he felt when watched by the white officers at the field. And yet this old man had neither power, prestige, rank nor technique. Nothing that could rid him of this terrible feeling. He watched him, seeing his face struggle to express a turmoil of feeling.

"What you mean, son? What you talking 'bout . . . ?"

"Go away. Go tell your tales to the white folks."

"But I didn't mean nothing like that. . . . I . . . I wasn't tryin' to hurt your feelings. . . ."

"Please. Get the hell away from me!"

"But I didn't, son. I didn't mean all them things a-tall."

Todd shook as with a chill, searching Jefferson's face for a trace of the mockery he had seen there. But now the face was somber and tired and old. He was confused. He could not be sure that there had ever been laughter there, that Jefferson had ever really laughed in his whole life. He saw Jefferson reach out to touch him and shrank away, wondering if anything except the pain, now causing his vision to waver, was real. Perhaps he had imagined it all.

"Don't let it get you down, son," the voice said pensively.

He heard Jefferson sigh wearily, as though he felt more than he could say. His anger ebbed, leaving only the pain.

"I'm sorry," he mumbled.

"You just wore out with pain, was all. . . ."

He saw him through a blur, smiling. And for a second he felt the embarrassed silence of understanding flutter between them.

"What you was doin' flyin' over this section, son? Wasn't you scared they might shoot you for a cow?"

Todd tensed. Was he being laughed at again? But before he could decide, the pain shook him and a part of him was lying calmly behind the screen of pain that had fallen between them, recalling the first time he had ever seen a plane. It was as though an endless series of hangars had been shaken ajar in the air base of his memory and from each, like a young wasp emerging from its cell, arose the memory of a plane.

The first time I ever saw a plane I was very small and planes were new in the world. I was four-and-a-half and the only plane that I had ever seen was a model suspended from the ceiling of the automobile exhibit at the State Fair. But I did not know that it was only a model. I did not know how large a real plane was, nor how expensive. To me it was a fascinating toy, complete in itself, which my mother said could only be owned by rich little white boys. I stood rigid with admiration, my head straining backwards as I watched the gray little plane describing arcs above the gleaming tops of the automobiles. And I vowed that, rich or poor, someday I would own such a toy. My mother had to drag me out of the exhibit and not even the merry-go-round, the Ferris wheel, or the racing horses could hold my attention for the rest of the Fair. I was too busy imitating the tiny drone of the plane with my lips, and imitating with my hands the motion, swift and circling, that it made in flight.

After that I no longer used the pieces of lumber that lay about our back yard to construct wagons and autos . . . now it was used for airplanes. I built biplanes, using pieces of board for wings, a small box for the fuselage, another piece of wood for the rudder. The trip to the Fair had brought something new into my small world. I asked my mother repeatedly when the Fair would come back again. I'd lie in the grass and watch the sky, and each fighting bird became a soaring plane. I would have been good a year just to have seen a plane again. I became a nuisance to everyone with my questions about airplanes. But planes were new to the old folks, too, and there was little that they could tell me. Only my uncle knew some of the answers. And better still, he could carve propellers from pieces of wood that would whirl rapidly in the wind, wobbling noisily upon oiled nails.

I wanted a plane more than I'd wanted anything; more than I wanted the red wagon with rubber tires, more than the train that ran on a track with its train of cars. I asked my mother over and over again:

"Mamma?"

"What do you want, boy?" she'd say.

"Mamma, will you get mad if I ask you?" I'd say.

"What do you want now? I ain't got time to be answering a lot of fool questions. What you want?"

"Mamma, when you gonna get me one . . . ?" I'd ask.

"Get you one what?" she'd say.

"You know, Momma; what I been asking you. . . ."

"Boy," she'd say, "if you don't want a spanking you better come on an' tell me what you talking about so I can get on with my work."

"Aw, Mamma, you know. . . ."

"What I just tell you?" she'd say.

"I mean when you gonna buy me a airplane."

"AIRPLANE! Boy, is you crazy? How many times I have to tell you to stop that foolishness. I done told you them things cost too much. I bet I'm gon' wham the living daylight out of you if you don't quit worrying me 'bout them things!"

But this did not stop me, and a few days later I'd try all over again.

Then one day a strange thing happened. It was spring and for some reason I had been hot and irritable all morning. It was a beautiful spring. I could feel it as I played barefoot in the backyard. Blossoms hung from the thorny black locust trees like clusters of fragrant white grapes. Butterflies flickered in the sunlight above the short new dew-wet grass. I had gone in the house for bread and butter and coming out I heard a steady unfamiliar drone. It was unlike anything I had ever heard before. I tried to place the sound. It was no use. It was a sensation like that I had when searching for my father's watch, heard ticking unseen in a room. It made me feel as though I had forgotten to perform some task that my mother had ordered . . . then I located it, overhead. In the sky, flying quite low and about a hundred yards off was a plane! It came so slowly that it seemed barely to move. My mouth hung wide; my bread and butter fell into the dirt. I wanted to jump up and down and cheer. And when the idea struck I trembled with excitement: "Some little white boy's plane's done flew away and all I got to do is stretch out my hands and it'll be mine!" It was a little plane like that at the Fair, flying no higher than the eaves of our roof. Seeing it come steadily forward I felt the world grow warm with promise. I opened the screen and climbed over it and clung there, waiting. I would catch the plane as it came over and swing down fast and run into the house before anyone could see me. Then no one could come to claim the plane. It droned nearer. Then when it hung like a silver cross in the blue directly above me I stretched out my hand and grabbed. It was like sticking my finger through a soap bubble. The plane flew on, as though I had simply blown my breath after it. I grabbed again, frantically, trying to catch the tail. My fingers clutched the air and disappointment surged tight and hard in my throat. Giving one last desperate grasp, I strained forward. My fingers ripped from the screen. I was falling. The ground burst hard against me. I drummed the earth with my heels and when my breath returned, I lay there bawling.

My mother rushed through the door.

"What's the matter, chile! What on earth is wrong with you?"

"It's gone! It's gone!"

"What gone?"

"The airplane . . ."

"Airplane?"

"Yessum, jus' like the one at the Fair. . . . I . . . I tried to stop it an' it kep' right on going. . . ."

"When, boy?"

"Just now," I cried, through my tears.

"Where it go, boy, what way?"

"Yonder, there . . ."

She scanned the sky, her arms akimbo and her checkered apron flapping in the wind as I pointed to the fading plane. Finally she looked down at me, slowly shaking her head.

"It's gone! It's gone!" I cried.

"Boy, is you a fool?" she said. "Don't you see that there's a real airplane 'stead of one of them toy ones?"

"Real . . . ?" I forgot to cry. "Real?"

"Yass, real. Don't you know that thing you reaching for is bigger'n a auto? You here trying to reach for it and I bet it's flying 'bout two hundred miles higher'n this roof." She was disgusted with me. "You come on in this house before somebody else sees what a fool you done turned out to be. You must think these here lil ole arms of you'n is mighty long. . . ."

I was carried into the house and undressed for bed and the doctor was called. I cried bitterly, as much from the disappointment of finding the plane so far beyond my reach as from the pain.

When the doctor came I heard my mother telling him about the plane and asking if anything was wrong with my mind. He explained that I had had a fever for several hours. But I was kept in bed for a week and I constantly saw the plane in my sleep, flying just beyond my fingertips, sailing so slowly that it seemed barely to move. And each time I'd reach out to grab it I'd miss and through each dream I'd hear my grandma warning:

> *Young man, young man,*
> *Yo' arms too short*
> *To box with God. . . .*

"Hey, son!"

At first he did not know where he was and looked at the old man pointing, with blurred eyes.

"Ain't that one of you-all's airplanes coming after you?"

As his vision cleared he saw a small black shape above a distant field, soaring through waves of heat. But he could not be sure and with the pain he feared that somehow a horrible recurring fantasy of being split in twain by the whirling blades of a propeller had come true.

"You think he sees us?" he heard.

"See? I hope so."

"He's coming like a bat outa hell!"

Straining, he heard the faint sound of a motor and hoped it would soon be over.

"How you feeling?"

"Like a nightmare," he said.

"Hey, he's done curved back the other way!"

"Maybe he saw us," he said. "Maybe he's gone to send out the ambulance and ground crew." And, he thought with despair, maybe he didn't even see us.

"Where did you send the boy?"

"Down to Mister Graves," Jefferson said. "Man what owns this land."

"Do you think he phoned?"

Jefferson looked at him quickly.

"Aw sho'. Dabney Graves is got a bad name on accounta them killings but he'll call though. . . ."

"What killings?"

"Them five fellers . . . ain't you heard?" he asked with surprise.

"No."

"Everybody knows 'bout Dabney Graves, especially the colored. He done killed enough of us."

Todd had the sensation of being caught in a white neighborhood after dark.

"What did they do?" he asked.

"Thought they was men," Jefferson said. "An' some he owed money, like he do me. . . ."

"But why do you stay here?"

"You black, son."

"I know, but . . ."

"You have to come by the white folks, too."

He turned away from Jefferson's eyes, at once consoled and accused. And I'll have to come by them soon, he thought with despair. Closing his eyes, he heard Jefferson's voice as the sun burned blood-red upon his lips.

"I got nowhere to go," Jefferson said, "an' they'd come after me if I did. But Dabney Graves is a funny fellow. He's all the time making jokes. He can be mean as hell, then he's liable to turn right around and back the colored against the white folks. I seen him do it. But me, I hates him for that more'n anything else. 'Cause just as soon as he gits tired helping a man he don't care what happens to him. He just leaves him stone cold. And then the other white folks is double hard on anybody he done helped. For him it's just a joke. He don't give a hilla beans for nobody—but hisself. . . ."

Todd listened to the thread of detachment in the old man's voice. It was as though he held his words arm's length before him to avoid their destructive meaning.

"He'd just as soon do you a favor and then turn right around and have you strung up. Me, I stays outa his way 'cause down here that's what you gotta do."

If my ankle would only ease for a while, he thought. The closer I spin toward the earth the blacker I become, flashed through his mind. Sweat ran into his eyes and he was sure that he would never see the plane if his head continued whirling. He tried to see Jefferson, what it was that Jefferson held in his hand? It was a little black man, another Jefferson! A little black Jefferson that shook with fits of belly-laughter while the other Jefferson looked on with detachment. Then Jefferson looked up from the thing in his hand and turned to speak, but Todd was far away, searching the sky for a plane in a hot dry land on a day and age he had long forgotten. He was going mysteriously with his mother through empty streets where black faces peered from behind drawn shades and someone was rapping at a window and he was looking back to see a hand and a frightened face frantically beckoning from a cracked door and his mother was looking down the empty perspective of the street and shaking her head and hurrying him along and at first it was only a flash he saw and a motor was droning as through the sun-glare he saw it gleaming silver as it circled and he was seeing a burst like a puff of white smoke and hearing his mother yell, Come along, boy, I got no time for them fool airplanes, I got no time, and he saw it a second time, the plane flying high, and the burst appeared suddenly and fell slowly, billowing out and sparkling like fireworks and he was watching and being hurried along as the air filled with a flurry of white pinwheeling cards that caught in the wind and scattered over the rooftops and into the gutters and a woman was running and snatching a card and reading it and screaming and he darted into the shower, grabbing as in winter he grabbed for snowflakes and bounding away at his mother's, Come on here, boy! Come on, I say! and he was watching as she took the card away, seeing her face grow puzzled and turning taut as her voice quavered, "Niggers Stay From The Polls," and died to a moan of terror as he saw the eyeless sockets of a white hood staring at him from the card and above he saw the plane spiraling gracefully, agleam in the sun like a fiery sword. And seeing it soar he was caught, transfixed between a terrible horror and a horrible fascination.

The sun was not so high now, and Jefferson was calling and gradually he saw three figures moving across the curving roll of the field.

"Look like some doctors, all dressed in white," said Jefferson.

They're coming at last, Todd thought. And he felt such a release of tension within him that he thought he would faint. But no sooner did he close his eyes than he was seized and he was struggling with three white men who were forcing his arms into some kind of coat. It was too much for him, his arms were pinned to his sides and as the pain blazed in his eyes, he realized that it was a straitjacket. What filthy joke was this?

"That oughta hold him, Mister Graves," he heard.

His total energies seemed focused in his eyes as he searched their faces. That was Graves; the other two wore hospital uniforms. He was poised between two poles of fear and hate as he heard the one called Graves saying, "He looks kinda purty in that there suit, boys. I'm glad you dropped by."

"This boy ain't crazy, Mister Graves," one of the others said. "He needs a doctor, not us. Don't see how you led us way out here anyway. It might be a joke to you, but your cousin Rudolph liable to kill somebody. White folks or niggers, don't make no difference. . . ."

Todd saw the man turn red with anger. Graves looked down upon him, chuckling.

"This nigguh belongs in a straitjacket, too, boys. I knowed that the minit

Jeff's kid said something 'bout a nigguh flyer. You all know you cain't let the nigguh git up that high without his going crazy. The nigguh brain ain't built right for high altitudes. . . ."

Todd watched the drawling red face, feeling that all the unnamed horror and obscenities that he had ever imagined stood materialized before him.

"Let's git outta here," one of the attendants said.

Todd saw the other reach toward him, realizing for the first time that he lay upon a stretcher as he yelled.

"Don't put your hands on me!"

They drew back, surprised.

"What's that you say, nigguh?" asked Graves.

He did not answer and thought that Graves's foot was aimed at his head. It landed on his chest and he could hardly breathe. He coughed helplessly, seeing Graves's lips stretch taut over his yellow teeth, and tried to shift his head. It was as though a half-dead fly was dragging slowly across his face and a bomb seemed to burst within him. Blasts of hot, hysterical laughter tore from his chest, causing his eyes to pop and he felt that the veins in his neck would surely burst. And then a part of him stood behind it all, watching the surprise in Graves's red face and his own hysteria. He thought he would never stop, he would laugh himself to death. It rang in his ears like Jefferson's laughter and he looked for him, centering his eyes desperately upon his face, as though somehow he had become his sole salvation in an insane world of outrage and humiliation. It brought a certain relief. He was suddenly aware that although his body was still contorted it was an echo that no longer rang in his ears. He heard Jefferson's voice with gratitude.

"Mister Graves, the Army done tole him not to leave his airplane."

"Nigguh, Army or no, you gittin' off my land! That airplane can stay 'cause it was paid for by taxpayers' money. But you gittin' off. An' dead or alive, it don't make no difference to me."

Todd was beyond it now, lost in a world of anguish.

"Jeff," Graves said, "you and Teddy come and grab holt. I want you to take this here black eagle over to that nigguh airfield and leave him."

Jefferson and the boy approached him silently. He looked away, realizing and doubting at once that only they could release him from his overpowering sense of isolation.

They bent for the stretcher. One of the attendants moved toward Teddy.

"Think you can manage it, boy?"

"I think I can, suh," Teddy said.

"Well, you better go behind then, and let yo' pa go ahead so's to keep that leg elevated."

He saw the white men walking ahead as Jefferson and the boy carried him along in silence. Then they were pausing and he felt a hand wiping his face; then he was moving again. And it was as though he had been lifted out of his isolation, back into the world of men. A new current of communication flowed between the man and boy and himself. They moved him gently. Far away he heard a mockingbird liquidly calling. He raised his eyes, seeing a buzzard poised unmoving in space. For a moment the whole afternoon seemed suspended and he waited for the horror to seize him again. Then like a song within his head he heard the boy's soft humming and saw the dark bird glide into the sun and glow like a bird of flaming gold.

HARRISON BERGERON

KURT VONNEGUT, JR.

The year was 2081, and everybody was finally equal. They weren't only equal before God and the law. They were equal every which way. Nobody was smarter than anybody else. Nobody was better looking than anybody else. Nobody was stronger or quicker than anybody else. All this equality was due to the 211th, 212th, and 213th Amendments to the Constitution, and to the unceasing vigilance of agents of the United States Handicapper General.

Some things about living still weren't quite right, though. April, for instance, still drove people crazy by not being springtime. And it was in that clammy month that the H-G men took George and Hazel Bergeron's fourteen-year-old son, Harrison, away.

It was tragic, all right, but George and Hazel couldn't think about it very hard. Hazel had a perfectly average intelligence, which meant she couldn't think about anything except in short bursts. And George, while his intelligence was way above normal, had a little mental handicap radio in his ear. He was required by law to wear it at all times. It was tuned to a government transmitter. Every twenty seconds or so, the transmitter would send out some sharp noise to keep people like George from taking unfair advantage of their brains.

George and Hazel were watching television. There were tears on Hazel's cheeks, but she'd forgotten for the moment what they were about.

On the television screen were ballerinas.

A buzzer sounded in George's head. His thoughts fled in panic, like bandits from a burglar alarm.

"That was a real pretty dance, that dance they just did," said Hazel.

"Huh?" said George.

"That dance—it was nice," said Hazel.

"Yup," said George. He tried to think a little about the ballerinas. They weren't really very good—no better than anybody else would have been, anyway. They were burdened with sash-weights and bags of birdshot, and their faces were masked, so that no one, seeing a free and graceful gesture or a pretty face, would feel like something the cat drug in. George was toying with the vague notion that maybe dancers shouldn't be handicapped. But he didn't get very far with it before another noise in his ear radio scattered his thoughts.

George winced. So did two out of the eight ballerinas.

Hazel saw him wince. Having no mental handicap herself, she had to ask George what the latest sound had been.

"Sounded like somebody hitting a milk bottle with a ball peen hammer," said George.

"I'd think it would be real interesting, hearing all the different sounds," said Hazel, a little envious. "All the things they think up."

"Um," said George.

"Only, if I was Handicapper General, you know what I would do?" said Hazel. Hazel, as a matter of fact, bore a strong resemblance to the Handicapper General, a woman named Diana Moon Glampers. "If I was Diana Moon Glampers," said Hazel, "I'd have chimes on Sunday—just chimes. Kind of in honor of religion."

"I could think, if it was just chimes," said George.

"Well—maybe make 'em real loud," said Hazel. "I think I'd make a good Handicapper General."

"Good as anybody else," said George.

"Who knows better'n I do what normal is?" said Hazel.

"Right," said George. He began to think glimmeringly about his abnormal son who was now in jail, about Harrison, but a twenty-one-gun salute in his head stopped that.

"Boy!" said Hazel, "that was a doozy, wasn't it?"

It was such a doozy that George was white and trembling, and tears stood on the rims of his red eyes. Two of the eight ballerinas had collapsed to the studio floor, were holding their temples.

"All of a sudden you look so tired," said Hazel. "Why don't you stretch out on the sofa, so's you can rest your handicap bag on the pillows, honeybunch." She was referring to the forty-seven pounds of birdshot in a canvas bag, which was padlocked around George's neck. "Go on and rest the bag for a little while," she said. "I don't care if you're not equal to me for a while."

George weighed the bag with his hands. "I don't mind it," he said. "I don't notice it any more. It's just a part of me."

"You been so tired lately—kind of wore out," said Hazel. "If there was just some way we could make a little hole in the bottom of the bag, and just take out a few of them lead balls. Just a few."

"Two years in prison and two thousand dollars fine for every ball I took out," said George. "I don't call that a bargain."

"If you could just take a few out when you came home from work," said Hazel. "I mean—you don't compete with anybody around here. You just set around."

"If I tried to get away with it," said George, "then other people'd get away with it—and pretty soon we'd be right back to the dark ages again, with everybody competing against everybody else. You wouldn't like that, would you?"

"I'd hate it," said Hazel.

"There you are," said George. "The minute people start cheating on laws, what do you think happens to society?"

If Hazel hadn't been able to come up with an answer to this question, George couldn't have supplied one. A siren was going off in his head.

"Reckon it'd fall apart," said Hazel.

"What would?" said George blankly.

"Society," said Hazel uncertainly. "Wasn't that what you just said?"

"Who knows?" said George.

The television program was suddenly interrupted for a news bulletin. It wasn't clear at first as to what the bulletin was about, since the announcer, like all announcers, had a serious speech impediment. For about half a minute, and in a state of high excitement, the announcer tried to say, "Ladies and gentlemen—"

He finally gave up, handed the bulletin to a ballerina to read.

"That's all right—" Hazel said of the announcer, "he tried. That's the big thing. He tried to do the best he could with what God gave him. He should get a nice raise for trying so hard."

"Ladies and gentlemen—" said the ballerina, reading the bulletin. She must have been extraordinarily beautiful, because the mask she wore was hideous. And it was easy to see that she was the strongest and most graceful of all the dancers, for her handicap bags were as big as those worn by two-hundred-pound men.

And she had to apologize at once for her voice, which was a very unfair voice for a woman to use. Her voice was a warm, luminous, timeless melody. "Excuse me—" she said, and she began again, making her voice absolutely uncompetitive.

"Harrison Bergeron, age fourteen," she said in a grackle squawk, "has just escaped from jail, where he was held on suspicion of plotting to overthrow the government. He is a genius and an athlete, is under-handicapped, and should be regarded as extremely dangerous."

A police photograph of Harrison Bergeron was flashed on the screen—upside down, then sideways, upside down again, then right side up. The picture showed the full length of Harrison against a background calibrated in feet and inches. He was exactly seven feet tall.

The rest of Harrison's appearance was Halloween and hardware. Nobody had ever born heavier handicaps. He had outgrown hindrances faster than the H-G men could think them up. Instead of a little ear radio for a mental handicap, he wore a tremendous pair of earphones, and spectacles with thick wavy lenses. The spectacles were intended to make him not only half blind, but to give him whanging headaches besides.

Scrap metal was hung all over him. Ordinarily, there was a certain symmetry, a military neatness to the handicaps issued to strong people, but Harrison looked like a walking junkyard. In the race of life, Harrison carried three hundred pounds.

And to offset his good looks, the H-G men required that he wear at all times a red rubber ball for a nose, keep his eyebrows shaved off, and cover his even white teeth with black caps at snaggle-tooth random.

"If you see this boy," said the ballerina, "do not—I repeat, do not—try to reason with him."

There was the shriek of a door being torn from its hinges.

Screams and barking cries of consternation came from the television set. The photograph of Harrison Bergeron on the screen jumped again and again, as though dancing to the tune of an earthquake.

George Bergeron correctly identified the earthquake, and well he might have—for many was the time his own home had danced to the same crashing tune. "My God—" said George, "that must be Harrison!"

The realization was blasted from his mind instantly by the sound of an automobile collision in his head.

When George could open his eyes again, the photograph of Harrison was gone. A living, breathing Harrison filled the screen.

Clanking, clownish, and huge, Harrison stood in the center of the studio. The knob of the uprooted studio door was still in his hand. Ballerinas, technicians, musicians, and announcers cowered on their knees before him, expecting to die.

"I am the Emperor!" cried Harrison. "Do you hear? I am the Emperor! Everybody must do what I say at once!" He stamped his foot and the studio shook.

"Even as I stand here—" he bellowed, "crippled, hobbled, sickened—I am a greater ruler than any man who ever lived! Now watch me become what I can become!"

Harrison tore the straps of his handicap harness like wet tissue paper, tore straps guaranteed to support five thousand pounds.

Harrison's scrap-iron handicaps crashed to the floor.

Harrison thrust his thumbs under the bar of the padlock that secured his head harness. The bar snapped like celery. Harrison smashed his headphones and spectacles against the wall.

He flung away his rubber-ball nose, revealed a man that would have awed Thor, the god of thunder.

"I shall now select my Empress!" he said, looking down on the cowering people. "Let the first woman who dares rise to her feet claim her mate and her throne!"

A moment passed, and then a ballerina arose, swaying like a willow.

Harrison plucked the mental handicap away from her ear, snapped off her physical handicaps with marvellous delicacy. Last of all, he removed her mask.

She was blindingly beautiful.

"Now—" said Harrison, taking her hand, "shall we show the people the meaning of the word dance? Music!" he commanded.

The musicians scrambled back into their chairs, and Harrison stripped them of their handicaps, too. "Play your best," he told them, "and I'll make you barons and dukes and earls."

The music began. It was normal at first—cheap, silly, false. But Harrison snatched two musicians from their chairs, waved them like batons as he sang the music as he wanted it played. He slammed them back into their chairs.

The music began again and was much improved.

Harrison and his Empress merely listened to the music for a while—listened gravely, as though synchronizing their heartbeats with it.

They shifted their weights to their toes.

Harrison placed his big hands on the girl's tiny waist, letting her sense the weightlessness that would soon be hers.

And then, in an explosion of joy and grace, into the air they sprang!

Not only were the laws of the land abandoned, but the law of gravity and the laws of motion as well.

They reeled, whirled, swiveled, flounced, capered, gamboled, and spun.

They leaped like deer on the moon.

The studio ceiling was thirty feet high, but each leap brought the dancers nearer to it.

It became their obvious intention to kiss the ceiling.

They kissed it.

And then, neutralizing gravity with love and pure will, they remained suspended in air inches below the ceiling, and they kissed each other for a long, long time.

It was then that Diana Moon Glampers, the Handicapper General, came into the studio with a double-barreled ten-gauge shotgun. She fired twice, and the Emperor and the Empress were dead before they hit the floor.

Diana Moon Glampers loaded the gun again. She aimed it at the musicians and told them they had ten seconds to get their handicaps back on.

It was then that the Bergerons' television tube burned out.

Hazel turned to comment about the blackout to George. But George had gone out into the kitchen for a can of beer.

George came back in with the beer, paused while a handicap signal shook him up. And then he sat down again. "You been crying?" he said to Hazel.

"Yup, she said.

"What about?" he said.

"I forget," she said. "Something real sad on television."

"What was it?" he said.

"It's all kind of mixed up in my mind," said Hazel.

"Forget sad things," said George.

"I always do," said Hazel.

"That's my girl," said George. He winced. There was the sound of a rivetting gun in his head.

"Gee—I could tell that one was a doozy," said Hazel.

"You can say that again," said George.

"Gee—" said Hazel, "I could tell that one was a doozy."

In Another Country

ERNEST HEMINGWAY

In the fall the war was always there, but we did not go to it any more. It was cold in the fall in Milan and the dark came very early. Then the electric lights came on, and it was pleasant along the streets looking in the windows. There was much game hanging outside the shops, and the snow powdered in the fur of the foxes and the wind blew their tails. The deer hung stiff and heavy and empty, and small birds blew in the wind and the wind turned their feathers. It was a cold fall and the wind came down from the mountains.

We were all at the hospital every afternoon, and there were different ways of walking across the town through the dusk to the hospital. Two of the ways were alongside canals, but they were long. Always, though, you crossed a bridge across a canal to enter the hospital. There was a choice of three bridges. On one of them a woman sold roasted chestnuts. It was warm, standing in front of her charcoal fire, and the chestnuts were warm afterward in your pocket. The hospital was very old and very beautiful, and you entered through a gate and walked across a courtyard and out a gate on the other side. There were usually funerals starting from the courtyard. Beyond the old hospital were the new brick pavilions, and there we met every afternoon and were all very polite and interested in what was the matter, and sat in the machines that were to make so much difference.

The doctor came up to the machine where I was sitting and said: "What did you like best to do before the war? Did you practise a sport?"

I said: "Yes, football."

"Good," he said. "You will be able to play football again better than ever."

My knee did not bend and the leg dropped straight from the knee to the ankle without a calf, and the machine was to bend the knee and make it move as in riding a tricycle. But it did not bend yet, and instead the machine lurched when it came to the bending part. The doctor said: "That will all pass. You are a fortunate young man. You will play football again like a champion."

In the next machine was a major who had a little hand like a baby's. He winked at me when the doctor examined his hand, which was between two leather straps that bounced up and flapped the stiff fingers, and said: "And will I too play football, captain-doctor?" He had been a very great fencer, and before the war the greatest fencer in Italy.

The doctor went to his office in a back room and brought a photograph which showed a hand that had been withered almost as small as the major's, before it had taken a machine course, and after was a little larger. The major held the photograph with his good hand and looked at it very carefully. "A wound?" he asked.

"An industrial accident," the doctor said.

"Very interesting, very interesting," the major said, and handed it back to the doctor.

"You have confidence?"

"No," said the major.

There were three boys who came each day who were about the same age I was. They were all three from Milan, and one of them was to be a lawyer, and one was to be a painter, and one had intended to be a soldier, and after we were finished with the machines, sometimes we walked back together to the Café Cova, which was next door to the Scala. We walked the short way through the communist quarter because we were four together. The people hated us because we were officers, and from a wine-shop some one called out, "A basso gli ufficiali!" as we passed. Another boy who walked with us sometimes and made us five wore a black silk handkerchief across his face because he had no nose then and his face was to be rebuilt. He had gone out to the front from the military academy and been wounded within an hour after he had gone into the front line for the first time. They rebuilt his face, but he came from a very old family and they could never get the nose exactly right. He went to South America and worked in a bank. But this was a long time ago, and then we did not any of us know how it was going to be afterward. We only knew then that there was always the war, but that we were not going to it any more.

We all had the same medals, except the boy with the black silk bandage across his face, and he had not been at the front long enough to get any medals. The tall boy with a very pale face who was to be a lawyer had been a lieutenant of Arditi and had three medals of the sort we each had only one of. He had lived a very long time with death and was a little detached. We were all a little detached, and there was nothing that held us together except that we met every afternoon at the hospital. Although, as we walked to the Cova through the tough part of town, walking in the dark, with light and singing coming out of the wine-shops, and sometimes having to walk into the street when the men and women would crowd together on the sidewalk so that we would have had to jostle them to get by, we felt held together by there being something that had happened that they, the people who disliked us, did not understand.

We ourselves all understood the Cova, where it was rich and warm and not too brightly lighted, and noisy and smoky at certain hours, and there were always girls at the tables and the illustrated papers on a rack on the wall. The girls at the Cova were very patriotic, and I found that the most patriotic people in Italy were the café girls—and I believe they are still patriotic.

The boys at first were very polite about my medals and asked me what I had done to get them. I showed them the papers, which were written in very beautiful language and full of *fratellanza* and *abnegazione,* but which really said, with the adjectives removed, that I had been given the medals because I was an American. After that their manner changed a little toward me, although

I was their friend against outsiders. I was a friend, but I was never really one of them after they had read the citations, because it had been different with them and they had done very different things to get their medals. I had been wounded, it was true; but we all knew that being wounded, after all, was really an accident. I was never ashamed of the ribbons, though, and sometimes, after the cocktail hour, I would imagine myself having done all the things they had done to get their medals; but walking home at night through the empty streets with the cold wind and all the shops closed, trying to keep near the street lights, I knew that I would never have done such things, and I was very much afraid to die, and often lay in bed at night by myself, afraid to die and wondering how I would be when I went back to the front again.

The three with the medals were like hunting-hawks; and I was not a hawk, although I might seem a hawk to those who had never hunted; they, the three, knew better and so we drifted apart. But I stayed good friends with the boy who had been wounded his first day at the front, because he would never know now how he would have turned out; so he could never be accepted either, and I liked him because I thought perhaps he would not have turned out to be a hawk either.

The major, who had been the great fencer, did not believe in bravery, and spent much time while we sat in the machines correcting my grammar. He had complimented me on how I spoke Italian, and we talked together very easily. One day I had said that Italian seemed such an easy language to me that I could not take a great interest in it; everything was so easy to say. "Ah, yes," the major said. "Why, then, do you not take up the use of grammar?" So we took up the use of grammar, and soon Italian was such a difficult language that I was afraid to talk to him until I had the grammar straight in my mind.

The major came very regularly to the hospital. I do not think he ever missed a day, although I am sure he did not believe in the machines. There was a time when none of us believed in the machines, and one day the major said it was all nonsense. The machines were new then and it was we who were to prove them. It was an idiotic idea, he said, "a theory, like another." I had not learned my grammar, and he said I was a stupid impossible disgrace, and he was a fool to have bothered with me. He was a small man and he sat straight up in his chair with his right hand thrust into the machine and looked straight ahead at the wall while the straps thumped up and down with his fingers in them.

"What will you do when the war is over if it is over?" he asked me. "Speak grammatically!"

"I will go to the States."

"Are you married?"

"No, but I hope to be."

"The more of a fool you are," he said. He seemed very angry. "A man must not marry."

"Why, Signor Maggiore?"

"Don't call me 'Signor Maggiore.' "

"Why must not a man marry?"

"He cannot marry. He cannot marry," he said angrily. "If he is to lose everything, he should not place himself in a position to lose that. He should not place himself in a position to lose. He should find things he cannot lose."

He spoke very angrily and bitterly, and looked straight ahead while he talked.

"But why should he necessarily lose it?"

"He'll lose it," the major said. He was looking at the wall. Then he looked down at the machine and jerked his little hand out from between the straps and slapped it hard against his thigh. "He'll lose it," he almost shouted. "Don't argue with me!" Then he called to the attendant who ran the machines. "Come and turn this damned thing off."

He went back into the other room for the light treatment and the massage. Then I heard him ask the doctor if he might use his telephone and he shut the door. When he came back into the room, I was sitting in another machine. He was wearing his cape and had his cap on, and he came directly toward my machine and put his arm on my shoulder.

"I am so sorry," he said, and patted me on the shoulder with his good hand. "I would not be rude. My wife has just died. You must forgive me."

"Oh—" I said, feeling sick for him. "I am *so* sorry."

He stood there biting his lower lip. "It is very difficult," he said. "I cannot resign myself."

He looked straight past me and out through the window. Then he began to cry. "I am utterly unable to resign myself," he said and choked. And then crying, his head up looking at nothing, carrying himself straight and soldierly, with tears on both his cheeks and biting his lips, he walked past the machines and out the door.

The doctor told me that the major's wife, who was very young and whom he had not married until he was definitely invalided out of the war, had died of pneumonia. She had been sick only a few days. No one expected her to die. The major did not come to the hospital for three days. Then he came at the usual hour, wearing a black band on the sleeve of his uniform. When he came back, there were large framed photographs around the wall, of all sorts of wounds before and after they had been cured by the machines. In front of the machine the major used were three photographs of hands like his that were completely restored. I do not know where the doctor got them. I always understood we were the first to use the machines. The photographs did not make much difference to the major because he only looked out of the window.

Jean Beicke

WILLIAM CARLOS WILLIAMS

During a time like this, they kid a lot among the doctors and nurses on the obstetrical floor because of the rushing business in new babies that's pretty nearly always going on up there. It's the Depression, they say, nobody has any money so they stay home nights. But one bad result of this is that in the children's ward, another floor up, you see a lot of unwanted children.

The parents get them into the place under all sorts of pretexts. For instance, we have two premature brats, Navarro and Cryschka, one a boy and one a girl; the mother died when Cryschka was born, I think. We got them within a few days of each other, one weighing four pounds and one a few ounces more. They dropped down below four pounds before we got them going but there they are; we had a lot of fun betting on their daily gains in weight but we still have them. They're in pretty good shape though now. Most of the kids that are left that way get along swell. The nurses grow attached to them and get a real thrill when they begin to pick up. It's great to see. And the parents sometimes don't even come to visit them, afraid we'll grab them and make them take the kids out, I suppose.

A funny one is a little Hungarian Gypsy girl that's been up there for the past month. She was about eight weeks old maybe when they brought her in with something on her lower lip that looked like a chancre. Everyone was interested but the Wassermann was negative. It turned out finally to be nothing but a peculiarly situated birthmark. But that kid is still there too. Nobody can find the parents. Maybe they'll turn up some day.

Even when we do get rid of them, they often come back in a week or so— sometimes in terrible condition, full of impetigo, down in weight—everything we'd done for them to do over again. I think it's deliberate neglect in most cases. That's what happened to this little Gypsy. The nurse was funny after the mother had left the second time. I couldn't speak to her, she said. I just couldn't say a word I was so mad. I wanted to slap her.

We had a couple of Irish girls a while back named Cowley. One was a red head with beautiful wavy hair and the other a straight haired blonde. They really were good looking and not infants at all. I should say they must have been two and three years old approximately. I can't imagine how the parents could have abandoned them. But they did. I think they were habitual drunkards and may have had to beat it besides on short notice. No fault of theirs maybe.

But all these are, after all, not the kind of kids I have in mind. The ones I mean are those they bring in stinking dirty, and I mean stinking. The poor brats are almost dead sometimes, just living skeletons, almost, wrapped in rags, their heads caked with dirt, their eyes stuck together with pus and their legs all excoriated from the dirty diapers no one has had the interest to take off them regularly. One poor little pot we have now with a thin purplish skin and big veins standing out all over its head had a big sore place in the fold of its neck under the chin. The nurse told me that when she started to undress it it had on a shirt with a neckband that rubbed right into that place. Just dirt. The mother gave a story of having had it in some sort of home in Paterson. We couldn't get it straight. We never try. What the hell? We take 'em and try to make something out of them.

Sometimes, you'd be surprised, some doctor has given the parents a ride before they bring the child to the clinic. You wouldn't believe it. They clean 'em out, maybe for twenty-five dollars—they maybe had to borrow—and then tell 'em to move on. It happens. Men we all know too. Pretty bad. But what can you do?

And sometimes the kids are not only dirty and neglected but sick, ready to die. You ought to see those nurses work. You'd think it was the brat of their best friend. They handle those kids as if they were worth a million dollars. Not that some nurses aren't better than others but in general they break their hearts over those kids, many times, when I, for one, wish they'd never get well.

I often kid the girls. Why not? I look at some miserable specimens they've dolled up for me when I make the rounds in the morning and I tell them: Give it an enema, maybe it will get well and grow up into a cheap prostitute or something. The country needs you, brat. I once proposed that we have a mock wedding between a born garbage hustler we'd saved and a little female with a fresh mug on her that would make anybody smile.

Poor kids! You really wonder sometimes if medicine isn't all wrong to try to do anything for them at all. You actually want to see them pass out, especially when they're deformed or—they're awful sometimes. Every one has rickets in an advanced form, scurvy too, flat chests, spindly arms and legs. They come in with pneumonia, a temperature of a hundred and six, maybe, and before you can do a thing, they're dead.

This little Jean Beicke was like that. She was about the worst you'd expect to find anywhere. Eleven months old. Lying on the examining table with a blanket half way up her body, stripped, lying there, you'd think it a five months baby, just about that long. But when the nurse took the blanket away, her legs kept on going for a good eight inches longer. I couldn't get used to it. I covered her up and asked two of the men to guess how long she was. Both guessed at least half a foot too short. One thing that helped the illusion besides her small face was her arms. They came about to her hips. I don't know what made that. They should come down to her thighs, you know.

She was just skin and bones but her eyes were good and she looked straight at you. Only if you touched her anywhere, she started to whine and then cry with a shrieking, distressing sort of cry that no one wanted to hear. We handled her as gently as we knew how but she had to cry just the same.

She was one of the damnedest looking kids I've ever seen. Her head was all up in front and flat behind, I suppose from lying on the back of her head so long the weight of it and the softness of the bones from the rickets had just flattened it out and pushed it up forward. And her legs and arms seemed loose on her like the arms and legs of some cheap dolls. You could bend her feet up on her shins absolutely flat—but there was no real deformity, just all loosened up. Nobody was with her when I saw her though her mother had brought her in.

It was about ten in the evening, the interne had asked me to see her because she had a stiff neck, and how! and there was some thought of meningitis—perhaps infantile paralysis. Anyhow, they didn't want her to go through the night without at least a lumbar puncture if she needed it. She had a fierce cough and a fairly high fever. I made it out to be a case of broncho-pneumonia with meningismus but no true involvement of the central nervous system. Besides she had inflamed ear drums.

I wanted to incise the drums, especially the left, and would have done it only the night superintendent came along just then and made me call the ear man on service. You know. She also looked to see if we had an operative release from the parents. There was. So I went home, the ear man came in a while later and opened the ears—a little bloody serum from both sides and that was that.

Next day we did a lumbar puncture, tapped the spine that is, and found clear fluid with a few lymphocytes in it, nothing diagnostic. The X-ray of the chest clinched the diagnosis of broncho-pneumonia, there was an extensive involvement. She was pretty sick. We all expected her to die from exhaustion before she'd gone very far.

I had to laugh every time I looked at the brat after that, she was such a funny looking one but one thing that kept her from being a total loss was that she did eat. Boy! how that kid could eat! As sick as she was she took her grub right on time every three hours, a big eight ounce bottle of whole milk and digested it perfectly. In this depression you got to be such a hungry baby, I heard the nurse say to her once. It's a sign of intelligence, I told her. But anyway, we all got to be crazy about Jean. She'd just lie there and eat and sleep. Or she'd lie and look straight in front of her by the hour. Her eyes were blue, a pale sort of blue. But if you went to touch her, she'd begin to scream. We just didn't, that's all, unless we absolutely had to. And she began to gain in weight. Can you imagine that? I suppose she had been so terribly run down that food, real food, was an entirely new experience to her. Anyway she took her food and gained on it though her temperature continued to run steadily around between a hundred and three and a hundred and four for the first eight or ten days. We were surprised.

When we were expecting her to begin to show improvement, however, she didn't. We did another lumbar puncture and found fewer cells. That was fine and the second X-ray of the chest showed it somewhat improved also. That wasn't so good though, because the temperature still kept up and we had no way to account for it. I looked at the ears again and thought they ought to be opened once more. The ear man disagreed but I kept after him and next day he did it to please me. He didn't get anything but a drop of serum on either side.

Well, Jean didn't get well. We did everything we knew how to do except the right thing. She carried on for another two—no I think it was three—weeks longer. A couple of times her temperature shot up to a hundred and eight. Of course we knew then it was the end. We went over her six or eight times, three or four of us, one after the other, and nobody thought to take an X-ray of the mastoid regions. It was dumb, if you want to say it, but there wasn't a sign of anything but the history of the case to point to it. The ears had been opened early, they had been watched carefully, there was no discharge to speak of at any time and from the external examination, the mastoid processes showed no change from the normal. But that's what she died of, acute purulent mastoiditis of the left side, going on to involvement of the left lateral sinus and finally the meninges. We might, however, have taken a culture of the pus when the ear was first opened and I shall always, after this, in suspicious cases. I have been told since that if you get a virulent bug like the streptococcus mucosus capsulatus it's wise at least to go in behind the ear for drainage if the temperature keeps up. Anyhow she died.

I went in when she was just lying there gasping. Somehow or other, I hated to see that kid go. Everybody felt rotten. She was such a scrawny, misshapen, worthless piece of humanity that I had said many times that somebody ought to chuck her in the garbage chute—but after a month watching her suck up her milk and thrive on it—and to see those alert blue eyes in that face—well, it wasn't pleasant. Her mother was sitting by the bed crying quietly when I came in, the morning of the last day. She was a young woman, didn't look more than a girl, she just sat there looking at the child and crying without a sound.

I expected her to begin to ask me questions with that look on her face all doctors hate—but she didn't. I put my hand on her shoulder and told her we had done everything we knew how to do for Jean but that we really didn't know what, finally, was killing her. The woman didn't make any sign of hearing me. Just sat there looking in between the bars of the crib. So after a moment watching the poor kid beside her, I turned to the infant in the next crib to go on with my rounds. There was an older woman there looking in at that baby also—no better off than Jean, surely. I spoke to her, thinking she was the mother of this one, but she wasn't.

Before I could say anything, she told me she was the older sister of Jean's mother and that she knew that Jean was dying and that it was a good thing. That gave me an idea—I hated to talk to Jean's mother herself—so I beckoned the woman to come out into the hall with me.

I'm glad she's going to die, she said. She's got two others home, older, and her husband has run off with another woman. It's better off dead—never was any good anyway. You know her husband came down from Canada about a year and a half ago. She seen him and asked him to come back and live with her and the children. He come back just long enough to get her pregnant with this one then he left her again and went back to the other woman. And I suppose knowing she was pregnant, and suffering, and having no money and nowhere to get it, she was worrying and this one never was formed right. I seen it as soon as it was born. I guess the condition she was in was the cause. She's got enough to worry about now without this one. The husband's gone to Canada again and we can't get a thing out of him. I been keeping them, but we can't do much more. She'd work if she could find anything but what can you do with three kids in times like this? She's got a boy nine years old but her mother-in-law sneaked it away from her and now he's with his father in Canada. She worries about him too, but that don't do no good.

Listen, I said, I want to ask you something. Do you think she'd let us do an autopsy on Jean if she dies? I hate to speak to her of such a thing now but to tell you the truth, we've worked hard on that poor child and we don't exactly know what is the trouble. We know that she's had pneumonia but that's been getting well. Would you take it up with her for me, if—of course—she dies.

Oh, she's gonna die all right, said the woman. Sure, I will. If you can learn anything, it's only right. I'll see that you get the chance. She won't make any kick, I'll tell her.

Thanks, I said.

The infant died about five in the afternoon. The pathologist was dog-tired from a lot of extra work he'd had to do due to the absence of his assistant on her vacation so he put off the autopsy till next morning. They packed the body in ice in one of the service hoppers. It worked perfectly.

Next morning they did the postmortem. I couldn't get the nurse to go down to it. I may be a sap, she said, but I can't do it, that's all. I can't. Not when I've taken care of them. I feel as if they're my own.

I was amazed to see how completely the lungs had cleared up. They were almost normal except for a very small patch of residual pneumonia here and there which really amounted to nothing. Chest and abdomen were in excellent shape, otherwise, throughout—not a thing aside from the negligible pneumonia. Then he opened the head.

It seemed to me the poor kid's convolutions were unusually well developed. I kept thinking it's incredible that that complicated mechanism of the brain has come into being just for this. I never can quite get used to an autopsy.

The first evidence of the real trouble—for there had been no gross evidence of meningitis—was when the pathologist took the brain in his hand and made the long steady cut which opened up the left lateral ventricle. There was just a faint color of pus on the bulb of the choroid plexus there. Then the diagnosis all cleared up quickly. The left lateral sinus was completely thrombosed and on going into the left temporal bone from the inside the mastoid process was all broken down.

I called up the ear man and he came down at once. A clear miss, he said. I think if we'd gone in there earlier, we'd have saved her.

For what? said I. Vote the straight Communist ticket.

Would it make us any dumber? said the ear man.

TO HELL WITH DYING

ALICE WALKER

"To hell with dying," my father would say, "these children want Mr. Sweet!"

Mr. Sweet was a diabetic and an alcoholic and a guitar player and lived down the road from us on a neglected cotton farm. My older brothers and sisters got the most benefit from Mr. Sweet, for when they were growing up he had quite a few years ahead of him and so was capable of being called back from the brink of death any number of times—whenever the voice of my father reached him as he lay expiring. . . . "To hell with dying, man," my father would say, pushing the wife away from the bedside (in tears although she knew the death was not necessarily the last one unless Mr. Sweet really wanted it to be), "the children want Mr. Sweet!" And they did want him, for at a signal from Father they would come crowding around the bed and throw themselves on the covers and whoever was the smallest at the time would kiss him all over his wrinkled brown face and begin to tickle him so that he would laugh all down in his stomach, and his moustache which was long and sort of straggly, would shake like Spanish moss and was also that color.

Mr. Sweet had been ambitious as a boy, wanted to be a doctor or lawyer or sailor, only to find that black men fare better if they are not. Since he could be none of those things he turned to fishing as his only earnest career and playing the guitar as his only claim to doing anything extraordinarily well. His son, the only one that he and his wife, Miss Mary, had, was shiftless as the day is long and spent money as if he were trying to see the bottom of the mint, which Mr. Sweet would tell him was the clean brown palm of his hand. Miss Mary loved her "baby," however, and worked hard to get him the "li'l necessaries" of life, which turned out mostly to be women.

Mr. Sweet was a tall, thinnish man with thick kinky hair going dead white. He was dark brown, his eyes were very squinty and sort of bluish, and he chewed Brown Mule tobacco. He was constantly on the verge of being blind drunk, for he brewed his own liquor and was not in the least a stingy sort of man, and was always very melancholy and sad, though frequently when he was "feelin' good" he'd dance around the yard with us, usually keeling over just as my mother came to see what the commotion was.

Toward all of us children he was very kind, and had the grace to be shy with us, which is unusual in grown-ups. He had great respect for my mother for she never held his drunkenness against him and would let us play with him even when he was about to fall in the fireplace from drink. Although Mr. Sweet would sometimes lose complete or nearly complete control of his head and neck so that he would loll in his chair, his mind remained strangely acute and his speech not too affected. His ability to be drunk and sober at the same time made him an ideal playmate, for he was as weak as we were and we could usually best him in wrestling, all the while keeping a fairly coherent conversation going.

We never felt anything of Mr. Sweet's age when we played with him. We loved his wrinkles and would draw some on our brows to be like him, and his white hair was my special treasure and he knew it and would never come to visit us just after he had had his hair cut off at the barbershop. Once he came to our house for something, probably to see my father about fertilizer for his crops, for although he never paid the slightest attention to his crops he liked to know what things would be best to use on them if he ever did. Anyhow, he had not come with his hair since he had just had it shaved off at the barbershop. He wore a huge straw hat to keep off the sun and also to keep his head away from me. But as soon as I saw him I ran up and demanded that he take me up and kiss me, with his funny beard which smelled so strongly of tobacco. Looking forward to burying my small fingers into his woolly hair I threw away his hat only to find he had done something to his hair, that it was no longer there! I let out a squall which made my mother think that Mr. Sweet had finally dropped me in the well or something and from that day I've been wary of men in hats. However, not long after, Mr. Sweet showed up with his hair grown out and just as white and kinky and impenetrable as it ever was.

Mr. Sweet used to call me his princess, and I believed it. He made me feel pretty at five and six, and simply outrageously devastating at the blazing age of eight and a half. When he came to our house with his guitar the whole family would stop whatever they were doing to sit around him and listen to him play. He liked to play "Sweet Georgia Brown," that was what he called me sometimes, and also he liked to play "Caldonia" and all sorts of sweet, sad, wonderful songs which he sometimes made up. It was from one of these songs that I learned that he had had to marry Miss Mary when he had in fact loved somebody else (now living in Chi'-ca-go or, De-stroy, Michigan). He was not sure that Joe Lee, her "baby," was also his baby. Sometimes he would cry and that was an indication that he was about to die again. And so we would all get prepared, for we were sure to be called upon.

I was seven the first time I remember actually participating in one of Mr. Sweet's "revivals"—my parents told me I had participated before, I had been the one chosen to kiss him and tickle him long before I knew the rite of Mr. Sweet's rehabilitation. He had come to our house, it was a few years after his wife's death, and he was very sad, and also, typically, very drunk. He sat on the floor next to me and my older brother, the rest of the children were grown-up and lived elsewhere, and began to play his guitar and cry. I held his woolly head in my arms and wished I could have been old enough to have been the woman he loved so much and that I had not been lost years and years ago.

When he was leaving my mother said to us that we'd better sleep light that night for we'd probably have to go over to Mr. Sweet's before daylight. And we did. For soon after we had gone to bed one of the neighbors knocked on our door and called my father and said that Mr. Sweet was sinking fast and if we wanted to get in a word before the crossover he'd better shake a leg and get over to Mr. Sweet's house. All the neighbors knew to come to our house if something was wrong with Mr. Sweet, but they did not know how we always managed to make him well, or at least stop him from dying, when he was often so near death. As soon as we heard the cry we got up, my brother and I and my mother and father, and put on our clothes. We hurried out of the house and down the road for we were always afraid that we might someday be too late and Mr. Sweet would get tired of dallying.

When we got to the house, a very poor shack really, we found the front room full of neighbors and relatives and someone met us at the door and said that it was all very sad that old Mr. Sweet Little (for Little was his family name although we mostly ignored it) was about to kick the bucket. My parents were advised not to take my brother and me into the "death-room" seeing we were so young and all, but we were so much more accustomed to the death-room than he that we ignored him and dashed in without giving his warning a second thought. I was almost in tears, for these deaths upset me fearfully, and the thought of how much depended on me and my brother (who was such a ham most of the time) made me very nervous.

The doctor was bending over the bed and turned back to tell us for at least the tenth time in the history of my family that alas, old Mr. Sweet Little was dying and that the children had best not see the face of implacable death (I didn't know what "implacable" was, but whatever it was, Mr. Sweet was not!). My father pushed him rather abruptly out of the way saying as he always did and very loudly for he was saying it to Mr. Sweet, "To hell with dying, man, these children want Mr. Sweet!" which was my cue to throw myself upon the bed and kiss Mr. Sweet all around the whiskers and under the eyes and around the collar of his nightshirt where he smelled so strongly of all sorts of things, mostly liniment.

I was very good at bringing him around, for as soon as I saw that he was struggling to open his eyes I knew he was going to be all right and so could finish my revival sure of success. As soon as his eyes were open he would begin to smile and that way I knew that I had surely won. Once though I got a tremendous scare for he could not open his eyes and later I learned that he had had a stroke and that one side of his face was stiff and hard to get into motion. When he began to smile I could tickle him in earnest for I was sure that nothing would get in the way of his laughter, although once he began to cough so hard that he almost threw me off his stomach, but that was when I was very small, little more than a baby, and my bushy hair had gotten in his nose.

When we were sure he would listen to us we would ask him why he was in bed and when he was coming to see us again and could we play with his guitar which more than likely would be leaning against the bed. His eyes would get all misty and he would sometimes cry out loud, but we never let it embarrass us for he knew that we loved him and that we sometimes cried too for no reason. My parents would leave the room to just the three of us; Mr. Sweet, by that time, would be propped up in bed with a number of pillows behind his head and with me sitting and lying on his shoulder and along his chest. Even when he had trouble breathing he would not ask me to get down. Looking into my eyes he would shake his white head and run a scratchy old finger all around my hairline, which was rather low down nearly to my eyebrows and for which some people said I looked like a baby monkey.

My brother was very generous in all this, he let me do all the revivaling—he had done it for years before I was born and so was glad to be able to pass it on to someone new. What he would do while I talked to Mr. Sweet was pretend to play the guitar, in fact pretend that he was a young version of Mr. Sweet, and it always made Mr. Sweet glad to think that someone wanted to be like him—of course we did not know this then, we played the thing by ear, and whatever he seemed to like, we did. We were desperately afraid that he was just going to take off one day and leave us.

It did not occur to us that we were doing anything special; we had not learned that death was final when it did come. We thought nothing of triumphing over it so many times, and in fact became a trifle contemptuous of people who let themselves be carried away. It did not occur to us that if our own father had been dying we could not have stopped it, that Mr. Sweet was the only person over whom we had power.

When Mr. Sweet was in his eighties I was a young lady studying away in a university many miles from home. I saw him whenever I went home, but he was never on the verge of dying that I could tell and I began to feel that my anxiety for his health and psychological well-being was unnecessary. By this time he not only had a moustache but a long flowing snow-white beard which I loved and combed and braided for hours. He was still a very heavy drinker and was like an old Chinese opium-user, very peaceful, fragile, gentle, and the only jarring note about him was his old steel guitar which he still played in the old sad, sweet, downhome blues way.

On Mr. Sweet's ninetieth birthday I was finishing my doctorate in Massachusetts and had been making arrangements to go home for several weeks' rest. That morning I got a telegram telling me that Mr. Sweet was dying again and could I please drop everything and come home. Of course I could. My dissertation could wait and my teachers would understand when I explained to them when I got back. I ran to the phone, called the airport, and within four hours I was speeding along the dusty road to Mr. Sweet's.

The house was more dilapidated than when I was last there, barely a shack, but it was overgrown with yellow roses which my family had planted many years ago. The air was heavy and sweet and very peaceful. I felt strange walking through the gate and up the old rickety steps. But the strangeness left me as I caught sight of the long white beard I loved so well flowing down the thin body over the familiar quilt coverlet. Mr. Sweet!

His eyes were closed tight and his hands, crossed over his stomach, were thin and delicate, no longer rough and scratchy. I remembered how always before I had run and jumped up on him just anywhere; now I knew he would not be able to support my weight. I looked around at my parents, and was surprised to see that my father and mother also looked old and frail. My father, his own hair very gray, leaned over the quietly sleeping old man who, incidentally, smelled still of wine and tobacco, and said as he'd done so many times, "To hell with dying, man! My daughter is home to see Mr. Sweet!" My brother had not been able to come as he was in the war in Asia. I bent down and gently stroked the closed eyes and gradually they began to open. The closed, wine-stained lips twitched a little, then parted in a warm, slightly embarrassed smile. Mr. Sweet could see me and he recognized me and his eyes looked very spry and twinkly for a moment. I put my head down on the pillow next to his and we just looked at each other for a long time. Then he began to trace my peculiar hairline with a thin, smooth finger. I closed my eyes when his finger halted above my ear (he used to rejoice at the dirt in my ears when I was little), his hand stayed cupped around my cheek. When I opened my eyes, sure I had reached him in time, his were closed.

Even at twenty-four how could I believe that I had failed? that Mr. Sweet was really gone? He had never gone before. But when I looked up at my parents I saw that they were holding back tears. They had loved him dearly. He was like a piece of rare and delicate china which was always being saved from breaking and which finally fell. I looked long at the old face, the wrinkled forehead, the red lips, the hands that still reached out to me. Soon I felt my father pushing something cool into my hands. It was Mr. Sweet's guitar. He had asked them months before to give it to me, he had known that even if I came next time he would not be able to respond in the old way. He did not want me to feel that my trip had been for nothing.

The old guitar! I plucked the strings, hummed "Sweet Georgia Brown." The magic of Mr. Sweet lingered still in the cool steel box. Through the window I could catch the fragrant delicate scent of tender yellow roses. The man on the high old-fashioned bed with the quilt coverlet and the flowing white beard had been my first love.

*The Boarding House

JAMES JOYCE

Mrs Mooney was a butcher's daughter. She was a woman who was quite able to keep things to herself: a determined woman. She had married her father's foreman and opened a butcher's shop near Spring Gardens. But as soon as his father-in-law was dead Mr Mooney began to go to the devil. He drank, plundered the till, ran headlong into debt. It was no use making him take the pledge: he was sure to break out again a few days after. By fighting his wife in the presence of customers and by buying bad meat he ruined his business. One night he went for his wife with the cleaver and she had to sleep in a neighbour's house.

After that they lived apart. She went to the priest and got a separation from him with care of the children. She would give him neither money nor food nor house-room; and so he was obliged to enlist himself as a sheriff's man. He was a shabby stooped little drunkard with a white face and a white moustache and white eyebrows, pencilled above his little eyes, which were pink-veined and raw; and all day long he sat in the bailiff's room, waiting to be put on a job. Mrs Mooney, who had taken what remained of her money out of the butcher business and set up a boarding house in Hardwicke Street, was a big imposing woman. Her house had a floating population made up of tourists from Liverpool and the Isle of Man and, occasionally, *artistes* from the music halls. Its resident population was made up of clerks from the city. She governed her house cunningly and firmly, knew when to give credit, when to be stern and when to let things pass. All the resident young men spoke of her as *The Madam.*

Mrs Mooney's young men paid fifteen shillings a week for board and lodgings (beer or stout at dinner excluded). They shared in common tastes and occupations and for this reason they were very chummy with one another.

They discussed with one another the chances of favourites and outsiders. Jack Mooney, the Madam's son, who was clerk to a commission agent in Fleet Street, had the reputation of being a hard case. He was fond of using soldiers' obscenities: usually he came home in the small hours. When he met his friends he had always a good one to tell them and he was always sure to be on to a good thing—that is to say, a likely horse or a likely *artiste*. He was also handy with the mits and sang comic songs. On Sunday nights there would often be a reunion in Mrs Mooney's front drawing-room. The music-hall *artistes* would oblige; and Sheridan played waltzes and polkas and vamped accompaniments. Polly Mooney, the Madam's daughter, would also sing. She sang:

> *I'm a . . . naughty girl.*
> *You needn't sham:*
> *You know I am.*

Polly was a slim girl of nineteen, she had light soft hair and a small full mouth. Her eyes, which were grey with a shade of green through them, had a habit of glancing upwards when she spoke with anyone, which made her look like a little perverse madonna. Mrs Mooney had first sent her daughter to be a typist in a corn-factor's office but, as a disreputable sheriff's man used to come every other day to the office, asking to be allowed to say a word to his daughter, she had taken her daughter home again and set her to do housework. As Polly was very lively the intention was to give her the run of the young men. Besides, young men like to feel that there is a young woman not very far away. Polly, of course, flirted with the young men but Mrs Mooney, who was a shrewd judge, knew that the young men were only passing the time away: none of them meant business. Things went on so for a long time and Mrs Mooney began to think of sending Polly back to typewriting when she noticed that something was going on between Polly and one of the young men. She watched the pair and kept her own counsel.

Polly knew that she was being watched, but still her mother's persistent silence could not be misunderstood. There had been no open complicity between mother and daughter, no open understanding but, though people in the house began to talk of the affair, still Mrs Mooney did not intervene. Polly began to grow a little strange in her manner and the young man was evidently perturbed. At last, when she judged it to be the right moment, Mrs Mooney intervened. She dealt with moral problems as a cleaver deals with meat: and in this case she had made up her mind.

It was a bright Sunday morning of early summer, promising heat, but with a fresh breeze blowing. All the windows of the boarding house were open and the lace curtains ballooned gently towards the street beneath the raised sashes. The belfry of George's Church sent out constant peals and worshippers, singly or in groups, traversed the little circus before the church, revealing their purpose by their self-contained demeanour no less than by the little volumes in their gloved hands. Breakfast was over in the boarding house and the table of the breakfast-room was covered with plates on which lay yellow streaks of eggs with morsels of bacon-fat and bacon-rind. Mrs Mooney sat in the straw arm-chair and watched the servant Mary remove the breakfast things. She made Mary collect the crusts and pieces of broken bread to help to make Tuesday's bread-pudding. When the table was cleared, the broken bread collected, the sugar and butter safe under lock and key, she began to reconstruct the interview which she had had the night before with Polly. Things were as she had suspected: she had been frank in her questions and Polly had been frank in her answers. Both had been somewhat awkward, of course. She had been made awkward by her not wishing to receive the news in too cavalier a fashion or to seem to have connived and Polly had been made awkward not merely because allusions of that kind always made her awkward but also because she did not wish it to be thought that in her wise innocence she had divined the intention behind her mother's tolerance.

Mrs Mooney glanced instinctively at the little gilt clock on the mantelpiece as soon as she had become aware through her revery that the bells of George's Church had stopped ringing. It was seventeen minutes past eleven: she would have lots of time to have the matter out with Mr Doran and then catch short twelve at Marlborough Street. She was sure she would win. To begin with she had all the weight of social opinion on her side: she was an outraged mother. She had allowed him to live beneath her roof, assuming that he was a man of honour, and he had simply abused her hospitality. He was thirty-four or thirty-five years of age, so that youth could not be pleaded as his excuse; nor could ignorance be his excuse since he was a man who had seen something of the world. He had simply taken advantage of Polly's youth and inexperience: that was evident. The question was: What reparation would he make?

There must be reparation made in such cases. It is all very well for the man: he can go his ways as if nothing had happened, having had his moment of pleasure, but the girl has to bear the brunt. Some mothers would be content to patch up such an affair for a sum of money; she had known cases of it. But she would not do so. For her only one reparation could make up for the loss of her daughter's honour: marriage.

She counted all her cards again before sending Mary up to Mr Doran's room to say that she wished to speak with him. She felt sure she would win. He was a serious young man, not rakish or loud-voiced like the others. If it had been Mr Sheridan or Mr Meade or Bantam Lyons her task would have been much harder. She did not think he would face publicity. All the lodgers in the house knew something of the affair; details had been invented by some. Besides, he had been employed for thirteen years in a great Catholic wine-merchant's office and publicity would mean for him, perhaps, the loss of his sit. Whereas if he agreed all might be well. She know he had a good screw for one thing and she suspected he had a bit of stuff put by.

Nearly the half-hour! She stood up and surveyed herself in the pier-glass. The decisive expression of her great florid face satisfied her and she thought of some mothers she knew who could not get their daughters off their hands.

Mr Doran was very anxious indeed this Sunday morning. He had made two attempts to shave but his hand had been so unsteady that he had been obliged to desist. Three days' reddish beard fringed his jaws and every two or three minutes a mist gathered on his glasses so that he had to take them off and polish them with his pocket-handkerchief. The recollection of his confession of the night before was a cause of acute pain to him; the priest had drawn out every ridiculous detail of the affair and in the end had so magnified his sin that he was almost thankful at being afforded a loophole of reparation. The harm was done. What could he do now but marry her or run away? He could not brazen it out. The affair would be sure to be talked of and his employer would be certain to hear of it. Dublin is such a small city: everyone knows everyone else's business. He felt his heart leap warmly in his throat as he heard in his excited imagination old Mr Leonard calling out in his rasping voice: *Send Mr Doran here, please.*

All his long years of service gone for nothing! All his industry and diligence thrown away! As a young man he had sown his wild oats, of course; he had boasted of his free-thinking and denied the existence of God to his companions in public-houses. But that was all passed and done with . . . nearly. He still bought a copy of *Reynolds's Newspaper* every week but he attended to his religious duties and for nine-tenths of the year lived a regular life. He had money enough to settle down on; it was not that. But the family would look down on her. First of all there was her disreputable father and then her mother's boarding house was beginning to get a certain fame. He had a notion that he was being had. He could imagine his friends talking of the affair and laughing. She *was* a little vulgar; some times she said *I seen* and *If I had've known*. But what would grammar matter if he really loved her? He could not make up his mind whether to like her or despise her for what she had done. Of course, he had done it too. His instinct urged him to remain free, not to marry. Once you are married you are done for, it said.

While he was sitting helplessly on the side of the bed in shirt and trousers she tapped lightly at his door and entered. She told him all, that she had made a clean breast of it to her mother and that her mother would speak with him that morning. She cried and threw her arms round his neck, saying:

—O Bob! Bob! What am I to do? What am I to do at all?

She would put an end to herself, she said.

He comforted her feebly, telling her not to cry, that it would be all right, never fear. He felt against his shirt the agitation of her bosom.

It was not altogether his fault that it had happened. He remembered well, with the curious patient memory of the celibate, the first casual caresses her dress, her breath, her fingers had given him. Then late one night as he was undressing for bed she had tapped at his door, timidly. She wanted to relight her candle at his for hers had been blown out by a gust. It was her bath night. She wore a loose open combing-jacket of printed flannel. Her white instep shone in the opening of her furry slippers and the blood glowed warmly behind her perfumed skin. From her hands and wrists too as she lit and steadied her candle a faint perfume arose.

On nights when he came in very late it was she who warmed up his dinner. He scarcely knew what he was eating, feeling her beside him alone, at night, in the sleeping house. And her thoughtfulness! If the night was anyway cold or wet or windy there was sure to be a little tumbler of punch ready for him. Perhaps they could be happy together. . . .

They used to go upstairs together on tiptoe, each with a candle, and on the third landing exchange reluctant good-nights. They used to kiss. He remembered well her eyes, the touch of her hand and his delirium. . . .

But delirium passes. He echoed her phrase, applying it to himself: *What am I to do?* The instinct of the celibate warned him to hold back. But the sin was there; even his sense of honour told him that reparation must be made for such a sin.

While he was sitting with her on the side of the bed Mary came to the door and said that the missus wanted to see him in the parlour. He stood up to put on his coat and waistcoat, more helpless than ever. When he was dressed he went over to her to comfort her. It would be all right, never fear. He left her crying on the bed and moaning softly: *O my God!*

Going down the stairs his glasses became so dimmed with moisture that he had to take them off and polish them. He longed to ascend through the roof and fly away to another country where he would never hear again of his trouble, and yet a force pushed him downstairs step by step. The implacable faces of his employer and of the Madam stared upon his discomfiture. On the last flight of stairs he passed Jack Mooney who was coming up from the pantry nursing two bottles of *Bass.* They saluted coldly; and the lover's eyes rested for a second or two on a thick bulldog face and a pair of thick short arms. When he reached the foot of the staircase he glanced up and saw Jack regarding him from the door of the return-room.

Suddenly he remembered the night when one of the music-hall *artistes*, a little blond Londoner, had made a rather free allusion to Polly. The reunion had been almost broken up on account of Jack's violence. Everyone tried to quiet him. The music-hall *artiste*, a little paler than usual, kept smiling and saying that there was no harm meant: but Jack kept shouting at him that if any fellow tried that sort of game on with *his* sister he'd bloody well put his teeth down his throat, so he would.

. . . .

Polly sat for a little time on the side of the bed, crying. Then she dried her eyes and went over to the looking-glass. She dipped the end of the towel in the water-jug and refreshed her eyes with the cool water. She looked at herself in profile and readjusted a hairpin above her ear. Then she went back to the bed again and sat at the foot. She regarded the pillows for a long time and the sight of them awakened in her mind secret amiable memories. She rested the nape of her neck against the cool iron bed-rail and fell into a revery. There was no longer any perturbation visible on her face.

She waited on patiently, almost cheerfully, without alarm, her memories gradually giving place to hopes and visions of the future. Her hopes and visions were so intricate that she no longer saw the white pillows on which her gaze was fixed or remembered that she was waiting for anything.

At last she heard her mother calling. She started to her feet and ran to the banisters.

—Polly! Polly!

—Yes, mamma?

—Come down, dear. Mr Doran wants to speak to you. Then she remembered what she had been waiting for.

THE NEW VILLA

ANTON CHEKHOV

1

Two miles from the village of Obrutchanovo a huge bridge was being built. From the village, which stood up high on the steep river-bank, its trellis-like skeleton could be seen, and in foggy weather and on still winter days, when its delicate iron girders and all the scaffolding around was covered with hoar frost, it presented a picturesque and even fantastic spectacle. Kutcherov, the engineer who was building the bridge, a stout, broad-shouldered, bearded man in a soft crumpled cap drove through the village in his racing droshky or his open carriage. Now and then on holidays navvies working on the bridge would come to the village; they begged for alms, laughed at the women, and sometimes carried off something. But that was rare; as a rule the days passed quietly and peacefully as though no bridge-building were going on, and only in the evening, when camp fires gleamed near the bridge, the wind faintly wafted the songs of the navvies. And by day there was sometimes the mournful clang of metal, don-don-don.

It happened that the engineer's wife came to see him. She was pleased with the river-banks and the gorgeous view over the green valley with trees, churches, flocks, and she began begging her husband to buy a small piece of ground and to build them a cottage on it. Her husband agreed. They bought sixty acres of land, and on the high bank in a field, where in earlier days the cows of Obrutchanovo used to wander, they built a pretty house of two storeys with a terrace and a verandah, with a tower and a flagstaff on which a flag fluttered on Sundays—they built it in about three months, and then all the winter they were planting big trees, and when spring came and everything began to be green there were already avenues to the new house, a gardener and two labourers in white aprons were digging near it, there was a little fountain, and a globe of looking-glass flashed so brilliantly that it was painful to look at. The house had already been named the New Villa.

On a bright, warm morning at the end of May two horses were brought to Obrutchanovo to the village blacksmith, Rodion Petrov. They came from the New Villa. The horses were sleek, graceful beasts, as white as snow, and strikingly alike.

"Perfect swans!" said Rodion, gazing at them with reverent admiration.

His wife Stepanida, his children and grandchildren came out into the street to look at them. By degrees a crowd collected. The Lytchkovs, father and son, both men with swollen faces and entirely beardless, came up bareheaded. Kozov, a tall, thin old man with a long, narrow beard, came up leaning on a stick with a crook handle: he kept winking with his crafty eyes and smiling ironically as though he knew something.

"It's only that they are white; what is there in them?" he said. "Put mine on oats, and they will be just as sleek. They ought to be in a plough and with a whip, too. . . ."

The coachman simply looked at him with disdain, but did not utter a word. And afterwards, while they were blowing up the fire at the forge, the coachman talked while he smoked cigarettes. The peasants learned from him various details: his employers were wealthy people; his mistress, Elena Ivanovna, had till her marriage lived in Moscow in a poor way as a governess; she was kind-hearted, compassionate, and fond of helping the poor. On the new estate, he told them, they were not going to plough or to sow, but simply to live for their pleasure, live only to breathe the fresh air. When he had finished and led the horses back a crowd of boys followed him, the dogs barked, and Kozov, looking after him, winked sarcastically.

"Landowners, too-oo!" he said. "They have built a house and set up horses, but I bet they are nobodies—landowners, too-oo."

Kozov for some reason took a dislike from the first to the new house, to the white horses, and to the handsome, well-fed coachman. Kozov was a solitary man, a widower; he had a dreary life (he was prevented from working by a disease which he sometimes called a rupture and sometimes worms); he was maintained by his son, who worked at a confectioner's in Harkov and sent him money; and from early morning till evening he sauntered at leisure about the river or about the village; if he saw, for instance, a peasant carting a log, or fishing, he would say: "That log's dry wood—it is rotten," or, "They won't bite in weather like this." In times of drought he would declare that there would not be a drop of rain till the frost came; and when the rains came he would say that everything would rot in the fields, that everything was ruined. And as he said these things he would wink as though he knew something.

At the New Villa they burned Bengal lights and sent up fireworks in the evenings, and a sailing-boat with red lanterns floated by Obrutchanovo. One morning the engineer's wife, Elena Ivanovna, and her little daughter drove to the village in a carriage with yellow wheels and a pair of dark bay ponies; both mother and daughter were wearing broadbrimmed straw hats, bent down over their ears.

This was exactly at the time when they were carting manure, and the blacksmith Rodion, a tall, gaunt old man, bareheaded and barefooted, was standing near his dirty and repulsive-looking cart and, flustered, looked at the ponies, and it was evident by his face that he had never seen such little horses before.

"The Kutcherov lady has come!" was whispered around. "Look, the Kutcherov lady has come!"

Elena Ivanovna looked at the huts as though she were selecting one, and then stopped at the very poorest, at the windows of which there were so many children's heads—flaxen, red, and dark. Stepanida, Rodion's wife, a stout woman, came running out of the hut; her kerchief slipped off her grey head; she looked at the carriage facing the sun, and her face smiled and wrinkled up as though she were blind.

"This is for your children," said Elena Ivanovna, and she gave her three roubles.

Stepanida suddenly burst into tears and bowed down to the ground. Rodion, too, flopped to the ground, displaying his brownish bald head, and as he did so he almost caught his wife in the ribs with the fork. Elena Ivanovna was overcome with confusion and drove back.

2

The Lytchkovs, father and son, caught in their meadows two cart-horses, a pony, and a broad-faced Aalhaus bull-calf, and with the help of redheaded Volodka, son of the blacksmith Rodion, drove them to the village. They called the village elder, collected witnesses, and went to look at the damage.

"All right, let 'em!" said Kozov, winking, "le-et 'em! Let them get out of it if they can, the engineers! Do you think there is no such thing as law? All right! Send for the police inspector, draw up a statement! . . ."

"Draw up a statement," repeated Volodka.

"I don't want to let this pass!" shouted the younger Lytchkov. He shouted louder and louder, and his beardless face seemed to be more and more swollen. "They've set up a nice fashion! Leave them free, and they will ruin all the meadows! You've no sort of right to ill-treat people! We are not serfs now!"

"We are not serfs now!" repeated Volodka.

"We got on all right without a bridge," said the elder Lytchkov gloomily; "we did not ask for it. What do we want a bridge for? We don't want it!"

"Brothers, good Christians, we cannot leave it like this!"

"All right, let 'em!" said Kozov, winking. "Let them get out of it if they can! Landowners, indeed!"

They went back to the village, and as they walked the younger Lytchkov beat himself on the breast with his fist and shouted all the way, and Volodka shouted, too, repeating his words. And meanwhile quite a crowd had gathered in the village round the thoroughbred bull-calf and the horses. The bull-calf was embarrassed and looked up from under his brows, but suddenly lowered his muzzle to the ground and took to his heels, kicking up his hind legs; Kozov was frightened and waved his stick at him, and they all burst out laughing. Then they locked up the beasts and waited.

In the evening the engineer sent five roubles for the damage, and the two horses, the pony and the bull-calf, without being fed or given water, returned home, their heads hanging with a guilty air as though they were convicted criminals.

On getting the five roubles the Lytchkovs, father and son, the village elder and Volodka, punted over the river in a boat and went to a hamlet on the other side where there was a tavern, and there had a long carousal. Their singing and the shouting of the younger Lytchkov could be heard from the village. Their women were uneasy and did not sleep all night. Rodion did not sleep either.

"It's a bad business," he said, sighing and turning from side to side. "The gentleman will be angry, and then there will be trouble. . . . They have insulted the gentleman. . . . Oh, they've insulted him. It's a bad business. . . ."

It happened that the peasants, Rodion amongst them, went into their forest to divide the clearings for mowing, and as they were returning home they were met by the engineer. He was wearing a red cotton shirt and high boots; a setter dog with its long tongue hanging out, followed behind him.

"Good-day, brothers," he said.

The peasants stopped and took off their hats.

"I have long wanted to have a talk with you, friends," he went on. "This is what it is. Ever since the early spring your cattle have been in my copse and garden every day. Everything is trampled down; the pigs have rooted up the meadow, are ruining everything in the kitchen garden, and all the undergrowth in the copse is destroyed. There is no getting on with your herdsmen; one asks them civilly, and they are rude. Damage is done on my estate every day and I do nothing—I don't fine you or make a complaint; meanwhile you impounded my horses and my bull-calf and exacted five roubles. Was that right? Is that neighbourly?" he went on, and his face was so soft and persuasive, and his expression was not forbidding. "Is that the way decent people behave? A week ago one of your people cut down two oak saplings in my copse. You have dug up the road to Eresnevo, and now I have to go two miles round. Why do you injure me at every step? What harm have I done you? For God's sake, tell me! My wife and I do our utmost to live with you in peace and harmony; we help the peasants as we can. My wife is a kind, warmhearted woman; she never refuses you help. That is her dream—to be of use to you and your children. You reward us with evil for our good. You are unjust, my friends. Think of that. I ask you earnestly to think it over. We treat you humanely; repay us in the same coin."

He turned and went away. The peasants stood a little longer, put on their caps and walked away. Rodion, who always understood everything that was said to him in some peculiar way of his own, heaved a sigh and said:

"We must pay. 'Repay in coin, my friends' . . . he said."

They walked to the village in silence. On reaching home Rodion said his prayer, took off his boots, and sat down on the bench beside his wife. Stepanida and he always sat side by side when they were at home, and always walked side by side in the street; they ate and they drank and they slept always together, and the older they grew the more they loved one another. It was hot and crowded in their hut, and there were children everywhere—on the floors, in the windows, on the stove. . . . In spite of her advanced years Stepanida was still bearing children, and now, looking at the crowd of children, it was hard to distinguish which were Rodion's and which were Volodka's. Volodka's wife, Lukerya, a plain young woman with prominent eyes and a nose like the beak of a bird, was kneading dough in a tub; Volodka was sitting on the stove with his legs hanging.

"On the road near Nikita's buckwheat . . . the engineer with his dog . . ." Rodion began, after a rest, scratching his ribs and his elbow. " 'You must pay,' says he . . . 'coin,' says he. . . . Coin or no coin, we shall have to collect ten kopecks from every hut. We've offended the gentleman very much. I am sorry for him. . . ."

"We've lived without a bridge," said Volodka, not looking at anyone, "and we don't want one."

"What next; the bridge is a government business."

"We don't want it."

"Your opinion is not asked. What is it to you?"

" 'Your opinion is not asked,' " Volodka mimicked him. "We don't want to drive anywhere; what do we want with a bridge? If we have to, we can cross by the boat."

Someone from the yard outside knocked at the window so violently that it seemed to shake the whole hut.

"Is Volodka at home?" he heard the voice of the younger Lytchkov. "Volodka, come out, come along."

Volodka jumped down off the stove and began looking for his cap.

"Don't go, Volodka," said Rodion diffidently. "Don't go with them, son. You are foolish, like a little child; they will teach you no good; don't go!"

"Don't go, son," said Stepanida, and she blinked as though about to shed tears. "I bet they are calling you to the tavern."

" 'To the tavern,' " Volodka mimicked.

"You'll come back drunk again, you currish Herod," said Lukerya, looking at him angrily. "Go along, go along, and may you burn up with vodka, you tailless Satan!"

"You hold your tongue," shouted Volodka.

"They've married me to a fool, they've ruined me, a luckless orphan, you redheaded drunkard . . ." wailed Lukerya, wiping her face with a hand covered with dough. "I wish I had never set eyes on you."

Volodka gave her a blow on the ear and went off.

3

Elena Ivanovna and her little daughter visited the village on foot. They were out for a walk. It was a Sunday, and the peasant women and girls were walking up and down the street in their brightly-coloured dresses. Rodion and Stepanida, sitting side by side at their door, bowed and smiled to Elena Ivanovna and her little daughter as to acquaintances. From the windows more than a dozen children stared at them; their faces expressed amazement and curiosity, and they could be heard whispering:

"The Kutcherov lady has come! The Kutcherov lady!"

"Good-morning," said Elena Ivanovna, and she stopped; she paused, and then asked: "Well, how are you getting on?"

"We get along all right, thank God," answered Rodion, speaking rapidly. "To be sure we get along."

"The life we lead!" smiled Stepanida. "You can see our poverty yourself, dear lady! The family is fourteen souls in all, and only two breadwinners. We are supposed to be blacksmiths, but when they bring us a horse to shoe we have no coal, nothing to buy it with. We are worried to death, lady," she went on, and laughed. "Oh, oh, we are worried to death."

Elena Ivanovna sat down at the entrance and, putting her arm round her little girl, pondered something, and judging from the little girl's expression, melancholy thoughts were straying through her mind, too; as she brooded she played with the sumptuous lace on the parasol she had taken out of her mother's hands.

"Poverty," said Rodion, "a great deal of anxiety—you see no end to it. Here, God sends no rain . . . our life is not easy, there is no denying it."

"You have a hard time in this life," said Elena Ivanovna, "but in the other world you will be happy."

Rodion did not understand her, and simply coughed into his clenched hand by way of reply. Stepanida said:

"Dear lady, the rich men will be all right in the next world, too. The rich put up candles, pay for services; the rich give to beggars, but what can the poor man do? He has no time to make the sign of the cross. He is the beggar of beggars himself; how can he think of his soul? And many sins come from poverty; from trouble we snarl at one another like dogs, we haven't a good word to say to one another, and all sorts of things happen, dear lady—God forbid! It seems we have no luck in this world nor the next. All the luck has fallen to the rich."

She spoke gaily; she was evidently used to talking of her hard life. And Rodion smiled, too; he was pleased that his old woman was so clever, so ready of speech.

"It is only on the surface that the rich seem to be happy," said Elena Ivanovna. "Every man has his sorrow. Here my husband and I do not live poorly, we have means, but are we happy? I am young, but I have had four children; my children are always being ill. I am ill, too, and constantly being doctored."

"And what is your illness?" asked Rodion.

"A woman's complaint. I get no sleep; a continual headache gives me no peace. Here I am sitting and talking, but my head is bad, I am weak all over, and I should prefer the hardest labour to such a condition. My soul, too, is troubled; I am in continual fear for my children, my husband. Every family has its own trouble of some sort; we have ours. I am not of noble birth. My grandfather was a simple peasant, my father was a tradesman in Moscow; he was a plain, uneducated man, too, while my husband's parents were wealthy and distinguished. They did not want him to marry me, but he disobeyed them, quarrelled with them, and they have not forgiven us to this day. That worries my husband; it troubles him and keeps him in constant agitation; he loves his mother, loves her dearly. So I am uneasy, too, my soul is in pain."

Peasants, men and women, were by now standing round Rodion's hut and listening. Kozov came up, too, and stood twitching his long, narrow beard. The Lytchkovs, father and son, drew near.

"And say what you like, one cannot be happy and satisfied if one does not feel in one's proper place." Elena Ivanovna went on. "Each of you has his strip of land, each of you works and knows what he is working for; my husband builds bridges—in short, everyone has his place, while I, I simply walk about. I have not my bit to work. I don't work, and feel as though I were an outsider. I am saying all this that you may not judge from outward appearances; if a man is expensively dressed and has means it does not prove that he is satisfied with his life."

She got up to go away and took her daughter by the hand.

"I like your place here very much," she said, and smiled, and from that faint, diffident smile one could tell how unwell she really was, how young and how pretty; she had a pale, thinnish face with dark eyebrows and fair hair. And the little girl was just such another as her mother: thin, fair, and slender. There was a fragrance of scent about them.

"I like the river and the forest and the village," Elena Ivanovna went on; "I could live here all my life, and I feel as though here I should get strong and find my place. I want to help you—I want to dreadfully—to be of use, to be a real friend to you. I know your need, and what I don't know I feel, my heart guesses. I am sick, feeble, and for me perhaps it is not possible to change my life as I would. But I have children. I will try to bring them up that they may be of use to you, may love you. I shall impress upon them continually that their life does not belong to them, but to you. Only I beg you earnestly, I beseech you, trust us, live in friendship with us. My husband is a kind, good man. Don't worry him, don't irritate him. He is sensitive to every trifle, and yesterday, for instance, your cattle were in our vegetable garden, and one of your people broke down the fence to the bee-hives, and such an attitude to us drives my husband to despair. I beg you," she went on in an imploring voice, and she clasped her hands on her bosom—"I beg you to treat us as good neighbours; let us live in peace! There is a saying, you know, that even a bad peace is better than a good quarrel, and, 'Don't buy property, but buy neighbours.' I repeat my husband is a kind man and good; if all goes well we promise to do everything in our power for you; we will mend the roads, we will build a school for your children. I promise you."

"Of course we thank you humbly, lady," said Lytchkov the father, looking at the ground; "you are educated people; it is for you to know best. Only, you see, Voronov, a rich peasant at Eresnevo, promised to build a school; he, too, said, 'I will do this for you,' 'I will do that for you,' and he only put up the framework and refused to go on. And then they made the peasants put the roof on and finish it; it cost them a thousand roubles. Voronov did not care; he only stroked his beard, but the peasants felt it a bit hard."

"That was a crow, but now there's a rook, too," said Kozov, and he winked. There was the sound of laughter.

"We don't want a school," said Volodka sullenly. "Our children go to Petrovskoe, and they can go on going there; we don't want it."

Elena Ivanovna seemed suddenly intimidated; her face looked paler and thinner, she shrank into herself as though she had been touched with something coarse, and walked away without uttering another word. And she walked more and more quickly, without looking round.

"Lady," said Rodion, walking after her, "lady, wait a bit; hear what I would say to you."

He followed her without his cap, and spoke softly as though begging.

"Lady, wait and hear what I will say to you."

They had walked out of the village, and Elena Ivanovna stopped beside a cart in the shade of an old mountain ash.

"Don't be offended, lady," said Rodion. "What does it mean? Have patience. Have patience for a couple of years. You will live here, you will have patience, and it will all come round. Our folks are good and peaceable; there's no harm in them; it's God's truth I'm telling you. Don't mind Kozov and the Lytchkovs, and don't mind Volodka. He's a fool; he listens to the first that speaks. The others are quiet folks; they are silent. Some would be glad, you know, to say a word from the heart and to stand up for themselves, but cannot. They have a heart and a conscience, but no tongue. Don't be offended . . . have patience. . . . What does it matter?"

Elena Ivanovna looked at the broad, tranquil river, pondering, and tears flowed down her cheeks. And Rodion was troubled by those tears; he almost cried himself.

"Never mind . . ." he muttered. "Have patience for a couple of years. You can have the school, you can have the roads, only not all at once. If you went, let us say, to sow corn on that mound you would first have to weed it out, to pick out all the stones, and then to plough, and work and work . . . and with the people, you see, it is the same . . . you must work and work until you overcome them."

The crowd had moved away from Rodion's hut, and was coming along the street towards the mountain ash. They began singing songs and playing the concertina, and they kept coming closer and closer. . . .

"Mamma, let us go away from here," said the little girl, huddling up to her mother, pale and shaking all over; "let us go away, mamma!"

"Where?"

"To Moscow. . . . Let us go, mamma."

The child began crying.

Rodion was utterly overcome; his face broke into profuse perspiration; he took out of his pocket a little crooked cucumber, like a half-moon, covered with crumbs of rye bread, and began thrusting it into the little girl's hands.

"Come, come," he muttered, scowling severely; "take the little cucumber, eat it up. . . . You mustn't cry. Mamma will whip you. . . . She'll tell your father of you when you get home. Come, come. . . ."

They walked on, and he still followed behind them, wanting to say something friendly and persuasive to them. And seeing that they were both absorbed in their own thoughts and their own griefs, and not noticing him, he stopped and, shading his eyes from the sun, looked after them for a long time till they disappeared into their copse.

4

The engineer seemed to grow irritable and petty, and in every trivial incident saw an act of robbery or outrage. His gate was kept bolted even by day, and at night two watchmen walked up and down the garden beating a board; and they gave up employing anyone from Obrutchanovo as a labourer. As ill-luck would have it someone (either a peasant or one of the workmen) took the new wheels off the cart and replaced them by old ones, then soon afterwards two bridles and a pair of pincers were carried off, and murmurs arose even in the village. People began to say that a search should be made at the Lytchkovs' and at Volodka's, and then the bridles and the pincers were found under the hedge in the engineer's garden; someone had thrown them down there.

It happened that the peasants were coming in a crowd out of the forest, and again they met the engineer on the road. He stopped, and without wishing them good-day he began, looking angrily first at one, then at another:

"I have begged you not to gather mushrooms in the park and near the yard, but to leave them for my wife and children, but your girls come before daybreak and there is not a mushroom left. . . . Whether one asks you or not it maks no difference. Entreaties, and friendliness, and persuasion I see are all useless."

He fixed his indignant eyes on Rodion and went on:

"My wife and I behaved to you as human beings, as to our equals, and you? But what's the use of talking! It will end by our looking down upon you. There is nothing left!"

And making an effort to restrain his anger, not to say too much, he turned and went on.

On getting home Rodion said his prayer, took off his boots, and sat down beside his wife.

"Yes . . ." he began with a sigh. "We were walking along just now, and Mr. Kutcherov met us. . . . Yes. . . . He saw the girls at daybreak. . . . 'Why don't they bring mushrooms,' he said . . . 'to my wife and children?' he said. . . . And then he looked at me and he said: 'I and my wife will look after you,' he said. I wanted to fall down at his feet, but I hadn't the courage. . . . God give him health. . . . God bless him! . . ."

Stepanida crossed herself and sighed.

"They are kind, simple-hearted people," Rodion went on, " 'We shall look after you.' . . . He promised me that before everyone. In our old age . . . it wouldn't be a bad thing. . . . I should always pray for them. . . . Holy Mother, bless them. . . ."

The Feast of the Exaltation of the Cross, the fourteenth of September, was the festival of the village church. The Lytchkovs, father and son, went across the river early in the morning and returned to dinner drunk; they spent a long time going about the village, alternately singing and swearing; then they had a fight and went to the New Villa to complain. First Lytchkov the father went into the yard with a long ashen stick in his hands. He stopped irresolutely and took off his hat. Just at that moment the engineer and his family were sitting on the verandah, drinking tea.

"What do you want?" shouted the engineer.

"Your honour . . . " Lytchkov began, and burst into tears. "Show the Divine mercy, protect me . . . my son makes my life a misery . . . your honour. . . ."

Lytchkov the son walked up, too; he, too, was bareheaded and had a stick in his hand; he stopped and fixed his drunken senseless eyes on the verandah.

"It is not my business to settle your affairs," said the engineer. "Go to the rural captain or the police officer."

"I have been everywhere. . . . I have lodged a petition . . ." said Lytchkov the father, and he sobbed. "Where can I go now? He can kill me now, it seems. He can do anything. Is that the way to treat a father? A father?"

He raised his stick and hit his son on the head; the son raised his stick and struck the father just on his bald patch such a blow that the stick bounced back. The father did not even flinch, but hit his son again and again on the head. And so they stood and kept hitting one another on the head, and it looked not so much like a fight as some sort of a game. And peasants, men and women, stood in a crowd at the gate and looked into the garden, and the faces of all were grave. They were the peasants who had come to greet them for the holiday, but seeing the Lytchkovs, they were ashamed and did not go in.

The next morning Elena Ivanovna went with the children to Moscow. And there was a rumour that the engineer was selling his house. . . .

5

The peasants had long ago grown used to the sight of the bridge, and it was difficult to imagine the river at that place without a bridge. The heap of rubble left from the building of it had long been overgrown with grass, the navvies were forgotten, and instead of the strains of the "Dubinushka" that they used to sing, the peasants heard almost every hour the sounds of a passing train.

The New Villa has long ago been sold; now it belongs to a government clerk who comes here from the town for the holidays with his family, drinks tea on the terrace, and then goes back to the town again. He wears a cockade on his cap; he talks and clears his throat as though he were a very important official, though he is only of the rank of a collegiate secretary, and when the peasants bow he makes no response.

In Obrutchanovo everyone has grown older; Kozov is dead. In Rodion's hut there are even more children. Volodka has grown a long red beard. They are still as poor as ever.

In the early spring the Obrutchanovo peasants were sawing wood near the station. And after work they were going home; they walked without haste one after the other. Broad saws curved over their shoulders; the sun was reflected in them. The nightingales were singing in the bushes on the bank, larks were trilling in the heavens. It was quiet at the New Villa; there was not a soul there, and only golden pigeons—golden because the sunlight was streaming upon them—were flying over the house. All of them—Rodion, the two Lytch-kovs, and Volodka—thought of the white horses, the little ponies, the fireworks, the boat with the lanterns; they remembered how the engineer's wife, so beautiful and so grandly dressed, had come into the village and talked to them in such a friendly way. And it seemed as though all that had never been; it was like a dream or a fairy-tale.

They trudged along, tired out, and mused as they went. . . . In their village, they mused, the people were good, quiet, sensible, fearing God, and Elena Ivanovna, too, was quiet, kind, and gentle; it made one sad to look at her, but why had they not got on together? Why had they parted like enemies? How was it that some mist had shrouded from their eyes what mattered most, and had let them see nothing but damage done by cattle, bridles, pincers, and all those trivial things which now, as they remembered them, seemed so non-sensical? How was it that with the new owner they lived in peace, and yet had been on bad terms with the engineer?

And not knowing what answer to make to these questions they were all silent except Volodka, who muttered something.

"What is it?" Rodion asked.

"We lived without a bridge . . ." said Volodka gloomily. "We lived without a bridge, and did not ask for one . . . and we don't want it. . . ."

No one answered him and they walked on in silence with drooping heads.

*A COUNTRY DOCTOR

FRANZ KAFKA

I was in great perplexity; I had to start on an urgent journey; a seriously ill patient was waiting for me in a village ten miles off; a thick blizzard of snow filled all the wide spaces between him and me; I had a gig, a light gig with big wheels, exactly right for our country roads; muffed in furs, my bag of instruments in my hand, I was in the courtyard all ready for the journey; but there was no horse to be had, no horse. My own horse had died in the night, worn out by the fatigues of this icy winter; my servant girl was now running round the village trying to borrow a horse; but it was hopeless, I knew it, and I stood there forlornly, with the snow gathering more and more thickly upon me, more and more unable to move. In the gateway the girl appeared, alone, and waved the lantern; of course, who would lend a horse at this time for such a journey? I strode through the courtway once more; I could see no way out; in my confused distress I kicked at the dilapidated door of the year-long uninhabited pigsty. It flew open and flapped to and fro on its hinges. A steam and smell as of horses came out of it. A dim stable lantern was swinging inside from a rope. A man, crouching on his hams in that low space, showed an open blue-eyed face. "Shall I yoke up?" he asked, crawling out on all fours. I did not know what to say and merely stooped down to see what else was in the sty. The servant girl standing beside me. "You never know what you're going to find in your own house," she said, and we both laughed. "Hey there, Brother, hey there, Sister!" called the groom, and two horses, enormous creatures with powerful flanks, one after the other, their legs tucked close to their bodies, each well-shaped head lowered like a camel's, by sheer strength of buttocking squeezed out through the door hole which they filled entirely. But at once they were standing up, with their long legs and their bodies steaming thickly. "Give him a hand," I said, and the willing girl hurried to help the groom with the harnessing. Yet hardly was she beside him when the groom clipped hold of her and pushed his face against hers. She screamed and fled back to me; on her cheek stood out in red the marks of two rows of teeth. "You brute," I yelled in fury, "do you want a whipping?" but in the same moment reflected that the man was a stranger; that I did not know where he came from, and that of his own free will he was helping me out when everyone else had failed me. As if he knew my thoughts he took no offense at my threat but, still busied with the horses, only turned round once towards me. "Get in," he said then, and indeed: everything was ready. A magnificent pair of horses, I observed, such as I had never sat behind, and I climbed in happily. "But I'll drive, you don't know the way," I said. "Of course," said he, "I'm not coming with you anyway, I'm staying with Rose." "No," shrieked Rose, fleeing into the house with a justified presentiment that her fate was inescapable; I heard the door chain rattle as she put it up; I heard the key turn in the lock; I could see, moreover, how she put out the lights in the entrance hall and in further flight all through the rooms to keep herself from being discovered. "You're coming with me," I said to the groom, "or I won't go, urgent as my journey is. I'm not thinking of paying for it by handing the girl over to you." "Gee up!" he said; clapped his hands; the gig whirled off like a log in a freshet; I could just hear the door of my house splitting and bursting as the groom charged at it and then I was deafened and blinded by a storming rush that steadily buffeted all my senses. But this only for a moment, since, as if my patient's farmyard had opened out just before my courtyard gate, I was already there; the horses had come quietly to a standstill; the blizzard had stopped; the moonlight all around; my patient's parents hurried out of the house, his sister behind them; I was almost lifted out of the gig; from their confused ejaculations I gathered not a word; in the sick room the air was almost unbreathable; the neglected stove was smoking; I wanted to push open a window; but first I had to look at my patient. Gaunt, without any fever, not cold, not warm, with vacant eyes, without a shirt, the youngster heaved himself up from the feather bedding, threw his arms around my neck and whispered in my ear: "Doctor, let me die." I glanced round the room; no one had heard it; the parents were leaning forward in silence waiting for my verdict; the sister had set a chair for my handbag; I opened the bag and hunted among my instruments; the boy kept clutching at me from his bed to remind me of his entreaty; I picked up a pair of tweezers, examined them in the candlelight and laid them down again. "Yes," I thought blasphemously, "in cases like this the gods are helpful, send the missing horse, add to it a second because of the urgency, and to crown everything bestow even a groom—" And only now did I remember Rose again; what was I to do, how could I rescue her, how could I pull her away from under that groom at ten miles' distance, with a team of horses I couldn't control. These horses, now, they had somehow slipped the reins loose, pushed the window open from the outside, I did not know how; each of them had stuck a head in at a window and, quite unmoved by the startled cries of the family, stood eyeing the patient. "Better go back at once," I thought, as if the horses were summoning me to the return journey, yet I permitted the patient's sister, who fancied that I was dazed by the heat, to take my fur coat from me. A glass of rum was poured out for me, the old man clapped me on the shoulder, a familiarity justified by this offer of his treasure. I shook my head; in the narrow confines of the old man's thoughts I felt ill; that was my only reason for refusing the drink. The mother stood by the bedside and cajoled me towards it. I yielded, and, while one of the horses whinnied loudly to the ceiling, laid my head to the boy's breast, which shivered under my wet beard. I confirmed what I already knew; the boy was quite sound, something a little wrong with his circulation, saturated with coffee by his solicitous mother, but sound and best turned out of bed with one shove. I am no world reformer and so I let him lie. I was the district doctor and I did my duty to the uttermost, to the point where it became almost too much. I was badly paid and yet generous and helpful to the poor. I had still to see that Rose was all right, and then the boy might have his way and I wanted to die too. What was I doing there in that endless winter! My horse was dead, and not a single person in the village would lend me another. I had to get my team out of the pigsty; if they hadn't chanced to be horses I should have had to travel with swine. That was how it was. And I nodded to the family. They knew nothing about it, and, had they known, would not have believed it. To write prescriptions is easy, but to come to an understanding with people is hard. Well, this should be the end of my visit, I had once more been called out needlessly, I was used to that, the whole district made my life a torment with my night bell, but that I should have to sacrifice Rose this time as well, the pretty girl who had lived in my house for years almost without my noticing her—that sacrifice was too much to ask, and I had somehow to get it reasoned out in my head with the help of what craft I could muster, in order not to let fly at this family, which with the best will in the world could not restore Rose to me. But as I shut my bag and put an arm out for my fur coat, the family meanwhile standing together, the father sniffing at the glass of rum in his hand, the mother, apparently disappointed in me—why, what do people expect?—biting her lips with tears in her eyes, the sister fluttering a blood-soaked towel, I was somehow ready to admit conditionally that the boy might be ill after all. I went towards him, he welcomed me smiling as if I were bringing him the most nourishing invalid broth—ah, now both horses were whinnying together; the noise, I suppose, was ordained by heaven to assist my examination of the patient—and this time I discovered that the boy was indeed ill. In his right side, near the hip, was an open wound as big as the palm of my hand. Rose-red, in many variations of shade, dark in the hollows, lighter at the edges, softly granulated, with irregular clots of blood, open as a surface mine to the daylight. That was how it looked from a distance. But on a closer inspection there was another complication. I could not help a low whistle of surprise. Worms, as thick and as long as my little finger, themselves rose-red and blood-spotted as well, were wriggling from their fastness in the interior of the wound towards the light, with small white heads and many little legs. Poor boy, you were past helping. I had discovered your great wound; this blossom in your side was destroying you. The family was pleased; they saw me busying myself; the sister told the mother, the mother the father, the father told several guests who were coming in, through the moonlight at the open door, walking on tiptoe, keeping their balance with outstretched arms. "Will you save me?" whispered the boy with a sob, quite blinded by the life within his wound. That is what people are like in my district. Always expecting the impossible from the doctor. They have lost their ancient beliefs; the parson sits at home and unravels his vestments, one after another; but the doctor is supposed to be omnipotent with his merciful surgeon's hand. Well, as it pleases them; I have not thrust my services on them; if they misuse me for sacred ends, I let that happen to me too; what better do I want, old country doctor that I am, bereft of my servant girl! And so they came, the family and the village elders, and stripped my clothes off me; a school choir with the teacher at the head of it stood before the house and sang these words to an utterly simple tune:

> Strip his clothes off, then he'll heal us,
> If he doesn't, kill him dead!
> Only a doctor, only a doctor.

Then my clothes were off and I looked at the people quietly, my fingers in my beard and my head cocked to one side. I was altogether composed and equal to the situation and remained so, although it was no help to me, since they now took me by the head and feet and carried me to the bed. They laid me down in it next to the wall, on the side of the wound. Then they all left the room; the door was shut; the singing stopped; clouds covered the moon; the bedding was warm around me; the horses' heads in the opened windows wavered like shadows. "Do you know," said a voice in my ear, "I have very little confidence in you. Why, you were only blown in here, you didn't come on your own feet. Instead of helping me, you're cramping me on my death bed. What I'd like best is to scratch your eyes out." "Right," I said, "it's a shame. And yet I am a doctor. What am I to do? Believe me, it is not too easy for me either." "Am I supposed to be content with this apology? Oh, I must be, I can't help it. I always have to put up with things. A fine wound is all I brought into the world; that was my sole endowment." My young friend," said I, "your mistake is: you have not a wide enough view. I have been in all the sickrooms, far and wide, and I tell you: your wound is not so bad. Done in a tight corner with two strokes of the ax. Many a one proffers his side and can hardly hear the ax in the forest, far less that it is coming nearer to him." "Is that really so, or are you deluding me in my fever?" "It is really so, take the word of honor of an official doctor." And he took it and lay still. But now it was time for me to think of escaping. The horses were still standing faithfully in their places. My clothes, my fur coat, my bag were quickly collected; I didn't want to waste time dressing; if the horses raced home as they had come, I should only be springing, as it were, out of this bed into my own. Obediently a horse backed away from the window; I threw my bundle into the gig; the fur coat missed its mark and was caught on a hook only by the sleeve. Good enough. I swung myself on to the horse. With the reins loosely trailing, one horse barely fastened to the other, the gig swaying behind, my fur coat last of all in the snow. "Geeup!" I said, but there was no galloping; slowly, like old men, we crawled through the snowy wastes; a long time echoed behind us the new but faulty song of the children:

> O be joyful, all you patients,
> The doctor's laid in bed beside you!

Never shall I reach home at this rate; my flourishing practice is done for; my successor is robbing me, but in vain, for he cannot take my place; in my house the disgusting groom is raging; Rose is the victim; I do not want to think about it any more. Naked, exposed to the frost of this most unhappy of ages, with an earthly vehicle, unearthly horses, old man that I am, I wander astray. My fur coat is hanging from the back of the gig, but I cannot reach it, and none of my limber pack of patients lifts a finger. Betrayed! Betrayed! A false alarm on the night bell once answered—it cannot be made good, not ever.

Twentieth-Century Causes

BETRAYALS AND LOYALTIES

It has been said more than once that twentieth century men and women have had to find, anew and for themselves, something to live by. The classic choices have been religion, a social cause, national patriotism, some mixture of those three, or personal ethical systems. One prime difficulty among many, in our century, has been the fact that social causes attractive in theory have turned out to be ruinous in reality. Ends have been used to justify the most terrible of means. Doctrines pointing to the emancipation of man have resulted in practical enslavement. History indicates undeniably that "causes," however high or noble, can become abstract, rigid, and ideological— to the point of erasing individual human beings and their living values. Such situations almost invite honest deviation from ideals. But no matter what the "cause," betrayals will occur out of nonidealistic or dishonest motives: the old familiar drives for status, power, revenge, or monetary gain.

No one has defined these issues more clearly than those recent writers who are themselves inheritors of the humanistic values of the past. It is writers of this persuasion whom we shall read in this final section. Traces of a twentieth century movement called "existentialism" appear in some stories in this group. There is an emphasis on situations involving responsible, individual choice despite awareness of absurdity in the human condition. Treatment of character or of a fictional character's "past" is less causal or documentary than in much earlier fiction.

We have seen that fiction is a means by which we can correct, repair, enlarge, or limit, our sense of human reality. Good fiction will never limit our comprehension but will instead expand our imaginative and emotional capacities. In a sense, we live by "fictions"— images of the desirable or undesirable qualities in living, of the things worth our rejecting or worth our seeking and achieving. We

297

cannot live humanly without awareness of the positive—and negative —alternatives open to us. In this seeking, good fiction is a main resource.

Guests of the Nation[1]

FRANK O'CONNOR

1

At dusk the big Englishman, Belcher, would shift his long legs out of the ashes and say "Well, chums, what about it?" and Noble or me would say "All right, chum" (for we had picked up some of their curious expressions), and the little Englishman, Hawkins, would light the lamp and bring out the cards. Sometimes Jeremiah Donovan would come up and supervise the game and get excited over Hawkins's cards, which he always played badly, and shout at him as if he was one of our own "Ah, you divil, you, why didn't you play the tray?"

But ordinarily Jeremiah was a sober and contented poor devil like the big Englishman, Belcher, and was looked up to only because he was a fair hand at documents, though he was slow enough even with them. He wore a small cloth hat and big gaiters over his long pants, and you seldom saw him with his hands out of his pockets. He reddened when you talked to him, tilting from toe to heel and back, and looking down all the time at his big farmer's feet. Noble and me used to make fun of his broad accent, because we were from the town.

I couldn't at the time see the point of me and Noble guarding Belcher and Hawkins at all, for it was my belief that you could have planted that pair down anywhere from this to Claregalway and they'd have taken root there like a native weed. I never in my short experience seen two men to take to the country as they did.

They were handed on to us by the Second Battalion when the search for

[1]Time of action: the Anglo-Irish war of the twentieth century, which ended "officially" with the creation of the Irish Free State in 1921–22. Settlement of "the Irish question" was an issue in England for hundreds of years. From the Irish point of view, it was "the English question" and is still a live issue.

them became too hot, and Noble and myself, being young, took over with a natural feeling of responsibility, but Hawkins made us look like fools when he showed that he knew the country better than we did.

"You're the bloke they calls Bonaparte," he says to me. "Mary Brigid O'Connell told me to ask you what you done with the pair of her brother's socks you borrowed."

For it seemed, as they explained it, that the Second used to have little evenings, and some of the girls of the neighbourhood turned in, and, seeing they were such decent chaps, our fellows couldn't leave the two Englishmen out of them. Hawkins learned to dance "The Walls of Limerick," "The Siege of Ennis," and "The Waves of Tory" as well as any of them, though, naturally, he couldn't return the compliment, because our lads at that time did not dance foreign dances on principle.

So whatever privileges Belcher and Hawkins had with the Second they just naturally took with us, and after the first day or two we gave up all pretence of keeping a close eye on them. Not that they could have got far, for they had accents you could cut with a knife and wore khaki tunics and overcoats with civilian pants and boots. But it's my belief that they never had any idea of escaping and were quite content to be where they were.

It was a treat to see how Belcher got off with the old woman of the house where we were staying. She was a great warrant to scold, and cranky even with us, but before ever she had a chance of giving our guests, as I may call them, a lick of her tongue, Belcher had made her his friend for life. She was breaking sticks, and Belcher, who hadn't been more than ten minutes in the house, jumped up from his seat and went over to her.

"Allow me, madam," he says, smiling his queer little smile, "please allow me"; and he takes the bloody hatchet. She was struck too paralytic to speak, and after that, Belcher would be at her heels, carrying a bucket, a basket, or a load of turf, as the case might be. As Noble said, he got into looking before she leapt, and hot water, or any little thing she wanted, Belcher would have it ready for her. For such a huge man (and though I am five foot ten myself I had to look up at him) he had an uncommon shortness—or should I say lack?—of speech. It took us some time to get used to him, walking in and out, like a ghost, without a word. Especially because Hawkins talked enough for a platoon, it was strange to hear big Belcher with his toes in the ashes come out with a solitary "Excuse me, chum," or "That's right, chum." His one and only passion was cards, and I will say for him that he was a good card-player. He could have fleeced myself and Noble, but whatever we lost to him Hawkins lost to us, and Hawkins played with the money Belcher gave him.

Hawkins lost to us because he had too much old gab, and we probably lost to Belcher for the same reason. Hawkins and Noble would spit at one another about religion into the early hours of the morning, and Hawkins worried the soul out of Noble, whose brother was a priest, with a string of questions that would puzzle a cardinal. To make it worse, even in treating of holy subjects, Hawkins had a deplorable tongue. I never in all my career met a man who could mix such a variety of cursing and bad language into an argument. He was a terrible man, and a fright to argue. He never did a stroke of work, and when he had no one else to talk to, he got stuck in the old woman.

He met his match in her, for one day when he tried to get her to complain profanely of the drought, she gave him a great come-down by blaming it entirely on Jupiter Pluvius (a deity neither Hawkins nor I had ever heard of, though Noble said that among the pagans it was believed that he had something to do with the rain). Another day he was swearing at the capitalists for starting the German war when the old lady laid down her iron, puckered up her little crab's mouth, and said: "Mr. Hawkins, you can say what you like about the war, and think you'll deceive me because I'm only a simple poor country-woman, but I know what started the war. It was the Italian Count that stole the heathen divinity out of the temple in Japan. Believe me, Mr. Hawkins, nothing but sorrow and want can follow the people that disturb the hidden powers."

A queer old girl, all right.

2

We had our tea one evening, and Hawkins lit the lamp and we all sat into cards. Jeremiah Donovan came in too, and sat down and watched us for a while, and it suddenly struck me that he had no great love for the two Englishmen. It came as a great surprise to me, because I hadn't noticed anything about him before.

Late in the evening a really terrible argument blew up between Hawkins and Noble, about capitalists and priests and love of your country.

"The capitalists," says Hawkins with an angry gulp, "pays the priests to tell you about the next world so as you won't notice what the bastards are up to in this."

"Nonsense, man!" says Noble, losing his temper. "Before ever a capitalist was thought of, people believed in the next world."

Hawkins stood up as though he was preaching a sermon.

"Oh, they did, did they?" he says with a sneer. "They believed all the things you believe, isn't that what you mean? And you believe that God created Adam, and Adam created Shem, and Shem created Jehoshophat. You believe all that silly old fairytale about Eve and Eden and the apple. Well, listen to me, chum. If you're entitled to hold a silly belief like that, I'm entitled to hold my silly belief—which is that the first thing your God created was a bleeding capitalist, with morality and Rolls-Royce complete. Am I right, chum?" he says to Belcher.

"You're right, chum," says Belcher with his amused smile, and got up from the table to stretch his long legs into the fire and stroke his moustache. So, seeing that Jeremiah Donovan was going, and that there was no knowing when the argument about religion would be over, I went out with him. We strolled down to the village together, and then he stopped and started blushing and mumbling and saying I ought to be behind, keeping guard on the prisoners. I didn't like the tone he took with me, and anyway I was bored with life in the cottage, so I replied by asking him what the hell we wanted guarding them at all for. I told him I'd talked it over with Noble, and that we'd both rather be out with a fighting column.

"What use are those fellows to us?" says I.

He looked at me in surprise and said: "I thought you knew we were keeping them as hostages."

"Hostages?" I said.

"The enemy have prisoners belonging to us," he says, "and now they're talking of shooting them. If they shoot our prisoners, we'll shoot theirs."

"Shoot them?" I said.

"What else did you think we were keeping them for?" he says.

"Wasn't it very unforeseen of you not to warn Noble and myself of that in the beginning?" I said.

"How was it?" says he. "You might have known it."

"We couldn't know it, Jeremiah Donovan," says I. "How could we when they were on our hands so long?"

"The enemy have our prisoners as long and longer," says he.

"That's not the same thing at all," says I.

"What difference is there?" says he.

I couldn't tell him, because I knew he wouldn't understand. If it was only an old dog that was going to the vet's, you'd try and not get too fond of him, but Jeremiah Donovan wasn't a man that would ever be in danger of that.

"And when is this thing going to be decided?" says I.

"We might hear tonight," he says. "Or tomorrow or the next day at latest. So if it's only hanging round here that's a trouble to you, you'll be free soon enough."

It wasn't the hanging round that was a trouble to me at all by this time. I had worse things to worry about. When I got back to the cottage the argument was still on. Hawkins was holding forth in his best style, maintaining that there was no next world, and Noble was maintaining that there was; but I could see that Hawkins had had the best of it.

"Do you know what, chum?" he was saying with a saucy smile. "I think you're just as big a bleeding unbeliever as I am. You say you believe in the next world, and you know just as much about the next world as I do, which is sweet damn-all. What's heaven? You don't know. Where's heaven? You don't know. You know sweet damn-all! I ask you again, do they wear wings?"

"Very well, then," says Noble, "they do. Is that enough for you? They do wear wings."

"Where do they get them, then? Who makes them? Have they a factory for wings? Have they a sort of store where you hands in your chit and takes your bleeding wings?"

"You're an impossible man to argue with," says Noble. "Now, listen to me—" And they were off again.

It was long after midnight when we locked up and went to bed. As I blew out the candle I told Noble what Jeremiah Donovan was after telling me. Noble took it very quietly. When we'd been in bed about an hour he asked me did I think we ought to tell the Englishmen. I didn't think we should, because it was more than likely that the English wouldn't shoot our men, and even if they did, the brigade officers, who were always up and down with the Second Battalion and knew the Englishmen well, wouldn't be likely to want them plugged. "I think so too," says Noble. "It would be great cruelty to put the wind up them now."

"It was very unforeseen of Jeremiah Donovan anyhow," says I.

It was next morning that we found it so hard to face Belcher and Hawkins. We went about the house all day scarcely saying a word. Belcher didn't seem to notice; he was stretched into the ashes as usual, with his usual look of waiting in quietness for something unforeseen to happen, but Hawkins noticed and put it down to Noble's being beaten in the argument of the night before.

"Why can't you take a discussion in the proper spirit?" he says severely. "You and your Adam and Eve! I'm a Communist, that's what I am. Communist or anarchist, it all comes to much the same thing." And for hours he went round the house, muttering when the fit took him. "Adam and Eve! Adam and Eve! Nothing better to do with their time than picking bleeding apples!"

3

I don't know how we got through that day, but I was very glad when it was over, the tea things were cleared away, and Belcher said in his peaceable way: "Well, chums, what about it?" We sat round the table and Hawkins took out the cards, and just then I heard Jeremiah Donovan's footstep on the path and a dark presentiment crossed my mind. I rose from the table and caught him before he reached the door.

"What do you want?" I asked.

"I want those two soldier friends of yours," he says, getting red.

"Is that the way, Jeremiah Donovan?" I asked.

"That's the way. There were four of our lads shot this morning, one of them a boy of sixteen."

"That's bad," I said.

At that moment Noble followed me out, and the three of us walked down the path together, talking in whispers. Feeney, the local intelligence officer, was standing by the gate.

"What are you going to do about it?" I asked Jeremiah Donovan.

"I want you and Noble to get them out; tell them they're being shifted again; that'll be the quietest way."

"Leave me out of that," says Noble under his breath.

Jeremiah Donovan looks at him hard.

"All right," he says. "You and Feeney get a few tools from the shed and dig a hole by the far end of the bog. Bonaparte and myself will be after you. Don't let anyone see you with the tools. I wouldn't like it to go beyond ourselves."

We saw Feeney and Noble go round to the shed and went in ourselves. I left Jeremiah Donovan to do the explanations. He told them that he had orders to send them back to the Second Batallion. Hawkins let out a mouthful of curses, and you could see that though Belcher didn't say anything, he was a bit upset too. The old woman was for having them stay in spite of us, and she didn't stop advising them until Jeremiah Donovan lost his temper and turned on her. He had a nasty temper, I noticed. It was pitch-dark in the cottage by this time, but no one thought of lighting the lamp, and in the darkness the two Englishmen fetched their topcoats and said good-bye to the old woman.

"Just as a man makes a home of a bleeding place, some bastard at headquarters thinks you're too cushy and shunts you off," says Hawkins, shaking her hand.

"A thousand thanks, madam," says Belcher. "A thousand thanks for everything"—as though he'd made it up.

We went round to the back of the house and down towards the bog. It was only then that Jeremiah Donovan told them. He was shaking with excitement.

"There were four of our fellows shot in Cork this morning and now you're to be shot as a reprisal."

"What are you talking about?" snaps Hawkins. "It's bad enough being mucked about as we are without having to put up with your funny jokes."

"It isn't a joke," says Donovan. "I'm sorry, Hawkins, but it's true," and begins on the usual rigmarole about duty and how unpleasant it is.

I never noticed that people who talk a lot about duty find it much of a trouble to them.

"Oh, cut it out!" says Hawkins.

"Ask Bonaparte," says Donovan, seeing that Hawkins isn't taking him seriously. "Isn't it true, Bonaparte?"

"It is," I say, and Hawkins stops.

"Ah, for Christ's sake, chum!"

"I mean it, chum," I say.

"You don't sound as if you mean it."

"If he doesn't mean it, I do," says Donovan, working himself up.

"What have you against me, Jeremiah Donovan?"

"I never said I had anything against you. But why did your people take out four of our prisoners and shoot them in cold blood?"

He took Hawkins by the arm and dragged him on, but it was impossible to make him understand that we were in earnest. I had the Smith and Wesson in my pocket and I kept fingering it and wondering what I'd do if they put up a fight for it or ran, and wishing to God they'd do one or the other. I knew if they did run for it, that I'd never fire on them. Hawkins wanted to know was Noble in it, and when we said yes, he asked us why Noble wanted to plug him. Why did any of us want to plug him? What had he done to us? Weren't we all chums? Didn't we understand him and didn't he understand us? Did we imagine for an instant that he'd shoot us for all the so-and-so officers in the so-and-so British Army?

By this time we'd reached the bog, and I was so sick I couldn't even answer him. We walked along the edge of it in the darkness, and every now and then Hawkins would call a halt and begin all over again, as if he was wound up, about our being chums, and I knew that nothing but the sight of the grave would convince him that we had to do it. And all the time I was hoping that something would happen; that they'd run for it or that Noble would take over the responsibility from me. I had the feeling that it was worse on Noble than on me.

<h1 style="text-align:center">4</h1>

At last we saw the lantern in the distance and made towards it. Noble was carrying it, and Feeney was standing somewhere in the darkness behind him, and the picture of them so still and silent in the bogland brought it home to me that we were in earnest, and banished the last bit of hope I had.

Belcher, on recognizing Noble, said: "Hallo, chum," in his quiet way, but Hawkins flew at him at once, and the argument began all over again, only this time Noble had nothing to say for himself and stood with his head down, holding the lantern between his legs.

It was Jeremiah Donovan who did the answering. For the twentieth time, as though it was haunting his mind, Hawkins asked if anybody thought he'd shoot Noble.

"Yes, you would," says Jeremiah Donovan.

"No, I wouldn't, damn you!"

"You would, because you'd know you'd be shot for not doing it."

"I wouldn't, not if I was to be shot twenty times over. I wouldn't shoot a pal. And Belcher wouldn't—isn't that right, Belcher?"

"That's right, chum," Belcher said, but more by way of answering the question than of joining in the argument. Belcher sounded as though whatever unforeseen thing he'd always been waiting for had come at last.

"Anyway, who says Noble would be shot if I wasn't? What do you think I'd do if I was in his place, out in the middle of a blasted bog?"

"What would you do?" asks Donovan.

"I'd go with him wherever he was going, of course. Share my last bob with him and stick by him through thick and thin. No one can ever say of me that I let down a pal."

"We had enough of this," says Jeremiah Donovan, cocking his revolver. "Is there any message you want to send?"

"No, there isn't."

"Do you want to say your prayers?"

Hawkins came out with a cold-blooded remark that even shocked me and turned on Noble again.

"Listen to me, Noble," he says. "You and me are chums. You can't come over to my side, so I'll come over to your side. That show you I mean what I say? Give me a rifle and I'll go along with you and the other lads."

Nobody answered him. We knew that was no way out.

"Hear what I'm saying?" he says. "I'm through with it. I'm a deserter or anything else you like. I don't believe in your stuff, but it's no worse than mine. That satisfy you?"

Noble raised his head, but Donovan began to speak and he lowered it again without replying.

"For the last time, have you any messages to send?" says Donovan in a cold, excited sort of voice.

"Shut up, Donovan! You don't understand me, but these lads do. They're not the sort to make a pal and kill a pal. They're not the tools of any capitalist."

I alone of the crowd saw Donovan raise his Webley to the back of Hawkins's neck, and as he did so I shut my eyes and tried to pray. Hawkins had begun to say something else when Donovan fired, and as I opened my eyes at the bang, I saw Hawkins stagger at the knees and lie out flat at Noble's feet, slowly and as quiet as a kid falling asleep, with the lantern-light on his lean legs and bright farmer's boots. We all stood very still, watching him settle out in the last agony.

Then Belcher took out a handkerchief and began to tie it about his own eyes (in our excitement we'd forgotten to do the same for Hawkins), and, seeing it wasn't big enough, turned and asked for the loan of mine. I gave it to him and he knotted the two together and pointed with his foot at Hawkins.

"He's not quite dead," he says. "Better give him another."

Sure enough, Hawkins's left knee is beginning to rise. I bend down and put my gun to his head; then, recollecting myself, I get up again. Belcher understands what's in my mind.

"Give him his first," he says. "I don't mind. Poor bastard, we don't know what's happening to him now."

I knelt and fired. By this time I didn't seem to know what I was doing. Belcher, who was fumbling a bit awkwardly with the handkerchiefs, came out with a laugh as he heard the shot. It was the first time I heard him laugh and it sent a shudder down my back; it sounded so unnatural.

"Poor bugger!" he said quietly. "And last night he was so curious about it all. It's very queer, chums, I always think. Now he knows as much about it as they'll ever let him know, and last night he was all in the dark."

Donovan helped him to tie the handkerchiefs about his eyes. "Thanks, chum," he said. Donovan asked if there were any messages he wanted sent.

"No, chum," he says. "Not for me. If any of you would like to write to Hawkins's mother, you'll find a letter from her in his pocket. He and his mother were great chums. But my missus left me eight years ago. Went away with another fellow and took the kid with her. I like the feeling of a home, as you may have noticed, but I couldn't start again after that."

It was an extraordinary thing, but in those few minutes Belcher said more than in all the weeks before. It was just as if the sound of the shot had started a flood of talk in him and he could go on the whole night like that, quite happily, talking about himself. We stood round like fools now that he couldn't see us any longer. Donovan looked at Noble, and Noble shook his head. Then Donovan raised his Webley, and at that moment Belcher gives his queer laugh again. He may have thought we were talking about him, or perhaps he noticed the same thing I'd noticed and couldn't understand it.

"Excuse me, chums," he says. "I feel I'm talking the hell of a lot, and so silly, about my being so handy about a house and things like that. But this thing came on me suddenly. You'll forgive me, I'm sure."

"You don't want to say a prayer?" asks Donovan.

"No, chum," he says. "I don't think it would help. I'm ready, and you boys want to get it over."

"You understand that we're only doing our duty?" says Donovan.

Belcher's head was raised like a blind man's, so that you could only see his chin and the tip of his nose in the lantern-light.

"I never could make out what duty was myself," he said. "I think you're all good lads, if that's what you mean. I'm not complaining."

Noble, just as if he couldn't bear any more of it, raised his fist at Donovan, and in a flash Donovan raised his gun and fired. The big man went over like a sack of meal, and this time there was no need of a second shot.

I don't remember much about the burying, but that it was worse than all the rest because we had to carry them to the grave. It was all mad lonely with nothing but a patch of lantern-light between ourselves and the dark, and birds hooting and screeching all round, disturbed by the guns. Noble went through Hawkins's belongings to find the letter from his mother, and then joined his hands together. He did the same with Belcher. Then, when we'd filled in the grave, we separated from Jeremiah Donovan and Feeney and took our tools back to the shed. All the way we didn't speak a word. The kitchen was dark and cold as we'd left it, and the old woman was sitting over the hearth, saying her beads. We walked past her into the room, and Noble struck a match to light the lamp. She rose quietly and came to the doorway with all her cantankerousness gone.

"What did ye do with them?" she asked in a whisper, and Noble started so that the match went out in his hand.

"What's that?" he asked without turning round.

"I heard ye," she said.

"What did you hear?" asked Noble.

"I heard ye. Do ye think I didn't hear ye, putting the spade back in the houseen?"

Noble struck another match and this time the lamp lit for him.

"Was that what ye did to them?" she asked.

Then, by God, in the very doorway, she fell on her knees and began praying, and after looking at her for a minute or two Noble did the same by the fireplace. I pushed my way out past her and left them at it. I stood at the door, watching the stars and listening to the shrieking of the birds dying out over the bogs. It is so strange what you feel at times like that that you can't describe it. Noble says he saw everything ten times the size, as though there were nothing in the whole world but that little patch of bog with the two Englishmen stiffening into it, but with me it was as if the patch of bog where the Englishmen were was a million miles away, and even Noble and the old woman, mumbling behind me, and the birds and the bloody stars were all far away, and I was somehow very small and very lost and lonely like a child astray in the snow. And anything that happened to me afterwards, I never felt the same about again.

Please Don't Kill Anything

ARTHUR MILLER

That beach was golden toward sundown. The bathers had all gone home when the wind got brisk. Gulls were diving just beyond the breakers. On the horizon they could see four stubby fishing boats moving in a line. Then she turned toward the right and saw the two parked trucks and the fishermen hauling on a net. "Let's see if they caught anything," she said, with the swift surge of wonder that swept through her at any new sight.

The trucks were battered and rusty, with open backs, and the one they came upon had about twenty-five big, sand-sprinkled bass and small bluefish piled at the tailgate. A man in his sixties was sitting on the truck, holding a rope that was wound around a winch at his side. He nodded to them pleasantly and drew on the rope to keep it wound tightly around the turning winch. At the water's edge another man kept watch over the net, piling it in a heap as it was drawn out of the water.

Sam glanced at the fish as they arrived at the truck and knew she would be startled. She saw them, and her eyes widened, but she even tried to smile in congratulation to the old man who drew on the rope, and she said, "You catch all these?"

"Yup," he said, and his eyes warmed at her beauty.

"These are all dead, aren't they," she said.

"Oh, ya," the old man said.

She had an excitement in her eyes as she looked, it seemed, at each individual fish to be sure it wasn't moving. Sam started talking to the old man about the probability of a good catch in the net now coming into shore, and she was drawn into the conversation, and he was relieved that her eyes, the color of the blue sea, were calmed.

But now the old man moved a lever, and the winch speeded up with a rising whine, and he was exerting himself to keep the rope taut. The winch on the other truck also turned faster, and the two net-tenders on the beach moved rapidly from the trucks to the edge of the water, hurriedly piling up the incoming net. Now they could see the curving line of cork floats only a few yards away in the water.

"Why do you pull so fast?" Sam asked the old man. "Are they fighting the net?"

"Naw," the old man said, "just want to keep her taut so they mightn't jump over and git away."

The waves were breaking into the net now, but they could not yet see any fish. She put her two hands up to her cheeks and said, "Oh, now they know they're caught!" She laughed. "Each one is wondering what happened!" He was glad she was making fun of herself even if her eyes were fixed in fear on the submerged net. She glanced up at her husband and said, "Oh, dear, they're going to be caught now."

He started to explain, but she quickly went on. "I know it's all right as long as they're eaten. They're going to eat them, aren't they?"

"They'll sell them to the fish stores," he said softly, so the old man at the winch wouldn't hear. "They'll feed people."

"Yes," she said, like a child reassured. "I'll watch it. I'm watching it," she almost announced to him. But in her something was holding its breath.

A wave receded then, and with one pull the bag of the net was drawn out of the surf. Voices sounded from both trucks; it wasn't much of a catch. She saw the tails of small bluefish writhing up through the net ("They're standing on their heads!"), and a great bass flopping, and sea robins trying to stretch their curved umber wings, and one flounder lying in the midst of this tangled rubble of the sea. She kept pointing here and there at a fish that had suddenly jerked or flopped over, and called out, "There's one! There's another one!"—meaning they were not dead yet and, he knew, must be rescued.

The men opened the net and pulled out the bass and some bluefish, tossing the sea robins onto the sand and the flounder, and two blowfish, which immediately began to swell. She turned to the old man on the truck and, trying to smile, she called to him with a sharpness in her voice, almost a cry, "Don't you take those?"

He drew an old man's warmth from the glow of her face and the startling shape of her body under the striped jersey and the beige slacks. "They're no good, ma'am," he said.

"Well, don't you put them back?"

The old man seemed to hesitate as though some memory of guilt had crossed his mind. "Sure. We put them back"—and sat there watching his partner, who was picking good fish out of the net and tossing the winged fish right and left onto the sand.

There were now about fifty sea robins on the beach, some of them gulping, some perfectly still. Sam could feel the tension rising in her, and he walked over to the nearest fish and, feeling a tremor of repugnance, picked it up and threw it into the waves and came back to her. The pulse of its life was still in his fingers. "If I had something to hold them with," she began.

"You can't throw all those fish back," he said.

"But they're alive!" she said, desperately trying to smile and not to separate herself from him.

"No, they're dead. Most of them are dead, sweet."

"Are they dead?" she turned and asked the old man.

"No, they ain't dead. Most."

"Would they live again if they had water?"

"Oh, sure, they come to," he said, trying to assuage her but not moving from his place.

She took off one sandal and went to a fish that was writhing and tried to flip it into the water, but it slipped away. Sam came over and picked it up and flung it into the sea. He was laughing now, and she kept saying, "I'm sorry. But if they're alive . . . !"

"It's all right," he said, "but they're mostly dead by now. Look." And he picked up one that was motionless; it felt flabby. He threw it into the water, and it arched itself as it struck, and she cried out, "There! It's swimming!"

Defeated and grinning, now that he saw the fishermen watching him with smiles on their faces, he went about throwing all the sea robins back into the water. He sensed that even with their smiles the men were somehow held by her insistence, and as he threw the slimy fish in one by one he saw each fish separately, each straining for its quart of sea, and he was no longer ashamed. And there were two fish left, both sea robins with white bellies and stiff umber wings and the beginnings of legs sprouting from both sides of their necks. They were motionless on their backs. He did not bend to pick them up because she seemed prepared to sacrifice them, and he went back to her, feeling, somehow, that if he let those two die on the beach she might come to terms with this kind of waste. For he had had to open the window at home, once, to let out a moth, which ordinarily he would have swatted, and while part of his heart worshiped her fierce tenderness toward all that lived, another part knew that she must come to understand that she did not die with the moths and the spiders and the fledgling birds and, now, with these fish. But it was also that he wished the fishermen to see that she was not quite so fanatic as to require these two last, obviously dead, sea robins to be given their chance.

He stood beside her again, waiting. He smiled and said, "You got a job cut out for yourself. There's twenty-five miles of beach we can cruise, throwing back fish." She laughed and drew his head down and kissed him, and he hugged her, and she said, "Just those two. Go on, Sam. They might be alive."

He laughed again and picked up one of the fish, knowing that it was even more unjust for two to die when fifty had been saved, and as he tossed it to the waves a dog appeared. It was a big, brown retriever with sea-matted hair, and it leaped into the waves and dipped its head into the water, raised up with the sea robin gently cradled in its mouth, and came back with great pride to lay it carefully at Sam's feet. "God, look how gently he brings it back!" Sam said.

"Oh, dear!" She laughed and bent toward the stern face of the buff-eyed dog. The dog returned her a look of athletic determination. "You mustn't do that!" Helplessly she looked at Sam, who picked up the fish and threw it back. Again the dog leaped in and retrieved it and now with enormous élan and pride nearly danced back to Sam, laid it at his feet, and stood waiting for the next throw, its legs trembling with eagerness.

"Well?" he said to her. "There you are. There's a whole conspiracy against these two fish. This guy was trained to help man; man has to eat and something's got to die, puss . . ."

As he spoke a silvery minnow slid out of the mouth of the sea robin at his feet. "Look at that now!" he yelled. "See? What about *that* little fish?"

"Yes!" she said, like an admission.

"You see? The victims make other victims."

"Well, hurry, throw it back anyway."

"But this character keeps bringing it back. This fish is doomed," he said, and they were both laughing, but she had in her head a clock which was telling her that every second counted, and she started to bend toward the fish at his feet despite her repugnance at touching it. He moved her hand away and picked it up, threw it, and when the dog turned and went into the water for it, he ran a few yards along the beach to the other fish and threw it in.

"Now," he said a little breathlessly as the dog returned with the first fish, "now there's one. This is a positively doomed fish on the principle that man has to eat and this dog is part of the scheme to feed him." But now even he could not take his eyes from the fish, which had taken to breathing rapidly, what with the shocks of being thrown into the water and being picked up by the dog and flying through the brisk wind. "This fish wishes you'd let it die in peace!" He laughed.

She looked around almost frantically, still smiling and laughing with him, and saw a stick and ran, ran with the dancer's leaping stride, and the dog glanced at her, then watched her as she waved the stick and called to him. She threw it into the sea, and the dog streaked into the water after it; and Sam picked up the last fish quickly and flung it, and it arched with life as it slid into a wave.

The beach was now clean, and the fishermen were busy stowing their nets, and the two walked away toward the road. "I'm sorry, Sam, but they were alive, and if nobody's going to eat them . . ."

"Well, the tide would have taken them out dead, puss, and they'd have been eaten by other fish. They wouldn't have been wasted."

"Yes," she said.

They walked, holding each other by the hand, and she was silent. He felt a great happiness opening in him that she had laid his hand on the fish which were now swimming in the sea because he had lifted them. Now she looked up at him like a little girl, with that naked wonder in her face, even as she was smiling in the way of a grown woman, and she said, "But some of them might live now till they're old."

"And then they'll die," he said.

"But at least they'll live as long as they can." And she laughed with the woman part of her that knew of absurdities.

"That's right," he said, "they'll live to a ripe old age and grow prosperous and dignified . . ."

She burst out laughing. "And see their children grown up!"

He kissed her on her lips, blessing her and her wish. "Oh, how I love you," she said with tears in her eyes. Then they walked home.

THE GUEST

ALBERT CAMUS

The schoolmaster was watching the two men climb toward him. One was on horseback, the other on foot. They had not yet tackled the abrupt rise leading to the schoolhouse built on the hillside. They were toiling onward, making slow progress in the snow, among the stones, on the vast expanse of the high, deserted plateau. From time to time the horse stumbled. Without hearing anything yet, he could see the breath issuing from the horse's nostrils. One of the men, at least, knew the region. They were following the trail although it had disappeared days ago under a layer of dirty white snow. The schoolmaster calculated that it would take them half an hour to get onto the hill. It was cold; he went back into the school to get a sweater.

He crossed the empty, frigid classroom. On the blackboard the four rivers of France, drawn with four different colored chalks, had been flowing toward their estuaries for the past three days. Snow had suddenly fallen in mid-October after eight months of drought without the transition of rain, and the twenty pupils, more or less, who lived in the villages scattered over the plateau had stopped coming. With fair weather they would return. Daru now heated only the single room that was his lodging, adjoining the classroom and giving also onto the plateau to the east. Like the class windows, his window looked to the south too. On that side the school was a few kilometers from the point where the plateau began to slope toward the south. In clear weather could be seen the purple mass of the mountain range where the gap opened onto the desert.

Somewhat warmed, Daru returned to the window from which he had first seen the two men. They were no longer visible. Hence they must have tackled the rise. The sky was not so dark, for the snow had stopped falling during the night. The morning had opened with a dirty light which had scarcely become brighter as the ceiling of clouds lifted. At two in the afternoon it seemed as if the day were merely beginning. But still this was better than those three days when the thick snow was falling amidst unbroken darkness with little gusts of wind that rattled the double door of the classroom. Then Daru had spent long hours in his room, leaving it only to go to the shed and feed the chickens or get some coal. Fortunately the delivery truck fromTadjid, the nearest village to the north, had brought his supplies two days before the blizzard. It would return in forty-eight hours.

Besides, he had enough to resist a siege, for the little room was cluttered with bags of wheat that the administration left as a stock to distribute to those of his pupils whose families had suffered from the drought. Actually they had all been victims because they were all poor. Every day Daru would distribute a ration to the children. They had missed it, he knew, during these bad days. Possibly one of the fathers or big brothers would come this afternoon and he could supply them with grain. It was just a matter of carrying them over to the next harvest. Now shiploads of wheat were arriving from France and the worst was over. But it would be hard to forget that poverty, that army of ragged ghosts wandering in the sunlight, the plateaus burned to a cinder month after month, the earth shriveled up little by little, literally scorched, every stone bursting into dust under one's foot. The sheep had died then by thousands and even a few men, here and there, sometimes without anyone's knowing.

In contrast with such poverty, he who lived almost like a monk in his remote schoolhouse, nonetheless satisfied with the little he had and with the rough life, had felt like a lord with his white-washed walls, his narrow couch, his unpainted shelves, his well, and his weekly provision of water and food. And suddenly this snow, without warning, without the foretaste of rain. This is the way the region was, cruel to live in, even without men—who didn't help matters either. But Daru had been born here. Everywhere else, he felt exiled.

He stepped out onto the terrace in front of the schoolhouse. The two men were now halfway up the slope. He recognized the horseman as Balducci, the old gendarme he had known for a long time. Balducci was holding on the end of a rope an Arab who was walking behind him with hands bound and head lowered. The gendarme waved a greeting to which Daru did not reply, lost as he was in contemplation of the Arab dressed in a faded blue jellaba, his feet in sandals but covered with socks of heavy raw wool, his head surmounted by a narrow, short *chèche*. They were approaching. Balducci was holding back his horse in order not to hurt the Arab, and the group was advancing slowly.

Within earshot, Balducci shouted: "One hour to do the three kilometers from El Ameur!" Daru did not answer. Short and square in his thick sweater, he watched them climb. Not once had the Arab raised his head. "Hello," said Daru when they got up onto the terrace. "Come in and warm up." Balducci painfully got down from his horse without letting go the rope. From under his bristling mustache he smiled at the schoolmaster. His little dark eyes, deep-set under a tanned forehead, and his mouth surrounded with wrinkles made him look attentive and studious. Daru took the bridle, led the horse to the shed, and came back to the two men, who were now waiting for him in the school. He led them into his room. "I am going to heat up the classroom," he said. "We'll be more comfortable there." When he entered the room again, Balducci was on the couch. He had undone the rope tying him to the Arab, who had squatted near the stove. His hands still bound, the *chèche* pushed back on his head, he was looking toward the window. At first Daru noticed only his huge lips, fat, smooth, almost Negroid; yet his nose was straight, his eyes were dark and full of fever. The *chèche* revealed an obstinate forehead and, under the weathered skin now rather discolored by the cold, the whole face had a restless and rebellious look that struck Daru when the Arab, turning his face toward him, looked him straight in the eyes. "Go into the other room," said the schoolmaster, "and I'll make you some mint tea." "Thanks," Balducci said. "What a chore! How I long for retirement." And addressing his prisoner in Arabic:

"Come on, you." The Arab got up and, slowly, holding his bound wrists in front of him, went into the classroom.

With the tea, Daru brought a chair. But Balducci was already enthroned on the nearest pupil's desk and the Arab had squatted against the teacher's platform facing the stove, which stood between the desk and the window. When he held out the glass of tea to the prisoner, Daru hesitated at the sight of his bound hands. "He might perhaps be untied." "Sure," said Balducci. "That was for the trip." He started to get to his feet. But Daru, setting the glass on the floor, had knelt beside the Arab. Without saying anything, the Arab watched him with his feverish eyes. Once his hands were free, he rubbed his swollen wrists against each other, took the glass of tea, and sucked up the burning liquid in swift little sips.

"Good," said Daru. "And where are you headed?"

Balducci withdrew his mustache from the tea. "Here, son."

"Odd pupils! And you're spending the night?"

"No. I'm going back to El Ameur. And you will deliver this fellow to Tinguit. He is expected at police headquarters."

Balducci was looking at Daru with a friendly little smile.

"What's this story?" asked the schoolmaster. "Are you pulling my leg?"

"No, son. Those are the orders."

"The orders? I'm not . . ." Daru hesitated, not wanting to hurt the old Corsican. "I mean, that's not my job."

"What! What's the meaning of that? In wartime people do all kinds of jobs."

"Then I'll wait for the declaration of war!"

Balducci nodded.

"O.K. But the orders exist and they concern you too. Things are brewing, it appears. There is talk of a forthcoming revolt. We are mobilized, in a way."

Daru still had his obstinate look.

"Listen, son," Balducci said. "I like you and you must understand. There's only a dozen of us at El Ameur to patrol throughout the whole territory of a small department and I must get back in a hurry. I was told to hand this guy over to you and return without delay. He couldn't be kept there. His village was beginning to stir; they wanted to take him back. You must take him to Tinguit tomorrow before the day is over. Twenty kilometers shouldn't faze a husky fellow like you. After that, all will be over. You'll come back to your pupils and your comfortable life."

Behind the wall the horse could be heard snorting and pawing the earth. Daru was looking out the window. Decidedly, the weather was clearing and the light was increasing over the snowy plateau. When all the snow was melted, the sun would take over again and once more would burn the fields of stone. For days, still, the unchanging sky would shed its dry light on the solitary expanse where nothing had any connection with man.

"After all," he said, turning around toward Balducci, "what did he do?" And, before the gendarme had opened his mouth, he asked: "Does he speak French?"

"No, not a word. We had been looking for him for a month, but they were hiding him. He killed his cousin."

"Is he against us?"

"I don't think so. But you can never be sure."

"Why did he kill?"

"A family squabble, I think. One owed the other grain, it seems. It's not at all clear. In short, he killed his cousin with a billhook. You know, like a sheep, *kreezk!*"

Balducci made the gesture of drawing a blade across his throat and the Arab, his attention attracted, watched him with a sort of anxiety. Daru felt a sudden wrath against the man, against all men with their rotten spite, their tireless hates, their blood lust.

But the kettle was singing on the stove. He served Balducci more tea, hesitated, then served the Arab again, who, a second time, drank avidly. His raised arms made the jellaba fall open and the schoolmaster saw his thin, muscular chest.

"Thanks, kid," Balducci said. "And now, I'm off."

He got up and went toward the Arab, taking a small rope from his pocket.

"What are you doing?" Daru asked dryly.

Balducci, disconcerted, showed him the rope.

"Don't bother."

The old gendarme hesitated. "It's up to you. Of course, you are armed?"

"I have my shotgun."

"Where?"

"In the trunk."

"You ought to have it near your bed."

"Why? I have nothing to fear."

"You're crazy, son. If there's an uprising, no one is safe, we're all in the same boat."

"I'll defend myself. I'll have time to see them coming."

Balducci began to laugh, then suddenly the mustache covered the white teeth.

"You'll have time? O.K. That's just what I was saying. You have always been a little cracked. That's why I like you, my son was like that."

At the same time he took out his revolver and put it on the desk.

"Keep it; I don't need two weapons from here to El Ameur."

The revolver shone against the black paint of the table. When the gendarme turned toward him, the schoolmaster caught the smell of leather and horseflesh.

"Listen, Balducci," Daru said suddenly, "every bit of this disgusts me, and first of all your fellow here. But I won't hand him over. Fight, yes, if I have to. But not that."

The old gendarme stood in front of him and looked at him severely.

"You're being a fool," he said slowly. "I don't like it either. You don't get used to putting a rope on a man even after years of it, and you're even ashamed —yes, ashamed. But you can't let them have their way."

"I won't hand him over," Daru said again.

"It's an order, son, and I repeat it."

"That's right. Repeat to them what I've said to you: I won't hand him over."

Balducci made a visible effort to reflect. He looked at the Arab and at Daru. At last he decided.

"No, I won't tell them anything. If you want to drop us, go ahead; I'll not denounce you. I have an order to deliver the prisoner and I'm doing so. And now you'll just sign this paper for me."

"There's no need. I'll not deny that you left him with me."

"Don't be mean with me. I know you'll tell the truth. You're from hereabouts and you are a man. But you must sign, that's the rule."

Daru opened his drawer, took out a little square bottle of purple ink, the red wooden penholder with the "sergeant-major" pen he used for making models of penmanship, and signed. The gendarme carefully folded the paper and put it into his wallet. Then he moved toward the door.

"I'll see you off," Daru said.

"No," said Balducci. "There's no use being polite. You insulted me."

He looked at the Arab, motionless in the same spot, sniffed peevishly, and turned away toward the door. "Good-by, son," he said. The door shut behind him. Balducci appeared suddenly outside the window and then disappeared. His footsteps were muffled by the snow. The horse stirred on the other side of the wall and several chickens fluttered in fright. A moment later Balducci reappeared outside the window leading the horse by the bridle. He walked toward the little rise without turning around and disappeared from sight with the horse following him. A big stone could be heard bouncing down. Daru walked back toward the prisoner, who, without stirring, never took his eyes off him. "Wait," the schoolmaster said in Arabic and went toward the bedroom. As he was going through the door, he had a second thought, went to the desk, took the revolver, and stuck it in his pocket. Then, without looking back, he went into his room.

For some time he lay on his couch watching the sky gradually close over, listening to the silence. It was this silence that had seemed painful to him during the first days here, after the war. He had requested a post in the little town at the base of the foothills separating the upper plateaus from the desert. There, rocky walls, green and black to the north, pink and lavender to the south, marked the frontier of eternal summer. He had been named to a post farther north, on the plateau itself. In the beginning, the solitude and the silence had been hard for him on these wastelands peopled only by stones. Occasionally, furrows suggested cultivation, but they had been dug to uncover a certain kind of stone good for building. The only plowing here was to harvest rocks. Elsewhere a thin layer of soil accumulated in the hollows would be scraped out to enrich paltry village gardens. This is the way it was: bare rock covered three quarters of the region. Towns sprang up, flourished, then disappeared; men came by, loved one another or fought bitterly, then died. No one in this desert, neither he nor his guest, mattered. And yet, outside this desert neither of them, Daru knew, could have really lived.

When he got up, no noise came from the classroom. He was amazed at the unmixed joy he derived from the mere thought that the Arab might have fled and that he would be alone with no decision to make. But the prisoner was there. He had merely stretched out between the stove and the desk. With eyes open, he was staring at the ceiling. In that position, his thick lips were particularly noticeable, giving him a pouting look. "Come," said Daru. The Arab got up and followed him. In the bedroom, the schoolmaster pointed to a chair near the table under the window. The Arab sat down without taking his eyes off Daru.

"Are you hungry?"

"Yes," the prisoner said.

Daru set the table for two. He took flour and oil, shaped a cake in a frying-pan, and lighted the little stove that functioned on bottled gas. While the cake was cooking, he went out to the shed to get cheese, eggs, dates, and condensed milk. When the cake was done he set it on the window sill to cool, heated some condensed milk diluted with water, and beat up the eggs into an omelette. In one of his motions he knocked against the revolver stuck in his right pocket. He set the bowl down, went into the classroom, and put the revolver in his desk drawer. When he came back to the room, night was falling. He put on the light and served the Arab. "Eat," he said. The Arab took a piece of the cake, lifted it eagerly to his mouth, and stopped short.

"And you?" he asked.

"After you. I'll eat too."

The thick lips opened slightly. The Arab hesitated, then bit into the cake determinedly.

The meal over, the Arab looked at the schoolmaster. "Are you the judge?"

"No, I'm simply keeping you until tomorrow."

"Why do you eat with me?"

"I'm hungry."

The Arab fell silent. Daru got up and went out. He brought back a folding bed from the shed, set it up between the table and the stove, perpendicular to his own bed. From a large suitcase which, upright in a corner, served as a shelf for papers, he took two blankets and arranged them on the camp bed. Then he stopped, felt useless, and sat down on his bed. There was nothing more to do or to get ready. He had to look at this man. He looked at him, therefore, trying to imagine his face bursting with rage. He couldn't do so. He could see nothing but the dark yet shining eyes and the animal mouth.

"Why did you kill him?" he asked in a voice whose hostile tone surprised him.

The Arab looked away.

"He ran away. I ran after him."

He raised his eyes to Daru again and they were full of a sort of woeful interrogation. "Now what will they do to me?"

"Are you afraid?"

He stiffened, turning his eyes away.

"Are you sorry?"

The Arab stared at him openmouthed. Obviously he did not understand. Daru's annoyance was growing. At the same time he felt awkward and self-conscious with his big body wedged between the two beds.

"Lie down there," he said impatiently. "That's your bed."

The Arab didn't move. He called to Daru:

"Tell me!"

The schoolmaster looked at him.

"Is the gendarme coming back tomorrow?"

"I don't know."

"Are you coming with us?"

"I don't know. Why?"

The prisoner got up and stretched out on top of the blankets, his feet toward the window. The light from the electric bulb shone straight into his eyes and he closed them at once.

"Why?" Daru repeated, standing beside the bed.

The Arab opened his eyes under the blinding light and looked at him, trying not to blink.

"Come with us," he said.

In the middle of the night, Daru was still not asleep. He had gone to bed after undressing completely; he generally slept naked. But when he suddenly realized that he had nothing on, he hesitated. He felt vulnerable and the temptation came to him to put his clothes back on. Then he shrugged his shoulders; after all, he wasn't a child and, if need be, he could break his adversary in two. From his bed he could observe him, lying on his back, still motionless with his eyes closed under the harsh light. When Daru turned out the light, the darkness seemed to coagulate all of a sudden. Little by little, the night came back to life in the window where the starless sky was stirring gently. The schoolmaster soon made out the body lying at his feet. The Arab still did not move, but his eyes seemed open. A faint wind was prowling around the schoolhouse. Perhaps it would drive away the clouds and the sun would reappear.

During the night the wind increased. The hens fluttered a little and then were silent. The Arab turned over on his side with his back to Daru, who thought he heard him moan. Then he listened for his guest's breathing, become heavier and more regular. He listened to that breath so close to him and mused without being able to go to sleep. In this room where he had been sleeping alone for a year, this presence bothered him. But it bothered him also by imposing on him a sort of brotherhood he knew well but refused to accept in the present circumstances. Men who share the same rooms, soldiers or prisoners, develop a strange alliance as if, having cast off their armor with their clothing, they fraternized every evening, over and above their differences, in the ancient community of dream and fatigue. But Daru shook himself; he didn't like such musings, and it was essential to sleep.

A little later, however, when the Arab stirred slightly, the schoolmaster was still not asleep. When the prisoner made a second move, he stiffened, on the alert. The Arab was lifting himself slowly on his arms with almost the motion of a sleepwalker. Seated upright in bed, he waited motionless without turning his head toward Daru, as if he were listening attentively. Daru did not stir; it had just occurred to him that the revolver was still in the drawer of his desk. It was better to act at once. Yet he continued to observe the prisoner, who, with the same slithery motion, put his feet on the ground, waited again, then began to stand up slowly. Daru was about to call out to him when the Arab began to walk, in a quite natural but extraordinarily silent way. He was heading toward the door at the end of the room that opened into the shed. He lifted the latch with precaution and went out, pushing the door behind him but without shutting it. Daru had not stirred. "He is running away," he merely thought. "Good riddance!" Yet he listened attentively. The hens were not fluttering; the guest must be on the plateau. A faint sound of water reached him, and he didn't know what it was until the Arab again stood framed in the doorway, closed the door carefully, and came back to bed without a sound. Then Daru turned his back on him and fell asleep. Still later he seemed, from the depths of his sleep, to hear furtive steps around the schoolhouse. "I'm dreaming! I'm dreaming!" he repeated to himself. And he went on sleeping.

When he awoke, the sky was clear; the loose window let in a cold, pure air. The Arab was asleep, hunched up under the blankets now, his mouth open, utterly relaxed. But when Daru shook him, he started dreadfully, staring at Daru with wild eyes as if he had never seen him and such a frightened expression that the schoolmaster stepped back. "Don't be afraid. It's me. You must eat." The Arab nodded his head and said yes. Calm had returned to his face, but his expression was vacant and listless.

The coffee was ready. They drank it seated together on the folding bed as they munched their pieces of the cake. Then Daru led the Arab under the shed and showed him the faucet where he washed. He went back into the room, folded the blankets and the bed, made his own bed and put the room in order. Then he went through the classroom and out onto the terrace. The sun was already rising in the blue sky; a soft, bright light was bathing the deserted plateau. On the ridge the snow was melting in spots. The stones were about to reappear. Crouched on the edge of the plateau, the schoolmaster looked at the deserted expanse. He thought of Balducci. He had hurt him, for he had sent him off in a way as if he didn't want to be associated with him. He could still hear the gendarme's farewell and, without knowing why, he felt strangely empty and vulnerable. At that moment, from the other side of the schoolhouse, the prisoner coughed. Daru listened to him almost despite himself and then, furious, threw a pebble that whistled through the air before sinking into the snow. That man's stupid crime revolted him, but to hand him over was contrary to honor. Merely thinking of it made him smart with humiliation. And he cursed at one and the same time his own people who had sent him this Arab and the Arab too who had dared to kill and not managed to get away. Daru got up, walked in a circle on the terrace, waited motionless, and then went back into the schoolhouse.

The Arab, leaning over the cement floor of the shed, was washing his teeth with two fingers. Daru looked at him and said: "Come." He went back into the room ahead of the prisoner. He slipped a hunting-jacket on over his sweater and put on walking-shoes. Standing, he waited until the Arab had put on his *chèche* and sandals. They went into the classroom and the schoolmaster pointed to the exit, saying: "Go ahead." The fellow didn't budge. "I'm coming," said Daru. The Arab went out. Daru went back into the room and made a package of pieces of rusk, dates, and sugar. In the classroom, before going out, he hesitated a second in front of his desk, then crossed the threshold and locked the door. "That's the way," he said. He started toward the east, followed by the prisoner. But, a short distance from the schoolhouse, he thought he heard a slight sound behind them. He retraced his steps and examined the surroundings of the house; there was no one there. The Arab watched him without seeming to understand. "Come on," said Daru.

They walked for an hour and rested beside a sharp peak of limestone. The snow was melting faster and faster and the sun was drinking up the puddles at once, rapidly cleaning the plateau, which gradually dried and vibrated like the air itself. When they resumed walking, the ground rang under their feet. From time to time a bird rent the space in front of them with a joyful cry. Daru breathed in deeply the fresh morning light. He felt a sort of rapture before the vast familiar expanse, now almost entirely yellow under its dome of blue sky. They walked an hour more, descending toward the south. They reached a level height made up of crumbly rocks. From there on, the plateau sloped down, eastward, toward a low plain where there were a few spindly trees and, to the south, toward outcroppings of rock that gave the landscape a chaotic look.

Daru surveyed the two directions. There was nothing but the sky on the horizon. Not a man could be seen. He turned toward the Arab, who was looking at him blankly. Daru held out the package to him. "Take it," he said. "There are dates, bread, and sugar. You can hold out for two days. Here are a thousand francs too." The Arab took the package and the money but kept his full hands at chest level as if he didn't know what to do with what was being given him. "Now look," the schoolmaster said as he pointed in the direction of the east, "there's the way to Tinguit. You have a two-hour walk. At Tinguit you'll find the administration and the police. They are expecting you." The Arab looked toward the east, still holding the package and the money against his chest. Daru took his elbow and turned him rather roughly toward the south. At the foot of the height on which they stood could be seen a faint path. "That's the trail across the plateau. In a day's walk from here you'll find pasturelands and the first nomads. They'll take you in and shelter you according to their law." The Arab had now turned toward Daru and a sort of panic was visible in his expression. "Listen," he said. Daru shook his head: "No, be quiet. Now I'm leaving you." He turned his back on him, took two long steps in the direction of the school, looked hesitantly at the motionless Arab, and started off again. For a few minutes he heard nothing but his own step resounding on the cold ground and did not turn his head. A moment later, however, he turned around. The Arab was still there on the edge of the hill, his arms hanging now, and he was looking at the schoolmaster. Daru felt something rise in his throat. But he swore with impatience, waved vaguely, and started off again. He had already gone some distance when he again stopped and looked. There was no longer anyone on the hill.

Daru hesitated. The sun was now rather high in the sky and was beginning to beat down on his head. The schoolmaster retraced his steps, at first somewhat uncertainly, then with decision. When he reached the little hill, he was bathed in sweat. He climbed it as fast as he could and stopped, out of breath, at the top. The rock-fields to the south stood out sharply against the blue sky, but on the plain to the east a steamy heat was already rising. And in that slight haze, Daru, with heavy heart, made out the Arab walking slowly on the road to prison.

A little later, standing before the window of the classroom, the schoolmaster was watching the clear light bathing the whole surface of the plateau, but he hardly saw it. Behind him on the blackboard, among the winding French rivers, sprawled the clumsily chalked-up words he had just read: "You handed over our brother. You will pay for this." Daru looked at the sky, the plateau, and, beyond, the invisible lands stretching all the way to the sea. In this vast landscape he had loved so much, he was alone.

*FLOWERING JUDAS

KATHERINE ANNE PORTER

Braggioni sits heaped upon the edge of a straight-backed chair much too small for him, and sings to Laura in a furry, mournful voice. Laura has begun to find reasons for avoiding her own house until the latest possible moment, for Braggioni is there almost every night. No matter how late she is, he will be sitting there with a surly, waiting expression, pulling at his kinky yellow hair, thumbing the strings of his guitar, snarling a tune under his breath. Lupe the Indian maid meets Laura at the door, and says with a flicker of a glance towards the upper room, "He waits."

Laura wishes to lie down, she is tired of her hairpins and the feel of her long tight sleeves, but she says to him, "Have you a new song for me this evening?" If he says yes, she asks him to sing it. If he says no, she remembers his favorite one, and asks him to sing it again. Lupe brings her a cup of chocolate and a plate of rice, and Laura eats at the small table under the lamp, first inviting Braggioni, whose answer is always the same: "I have eaten, and besides, chocolate thickens the voice."

Laura says, "Sing, then," and Braggioni heaves himself into song. He scratches the guitar familiarly as though it were a pet animal, and sings passionately off key, taking the high notes in a prolonged painful squeal. Laura, who haunts the markets listening to the ballad singers, and stops every day to hear the blind boy playing his reed-flute in Sixteenth of September Street, listens to Braggioni with pitiless courtesy, because she dares not smile at his miserable performance. Nobody dares to smile at him. Braggioni is cruel to everyone, with a kind of specialized insolence, but he is so vain of his talents, and so sensitive to slights, it would require a cruelty and vanity greater than his own to lay a finger on the vast cureless wound of his self-esteem. It would require courage, too, for it is dangerous to offend him, and nobody has this courage.

Braggioni loves himself with such tenderness and amplitude and eternal charity that his followers—for he is a leader of men, a skilled revolutionist, and his skin has been punctured in honorable warfare—warm themselves in the reflected glow, and say to each other: "He has a real nobility, a love of humanity raised above mere personal affections." The excess of this self-love has flowed out, inconveniently for her, over Laura, who, with so many others, owes her comfortable situation and her salary to him. When he is in a very good humor, he tells her, "I am tempted to forgive you for being a *gringa. Gringita!*" and Laura, burning, imagines herself leaning forward suddenly, and with a sound back-handed slap wiping the suety smile from his face. If he notices her eyes at these moments he gives no sign.

She knows what Braggioni would offer her, and she must resist tenaciously without appearing to resist, and if she could avoid it she would not admit even to herself the slow drift of his intention. During these long evenings which have spoiled a long month for her, she sits in her deep chair with an open book on her knees, resting her eyes on the consoling rigidity of the printed page when the sight and sound of Braggioni singing threaten to identify themselves with all her remembered afflictions and to add their weight to her uneasy premonitions of the future. The gluttonous bulk of Braggioni has become a symbol of her many disillusions, for a revolutionist should be lean, animated by heroic faith, a vessel of abstract virtues. This is nonsense, she knows it now and is ashamed of it. Revolution must have leaders, and leadership is a career for energetic men. She is, her comrades tell her, full of romantic error, for what she defines as cynicism in them is merely "a developed sense of reality." She is almost too willing to say, "I am wrong, I suppose I don't really understand the principles," and afterward she makes a secret truce with herself, determined not to surrender her will to such expedient logic. But she cannot help feeling that she has been betrayed irreparably by the disunion between her way of living and her feeling of what life should be, and at times she is almost contented to rest in this sense of grievance as a private store of consolation. Sometimes she wishes to run away, but she stays. Now she longs to fly out of this room, down the narrow stairs, and into the street where the houses lean together like conspirators under a single mottled lamp, and leave Braggioni singing to himself.

Instead she looks at Braggioni, frankly and clearly, like a good child who understands the rules of behavior. Her knees cling together under sound blue serge, and her round white collar is not purposely nun-like. She wears the uniform of an idea, and has renounced vanities. She was born Roman Catholic, and in spite of her fear of being seen by someone who might make a scandal of it, she slips now and again into some crumbling little church, kneels on the chilly stone, and says a Hail Mary on the gold rosary she bought in Tehuantepec. It is no good and she ends by examining the altar with its tinsel flowers and ragged brocades, and feels tender about the battered doll-shape of some male saint whose white, lace-trimmed drawers hang limply around his ankles below the hieratic dignity of his velvet robe. She has encased herself in a set of principles derived from her early training, leaving no detail of gesture or of personal taste untouched, and for this reason she will not wear lace made on machines. This is her private heresy, for in her special group the machine is sacred, and will be the salvation of the workers. She loves fine lace, and there is a tiny edge of fluted cobweb on this collar, which is one of twenty precisely alike, folded in blue tissue paper in the upper drawer of her clothes chest.

Braggioni catches her glance solidly as if he had been waiting for it, leans forward, balancing his paunch between his spread knees, and sings with tremendous emphasis, weighing his words. He has, the song relates, no father and no mother, nor even a friend to console him; lonely as a wave of the sea he comes and goes, lonely as a wave. His mouth opens round and yearns sideways, his balloon cheeks grow oily with the labor of song. He bulges marvelously in his expensive garments. Over his lavender collar, crushed upon a purple necktie, held by a diamond hoop: over his ammunition belt of tooled leather worked in silver, buckled cruelly around his gasping middle: over the tops of his glossy yellow shoes Braggioni swells with ominous ripeness, his mauve silk hose stretched taut, his ankles bound with the stout leather thongs of his shoes.

When he stretches his eyelids at Laura she notes again that his eyes are the true tawny yellow cat's eyes. He is rich, not in money, he tells her, but in power, and this power brings with it the blameless ownership of things, and the right to indulge his love of small luxuries. "I have a taste for the elegant refinements," he said once, flourishing a yellow silk handkerchief before her nose. "Smell that? It is Jockey Club, imported from New York." Nonetheless he is wounded by life. He will say so presently. "It is true everything turns to dust in the hand, to gall on the tongue." He sighs and his leather belt creaks like a saddle girth. "I am disappointed in everything as it comes. Everything." He shakes his head. "You, poor thing, you will be disappointed too. You are born for it. We are more alike than you realize in some things. Wait and see. Some day you will remember what I have told you, you will know that Braggioni was your friend."

Laura feels a slow chill, a purely physical sense of danger, a warning in her blood that violence, mutilation, a shocking death, wait for her with lessening patience. She has translated this fear into something homely, immediate, and sometimes hesitates before crossing the street. "My personal fate is nothing, except as the testimony of a mental attitude," she reminds herself, quoting from some forgotten philosophic primer, and is sensible enough to add, "Anyhow, I shall not be killed by an automobile if I can help it."

"It may be true I am as corrupt, in another way, as Braggioni," she thinks in spite of herself, "as callous, as incomplete," and if this is so, any kind of death seems preferable. Still she sits quietly, she does not run. Where could she go? Uninvited she has promised herself to this place; she can no longer imagine herself as living in another country, and there is no pleasure in remembering her life before she came here.

Precisely what is the nature of this devotion, its true motives, and what are its obligations? Laura cannot say. She spends part of her days in Xochimilco, near by, teaching Indian children to say in English, "The cat is on the mat." When she appears in the classroom they crowd about her with smiles on their wise, innocent, clay-colored faces, crying, "Good morning, my titcher!" in immaculate voices, and they make of her desk a fresh garden of flowers every day.

During her leisure she goes to union meetings and listens to busy important voices quarreling over tactics, methods, internal politics. She visits the prisoners of her own political faith in their cells, where they entertain themselves with counting cockroaches, repenting of their indiscretions, composing their memoirs, writing out manifestoes and plans for their comrades who are still walking about free, hands in pockets, sniffing fresh air. Laura brings them food and cigarettes and a little money, and she brings messages disguised in equivocal phrases from the men outside who dare not set foot in the prison for fear of disappearing into the cells kept empty for them. If the prisoners confuse night and day, and complain, "Dear little Laura, time doesn't pass in this infernal hole, and I won't know when it is time to sleep unless I have a reminder," she brings them their favorite narcotics, and says in a tone that does not wound them with pity, "Tonight will really be night for you," and though her Spanish amuses them, they find her comforting, useful. If they lose patience and all faith, and curse the slowness of their friends in coming to their rescue with money and influence, they trust her not to repeat everything, and if she inquires, "Where do you think we can find money, or influence?" they are certain to answer, "Well, there is Braggioni, why doesn't he do something?"

She smuggles letters from headquarters to men hiding from firing squads in back streets in mildewed houses, where they sit in tumbled beds and talk bitterly as if all Mexico were at their heels, when Laura knows positively they might appear at the band concert in the Alameda on Sunday morning, and no one would notice them. But Braggioni says, "Let them sweat a little. The next time they may be careful. It is very restful to have them out of the way for a while." She is not afraid to knock on any door in any street after midnight, and enter in the darkness, and say to one of these men who is really in danger: "They will be looking for you—seriously—tomorrow morning after six. Here is some money from Vicente. Go to Vera Cruz and wait."

She borrows money from the Roumanian agitator to give to his bitter enemy the Polish agitator. The favor of Braggioni is their disputed territory, and Braggioni holds the balance nicely, for he can use them both. The Polish agitator talks love to her over café tables, hoping to exploit what he believes is her secret sentimental preference for him, and he gives her misinformation which he begs her to repeat as the solemn truth to certain persons. The Roumanian is more adroit. He is generous with his money in all good causes, and lies to her with an air of ingenuous candor, as if he were her good friend and confidant. She never repeats anything they may say. Braggioni never asks questions. He has other ways to discover all that he wishes to know about them.

Nobody touches her, but all praise her gray eyes, and the soft, round under lip which promises gayety, yet is always grave, nearly always firmly closed: and they cannot understand why she is in Mexico. She walks back and forth on her errands, with puzzled eyebrows, carrying her little folder of drawings and music and school papers. No dancer dances more beautifully than Laura walks, and she inspires some amusing, unexpected ardors, which cause little gossip, because nothing comes of them. A young captain who had been a soldier in Zapata's army attempted, during a horseback ride near Cuernavaca, to express his desire for her with the noble simplicity befitting a rude folk-hero: but gently, because he was gentle. This gentleness was his defeat, for when he alighted, and removed her foot from the stirrup, and essayed to draw her down into his arms, her horse, ordinarily a tame one, shied fiercely, reared and plunged away. The young hero's horse careened blindly after his stable-mate, and the hero did not return to the hotel until rather late that evening. At breakfast he came to her table in full charro dress, gray buckskin jacket and trousers with strings of silver buttons down the leg, and he was in a humorous, careless mood. "May I sit with you?" and "You are a wonderful rider. I was terrified that you might be thrown and dragged. I should never have forgiven myself. But I cannot admire you enough for your riding!"

"I learned to ride in Arizona," said Laura.

"If you will ride with me again this morning, I promise you a horse that will not shy with you," he said. But Laura remembered that she must return to Mexico City at noon.

Next morning the children made a celebration and spent their playtime writing on the blackboard, "We lov ar ticher," and with tinted chalks they drew wreaths of flowers around the words. The young hero wrote her a letter: "I am a very foolish, wasteful, impulsive man. I should have first said I love you, and then you would not have run away. But you shall see me again." Laura thought, "I must send him a box of colored crayons," but she was trying to forgive herself for having spurred her horse at the wrong moment.

A brown, shock-haired youth came and stood in her patio one night and sang like a lost soul for two hours, but Laura could think of nothing to do about it. The moonlight spread a wash of gauzy silver over the clear spaces of the garden, and the shadows were cobalt blue. The scarlet blossoms of the Judas tree were dull purple, and the names of the colors repeated themselves automatically in her mind, while she watched not the boy, but his shadow, fallen like a dark garment across the fountain rim, trailing in the water. Lupe came silently and whispered expert counsel in her ear: "If you will throw him one little flower, he will sing another song or two and go away." Laura threw the flower, and he sang a last song and went away with the flower tucked in the band of his hat. Lupe said, "He is one of the organizers of the Typographers Union, and before that he sold corridos in the Merced market, and before that he came from Guanajuato, where I was born. I would not trust any man, but I trust least those from Guanajuato."

She did not tell Laura that he would be back again the next night, and the next, nor that he would follow her at a certain fixed distance around the Merced market, through the Zócolo, up Francisco I. Madero Avenue, and so along the Paseo de la Reforma to Chapultepec Park, and into the Philosopher's Footpath, still with that flower withering in his hat, and an indivisible attention in his eyes.

Now Laura is accustomed to him, it means nothing except that he is nineteen years old and is observing a convention with all propriety, as though it were founded on a law of nature, which in the end it might very well prove to be. He is beginning to write poems which he prints on a wooden press, and he leaves them stuck like handbills in her door. She is pleasantly disturbed by the abstract, unhurried watchfulness of his black eyes which will in time turn easily towards another object. She tells herself that throwing the flower was a mistake, for she is twenty-two years old and knows better; but she refuses to regret it, and persuades herself that her negation of all external events as they occur is a sign that she is gradually perfecting herself in the stoicism she strives to cultivate against that disaster she fears, though she cannot name it.

She is not at home in the world. Every day she teaches children who remain strangers to her, though she loves their tender round hands and their charming opportunistic savagery. She knocks at unfamiliar doors not knowing whether a friend or a stranger shall answer, and even if a known face emerges from the sour gloom of that unknown interior, still it is the face of a stranger. No matter what this stranger says to her, nor what her message to him, the very cells of her flesh reject knowledge and kinship in one monotonous word. No. No. No. She draws her strength from this one holy talismanic word which does not suffer her to be led into evil. Denying everything, she may walk anywhere in safety, she looks at everything without amazement.

No, repeats this firm unchanging voice of her blood; and she looks at Braggioni without amazement. He is a great man, he wishes to impress this simple girl who covers her great round breasts with thick dark cloth, and who hides long, invaluably beautiful legs under a heavy skirt. She is almost thin except for the incomprehensible fullness of her breasts, like a nursing mother's, and Braggioni, who considers himself a judge of women, speculates again on the puzzle of her notorious virginity, and takes the liberty of speech which she permits without a sign of modesty, indeed, without any sort of sign, which is disconcerting.

"You think you are so cold, *gringita!* Wait and see. You will surprise yourself some day! May I be there to advise you!" He stretches his eyelids at her, and his ill-humored cat's eyes waver in a separate glance for the two points of light marking the opposite ends of a smoothly drawn path between the swollen curve of her breasts. He is not put off by that blue serge, nor by her resolutely fixed gaze. There is all the time in the world. His cheeks are bellying with the wind of song. "O girl with the dark eyes," he sings, and reconsiders. "But yours are not dark. I can change all that. O girl with the green eyes, you have stolen my heart away!" Then his mind wanders to the song, and Laura feels the weight of his attention being shifted elsewhere. Singing thus, he seems harmless, he is quite harmless, there is nothing to do but sit patiently and say "No," when the moment comes. She draws a full breath, and her mind wanders also, but not far. She dares not wander too far.

Not for nothing has Braggioni taken pains to be a good revolutionist and a professional lover of humanity. He will never die of it. He has the malice, the cleverness, the wickedness, the sharpness of wit, the hardness of heart, stipulated for loving the world profitably. *He will never die of it.* He will live to see himself kicked out from his feeding trough by other hungry world-saviours. Traditionally he must sing in spite of his life which drives him to bloodshed, he tells Laura, for his father was a Tuscany peasant who drifted to Yucatan and married a Maya woman: a woman of race, an aristocrat. They gave him the love and knowledge of music, thus: and under the rip of his thumbnail, the strings of the instrument complain like exposed nerves.

Once he was called Delgadito by all the girls and married women who ran after him; he was so scrawny all his bones showed under his thin cotton clothing, and he could squeeze his emptiness to the very backbone with his two hands. He was a poet and the revolution was only a dream then; too many women loved him and sapped away his youth, and he could never find enough to eat anywhere, anywhere! Now he is a leader of men, crafty men who whisper in his ear, hungry men who wait for hours outside his office for a word with him, emaciated men with wild faces who waylay him at the street gate with a timid, "Comrade, let me tell you . . ." and they blow the foul breath from their empty stomachs in his face.

He is always sympathetic. He gives them handfuls of small coins from his own pocket, he promises them work, there will be demonstrations, they must join the unions and attend the meetings, above all they must be on the watch for spies. They are closer to him than his own brothers, without them he can do nothing—until tomorrow, comrade!

Until tomorrow. "They are stupid, they are lazy, they are treacherous, they would cut my throat for nothing," he says to Laura. He has good food and abundant drink, he hires an automobile and drives in the Paseo on Sunday morning, and enjoys plenty of sleep in a soft bed beside a wife who dares not disturb him; and he sits pampering his bones in easy billows of fat, singing to Laura, who knows and thinks these things about him. When he was fifteen, he tried to drown himself because he loved a girl, his first love, and she laughed at him. "A thousand women have paid for that," and his tight little mouth turns down at the corners. Now he perfumes his hair with Jockey Club, and confides to Laura: "One woman is really as good as another for me, in the dark. I prefer them all."

His wife organizes unions among the girls in the cigarette factories, and walks in picket lines, and even speaks at meetings in the evening. But she cannot be brought to acknowledge the benefits of true liberty. "I tell her I must have my freedom, net. She does not understand my point of view." Laura has heard this many times. Braggioni scratches the guitar and meditates. "She is an instinctively virtuous woman, pure gold, no doubt of that. If she were not, I should lock her up, and she knows it."

His wife, who works so hard for the good of the factory girls, employs part of her leisure lying on the floor weeping because there are so many women in the world, and only one husband for her, and she never knows where nor when to look for him. He told her: "Unless you can learn to cry when I am not here, I must go away for good." That day he went away and took a room at the Hotel Madrid.

It is this month of separation for the sake of higher principles that has been spoiled not only for Mrs. Braggioni, whose sense of reality is beyond criticism, but for Laura, who feels herself bogged in a nightmare. Tonight Laura envies Mrs. Braggioni, who is alone, and free to weep as much as she pleases about a concrete wrong. Laura has just come from a visit to the prison, and she is waiting for tomorrow with a bitter anxiety as if tomorrow may not come, but time may be caught immovably in this hour, with herself transfixed, Braggioni singing on forever, and Eugenio's body not yet discovered by the guard.

Braggioni says: "Are you going to sleep?" Almost before she can shake her head, he begins telling her about the May-day disturbances coming on in Morelia, for the Catholics hold a festival in honor of the Blessed Virgin, and the Socialists celebrate their martyrs on that day. "There will be two independent processions, starting from either end of town, and they will march until they meet, and the rest depends . . ." He asks her to oil and load his pistols. Standing up, he unbuckles his ammunition belt, and spreads it laden across her knees. Laura sits with the shells slipping through the cleaning cloth dipped in oil, and he says again he cannot understand why she works so hard for the revolutionary idea unless she loves some man who is in it. "Are you not in love with someone?" "No," says Laura. "And no one is in love with you?" "No." "Then it is your own fault. No woman need go begging. Why, what is the matter with you? The legless beggar woman in the Alameda has a perfectly faithful lover. Did you know that?"

Laura peers down the pistol barrel and says nothing, but a long, slow faintness rises and subsides in her; Braggioni curves his swollen fingers around the throat of the guitar and softly smothers the music out of it, and when she hears him again he seems to have forgotten her, and is speaking in the hypnotic voice he uses when talking in small rooms to a listening, close-gathered crowd. Some day this world, now seemingly so composed and eternal, to the edges of every sea shall be merely a tangle of gaping trenches, of crashing walls and broken bodies. Everything must be torn from its accustomed place where it has rotted for centuries, hurled skyward and distributed, cast down again clean as rain, without separate identity. Nothing shall survive that the stiffened hands of poverty have created for the rich and no one shall be left alive except the elect spirits destined to procreate a new world cleansed of cruelty and injustice, ruled by benevolent anarchy: "Pistols are good, I love them, cannon are even better, but in the end I pin my faith to good dynamite," he concludes, and strokes the pistol lying in her hands. "Once I dreamed of destroying this city, in case it offered resistance to General Ortiz, but it fell into his hands like an overripe pear."

He is made restless by his own words, rises and stands waiting. Laura holds up the belt to him: "Put that on, and go kill somebody in Morelia, and you will be happier," she says softly. The presence of death in the room makes her bold. "Today, I found Eugenio going into a stupor. He refused to allow me to call the prison doctor. He had taken all the tablets I brought him yesterday. He said he took them because he was bored."

"He is a fool, and his death is his own business," says Braggioni, fastening his belt carefully.

"I told him if he had waited only a little while longer, you would have got him set free," says Laura. "He said he did not want to wait."

"He is a fool and we are well rid of him," says Braggioni, reaching for his hat.

He goes away. Laura knows his mood has changed, she will not see him any more for a while. He will send word when he needs her to go on errands into strange streets, to speak to the strange faces that will appear, like clay masks with the power of human speech, to mutter their thanks to Braggioni for his help. Now she is free, and she thinks, I must run while there is time. But she does not go.

Braggioni enters his own house where for a month his wife has spent many hours every night weeping and tangling her hair upon her pillow. She is weeping now, and she weeps more at the sight of him, the cause of all her sorrows. He looks about the room. Nothing is changed, the smells are good and familiar, he is well acquainted with the woman who comes toward him with no reproach except grief on her face. He says to her tenderly: "You are so good, please don't cry any more, you dear good creature." She says, "Are you tired, my angel? Sit here and I will wash your feet." She brings a bowl of water, and kneeling, unlaces his shoes, and when from her knees she raises her sad eyes under her blackened lids, he is sorry for everything, and bursts into tears. "Ah, yes, I am hungry, I am tired, let us eat something together," he says, between sobs. His wife leans her head on his arm and says, "Forgive me!" and this time he is refreshed by the solemn, endless rain of her tears.

Laura takes off her serge dress and puts on a white linen nightgown and goes to bed. She turns her head a little to one side, and lying still, reminds herself that it is time to sleep. Numbers tick in her brain like little clocks, soundless doors close of themselves around her. If you would sleep, you must not remember anything, the children will say tomorrow, good morning, my teacher, the poor prisoners who come every day bringing flowers to their jailor. 1–2–3–4–5—it is monstrous to confuse love with revolution, night with day, life with death—ah, Eugenio!

The tolling of the midnight bell is a signal, but what does it mean? Get up, Laura, and follow me: come out of your sleep, out of your bed, out of this strange house. What are you doing in this house? Without a word, without fear she rose and reached for Eugenio's hand, but he eluded her with a sharp, sly smile and drifted away. This is not all, you shall see—Murderer, he said, follow me, I will show you a new country, but it is far away and we must hurry. No, said Laura, not unless you take my hand, no; and she clung first to the stair rail, and then to the topmost branch of the Judas tree that bent down slowly and set her upon the earth, and then to the rocky ledge of a cliff, and then to the jagged wave of a sea that was not water but a desert of crumbling stone. Where are you taking me, she asked in wonder but without fear. To death, and it is a long way off, and we must hurry, said Eugenio. No, said Laura, not unless you take my hand. Then eat these flowers, poor prisoner, said Eugenio in a voice of pity, take and eat: and from the Judas tree he stripped the warm bleeding flowers, and held them to her lips. She saw that his hand was fleshless, a cluster of small white petrified branches, and his eye sockets were without light, but she ate the flowers greedily for they satisfied both hunger and thirst. Murderer! said Eugenio, and Cannibal! This is my body and my blood. Laura cried No! and at the sound of her own voice, she awoke trembling, and was afraid to sleep again.

*DELTA AUTUMN

WILLIAM FAULKNER

Soon now they would enter the Delta. The sensation was familiar to him. It had been renewed like this each last week in November for more than fifty years—the last hill, at the foot of which the rich unbroken alluvial flatness began as the sea began at the base of its cliffs, dissolving away beneath the unhurried November rain as the sea itself would dissolve away.

At first they had come in wagons: the guns, the bedding, the dogs, the food, the whisky, the keen heart-lifting anticipation of hunting; the young men who could drive all night and all the following day in the cold rain and pitch a camp in the rain and sleep in the wet blankets and rise at daylight the next morning and hunt. There had been bear then. A man shot a doe or a fawn as quickly as he did a buck, and in the afternoons they shot wild turkey with pistols to test their stalking skill and markmanship, feeding all but the breast to the dogs. But that time was gone now. Now they went in cars, driving faster and faster each year because the roads were better and they had farther and farther to drive, the territory in which game still existed drawing yearly inward as his life was drawing inward, until now he was the last of those who had once made the journey in wagons without feeling it and now those who accompanied him were the sons and even grandsons of the men who had ridden for twenty-four hours in the rain or sleet behind the steaming mules. They called him 'Uncle Ike' now, and he no longer told anyone how near eighty he actually was because he knew as well as they did that he no longer had any business making such expeditions, even by car.

In fact, each time now, on that first night in camp, lying aching and sleepless in the harsh blankets, his blood only faintly warmed by the single thin whisky-and-water which he allowed himself, he would tell himself that this would be his last. But he would stand that trip—he still shot almost as well as he ever had, still killed almost as much of the game he saw as he ever killed; he no longer even knew how many deer had fallen before his gun—and the fierce long heat of the next summer would renew him. Then November would come again, and again in the car with two of the sons of his old companions, whom he had taught not only how to distinguish between the prints left by a buck or a doe but between the sound they made in moving, he would look ahead past the jerking arc of the windshield wiper and see the land flatten suddenly and swoop, dissolving away beneath the rain as the sea itself would dissolve, and he would say, "Well, boys, there it is again."

This time though, he didn't have time to speak. The driver of the car stopped it, slamming it to a skidding halt on the greasy pavement without warning, actually flinging the two passengers forward until they caught themselves with their braced hands against the dash. "What the hell, Roth!" the man in the middle said. "Can't you whistle first when you do that? Hurt you, Uncle Ike?"

"No," the old man said. "What's the matter?" The driver didn't answer. Still leaning forward, the old man looked sharply past the face of the man between them, at the face of his kinsman. It was the youngest face of them all, aquiline, saturnine, a little ruthless, the face of his ancestor too, tempered a little, altered a little, stating sombrely through the streaming windshield across which the twin wipers flicked and flicked.

"I didn't intend to come back in here this time," he said suddenly and harshly.

"You said that back in Jefferson last week," the old man said. "Then you changed your mind. Have you changed it again? This aint a very good time to———"

"Oh, Roth's coming," the man in the middle said. His name was Legate. He seemed to be speaking to no one, as he was looking at neither of them. "If it was just a buck he was coming all this distance for, now. But he's got a doe in here. Of course a old man like Uncle Ike cant be interested in no doe, not one that walks on two legs—when she's standing up, that is. Pretty light-colored, too. The one he was after them nights last fall when he said he was coon-hunting, Uncle Ike. The one I figured maybe he was still running when he was gone all that month last January. But of course a old man like Uncle Ike aint got no interest in nothing like that." He chortled, still looking at no one, not completely jeering.

"What?" the old man said. "What's that?" But he had not even so much as glanced at Legate. He was still watching his kinsman's face. The eyes behind the spectacles were the blurred eyes of an old man, but they were quite sharp too; eyes which could still see a gun-barrel and what ran beyond it as well as any of them could. He was remembering himself now: how last year, during the final stage by motor boat in to where they camped, a box of food had been lost overboard and how on the next day his kinsman had gone back to the nearest town for supplies and had been gone overnight. And when he did return, something had happened to him. He would go into the woods with his rifle each dawn when the others went, but the old man, watching him, knew that he was not hunting. "All right," he said. "Take me and Will on to shelter where we can wait for the truck, and you can go on back."

"I'm going in," the other said harshly. "Dont worry. Because this will be the last of it."

"The last of deer hunting, or of doe hunting?" Legate said. This time the old man paid no attention to him even by speech. He still watched the young man's savage and brooding face.

"Why?" he said.

"After Hitler gets through with it? Or Smith or Jones or Roosevelt or Willkie or whatever he will call himself in this country?"

"We'll stop him in this country," Legate said. "Even if he calls himself George Washington."

"How?" Edmonds said. "By singing God bless America in bars at midnight and wearing dime-store flags in our lapels?"

"So that's what's worrying you," the old man said. "I aint noticed this country being short of defenders yet, when it needed them. You did some of it yourself twenty-odd years ago, before you were a grown man even. This country is a little mite stronger than any one man or group of men, outside of it or even inside of it either. I reckon, when the time comes and some of you have done got tired of hollering we are whipped if we dont go to war and some more are hollering we are whipped if we do, it will cope with one Austrian paper-hanger, no matter what he will be calling himself. My pappy and some other better men than any of them you named tried once to tear it in two with a war, and they failed."

"And what have you got left?" the other said. "Half the people without jobs and half the factories closed by strikes. Half the people on public dole that wont work and half that couldn't work even if they would. Too much cotton and corn and hogs, and not enough for people to eat and wear. The country full of people to tell a man how he cant raise his own cotton whether he will or wont, and Sally Rand with a sergeant's stripes and not even the fan couldn't fill the army rolls. Too much not-butter and not even the guns————"

"We got a deer camp—if we ever get to it," Legate said. "Not to mention does."

"It's a good time to mention does," the old man said. "Does and fawns both. The only fighting anywhere that ever had anything of God's blessing on it has been when men fought to protect does and fawns. If it's going to come to fighting, that's a good thing to mention and remember too."

"Haven't you discovered in—how many years more than seventy is it?—that women and children are one thing there's never any scarcity of?" Edmonds said.

"Maybe that's why all I am worrying about right now is that ten miles of river we still have got to run before we can make camp," the old man said. "So let's get on."

They went on. Soon they were going fast again, as Edmonds always drove, consulting neither of them about the speed just as he had given neither of them any warning when he slammed the car to stop. The old man relaxed again. He watched, as he did each recurrent November while more than sixty of them passed, the land which he had seen change. At first there had been only the old towns along the River and the old towns along the hills, from each of which the planters with their gangs of slaves and then of hired laborers had wrested from the impenetrable jungle of water-standing cane and cypress, gum and holly and oak and ash, cotton patches which as the years passed became fields and then plantations. The paths made by deer and bear became roads and then highways, with towns in turn springing up along them and along the rivers Tallahatchie and Sunflower which joined and became the Yazoo, the River of the Dead of the Choctaws—the thick, slow, black, unsunned streams almost without current, which once each year ceased to flow at all and then reversed, spreading, drowning the rich land and subsiding again, leaving it still richer.

Most of that was gone now. Now a man drove two hundred miles from Jefferson before he found wilderness to hunt in. Now the land lay open from the cradling hills on the East to the rampart of levee on the West, standing horseman-tall with cotton for the world's looms—the rich black land, imponderable and vast, fecund up to the very doorsteps of the negroes who worked it and of the white men who owned it; which exhausted the hunting life of a dog in one year, the working life of a mule in five and of a man in twenty—the land in which neon flashed past them from the little countless towns and countless shining this-year's automobiles sped past them on the broad plumb-ruled highways, yet in which the only permanent mark of man's occupation seemed to be the tremendous gins, constructed in sections of sheet iron and in a week's time though they were, since no man, millionaire though he be, would build more than a roof and walls to shelter the camping equipment he lived from when he knew that once each ten years or so his house would be flooded to the second storey and all within it ruined;—the land across which there came now no scream of panther but instead the long hooting of locomotives: trains of incredible length and drawn by a single engine, since there was no gradient anywhere and no elevation save those raised by forgotten aboriginal hands as refuges from the yearly water and used by their Indian successors to sepulchre their fathers' bones, and all that remained of that old time were the Indian names on the little towns and usually pertaining to water—Aluschaskuna, Tillatoba, Homochitto, Yazoo.

By early afternoon, they were on water. At the last little Indian-named town at the end of pavement they waited until the other car and the two trucks—the one carrying the bedding and tents and food, the other the horses—overtook them. They left the concrete and, after another mile or so, the gravel too. In caravan they ground on through the ceaselessly dissolving afternoon, with skid-chains on the wheels now, lurching and splashing and sliding among the ruts, until presently it seemed to him that the retrograde of his remembering had gained an inverse velocity from their own slow progress, that the land had retreated not in minutes from the last spread of gravel but in years, decades, back toward what it had been when he first knew it: the road they now followed once more the ancient pathway of bear and deer, the diminishing fields they now passed once more scooped punily and terrifically by axe and saw and mule-drawn plow from the wilderness' flank, out of the brooding and immemorial tangle, in place of ruthless mile-wide parallelograms wrought by ditching the dyking machinery.

They reached the river landing and unloaded, the horses to go overland down stream to a point opposite the camp and swim the river, themselves and the bedding and food and dogs and guns in the motor launch. It was himself, though no horseman, no farmer, not even a countryman save by his distant birth and boyhood, who coaxed and soothed the two horses, drawing them by his own single frail hand until, backing, filling, trembling a little, they surged, halted, then sprang scrambling down from the truck, possessing no affinity for them as creatures, beasts, but being merely insulated by his years and time from the corruption of steel and oiled moving parts which tainted the others.

Then, his old hammer double gun which was only twelve years younger than he standing between his knees, he watched even the last puny marks of man—cabin, clearing, the small and irregular fields which a year ago were jungle and in which the skeleton stalks of this year's cotton stood almost as tall and rank as the old cane had stood, as if man had had to marry his planting to the wilderness in order to conquer it—fall away and vanish. The twin banks marched with wilderness as he remembered it—the tangle of brier and cane impenetrable even to sight twenty feet away, the tall tremendous soaring of oak and gum and ash and hickory which had rung to no axe save the hunter's, had echoed to no machinery save the beat of old-time steam boats traversing it or to the snarling of launches like their own of people going into it to dwell for a week or two weeks because it was still wilderness. There was some of it left, although now it was two hundred miles from Jefferson when once it had been thirty. He had watched it, not being conquered, destroyed, so much as retreating since its purpose was served now and its time an outmoded time, retreating southward through this inverted-apex, this ∇-shaped section of earth between hills and River until what was left of it seemed now to be gathered and for the time arrested in one tremendous density of brooding and inscrutable impenetrability at the ultimate funnelling tip.

They reached the site of their last-year's camp with still two hours left of light. "You go on over under that driest tree and set down," Legate told him. "—if you can find it. Me and these other young boys will do this." He did neither. He was not tired yet. That would come later. *Maybe it wont come at all this time,* he thought, as he had thought at this point each November for the last five or six of them. *Maybe I will go out on stand in the morning too;* knowing that he would not, not even if he took the advice and sat down under the driest shelter and did nothing until camp was made and supper cooked. Because it would not be the fatigue. It would be because he would not sleep tonight but would lie instead wakeful and peaceful on the cot amid the tent-filling snoring and the rain's whisper as he always did on the first night in camp; peaceful, without regret or fretting, telling himself that was all right too, who didn't have so many of them left as to waste one sleeping.

In his slicker he directed the unloading of the boat—the tents, the stove, the bedding, the food for themselves and the dogs until there should be meat in camp. He sent two of the negroes to cut firewood; he had the cook-tent raised and the stove up and a fire going and supper cooking while the big tent was still being staked down. Then in the beginning of dusk he crossed in the boat to where the horses waited, backing and snorting at the water. He took the lead-ropes and with no more weight than that and his voice, he drew them down into the water and held them beside the boat with only their heads above the surface, as though they actually were suspended from his frail and strengthless old man's hands, while the boat recrossed and each horse in turn lay prone in the shallows, panting and trembling, its eyes rolling in the dusk, until the same weightless hand and unraised voice gathered it surging upward, splashing and thrashing up the bank.

Then the meal was ready. The last of light was gone now save the thin stain of it snared somewhere between the river's surface and the rain. He had the single glass of thin whisky-and-water, then, standing in the churned mud beneath the stretched tarpaulin, he said grace over the fried slabs of pork, the hot soft shapeless bread, the canned beans and molasses and coffee in iron plates and cups,—the town food, brought along with them—then covered himself again, the others following. "Eat," he said. "Eat it all up. I dont want a piece of town meat in camp after breakfast tomorrow. Then you boys will hunt. You'll have to. When I first started hunting in this bottom sixty years ago with old General Compson and Major de Spain and Roth's grandfather and Will Legate's too, Major de Spain wouldn't allow but two pieces of foreign grub in his camp. That was one side of pork and one ham of beef. And not to eat for the first supper and breakfast neither. It was to save until along toward the end of camp when everybody was so sick of bear meat and coon and venison that we couldn't even look at it."

"I thought Uncle Ike was going to say the pork and beef was for the dogs," Legate said, chewing. "But that's right; I remember. You just shot the dogs a mess of wild turkey every evening when they got tired of deer guts."

"Times are different now," another said. "There was game here then."

"Yes," the old man said quietly. "There was game here then."

"Besides, they shot does then too," Legate said. "As it is now, we aint got but one doe-hunter in———"

"And better men hunted it," Edmonds said. He stood at the end of the rough plank table, eating rapidly and steadily as the others ate. But again the old man looked sharply across at the sullen, handsome, brooding face which appeared now darker and more sullen still in the light of the smoky lantern. "Go on. Say it."

"I didn't say that," the old man said. "There are good men everywhere, at all times. Most men are. Some are just unlucky, because most men are a little better than their circumstances give them a chance to be. And I've known some that even the circumstances couldn't stop."

"Well, I wouldn't say—" Legate said.

"So you've lived almost eighty years," Edmonds said. "And that's what you finally learned about the other animals you lived among. I suppose the question to ask you is, where have you been all the time you were dead?"

There was a silence; for the instant even Legate's jaw stopped chewing while he gaped at Edmonds. "Well, by God, Roth—" the third speaker said. But it was the old man who spoke, his voice still peaceful and untroubled and merely grave:

"Maybe so," he said. "But if being what you call alive would have learned me any different, I reckon I'm satisfied, wherever it was I've been."

"Well, I wouldn't say that Roth—" Legate said.

The third speaker was still leaning forward a little over the table, looking at Edmonds. "Meaning that it's only because folks happen to be watching him that a man behaves at all," he said. "Is that it?"

"Yes," Edmonds said. "A man in a blue coat, with a badge on it watching him. Maybe just the badge."

"I deny that," the old man said. "I don't———"

The other two paid no attention to him. Even Legate was listening to them for the moment, his mouth still full of food and still open a little, his knife with another lump of something balanced on the tip of the blade arrested halfway to his mouth. "I'm glad I dont have your opinion of folks," the third speaker said. "I take it you include yourself."

"I see," Edmonds said. "You prefer Uncle Ike's opinion of circumstances. All right. Who makes the circumstances?"

"Luck,"the third said. "Chance. Happen-so. I see what you are getting at. But that's just what Uncle Ike said: that now and then, maybe most of the time, man is a little better than the net result of his and his neighbors' doings, when he gets the chance to be."

This time Legate swallowed first. He was not to be stopped this time. "Well, I wouldn't say that Roth Edmonds can hunt one doe every day and night for two weeks and was a poor hunter or a unlucky one neither. A man that still have the same doe left to hunt on again next year———"

"Have some meat," the man next to him said.

"—aint no unlucky—What?" Legate said.

"Have some meat." The other offered the dish.

"I got some," Legate said.

"Have some more," the third speaker said. "You and Roth Edmonds both. Have a heap of it. Clapping your jaws together that way with nothing to break the shock." Someone chortled. Then they all laughed, with relief, the tension broken. But the old man was speaking, even into the laughter, in that peaceful and still untroubled voice:

"I still believe. I see proof everywhere. I grant that man made a heap of his circumstances, him and his living neighbors between them. He even inherited some of them already made, already almost ruined even. A while ago Henry Wyatt there said how there used to be more game here. There was. So much that we even killed does. I seem to remember Will Legate mentioning that too—" Someone laughed, a single guffaw, stillborn. It ceased and they all listened, gravely, looking down at their plates. Edmonds was drinking his coffee, sullen, brooding, inattentive.

"Some folks still kill does," Wyatt said. "There wont be just one buck hanging in this bottom tomorrow night without any head to fit it."

"I didn't say all men," the old man said. "I said most men. And not just because there is a man with a badge to watch us. We probably wont even see him unless maybe he will stop here about noon tomorrow and eat dinner with us and check our licenses————"

"We dont kill does because if we did kill does in a few years there wouldn't even be any bucks left to kill, Uncle Ike," Wyatt said.

"According to Roth yonder, that's one thing we wont never have to worry about," the old man said. "He said on the way here this morning that does and fawns—I believe he said women and children—are two things this world aint ever lacked. But that aint all of it," he said. "That's just the mind's reason a man has to give himself because the heart dont always have time to bother with thinking up words that fit together. God created man and He created the world for him to live in and I reckon He created the kind of world He would have wanted to live in if He had been a man—the ground to walk on, the big woods, the trees and the water, and the game to live in it. And maybe He didn't put the desire to hunt and kill game in man but I reckon He knew it was going to be there, that man was going to teach it to himself, since he wasn't quite God himself yet————"

"When will he be?" Wyatt said.

"I think that every man and woman, at the instant when it dont even matter whether they marry or not, I think that whether they marry then or afterward or dont never, at that instant the two of them together were God."

"Then there are some Gods in this world I wouldn't want to touch, and with a damn long stick," Edmonds said. He set his coffee cup down and looked at Wyatt. "And that includes myself, if that's what you want to know. I'm going to bed." He was gone. There was a general movement among the others. But it ceased and they stood again about the table, not looking at the old man, apparently held there yet by his quiet and peaceful voice as the heads of the swimming horses had been held above the water by his weightless hand. The three negroes—the cook and his helper and old Isham—were sitting quietly in the entrance of the kitchen tent, listening too, the three faces dark and motionless and musing.

"He put them both here: man, and the game he would follow and kill, foreknowing it. I believe He said, 'So be it.' I reckon He even foreknew the end. But He said, 'I will give him his chance. I will give him warning and foreknowledge too, along with the desire to follow and the power to slay. The woods and fields he ravages and the game he devastates will be the consequence and signature of his crime and guilt, and his punishment.'—Bed time," he said. His voice and inflection did not change at all. "Breakfast at four oclock, Isham. We want meat on the ground by sunup time."

There was a good fire in the sheet-iron heater; the tent was warm and was beginning to dry out, except for the mud underfoot. Edmonds was already rolled into his blankets, motionless, his face to the wall. Isham had made up his bed too—the strong, battered iron cot, the stained mattress which was not quite soft enough, the worn, often-washed blankets which as the years passed were less and less warm enough. But the tent was warm; presently, when the kitchen was cleaned up and readied for breakfast, the young negro would come in to lie down before the heater, where he could be roused to put fresh wood into it from time to time. And then, he knew now he would not sleep tonight anyway; he no longer needed to tell himself that perhaps he would. But it was all right now. The day was ended now and night faced him, but alarmless, empty of fret. *Maybe I came for this,* he thought: *Not to hunt, but for this. I would come anyway, even if only to go back home tomorrow.* Wearing only his bagging woolen underwear, his spectacles folded away in the worn case beneath the pillow where he could reach them readily and his lean body fitted easily into the old worn groove of mattress and blankets, he lay on his back, his hands crossed on his breast and his eyes closed while the others undressed and went to bed and the last of the sporadic talking died into snoring. Then he opened his eyes and lay peaceful and quiet as a child, looking up at the motionless belly of rain-murmured canvas upon which the glow of the heater was dying slowly away and would fade still further until the young negro, lying on two planks before it, would sit up and stoke it and lie back down again.

They had a house once. That was sixty years ago, when the Big Bottom was only thirty miles from Jefferson and old Major de Spain, who had been his father's cavalry commander in '61 and '2 and '3 and '4, and his cousin (his older brother; his father too) had taken him into the woods for the first time. Old Sam Fathers was alive then, born in slavery, son of a Negro slave and a Chickasaw chief, who had taught him how to shoot, not only when to shoot but when not to; such a November dawn as tomorrow would be and the old man led him straight to the great cypress and he had known the buck would pass exactly there because there was something running in Sam Fathers' veins which ran in the veins of the buck too, and they stood there against the tremendous trunk, the old man of seventy and the boy of twelve, and there was nothing save the dawn until suddenly the buck was there, smoke-colored out of nothing, magnificent with speed: and Sam Fathers said, 'Now. Shoot quick and shoot slow:' and the gun levelled rapidly without haste and crashed and he walked to the buck lying still intact and still in the shape of that magnificent speed and bled it with Sam's knife and Sam dipped his hands into the hot blood and marked his face forever while he stood trying not to tremble, humbly and with pride too though the boy of twelve had been unable to phrase it then: *I slew you; my bearing must not shame your quitting life. My conduct forever onward must become your death;* marking him for that and for more than that: that day and himself and McCaslin juxtaposed not against the wilderness but against the tamed land, the old wrong and shame itself, in repudiation and denial at least of the land and the wrong and shame even if he couldn't cure the wrong and eradicate the shame, who at fourteen when he learned of it had believed he could do both when he became competent and when at twenty-one he became competent he knew that he could do neither but at least he could repudiate the wrong and shame, at least in principle, and at least the land itself in fact, for his son at least: and did, thought he had: then (married then) in a rented cubicle in a back-street stock-traders' boarding-house, the first and last time he ever saw her naked body, himself and his wife juxtaposed in their turn against that same land, that same wrong and shame from whose regret and grief he would at least save and free his son and, saving and freeing his son, lost him. They had the house then. That roof, the two weeks of each November which they spent under it, had become his home. Although since that time they had lived during the two fall weeks in tents and not always in the same place two years in succession and now his companions were the sons and even the grandsons of them with whom he had lived in the house and for almost fifty years now the house itself had not even existed, the conviction, the sense and feeling of home, had been merely trans-ferred into the canvas. He owned a house in Jefferson, a good house though small, where he had had a wife and lived with her and lost her, ay, lost her even though he had lost her in the rented cubicle before he and his old clever dipsomaniac partner had finished the house for them to move into it: but lost her, because she loved him. But women hope for so much. They never live too long to still believe that anything within the scope of their passionate wanting is likewise within the range of their passionate hope: and it was still kept for him by his dead wife's widowed niece and her children and he was comfortable in it, his wants and needs and even the small trying harmless crochets of an old man looked after by blood at least related to the blood which he had elected out of all the earth to cherish. But he spent the time within those walls waiting for November, because even this tent with its muddy floor and the bed which was not wide enough nor soft enough nor even warm enough, was his home and these men, some of whom he only saw during these two November weeks and not one of whom even bore any name he used to know—De Spain and Compson and Ewell and Hogganbeck—were more his kin than any. Because this was his land————

The shadow of the youngest negro loomed. It soared, blotting the heater's dying glow from the ceiling, the wood billets thumping into the iron maw until the glow, the flame, leaped high and bright across the canvas. But the negro's shadow still remained, by its length and breadth, standing, since it covered most of the ceiling, until after a moment he raised himself on one elbow to look. It was not the negro, it was his kinsman; when he spoke the other turned sharp against the red firelight the sullen and ruthless profile.

"Nothing," Edmonds said. "Go on back to sleep."

"Since Will Legate mentioned it," McCaslin said, "I remember you had some trouble sleeping in here last fall too. Only you called it coon-hunting then. Or was it Will Legate called it that?" The other didn't answer. Then he turned and went back to his bed. McCaslin, still propped on his elbow, watched until the other's shadow sank down the wall and vanished, became one with the mass of sleeping shadows. "That's right," he said. "Try to get some sleep. We must have meat in camp tomorrow. You can do all the setting up you want to after that." He lay down again, his hands crossed again on his breast, watching the glow of the heater on the canvas ceiling. It was steady again now, the fresh wood accepted, being assimilated; soon it would begin to fade again, taking with it the last echo of that sudden upflare of a young man's passion and unrest. Let him lie awake for a little while, he thought; He will lie still some day for a long time without even dissatisfaction to disturb him. And lying awake here, in these surroundings, would soothe him if anything could, if anything could soothe a man just forty years old. Yes, he thought; Forty years old or thirty, or even the trembling and sleepless ardor of a boy; already the tent, the rain-murmured canvas globe, was once more filled with it. He lay on his back, his eyes closed, his breathing quiet and peaceful as a child's, listening to it— that silence which was never silence but was myriad. He could almost see it, tremendous, primeval, looming, musing downward upon this puny evanescent clutter of human sojourn which after a single brief week would vanish and in another week would be completely healed, traceless in the unmarked solitude. Because it was his land, although he had never owned a foot of it. He had never wanted to, not even after he saw plain its ultimate doom, watching it retreat year by year before the onslaught of axe and saw and log-lines and then dynamite and tractor plows, because it belonged to no man. It belonged to all; they had only to use it well, humbly and with pride. Then suddenly he knew why he had never wanted to own any of it, arrest at least that much of what people called progress, measure his longevity at least against that much of its ultimate fate. It was because there was just exactly enough of it. He seemed to see the two of them—himself and the wilderness—as coevals, his own span as a hunter, a woodsman, not contemporary with his first breath but transmitted to him, assumed by him gladly, humbly, with joy and pride, from that old Major de Spain and that old Sam Fathers who had taught him to hunt, the two spans running out together, not toward oblivion, nothingness, but into a dimension free of both time and space where once more the untreed land warped and wrung to mathematical squares of rank cotton for the frantic old-world people to turn into shells to shoot at one another, would find ample room for both—the names, the faces of the old men he had known and loved and for a little while outlived, moving again among the shades of tall unaxed trees and sightless brakes where the wild strong immortal game ran forever before the tireless belling immortal hounds, falling and rising phoenix-like to the soundless guns.

He had been asleep. The lantern was lighted now. Outside in the darkness the oldest negro, Isham, was beating a spoon against the bottom of a tin pan and crying, "Raise up and get yo foa clock coffy. Raise up and get yo foa clock coffy," and the tent was full of low talk and of men dressing, and Legate's voice, repeating: "Get out of here now and let Uncle Ike sleep. If you wake him up, he'll go out with us. And he aint got any business in the woods this morning."

So he didn't move. He lay with his eyes closed, his breathing gentle and peaceful, and heard them one by one leave the tent. He listened to the breakfast sounds from the table beneath the tarpaulin and heard them depart—the horses, the dogs, the last voice until it died away and there was only the sounds of the negroes clearing breakfast away. After a while he might possibly even hear the first faint clear cry of the first hound ring through the wet woods from where the buck had bedded, then he would go back to sleep again—

The tent-flap swung in and fell. Something jarred sharply against the end of the cot and a hand grasped his knee through the blanket before he could open his eyes. It was Edmonds, carrying a shotgun in place of his rifle. He spoke in a harsh, rapid voice:

"Sorry to wake you. There will be a———"

"I was awake," McCaslin said. "Are you going to shoot that shotgun today?"

"You just told me last night you want meat," Edmonds said. "There will be a———"

"Since when did you start having trouble getting meat with your rifle?"

"All right," the other said, with that harsh, restrained, furious impatience. Then McCaslin saw in his hand a thick oblong: an envelope. "There will be a message here some time this morning, looking for me. Maybe it wont come. If it does, give the messenger this and tell h— say I said No."

"A what?" McCaslin said. "Tell who?" He half rose onto his elbow as Edmonds jerked the envelope onto the blanket, already turning toward the entrance, the envelope striking solid and heavy and without noise and already sliding from the bed until McCaslin caught it, divining by feel through the paper as instantaneously and conclusively as if he had opened the envelope and looked, the thick sheaf of banknotes. "Wait," he said. "Wait:"—more than the blood kinsman, more even than the senior in years, so that the other paused, the canvas lifted, looking back, and McCaslin saw that outside it was already day. "Tell her No," he said. "Tell her." They stared at one another—the old face, wan, sleep-raddled above the tumbled bed, the dark and sullen younger one at once furious and cold. "Will Legate was right. This is what you called coon-hunting. And now this." He didn't raise the envelope. He made no motion, no gesture to indicate it. "What did you promise her that you haven't the courage to face her and retract?"

"Nothing!" the other said. "Nothing! This is all of it. Tell her I said No." He was gone. The tent flap lifted on an in-waft of faint light and the constant murmur of rain, and fell again, leaving the old man still half-raised onto one elbow, the envelope clutched in the other shaking hand. Afterward it seemed to him that he had begun to hear the approaching boat almost immediately, before the other could have got out of sight even. It seemed to him that there had been no interval whatever: the tent flap falling on the same out-waft of faint and rain-filled light like the suspiration and expiration of the same breath and then in the next second lifted again—the mounting snarl of the outboard engine, increasing, nearer and nearer and louder and louder then cut short off, ceasing with the absolute instantaneity of a blown-out candle, into the lap and plop of water under the bows as the skiff slid in to the bank, the youngest negro, the youth, raising the tent flap beyond which for that instant he saw the boat—a small skiff with a negro man sitting in the stern beside the up-slanted motor—then the woman entering, in a man's hat and a man's slicker and rubber boots, carrying the blanket-swaddled bundle on one arm and holding the edge of the unbuttoned raincoat over it with the other hand: and bringing something else, something intangible, an effluvium which he knew he would recognise in a moment because Isham had already told him, warned him, by sending the young negro to the tent to announce the visitor instead of coming himself, the flap falling at last on the young negro and they were alone—the face indistinct and as yet only young and with dark eyes, queerly colorless but not ill and not that of a country woman despite the garments she wore, looking down at him where he sat upright on the cot now, clutching the envelope, the soiled undergarment bagging about him and the twisted blankets huddled about his hips.

"Is that his?" he cried. "Dont lie to me!"

"Yes," she said. "He's gone."

"Yes. He's gone. You wont jump him here. Not this time. I dont reckon even you expected that. He left you this. Here." He fumbled at the envelope. It was not to pick it up, because it was still in his hand; he had never put it down. It was as if he had to fumble somehow to co-ordinate physically his heretofore obedient hand with what his brain was commanding of it, as if he had never performed such an action before, extending the envelope at last, saying again, "Here. Take it. Take it:" until he became aware of her eyes, or not the eyes so much as the look, the regard fixed now on his face with that immersed contemplation, that bottomless and intent candor, of a child. If she had ever seen either the envelope or his movement to extend it, she did not show it.

"You're Uncle Isaac," she said.

"Yes," he said. "But never mind that. Here. Take it. He said to tell you No." She looked at the envelope, then she took it. It was sealed and bore no superscription. Nevertheless, even after she glanced at the front of it, he watched her hold it in the one free hand and tear the corner off with her teeth and manage to rip it open and tilt the neat sheaf of bound notes onto the blanket without even glancing at them and look into the empty envelope and take the edge between her teeth and tear it completely open before she crumpled and dropped it.

"That's just money," she said.

"What did you expect? What else did you expect? You have known him long enough or at least often enough to have got that child, and you dont know him any better than that?"

"Not very often. Not very long. Just that week here last fall, and in January he sent for me and we went West, to New Mexico. We were there six weeks, where I could at least sleep in the same apartment where I cooked for him and looked after his clothes————"

"But not marriage," he said. "Not marriage. He didn't promise you that. Dont lie to me. He didn't have to."

"No. He didn't have to. I didn't ask him to. I knew what I was doing. I knew that to begin with, long before honor I imagine he called it told him the time had come to tell me in so many words what his code I suppose he would call it would forbid him forever to do. And we agreed. Then we agreed again before he left New Mexico, to make sure. That that would be all of it. I believed him. No, I dont mean that; I mean I believed myself. I wasn't even listening to him anymore by then because by that time it had been a long time since he had had anything else to tell me for me to have to hear. By then I wasn't even listening enough to ask him to please stop talking. I was listening to myself. And I believed it. I must have believed it. I dont see how I could have helped but believe it, because he was gone then as we had agreed and he didn't write as we had agreed, just the money came to the bank in Vicksburg in my name but coming from nobody as we had agreed. So I must have believed it. I even wrote him last month to make sure again and the letter came back unopened and I was sure. So I left the hospital and rented myself a room to live in until the deer season opened so I could make sure myself and I was waiting beside the road yesterday when your car passed and he saw me and so I was sure."

"Then what do you want?" he said. "What do you want? What do you expect?"

"Yes," she said. And while he glared at her, his white hair awry from the pillow and his eyes, lacking the spectacles to focus them, blurred and irisless and apparently pupilless, he saw again that grave, intent, speculative and detached fixity like a child watching him. "His great great—Wait a minute.—great great *great* grandfather was your grandfather. McCaslin. Only it got to be Edmonds. Only it got to be more than that. Your cousin McCaslin was there that day when your father and Uncle Buddy won Tennie from Mr Beauchamp for the one that had no name but Terrel so you called him Tomey's Terrel, to marry. But after that it got to be Edmonds." She regarded him, almost peacefully, with that unwinking and heatless fixity—the dark wide bottomless eyes in the face's dead and toneless pallor which to the old man looked anything but dead, but young and incredibly and even ineradicably alive—as though she were not only not looking at anything, she was not even speaking to anyone but herself. "I would have made a man of him. He's not a man yet. You spoiled him. You, and Uncle Lucas and Aunt Mollie. But mostly you."

"Me?" he said. "Me?"

"Yes. When you gave to his grandfather that land which didn't belong to him, not even half of it by will or even law."

"And never mind that too," he said. "Never mind that too. You," he said. "You sound like you have been to college even. You sound almost like a Northerner even, not like the draggle-tailed women of these Delta peckerwoods. Yet you meet a man on the street one afternoon just because a box of groceries happened to fall out of a boat. And a month later you go off with him and live with him until he got a child on you: and then, by your own statement, you sat there while he took his hat and said goodbye and walked out. Even a Delta peckerwood would look after even a draggle-tail better than that. Haven't you got any folks at all?"

"Yes," she said. "I was living with one of them. My aunt, in Vicksburg. I came to live with her two years ago when my father died; we lived in Indianapolis then. But I got a job, teaching school here in Aluschaskuna, because my aunt was a widow, with a big family, taking in washing to sup————"

"Took in what?" he said. "Took in washing?" He sprang, still seated even, flinging himself backward onto one arm, awry-haired, glaring. Now he understood what it was she had brought into the tent with her, what old Isham had already told him by sending the youth to bring her in to him—the pale lips, the skin pallid and dead-looking yet not ill, the dark and tragic and foreknowing eyes. *Maybe in a thousand or two thousand years in America,* he thought.

But not now! Not now! He cried, not loud, in a voice of amazement, pity, and outrage: "You're a nigger!"

"Yes," she said. "James Beauchamp—you called him Tennie's Jim though he had a name—was my grandfather. I said you were Uncle Isaac."

"And he knows?"

"No," she said. "What good would that have done?"

"But you did," he cried. "But you did. Then what do you expect here?"

"Nothing."

"Then why did you come here? You said you were waiting in Aluschaskuna yesterday and he saw you. Why did you come this morning?"

"I'm going back North. Back home. My cousin brought me up the day before yesterday in his boat. He's going to take me on to Leland to get the train."

"Then go," he said. Then he cried again in that thin not loud and grieving voice: "Get out of here! I can do nothing for you! Cant nobody do nothing for you!" She moved; she was not looking at him again, toward the entrance. "Wait," he said. She paused again, obediently still, turning. He took up the sheaf of banknotes and laid it on the blanket at the foot of the cot and drew his hand back beneath the blanket. "There," he said.

Now she looked at the money, for the first time, one brief blank glance, then away again. "I dont need it. He gave me money last winter. Besides the money he sent to Vicksburg. Provided. Honor and code too. That was all arranged."

"Take it," he said. His voice began to rise again, but he stopped it. "Take it out of my tent." She came back to the cot and took up the money; whereupon once more he said, "Wait:" although she had not turned, still stooping, and he put out his hand. But, sitting, he could not complete the reach until she moved her hand, the single hand which held the money, until he touched it. He didn't grasp it, he merely touched it—the gnarled, bloodless, bone-light bone-dry old man's fingers touching for a second the smooth young flesh where the strong old blood ran after its long lost journey back to home. "Tennie's Jim," he said. "Tennie's Jim." He drew the hand back beneath the blanket again: he said harshly now: "It's a boy, I reckon. They usually are, except that one that was its own mother too."

"Yes," she said. "It's a boy." She stood for a moment longer, looking at him. Just for an instant her free hand moved as though she were about to lift the edge of the raincoat away from the child's face. But she did not. She turned again when once more he said Wait and moved beneath the blanket.

"Turn your back," he said. "I am going to get up. I aint got my pants on." Then he could not get up. He sat in the huddled blanket, shaking, while again she turned and looked down at him in dark interrogation. "There," he said harshly, in the thin and shaking old man's voice. "On the nail there. The tent-pole."

"What?" she said.

"The horn!" he said harshly. "The horn." She went and got it, thrust the money into the slicker's side pocket as if it were a rag, a soiled handkerchief, and lifted down the horn, the one which General Compson had left him in his will, covered with the unbroken skin from a buck's shank and bound with silver.

"What?" she said.

"It's his. Take it."

"Oh," she said. "Yes. Thank you."

"Yes," he said, harshly, rapidly, but not so harsh now and soon not harsh at all but just rapid, urgent, until he knew that his voice was running away with him and he had neither intended it nor could stop it: "That's right. Go back North. Marry: a man in your own race. That's the only salvation for you —for a while yet, maybe a long while yet. We will have to wait. Marry a black man. You are young, handsome, almost white; you could find a black man who would see in you what it was you saw in him, who would ask nothing of you and expect less and get even still less than that, if it's revenge you want. Then you will forget all this, forget it ever happened, that he ever existed—" until he could stop it at last and did, sitting there in his huddle of blankets during the instant when, without moving at all, she blazed silently down at him. Then that was gone too. She stood in the gleaming and still dripping slicker, looking quietly down at him from under the sodden hat.

"Old man," she said, "have you lived so long and forgotten so much that you dont remember anything you ever knew or felt or even heard about love?"

Then she was gone too. The waft of light and the murmur of the constant rain flowed into the tent and then out again as the flap fell. Lying back once more, trembling, panting, the blanket huddled to his chin and his hands crossed on his breast, he listened to the pop and snarl, the mounting then fading whine of the motor until it died away and once again the tent held only silence and the sound of rain. And cold too: he lay shaking faintly and steadily in it, rigid save for the shaking. This Delta, he thought: This Delta. *This land which man has deswamped and denuded and derivered in two generations so that white men can own plantations and commute every night to Memphis and black men own plantations and ride in jim crow cars to Chicago to live in millionaires' mansions on Lakeshore Drive, where white men rent farms and live like niggers and niggers crop on shares and live like animals, where cotton is planted and grows man-tall in the very cracks of the sidewalks, and usury and mortgage and bankruptcy and measureless wealth, Chinese and African and Aryan and Jew, all breed and spawn together until no man has time to say which one is which nor cares. . . .* No wonder the ruined woods I used to know dont cry for retribution! he thought: The people who have destroyed it will accomplish its revenge.

The tent flap jerked rapidly in and fell. He did not move save to turn his head and open his eyes. It was Legate. He went quickly to Edmonds' bed and stooped, rummaging hurriedly among the still-tumbled blankets.

"What is it?" he said.

"Looking for Roth's knife," Legate said. "I come back to get a horse. We got a deer on the ground." He rose, the knife in his hand, and hurried toward the entrance.

"Who killed it?" McCaslin said. "Was it Roth?"

"Yes," Legate said, raising the flap.

"Wait," McCaslin said. He moved, suddenly, onto his elbow. "What was it?" Legate paused for an instant beneath the lifted flap. He did not look back.

"Just a deer, Uncle Ike," he said impatiently. "Nothing extra." He was gone; again the flap fell behind him, wafting out of the tent again the faint light and the constant and grieving rain. McCaslin lay back down, the blanket once more drawn to his chin, his crossed hands once more weightless on his breast in the empty tent.

"It was a doe," he said.

This Morning,
This Evening,
So Soon

JAMES BALDWIN

"You are full of nightmares," Harriet tells me. She is in her dressing gown and has cream all over her face. She and my older sister, Louisa, are going out to be girls together. I suppose they have many things to talk about—they have *me* to talk about, certainly—and they do not want my presence. I have been given a bachelor's evening. The director of the film which has brought us such incredible and troubling riches will be along later to take me out to dinner.

I watch her face. I know that it is quite impossible for her to be as untroubled as she seems. Her self-control is mainly for my benefit—my benefit, and Paul's. Harriet comes from orderly and progressive Sweden and has reacted against all the advanced doctrines to which she has been exposed by becoming steadily and beautifully old-fashioned. We never fought in front of Paul, not even when he was a baby. Harriet does not so much believe in protecting children as she does in helping them to build a foundation on which they can build and build again, each time life's high-flying steel ball knocks down everything they have built.

Whenever I become upset, Harriet becomes very cheerful and composed. I think she began to learn how to do this over eight years ago, when I returned from my only visit to America. Now, perhaps, it has become something she could not control if she wished to. This morning, at breakfast, when I yelled at

Paul, she averted Paul's tears and my own guilt by looking up and saying, "My God, your father is cranky this morning, isn't he?"

Paul's attention was immediately distracted from his wounds, and the unjust inflicter of those wounds, to his mother's laughter. He watched her.

"It is because he is afraid they will not like his songs in New York. Your father is an *artiste, mon chou,* and they are very mysterious people, *les artistes.* Millions of people are waiting for him in New York, they are begging him to come, and they will give him a *lot* of money, but he is afraid they will not like him. Tell him he is wrong."

She succeeded in rekindling Paul's excitement about places he has never seen. I was also, at once, reinvested with all my glamour. I think it is sometimes extremely difficult for Paul to realize that the face he sees on record sleeves and in the newspapers and on the screen is nothing more or less than the face of his father—who sometimes yells at him. Of course, since he is only seven—going on eight, he will be eight years old this winter—he cannot know that I am baffled, too.

"Of course, you are wrong, you are silly," he said with passion—and caused me to smile. His English is strongly accented and is not, in fact, as good as his French, for he speaks French all day at school. French is really his first language, the first he ever heard. "You are the greatest singer in France"— sounding exactly as he must sound when he makes this pronouncement to his schoolmates—"the greatest *American* singer"—this concession was so gracefully made that it was not a concession at all, it added inches to my stature, America being only a glamorous word for Paul. It is the place from which his father came, and to which he now is going, a place which very few people have ever seen. But his aunt is one of them and he looked over at her. "Mme. Dumont says so, and she says he is a *great actor, too.*" Louisa nodded, smiling. "And she has seen *Les Fauves Nous Attendent*—five times!" This clinched it, of course. Mme. Dumont is our concierge and she has known Paul all his life. I suppose he will not begin to doubt anything she says until he begins to doubt everything.

He looked over at me again. "So you are wrong to be afraid."

"I was wrong to yell at you, too. I won't yell at you any more today."

"All right." He was very grave.

Louisa poured more coffee. "He's going to knock them dead in New York. You'll see."

"*Mais bien sûr,*" said Paul, doubtfully. He does not quite know what "knock them dead" means, though he was sure, from her tone, that she must have been agreeing with him. He does not quite understand this aunt, whom he met for the first time two months ago, when she arrived to spend the summer with us. Her accent is entirely different from anything he has ever heard. He does not really understand why, since she is my sister and his aunt, she should be unable to speak French.

Harriet, Louisa, and I looked at each other and smiled. "Knock them dead," said Harriet, "means *d'avoir un succès fou.* But you will soon pick up all the American expressions." She looked at me and laughed. "So will I."

"That's what he's afraid of." Louisa grinned. "We have *got* some expressions, believe me. Don't let anybody ever tell you America hasn't got a culture. Our culture is as thick as clabber milk."

"Ah," Harriet answered, "I know. I know."

"I'm going to be practicing later," I told Paul.

His face lit up. *"Bon."* This meant that, later, he would come into my study and lie on the floor with his papers and crayons while I worked out with the piano and the tape recorder. He knew that I was offering this as an olive branch. All things considered, we get on pretty well, my son and I.

He looked over at Louisa again. She held a coffee cup in one hand and a cigarette in the other; and something about her baffled him. It was early, so she had not yet put on her face. Her short, thick, graying hair was rougher than usual, almost as rough as my own—later, she would be going to the hairdresser's; she is fairer than I, and better-looking; Louisa, in fact, caught all the looks in the family. Paul knows that she is my older sister and that she helped to raise me, though he does not, of course, know what this means. He knows that she is a schoolteacher in the *American* South, which is not, for some reason, the same place as South America. I could see him trying to fit all these exotic details together into a pattern which would explain her strangeness—strangeness of accent, strangeness of manner. In comparison with the people he has always known, Louisa must seem, for all her generosity and laughter and affection, peculiarly uncertain of herself, peculiarly hostile and embattled.

I wondered what he would think of his Uncle Norman, older and much blacker than I, who lives near the Alabama town in which we were born. Norman will meet us at the boat.

Now Harriet repeats, "Nightmares, nightmares. Nothing ever turns out as badly as you think it will—in fact," she adds laughing, "I am happy to say that that would scarcely be possible."

Her eyes seek mine in the mirror—dark-blue eyes, pale skin, black hair. I had always thought of Sweden as being populated entirely by blondes, and I thought that Harriet was abnormally dark for a Swedish girl. But when we visited Sweden, I found out differently. "It is all a great racial salad, Europe, that is why I am sure that I will never understand your country," Harriet said. That was in the days when we never imagined that we would be going to it.

I wonder what she is really thinking. Still, she is right, in two days we will be on a boat, and there is simply no point in carrying around my load of apprehension. I sit down on the bed, watching her fix her face. I realize that I am going to miss this old-fashioned bedroom. For years, we've talked about throwing out the old junk which came with the apartment and replacing it with less massive, modern furniture. But we never have.

"Oh, everything will probably work out," I say. "I've been in a bad mood all day long. I just can't sing any more." We both laugh. She reaches for a wad of tissues and begins wiping off the cream. "I wonder how Paul will like it, if he'll make friends—that's all."

"Paul will like any place where you are, where we are. Don't you worry about Paul."

Paul has never been called any names, so far. Only, once he asked us what the word *métis* meant and Harriet explained to him that it meant mixed blood, adding that the blood of just about everybody in the world was mixed by now. Mme. Dumont contributed bawdy and detailed corroboration from her own family tree, the roots of which were somewhere in Corsica; the moral of the story, as she told it, was that women were weak, men incorrigible, and *le bon Dieu* appallingly clever. Mme. Dumont's version is the version I prefer, but it may not be, for Paul, the most utilitarian.

Harriet rises from the dressing table and comes over to sit in my lap. I fall back with her on the bed, and she smiles down into my face.

"Now, don't worry," she tells me, "please try not to worry. Whatever is coming, we will manage it all very well, you will see. We have each other and we have our son and we know what we want. So, we are luckier than most people."

I kiss her on the chin. "I'm luckier than most men."

"I'm a very lucky woman, too."

And for a moment we are silent, alone in our room, which we have shared so long. The slight rise and fall of Harriet's breathing creates an intermittent pressure against my chest, and I think how, if I had never left America, I would never have met her and would never have established a life of my own, would never have entered my own life. For everyone's life begins on a level where races, armies, and churches stop. And yet everyone's life is always shaped by races, churches, and armies; races, churches, armies menace, and have taken, many lives. If Harriet had been born in America, it would have taken her a long time, perhaps forever, to look on me as a man like other men; if I had met her in America, I would never have been able to look on her as a woman like all other women. The habits of public rage and power would also have been our private compulsions, and would have blinded our eyes. We would never have been able to love each other. And Paul would never have been born.

Perhaps, if I had stayed in America, I would have found another woman and had another son. But that other woman, that other son are in the limbo of vanished possibilities. I might also have become something else, instead of an actor-singer, perhaps a lawyer, like my brother, or a teacher, like my sister. But no, I am what I have become and this woman beside me is my wife, and I love her. All the sons I might have had mean nothing, since I *have* a son, I named him, Paul, for my father, and I love him.

I think of all the things I have seen destroyed in America, all the things that I have lost there, all the threats it holds for me and mine.

I grin up at Harriet. "Do you love me?"

"Of course not. I simply have been madly plotting to get to America all these years."

"What a patient wench you are."

"The Swedes are very patient."

She kisses me again and stands up. Louisa comes in, also in a dressing gown.

"I hope you two aren't sitting in here yakking about the *subject.*" She looks at me. "My, you are the sorriest-looking celebrity I've ever seen. I've always wondered why people like you hired press agents. Now I know." She goes to Harriet's dressing table. "Honey, do you mind if I borrow some of that *mad* nail polish?"

Harriet goes over to the dressing table. "I'm not sure I know *which* mad nail polish you mean."

Harriet and Louisa, somewhat to my surprise, get on very well. Each seems to find the other full of the weirdest and most delightful surprises. Harriet has been teaching Louisa French and Swedish expressions, and Louisa has been teaching Harriet some of the saltier expressions of the black South. Whenever one of them is not playing straight man to the other's accent, they become involved in long speculations as to how a language reveals the history and the attitudes of a people. They discovered that all the European languages contain a phrase equivalent to "to work like a nigger." ("Of course," says Louisa, "they've had black men working for them for a long time.") "Language is experience and language is power," says Louisa, after regretting that she does not know any of the African dialects. "That's what I keep trying to tell those dicty bastards down South. They get their own experience into the language, we'll have a great language. But, no, they all want to talk like white folks." Then she leans forward, grasping Harriet by the knee. "I tell them, honey, white folks ain't saying *nothing.* Not a thing are they saying—and *some* of them know it, they *need* what you got, the whole world needs it." Then she leans back, in disgust. "You think they listen to me? Indeed they do not. They just go right on, trying to talk like white folks." She leans forward again, in tremendous indignation. "You know some of them folks are *ashamed* of Mahalia Jackson? *Ashamed* of her, one of the greatest singers alive! They think she's common." Then she looks about the room as though she held a bottle in her hand and were looking for a skull to crack.

I think it is because Louisa has never been able to talk like this to any white person before. All the white people she has ever met needed, in one way or another, to be reassured, consoled, to have their consciences pricked but not blasted; could not, could not afford to hear a truth which would shatter, irrevocably, their image of themselves. It is astonishing the lengths to which a person, or a people, will go in order to avoid a truthful mirror. But Harriet's necessity is precisely the opposite: it is of the utmost importance that she learn everything that Louisa can tell her, and then learn more, much more. Harriet is really trying to learn from Louisa how best to protect her husband and her son. This is why they are going out alone tonight. They will have, tonight, as it were, a final council of war. I may be moody, but they, thank God, are practical.

Now Louisa turns to me while Harriet rummages about on the dressing table. "What time is Vidal coming for you?"

"Oh, around seven-thirty, eight o'clock. He says he's reserved tables for us in some very chic place, but he won't say where." Louisa wriggles her shoulders, raises her eyebrows, and does a tiny bump and grind. I laugh. "That's right. And then I guess we'll go out and get drunk."

"I hope to God you do. You've been about as cheerful as a cemetery these last few days. And, that way, your hangover will keep you from bugging us tomorrow."

"What about *your* hangovers? I know the way you girls drink."

"Well, we'll be paying for our own drinks," says Harriet, "so I don't think we'll have that problem. But *you're* going to be feted, like an international movie star."

"You sure you don't want to change your mind and come out with Vidal and me?"

"We're sure," Louisa says. She looks down at me and gives a small, amused grunt. "An international movie star. And I used to change your diapers. I'll be damned." She is grave for a moment. "Mama'd be proud of you, you know that?" We look at each other and the air between us is charged with secrets which not even Harriet will ever know. "Now, get the hell out of here, so we can get dressed."

"I'll take Paul on down to Mme. Dumont's."

Paul is to have supper with her children and spend the night there.

"For the last time," says Mme. Dumont and she rubs her hand over Paul's violently curly black hair. *"Tu vas nous manquer, tu sais?"* Then she looks up at me and laughs. "He doesn't care. He is only interested in seeing the big ship and all the wonders of New York. Children are never sad to make journeys."

"I would be very sad to go," says Paul, politely, "but my father must go to New York to work and he wants me to come with him."

Over his head, Mme. Dumont and I smile at each other. *"Il est malin, ton gosse!"* She looks down at him again. "And do you think, my little diplomat, that you will like New York?"

"We aren't only going to New York," Paul answers, "we are going to California, too."

"Well, do you think you will like California?"

Paul looks at me. "I don't know. If we don't like it, we'll come back."

"So simple. Just like that," says Mme. Dumont. She looks at me. "It is the best way to look at life. Do come back. You know, we feel that you belong to us, too, here in France."

"I hope you do," I say. "I hope you do. I have always felt—always felt at home here." I bend down and Paul and I kiss each other on the cheek. We have always done so—but will we be able to do so in America? American fathers never kiss American sons. I straighten, my hand on Paul's shoulder. "You be good. I'll pick you up for breakfast, or, if you get up first you come and pick me up and we can hang out together tomorrow, while your *Maman* and your Aunt Louisa finish packing. They won't want two men hanging around the house."

"D'accord. Where shall we hang out?" On the last two words he stumbles a little and imitates me.

"Maybe we can go to the zoo, I don't know. And I'll take you to lunch at the Eiffel Tower, would you like that?"

"Oh, yes," he says, "I'd love that." When he is pleased, he seems to glow. All the energy of his small, tough, concentrated being charges an unseen battery and adds an incredible luster to his eyes, which are large and dark brown

—like mine—and to his skin, which always reminds me of the colors of honey and the fires of the sun.

"OK, then." I shake hands with Mme. Dumont. *"Bonsoir, Madame."* I ring for the elevator, staring at Paul. *"Ciao, Pauli."*

"Bonsoir, Papa."

And Mme. Dumont takes him inside.

Upstairs, Harriet and Louisa are finally powdered, perfumed, and jeweled, and ready to go: dry martinis at the Ritz, supper, "in some *very* expensive little place," says Harriet, and perhaps the Folies Bergère afterwards. "A real cornball, tourist evening," says Louisa. "I'm working on the theory that if I can get Harriet to act like an American now, she won't have so much trouble later."

"I very much doubt," Harriet says, "that I will be able to endure the Folies Bergère for three solid hours."

"Oh, then we'll duck across town to Harry's New York bar and drink mint juleps," says Louisa.

I realize that, quite apart from everything else, Louisa is having as much fun as she has ever had in her life before. Perhaps she, too, will be sad to leave Paris, even though she has only known it for such a short time.

"Do people drink those in New York?" Harriet asks. I think she is making a list of the things people do or do not do in New York.

"Some people do." Louisa winks at me. "Do you realize that this Swedish chick's picked up an Alabama drawl?"

We laugh together. The elevator chugs to a landing.

"We'll stop and say good night to Paul," Harriet says. She kisses me. "Give our best to Vidal."

"Right. Have a good time. Don't let any Frenchmen run off with Louisa."

"I did not come to Paris to be protected, and if I had, this wild chick *you* married couldn't do it. I just *might* upset everybody and come home with a French count." She presses the elevator button and the cage goes down.

I walk back into our dismantled apartment. It stinks of departure. There are bags and crates in the hall, which will be taken away tomorrow, there are no books in the bookcases, the kitchen looks as though we never cooked a meal there, never dawdled there, in the early morning or late at night, over coffee. Presently, I must shower and shave but now I pour myself a drink and light a cigarette and step out on our balcony. It is dusk, the brilliant light of Paris is beginning to fade, and the green of the trees is darkening.

I have lived in this city for twelve years. This apartment is on the top floor of a corner building. We look out over the trees and the roof tops to the Champ de Mars, where the Eiffel Tower stands. Beyond this field is the river, which I have crossed so often, in so many states of mind. I have crossed every bridge in Paris, I have walked along every *quai.* I know the river as one finally knows a friend, know it when it is black, guarding all the lights of Paris in its depths, and seeming, in its vast silence, to be communing with the dead who lie beneath it; when it is yellow, evil, and roaring, giving a rough time to tugboats and barges, and causing people to remember that it has been known to rise, it has been known to kill; when it is peaceful, a slick, dark, dirty green, playing host to rowboats and *les bateaux mouches* and throwing up from time to time an extremely unhealthy fish. The men who stand along the *quais* all summer with their fishing lines gratefully accept the slimy object and throw it in a rusty can. I have always wondered who eats those fish.

And I walk up and down, up and down, glad to be alone.

It is August, the month when all Parisians desert Paris and one has to walk miles to find a barbershop or a laundry open in some tree-shadowed, silent side street. There is a single person on the avenue, a paratrooper walking toward École Militaire. He is also walking, almost certainly, and rather sooner than later, toward Algeria. I have a friend, a good-natured boy who was always hanging around the clubs in which I worked in the old days, who has just returned from Algeria, with a recurring, debilitating fever, and minus one eye. The government has set his pension at the sum, arbitrary if not occult, of fifty-three thousand francs every three months. Of course, it is quite impossible to live on this amount of money without working—but who will hire a half-blind invalid? This boy has been spoiled forever, long before his thirtieth birthday, and there are thousands like him all over France.

And there are fewer Algerians to be found on the streets of Paris now. The rug sellers, the peanut vendors, the postcard peddlers and money-changers have vanished. The boys I used to know during my first years in Paris are scattered—or corralled—the Lord knows where.

Most of them had no money. They lived three and four together in rooms with a single skylight, a single hard cot, or in buildings that seemed abandoned, with cardboard in the windows, with erratic plumbing in a wet, cobblestoned yard, in dark, dead-end alleys, or on the outer, chilling heights of Paris.

The Arab cafés are closed—those dark, acrid cafés in which I used to meet with them to drink tea, to get high on hashish, to listen to the obsessive, stringed music which has no relation to any beat, any time, that I have ever known. I once thought of the North Africans as my brothers and that is why I went to their cafés. They were very friendly to me, perhaps one or two of them remained really fond of me even after I could no longer afford to smoke Lucky Strikes and after my collection of American sport shirts had vanished —mostly into their wardrobes. They seemed to feel that they had every right to them, since I could only have wrested these things from the world by cunning—it meant nothing to say that I had had no choice in the matter; perhaps I had wrested these things from the world by treason, by refusing to be identified with the misery of my people. Perhaps, indeed, I identified myself with those who were responsible for this misery.

And this was true. Their rage, the only note in all their music which I could not fail to recognize, to which I responded, yet had the effect of setting us more than ever at a division. They were perfectly prepared to drive all Frenchmen into the sea, and to level the city of Paris. But I could not hate the French, because they left me alone. And I love Paris, I will always love it, it is the city which saved my life. It saved my life by allowing me to find out who I am.

It was on a bridge, one tremendous, April morning, that I knew I had fallen in love. Harriet and I were walking hand in hand. The bridge was the Pont

Royal, just before us was the great *horloge,* high and lifted up, saying ten to ten; beyond this, the golden statue of Joan of Arc, with her sword uplifted. Harriet and I were silent, for we had been quarreling about something. Now, when I look back, I think we had reached that state when an affair must either end or become something more than an affair.

I looked sideways at Harriet's face, which was still. Her dark-blue eyes were narrowed against the sun, and her full, pink lips were still slightly sulky, like a child's. In those days, she hardly ever wore make-up. I was in my shirt sleeves. Her face made me want to laugh and run my hand over her short dark hair. I wanted to pull her to me and say, *Baby, don't be mad at me,* and at that moment something tugged at my heart and made me catch my breath. There were millions of people all around us, but I was alone with Harriet. She was alone with me. Never, in all my life, until that moment, had I been alone with anyone. The world had always been with us, between us, defeating the quarrel we could not achieve, and making love impossible. During all the years of my life, until that moment, I had carried the menacing, the hostile, killing world with me everywhere. No matter what I was doing or saying or feeling, one eye had always been on the world—that world which I had learned to distrust almost as soon as I learned my name, that world on which I knew one could never turn one's back, the white man's world. And for the first time in my life I was free of it; it had not existed for me; I had been quarreling with my girl. It was our quarrel, it was entirely between us, it had nothing to do with anyone else in the world. For the first time in my life I had not been afraid of the patriotism of the mindless, in uniform or out, who would beat me up and treat the woman who was with me as though she were the lowest of untouchables. For the first time in my life I felt that no force jeopardized my right, my power, to possess and to protect a woman; for the first time, the first time, felt that the woman was not, in her own eyes or in the eyes of the world, degraded by my presence.

The sun fell over everything, like a blessing, people were moving all about us, I will never forget the feeling of Harriet's small hand in mine, dry and trusting, and I turned to her, slowing our pace. She looked up at me with her enormous, blue eyes, and she seemed to wait. I said, *"Harriet. Harriet. Tu sais, il y a quelque chose de très grave qui m'est arrivé. Je t'aime. Je t'aime. Tu me comprends,* or shall I say it in English?"

This was eight years ago, shortly before my first and only visit home.

That was when my mother died. I stayed in America for three months. When I came back, Harriet thought that the change in me was due to my grief —I was very silent, very thin. But it had not been my mother's death which accounted for the change. I had known that my mother was going to die. I had not known what America would be like for me after nearly four years away.

I remember standing at the rail and watching the distance between myself and Le Havre increase. Hands fell, ceasing to wave, handkerchiefs ceased to flutter, people turned away, they mounted their bicycles or got into their cars and rode off. Soon, Le Havre was nothing but a blur. I thought of Harriet, already miles from me in Paris, and I pressed my lips tightly together in order not to cry.

Then, as Europe dropped below the water, as the days passed and passed, as we left behind us the skies of Europe and the eyes of everyone on the ship began, so to speak, to refocus, waiting for the first glimpse of America, my apprehension began to give way to a secret joy, a checked anticipation. I thought of such details as showers, which are rare in Paris, and I thought of such things as rich, cold, American milk and heavy, chocolate cake. I wondered about my friends, wondered if I had any left, and wondered if they would be glad to see me.

The Americans on the boat did not seem to be so bad, but I was fascinated, after such a long absence from it, by the nature of their friendliness. It was a friendliness which did not suggest, and was not intended to suggest, any possibility of friendship. Unlike Europeans, they dropped titles and used first names almost at once, leaving themselves, unlike the Europeans, with nowhere thereafter to go. Once one had become "Pete" or "Jane" or "Bill" all that could decently be known was known and any suggestion that there might be further depths, a person, so to speak, behind the name, was taken as a violation of that privacy which did not, paradoxically, since they trusted it so little, seem to exist among Americans. They apparently equated privacy with the unspeakable things they did in the bathroom or the bedroom, which they related only to the analyst, and then read about in the pages of best sellers. There was an eerie and unnerving irreality about everything they said and did, as though they were all members of the same team and were acting on orders from some invincibly cheerful and tirelessly inventive coach. I was fascinated by it. I found it oddly moving, but I cannot say that I was displeased. It had not occurred to me before that Americans, who had never treated me with any respect, had no respect for each other.

On the last night but one, there was a gala in the big ballroom and I sang. It had been a long time since I had sung before so many Americans. My audience had mainly been penniless French students, in the weird, Left Bank bistros I worked in those days. Still, I was a great hit with them and by this time I had become enough of a drawing card, in the Latin Quarter and in St. Germain des Prés, to have attracted a couple of critics, to have had my picture in *France-soir,* and to have acquired a legal work permit which allowed me to make a little more money. Just the same, no matter how industrious and brilliant some of the musicians had been, or how devoted my audience, they did not know, they could not know, what my songs came out of. They did not know what was funny about it. It was impossible to translate: It damn well better be funny, or Laughing to keep from crying, or What did *I* do to be so black and blue?

The moment I stepped out on the floor, they began to smile, something opened in them, they were ready to be pleased. I found in their faces, as they watched me, smiling, waiting, an artless relief, a profound reassurance. Nothing was more familiar to them than the sight of a dark boy, singing, and there were few things on earth more necessary. It was under cover of darkness, my own darkness, that I could sing for them of the joys, passions, and terrors they smuggled about with them like steadily depreciating contraband. Under cover of the midnight fiction that I was unlike them because I was black, they could stealthily gaze at those treasures which they had been mysteriously forbidden to possess and were never permitted to declare.

I sang *I'm Coming, Virginia,* and *Take This Hammer,* and *Precious Lord.* They wouldn't let me go and I came back and sang a couple of the oldest blues I knew. Then someone asked me to sing *Swanee River,* and I did, astonished that I could, astonished that this song, which I had put down long ago, should have the power to move me. Then, if only, perhaps, to make the record complete, I wanted to sing *Strange Fruit,* but, on this number, no one can surpass the great, tormented Billie Holiday. So I finished with *Great Getting-Up Morning* and I guess I can say that if I didn't stop the show I certainly ended it. I got a big hand and I drank at a few tables and I danced with a few girls.

After one more day and one more night, the boat landed in New York. I woke up, I was bright awake at once, and I thought, *We're here.* I turned on all the lights in my small cabin and I stared into the mirror as though I were committing my face to memory. I took a shower and I took a long time shaving and I dressed myself very carefully. I walked the long ship corridors to the dining room, looking at the luggage piled high before the elevators and beside the steps. The dining room was nearly half empty and full of a quick and joyous excitement which depressed me even more. People ate quickly, chattering to each other, anxious to get upstairs and go on deck. Was it my imagination or was it true that they seemed to avoid my eyes? A few people waved and smiled, but let me pass; perhaps it would have made them uncomfortable, this morning, to try to share their excitement with me; perhaps they did not want to know whether or not it was possible for me to share it. I walked to my table and sat down. I munched toast as dry as paper and drank a pot of coffee. Then I tipped my waiter, who bowed and smiled and called me "sir" and said that he hoped to see me on the boat again. "I hope so, too," I said.

And was it true, or was it my imagination, that a flash of wondering comprehension, a flicker of wry sympathy, then appeared in the waiter's eyes? I walked upstairs to the deck.

There was a breeze from the water but the sun was hot and made me remember how ugly New York summers could be. All of the deck chairs had been taken away and people milled about in the space where the deck chairs had been, moved from one side of the ship to the other, clambered up and down the steps, crowded the rails, and they were busy taking photographs— of the harbor, of each other, of the sea, of the gulls. I walked slowly along the deck, and an impulse stronger than myself drove me to the rail. There it was, the great, unfinished city, with all its towers blazing in the sun. It came toward us slowly and patiently, like some enormous, cunning, and murderous beast, ready to devour, impossible to escape. I watched it come closer and I listened to the people around me, to their excitement and their pleasure. There was no doubt that it was real. I watched their shining faces and wondered if I were mad. For a moment I longed, with all my heart, to be able to feel whatever they were feeling, if only to know what such a feeling was like. As the boat moved slowly into the harbor, they were being moved into safety. It was only I who was being floated into danger. I turned my head, looking for

Europe, but all that stretched behind me was the sky, thick with gulls. I moved away from the rail. A big, sandy-haired man held his daughter on his shoulders, showing her the Statue of Liberty. I would never know what this statue meant to others, she had always been an ugly joke for me. And the American flag was flying from the top of the ship, above my head. I had seen the French flag drive the French into the most unspeakable frenzies, I had seen the flag which was nominally mine used to dignify the vilest purposes: now I would never, as long as I lived, know what others saw when they saw a flag. "There's no place like home," said a voice close by, and I thought, *There damn sure isn't.* I decided to go back to my cabin and have a drink.

There was a cablegram from Harriet in my cabin. It said: Be good. Be quick. I'm waiting. I folded it carefully and put it in my breast pocket. Then I wondered if I would ever get back to her. How long would it take me to earn the money to get out of this land? Sweat broke out on my forehead and I poured myself some whisky from my nearly empty bottle. I paced the tiny cabin. It was silent. There was no one down in the cabins now.

I was not sober when I faced the uniforms in the first-class lounge. There were two of them; they were not unfriendly. They looked at my passport, they looked at me. "You've been away a long time," said one of them.

"Yes," I said, "it's been a while."

"What did you do over there all that time?"—with a grin meant to hide more than it revealed, which hideously revealed more than it could hide.

I said, "I'm a singer," and the room seemed to rock around me. I held on to what I hoped was a calm, open smile. I had not had to deal with these faces in so long that I had forgotten how to do it. I had once known how to pitch my voice precisely between curtness and servility, and known what razor's edge of a pickaninny's smile would turn away wrath. But I had forgotten all the tricks on which my life had once depended. Once I had been an expert at baffling these people, at setting their teeth on edge, and dancing just outside the trap laid for me. But I was not an expert now. These faces were no longer merely the faces of two white men, who were my enemies. They were the faces of two white people whom I did not understand, and I could no longer plan my moves in accordance with what I knew of their cowardice and their needs and their strategy. That moment on the bridge had undone me forever.

"That's right," said one of them, "that's what it says, right here on the passport. Never heard of you, though." They looked up at me. "Did you do a lot of singing over there?"

"Some."

"What kind—concerts?"

"No." I wondered what I looked like, sounded like. I could tell nothing from their eyes. "I worked a few night clubs."

"Night clubs, eh? I guess they liked you over there."

"Yes," I said, "they seemed to like me all right."

"Well"—and my passport was stamped and handed back to me—"let's hope they like you over here."

"Thanks." They laughed—was it at me, or was it my imagination? and I picked up the one bag I was carrying and threw my trench coat over one shoulder and walked out of the first-class lounge. I stood in the slow-moving, murmuring line which led to the gangplank. I looked straight ahead and watched heads, smiling faces, step up to the shadow of the gangplank awning and then swiftly descend out of sight. I put my passport back in my breast pocket—*Be quick. I'm waiting*—and I held my landing card in my hand. Then, suddenly, there I was, standing on the edge of the boat, staring down the long ramp to the ground. At the end of the plank, on the ground, stood a heavy man in a uniform. His cap was pushed back from his gray hair and his face was red and wet. He looked up at me. This was the face I remembered, the face of my nightmares; perhaps hatred had caused me to know this face better than I would ever know the face of any lover. "Come on, boy," he cried, "come on, come on!"

And I almost smiled. I was home. I touched my breast pocket. I thought of a song I sometimes sang. *When will I ever get to be a man?* I came down the gangplank, stumbling a little, and gave the man my landing card.

Much later in the day, a customs inspector checked my baggage and waved me away. I picked up my bags and started walking down the long stretch which led to the gate, to the city.

And I heard someone call my name.

I looked up and saw Louisa running toward me. I dropped my bags and grabbed her in my arms and tears came to my eyes and rolled down my face. I did not know whether the tears were for joy at seeing her, or from rage, or both.

"How are you? How are you? You look wonderful, but, oh, haven't you lost weight? It's wonderful to see you again."

I wiped my eyes. "It's wonderful to see you, too, I bet you thought I was never coming back."

Louisa laughed. "I wouldn't have blamed you if you hadn't. These people are just as corny as ever, I swear I don't believe there's any hope for them. How's your French? Lord, when I think that it was I who studied French and now I can't speak a word. And you never went near it and you probably speak it like a native."

I grinned. *"Pas mal. Je me défends pas mal."* We started down the wide steps into the street. "My God," I said. "New York." I was not aware of its towers now. We were in the shadow of the elevated highway but the thing which most struck me was neither light nor shade, but noise. It came from a million things at once, from trucks and tires and clutches and brakes and doors; from machines shuttling and stamping and rolling and cutting and pressing; from the building of tunnels, the checking of gas mains, the laying of wires, the digging of foundations; from the chattering of rivets, the scream of the pile driver, the clanging of great shovels; from the battering down and the raising up of walls; from millions of radios and television sets and juke-boxes. The human voices distinguished themselves from the roar only by their note of strain and hostility. Another fleshy man, uniformed and red-faced, hailed a cab for us and touched his cap politely but could only manage a peremptory growl: "Right this way, miss. Step up, sir." He slammed the cab door behind us. Louisa directed the driver to the New Yorker Hotel.

"Do they take us there?"

She looked at me. "They got laws in New York, honey, it'd be the easiest thing in the world to spend all your time in court. But over at the New Yorker, I believe they've already got the message." She took my arm. "You see? In spite of all this chopping and booming, this place hasn't really changed very much. You still can't hear yourself talk."

And I thought to myself, Maybe that's the point.

Early the next morning we checked out of the hotel and took the plane for Alabama.

I am just stepping out of the shower when I hear the bell ring. I dry myself hurriedly and put on a bathrobe. It is Vidal, of course, and very elegant he is, too, with his bushy gray hair quite lustrous, his swarthy, cynical, gypsylike face shaved and lotioned. Usually he looks just any old way. But tonight his brief bulk is contained in a dark-blue suit and he has an ironical pearl stickpin in his blue tie.

"Come in, make yourself a drink. I'll be with you in a second."

"I am, *hélas!,* on time. I trust you will forgive me for my thoughtlessness."

But I am already back in the bathroom. Vidal puts on a record: Mahalia Jackson, singing *I'm Going to Live the Life I Sing About in My Song.*

When I am dressed, I find him sitting in a chair before the open window. The daylight is gone, but it is not exactly dark. The trees are black now against the darkening sky. The lights in windows and the lights of motorcars are yellow and ringed. The street lights have not yet been turned on. It is as though, out of deference to the departed day, Paris waited a decent interval before assigning her role to a more theatrical but inferior performer.

Vidal is drinking a whisky and soda. I pour myself a drink. He watches me.

"Well. How are you, my friend? You are nearly gone. Are you happy to be leaving us?"

"No." I say this with more force than I had intended. Vidal raises his eyebrows, looking amused and distant. "I never really intended to go back there. I certainly never intended to raise my kid there—"

"*Mais, mon cher,*" Vidal says, calmly, "you are an intelligent man, you must have known that you would probably be returning one day." He pauses. "And, as for Pauli—did it never occur to you that he might wish one day to see the country in which his father and his father's fathers were born?"

"To do that, really, he'd have to go to Africa."

"America will always mean more to him than Africa, you know that."

"I don't know." I throw my drink down and pour myself another. "Why should he want to cross all that water just to be called a nigger? America never gave him anything."

"It gave him his father."

I look at him. "You mean, his father escaped."

Vidal throws back his head and laughs. If Vidal likes you, he is certain to laugh at you and his laughter can be very unnerving. But the look, the silence which follows this laughter can be very unnerving, too. And, now, in the silence, he asks me, "Do you really think that you have escaped anything? Come. I know you for a better man than that." He walks to the table which holds the liquor. "In that movie of ours which has made you so famous, and, as I now see, so troubled, what are you playing, after all? What is the tragedy of this half-breed troubadour if not, precisely, that he has taken all the possible roads to escape and that all these roads have failed him?" He pauses, with the bottle in one hand, and looks at me. "Do you remember the trouble I had to get a performance out of you? How you hated me, you sometimes looked as though you wanted to shoot me! And do you remember when the role of Chico began to come alive?" He pours his drink. "Think back, remember. I am a very great director, *mais pardon!* I could not have got such a performance out of anyone but you. And what were you thinking of, what was in your mind, what nightmare were you living with when you began, at last, to play the role—truthfully?" He walks back to his seat.

Chico, in the film, is the son of a Martinique woman and a French *colon* who hates both his mother and his father. He flees from the island to the capital, carrying his hatred with him. This hatred has now grown, naturally, to include all dark women and all white men, in a word, everyone. He descends into the underworld of Paris, where he dies. *Les fauves*—the wild beasts—refers to the life he has fled and to the life which engulfs him. When I agreed to do the role, I felt that I could probably achieve it by bearing in mind the North Africans I had watched in Paris for so long. But this did not please Vidal. The blowup came while we were rehearsing a fairly simple, straightforward scene. Chico goes into a sleazy Pigalle dance hall to beg the French owner for a particularly humiliating job. And this Frenchman reminds him of his father.

"You are playing this boy as though you thought of him as the noble savage," Vidal said, icily. *"Ça vient d'où*—all these ghastly mannerisms you are using all the time?"

Everyone fell silent, for Vidal rarely spoke this way. This silence told me that everyone, the actor with whom I was playing the scene and all the people in the "dance hall," shared Vidal's opinion of my performance and was relieved that he was going to do something about it. I was humiliated and too angry to speak; but perhaps I also felt, at the very bottom of my heart, a certain relief, an unwilling respect.

"You are doing it all wrong," he said, more gently. Then, "Come, let us have a drink together."

We walked into his office. He took a bottle and two glasses out of his desk. "Forgive me, but you put me in mind of some of those English *lady* actresses who love to play *putain* as long as it is always absolutely clear to the audience that they are really ladies. So perhaps they read a book, not usually, *hélas!*, *Fanny Hill,* and they have their chauffeurs drive them through Soho once or twice—and they come to the stage with a performance so absolutely loaded with detail, every bit of it meaningless, that there can be no doubt that they are acting. It is what the British call a triumph." He poured two cognacs. "That is what you are doing. Why? Who do you think this boy is, what do you think he is feeling, when he asks for this job?" He watched me carefully and I bitterly resented his look. "You come from America. The situation is not so pretty there for boys like you. I know you may not have been as poor as—as some—but is it really impossible for you to understand what a boy like Chico feels? Have you never, yourself, been in a similar position?"

I hated him for asking the question because I knew he knew the answer to it. "I would have had to be a very lucky black man not to have been in such a position."

"You would have had to be a very lucky *man.*"

"Oh, God," I said, "please don't give me any of this equality-in-anguish business."

"It is perfectly possible," he said, sharply, "that there is not another kind."

Then he was silent. He sat down behind his desk. He cut a cigar and lit it, puffing up clouds of smoke, as though to prevent us from seeing each other too clearly. "Consider this," he said. "I am a French director who has never seen your country. I have never done you any harm, except, perhaps, historically—I mean, because I am white—but I cannot be blamed for that—"

"But *I* can be," I said, "and I am! I've never understood why, if *I* have to pay for the history written in the color of my skin, *you* should get off scot-free!" But I was surprised at my vehemence, I had not known I was going to say these things, and by the fact that I was trembling and from the way he looked at me I knew that, from a professional point of view anyway, I was playing into his hands.

"What makes you think I *do?*" His face looked weary and stern. "I am a Frenchman. Look at France. You think that I—we—are not paying for our history?" He walked to the window, staring out at the rather grim little town in which the studio was located. "If it is revenge that you want, well, then, let me tell you, you will have it. You will probably have it, whether you want it or not, our stupidity will make it inevitable." He turned back into the room. "But I beg you not to confuse me with the happy people of your country, who scarcely know that there is such a thing as history and so, naturally, imagine that they can escape, as you put it, scot-free. That is what you are doing, that is what I was about to say. I was about to say that I am a French director and I have never been in your country and I have never done you any harm—but you are not talking to that man, in this room, now. You are not talking to Jean Luc Vidal, but to some other white man, whom you remember, who has nothing to do with me." He paused and went back to his desk. "Oh, most of the time you are not like this, I know. But it is there all the time, it must be, because when you are upset, this is what comes out. So you are not playing Chico truthfully, you are lying about him, and I will not let you do it. When you go back, now, and play this scene again, I want you to remember what has just happened in this room. You brought your past into this room. That is what Chico does when he walks into the dance hall. The Frenchman whom he begs for a job is not merely a Frenchman—he is the father who disowned and betrayed him and all the Frenchmen whom he hates." He smiled and poured me another cognac. "Ah! If it were not for *my* history, I would not have so much trouble to get the truth out of you." He looked into my face, half smiling. "And you, you are angry—are you not?—that I *ask* you for the truth. You think I have no right to ask." Then he said something which he knew would enrage me. "Who are you then, and what good has it done you to come to France, and how will you raise your son? Will you teach him never to tell the truth to anyone?" And he moved behind his desk and looked at me, as though from behind a barricade.

"You have no right to talk to me this way."

"Oh, yes, I do," he said. "I have a film to make and a reputation to maintain and I am going to get a performance out of you." He looked at his watch. "Let us go back to work."

I watch him now, sitting quietly in my living room, tough, cynical, crafty old Frenchman, and I wonder if he knows that the nightmare at the bottom of my mind, as I played the role of Chico, was all the possible fates of Paul. This is but another way of saying that I relived the disasters which had nearly undone me; but, because I was thinking of Paul, I discovered that I did not want my son ever to feel toward me as I had felt toward my own father. He had died when I was eleven, but I had watched the humiliations he had to bear, and I had pitied him. But was there not, in that pity, however painfully and unwillingly, also some contempt? For how could I *know* what he had borne? I knew only that I was his son. However he had loved me, whatever he had borne, I, his son, was despised. Even had he lived, he could have done nothing to prevent it, nothing to protect me. The best that he could hope to do was to prepare me for it; and even at that he had failed. How can one be prepared for the spittle in the face, all the tireless ingenuity which goes into the spite and fear of small, unutterably miserable people, whose greatest terror is the singular identity, whose joy, whose safety, is entirely dependent on the humiliation and anguish of others?

But for Paul, I swore it, such a day would never come. I would throw my life and my work between Paul and the nightmare of the world. I would make it impossible for the world to treat Paul as it had treated my father and me.

Mahalia's record ends. Vidal rises to turn it over. "Well?" He looks at me very affectionately. "Your nightmares, please!"

"Oh, I was thinking of that summer I spent in Alabama, when my mother died." I stop. "You know, but when we finally filmed that bar scene, I was thinking of New York. I was scared in Alabama, but I almost went crazy in New York. I was sure I'd never make it back here—back here to Harriet. And I knew if I didn't, it was going to be the end of me." Now Mahalia is singing *When the Saints Go Marching In.* "I got a job in the town as an elevator boy, in the town's big department store. It was a special favor, one of my father's white friends got it for me. For a long time, in the South, we all—depended—on the —*kindness*—of white friends." I take out a handkerchief and wipe my face. "But this man didn't like me. I guess I didn't seem grateful enough, wasn't enough like my father, what he thought my father was. And I couldn't get used to the town again, I'd been away too long, I hated it. It's a terrible town, anyway, the whole thing looks as though it's been built around a jailhouse. There's a room in the courthouse, a room where they beat you up. Maybe you're walking along the street one night, it's usually at night, but it happens in the daytime, too. And the police car comes up behind you and the cop says, 'Hey, boy. Come on over here.' So you go on over. He says, 'Boy, I believe you're drunk.' And, you see, if you say, 'No, no sir,' he'll beat you because you're calling him a liar. And if you say anything else, unless it's something to make him laugh, he'll take you in and beat you, just for fun. The trick is to think of some way for them to have their fun without beating you up."

The street lights of Paris click on and turn all the green leaves silver. "Or to go along with the ways *they* dream up. And they'll do anything, anything at all, to prove that you're no better than a dog and to make you feel like one. And they hated me because I'd been North and I'd been to Europe. People kept saying, I hope you didn't bring no foreign notions back here with you, boy. And I'd say, 'No sir,' or 'No ma'am,' but I never said it right. And there was a time, all of them remembered it, when I *had* said it right. But now they could tell that I despised them—I guess, no matter what, I wanted them to know that I despised them. But I didn't despise them any more than everyone else did, only the others never let it show. They knew how to keep the white folks happy, and it was easy—you just had to keep them feeling like they were God's favor to the universe. They'd walk around with great, big, foolish grins on their faces and the colored folks loved to see this, because they hated them so much. 'Just look at So-and-So,' somebody'd say. 'His white is *on* him today.' And when we didn't hate them, we pitied them. In America, that's usually what it means to have a white friend. You pity the poor bastard because he was born believing the world's a great place to be, and you know it's not, and you can see that he's going to have a terrible time getting used to this idea, if he *ever* gets used to it."

Then I think of Paul again, those eyes which still imagine that I can do anything, that skin, the color of honey and fire, his jet-black, curly hair. I look out at Paris again, and I listen to Mahalia. "Maybe it's better to have the terrible times first. I don't know. Maybe, then, you can have, *if* you live, a better life, a real life, because you had to fight so hard to get it away—you know?—from the mad dog who held it in his teeth. But then your life has all those tooth marks, too, all those tatters, and all that blood." I walk to the bottle and raise it. "One for the road?"

"Thank you," says Vidal.

I pour us a drink, and he watches me. I have never talked so much before, not about those things anyway. I know that Vidal has nightmares, because he knows so much about them, but he has never told me what his are. I think that he probably does not talk about his nightmares any more. I know that the war cost him his wife and his son, and that he was in prison in Germany. He very rarely refers to it. He has a married daughter who lives in England, and he rarely speaks of her. He is like a man who has learned to live on what is left of an enormous fortune.

We are silent for a moment.

"Please go on," he says, with a smile. "I am curious about the reality behind the reality of your performance."

"My sister, Louisa, never married," I say, abruptly, "because, once, years ago, she and the boy she was going with and two friends of theirs were out driving in a car and the police stopped them. The girl who was with them was very fair and the police pretended not to believe her when she said she was colored. They made her get out and stand in front of the headlights of the car and pull down her pants and raise her dress—they said that was the only way they could be sure. And you can imagine what they said, and what they did—and they were lucky, at that, that it didn't go any further. But none of the men could do anthing about it. Louisa couldn't face that boy again, and I guess he couldn't face her." Now it is really growing dark in the room and I cross to the light switch. "You know, I know what that boy felt, I've felt it. They want you to feel that you're not a man, maybe that's the only way they can feel like men, I don't know. I walked around New York with Harriet's cablegram in my pocket as though it were some atomic secret, in *code,* and they'd kill me if they ever found out what it meant. You know, there's something wrong with people like that. And thank God Harriet was here, she *proved* that the world was bigger than the world they wanted me to live in, I *had* to get back here, get to a place where people were too busy with their own lives, *their private lives,* to make fantasies about mine, to set up walls around mine." I look at him. The light in the room has made the night outside blue-black and golden and the great searchlight of the Eiffel Tower is turning in the sky. "That's what it's like in America, for me, anyway. I always feel that I don't exist there, except in someone else's—usually dirty—mind. I don't know if you know what that means, but I do, and I don't want to put Harriet through that and I don't want to raise Paul there."

"Well," he says at last, "you are not required to remain in America forever, are you? You will sing in that elegant club which apparently feels that it cannot, much longer, so much as open its doors without you, and you will probably accept the movie offer, you would be very foolish not to. You will make a lot of money. Then, one day, you will remember that airlines and steamship companies are still in business and that France still exists. *That* will certainly be cause for astonishment."

Vidal was a Gaullist before de Gaulle came to power. But he regrets the manner of de Gaulle's rise and he is worried about de Gaulle's regime. "It is not the fault of *mon général,*" he sometimes says, sadly. "Perhaps it is history's fault. I *suppose* it must be history which always arranges to bill a civilization at the very instant it is least prepared to pay."

Now he rises and walks out on the balcony, as though to reassure himself of the reality of Paris. Mahalia is singing *Didn't It Rain?* I walk out and stand beside him.

"You are a good boy—Chico," he says. I laugh. "You believe in love. You do not know all the things love cannot do, but"—he smiles—"love will teach you that."

We go, after dinner, to a Left Bank discothèque which can charge outrageous prices because Marlon Brando wandered in there one night. By accident, according to Vidal. "Do you know how many people in Paris are becoming rich—to say nothing of those, *hélas!,* who are going broke—on the off chance that Marlon Brando will lose his way again?"

He has not, presumably, lost his way tonight, but the discothèque is crowded with those strangely faceless people who are part of the night life of all great cities, and who always arrive, moments, hours, or decades late, on the spot made notorious by an event or a movement or a handful of personalities. So here are American boys, anything but beardless, scratching around for Hemingway; American girls titillating themselves with Frenchmen and existentialism, while waiting for the American boys to shave off their beards; French painters, busily pursuing the revolution which ended thirty years ago; and the young, bored, perverted, American *arrivistes* who are buying their way into the art world via flattery and liquor, and the production of canvases as arid as their greedy little faces. Here are boys, of all nations, one step above the pimp, who are occasionally walked across a stage or trotted before a camera. And the girls, their enemies, whose faces are sometimes seen in ads, one of whom will surely have a tantrum before the evening is out.

In a corner, as usual, surrounded, as usual, by smiling young men, sits the drunken blonde woman who was once the mistress of a famous, dead painter. She is a figure of some importance in the art world, and so rarely has to pay for either her drinks or her lovers. An older Frenchman, who was once a famous director, is playing *quatre cent vingt-et-un* with the woman behind the cash register. He nods pleasantly to Vidal and me as we enter, but makes no move to join us, and I respect him for this. Vidal and I are obviously cast tonight in the role vacated by Brando: our entrance justifies the prices and sends a kind of shiver through the room. It is marvelous to watch the face of the waiter as he approaches, all smiles and deference and grace, not so much honored by our presence as achieving his reality from it; excellence, he seems to be saying, gravitates naturally toward excellence. We order two whiskey and sodas. I know why Vidal sometimes comes here. He is lonely. I do not think that he expects ever to love one woman again, and so he distracts himself with many.

Since this is a discothèque, jazz is blaring from the walls and record sleeves are scattered about with a devastating carelessness. Two of them are mine and no doubt, presently, someone will play the recording of the songs I sang in the film.

"I thought," says Vidal, with a malicious little smile, "that your farewell to Paris would not be complete without a brief exposure to the perils of fame. Perhaps it will help prepare you for America, where, I am told, the populace is yet more carnivorous than it is here."

I can see that one of the vacant models is preparing herself to come to our table and ask for an autograph, hoping, since she is pretty—she has, that is, the usual female equipment, dramatized in the usual, modern way—to be invited for a drink. Should the maneuver succeed, one of her boy friends or girl friends will contrive to come by the table, asking for a light or a pencil or a lipstick, and it will be extremely difficult not to invite this person to join us, too. Before the evening ends, we will be surrounded. I don't, now, know what I expected of fame, but I suppose it never occurred to me that the light could be just as dangerous, just as killing, as the dark.

"Well, let's make it brief," I tell him. "Sometimes I wish that you weren't quite so fond of me."

He laughs. "There are some very interesting people here tonight. Look."

Across the room from us, and now staring at our table, are a group of American Negro students, who are probably visiting Paris for the first time. There are four of them, two boys and two girls, and I suppose that they must be in their late teens or early twenties. One of the boys, a gleaming, curly-haired, golden-brown type—the color of his mother's fried chicken—is carrying a guitar. When they realize we have noticed them, they smile and wave—wave as though I were one of their possessions, as, indeed, I am. Golden-brown is a mime. He raises his guitar, drops his shoulders, and his face falls into the lugubrious lines of Chico's face as he approaches death. He strums a little of the film's theme music, and I laugh and the table laughs. It is as though we were all back home and had met for a moment, on a Sunday morning, say, before a church or a poolroom or a barbershop.

And they have created a sensation in the discothèque, naturally, having managed, with no effort whatever, to outwit all the gleaming boys and girls. Their table, which had been of no interest only a moment before, has now become the focus of a rather pathetic attention; their smiles have made it possible for the others to smile, and to nod in our direction.

"Oh," says Vidal, "he does that far better than you ever did, perhaps I will make him a star."

"Feel free, *m'sieu, le bon Dieu,* I got mine." But I can see that his attention has really been caught by one of the girls, slim, tense, and dark, who seems, though it is hard to know how one senses such things, to be treated by the others with a special respect. And, in fact, the table now seems to be having a council of war, to be demanding her opinion or her cooperation. She listens, frowning, laughing; the quality, the force of her intelligence causes her face to keep changing all the time, as though a light played on it. And, presently, with a gesture she might once have used to scatter feed to chickens, she scoops up from the floor one of those dangling rag bags women love to carry. She holds it loosely by the drawstrings, so that it is banging somewhere around her ankle, and walks over to our table. She has an honest, forthright walk, entirely unlike the calculated, pelvic workout by means of which most women get about. She is small, but sturdily, economically, put together.

As she reaches our table, Vidal and I rise, and this throws her for a second. (It has been a long time since I have seen such an attractive girl.)

Also, everyone, of course, is watching us. It is really a quite curious moment. They have put on the record of Chico singing a sad, angry Martinique ballad; my own voice is coming at us from the walls as the girl looks from Vidal to me, and smiles.

"I guess you know," she says, "we weren't *about* to let you get out of here without bugging you just a little bit. We've only been in Paris just a couple of days and we thought for sure that we wouldn't have a chance of running into you anywhere, because it's in all the papers that you're coming home."

"Yes," I say, "yes. I'm leaving the day after tomorrow."

"Oh!" She grins. "Then we really *are* lucky." I find that I have almost forgotten the urchin-like grin of a colored girl. "I guess, before I keep babbling on, I'd better introduce myself. My name is Ada Holmes."

We shake hands. "This is Monsieur Vidal, the director of the film."

"I'm very honored to meet you, sir."

"Will you join us for a moment? Won't you sit down?" And Vidal pulls a chair out for her.

But she frowns contritely. "I really ought to get back to my friends." She looks at me. "I really just came over to say, for myself and all the kids, that we've got your records and we've seen your movie, and it means so much to us"—and she laughs, breathlessly, nervously, it is somehow more moving than tears—"more than I can say. Much more. And we wanted to know if you and your friend"—she looks at Vidal—"your *director,* Monsieur Vidal, would allow us to buy you a drink? We'd be very honored if you would."

'It is we who are honored," says Vidal, promptly, "*and* grateful. We were getting terribly bored with one another, thank God you came along."

The three of us laugh, and we cross the room.

The three at the table rise, and Ada makes the introductions. The other girl, taller and paler than Ada, is named Ruth. One of the boys is named Talley—"short for Talliafero"—and Golden-brown's name is Pete. "Man," he tells me, "I dig you the most. You tore me up, baby, tore me *up.*"

"You tore up a lot of people," Talley says, cryptically, and he and Ruth laugh. Vidal does not know, but I do, that Talley is probably referring to white people.

They are from New Orleans and Tallahassee and North Carolina; are college students, and met on the boat. They have been in Europe all summer, in Italy and Spain, but are only just getting to Paris.

"We meant to come sooner," says Ada, "but we could never make up our minds to leave a place. I thought we'd never pry Ruth loose from Venice."

"I resigned myself," says Pete, "and just sat in the Piazza San Marco, drinking gin fizz and being photographed with the pigeons, while Ruth had herself driven *all* up and down the Grand Canal." He looks at Ruth. "Finally, thank heaven, it rained."

"She was working off her hostilities," says Ada, with a grin. "We thought we might as well let her do it in Venice, the opportunities in North Carolina are really terribly limited."

"There are some very upset people walking around down there," Ruth says, "and a couple of tours around the Grand Canal might do them a world of good."

Pete laughs. "Can't you just see Ruth escorting them to the edge of the water?"

"I haven't lifted my hand in anger yet," Ruth says, "but, oh, Lord," and she laughs, clenching and unclenching her fists.

"You haven't been back for a long time, have you?" Talley asks me.

"Eight years. I haven't really lived there for twelve years."

Pete whistles. "I fear you are in for some surprises, my friend. There have been some changes made." Then, "Are you afraid?"

"A little."

"We all are," says Ada, "that's why I was so glad to get away for a little while."

"Then you haven't been back since Black Monday," Talley says. He laughs.

"That's how it's gone down in Confederate history." He turns to Vidal. "What do people think about it here?"

Vidal smiles, delighted. "It seems extraordinarily infantile behavior, even for Americans, from whom, I must say, I have never expected very much in the way of maturity." Everyone at the table laughs. Vidal goes on. "But I cannot really talk about it, I do not understand it. I have never really understood Americans; I am an old man now, and I suppose I never will. There is something very nice about them, something very winning, but they seem so ignorant—so ignorant of life. Perhaps it is strange, but the only people from your country with whom I have ever made contact are black people—like my good friend, my discovery, here," and he slaps me on the shoulder. "Perhaps it is because we, in Europe, whatever else we do not know, or have forgotten, know about suffering. We have suffered here. You have suffered, too. But most Americans do not yet know what anguish is. It is too bad, because the life of the West is in their hands." He turns to Ada. "I cannot help saying that I think it is a scandal—and we may all pay very dearly for it—that a civilized nation should elect to represent it a man who is so simple that he thinks the world is simple." And silence falls at the table and the four young faces stare at him.

"Well," says Pete, at last, turning to me, "you won't be bored, man, when you get back there."

"It's much too nice a night," I say, "to stay cooped up in this place, where all I can hear is my own records." We laugh. "Why don't we get out of here and find a sidewalk café?" I tap Pete's guitar. "Maybe we can find out if you've got any talent."

"Oh, talent I've got," says Pete, "but character, man, I'm lacking."

So, after some confusion about the bill, for which Vidal has already made himself responsible, we walk out into the Paris night. It is very strange to feel that, very soon now, these boulevards will not exist for me. People will be walking up and down, as they are tonight, and lovers will be murmuring in the black shadows of the plane trees, and there will be these same still figures on the benches or in the parks—but they will not exist for me, I will not be here. For a long while Paris will no longer exist for me, except in my mind; and only in the minds of some people will I exist any longer for Paris. After departure, only invisible things are left, perhaps the life of the world is held together by invisible chains of memory and loss and love. So many things, so many people, depart! And we can only repossess them in our minds. Perhaps this is what the old folks meant, what my mother and my father meant, when they counseled us to keep the faith.

We have taken a table at the Deux Magots and Pete strums on his guitar and begins to play this song:

> *Preach the word, preach the word, preach the word!*
> *If I never, never see you any more.*
> *Preach the word, preach the word.*
> *And I'll meet you on Canaan's shore.*

He has a strong, clear, boyish voice, like a young preacher's, and he is smiling as he sings his song. Ada and I look at each other and grin, and Vidal is smiling. The waiter looks a little worried, for we are already beginning to attract a crowd, but it is a summer night, the gendarmes on the corner do not seem to mind, and there will be time, anyway, to stop us.

Pete was not there, none of us were, the first time this song was needed; and no one now alive can imagine what that time was like. But the song has come down the bloodstained ages. I suppose this to mean that the song is still needed, still has its work to do.

The others are all, visibly, very proud of Pete; and we all join him, and people stop to listen:

> *Testify! Testify!*
> *If I never, never see you any more!*
> *Testify! Testify!*
> *I'll meet you on Cannan's shore!*

In the crowd that has gathered to listen to us, I see a face I know, the face of a North African prize fighter, who is no longer in the ring. I used to know him well in the old days, but have not seen him for a long time. He looks quite well, his face is shining, he is quite decently dressed. And something about the way he holds himself, not quite looking at our table, tells me that he has seen me, but does not want to risk a rebuff. So I call him. "Boona!"

And he turns, smiling, and comes loping over to our table, his hands in his pockets. Pete is still singing and Ada and Vidal have taken off on a conversation of their own. Ruth and Talley look curiously, expectantly, at Boona. Now that I have called him over, I feel somewhat uneasy. I realize that I do not know what he is doing now, or how he will get along with any of these people, and I can see in his eyes that he is delighted to be in the presence of two young girls. There are virtually no North African women in Paris, and not even the dirty, rat-faced girls who live, apparently, in cafés are willing to go with an Arab. So Boona is always looking for a girl, and because he is so deprived and because he is not Western, his techniques can be very unsettling. I know he is relieved that the girls are not French and not white. He looks briefly at Vidal and Ada. Vidal, also, though for different reasons, is always looking for a girl.

But Boona has always been very nice to me. Perhaps I am sorry that I called him over, but I did not want to snub him.

He clasps one hand to the side of my head, as is his habit. *"Comment vas-tu, mon frère?* I have not see you, oh, for long time." And he asks me, as in the old days, "You all right? Nobody bother you?" And he laughs. "Ah! *Tu as fait le chemin, toi!* Now you are *vedette*, big star—wonderful!" He looks around the table, made a little uncomfortable by the silence that has fallen, now that Pete has stopped singing. "I have seen you in the movies—you know?—and I tell everybody, I know *him!*" He points to me, and laughs, and Ruth and Talley laugh with him. "That's right, man, you make me real proud, you make me cry!"

"Boona, I want you to meet some friends of mine." And I go round the table: "Ruth, Talley, Ada, Pete"—and he bows and shakes hands, his dark eyes gleaming with pleasure—"*et Monsieur Vidal, le metteur en scène du film qui t'a arraché des larmes.*"

"*Enchanté.*" But his attitude toward Vidal is colder, more distrustful. "Of course I have heard of Monsieur Vidal. He is the director of many films, many of them made me cry." This last statement is utterly, even insolently, insincere.

But Vidal, I think, is relieved that I will now be forced to speak to Boona and will leave him alone with Ada.

"Sit down," I say, "have a drink with us, let me have your news. What's been happening with you, what are you doing with yourself these days?"

"Ah," he sits down, "nothing very brilliant, my brother." He looks at me quickly, with a little smile. "You know, we have been having hard times here."

"Where are you from?" Ada asks him.

His brilliant eyes take her in entirely, but she does not flinch. "I am from Tunis." He says it proudly, with a little smile.

"From Tunis. I have never been to Africa, I would love to go one day."

He laughs. "Africa is a big place. Very big. There are many countries in Africa, many"—he looks briefly at Vidal—"different kinds of people, many colonies."

"But Tunis," she continues, in her innocence, "is free? Freedom is happening all over Africa. That's why I would like to go there."

"I have not been back for a long time," says Boona, "but all the news I get from Tunis, from my people, is not good."

"Wouldn't you like to go back?" Ruth asks.

Again he looks at Vidal. "That is not so easy."

Vidal smiles. "You know what I would like to do? There's a wonderful Spanish place not far from here, where we can listen to live music and dance a little." He turns to Ada. "Would you like that?"

He is leaving it up to me to get rid of Boona, and it is, of course, precisely for this reason that I cannot do it. Besides, it is no longer so simple.

"Oh, I'd love that," says Ada, and she turns to Boona. "Won't you come, too?"

"Thank you, mam'selle," he says, softly, and his tongue flicks briefly over his lower lip, and he smiles. He is very moved, people are not often nice to him.

In the Spanish place there are indeed a couple of Spanish guitars, drums, castanets, and a piano, but the uses to which these are being put carry one back, as Pete puts it, to the levee. "These are the wailingest Spanish cats I ever heard," says Ruth. "They didn't learn how to do this in Spain, no, they didn't, they been rambling. You ever hear anything like this going on in Spain?" Talley takes her out on the dance floor, which is already crowded. A very handsome Frenchwoman is dancing with an enormous, handsome black man, who seems to be her lover, who seems to have taught her how to dance. Apparently, they are known to the musicians, who egg them on with small cries of "*Olé!*" It is a very good-natured crowd, mostly foreigners, Spaniards, Swedes, Greeks. Boona takes Ada out on the dance floor while Vidal is answering some questions put to him by Pete on the entertainment situation in France. Vidal looks a little put out, and I am amused.

We are there for perhaps an hour, dancing, talking, and I am, at last, a little drunk. In spite of Boona, who is a very good and tireless dancer, Vidal continues his pursuit of Ada, and I begin to wonder if he will make it and I begin to wonder if I want him to.

I am still puzzling out my reaction when Pete, who has disappeared, comes in through the front door, catches my eye, and signals to me. I leave the table and follow him into the streets.

He looks very upset. "I don't want to bug you, man," he says, "but I fear your boy has goofed."

I know he is not joking. I think he is probably angry at Vidal because of Ada, and I wonder what I can do about it and why he should be telling me.

I stare at him, gravely, and he says, "It looks like he stole some money."

"Stole *money*? Who, Vidal?"

And then, of course, I get it, in the split second before he says, impatiently, "No, are you kidding? Your friend, the Tunisian."

I do not know what to say or what to do, and so I temporize with questions. All the time I am wondering if this can be true and what I can do about it if it is. The trouble is, I know that Boona steals, he would probably not be alive if he didn't, but I cannot say so to these children, who probably still imagine that everyone who steals is a thief. But he has never, to my knowledge, stolen from a friend. It seems unlike him. I have always thought of him as being better than that, and smarter than that. And so I cannot believe it, but neither can I doubt it. I do not know anything about Boona's life, these days. This causes me to realize that I do not really know much about Boona.

"Who did he steal it from?"

"From Ada. Out of her bag."

"How much?"

"Ten dollars. It's not an awful lot of money, but"—he grimaces—"none of us *have* an awful lot of money."

"I know." The dark side street on which we stand is nearly empty. The only sound on the street is the muffled music of the Spanish club.

"How do you know it was Boona?"

He anticipates my own unspoken rejoinder. "Who else could it be? Besides—somebody *saw* him do it."

"Somebody saw him?"

"Yes."

I do not ask him who this person is, for fear that he will say it is Vidal.

"Well," I say, "I'll try to get it back." I think that I will take Boona aside and then replace the money myself. "Was it in dollars or in francs?"

"In francs."

I have no dollars and this makes it easier. I do not know how I can possibly face Boona and accuse him of stealing money from my friends. I would rather give him the benefit of even the faintest doubt. But, "Who saw him?" I ask.

"Talley. But we didn't want to make a thing about it—"

"Does Ada know it's gone?"

"Yes." He looks at me helplessly. "I know this makes you feel pretty bad, but we thought we'd better tell you, rather than"—lamely—"anybody else."

Now, Ada comes out of the club, carrying her ridiculous handbag, and with her face all knotted and sad. "Oh," she says, "I hate to cause all this trouble, it's not worth it, not for ten lousy dollars." I am astonished to see that she has been weeping, and tears come to her eyes now.

I put my arm around her shoulder. "Come on, now. You're not causing anybody any trouble and, anyway, it's nothing to cry about."

"It isn't your fault, Ada," Pete says, miserably.

"Oh, I ought to get a sensible handbag," she says, "like you're always telling me to do," and she laughs a little, then looks at me. "Please don't try to do anything about it. Let's just forget it."

"What's happening inside?" I ask her.

"Nothing. They're just talking. I think Mr. Vidal is dancing with Ruth. He's a great dancer, that little Frenchman."

"He's a great talker, too," Pete says.

"Oh, he doesn't mean anything," says Ada, "he's just having fun. He probably doesn't get a chance to talk to many American girls."

"He certainly made up for lost time tonight."

"Look," I say, "if Talley and Boona are alone, maybe you better go back in. We'll be in in a minute. Let's try to keep this as quiet as we can."

"Yeah," he says, "okay. We're going soon anyway, okay?"

"Yes," she tells him, "right away."

But as he turns away, Boona and Talley step out into the street, and it is clear that Talley feels that he has Boona under arrest. I almost laugh, the whole thing is beginning to resemble one of those mad French farces with people flying in and out of doors; but Boona comes straight to me.

"They say I stole money, my friend. You know me, you are the only one here who knows me, you know I would not do such a thing."

I look at him and I do not know what to say. Ada looks at him with her eyes full of tears and looks away. I take Boona's arm.

"We'll be back in a minute," I say. We walk a few paces up the dark, silent street.

"'She say I take her money," he says. He, too, looks as though he is about to weep—but I do not know for which reason. "You know me, you know me almost twelve years, you think I do such a thing?"

Talley saw you, I want to say, but I cannot say it. Perhaps Talley only thought he saw him. Perhaps it is easy to see a boy who looks like Boona with his hand in an American girl's purse.

"If you not believe me," he says, "search me. Search me!" And he opens his arms wide, theatrically, and now there are tears standing in his eyes.

I do not know what his tears mean, but I certainly cannot search him. I want to say, I know you steal, I know you have to steal. Perhaps you took the money out of this girl's purse in order to eat tomorrow, in order not to be thrown into the streets tonight, in order to stay out of jail. This girl means nothing to you, after all, she is only an American, an American like me. Perhaps, I suddenly think, no girl means anything to you, or ever will again, they have beaten you too hard and kept you in the gutter too long. And I also think, If you would steal from her, then of course you would lie to me, neither of us means anything to you; perhaps, in your eyes, we are simply luckier gangsters in a world which is run by gangsters. But I cannot say any of these things to Boona. I cannot say, Tell me the truth, nobody cares about the money any more.

So I say, "Of course I will not search you." And I realize that he knew that I would not.

"I think it is that Frenchman who says I am a thief. They think we all are thieves." His eyes are bright and bitter. He looks over my shoulder. "They have all come out of the club now."

I look around and they are all there, in a little dark knot on the sidewalk.

"Don't worry," I say. "It doesn't matter."

"You believe me? My brother?" And his eyes look into mine with a terrible intensity.

"Yes," I force myself to say, "yes, of course, I believe you. Someone made a mistake, that's all."

"You know, the way American girls run around, they have their sack open all the time, she could lose the money anywhere. Why she blame me? Because I come from Africa?" Tears are glittering on his face. "Here she come now."

And Ada comes up the street with her straight, determined walk. She walks straight to Boona and takes his hand. "I am sorry," she says, "for everything that happened. Please believe me. It isn't worth all this fuss. I'm sure you're a very nice person, and"—she falters—"I must have lost the money, I'm sure I lost it." She looks at him. "It isn't worth hurting your feelings, and I'm terribly sorry about it."

"I no take your money," he says. "Really, truly, I no take it. Ask him"—pointing to me, grabbing me by the arm, shaking me—"he know me for years, he will tell you that I never, never steal!"

"I'm sure," she says. "I'm sure."

I take Boona by the arm again. "Let's forget it. Let's forget it all. We're all going home now, and one of these days we'll have a drink again and we'll forget all about it, all right?"

"Yes," says Ada, "let us forget it." And she holds out her hand.

Boona takes it, wonderingly. His eyes take her in again. "You are a very nice girl. Really. A very nice girl."

"I'm sure you're a nice person, too." She pauses. "Goodnight."

"Goodnight," he says, after a long silence.

Then he kisses me on both cheeks. *"Au revoir, mon frère."*

"Au revoir, Boona."

After a moment we turn and walk away, leaving him standing there.

"Did he take it?" asks Vidal.

"I tell you, I *saw* him," says Talley.

"Well," I say, "it doesn't matter now." I look back and see Boona's stocky figure disappearing down the street.

"No," says Ada, "it doesn't matter." She looks up. "It's almost morning."

"I would gladly," says Vidal, stammering, "gladly—"

But she is herself again. "I wouldn't think of it. We had a wonderful time tonight, a wonderful time, and I wouldn't think of it." She turns to me with that urchin-like grin. "It was wonderful meeting you. I hope you won't have too much trouble getting used to the States again."

"Oh, I don't think I will," I say. And then, "I hope you won't."

"No," she says, "I don't think anything they can do will surprise me any more."

"Which way are we all going?" asks Vidal. "I hope someone will share my taxi with me."

But he lives in the sixteenth arrondissement, which is not in anyone's direction. We walk him to the line of cabs standing under the clock at Odéon.

And we look each other in the face, in the growing morning light. His face looks weary and lined and lonely. He puts both hands on my shoulders and then puts one hand on the nape of my neck. "Do not forget me, Chico," he says. "You must come back and see us, one of these days. Many of us depend on you for many things."

"I'll be back," I say. "I'll never forget you."

He raises his eyebrows and smiles. *"Alors, adieu."*

"Adieu, Vidal."

"I was happy to meet all of you," he says. He looks at Ada. "Perhaps we will meet again before you leave."

"Perhaps," she says. "Goodby, Monsieur Vidal."

"Goodby."

Vidal's cab drives away. "I also leave you now," I say. "I must go home and wake up my son and prepare for our journey."

I leave them standing on the corner, under the clock, which points to six. They look very strange and lost and determined, the four of them. Just before my cab turns off the boulevard, I wave to them and they wave back.

Mme. Dumont is in the hall, mopping the floor.

"Did all my family get home?" I ask. I feel very cheerful, I do not know why.

"Yes," she says, "they are all here. Paul is still sleeping."

"May I go in and get him?"

She looks at me in surprise. "Of course."

So I walk into her apartment and walk into the room where Paul lies sleeping. I stand over his bed for a long time.

Perhaps my thoughts traveled—travel through to him. He opens his eyes and smiles up at me. He puts a fist to his eyes and raises his arms. *"Bonjour, Papa."*

I lift him up. *"Bonjour.* How do you feel today?"

"Oh, I don't know yet," he says.

I laugh. I put him on my shoulder and walk out into the hall. Mme. Dumont looks up at him with her radiant, aging face.

"Ah," she says, "you are going on a journey! How does it feel?"

"He doesn't know yet," I tell her. I walk to the elevator door and open it, dropping Paul down to the crook of my arm.

She laughs again. "He will know later. What a journey! *Jusqu'au nouveau monde!"*

I open the cage and we step inside. "Yes," I say, "all the way to the new world." I press the button and the cage, holding my son and me, goes up.

"Two Soldiers"

Problems *(1) Carry out the rereading and analysis of humor recommended in the third paragraph on page 17. A good story will not be ruined by rereading or by a reasonable amount of analysis. The reader's skill in noticing various qualities of writing will increase in the only way such skill can increase.*

(2) "Two Soldiers" contains relatively little "action" in its first part. "Action" picks up when the younger brother leaves home. Is the first part necessary, then? If it were omitted or reduced, what difference would such a change make? To answer this question, it is necessary to ask what is achieved in the first part of the story and whether this is necessary for effects achieved later.

Question *Can you find in this story an example of (a) humor arising from situation alone? (b) humor arising from character? (c) humor arising from the language used?*

"Tell Me How Long the Train's Been Gone"

Problems *(1) Consider the frequency of such phrases as our father, our mother. What are the meanings and effects of this repetition? We suggest that such phrases in this story carry strong feelings close to the center of what Baldwin is trying to communicate: perhaps a feeling about family and about family attitudes that would need to exist in a world that could gain this author's affection and respect.*

(2) A quick sampling of diction (words, vocabulary) in "Tell Me How Long the Train's Been Gone" was made as part of the comment about that story. The inquiry as to contrasts in diction between that story and "Two Soldiers" can be extended to take in the entirety of each story. Present your findings in a paper of your own. Your data will be the diction in the two stories. Your conclusions will be your own, based on the data.

(3) In commenting on "Tell Me How Long" we indicated that an author may organize a story by summarizing certain events and by presenting other events in a dramatic or second-by-second way, for added emphasis. Do an analysis of "Tell Me How Long" in such a way as to show which events received major emphasis and which received a lesser emphasis. What can you learn from this project about the way in which Baldwin constructed his story? Report your findings in a paper.

"A Sick Call"

Questions *Like much good literature, "A Sick Call" presses questions upon the reader which throw him back upon his attitudes and his knowledge of himself. Among such questions are these:*

(1) Is it possible to respect a person whose beliefs on an important matter are wholly different from mine?

(2) What capacity do I possess for being objective about people whose actions or opinions differ from mine?

(3) Do I tend to judge people by the labels they wear

("priest," "young husband"), or by their single acts, or by their total behavior as I know it?

(4) Does the end justify the means? If so, under what conditions? If not, why not?

(5) Do I prefer an ethically complex or ethically simple view of life?

(6) Do I sometimes insist upon the ethically simple view with little reason?

"File and Forget"	**Question**	*Note the reference, in a letter from one Clint Jordon, to "old Willa Cather" and her decision of some kind concerning the use of her middle name. Mr. Jordon reports the middle name as Seibert. Is he correct?*

"The Lift That Went Down into Hell"   **Problems**

(1) Write a brief report in which you attempt to define, through fresh examples: (a) traditional symbolism; (b) traditional symbolism modified in a special way by the author, as Lagerkvist makes his own special characterization of the Devil in "The Lift That Went Down into Hell."

(2) The environment of Hell in "Lift" provides an ironic meaning for many descriptive details that would otherwise be commonplace realism. Find a dozen details in that story which take on an edge of ironic meaning simply because of the environment, and show what these meanings are.

Stories in the first group   **Problems**

(1) If you will recall now the five stories in this section, you will see that in each instance you—as reader—came to know and understand things which the characters themselves did not know or understand. The ironic knowledge was the source not only of pleasure but also of specific meanings carried by the story. Such meanings are not "read into" the story, but are there by intention, for the skilled reader to discover. Read one story not discussed in this introductory Section. Make notes on the first signs of the author's attitude you find, and notes on the things you are led to know or understand which characters in the story do not know or understand. Read another story, making notes of the same kind. Then write a report in which you explain (a) the means by which the author's attitudes are revealed and (b) the nature and extent of the dramatic irony in each story. Add a comment as to which story, in your opinion, makes the most forceful use of dramatic irony.

(2) Curiosity is somewhat like a Chinese box. Each question gives way to a new question. Recall how, in the Faulkner story, "Two Soldiers," the brothers hear first about Pearl Harbor, then become worried (the older brother) and puzzled (the younger), after which the older brother leaves, and then the younger acts. At each stage, the reader is curious about a new event related causally to earlier events and earlier knowledge. Gradually he is led into the heart of the story by a series of questions which the story places in his mind. Such questions are called "narrative questions." Compare the functions of curiosity and "caring" in two other stories you have read so far.

(3) Write a brief report on the speech (language) and thought of the younger brother in "Two Soldiers," whose use of language is the most fundamental source of concrete reality

in that story. In your report, try to show how it is that the younger brother is able, with seeming naturalness, to mention so very many details of his environment and his experiences. This project will reveal more about the uses of first-person narrative than any amount of theory will. If you want to write, this project will help you see some "how-to-do-it" possibilities.

(4) Choose a story not discussed in this introductory section. Then write a brief report on it as a symbol of meanings which lie outside the story. That is, what bearings does the story have on phases of human experience you know about or can think of? On human problems and issues and values?

"The Blue Hotel"   **Questions**   (1) There is a surprise in the ending of this story. What is it? What is its significance? What does this knowledge do to your view of the stranger who is supposed to have "started" all the trouble, and to your view of his fate? Has the author established a probability that the stranger would meet much the same fate anyway?

(2) The hotelkeeper, the father, acts according to more than one abstract or ideal code of conduct. What are these codes? Do human beings, to your knowledge, adopt codes of behavior and follow them as mechanically as the hotelkeeper does? What is the author's probable intention in portraying the hotelkeeper as a keeper of codes? As a man who changes from one code to another?

(3) Does this story seem to convey any generally applicable "truth" about human affairs, or does it seem confined to questions of what will happen next and to the humorous antics of the stranger?

(4) Do you know what the social status of gamblers was in the early West? Is there any clue in the story itself?

"Heart of Darkness"   **Questions**   (1) What can you learn from "Heart of Darkness" about the world of commerce and colonialism as it existed at the time represented in the story? In answering this question, try to report as many cause-and-effect relations as you feel are represented In the story.

(2) Write as complete a report as you can on the functions of Marlow in "Heart of Darkness"—that is, the uses to which the author puts this character as a carrier of meaning and a technical convenience.

(3) What can you infer about Conrad's view of the black men and women that Marlow observes in Africa? Support your generalizations with illustrative examples from the text.

"Hodel"   **Glossary**   This glossary for "Hodel" was assembled, with permission, from a longer glossary prepared for stories of Sholom Aleichem in The Old Country. Some of the spellings in these stories are given phonetically as they occurred in popular usage; correct transliterated spellings are shown in parentheses. Bracketed information is taken from other portions of the longer glossary.

datcha: Summer cottage in the country.

Hashono Rabo   (Hoshana Rabbah): The seventh day of Succoth (Feast of Booths).

knishes: Potato or kasha [groats] dumpling, fried or baked.

Medresh (Midrash): *A body of exegetical literature, devotional and ethical in character, which attempts to illuminate the literal text of the Bible with its inner meanings. The* Midrash *is constantly cited by pious and learned Jews in Scriptural and Talmudic disputation.*

Reb: *Mister.*

shlimazl: *An incompetent person, one who has perpetual bad luck. Everything happens to him.*

shofar: *Ram's horn blown in the synagogue at services on* Rosh Hashanah *[the Jewish New Year, celebrated in September] and* Yom Kippur *[Day of Atonement, the most important Jewish religious holiday, which takes place eight days after Rosh Hashanah].*

succah: *A booth made of fresh green branches in which pious Jews celebrate the Feast of Tabernacles. This is done symbolically to recall the forty days' wandering—"that your generations may know that I made the children of Israel to dwell in booths, when I brought them out of the land of Egypt."*

Succos (Succoth): *The Feast of Tabernacles, survival of the ancient festival on which male Jews were required to go on a pilgrimage to the Temple in Jerusalem. Lasts nine days and begins on the 15th day of the seventh lunar month of Tishri (September-October).*

"The Boarding House"

Comment *We note that the most definitive edition of* Dubliners *(1967) avoids certain conventional uses of periods and quotes. This version, preferred by the editors, in various ways restores Joyce's original text.*

Questions *(1) Can you detect in this story any sign of the author's attitudes toward the mother, the daughter, the father, or Mr Doran? How are these attitudes conveyed if they are here? What is the difficulty in being sure that these attitudes are those of the author?*

(2) Compare "The Boarding House" with "In Another Country" and with "Everything That Rises Must Converge" in respect to the objectivity of the method or technique. Compare all three in respect to the ease or difficulty of discovering the author's probable attitudes toward characters and events.

"A Country Doctor"

Questions *(1) To achieve perspective on this story, which is heavily symbolic, work out some preliminary answers to the following question: What would you say are the typical problems of a doctor's life? Think of physical necessities, problems of time, problems of "duty," possible attitudes and expectations of patients and their families. Think also of specifically professional problems, such as those of diagnosis. Think also of possible ways in which any person might like to spend his time, apart from the demands of a profession. Then reread the story with the ideas in mind which you have worked out. Can you discover that the doctor in the story faces any typical problems?*

(2) What degree of success does the doctor in the story experience? What personal and professional frustrations seem to be most troublesome? What is the nature of the patient's illness? of his wound?

(3) What symbols can you find in this story which seem to be Christian in origin? How are they used?

(4) Can you discover any likelihood that doctor and patient are in any way to be equated—to be regarded, in other words, as having either similar problems or a similar fate?

(5) The doctor leads a busy mental life, with thoughts ranging from the practical "conscious" level to thoughts, feelings, and wants which may be half-realized or even below the threshold of conscious awareness. What conflicts within the doctor are suggested by this material in the story? Particularly, what are the wants and the fears? Is all this dreamlike material a fair symbol of man's mental life?

(6) What of the environment in which the doctor lives and works? Include in your thought about this the physical environment, the patient and family, the other live creatures, and especially the weather. Is this environment friendly, unfriendly, or just neutrally accidental?

(7) Is the doctor a fair symbol of man's life and work in the world we know?

(8) Is there, possibly, a humorous element in the author's attitude? What effect does it have?

"Flowering Judas"

Questions (1) Reread the first three paragraphs of this story closely, and notice that detail is reported as follows:
  (a) in the dramatic present: "Braggioni sits heaped upon the edge of a straight-backed chair . . ."
  (b) in summary narrative: "No matter how late she is, he will be sitting there . . ." and "Laura, who haunts the markets listening to the ballad singers, and stops every day . . ."
After identifying these two ways of reporting events, and after noting the frequent shifting from the one to the other, fix also in your mind the fact that the author makes a constant use of the progressive tense: "Braggioni sits, Laura says, Laura wishes to lie down, Laura haunts the marketplace and stops every day," etc. With these technical features in mind, read into the story again. What effects do you suppose are achieved by the steady use of the present progressive tense and the shifting from dramatic present to summary narrative and back again?

(2) In the last paragraph of "Flowering Judas" the tense changes suddenly and sharply from present progressive, which has been used throughout the story, to past: "Without a word, without fear she rose and reached for Eugenio's hand . . ." What effects are achieved by this sudden use of the past tense after the reader's long immersion in the present tense? (The best way to answer this question is to read up to and through this transition yourself.)

(3) Make a short list of all the ways in which Laura can feel that something or someone has betrayed her or proved undependable. Make another short list of all the ways in which Laura may feel that she herself has betrayed something or someone. Does this combination of hurt and guilt in Laura justify, in your opinion, the condition of near-paralysis in which she finds herself?

(4) Is Laura's condition of being partly hurt and partly guilty a just symbol of any kind of individual or group life in our time? Would you say that Laura is mainly a symbol of "fear of life, wish for death," or of "the barrenness of causes"?

(5) Is it possible, in your opinion, for a human being to be so

preoccupied with either fear or guilt or a cause that he is unaware of his surroundings or of danger?

(6) Laura is more aware of some kinds of "danger" than of others. What are these "dangers" and what do they show you about Laura?

(7) In what ways are the major sources of security in our times mirrored in "Flowering Judas"? Is the Judas tree a symbol of multiple or single betrayal?

(8) What are the attitudes of Braggioni to the "causes" he serves?

"Delta Autumn" Questions (1) You may be aided in reading this story if you are informed that Uncle Ike McCaslin and Roth Edmonds and the girl in the story are all distantly related. Uncle Ike's aunt married an Edmonds. Uncle Ike's grandfather is one of the girl's ancestors. (See Faulkner's Go Down, Moses.) Ike has refused an inheritance which therefore passed to the Edmonds branch of the family, the refusal being based on idealistic grounds— that is, unwillingness to accept property developed through slavery. Roth Edmonds and Ike differ in this story on a question involving idealism. What is the question?

(2) The wilderness has special symbolic meanings for Uncle Ike McCaslin. What are these meanings?

(3) It has been said that Faulkner, as a writer of fiction, is especially interested in presenting the view that the past is implicit in the present. Can you find this point of view in "Delta Autumn"?

(4) What views of religion are expressed in this story?

(5) Can you find in this story, which carries references to Hitler and World War II, any kind of forecast of the human future in the delta country?

(6) Can you think of any reason why Roth Edmonds, in this story, is inclined to argue that man will do the right thing only because someone may be watching? Do you agree with this point of view?

(7) From images used, from wording, and from connotations of words, what can you discover about the author's views of modern life, including business and work?

(8) Did the girl go to the camp to get money, to let Roth Edmonds see his son, or for what reason?

(9) What is the author's apparent attitude toward the girl? What is Ike McCaslin's apparent attitude?

The Authors:

Sholom Aleichem (1859–1916) Sholom Aleichem, the pen name of Solomon Rabinowitz, means "Peace be unto you" and is used informally and familiarly as a greeting between Jews.

James Baldwin (b. 1924)

Morley Callaghan (b. 1903)

Albert Camus	*(1913–1960)*
Anton Chekhov	*(1860–1904)*
Joseph Conrad	*(1857–1924)*
Stephen Crane	*(1871–1900)*
Ralph Ellison	*(b. 1914)*
William Faulkner	*(1897–1962)*
Ernest Hemingway	*(1898–1961)*
Paul Horgan	*(b. 1903)*
James Joyce	*(1882–1941)*
Franz Kafka	*(1883–1924)*
Pär Lagerkvist	*(b. 1891)*
Bernard Malamud	*(b. 1914)*
Alice Marriott	*(b. 1910)*
Arthur Miller	*(b. 1915)*
N. Scott Momaday	*(b. 1934)*
Flannery O'Connor	*(1925–1964)*
Frank O'Connor	*(1903–1966) A pseudonym for Michael O'Donovan*
Alan Paton	*(b. 1903)*
Katherine Anne Porter	*(b. 1890)*
James Thurber	*(1894–1961)*
Jean Toomer	*(1894–1967)*
Kurt Vonnegut, Jr.	*(b. 1922)*
Alice Walker	*(b. 1944)*
William Carlos Williams	*(1883–1963)*

POETRY

The Art of Reading Poetry

Generally speaking, poetry has no subject matter distinct from that of prose. At certain periods in the past there may seem to have been a difference, when the reading public valued most highly the lofty "poetical" poems devoted to vast thoughts, extravagant emotions, or events such as ordinary mortals rarely encounter, all presented in dignified formal language. But this has never been the exclusive province of poetry. Homer wrote of great heroes having great adventures, but those heroes also cooked and ate their supper, and Homer described that too. Six hundred years ago Chaucer wrote a complaint to his purse (empty) in verse; a century ago Emily Dickinson wrote a poem about a common house fly and (in the same poem) human death. Shakespeare's characters and Chaucer's stories sometimes used verse to say what is even today nearly unprintable. These are random instances. Conceivably, anything of interest to men and women may furnish a subject for the poet, and he may employ almost every variety of language.

In form, too, the range of poetry is wide. At one end of its spectrum the distinction between verse and prose cannot be clearly drawn. Some "poetic prose" might well have been printed in lines of verse, as may be seen in the following apostrophe to death, which, originally written and printed as prose, concludes a History of the World which Sir Walter Ralegh wrote from prison.

O eloquent, just and mighty death,
Whom none could advise, thou hast persuaded;
What none hath presumed, thou hast done;
And whom all the world hath flattered, thou
Hast cast out of the world and despised:

> Thou hast drawn together all the extravagant greatness,
> All the pride, cruelty and ambition of man,
> And covered all over with two narrow words:
> Hic jacet.

Broken into lines here but otherwise unchanged, the prose reads quite naturally as verse. The generalized thoughts of death may well have been heightened into poetry by Ralegh's awareness of his own tenuous hold upon life though he utters no word of that (he was eventually executed).

It would be even easier to find passages of reputable modern free verse that would pass unnoticed as prose if they were so printed. Yet, such instances notwithstanding and although it is sometimes relative rather than absolute, there does exist a difference between prose and poetry, a difference deriving from two sources. One source is a special attitude of the writer or some feeling towards his subject—whatever that subject may be—that demands a heightening of his language; the other is man's natural feeling for rhythm in general and hence, on occasion, for rhythmical language.

RHYTHM AND PATTERN

Intensification of experience through rhythm is as old as the human race. We know this from such group activities as the rhythmic chants that, alone or accompanied by bodily movements, have always been a ritual part equally of religious ceremony and of children's games. But rhythm is not a group phenomenon only; it is instinctive in individual man and in its simplest and most habitual forms is not necessarily an intensifier of anything. It may in fact be the reverse. We walk and breathe rhythmically. Though we can do both unrhythmically for a short time if we try, the moment we relax our attention the rhythm returns. A perfectly simple and regular rhythm, however, quickly becomes intolerable if we focus conscious attention upon it. If we sit in a room with a loudly ticking clock, we find ourselves unconsciously varying the sound by thinking we hear tick-tock, though the actual sounds are identical. But tick-tock also is too simple, and soon, to avoid unbearable monotony, we have to stop listening or remove the clock. Rhythm rides us unpleasantly or else anesthetizes us, unless we succeed in riding it—in manipulating it, that is, to suit our own will. That is why in imagination we tend to hear a tune or words to vary the mechanical rhythms of a clock or a railroad train. In good poetry the rhythm cannot be mechanical or simple but must be flexible and varied.

An analogy will illustrate this. Poetry, it has been said, is to prose what dancing is to walking. Though sometimes we stroll for pleasure, ordinarily walking is a means to an end: we walk, scarcely aware of the physical sensation of walking, in order to get somewhere, the sooner the better. But we dance to stay where we are, enjoying the repetitive yet varied flowing of one movement into another, and enjoying the harmony between our own movements and that of the music and of our partner. Prose is often read quickly to see how the story comes out or to learn all the facts. But just as one cannot properly hurry through a dance, so one cannot read poetry in a hurry, with muscles taut, ready to go somewhere. It should be read with at least a little leisure and either actually aloud or with the imagined sound present to the mind's ear. To a really good dancer, the music—itself full of rhythmic and melodic variety—becomes a basis for further variations of turn, whirl and syncopation; he anticipates, delays, whirls, then returns just in time to pick up the beat again. The conventional rules of versification (see pp. 638-639) provide for poetry the elementary dá-di-dá or tick-tock against which these variations are played. Though some writers of third-rate verse and some sing-song readers never get much beyond this mechanical regularity, the rhythm and music of good poetry are as far beyond it in gracefulness, expressiveness, and variety as the fine dancer is beyond the clodhopper who can only keep time. Good poetry, in short, like good dancing, is a satisfying expression of freedom within the bounds of a convention or a form.

If anyone doubts the importance of rhythm, as well as other effects of sound, among the fused elements that make up a poem, he may find an illustration in a common nursery rhyme. Few people who have once known it ever forget the old rhyme about "Pease porridge hot, Pease porridge cold." Yet it seems odd that a grown-up should remember these useless verses when he has forgotten a thousand more interesting, more personal, and more important things that he knew as a child. Frequent repetition is only part of the answer, for he has forgotten many things that he has heard or repeated much oftener. The attraction cannot be in the meaning, for that is so slight as to be almost non-existent. Though a man may remember the lines for seventy years, he probably does not even know what pease porridge (perhaps a near relation of split pea soup) is; and he certainly does not care whether it is hot or cold, since he does not expect to eat it. This is a surprising phenomenon: the almost universal memory, surviving through a lifetime out of the welter of things once known and forgotten, of a trivial statement about an uninteresting and unidentified food.

The explanation is simply that it is good poetry, of a small sort and on its own level. It satisfies, for one thing, the natural liking for a rhythm that is both strongly marked and varied. Though comparatively simple, the rhythm of "Pease Porridge" has surprising variety: no two lines of the stanza are exactly alike. The sounds, moreover, are appropriate, for they are inextricably interwoven with what little meaning there is. The key words hot and cold are emphasized by pauses and rhyme. Hot is a light quick word, whose sounds cannot be prolonged (try prolonging a t sound or even a short o sound); it easily coalesces with its meaning: we drop the word as quickly as we would a hot object. Cold, on the other hand, is a long slow syllable, and solid—like congealed porridge, one might almost say. A diagram may be unpoetical but will show something of what is meant.

■ The stresses and timing:

Pease/porridge/hot
Pease/porridge/cold
Pease/porridge/in the/pot
Nine/days/old

■ The tune: a rising inflection in lines 1 and 3 with staccato endings, a falling in lines 2 and 4 with prolonged endings.

Pease porridge hot
Pease porridge cold
Pease porridge in the pot
Nine days old

In poetry, rhythm is usually reinforced, as it is here, by other effects of sound. The poet may employ rhyme to mark the ends of lines, and he nearly always makes use of other kinds of repetition, such as assonance and alliteration (see the Glossary beginning on page 639). Like rhythm itself, these effects develop out of a natural liking for repetitive echoes. Any child would prefer "Ring a round a Rosy" to "Make a circle about Rosie." Such patterns, used more subtly and interwoven with the meaning of a poem, appeal equally to the maturer mind and ear. In the lines

> And malt does more than Milton can
> To justify God's ways to man,

the poet Housman preferred malt to ale because its alliteration sharpened the absurd contrast between ale and Milton (who announced in Paradise Lost that his purpose was "to justify the ways of God to Men"). In these lines, rhyme, meter, and alliteration combine to heighten the writer's cynical and witty statement that only when a man is drunk can he think well of the universe.

In good verse the irregular patterns of alliteration and assonance and the more regular rhythmic beats within the line are bound together in larger rhythmic and structural units. Neither the sense nor the sound pattern of the opening of "Pease porridge" is complete till the fourth line ends; and here again the nursery rhyme illustrates a principle of poetic structure, the close of the stanza bringing to rest a movement of tune, rhythm, and thought which began four lines earlier. Rhyme too, in its usual place at the ends of lines, helps in creating this larger pattern. Almost endless combinations of verse forms are available to the poet, as the reader may come to realize from even the limited number of poems in this volume.

FORM, SYMBOL, AND MEANING

Everyone has experienced the pleasure and pride of having something perfectly shipshape: rows of extra-straight, fine-growing corn in a field; tools all in order, bright and sharp; bureau drawer or desk reorganized so that its former chaos is transformed into perfect and intelligible order. One dwells upon such things with more satisfaction than their convenience or profit alone will account for. A man likes to go out and look at such a field though looking will not increase its yield or bring him in more money; the sight may give him pleasure even if the field belongs to someone else.

Most of life, however, is not a well arranged bureau drawer. Hence, the function of poetry is possibly best described by those who explain it as an imaginative means of creating order out of chaos. Existence, whether on its everyday level or at its most intense, has always been chaotic and fragmentary. One desire, one loyalty, runs counter to another; claims conflict with claims, problems remain insoluble; the future is always uncertain; we never know the whole of anything: these are the inevitable conditions of life. Poetry does not disguise them, is not a device for wish-fulfillment or escape. But by subjecting some aspect of reality to poetic form, to a poetic mode of order, the poet isolates it and focuses upon it sharply, presenting for our imaginative contemplation one experience complete and unconfused by irrelevancies, to be dwelt upon till its full significance is both realized and felt. It becomes then a concrete symbol of the idea of order itself.

All good poetry is characterized by intensity, but this does not mean that it always deals with or expresses an intensely emotional aspect of life. It may do this, as does Milton's sonnet on a massacre (see page 523). Or it may simply capture a transient moment such as that in which Robert Frost saw a colt in a field frightened by its first snowstorm. The vivid moment of interest in the colt's fright and the visual image of it running wildly in the snow were intense enough to make a poem ("The Runaway," page 582). The poet Sir John Suckling mockingly boasts of faithfulness to his current lady and half promises—provided the lady is accommodating —to continue in love for three days more:

> Out upon it! I have lov'd
>   Three whole days together;
> And am like to love three more,
>   If it prove fair weather.
>
> Time shall moult away his wings,
>   Ere he shall discover
> In the whole wide world again
>   Such a constant lover.
>
> But the spite on 't is, no praise
>   Is due at all to me:
> Love with me had made no stays,
>   Had it any been but she.
>
> Had it any been but she,
>   And that very face,
> There had been at least ere this
>   A dozen dozen in her place.

Not much intensity of love here, obviously. And no important joy or suffering. What we have, instead, is witty mockery outdoing itself in each reversal; a boast, followed by retraction and a double-edged compliment to a court lady, all heightened by fine precision and neatness of phrase and form—an intensity of zest in poetic workmanship, not of raw emotion. Yet it is not without meaning, for in mocking himself so coolly Lovelace also indirectly mocks his society and our own: though poet and lady are now several centuries dead, the young man is any young man anywhere "playing the field" and at the same time showing a poetic-ironic consciousness of what he is doing.

Thus the poet, through his perception of the inner meaning of things and by his power over language, succeeds in communicating the otherwise incommunicable and in bringing to full realization experience that, in our preoccupation with daily routine, daily desires, and daily chaos, ordinarily slips by us as an undifferentiated part of that routine and chaos.

THE POET'S LANGUAGE

Like most objects that are used a great deal, words are subject to two somewhat contrary processes. They become freighted with innumerable associations of all sorts—which means they become rich in their power of suggestion. Yet they also become defaced and dull, their distinguishing features rubbed flat by careless, half-accurate everyday use. What the poet does through his fresh awareness of language is to bring us its inherited load of richness and at the same time to clear away the incrustations of careless use, so that his words have the value of both fresh bright newness and old rich association.

For example, the expression "glamorous eyes" one would think is pretty stale; it has long been a sentimental cliché fit only for the cover of a Hollywood maga-zine, if that. But the poet de la Mare uses it. He precedes it, however, by "stare," a hard unsentimental word, rather than the expected softer "gaze;" and he em-ploys it to describe not a woman but a moth hovering about a candle: the moth "stares from her glamorous eyes." The worn-out coin "glamorous" is here new-minted, with its cheap associations dusted off by "stares" and by the reader's memory of bug eyes, yet with its original powerful associations remaining. This is a typical example, all the more typical because so small and unspectacular, of a poet's handling of language. It may help to show how alert and unhurried the reader must be to catch the full force of a good poem.

When Coleridge said that good prose consists of "words in the best order" and poetry of "the best words in the best order," he was perhaps casting a needless slur upon prose. The point underlying his distinction, however, is this: when words are arranged metrically, the rhythm and the accompanying pauses—which are more marked in poetry than in prose—give more than ordinary prominence to each individual word or phrase and send the reader's mind, during the pause, rolling back for an instant over the phrase just past. That means that the words must be worth the prominence they receive; otherwise they will seem excessively dull or foolish. There is nothing wrong in prose with the phrase "When he called me on the telephone. . . ." But if a song writer should write, as one did (approximately, if not exactly),

> When he called me-e-e
> On the telephone,

he needs a very good tune to cover up the flatness of words that have been made conspicuous, syllable for syllable, by rhythm and pause.

IMAGERY, SYMBOL, METAPHOR, AND MEANING

The analogy drawn earlier between poetry and dancing falls short in one impor-tant particular, for aside from ballets that act out a story or certain folk dances that symbolize an activity such as fighting or harvesting, dancing has no specific "meaning," whereas poetry has. Words have meaning which the poet could not suppress if he wished to; even in nonsense verse or half-nonsensical nursery rhymes hints and fragments of meaning persist. A poem therefore is clearly not just an organized pattern of linguistic sounds; it is first of all an organization of meaning. Often the overt meaning is immediately clear, as it is in the poem of Suckling quoted earlier; but not infrequently, though most of the words will be common ones, the inexperienced reader will have difficulty in making out even the literal sense of a poem. This is in part because the poet will not weaken the impact of what he writes by inserting routine explanations that have not enough interest in themselves to deserve the prominence of rhythm and that would sound unpleasantly flat in verse. He may therefore leave explanatory matter for the reader to figure out. With a little practice the reader becomes mentally agile enough to do this most of the time without much trouble. His reward comes in finding the poem a packed piece, free of inessentials and dullness.

A celebrated and rather extreme modern instance of a gap left for the reader to supply occurs in T. S. Eliot's "The Love Song of J. Alfred Prufrock," when Prufrock interrupts his inner soliloquy. Should he, he has been asking himself, propose marriage (or possibly an affair) to a woman? As he wonders what he might say to her, he breaks off abruptly with

> I should have been a pair of ragged claws
> Scuttling across the floors of silent seas.

The reader is left to understand from this that, brought face to face with the thought of actually proposing to a woman, Prufrock recognizes that his nature is solitary, that he is incapable of coming out of his shell (the everyday trite version of the "ragged claws" image). By comparison with the average man, Prufrock might have explained, he is like a lobster which, as every elementary student of biology knows, wears its skeleton on the outside as protective covering and is a cold-blooded creature living a lonely life at the bottom of the sea (the poem was written before Rachel Carson and more recent writers had removed some of the solitude from the sea-bottom). Instead of explaining all this at length, the poet takes for granted that his reader has a mind sufficiently agile to understand. It is the kind of symbol that every mind employs in musing. By presenting it without explanation, Eliot gains realism and a striking dramatic effect, at the same time avoiding dull exposition.

The concentration and the force of poetry are achieved, as this illustration from "Prufrock" suggests, in great measure through imagery and figurative language. Concrete words that call up images of sight, touch, sound, movement, heat or cold almost always make a stronger impression than abstract or generalized language. The word motherhood is likely to pass through the mind without leaving a stir, whereas "my mother in the kitchen" may stir memories, pictures, and feelings too numerous to list. Part of the poet's power lies in his ability to choose images that will most vividly communicate the experience he writes of.

Much of the concrete image-making language of poetry is figurative: it communicates a truth or an idea or emotion, that is, without itself being literally true. The image in "Prufrock" is such a figure. We do not suppose Prufrock literally wished to be a lobster; and besides, claws do not scuttle by themselves without the rest of the body.

Poets, and many non-poets too, think naturally in such images; it is not in the least a forced way of writing. Even in ordinary conversation we use figures as a kind of emphatic shorthand. One man, we say, is "down to earth;" another "has his head in the clouds." The expressions are unoriginal and overworked, yet even so they tell more, and tell it more forcefully, than if we said, literally, that the men were "practical" and "impractical." To supplement "impractical" with all the addi-

tional implications of "head in the clouds" without using figurative language would require several sentences at least; and the long literal statement would still lack the force and vividness of the figurative one.

LITERARY ALLUSION

Many poetic allusions have this same value of saying much in little, though they are sometimes an obstacle to immediate understanding. In former times, the stories of Greek mythology were as familiar to children as stories of Spacemen or Martians are today, and Greek myth is particularly rich in natural symbolic meaning. Assuming that everyone knows the story of Helen and the Trojan war—a story that has long been, among other things, a classic symbol of the destructive power of feminine beauty—one modern poet, seeing an unknown woman walk by, exclaims: "Now I know what Helen was!" After that, he does not need to describe the passing beauty. Another poet pays a double-edged tribute to the woman he loves: "Was there another Troy for her to burn?" The mere name of Helen and the image of Troy burning (if one knows the story of the daughter of Zeus and Leda and of the nine years' siege of Troy and the tenth year of looting and burning) are explosive capsules in which is concentrated a whole world of experience past and present. That is why, though a reader is often inconvenienced and sometimes irritated by having to look up unfamiliar allusions, in the long run we do not ask the poet to reduce his circle of reference to our smaller or different experience but, instead, find it worthwhile to try to extend our own. If the poet had to give up Helen and Troy, he could not convey with any such richness of suggestion, or such force and concentration, the combination of beauty, power, danger, and destruction—along with the reminder that some problems of man are as old as history—represented by the ancient story.

The name of Ulysses (Odysseus) is still a tremendous piece of shorthand if we know the Odyssey. *James Joyce took advantage of Homer when he wrote the twentieth century's most celebrated novel,* Ulysses. *So did a less famous novelist who named a book about Iowa* The Odyssey of a Nice Girl. *When Tennyson wrote of Ulysses (page 496) as a particular man with an urge to travel, he was also writing about man's eternal desire for knowledge and experience, a desire that is deep at the roots of civilization. Tennyson could say this and many other things at once because the name from the ancient story telescopes a great world of meaning. It also keeps us reminded of the long view, reminded that man's search began with pre-history and may possibly still, with care and some luck, have a future.*

THE READER'S RESPONSIBILITY

Poetry, like music, is meant to be revisited; it is not composed for a single reading or hearing. This follows from the mood in which it originates, the impulse to "dwell upon" something, to experience fully whatever it is the poem represents. A poem therefore may have many layers of significance; in saying one thing it often, as with Tennyson's "Ulysses," indirectly says other more general or more universal things. The first reading of a poem may therefore be little more than an aerial tour from which one gets a preliminary rough map of the region. Real exploration often begins only with the second reading. Housman opened his poem ''To an Athlete Dying Young'' with these stanzas (for the whole poem, see page 432):

The time you won your town the race
We chaired you through the market-place;
Man and boy stood cheering by,
And home we brought you shoulder-high.

Today, the road all runners come,
Shoulder-high we bring you home,
And set you at your threshold down,
Townsman of a stiller town.

The outline of this poem is simple enough to be grasped immediately. Every reader knows (if only from the title) that the runner has died. But at first he may not notice that the funeral is described in the same images as the triumph, or see how the images that are literally true in the first stanza become metaphorical in the second. Town, runner, home, being carried on others' shoulders are all repeated; only, in the second stanza, it is the road ''all runners'' travel, and the town is ''stiller,'' the ''cheering'' gone. Death has not been mentioned. For the reader, the poet's view of the peak of life and its extinction presented thus through almost identical images— images perfectly appropriate to both—breaks down some of the rigid categories in which he ordinarily thinks of triumph, life, and death. And though he comes away with no definable new truth, the reader finds himself seeing all with a wider, if ironical, vision—but only on a second or third reading. Yet this is a relatively simple and clear poem. Rereading and (as we emphasized earlier) leisurely, deliberate reading are essential so that each thing said may reverberate in the mind. In reading any poetry that amounts to anything, the reader must let it reverberate.

Note   Brief explanations of certain proper names and unusual words or allusions are given in the text, as a rule only for words and names not adequately covered in standard college dictionaries. Longer explanations, discussions, and interpretations for some but not all of the poems appear separately in the Notes and Comments on Poetry (pp. 642-671). These vary in length and fullness, the assumption being that readers can profit from examples of critcal interpretation but should also be left free to interpret much of their reading for themselves.

A short discussion of versification and a glossary of terms will be found on pages 638-642.

Transition to Poetry

CHARACTERS

The poems in this first group are for the most part character sketches, a type of writing that commonly employs prose. Not conspicuously "poetical," their style is apt to be informal and conversational. In some the tone is cool and objective; the writer may use verse form not to express emotion but to give what he says a neat, crisp outline, to point up a few words or thoughts, or to make each detail stand out with emphasis.

Some of the poems present an individual, some a type. Several sum up a lifetime's knowledge of a person in a few lines. All were written by poets who saw and judged for themselves, hence they are free from the "stock response." Barker writes affectionately about his mother, Yeats about the woman he loved for many years. But there is no ideal, standard, or ready-made mother or lover in the group.

Note *An asterisk (*) before a title or a poet's name signifies that notes on that poem or poet can be found in the supplementary material beginning on page 642.*

*Richard Cory

EDWIN ARLINGTON ROBINSON

Whenever Richard Cory went down town,
We people on the pavement looked at him:
He was a gentleman from sole to crown,
Clean favored, and imperially slim.

And he was always quietly arrayed,
And he was always human when he talked;
But still he fluttered pulses when he said,
"Good-morning," and he glittered when he walked.

And he was rich—yes, richer than a king—
And admirably schooled in every grace: 10
In fine, we thought that he was everything
To make us wish that we were in his place.

So on we worked, and waited for the light,
And went without the meat, and cursed the bread;
And Richard Cory, one calm summer night,
Went home and put a bullet through his head.

Mr. Flood's Party

EDWIN ARLINGTON ROBINSON

Old Eben Flood, climbing alone one night
Over the hill between the town below
And the forsaken upland hermitage
That held as much as he should ever know
On earth again of home, paused warily.
The road was his with not a native near;
And Eben, having leisure, said aloud,
For no man else in Tilbury Town to hear:

"Well, Mr. Flood, we have the harvest moon
Again, and we may not have many more;   10
The bird is on the wing, the poet says,
And you and I have said it here before.
Drink to the bird." He raised up to the light
The jug that he had gone so far to fill,
And answered huskily: "Well, Mr. Flood,
Since you propose it, I believe I will."

Alone, as if enduring to the end
A valiant armor of scarred hopes outworn,
He stood there in the middle of the road
Like Roland's ghost winding a silent horn.   20
Below him, in the town among the trees,
Where friends of other days had honored him,
A phantom salutation of the dead
Rang thinly till old Eben's eyes were dim.

Then, as a mother lays her sleeping child
Down tenderly, fearing it may awake,
He set the jug down slowly at his feet
With trembling care, knowing that most things break;
And only when assured that on firm earth
It stood, as the uncertain lives of men   30
Assuredly did not, he paced away,
And with his hand extended paused again:

"Well, Mr. Flood, we have not met like this
In a long time; and many a change has come
To both of us, I fear, since last it was
We had a drop together. Welcome home!"
Convivially returning with himself,
Again he raised the jug up to the light;
And with an acquiescent quaver said:
"Well, Mr. Flood, if you insist, I might.   40

"Only a very little, Mr. Flood—
For auld lang syne. No more, sir; that will do."
So, for the time, apparently it did,
And Eben evidently thought so too;
For soon amid the silver loneliness
Of night he lifted up his voice and sang,
Secure, with only two moons listening,
Until the whole harmonious landscape rang—

"For auld lang syne." The weary throat gave out,
The last word wavered; and the song being done,   50
He raised again the jug regretfully
And shook his head, and was again alone.
There was not much that was ahead of him,
And there was nothing in the town below—
Where strangers would have shut the many doors
That many friends had opened long ago.

_l. 20. Roland: Treacherously attacked, the medieval French hero refused to sound his horn
to summon aid till he lay dying._

Miniver Cheevy

EDWIN ARLINGTON ROBINSON

Miniver Cheevy, child of scorn,
   Grew lean while he assailed the seasons;
He wept that he was ever born,
   And he had reasons.

Miniver loved the days of old
   When swords were bright and steeds were prancing;
The vision of a warrior bold
   Would set him dancing.

Miniver sighed for what was not,
   And dreamed, and rested from his labors;   10
He dreamed of Thebes and Camelot,
   And Priam's neighbors.

Miniver mourned the ripe renown
That made so many a name so fragrant;
He mourned Romance, now on the town,
   And Art, a vagrant.

Miniver loved the Medici,
   Albeit he had never seen one;
He would have sinned incessantly
   Could he have been one.   20

Miniver cursed the commonplace
   And eyed a khaki suit with loathing;
He missed the mediaeval grace
   Of iron clothing.

Miniver scorned the gold he sought,
   But sore annoyed was he without it;
Miniver thought, and thought, and thought,
   And thought about it.

Miniver Cheevy, born too late,
   Scratched his head and kept on thinking;   30
Miniver coughed, and called it fate,
And kept on drinking.

---

l. 15. on the town: On relief or welfare.

Museums

LOUIS MACNEICE

Museums offer us, running from among the buses,
A centrally heated refuge, parquet floors and sarcophaguses,
Into whose tall fake porches we hurry without a sound
Like a beetle under a brick that lies, useless, on the ground.
Warmed and cajoled by the silence the cowed cypher revives,
Mirrors himself in the cases of pots, paces himself by marble lives,
Makes believe it was he that was the glory that was Rome,
Soft on his cheek the nimbus of other people's martyrdom,
And then returns to the street, his mind an arena where sprawls
Any number of consumptive Keatses and dying Gauls.

---

l. 3. fake porches: Modern imitations of Greek or Roman architecture.

nobody loses all the time

e. e. cummings

nobody loses all the time

i had an uncle named
Sol who was a born failure and
nearly everybody said he should have gone
into vaudeville perhaps because my Uncle Sol could
sing McCann He Was A Diver on Xmas Eve like Hell Itself which
may or may not account for the fact that my Uncle

Sol indulged in that possibly most inexcusable
of all to use a highfalootin phrase
luxuries that is or to   10
wit farming and be
it needlessly
added

my Uncle Sol's farm
failed because the chickens
ate the vegetables so
my Uncle Sol had a
chicken farm till the
skunks ate the chickens when

my Uncle Sol   20
had a skunk farm but
the skunks caught cold and
died and so
my Uncle Sol imitated the
skunks in a subtle manner

or by drowning himself in the watertank
but somebody who'd given my Uncle Sol a Victor
Victrola and records while he lived presented to
him upon the auspicious occasion of his decease a
scrumptious not to mention splendiferous funeral with   30
tall boys in black gloves and flowers and everything and

i remember we all cried like the Missouri
when my Uncle Sol's coffin lurched because
somebody pressed a button
(and down went
my Uncle
Sol

and started a worm farm)

SONNET

To My Mother

GEORGE BARKER

Most near, most dear, most loved and most far,
Under the window where I often found her
Sitting as huge as Asia, seismic with laughter,
Gin and chicken helpless in her Irish hand,
Irresistible as Rabelais, but most tender for
The lame dogs and hurt birds that surround her,—
She is a procession no one can follow after
But be like a little dog following a brass band.

She will not glance up at the bomber, or condescend
To drop her gin and scuttle to a cellar,   10
But lean on the mahogany table like a mountain
Whom only faith can move, and so I send
O all my faith and all my love to tell her
That she will move from mourning into morning.

l. 5. Rabelais: Sixteenth-century author of racy satiric tales of the giant Gargantua.

*Lucinda Matlock

EDGAR LEE MASTERS

I went to the dances at Chandlerville,
And played snap-out at Winchester.
One time we changed partners,
Driving home in the moonlight of middle June,
And then I found Davis.
We were married and lived together for seventy years,
Enjoying, working, raising the twelve children,
Eight of whom we lost
Ere I had reached the age of sixty.
I spun, I wove, I kept the house, I nursed the sick.   10
I made the garden, and for holiday
Rambled over the fields where sang the larks,
And by Spoon River gathering many a shell,
And many a flower and medicinal weed—
Shouting to the wooded hills, singing to the green valleys.
At ninety-six I had lived enough, that is all,
And passed to a sweet repose.
What is this I hear of sorrow and weariness,
Anger, discontent and drooping hopes?
Degenerate sons and daughters,   20
Life is too strong for you—
It takes life to love Life.

*My Last Duchess

ROBERT BROWNING

Ferrara

That's my last Duchess painted on the wall,
Looking as if she were alive. I call
That piece a wonder, now: Frà Pandolf's hands
Worked busily a day, and there she stands.
Will't please you sit and look at her? I said
"Frà Pandolf" by design, for never read
Strangers like you that pictured countenance,
The depth and passion of its earnest glance,
But to myself they turned (since none puts by

The curtain I have drawn for you, but I)   10
And seemed as they would ask me, if they durst,
How such a glance came there; so, not the first
Are you to turn and ask thus. Sir, 'twas not
Her husband's presence only, called that spot
Of joy into the Duchess' cheek: perhaps
Frà Pandolf chanced to say "Her mantle laps
Over my lady's wrist too much," or "Paint
Must never hope to reproduce the faint
Half-flush that dies along her throat:" such stuff
Was courtesy, she thought, and cause enough   20
For calling up that spot of joy. She had
A heart—how shall I say?—too soon made glad,
Too easily impressed; she liked whate'er
She looked on, and her looks went everywhere.
Sir, 'twas all one! My favour at her breast,
The dropping of the daylight in the West,
The bough of cherries some officious fool
Broke in the orchard for her, the white mule
She rode with round the terrace—all and each
Would draw from her alike the approving speech,   30
Or blush, at least. She thanked men,—good! but thanked
Somehow—I know not how—as if she ranked
My gift of a nine-hundred-years-old name
With anybody's gift. Who'd stoop to blame
This sort of trifling? Even had you skill
In speech—(which I have not)—to make your will
Quite clear to such an one, and say, "Just this
Or that in you disgusts me; here you miss,
Or there exceed the mark"—and if she let
Herself be lessoned so, nor plainly set   40
Her wits to yours, forsooth, and made excuse,
—E'en then would be some stooping; and I choose
Never to stoop. Oh sir, she smiled, no doubt,
Whene'er I passed her; but who passed without
Much the same smile? This grew; I gave commands;
Then all smiles stopped together. There she stands
As if alive. Will 't please you rise? We'll meet
The company below, then. I repeat,
The Count your master's known munificence
Is ample warrant that no just pretense   50
Of mine for dowry will be disallowed;
Though his fair daughter's self, as I avowed
At starting, is my object. Nay, we'll go
Together down, sir. Notice Neptune, though,
Taming a sea-horse, thought a rarity,
Which Claus of Innsbruck cast in bronze for me!

Soliloquy of the Spanish Cloister

ROBERT BROWNING

Gr-r-r—there go, my heart's abhorrence!
　　Water your damned flower-pots, do!
If hate killed men, Brother Lawrence,
　　God's blood, would not mine kill you!
What? your myrtle-bush wants trimming?
　　Oh, that rose has prior claims—
Needs its leaden vase filled brimming?
　　Hell dry you up with its flames!

At the meal we sit together:
　　Salve tibi! I must hear   10
Wise talk of the kind of weather,
　　Sort of season, time of year:
Not a plenteous cork-crop: scarcely
　　Dare we hope oak-galls, I doubt:
What's the Latin name for "parsley"?
　　What's the Greek name for Swine's Snout?

Whew! We'll have our platter burnished,
　　Laid with care on our own shelf!
With a fire-new spoon we're furnished,
　　And a goblet for ourself,   20
Rinsed like something sacrificial
　　Ere 'tis fit to touch our chaps—
Marked with L for our initial!
　　(He-he! There his lily snaps!)

Saint, forsooth! While brown Dolores
　　Squats outside the Convent bank
With Sanchicha, telling stories,
　　Steeping tresses in the tank,
Blue-black, lustrous, thick like horse-hairs,
　　—Can't I see his dead eye glow,   30
Bright as 'twere a Barbary corsair's?
　　(That is, if he'd let it show!)

When he finishes refection,
　　Knife and fork he never lays
Cross-wise, to my recollection,
　　As do I, in Jesu's praise.

---

l. 10. Salve tibi!: *Hail to thee!*

I the Trinity illustrate,
  Drinking watered orange-pulp—
In three sips the Arian frustrate;
  While he drains his at one gulp.   40

Oh, those melons! If he's able
  We're to have a feast! so nice!
One goes to the Abbot's table,
  All of us get each a slice.
How go on your flowers? None double?
  Not one fruit-sort can you spy?
Strange!—And I, too, at such trouble
  Keep them close-nipped on the sly!

There's a great text in Galatians,
  Once you trip on it, entails   50
Twenty-nine distinct damnations,
  One sure, if another fails:
If I trip him just-a-dying,
  Sure of heaven as sure can be,
Spin him round and send him flying
  Off to hell, a Manichee?

Or, my scrofulous French novel
  On grey paper with blunt type!
Simply glance at it, you grovel
  Hand and foot in Belial's gripe: 60
If I double down its pages
  At the woeful sixteenth print,
When he gathers his greengages,
  Ope a sieve and slip it in't?

Or, there's Satan!—one might venture
  Pledge one's soul to him, yet leave
Such a flaw in the indenture
  As he'd miss till, past retrieve,
Blasted lay that rose-acacia
  We're so proud of! *Hy, Zy, Hine* . . .   70
'St, there's Vespers! *Plena gratia,*
  Ave, Virgo! G-r-r-r—you swine!

---

ll. 37–39. The Arian heresy maintained that Christ is inferior to God, in opposition to the Trinitarian doctrine of the equality of the Three Persons of the Trinity.
l. 46. fruit-sort: Pistillate, i.e., flowers from which fruit will be developed, as distinguished from staminate flowers, which produce the pollen.
l. 64. Sieve: A kind of basket used for produce.
l. 70. Hy, Zy, Hine: Words still unexplained; possibly the beginning of a spell invoking Satan.
ll. 71–72. Plena . . . : Hail, Virgin, full of grace!

*Her Praise

WILLIAM BUTLER YEATS

She is foremost of those that I would hear praised.
I have gone about the house, gone up and down
As a man does who has published a new book,
Or a young girl dressed out in her new gown,
And though I have turned the talk by hook or crook
Until her praise should be the uppermost theme,
A woman spoke of some new tale she had read,
A man confusedly in a half dream
As though some other name ran in his head.
She is foremost of those that I would hear praised.   10
I will talk no more of books or the long war
But walk by the dry thorn until I have found
Some beggar sheltering from the wind, and there
Manage the talk until her name come round.
If there be rags enough he will know her name
And be well pleased remembering it, for in the old days,
Though she had young men's praise and old men's blame,
Among the poor both old and young gave her praise.

No Second Troy

WILLIAM BUTLER YEATS

Why should I blame her that she filled my days
With misery, or that she would of late
Have taught to ignorant men most violent ways,
Or hurled the little streets upon the great,
Had they but courage equal to desire?
What could have made her peaceful with a mind
That nobleness made simple as a fire,
With beauty like a tightened bow, a kind
That is not natural in an age like this,
Being high and solitary and most stern?   10
Why, what could she have done, being what she is?
Was there another Troy for her to burn?

That the Night Come

WILLIAM BUTLER YEATS

She lived in storm and strife,
Her soul had such desire
For what proud death may bring
That it could not endure
The common good of life,
But lived as 'twere a king
That packed his marriage day
With banneret and pennon,
Trumpet and kettledrum,
And the outrageous cannon,   10
To bundle time away
That the night come.

NARRATIVES

Each of the poems in the following group tells a story. Although the term narrative *is most often associated today with prose, and although character and story are staple materials of prose fiction, historically verse narrative is believed to be older than prose narrative. The ancient Homeric epic stories, for example, are in early Greek verse.*

The first narrative in the present selection, "The Death of the Hired Man," might today have been written as a short story in prose emphasizing character and attitudes rather than plot, or it might have been a one-act play in which three characters are delineated through the conversation of two of them. Of the narrative poems in this collection, this one is the most clearly transitional between prose and poetry. The poems that follow it are a selection of the more stylized old popular ballads and of later narratives influenced by them (a further account of ballads will be found in the Notes (pp. 643–644).

The Death of the Hired Man

ROBERT FROST

Mary sat musing on the lamp-flame at the table,
Waiting for Warren. When she heard his step,
She ran on tiptoe down the darkened passage
To meet him in the doorway with the news
And put him on his guard. "Silas is back."
She pushed him outward with her through the door
And shut it after her. "Be kind," she said.
She took the market things from Warren's arms
And set them on the porch, then drew him down
To sit beside her on the wooden steps.   10

"When was I ever anything but kind to him?
But I'll not have the fellow back," he said.
"I told him so last haying, didn't I?
If he left then, I said, that ended it.
What good is he? Who else will harbor him
At his age for the little he can do?
What help he is there's no depending on.
Off he goes always when I need him most.
He thinks he ought to earn a little pay,
Enough at least to buy tobacco with,   20
So he won't have to beg and be beholden.
'All right,' I say, 'I can't afford to pay
Any fixed wages, though I wish I could.'
'Someone else can.' 'Then someone else will have to.'
I shouldn't mind his bettering himself
If that was what it was. You can be certain,
When he begins like that, there's someone at him
Trying to coax him off with pocket money—
In haying time, when any help is scarce.
In winter he comes back to us. I'm done."   30

"Sh! not so loud: he'll hear you," Mary said.

"I want him to: he'll have to soon or late."

"He's worn out. He's asleep beside the stove.
When I came up from Rowe's I found him here,
Huddled against the barn door fast asleep,
A miserable sight, and frightening, too—
You needn't smile—I didn't recognize him—

I wasn't looking for him—and he's changed.
Wait till you see."

        "Where did you say he'd been?"

"He didn't say. I dragged him to the house,   40
And gave him tea and tried to make him smoke.
I tried to make him talk about his travels.
Nothing would do: he just kept nodding off."

"What did he say? Did he say anything?"

"But little."

        "Anything? Mary, confess
He said he'd come to ditch the meadow for me."

"Warren!"

        "But did he? I just want to know."

"Of course he did. What would you have him say?
Surely you wouldn't grudge the poor old man
Some humble way to save his self-respect.   50
He added, if you really care to know,
He meant to clear the upper pasture, too.
That sounds like something you have heard before?
Warren, I wish you could have heard the way
He jumbled everything. I stopped to look
Two or three times—he made me feel so queer—
To see if he was talking in his sleep.
He ran on Harold Wilson—you remember—
The boy you had in haying four years since.
He's finished school, and teaching in his college.   60
Silas declares you'll have to get him back.
He says they two will make a team for work:
Between them they will lay this farm as smooth!
The way he mixed that in with other things.
He thinks young Wilson a likely lad, though daft
On education—you know how they fought
All through July under the blazing sun,
Silas up on the cart to build the load,
Harold along beside to pitch it on."

"Yes, I took care to keep well out of earshot."   70

"Well, those days trouble Silas like a dream.
You wouldn't think they would. How some things linger!
Harold's young college-boy's assurance piqued him.
After so many years he still keeps finding
Good arguments he sees he might have used.
I sympathize. I know just how it feels
To think of the right thing to say too late.
Harold's associated in his mind with Latin.
He asked me what I thought of Harold's saying
He studied Latin, like the violin,   80
Because he liked it—that an argument!
He said he couldn't make the boy believe
He could find water with a hazel prong—
Which showed how much good school had ever done him.
He wanted to go over that. But most of all
He thinks if he could have another chance
To teach him how to build a load of hay—"

"I know, that's Silas' one accomplishment.
He bundles every forkful in its place,
And tags and numbers it for future reference,   90
So he can find and easily dislodge it
In the unloading. Silas does that well.
He takes it out in bunches like big birds' nests.
You never see him standing on the hay
He's trying to lift, straining to lift himself."

"He thinks if he could teach him that, he'd be
Some good perhaps to someone in the world.
He hates to see a boy the fool of books.
Poor Silas, so concerned for other folk,
And nothing to look backward to with pride,   100
And nothing to look forward to with hope,
So now and never any different."

Part of a moon was falling down the west,
Dragging the whole sky with it to the hills.
Its light poured softly in her lap. She saw it
And spread her apron to it. She put out her hand
Among the harplike morning-glory strings,
Taut with the dew from garden bed to eaves,
As if she played unheard some tenderness
That wrought on him beside her in the night.   110
"Warren," she said, "he has come home to die:
You needn't be afraid he'll leave you this time."
"Home," he mocked gently.

"Yes, what else but home?
It all depends on what you mean by home.
Of course he's nothing to us, any more
Than was the hound that came a stranger to us
Out of the woods, worn out upon the trail."

"Home is the place where, when you have to go there,
They have to take you in."

             "I should have called it
Something you somehow haven't to deserve."   120

Warren leaned out and took a step or two,
Picked up a little stick, and brought it back
And broke it in his hand and tossed it by.
'Silas has better claim on us you think
Than on his brother? Thirteen little miles
As the road winds would bring him to his door.
Silas has walked that far no doubt today.
Why didn't he go there? His brother's rich,
A somebody—director in the bank.'

"He never told us that."

             "We know it though."   130

"I think his brother ought to help, of course.
I'll see to that if there is need. He ought of right
To take him in, and might be willing to—
He may be better than appearances.
But have some pity on Silas. Do you think
If he had any pride in claiming kin
Or anything he looked for from his brother,
He'd keep so still about him all this time?"

"I wonder what's between them."

             "I can tell you.
Silas is what he is—we wouldn't mind him—   140
But just the kind that kinsfolk can't abide.
He never did a thing so very bad.
He don't know why he isn't quite as good
As anybody. Worthless though he is,
He won't be made ashamed to please his brother."

"*I* can't think Si ever hurt any one."

"No, but he hurt my heart the way he lay
And rolled his old head on that sharp-edged chair-back.
He wouldn't let me put him on the lounge.
You must go in and see what you can do.   150
I made the bed up for him there tonight.
You'll be surprised at him—how much he's broken.
His working days are done; I'm sure of it."

"I'd not be in a hurry to say that."

"I haven't been. Go, look, see for yourself.
But, Warren, please remember how it is:
He's come to help you ditch the meadow.
He has a plan. You mustn't laugh at him.
He may not speak of it, and then he may.
I'll sit and see if that small sailing cloud   160
Will hit or miss the moon."

                    It hit the moon.
Then there were three there, making a dim row,
The moon, the little silver cloud, and she.

Warren returned—too soon, it seemed to her,
Slipped to her side, caught up her hand and waited.

"Warren?" she questioned.

                    "Dead," was all he answered.

*Bonny Barbara Allan

Anonymous

It was in and about the Martinmas time,
    When the green leaves were a falling,
That Sir John Graeme, in the West Country,
    Fell in love with Barbara Allan.

He sent his man down through the town,
    To the place where she was dwelling:
"O haste and come to my master dear,
    Gin ye be Barbara Allan."

---

l. 1. Martinmas: November 11.
l. 8. gin: If.

O hooly, hooly rose she up,
   To the place where he was lying,
And when she drew the curtain by,
   "Young man, I think you're dying."   10

"O it's I'm sick, and very, very sick,
   And 't is a' for Barbara Allan:"
"O the better for me ye 's never be,
   Tho your heart's blood were a spilling.

"O dinna ye mind, young man," said she,
   "When ye was in the tavern a drinking,
That ye made the healths gae round and round,
   And slighted Barbara Allan?"   20

He turned his face unto the wall,
   And death was with him dealing:
"Adieu, adieu, my dear friends all,
   And be kind to Barbara Allan."

And slowly, slowly raise she up,
   And slowly, slowly left him,
And sighing said, she could not stay,
   Since death of life had reft him.

She had not gane a mile but twa,
   When she heard the dead-bell ringing,   30
And every jow that the dead-bell geid,
   It cry'd, Woe to Barbara Allan!

"O Mother, mother, make my bed!
   O make it saft and narrow!
Since my love died for me to-day,
   I'll die for him to-morrow."

---

l. 9. hooly: Slowly.
l. 31. jow: Stroke. geid: gave.

Marie Hamilton

Anonymous

Word's gane to the kitchen,
   And word's gane to the ha,
That Marie Hamilton gangs wi bairn
   To the hichest Stewart of a'.

He's courted her in the kitchen,
   He's courted her in the ha,
He's courted her in the laigh cellar,
   And that was warst of a'.

She's tyed it in her apron
   And she's thrown it in the sea;   10
Says, "Sink ye, swim ye, bonny wee babe!
   You'l neer get mair o me."

Down then cam the auld queen,
   Goud tassels tying her hair:
"O Marie, where's the bonny wee babe
   That I heard greet sae sair?"

"There was never a babe intill my room,
   As little designs to be;
It was but a touch o my sair side,
   Come oer my fair bodie."   20

"O Marie, put on your robes o black,
   Or else your robes o brown,
For ye maun gang wi me the night,
   To see fair Edinbro town."

"I winna put on my robes o black,
   Nor yet my robes o brown;
But I'll put on my robes o white,
   To shine through Edinbro town."

---

l. 3. gangs wi bairn: Is pregnant.
l. 4. The Stewarts were the royal family of Scotland.
l. 7. laigh: Low.
l. 14. goud: Gold.
l. 16. greet: Weep.

When she gaed up the Cannogate,
  She laughed loud laughters three;
But whan she cam down the Cannogate
  The tear blinded her ee.

When she gaed up the Parliament stair,
  The heel cam aff her shee;
And lang or she cam down again
  She was condemned to dee.

When she cam down the Cannogate,
  The Cannogate sae free,
Many a ladie lookd oer her window,
  Weeping for this ladie.

"Ye need nae weep for me," she says,
  "Ye need nae weep for me;
For had I not slain mine own sweet babe,
  This death I wadna dee.

"Bring me a bottle of wine," she says,
  "The best that eer ye hae,
That I may drink to my weil-wishers,
  And they may drink to me.

"Here's a health to the jolly sailors,
  That sail upon the main;
Let them never let on to my father and mother
  But what I'm coming hame.

"Here's a health to the jolly sailors,
  That sail upon the sea;
Let them never let on to my father and mother
  That I cam here to dee.

"Oh little did my mother think,
  The day she cradled me,
What lands I was to travel through,
  What death I was to dee.

"Oh little did my father think,
  The day he held up me,
What lands I was to travel though,
  What death I was to dee.

30

40

50

60

---

l. 29. Cannogate: Street leading from the palace to the Parliament House.

"Last night I washd the queens feet,
    And gently laid her down;
And a' the thanks I've gotten the nicht
    To be hangd in Edinbro town!

"Last nicht there was four Maries,
    The nicht there'll be but three;   70
There was Marie Seton, and Marie Beton,
    And Marie Carmichael, and me."

Johnie Armstrong

Anonymous

There dwelt a man in faire Westmerland,
    Ionnë Armestrong men did him call,
He had nither lands nor rents coming in,
    Yet he kept eight score men in his hall.

He had horse and harness for them all,
    Goodly steeds were all milke-white;
O the golden bands an about their necks
    And their weapons, they were all alike.

Newes then was brought unto the king
    That there was sicke a won as hee,   10
That livëd lyke a bold out-law,
    And robbëd all the north country.

The king he writt an a letter then,
    A letter which was large and long;
He signëd it with his owne hand,
    And he promised to doe him no wrong.

When this letter came Ionnë untill,
    His heart it was as bylthe as birds on the tree:
"Never was I sent for before any king,
    My father, my grandfather, nor none but mee.   20

"And if wee goe the king before,
    I would we went most orderly;
Every man of you shall have his scarlet cloak,
    Laced with silver laces three.

I. 10. sicke: Such.

"Every won of you shall have his velvett coat,
    Laced with sillver lace so white;
O the golden bands an about your necks,
    Black hatts, white feathers, all alyke."

By the morrow morninge at ten of the clock,
    Towards Edenburough gon was hee,   30
And with him all his eight score men;
    Good lord, it was a goodly sight for to see!

When Ionnë came befower the king,
    He fell downe on his knee;
"O pardon, my soveraine leige," he said,
    "O pardon my eight score men and mee!"

"Thou shalt have no pardon, thou traytor strong,
    For thy eight score men nor thee;
For to-morrow morning by ten of the clock,
    Both thou and them shall hang on the gallow-tree."   40

But Ionnë looked over his left shoulder,
    Good Lord, what a grevious look looked hee!
Saying, "Asking grace of a graceles face—
    Why there is none for you nor me."

But Ionnë had a bright sword by his side,
    And it was made of the mettle so free,
That had not the king stept his foot aside,
    He had smitten his head from his faire boddë.

Saying, "Fight on, my merry men all,
    And see that none of you be taine;   50
For rather than men shall say we were hanged,
    Let them report how we were slaine."

Then, God wott, faire Eddenburrough rose,
    And so besett poore Ionnë rounde,
That fowerscore and tenn of Ionnës best men
    Lay gasping all upon the ground.

Then like a mad man Ionnë laide about,
    And like a mad man then fought hee,
Untill a falce Scot came Ionnë behinde,
    And runn him through the faire boddee.   60

Saying, "Fight on, my merry men all,
    And see that none of you be taine;
For I will stand by and bleed but awhile,
    And then will I come and fight againe."

Newes then was brought to young Ionnë Armestrong,
    As he stood by his nurses knee.
Who vowed if ere he lived for to be a man,
    O the treacherous Scots revengd hee 'd be.

Sir Patrick Spence

Anonymous

The king sits in Dumferling toune,
    Drinking the blude-reid wine:
"O whar will I get guid sailor,
    To sail this schip of mine?"

Up and spak an eldern knicht,
    Sat at the kings richt kne:
"Sir Patrick Spence is the best sailor,
    That sails upon the se."

The king has written a braid letter,
    And signd it wi his hand,   10
And sent it to Sir Patrick Spence,
    Was walking on the sand.

The first line that Sir Patrick red,
    A loud lauch lauchèd he;
The next line that Sir Patrick red,
    The teir blinded his ee.

"O wha is this has don this deid,
    This ill deid don to me,
To send me out this time o' the yeir,
    To sail upon the se!   20

l. 9. braid: Broad.
l. 14. lauch: Laugh.

"Mak hast, mak haste, my mirry men all,
   Our guid schip sails the morne."
"O say na sae, my master deir,
   For I feir a deadlie storme.

"Late late yestreen I saw the new moone,
   Wi the auld moone in hir arme,
And I feir, I feir, my deir master,
   That we will cum to harme."

O our Scots nobles wer richt laith
   To weet their cork-heild schoone;   30
Bot lang owre a' the play wer playd,
   Their hats they swam aboone.

O lang, lang may their ladies sit,
   Wi thair fans into their hand,
Or eir they se Sir Patrick Spence
   Cum sailing to the land.

O lang, lang may the ladies stand,
   Wi thair gold kems in their hair,
Waiting for thair ain deir lords,
   For they 'll se thame na mair.   40

Haf owre, haf owre to Aberdour,
   It's fiftie fadom deip,
And thair lies guid Sir Patrick Spence,
Wi the Scots lords at his feit.

---

l. 29. laith: Loath.
l. 32. aboone: Above.

The Twa Corbies

Anonymous

As I was walking all alane,
I herd twa corbies making a mane;
The tane unto the t' other say,
"Where sall we gang and dine to-day?"

"In behint yon auld fail dyke,
I wot there lies a new slain knight;
And naebody kens that he lies there,
But his hawk, his hound, and lady fair.

"His hound is to the hunting gane,
His hawk to fetch the wild-fowl hame,   10
His lady's ta'en another mate,
So we may mak our dinner sweet.

"Ye'll sit on his white hause-bane,
And I'll pike out his bonny blue een;
Wi ae lock o his gowden hair
We'll theek our nest when it grows bare.

"Mony a one for him makes mane,
But nane sall ken where he is gane;
Oer his white banes when they are bare,
The wind sall blaw for evermair."   20

---

l. 2. corbies: Ravens or crows. mane: Moan, lament.
l. 5. fail: Turf.
l. 7. kens: Knows.
l. 13. hause-bane: Neck bone.
l. 16. theek: Thatch.

[*Back and side go bare, go bare*]

[from *GAMMER GURTON'S NEEDLE*]

Anonymous, Sixteenth Century

Back and side go bare, go bare,
  Both foot and hand go cold;
But, belly, God send thee good ale enough,
  Whether it be new or old.

I cannot eat but little meat,
   My stomach is not good;
But sure I think that I can drink
   With him that wears a hood.
Though I go bare, take ye no care,
   I am nothing a-cold;   10
I stuff my skin so full within
   Of jolly good ale and old.

   Back and side go bare, go bare, etc.

I love no roast but a nutbrown toast,
   And a crab laid in the fire;
A little bread shall do me stead,
   Much bread I not desire.
No frost nor snow, no wind, I trow,
   Can hurt me if I would,
I am so wrapt, and throughly lapt   20
   Of jolly good ale and old.

   Back and side go bare, go bare, etc.

And Tib my wife, that as her life
   Loveth well good ale to seek,
Full oft drinks she, till ye may see
   The tears run down her cheek.
Then doth she troll to me the bowl,
   Even as a maltworm should;
And saith, "Sweetheart, I took my part
   Of this jolly good ale and old."   30

   Back and side go bare, go bare, etc.

Now let them drink, till they nod and wink,
   Even as good fellows should do;
They shall not miss to have the bliss
   Good ale doth bring men to.
And all poor souls that have scourèd bowls,
   Or have them lustily trolled,
God save the lives of them and their wives,
   Whether they be young or old.

   Back and side go bare, go bare, etc.   40

---

l. 8. him that wears a hood: A friar.
l. 14. nutbrown toast: Toast soaked in ale.
l. 15. crab: Crab apple.
l. 27. troll: Pass around.
l. 28. maltworm: Drunkard.
l. 36. scoured: Emptied.

Proud Maisie

[from THE HEART OF MIDLOTHIAN]

SIR WALTER SCOTT

Proud Maisie is in the wood,
  Walking so early;
Sweet Robin sits on the bush,
  Singing so rarely.

"Tell me, thou bonny bird,
  When shall I marry me?"—
"When six braw gentlemen
  Kirkward shall carry ye."

"Who makes the bridal bed,
  Birdie, say truly?"—
"The grey-headed sexton
  That delves the grave duly.   10

"The glow-worm o'er grave and stone
  Shall light thee steady.
The owl from the steeple sing,
  'Welcome, proud lady.' "

---

l. 7. braw: Fine.

*The Ballad of Late Annie

GWENDOLYN BROOKS

Late Annie in her bower lay,
Though sun was up and spinning.
The blush-brown shoulder was so bare,
Blush-brown lip was winning.

Out then shrieked the mother-dear,
"Be I to fetch and carry?
Get a broom to whish the doors
Or get a man to marry."

"Men there were and men there be
But never men so many   10
Chief enough to marry me,"
Thought the proud late Annie.

"Whom I raise shades before
Must be gist and lacquer.
With melted opals for my milk,
Pearl-leaf for my cracker."

*Slim in Hell

STERLING A. BROWN

1

Slim Greer went to heaven;
    St. Peter said, "Slim,
You been a right good boy."
    An' he winked at him.

        "You been a travelin' rascal
            In yo' day.
        You kin roam once mo';
            Den you comes to stay.

"Put dese wings on yo' shoulders,
    An' save yo' feet."   10
Slim grin, and he speak up,
    "Thankye, Pete."

        Den Peter say, "Go
            To Hell an' see,
        All dat is doing, and
            Report to me.

"Be sure to remember
    How everything go."
Slim say, "I be seein' yuh
    On de late watch, bo."   20

        Slim got to cavortin'
            Swell as you choose
        Like Lindy in de Spirit
            Of St. Louis Blues.

He flew an' he flew,
　　Till at last he hit
A hangar wid de sign readin'
　　DIS IS IT.

　　　　Den he parked his wings
　　　　　An' strolled aroun',　　　　　　　　　　30
　　　　Gittin' used to his feet
　　　　　On de solid ground.

2

Big bloodhound came aroarin'
　　Like Niagry Falls,
Sicked on by white devils
　　In overhalls.

Now Slim warn't scared,
　　Cross my heart, it's a fac',
An de dog went on a bayin'
　　Some po' devil's track.　　　　　　　　　　　40

　　　　Den Slim saw a mansion
　　　　　An' walked right in;
　　　　De Devil looked up
　　　　　Wid a sickly grin.

"Suttinly didn't look
　　Fo' you, Mr. Greer,
How it happens you comes
　　To visit here?"

　　　　Slim say—"Oh, jes' thought
　　　　　I'd drap by a spell."　　　　　　　　　50
　　　　"Feel at home, seh, an' here's
　　　　　De keys to hell."

Den he took Slim around
　　An' showed him people
Raisin' hell as high as
　　De First Church Steeple.

　　　　Lots of folks fightin'
　　　　　At de roulette wheel,
　　　　Like old Rampart Street,
　　　　　Or leastwise Beale.　　　　　　　　　60

Showed him bawdy houses
    An' cabarets,
Slim thought of New Orleans
    An Memphis days.

        Each devil was busy
            Wid a devilish broad,
        An' Slim cried, "Lawdy,
            Lawd, Lawd, Lawd."

Took him in a room
    Where Slim see   70
De preacher wid a brownskin
    On each knee.

        Showed him giant stills,
            Going everywhere,
        Wid a passel of devils
            Stretched dead drunk there.

Den he took him to de furnace
    Dat some devils was firing,
Hot as hell, an' Slim start
    A mean presspirin'.   80

        White devils wid pitchforks
            Threw black devils on,
        Slim thought he'd better
            Be gittin' along.

An' he say—"Dis makes
    Me think of home—
Vicksburg, Little Rock, Jackson,
    Waco and Rome."

        Den de devil gave Slim
            De big Ha-Ha;   90
        An' turned into a cracker,
            Wid a sherriff's star.

Slim ran fo' his wings,
    Lit out from de groun'
Hauled it back to St. Peter,
    Safety boun'.

---

l. 91. cracker: Southern "poor white."

3

St. Peter said, "Well,
    You got back quick.
How's de devil? An' what's
    His latest trick?"   100

An' Slim say, "Peter,
    I really cain't tell,
The place was Dixie
    That I took for hell."

Then Peter say, "You must
    Be crazy, I vow,
Where'n hell dja think Hell *was,*
    Anyhow?

"Git on back to de yearth,
    Cause I got de fear,   110
You'se a leetle too dumb,
    Fo' to stay up here . . ."

*[O What is that Sound]

W. H. AUDEN

O what is that sound which so thrills the ear
    Down in the valley drumming, drumming?
Only the scarlet soldiers, dear,
    The soldiers coming.

O what is that light I see flashing so clear
    Over the distance brightly, brightly?
Only the sun on their weapons, dear,
    As they step lightly.

O what are they doing with all that gear,
    What are they doing this morning, this morning?   10
Only their usual manoeuvres, dear,
    Or perhaps a warning.

O why have they left the road down there,
    Why are they suddenly wheeling, wheeling?
Perhaps a change in their orders, dear.
    Why are you kneeling?

O haven't they stopped for the doctor's care,
   Haven't they reined their horses, their horses?
Why, they are none of them wounded, dear,
   None of these forces.   20

O is it the parson they want, with white hair,
   Is it the parson, is it, is it?
No, they are passing his gateway, dear,
   Without a visit.

O it must be the farmer who lives so near.
   It must be the farmer so cunning, so cunning?
They have passed the farmyard already, dear,
   And now they are running.

O where are you going? Stay with me here!
   Were the vows you swore deceiving, deceiving?   30
No, I promised to love you, dear,
   But I must be leaving.

O it's broken the lock and splintered the door,
   O it's the gate where they're turning, turning;
Their boots are heavy on the floor
   And their eyes are burning.

*The Castaway

WILLIAM COWPER

Obscurest night involv'd the sky,
   Th' Atlantic billows roar'd,
When such a destin'd wretch as I,
   Wash'd headlong from on board,
Of friends, of hope, of all bereft,
His floating home for ever left.

No braver chief could Albion boast
   Than he with whom he went,
Nor ever ship left Albion's coast,
   With warmer wishes sent.   10
He lov'd them both, but both in vain,
Nor him beheld, nor her again.

Not long beneath the whelming brine,
    Expert to swim, he lay;
Nor soon he felt his strength decline,
    Or courage die away;
But wag'd with death a lasting strife,
Supported by despair of life.

He shouted: nor his friends had failed
    To check the vessel's course,   20
But so the furious blast prevail'd,
    That, pitiless perforce,
They left their outcast mate behind,
And scudded still before the wind.

Some succor yet they could afford;
    And, such as storms allow,
The cask, the coop, the floated cord,
    Delay'd not to bestow,
But he (they knew) nor ship, nor shore,
Whate'er they gave, should visit more.   30

Nor, cruel as it seem'd, could he
    Their haste himself condemn,
Aware that flight, in such a sea,
    Alone could rescue them;
Yet bitter felt it still to die
Deserted, and his friends so nigh.

He long survives, who lives an hour
    In ocean, self-upheld;
And so long he, with unspent pow'r,
    His destiny repell'd;   40
And ever, as the minutes flew,
Entreated help, or cried—Adieu!

At length, his transient respite past,
    His comrades, who before
Had heard his voice in ev'ry blast,
    Could catch the sound no more.
For then, by toil subdued, he drank
The stifling wave, and then he sank.

No poet wept him; but the page
    Of narrative sincere,   50
That tells his name, his worth, his age,
    Is wet with Anson's tear.
And tears by bards or heroes shed
Alike immortalize the dead.

I therefore purpose not, or dream,
   Descanting on his fate,
To give the melancholy theme
   A more enduring date:
But misery still delights to trace
Its 'semblance in another's case.   60

No voice divine the storm allay'd,
   No light propitious shone;
When, snatch'd from all effectual aid,
   We perish'd, each alone:
But I beneath a rougher sea,
And whelm'd in deeper gulphs than he.

*The Host of the Air

WILLIAM BUTLER YEATS

O'Driscoll drove with a song
The wild duck and the drake
From the tall and the tufted reeds
Of the drear Hart Lake.

And he saw how the reeds grew dark
At the coming of night-tide,
And dreamed of the long dim hair
Of Bridget his bride.

He heard while he sang and dreamed
A piper piping away,   10
And never was piping so sad,
And never was piping so gay.

And he saw young men and young girls
Who danced on a level place,
And Bridget his bride among them,
With a sad and a gay face.

The dancers crowded about him.
And many a sweet thing said,
And a young man brought him red wine
And a young girl white bread.   20

But Bridget drew him by the sleeve,
Away from the merry bands,
To old men playing at cards
With a twinkling of ancient hands.

The bread and the wine had a doom,
For these were the host of the air;
He sat and played in a dream
Of her long dim hair.

He played with the merry old men
And thought not of evil chance,   30
Until one bore Bridget his bride
Away from the merry dance.

He bore her away in his arms,
The handsomest young man there,
And his neck and his breast and his arms
Were drowned in her long dim hair.

O'Driscoll scattered the cards
And out of his dream awoke:
Old men and young men and young girls
Were gone like a drifting smoke;   40

But he heard high up in the air
A piper piping away,
And never was piping so sad,
And never was piping so gay.

The Three Beggars

WILLIAM BUTLER YEATS

"Though to my feathers in the wet,
I have stood here from break of day,
I have not found a thing to eat,
For only rubbish comes my way.
Am I to live on lebeen-lone?"
Muttered the old crane of Gort.
"For all my pains on lebeen-lone?"

l. 5. *lebeen*: Minnows.
l. 6. *Gort*: A village in Galway, Ireland.

King Guaire walked amid his court
The palace-yard and river-side
And there to three old beggars said,   10
"You that have wandered far and wide
Can ravel out what's in my head.
Do men who least desire get most,
Or get the most who most desire?"
A beggar said, "They get the most
Whom man or devil cannot tire,
And what could make their muscles taut
Unless desire had made them so?"
But Guaire laughed with secret thought,
"If that be true as it seems true,   20
One of you three is a rich man,
For he shall have a thousand pounds
Who is first asleep, if but he can
Sleep before the third noon sounds."
And thereon, merry as a bird
With his old thoughts, King Guaire went
From river-side and palace-yard
And left them to their argument.
"And if I win," one beggar said,
"Though I am old I shall persuade   30
A pretty girl to share my bed";
The second: "I shall learn a trade";
The third: "I'll hurry to the course
Among the other gentlemen,
And lay it all upon a horse";
The second: "I have thought again:
A farmer has more dignity."
One to another sighed and cried:
The exorbitant dreams of beggary,
That idleness had borne to pride,   40
Sang through their teeth from noon to noon;
And when the second twilight brought
The frenzy of the beggars' moon
None closed his blood-shot eyes but sought
To keep his fellows from their sleep;
All shouted till their anger grew
And they were whirling in a heap.

They mauled and bit the whole night through;
They mauled and bit till the day shone;
They mauled and bit through all that day   50
And till another night had gone,
Or if they made a moment's stay
They sat upon their heels to rail,

And when old Guaire came and stood
Before the three to end this tale,
They were commingling lice and blood.
"Time's up," he cried, and all the three
With blood-shot eyes upon him stared.
"Time's up," he cried, and all the three
Fell down upon the dust and snored.   60

"Maybe I shall be lucky yet,
Now they are silent," said the crane.
"Though to my feathers in the wet
I've stood as I were made of stone
And seen the rubbish run about,
It's certain there are trout somewhere
And maybe I shall take a trout
If but I do not seem to care."

Techniques

IMAGE, PATTERN, AND RHYTHM

The way in which a thing is said greatly affects both its meaning and the effective communication of that meaning. For in poetry the means and the end are inseparable; some would say even that the means and end are one and the same. In this section are grouped a few poems notable for their imagery, pattern, and rhythm. Obviously, examples equally good will be found elsewhere, and the reader who is developing an awareness of the values of poetry will be alert to their presence in other poems and to their function as means or ends wherever they occur.

Occasionally the force of a poem may depend almost entirely on the effect of a single image (or two or three related or contrasted images) presented in vivid and concentrated language. The first five poems in the group may be considered in this light. Imagery, however, may also be a formal unifying feature in longer poems, where it creates a pattern, somewhat analogous to recurring phrases in music or repeated colors and forms in a patterned rug. For a pattern of this sort, few poems exhibit greater skill than Housman's "To an Athlete Dying Young." Other instances occur in "Colonel Fantock" and H.D.'s "Lethe," where not only the pattern of imagery but even that of repetitive syntax is essential in establishing the meaning and mood.

Assonance and alliteration also (see Glossary, p. 639), along with rhyme, frequently have a structural function in unifying the poem. For these, "Kubla Khan" and Hopkins's "Fragment" provide two examples out of many that will be found elsewhere.

Again, rhythm, already discussed in the introductory remarks, is an equally important element in verse. Until the present century, nearly all English poems were composed in a rhythmic accentual-syllabic verse arranged according to established patterns on a fairly strict system (the poet, however, was always at liberty to vary it in many ways).

429

As these metrical patterns are somewhat technical, they have been set forth briefly in a separate section, which may profitably be taken up at this time (see "Versification," pp. 638–639). Since about 1910 or 1915, however, a good deal of writing has been done in "free verse," which has a looser rhythm for which no generally agreed principles have been formulated. The first three poems here employ free verse, as do many among the modern poems in "Recent Modes" (pages 613–637). The best means of becoming aware of the rhythm in these poems is by reading them aloud, trying to give full value to the natural rising and falling inflections of the voice and to the pauses both within and at the ends of lines. Important modern poetry has been written in both free and conventional verse, often with each influencing the other.

Fog

CARL SANDBURG

The fog comes
on little cat feet.

It sits looking
over harbor and city
on silent haunches
and then moves on.

Autumn

T. E. HULME

A touch of cold in the Autumn night—
I walked abroad,
And saw the ruddy moon lean over a hedge
Like a red-faced farmer,
I did not stop to speak, but nodded,
And round about were the wistful stars
With white faces like town children.

The Embankment

(The fantasia of a fallen gentleman on a cold, bitter night)

T. E. HULME

Once, in finesse of fiddles found I ecstasy,
In the flash of gold heels on the hard pavement.
Now see I
That warmth's the very stuff of poesy.
Oh, God, make small
The old star-eaten blanket of the sky,
That I may fold it round me and in comfort lie.

Title: The embankment along the River Thames in London.

The Balloon of the Mind

WILLIAM BUTLER YEATS

Hands, do what you're bid:
Bring the balloon of the mind
That bellies and drags in the wind
Into its narrow shed.

*[fragment]

GERARD MANLEY HOPKINS

Strike, churl; hurl, cheerless wind, then; heltering hail
May's beauty massacre and wispèd wild clouds grow
Out on the giant air; tell Summer No,
Bid joy back, have at the harvest, keep Hope pale.

*To an Athlete Dying Young

A. E. HOUSMAN

The time you won your town the race
We chaired you through the market-place;
Man and boy stood cheering by,
And home we brought you shoulder-high.

Today, the road all runners come,
Shoulder-high we bring you home,
And set you at your threshold down,
Townsman of a stiller town.

Smart lad, to slip betimes away
From fields where glory does not stay   10
And early though the laurel grows
It withers quicker than the rose.

Eyes the shady night has shut
Cannot see the record cut,
And silence sounds no worse than cheers
After earth has stopped the ears:

Now you will not swell the rout
Of lads that wore their honors out,
Runners whom renown outran
And the name died before the man.   20

So set, before its echoes fade,
The fleet foot on the sill of shade,
And hold to the low lintel up
The still-defended challenge-cup.

And round that early-laureled head
Will flock to gaze the strengthless dead,
And find unwithered on its curls
The garland briefer than a girl's.

*Lethe

H. D. (HILDA DOOLITTLE)

Nor skin hide nor fleece
    Shall cover you,
Nor curtain of crimson nor fine
Shelter of cedar-wood be over you,
    Nor the fir-tree
    Nor the pine.

Nor sight of whin nor gorse
    Nor river-yew,
Nor fragrance of flowering bush,
Nor wailing of reed-bird to waken you,   10
    Nor of linnet,
    Nor of thrush.

Nor word nor touch nor sight
    Of lover, you
Shall long through the night but for this:
The roll of the full tide to cover you
    Without question,
    Without kiss.

*a pretty a day

e. e. cummings

a pretty a day
(and every fades)
is here and away
(but born are maids
to flower an hour
in all,all)

o yes to flower
until so blithe
a doer a wooer
some limber and lithe   10
some very fine mower
a tall;tall

some jerry so very
(and nellie and fan)
some handsomest harry
(and sally and nan
they tremble and cower
so pale:pale)

for betty was born
to never say nay   20
but lucy could learn
and lily could pray
and fewer were shyer
than doll.   doll

Question

MAY SWENSON

Body my house
my horse my hound
what will I do
when you are fallen

Where will I sleep
How will I ride
What will I hunt

Where can I go
without my mount
all eager and quick   10
How will I know

in thicket ahead
is danger or treasure
when Body my good
bright dog is dead

How will it be
To lie in the sky
without roof or door
and wind for an eye

With cloud for shift   20
How will I hide?

---

l. 20. shift: Chemise, a woman's loose one-piece undergarment or dress.

*Kubla Khan

SAMUEL TAYLOR COLERIDGE

In Xanadu did Kubla Khan
A stately pleasure-dome decree:
Where Alph, the sacred river, ran
Through caverns measureless to man
   Down to a sunless sea.
So twice five miles of fertile ground
With walls and towers were girdled round:
And there were gardens bright with sinuous rills,
Where blossomed many an incense-bearing tree;
And here were forests ancient as the hills,   10
Enfolding sunny spots of greenery.

But oh! that deep romantic chasm which slanted
Down the green hill athwart a cedarn cover!
A savage place! as holy and enchanted
As e'er beneath a waning moon was haunted
By woman wailing for her demon-lover!
And from this chasm, with ceaseless turmoil seething,
As if this earth in fast thick pants were breathing,
A mighty fountain momently was forced:
Amid whose swift half-intermitted burst   20
Huge fragments vaulted like rebounding hail,
Or chaffy grain beneath the thresher's flail:
And 'mid these dancing rocks at once and ever
It flung up momently the sacred river.
Five miles meandering with a mazy motion
Through wood and dale the sacred river ran,
Then reached the caverns measureless to man,
And sank in tumult to a lifeless ocean:
And 'mid this tumult Kubla heard from far
Ancestral voices prophesying war!   30
   The shadow of the dome of pleasure
   Floated midway on the waves;
   Where was heard the mingled measure
   From the fountain and the caves.
It was a miracle of rare device,
A sunny pleasure-dome with caves of ice!

   A damsel with a dulcimer
   In a vision once I saw:
   It was an Abyssinian maid,
   And on her dulcimer she played,   40

Singing of Mount Abora.
Could I revive within me
Her symphony and song,
To such a deep delight 'twould win me,
That with music loud and long,
I would build that dome in air,
That sunny dome! those caves of ice!
And all who heard should see them there,
And all should cry, Beware! Beware!
His flashing eyes, his floating hair!   50
Weave a circle round him thrice,
And close your eyes with holy dread,
For he on honey-dew hath fed,
And drunk the milk of Paradise.

*Birds at Winter Nightfall

TRIOLET

THOMAS HARDY

Around the house the flakes fly faster,
And all the berries now are gone
From holly and cotonea-aster
Around the house. The flakes fly!—faster
Shutting indoors that crumb-outcaster
We used to see upon the lawn
Around the house. The flakes fly faster,
And all the berries now are gone!

*Triolet

ROBERT BRIDGES

When first we met we did not guess
That Love would prove so hard a master;
Of more than common friendliness
When first we met we did not guess.
Who could foretell this sore distress,
This irretrievable disaster
When first we met?—We did not guess
That Love would prove so hard a master.

*Colonel Fantock

(to Osbert and Sacheverell)

EDITH SITWELL

Thus spoke the lady underneath the trees:
I was a member of a family
Whose legend was of hunting—(all the rare
And unattainable brightness of the air)—
A race whose fabled skill in falconry
Was used on the small songbirds and a winged
And blinded Destiny. . . . I think that only
Winged ones know the highest eyrie is so lonely.
There in a land, austere and elegant,
The castle seemed an arabesque in music;   10
We moved in an hallucination born
Of silence, which like music gave us lotus
To eat, perfuming lips and our long eyelids
As we trailed over the sad summer grass,
Or sat beneath a smooth and mournful tree.

And Time passed, suavely, imperceptibly.

But Dagobert and Peregrine and I
Were children then; we walked like shy gazelles
Among the music of the thin flower-bells.
And life still held some promise—never ask   20
Of what—but life seemed less a stranger then,
Than ever after in this cold existence.
I always was a little outside life—
And so the things we touch could comfort me;
I loved the shy dreams we could hear and see—
For I was like one dead, like a small ghost,
A little cold air wandering and lost.

All day within the straw-roofed arabesque
Of the towered castle and the sleepy gardens wandered
We; those delicate paladins, the waves   30
Told us fantastic legends that we pondered.

And the soft leaves were breasted like a dove,
Crooning old mournful tales of untrue love.

When night came, sounding like the growth of trees,
My great-grandmother bent to say good night,
And the enchanted moonlight seemed transformed

Into the silvery tinkling of an old
And gentle music-box that played a tune
Of Circean enchantments and far seas;
Her voice was lulling like the splash of these.   40
When she had given me her good-night kiss,
There, in her lengthened shadow, I saw this
Old military ghost with May-fly whiskers—
Poor harmless creature, blown by the cold wind,
Boasting of unseen unreal victories
To a harsh unbelieving world unkind:
For all the battles that this warrior fought
Were with cold poverty and helpless age—
His spoils were shelters from the winter's rage.
And so forever through his braggart voice,   50
Through all that martial trumpet's sound, his soul
Wept with a little sound so pitiful,
Knowing that he is outside life forever
With no one that will warm or comfort him. . . .
He is not even dead, but Death's buffoon
On a bare stage, a shrunken pantaloon.
His military banner never fell,
Nor his account of victories, the stories
Of old apocryphal misfortunes, glories
Which comforted his heart in later life   60
When he was the Napoleon of the schoolroom
And all the victories he gained were over
Little boys who would not learn to spell.

All day within the sweet and ancient gardens
He had my childish self for audience—
Whose body flat and strange, whose pale straight hair
Made me appear as though I had been drowned—
(We all have the remote air of a legend)—
And Dagobert my brother, whose large strength,
Great body, and grave beauty still reflect   70
The Angevin dead kings from whom we spring;
And sweet as the young tender winds that stir
In thickets when the earliest flower-bells sing
Upon the boughs was his just character;
And Peregrine the youngest with a naïve
Shy grace like a faun's, whose slant eyes seemed
The warm green light beneath eternal boughs.
His hair was like the fronds of feathers, life
In him was changing ever, springing fresh
As the dark songs of birds . . . the furry warmth   80
And purring sound of fires was in his voice,
Which never failed to warm and comfort me.

And there were haunted summers in Troy Park
When all the stillness budded into leaves;
We listened, like Ophelia drowned in blond
And fluid hair, beneath stag-antlered trees;
Then in the ancient park the country-pleasant
Shadows fell as brown as any pheasant,
And Colonel Fantock seemed like one of these.
Sometimes for comfort in the castle kitchen   90
He drowsed, where with a sweet and velvet lip
The snapdragons within the fire
Of their red summer never tire.
And Colonel Fantock liked our company;
For us he wandered over each old lie,
Changing the flowering hawthorn, full of bees,
Into the silver helm of Hercules,
For us defended Troy from the top stair
Outside the nursery, when the calm full moon
Was like the sound within the growth of trees.   100

But then came one cruel day in deepest June,
When pink flowers seemed a sweet Mozartian tune,
And Colonel Fantock pondered o'er a book.
A gay voice like a honeysuckle nook—
So sweet—said, "It is Colonel Fantock's age
Which makes him babble." . . . Blown by winter's rage,
The poor old man then knew his creeping fate,
The darkening shadow that would take his sight
And hearing; and he thought of his saved pence
Which scarce would rent a grave . . . That youthful voice   110
Was a dark bell which ever clanged "Too late"—
A creeping shadow that would steal from him
Even the little boys who would not spell—
His only prisoners. . . . On that June day
Cold Death had taken his first citadel.

Themes

Insight into poetry can be enriched by observing and comparing different treatments of the same or similar objects. By such comparison we increase our awareness of how much there is to be said on any important subject. We also gain greatly in our power to discriminate fine shades of meaning, feeling, and attitude, and to appreciate the variety of means by which those meanings and feelings are conveyed. The more sharply we perceive the how of a poem, the more fully we feel the distinctive force of its what. The following groups of poems deal in a great variety of ways with seven themes that have been of enduring concern to men and women:

- Love

- Death

- Man, Machine, and Society

- Man and Nature

- Time, Space, and Mutability

- On the Meaning of Life

- Religion

LOVE

*[Who would have thought]

THOMAS HOWELL

Who would have thought that face of thine
   Had been so full of doubleness?
Or else within those crystal eyne
   Had rest so much unstableness?
Thy face so fair, thy look so strange,
Who would have thought so full of change?

---

l. 3. eyne: Eyes.

[Brown is my Love]

Anonymous, 1597

   Brown is my Love, but graceful:
   And each renownëd whiteness
Matched with thy lovely brown loseth its brightness.

   Fair is my Love, but scornful:
   Yet have I seen despisëd
Dainty white lilies, and sad flowers well prizëd.

---

l. 6. sad: Dark, somber.

[O western wind, when wilt thou blow]

Anonymous, Sixteenth Century

O western wind, when wilt thou blow,
That the small rain down can rain?
Christ, if my love were in my arms
And I in my bed again!

[*Thou sleepest fast*]

Anonymous, c. 1550

Thou sleepest fast, and I with woeful heart
  Stand here alone sighing and cannot fly:
Thou sleepest fast, when cruel Love his dart
  On me doth cast, alas, so painfully!
Thou sleepest fast, and I, all full of smart,
  To thee, my foe, in vain do call and cry:
And yet, methinkes, though thou sleepest fast
Thou dreamest still which way my life to wast.

---

l. 8. wast: Waste.

To a Lady to Answer Directly with Yea or Nay

SIR THOMAS WYATT

Madam, withouten many words,
  Once, I am sure, ye will or no:
And if ye will, then leave your bords
  And use your wit and show it so:
And with a beck ye shall me call;
  And if of one, that burneth alway,
Ye have any pity at all.
  Answer him fair with yea, or nay.
If it be yea, I shall be fain;
  If it be nay, friends as before;   10
Ye shall another man obtain,
  And I mine own and yours no more.

---

l. 3. bords: Jests, games.

*The Lover Showeth How He Is Forsaken of Such as He Sometime Enjoyed

SIR THOMAS WYATT

They flee from me, that sometime did me seek
With naked foot, stalking in my chamber.
I have seen them gentle, tame, and meek,
That now are wild, and do not remember
That sometime they put themselves in danger
To take bread at my hand; and now they range
Busily seeking with a continual change.

Thanked be fortune it hath been otherwise
Twenty times better; but once, in special,
In thin array, after a pleasant guise,   10
When her loose gown from her shoulders did fall,
And she me caught in her arms long and small,
Therewith all sweetly did me kiss,
And softly said: "Dear heart, how like you this?"

It was no dream: I lay broad waking
But all is turned, thorough my gentleness,
Into a strange fashion of forsaking;
And I have leave to go of her goodness:
And she also to use newfangleness.
But since that I so kindly am served,   20
I would fain know what she hath deserved.

_____
l. 1. sometime: Formerly.

Song

GEORGE PEELE

Whenas the rye reach to the chin,
And chopcherry, chopcherry ripe within,
Strawberries swimming in the cream,
And schoolboys playing in the stream;
Then oh, then oh, then oh, my true Love said,
Till that time come again
She could not live a maid.

_____
l. 2. chopcherry: A game for the cherry season.

*The Passionate Shepherd to His Love

CHRISTOPHER MARLOWE

Come live with me and be my Love,
And we will all the pleasures prove
That valleys, groves, hills, and fields,
Woods, or steepy mountains yields.

And we will sit upon the rocks
Seeing the shepherds feed their flocks,
By shallow rivers, to whose falls
Melodious birds sing madrigals.

And I will make thee beds of roses,
And a thousand fragrant posies,   10
A cap of flowers, and a kirtle
Embroidered all with leaves of myrtle;

A gown made of the finest wool,
Which from our pretty lambs we pull;
Fair linëd slippers for the cold,
With buckles of the purest gold;

A belt of straw and ivy buds
With coral clasps and amber studs:
And if these pleasures may thee move,
Come live with me, and be my Love.   20

The shepherd swains shall dance and sing
For thy delight each May morning:
If these delights thy mind may move,
Then live with me and be my Love.

---

l. 11. kirtle: Gown.

The Nymph's Reply to the Shepherd

? SIR WALTER RALEGH

If all the world and love were young,
And truth in every shepherd's tongue,
These pretty pleasures might me move
To live with thee and be thy Love.

Time drives the flocks from field to fold,
When rivers rage and rocks grow cold;
And Philomel becometh dumb;
The rest complains of cares to come.

The flowers do fade, and wanton fields
To wayward winter reckoning yields:　　　　　　　　　　　10
A honey tongue, a heart of gall,
Is fancy's spring, but sorrow's fall.

Thy gowns, thy shoes, thy beds of roses,
Thy cap, thy kirtle, and thy posies
Soon break, soon wither, soon forgotten,
In folly ripe, in reason rotten.

Thy belt of straw and ivy buds,
Thy coral clasps and amber studs,
All these in me no means can move
To come to thee and be thy Love.　　　　　　　　　　　20

But could youth last, and love still breed,
Had joys no date, nor age no need,
Then these delights my mind might move
To live with thee and be thy Love.

---

l. 7. Philomel: A name for the nightingale derived from the Greek story of Philomela, Procne, and Tereus.
l. 21. still: Always, constantly.
l. 22. date: Terminal date, termination.

[*Still to be neat*]

BEN JONSON

Still to be neat, still to be drest,
As you were going to a feast;
Still to be powder'd, still perfum'd;—
Lady, it is to be presum'd,
Though art's hid causes are not found.
All is not sweet, all is not sound.

Give me a look, give me a face,
That makes simplicity a grace;
Robes loosely flowing, hair as free:
Such sweet neglect more taketh me　　　　　　　　　　　10
Than all th' adulteries of art;
They strike mine eyes, but not my heart.

*Upon Julia's Clothes

ROBERT HERRICK

When as in silks my *Julia* goes,
Then, then (methinks) how sweetly flowes
That liquefaction of her clothes.

Next, when I cast mine eyes and see
That brave Vibration each way free;
O how that glittering taketh me!

Idolatry

ARNA BONTEMPS

You have been good to me, I give you this:
The arms of lovers empty as our own,
Marble lips sustaining one long kiss
And the hard sound of hammers breaking stone.

For I will build a chapel in the place
Where our love died and I will journey there
To make a sign and kneel before your face
And set an old bell tolling on the air.

[Shall I, wasting in despair]

GEORGE WITHER

Shall I, wasting in despair,
Die, because a woman's fair?
Or make pale my cheeks with care,
'Cause another's rosy are?
Be she fairer than the day,
Or the flowery meads in May!
    If she be not so to me,
    What care I how fair she be?

Should my heart be griev'd, or pin'd,
'Cause I see a woman kind?   10
Or a well disposed nature
Joined with a lovely feature?
Be she meeker, kinder than
Turtle dove, or pelican!
    If she be not so to me,
    What care I how kind she be?

Shall a woman's virtues move
Me to perish for her love?
Or, her well deserving known,
Make me quite forget mine own?   20
Be she with that goodness blest,
Which may gain her, name of best!
    If she be not such to me,
    What care I how good she be?

'Cause her fortune seems too high,
Shall I play the fool, and die?
Those that bear a noble mind,
Where they want of riches find,
Think "What, with them, they would do,
That, without them, dare to woo!"   30
    And unless that mind I see,
    What care I though great she be?

Great, or good, or kind, or fair,
I will ne'er the more despair!
If she love me (this believe!)
I will die, ere she shall grieve!
If she slight me, when I woo,
I can scorn, and let her go!
    For if she be not for me,
    What care I for whom she be?   40

----

l. 14. The female pelican was once believed to feed her young with her own blood.

[*Why so pale and wan, fond lover?*]

SIR JOHN SUCKLING

Why so pale and wan, fond lover?
   Prithee, why so pale?
Will, when looking well can't move her,
   Looking ill prevail?
   Prithee, why so pale?

Why so dull and mute, young sinner?
   Prithee, why so mute?
Will, when speaking well can't win her,
   Saying nothing do 't?
   Prithee, why so mute?   10

Quit, quit, for shame, this will not move:
   This cannot take her.
If of herself she will not love,
   Nothing can make her:
   The devil take her!

To Lucasta, on Going to the Wars

RICHARD LOVELACE

Tell me not, Sweet, I am unkind,
   That from the Nunnery
Of thy chaste breast, and quiet mind,
   To War and Arms I fly.

True; a new Mistress now I chase,
   The first Foe in the Field;
And with a stronger Faith embrace
   A Sword, a Horse, a Shield

Yet this Inconstancy is such,
   As you too shall adore;   10
I could not love thee, Dear, so much,
   Lov'd I not Honour more.

[What shall I do when the Summer troubles]

EMILY DICKINSON

What shall I do when the Summer troubles—
What, when the Rose is ripe—
What when the Eggs fly off in Music
From the Maple Keep?

What shall I do when the Skies a'chirrup
Drop a Tune on me—
When the Bee hangs all Noon in the Buttercup
What will become of me?

Oh, when the Squirrel fills His Pockets
And the Berries stare   10
How can I bear their jocund Faces
Thou from Here, so far?

'Twouldn't afflict a Robin—
All His Goods have Wings—
I—do not fly, so wherefore
My Perennial Things?

[The Soul selects her own Society]

EMILY DICKINSON

The Soul selects her own Society—
Then—shuts the Door—
To her divine Majority—
Present no more—

Unmoved—she notes the Chariots—pausing—
At her low Gate—
Unmoved—an Emperor be kneeling
Upon her Mat—

I've known her—from an ample nation—
Choose One—   10
Then—close the Valves of her attention—
Like Stone—

The River-Merchant's Wife: A Letter

EZRA POUND

While my hair was still cut straight across my forehead
Played I about the front gate, pulling flowers.
You came by on bamboo stilts, playing horse,
You walked about my seat, playing with blue plums.
And we went on living in the village of Chokan:
Two small people, without dislike or suspicion.

At fourteen I married My Lord you.
I never laughed, being bashful.
Lowering my head, I looked at the wall.
Called to, a thousand times, I never looked back.   10

At fifteen I stopped scowling,
I desired my dust to be mingled with yours
Forever and forever and forever.
Why should I climb the look out?

At sixteen you departed.
You went into far Ku-to-yen, by the river of swirling eddies.
And you have been gone five months.
The monkeys make sorrowful noise overhead.
You dragged your feet when you went out.
By the gate now, the moss is grown, the different mosses,   20
Too deep to clear them away!
The leaves fall early this autumn, in wind.
The paired butterflies are already yellow with August
Over the grass in the West garden;
They hurt me. I grow older.
If you are coming down through the narrows of the river Kiang,
Please let me know beforehand,
And I will come out to meet you
          As far as Cho-fu-Sa.

Title: According to Pound, this poem is from the Chinese of Rihaku (eighth century A.D.).

The Old-Marrieds

GWENDOLYN BROOKS

But in the crowding darkness not a word did they say.
Though the pretty-coated birds had piped so lightly all the day.
And he had seen the lovers in the little side streets.
And she had heard the morning stories clogged with sweets.
It was quite a time for loving. It was midnight. It was May.
But in the crowding darkness not a word did they say.

The Lovepet

TED HUGHES

Was it an animal? Was it a bird?
She stroked it. He spoke to it softly.
She made her voice its happy forest.
He brought it out with sugarlump smiles.
Soon it was licking their kisses.

She gave it the strings of her voice, which it swallowed.
He gave it the blood of his face, it grew eager.
She gave it the licorice of her mouth, it began to thrive.
He opened the aniseed of his future
And it bit and gulped, grew vicious, snatched   10
The focus of his eyes.
She gave it the steadiness of her hand.
He gave it the strength of his spine, it ate everything.

It began to cry. What could they give it?
They gave it their calendars, it bolted their diaries.
They gave it their sleep, it gobbled their dreams.
Even while they slept,
It ate their bodyskin and the muscle beneath.
They gave it vows, its teeth clashed its starvation
Through every word they uttered.   20

It found snakes under the floor, it ate them.
It found a spider horror
In their palms and ate it.

They gave it double smiles and blank silence.
It chewed holes in their carpets.
They gave it logic.

It ate the color of their hair.
They gave it every argument that would come.
They gave it shouting and yelling, they meant it.
It ate the faces of their children.   30

They gave it their photograph albums, they gave it their records.
It ate the color of the sun.
They gave it a thousand letters, they gave it money.
It ate their future complete, it waited for them,
Staring and starving.
They gave it screams, it had gone too far.
It ate into their brains.
It ate the roof.
It ate lonely stone, it ate wind, crying famine.
It went furiously off.   40

They wept, they called it back, it could have everything.
It stripped out their nerves, chewed, chewed flavorless.
It bit at their numb bodies, they did not resist.
It bit into their blank brains, they hardly knew.

It moved bellowing
Through a ruin of starlight and crockery.

It drew slowly off, they could not move.

It went far away, they could not speak.

Only their tears moved.

Guitar Recitativos, No. III

A. R. AMMONS

I'm tired of the you-and-me thing
I am for more research into the nature of the amorous bond
the discovery of catalysts for speeding-up, wearing out, and getting it over
    with
or for slowing it down to allow long intervals of looseness

Baby, there are times when the mixture becomes immiscible
and other times we get so stirred up I can't tell
whether I'm you or me
and then I have this fear of a surprising reaction in which
we both turn into something else

powdery or gaseous or slightly metallic   10
What I mean is this whole relationship is, lacking further
knowledge, risky: while there's still time, why
don't you get yourself together and I'll

get myself together and then we'll sort of shy out
of each other's gravitational field, unstring the
electromagnetism, and then sort of just drop this
whole orientation, baby

DEATH

A Lyke-Wake Dirge

Anonymous, Sixteenth Century(?)

This ae nighte, this ae nighte,
  —*Every nighte and alle,*
Fire and fleet and candle-lighte,
  And Christe receive thy saule.

When thou from hence away art past,
  —*Every nighte and alle,*
To Whinny-muir thou com'st at last:
  And Christe receive thy saule.

If ever thou gavest hosen and shoon,
  —*Every nighte and alle,*   10
Sit thee down and put them on:
  And Christe receive thy saule.

Title: Lyke: Body.
l. 1. ae: One.
l. 3. fleet: Perhaps a paved floor, but the meaning of the word here is not certainly known.
l. 7. Whinny-muir: A moor covered with whin (gorse, furze), a shrub in which sharp spines take the place of leaves.
l. 9. hosen and shoon: Hose and shoes.

If hosen and shoon thou ne'er gav'st nane
   —Every nighte and alle,
The whinnes sall prick thee to the bare bane;
   And Christe receive thy saule.

From Brig o' Dread when thou may'st pass,
   —Every nighte and alle,
To Purgatory fire thou com'st at last;
   And Christe receive thy saule.   20

If ever thou gavest meat or drink,
   —Every nighte and alle,
The fire sall never make thee shrink;
   And Christe receive thy saule.

If meat or drink thou ne'er gav'st nane,
   —Every nighte and alle,
The fire will burn thee to the bare bane;
   And Christe receive thy saule.

This ae nighte, this ae nighte,
   —Every nighte and alle,   30
Fire and fleet and candle-lighte,
   And Christe receive thy saule.

---

l. 13. nane: None.
l. 15. bane: Bone.
l. 17. Brig: Bridge.

[*Fear no more*]

WILLIAM SHAKESPEARE

Fear no more the heat o' the' sun,
   Nor the furious winter's rages;
Thou thy worldly task hast done,
   Home art gone, and ta'en thy wages:
Golden lads and girls all must,
As chimney-sweepers, come to dust.

Fear no more the frown o' th' great;
   Thou art past the tyrant's stroke;
Care no more to clothe and eat;
   To thee the reed is as the oak: 10
The sceptre, learning, physic, must
All follow this, and come to dust.

Fear no more the lightning-flash,
    Nor th' all-dreaded thunder-stone;
Fear not slander, censure rash;
    Thou hast finish'd joy and moan:
All lovers young, all lovers must
Consign to thee, and come to dust.

No exorciser harm thee!
    Nor no witchcraft charm thee!   20
Ghost unlaid forbear thee!
    Nothing ill come near thee!
Quiet consummation have;
And renowned be thy grave!

*[Full fathom five]

WILLIAM SHAKESPEARE

Full fathom five thy father lies;
    Of his bones are coral made;
Those are pearls that were his eyes;
    Nothing of him that doth fade
But doth suffer a sea change
Into something rich and strange.
Sea-nymphs hourly ring his knell:
                                    Ding-dong!
Hark! now I hear them,—Ding-dong, bell!

[A slumber did my spirit seal]

WILLIAM WORDSWORTH

A slumber did my spirit seal;
    I had no human fears:
She seemed a thing that could not feel
    The touch of earthly years.

No motion has she now, no force;
    She neither hears nor sees;
Rolled round in earth's diurnal course,
    With rocks, and stones, and trees.

*Bredon Hill

A. E. HOUSMAN

In summertime on Bredon
   The bells they sound so clear;
Round both the shires they ring them
   In steeples far and near,
   A happy noise to hear.

Here of a Sunday morning
   My love and I would lie,
And see the coloured counties,
   And hear the larks so high
   About us in the sky.   10

The bells would ring to call her
   In valleys miles away:
"Come all to church, good people;
   Good people, come and pray."
   But here my love would stay.

And I would turn and answer
   Among the springing thyme,
"Oh, peal upon our wedding,
   And we will hear the chime,
   And come to church in time."   20

But when the snows at Christmas
   On Bredon top were strown,
My love rose up so early
   And stole out unbeknown
   And went to church alone.

They tolled the one bell only,
   Groom there was none to see,
The mourners followed after,
   And so to church went she,
   And would not wait for me.   30

The bells they sound on Bredon,
   And still the steeples hum.
"Come all to church, good people,"—
   Oh, noisy bells, be dumb;
   I hear you, I will come.

[*The rain, it streams on stone and hillock*]

A. E. HOUSMAN

The rain, it streams on stone and hillock,
    The boot clings to the clay.
Since all is done that's due and right
Let's home; and now, my lad, good-night,
    For I must turn away.

Good-night, my lad, for nought's eternal;
    No league of ours, for sure.
To-morrow I shall miss you less,
And ache of heart and heaviness
    Are things that time should cure.   10

Over the hill the highway marches
    And what's beyond is wide:
Oh soon enough will pine to nought
Remembrance and the faithful thought
    That sits the grave beside.

The skies, they are not always raining
    Nor grey the twelvemonth through;
And I shall meet good days and mirth,
And range the lovely lands of earth
    With friends no worse than you.   20

But oh, my man, the house is fallen
    That none can build again;
My man, how full of joy and woe
Your mother bore you years ago
    To-night to lie in the rain.

*The House

WALTER DE LA MARE

    'Mother, it's such a lonely house,'
The child cried; and the wind sighed.
    'A narrow but a lovely house,'
        The mother replied.

'Child, it is such a narrow house,'
  The ghost cried; and the wind sighed.
  'A narrow and a lonely house,'
    The withering grass replied.

The Listeners

WALTER DE LA MARE

"Is there anybody there?" said the Traveller,
  Knocking on the moonlit door;
And his horse in the silence champed the grasses
  Of the forest's ferny floor:
And a bird flew up out of the turret,
  Above the Traveller's head:
And he smote upon the door again a second time;
  "Is there anybody there?" he said.
But no one descended to the Traveller;
  No head from the leaf-fringed sill   10
Leaned over and looked into his gray eyes,
  Where he stood perplexed and still.
But only a host of phantom listeners
  That dwelt in the lone house then
Stood listening in the quiet of the moonlight
  To that voice from the world of men:
Stood thronging the faint moonbeams on the dark stair,
  That goes down to the empty hall,
Hearkening in an air stirred and shaken
  By the lonely Traveller's call.   20
And he felt in his heart their strangeness,
  Their stillness answering his cry,
While his horse moved, cropping the dark turf,
  'Neath the starred and leafy sky;
For he suddenly smote on the door, even
  Louder, and lifted his head:—
"Tell them I came, and no one answered,
  That I kept my word," he said.
Never the least stir made the listeners,
  Though every word he spake   30
Fell echoing through the shadowiness of the still house
  From the one man left awake:
Ay, they heard his foot upon the stirrup,
  And the sound of iron on stone,
And how the silence surged softly backward,
  When the plunging hoofs were gone.

The Ghost

WALTER DE LA MARE

"Who knocks?" "I, who was beautiful,
Beyond all dreams to restore,
I, from the roots of the dark thorn am hither,
And knock on the door."

"Who speaks?" "I—once was my speech
Sweet as the bird's on the air,
When echo lurks by the waters to heed;
'Tis I speak thee fair."

"Dark is the hour!" "Ay, and cold."
"Lone is my house." "Ah, but mine?"   10
"Sight, touch, lips, eyes yearned in vain."
"Long dead these to thine . . ."

Silence. Still faint on the porch
Brake the flames of the stars.
In gloom groped a hope-wearied hand
Over keys, bolts, and bars.

A face peered. All the grey night
    In chaos of vacancy shone;
Nought but vast sorrow was there—
    The sweet cheat gone.   20

*The Old Men

WALTER DE LA MARE

Old and alone, sit we,
    Caged, riddle-rid men;
Lost to Earth's "Listen!" and "See!"
    Thought's "Wherefore?" and "When?"

Only far memories stray
    Of a past once lovely, but now
Wasted and faded away,
    Like green leaves from the bough.

Vast broods the silence of night,
    The ruinous moon   10
Lifts on our faces her light,
    Whence all dreaming is gone.

We speak not; trembles each head;
    In their sockets our eyes are still;
Desire as cold as the dead;
    Without wonder or will.

And One, with a lanthorn, draws near,
    At clash with the moon in our eyes:
"Where art thou?" he asks: "I am here,"
    One by one we arise.   20

And none lifts a hand to withhold
    A friend from the touch of that foe:
Heart cries unto heart, "Thou art old!"
    Yet, reluctant, we go.

*The Death of a Soldier

WALLACE STEVENS

Life contracts and death is expected,
As in a season of autumn.
The soldier falls.

He does not become a three-days personage,
Imposing his separation,
Calling for pomp.

Death is absolute and without memorial,
As in a season of autumn,
When the wind stops,

When the wind stops and, over the heavens,   10
The clouds go, nevertheless,
In their direction.

Bells for John Whiteside's Daughter

JOHN CROWE RANSOM

There was such speed in her little body,
And such lightness in her footfall,
It is no wonder her brown study
Astonishes us all.

Her wars were bruited in our high window.
We looked among orchard trees and beyond
Where she took arms against her shadow,
Or harried unto the pond

The lazy geese, like a snow cloud
Dripping their snow on the green grass,   10
Tricking and stopping, sleepy and proud,
Who cried in goose, Alas,

For the tireless heart within the little
Lady with rod that made them rise
From their noon apple-dreams, and scuttle
Goose-fashion under the skies!

But now go the bells, and we are ready,
In one house we are sternly stopped
To say we are vexed at her brown study,
Lying so primly propped.   20

MAN, MACHINE, AND SOCIETY

*The Chimney Sweeper

[from SONGS OF INNOCENCE]

WILLIAM BLAKE

When my mother died I was very young,
And my father sold me while yet my tongue
Could scarcely cry " 'weep! 'weep! 'weep! 'weep!"
So your chimneys I sweep & in soot I sleep.

There's little Tom Dacre, who cried when his head,
That curl'd like a lamb's back, was shav'd: so I said,
"Hush, Tom! never mind it, for when your head's bare
You know that the soot cannot spoil your white hair."

And so he was quiet, & that very night,
As Tom was a-sleeping, he had such a sight!   10
That thousands of sweepers, Dick, Joe, Ned & Jack,
Were all of them lock'd up in coffins of black.

And by came an Angel who had a bright key,
And he open'd the coffins & set them all free;
Then down a green plain leaping, laughing, they run,
And wash in a river, and shine in the Sun.

Then naked & white, all their bags left behind,
They rise upon clouds, and sport in the wind;
And the Angel told Tom, if he'd be a good boy,
He'd have God for his father, & never want joy.   20

And so Tom awoke; and we rose in the dark,
And got with our bags & our brushes to work,
Tho' the morning was cold, Tom was happy & warm;
So if all do their duty they need not fear harm.

London

WILLIAM BLAKE

I wander thro' each charter'd street,
Near where the charter'd Thames does flow,
And mark in every face I meet
Marks of weakness, marks of woe.

In every cry of every Man,
In every Infant's cry of fear,
In every voice, in every ban,
The mind-forg'd manacles I hear.

How the Chimney-sweeper's cry
Every black'ning church appalls;   10
And the hapless Soldier's sigh
Runs in blood down Palace walls.

But most thro' midnight streets I hear
How the youthful Harlot's curse
Blasts the newborn Infant's tear,
And blights with plagues the Marriage hearse.

from *Milton*

WILLIAM BLAKE

And did those feet in ancient time
   Walk upon England's mountains green?
And was the holy Lamb of God
   On England's pleasant pastures seen?

And did the Countenance Divine
   Shine forth upon our clouded hills?
And was Jerusalem builded here
   Among these dark Satanic Mills?

Bring me my Bow of burning gold:
   Bring me my Arrows of desire: 10
Bring me my Spear: O clouds unfold!
   Bring me my chariot of fire.

I will not cease from Mental Fight,
   Nor shall my Sword sleep in my hand
Till we have built Jerusalem
   In England's green & pleasant Land.

*Lament of the Frontier Guard

EZRA POUND

By the North Gate, the wind blows full of sand,
Lonely from the beginning of time until now!
Trees fall, the grass goes yellow with autumn.
I climb the towers and towers to watch out the barbarous land:
Desolate castle, the sky, the wide desert.
There is no wall left to this village.
Bones white with a thousand frosts,
High heaps, covered with trees and grass;
Who brought this to pass?
Who has brought the flaming imperial anger?   10
Who has brought the army with drums and with kettle-drums?
Barbarous kings.
A gracious spring, turned to blood-ravenous autumn,
A turmoil of wars-men, spread over the middle kingdom,
Three hundred and sixty thousand,

And sorrow, sorrow like rain.
Sorrow to go, and sorrow, sorrow returning.
Desolate, desolate fields,
And no children of warfare upon them,
    No longer the men for offence and defence.   20
Ah, how shall you know the dreary sorrow at the North Gate
With Rihoku's name forgotten,
And we guardsmen fed to the tigers.

—BY RIHAKU

To a Locomotive in Winter

WALT WHITMAN

Thee for my recitative,
Thee in the driving storm even as now, the snow, the winter-day declining,
Thee in thy panoply, thy measur'd dual throbbing and thy beat convulsive,
Thy black cylindric body, golden brass and silvery steel,
Thy ponderous side-bars, parallel and connecting rods, gyrating, shuttling
    at thy sides,
Thy metrical, now swelling pant and roar, now tapering in the distance,
Thy great protruding head-light fix'd in front,
Thy long, pale, floating vapor-pennants, tinged with delicate purple,
The dense and murky clouds out-belching from thy smoke-stack,
Thy knitted frame, thy springs and valves, the tremulous twinkle of thy
    wheels,   10
Thy train of cars behind, obedient, merrily following,
Through gale or calm, now swift, now slack, yet steadily careering;
Type of the modern—emblem of motion and power—pulse of the continent,
For once come serve the Muse and merge in verse, even as here I see thee,
With storm and buffeting gusts of wind and falling snow,
By day thy warning ringing bell to sound its notes,
By night thy silent signal lamps to swing.

Fierce-throated beauty!
Roll through my chant with all thy lawless music, thy swinging lamps at
    night,
Thy madly-whistled laughter, echoing, rumbling like an earthquake, rousing
    all,   20
Law of thyself complete, thine own track firmly holding,
(No sweetness debonair of tearful harp or glib piano thine,)
Thy trills of shrieks by rocks and hills return'd,
Launch'd o'er the prairies wide, across the lakes,
To the free skies unpent and glad and strong.

Limited

CARL SANDBURG

I am riding on a limited express, one of the crack trains of the nation.
Hurtling across the prairie into blue haze and dark air go fifteen all-steel
    coaches holding a thousand people.
(All the coaches shall be scrap and rust and all the men and women
    laughing in the diners and sleepers shall pass to ashes.)
I ask a man in the smoker where he is going and he answers: "Omaha."

The Unknown Citizen

W. H. AUDEN

(TO JS/07/M/378
THIS MARBLE MONUMENT
IS ERECTED BY THE STATE)

He was found by the Bureau of Statistics to be
One against whom there was no official complaint,
And all the reports on his conduct agree
That, in the modern sense of an old-fashioned word, he was a saint,
For in everything he did he served the Greater Community.
Except for the War till the day he retired
He worked in a factory and never got fired,
But satisfied his employers, Fudge Motors Inc.
Yet he wasn't a scab or odd in his views,
For his Union reports that he paid his dues,   10
(Our report on his Union shows it was sound)
And our Social Psychology workers found
That he was popular with his mates and liked a drink.
The Press are convinced that he bought a paper every day
And that his reactions to advertisements were normal in every way.
Policies taken out in his name prove that he was fully insured,
And his Health-card shows he was once in hospital but left it cured.
Both Producers Research and High-Grade Living declare
He was fully sensible to the advantages of the Instalment Plan
And had everything necessary to the Modern Man,   20
A phonograph, a radio, a car and a frigidaire.
Our researchers into Public Opinion are content
That he held the proper opinions for the time of year;
When there was peace, he was for peace; when there was war, he went.

He was married and added five children to the population,
Which our Eugenist says was the right number for a parent of his
  generation,
And our teachers report that he never interfered with their education.
Was he free? Was he happy? The question is absurd:
Had anything been wrong, we should certainly have heard.

*Pot-Luck Among the Casuals

MARSDEN HARTLEY

A dog came loping to his side:
"have you any of a speechless bone?"
"no—but I have foul weathers in
my head,
and why should you want another one?
you who are all but wrack of bone
and nearly dead.
why every wind plays tunes upon
your ribs; the birds could build a nest
in the hollow of your spine;   10
who is it fed you on broken stone,
you walking, pallid skeleton?"

He gave him hunk of what he had,
" 'tis good enough for me; none," or so he said,
"when you want to go, is sweeter,
from worse to something better;
bone will maybe sharpen teeth
but makes pain sharper underneath;
a bowl of downright summer blood
would do you heaps of good."   20

The dog looked up to him and said,
"save me, save me from a speedy grave,
give anything of what you have";
he gave two hunks of what he little had
it was as if his jaw would crack
it felt so good;
a smile came out of canine face
and fairly shamed the listless place;
a dog that wants is tragical to see;
we're used to men that get that way.   30

*Bagpipe Music

LOUIS MACNEICE

It's no go the merry-go-round, it's no go the rickshaw,
All we want is a limousine and ticket for the peepshow.
Their knickers are made of crêpe-de-chine, their shoes are made of python,
Their halls are lined with tiger rugs and their walls with heads of bison.

John MacDonald found a corpse, put it under the sofa,
Waited till it came to life and hit it with a poker,
Sold its eyes for souvenirs, sold its blood for whiskey,
Kept its bones for dumb-bells to use when he was fifty.

It's no go the Yogi-Man, it's no go Blavatsky,
All we want is a bank balance and a bit of skirt in a taxi.   10

Annie MacDougall went to milk, caught her foot in the heather,
Woke to hear a dance record playing of Old Vienna.
It's no go your maidenheads, it's no go your culture,
All we want is a Dunlop tyre and the devil mend the puncture.

The Laird o'Phelps spent Hogmannay declaring he was sober;
Counted his feet to prove the fact and found he had one foot over.
Mrs. Carmichael had her fifth, looked at the job with repulsion,
Said to the midwife "Take it away; I'm through with overproduction."

It's no go the gossip column, it's no go the Ceilidh,
All we want is a mother's help and a sugarstick for the baby.   20

Willie Murray cut his thumb, couldn't count the damage,
Took the hide of an Ayrshire cow and used it for a bandage.
His brother caught three hundred cran when the seas were lavish,
Threw the bleeders back in the sea and went upon the parish.

It's no go the Herring Board, it's no go the Bible,
All we want is a packet of fags when our hands are idle.

It's no go the picture palace, it's no go the stadium,
It's no go the country cot with a pot of pink geraniums.
It's no go the Government grants, it's no go the elections,
Sit on your arse for fifty years and hang your hat on a pension.   30

---

l. 15. Hogmannay: New Year's Eve in Scotland.
l. 19. Ceilidh (pron. Kaily): A social gathering.
l. 23. cran: Unit of measure for herring.

It's no go my honey love, it's no go my poppet;
Work your hands from day to day, the winds will blow the profit.
The glass is falling hour by hour, the glass will fall for ever,
But if you break the bloody glass you won't hold up the weather.

Sunday Morning

LOUIS MACNEICE

Down the road some one is practising scales,
The notes like little fishes vanish with a wink of tails,
Man's heart expands to tinker with his car
For this is Sunday morning, Fate's great bazaar;
Regard these means as ends, concentrate on this Now,
And you may grow to music or drive beyond Hindhead anyhow,
Take corners on two wheels until you go so fast
That you can clutch a fringe or two of the windy past,
That you can abstract this day and make it to the week of time
A small eternity, a sonnet self-contained in rhyme.   10

But listen, up the road, something gulps, the church spire
Opens its eight bells out, skulls' mouths which will not tire
To tell how there is no music or movement that ensures
Escape from the weekday time. Which deadens and endures.

I, Too

LANGSTON HUGHES

I, too, sing America.

I am the darker brother.
They send me to eat in the kitchen
When company comes,
But I laugh,
And eat well,
And grow strong.

Tomorrow,
I'll be at the table
When company comes.
Nobody'll dare
Say to me,
"Eat in the kitchen,"
Then.

Besides,
They'll see how beautiful I am
And be ashamed—

I, too, am America.

10

Without Benefit of Declaration

LANGSTON HUGHES

Listen here, Joe
Don't you know
That tomorrow
You got to go
Out yonder where
The steel winds blow?

Listen here, kid,
It's been said
Tomorrow you'll be dead
Out there where
The snow is lead.

10

Don't ask me why.
Just go ahead and die.
Hidden from the sky
Out yonder you'll lie:
A medal to your family—
In exchange for
A guy

Mama, don't cry.

Anybody
Better than
Nobody.

In the barren dusk
Even the snake
That spirals
Terror on the sand—

Better than nobody
In this lonely
Land.   10

Mose

STERLING A. BROWN

Mose is black and evil
And damns his luck
Driving Master Schwartz's
Big coal truck.

He's got no gal,
He's got no jack,
No fancy silk shirts
For his back.

But summer evenings,
Hard luck Mose   10
Goes in for all
The fun he knows.

On the corner kerb
With a sad quartette
His tenor peals
Like a clarinet.

O hit it Moses
Sing att thing
But Mose's mind
Goes wandering;—   20

And to the stars
Over the town
Floats, from a good man
Way, way down—

A soft song, filled
With a misery
Older than Mose
Will ever be.

The Inquisitors

ROBINSON JEFFERS

Coming around a corner of the dark trail . . . what was wrong with the
   valley?
Azevedo checked his horse and sat staring: it was all changed. It was
   occupied. There were three hills
Where none had been: and firelight flickered red on their knees between
   them: if they were hills:
They were more like Red Indians around a camp-fire, grave and dark,
   mountain-high, hams on heels
Squatting around a little fire of hundred-foot logs. Azevedo remembers he
   felt an icebrook
Glide on his spine; he slipped down from the saddle and hid
In the brush by the trail, above the black redwood forest. There was the
   Little Sur South Fork,
Its forest valley; the man had come in at nightfall over Bowcher's Gap, and
   a high moon hunted
Through running clouds. He heard the rumble of a voice, heavy not loud,
   saying, "I gathered some,
You can inspect them." One of the hills moved a huge hand   10
And poured its contents on a table-topped rock that stood in the firelight;
   men and women fell out;
Some crawled and some lay quiet; the hills leaned to eye them. One said:
   "It seems hardly possible
Such fragile creatures could be so noxious." Another answered

"True, but we've seen. But it is only recently they have the power." The third answered. "That bomb?"

"Oh," he said, "—and the rest." He reached across and picked up one of the mites from the rock, and held it

Close to his eyes, and very carefully with finger and thumbnail peeled it: by chance a young female

With long black hair: it was too helpless even to scream. He held it by one white leg and stared at it:

"I can see nothing strange: only so fragile."

The third hill answered, "We suppose it is something

Inside the head." Then the other split the skull with his thumbnail, squinting his eyes and peering, and said,   20

"A drop of marrow. How could that spoil the earth?" "Nevertheless," he answered,

"They have that bomb. The blasts and the fires are nothing: freckles on the earth: the emanations

Might set the whole planet into a tricky fever

And destroy much." "Themselves," he answered. "Let them. Why not?" "No," he answered, "life."

Azevedo

Still watched in horror, and all three of the hills

Picked little animals from the rock, peeled them and cracked them, or toasted them

On the red coals, or split their bodies from the crotch upward

To stare inside. They said, "It remains a mystery. However," they said,

"It is not likely they can destroy all life: the planet is capacious. Life would surely grow up again

From grubs in the soil, or the newt and toad level, and be beautiful again. And again perhaps break its legs   30

On its own cleverness: who can forecast the future?" The speaker yawned, and with his flat hand

Brushed the rock clean; the three slowly stood up,

Taller than Pico Blanco into the sky, their Indian-beaked heads in the moon-cloud,

And trampled their watchfire out and went away southward, stepping across the Ventana mountains.

MAN AND NATURE

[Sumer is icumen in]

Anonymous, probably late Thirteenth Century

> Sumer is icumen in,
>> Lhudë sing cuccu!
>
> Growëth sed and bloweth med
>> And springth the wodë nu.
>>> Sing cuccu!
>
> Awë bleteth after lomb,
>> Lhouth after calvë cu
>
> Bulluc sterteth, buckë verteth.
>> Murie sing cuccu!
>>> Cuccu, cuccu,   10
>
> Wel singës thu, cuccu
>> Ne swik thu naver nu!
>
> Sing cuccu nu, Sing cuccu!
> Sing cuccu, Sing cuccu, nu!

l. 2. Lhudë: Loud.
l. 3. sed: Seed. bloweth med: Blossoms [the] meadow.
l. 4. wodë: Wood. nu: Now.
l. 6. Awë: Ewe.
l. 7. Lhouth: Loweth or Lows. cu: Cow.
l. 8. sterteth: Leaps. verteth: Probably veers or starts.
l. 9. murie: Merrily.
l. 12. swik: Cease.

Ancient Music

EZRA POUND

> Winter is icummen in,
> Lhude sing Goddamm,
> Raineth drop and staineth slop,
> And how the wind doth ramm!
>> Sing: Goddamm.

Skiddeth bus and sloppeth us,
An ague hath my ham.
Freezeth river, turneth liver,
          Damn you, sing: Goddamm.
Goddamm, Goddamm, 'tis why I am, Goddamm,   10

          So 'gainst the winter's balm.
Sing goddamm, damm, sing Goddamm,
Sing goddamm, sing goddamm, DAMM.

*Spring

WILLIAM SHAKESPEARE

When daisies pied and violets blue
    And lady-smocks all silver-white
And cuckoo-buds of yellow hue
    Do paint the meadows with delight,
The cuckoo then, on every tree,
Mocks married men; for thus sings he,
          Cuckoo;
Cuckoo, cuckoo: O, word of fear,
Unpleasing to a married ear!

When shepherds pipe on oaten straws   10
    And merry larks are plowmen's clocks,
When turtles tread, and rooks, and daws,
    And maidens bleach their summer smocks,
The cuckoo then, on every tree,
Mocks married men; for thus sings he,
          Cuckoo;
Cuckoo, cuckoo: O, word of fear,
Unpleasing to a married ear!

---

l. 2. lady-smocks: A white-flowered plant of the cress family.
l. 3. The name cuckoo-flower *was applied to several different species of plant.*
l. 12. turtles: Turtle-doves. tread: *Mate.*

Winter

WILLIAM SHAKESPEARE

When icicles hang by the wall,
   And Dick the shepherd blows his nail,
And Tom bears logs into the hall,
   And milk comes frozen home in pail,
When blood is nipp'd, and ways be foul,
Then nightly sings the staring owl,
           Tu-who;
Tu-whit, tu-who—a merry note,
While greasy Joan doth keel the pot.

When all aloud the wind doth blow,   10
   And coughing drowns the parson's saw,
And birds sit brooding in the snow,
   And Marian's nose looks red and raw,
When roasted crabs hiss in the bowl,
Then nightly sings the staring owl,
           Tu-who;
Tu-whit, tu-who—a merry note,
While greasy Joan doth keel the pot.

---

l. 2. blows his nail: Lounges around with nothing to do.
l. 9. keel: Cool.
l. 14. crabs: Crabapples, used to flavor a bowl of ale.

The Garden

ANDREW MARVELL

I

How vainly men themselves amaze
To win the Palm, the Oke, or Bayes;
And their uncessant Labours see
Crown'd from some single Herb or Tree,
Whose short and narrow verged Shade
Does prudently their Toyles upbraid;
While all Flow'rs and all Trees do close
To weave the Garlands of repose.

II

Fair quiet, have I found thee here,
And Innocence thy Sister dear!   10
Mistaken long, I sought you then
In busie Companies of Men.
Your sacred Plants, if here below,
Only among the Plants will grow.
Society is all but rude,
To this delicious Solitude.

III

No white nor red was ever seen
So am'rous as this lovely green.
Fond Lovers, cruel as their Flame,
Cut in these Trees their Mistress name.   20
Little, Alas, they know, or heed,
How far these Beauties Hers exceed!
Fair Trees! where s'eer your barkes I wound,
No Name shall but your own be found.

IV

When we have run our Passions heat,
Love hither makes his best retreat.
The *Gods,* that mortal Beauty chase,
Still in a Tree did end their race.
Apollo hunted *Daphne* so,
Only that She might Laurel grow.   30
And *Pan* did after *Syrinx* speed,
Not as a Nymph, but for a Reed.

V

What wond'rous Life is this I lead!
Ripe Apples drop about my head;
The Luscious Clusters of the Vine
Upon my Mouth do crush their Wine;
The Nectaren, and curious Peach,
Into my hands themselves do reach;
Stumbling on Melons, as I pass,
Insnar'd with Flow'rs, I fall on Grass.   40

VI

Mean while the Mind, from pleasure less,
Withdraws into its happiness:
The Mind, that Ocean where each kind
Does streight its own resemblance find;
Yet it creates, transcending these,
Far other Worlds, and other Seas;
Annihilating all that's made
To a green Thought in a green Shade.

VII

Here at the Fountains sliding foot,
Or at some Fruit-trees mossy root,   50
Casting the Bodies Vest aside,
My Soul into the boughs does glide:
There like a Bird it sits, and sings,
Then whets, and combs its silver Wings;
And, till prepar'd for longer flight,
Waves in its Plumes the various Light.

VIII

Such was that happy Garden-state,
While Man there walk'd without a Mate:
After a Place so pure, and sweet,
What other Help could yet be meet!   60
But 'twas beyond a Mortal's share
To wander solitary there:
Two Paradises 'twere in one
To live in Paradise alone.

IX

How well the skillful Gardner drew
Of flow'rs and herbes this Dial new;
Where from above the milder Sun
Does through a fragrant Zodiak run;
And, as it works, th'industrious Bee
Computes its time as well as we.   70
How could such sweet and wholesome Hours
Be reckon'd but with herbs and flow'rs!

*The Mower Against Gardens

ANDREW MARVELL

Luxurious Man, to bring his Vice in use,
    Did after him the World seduce:
And from the fields the Flow'rs and Plants allure,
    Where Nature was most plain and pure.
He first enclos'd within the Gardens square
    A dead and standing pool of Air:
And a more luscious Earth for them did knead,
    Which stupifi'd them while it fed.
The Pink grew then as double as his Mind;
    The nutriment did change the kind.   10
With strange perfumes he did the Roses taint.
    And Flow'rs themselves were taught to paint.
The Tulip, white, did for complexion seek;
    And learn'd to interline its cheek:
Its Onion root they then so high did hold,
    That one was for a Meadow sold.
Another World was search'd, through Oceans new,
    To find the *Marvel of Peru*.
And yet these Rarities might be allow'd,
    To Man, that sov'raign thing and proud;   20
Had he not dealt between the Bark and Tree,
    Forbidden mixtures there to see.
No Plant now knew the Stock from which it came;
    He grafts upon the Wild the Tame:
That the uncertain and adult'rate fruit
    Might put the Palate in dispute.
His green *Seraglio* has its Eunuchs too;
    Lest any Tyrant him out-doe.
And in the Cherry he does Nature vex,
    To procreate without a Sex.   30
'Tis all enforc'd; the Fountain and the Grot;
    While the sweet Fields do lye forgot:
Where willing Nature does to all dispence
    A wild and fragrant Innocence:
And *Fauns* and *Faryes* do the Meadows till,
    More by their presence then their skill.
Their Statues polish'd by some ancient hand,
    May to adorn the Gardens stand:
But howso'ere the Figures do excel,
    The *Gods* themselves with us do dwell.   40

*November

ROBERT BRIDGES

The lonely season in lonely lands, when fled
Are half the birds, and mists lie low, and the sun
Is rarely seen, nor strayeth far from his bed;
The short days pass unwelcomed one by one.

Out by the ricks the mantled engine stands
Crestfallen, deserted,—for now all hands
Are told to the plough,—and ere it is dawn appear
The teams following and crossing far and near,
As hour by hour they broaden the brown bands
Of the striped fields; and behind them firk and prance   10
The heavy rooks, and daws grey-pated dance:
As awhile, surmounting a crest, in sharp outline
(A miniature of toil, a gem's design,)
They are pictured, horses and men, or now near by
Above the lane they shout lifting the share,
By the trim hedgerow bloom'd with purple air;
Where, under the thorns, dead leaves in huddle lie
Packed by the gales of Autumn, and in and out
The small wrens glide
With a happy note of cheer,   20
And yellow amorets flutter above and about,
Gay, familiar in fear.

And now, if the night shall be cold, across the sky
Linnets and twites, in small flocks helter-skelter,
All the afternoon to the gardens fly,
From thistle-pastures hurrying to gain the shelter
Of American rhododendron or cherry-laurel:
And here and there, near chilly setting of sun,
In an isolated tree a congregation
Of starlings chatter and chide,   30
Thickset as summer leaves, in garrulous quarrel:
Suddenly they hush as one,—
The tree top springs,—
And off, with a whirr of wings,
They fly by the score

---

l. 10. firk: Hasten or be frisky.
l. 11. Rooks and daws resemble crows.
l. 15. share: Plowshare.
l. 16. bloom'd: Silvered over with autumn haze.
l. 24. twites or twite finches: Another kind of finch or linnet.

To the holly—thicket, and there with myriads more
Dispute for the roosts; and from the unseen nation
A babel of tongues, like running water unceasing,
Makes live the wood, the flocking cries increasing,
Wrangling discordantly, incessantly,   40
While falls the night on them self-occupied;
The long dark night, that lengthens slow,
Deepening with Winter to starve grass and tree,
And soon to bury in snow
The Earth, that sleeping 'neath her frozen stole,
Shall dream a dream crept from the sunless pole
Of how her end shall be.

*Nightingales

ROBERT BRIDGES

Beautiful must be the mountains whence ye come,
And bright in the fruitful valleys the streams, wherefrom
    Ye learn your song:
    Where are those starry woods? O might I wander there,
    Among the flowers, which in that heavenly air
        Bloom the year long!

    Nay, barren are those mountains and spent the streams:
    Our song is the voice of desire, that haunts our dreams
        A throe of the heart,
Whose pining visions dim, forbidden hopes profound,   10
    No dying cadence nor long sigh can sound,
        For all our art.

    Alone, aloud in the raptured ear of men
    We pour our dark nocturnal secret; and then,
        As night is withdrawn
    From these sweet-springing meads and bursting boughs of May,
        Dream, while the innumerable choir of day
            Welcome the dawn.

Under Cover

ABBIE HUSTON EVANS

Rain with the old sound, with the country sough
From fields and meadows overpast and trees
That strip it into whip-lash, I hear now
Beat on this hill and cut about its knees.
Now while the lithe wind turns and springs again
On the spent tree, and rain floods down the glass,
I hear the sounds earth knew before we men
Came on, and shall know after we shall pass.
While ancient rumor rising to a shriek
Comes in to tell of matters we forget,   10
I am one more of the beasts of the field in bleak
Ecstatic cover, huddled from the wet.
   So stands the ox, so crouches now the mole,
   So sits the dry woodpecker in his hole.

Euroclydon

ABBIE HUSTON EVANS

The east-northeaster pounds the coast tonight,
Thudding and grinding at the knees of islands;
It sets the bell-buoys clanging and calls out
The gruff storm-warnings up and down the coast.
—So this, none else, was Paul's Euroclydon,
That old tempestuous wind that leaped from Crete
And heaped the seas up till they broke the ship,
But not the man.—Pull out the Book again:
"When the south wind blew softly—" (O sweet words,
The spring is in them. Hark!)—"we loosed from Crete."   10
I sit and listen while Euroclydon,
That old storm-wind that had a name of its own
Two thousand years before I yet had mine,
Pelts on my pane with blizzard snow like grit,
Shrieks down my chimney, grips my house foursquare,
And pants against my door.
                  Old tiger, hail!

Title: The Greek name for a tempestuous northeast wind in the Mediterranean.
ll. 8–10. The New Testament (Acts 27) describes the shipwreck of the Apostle Paul.

The Gallows

EDWARD THOMAS

There was a weasel lived in the sun
With all his family,
Till a keeper shot him with his gun
And hung him up on a tree,
Where he swings in the wind and rain
In the sun and in the snow,
Without pleasure, without pain,
On the dead oak tree bough.

There was a crow who was no sleeper,
But a thief and a murderer   10
Till a very late hour; and this keeper
Made him one of the things that were,
To hang and flap in rain and wind
In the sun and in the snow.
There are no more sins to be sinned
On the dead oak tree bough.

There was a magpie, too,
Had a long tongue and a long tail;
He could both talk and do—
But what did that avail?   20
He, too, flaps in the wind and rain
Alongside weasel and crow,
Without pleasure, without pain,
On the dead oak tree bough.

And many other beasts
And birds, skin, bone, and feather,
Have been taken from their feasts
And hung up there together.
To swing and have endless leisure
In the sun and in the snow,   30
Without pain, without pleasure,
On the dead oak tree bough.

Out in the Dark

EDWARD THOMAS

Out in the dark over the snow
The fallow fawns invisible go
With the fallow doe;
And the winds blow
Fast as the stars are slow.

Stealthily the dark haunts round
And, when the lamp goes, without sound
At a swifter bound
Than the swiftest hound,
Arrives, and all else is drowned;   10

And I and star and wind and deer,
Are in the dark together,—near,
Yet far,—and fear
Drums on my ear
In that sage company drear.

How weak and little is the light,
All the universe of sight,
Love and delight,
Before the might,
If you love it not, of night.   20

———————
l. 2. The fallow deer is a small pale-yellow European deer.

The Hermit

WILLIAM H. DAVIES

What moves that lonely man is not the boom
    Of waves that break against the cliff so strong;
Nor roar of thunder, when that traveling voice
    Is caught by rocks that carry far along.

'Tis not the groan of oak tree in its prime,
    When lightning strikes its solid heart to dust;
Nor frozen pond when, melted by the sun,
    It suddenly doth break its sparkling crust.

What moves that man is when the blind bat taps
   His window when he sits alone at night;   10
Or when the small bird sounds like some great beast
   Among the dead, dry leaves so frail and light.

Or when the moths on his night-pillow beat
   Such heavy blows he fears they'll break his bones;
Or when a mouse inside the papered walls,
   Comes like a tiger crunching through the stones.

[I hear the cries of evening]

STEPHEN SPENDER

I hear the cries of evening, while the paw
Of dark, creeps up the turf:
Sheep bleating, swaying gulls' cry, the rook's "Caw,"
The hammering surf.

I am inconstant, yet this constancy
Of natural rest, pulls at my heart;
Town-bred, I feel the roots of each earth-cry
Tear me apart.

These are the creakings of the dusty day
When the dog Night bites sharp,   10
These fingers grip my soul and tear away
And pluck me like a harp.

I feel the huge sphere turn, the great wheel sing
While beasts move to their ease:
Sheep's love, gulls' peace—I feel my chattering
Uncared by these.

*The Yachts

WILLIAM CARLOS WILLIAMS

The Yachts
contend in a sea which the land partly encloses
shielding them from the too heavy blows
of an ungoverned ocean which when it chooses

tortures the biggest hulls, the best man knows
to pit against its beatings, and sinks them pitilessly.
Mothlike in mists, scintillant in the minute

brilliance of cloudless days, with broad bellying sails
they glide to the wind tossing green water
from their sharp prows while over them the crew crawls   10

ant-like, solictiously grooming them, releasing,
making fast as they turn, lean far over and having
caught the wind again, side by side, head for the mark.

In a well guarded arena of open water surrounded by
lesser and greater craft which, sycophant, lumbering
and flittering follow them, they appear youthful, rare

as the light of a happy eye, live with the grace
of all that in the mind is feckless, free and
naturally to be desired. Now the sea which holds them

is moody, lapping their glossy sides, as if feeling   20
for some slightest flaw but fails completely.
Today no race. Then the wind comes again. The yachts

move, jockeying for a start, the signal is set and they
are off. Now the waves strike at them but they are too
well made, they slip through, though they take in canvas.

Arms with hands grasping seek to clutch at the prows.
Bodies thrown recklessly in the way are cut aside.
It is a sea of faces about them in agony, in despair

until the horror of the race dawns staggering the mind,
the whole sea become an entanglement of watery bodies   30
lost to the world bearing what they cannot hold. Broken,

beaten, desolate, reaching from the dead to be taken up
they cry out, failing, failing! their cries rising
in waves still as the skillful yachts pass over.

Spring and All

WILLIAM CARLOS WILLIAMS

By the road to the contagious hospital
under the surge of the blue
mottled clouds driven from the
northeast—a cold wind. Beyond, the
waste of broad, muddy fields
brown with dried weeds, standing and fallen

patches of standing water
the scattering of tall trees

All along the road the reddish
purplish, forked, upstanding, twiggy   10
stuff of bushes and small trees
with dead, brown leaves under them
leafless vines—

Lifeless in appearance, sluggish
dazed spring approaches—

They enter the new world naked,
cold, uncertain of all
save that they enter. All about them
the cold, familiar wind—

Now the grass, tomorrow   20
the stiff curl of wildcarrot leaf
One by one objects are defined—
It quickens: clarity, outline of leaf

But now the stark dignity of
entrance—Still, the profound change
has come upon them: rooted, they
grip down and begin to awaken

The Bear

N. SCOTT MOMADAY

What ruse of vision,
escarping the wall of leaves,
    rending incision
into countless surfaces,

    would cull and color
his somnolence, whose old age
    has outworn valor,
all but the fact of courage?

    Seen, he does not come,
move, but seems forever there,
    dimensionless, dumb,
in the windless noon's hot glare.

    More scarred than others
these years since the trap maimed him,
    pain slants his withers,
drawing up the crooked limb.

    Then he is gone, whole,
without urgency, from sight,
    as buzzards control,
imperceptibly, their flight.

Song of the Black Bear

Anonymous, Navajo

My moccasins are black obsidian,
My leggings are black obsidian,
My shirt is black obsidian.
I am girded with a black arrowsnake.
Black snakes go up from my head.
With zigzag lightning darting from the ends of my feet I step.
With zigzag lightning streaming out from my knees I step,
With zigzag lightning streaming from the tip of my tongue I speak.
Now a disk of pollen rests on the crown of my head.
Gray arrowsnakes and rattlesnakes eat it.   10

Black obsidian and zigzag lightning streams out from me in four ways,
Where they strike the earth, bad things, bad talk does not like it.
It causes the missiles to spread out.
Long Life, something frightful I am.
Now I am.

There is danger where I move my feet.
I am whirlwind.
There is danger when I move my feet.
I am a gray bear.
When I walk, where I step, lightning flies from me,   20
Where I walk, one to be feared [I am].

Where I walk, Long Life.
One to be feared I am.
There is danger where I walk.

TIME, SPACE, AND MUTABILITY

*To Daffodils

ROBERT HERRICK

Fair Daffodils, we weep to see
    You haste away so soon:
As yet the early-rising Sun
    Has not attain'd his noon.

    Stay, stay,
Until the hasting day
    Has run
    But to the even-song;
And, having pray'd together, we
    Will go with you along.   10

We have short time to stay, as you,
    We have as short a Spring!
As quick a growth to meet decay
    As you, or any thing.
    We die,

As your hours do, and dry
    Away
Like to the Summer's rain;
Or as the pearls of morning's dew
    Ne'er to be found again.   20

To the Virgins, To Make Much of Time

ROBERT HERRICK

Gather ye Rose-buds while ye may,
    Old Time is still a flying:
And this same flower that smiles to day,
    To morrow will be dying.

The glorious Lamp of Heaven, the Sun,
    The higher he's a getting;
The sooner will his Race be run,
    And neerer he's to Setting.

That Age is best, which is the first,
    When Youth and Blood are warmer;   10
But being spent, the worse, and worst
    Times, still succeed the former.

Then be not coy, but use your time;
    And while ye may, goe marry:
For having lost but once your prime,
    You may for ever tarry.

Blue Girls

JOHN CROWE RANSOM

Twirling your blue skirts, travelling the sward
Under the towers of your seminary,
Go listen to your teachers old and contrary
Without believing a word.

Tie the white fillets then about your hair
And think no more of what will come to pass
Than bluebirds that go walking on the grass
And chattering on the air.

Practise your beauty, blue girls, before it fail;
And I will cry with my loud lips and publish   10
Beauty which all our power shall never establish,
It is so frail.

For I could tell you a story which is true;
I know a lady with a terrible tongue,
Blear eyes fallen from blue,
All her perfections tarnished—yet it is not long
Since she was lovelier than any of you.

*To His Coy Mistress

ANDREW MARVELL

Had we but World enough, and Time,
This coyness Lady were no crime.
We would sit down, and think which way
To walk, and pass our long Loves Day.
Thou by the *Indian Ganges* side
Should'st Rubies find: I by the Tide
Of *Humber* would complain. I would
Love you ten years before the Flood:
And you should if you please refuse
Till the Conversion of the *Jews.*   10
My vegetable Love should grow
Vaster than Empires, and more slow.
An hundred years should go to praise
Thine Eyes, and on thy Forehead Gaze.
Two hundred to adore each Breast:
But thirty thousand to the rest.
An Age at least to every part,
And the last Age should show your Heart.
For Lady you deserve this State;
Nor would I love at lower rate.   20
    But at my back I alwaies hear
Times wingèd Chariot hurrying near:
And yonder all before us lye
Desarts of vast Eternity.

Thy Beauty shall no more be found,
Nor, in thy marble Vault, shall sound
My echoing Song: then Worms shall try
That long preserv'd Virginity:
And your quaint Honour turn to dust;
And into ashes all my Lust.   30
The Grave's a fine and private place,
But none I think do there embrace.
  Now therefore, while the youthful hew
Sits on thy skin like morning dew,
And while thy willing Soul transpires
At every pore with instant Fires,
Now let us sport while we may;
And now, like am'rous birds of prey,
Rather at once our Time devour,
Than languish in his slow-chapt pow'r.   40
Let us roll all our Strength, and all
Our Sweetness, up into one Ball;
And tear our Pleasures with rough strife,
Thorough the Iron gates of Life.
Thus, though we cannot make our Sun
Stand still, yet we will make him run.

---

l. 35. transpires: Breathes forth.
l. 44. thorough: Through.

*You, Andrew Marvell

ARCHIBALD MACLEISH

And here face down beneath the sun
And here upon the earth's noonward height
To feel the always coming on
The always rising of the night

To feel creep up the curving east
The earthy chill of dusk and slow
Upon those under lands the vast
And everclimbing shadow grow

And strange at Ecbatan the trees
Take leaf by leaf the evening strange   10
The flooding dark about their knees
The mountains over Persia change

---

l. 9. Ecbatan: Ancient name of the Persian city of Hamadan.

And now at Kermanshah the gate
Dark empty and the withered grass
And through the twilight now the late
Few travelers in the westward pass

And Baghdad darken and the bridge
Across the silent river gone
And through Arabia the edge
Of evening widen and steal on   20

And deepen on Palmyra's street
The wheel rut in the ruined stone
And Lebanon fade out and Crete
High through the clouds and overblown

And over Sicily the air
Still flashing with the landward gulls
And loom and slowly disappear
The sails above the shadowy hulls

And spain go under and the shore
Of Africa the gilded sand   30
And evening vanish and no more
The low pale light across that land

Nor now the long light on the sea
And here face downward in the sun
To feel how swift how secretly
The shadow of the night comes on . . .

---

l. 13. Kermanshah: Persian city west of Hamadan.
l. 16. westward pass: Probably the Zagros Gate, a pass west of Kermanshah.
l. 21. Palmyra: Ancient caravan center, with ruins of various past epochs.

*Mutability

WILLIAM WORDSWORTH

From low to high doth dissolution climb,
And sink from high to low, along a scale
Of awful notes, whose concord shall not fail;
A musical but melancholy chime,
Which they can hear who meddle not with crime,
Nor avarice, nor over-anxious care.

Truth fails not; but her outward forms that bear
The longest date do melt like frosty rime,
That in the morning whitened hill and plain
And is no more; drop like the tower sublime   10
Of yesterday, which royally did wear
His crown of weeds, but could not even sustain
Some casual shout that broke the silent air,
Or the unimaginable touch of Time.

Close Your Eyes!

ARNA BONTEMPS

Go through the gates with closed eyes.
Stand erect and let your black face front the west.
Drop the axe and leave the timber where it lies;
A woodman on the hill must have his rest.

Go where leaves are lying brown and wet.
Forget her warm arms and her breast who mothered you,
And every face you ever loved forget.
Close your eyes; walk bravely through.

The force that through the green fuse drives

DYLAN THOMAS

The force that through the green fuse drives the flower
Drives my green age; that blasts the roots of trees
Is my destroyer.
And I am dumb to tell the crooked rose
My youth is bent by the same wintry fever.

The force that drives the water through the rocks
Drives my red blood; that dries the mouthing streams
Turns mine to wax.
And I am dumb to mouth unto my veins
How at the mountain spring the same mouth sucks.   10

The hand that whirls the water in the pool
Stirs the quicksand; that ropes the blowing wind
Hauls my shroud sail.
And I am dumb to tell the hanging man
How of my clay is made the hangman's lime.

The lips of time leech to the fountain head;
Love drips and gathers, but the fallen blood
Shall calm her sores.
And I am dumb to tell a weather's wind
How time has ticked a heaven round the stars.   20

And I am dumb to tell the lover's tomb
How at my sheet goes the same crooked worm.

*Fern Hill

DYLAN THOMAS

Now as I was young and easy under the apple boughs
About the lilting house and happy as the grass was green,
   The night above the dingle starry,
      Time let me hail and climb
   Golden in the heydays of his eyes,
And honoured among wagons I was prince of the apple towns
And once below a time I lordly had the trees and leaves
      Trail with daisies and barley
   Down the rivers of the windfall light.

And as I was green and carefree, famous among the barns   10
About the happy yard and singing as the farm was home,
   In the sun that is young once only,
      Time let me play and be
   Golden in the mercy of his means,
And green and golden I was huntsman and herdsman, the calves
Sang to my horn, the foxes on the hills barked clear and cold,
      And the sabbath rang slowly
   In the pebbles of the holy streams.

All the sun long it was running, it was lovely, the hay
Fields high as the house, the tunes from the chimneys, it was air   20
   And playing, lovely and watery
     And fire green as grass.
   And nightly under the simple stars
As I rode to sleep the owls were bearing the farm away,
All the moon long I heard, blessed among stables, the nightjars
   Flying with the ricks, and the horses
     Flashing into the dark.

And then to awake, and the farm, like a wanderer white
With the dew, come back, the cock on his shoulder: it was all
   Shining, it was Adam and maiden,   30
     The sky gathered again
   And the sun grew round that very day.
So it must have been after the birth of the simple light
In the first, spinning place, the spellbound horses walking warm
   Out of the whinnying green stable
     On to the fields of praise.

And honoured among foxes and pheasants by the gay house
Under the new made clouds and happy as the heart was long,
   In the sun born over and over,
     I ran my heedless ways,   40
   My wishes raced through the house high hay
And nothing I cared, at my sky blue trades, that time allows
In all his tuneful turning so few and such morning songs
   Before the children green and golden
     Follow him out of grace,

Nothing I cared, in the lamb white days, that time would take me
Up to the swallow thronged loft by the shadow of my hand,
   In the moon that is always rising,
     Nor that riding to sleep
   I should hear him fly with the high fields   50
And wake to the farm forever fled from the childless land.
Oh as I was young and easy in the mercy of his means,
   Time held me green and dying
Though I sang in my chains like the sea.

---

l. 25. nightjars: Birds related to the whippoorwills.

ON THE MEANING OF LIFE

The selections in the following group are not formal philosophical poems, but directly or indirectly they touch upon philosophy, raising such questions as whether life is worth living, how or whether man can make his life truly meaningful, whether the universe has any purpose. Many poems in other groups deal with these questions also; they range from the lightness of Herrick's carpe diem *poem (p. 489) to the magnitude of Yeats's "Among School Children" (page 578).*

*Ulysses

ALFRED, LORD TENNYSON

It little profits that an idle king,
By this still hearth, among these barren crags,
Match'd with an aged wife, I mete and dole
Unequal laws unto a savage race,
That hoard, and sleep, and feed, and know not me.
I cannot rest from travel: I will drink
Life to the lees: all times I have enjoy'd
Greatly, have suffer'd greatly, both with those
That loved me, and alone; on shore, and when
Thro' scudding drifts the rainy Hyades   10
Vext the dim sea, I am become a name;
For always roaming with a hungry heart
Much have I seen and known; cities of men
And manners, climates, councils, governments,
Myself not least, but honour'd of them all;
And drunk delight of battle with my peers,
Far on the ringing plains of windy Troy.
I am a part of all that I have met;
Yet all experience is an arch wherethro'
Gleams that untravel'd world, whose margin fades   20
For ever and for ever when I move.
How dull it is to pause, to make an end,
To rust unburnish'd, not to shine in use!
As tho' to breathe were life. Life piled on life

Were all too little, and of one to me
Little remains: but every hour is saved
From that eternal silence, something more,
A bringer of new things; and vile it were
For some three suns to store and hoard myself,
And this gray spirit yearning in desire   30
To follow knowledge like a singing star,
Beyond the utmost bound of human thought.
    This is my son, mine own Telemachus,
To whom I leave the sceptre and the isle—
Well-loved of me, discerning to fulfill
This labour, by slow prudence to make mild
A rugged people, and thro' soft degrees
Subdue them to the useful and the good.
Most blameless is he, centered in the sphere
Of common duties, decent not to fail   40
In offices of tenderness, and pay
Meet adoration to my household gods,
When I am gone. He works his work, I mine.

    There lies the port; the vessel puffs her sail:
There gloom the dark broad seas. My mariners,
Souls that have toil'd, and wrought, and thought with me—
That ever with a frolic welcome took
The thunder and the sunshine, and opposed
Free hearts, free foreheads—you and I are old;
Old age hath yet his honour and his toil;   50
Death closes all: but something ere the end,
Some work of noble note, may yet be done,
Not unbecoming men that strove with Gods.
The lights begin to twinkle from the rocks:
The long day wanes: the slow moon climbs: the deep
Moans round with many voices. Come, my friends,
'T is not too late to seek a newer world.
Push off, and sitting well in order smite
The sounding furrows; for my purpose holds
To sail beyond the sunset, and the baths   60
Of all the western stars, until I die.
It may be that the gulfs will wash us down:
It may be we shall touch the Happy Isles,
And see the great Achilles, whom we knew.
Tho' much is taken, much abides; and tho'
We are not now that strength which in old days
Moved earth and heaven, that which we are, we are;
One equal temper of heroic hearts,
Made weak by time and fate, but strong in will
To strive, to seek, to find, and not to yield.   70

*The Lotos-Eaters

ALFRED, LORD TENNYSON

"Courage!" he said, and pointed toward the land,
"This mounting wave will roll us shoreward soon."
In the afternoon they came unto a land
In which it seemèd always afternoon.
All round the coast the languid air did swoon,
Breathing like one that hath a weary dream.
Full-faced above the valley stood the moon;
And like a downward smoke, the slender stream
Along the cliff to fall and pause and fall did seem.

A land of streams! some, like a downward smoke,   10
Slow-dropping veils of thinnest lawn, did go;
And some thro' wavering lights and shadows broke,
Rolling a slumbrous sheet of foam below.
They saw the gleaming river seaward flow
From the inner land: far off, three mountaintops,
Three silent pinnacles of aged snow,
Stood sunset-flush'd: and, dew'd with showery drops,
Up-clomb the shadowy pine above the woven corpse.

The charmèd sunset linger'd low adown
In the red West: thro' mountain clefts the dale   20
Was seen far inland, and the yellow down
Border'd with palm, and many a winding vale
And meadow, set with slender galingale;
A land where all things always seem'd the same!
And round about the keel with faces pale,
Dark faces pale against that rosy flame,
The mild-eyed melancholy Lotos-eaters came.

Branches they bore of that enchanted stem,
Laden with flower and fruit, whereof they gave
To each, but whoso did receive of them   30
And taste, to him the gushing of the wave
Far far away did seem to mourn and rave
On alien shores; and if his fellow spake,
His voice was thin, as voices from the grave;
And deep-asleep he seem'd, yet all awake,
And music in his ears his beating heart did make.

---

l. 21. down: Open hilly land.

They sat them down upon the yellow sand,
Between the sun and moon upon the shore;
And sweet it was to dream of Fatherland,
Of child, and wife, and slave; but evermore   40
Most weary seem'd the sea, weary the oar,
Weary the wandering fields of barren foam.
Then someone said, "We will return no more,"
And all at once they sang, "Our island home
Is far beyond the wave; we will no longer roam."

CHORIC SONG
I

There is sweet music here that softer falls
Than petals from blown roses on the grass,
Or night-dews on still waters between walls
Of shadowy granite, in a gleaming pass;
Music that gentlier on the spirit lies,   50
Than tir'd eyelids upon tir'd eyes;
Music that brings sweet sleep down from the blissful skies.
Here are cool mosses deep,
And thro' the moss the ivies creep,
And in the stream the long-leaved flowers weep,
And from the craggy ledge the poppy hangs in sleep.

II

Why are we weigh'd upon with heaviness,
And utterly consumed with sharp distress,
While all things else have rest from weariness?
All things have rest: why should we toil alone,   60
We only toil, who are the first of things,
And make perpetual moan,
Still from one sorrow to another thrown:
Nor ever fold our wings,
And cease from wanderings,
Nor steep our brows in slumber's holy balm;
Nor harken what the inner spirit sings,
"There is no joy but calm!"
Why should we only toil, the roof and crown of things?

III

Lo! in the middle of the wood,   70
The folded leaf is woo'd from out the bud
With winds upon the branch, and there
Grows green and broad, and takes no care,
Sun-steep'd at noon, and in the moon

Nightly dew-fed; and turning yellow
Falls, and floats adown the air.
Lo! sweeten'd with the summer light,
The full-juiced apple, waxing over-mellow,
Drops in a silent autumn night.
All its allotted length of days,   80
The flower ripens in its place,
Ripens and fades, and falls, and hath no toil,
Fast-rooted in the fruitful soil.

IV

Hateful is the dark-blue sky,
Vaulted o'er the dark-blue sea.
Death is the end of life; ah, why
Should life all labour be?
Let us alone. Time driveth onward fast,
And in a little while our lips are dumb.
Let us alone. What is it that will last?   90
All things are taken from us, and become
Portions and parcels of the dreadful Past.
Let us alone. What pleasure can we have
To war with evil? Is there any peace
In ever climbing up the climbing wave?
All things have rest, and ripen toward the grave
In silence; ripen, fall, and cease:
Give us long rest or death, dark death, or dreamful ease.

V

How sweet it were, hearing the downward stream
With half-shut eyes to seem   100
Falling asleep in a half-dream!
To dream and dream, like yonder amber light,
Which will not leave the myrrh-bush on the height;
To hear each other's whispered speech;
Eating the Lotos day by day,
To watch the crisping ripples on the beach,
And tender curving lines of creamy spray;
To lend our hearts and spirits wholly
To the influence of mild-minded melancholy;
To muse and brood and live again in memory,   110
With those old faces of our infancy
Heap'd over with a mound of grass,
Two handfuls of white dust, shut in an urn of brass!

---

l. 106. crisping: Curling.

VI

Dear is the memory of our wedded lives,
And dear the last embraces of our wives
And their warm tears; but all hath suffered change:
For surely now our household hearths are cold:
Our sons inherit us: our looks are strange:
And we should come like ghosts to trouble joy.
Or else the island princes over-bold   120
Have eat our substance, and the minstrel sings
Before them of the ten years' war in Troy,
And our great deeds, as half-forgotten things.
Is there confusion in the little isle?
Let what is broken so remain.
The gods are hard to reconcile:
'Tis hard to settle order once again.
There *is* confusion worse than death,
Trouble on trouble, pain on pain,
Long labour unto aged breath,   130
Sore task to hearts worn out by many wars
And eyes grown dim with gazing on the pilot-stars.

VII

But, propt on beds of amaranth and moly,
How sweet (while warm airs lull us, blowing lowly)
With half-dropt eyelid still,
Beneath a heaven dark and holy,
To watch the long bright river drawing slowly
His waters from the purple hill—
To hear the dewy echoes calling
From cave to cave thro' the thick-twined vine—   140
To watch the emerald-coloured water falling
Thro' many a wov'n acanthus-wreath divine!
Only to hear and see the far-off sparkling brine,
Only to hear were sweet, stretch'd out beneath the pine.

VIII

The Lotos blooms below the barren peak:
The Lotos blows by every winding creek:
All day the wind breathes low with mellower tone:
Thro' every hollow cave and alley lone
Round and round the spicy downs the yellow Lotos-dust is blown
We have had enough of action, and of motion we,   150
Roll'd to starboard, roll'd to larboard, when the surge was seething free,
Where the wallowing monster spouted his foam-fountains in the sea

Let us swear an oath, and keep it with an equal mind,
In the hollow Lotos-land to live and lie reclined
On the hills like Gods together, careless of mankind.
For they lie beside their nectar, and the bolts are hurl'd
Far below them in the valleys, and the clouds are lightly curl'd
Round their golden houses, girdled with the gleaming world:
Where they smile in secret, looking over wasted lands,
Blight and famine, plague and earthquake, roaring deeps and fiery
    sands,   160
Clanging fights, and flaming towns, and sinking ships, and praying hands.
But they smile, they find a music centred in a doleful song
Steaming up, a lamentation and an ancient tale of wrong,
Chanted from an ill-used race of men that cleave the soil,
Like a tale of little meaning tho' the words are strong;
Sow the seed, and reap the harvest with enduring toil,
Storing yearly little dues of wheat, and wine and oil;
Till they perish and they suffer—some, 'tis whisper'd—down in hell
Suffer endless anguish, others in Elysian valleys dwell,
Resting weary limbs at last on beds of asphodel.   170
Surely, surely, slumber is more sweet than toil, the shore
Than labour in the deep mid-ocean, wind and wave and oar;
O rest ye, brother mariners, we will not wander more.

Dover Beach

MATTHEW ARNOLD

The sea is calm to-night.
The tide is full, the moon lies fair
Upon the straits;—on the French coast the light
Gleams and is gone; the cliffs of England stand,
Glimmering and vast, out in the tranquil bay.
Come to the window, sweet is the night-air!

Only, from the long line of spray
Where the sea meets the moon-blanch'd land,
Listen! you hear the grating roar
Of pebbles which the waves draw back, and fling,   10
At their return, up the high strand,
Begin, and cease, and then again begin,
With tremulous cadence slow, and bring
The eternal note of sadness in.

Sophocles long ago
Heard it on the Aegaean, and it brought
Into his mind the turbid ebb and flow
Of human misery; we
Find also in the sound a thought,
Hearing it by this distant northern sea.   20

The Sea of Faith
Was once, too, at the full, and round earth's shore
Lay like the folds of a bright girdle furl'd
But now I only hear
Its melancholy, long, withdrawing roar,
Retreating, to the breath
Of the night-wind, down the vast edges drear
And naked shingles of the world.

      Ah, love, let us be true
To one another! for the world, which seems   30
To lie before us like a land of dreams,
So various, so beautiful, so new,
Hath really neither joy, nor love, nor light,
Nor certitude, nor peace, nor help for pain;
And we are here as on a darkling plain
Swept with confused alarms of struggle and flight,
Where ignorant armies clash by night.

[A loss of something ever felt I]

EMILY DICKINSON

A loss of something ever felt I—
The first that I could recollect
Bereft I was—of what I knew not
Too young that any should suspect

A Mourner walked among the children
I notwithstanding went about
As one bemoaning a Dominion
Itself the only Prince cast out—

Elder, Today, a session wiser
And fainter, too, as Wiseness is—   10
I find myself still softly searching
For my Delinquent Palaces—

And a Suspicion, like a Finger
Touches my Forehead now and then
That I am looking oppositely
For the site of the Kingdom of Heaven—

[*Finding is the first Act*]

EMILY DICKINSON

Finding is the first Act
The second, loss,
Third, Expedition for
the "Golden Fleece"

Fourth, no Discovery—
Fifth, no Crew—
Finally, no Golden Fleece—
Jason—sham—too.

[*The wayfarer*]

STEPHEN CRANE

The wayfarer,
Perceiving the pathway to truth,
Was struck with astonishment.
It was thickly grown with weeds.
"Ha," he said,
"I see that none has passed here
In a long time."
Later he saw that each weed
Was a singular knife.
"Well," he mumbled at last,   10
"Doubtless there are other roads."

[*A man said to the Universe*]

STEPHEN CRANE

A man said to the Universe:
"Sir, I exist!"
"However," replied the universe,
"The fact has not created in me
"A sense of obligation."

Waiting Both

THOMAS HARDY

A star looks down at me,
And says: "Here I and you
Stand, each in our degree.
What do you mean to do,—
        Mean to do?"

I say: "For all I know,
Wait, and let Time go by,
Till my change come."—"Just so,"
The star says: "So mean I:—
        So mean I."   10

By the Earth's Corpse

THOMAS HARDY

I

"O Lord, why grievest Thou?—
    Since Life has ceased to be
Upon this globe, now cold
    As lunar land and sea,
And humankind, and fowl, and fur
    Are gone eternally,
All is the same to Thee as ere
    They knew mortality."

II

"O, Time," replied the Lord,
   "Thou readest me ill, I ween;   10
Were all *the same,* I should not grieve
   At that late earthly scene,
Now blestly past—though planned by me
   With interest close and keen!—
Nay, nay: things now are *not* the same
   As they have earlier been.

III

"Written indelibly
On my eternal mind
Are all the wrongs endured
By Earth's poor patient kind,   20
Which my too oft unconscious hand
   Let enter undesigned.
No god can cancel deeds foredone,
   Or thy old coils unwind!

IV

"As when in Nöe's days,
   I whelmed the plains with sea,
So at this last, when flesh
   And herb but fossils be,
And, all extinct, their piteous dust
   Revolves obliviously,   30
That I made Earth, and life, and man,
   It still repenteth me!''

The Life of Man

FRANCIS BACON

The world's a bubble, and the life of man
        Less than a span:
In his conception wretched, from the womb
        So to the tomb;
Curst from his cradle, and brought up to years
        With cares and fears.
Who then to frail mortality shall trust,
But limns the water, or but writes in dust.

Yet since with sorrow here we live oppressed,
      What life is best?   10
Courts are but only superficial schools
      To dandle fools:
The rural parts are turned into a den
      Of savage men:
And where's a city from all vice so free,
But may be termed the worst of all the three?

Domestic cares afflict the husband's bed,
      Or pains his head:
Those that live single, take it for a curse,
      Or do things worse: 20
Some would have children; those that have them, moan
      Or wish them gone:
What is it, then, to have, or have no wife,
But single thraldom, or a double strife?

Our own affections still at home to please
      Is a disease:
To cross the seas to any foreign soil,
      Perils and toil:
Wars with their noise affright us; when they cease,
      We're worse in peace;—   30
What then remains, but that we still should cry
Not to be born, or, being born, to die?

---

l. 11. Courts: Royal (not legal) courts.

[*When smoke stood up from Ludlow*]

A. E. HOUSMAN

When smoke stood up from Ludlow,
   And mist blew off from Teme,
And blithe afield to plowing
   Against the morning beam
   I strode beside my team,

The blackbird in the coppice
   Looked out to see me stride,
And hearkened as I whistled
   The trampling team beside,
   And fluted and replied: 10

"Lie down, lie down, young yeoman;
   What use to rise and rise?
Rise man a thousand mornings
   Yet down at last he lies,
   And then the man is wise."

I heard the tune he sang me,
   And spied his yellow bill;
I picked a stone and aimed it
   And threw it with a will:
   Then the bird was still.   20

Then my soul within me
   Took up the blackbird's strain,
And still beside the horses
   Along the dewy lane
   It sang the song again:

"Lie down, lie down, young yeoman;
   The sun moves always west;
The road one treads to labour
   Will lead one home to rest,
   And that will be the best."   30

*Musée des Beaux Arts

W. H. AUDEN

About suffering they were never wrong,
The Old Masters: how well they understood
Its human position; how it takes place
While someone else is eating or opening a window or just walking dully
   along;
How, when the aged are reverently, passionately waiting
For the miraculous birth, there always must be
Children who did not specially want it to happen, skating
On a pond at the edge of the wood:
They never forgot
That even the dreadful martyrdom must run its course   10
Anyhow in a corner, some untidy spot
Where the dogs go on with their doggy life and the torturer's horse
Scratches its innocent behind on a tree.

In Brueghel's *Icarus*, for instance: how everything turns away
Quite leisurely from the disaster; the ploughman may
Have heard the splash, the forsaken cry,
But for him it was not an important failure; the sun shone
As it had to on the white legs disappearing into the green
Water; and the expensive delicate ship that must have seen
Something amazing, a boy falling out of the sky,   20
Had somewhere to get to and sailed calmly on.

The Treehouse

JAMES A. EMANUEL

To every man
His treehouse,
A green splice in the humping years,
Spartan with narrow cot
And prickly door.

To every man
His twilight flash
Of luminous recall
   of tiptoe years
   in leaf-stung flight;   10
   of days of squirm and bite
   that waved antennas through the grass;
   of nights
   when every moving thing
   was girlshaped,
   expectantly turning.

To every man
His house below
And his house above—
With perilous stairs   20
Between.

*If the Stars Should Fall

SAMUEL ALLEN

Again the day
The low bleak day of the stricken years
And now the years.

The huge slow grief drives on
And I wonder why
And I grow cold
And care less
And less and less I care.

If the stars should fall,
I grant them privilege;   10
Or if the stars should rise to a brighter flame
The mighty dog, the buckled Orion
To excellent purposes appear to gain—
I should renew their privilege
To fall down.

It is all to me the same
The same to me
I say the great Gods, all of them,
All—cold, pitiless—
Let them fall down   20
Let them buckle and drop.

RELIGION

*Following are but a few of many poems in this volume which deal
with religion; see particularly those of Gerard Manley Hopkins (pp.
569–571). Donne and Herbert were intensely religious; in his lifetime
Donne was more celebrated as a preacher than as a poet. Housman,
on th eother hand, was an atheist but retained a love of the Bible and
a reverence for the goodness of Jesus, as well as some sympathy
for the Church of England. In the "Easter Hymn" he writes rather as
an agnostic, as one who does not know whether or not Christ rose
from the dead.*

Peace

GEORGE HERBERT

Sweet Peace, where dost thou dwell? I humbly crave,
    Let me once know.
  I sought thee in a secret cave,
    And ask'd, if Peace were there.
A hollow wind did seem to answer, No:
    Go seek elsewhere.

I did; and going did a rainbow note:
    Surely, thought I,
  This is the lace of Peace's coat:
    I will search out the matter.   10
But while I lookt the clouds immediately
    Did break and scatter.

Then went I to a garden and did spy
    A gallant flower,
  The Crown Imperiall: Sure, said I,
    Peace at the root must dwell.
But when I digg'd, I saw a worm devoure
    What show'd so well.

At length I met a rev'rend good old man;
    Whom when for Peace   20
  I did demand, he thus began:
    There was a Prince of old
At Salem dwelt, who liv'd with good increase
    Of flock and fold.

He sweetly liv'd; yet sweetnesse did not save
    His life from foes.
  But after death out of His grave
    There sprang twelve stalks of wheat;
Which many wond'ring at, got some of those
    To plant and set.   30

---

l. 15. Crown Imperiall: Fritillaria imperialis, *a spring-blooming plant with clusters of pendent, bell-shaped flowers.*
l. 22ff. Prince . . . Salem: Melchisedec, "King of Salem, which is, King of peace," in the Old Testament blessed Abraham, and was later represented as prefiguring Christ.
l. 28. twelve stalks of wheat: The twelve Apostles.

It prosper'd strangely, and did soon disperse
    Through all the earth:
      For they that taste it do rehearse,
        That vertue lies therein;
A secret vertue bringing peace and mirth
      By flight of sinne.

Take of this grain, which in my garden grows,
    And grows for you;
      Make bread of it: and that repose
        And peace, which ev'ry where   40
With so much earnestness you do pursue
      Is only there.

The Pulley

GEORGE HERBERT

    When God at first made man,
Having a glass of blessings standing by;
Let us (said he) poure on him all we can:
Let the worlds riches, which dispered lie,
    Contract into a span.

    So strength first made a way;
Then beautie flow'd, then wisdome, honour, pleasure:
When almost all was out, God made a stay,
Perceiving that alone of all his treasure
    Rest in the bottome lay.   10

    For if I should (said he)
Bestow this jewell also on my creature,
He would adore my gifts instead of me,
And rest in Nature, not the God of Nature:
    So both should losers be.

    Yet let him keep the rest,
But keep them with repining restlessnesse:
Let him be rich and wearie, that at least,
If goodnesse leade him not, yet wearinesse   20
    May tosse him to my breast.

*Easter Hymn

A. E. HOUSMAN

If in that Syrian garden, ages slain,
You sleep, and know not you are dead in vain,
Nor even in dreams behold how dark and bright
Ascends in smoke and fire by day and night
The hate you died to quench and could but fan,
Sleep well and see no morning, son of man.

But if, the grave rent and the stone rolled by,
At the right hand of majesty on high
You sit, and sitting so remember yet
Your tears, your agony and bloody sweat,   10
Your cross and passion and the life you gave,
Bow hither out of heaven and see and save.

*The Flight in the Desert

BROTHER ANTONINUS (WILLIAM EVERSON)

The last settlement scraggled out with a barbed wire fence
And fell from sight. They crossed coyote country:
Mesquite, sage, the bunchgrass knotted in patches;
And there the prairie dog yapped in the valley;
And on the high plateau the short-armed badger
Delved his clay. But beyond that the desert,
Raw, unslakable, its perjured dominion wholly contained
In the sun's remorseless mandate, where the dim trail
Died ahead in the watery horizon: God knows where.

And there the failures: skull of the ox,   10
Where the animal terror trembled on in the hollowed eyes;
The catastrophic wheel, split, sandbedded;
And the sad jawbone of a horse. These the denials
Of the retributive tribes, fiercer than pestilence,
Whose scrupulous realm this was.

Only the burro took no notice: the forefoot
Placed with the nice particularity of one
To whom the evil of the day is wholly sufficient.
Even the jocular ears marked time.

But they, the man and the anxious woman,   20
Who stared pinch-eyed into the settling sun,
They went forward into its denseness
All apprehensive, and would many a time have turned
But for what they carried. That brought them on.
In the gritty blanket they bore the world's great risk,
And knew it; and kept it covered, near to the blind heart,
That hugs in a bad hour its sweetest need,
Possessed against the drawn night
That comes now, over the dead arroyos,
Cold and acrid and black.   30

This was the first of his goings forth into the wilderness of the world.
There was much to follow: much of portent, much of dread.
But what was so meek then and so mere, so slight and strengthless,
(Too tender, almost, to be touched)—what they nervously guarded
Guarded them. As we, each day, from the lifted chalice,
That strengthless Bread the mildest tongue subsumes,
To be taken out in the blatant kingdom,
Where Herod sweats, and his deft henchmen
Riffle the tabloids—that keeps us.

Over the campfire the desert moon   40
Slivers the west, too chaste and cleanly
To mean hard luck. The man rattles the skillet
To take the raw edge off the silence;
The woman lifts up her heart; the Infant
Knuckles the generous breast, and feeds.

Forms

Shifting the focus of his attention from the content of poetry to its form, the reader will discover several discrete patterns. The ballad is the simplest and most native of English poetic forms, but, as a "story" or narrative form, it has been represented in an earlier group in this volume (pp. 403–428). The lyric too is often called a form, but except where it refers to the earliest times, when lyrics were composed exclusively to be sung, not spoken or read, the term has become a catch-all for a large and various assortment of short, or at least not-long poems; it therefore scarcely repays study as a separate form (probably more than half the poems in this volume are "lyrics" in one sense or another, and the song-like quality of some of them will be apparent).

THE SONNET

The sonnet, ode, and elegy, represented here, are the most important of the other poetic forms in English, apart from the book-length epic or other long narrative.

The sonnet was introduced into England in the sixteenth century, mainly as a result of the vogue of the Italian love sonnets of Petrarch.

Though there have been many variations, the two chief sonnet forms in English poetry are known as the Italian and the English or Shakespearean.

Both consist of fourteen lines of iambic pentameter. For the Italian form, the poet chooses a two-part subject, involving perhaps a question and answer or some other shift of thought or mood that will fit into a two-part form. The first eight lines, or octave, are held together in a fixed rhyme scheme (a b b a, a b b a). With the "turn" of subject comes a change of rhyme in the sestet (the last six lines), where the poet has a freer choice. The rhyme may be c d e c d e or any of several other arrangements. Donne's religious sonnet in the preceding section (page 411). "At the round earth's imagined corners," illustrates a use of the turn perfectly. In the declamatory octave he welcomes the end of the world and the Day of Judgment; in the sestet he changes his mind. Reflecting, he asks for delay; he is not yet fit for the Judgment. Many sonnets in English, such as those of Milton, employ the Italian rhyme scheme without quite such a clearly marked and exactly placed turn of thought.

The "English" form has been used most notably by Shakespeare. It consists of three quatrains of alternate rhyme (a b a b, c d c d, e f e f), followed by a couplet. Sometimes the Shakespearean sonnet follows a two-part scheme of thought like the Italian; often it does not.

In the Elizabethan age, many poets wrote "sonnet sequences," series of independent sonnets dealing with one subject or connected by a thread of story, usually about the poet's real or imagined love. Those of Shakespeare belong to such a sequence.

For additional sonnets, see those of Donne in the preceding section, Wordsworth's "Mutability" (pp. 492–493), several by Hopkins (pp. 570–571), and Hayden's "Frederick Douglass" (p. 605).

A Renouncing of Love

SIR THOMAS WYATT

Farewell, Love, and all thy laws for ever;
Thy baited hooks shall tangle me no more:
Senec and Plato call me from thy lore,
To perfect wealth, my wit for to endeavour;
In blind errour when I did persever,
Thy sharp repulse, that pricketh aye so sore,
Taught me in trifles that I set no store;

---

l. 3. Senec: Seneca, the Roman philosopher.
l. 7. Taught me that I should set no store in trifles.

But 'scape forth thence, since liberty is lever:
Therefore, farewell, go trouble younger hearts,
And in me claim no more authority;   10
With idle youth go use thy property,
And theron spend thy many brittle darts:
    For hitherto though I have lost my time,
    Me list no longer rotten boughs to climb.

---

l. 8. lever: More desirable.

*[Since there's no help, come let us kiss and part]

MICHAEL DRAYTON

Since there's no help, come let us kiss and part;
Nay, I have done, you get no more of me,
And I am glad, yea glad with all my heart
That thus so cleanly I myself can free;
Shake hands for ever, cancel all our vows,
And when we meet at any time again,
Be it not seen in either of our brows
That we one jot of former love retain.
Now at the last gasp of love's latest breath,
When, his pulse failing, passion speechless lies,   10
When faith is kneeling by his bed of death,
And innocence is closing up his eyes,
    Now if thou wouldst, when all have given him over,
    From death to life thou mightst him yet recover.

*Sonnets

WILLIAM SHAKESPEARE

SONNET 18

Shall I compare thee to a summer's day?
Thou art more lovely and more temperate:
Rough winds do shake the darling buds of May,
And summer's lease hath all too short a date:
Sometime too hot the eye of heaven shines,
And often is his gold complexion dimm'd;
And every fair from fair sometime declines,

By chance, or nature's changing course untrimm'd;
But thy eternal summer shall not fade,
Nor lose possession of that fair thou ow'st,   10
Nor shall Death brag thou wander'st in his shade,
When in eternal lines to time thou grow'st;
    So long as men can breathe, or eyes can see,
    So long lives this, and this gives life to thee.

----

l. 10. ow'st: Ownest.

SONNET 29

When in disgrace with fortune and men's eyes
I all alone beweep my outcast state,
And trouble deaf heaven with my bootless cries,
And look upon myself, and curse my fate,
Wishing me like to one more rich in hope,
Featur'd like him, like him with friends possess'd,
Desiring this man's art, and that man's scope,
With what I most enjoy contented least;
Yet in these thoughts myself almost despising,
Haply I think on thee,—and then my state,   10
Like to the lark at break of day arising
From sullen earth, sings hymns at heaven's gate;
    For thy sweet love remember'd such wealth brings
    That then I scorn to change my state with kings.

SONNET 30

When to the sessions of sweet silent thought
I summon up remembrance of things past,
I sigh the lack of many a thing I sought,
And with old woes new wail my dear time's waste:
Then can I drown an eye, unus'd to flow,
For precious friends hid in death's dateless night,
And weep afresh love's long since cancell'd woe,
And moan th' expense of many a vanish'd sight:
Then can I grieve at grievances foregone,
And heavily from woe to woe tell o'er   10
The sad account of fore-bemoaned moan,
Which I new pay as if not paid before.
    But if the while I think on thee, dear friend,
    All losses are restor'd and sorrows end.

SONNET 33

Full many a glorious morning have I seen
Flatter the mountain-tops with sovereign eye,
Kissing with golden face the meadows green,

Gilding pale streams with heavenly alchemy;
Anon permit the basest clouds to ride
With ugly rack on his celestial face,
And from the forlorn world his visage hide,
Stealing unseen to west with this disgrace.
Even so my sun one early morn did shine
With all-triumphant splendour on my brow;   10
But, out; alack! he was but one hour mine,
The region cloud hath mask'd him from me now.
    Yet him for this my love no whit disdaineth;
    Suns of the world may stain when heaven's sun staineth.

---

l. 6. rack: A wind-driven mass of high clouds.
l. 14. stain: Become darkened.

SONNET 65

Since brass, nor stone, nor earth, nor boundless sea,
But sad mortality o'er-sways their power,
How with this rage shall beauty hold a plea,
Whose action is no stronger than a flower?
O! how shall summer's honey breath hold out
Against the wrackful siege of batt'ring days,
When rocks impregnable are not so stout,
Nor gates of steel so strong, but Time decays?
O fearful meditation! where, alack,
Shall Time's best jewel from Time's chest lie hid?   10
Or what strong hand can hold his swift foot back?
Or who his spoil of beauty can forbid?
    O! none, unless this miracle have might,
    That in black ink my love may still shine bright.

SONNET 71

No longer mourn for me when I am dead
Than you shall hear the surly sullen bell
Give warning to the world that I am fled
From this vile world, with vilest worms to dwell:
Nay, if you read this line, remember not
The hand that writ it; for I love you so,
That I in your sweet thoughts would be forgot,
If thinking on me then should make you woe.
O! if, I say, you look upon this verse,
When I perhaps compounded am with clay,   10
Do not so much as my poor name rehearse,
But let your love even with my life decay;
    Lest the wise world should look into your moan,
    And mock you with me after I am gone.

SONNET 73

That time of year thou mayst in me behold
When yellow leaves, or none, or few, do hang
Upon those boughs which shake against the cold,
Bare ruin'd choirs, where late the sweet birds sang.
In me thou see'st the twilight of such day
As after sunset fadeth in the west,
Which by and by black night doth take away,
Death's second self, that seals up all in rest.
In me thou see'st the glowing of such fire
That on the ashes of his youth doth lie,   10
As the death-bed whereon it must expire,
Consum'd with that which it was nourish'd by.
  This thou perceiv'st, which makes thy love more strong,
  To love that well which thou must leave ere long.

SONNET 106

When in the chronicle of wasted time
I see descriptions of the fairest wights,
And beauty making beautiful old rime,
In praise of ladies dead and lovely knights;
Then, in the blazon of sweet beauty's best,
Of hand, of foot, of lip, of eye, of brow,
I see their antique pen would have express'd
Even such a beauty as you master now.
So all their praises are but prophecies
Of this our time, all you prefiguring;   10
And, for they look'd but with divining eyes,
They had not skill enough your worth to sing:
  For we, which now behold these present days,
  Have eyes to wonder, but lack tongues to praise.

SONNET 116

Let me not to the marriage of true minds
Admit impediments. Love is not love
Which alters when it alteration finds,
Or bends with the remover to remove:
O, no! it is an ever-fixed mark
That looks on tempests and is never shaken;
It is the star to every wand'ring bark,
Whose worth's unknown, although his height be taken.
Love's not Time's fool, though rosy lips and cheeks
Within his bending sickle's compass come;   10
Love alters not with his brief hours and weeks,
But bears it out even to the edge of doom.
  If this be error, and upon me prov'd.
  I never writ, nor no man ever lov'd.

*[When I consider how my light is spent]

JOHN MILTON

When I consider how my light is spent,
Ere half my days, in this dark world and wide,
And that one Talent which is death to hide,
Lodg'd with me useless, though my Soul more bent
To serve therewith my Maker, and present
My true account, least he returning chide,
Doth God exact day-labour, light deny'd,
I fondly ask; But patience to prevent
That murmur, soon replies, God doth not need
Either man's work or his own gifts, who best   10
Bear his milde yoak, they serve him best, his State
Is Kingly. Thousands at his bidding speed
And post o're Land and Ocean without rest:
They also serve who only stand and waite.

---

l. 6. *least:* Lest.
l. 8. *fondly:* Foolishly.

*On the Late Massacre in Piedmont

JOHN MILTON

Avenge O Lord thy slaughter'd Saints, whose bones
Lie scatter'd on the Alpine mountains cold,
Ev'n them who kept thy truth so pure of old
When all our Fathers worship't Stocks and Stones,
Forget not: in thy book record their groanes
Who were thy Sheep and in their antient Fold
Slayn by the bloody *Piemontese* that roll'd
Mother with Infant down the Rocks. Their moans
The Vales redoubl'd to the Hills, and they
To Heav'n. Their martyr'd blood and ashes sow   10
O're all th' *Italian* fields where still doth sway
The triple Tyrant: that from these may grow
A hunder'd-fold, who having learnt thy way
Early may fly the *Babylonian* woe.

---

l. 12. *triple Tyrant:* The pope, who wears a triple-crowned tiara.

Composed Upon Westminster Bridge, September 3, 1802

WILLIAM WORDSWORTH

Earth has not anything to show more fair:
Dull would he be of soul who could pass by
A sight so touching in its majesty:
This City now doth, like a garment, wear
The beauty of the morning; silent, bare,
Ships, towers, domes, theatres, and temples lie
Open unto the fields, and to the sky;
All bright and glittering in the smokeless air.
Never did sun more beautifully steep
In his first splendour, valley, rock, or hill;   10
Ne'er saw I, never felt, a calm so deep!
The river glideth at his own sweet will:
Dear God! the very houses seem asleep;
And all that mighty heart is lying still!

[The world is too much with us]

WILLIAM WORDSWORTH

The world is too much with us; late and soon,
Getting and spending, we lay waste our powers:
Little we see in Nature that is ours;
We have given our hearts away, a sordid boon!
This Sea that bares her bosom to the moon;
The winds that will be howling at all hours,
And are up-gathered now like sleeping flowers;
For this, for everything, we are out of tune;
It moves us not.—Great God! I'd rather be
A Pagan suckled in a creed outworn;   10
So might I, standing on this pleasant lea,
Have glimpses that would make me less forlorn;
Have sight of Proteus rising from the sea;
Or hear old Triton blow his wreathèd horn.

_____

ll. 13–14. Proteus and Triton: Sea gods of classical mythology.

England in 1819

PERCY BYSSHE SHELLEY

An old, mad, blind, despised and dying king;
Princes, the dregs of their dull race, who flow
Through public scorn—mud from a muddy spring;
Rulers, who neither see, nor feel, nor know,
But leech-like to their fainting country cling,
Till they drop, blind in blood, without a blow;
A people starved and stabbed in the untilled field;
An army which liberticide and prey
Makes as a two-edged sword to all who wield;
Golden and sanguine laws which tempt and slay;   10
Religion Christless, Godless—a book sealed;
A Senate—Time's worst statute unrepealed,
Are graves from which a glorious Phantom may
Burst to illumine our tempestuous day.

---

l. 1. king: George III.
l. 12. statute unrepealed: Discriminatory laws against Catholics.

Ozymandias

PERCY BYSSHE SHELLEY

I met a traveler from an antique land
Who said: Two vast and trunkless legs of stone
Stand in the desert. Near them, on the sand,
Half sunk, a shattered visage lies, whose frown,
And wrinkled lip, and sneer of cold command,
Tell that its sculptor well those passions read
Which yet survive, stamped on these lifeless things,
The hand that mocked them, and the heart that fed;
And on the pedestal these words appear:
"My name is Ozymandias, king of kings: 10
Look on my works, ye Mighty, and despair!"
Nothing beside remains. Round the decay
Of that colossal wreck, boundless and bare
The lone and level sands stretch far away.

*Sonnet 23

[from *THE GROWTH OF LOVE*]

ROBERT BRIDGES

O weary pilgrims, chanting of your woe,
That turn your eyes to all the peaks that shine,
Hailing in each the citadel divine
The which ye thought to have enter'd long ago;
Until at length your feeble steps and slow
Falter upon the threshold of the shrine,
And your hearts overburden'd doubt in fine
Whether it be Jerusalem or no:
Dishearten'd pilgrims, I am one of you;
For, having worshipp'd many a barren face,   10
I scarce now greet the goal I journey'd to:
I stand a pagan in the holy place;
Beneath the lamp of truth I am found untrue,
And question with the God that I embrace.

THE ODE

Odes and elegies are serious poems, dignified and rather slow in movement. As a rule, they are longer and more reflective than most lyric poems. The subject of an ode may be anything that has sufficient magnitude to warrant its lofty tone and its frequently formal treatment. The verse form varies. Some English odes follow more or less closely the structure of the Greek odes of Pindar, others have irregular rhyme and stanza, and still others employ regular stanzas of various kinds.

Several of the greatest English odes will be found among the selections from Keats (pp. 561–568).

*Ode

INTIMATIONS OF IMMORTALITY FROM RECOLLECTIONS OF EARLY CHILDHOOD

WILLIAM WORDSWORTH

The Child is father of the Man;
And I could wish my days to be
Bound each to each by natural piety.

I

There was a time when meadow, grove, and stream,
   The earth, and every common sight,
     To me did seem
   Appareled in celestial light,
The glory and the freshness of a dream.
It is not now as it hath been of yore;—
   Turn whersoe'er I may,
     By night or day,
The things which I have seen I now can see no more.

II

   The Rainbow comes and goes,   10
   And lovely is the Rose;
   The Moon doth with delight
Look round her when the heavens are bare;
   Waters on a starry night
   Are beautiful and fair;
  The sunshine is a glorious birth;
  But yet I know, where'er I go,
That there hath passed away a glory from the earth.

III

Now, while the birds thus sing a joyous song,
   And while the young lambs bound   20
     As to the tabor's sound,
To me alone there came a thought of grief:
A timely utterance gave that thought relief,
     And I again am strong:
The cataracts blow their trumpets from the steep;
No more shall grief of mine the season wrong;
I hear the Echoes through the mountains throng,
The Winds come to me from the fields of sleep,

And all the earth is gay;
  Land and sea   30
 Give themselves up to jollity,
  And with the heart of May
 Doth every Beast keep holiday;—
  Thou Child of Joy,
Shout round me, let me hear thy shouts, thou happy Shepherd-boy!

IV

Ye blessèd Creatures, I have heard the call
  Ye to each other make; I see
The heavens laugh with you in your jubilee;
  My heart is at your festival,
  My head hath its coronal,   40
The fulness of your bliss, I feel—I feel it all.
  Oh evil day! if I were sullen
  While Earth herself is adorning,
   This sweet May-morning,
  And the Children are culling
   On every side,
  In a thousand valleys far and wide,
  Fresh flowers; while the sun shines warm,
And the Babe leaps up on his Mother's arm:—
  I hear, I hear, with joy I hear!   50
  —But there's a Tree, of many, one,
A single Field which I have looked upon,
Both of them speak of something that is gone:
  The Pansy at my feet
  Doth the same tale repeat:
Whither is fled the visionary gleam?
Where is it now, the glory and the dream?

V

Our birth is but a sleep and a forgetting:
The Soul that rises with us, our life's Star,
  Hath had elsewhere its setting,   60
  And cometh from afar:
  Not in entire forgetfulness,
  And not in utter nakedness,
But trailing clouds of glory do we come
  From God, who is our home:
Heaven lies about us in our infancy!
Shades of the prison-house begin to close
  Upon the growing Boy,
   But He

Beholds the light, and whence it flows,
    He sees it in his joy;
The Youth, who daily farther from the east
    Must travel, still is Nature's Priest,
    And by the vision splendid
    Is on his way attended;
At length the Man perceives it die away,
And fade into the light of common day.   70

VI

Earth fills her lap with pleasures of her own;
Yearnings she hath in her own natural kind,
And, even with something of a Mother's mind,   80
    And no unworthy aim,
    The homely Nurse doth all she can
To make her Foster-child, her Inmate Man,
    Forget the glories he hath known,
And that imperial palace whence he came.

VII

Behold the Child among his new-born blisses,
A six years' Darling of a pigmy size!
See, where 'mid work of his own hand he lies,
Fretted by sallies of his mother's kisses,
With light upon him from his father's eyes!   90
See, at his feet, some little plan or chart,
Some fragment from his dream of human life,
Shaped by himself with newly-learned art;
    A wedding or a festival,
    A mourning or a funeral;
      And this hath now his heart,
    And unto this he frames his song:
      Then will he fit his tongue
To dialogues of business, love, or strife;
    But it will not be long   100
    Ere this be thrown aside,
    And with new joy and pride
The little Actor cons another part;
Filling from time to time his "humorous stage"
With all the Persons, down to palsied Age,
That Life brings with her in her equipage;
    As if his whole vocation
    Were endless imitation.

VIII

Thou, whose exterior semblance doth belie
    Thy Soul's immensity;   110
Thou best Philosopher, who yet dost keep
Thy heritage, thou Eye among the blind,
That, deaf and silent, read'st the eternal deep,
Haunted for ever by the eternal mind,—
    Mighty Prophet! Seer blest!
    On whom those truths do rest,
Which we are toiling all our lives to find,
In darkness lost, the darkness of the grave;
Thou, over whom thy Immortality
Broods like the Day, a Master o'er a Slave,   120
A Presence which is not to be put by;
Thou little Child, yet glorious in the might
Of heaven-born freedom on thy being's height,
Why with such earnest pains dost thou provoke
The years to bring the inevitable yoke,
Thus blindly with thy blessedness at strife?
Full soon thy Soul shall have her earthly freight,
And custom lie upon thee with a weight,
Heavy as frost, and deep almost as life!

IX

    O joy! that in our embers   130
    Is something that doth live,
    That nature yet remembers
    What was so fugitive!
The thought of our past years in me doth breed
Perpetual benediction: not indeed
For that which is most worthy to be blest;
Delight and liberty, the simple creed
Of Childhood, whether busy or at rest,
With new-fledged hope still fluttering in his breast:—
    Not for these I raise   140
    The song of thanks and praise;
    But for those obstinate questionings
    Of sense and outward things,
    Fallings from us, vanishings;
    Blank misgivings of a Creature
Moving about in worlds not realised,
High instincts before which our mortal Nature
Did tremble like a guilty Thing surprised:
    But for those first affections,
    Those shadowy recollections,   150

Which, be they what they may,
Are yet the fountain-light of all our day,
Are yet a master-light of all our seeing;
     Uphold us, cherish, and have power to make
Our noisy years seem moments in the being
Of the eternal Silence: truths that wake,
      To perish never:
Which neither listlessness, nor mad endeavour,
      Nor Man nor Boy,
Nor all that is at enmity with joy,   160
Can utterly abolish or destroy!
     Hence in a season of calm weather
      Though inland far we be,
Our Souls have sight of that immortal sea
     Which brought us hither,
     Can in a moment travel thither,
And see the Children sport upon the shore,
And hear the mighty waters rolling evermore.

X

Then sing, ye Birds, sing, sing a joyous song!
     And let the young Lambs bound   170
     As to the tabor's sound!
We in thought will join your throng.
     Ye that pipe and ye that play,
     Ye that through your hearts today
      Feel the gladness of the May!
What though the radiance which was once so bright
Be now for ever taken from my sight,
     Though nothing can bring back the hour
Of splendour in the grass, of glory in the flower;
     We will grieve not, rather find   180
     Strength in what remains behind;
     In the primal sympathy
     Which having been must ever be;
     In the soothing thoughts that spring
     Out of human suffering;
     In the faith that looks through death,
In years that bring the philosophic mind.

XI

And O, ye Fountains, Meadows, Hills, and Groves,
Forebode not any severing of our loves!
Yet in my heart of hearts I feel your might;   190
I only have relinquished one delight

To live beneath your more habitual sway.
I love the Brooks which down their channels fret,
Even more than when I tripped lightly as they;
The innocent brightness of a new-born Day
      Is lovely yet;
The Clouds that gather round the setting sun
Do take a sober colouring from an eye
That hath kept watch o'er man's mortality;
Another race hath been, and other palms are won.   200
Thanks to the human heart by which we live,
Thanks to its tenderness, its joys, and fears,
To me the meanest flower that blows can give
Thoughts that do often lie too deep for tears.

*Dejection: An Ode

[Written April 4, 1802]

SAMUEL TAYLOR COLERIDGE

Late, late yestreen I saw the new Moon,
With the old Moon in her arms;
And I fear, I fear, my Master dear!
We shall have a deadly storm.

—BALLAD OF SIR PATRICK SPENCE

I

Well! If the Bard was weather-wise, who made
  The grand old ballad of Sir Patrick Spence,
  This night, so tranquil now, will not go hence
Unroused by winds, that ply a busier trade
Than those which mould yon cloud in lazy flakes,
Or the dull sobbing draft, that moans and rakes
Upon the strings of this Aeolian lute,
    Which better far were mute.
  For lo! the New-moon winter-bright!
  And overspread with phantom light,   10
  (With swimming phantom light o'erspread
  But rimmed and circled by a silver thread)
I see the old Moon in her lap, foretelling
  The coming-on of rain and squally blast.
And oh! that even now the gust were swelling,
  And the slant night-shower driving loud and fast!

Those sounds which oft have raised me, whilst they awed,
  And sent my soul abroad,
Might now perhaps their wonted impulse give,
Might startle this dull pain, and make it move and live!   20

II

A grief without a pang, void, dark, and drear,
 A stifled, drowsy, unimpassioned grief,
 Which finds no natural outlet, no relief,
  In word, or sigh, or tear—
O Lady! in this wan and heartless mood,
To other thoughts by yonder throstle woo'd,
 All this long eve, so balmy and serene,
Have I been gazing on the western sky,
 And its peculiar tint of yellow green:
And still I gaze—and with how blank an eye!   30
And those thin clouds above, in flakes and bars,
That give away their motion to the stars;
Those stars, that glide behind them or between,
Now sparkling, now bedimmed, but always seen:
Yon crescent Moon, as fixed as if it grew
In its own cloudless, starless lake of blue;
I see them all so excellently fair,
I see, not feel, how beautiful they are!

III

 My genial spirits fail;
  And what can these avail   40
To lift the smothering weight from off my breast?
  It were a vain endeavour,
  Though I should gaze for ever
On that green light that lingers in the west:
I may not hope from outward forms to win
The passion and the life, whose fountains are within.

IV

O Lady! we receive but what we give,
And in our life alone does Nature live:
Ours is her wedding garment, ours her shroud!
 And would we aught behold, of higher worth,   50
Than that inanimate cold world allowed
To the poor loveless ever-anxious crowd,
 Ah! from the soul itself must issue forth

A light, a glory, a fair luminous cloud
    Enveloping the Earth—
And from the soul itself must there be sent
  A sweet and potent voice, of its own birth,
Of all sweet sounds the life and element!

V

O pure of heart! thou need'st not ask of me
What this strong music in the soul may be!   60
What, and wherein it doth exist,
This light, this glory, this fair luminous mist,
This beautiful and beauty-making power.
  Joy, virtuous Lady! Joy that ne'er was given,
Save to the pure, and in their purest hour,
Life, and Life's effluence, cloud at once and shower,
Joy, Lady! is the spirit and the power,
Which wedding Nature to us gives in dower
  A new Earth and new Heaven,
Undreamt of by the sensual and the proud   70
Joy is the sweet voice, Joy the luminous cloud—
    We in ourselves rejoice!
And thence flows all that charms or ear or sight,
  All melodies the echoes of that voice,
All colours a suffusion from that light.

VI

There was a time when, though my path was rough,
  This joy within me dallied with distress,
And all misfortunes were but as the stuff
  Whence Fancy made me dreams of happiness:
For hope grew round me, like the twining vine,   80
And fruits, and foliage, not my own, seemed mine.
But now afflictions bow me down to earth:
Nor care I that they rob me of my mirth;
    But oh! each visitation
Suspends what nature gave me at my birth,
  My shaping spirit of Imagination.
For not to think of what I needs must feel,
  But to be still and patient, all I can;
And haply by abstruse research to steal
  From my own nature all the natural man—   90
  This was my sole resource, my only plan:
Till that which suits a part infects the whole,
And now is almost grown the habit of my soul.

VII

Hence, viper thoughts, that coil around my mind,
    Reality's dark dream!
I turn from you, and listen to the wind,
  Which long has raved unnoticed. What a scream
Of agony by torture lengthened out
That lute sent forth! Thou Wind, that rav'st without,
  Bare crag, or mountain-tairn, or blasted tree,   100
Or pine-grove whither woodman never clomb,
Or lonely house, long held the witches' home,
  Methinks were fitter instruments for thee,
Mad Lutanist! who in this month of showers,
Of dark-brown gardens, and of peeping flowers,
Mak'st Devils' yule, with worse than wintry song,
The blossoms, buds, and timorous leaves among.
  Thou Actor, perfect in all tragic sounds!
Thou mighty Poet, e'en to frenzy bold!
    What tell'st thou now about?   110
     'Tis of the rushing of an host in rout,
  With groans, of trampled men, with smarting wounds—
At once they groan with pain, and shudder with the cold!
But hush! there is a pause of deepest silence!
  And all that noise, as of a rushing crowd,
With groans, and tremulous shudderings—all is over—
  It tells another tale, with sounds less deep and loud!
    A tale of less affright,
    And tempered with delight,
As Otway's self had framed the tender lay,—   120
    'Tis of a little child
    Upon a lonesome wild,
Not far from home, but she hath lost her way:
And now moans low in bitter grief and fear,
And now screams loud, and hopes to make her mother hear.

VIII

'Tis midnight, but small thoughts have I of sleep:
Full seldom may my friend such vigils keep!
Visit her, gentle Sleep! with wings of healing,
  And may this storm be but a mountain-birth,
May all the stars hang bright above her dwelling,   130
  Silent as though they watched the sleeping Earth!
    With light heart may she rise,
    Gay fancy, cheerful eyes,
  Joy lift her spirit, joy attune her voice;
To her may all things live, from pole to pole,

Their life the eddying of her living soul!
   O simple spirit, guided from above,
Dear Lady. friend devoutest of my choice,
Thus mayest thou ever, evermore rejoice.

*Ode to the West Wind

PERCY BYSSHE SHELLEY

1

O wild West Wind, thou breath of Autumn's being,
Thou, from whose unseen presence the leaves dead
Are driven, like ghosts from an enchanter fleeting,

Yellow, and black, and pale, and hectic red,
Pestilence-stricken multitudes: O thou,
Who chariotest to their dark wintry bed

The wingèd seeds, where they lie cold and low,
Each like a corpse within its grave, until
Thine azure sister of the Spring shall blow

Her clarion o'er the dreaming earth, and fill   10
(Driving sweet buds like flocks to feed in air)
With living hues and odors plain and hill:

Wild Spirit, which art moving everywhere;
Destroyer and preserver; hear! oh hear!

2

Thou on whose stream, mid the steep sky's commotion,
Loose clouds like earth's decaying leaves are shed,
Shook from the tangled boughs of Heaven and Ocean,

Angels of rain and lightning: there are spread
On the blue surface of thine aëry surge,
Like the bright hair uplifted from the head   20

Of some fierce Maenad, even from the dim verge
Of the horizon to the zenith's height,
The locks of the approaching storm. Thou dirge

Of the dying year, to which this closing night
Will be the dome of a vast sepulchre,
Vaulted with all thy congregated might

Of vapours, from whose solid atmosphere
Black rain, and fire, and hail will burst: oh, hear!

3

Thou who didst waken from his summer dreams
The blue Mediterranean, where he lay,   30
Lulled by the coil of his crystàlline streams,

Beside a pumice isle in Baiae's bay,
And saw in sleep old palaces and towers
Quivering within the wave's intenser day,

All overgrown with azure moss and flowers
So sweet, the sense faints picturing them! Thou
For whose path the Atlantic's level powers

Cleave themselves into chasms, while far below
The sea-blooms and the oozy woods which wear
The sapless foliage of the ocean, know   40

Thy voice, and suddenly grow gray with fear,
And tremble and despoil themselves: oh, hear!

4

If I were a dead leaf thou mightest bear;
If I were a swift cloud to fly with thee;
A wave to pant beneath thy power, and share

The impulse of thy strength, only less free
Than thou, O uncontrollable! If even
I were as in my boyhood, and could be

The comrade of thy wanderings over Heaven,
As then, when to outstrip thy skiey speed   50
Scarce seemed a vision; I would ne'er have striven

As thus with thee in prayer in my sore need.
Oh, lift me as a wave, a leaf, a cloud!
I fall upon the thorns of life! I bleed!

A heavy weight of hours has chained and bowed
One too like thee—tameless, and swift, and proud.

5

Make me thy lyre, even as the forest is:
What if my leaves are falling like its own!
The tumult of thy mighty harmonies

Will take from both a deep, autumnal tone,   60
Sweet though in sadness. Be thou, Spirit fierce,
My spirit! Be thou me, impetuous one!

Drive my dead thoughts over the universe
Like withered leaves to quicken a new birth!
And, by the incantation of this verse,

Scatter, as from an unextinguished hearth
Ashes and sparks, my words among mankind!
Be through my lips to unawakened earth

The trumpet of a prophecy! O, Wind,
If Winter comes, can Spring be far behind?   70

THE ELEGY

---

*An elegy usually both laments and praises the dead. Some English
elegies adopt the conventions of pastoral poetry, using as a background nature and the life of shepherds, with idealized and conven-
tionalized scenes and classical names. Though pastoral elegies are
artificial in this borrowing of elements from classical poetry, they
nevertheless tend to follow the natural course of human experience.
When someone dies young or in his prime, the first feeling of the
mourner is of irreparable loss and irreconcilable grief. Why should
death, he feels, have prematurely taken this particular person? Why
was the loss not prevented? Then, if the speaker is not overwhelmed
by a shattering grief (if he is a friend, perhaps, and not a lover) his
next thought may be of himself: "It might as easily have happened
to me." This leads him to an examination of his own goals and way
of life. Finally, his thought returns to the dead, but with the passing
of time he has become more reconciled and may turn to faith or
some sort of hope: the friend, after all, is not really dead, or has not
died in vain.*

*The conventional pattern of the elegy, then, like the normal course of
a sorrow in real life, runs through three stages: (1) the irreconcilable
cry: Weep, he is gone forever. Why did this have to happen?; (2)
taking stock of oneself, and sometimes more broadly of the world of*

living; (3) the reconciliation: Do not weep; he is not really dead; something of value survives, and life must go on. "Lycidas" is the one example here of the classical elegy. The others that follow represent deliberate departures from it.

*Lycidas

JOHN MILTON

In this Monody the Author bewails a learned Friend, unfortunatly drown'd in his Passage from Chester on the Irish Seas, 1637. And by occasion fortels the ruine of our corrupted clergy then in their height.

Yet once more, O ye Laurels, and once more
Ye Myrtles brown, with Ivy never-sear,
I com to pluck your Berries harsh and crude,
And with forc'd fingers rude,
Shatter your leaves before the mellowing year.
Bitter constraint, and sad occasion dear,
Compels me to disturb your season due:
For *Lycidas* is dead, dead ere his prime
Young *Lycidas*, and hath not left his peer:
Who would not sing for *Lycidas?* he knew   10
Himself to sing, and build the lofty rhyme
He must not flote upon his watry bear
Unwept, and welter to the parching wind,
Without the meed of som melodious tear.
   Begin then, Sisters of the sacred well,
That from beneath the seat of *Jove* doth spring,
Begin, and somwhat loudly sweep the string.
Hence with denial vain, and coy excuse,
So may some gentle Muse
With lucky words favour my destin'd Urn,   20
And as he passes turn,
And bid fair peace be to my sable shrowd.
For we were nurst upon the self-same hill,
Fed the same flock, by fountain, shade, and rill.
   Together both, ere the high Lawns appear'd

---

l. 12. bear: Bier.
l. 15. Sisters . . . : The Muses.

Under the opening eye-lids of the morn,
We drove a field, and both together heard
What time the Gray-fly winds her sultry horn,
Batt'ning our flocks with the fresh dews of night,
Oft till the Star that rose, at Ev'ning, bright   30
Toward Heav'ns descent had slop'd his westering wheel.
Mean while the Rural ditties were not mute,
Temper'd to th'Oaten Flute;
Rough *Satyrs* danc'd, and *Fauns* with clov'n heel,
From the glad sound would not be absent long,
And old *Damaetas* lov'd to hear our song.
    But O the heavy change, now thou art gon,
Now thou art gon, and never must return!
Thee Shepherd, thee the Woods, and desert Caves,
With wilde Thyme and the gadding Vine o'regrown,   40
And all their echoes mourn.
The Willows, and the Hazle Copses green,
Shall now no more be seen,
Fanning their joyous Leaves to thy soft layes.
As killing as the Canker to the Rose,
Or Taint-worm to the weanling Herds that graze,
Or Frost to Flowers, that their gay wardrop wear,
When first the White thorn blows;
Such, *Lycidas*, thy loss to Shepherds ear.
    Where were ye Nymphs when the remorseless deep   50
Clos'd o're the head of your lov'd *Lycidas*?
For neither were ye playing on the steep,
Where your old *Bards*, the famous *Druids* ly,
Nor on the shaggy top of *Mona* high,
Nor yet where *Deva* spreads her wisard stream:
Ay me, I fondly dream!
Had ye bin there—for what could that have don?
What could the Muse her self that *Orpheus* bore,
The Muse her self, for her inchanting son
Whom Universal nature did lament,   60
When by the rout that made the hideous roar,
His goary visage down the stream was sent,
Down the swift *Hebrus* to the *Lesbian* shore.
    Alas! What boots it with uncessant care
To tend the homely slighted Shepherds trade,
And strictly meditate the thankles Muse,
Were it not better don as others use,
To sport with *Amaryllis* in the shade,
Or with the tangles of *Neaera's* hair?

---

l. 48. White thorn: Hawthorn.
l. 54. Mona: Island of Anglesey, near which King had drowned.
l. 55. Deva: The river Dee.

Fame is the spur that the clear spirit doth raise   70
(That last infirmity of Noble mind)
To scorn delights, and live laborious dayes;
But the fair Guerdon when we hope to find,
And think to burst out into sudden blaze,
Comes the blind *Fury* with th'abhorred shears,
And slits the thin spun life. But not the praise,
Phoebus repli'd, and touch'd my trembling ears;
Fame is no plant that grows on mortal soil,
Nor in the glistering foil
Set off to th' world, nor in broad rumour lies,   80
But lives and spreds aloft by those pure eyes,
And perfet witnes of all judging *Jove;*
As he pronounces lastly on each deed,
Of so much fame in Heav'n expect thy meed.
     O Fountain *Arethuse,* and thou honour'd floud,
Smooth-sliding *Mincius,* crown'd with vocall reeds,
That strain I heard was of a higher mood:
But now my Oate proceeds,
And listens to the Herald of the Sea
That came in *Neptune's* plea,   90
He ask'd the Waves, and ask'd the Fellon winds,
What hard mishap hath doom'd this gentle swain?
And question'd every gust of rugged wings
That blows from off each beaked Promontory,
They knew not of his story,
And sage *Hippotades* their answer brings,
That not a blast was from his dungeon stray'd,
The Ayr was calm, and on the level brine,
Sleek *Panope* with all her sisters play'd.
It was that fatall and perfidious Bark   100
Built in th'eclipse, and rigg'd with curses dark,
That sunk so low that sacred head of thine.
     Next *Camus,* reverend Sire, went footing slow,
His Mantle hairy, and his Bonnet sedge,
Inwrought with figures dim, and on the edge
Like to that sanguine flower inscrib'd with woe.
Ah; Who hath reft (quoth he) my dearest pledge?
Last came, and last did go,
The Pilot of the *Galilean* lake,
Two massy Keyes he bore of metals twain,   110
(The Golden opes, the Iron shuts amain)

---

l. 79. glistering foil: Glittering gold foil.
l. 85. Arethuse: Fountain in Sicily associated with the Greek pastoral poet Theocritus.
l. 86. Mincius: River associated with Virgil, who wrote Latin pastoral poetry.
l. 96. Hippotades: Aeolus, god of the winds.
l. 99. Panope: A sea nymph.
l. 103. Camus: The river Cam, from which Cambridge receives its name.

He shook his Miter'd locks, and stern bespake,
How well could I have spar'd for thee, young swain,
Anow of such as for their bellies sake,
Creep and intrude, and climb into the fold?
Of other care they little reck'ning make,
Then how to scramble at the shearers feast,
And shove away the worthy bidden guest.
Blind mouthes! that scarce themselves know how to hold
A Sheep-hook, or have learn'd ought els the least   120
That to the faithful herdmans art belongs!
What recks it them? What need they? They are sped;
And when they list, their lean and flashy songs
Grate on their scrannel Pipes of wretched straw,
The hungry Sheep look up, and are not fed,
But swoln with wind, and the rank mist they draw,
Rot inwardly, and foul contagion spread:
Besides what the grim Woolf with privy paw
Daily devours apace, and nothing sed,
But that two-handed engine at the door,   130
Stands ready to smite once, and smite no more.
    Return *Alpheus*, the dread voice is past,
That shrunk thy streams; Return *Sicilian* Muse,
And call the Vales, and bid them hither cast
Their Bels, and Flourets of a thousand hues.
Ye valleys low where the milde whispers use,
Of shades and wanton winds, and gushing brooks,
On whose fresh lap the swart Star sparely looks,
Throw hither all your quaint enameld eyes,
That on the green terf suck the honied showres,   140
And purple all the ground with vernal flowres.
Bring the rathe Primrose that forsaken dies.
The tufted Crow-toe, and pale Gessamine,
The white Pink, and the Pansie freakt with jeat,
The glowing Violet,
The Musk-rose, and the well attir'd Woodbine.
With Cowslips wan that hang the pensive hed,
And every flower that sad embroidery wears:
Bid *Amaranthus* all his beauty shed,
And Daffadillies fill their cups with tears,   150
To strew the Laureat Herse where *Lycid* lies.
For so to interpose a little ease,

---

l. 114. Anow: Enough.
l. 124. scrannel: Thin and discordant.
l. 128. privy: Furtive, private.
l. 138. swart Star: Sirius, the Dog Star, whose name means "scorching."
l. 142. rathe: Early.
l. 143. Crow-toe: Crowfoot, ranunculus.
l. 144. freakt: Streaked.

Let our frail thoughts dally with false surmise.
Ay me! Whilst thee the shores, and sounding Seas
Wash far away, where ere thy bones are hurld,
Whether beyond the stormy *Hebrides*,
Where thou perhaps under the whelming tide
Visit'st the bottom of the monstrous world;
Or whether thou to our moist vows deny'd,
Sleep'st by the fable of *Bellerus* old,   160
Where the great vision of the guarded Mount
Looks toward *Namancos* and *Bayona's* hold;
Look homeward Angel now, and melt with ruth.
And, O ye *Dolphins*, waft the haples youth.
   Weep no more, woful Shepherds weep no more,
For *Lycidas* your sorrow is not dead,
Sunk though he be beneath the watry floar,
So sinks the day-star in the Ocean bed,
And yet anon repairs his drooping head,
And tricks his beams, and with new spangled Ore,   170
Flames in the forehead of the morning sky:
So *Lycidas* sunk low, but mounted high,
Through the dear might of him that walk'd the waves
Where other groves, and other streams along,
With *Nectar* pure his oozy Lock's he laves,
And hears the unexpressive nuptiall Song,
In the blest Kingdoms meek of joy and love.
There entertain him all the Saints above,
In solemn troops, and sweet Societies
That sing, and singing in their glory move,   180
And wipe the tears for ever from his eyes.
Now *Lycidas* the Shepherds weep no more;
Hence forth thou art the Genius of the shore,
In thy large recompense, and shalt be good
To all that wander in that perilous flood.
   Thus sang the uncouth Swain to th'Okes and rills,
While the still morn went out with Sandals gray,
He touch'd the tender stops of various Quills,
With eager thought warbling his *Dorick* lay:
And now the Sun had stretch'd out all the hills,   190
And now was dropt into the Western bay;
At last he rose, and twitch'd his Mantle blew:
To morrow to fresh Woods, and Pastures new.

---

l. 168. day-star: Sun.
l. 173. Matt. xiv. 25–33.
l. 183. Genius: Guardian spirit.
l. 186. uncouth: Unknown or rustic.
l. 189. Dorick: The dialect of Greek pastoral poetry.

Elegy Written in a Country Churchyard

THOMAS GRAY

The Curfew tolls the knell of parting day,
The lowing herd wind slowly o'er the lea,
The plowman homeward plods his weary way,
And leaves the world to darkness and to me.

Now fades the glimmering landscape on the sight,
And all the air a solemn stillness holds,
Save where the beetle wheels his droning flight,
And drowsy tinklings lull the distant folds;

Save that from yonder ivy-mantled tower
The moping owl does to the moon complain   10
Of such as, wandering near her secret bower,
Molest her ancient solitary reign.

Beneath those rugged elms, that yew-tree's shade,
Where heaves the turf in many a mouldering heap,
Each in his narrow cell forever laid,
The rude Forefathers of the hamlet sleep.

The breezy call of incense-breathing Morn,
The swallow twittering from the straw-built shed,
The cock's shrill clarion, or the echoing horn,
No more shall rouse them from their lowly bed.   20

For them no more the blazing hearth shall burn,
Or busy housewife ply her evening care:
No children run to lisp their sire's return,
Or climb his knees the envied kiss to share.

Oft did the harvest to their sickle yield,
Their furrow oft the stubborn glebe has broke;
How jocund did they drive their team afield!
How bowed the woods beneath their sturdy stroke!

Let not Ambition mock their useful toil,
Their homely joys, and destiny obscure;   30
Nor Grandeur hear with a disdainful smile
The short and simple annals of the poor.

The boast of heraldry, the pomp of power,
And all that beauty, all that wealth e'er gave,
Awaits alike the inevitable hour.
The paths of glory lead but to the grave.

Nor you, ye Proud, impute to These the fault,
If Memory o'er their Tomb no Trophies raise,
Where through the long-drawn aisle and fretted vault
The pealing anthem swells the note of praise.   40

Can storied urn or animated bust
Back to its mansion call the fleeting breath?
Can Honour's voice provoke the silent dust,
Or Flattery soothe the dull cold ear of Death?

Perhaps in this neglected spot is laid
Some heart once pregnant with celestial fire;
Hands, that the rod of empire might have swayed,
Or waked to extasy the living lyre.

But Knowledge to their eyes her ample page
Rich with the spoils of time did ne'er unroll;   50
Chill Penury repressed their noble rage,
And froze the genial current of the soul.

Full many a gem of purest ray serene,
The dark unfathomed caves of ocean bear:
Full many a flower is born to blush unseen,
And waste its sweetness on the desert air.

Some village-Hampden, that with dauntless breast
The little Tyrant of his fields withstood;
Some mute, inglorious Milton here may rest,
Some Cromwell guiltless of his country's blood.   60

The applause of listening senates to command,
The threats of pain and ruin to despise,
To scatter plenty o'er a smiling land,
And read their history in a nation's eyes,

Their lot forbad: nor circumscribed alone
Their growing virtues, but their crimes confined;
Forbad to wade through slaughter to a throne,
And shut the gates of mercy on mankind;

The struggling pangs of conscious truth to hide,
To quench the blushes of ingenuous shame,   70
Or heap the shrine of Luxury and Pride
With incense kindled at the Muse's flame.

---

l. 43. provoke: Call forth.
l. 51. rage: Enthusiasm.
l. 57. John Hampden, 17th-century statesman, opponent of Charles I.

Far from the madding crowd's ignoble strife,
Their sober wishes never learned to stray;
They kept the noiseless tenor of their way.

Yet ev'n these bones from insult to protect,
Along the cool sequestered vale of life
Some frail memorial still erected nigh,
With uncouth rhymes and shapeless sculpture decked,
Implores the passing tribute of a sigh.   80

Their name, their years, spelt by the unlettered Muse,
The place of fame and elegy supply;
And many a holy text around she strews,
That teach the rustic moralist to die.

For who, to dumb Forgetfulness a prey,
This pleasing anxious being e'er resigned,
Left the warm precincts of the cheerful day,
Nor cast one longing lingering look behind?

On some fond breast the parting soul relies,
Some pious drops the closing eye requires;   90
Ev'n from the tomb the voice of Nature cries,
Ev'n in our Ashes live their wonted Fires.

For thee who, mindful of the unhonoured Dead,
Dost in these lines their artless tale relate;
If chance, by lonely contemplation led,
Some kindred Spirit shall inquire thy fate,

Haply some hoary-headed Swain may say,
"Oft have we seen him at the peep of dawn
Brushing with hasty steps the dews away,
To meet the sun upon the upland lawn.   100

"There at the foot of yonder nodding beech
That wreathes its old fantastic roots so high,
His listless length at noontide would he stretch,
And pore upon the brook that babbles by.

"Hard by yon wood, now smiling as in scorn,
Muttering his wayward fancies he would rove;
Now drooping, woeful wan, like one forlorn,
Or crazed with care, or crossed in hopeless love.

"One morn I missed him on the customed hill,
Along the heath, and near his favourite tree;   110
Another came; nor yet beside the rill,
Nor up the lawn, nor at the wood was he;

"The next with dirges due in sad array,
Slow through the church-way path we saw him borne.
Approach and read (for thou canst read) the lay,
Graved on the stone beneath yon agèd thorn."

THE EPITAPH

Here rests his head upon the lap of Earth,
A Youth to Fortune and to Fame unknown.
Fair Science frowned not on his humble birth,
And Melancholy marked him for her own.   120

Large was his bounty, and his soul sincere,
Heaven did a recompense as largely send:
He gave to Misery all he had, a tear,
He gained from Heaven ('twas all he wished) a friend.

No farther seek his merits to disclose,
Or draw his frailties from their dread abode,
(There they alike in trembling hope repose,)
The bosom of his Father and his God.

In Memory of W. B. Yeats

(*d. Jan. 1939*)

W. H. AUDEN

1

He disappeared in the dead of winter:
The brooks were frozen, the airports almost deserted,
And snow disfigured the public statues;
The mercury sank in the mouth of the dying day.
What instruments we have agree
The day of his death was a dark cold day.

Far from his illness
The wolves ran on through the evergreen forests,
The peasant river was untempted by the fashionable quays;
By mourning tongues   10
The death of the poet was kept from his poems.

But for him it was his last afternoon as himself,
An afternoon of nurses and rumours;
The provinces of his body revolted,
The squares of his mind were empty,
Silence invaded the suburbs,
The current of his feeling failed: he became his admirers.

Now he is scattered among a hundred cities
And wholly given over to unfamiliar affections;
To find his happiness in another kind of wood   20
And be punished under a foreign code of conscience.
The words of a dead man
Are modified in the guts of the living.

But in the importance and noise of to-morrow
When the brokers are roaring like beasts on the floor of the Bourse,
And the poor have the sufferings to which they are fairly accustomed,
And each in the cell of himself is almost convinced of his freedom,
A few thousand will think of this day
As one thinks of a day when one did something slightly unusual.
What instruments we have agree   30
The day of his death was a dark cold day.

2

You were silly like us; your gift survived it all:
The parish of rich women, physical decay,
Yourself. Mad Ireland hurt you into poetry.
Now Ireland has her madness and her weather still,
For poetry makes nothing happen: it survives
In the valley of its making where executives
Would never want to tamper, flows on south
From ranches of isolation and the busy griefs,
Raw towns that we believe and die in; it survives,   40
A way of happening, a mouth.

3

Earth, receive an honoured guest:
William Yeats is laid to rest.
Let the Irish vessel lie
Emptied of its poetry.

In the nightmare of the dark
All the dogs of Europe bark,
And the living nations wait,   50
Each sequestered in its hate;

Intellectual disgrace
Stares from every human face,
And the seas of pity lie
Locked and frozen in each eye.

Follow, poet, follow right
To the bottom of the night,
With your unconstraining voice
Still persuade us to rejoice;

With the farming of a verse   60
Make a vineyard of the curse,
Sing of human unsuccess
In a rapture of distress;

In the deserts of the heart
Let the healing fountain start,
In the prison of his days
Teach the free man how to praise.

*After the Funeral
(In memory of Ann Jones)

DYLAN THOMAS

After the funeral, mule praises, brays,
Windshake of sailshaped ears, muffle-toed tap
Tap happily of one peg in the thick
Grave's foot, blinds down the lids, the teeth in black,
The spittled eyes, the salt ponds in the sleeves,
Morning smack of the spade that wakes up sleep,
Shakes a desolate boy who slits his throat
In the dark of the coffin and sheds dry leaves.
That breaks one bone to light with a judgment clout,
After the feast of tear-stuffed time and thistles   10
In a room with a stuffed fox and a stale fern,
I stand, for this memorial's sake, alone
In the snivelling hours with dead, humped Ann
Whose hooded, fountain heart once fell in puddles
Round the parched worlds of Wales and drowned each sun
(Though this for her is a monstrous image blindly
Magnified out of praise; her death was a still drop;
She would not have me sinking in the holy
Flood of her heart's fame; she would lie dumb and deep
And need no druid of her broken body).   20
But I, Ann's bard on a raised hearth, call all
The seas to service that her wood-tongued virtue
Babble like a bellbuoy over the hymning heads,
Bow down the walls of the ferned and foxy woods

That her love sing and swing through a brown chapel,
Bless her bent spirit with four, crossing birds.
Her flesh was meek as milk, but this skyward statue
With the wild breast and blessed and giant skull
Is carved from her in a room with a wet window
In a fiercely mourning house in a crooked year.   30
I know her scrubbed and sour humble hands
Lie with religion in their cramp, her threadbare
Whisper in a damp word, her wits drilled hollow,
Her fist of a face died clenched on a round pain;
And sculptured Ann is seventy years of stone.
These cloud-sopped, marble hands, this monumental
Argument of the hewn voice, gesture and psalm
Storm me forever over her grave until
The stuffed lung of the fox twitch and cry Love
And the strutting fern lay seeds on the black sill.   40

Eleven Representative Poets

NOTE *For biographical information and other works by these poets, consult the 'notes' beginning on page 656.*

*JOHN DONNE

The Bait

Come live with me, and be my love,
And we will some new pleasures prove
Of golden sands, and crystal brooks,
With silken lines, and silver hooks.

There will the river whispering run
Warm'd by thy eyes, more than the sun;
And there the enamour'd fish will stay
Begging themselves they may betray.

When thou wilt swim in that live bath,
Each fish, which every channel hath,　　　　　　　　　10
Will amorously to thee swim,
Gladder to catch thee, than thou him.

If thou to be so seen be'st loath
By Sun, or Moon, thou dark'nest both,
And if myself have leave to see,
I need not their light, having thee.

Let others freeze with angling reeds,
And cut their legs with shells and weeds,
Or treacherously poor fish beset,
With strangling snare, or windowy net:

Let coarse bold hands, from slimy nest
The bedded fish in banks out-wrest;
Or curious traitors, sleave-silk flies,
Bewitch poor fishes' wand'ring eyes.

For thee, thou need'st no such deceit,
For thou thyself art thine own bait;
That fish that is not catch'd thereby,
Alas, is wiser far than I.

20

---

l. 17. reeds: Rods.
l. 23. sleave-silk flies: Artificial flies made of floss or raw silk.

*Song

Go and catch a falling star,
  Get with child a mandrake root,
Tell me where all past years are,
  Or who cleft the Devil's foot,
Teach me to hear mermaids singing,
Or to keep off envy's stinging,
        And find
        What wind
Serves to advance an honest mind.

If thou be'st born to strange sights,
  Things invisible to see,
Ride ten thousand days and nights,
  Till age snow white hairs on thee;
Thou, when thou return'st, wilt tell me
All strange wonders that befell thee,
        And swear
        Nowhere
Lives a woman true, and fair.

10

If thou findest one, let me know,
   Such a pilgrimage were sweet;—   20
Yet do not, I would not go,
   Though at next door we might meet;
Though she were true, when you met her,
And last, till you write your letter,
         Yet she
         Will be
False, ere I come, to two, or three.

*The Indifferent

I can love both fair and brown,
Her whom abundance melts, and her whom want betrays,
Her who loves loneness best, and her who masks and plays,
Her whom the country form'd, and whom the town,
Her who believes, and her who tries,
Her who still weeps with spongy eyes,
And her who is dry cork and never cries;
I can love her, and her, and you, and you,
I can love any, so she be not true.
Will no other vice content you?   10
Will it not serve your turn to do as did your mothers?
Or have you all old vices spent, and now would find out others?
Or doth a fear, that men are true, torment you?
O we are not, be not you so.
Let me, and do you, twenty know.
Rob me, but bind me not, and let me go.
Must I, who came to travel thorough you,
Grow your fix'd subject, because you are true?

Venus heard me sigh this song,
And by love's sweetest part, variety, she swore   20
She heard not this till now; and that it should be so no more.
She went, examin'd, and return'd ere long,
And said, "Alas, some two or three
Poor heretics in love there be,
Which think to stablish dangerous constancy.
But I have told them: 'Since you will be true,
You shall be true to them, who are false to you!' "

---

l. 1. fair and brown: Blonde and brunette.

*The Funeral

Whoever comes to shroud me, do not harm
    Nor question much
That subtle wreath of hair, which crowns my arm;
The mystery, the sign, you must not touch,
    For 'tis my outward Soul,
Viceroy to that, which then to heaven being gone,
    Will leave this to control,
And keep these limbs, her provinces, from dissolution.

For if the sinewy thread my brain lets fall
    Through every part,   10
Can tie those parts, and make me one of all;
These hairs which upward grew, and strength and art
    Have from a better brain,
Can better do it; except she meant that I
    By this should know my pain,
As prisoners then are manacled, when they're condemn'd to die.

Whate'er she meant by it, bury it with me,
    For since I am
Love's martyr, it might breed idolatry
If into others' hands these relics came;   20
    As 'twas humility
To afford to it all that a soul can do,
    So, 'tis some bravery,
That since you would save none of me, I bury some of you.

---

l. 9. sinewy thread: The nervous system.
l. 23. bravery: Boldness.

*The Good-Morrow

I wonder, by my troth, what thou and I
Did, till we loved? Were we not wean'd till then?
But suck'd on country pleasures, childishly?
Or snorted we in the Seven Sleepers' den?
'Twas so; but this, all pleasures fancies be:
If ever any beauty I did see,
Which I desir'd, and got, 'twas but a dream of thee.

---

l. 5. but: Except for.

And now good-morrow to our waking souls,
Which watch not one another out of fear;
For love, all love of other sights controls,   10
And makes one little room, an everywhere.
Let sea-discoverers to new worlds have gone,
Let maps to others, worlds on worlds have shown,
Let us possess one world, each hath one, and is one.

My face in thine eye, thine in mine appears,
And true plain hearts do in the faces rest;
Where can we find two better hemispheres,
Without sharp North, without declining West?
Whatever dies, was not mix'd equally;
If our two loves be one, or, thou and I   20
Love so alike, that none do slacken, none can die.

---

l. 21. none: Neither.

*The Anniversary

All Kings, and all their favourites,
    All glory of honours, beauties, wits,
The Sun itself, which makes times, as they pass,
Is elder by a year, now, than it was
When thou and I first one another saw:
All other things to their destruction draw,
    Only our love hath no decay;
This, no tommorow hath, nor yesterday;
Running it never runs from us away,
But truly keeps his first, last, everlasting day .   10

    Two graves must hide thine and my corse;
    If one might, death were no divorce:
Alas, as well as other Princes, we
(Who Prince enough in one another be)
Must leave at last in death, these eyes, and ears,
Oft fed with true oaths, and with sweet salt tears;
    But souls where nothing dwells but love
(All other thoughts being inmates) then shall prove
This, or a love increasèd there above,
When bodies to their graves, souls from their graves remove.   20

---

l. 11. corse: Corpse.
l. 18. inmates: Lodgers, not permanent dwellers. prove: Test out, or experience.

And then we shall be throughly blest,
    But we no more than all the rest;
Here upon earth, we are Kings, and none but we
Can be such kings, nor of such subjects be:
Who is so safe as we, where none can do
Treason to us, except one of us two?
    True and false fears let us refrain,
Let us love nobly, and live, and add again
Years and years unto years, till we attain
To write threescore; this is the second of our reign.   30

*The Canonization

For God's sake hold your tongue, and let me love,
    Or chide my palsy, or my gout,
My five gray hairs, or ruin'd fortune flout,
With wealth your state, your mind with arts improve,
      Take you a course, get you a place,
      Observe his honour, or his grace,
Or the King's real, or his stamped face
      Contemplate; what you will, approve,
      So you will let me love.

Alas, alas, who's injured by my love?   10
    What merchant's ships have my sighs drown'd?
Who says my tears have overflow'd his ground?
When did my colds a forward spring remove?
      When did the heats which my veins fill
      Add one man to the plaguy bill?
Soldiers find wars, and lawyers find out still
      Litigious men, which quarrels move,
      Though she and I do love.

Call us what you will, we are made such by love;
    Call her one, me another fly,   20
We are tapers too, and at our own cost die,
And we in us find the Eagle and the Dove.
      The Phoenix riddle hath more wit
      By us; we two being one, are it.
So to one neutral thing both sexes fit,
      We die and rise the same, and prove
      Mysterious by this love.

---

l. 5. course: Either a course of study or a career.
place: A job, at court (or elsewhere).
ll. 13–14. colds . . . heats: Chills and fevers of love.
l. 15. plaguy bill: Published list of those who have died of plague.
l. 22. Eagle . . . Dove: Strength and gentleness.

We can die by it, if not live by love.
   And if unfit for tombs and hearse
Our legend be, it will be fit for verse;   30
And if no piece of chronicle we prove,
     We'll build in sonnets pretty rooms;
     As well a well-wrought urn becomes
The greatest ashes, as half-acre tombs,
   And by these hymns, all shall approve
   Us *canoniz'd* for Love;

And thus invoke us: "You, whom reverend love
   Made one another's hermitage;
You, to whome love was peace, that now is rage;
Who did the whole world's soul contract, and drove   40
   Into the glasses of your eyes
   (So made such mirrors, and such spies,
That they did all to you epitomize)
   Countries, towns, courts: beg from above
   A pattern of your love!"

*WILLIAM BLAKE

The Clod and the Pebble

"Love seeketh not Itself to please,
   Nor for itself hath any care, ·
But for another gives its ease,
   And builds a Heaven in Hell's despair."

So sung a little Clod of Clay
   Trodden with the cattle's feet,
But a Pebble of the brook
   Warbled out these metres meet:

"Love seeketh only Self to please,
   To bind another to Its delight,   10
Joys in another's loss of ease,
   And builds a Hell in Heaven's despite."

*The Tyger

Tyger! Tyger! burning bright
In the forests of the night,
What immortal hand or eye
Could frame thy fearful symmetry?

In what distant deeps or skies
Burnt the fire of thine eyes?
On what wings dare he aspire?
What the hand dare seize the fire?

And what shoulder, & what art,
Could twist the sinews of thy heart?   10
And when thy heart began to beat,
What dread hand? & what dread feet?

What the hammer? what the chain?
In what furnace was thy brain?
What the anvil? what dread grasp
Dare its deadly terrors clasp?

When the stars threw down their spears,
And water'd heaven with their tears,
Did he smile his work to see?
Did he who made the Lamb make thee?   20

Tyger! Tyger! burning bright
In the forests of the night,
What immortal hand or eye,
Dare frame thy fearful symmetry?

*Mad Song

The wild winds weep,
And the night is a-cold;
Come hither, Sleep,
And my griefs unfold:
But lo! the morning peeps
Over the eastern steeps,
And the rustling birds of dawn
The earth do scorn.

Lo! to the vault
Of paved heaven,   10
With sorrow fraught
My notes are driven:
They strike the ear of night,
Make weep the eyes of day;
They make mad the roaring winds,
And with tempests play.

Like a fiend in a cloud,
With howling woe,
After night I do crowd,
And with night will go;   20
I turn my back to the east,
From whence comforts have increas'd;
For light doth seize my brain
With frantic pain.

A Poison Tree

I was angry with my friend:
I told my wrath, my wrath did end.
I was angry with my foe:
I told it not, my wrath did grow.

And I water'd it in fears,
Night & morning with my tears;
And I sunned it with smiles,
And with soft deceitful wiles.

And it grew both day and night,
Till it bore an apple bright;   10
And my foe beheld it shine,
And he knew that it was mine,

And into my garden stole
When the night had veil'd the pole:
In the morning glad I see
My foe outstretch'd beneath the tree.

The Garden of Love

I went to the Garden of Love,
And saw what I never had seen:
A Chapel was built in the midst,
Where I used to play on the green.

And the gates of this Chapel were shut,
And 'Thou shalt not' writ over the door;
So I turn'd to the Garden of Love
That so many sweet flowers bore;

And I saw it was fillèd with graves,
And tomb-stones where flowers should be;   10
And Priests in black gowns were walking their rounds,
And binding with briars my joys & desires.

The Human Abstract

Pity would be no more
If we did not make somebody Poor;
And Mercy no more could be
If all were as happy as we.

And mutual fear brings peace,
Till the selfish loves increase;
Then Cruelty knits a snare,
And spreads his baits with care.

He sits down with holy fears,
And waters the ground with tears;   10
Then Humility takes its root
Underneath his foot.

Soon spreads the dismal shade
Of Mystery over his head;
And the Caterpiller and Fly
Feed on the Mystery.

And it bears the fruit of Deceit,
Ruddy and sweet to eat;
And the Raven his nest has made
In its thickest shade.   20

The Gods of the earth and sea
Sought thro' Nature to find this Tree;
But their search was all in vain:
There grows one in the Human Brain.

*from *Auguries of Innocence*

To see a World in a Grain of Sand,
    And a Heaven in a Wild Flower,
Hold Infinity in the palm of your hand,
    And Eternity in an hour.

*JOHN KEATS

La Belle Dame sans Merci

O what can ail thee, knight-at-arms,
    Alone and palely loitering?
The sedge has wither'd from the lake,
    And no birds sing.

O what can ail thee, knight-at-arms!
    So haggard and so woe-begone?
The squirrel's granary is full,
    And the harvest's done.

I see a lily on thy brow,
    With anguish moist and fever dew,   10
And on thy cheeks a fading rose
    Fast withereth too.

I met a lady in the meads,
    Full beautiful—a faery's child,
Her hair was long, her foot was light,
    And her eyes were wild.

I made a garland for her head,
  And bracelets too, and fragrant zone;
She look'd at me as she did love,
  And made sweet moan.   20

I set her on my pacing steed,
  And nothing else saw all day long,
For sidelong would she bend, and sing
  A faery's song.

She found me roots of relish sweet,
  And honey wild, and manna dew,
And sure in language strange she said—
  "I love thee true."

She took me to her elfin grot,
  And there she wept, and sigh'd full sore,   30
And there I shut her wild wild eyes
  With kisses four.

And there she lulled me asleep,
  And there I dream'd—Ah! woe betide!
The latest dream I ever dream'd
  On the cold hill side.

I saw pale kings and princes too,
  Pale warriors, death-pale were they all;
They cried—"La Belle Dame sans Merci
  Hath thee in thrall!"   40

I saw their starv'd lips in the gloam
  With horrid warning gaped wide,
And I awoke and found me here,
  On the cold hill's side.

And this is why I sojourn here,
  Alone and palely loitering,
Though the sedge has wither'd from the lake,
  And no birds sing.

_____

l. 18. fragrant zone: Girdle, presumably of flowers.

[When I have fears
that I may cease to be]

When I have fears that I may cease to be
   Before my pen has glean'd my teeming brain,
Before high-piled books, in charact'ry,
   Hold like rich garners the full-ripen'd grain;
When I behold, upon the night's starr'd face,
   Huge cloudy symbols of a high romance,
And think that I may never live to trace
   Their shadows, with the magic hand of chance;
And when I feel, fair creature of an hour!
   That I shall never look upon thee more,   10
Never have relish in the faery power
   Of unreflecting love!—then on the shore
Of the wide world I stand alone, and think
Till love and fame to nothingness do sink.

*On First Looking into Chapman's Homer

Much have I travell'd in the realms of gold,
   And many goodly states and kingdoms seen;
Round many western islands have I been
Which bards in fealty to Apollo hold.
Oft of one wide expanse had I been told
   That deep-brow'd Homer ruled as his demesne;
   Yet did I never breathe its pure serene
Till I heard Chapman speak out loud and bold;
Then felt I like some watcher of the skies
   When a new planet swims into his ken;   10
Or like stout Cortez when with eagle eyes
   He star'd at the Pacific—and all his men
Look'd at each other with a wild surmise—
   Silent, upon a peak in Darien.

---

l. 11. Cortez: A mistake for Balboa.

*Ode to a Nightingale

1

My heart aches, and a drowsy numbness pains
  My sense, as though of hemlock I had drunk,
Or emptied some dull opiate to the drains
  One minute past, and Lethe-wards had sunk:
'Tis not through envy of thy happy lot,
  But being too happy in thine happiness,—
    That thou, light-winged Dryad of the trees,
      In some melodious plot
  Of beechen green, and shadows numberless,
    Singest of summer in full-throated ease.   10

2

O, for a draught of vintage! that hath been
  Cool'd a long age in the deep-delved earth,
Tasting of Flora and the country green,
  Dance, and Provençal song, and sunburnt mirth!
O for a beaker full of the warm South,
  Full of the true, the blushful Hippocrene,
    With beaded bubbles winking at the brim,
      And purple-stained mouth;
  That I might drink, and leave the world unseen,
    And with thee fade away into the forest dim: 20

3

Fade far away, dissolve, and quite forget
  What thou among the leaves hast never known,
The weariness, the fever, and the fret
  Here, where men sit and hear each other groan;
Where palsy shakes a few, sad, last gray hairs,
  Where youth grows pale, and spectre-thin, and dies;
    Where but to think is to be full of sorrow
      And leaden-eyed despairs,
  Where Beauty cannot keep her lustrous eyes,
    Or new Love pine at them beyond tomorrow.   30

4

Away! away! for I will fly to thee,
  Not charioted by Bacchus and his pards,
But on the viewless wings of Poesy,

Though the dull brain perplexes and retards:
Already with thee! tender is the night,
  And haply the Queen-Moon is on her throne,
    Cluster'd around by all her starry Fays;
      But here there is no light,
  Save what from heaven is with the breezes blown
    Through verdurous glooms and winding mossy ways.   40

5

I cannot see what flowers are at my feet,
  Nor what soft incense hangs upon the boughs,
But, in embalmed darkness, guess each sweet
  Wherewith the seasonable month endows
The grass, the thicket, and the fruit-tree wild;
  White hawthorn, and the pastoral eglantine;
    Fast fading violets cover'd up in leaves;
      And mid-May's eldest child,
  The coming musk-rose, full of dewy wine,
    The murmurous haunt of flies on summer eves.   50

6

Darkling I listen; and, for many a time
  I have been half in love with easeful Death,
Call'd him soft names in many a mused rhyme,
  To take into the air my quiet breath;
Now more than ever seems it rich to die,
  To cease upon the midnight with no pain,
    While thou art pouring forth thy soul abroad
      In such an ecstasy!
  Still wouldst thou sing, and I have ears in vain—
    To thy requiem become a sod.   60

7

Thou wast not born for death, immortal Bird!
  No hungry generations tread thee down;
The voice I hear this passing night was heard
  In ancient days by emperor and clown:
Perhaps the self-same song that found a path
  Through the sad heart of Ruth, when, sick for home,
    She stood in tears amid the alien corn;
      The same that oft-times hath
  Charm'd magic casements, opening on the foam
    Of perilous seas, in faery lands forlorn.   70

Forlorn! the very word is like a bell
   To toll me back from thee to my sole self!
Adieu! the fancy cannot cheat so well
   As she is fam'd to do, deceiving elf.
Adieu! adieu! thy plaintive anthem fades
   Past the near meadows, over the still stream,
      Up the hill-side; and now 't is buried deep
       In the next valley-glades:
Was it a vision, or a waking dream?
   Fled is that music:—Do I wake or sleep?   80

*Ode on a Grecian Urn

1

Thou still unravish'd bride of quietness,
   Thou foster-child of silence and slow time,
Sylvan historian, who canst thus express
   A flowery tale more sweetly than our rhyme:
What leaf-fring'd legend haunts about thy shape
   Of deities or mortals, or of both,
      In Tempe or the dales of Arcady?
What men or gods are these? What maidens loth?
   What mad pursuit? What struggle to escape?
      What pipes and timbrels? What wild ecstasy?   10

2

Heard melodies are sweet, but those unheard
   Are sweeter; therefore, ye soft pipes, play on;
Not to the sensual ear, but, more endeared,
   Pipe to the spirit ditties of no tone:
Fair youth, beneath the trees, thou canst not leave
   Thy song, nor ever can those trees be bare;
      Bold Lover, never, never canst thou kiss,
Though winning near the goal—yet, do not grieve;
   She cannot fade, though thou hast not thy bliss,
      For ever wilt thou love, and she be fair!   20

3

Ah, happy, happy boughs! that cannot shed
   Your leaves, nor ever bid the Spring adieu;
And, happy melodist, unwearied,

For ever piping songs for ever new;
More happy love! more happy, happy love!
  For ever warm and still to be enjoyed,
    For ever panting, and for ever young;
All breathing human passion far above,
  That leaves a heart high-sorrowful and cloy'd,
    A burning forehead, and a parching tongue.   30

4

Who are these coming to the sacrifice?
  To what green altar, O mysterious priest,
Lead'st thou that heifer lowing at the skies,
  And all her silken flanks with garlands drest?
What little town by river or sea shore,
  Or mountain-built with peaceful citadel,
    Is emptied of this folk, this pious morn?
And, little town, thy streets for evermore
  Will silent be; and not a soul to tell
    Why thou art desolate, can e'er return.   40

5

O Attic shape! Fair attitude! with brede
  Of marble men and maidens overwrought,
With forest branches and the trodden weed;
  Thou, silent form, dost tease us out of thought
As doth eternity: Cold Pastoral!
  When old age shall this generation waste,
    Thou shalt remain, in midst of other woe
Than ours, a friend to man, to whom thou say'st,
  Beauty is truth, truth beauty,—that is all
    Ye know on earth, and all ye need to know.   50

---

l. 41. brede: Embroidery.

*To Autumn

1

Season of mists and mellow fruitfulness,
   Close bosom-friend of the maturing sun;
Conspiring with him how to load and bless
     With fruit the vines that round the thatch-eaves run;
To bend with apples the moss'd cottage-trees,
   And fill all fruit with ripeness to the core;
     To swell the gourd, and plump the hazel shells
With a sweet kernel; to set budding more,
   And still more, later flowers for the bees,
     Until they think warm days will never cease,   10
     For Summer has o'er-brimm'd their clammy cells.

2

Who hath not seen thee oft amid thy store?
   Sometimes whoever seeks abroad may find
Thee sitting careless on a granary floor,
   Thy hair soft-lifted by the winnowing wind;
Or on a half-reap'd furrow sound sleep,
   Drows'd with the fume of poppies, while thy hook
     Spares the next swath and all its twined flowers:
And sometimes like a gleaner thou dost keep
   Steady thy laden head across a brook;   20
   Or by a cyder-press, with patient look,
     Thou watchest the last oozings hours by hours.

3

Where are the songs of Spring? Ay, where are they?
   Think not of them, thou hast thy music too,—
While barred clouds bloom the soft-dying day,
   And touch the stubble-plains with rosy hue;
Then in a wailful choir the small gnats mourn
   Among the river shallows, borne aloft
     Or sinking as the light wind lives or dies;
And full-grown lambs loud bleat from hilly bourn;   30
   Hedge-crickets sing; and now with treble soft
   The redbreast whistles from a garden-croft;
     And gathering swallows twitter in the skies.

*GERARD MANLEY HOPKINS

*Heaven-Haven

A Nun Takes the Veil

I have desired to go
   Where springs not fail,
To fields where flies no sharp and sided hail
   And a few lilies blow.

And I have asked to be
   Where no storms come,
Where the green swell is in the havens dumb,
   And out of the swing of the sea.

*Pied Beauty

Glory be to God for dappled things—
   For skies of couple-colour as a brinded cow;
     For rose-moles all in stipple upon trout that swim;
Fresh-firecoal chestnut-falls; finches' wings;
   Landscape plotted and pieced—fold, fallow, and plough;
   And all trades, their gear and tackle and trim.

All things counter, original, spare, strange;
   Whatever is fickle, freckled (who knows how?)
     With swift, slow; sweet, sour; adazzle, dim;
He fathers-forth whose beauty is past change: 10
     Praise him.

*The Windhover

To Christ Our Lord

I caught this morning morning's minion, king-
   dom of daylight's dauphin, dapple-dawn-drawn Falcon, in his riding
   Of the rolling level underneath him steady air, and striding
High there, how he rung upon the rein of a wimpling wing

In his ectasy! then off, off forth on swing,
  As a skate's heel sweeps smooth on a bow-bend: the hurl and gliding
  Rebuffed the big wind. My heart in hiding
Stirred for a bird,—the achieve of, the mastery of the thing!

Brute beauty and valour and act, oh, air, pride, plume, here
  Buckle! And the fire that breaks from thee then, a billion   10
  Times told lovelier, more dangerous, O my chevalier!

No wonder of it: shéer plód makes plough down sillion
Shine, and blue-bleak embers, ah my dear,
  Fall, gall themselves, and gash gold-vermilion.

Spring and Fall: to a young child

Margaret, are you grieving
Over Goldengrove unleaving?
Leaves, like the things of man, you
With your fresh thoughts care for, can you?
Ah! as the heart grows older
It will come to such sights colder
By and by, nor spare a sigh
Though worlds of wanwood leafmeal lie;
And yet you will weep and know why.
Now no matter, child, the name: 10
Sorrow's springs are the same.
Nor mouth had, no nor mind, expressed
What heart heard of, ghost guessed:
It is the blight man was born for,
It is Margaret you mourn for.

*[No worst, there is none]

No worst, there is none. Pitched past pitch of grief,
More pangs will, schooled at forepangs, wilder wring.
Comforter, where, where is your comforting?
Mary, mother of us, where is your relief?
My cries heave, herds-long; huddle in a main, a chief
Woe, world-sorrow; on an age-old anvil wince and sing—
Then lull, then leave off. Fury had shrieked "No ling-
ering! Let me be fell: force I must be brief."

O the mind, mind has mountains; cliffs of fall
Frightful, sheer, no-man-fathomed. Hold them cheap   10
May who ne'er hung there. Nor does long our small
Durance deal with that steep or deep. Here! creep,
Wretch, under a comfort serves in a whirlwind: all
Life death does end and each day dies with sleep.

*[Thou art indeed just, Lord]

*Justus quidem tu es, Domine, si
disputem tecum: verumtamen
justa loquar ad te: Quare via
impiorum prosperatur? &c.*

Thou art indeed just, Lord, if I contend
With thee; but, sir, so what I plead is just.
Why do sinners' ways prosper? and why must
Disappointment all I endeavor end?
   Wert thou my enemy, O thou my friend,
How wouldst thou worse, I wonder, than thou dost
Defeat, thwart me? Oh, the sots and thralls of lust
Do in spare hours more thrive than I that spend,
Sir, life upon thy cause. See, banks and brakes
Now, leavèd how thick! lacèd they are again   10
With fretty chervil, look, and fresh wind shakes
Them; birds build—but not I build; no, but strain,
Time's eunuch, and not breed one work that wakes.
Mine, O thou lord of life, send my roots rain.

*THOMAS HARDY

I Said to Love

   I said to Love,
"It is not now as in old days
When men adored thee and thy ways
   All else above;

Named thee the Boy, the Bright, the One
Who spread a heaven beneath the sun,"
      I said to Love.

      I said to him,
"We now know more of thee than then;
We were but weak in judgment when,   10
      With hearts abrim,
We clamoured thee that thou would'st please
Inflict on us thine agonies,"
      I said to him.

      I said to Love,
"Thou art not young, thou art not fair,
No elfin darts, no cherub air,
      Nor swan, nor dove
Are thine; but features pitiless,
And iron daggers of distress,"   20
      I said to Love.

      "Depart then, Love! . . .
—Man's race shall perish, threatened thou,
Without thy kindling coupling-vow?
The age to come the man of now
      Know nothing of?—
We fear not such a threat from thee;
We are too old in apathy!
Mankind shall cease.—So let it be,"
      I said to Love.   30

The Darkling Thrush

I leant upon a coppice gate
      When Frost was spectre-gray,
And Winter's dregs made desolate
      The weakening eye of day.
The tangled bine-stems scored the sky
      Like strings of broken lyres,
And all mankind that haunted nigh
      Had sought their household fires.

The land's sharp features seemed to be
      The Century's corpse outleant,   10
His crypt the cloudy canopy,
      The wind his death-lament.

The ancient pulse of germ and birth
      Was shrunken hard and dry,
And every spirit upon earth
      Seemed fervourless as I.

At once a voice arose among
      The bleak twigs overhead
In a full-hearted evensong
      Of joy illimited;   20
An aged thrush, frail, gaunt, and small,
      In blast-beruffled plume,
Had chosen thus to fling his soul
      Upon the growing gloom.

So little cause for carollings
      Of such ecstatic sound
Was written on terrestrial things
      Afar or nigh around,
That I could think there trembled through
      His happy good-night air   30
Some blessed Hope, whereof he knew
      And I was unaware.

In Tenebris

I

*Percussus sum sicut foenum, et
aruit cor meum.*

      Wintertime nighs;
But my bereavement-pain
It cannot bring again:
      Twice no one dies.

      Flower-petals flee;
But, since it once hath been,
No more that severing scene
      Can harrow me.

      Birds faint in dread:
I shall not lose old strength   10
In the lone frost's black length:
      Strength long since fled!

Title: In Darkness.
*Epigraph: "My heart is smitten, and withered like grass" (Psalms, cii. 4. King James
version).*

Leaves freeze to dun;
But friends can not turn cold
This season as of old
        For him with none.

Tempests may scath;
But love can not make smart
Again this year his heart
        Who no heart hath.   20

Black is night's cope;
But death will not appal
One who, past doubtings all,
        Waits in unhope.

He Abjures Love

At last I put off love,
    For twice ten years
The daysman of my thought,
    And hope, and doing;
Being ashamed thereof,
    And faint of fears
And desolations, wrought
    In his pursuing,

Since first in youthtime those
    Disquietings   10
That heart-enslavement brings
    To hale and hoary,
Became my housefellows,
    And, fool and blind,
I turned from kith and kind
    To give him glory.

I was as children be
    Who have no care;
I did not shrink or sigh,
    I did not sicken;   20
But lo, Love beckoned me.
    And I was bare,
And poor, and starved, and dry,
    And fever-stricken.

Too many times ablaze
   With fatuous fires,
Enkindled by his wiles
   To new embraces,
Did I, by wilful ways
   And baseless ires,   30
Return the anxious smiles
   Of friendly faces.

No more will now rate I
   The common rare,
The midnight drizzle dew,
   The gray hour golden,
The wind a yearning cry,
   The faulty fair,
Things dreamt, of comelier hue
   Than things beholden! . . .   40

—I speak as one who plumbs
   Life's dim profound,
One who at length can sound
   Clear views and certain.
But—after love what comes?
   A scene that lours,
A few sad vacant hours,
   And then, the Curtain.

*Channel Firing

That night your great guns, unawares,
Shook all our coffins as we lay,
And broke the chancel window-squares,
We thought it was the Judgment-day

And sat upright. While drearisome
Arose the howl of wakened hounds:
The mouse let fall the altar-crumb,
The worms drew back into the mounds,

The glebe cow drooled. Till God called, "No;
It's gunnery practice out at sea   10
Just as before you went below;
The world is as it used to be:

"All nations striving strong to make
Red war yet redder. Mad as hatters
They do no more for Christés sake
Than you who are helpless in such matters.

"That this is not the judgment-hour
For some of them's a blessed thing,
For if it were they'd have to scour
Hell's floor for so much threatening. . . .   20

"Ha, ha. It will be warmer when
I blow the trumpet (if indeed
I ever do; for you are men,
And rest eternal sorely need)."

So down we lay again. "I wonder,
Will the world ever saner be,"
Said one, "than when He sent us under
In our indifferent century!"

And many a skeleton shook his head.
"Instead of preaching forty year,"   30
My neighbour Parson Thirdly said,
"I wish I had stuck to pipes and beer."

Again the guns disturbed the hour,
Roaring their readiness to avenge,
As far inland as Stourton Tower,
And Camelot, and starlit Stonehenge.

April 1914

The Oxen

Christmas Eve, and twelve of the clock.
    "Now they are all on their knees,"
An elder said as we sat in a flock
    By the embers in hearthside ease.

We pictured the meek mild creatures where
    They dwelt in their strawy pen,
Nor did it occur to one of us there
    To doubt they were kneeling then.

So fair a fancy few would weave
    In these years! Yet, I feel,   10
If someone said on Christmas Eve,
    "Come; see the oxen kneel

"In the lonely barton by yonder coomb
   Our childhood used to know,"
I should go with him in the gloom,
   Hoping it might be so.

*WILLIAM BUTLER YEATS

*The Magi

Now as at all times I can see in the mind's eye,
In their stiff, painted clothes, the pale unsatisfied ones
Appear and disappear in the blue depth of the sky
With all their ancient faces like rain-beaten stones,
And all their helms of silver hovering side by side,
And all their eyes still fixed, hoping to find once more,
Being by Calvary's turbulence unsatisfied,
The uncontrollable mystery on the bestial floor.

*The Second Coming

Turning and turning in the widening gyre
The falcon cannot hear the falconer;
Things fall apart; the centre cannot hold;
Mere anachy is loosed upon the world,
The blood-dimmed tide is loosed, and everywhere
The ceremony of innocence is drowned;
The best lack all conviction, while the worst
Are full of passionate intensity.

Surely some revelation is at hand;
Surely the Second Coming is at hand.   10
The Second Coming! Hardly are those words out
When a vast image out of *Spiritus Mundi*
Troubles my sight: somewhere in sands of the desert
A shape with lion body and the head of a man,
A gaze blank and pitiless as the sun,
Is moving its slow thighs, while all about it

Reel shadows of the indignant desert birds.
The darkness drops again; but now I know
That twenty centuries of stony sleep
Were vexed to nightmare by a rocking cradle,   20
And what rough beast, its hour come round at last,
Slouches towards Bethlehem to be born?

*The Cold Heaven

Suddenly I saw the cold and rook-delighting heaven
That seemed as though ice burned and was but the more ice,
And thereupon imagination and heart were driven
So wild that every casual thought of that and this
Vanished, and left but memories, that should be out of season
With the hot blood of youth, of love crossed long ago;
And I took all the blame out of all sense and reason,
Until I cried and trembled and rocked to and fro,
Riddled with light. Ah! when the ghost begins to quicken,
Confusion of the death-bed over, is it sent   10
Out naked on the roads, as the books say, and stricken
By the injustice of the skies for punishment?

*Among School Children

I

I walk through the long schoolroom questioning;
A kind old nun in a white hood replies;
The children learn to cipher and to sing,
To study reading-books and histories,
To cut and sew, be neat in everything
In the best modern way—the children's eyes
In momentary wonder stare upon
A sixty-year-old smiling public man.

II

I dream of a Ledaean body, bent
Above a sinking fire, a tale that she   10
Told of a harsh reproof, or trivial event
That changed some childish day to tragedy—

---

l. 9. Ledaean: Referring to Helen, daughter of Leda.

Told, and it seemed that our two natures blent
Into a sphere from youthful sympathy,
Or else, to alter Plato's parable,
Into the yolk and white of the one shell.

III

And thinking of that fit of grief or rage
I look upon one child or t'other there
And wonder if she stood so at that age—
For even daughters of the swan can share   20
Something of every paddler's heritage—
And had that colour upon cheek or hair,
And thereupon my heart is driven wild:
She stands before me as a living child.

IV

Her present image floats into the mind—
Did Quattrocento finger fashion it
Hollow of cheek as though it drank the wind
And took a mess of shadows for its meat?
And I though never of Ledaean kind
Had pretty plumage once—enough of that,   30
Better to smile on all that smile, and show
There is a comfortable kind of old scarecrow.

V

What youthful mother, a shape upon her lap
Honey of generation had betrayed,
And that must sleep, shriek, struggle to escape
As recollection or the drug decide,
Would think her son, did she but see that shape
With sixty or more winters on its head,
A compensation for the pang of his birth,
Or the uncertainty of his setting forth?   40

VI

Plato thought nature but a spume that plays
Upon a ghostly paradigm of things;
Solider Aristotle played the taws
Upon the bottom of a king of kings;
World-famous golden-thighed Pythagoras

---

l. 43. taws: Whips.

Fingered upon a fiddle-stick or strings
What a star sang and careless Muses heard:
Old clothes upon old sticks to scare a bird.

VII

Both nuns and mothers worship images,
But those the candles light are not as those   50
That animate a mother's reveries,
But keep a marble or a bronze repose.
And yet they too break hearts—O Presences
That passion, piety or affection knows,
And that all heavenly glory symbolise—
O self-born mockers of man's enterprise;

VIII

Labour is blossoming or dancing where
The body is not bruised to pleasure soul,
Nor beauty born out of its own despair,
Nor blear-eyed wisdom out of midnight oil.   60
O chestnut tree, great-rooted blossomer,
Are you the leaf, the blossom or the bole?
O body swayed to music, O brightening glance,
How can we know the dancer from the dance?

Meru

Civilisation is hooped together, brought
Under a rule, under the semblance of peace
By manifold illusion; but man's life is thought,
And he, despite his terror, cannot cease
Ravening through century after century,
Ravening, raging, and uprooting that he may come
Into the desolation of reality:
Egypt and Greece, good-bye, and good-bye, Rome!
Hermits upon Mount Meru or Everest,
Caverned in night under the drifted snow,   10
Or where that snow and winter's dreadful blast
Beat down upon their naked bodies, know
That day brings round the night, that before dawn
His glory and his monuments are gone.

Title: A mythical high mountain at the center of the world, dwelling place of the god Vishnu, who has gone through many incarnations.

*Lapis Lazuli

(for Harry Clifton)

I have heard that hysterical women say
They are sick of the palette and fiddle-bow,
Of poets that are always gay,
For everybody knows or else should know
That if nothing drastic is done
Aeroplane and Zeppelin will come out,
Pitch like King Billy bomb-balls in
Until the town lie beaten flat.

All perform their tragic play,
There struts Hamlet, there is Lear,   10
That's Ophelia, that Cordelia;
Yet they, should the last scene be there,
The great stage curtain about to drop,
If worthy their prominent part in the play,
Do not break up their lines to weep.
They know that Hamlet and Lear are gay;
Gaiety transfiguring all that dread.
All men have aimed at, found and lost;
Black out; Heaven blazing into the head:
Tragedy wrought to its uttermost.   20
Though Hamlet rambles and Lear rages,
And all the drop-scenes drop at once
Upon a hundred thousand stages,
It cannot grow by an inch or an ounce.

On their own feet they came, or on shipboard,
Camel-back, horse-back, ass-back, mule-back,
Old civilisations put to the sword.
Then they and their wisdom went to rack:
No handiwork of Callimachus,
Who handled marble as if it were bronze,   30
Made draperies that seemed to rise
When sea-wind swept the corner, stands;
His long lamp-chimney shaped like the stem
Of a slender palm, stood but a day;
All things fall and are built again,
And those that build them again are gay.

Two Chinamen, behind them a third,
Are carved in lapis lazuli,
Over them flies a long-legged bird,

A symbol of longevity;   40
The third, doubtless a serving-man,
Carries a musical instrument.
Every discoloration of the stone,
Every accidental crack or dent,
Seems a water-course or an avalanche,
Or lofty slope where it still snows
Though doubtless plum or cherry-branch
Sweetens the little half-way house
Those Chinamen climb towards, and I
Delight to imagine them seated there;   50
There, on the mountain and the sky,
On all the tragic scene they stare.
One asks for mournful melodies;
Accomplished fingers begin to play.
Their eyes mid many wrinkles, their eyes,
Their ancient, glittering eyes, are gay.

*ROBERT FROST

The Runaway

Once when the snow of the year was beginning to fall,
We stopped by a mountain pasture to say, "Whose colt?"
A little Morgan had one forefoot on the wall,
The other curled at his breast. He dipped his head
And snorted at us. And then he had to bolt.
We heard the miniature thunder where he fled,
And we saw him, or thought we saw him, dim and gray,
Like a shadow against the curtain of falling flakes.
"I think the little fellow's afraid of the snow.
He isn't winter-broken. It isn't play   10
With the little fellow at all. He's running away.
I doubt if even his mother could tell him, 'Sakes,
It's only weather.' He'd think she didn't know!
Where is his mother? He can't be out alone."
And now he comes again with a clatter of stone,
And mounts the wall again with whited eyes
And all his tail that isn't hair up straight.

He shudders his coat as if to throw off flies.
"Whoever it is that leaves him out so late,
When other creatures have gone to stall and bin,   20
Ought to be told to come and take him in."

Dust of Snow

The way a crow
Shook down on me
The dust of snow
From a hemlock tree

Has given my heart
A change of mood
And saved some part
Of a day I had rued.

After Apple-Picking

My long two-pointed ladder's sticking through a tree
Toward heaven still,
And there's a barrel that I didn't fill
Beside it, and there may be two or three
Apples I didn't pick upon some bough.
But I am done with apple-picking now.
Essence of winter sleep is on the night,
The scent of apples: I am drowsing off.
I cannot rub the strangeness from my sight
I got from looking through a pane of glass   10
I skimmed this morning from the drinking trough
And held against the world of hoary grass.
It melted, and I let it fall and break.
But I was well
Upon my way to sleep before it fell,
And I could tell
What form my dreaming was about to take.
Magnified apples appear and disappear,
Stem end and blossom end,
And every fleck of russet showing clear.   20
My instep arch not only keeps the ache,
It keeps the pressure of a ladder-round.
I feel the ladder sway as the boughs bend.

And I keep hearing from the cellar bin
The rumbling sound
Of load on load of apples coming in.
For I have had too much
Of apple-picking: I am overtired
Of the great harvest I myself desired.
There were ten thousand thousand fruit to touch,   30
Cherish in hand, lift down, and not let fall.
For all
That struck the earth,
No matter if not bruised or spiked with stubble,
Went surely to the cider-apple heap
As of no worth.
One can see what will trouble
This sleep of mine, whatever sleep it is.
Were he not gone,
The woodchuck could say whether it's like his   40
Long sleep, as I describe its coming on,
Or just some human sleep.

Nothing Gold Can Stay

Nature's first green is gold,
Her hardest hue to hold.
Her early leaf's a flower;
But only so an hour.

Then leaf subsides to leaf.
So Eden sank to grief,
So dawn goes down to day.
Nothing gold can stay.

Fire and Ice

Some say the world wlli end in fire,
Some say in ice.
From what I've tasted of desire
I hold with those who favor fire.
But if it had to perish twice,
I think I know enough of hate
To say that for destruction ice
Is also great
And would suffice.

Desert Places

Snow falling and night falling fast, oh, fast
In a field I looked into going past,
And the ground almost covered smooth in snow,
But a few weeds and stubble showing last.

The woods around it have it—it is theirs.
All animals are smothered in their lairs.
I am too absent-spirited to count;
The loneliness includes me unawares.

And lonely as it is, that loneliness
Will be more lonely ere it will be less—   10
A blanker whiteness of benighted snow
With no expression, nothing to express.

They cannot scare me with their empty spaces
Between stars—on stars where no human race is.
I have it in me so much nearer home
To scare myself with my own desert places.

*T. S. ELIOT

*The Love Song of J. Alfred Prufrock

*S'io credesse che mia risposta fosse
A persona che mai tornasse al mondo,
Questa fiamma staria senza più scosse.
Ma per ciò cche giammai di questo fondo
Non tornò vivo alcun, s'i'odo il vero,
Senza tema d'infamia ti rispondo.*

Let us go then, you and I,
When the evening is spread out against the sky
Like a patient etherised upon a table;
Let us go, through certain half-deserted streets,
The muttering retreats
Of restless nights in one-night cheap hotels

And sawdust restaurants with oyster-shells:
Streets that follow like a tedious argument
Of insidious intent
To lead you to an overwhelming question . . .   10
Oh, do not ask, "What is it?"
Let us go and make our visit.

    In the room the women come and go
Talking of Michelangelo.

    The yellow fog that rubs its back upon the window-panes,
The yellow smoke that rubs its muzzle on the window-panes,
Licked its tongue into the corners of the evening,
Lingered upon the pools that stand in drains,
Let fall upon its back the soot that falls from chimneys,
Slipped by the terrace, made a sudden leap,   20
And seeing that it was a soft October night,
Curled once about the house, and fell asleep.

    And indeed there will be time
For the yellow smoke that slides along the street
Rubbing its back upon the window-panes;
There will be time, there will be time
To prepare a face to meet the faces that you meet;
There will be time to murder and create,
And time for all the works and days of hands
That lift and drop a question on your plate;   30
Time for you and time for me,
And time yet for a hundred indecisions,
And for a hundred visions and revisions,
Before the taking of a toast and tea.

    In the room the women come and go
Talking of Michelangelo.

    And indeed there will be time
To wonder, "Do I dare?" and, "Do I dare?"
Time to turn back and descend the stair,
With a bald spot in the middle of my hair—   40
(They will say: "How his hair is growing thin!")
My morning coat, my collar mounting firmly to the chin,
My necktie rich and modest, but asserted by a simple pin—
(They will say: "But how his arms and legs are thin!")
Do I dare
Disturb the universe?
In a minute there is time
For decisions and revisions which a minute will reverse.

For I have known them all already, known them all—
Have known the evenings, mornings, afternoons,   50
I have measured out my life with coffee spoons;
I know the voices dying with a dying fall
Beneath the music from a farther room.
    So how should I presume?

And I have known the eyes already, known them all—
The eyes that fix you in a formulated phrase,
And when I am formulated, sprawling on a pin,
When I am pinned and wriggling on the wall,
Then how should I begin
To spit out all the butt-ends of my days and ways?   60
    And how should I presume?

And I have known the arms already, known them all—
Arms that are braceleted and white and bare
(But in the lamplight, downed with light brown hair!)
Is it perfume from a dress
That makes me so digress?
Arms that lie along a table, or wrap about a shawl.
    And should I then presume?
    And how should I begin?

      . . . . .

Shall I say, I have gone at dusk through narrow streets   70
And watched the smoke that rises from the pipes
Of lonely men in shirt-sleeves, leaning out of windows? . . .

    I should have been a pair of ragged claws
Scuttling across the floors of silent seas.

      . . . . .

And the afternoon, the evening, sleeps so peacefully!
Smoothed by long fingers,
Asleep . . . tired . . . or it malingers,
Stretched on the floor, here beside you and me.
Should I, after tea and cakes and ices,
Have the strength to force the moment to its crisis?   80
But though I have wept and fasted, wept and prayed,
Though I have seen my head (grown slightly bald) brought in upon a platter,
I am no prophet—and here's no great matter;
I have seen the moment of my greatness flicker,
And I have seen the eternal Footman hold my coat, and snicker,
And in short, I was afraid.

    And would it have been worth it, after all,
After the cups, the marmalade, the tea,
Among the porcelain, among some talk of you and me,

Would it have been worth while,   90
To have bitten off the matter with a smile,
To have squeezed the universe into a ball
To roll it towards some overwhelming question,
To say: "I am Lazarus, come from the dead,
Come back to tell you all, I shall tell you all"—
If one, settling a pillow by her head,
    Should say: "That is not what I meant at all.
    That is not it, at all."

    And would it have been worth it, after all,
Would it have been worth while,   100
After the sunsets and the dooryards and the sprinkled streets,
After the novels, after the teacups, after the skirts that trail along the floor—
And this, and so much more?—
It is impossible to say just what I mean!
But as if a magic lantern threw the nerves in patterns on a screen:
Would it have been worth while
If one, settling a pillow or throwing off a shawl,
And turning toward the window, should say:
    "That is not it at all,
    That is not what I meant, at all."   110

                                    .   .   .   .   .

No! I am not Prince Hamlet, nor was meant to be;
Am an attendant lord, one that will do
To swell a progress, start a scene or two,
Advise the prince; no doubt, an easy tool,
Deferential, glad to be of use,
Politic, cautious, and meticulous;
Full of high sentence, but a bit obtuse;
At times, indeed, almost ridiculous—
Almost, at times, the Fool.

    I grow old . . . I grow old . . .   120
I shall wear the bottoms of my trousers rolled.

    Shall I part my hair behind? Do I dare to eat a peach?
I shall wear white flannel trousers, and walk upon the beach.
I have heard the mermaids singing, each to each.

    I do not think that they will sing to me.

    I have seen them riding seaward on the waves
Combing the white hair of the waves blown back
When the wind blows the water white and black.
    We have lingered in the chambers of the sea
By sea-girls wreathed with seaweed red and brown   130
Till human voices wake us, and we drown.

*Rhapsody on a Windy Night

Twelve o'clock.
Along the reaches of the street
Held in a lunar synthesis,
Whispering lunar incantations
Dissolve the floors of memory
And all its clear relations,
Its divisions and precisions.
Every street lamp that I pass
Beats like a fatalistic drum,
And through the spaces of the dark 10
Midnight shakes the memory
As a madman shakes a dead geranium.

Half-past one,
The street-lamp sputtered,
The street-lamp muttered,
The street-lamp said, 'Regard that woman
Who hesitates toward you in the light of the door
Which opens on her like a grin.
You see the border of her dress
Is torn and stained with sand, 20
And you see the corner of her eye
Twists like a crooked pin.'

The memory throws up high and dry
A crowd of twisted things;
A twisted branch upon the beach
Eaten smooth, and polished
As if the world gave up
The secret of its skeleton,
Stiff and white.
A broken spring in a factory yard, 30
Rust that clings to the form that the strength has left
Hard and curled and ready to snap.

Half-past two,
The street-lamp said,
'Remark the cat which flattens itself in the gutter,
Slips out its tongue
And devours a morsel of rancid butter.'
So the hand of the child, automatic,
Slipped out and pocketed a toy that was running along the quay.
I could see nothing behind that child's eye. 40
I have seen eyes in the street

Trying to peer through lighted shutters,
And a crab one afternoon in a pool,
An old crab with barnacles on his back,
Gripped the end of a stick which I held him.

Half-past three,
The lamp sputtered,
The lamp muttered in the dark.
The lamp hummed:
'Regard the moon,   50
La lune ne garde aucune rancune,
She winks a feeble eye,
She smiles into corners.
She smooths the hair of the grass.
The moon has lost her memory.
A washed-out smallpox cracks her face,
Her hand twists a paper rose,
That smells of dust and eau de Cologne,
She is alone
With all the old nocturnal smells   60
That cross and cross across her brain.'
The reminiscence comes
Of sunless dry geraniums
And dust in crevices,
Smells of chestnuts in the street,
And female smells in shuttered rooms,
And cigarettes in corridors
And cocktail smells in bars.

The lamp said,
'Four o'clock,   70
Here is the number on the door.
Memory!
You have the key,
The little lamp spreads a ring on the stair.
Mount.
The bed is open; the tooth-brush hangs on the wall,
Put your shoes at the door, sleep, prepare for life.'

The last twist of the knife.

*Journey of the Magi

'A cold coming we had of it,
Just the worst time of the year
For a journey, and such a long journey:
The ways deep and the weather sharp,
The very dead of winter.'
And the camels galled, sore-footed, refractory,
Lying down in the melting snow.
There were times we regretted
The summer palaces on slopes, the terraces,
And the silken girls bringing sherbet.   10
Then the camel men cursing and grumbling
And running away, and wanting their liquor and women,
And the night-fires going out, and the lack of shelters,
And the cities hostile and the towns unfriendly
And the villages dirty and charging high prices:
A hard time we had of it.
At the end we preferred to travel all night,
Sleeping in snatches,
With the voices singing in our ears, saying
That this was all folly.   20

Then at dawn we came down to a temperate valley,
Wet, below the snow line, smelling of vegetation;
With a running stream and a water-mill beating the darkness,
And three trees on the low sky.
And an old white horse galloped away in the meadow.
Then we came to a tavern with vine-leaves over the lintel,
Six hands at an open door dicing for pieces of silver,
And feet kicking the empty wine-skins.
But there was no information, and so we continued
And arrived at evening, not a moment too soon   30
Finding the place; it was (you may say) satisfactory.

All this was a long time ago, I remember,
And I would do it again, but set down
This set down
This: were we led all that way for
Birth or Death? There was a Birth, certainly,
We had evidence and no doubt. I had seen birth and death,
But had thought they were different; this Birth was
Hard and bitter agony for us, like Death, our death.
We returned to our places, these Kingdoms,   40
But no longer at ease here, in the old dispensation,
With an alien people clutching their gods.
I should be glad of another death.

*WALLACE STEVENS

*Peter Quince at the Clavier

I

Just as my fingers on these keys
Make music, so the self-same sounds
On my spirit make a music, too.

Music is feeling, then, not sound;
And thus it is that what I feel,
Here in this room, desiring you,

Thinking of your blue-shadowed silk,
Is music. It is like the strain
Waked in the elders by Susanna.

Of a green evening, clear and warm,   10
She bathed in her still garden, while
The red-eyed elders watching, felt

The basses of their beings throb
In witching chords, and their thin blood
Pulse pizzicati of Hosanna.

II

In the green water, clear and warm,
Susanna lay.
She searched
The touch of springs,
And found   20
Concealed imaginings.
She sighed,
For so much melody.

Upon the bank, she stood
In the cool
Of spent emotions.
She felt, among the leaves,
The dew
Of old devotions.

She walked upon the grass,
Still quavering.
The winds were like her maids,
On timid feet,
Fetching her woven scarves,
Yet wavering.   30

A breath upon her hand
Muted the night.
She turned—
A cymbal crashed,
And roaring horns.   40

III

Soon, with a noise like tambourines,
Came her attendant Byzantines.

They wondered why Susanna cried
Against the elders by her side;

And as they whispered, the refrain
Was like a willow swept by rain.

Anon, their lamps' uplifted flame
Revealed Susanna and her shame.

And then, the simpering Byzantines
Fled, with a noise like tambourines.   50

IV

Beauty is momentary in the mind—
The fitful tracing of a portal;
But in the flesh it is immortal.

The body dies; the body's beauty lives.
So evenings die, in their green going,
A wave, interminably flowing.
So gardens die, their meek breath scenting
The cowl of winter, done repenting.
So maidens die, to the auroral
Celebration of a maiden's choral.   60

Susanna's music touched the bawdy strings
Of those white elders; but, escaping,
Left only Death's ironic scraping.
Now, in its immortality, it plays
On the clear viol of her memory,
And makes a constant sacrament of praise.

*Domination of Black

At night, by the fire,
The colors of the bushes
And of the fallen leaves,
Repeating themselves,
Turned in the room,
Like the leaves themselves
Turning in the wind.
Yes: but the color of the heavy hemlocks
Came striding.
And I remembered the cry of the peacocks.   10

The colors of their tails
Were like the leaves themselves
Turning in the wind,
In the twilight wind.
They swept over the room,
Just as they flew from the boughs of the hemlocks
Down to the ground.
I heard them cry—the peacocks.
Was it a cry against the twilight
Or against the leaves themselves   20
Turning in the wind,
Turning as the flames
Turned in the fire,
Turning as the tails of the peacocks
Turned in the loud fire,
Loud as the hemlocks
Full of the cry of the peacocks?
Or was it a cry against the hemlocks?

Out of the window,
I saw how the planets gathered   30
Like the leaves themselves
Turning in the wind.
I saw how the night came,
Came striding like the color of the heavy hemlocks.
I felt afraid.
And I remembered the cry of the peacocks.

The Snow Man

One must have a mind of winter
To regard the frost and the boughs
Of the pine-trees crusted with snow;

And have been cold a long time
To behold the junipers shagged with ice,
The spruces rough in the distant glitter

Of the January sun; and not to think
Of any misery in the sound of the wind,
In the sound of a few leaves,

Which is the sound of the land   10
Full of the same wind
That is blowing in the same bare place

For the listener, who listens in the snow,
And, nothing himself, beholds
Nothing that is not there and the nothing that is.

*Sunday Morning

I

Complacencies of the peignoir, and late
Coffee and oranges in a sunny chair,
And the green freedom of a cockatoo
Upon a rug mingle to dissipate
The holy hush of ancient sacrifice.
She dreams a little, and she feels the dark
Encroachment of that old catastrophe,
As a calm darkens among water-lights.
The pungent oranges and bright, green wings
Seem things in some procession of the dead,   10
Winding across wide water, without sound.
The day is like wide water, without sound,
Stilled for the passing of her dreaming feet
Over the seas, to silent Palestine,
Dominion of the blood and sepulchre.

II

Why should she give her bounty to the dead?
What is divinity if it can come
Only in silent shadows and in dreams?
Shall she not find in comforts of the sun,
In pungent fruit and bright, green wings, or else   20
In any balm or beauty of the earth,
Things to be cherished like the thought of heaven?
Divinity must live within herself:
Passions of rain, or moods in falling snow;
Grievings in loneliness, or unsubdued
Elations when the forest blooms; gusty
Emotions on wet roads on autumn nights;
All pleasures and all pains, remembering
The bough of summer and the winter branch.
These are the measures destined for her soul.   30

III

Jove in the clouds had his inhuman birth.
No mother suckled him, no sweet land gave
Large-mannered motions to his mythy mind.
He moved among us, as a muttering king,
Magnificent, would move among his hinds,
Until our blood, commingling, virginal,
With heaven, brought such requital to desire
The very hinds discerned it, in a star.
Shall our blood fail? Or shall it come to be
The blood of paradise? And shall the earth   40
Seem all of paradise that we shall know?
The sky will be much friendlier then than now,
A part of labor and a part of pain,
And next in glory to enduring love,
Not this dividing and indifferent blue.

IV

She says, "I am content when wakened birds,
Before they fly, test the reality
Of misty fields, by their sweet questionings;
But when the birds are gone, and their warm fields
Return no more, where, then, is paradise?"   50
There is not any haunt of prophecy,
Nor any old chimera of the grave,
Neither the golden underground, nor isle
Melodious, whose spirits gat them home,
Nor visionary south, nor cloudy palm

Remote on heaven's hill, that has endured
As April's green endures; or will endure
Like her remembrance of awakened birds,
Or her desire for June and evening, tipped
By the consummation of the swallow's wings.   60

V

She says, "But in contentment I still feel
The need of some imperishable bliss."
Death is the mother of beauty; hence from her,
Alone, shall come fulfillment to our dreams
And our desires. Although she strews the leaves ·
Of sure obliteration on our paths,
The path sick sorrow took, the many paths
Where triumph rang its brassy phrase, or love
Whispered a little out of tenderness,
She makes the willow shiver in the sun   70
For maidens who were wont to sit and gaze
Upon the grass, relinquished to their feet.
She causes boys to pile new plums and pears
On disregarded plate. The maidens taste
And stray impassioned in the littering leaves.

VI

Is there no change of death in paradise?
Does ripe fruit never fall? Or do the boughs
Hang always heavy in that perfect sky,
Unchanging, yet so like our perishing earth,
With rivers like our own that seek for seas   80
They never find, the same receding shores
That never touch with inarticulate pang?
Why set the pear upon those river-banks
Or spice the shores with odors of the plum?
Alas, that they should wear our colors there,
The silken weavings of our afternoons,
And pick the strings of our insipid lutes!
Death is the mother of beauty, mystical,
Within whose burning bosom we devise
Our earthly mothers waiting, sleeplessly.   90

VII

Supple and turbulent, a ring of men
Shall chant in orgy on a summer morn
Their boisterous devotion to the sun,

Not as a god, but as a god might be,
Naked among them, like a savage source.
Their chant shall be a chant of paradise,
Out of their blood, returning to the sky;
And in their chant shall enter, voice by voice,
The windy lake wherein their lord delights,
The trees, like serafin, and echoing hills,   100
That choir among themselves long afterward.
They shall know well the heavenly fellowship
Of men that perish and of summer morn.
And whence they came and whither they shall go
The dew upon their feet shall manifest.

VIII

She hears, upon that water without sound,
A voice that cries, "The tomb in Palestine
Is not the porch of spirits lingering.
It is the grave of Jesus, where he lay."
We live in an old chaos of the sun,   110
Or old dependency of day and night,
Or island solitude, unsponsored, free,
Of that wide water, inescapable.
Deer walk upon our mountains, and the quail
Whistle about us their spontaneous cries;
Sweet berries ripen in the wilderness;
And, in the isolation of the sky,
At evening, casual flocks of pigeons make
Ambiguous undulations as they sink,
Downward to darkness, on extended wings.   120

*The Idea of Order at Key West

She sang beyond the genius of the sea.
The water never formed to mind or voice,
Like a body wholly body, fluttering
Its empty sleeves; and yet its mimic motion
Made constant cry, caused constantly a cry,
That was not ours although we understood,
Inhuman, of the veritable ocean.

The sea was not a mask. No more was she.
The song and water were not medleyed sound
Even if what she sang was what she heard,   10
Since what she sang was uttered word by word.

It may be that in all her phrases stirred
The grinding water and the gasping wind;
But it was she and not the sea we heard.

For she was maker of the song she sang.
The ever-hooded, tragic-gestured sea
Was merely a place by which she walked to sing.
Whose spirit is this? we said, because we knew
It was the spirit that we sought and knew
That we should ask this often as she sang.   20

If it was only the dark voice of the sea
That rose, or even colored by many waves;
If it was only the outer voice of sky
And cloud, of the sunken coral water-walled,
However clear, it would have been deep air,
The heaving speech of air, a summer sound
Repeated in a summer without end
And sound alone. But it was more than that,
More even than her voice, and ours, among
The meaningless plungings of water and the wind,   30
Theatrical distances, bronze shadows heaped
On high horizons, mountainous atmospheres
Of sky and sea.
                        It was her voice that made
The sky acutest at its vanishing.
She measured to the hour its solitude.
She was the single artificer of the world
In which she sang. And when she sang, the sea,
Whatever self it had, became the self
That was her song, for she was the maker. Then we,
As we beheld her striding there alone,   40
Knew that there never was a world for her
Except the one she sang and, singing, made.

Ramon Fernandez, tell me, if you know,
Why, when the singing ended and we turned
Toward the town, tell why the glassy lights,
The lights in the fishing boats at anchor there,
As the night descended, tilting in the air,
Mastered the night and portioned out the sea,
Fixing emblazoned zones and fiery poles,
Arranging, deepening, enchanting night.   50
Oh! Blessed rage for order, pale Ramon,
The maker's rage to order words of the sea,
Words of the fragrant portals, dimly-starred,
And of ourselves and of our origins,
In ghostlier demarcations, keener sounds.

A Rabbit as King of the Ghosts

The difficulty to think at the end of day,
When the shapeless shadow covers the sun
And nothing is left except light on your fur—

There was the cat slopping its milk all day,
Fat cat, red tongue, green mind, white milk
And August the most peaceful month.

To be, in the grass, in the peacefullest time,
Without that monument of cat,
The cat forgotten in the moon;

And to feel that the light is a rabbit-light,   10
In which everything is meant for you
And nothing need be explained;

Then there is nothing to think of. It comes of itself;
And east rushes west and west rushes down,
No matter. The grass is full

And full of yourself. The trees around are for you,
The whole of the wideness of night is for you,
A self that touches all edges,

You become a self that fills the four corners of night.
The red cat hides away in the fur-light   20
And there you are humped high, humped up,

You are humped higher and higher, black as stone—
You sit with your head like a carving in space
And the little green cat is a bug in the grass.

*ROBERT HAYDEN

*Middle Passage

I

Jesús, Estrella, Esperanza, Mercy:

Sails flashing to the wind like weapons,
sharks following the moans the fever and the dying;
horror the corposant and compass rose.

Middle Passage:
     voyage through death
          to life upon these shores.

"10 April 1800—
Blacks rebellions. Crew uneasy. Our linguist says
their moaning is a prayer for death,
ours and their own. Some try to starve themselves.
Lost three this morning leaped with crazy laughter
to the waiting sharks, sang as they went under."

Desire, Adventure, Tartar, Ann:

Standing to America, bringing home
black gold, black ivory, black seed.

    Deep in the festering hold thy father lies,
    of his bones New England pews are made,
    those are altar lights that were his eyes.

Jesus Saviour Pilot Me
Over Life's Tempestuous Sea

We pray that Thou wilt grant, O Lord,
safe passage to our vessels bringing
heathen souls unto Thy chastening.

Jesus Saviour

    "8 bells. I cannot sleep, for I am sick
with fear, but writing eases fear a little
since still my eyes can see these words take shape
upon the page & so I write, as one
would turn to exorcism. 4 days scudding,

but now the sea is calm again. Misfortune
follows in our wake like sharks (our grinning
tutelary gods). Which one of us
has killed an albatross? A plague among
our blacks—Ophthalmia: blindness—& we
have jettisoned the blind to no avail.
It spreads, the terrifying sickness spreads.
Its claws have scratched sight from the Capt.'s eyes
& there is blindness in the fo'c'sle
& we must sail 3 weeks before we come   40
to port."

   What port awaits us, Davy Jones'
   or home? I've heard of slavers drifting, drifting,
   playthings of wind and storm and chance, their crews
   gone blind, the jungle hatred
   crawling up on deck.

Thou Who Walked On Galilee

   "Deponent further sayeth *The Bella J*
   left the Guinea Coast
   with cargo of five hundred blacks and odd   50
   for the barracoons of Florida:

   "That there was hardly room 'tween-decks for half
   the sweltering cattle stowed spoon-fashion there;
   that some went mad of thirst and tore their flesh
   and sucked the blood:

   "That Crew and Captain lusted with the comeliest
   of the savage girls kept naked in the cabins;
   that there was one they called The Guinea Rose
   and they cast lots and fought to lie with her:

   "That when the Bo's'n piped all hands, the flames   60
   spreading from starboard already were beyond
   control, the negroes howling and their chains
   entangled with the flames:

   "That the burning blacks could not be reached,
   that the Crew abandoned ship,
   leaving their shrieking negresses behind,
   that the Captain perished drunken with the wenches:

   "Further Deponent sayeth not."

Pilot Oh Pilot Me

II

Aye, lad, and I have seen those factories,   70
Gambia, Rio Pongo, Calabar;
have watched the artful mongos baiting traps
of war wherein the victor and the vanquished

Were caught as prizes for our barracoons.
Have seen the nigger kings whose vanity
and greed turned wild black hides of Fellatah,
Mandingo, Ibo, Kru to gold for us.

And there was one—King Anthracite we named him—
fetish face beneath French parasols
of brass and orange velvet, impudent mouth   80
whose cups were carven skulls of enemies:

He'd honor us with drum and feast and conjo
and palm-oil-glistening wenches deft in love,
and for tin crowns that shone with paste,
red calico and German-silver trinkets

Would have the drums talk war and send
his warriors to burn the sleeping villages
and kill the sick and old and lead the young
in coffles to our factories.

Twenty years a trader, twenty years,   90
for there was wealth aplenty to be harvested
from those black fields, and I'd be trading still
but for the fevers melting down my bones.

III

Shuttles in the rocking loom of history,
the dark ships move, the dark ships move,
their bright ironical names
like jests of kindness on a murderer's mouth;
plough through thrashing glister toward
fata morgana's lucent melting shore,
weave toward New World littorals that are   100
mirage and myth and actual shore.

Voyage through death,
                    voyage whose chartings are unlove.

A charnel stench, effluvium of living death

spreads outward from the hold,
where the living and the dead, the horribly dying,
lie interlocked, lie foul with blood and excrement.

Deep in the festering hold thy father lies,
the corpse of mercy rots with him,
rats eat love's rotten gelid eyes.   110

But, oh, the living look at you
with human eyes whose suffering accuses you,
whose hatred reaches through the swill of dark
to strike you like a leper's claw.

You cannot stare that hatred down
or chain the fear that stalks the watches
and breathes on you its fetid scorching breath;
cannot kill the deep immortal human wish,
the timeless will.

"But for the storm that flung up barriers   120
of wind and wave, *The Amistad,* señores,
would have reached the port of Príncipe in two,
three days at most; but for the storm we should
have been prepared for what befell.
Swift as the puma's leap it came. There was
that interval of moonless calm filled only
with the water's and the rigging's usual sounds,
then sudden movement, blows and snarling cries
and they had fallen on us with machete
and marlinspike. It was as though the very   130
air, the night itself were striking us.
Exhausted by the rigors of the storm,
we were no match for them. Our men went down
before the murderous Africans. Our loyal
Celestino ran from below with gun
and lantern and I saw, before the cane-
knife's wounding flash, Cinquez,
that surly brute who calls himself a prince,
directing, urging on the ghastly work.
He hacked the poor mulatto down, and then   140
he turned on me. The decks were slippery
when daylight finally came. It sickens me
to think of what I saw, of how these apes
threw overboard the butchered bodies of
our men, true Christians all, like so much jetsam.
Enough, enough. The rest is quickly told:
Cinquez was forced to spare the two of us

you see to steer the ship to Africa,
and we like phantoms doomed to rove the sea
voyaged east by day and west by night,   150
deceiving them, hoping for rescue,
prisoners on our own vessel, till
at length we drifted to the shores of this
your land, America, where we were freed
from our unspeakable misery. Now we
demand, good sirs, the extradition of
Cinquez and his accomplices to La
Havana. And it distresses us to know
there are so many here who seem inclined
to justify the mutiny of these blacks.   160
We find it paradoxical indeed
that you whose wealth, whose tree of liberty
are rooted in the labor of your slaves
should suffer the august John Quincy Adams
to speak with so much passion of the right
of chattel slaves to kill their lawful masters
and with his Roman rhetoric weave a hero's
garland for Cinquez. I tell you that
we are determined to return to Cuba
with our slaves and there see justice done. Cinquez—   170
or let us say 'the Prince'—Cinquez shall die."

The deep immortal human wish,
the timeless will:

Cinquez its deathless primaveral image,
life that transfigures many lives.

Voyage through death
                    to life upon these shores.

*Frederick Douglass

When it is finally ours, this freedom, this liberty, this beautiful
and terrible thing, needful to man as air,
usable as earth; when it belongs at last to all,
when it is truly instinct, brain matter, diastole, systole,
reflex action; when it is finally won; when it is more
than the gaudy mumbo jumbo of politicians:
this man, this Douglass, this former slave, this Negro
beaten to his knees, exiled, visioning a world
where none is lonely, none hunted, alien,

this man, superb in love and logic, this man   10
shall be remembered. Oh, not with statues' rhetoric,
not with legends and poems and wreaths of bronze alone,
but with the lives grown out of his life, the lives
fleshing his dream of the beautiful, needful thing.

Unidentified Flying Object

It's true Mattie Lee
has clean disappeared.
And shouldn't we notify
the sheriff? No use, Will
insists, no earthly use.

He was sleeping one off
under the trees that night,
he claims, and woke up when
the space-ship
landed—a silvery dome   10

with gassy-green and red-
hot-looking lights like eyes
that stared blinked stared.
Says he hid himself
in the bushes and watched,

shaking. Pretty soon
a hatch slides open, a ramp
glides forward like
a glowing tongue poked out.
And who or what is it   20

silently present there?
Same as if Will's
trying to peer through webs
and bars of gauzy glare
screening, distorting a shape

he sees yet cannot see.
But crazier than that
was when Mattie Lee
came running from her house
towards the thing.   30

She's wearing her sunflower hat
and the dress the lady she cooked
for gave her, and it's like
she's late for work the way
she scurries up the ramp.

And it seems to Will
that in its queer
shining, plain Mattie Lee's
transformed—is every teasing brown
he's ever wanted, never had.   40

He's fixing to shout, Come back,
Mattie Lee, come back;
but a heavy hand is over his mouth
when he hears her laugh
as she steps inside

without even a goodbye glance
around. The next Will knew,
the UFO rose in the air—
no blastoff roar, no flame,
he says—hung in the dark,   50

hovered, shimmered,
its eyes pulsing, then whirred
spiraling into the sky,
vanished as though
it had never been.

Will's tale anyhow.
All I'm certain of
is Mattie Lee's
nowhere to be found
and must have gone   60

off in a hurry. Left her doors
unlocked and the radio on
and a roast in the oven. Strange.
As for Will, he's a changed man,
not drinking nowadays and sad.

Mattie Lee's friends—
she's got no kinfolks, lived
alone—are worried, swear
Will was craving her
and she held herself too good   70

for him, being head of Mount
Nebo's usher board and such.
And some are hinting what I,
for one—well, never mind.
The talk is getting mean.

from *Words in the Mourning Time*

VII

voice in the wilderness

Know that love has chosen you
to live his crucial purposes.
Know that love has chosen you.
And will not pamper you nor spare;
demands obedience to all
the rigorous laws of risk,
does not pamper, will not spare.

Oh, master now love's instruments—
complex and not for the fearful,
simple and not for the foolish.   10
Master now love's instruments.

I who love you tell you this,
even as the pitiful killer waits for me,
I who love you tell you this.

A Plague of Starlings

(Fisk Campus)

Evenings I hear
the workmen fire
into the stiff
magnolia leaves,
routing the starlings
gathered noisy and
befouling there.

Their scissoring
terror like glass
coins spilling breaking   10

the birds explode
into mica sky
raggedly fall
to ground rigid
in clench of cold.

The spared return,
when the guns are through,
to the spoiled trees
like choiceless poor
to a dangerous   20
dwelling place,
chitter and quarrel
in the piercing dark
above the killed.

Mornings, I pick
my way past death's
black droppings:
on campus lawns
and streets
the troublesome   30
starlings
frost-salted lie,
troublesome still.

And if not careful
I shall tread
upon carcasses
carcasses when I
go mornings now
to lecture on
what Socrates,   40
the hemlock hour nigh,
told sorrowing
Phaedo and the rest
about the migratory
habits of the soul.

*ROBERT LOWELL

Rebellion

There was rebellion, father, when the mock
French windows slammed and you hove backward, rammed
Into your heirlooms, screens, a glass-cased clock,
The highboy quaking to its toes. You damned
My arm that cast your house upon your head
And broke the chimney flintlock on your skull.
Last night the moon was full:
I dreamed the dead
Caught at my knees and fell:
And it was well   10
With me, my father. Then
Behemoth and Leviathan
Devoured our mighty merchants. None could arm
Or put to sea. O father, on my farm
I added field to field
And I have sealed
An everlasting pact
With Dives to contract
The world that spreads in pain;
But the world spread   20
When the clubbed flintlock broke my father's brain.

As a Plane Tree by the Water

Darkness has called to darkness, and disgrace
Elbows about our windows in this planned
Babel of Boston where our money talks
And multiplies the darkness of a land
Of preparation where the Virgin walks
And roses spiral her enamelled face
Or fall to splinters on unwatered streets.
Our Lady of Babylon, go by, go by,
I was once the apple of your eye;
Flies, flies are on the plane tree, on the streets.   10

The flies, the flies, the flies of Babylon
Buzz in my ear-drums while the devil's long
Dirge of the people detonates the hour
For floating cities where his golden tongue
Enchants the masons of the Babel Tower
To raise tomorrow's city to the sun
That never sets upon these hell-fire streets
Of Boston, where the sunlight is a sword
Striking at the withholder of the Lord:
Flies, flies are on the plane tree, on the streets.   20

Flies strike the miraculous waters of the iced
Atlantic and the eyes of Bernadette
Who saw Our Lady standing in the cave
At Massabielle, saw her so squarely that
Her vision put out reason's eyes. The grave
Is open-mouthed and swallowed up in Christ.
O walls of Jericho! And all the streets
To our Atlantic wall are singing: "Sing,
Sing for the resurrection of the King."
Flies, flies are on the plane tree, on the streets.   30

---

l. 22. Bernadette: St. Bernadette Soubirous (1844–1879).

*Mr. Edwards and the Spider

I saw the spiders marching through the air,
Swimming from tree to tree that mildewed day
  In latter August when the hay
  Came creaking to the barn. But where
    The wind is westerly,
Where gnarled November makes the spiders fly
Into the apparitions of the sky,
  They purpose nothing but their ease and die
Urgently beating east to sunrise and the sea;

What are we in the hands of the great God?   10
It was in vain you set up thorn and briar
  In battle array against the fire
  And treason crackling in your blood;
    For the wild thorns grow tame
And will do nothing to oppose the flame;
Your lacerations tell the losing game
  You play against a sickness past your cure.
How will the hands be strong? How will the heart endure?

A very little thing, a little worm,
Or hourglass-blazoned spider, it is said,   20
    Can kill a tiger. Will the dead
    Hold up his mirror and affirm
        To the four winds the smell
    And flash of his authority? It's well
    If God who holds you to the pit of hell,
        Much as one holds a spider, will destroy,
Baffle and dissipate your soul. As a small boy

    On Windsor Marsh, I saw the spider die
    When thrown into the bowels of fierce fire:
        There's no long struggle, no desire   30
        To get up on its feet and fly—
        It stretches out its feet
    And dies. This is the sinner's last retreat;
    Yes, and no strength exerted on the heat
        Then sinews the abolished will, when sick
And full of burning, it will whistle on a brick.

    But who can plumb the sinking of that soul?
    Josiah Hawley, picture yourself cast
        Into a brick-kiln where the blast
        Fans your quick vitals to a coal—   40
            If measured by a glass,
    How long would it seem burning! Let there pass
    A minute, ten, ten trillion; but the blaze
    Is infinite, eternal: this is death,
To die and know it. This is the Black Widow, death.

Recent Modes

Modern trends in poetry date from the first quarter of the century and are so varied as to be unclassifiable. Some poets have continued to explore the possibilities of free verse as practiced earlier by Whitman and later by William Carlos Williams or, in a more restrained way, by Eliot, while others have recently returned to more or less traditional stanza forms and meter. A few—of whom the best known is Marianne Moore, the oldest writer in this final group—employ syllabic verse, verse without regularity of stress or beat but with a repetitive pattern based on the number of syllables in the line.

In theme and attitude the writers range from metaphysical or romantic to satiric, from light to serious, from academic or traditional to "beat," angry, or consciously neurotic. This century has produced heated discussion of the question of why poets continue to write rather more often about nature than about towns and machinery, when so many people now live in an urban and industrial environment. Are these poets, it is sometimes asked, simply refusing to face modern life as it is, or is there a sound and natural reason in human nature for their choice of subjects and imagery? We raise the question here but will not attempt to answer it categorically. Some have said, however, that the mechanical things which man himself can make, he can understand and deal with in equations or by strict reasoning, and that he does not need much imagination to deal with them once they are invented. His factories, however, cannot manufacture human beings, nature, or the powers and laws behind the world. These all-important and familiar yet half-unknown things he must deal with partly by imagination. Whether or not this is the reason, the fact is that even in modern poetry we usually see more of nature than we do of machines. Serious attempts, nevertheless, have been made to deal with specifically modern and urban themes, and some of these are presented here.

*MARIANNE MOORE

*No Swan So Fine

'No water so still as the
   dead fountains of Versailles.' No swan,
with swart blind look askance
and gondoliering legs, so fine
   as the chintz china one with fawn-
brown eyes and toothed gold
collar on to show whose bird it was.

Lodged in the Louis Fifteenth
   candelabrum-tree of cockscomb-
tinted buttons, dahlias,   10
sea-urchins, and everlastings,
   it perches on the branching foam
of polished sculptured
flowers—at ease and tall. The king is dead.

*Sojourn in the Whale

Trying to open locked doors with a sword, threading
   the points of needles, planting shade trees
   upside down; swallowed by the opaqueness of one whom the seas
love better than they love you, Ireland—

you have lived and lived on every kind of shortage.
   You have been compelled by hags to spin
   gold thread from straw and have heard men say: 'There is a feminine
temperament in direct contrast to

ours which makes her do these things. Circumscribed by a
   heritage of blindness and native   10
   incompetence, she will become wise and will be forced to give
in. Compelled by experience, she

will turn back; water seeks its own level': and you
   have smiled. 'Water in motion is far
   from level.' You have seen it, when obstacles happened to bar
the path, rise automatically.

*To a Steam Roller

The illustration
is nothing to you without the application.
　　You lack half wit. You crush all the particles down
　　　　into close conformity, and then walk back and forth on them.

Sparkling chips of rock
are crushed down to the level of the parent block.
　　Were not 'impersonal judgment in aesthetic
　　　　matters, a metaphysical impossibility,' you

might fairly achieve
it. As for butterflies, I can hardly conceive　　　　　　　　　　10
　　of one's attending upon you; but to question
　　　　the congruence of the complement is vain, if it exists.

ALAN STEPHENS

A Side-Gallery for Some Insects

1

Zonocerous variegatus
a grasshopper native to Africa

A moral apparatus—
gripping a fresh blade,
his black antennae cocked,

his eyes great hemispheres
of horn sprung from his shining
and variegated skull—he is

splashed with black, streaked
with scarlet, cobalt, white;
his shoulders plated yellow,

his wings under the gilt   10
netting a pale green:
these are the colors of his terrors

wrought into his exterior
where they belong, hardened
into enamels where they serve

steadily, to tell his enemies
"I am here: you will remember
I stink, and my flavor's foul . . ."

All this outside, he is
to himself, under the colors,   20
the sudden leap in the heat

the snap of wings in a stillness
breathed by his thousand pores
(his organs, buoyed in their casing,

bathed in a blood that's pale
and cool): spirit of innocent
acquaintance with this ground.

2

The kiss
a meditation

Of the prime sexual cloud
insects are crystalline, vivid
in their minute extremes.   30

Showers of crystals! Fireflies
in Siam assemble on trees
and flash so that each tree

lights up with its own rhythm;
the dances of other species,
the stridulations of the males,

caresses with antennae, the scent
of the emperor moth, aflow
for seven miles around him

declare the passion for a fate: 40
from a dread Indiscriminate
into a complex exigence

to drive and burn expertly,
eccentric, thorough and true, as
flicking the summer light

this way and that, a pair
of the diptera, ventral surfaces
together, mouthparts-touching,

will mate aloft; and she,
when they are done, sucks out   50
the contents of his body through his mouth

painstakingly; one imagines
her impersonal tenderness
for his definitive satisfaction.

3

A bizarre nymph of a mantis
under magnification

Air-shaken on his leaf,
mottled, glistening in the humors
of his birth, he finds a footing,

his gaze already entire
in the rigid facets, his black
gazelle horns still hardening: 60

each word is a lens—variously
I peer down where, below
meanings, he stands and quickens.

4

One of the mantises
"Homer, who was a poet of war, . . . knew it was the shield of
such happiness as is possible on earth."
—Santayana

The trim three-cornered head,
the body brought to an elegance
of elongations, the spiked

and heavy forearm tipped with
a surgical hook for the distracted
or the inattentive—in sandalwood

and light green his parts are one
deadly sanctity, twig-like
among the overlapping leaves.

5

A clear night sky

In the warm darkness the human
hesitates, before sleep; insects
emerge and glint about him

irregularly, cased in their tiny
destinies. The human passion
is to have a fate, but to have it

distantly burning. How well
he would sleep, encircled by his distinct
and well spaced energies—a zodiac.

70

80

Socrates Entranced

Supper and wine; but where
Is their friend Socrates?
Out on the thoroughfare;
One of his ectasies
Surprised the hale grotesque
While he passed through the dusk
Amongst the talkative
With whom he likes to live—

Who are like him, in bone,
Muscle, and busy veins
That feed their rootlets down
Over alert membranes
All eagerness to vary.
He finds them necessary.
Bent on the human noise
How excellent in poise

The grave Silenus head
Above the trampled ground
For a time quieted.
And once more to have found
In the conception there
The one man in dim air—

10

20

Once more, for the sake of thought,
Himself in passion, caught.

—And soon he will come in,
And with the wine and talk
The questioning begin;
Bewildered friends will balk,
Swerve, and perhaps agree,
Towards daybreak, sleepily;   30
With one exhausted friend
He'll go, time still to spend—

With them to his last day!
Near dusk he will have sent
The wailing women away,
And checked the friends' lament
So that they finally see
The citizen, as he
Adjusts to the city's will
A stiffening animal.   40

What I Will Think Of
As the White Dog Truth

I make out the white bulk in the dark—
the dog approaches at a quick pace
and goes by showing no interest in me,
and such is the quiet of the street
I hear the clicking of his toe-nails
on the blacktop, quick, business-like,
even half a block away, the sound
growing fainter very gradually
and already, while I keep an eye
on the wire-thin half rim of light   10
the moon shows in a sky jagged
with trees along the bottom—
already this encounter, the white bulk passing
in the dark, the diminishing click
of the toenails along the stretch
of silence back there, cannot be forced
not to have been, the lords of creation
themselves will have to submit to
its having been, if they should find it
some day blocking the way of a desire.   20

THEODORE ROETHKE

Epidermal Macabre

Indelicate is he who loathes
The aspect of his fleshy clothes,—
The flying fabric stitched on bone,
The vesture of the skeleton,
The garment neither fur nor hair,
The cloak of evil and despair,
The veil long violated by
Caresses of the hand and eye.
Yet such is my unseemliness:
I hate my epidermal dress,   10
The savage blood's obscenity,
The rags of my anatomy.
And willingly would I dispense
With false accouterments of sense,
To sleep immodestly, a most
Incarnadine and carnal ghost.

The Happy Three

Inside, my darling wife
Sharpened a butcher knife;
Sighed out her pure relief
    That I was gone.

When I had tried to clean
My papers up, between
Words skirting the obscene—
    She frowned her frown.

Shelves have a special use;
And Why muddy shoes   10
In with your underclothes?
    She asked, woman.

So I betook myself
With not one tiny laugh

To drink some half-and-half
   On the back lawn.

Who should come up right then,
But our goose, Marianne,
Having escaped her pen,
   Hunting the sun.   20

Named for a poetess,
(Whom I like none-the-less),
Her pure-white featheriness
   She paused to preen;

But when she pecked my toe,
My banked-up vertigo
Vanished like April snow;
   All rage was gone.

Then a close towhee, a
Phoebe not far away   30
Sang out audaciously
   Notes finely drawn.

Back to the house we ran,
Me, and dear Marianne—
Then we romped out again,
   Out again,
   Out again,
Three in the sun.

*Elegy

Her face like a rain-beaten stone on the day she rolled off
With the dark hearse, and enough flowers for an alderman,—
And so she was, in her way, Aunt Tilly.

Sighs, sighs, who says they have sequence?
Between the spirit and the flesh,—what war?
She never knew;
For she asked no quarter and gave none,
Who sat with the dead when the relatives left,
Who fed and tended the infirm, the mad, the epileptic,
And, with a harsh rasp of a laugh at herself,   10
Faced up to the worst.

I recall how she harried the children away all the late summer
From the one beautiful thing in her yard, the peachtree;
How she kept the wizened, the fallen, the misshapen for herself,
And picked and pickled the best, to be left on rickety doorsteps.

And yet she died in agony,
Her tongue, at the last, thick, black as an ox's.

Terror of cops, bill collectors, betrayers of the poor,—
I see you in some celestial supermarket,
Moving serenely among the leeks and cabbages,   20
Probing the squash,
Bearing down, with two steady eyes,
On the quaking butcher.

The Geranium

When I put her out, once, by the garbage pail,
She looked so limp and bedraggled,
So foolish and trusting, like a sick poodle,
Or a wizened aster in late September,
I brought her back in again
For a new routine—
Vitamins, water, and whatever
Sustenance seemed sensible
At the time: she'd lived
So long on gin, bobbie pins, half-smoked cigars, dead beer,   10
Her shriveled petals falling
On the faded carpet, the stale
Steak grease stuck to her fuzzy leaves.
(Dried-out, she creaked like a tulip.)

The things she endured!—
The dumb dames shrieking half the night
Or the two of us, alone, both seedy,
Me breathing booze at her,
She leaning out of her pot toward the window.

Near the end, she seemed almost to hear me—   20
And that was scary—
So when that snuffing cretin of a maid
Threw her, pot and all, into the trash-can,
I said nothing.

But I sacked the presumptuous hag the next week,
I was that lonely.

RICHARD WILBUR

Still, Citizen Sparrow

Still, citizen sparrow, this vulture which you call
Unnatural, let him but lumber again to air
Over the rotten office, let him bear
The carrion ballast up, and at the tall

Tip of the sky lie cruising. Then you'll see
That no more beautiful bird is in heaven's height,
No wider more placid wings, no watchfuller flight;
He shoulders nature there, the frightfully free,

The naked-headed one. Pardon him, you
Who dart in the orchard aisles, for it is he   10
Devours death, mocks mutability,
Has heart to make an end, keeps nature new.

Thinking of Noah, childheart, try to forget
How for so many bedlam hours his saw
Soured the song of birds with its wheezy gnaw,
And the slam of his hammer all the day beset

The people's ears. Forget that he could bear
To see the towns like coral under the keel,
And the fields so dismal deep. Try rather to feel
How high and weary it was, on the waters where   20

He rocked his only world, and everyone's.
Forgive the hero, you who would have died
Gladly with all you knew; he rode that tide
To Ararat; all men are Noah's sons.

Boy at the Window

Seeing the snowman standing all alone
In dusk and cold is more than he can bear.
The small boy weeps to hear the wind prepare
A night of gnashings and enormous moan.
His tearful sight can hardly reach to where
The pale-faced figure with bitumen eyes
Returns him such a god-forsaken stare
As outcast Adam gave to Paradise.

The man of snow is, nonetheless, content,
Having no wish to go inside and die.   10
Still, he is moved to see the youngster cry.
Though frozen water is his element,
He melts enough to drop from one soft eye
A trickle of the purest rain, a tear
For the child at the bright pane surrounded by
Such warmth, such light, such love, and so much fear.

REED WHITTEMORE

On the Suicide of a Friend

Some there are who are present at such occasions,
And conduct themselves with appropriate feeling and grace.
But they are the rare ones. Mostly the friends and relations
Are caught playing cards or eating miles from the place.
What happens on that dark river, or road, or mountain
Passes unnoticed as friend trumps loved one's ace.

Perhaps he knew this about them—worse, he did not,
And raged over the brink of that road or mountain
Thinking at least they'd remember before they forgot.
Either way, now he is dead and done with that lot.   10

The Party

They served tea in the sandpile, together with
Mudpies baked on the sidewalk.
After tea
The youngest said that he had had a good dinner,
The oldest dressed for a dance,
And they sallied forth together with watering pots
To moisten a rusted fire truck on account of it
Might rain.

I watched from my study,
Thought of my part in these contributions to world   10
Gaiety, and resolved
That the very least acknowledgment I could make
Would be to join them;
                        so we

All took our watering pots (filled with pies)
And poured tea on our dog. Then I kissed the children
And told them that when they grew up we would have
Real tea parties.

"That did be fun!" the youngest shouted, and ate pies
With wild surmise.   20

PHILIP LARKIN

Reasons for Attendance

The trumpet's voice, loud and authoritative,
Draws me a moment to the lighted glass
To watch the dancers—all under twenty-five—
Shifting intently, face to flushed face,
Solemnly on the beat of happiness.

—Or so I fancy, sensing the smoke and sweat,
The wonderful feel of girls. Why be out here?
But then, why be in there? Sex, yes, but what

Is sex? Surely, to think the lion's share
Of happiness is found by couples—sheer   10

Inaccuracy, as far as I'm concerned.
What calls me is that lifted, rough-tongued bell
(Art, if you like) whose individual sound
Insists I too am individual.
It speaks; I hear; others may hear as well,

But not for me, nor I for them; and so
With happiness. Therefore I stay outside,
Believing this; and they maul to and fro,
Believing that; and both are satisfied,
If no one has misjudged himself. Or lied.   20

Next, Please

Always too eager for the future, we
Pick up bad habits of expectancy.
Something is always approaching; every day
Till then we say,

Watching from a bluff the tiny, clear
Sparkling armada of promises draw near.
How slow they are! And how much time they waste,
Refusing to make haste!

Yet still they leave us holding wretched stalks
Of disappointment, for, though nothing balks   10
Each big approach, leaning with brasswork prinked,
Each rope distinct,

Flagged, and the figurehead with golden tits
Arching our way, it never anchors; it's
No sooner present than it turns to past.
Right to the last

We think each one will heave to and unload
All good into our lives, all we are owed
For waiting so devoutly and so long.
But we are wrong: 20

Only one ship is seeking us, a black-
Sailed unfamiliar, towing at her back
A huge and birdless silence. In her wake
No waters breed or break.

*LAWRENCE FERLINGHETTI

*Don't Let That Horse

Don't let that horse
        eat that violin
    cried Chagall's mother
            But he
    kept right on
            painting

And became famous
And kept on painting
        The Horse With Violin In Mouth
And when he finally finished it   10
he jumped up upon the horse
            and rode away
        waving the violin

And then with a low bow gave it
to the first naked nude he ran across

And there were no strings
        attached

Constantly Risking Absurdity

        Constantly risking absurdity
                and death
            whenever he performs
                above the heads
                        of his audience
        the poet like an acrobat
                climbs on rime
                    to a high wire of his own making
    and balancing on eyebeams
                    above a sea of faces   10
        paces his way
                    to the other side of day
            performing entrechats

                    and sleight-of-foot tricks
            and other high theatrics
                    and all without mistaking
            any thing
      for what it may not be
  For he's the super realist
                    who must perforce perceive   20
          taut truth
                    before the taking of each stance or step
in his supposed advance
                    toward the still higher perch
where Beauty stands and waits
          with gravity
                    to start her death-defying leap

And he
      a little charleychaplin man
                    who may or may not catch   30
      her fair eternal form
                    spreadeagled in the empty air
      of existence.

The Pennycandystore Beyond the El

The pennycandystore beyond the El
is where I first
            fell in love
                    with unreality
Jellybeans glowed in the semi-gloom
of that september afternoon
A cat upon the counter moved among
            the licorice sticks
            and tootsie rolls
            and Oh Boy Gum   10
Outside the leaves were falling as they died
A wind had blown away the sun

A girl ran in
Her hair was rainy
Her breasts were breathless in the little room

Outside the leaves were falling
            and they cried
                    Too soon! too soon!

*ALLEN GINSBERG

A Supermarket in California

What thoughts I have of you tonight, Walt Whitman, for I walked down the sidestreets under the trees with a headache self-conscious looking at the full moon.

In my hungry fatigue, and shopping for images, I went into the neon fruit supermarket, dreaming of your enumerations!

What peaches and what penumbras! Whole families shopping at night! Aisles full of husbands! Wives in the avocados, babies in the tomatoes!— and you, Garcia Lorca, what were you doing down by the watermelons?

I saw you, Walt Whitman, childless, lonely old grubber, poking among the meats in the refrigerator and eyeing the grocery boys.

I heard you asking questions of each: Who killed the pork chops? What price bananas? Are you my Angel?

I wandered in and out of the brilliant stacks of cans following you, and followed in my imagination by the store detective.

We strode down the open corridors together in our solitary fancy tasting artichokes, possessing every frozen delicacy, and never passing the cashier.

Where are we going, Walt Whitman? The doors close in an hour. Which way does your beard point tonight?

(I touch your book and dream of our odyssey in the supermarket and feel absurd.)

Will we walk all night through solitary streets? The trees add shade to shade, lights out in the houses, we'll both be lonely.   10

Will we stroll dreaming of the lost America of love past blue automobiles in driveways, home to our silent cottage?

Ah, dear father, graybeard, lonely old courage-teacher, what America did you have when Charon quit poling his ferry and you got out on a smoking bank and stood watching the boat disappear on the black waters of Lethe?

*GREGORY CORSO

A Race of Sound

Sounds are running a race the trek the climb the swim the pace
And voices are edging up to roars and close behind the closing of doors
    the thump of rabbits
And coming up in the stretch the howling of ghosts
The humming of birds and now voices are neck and neck
With the climb of vines and the trek of penguins
The swim of fish is third and moving in the inside thunder and bombs and
    in the back
        stretch the thud of coffins
        the fall of timber the sway of palms
Voices are leading are leading heaving and breathing speaking and singing
    fully in the clear but hold hold   10
From out of nowhere the wail of cats the chomp of carrots
A squeaky shoe challenges for the lead Oh what a race!
Here comes the drop of a pin the cawk of a parrot
The breaking of glass the scratch of an itch
The crowds are going wild! yelling and kicking and jumping
—so wild they win the race

A City Child's Day

(for Mr. Mason & Son)

No rooster wakes a child's city day
More likely an alarm clock
Yet whatever occasions it hail the dawn
Out into it he goes
Hands in pockets carefree and with glee
The gutter is his pastoral path
The fire hydrant his favorite toy
The pavement he walks covers perhaps
A trail that goes way back to a time of trees
When trees were plentiful when birds and beasts   10
When streams flowed and hills were visible
When Redmen lightly strode
And Dutchmen wore buckled hats and shoes

—Ah this walk is not new it is old
Ancient as the earth it covers
And older it grows

Grownups do not go where children go
At break of day their worlds split apart
Quite often it is night blends them
And even then sleep distinguishes them   20
Empty lots and stoops
Here the society of children gather
Boys may join the girls; most don't, yet he'd rather
They adorn and garland him he is their champion
He'll lead them to hopscotch and chalk writing
And awearied he'll sit with the fairest of them all
She with the regnant air of a queen will look away
As does he, like a proud Viking, from the writing on the wall

Fire is not fire but a magnificent truck
A shiny bell and uniformed men whose hats yell   30
With excitement and all that is wonderful
Away they siren even when the lights aren't green
Late noon falls like a heavy bassoon
Grownups pass by like sleepy shadows
No sound no word
And the big lady in the window, who is she?
She's carroty fingers and breadloaf arms!
Into aloneness he leaps and frightens a cat

O rare alley cat
Ever-bruised tom and ever-pregnant feline   40
Once so familiar and now in decline
No longer do you cuddle under parked cars
Climb in and out broken windows
And on fences meow to the stars

He runs he stops he kicks a can
He skips and over a hydrant he hops
It's time for the big boys to gather and play
He hurries he runs he knows the way
Just in time! they're choosing sides
They won't choose him he's still too small   50
Alone again
He runs he stops he picks up a stick
And floats it down a street running water
While his heart so like a clock
Tells him his day will soon be over

His exhaustion is lashed in crucifixional poses
Against buildings against cars against people
The day is changing the day is always changing
What happens to it when he goes home?
He's changing too   60
But why oh why does he feel for the worse?
What good the day if he's not good in it?
Left behind, demoted from his time,
He's unable to adhibit and nightcap his day
The Beginning remains unknown
The End remains unknown
This is his great sorrow
Day is all he knows
Not Night

WILLIAM J. HARRIS

Samantha Is My Negro Cat

Samantha is my
Negro cat.
Black with yellow eyes.
A big flat nose.
Thick features.
She came to me
from the street.
(A street nigger
with hairless ears.)
She's tough.   10
Been a mother too.
Has hard pink nipples.
(Yes, pink. She also has
a white spot on her neck.
She ain't pure. But
I don't care. I ain't no racist.)
She has a sad high ass.
Sway-back.
Not much to look at
but as affectionate   20

as any girl who's
had a hard time of it.
"Bums," said the vet
a little too objectively,
"always respond to love."

Samantha rubs against
me, sits across my
lap, purring her short-circuited purr.
(Hey, Doc, there's a wire loose
in her purr box.)   30

Lady, this man is
going to treat you better
than the rest.
(You say you've heard that one before.)
We'll comfort each other
in the evenings
after supper, when we stare
out on the
cold and dark street.

You Tell Me

You tell me
            that tree
—the oak
        with the
shrivelled limbs—
                    is a symbol
of suffering mankind.
Hell, baby,
            no goddam tree
sittin' in the night breeze
has had it as hard as me.

Persecuted, Betrayal, Volkswagen Blues

Oh, little green Volkswagen,
it's a pity you drove
out of my life.
I was told
by the automobile salesman,
whose eyes were miniature cigars,
you were the true type.

But who are you blinking
your turn signals for
now?   10

Maybe next time,
I'll buy a big American car.
At least they look like what they are.
You could at least have left
me a spare tire.
Just something to remember
you by.

I understand
how you had
to be independent.   20
Let no man behind your wheel.
But, OH, little green Volkswagen,
it's a pity you drove
out of my life.

Who are you opening
your sun roof for now?

Oh, little green Volkswagen,
it's a pity you drove
out of my life.

THOM GUNN

On the Move

'Man, you gotta Go.'

The blue jay scuffling in the bushes follows
Some hidden purpose, and the gust of birds
That spurts across the field, the wheeling swallows,
Have nested in the trees and undergrowth.
Seeking their instinct, or their poise, or both,
One moves with an uncertain violence
Under the dust thrown by a baffled sense
Or the dull thunder of approximate words.

On motorcycles, up the road, they come:
Small, black, as flies hanging in heat, the Boys,   10
Until the distance throws them forth, their hum
Bulges to thunder held by calf and thigh.
In goggles, donned impersonality,
In gleaming jackets trophied with the dust,
They strap in doubt—by hiding it, robust—
And almost hear a meaning in their noise.

Exact conclusion of their hardiness
Has no shape yet, but from known whereabouts
They ride, direction where the tires press.
They scare a flight of birds across the field: 20
Much that is natural, to the will must yield.
Men manufacture both machine and soul,
And use what they imperfectly control
To dare a future from the taken routes.

It is a part solution, after all.
One is not necessarily discord
On earth; or damned because, half animal,
One lacks direct instinct, because one wakes
Afloat on movement that divides and breaks.
One joins the movement in a valueless world   30
Choosing it, till, both hurler and the hurled,
One moves as well, always toward, toward.

A minute holds them, who have come to go:
The self-defined, astride the created will
They burst away; the towns they travel through
Are home for neither bird nor holiness,
For birds and saints complete their purposes.
At worst, one is in motion; and at best,
Reaching no absolute, in which to rest,
One is always nearer by not keeping still.   40

The Wheel of Fortune

Strapped helpless, monarchs and prelates, round they swung.
O mutability they cried, O perfect Wheel!
  The bishop dreamt of ruin while he dozed,
  A lover that his secrets were exposed,
And Lambert Simnel that he stirred the king's porridge.

Deeper they dream, disorder comes: high, low, are flung
Faster, limbs spinning. As the great Hub cracks they peel
  From off the Felloe of that even round.
  Bishop and lover sprawl upon the ground,
And Lambert Simnel stirs the under footman's porridge.   10

SYLVIA PLATH

*The Colossus

I shall never get you put together entirely,
Pieced, glued, and properly jointed.
Mule-bray, pig-grunt and bawdy cackles
Proceed from your great lips.
It's worse than a barnyard.

Perhaps you consider yourself an oracle,
Mouthpiece of the dead, or of some god or other.
Thirty years now I have laboured
To dredge the silt from your throat.
I am none the wiser.   10

Scaling little ladders with gluepots and pails of lysol
I crawl like an ant in mourning
Over the weedy acres of your brow
To mend the immense skull-plates and clear
The bald, white tumuli of your eyes.

A blue sky out of the Oresteia
Arches above us. O father, all by yourself
You are pithy and historical as the Roman Forum.
I open my lunch on a hill of black cypress.
Your fluted bones and acanthine hair are littered   20

In their old anarchy to the horizon-line.
It would take more than a lightning-stroke
To create such a ruin.
Nights, I squat in the cornucopia
Of your left ear, out of the wind,

Counting the red stars and those of plum-colour.
The sun rises under the pillar of your tongue.
My hours are married to shadow.
No longer do I listen for the scrape of a keel
On the blank stones of the landing.   30

Frog Autumn

Summer grows old, cold-blooded mother.
The insects are scant, skinny.
In these palustral homes we only
Croak and wither.

Mornings dissipate in somnolence.
The sun brightens tardily
Among the pithless reeds. Flies fail us.
The fen sickens.

Frost drops even the spider. Clearly
The genuis of plenitude   10
Houses himself elsewhere. Our folk thin
Lamentably.

---

l. 3. palustral: Marshy.

Versification

English versification is a complicated as well as controversial subject. The definitions given here consist merely of those most commonly applied. It should be remembered that the poet's ear is his final guide and that the established verse forms in English are full of variations.

The unit of traditional English verse is the foot, which ordinarily consists of either two or three syllables. The iambic foot, by far the most common of all, has two syllables with stress on the second (bĕtráy; hĕ laúghed); the trochaic, two syllables with stress on the first (wíckĕt; beát ĭt). The anapest consists of three syllables with stress on the last (ĭntĕrfére; ĭn ă stéw), and the dactyl of three with stress on the first (Flórĭdă). (This last, though regularly listed as a standard foot is so rare in English poetry that it may properly be ignored.) Ordinarily, one or another of these feet will predominate in a poem and the meter of the poem will be named accordingly: iambic pentameter, for example, if the standard foot is iambic and there are five feet to a line; or iambic hexameter if six to a line; tetrameter if four; trimeter if three; and so on.

Two other feet are common: the spondee, a foot made up of two stressed, and the pyrrhic, of two unstressed syllables. These are used, not as the meter for a whole poem, but as frequent variations from one of the standard meters. The standard ones themselves are to some extent interchangeable: a poem whose basic meter is iambic will usually contain some feet in which the stress is inverted and which are therefore trochaic; or it may contain an occasional anapestic foot, as well as spondees and pyrrhics.

The distinction between stressed and unstressed syllables is not a hard-and-fast one. In actual speech, syllables run the gamut from the syllabically almost nonexistent -tle in little to a strong and long one such as prowled. Poetry should be read with these varied shadings in mind and not in rigid categories of stressed and unstressed. A mechanical reading of the following lines of Wordsworth would give:

Ă slúm/bĕr díd / my̆ spír/ĭt seál;
Ĭ hád / nŏ hú/măn fears.

But such a reading kills the meaning. The lines should rather be read (with ' representing an intermediate degree of stress):

Ă slúm/bĕr dĭd / my̆ spír/ĭt seál;
Ĭ hád / nŏ hú/măn feárs.

or perhaps

Ĭ hád / nŏ hú/măn feárs.

Even this grossly oversimplifies what should be the real reading. For in the first line, my, though unstressed, and did, which stands where a stress is expected, have a great deal more weight than the opening syllable A or the -it of spirit. Every syllable in the line, in fact, has a slightly different degree of stress and pitch (varying as the voice is louder or softer, higher or lower) and a different duration. These lines are typical iambic verse with typical variations.

Anapestic verse is usually even more irregular. Byron began an account of a cavalry charge in anapests:

> The Assyr/ian came down/like a wolf/on the fold,
> And his co/horts were gleam/ing in pur/ple and gold.

These exceptionally regular lines are all very well while the horses are galloping, but to be durable for anything else, the meter requires a great deal of modification to prevent its galloping faster and faster, out of control. Auden's "O what is that Sound" (p. 422) employs anapestic meter with a great many restraining variations:

> O what/is that sound/which so thrills/the ear
> [˘ ˘] Down/in the val/ley drum/ming, drum/ming?

Trochaic verse is illustrated in Suckling's poem (p. 448):

> Why so/pale and/wan, fond/lover?
> Prithee,/why so/pale? [˘]

Some modern writers of what is called free verse have succeeded in producing poetic rhythms without employing any of the traditional metrical schemes. In reading, it is far more important to be able to avoid a deadly metrical sing-song than to be able to scan lines by rule; nevertheless, it is helpful to know something of the traditional meters, for they are the patterns that have run through the minds, consciously or subconsciously, of almost all earlier poets and of the majority even today.

Glossary of terms

Following are terms useful for studying and discussing poetry.

alliteration Correspondence of sounds at the beginning of syllables (usually accented syllables) that are close together: "The **pl**owman homeward **pl**ods his **w**eary **w**ay." Some writers confine the use of the term to consonant sounds and include initial repetition of vowels under assonance, q.v.

anapest (noun), anapestic (adj.), See the above notes on versification.

assonance Repetition of a vowel sound in consecutive or nearby words: "The **a**ngels keep their **a**ncient pl**a**ces."

ballad meter or ballad stanza These terms commonly designate a quatrain of alternating four- and three-stress lines, with the second and fourth rhyming (abcb). This is sometimes printed as a couplet of seven-foot lines. The term is also used for the same quatrain with alternate rhyme (abab).

blank verse	*Unrhymed iambic pentameter.*
caesura	*An internal pause in a line of verse, usually a pause required by the meaning.*
consonance	*Repetition of consonant sounds elsewhere than at the beginning of syllables: "Parched, he lurched to the bar."*
couplet	*A unit of two lines rhyming with each other; they are usually of the same length.*
dactyl	*(noun), dactylic (adj.). See the above notes on versification.*
dimeter	*A line consisting of two feet.*
elegy	*A poem of lamentation for the dead (formerly the term had a broader meaning).*
enjambment	*See* run-on line.
feminine ending	*An extra unstressed syllable at the end of an iambic or anapestic line.*
feminine rhyme	*See* rhyme.
foot	*See the above notes on versification.*
free verse	*Verse which follows no regular metrical scheme.*
heroic couplet	*Iambic pentameter rhyming in couplets. Some writers confine the use of the term to the "closed" couplet, in which the two rhyming lines form an independent unit of thought or a complete sentence.*
hexameter	*A line consisting of six feet.*
iamb	*(noun), iambic (adj.). See the above notes on versification.*
lyric	*Originally, a poem to be sung to the accompaniment of the lyre. The term has come to include, besides poems suitable for singing, a wide variety of forms: sonnets, odes, elegies, and poems in many different stanza arrangements. The lyric is usually short or of moderate length and is never primarily narrative or didactic. Directly or indirectly, it is subjective: that is, it is meant to convey emotions, attitudes, or states of mind.*
masculine rhyme	*See* rhyme.
metaphor	*A metaphor is an implied (not expressed) comparison between un-like things. "A shower of leaves" is a metaphor: leaves are essen-tially unlike rain, but one resemblance is seized upon. A metaphor*

may imply the comparison by taking for granted the identity of two things, as in this example where, by the mere use of the word shower, *the identity of leaves and rain is implied. Or the identity of unlike things may be stated outright as if it were a fact, as in saying, "Joe is a hog," in order to express vividly his greed. See* simile.

In recent years the term metaphor *has come to be used in a much broader sense for almost all nonliteral statement. It is even applied to language itself because, unlike such things as pictures, which can represent objects by imitating them, language is by nature symbolic. The word* hat, *for example, does not resemble a hat; it is an arbitrary sign, quite unlike the object, yet representing it.*

ode One of the longer forms of lyric, an ode is a lofty and dignified treatment of some theme. As originally developed in ancient Greece, its form was complex and somewhat rigid. An English ode may follow the classical pattern, or it may be written in either irregular or regular rhymed stanzas.

onomatopoeia The use of sounds that by imitation suggest the meaning, as in the words buzz, hiss, bubble. *This is a device more commonly discussed in the classroom than actually used by poets, for there are very few genuinely onomatopoetic words.*

ottava rima An eight-line stanza of iambic pentameter, rhyming abab...abcc.

pentameter A line consisting of five feet.

pyrrhic See the above notes on versification.

quatrain Any four-line stanza.

rhyme (or rime) In its broadest sense (rarely used) the term may refer to any repetition of the sounds of words. Commonly it means end-rhyme, repetition at the ends of lines. It consists usually in the matching of sounds beginning with an accented vowel and continuing to the end of the word: blow, go, haul, maul; dart, apart; destroy, joy. *These are masculine, or one-syllable rhymes, by far the most common in English verse.* Feminine or double rhyme *occurs in lines with feminine endings, when the last two syllables rhyme (reeling, peeling).* Triple or three-syllable rhyme *(bearable, wearable) is uncommon except in comic verse.* Internal rhyme *occurs when one or both rhymes are within the line instead of at the end:*

> We were the *first* that ever *burst*
> Into that silent sea.

run-on line (enjambment) A line in which the sense runs on to the following line without a noticeable pause, as in

> Dust to the dust! but the pure spirit shall flow
> Back to the burning fountain whence it came.

simile	*An expressed comparison between unlike things. A simile differs from a metaphor in being introduced by "like" or "as"; it is therefore a more nearly literal statement.*
sonnet	*See p. 517.*
Spenserian stanza	*A stanza of nine lines. The first eight are iambic pentameter, the ninth is hexameter. The rhyme is* ababbcbcc.
spondee	*(noun), spondaic (adj.). See the above notes on versification.*
terza rima	*A three-line stanza or group of lines in which the middle one is linked by rhyme to the following group.* aba/bcb/cdc, *and so on. For an example, see Shelley's "Ode to the West Wind."*
tetrameter	*A line consisting of four feet.*
trimeter	*A line consisting of three feet.*
trochee	*(noun), trochaic (adj.). See the above notes on versification.*

*NOTES AND COMMENTS ON POETRY

Transition to Poetry:

Characters

page 393   Robinson, "Richard Cory." *"The grass is always greener on the other side of the fence." "Wealth does not bring happiness." "Don't jump to conclusions about people, for every man is ultimately a mystery to his neighbors." "I'm just telling you what I know: this is how it happened in our village."—These are four different ways in which the poem has been summed up. If they are mutually exclusive or contradictory, then it is obvious that the reader should choose the interpretation that to him seems most in keeping with everything in the poem, and should be prepared to defend his reading against the others. Discussion of the poem might well center upon whether these different readings do tend to cancel each other out or whether they are reconcilable and may all play a part in the poem.*

page 398   Masters, "Lucinda Matlock." *In Spoon River Anthology, Masters undertook to represent the people of a Middle Western town by a series of imaginary epitaphs spoken by persons buried in the local cemetery. The free verse form and more particularly the frankness of some of the confessions created a furor when the work appeared in 1915. Now that the novelty has worn off, many critics consider the plan of the book more interesting than the execution.*

pages 398–399   Browning, "My Last Duchess." *This and the following selection from Browning are dramatic monologues: poems in which the author speaks through the mouth of someone not himself. A situation is created through which the character may reveal himself merely by talking.*

Browning finds subjects in incongruities of character for which the nobility and higher clergy of the Italian Renaissance were noted: unrestrained cruelty joined to a genuine love of beauty and art, implicit belief in the unworldly doctrines of the Church combined with a worldly acquisitive spirit or with most unchristian malice. These are the paradoxical elements out of which Browning aims to create believable characters in the two self-exposed persons represented here.

page 402   Yeats, "Her Praise." *The subject of this and the two following poems is Maud Gonne, a well-known and beautiful woman who devoted her life to the Irish revolutionary struggle against England. Yeats loved her for many years but did not always like her activities and opinions. In the third of these poems, by comparing her violent activities to a marriage celebration, Yeats appears to suggest that she was impelled by an unconscious wish for death.*

Narratives (Ballads)

pages 403–428   *Ballads were originally "songs that tell a story," composed orally, it is thought, and handed down through generations without any poet's name. These English and Scottish folk or "popular" ballads are simple in style and language. Frequently they employ repetition in the form of a question-and-answer formula through which the story is told, stock descriptive phrases, or a refrain. The story is usually presented in a single dramatic scene or in a series of detached scenes rather than by consecutive narrative. The ballads seldom explain motives and seldom express emotion directly. The listener's imagination and, when they are sung, the music must supply what the words leave unsaid. Though occasionally comic, the stories are most often violent and tragic.*

During the last two or more centuries, poets have found much to admire in these old ballads and have written "literary" ballads, not meant for actual song, in which some of the old simplicity and immediacy are revived. Both kinds of ballads are represented here, along with a few other poems that bear some resemblance to them.

page 408   **Anon. "Bonny Barbara Allan."** *This ballad combines stock ballad formulas ("She had not gane a mile but twa" and "make my bed," the latter as a token of approaching death) with unusually individual and complex motivation implied but not explained.*

page 418   Brooks, "The Ballad of Late Annie." *Like the preceding older one by Scott, this contemporary ballad by Gwendolyn Brooks is consciously founded on the folk ballad model. It forms part of her "Annie Allen" sequence, which won the Pulitzer Prize for poetry in 1949.*

page 419   Brown, "Slim in Hell." *Originally under the influence of the English tradition, the folk ballad began to establish itself as a native American growth, chiefly in rural regions—among negroes and mountain whites in the South, among cowboys in the West and lumbermen in the North. Later, sophisticated American poets adapted the form and employed it as Sterling Brown has done here, in one of the best examples of witty, comic but ultimately serious, ballad writing.*

page 422   Auden, "O What is that Sound." *As with the tall story of "Slim," Auden uses the ballad convention for a symbolic purpose. The poem was published in England in 1935, the year in which the office of Prime Minister fell to Neville Chamberlain and England's appeasement of Hitler got well under way.*

page 423   Cowper, "The Castaway." *The meaning of the two preceding poems, though not quite explicit, is clear once one knows the historical or racial situation to which each refers. This and most of the remaining narratives are less simple than even the sophisticated ballads. It is important to see both the surface and the submerged meanings, to understand how one reveals or is influenced by the other, and to appreciate the interweaving of the strands into a unified whole.*

The incident upon which Cowper's narrative is based was reported in Admiral George Anson's A Voyage Round the World *(see line 52). It is evident, however, that the poet is thinking of some other tragedy besides that of the drowned seaman. In the story of his death, Cowper saw an emblem of his own despair. A deeply religious and gentle man, he several times sank into a state of horror in which he believed his soul abandoned by God and doomed to Hell. Long struggles against despair won him some years of cheerful friendliness and sanity, but the dream in which a voice had once announced his doom continued to haunt him. "The Castaway" was written not long before his final descent into insanity. The seaman's story enabled him to express his despair with a degree of restraint and objectivity that gives the poem much of its symbolic power.*

page 425   Yeats, "The Host of the Air." *Yeats said this poem was founded on an old Irish folk ballad. The title refers to the "trooping fairies" of Irish legend, described by Yeats in* Irish Fairy and Folk Tales. *The name "Sidhe" (pronounced "shee"), he explained, in Gaelic means wind as well as fairies, and the Sidhe ride the wind. They take what size and shape they choose. They like to feast, fight, dance, and make love, and they play the most beautiful music. But they are inconstant and irresponsible. The story is probably clear as it stands, but originally Yeats included an explicit stanza in which O'Driscoll ran home, filled with dread, to find old women keening his dead wife. Yeats also explained that anyone who partakes of the fairies' food or drink "is glamoured and stolen by the fairies. This is why Bridget sets O'Driscoll to play cards."*

Techniques: Image, Pattern, and Rhythm

page 431   Hopkins, "fragment." *The lines exhibit several striking features. There are the metaphorical rather than literally descriptive epithets:* churl *for the wind,* giant *for the air,* helter *(borrowed from* helter-skelter*) for the hail. There is a resounding frequency and interlaced complexity of alliteration, assonance, and consonance (see Glossary, p. 639): such interrelated sounds, for example, as those in the first line:* churl, hurl, cheerless, hail. *Striking also is the use, throughout, of imperative verbs for statements that in content are purely descriptive, matter for which imperatives would ordinarily seem innapropriate or meaningless. The effect of all these unusual technical devices should be considered with reference to the feeling communicated about the storm.*

page 432   Housman, "To an Athlete Dying Young." *The first two stanzas, in which the words and images remain almost the same while the meaning is reversed, have been discussed in the introductory remarks on poetry (pp. 383–391). There is a great deal of other repetition throughout, much of it alliteration. A main feature of the poem, however, is its use of recurring imagery:*

the silence and cheers, for example, and the contrary-to-fact statement, made twice (lines 11–12, 27–28), that the laurel "withers quicker than the rose" (i.e., the athlete's supremacy is even shorter-lived than a girl's beauty). It may finally be felt that the whole statement of the poem—that the athlete is lucky to have died young—is not meant to be taken literally, since few athletes would in fact make that choice, but is simply a symbolic way of expressing regret at the brevity of youth, strength, and beauty.

line 11   laurel. *The evergreen European laurel or bay tree whose long-lasting leaves were used for the crown of victory.*

lines 21–28   *The scene here derives from the Greek conception of the world—or, as it was often thought to be, the house—of the dead, where the souls were "shades" (and cf. the "shady night," line 13).*

page 433   H. D. (Hilda Doolittle), "Lethe." *In Greek myth, Lethe is the river of forgetfulness in the world of the dead.*

The notable feature of this poem is its structure of negatives, or grammatical parallelism, and of duplicated or repetitive images, all of which contribute to the mood of a hopeless monotony of deprivation. "Whin" and "gorse" are different names for the same flowering shrub; cedar, fir, and pine all evergreens with needles, and so on. The "nor" formula names things only to take them away, leaving finally the one statement that is affirmative, "You shall long"; but then the thing that is longed for is itself negative—forgetfulness.

page 433   cummings, "a pretty a day." *This and the following poem illustrate swift movement secured by means of short lines and repeated sounds tumbling fast over each other. Even the rhymes and the punctuation affect the movement.*

pages 435–436   Coleridge, "Kubla Khan." *Coleridge had been reading from an old account of eastern travel (Purchas's* Pilgrimage*): "In Xamdu did Cublai Can build a stately Palace, encompassing sixteene miles of plaine ground with a wall, wherein are fertile meddowes, pleasant Springs, delightful Streames, . . . and in the middest thereof a sumptuous house of pleasure." Lines 1–36 describe the pleasure-grounds.*

The latter part is Coleridge's poetic explanation of why he had not completed the poem: he had lost his inspiration. In a vision, he says, he once heard music (that of the Abyssinian maid) which, if he could only revive it, would inspire him to create the scene of Kubla's paradise in such poetry as the world would listen to in awe. The magic circle, flashing eyes, and floating hair of the last lines are ancient conventional properties of divinely inspired poet-prophets.

Notice the extremely elaborate patterns of alliteration and assonance: Xan . . . Kubla Khan (pronounced like Can), dome decree, river ran, measure-man; pleasure . . . measureless, etc.

The poem is celebrated for its incantatory poetic music.

page 436   Hardy, "Birds at Winter Nightfall" and Bridges, "Triolet." *The triolet is one of the most rigid and artificial of all verse forms. Excellence consists in creating the illusion of freedom: of seeming, that is, to say what one wishes to say in the way one* wishes to say it, yet without breaking the boundaries of the form. A triolet consists of eight lines with only two rhymes. The whole first line is repeated as the fourth and again as the seventh line, the second is repeated as the eighth. Once the poet has composed his first two lines, therefore, he has very little leeway; yet he must not seem encumbered by the obligation to repeat and to rhyme so rigidly.

Both Hardy and Bridges disguise the prescribed repetitions by breaking up and altering the grammatical structure of the repeated lines. Aside from that, their two poems are in complete contrast. Hardy's is made up entirely of concrete imagery, used purely for its own sake, not either as background scene or as symbol (his "crumb-outcaster," incidentally, must be one of the most ingenious rhymes in English poetry but possibly for that very reason may be felt as a defect).

Bridges' triolet has no images at all and no sensuous words. Its dynamics consist in a progression from colorless commonplace monosyllables in which even the stressed words met and guess are almost characterless with their short—e vowels, through words stronger in meaning and sound, and longer— foretell, sore distress—to the climax of a line made up mainly of two words whose meanings are absolute and extreme, one of them a five-syllable word that stretches out into three of the four metrical feet: "This irretrievable disaster." The rhyme, for its full force, requires the usual British pronunciation of the long broad a (mahster and disahster). Through these architectonics of sound and sense, Bridges creates in eight strict and repetitive lines an arresting and quite profound statement about love.

pages
437–439

Sitwell, "Colonel Fantock." *Dame Edith Sitwell was descended from an ancient aristocratic English family, and her poetry often reflects this background. Much of her earlier work consists of experiments in elaborate patterns of rhythm, rhyme, assonance, and movement. She calls them "abstract" poems, though their titles are concrete enough: "Clowns' Houses" ("Beneath the flat and paper sky") and "Trio for Two Cats and a Trombone," for example.*

"Colonel Fantock" is one of the more serious of her earlier poems. In it she recalls her early life at "Troy Park" with her brothers Osbert and Sacheverell ("Dagobert and Peregrine," line 17) and sketches the character of the boys' tutor, "Colonel Fantock." The unity of the poem is one of mood rather than of subject or theme. The imagery should be closely studied for its effect on the mood.

lines
10–15

Observe especially here but also elsewhere the deliberate confusion of senses and facts: a castle that is like music; music and silence that are like the lotus flower "to eat," perfumed; grass and trees that are "sad" and "mournful"; and, later, the child who was like "a little cold air wandering" (line 27). The poet is using nonlogical language to convey experience that is real and vivid but for which factual and logical language is inadequate.

line 43

A picture of a May-fly in an encyclopedia will show perfectly the shape of the Colonel's whiskers. But why does the poet bring in the image of an airy, delicate flying creature when her subject is a superannuated military man who has taken a position as a tutor?

Consider the resemblances suggested between the old man and the poet herself as a child.

Notice the irregular off-and-on rhyme, which may be felt to strengthen the illusion of unplanned reverie over the past.

Themes:

Love

page 441   Howell, "Who would have thought." *This and several other poems in the group illustrate a vogue, during the sixteenth and seventeenth centuries, for cynical verses about women (the poets, of course, were men). In reading them, one becomes aware of the different attitudes that each represents— whether light, serious beneath a light surface, affectionate, bitter, etc.—and of the means by which each attitude is conveyed—as, for example, in Wyatt's "To a Lady to Answer Directly," where the downright, no-nonsense tone is due in part to an almost complete absence of adjectives and adverbs as well as to the direct yes-or-no statement.*

page 443   Wyatt, "The Lover Showeth How He Is Forsaken." *The image underlying the first stanza has been shown by Professor A. K. Moore to be probably that of a falcon:* flee *often meant* fly, gentle *was a common epithet for a female falcon, and falcons were often kept in their master's chamber. The women, then, who once came to the poet "gentle, tame, and meek" now have flown off like falcons reverting to the wild.*

Some writers have chosen to believe that the lady of the second and third stanzas is Fortune personified, instead of a flesh-and-blood woman; but in the light of the title as well as the poem as a whole, this reading may seem questionable.

page 444   Marlowe, "The Passionate Shepherd to His Love." *This is an example of the fashion for "pastoral" poetry in which artificial shepherds are presented in an artificial country setting. In such poetry the fields are never muddy, the shepherds never work, and life consists largely of love and conversation.*

page 446   Herrick, "Upon Julia's Clothes."

line 1   goes. *In Herrick's time the meaning of* go *was more specfic than it is now. It meant to walk.*

line 5   vibration. *Bentham in the eighteenth century described his walking for exercise as "vibrating."*

In neatly matched, contrasting tercets, Herrick describes the attraction of Julia's movements, first dressed, then undressed, using for witty contrast two words that then had scientific connotations, liquefaction *and* vibration.

Death

page 455   Shakespeare, "Full fathom five." *In this song, ding-dong is a "burden" or undersong, probably to be sung softly as an accompaniment while the other words are sung more distinctly.*

page 456   Housman, "Bredon Hill." *A successful poem seldom arises from the poet's attacking an important subject directly and squarely as a whole. More often it develops when an image, a line or two, or an oblique slant upon the subject occurs to the writer. "Bredon Hill" is a good poem in which to observe the result of this process. Its real subject, obviously, is the death of a girl and the grief of the lover who had hoped to marry her and now thinks he would like to die too. But the poet says little directly about this. Instead, he writes about the different ways of ringing church bells, about going or not going to church, and about sitting on a hill. The poem is thus less simple than it seems at a glance.*

pages 457–458 De la Mare, "The House" and poems following. *On the surface, de la Mare's poems may seem soft and conventionally romantic, with their mysterious horsemen, ghosts, and fairies. The softness, however, is deceptive; the poet offers no consolations, he glosses over nothing. Separation of mother and child, or of lovers, by death is irreparable, and there is no easy forgetting. The ghost returns, yet the living and dead do not really meet or meet only to be more lonely than before. Human nature is not idealized, and there is often a chilly hint of evil or malice at work behind the visible world.*

page 459 De la Mare, "The Old Men." *For the theme, cf. R. L. Stevenson's "Aes Triplex": "By the time a man gets well into the seventies, his continued existence is a mere miracle; and when he lays his old bones in bed for the night, there is an overwhelming probability that he will never see the day. Do the old men mind it, as a matter of fact? Why, no. . . . they hear of the death of people about their own age, or even younger, not as if it was a grisly warning, but with a simple childlike pleasure at having outlived someone else." De la Mare too knows how heartlessly self-centered the old can be.*

Almost every epithet will repay attention: "caged" (i.e., "lost to earth's listen *and* see"), *"riddle-rid" ("thought's wherefore? and when?), "in their sockets," "ruinous moon." The poem makes an exact, paraphrasable statement.*

page 460 Stevens, "The Death of a Soldier." *"Three-days personage" (line 4) refers to the customary three days between death and a home funeral, an interval in which the household revolves around the dead person, shades are drawn, voices are low, an emblem of flowers hangs at the door as a mark of mourning.*

Both in cadence and in grammatical structure the movement of the verse is continuous through the last two stanzas: feeling is created not through direct expression of it but objectively, through an opposition presented between stillness and motion, a soldier's death with no possibility even for a pause in the lives of others tó mourn.

Man, Machine, and Society pages 461–462 Blake, "The Chimney Sweeper." *The enforced employment of youngsters as "climbing boys" was widely condemned but still practiced in Blake's time.*

line 3 'weep: *a pun made from the lisped cry of the small "sweep" as he went through the streets calling out his occupation.*

pages 463–464 Pound, "Lament of the Frontier Guard." *"Rihoku," "Rihaku." The variant spellings are Pound's. He is using the Japanese name of the eighth century Chinese poet Li Po, whose poem Pound adapted or translated through the intermediary of notes by Ernest Fenellosa. The themes of war and a shrinking empire thus occur early and are recurrent in history.*

page 466 Hartley, "Pot-Luck Among the Casuals." *This poem grew out of the Depression of the 1930's. Hartley, though now known* as one of America's major painters (poetry being his second talent), was slow in achieving his reputation and himself suffered hardship during that period. In this dialogue between hungry man and hungry dog, the technical ambiguity of reference in the pronouns *he* and *his* is obviously part of what the poem is saying. Some readers feel that the generalization at the end weakens an otherwise fine poem.

Title. *"Casuals" are drifters, those subject to chance. In British and sometimes American usage the word refers to poor persons, vagrants, and migrant laborers.*

pages
467–468

MacNeice, "Bagpipe Music." *This poem treats the Depression with irony. Its theme is the irresponsibility of society in the face of both the Depression and the threat of Hitler. The scene is Scotland (hence the Scottish words). The title suggests not only the place but the tone—shrill, plaintive, and, like the cockeyed rhymes in the poem, off key.*

line 9 Mme. Blavatsky was a Theosophist leader. This cult and Yoga attracted a good many persons who were searching for salvation or truth or escape through mystical religions.

Man and Nature page 474 Shakespeare, "Spring." *This and the next poem form an ironical conclusion to the comedy* Love's Labor's Lost. *They are introduced as a "dialog" that two "learned men have compiled in praise of the owl and the cuckoo." The singers are the two seasons.*

The apparently simple poem is double-edged, for its pretty, cheerful picture of Spring is given a cynical twist. The song of the cuckoo is loved by the English as a sign of Spring. But it is a bird that lays its eggs in other birds' nests, and from this circumstance is derived the word cuckold, a mocking term for a man whose wife is unfaithful.

page 478 Marvell, "The Mower Against Gardens." *Marvell wrote a number of rural "mower" poems, in which the mower of fields celebrates nature, sometimes in conjunction with the theme of love. In this poem he speaks as the defender of untouched nature in opposition to cultivated gardens. He decries all that is artificial: walls or hedges; fertilizing, artificial breeding or crossing of plants; propagation by grafting; the breeding of a double flower from the single "Pink" (Dianthus); the recent craze for "broken colors," as striped or variegated shades were called in tulips, a craze so great that it caused wild financial speculation; the artificial breeding of sterile hybrids ("eunuchs," line 27; cf. the seedless grape and orange, which cannot be propagated by the "natural" means of seeds); importation of novel flowers (the Marvel-of-Peru or four o'clock, Mirabilis jalapa); and garden statuary.*

page 479 Bridges, "November." *The central part of this poem is full of sounds and activity of men and birds. But it is set within a contrasting frame that affects the state of mind in which, throughout, the poet sees and hears all the cheerful activity— a frame created by the opening stanza and by the final six lines in which the "November" of the opening foreshadows not only December but a vast and final geological December. This perspective alters all the value of the lively scene. A close reading of what is said about the birds may reveal still further meanings.*

page 480 Bridges, "Nightingales." *It has long been disputed whether the song of the nightingale (from the standpoint of the human listener) is sad or joyous. The Greek legend of Philomela suggests tragic associations, and Milton called the bird "most musicall, most melancholy." Others have called it "merry" or happy. This is the background of Bridges' double view.*

page 484 Williams, "The Yachts." *The concluding lines were probably written under the influence of Ruskin's memorable description of Turner's painting of a slave ship on the morning after a storm: the sharp angular waves scarcely distinguishable from limbs of dead and dying slaves who had been cast overboard.*

Time, Space, and Mutability

page 488 Herrick, "To Daffodils." *The theme here and in several of the following selections is that of* carpe diem, "seize the day" *—variations on "eat, drink, and be merry, for tomorrow we die."*

page 490 Marvell, "To His Coy Mistress."

lines 5–7 Ganges . . . Humber. *The lovers would begin their leisurely approach to each other from the opposite ends of the earth, the Humber being an English river.*

lines 21–22 *These are possibly the most celebrated lines in English poetry on the urgency of time.*

lines 39–40 -chapt: *from* chap. *meaning jaw. Let us devour time before he slowly devours us.*

pages 491–492 MacLeish, "You, Andrew Marvell." *As the title implies, this poem was inspired by the preceding one. MacLeish drops the love theme, however, and makes his poem entirely out of time and space.*

Perhaps the most notable feature of the poem is its grammatical structure: there is not one sentence. There is not even a subordinate clause or a finite verb until the last line, where a single dependent clause is hung upon an infinitive. Everywhere else, instead of verbs there are only infinitives depending on other infinitives, and participles and gerunds depending on infinitives: "To feel . . . chill . . . creep up . . . and . . . shadow grow . . . and . . . trees take leaf by leaf the evening . . . (to feel) . . . the mountains . . . change . . . and Baghdad darken . . . and Spain go under . . ." This linked structure is continuous and never reaches completion because there is no sentence, no end, no cessation of the movement of time. Thus the syntax itself is expressive of the theme.

MacLeish traces only half a revolution of the earth, and even that only in imagination, as he lies beneath the noonday sun somewhere in America, thinking of the edge of night approaching from the other side of the earth. Within these still moments in time and space, which frame the poem, he opens out the vastness and remoteness of past ages and distance. The place names, which mark the advance of the westward-moving shadow, are all rich in associations that go back through the Middle Ages to antiquity, and along with these names go many images suggesting evening and time past, such as the "earthy chill of dusk," the "ever-climbing shadow," and the "wheel rut in the ruined stone."

pages 492–493 Wordsworth, "Mutability."

A tower so old that weeds have grown on its roof, and so fragile that sound waves could destroy it.

pages
494–495

D. Thomas, "Fern Hill." *The theme is an obvious one, the brevity of childhood and its carefree joy. The poet recreates the joy even while he takes it away. Crudely expressed in prose, the thought runs something like this:*

As a boy, he and the farm were almost as one. Each day was fresh and full of delight. At night the farm vanished while he slept, only to appear again next morning as fresh and new as Eden. He had not thought that this would end, that all the while time held him prisoner, and that a night must quickly come when time would fly away with the farm—that is, with his childhood.

The poem is sprinkled with variations on set phrases from children's stories—"happy as the day is long," "once upon a time," "all the day long"—and with an extension of an ancient poetic device called the "transferred epithet," by which, for special effects, a descriptive word is attached, not to the object to which it logically applies, but to some other. Thomas carries this device to an extreme here and elsewhere, using it constantly instead of only occasionally: the house sings, the yard is happy, the boy is green, the stable is green and whinnies.

On the Meaning of Life

pages
496–497

Tennyson, "Ulysses." *In this dramatic monologue Tennyson writes of Ulysses (Odysseus) after the end of Homer's* Odyssey, *which had brought Ulysses home after a twenty years' absence, reunited him with his family after a fight with usurpers, and by implication ended "happily ever after." By rejecting this implied conclusion and providing a different one, Tennyson sets forth a philosophy of life.*

In the Odyssey, *the time of day that comes most often to mind is dawn, certainly the natural time for setting out on a journey in the ancient, pre-compass world. Yet Tennyson's Ulysses—and the poet is deliberate—sails at evening.*

line 4

savage race. *Ulysses' island kingdom of Ithaca was on the fringes rather than at the center of Greek culture.*

line 63

Happy Isles: *the Isles of the Blest in the western ocean, where heroes especially favored by the gods might live exempt from death.*

pages
498–502

Tennyson, "The Lotos-Eaters." *The subject is again from the* Odyssey, *the theme antithetical to that of* Ulysses. *In the land of the Lotos-Eaters, those who ate the lotus flower or fruit became languid and lost all desire for action (consider the implications of line 4, "a land in which it seemèd always afternoon"). The imagery throughout is significant for the mood, but that of line 95 particularly so: "ever climbing up the climbing wave" is a classic expression of futility. The sound and movement of the verse are also important. The first part is written in the Spenserian stanza (see p. 498, and notice the effect of the complicated rhyming and the extended last line).*

pages
508–509

Auden, "Musée des Beaux Arts." *Religious paintings of the Renaissance often contained figures of people and animals from everyday life that had little or nothing to do with the theme of the picture. These were painted with realistic and* sometimes humorous detail. *The same combination of the lofty and the commonplace occasionally appears in paintings of mythological subjects.*

line 14 Icarus. *According to Greek legend, Daedalus built wings by means of which he and his son Icarus escaped from the labyrinth in Crete. Icarus flew too close to the sun and fell and was drowned when the wax of his wings melted.*

page 510 Allen, "If the Stars Should Fall." *In the word* buckle *there is a play of two meanings: the hunter of Orion with buckled belt (line 12) and the Gods who may bend, break apart, and drop.*

This expression of gloom may derive from hopeless contemplation of racial problems, since the writer is a negro; but the central image of the poem carries it beyond any single problem into the region of cosmic hopelessness.

Religion page 515 Housman, "Easter Hymn." *Much of the tension in this poem is attributable to the syntax, suspense created by the periodic construction of the single sentence of which each stanza is composed. The date of the poem is not known, but Housman is clearly thinking of the modern war-ridden world, perhaps specifically the first World War.*

pages 515–516 Br. Antoninus, "The Flight in the Desert." *Taking belief for granted, Br. Antoninus recreates in modern terms the flight into Egypt of Mary and Joseph with the child Jesus, escaping from Herod's massacre of infants, of which they had received warning (see Matt. ii 13–23). The imagery, however, belongs not to Egypt but specifically to our American western desert (mesquite, prairie dog, coyote, etc.). The poem is in some respects comparable to Eliot's "Journey of the Magi" (see p. 591 and the note, p. 667), which probably influenced it.*

Forms:

The Sonnet page 519 Drayton, "Since there's no help." *This sonnet is remarkable for its unsentimental and modern tone, which comes in part from the high proportion of everyday, one-syllable words. But both style and mood change significantly with the turn of thought in the third quatrain.*

pages 519–522 Shakespeare, Sonnets. *Shakespeare's sonnets, it is believed, were composed in two sequences, but the order in which some belong is uncertain. Readers who are curious about the story behind them should read the whole series.*

page 520 Sonnets 29 and 30. *Both sonnets represent moods of depression, but they are clearly differentiated. The first is an almost paranoid state in which the poet feels as if everything in the world is against him, the other a mood of sadness and loss.*

No. 29 is characterized by unity and suspense attributable to the grammatical construction. No. 30 is a poem of emotions expressed through, and unified by, seemingly incongruous dry commercial and legal language. For example, in line 1, "sessions," used with "summon," in Shakespeare's day would have brought to mind the session or sitting of a court of law. "Dateless" (line 6), meaning "without fixed due date or date of termination" again suggests business or law; and "tell" (line 10) is to count (cf. the teller in a bank). The other similar words will be obvious to modern readers.

pages 520–521	Sonnet 33. *Note the single analogy that controls the language throughout.*

page 521	Sonnet 65.

line 6	batt'ring. *The association is with battering-rams, used in besieging a walled city. The first two quatrains play off against each other contrasting sets of images.*

page 523	Milton, "When I consider how my light is spent" (often referred to under the title "On His Blindness."

lines 3–7	*The reference here is to the parable of the "talents" (an ancient unit of money) in Matt. xxv.*

page 523	Milton, "On the Late Massacre in Piedmont." *The occasion of this sonnet was the Catholic persecution, in 1655, of an ancient Protestant sect in northern Italy.*

A good deal of the denunciatory solemnity of tone comes from the long and sonorous vowel sounds, particularly the long o's in the rhymes and elsewhere. More than most poems this demands to be read aloud, and with deliberation.

page 526	Bridges, "Sonnet 23." *The fact that the entire octave describes pilgrims to the Holy Land may cause a hasty reader to overlook the real subject, love—earthly, not heavenly love.*

The Ode

pages 527–532	Wordsworth, "Ode: Intimations of Immortality from Recollections of Early Childhood." *This "Ode" makes use of the neo-Platonic belief that the human soul exists in Heaven before being born on earth and that it brings with it into early life faint memories of its heavenly past. Such a notion fits well with the idealizing of childhood that followed from the wide popularity of the writings of Rousseau in the eighteenth century: the belief in the "natural goodness of man," which is the child's inheritance and which he loses only because of corrupted human institutions and the consequently faulty education he receives. Wordsworth describes the child as the wisest and best of mortals because the "clouds of glory" only gradually fade from his memory as the cares and evils of the world close around him.*

This idea leads further to the question of what the grown man can do. Must he simply mope over his lost childhood? Wordsworth's answer is no: through sympathetic devotion to nature and children, through experience and conscious reflection, he may arrive once more within sight and sound of that sea of immortality whence he came.

In form, the poem is one of the English irregular odes, with lines of varying length and irregularly placed rhyme.

Stanzas VII–VIII. The childs' play all has to do with imitation of grownup living: marriage, business, war, funerals. Why, the poet asks, is he in such haste to take on the "yoke" of maturity when he is so blessed as a child? Notice the elaborate suspended grammar of the single sentence that makes up most of Stanza VIII.

pages 532–536	Coleridge, "Dejection." *Coleridge and Wordsworth were intimate friends, and this ode is in part a reply to certain of the*

latter's ideas. Nature, Coleridge says, cannot be a true source of joy, which must come from harmony within ourselves. The inspiration that seems to come from without only mirrors our inner creative spirit. The poet's present dejection and poetic sterility have resulted from the loss of this inner joy. The ode is a much-revised version of a long verse-letter originally addressed to Sara Hutchinson (the "Lady" of line 65 and elsewhere), with whom Coleridge, trapped in an unhappy marriage to another woman, was hopelessly in love.

line 7 Aeolian lute: a stringed instrument so sensitive that when placed in an open window the currents of air will cause it to sound.

pages 536–538 Shelley, "Ode to the West Wind." *This is the most famous example in English verse of* terza rima *(see Glossary, p. 639), though the scheme is interrupted by a couplet marking the end of each division of the poem.*

The ode is notable also for its almost mathematical organization of imagery: the leaf presiding in Section 1, the cloud (with a reminder of the leaf) in 2, the wave (again with a reminder of leaf) in 3, the three united in 4, and a return to the leaf in the conclusion: the wind, meanwhile, presiding over everything. What is said by the imagery is another matter, here left for the reader's consideration.

The Elegy *pages 539–543* Milton, "Lycidas." *Milton mourns the death by shipwreck of Edward King, a young man whom he had known, probably not intimately, when both were students at Cambridge. He follows the tradition of the pastoral elegy, writing of himself and King as shepherds whose poems are songs sung to the accompaniment of "oaten flute" (a simple flute made from a hollow stem). But King had intended to become a clergyman, and so the other sense of pastor and pastoral enters into the poem too: King was to have been not only a poet but also a spiritual shepherd of a flock.*

lines 1–5 He is called upon to write this poem before his powers have matured.

lines 23–26 Milton translates the fact ("we went to college together") into its elaborate pastoral equivalent.

line 36 Damaetas. *Like "Lycidas," this name is common in pastoral poetry. The person meant by Milton is not known.*

line 58 Muse. *Calliope, the Muse of epic poetry, was the mother of Orpheus, legendary singer, inspirer of song, and leader of a Greek religious cult. According to one tradition, Maenads killed and dismembered him, and threw him into the stream. His head floated singing to Lesbos.*

line 75 blind Fury. *The Furies and the three Fates in mythology are not actually the same, though Milton identifies them here. Two Fates prepare and spin the thread of life; the third, Atropos the "inflexible" one, who is blindfold, cuts it.*

lines 89–90 Herald of the Sea. *Triton, a sea god, defends his father Neptune against the accusation of having drowned Lycidas.*

line 106 sanguine flower . . . *The youth Hyacinthus was loved but accidentally killed by Apollo. From his blood Apollo caused to spring up the hyacinth flower, whose petals were said to bear markings resembling the letters of the Greek word for "woe."*

line 109   The Pilot: *St. Peter, customarily represented in old paintings as carrying the keys of Heaven. He had been a fisherman on the Sea of Galilee and was with Jesus during a storm at sea. As the founder of the Church he may be called its first "pastor." As the first bishop of Rome, he is represented with a bishop's headdress ("Miter'd," line 112.)*

lines 113–31   *Milton attacks the English clergy.*

line 128   grim Woolf: *the Roman Catholic Church, endeavoring to win converts among Protestants.*

lines 130–131   *The "two-handed engine" has never been satisfactorily identified.*

line 132   Alpheus: *god of the river Alpheus and lover of Arethusa. He is associated here with pastoral poetry. In addressing him at this point, Milton returns to the theme with which the poem opened.*

lines 152–53   *The poet has imagined a suitable flowery funeral but now reminds himself that the body of Lycidas was never found.*

lines 160–63   *Bellerus, guarded mount, Namancos and Bayona. Land's End, the southwestern promontory of England; and St. Michael's Mount, near Land's End, which looks toward Spain (Namancos and Bayona). The Mount is supposed to be guarded by the Archangel Michael. Milton urges him to turn and look homeward, for the dangers are now domestic rather than foreign.*

line 164   Dolphins. *The Greek poet Arion was thrown overboard, according to Herodotus, and was carried to land by a dolphin. Milton may also have known of a Roman belief that spirits of the dead were borne by dolphins to the next world.*

pages 549–550   Thomas, "After the Funeral." *Dylan Thomas writes in a style not always easy to follow, for though he usually preserves the form of regular grammatical statements, the statements themselves are often nonlogical. The language is addressed directly to the imagination and the emotions, often bypassing the rational mind altogether. With Thomas more conspicuously than with most poets, the patterns of sound and imagery dominate the poem.*

"After the funeral" honors his aunt, Ann Jones, a poor, bent, hardworking old woman for whom the poet feels an affection that goes back to his boyhood. Its general outline is clear enough, but individual phrases sometimes telescope two or three images into one and therefore may puzzle the reader. In "Blinds down the lids" (line 4), for example, are telescoped the window blinds drawn down as a sign of mourning, the closed eyelids of the dead, which are "blinds" of another sort, and the coffin lid. The phrase just before this, "muffle-toed . . . one peg in the thick grave's foot," seems to fit both the perfunctory mourners, indifferent old people who themselves have one foot in the grave, and the nailing of the coffin lid.

Thomas first describes the funeral with its "mule praises," the stupid, perfunctory praise of those who do not recognize Ann's worth. But the sound of the spade "wakes" him back into his boyhood, so that he feels her death as he would have felt it then (lines 6–9). Afterwards, in her room with its stuffed fox and stale fern, he holds his own funeral service for her. The hearth of her room is now the "raised hearth" (line 21)—that is, the altar. He praises her in images beyond what she would have expected or thought suitable (lines 16–20). He calls upon the seas to make her inarticulate virtue "babble," and upon the "ferned and foxy woods" to make her love "sing and swing through a brown chapel" (which may be the woods or her room or both). And he blesses her with the sign of the cross made by flying birds. Then he describes her as she truly was—in contrast to the "mule praises" of the actual funeral. His praises are a monument ("this skyward statue"), and the monument is this poem that he is writing, which "storms" at him over her grave until by writing it he can bring to life again her love: "the stuffed fox cries Love and the stale fern is fertile."

For another elegy that in some ways resembles Thomas's, see that by Roethke, (p. 621).

Eleven Representative Poets:

John Donne

pages 551–557

Donne was a younger contemporary of Shakespeare, the chief of what Dr. Johnson named the "metaphysical" poets. His poetry is a remarkable blend of intellect and passion, of downright, everyday idiom and circuitous complexity. He employs many "conceits"—i.e., striking, often far-fetched figures of speech or comparisons drawn from unusual sources such as the scientific thought of his time.

For two of Donne's religious sonnets, see page 511. Most of his secular poems are believed to be the product of his earlier years.

page 552

"Song." It will be noted that in the first stanza Donne is passingly cynical about other things besides women. The poem should be read in the light of the next one, which shows the other side of the coin.

line 2

mandrake (mandragora): a plant that has been the subject of many superstitions. It has a forked root which is said to resemble the human form.

page 553

"The Indifferent." A modern editor, Theodore Redpath, suggests the following interpretations:

line 2

The woman "made amorous by living in luxury, and the woman who gives herself because she needs money."

line 5

believes (him) . . . tries (i.e., tests) (him).

line 17

travel. The older form of the same word is travail. A double meaning may be intended.

page 554

"The Funeral."

line 3

wreath of hair. Bracelets used to be made from a lock of a person's hair, woven or braided with strands of gold thread.

lines 12–13

The superior power of the bracelet is fancifully reasoned. Hair grows up from the brain, the nerves down; and the lady's brain that bore the hair was better than his. So surely this bracelet, after his death, will hold him together as a whole unified being better than the network of his nerves ever did—unless, he adds, she gave it to him only to remind him that he is still her prisoner.

line 22

The meaning is uncertain. It may be: "to confer on it all that a Soul can confer" (the suggestion is that of Redpath).

page 554   "The Good-Morrow."

line 4   According to tradition, the Seven Sleepers of Ephesus were seven Christians, in flight from persecution, who hid in a cave, were walled in, and slept till they were rescued two hundred years later.

line 19   not mixed equally. An old scientific belief held that compound substances whose elements are equally mixed are stable and cannot be dissolved.

page 555   "The Anniversary."

line 3   The "times" are hours, days, seasons, etc. It is not certain whether Donne meant "they" to refer to "Kings," or to "times." If the latter, he probably meant that though the sun is the cause of "times," the very passing of these times makes the sun itself older.

lines   The general meaning is that their loving souls will be even
18–20   happier after death.

page 556   "The Canonization."

line 7   stamped: on coins—i.e., pursue the King's favor, or pursue riches.

line 15   man. Some texts of the poem have more.

line 23   Phoenix: a bird in Egyptian mythology, of which only one exists. It lives 500 years, then consumes itself by fire, and from the ashes another rises. Since it reproduces itself, it may be considered as a union of both sexes.

lines   An almost identical thought is repeated three times in these
29–34   lines: if we are not important enough in a worldly way for a big funeral, a "half-acre tomb," or a place in history ("chronicle"), we shall at any rate be a fit subject for poems.

lines   The subject of "invoke" is "all" (line 35). "Beg" (line 44) is
36–45   imperative. Since the lovers are now canonized (have become saints), they are asked to intercede with heaven to send down a pattern by which others may have as perfect a love.

William Blake   pages   Blake earned his living as an engraver and was scarcely
                     557–561 known as a poet in his own day. Nearly all his poems were engraved, illustrated, and handcolored by himself, hence very few copies were circulated. His imagery often has the visual quality of the artist, not realistic but visionary—that is, both visual and symbolic.

page 558   "The Tyger." Ordinarily, lamb and tiger, used as symbols, are likely to represent good and evil or gentleness and ferocity. This is not quite what Blake meant. His tiger is terrifying but beautiful. He had never seen a real tiger, and his beast is rather a vision than a live animal. The meaning of the poem has been much disputed. The tiger is sometimes thought to represent divine Wrath, in contrast with Forgiveness of the lamb; or Experience in contrast with Innocence. In Blake's Songs of Innocence, the poem "The Lamb" asks much the same question ("Little Lamb, who made thee?"). The answer partly identifies the lamb with Jesus. "The Tyger" is the corresponding poem in Songs of Experience.

page 558 "Mad Song." "Tom-o'-Bedlam," or "mad" songs, were once fairly common, but Blake's is perhaps the only one that seems to penetrate convincingly into a deranged spirit.

"The Human Abstract." The poem attacks conventional religion, which Blake considered the modern center of hypocrisy and repression. Strongly anticlerical, he more than once portrayed the clergy as caterpillars (see line 15).

page 561 "Auguries of Innocence." These are unfinished and partly, unorganized lines, mainly couplets, never published by Blake himself. Only the first lines are printed here; the later ones tend to deteriorate into doggerel.

John Keats
pages 561–568 Keats is known for his delight in sensuous experience of all kinds—sights, sounds, colors, tactile sensation—and for his unusual mastery of the language for communicating it. He possessed a strong and critical intellect as well, through which he was bringing under firmer control his great gifts of experience and expression, when his work was cut short by illness and early death.

page 563 "On First Looking into Chapman's Homer." George Chapman's translation had appeared in 1598–1616. Pope's Homer superseded it in the eighteenth century and Keats was no doubt already familiar with that translation; but to the Romantic writers Pope seemed to have reduced Homer to polite drawing-room verse, whereas Chapman's version was felt to be heroic and noble.

page 564 "Ode to a Nightingale." The desire to escape sorrow and responsibility is a frequent theme in Keats's poetry; but it is always balanced by the recognition that there is no escape, that one must, after all, live in the real world and meet whatever comes (cf. "La Belle Dame sans Merci"). More than commonly susceptible to pleasure and more than commonly experienced in pain through much illness and early death running through his family, he often brings the two extremes together in his poetry.

line 14 Provençal song. From Provence came much of the lyric poetry of the Middle Ages.

line 26 Keats's brother Tom had died a few months before this was written.

lines 66–67 alien corn: a poetic epitome of part of the Old Testament book of Ruth. Note how this foreshadows the later "forlorn."

page 566 "Ode on a Grecian Urn." This is one of the most discussed, and perhaps over-discussed, of English poems, chiefly because of the closing statement about truth and beauty. As a universal principle, it seems to many people false, absurd, or immoral. By various ingenious explanations, critics have tried to rescue Keats from what appears to be a weak position. The question cannot be argued out here, but readers should keep in mind that Keats was using a commonplace as old as Plato, whose triad of values—the good, the true, and the beautiful— were regarded as approximately three aspects of the same thing. In a letter, Keats once wrote of the "truth" of creative imagination, "What the imagination seizes as Beauty must be truth—whether it existed before or not." This may throw some light on the poem. And Hazlitt, whom Keats admired, had said that "to the genuine artist, truth, nature, beauty are almost different names for the same thing." Though these statements do not fully explain the poem or necessarily validate its concluding lines, they suggest something of what people were thinking when they so often spoke of "truth and beauty" in connection with painting, sculpture, and poetry.

line 2   foster-child. *"Time" and "silence," though not the original creators (parents), were the foster-parents who had preserved the urn through the ages.*

Stanzas 2–3. *Art makes permanent and hence re-experience-able the experiences and emotions which in life are transitory.*

lines   dost tease: *taxes our thought or imagination beyond its capac-*
44–45   *ity, as does the attempt to imagine eternity.*

page 568   "To Autumn." *The atmosphere and mood of this poem may be profitably contrasted with that of Bridges' poem about autumn, "November" (p. 479).*

line 25   bloom. *Keats may have two different senses of this word in mind: the common one, having to do with blossoming; and the other, not quite as common but not at all unusual, meaning to cover with a soft, powdery silver, such as often appears as the "bloom" on plums and other fruit.*

line 28   *Some texts of the poem have* sallows (willows) *for* shallows.

Gerard Manley Hopkins   pages 569–571   *Hopkins' fame has been entirely posthumous, the first collection of his poems having appeared nearly thirty years after his death. Yet today he is sometimes considered a greater poet than the Victorian "giants" Tennyson and Browning. Hopkins was converted to Roman Catholicism while an undergraduate at Oxford and subsequently became a Jesuit priest. Nearly all religious in theme, his poetry is distinguished by emotional intensity, extreme individuality of language and imagery, and advanced metrical experiments.*

page 569   "Heaven-Haven."

line 3   sided. *"Hailstones are shaped like the cut of diamonds called brilliants [i.e., with numerous flat sides or facets]," Hopkins recorded in a notebook (this was a mistaken scientific observation made in the nineteenth century).*

The metrical change in the last line is onomatopoetic, by its own swing suggesting "the swing of the sea."

page 569   "Pied Beauty." *The imagery progresses from multitudinous variety in nature to duality (pairs of contrasts), and finally to unity.*

Title: pied: *piebald, of different colors, as spotted black and white. Here the poet means variegated. The theme might be summed up: Praise God, himself changeless yet the source of all change.*

line 4   *In his journal one autumn, Hopkins noted that the chestnuts that year were "as bright as coals or spots of vermilion."*

line 10   fathers-forth *is a verb,* He (God) *is its subject, and the preceding* all things, *etc., its object.*

"The Windhover."

Title: *The windhover is a small falcon, said to be named for its habit of hovering almost motionless, staying itself in the air with its head against the wind.*

The meaning of this sonnet has been much in dispute, but the interpretation given here is, in the editors' opinion, the only one that draws all the parts of the poem together into a coherent whole.

In the octave, the poet describes the bird of which he caught sight this morning. It is the favorite (minion), *the crown prince* (dauphin) *of the morning because of the beauty of its movement and its mastery over its element, the air. The poet's heart, which before had been stagnant and unwilling to feel anything* (in hiding), *was stirred by the bird's power and mastery.*

When the sestet opens, the individual bird has been universalized to stand for the whole of material creation or nature: "brute [i.e., animal] beauty . . . air, pride, plume." But as he contemplates it, this material world of nature, with all its beauty and power, seems to buckle, break open, collapse—like a structure that is burning from within. AND (the capitalization makes the word equivalent to "and behold!") through and beyond the material reality "breaks" the infinitely more beautiful, and more daring or dangerous, fire of the spirit of Christ (my chevalier), *whom the poet is now addressing directly. No wonder this happens, he says, for the most commonplace things break open to show inward beauty. The ordinary labor of ploughing breaks dull-colored earth into a shining furrow* (sillion) *of fresh soil (Hopkins's journal describes a recently ploughed hill "glistening with very bright newly turned sods"). And the coals of a fire (the English use very large chunks of coal in fireplaces) that seem dead on the outside* (blue-bleak embers) *fall open and show the still-bright fire* (gold-vermillion) *inside.*

This train of thought was common in Hopkins: the beauty of the material world stirred him for its own sake, then led him on to think of the spiritual beauty dwelling in or beyond the material.

line 4   rung upon the rein: *a term used in the training of a horse: at the end of a long rein the horse describes a circle. Here the falcon, using one wing as pivot, swings the circle.*

line 6   skate's heel . . . bow-bend: *another image of smooth circling, drawn from the art of skating.*

line 11   chevalier: *a term of honor: a chivalrous man, a knight. Here it is Christ, to whom the poem is addressed. Hopkins did not follow the modern custom of capitalizing nouns and pronouns referring to God or Christ (see the last sonnet of this group in which he addresses God as "sir").*

page 570   "No worst, there is none." *This and the next are two of the late, often called the "terrible" sonnets from their expression of an extreme spiritual despair, the causes of which are only partly known.*

page 571   "Thou art indeed just, Lord."

Justus quidem, etc. *from Jeremiah xii.1. Thou art indeed just,*

Lord, if I argue with thee: but yet I also speak just things to thee: Why do the ways of the impious prosper?

Thomas Hardy *pages 571–577* *Hardy is most widely known for his statements, in both verse and prose, of a pessimistic or fatalistic philosophy. In a great variety of ways, he expressed the belief that man might better not have evolved at all, not usually because of man's own evil nature but because fate, chance, the very constitution of the universe militate against his happiness. Occasionally, however, as in "The Darkling Thrush" and "The Oxen," he can at least imagine if not quite believe in a hope.*

page 575 *"Channel Firing." The place names at the end are associated with the far past, reminding us of all the centuries of human warfare.*

William Butler Yeats *pages 577–582* *Yeats is ranked by many critics as the greatest of the modern poets. He was an Irishman of Protestant Irish stock living in Catholic Ireland; a man with a wide range of interests, a poet with a wide range of styles, he became at first preeminent among the somewhat decadent English poets of the 1890's and again, in middle and old age (from about 1914 through the 1930's) preeminent among the rising generation of poets. Auden's elegy (p. 547) is the characteristically understated tribute of these younger men. Some of Yeats's best-known poems have been omitted from this selection because a full appreciation of them is almost impossible without a considerable knowledge of his other work. The reader who is interested in the little he finds here will find a great deal more in Yeats's collected poems and plays.*

For other poems by Yeats, see those on his love, pp. 402–403, and his narratives (pp. 425–428).

page 577 *"The Magi." Early in life Yeats had rejected most of the traditional beliefs of Christianity. Though the nominal subjects are the same, there is little basis for comparison between this and Eliot's "Journey of the Magi."*

The construction of Yeats's poem as a single sentence should be noticed. Further tension or suspense is produced by the interrupted order of words. In the first line, for example, the verb see *waits for its object till the end of the next line. In line 6,* to find *is suspended till its object,* mystery, *is reached two lines later; and, in the interval, even the phrase* being unsatisfied *(line 7) is interrupted by an inserted phrase. These scarcely noticeable grammatical tensions help to create the feeling that something important is being said and perhaps that something important is impending. The imagery and language contribute to the same effect, and these are worth study. The most striking word in the poem is* bestial, *which on the surface means only* belonging to beasts—*referring, that is, to the stable and manger where the Magi saw Jesus—but which nevertheless also conveys a strong suggestion of subhuman brutishness and violence.*

The individual parts of this poem are clear enough, but the whole seems somewhat mysterious. Compare it with the poem that follows.

page 577 "The Second Coming." *The title refers, of course, to the prophecy of Christ's second coming, but here the words are ironical. Yeats had a theory about historical cycles, each of about 2,000 years' duration, each an antithesis of the preceding, and each ushered in by a supernatural birth. The Greek era, by this theory, began with the birth of Helen of Troy, whose mother, Leda, was a mortal but whose father was Zeus appearing in the form of a swan. Next came the Christian era with the birth of Christ. A third, Yeats said, is now approaching. Sometimes he imagined it as better, sometimes as worse than our era. The Greek gods might return again; or, as he expressed it in his autobiography, there might come "after us the Savage God."*

The first stanza describes the state of the world as Yeats viewed it shortly after the close of World War I. A century earlier, after the Napoleonic Wars, Shelley had expressed the same thought in very similar terms in Prometheus Unbound:

> The good want power, but to weep barren tears.
> The powerful goodness want; worse need for them.
> The wise want love; and those who love want wisdom;
> And all best things are thus confused to ill.

line 12 Spiritus Mundi: *a "general store house of images which have ceased to be a property of any personality or spirit" (Yeats), much like the unconscious racial memory described by the philosophical psychoanalysist Jung.*

line 14 *The image here suggests a sphinx and a "brazen winged beast," as well as other combinations of man and beast such as the centaur, all of which Yeats wrote about elsewhere.*

page 578 "The Cold Heaven." *Like so many others of Yeats's poems, "The Cold Heaven" refers to his love (see poems in the first section.) But its essential subject is something broader, for it represents any moment when the cold light of truth suddenly breaks into one's consciousness to shatter a long illusion on which one's past life has been built.*

The poem, it will be noticed, is extremely subjective: all that happens is purely internal though much of the language is concrete. Consider how the effect of violence is produced in a poem in which nothing external can be said to happen.

page 578 "Among School Children." *While he was writing this poem, Yeats referred to it in a letter as his "curse upon old age." In the end, it became much more than that.*

The shape of the poem might be described in terms of Yeats's own image of a "gyre." It begins with a small commonplace event and spirals out in theme until at the end it raises questions almost too vast to be expressed clearly in language: What is reality or what constitutes value? The emotional energy that starts the widening spiral movement is sparked, once more, by the thought of Maud Gonne (see note to "Her Praise," p. 643). Because of this, an experience that begins as a cursory visit of inspection by Yeats, in his official capacity as an Irish senator, to a convent school, comes to engage all his power of feeling and thought, makes him wonder what he has given his life to, what others give their lives to—ultimately, what is worth giving one's life to.

Stanza II. Seeing the little girls in school, the poet is reminded of an occasion when "she" had once sat by the fire telling him a story of her childhood. He remembers it as a rare moment when he and she had felt united.

lines *The story of the origin of love in Plato's* Symposium. *Man,*
15–16 *originally whole, attacked the gods and for this was punished by Zeus, who split him in two "as you might divide an egg with a hair." Since then, the halves forever try to unite: "the pursuit of the whole is called love."*

line 26 *Quattrocento. Usually this would mean the fifteenth century. Yeats, however, may have meant the fourteenth and may have been thinking of pictures of Dante, whose "hollow face," he said, was "more plain to the mind's eye than any face but that of Christ." Maud Gonne's portraits show exaggeratedly hollow cheeks and eyes in her later years.*

line 28 *Mess here has nothing to do with untidiness; it means a quantity of food for a meal.*

lines *honey of generation. Yeats explained this as a legendary drug*
33–35 *that destroys the recollection of prenatal freedom. It therefore makes life tolerable while its effect lasts.*

The connection of Stanza VI with the preceding is made clear by Yeats's explanation of its meaning, "that even the greatest men are old scarecrows by the time their fame has come."

lines *These lines refer to Plato's theory of reality.*
41–42

lines *Aristotle was the tutor of Alexander the Great.*
43–44

lines *Pythagoras (who was believed by his followers to have golden*
45–47 *thighs) discovered the mathematical relation between the harmony of the octave and the length of strings. He therefore reasoned that the order of the whole universe consists of number. Applying the theory to the heavenly bodies produced the famous notion of the "music of the spheres" ("what a star sang," line 47).*

Stanza VII. The images worshiped by nuns are unchanging, those worshiped by mothers (their children) change; but both break the hearts of worshipers, Yeats says. Here he breaks off and addresses the images themselves as "Presences," bringing together the three devotions from the earlier stanzas: "passion" (Yeats's for his love), "piety" (the nuns to religion), "affection" (mothers for children). To the worshiper, these Presences symbolize "all heavenly glory." But in the end they only mock him, for in a sense they are not real but are "self-born," self-created: the value that man worships in them supposing it to be an objective value outside of himself, is only the value that he has subjectively bestowed upon them.

In the last stanza, the specific materials of the earlier part of the poem are still recognizable: the nun's asceticism (line 58), Maud Gonne's hollow beauty (line 59), his own wisdom that is not worth what it cost him (line 60); but these have grown far beyond their individual meaning and have become part of the universal question of values. The thought of the final stanza can be paraphrased only very crudely. It may be expressed in terms of ends and means: that the end cannot be separated from the means, that labor brings reward (blossoming, dancing) only when it is in itself reward. Or of the chestnut tree, the question is asked: Which is means—leaf, blossom, or bole—and which end? Which is the real, the essence?

Does the dancer exist only through the dance? The implied answer may be phrased even more abstractly: that there is no being except becoming.

A paraphrase is never more than an aid in approaching a poem, and here it is especially weak. In fact, here it is almost ruinous to the poem, because, quite apart from the feeling, the idea Yeats is getting at is something almost beyond the reach of logical thought. He could have described it in terms of his own very elaborate system of philosophical or semiphilosophical thought, but that required an entire book for him to explain, and we should need no less. Here he takes the poetic short cut, by which he suggests it to the imagination and emotions.

We shall not attempt to explain or describe the final poetic character and quality of "Among School Children" further than to call attention once more to the gyre-like structure of the poem and to the extraordinary style of Yeats, who can combine the most colloquial language and undignified imagery with the most dignified and remote in such a way as to create something quite different from either alone. Consider the homely and grotesque "comfortable kind of scarecrow," for example, and the "old clothes upon old sticks," in which the mere repetition of old before sticks helps transform the phrase from commonplace into poetry. The pattern of contrast between such phrases as these and very different ones like "a marble or a bronze repose" or the abstract apostrophe "O Presences," a contrast that runs through the poem almost to the end, contributes to produce the combined feeling of reality and importance in the poem. The dropping away of commonplace material toward the end is part of the gyre-like movement of the whole.

page 581　　"Lapis Lazuli." *Harry Clifton had given Yeats the carving described in the poem.*

line 4　　King Billy. *cf. "But King William threw his bomb-balls in," from an Irish song about the Battle of the Boyne. Yeats may have intended a double reference to Kaiser Wilhelm and the first World War.*

Callimachus (early 5th century, B.C.) is said to have been the first to use in sculpture a running drill as a major instrument, which made possible a flowing look in the drapery of a marble statue. Yet none of his work survives.

Robert Frost　　*pages 582–585*　　*After a slow start, Frost became one of the best-loved American poets of this century. He was also one of the most "native" American writers. Though born in San Francisco, he wrote almost always of farm life in New England. Many of his poems are simple and direct expressions of feeling or of folk (some critics would say folksy) wisdom. Others have overt symbolism and in still others, such as "After Apple Picking," the presence or absence of symbolic meaning has been much debated. Even at its least simple, however, his work does not approach in complexity that of most writers of this century.*

T. S. Eliot　　*pages 585–591*　　*Eliot has been one of the three or four most influential poets of the present century and an equally influential critic. He broke new ground in the use of urban imagery and in the development of a highly allusive and elliptical style. Writing at first as a sceptic, he later became convinced of man's* *need of religion, and when approaching the age of forty joined the church of England. Nearly all his later poems, of which* Journey of the Magi *is representative, are religious.*

page 585 *"The Love Song of J. Alfred Prufrock." Although interpretations of "Prufrock" vary in emphasis, the main outlines are familiar enough to be fairly well agreed upon. There will continue to be differences of opinion about details because, to a greater degree than most earlier poets, Eliot excludes mere explanation and omits transitions, just as the mind itself, in associating ideas, often seems to do.*

The epigraph comes from Dante's Inferno, Canto 27. *Guido da Montefeltro, one of the damned, has been asked about himself and speaks from out of a flame: "If I believed that my answer were to one who ever could return to the world, this flame should shake no more. But since, if what I hear is true, no one ever returned alive from this depth, without fear of infamy I answer you." The poet perhaps implies that what Prufrock (or the poem) says will be understood only by those who share his hell. What that hell is, appears gradually in the poem.*

In outline, the poem resembles a dramatic monologue of Browning, in which the speaker, placed in a specific situation, talks about the situation, and in so doing reveals his own character. Prufrock, however, does not speak to another character in the poem. He speaks nominally to an invisible companion but in reality as if to himself—his other or split self—but also possibly to the other Prufrocks of the world, who will understand him. The "you and I" of the opening and the "we," who share the same fate at the close, are appropriate to either or both of these interpretations.

The moment chosen for Prufrock's self-revelation is that of a decision. Shall he, or dare he propose to a woman (marriage probably, possibly an affair)? The answer is no, and so the "love song" of the title is ironic, for Prufrock is incapable of breaking through the barrier of his reserve, incapable of any genuine relationships with other human beings. The rise and fall of the merest possibility of action provides the structure or "plot" of his soliloquy. At the beginning he is irresolute: "Let us go (line 1) . . . and make our visit (line 12) . . . there will be time (line 23) . . . And indeed there will be time . . . to turn back (lines 37–40) . . . Do I dare disturb the universe? (lines 45–46) . . . should I then presume? And how should I begin?" (lines 68–69).

This see-saw of the will brings Prufrock to the point—almost —of thinking he really will make his proposal. The turning point of decision is not explicitly stated. It is reflected as if unconsciously in the imagery and even in the grammar, particularly in the shifting between indicative and subjunctive moods of the verbs. At his most hopeful moment, thinking in the regular future tense, he asks himself how he "shall" do it. Shall he say he does not want to be lonely all his life (lines 70–72)? He thinks of those streets of "one-night cheap hotels" (lines 4–6), where "lonely men in shirt-sleeves," with no home and nothing to do but look on at other people's lives, lean out of windows smoking pipes. Shall he say he does not wish to be one of these?

In this moment he comes closest to an affirmative decision; but the very contemplation of action as something he may in real life carry out brings an extreme revulsion. Retreating, he flees in spirit to the bottom of the sea; his real self is a subhuman "pair of ragged claws," a lobster that avoids impingement of the external world by wearing its skeleton on the outside. It is an image of the essentially cold solitary spirit. Prufrock's decision is crystallized in this instant. After his flight to the bottom of the sea he ceases to think of his choice in affirmative or future indicative verbs. He thinks in subjunctive and then in "contrary to fact" constructions: "Should I . . . have the strength (lines 79–88) . . . in short, I was afraid. And would it have been worth it, after all?" (lines 89–90). So the reader knows by the tenses and moods of verbs that the possible moment has gone by. The several-times-repeated question "Would it have been worth while?" is the dying fall of Prufrock's subsided will. It leads presently to his clear recognition: "No: I am not Prince Hamlet, nor was meant to be." Even Hamlet, without much will to act, acted finally. But not Prufrock. And he is not even the center of the piece, he reminds himself. He is no hero, no prophet, but "an attendant lord"—cautious, well-intentioned, at best an adviser, at worst almost a buffoon, but in either case a man on the fringe of life. So he will accept his fate and continue as he was, keeping up appearances and taking care of himself. But love is not for him. He knows its lure, at a distance only and with its back turned: the mermaids are "riding seaward" (lines 124–126).

At the end (as occasionally earlier) Prufrock speaks again in the plural. He has been talking of himself as "I." Now he returns to the "you and I" of the opening, since his plight is not unique. He has spoken as an individual, but the world contains others like him, and most people have a touch of Prufrock. His conclusion is therefore appropriately inclusive, though still framed in terms of his own experience. In our solitude "in the chambers of the sea," he says, "we" are capable of love ("by sea-girls wreathed"), but it is only a dream love. The approach of reality wakes us from the dream ("human voices wake us"), and at the touch of the real "we drown."

This is the outline of Prufrock's monologue, and through it his hell is defined. The imagery that runs through his mind completes the picture and makes vivid for the reader both his outer and his inner life. Possibly hell is too strong a word. Certainly it is strong for the elements of Prufrock's outer life: the social boredom, the women who chatter about art, the current novels, the innumerable teas, the measuring of one's life by that least of units the after-dinner coffee spoon. The word hell is appropriate, however, for the more significant internal imagery that presents him as a man paralyzed by self-distrust and agonizing self-consciousness.

These last terms are not those in which a psychologist would explain Prufrock's malaise. Eliot, however, is not psychoanalyzing Prufrock. What he presents is what it feels like to be Prufrock, not what is wrong with him or why it is wrong.

Most of what might be called the "subjective" images are concerned with stagnation or inaction, varying degrees of ill health, and the feeling of being split in two. The tone is set immediately by the apparently outrageous image of the evening sky as "a patient etherized upon a table"—pale, stagnant, and scarcely alive. The pools in drains, the cat-like fog, and the smoke are stagnant; the evening itself "malingers," psychological malaise disguising itself as physical.

Images revealing his self-consciousness (self-consciousness, of course, is a surface term for deeper things) range from petty anxieties of everyday life—thin hair, thin arms, thin legs that "they" will notice—to the greater, when the petty fear of servants who may snicker behind his back is magnified to the universal, the "eternal Footman" (line 85). More violent images express the extremes of his self-shattering consciousness. "The eyes that fix you," pin you to the wall like an insect specimen to be stared at as it dies, ejecting its insides at both ends in its death agony (lines 55–60). And scarcely less painful is Prufrock's feeling as if his whole nervous system were exposed, projected "in patterns on a screen" to be examined (line 105). There is the split-self in the image of John the Baptist: Prufrock has "seen" his own head brought in upon a platter (lines 82–83). Finally, there is the image that brings back the initial question from Dante. Supposing he did try to make a human contact, did tell "her" he was "Lazarus, come from the dead" to tell her "all" (lines 94–98). She would not understand. What have those in hell to say that those outside could understand?

Eliot has presented a dramatic picture of a man who from the outside is correct, well dressed, over-self-conscious, perhaps a trifle pathetic and a trifle absurd. But Prufrock knows he is all this, and the acceptance of this knowledge dignifies him. Moreover, his sufferings are real and in some degree universal. Eliot presents him, sufferings and all, in a dry tone; the man himself is a dry man.

The poem is a complex one and therefore many other meanings can be extracted from it or read into it. More could be said of the superficial society in which Prufrock lives. What we have given here, however, is the main thread that holds it all together.

lines 94–95
There are Biblical accounts of two different men named Lazarus who died. One was raised from the dead. The other was not, but Abraham was asked to let him return from the dead to testify. See Luke 16 and John 11–12.

line 117
high sentence: high thoughts. The phrase is borrowed from Chaucer's description of a scholar as thin as Prufrock.

line 121
trousers rolled. Robert H. Llewellyn furnished the key to this often misunderstood detail; he noted that trousers with cuffs had recently come into fashion. The word rolled was sometimes used for this. Here (as in lines 42–43, 123) Prufrock is concerned with wearing precisely the right clothes.

line 122
Peaches used to be considered indigestible.

page 589
"Rhapsody on a Windy Night."

line 51
The moon holds no malice.

page 591
"Journey of the Magi." The quotation marks at the beginning have no significance except as an acknowledgment that Eliot is using almost word for word the language of a sermon on the Nativity by the seventeenth-century bishop Lancelot Andrewes. Eliot quoted the passage elsewhere in an essay on Andrewes, commenting on the older writer's remarkable "sentences in which, before extracting all the spiritual meaning of a text, Andrewes forces a concrete presence upon us." Perhaps this is what Eliot too does in the apparently irrelevant concrete details he gives.

The specific subject is the journey of the Magi, and the ostensible theme is Birth. Yet the poem says at least as much about Death. Perhaps the underlying theme is the painful difficulty of bringing about in oneself a deep inner change, a difficulty so great as to make the birth of a new self seem more like a death.

Wallace Stevens *pages 592–600* Stevens' poetry is often difficult, yet not literary or learned in the usual sense: it does not bristle, as Eliot's does, with literary and mythological allusions or with obscure historical references. Its obscurity is owing to the character of Stevens' own mind, which is both philosophical and concrete, as well as highly imaginative. His scenes and images are apt to cling in the memory because of their extremely specific and unexpected character and their bright color. He writes from the humanistic philosophical position as opposed to Christian doctrine, and writes often of man's "blessed rage for order," which impels the imagination to creative activity.

page 592 "Peter Quince at the Clavier." Unlike most of Stevens' work, this poem does depend on external allusions. "Peter Quince," in the self-mocking title, is the name of the boorish clown in Midsummer Night's Dream who directs the play of Pyramus and Thisbe.

The story of Susanna is told in the Apocrypha. She was a beautiful and virtuous wife who went to bathe in her garden on a hot day, meanwhile sending her maids on an errand. Two lascivious elders, who had hidden themselves in the garden, tried to seduce her by threatening her with a false accusation. She refused them; they publicly swore they had found her lying with a young man, and she was condemned to death. The prophet Daniel, however, proved that they had lied; Susanna was saved and the elders were condemned instead.

The old story of Susanna has nothing to do with music; and her maids, of course, were not Byzantines.

page 594 "Domination of Black."

line 10 The cry of the peacock, in contrast with the beauty of its plumage, is a harsh, frightening scream.

page 595 "Sunday Morning." A Sunday morning, bright, lazy, and comfortable, becomes the background of a deeply felt debate between Christian and humanist values. "She" in the midst of this brightness is haunted by the dark thought of Christ's ancient sacrifice in Palestine. The poet asks why divinity should reside only there; why not here in one's living self, in the comfort, beauty—and sufferings too—of natural, not supernatural life? The Greek religion (Stanza III) began with supernaturalism, but it brought Jove to earth to become a somewhat human god. This so satisfied man's desires that the Christian imagination also—shepherds seeing the star of Bethlehem—brought God down to earth through the story of Jesus. Should heaven not, then, be a part of natural life instead of "this dividing and indifferent blue" of a supernatural religion?

Though "she" takes pleasure in natural life, in the birds (Stanza IV) while they are present, she still longs for the absolute, the permanent (when the birds are gone, where is

Paradise?). Nothing, he answers, is as permanent as nature itself is, through the change and recurrence of life and season: no heaven, no religion "has endured/as April's green endures." "Death is the mother of beauty," he says. If there is no change, how can there be life and beauty? If the apple is eternally ripe on the tree and never falls, how can buds and blossoms come; and how can blossoms grow into fruit without themselves dying? Through a vision of sun worshipers, he foresees a natural religion for the future, a belief which will accept the transitory as the only permanent; and in the end this message seems to reach "her." A voice says that the tomb in Palestine is not the entrance into eternal life; it is the simple grave of the human Jesus. We live in the natural changing world; and this is as it should be.

page 598   *"The Idea of Order at Key West." Irrelevant associations of a Florida resort town should not be allowed to creep into the mind, for when the poem was written, Key West retained much of its earlier character of a lonely outpost of sand, sea, sky, fishing boats, an occasional freighter, a sparse town. The poem is quiet and solitary.*

"She" in this poem is of course not an actual woman and probably not even a feminine symbolic figure; "she" is the Idea of Order itself.

line 43   *Stevens said he had chosen at random two common names that proved to be the name of a real person. However, Ramon Fernandez is a modern humanist philosopher with views not altogether unlike Stevens' own.*

Robert Hayden   pages 601–609   *Hayden is a contemporary poet of great versatility, master of a wide variety of themes, moods, and styles. The first two poems of his in this volume illustrate Hayden's concern with the origins, in slavery, of America's present racial problems. His tone ranges from the bitter irony of "Middle Passage," through the more conventionally poetic, to the updated folk-comic in such poems as "Unidentified Flying Object."*

page 601   *"Middle Passage." The title is the name of one of the main transatlantic routes of ships engaged in the African slave trade.*

lines 1 & 14   *the names of slave ships.*

lines 17–19   *a bitter parody on Shakespeare's song, "Full fathom five" (p. 455).*

lines 20–21   *a similar use of the opening lines of the familiar hymn.*

line 51   *barracoons: temporary pens or barracks for slaves.*

Part II deals with the means by which traders in Africa gained possession of slaves for export.

line 71   *African place names.*

lines 76–77   *African peoples.*

page 605   *"Frederick Douglass." Son of a slave woman and an unknown white father, Douglass escaped north from Maryland, became an eloquent lecturer for the Massachusetts Anti-Slavery*

Society, wrote several autobiographical books, and eventually, some years after the Civil War, was appointed minister to Haiti. He died in 1895.

Robert Lowell   *pages* *Lowell's background is in the New England tradition of "the*
                            610–612 *Lowells and Eliots." His poetry partly represents that tradition and partly rejects its values. Whatever his attitude towards it, his poetry is almost all rooted in this tradition.*

                page 611 *"Mr. Edwards and the Spider." Jonathan Edwards (1703–1758), the first great Calvinist writer and preacher of Colonial New England, is most widely remembered for his sermon "Sinners in the Hands of an Angry God." He was also a sensitive observer of nature, and at the age of twelve or thirteen wrote the earliest known observations on the "flying," or "balloon," spider.*

                line 28 *Windsor, Connecticut, was the birthplace of Edwards.*

                line 38 *Josiah Hawley was one of his chief opponents.*

Recent Modes   *page 614* *Moore. "No Swan So Fine." For many years Marianne Moore was a librarian. Often she seems to have leafed through weekly magazines or new books as they came in, lighting here and there upon odd items that struck her fancy and sparked her pen, making her seem like a kind of squirrel collector of choice oddities. Her own notes sometimes give the source of these bits of information, and our notes here derive mainly from hers.*

"There is no water so still as the dead fountains of Versailles.'" Percy Phillip, New York Times Magazine, *10th May 1931 (M. M.'s note).*

"A pair of Louis XV candelabra with Dresden figures of swans belonging to Lord Balfour" (M. M.'s note).

                page 614 *Moore, "Sojourn in the Whale." Consider the meaning of the ironies in this poem, beginning with the title, in the light of the recent history of Ireland and England.*

                lines 3–4 *"One whom the seas love" is of course England.*

                lines *The author notes that the quotation is from the* Literary Digest
                7–13 *but gives no date or context.*

                page 615 *Moore, "To a Steam Roller."*

                lines 7–8 *The author, who more often than not quotes from ephemeral or obscure sources, does not identify this one. Her quotations, in any case, are borrowed phrases and not allusions.*

                pages *Roethke, "Elegy." cf. Dylan Thomas's elegy on a similar theme,*
                621–622 *p. 549.*

                line 1 *In the "face like a rain-beaten stone" Roethke seems to be remembering the phrase in Yeats's* The Magi *(p. 577), but here, referring to a known human face, it of course has different connotations.*

                page 627 *Ferlinghetti, "Don't Let That Horse." Ferlinghetti, Ginsberg, and Corso are representative of the San Francisco "Beat" poets who came into prominence during the 1950's.*

lines 1–3   The paintings of Marc Chagall are characterized by fantastic juxtapositions of seemingly unrelated and unnaturally placed objects such as violins or horses—or bouquets of flowers——floating in the sky.

pages
636–637   Plath, "The Colossus."

line 16   Oresteia: *the group of Greek plays dealing with the story of Agamemnon, Clytemnestra, their son and daughter, and the slain lover Aegisthus.*

The Poets:

Samuel Allen *(b. 1917)*

A. R. Ammons *(b. 1926)*

Brother Antoninus (William Everson) *(b. 1912)*

Matthew Arnold *(1822–1888)*

W. H. Auden *(b. 1907)*

Francis Bacon *(1561–1626)*

George Barker *(b. 1913)*

William Blake *(1757–1827)*

Arna Bontemps *(b. 1902)*

Robert Bridges *(1844–1930)*

Gwendolyn Brooks *(b. 1917)*

Sterling A. Brown *(b. 1901)*

Robert Browning *(1812–1889)*

Samuel Taylor Coleridge *(1772–1834)*

Gregory Corso *(b. 1930)*

William Cowper *(1731–1800)*

Stephen Crane *(1870–1900)*

e. e. cummings *(1894–1962)*

William H. Davies *(1871–1940)*

Emily Dickinson *(1830–1886)*

John Donne *(1572–1631)*

Hilda Doolittle (H.D.) *(1886–1961)*

Michael Drayton *(1563–1631)*

T. S. Eliot *(1888–1965)*

James A. Emanuel *(b. 1921)*

Abbie Huston Evans *(b. 1881)*

Lawrence Ferlinghetti *(b. 1920)*

Robert Frost *(1874–1963)*

Allen Ginsberg *(b. 1926)*

Thomas Gray *(1716–1771)*

Thom Gunn *(b. 1929)*

Thomas Hardy *(1840–1928)*

William J. Harris *(contemporary)*

Marsden Hartley *(1877–1943)*

Robert Hayden *(b. 1913)*

George Herbert *(1593–1633)*

Robert Herrick *(1591–1674)*

Gerard Manley Hopkins *(1844–1889)*

A. E. Housman *(1859–1936)*

Thomas Howell *(16th Century)*

Langston Hughes *(1902–1967)*

Ted Hughes *(b. 1930)*

T. E. Hulme *(1883–1917)*

Robinson Jeffers *(1887–1962)*

Ben Jonson *(1572–1637)*

John Keats *(1795–1821)*

Philip Larkin *(b. 1922)*

Richard Lovelace *(1618–1657)*

Robert Lowell *(b. 1917)*

Archibald MacLeish *(b. 1892)*

Louis MacNeice *(1907–1963)*

Walter de la Mare *(1873–1956)*

Christopher Marlowe *(1564–1593)*

Andrew Marvell *(1621–1678)*

Edgar Lee Masters *(1869–1950)*

John Milton *(1608–1674)*

N. Scott Momaday *(b. 1934)*

Marianne Moore *(1887–1972)*

George Peele *(1588?–1597?)*

Sylvia Plath *(1932–1963)*

Ezra Pound *(b. 1885)*

Sir Walter Ralegh *(1552–1618)*

John Crowe Ransom *(b. 1888)*

Edwin Arlington Robinson
(1869–1935)

Theodore Roethke *(1908–1962)*

Carl Sandburg *(1878–1967)*

Sir Walter Scott *(1771–1832)*

William Shakespeare
(1564–1616)

Percy Bysshe Shelley
(1792–1822)

Edith Sitwell *(1887–1964)*

Stephen Spender *(b. 1909)*

Alan Stephens *(b. 1925)*

Wallace Stevens *(1879–1955)*

Sir John Suckling *(1609–1642)*

May Swenson *(b. 1919)*

Alfred, Lord Tennyson
(1809–1892)

Dylan Thomas *(1914–1953)*

Edward Thomas *(1878–1917)*

Walt Whitman *(1819–1891)*

Reed Whittemore *(b. 1919)*

Richard Wilbur *(b. 1921)*

William Carlos Williams
(1883–1963)

George Wither *(1588–1667)*

William Wordsworth
(1770–1850)

Sir Thomas Wyatt *(1503–1542)*

William Butler Yeats
(1865–1939)

DRAMA

The Art of Reading Plays

Plays are fiction just as short stories and novels are fiction. They are not life itself but they represent life in its various aspects and implications. Because fiction can imitate, typify, explore, imply, and generalize, it may be a truer representation of life than the raw material we find in newspaper and television reports. A play differs from other forms of fiction only in its methods of representing life, not in the substance it puts before us.

A play uses actors, costumes, makeup, lights, scenery, stage furniture, music, dance. It unfolds a story vividly before our eyes and ears. This is its advantage over other forms of fiction. But it also suffers from the disadvantage that it cannot comment directly on what it represents. Everything is set before us in words, action, and pictures; we cannot read the author's stage directions while we are watching the play.

The author does indeed comment on what he is representing, but his comment is found in the material he presents and in his manner of presentation, not in what he writes about the play. More than any other writer of fiction, he must economize on words and carefully select details. He must compress everything into two or three hours of stage time and bring it all out in sharp, carefully honed dialogue that, though highly artificial in form, is yet an imitation of human conversation.

There is no accurate nomenclature for classifying plays. For the purposes of this volume we may think of plays as ranging in tone from dark to light. The dark ones we may call tragedy. Tragedy, which faces up to human catastrophe, which "builds its shining citadel in the very centre of the enemy's country" (the words are Bertrand Russell's), lays stress on death as something imminent and inevitable, or as the end of a life filled with frustration, disappointment, disillusion.

Plays in the middle range present life as a thing of mixed or alternating sorrow and pleasure. Some of these we call tragicomedies; others, those that discuss certain specific problems or preoccupations or ideas, we call problem plays.

Comedies are at the lighter end of our tonal range. The essence of comedy is humor. It may be the intellectual verbal humor called wit. It may be found in the comedy of manners, with its mild ridicule of upper-class peculiarities; in satire, where the ridicule of human affairs becomes barbed; in situation comedy, which is the bringing together of incongruous characters in unlikely situations; or in farce, which usually depends on bodily humor, sometimes gross and ribald.

No matter the type of play, whenever it combines for us the pleasures of costume, lights, music, a few properties, and scenery, together with the power of human speech, we experience the genuine thrill of the theater. It is a unique feeling, one never to be forgotten.

We should not forego an opportunity to see a good play well performed, but we should also acquire a taste for reading plays. Sometimes, as with Antigone and Othello, we cannot well understand what we are seeing on the stage without previous study. Further, a play makes enjoyable reading because it presents a direct and economical version of its story. Finally, with a few hints from the playwright the reader can set the stage himself, clothe the characters in such costumes as he will, and read the speeches to himself with all the emphasis of which he is capable.

He can see the play in his mind's eye, hear it in his mind's ear.

Oedipus, King of Thebes, had the misfortune unknowingly to kill his father and marry his mother. When he discovered this, he put out his eyes and exiled himself. His wife/mother, Jocasta, committed suicide. Oedipus and Jocasta had two sons and two daughters. One son led an expedition against Thebes, now under the rule of Jocasta's brother, King Creon. As the present play, Antigone, opens, both sons are dead, but the disloyal son lies unburied outside the city. His sister, Antigone, is confronted with the same dilemma that many in our time feel they face: shall she obey a wicked decree promulgated by arrogant and arbitrary authority or shall she destroy herself in opposing it?

All plays are best performed, or at least visualized, in the kind of theater for which they were written. The ancient Greek theater in which Antigone *was originally performed had a bare, circular stage with a building to the rear and entrances left and right. The audience, perhaps as many as 15,000, sat on stone seats arranged in rows on a hillside, the whole not unlike the closed end of a large modern football stadium. The actors wore shoes that increased their height and masks that amplified their voices. The Chorus commented on the events of the play. Their leader, Choragos, also commented on the action and sometimes engaged in dialogue with the actors.*

Greek plays, religious in origin and spirit, were performed as part of an annual religious festival. The basic material of the plays was known to the audience. It was drawn from the stories of the Greek past: incidents connected with the Trojan War, for example, or King Agamemnon's return to his home after the war.

One aim of the playwright was to retell an incident in a new way without changing the essential story. Since religion and the state were but two aspects of the highly unified Greek culture, the citizen of Athens went to the plays not merely for excitement and intellectual diversion but also in a spirit of pious patriotism or patriotic piety. It was as though nowadays Americans would go to the theater early in the morning of an annual civic Play Week to see, that day, three tragedies on the landing of the Pilgrims at Plymouth, Washington at Valley Forge, and the assassination of Lincoln, plus one comedy on Rip Van Winkle.

Writers of the Greek tragedies discussed in their plays the profoundest questions of ethics and morality. Their underlying subject was the relation of man to the gods, or, as we might say today, the place of man in the universe. But since mankind has always considered ethics a part of religion, the Greek plays had much to say about how a human being should conduct his life. Thus Antigone is a story of one frail woman going to her death because she is convinced that the state, her opponent, is both tyrannical and immoral. In all but the circumstances and customs of performance, this is a modern play.

Note   An asterisk (*) before a title signifies that notes, problems, or questions on that play can be found in the supplementary material beginning on page 1111

*ANTIGONE

SOPHOCLES

*An English Version by Dudley
Fitts and Robert Fitzgerald*

SYNOPSIS

PROLOGUE	(Antigone, Ismene)	ODE III	(Chorus)
PARODOS	(Chorus)	SCENE IV	(Antigone, Creon, Chorus)
SCENE I	(Creon, Sentry, Chorus)	ODE IV	(Chorus)
ODE I	(Chorus)	SCENE V	(Teiresias, Creon, Chorus)
SCENE II	(Sentry, Creon, Antigone, Ismene, Chorus)	PAEAN	(Chorus)
ODE II	(Chorus)	EXODOS	(Messenger, Creon, Eurydice, Chorus)
SCENE III	(Haimon, Creon, Chorus)		

PERSONS REPRESENTED

ANTIGONE	TEIRESIAS
ISMENE	A SENTRY
EURYDICE	A MESSENGER
CREON	CHORUS
HAIMON	

SCENE

Before the palace of CREON, King of Thebes. A central double door, and two lateral doors. A platform extends the length of the façade, and from this platform three steps lead down into the "orchestra," or chorus-ground.   TIME: dawn of the day after the repulse of the Argive army from the assault on Thebes.

PROLOGUE

(ANTIGONE *and* ISMENE *enter from the central door of the Palace.*)

ANTIGONE   Ismene, dear sister,
You would think that we had already suffered enough
For the curse on Oedipus:
I cannot imagine any grief
That you and I have not gone through. And now—
Have they told you of the new decree of our King Creon?

ISMENE	I have heard nothing: I know
	That two sisters lost two brothers, a double death
	In a single hour; and I know that the Argive army
	Fled in the night; but beyond this, nothing.

ANTIGONE	I thought so. And that is why I wanted you
	To come out here with me. There is something we must do.

ISMENE	Why do you speak so strangely?

ANTIGONE	Listen, Ismene:
	Creon buried our brother Eteocles
	With military honors, gave him a soldier's funeral,
	And it was right that he should; but Polyneices,
	Who fought as bravely and died as miserably,—
	They say that Creon has sworn
	No one shall bury him, no one mourn for him,
	But his body must lie in the fields, a sweet treasure
	For carrion birds to find as they search for food.
	That is what they say, and our good Creon is coming here
	To announce it publicly; and the penalty—
	Stoning to death in the public square!

There it is,

And now you can prove what you are:
A true sister, or a traitor to your family.

ISMENE	Antigone, you are mad! What could I possibly do?

ANTIGONE	You must decide whether you will help me or not.

ISMENE	I do not understand you. Help you in what?

ANTIGONE	Ismene, I am going to bury him. Will you come?

ISMENE	Bury him! You have just said the new law forbids it.

ANTIGONE	He is my brother. And he is your brother, too.

ISMENE	But think of the danger! Think what Creon will do!

ANTIGONE	Creon is not strong enough to stand in my way.

ISMENE	Ah sister!
	Oedipus died, everyone hating him
	For what his own search brought to light, his eyes
	Ripped out by his own hand; and Iocaste died,
	His mother and wife at once: she twisted the cords
	That strangled her life; and our two brothers died,
	Each killed by the other's sword. And we are left:
	But oh, Antigone,
	Think how much more terrible than these
	Our own death would be if we should go against Creon
	And do what he has forbidden! We are only women,

We cannot fight with men, Antigone!
The law is strong, we must give in to the law
In this thing, and in worse. I beg the Dead
To forgive me, but I am helpless: I must yield
To those in authority. And I think it is dangerous business
To be always meddling.

ANTIGONE   If that is what you think,
I should not want you, even if you asked to come.
You have made your choice, you can be what you want to be.
But I will bury him; and if I must die,
I say that this crime is holy: I shall lie down
With him in death, and I shall be as dear
To him as he to me.
                          It is the dead,
Not the living, who make the longest demands:
We die for ever . . .
                          You may do as you like,
Since apparently the laws of the gods mean nothing to you.

ISMENE   They mean a great deal to me; but I have no strength
To break laws that were made for the public good.

ANTIGONE   That must be your excuse, I suppose. But as for me,
I will bury the brother I love.

ISMENE   Antigone,
I am so afraid for you!

ANTIGONE   You need not be:
You have yourself to consider, after all.

ISMENE   But no one must hear of this, you must tell no one!
I will keep it a secret, I promise!

ANTIGONE   Oh, tell it! Tell everyone!
Think how they'll hate you when it all comes out
If they learn that you knew about it all the time!

ISMENE   So fiery! You should be cold with fear.

ANTIGONE   Perhaps. But I am doing only what I must.

ISMENE   But can you do it? I say that you cannot.

ANTIGONE   Very well: when my strength gives out, I shall do no more.

ISMENE   Impossible things should not be tried at all.

ANTIGONE   Go away, Ismene:
I shall be hating you soon, and the dead will too,
For your words are hateful. Leave me my foolish plan:

I am not afraid of the danger; if it means death,
It will not be the worst of deaths—death without honor.

ISMENE   Go then, if you feel that you must.
You are unwise,
But a loyal friend indeed to those who love you.

(Exit into the Palace. ANTIGONE *goes off, L. Enter the* CHORUS.*)*

PARODOS

CHORUS   Now the long blade of the sun, lying   (STROPHE 1)
Level east to west, touches with glory
Thebes of the Seven Gates. Open, unlidded
Eye of golden day! O marching light
Across the eddy and rush of Dirce's stream,
Striking the white shields of the enemy
Thrown headlong backward from the blaze of morning!

CHORAGOS   Polyneices their commander
Roused them with windy phrases,
He the wild eagle screaming
Insults above our land,
His wings their shields of snow,
His crest their marshalled helms.

CHORUS   Against our seven gates in a yawning ring   (ANTISTROPHE 1)
The famished spears came onward in the night;
But before his jaws were sated with our blood,
Or pinefire took the garland of our towers,
He was thrown back; and as he turned, great Thebes—
No tender victim for his noisy power—
Rose like a dragon behind him, shouting war.

CHORAGOS   For God hates utterly
The bray of bragging tongues;
And when he beheld their smiling,
Their swagger of golden helms,
The frown of his thunder blasted
Their first man from our walls.

CHORUS   We heard his shout of triumph high in the air   (STROPHE 2)
Turn to a scream; far out in a flaming arc
He fell with his windy torch, and the earth struck him.
And others storming in fury no less than his
Found shock of death in the dusty joy of battle.

CHORAGOS   Seven captains at seven gates
Yielded their clanging arms to the god
That bends the battle-line and breaks it.

These two only, brothers in blood,
Face to face in matchless rage,
Mirroring each the other's death,
Clashed in long combat.

CHORUS But now in the beautiful morning of victory   (ANTISTROPHE 2)
Let Thebes of the many chariots sing for joy!
With hearts for dancing we'll take leave of war:
Our temples shall be sweet with hymns of praise,
And the long night shall echo with our chorus.

SCENE I

CHORAGOS But now at last our new King is coming:
Creon of Thebes, Menoikeus' son.
In this auspicious dawn of his reign
What are the new complexities
That shifting Fate has woven for him?
What is his counsel? Why has he summoned
The old men to hear him?

(*Enter* CREON *from the Palace, C. He addresses the* CHORUS *from the top step.*)

CREON Gentlemen: I have the honor to inform you that our Ship of
State, which recent storms have threatened to destroy, has
come safely to harbor at last, guided by the merciful wisdom
of Heaven. I have summoned you here this morning because I
know that I can depend upon you: your devotion to King Laïos
was absolute; you never hesitated in your duty to our late ruler
Oedipus; and when Oedipus died, your loyalty was transferred
to his children. Unfortunately, as you know, his two sons, the
princes Eteocles and Polyneices, have killed each other in
battle; and I, as the next in blood, have succeeded to the full
power of the throne.

I am aware, of course, that no Ruler can expect complete
loyalty from his subjects until he has been tested in office.
Nevertheless, I say to you at the very outset that I have nothing
but contempt for the kind of Governor who is afraid, for whatever reason, to follow the course that he knows is best for the
State; and as for the man who sets private friendship above the
public welfare,—I have no use for him, either. I call God to
witness that if I saw my country headed for ruin, I should not
be afraid to speak out plainly; and I need hardly remind you
that I would never have any dealings with an enemy of the
people. No one values friendship more highly than I; but we
must remember that friends made at the risk of wrecking our
Ship are not real friends at all.

These are my principles, at any rate, and that is why I have made the following decision concerning the sons of Oedipus: Eteocles, who died as a man should die, fighting for his country, is to be buried with full military honors, with all the ceremony that is usual when the greatest heroes die; but his brother Polyneices, who broke his exile to come back with fire and sword against his native city and the shrines of his fathers' gods, whose one idea was to spill the blood of his blood and sell his own people into slavery—Polyneices, I say, is to have no burial: no man is to touch him or say the least prayer for him; he shall lie on the plain, unburied; and the birds and the scavenging dogs can do with him whatever they like.

This is my command, and you can see the wisdom behind it. As long as I am King, no traitor is going to be honored with the loyal man. But whoever shows by word and deed that he is on the side of the State,—he shall have my respect while he is living, and my reverence when he is dead.

CHORAGOS   If that is your will, Creon son of Menoikeus,
You have the right to enforce it: we are yours.

CREON   That is my will. Take care that you do your part.

CHORAGOS   We are old men: let the younger ones carry it out.

CREON   I do not mean that: the sentries have been appointed.

CHORAGOS   Then what is it that you would have us do?

CREON   You will give no support to whoever breaks this law.

CHORAGOS   Only a crazy man is in love with death!

CREON   And death it is; yet money talks, and the wisest
Have sometimes been known to count a few coins too many.

(Enter SENTRY *from L.)*

SENTRY   I'll not say that I'm out of breath from running, King, because every time I stopped to think about what I have to tell you, I felt like going back. And all the time a voice kept saying, "You fool, don't you know you're walking straight into trouble?"; and then another voice: "Yes, but if you let somebody else get the news to Creon first, it will be even worse than that for you!" But good sense won out, at least I hope it was good sense, and here I am with a story that makes no sense at all; but I'll tell it anyhow, because, as they say, what's going to happen's going to happen, and—

CREON   Come to the point. What have you to say?

SENTRY   I did not do it. I did not see who did it. You must not punish me for what someone else has done.

CREON   A comprehensive defense! More effective, perhaps,
               If I knew its purpose. Come: what is it?

SENTRY   A dreadful thing . . . I don't know how to put it—

CREON   Out with it!

SENTRY   Well, then;
               The dead man—
                                 Polyneices—
               (Pause. The SENTRY is overcome, fumbles for words. CREON waits impassively.)
                                               out there—
                                                     someone,—
               New dust on the slimy flesh!
               (Pause. No sign from CREON)
                       Someone has given it burial that way, and
               Gone . . .
               (Long pause. CREON finally speaks with deadly control.)

CREON   And the man who dared do this?

SENTRY   I swear I
               Do not know! You must believe me!
                                           Listen:
               The ground was dry, not a sign of digging, no,
               Not a wheeltrack in the dust, no trace of anyone.
               It was when they relieved us this morning: and one of them,
               The corporal, pointed to it.
                                     There it was,
               The strangest—
                       Look:
               The body, just mounded over with light dust: you see?
               Not buried really, but as if they'd covered it
               Just enough for the ghost's peace. And no sign
               Of dogs or any wild animal that had been there.

               And then what a scene there was! Every man of us
               Accusing the other: we all proved the other man did it,
               We all had proof that we could not have done it.
               We were ready to take hot iron in our hands,
               Walk through fire, swear by all the gods,
               It was not I!
               I do not know who it was, but it was not I!
               (CREON's rage has been mounting steadily, but the SENTRY is too intent upon his story
               to notice it.)   And then, when this came to nothing, someone said
               A thing that silenced us and made us stare
               Down at the ground: you had to be told the news,
               And one of us had to do it! We threw the dice,
               And the bad luck fell on me. So here I am,
               No happier to be here than you are to have me:
               Nobody likes the man who brings bad news.

CHORAGOS I have been wondering, King: can it be that the gods have done this?

CREON Stop!
(*Furiously*) Must you doddering wrecks
Go out of your heads entirely? "The gods!"
Intolerable!
The gods favor this corpse? Why? How had he served them?
Tried to loot their temples, burn their images,
Yes, and the whole State, and its laws with it!
Is it your senile opinion that the gods love to honor bad men?
A pious thought!—
No, from the very beginning
There have been those who have whispered together,
Stiff-necked anarchists, putting their heads together,
Scheming against me in alleys. These are the men,
And they have bribed my own guard to do this thing.

(*Sententiously*) Money!
There's nothing in the world so demoralizing as money.
Down go your cities,
Homes gone, men gone, honest hearts corrupted,
Crookedness of all kinds, and all for money!
(*To* SENTRY) But you—!
I swear by God and by the throne of God,
The man who has done this thing shall pay for it!
Find that man, bring him here to me, or your death
Will be the least of your problems: I'll string you up
Alive, and there will be certain ways to make you
Discover your employer before you die;
And the process may teach you a lesson you seem to have
     missed:
The dearest profit is sometimes all too dear:
That depends on the source. Do you understand me?
A fortune won is often misfortune.

SENTRY King, may I speak?

CREON Your very voice distresses me.

SENTRY Are you sure that it is my voice, and not your conscience?

CREON By God, he wants to analyze me now!

SENTRY It is not what I say, but what has been done, that hurts you.

CREON You talk too much.

SENTRY Maybe; but I've done nothing.

CREON Sold your soul for some silver: that's all you've done.

SENTRY How dreadful it is when the right judge judges wrong!

CREON   Your figures of speech
               May entertain you now; but unless you bring me the man,
               You will get little profit from them in the end.
          (*Exit* CREON *into the Palace.*)

SENTRY   "Bring me the man"—!
               I'd like nothing better than bringing him the man!
               But bring him or not, you have seen the last of me here.
               At any rate, I am safe!
          (*Exit* SENTRY)

ODE 1

CHORUS   Numberless are the world's wonders, but none   (STROPHE 1)
               More wonderful than man; the stormgray sea
               Yields to his prows, the huge crests bear him high;
               Earth, holy and inexhaustible, is graven
               With shining furrows where his plows have gone
               Year after year, the timeless labor of stallions.

                                                          (ANTISTROPHE 1)
               The lightboned birds and beasts that cling to cover,
               The lithe fish lighting their reaches of dim water,
               All are taken, tamed in the net of his mind;
               The lion on the hill, the wild horse windy-maned,
               Resign to him; and his blunt yoke has broken
               The sultry shoulders of the mountain bull.

               Words also, and thought as rapid as air,   (STROPHE 2)
               He fashions to his good use; statecraft is his,
               And his the skill that deflects the arrows of snow,
               The spears of winter rain: from every wind
               He has made himself secure—from all but one:
               In the late wind of death he cannot stand.

                                                          (ANTISTROPHE 2)
               O clear intelligence, force beyond all measure!
               O fate of man, working both good and evil!
               When the laws are kept, how proudly his city stands!
               When the laws are broken, what of his city then?
               Never may the anarchic man find rest at my hearth,
               Never be it said that my thoughts are his thoughts.

SCENE II

          (*Re-enter* SENTRY *leading* ANTIGONE)

CHORAGOS   What does this mean? Surely this captive woman
               Is the Princess, Antigone. Why should she be taken?

SENTRY   Here is the one who did it! We caught her
           In the very act of burying him.—Where is Creon?

CHORAGOS   Just coming from the house.
  (Enter CREON, C.)

CREON   What has happened?
           Why have you come back so soon?

SENTRY   O King,
  (Expansively) A man should never be too sure of anything:
           I would have sworn
           That you'd not see me here again: your anger
           Frightened me so, and the things you threatened me with;
           But how could I tell then
           That I'd be able to solve the case so soon?

           No dice-throwing this time: I was only too glad to come!

           Here is this woman. She is the guilty one:
           We found her trying to bury him.
           Take her, then; question her; judge her as you will.
           I am through with the whole thing now, and glad of it.

CREON   But this is Antigone! Why have you brought her here?

SENTRY   She was burying him, I tell you!

CREON
  (Severely)   Is this the truth?

SENTRY   I saw her with my own eyes. Can I say more?

CREON   The details: come, tell me quickly!

SENTRY   It was like this:
           After those terrible threats of yours, King,
           We went back and brushed the dust away from the body.
           The flesh was soft by now, and stinking,
           So we sat on a hill to windward and kept guard.
           No napping this time! We kept each other awake.
           But nothing happened until the white round sun
           Whirled in the center of the round sky over us:
           Then, suddenly,
           A storm of dust roared up from the earth, and the sky
           Went out, the plain vanished with all its trees
           In the stinging dark. We closed our eyes and endured it.
           The whirlwind lasted a long time, but it passed;
           And then we looked, and there was Antigone!
           I have seen
           A mother bird come back to a stripped nest, heard
           Her crying bitterly a broken note or two
           For the young ones stolen. Just so, when this girl

Found the bare corpse, and all her love's work wasted,
She wept, and cried on heaven to damn the hands
That had done this thing.
                              And then she brought more dust
And sprinkled wine three times for her brother's ghost.

We ran and took her at once. She was not afraid,
Not even when we charged her with what she had done.
She denied nothing.
                              And this was a comfort to me,
And some uneasiness: for it is a good thing
To escape from death, but it is no great pleasure
To bring death to a friend.
                              Yet I always say
There is nothing so comfortable as your own safe skin!

CREON
(*Slowly, dangerously*)
                    And you, Antigone,
                    You with your head hanging,—do you confess this thing?

ANTIGONE   I do. I deny nothing.

CREON
(*To* SENTRY)   You may go.
(*Exit* SENTRY)
(*To* ANTIGONE)
                    Tell me, tell me briefly:
                    Had you heard my proclamation touching this matter?

ANTIGONE   It was public. Could I help hearing it?

CREON   And yet you dared defy the law.

ANTIGONE   I dared.
            It was not God's proclamation. That final Justice
            That rules the world below makes no such laws.

            Your edict, King, was strong,
            But all your strength is weakness itself against
            The immortal unrecorded laws of God.
            They are not merely now: they were, and shall be,
            Operative for ever, beyond man utterly.

            I knew I must die, even without your decree:
            I am only mortal. And if I must die
            Now, before it is my time to die,
            Surely this is no hardship: can anyone
            Living, as I live, with evil all about me,
            Think Death less than a friend? This death of mine
            Is of no importance; but if I had left my brother
            Lying in death unburied, I should have suffered.

Now I do not.
                        You smile at me. Ah Creon,
Think me a fool, if you like; but it may well be
That a fool convicts me of folly.

CHORAGOS   Like father, like daughter: both headstrong, deaf to reason!
She has never learned to yield.

CREON   She has much to learn.
The inflexible heart breaks first, the toughest iron
Cracks first, and the wildest horses bend their necks
At the pull of the smallest curb.
                                      Pride? In a slave?
This girl is guilty of a double insolence,
Breaking the given laws and boasting of it.
Who is the man here,
She or I, if this crime goes unpunished?
Sister's child, or more than sister's child,
Or closer yet in blood—she and her sister
Win bitter death for this!

(To SERVANTS)   Go, some of you,
Arrest Ismene. I accuse her equally.
Bring her: you will find her sniffling in the house there.

Her mind's a traitor: crimes kept in the dark
Cry for light, and the guardian brain shudders;
But how much worse than this
Is brazen boasting of barefaced anarchy!

ANTIGONE   Creon, what more do you want than my death?

CREON   Nothing.
That gives me everything.

ANTIGONE   Then I beg you: kill me.
This talking is a great weariness: your words
Are distasteful to me, and I am sure that mine
Seem so to you. And yet they should not seem so:
I should have praise and honor for what I have done.
All these men here would praise me
Were their lips not frozen shut with fear of you.

(Bitterly)   Ah the good fortune of kings,
Licensed to say and do whatever they please!

CREON   You are alone here in that opinion.

ANTIGONE   No, they are with me. But they keep their tongues in leash.

CREON   Maybe. But you are guilty, and they are not.

ANTIGONE   There is no guilt in reverence for the dead.

CREON	But Eteocles—was he not your brother too?
ANTIGONE	My brother too.
CREON	And you insult his memory?
ANTIGONE *(Softly)*	The dead man would not say that I insult it.
CREON	He would: for you honor a traitor as much as him.
ANTIGONE	His own brother, traitor or not, and equal in blood.
CREON	He made war on his country. Eteocles defended it.
ANTIGONE	Nevertheless, there are honors due all the dead.
CREON	But not the same for the wicked as for the just.
ANTIGONE	Ah Creon, Creon, Which of us can say what the gods hold wicked?
CREON	An enemy is an enemy, even dead.
ANTIGONE	It is my nature to join in love, not hate.
CREON *(Finally losing patience)*	Go join them, then; if you must have your love, Find it in hell!
CHORAGOS *(Enter ISMENE, guarded)*	But see, Ismene comes: Those tears are sisterly, the cloud That shadows her eyes rains down gentle sorrow.
CREON	You too, Ismene, Snake in my ordered house, sucking my blood Stealthily—and all the time I never knew That these two sisters were aiming at my throne! Ismene, Do you confess your share in this crime, or deny it? Answer me.
ISMENE	Yes, if she will let me say so. I am guilty.
ANTIGONE *(Coldly)*	No, Ismene. You have no right to say so. You would not help me, and I will not have you help me.
ISMENE	But now I know what you meant; and I am here To join you, to take my share of punishment.
ANTIGONE	The dead man and the gods who rule the dead Know whose act this was. Words are not friends.
ISMENE	Do you refuse me, Antigone? I want to die with you: I too have a duty that I must discharge to the dead.

ANTIGONE	You shall not lessen my death by sharing it.
ISMENE	What do I care for life when you are dead?
ANTIGONE	Ask Creon. You're always hanging on his opinions.
ISMENE	You are laughing at me. Why, Antigone?
ANTIGONE	It's a joyless laughter, Ismene.
ISMENE	But can I do nothing?
ANTIGONE	Yes. Save yourself. I shall not envy you. There are those who will praise you; I shall have honor, too.
ISMENE	But we are equally guilty!
ANTIGONE	No more, Ismene. You are alive, but I belong to Death.

CREON
(*To the* CHORUS)
        Gentlemen, I beg you to observe these girls:
        One has just now lost her mind; the other,
        It seems, has never had a mind at all.

ISMENE	Grief teaches the steadiest minds to waver, King.
CREON	Yours certainly did, when you assumed guilt with the guilty!
ISMENE	But how could I go on living without her?
CREON	You are. She is already dead.
ISMENE	But your own son's bride!
CREON	There are places enough for him to push his plow. I want no wicked women for my sons!
ISMENE	O dearest Haimon, how your father wrongs you!
CREON	I've had enough of your childish talk of marriage!
CHORAGOS	Do you really intend to steal this girl from your son?
CREON	No; Death will do that for me.
CHORAGOS	Then she must die?

CREON
(*Ironically*)   You dazzle me.
           —But enough of this talk!
(*To* GUARDS) You, there, take them away and guard them well:
        For they are but women, and even brave men run
        When they see Death coming.
(*Exeunt* ISMENE, ANTIGONE, *and* GUARDS)

ODE II

(STROPHE 1)

CHORUS   Fortunate is the man who has never tasted God's vengeance!
            Where once the anger of heaven has struck, that house is
                shaken
            For ever: damnation rises behind each child
            Like a wave cresting out of the black northeast,
            When the long darkness under sea roars up
            And bursts drumming death upon the windwhipped sand.

                                                    (ANTISTROPHE 1)
            I have seen this gathering sorrow from time long past
            Loom upon Oedipus' children: generation from generation
            Takes the compulsive rage of the enemy god.
            So lately this last flower of Oedipus' line
            Drank the sunlight! but now a passionate word
            And a handful of dust have closed up all its beauty.

                What mortal arrogance   (STROPHE 2)
                Transcends the wrath of Zeus?
            Sleep cannot lull him, nor the effortless long months
            Of the timeless gods: but he is young for ever,
            And his house is the shining day of high Olympos.
                All that is and shall be,
                And all the past, is his.
            No pride on earth is free of the curse of heaven.

                The straying dreams of men   (ANTISTROPHE 2)
                May bring them ghosts of joy:
            But as they drowse, the waking embers burn them;
            Or they walk with fixed eyes, as blind men walk.
            But the ancient wisdom speaks for our own time:
                Fate works most for woe
                With Folly's fairest show.
            Man's little pleasure is the spring of sorrow.

SCENE III

CHORAGOS   But here is Haimon, King, the last of all your sons.
            Is it grief for Antigone that brings him here,
            And bitterness at being robbed of his bride?

(*Enter* HAIMON)

CREON   We shall soon see, and no need of diviners.
                                                    —Son,
            You have heard my final judgment on that girl:
            Have you come here hating me, or have you come
            With deference and with love, whatever I do?

HAIMON   I am your son, father. You are my guide.
             You make things clear for me, and I obey you.
             No marriage means more to me than your continuing wisdom.

CREON   Good. That is the way to behave: subordinate
             Everything else, my son, to your father's will.
             This is what a man prays for, that he may get
             Sons attentive and dutiful in his house,
             Each one hating his father's enemies,
             Honoring his father's friends. But if his sons
             Fail him, if they turn out unprofitably,
             What has he fathered but trouble for himself
             And amusement for the malicious?

                                          So you are right
             Not to lose your head over this woman.
             Your pleasure with her would soon grow cold, Haimon,
             And then you'd have a hellcat in bed and elsewhere.
             Let her find her husband in Hell!
             Of all the people in this city, only she
             Has had contempt for my law and broken it.

             Do you want me to show myself weak before the people?
             Or to break my sworn word? No, and I will not.
             The woman dies.
             I suppose she'll plead "family ties." Well, let her.
             If I permit my own family to rebel,
             How shall I earn the world's obedience?
             Show me the man who keeps his house in hand,
             He's fit for public authority.

                                          I'll have no dealings
             With law-breakers, critics of the government:
             Whoever is chosen to govern should be obeyed—
             Must be obeyed, in all things, great and small,
             Just and unjust! O Haimon,
             The man who knows how to obey, and that man only,
             Knows how to give commands when the time comes.
             You can depend on him, no matter how fast
             The spears come: he's a good soldier, he'll stick it out.

             Anarchy, anarchy! Show me a greater evil!
             This is why cities tumble and the great houses rain down,
             This is what scatters armies!

             No, no: good lives are made so by discipline.
             We keep the laws then, and the lawmakers,
             And no woman shall seduce us. If we must lose,
             Let's lose to a man, at least! Is a woman stronger than we?

CHORAGOS   Unless time has rusted my wits,
             What you say, King, is said with point and dignity.

SOPHOCLES / Antigone   **693**

HAIMON

(*Boyishly earnest*)

Father:

Reason is God's crowning gift to man, and you are right
To warn me against losing mine. I cannot say—
I hope that I shall never want to say!—that you
Have reasoned badly. Yet there are other men
Who can reason, too; and their opinions might be helpful.
You are not in a position to know everything
That people say or do, or what they feel:
Your temper terrifies them—everyone
Will tell you only what you like to hear.
But I, at any rate, can listen; and I have heard them
Muttering and whispering in the dark about this girl.
They say no woman has ever, so unreasonably,
Died so shameful a death for a generous act:
"She covered her brother's body. It this indecent?
She kept him from dogs and vultures. Is this a crime?
Death?—She should have all the honor that we can give her!"

This is the way they talk out there in the city.

You must believe me:
Nothing is closer to me than your happiness.
What could be closer? Must not any son
Value his father's fortune as his father does his?
I beg you, do not be unchangeable:
Do not believe that you alone can be right.
The man who thinks that,
The man who maintains that only he has the power
To reason correctly, the gift to speak, the soul—
A man like that, when you know him, turns out empty.

It is not reason never to yield to reason!

In flood time you can see how some trees bend,
And because they bend, even their twigs are safe,
While stubborn trees are torn up, roots and all.
And the same thing happens in sailing:
Make your sheet fast, never slacken,—and over you go,
Head over heels and under: and there's your voyage.
Forget you are angry! Let yourself be moved!
I know I am young; but please let me say this:
The ideal condition
Would be, I admit, that men should be right by instinct;
But since we are all too likely to go astray,
The reasonable thing is to learn from those who can teach.

CHORAGOS   You will do well to listen to him, King,

If what he says is sensible. And you, Haimon,
Must listen to your father.—Both speak well.

CREON   You consider it right for a man of my years and experience
            To go to school to a boy?

HAIMON   It is not right
            If I am wrong. But if I am young, and right,
            What does my age matter?

CREON   You think it right to stand up for an anarchist?

HAIMON   Not at all. I pay no respect to criminals.

CREON   Then she is not a criminal?

HAIMON   The City would deny it, to a man.

CREON   And the City proposes to teach me how to rule?

HAIMON   Ah. Who is it that's talking like a boy now?

CREON   My voice is the one voice giving orders in this City!

HAIMON   It is no City if it takes orders from one voice.

CREON   The State is the King!

HAIMON
    (Pause)   Yes, if the State is a desert.
CREON   This boy, it seems, has sold out to a woman.

HAIMON   If you are a woman: my concern is only for you.

CREON   So? Your "concern"! In a public brawl with your father!

HAIMON   How about you, in a public brawl with justice?

CREON   With justice, when all that I do is within my rights?

HAIMON   You have no right to trample on God's right.

CREON
    (Completely out of control)
            Fool, adolescent fool! Taken in by a woman!

HAIMON   You'll never see me taken in by anything vile.

CREON   Every word you say is for her!

HAIMON
    (Quietly, darkly)   And for you.
            And for me. And for the gods under the earth.

CREON   You'll never marry her while she lives.

HAIMON   Then she must die.—But her death will cause another.

CREON   Another?
            Have you lost your senses? Is this an open threat?

HAIMON	There is no threat in speaking to emptiness.
CREON	I swear you'll regret this superior tone of yours! You are the empty one!
HAIMON	If you were not my father, I'd say you were perverse.
CREON	You girlstruck fool, don't play at words with me!
HAIMON	I am sorry. You prefer silence.
CREON	Now, by God—! I swear, by all the gods in heaven above us, You'll watch it, I swear you shall!
(To the SERVANTS)	Bring her out! Bring the woman out! Let her die before his eyes! Here, this instant, with her bridegroom beside her!
HAIMON	Not here, no; she will not die here, King. And you will never see my face again. Go on raving as long as you've a friend to endure you.
(Exit HAIMON)	
CHORAGOS	Gone, gone. Creon, a young man in a rage is dangerous!
CREON	Let him do, or dream to do, more than a man can. He shall not save these girls from death.
CHORAGOS	These girls? You have sentenced them both?
CREON	No, you are right. I will not kill the one whose hands are clean.
CHORAGOS	But Antigone?
CREON (Somberly)	I will carry her far away Out there in the wilderness, and lock her Living in a vault of stone. She shall have food, As the custom is, to absolve the State of her death. And then let her pray to the gods of hell: They are her only gods: Perhaps they will show her an escape from death, Or she may learn, though late, That piety shown the dead is pity in vain.
(Exit CREON)	

ODE III

CHORUS
Love, unconquerable   (STROPHE)
Waster of rich men, keeper
Of warm lights and all-night vigil
In the soft face of a girl:
Sea-wanderer, forest-visitor!
Even the pure Immortals cannot escape you,
And mortal man, in his one day's dusk,
Trembles before your glory.

Surely you swerve upon ruin   (ANTISTROPHE)
The just man's consenting heart,
As here you have made bright anger
Strike between father and son—
And none has conquered but Love!
A girl's glance working the will of heaven:
Pleasure to her alone who mocks us,
Merciless Aphrodite.

SCENE IV

CHORAGOS
(As ANTIGONE enters, guarded)
But I can no longer stand in awe of this,
Nor, seeing what I see, keep back my tears.
Here is Antigone, passing to that chamber
Where all find sleep at last.

ANTIGONE
Look upon me, friends, and pity me   (STROPHE 1)
Turning back at the night's edge to say
Good-by to the sun that shines for me no longer;
Now sleepy Death
Summons me down to Acheron, that cold shore:
There is no bridesong there, nor any music.

CHORUS
Yet not unpraised, not without a kind of honor,
You walk at last into the underworld;
Untouched by sickness, broken by no sword.
What woman has ever found your way to death?

ANTIGONE
How often I have heard the story of Niobe,   (ANTISTROPHE 1)
Tantalos' wretched daughter, how the stone
Clung fast about her, ivy-close: and they say
The rain falls endlessly
And sifting soft snow; her tears are never done.
I feel the loneliness of her death in mine.

CHORUS But she was born of heaven, and you
 Are woman, woman-born. If her death is yours,
 A mortal woman's, is this not for you
 Glory in our world and in the world beyond?

ANTIGONE You laugh at me. Ah, friends, friends,   (STROPHE 2)
 Can you not wait until I am dead? O Thebes,
 O men many-charioted, in love with Fortune,
 Dear springs of Dirce, sacred Theban grove,
 Be witnesses for me, denied all pity,
 Unjustly judged! and think a word of love
 For whose path turns
 Under dark earth, where there are no more tears.

CHORUS You have passed beyond human daring and come at last
 Into a place of stone where Justice sits.
 I cannot tell
 What shape of your father's guilt appears in this.

ANTIGONE You have touched it at last: that bridal bed   (ANTISTROPHE 2)
 Unspeakable, horror of son and mother mingling:
 Their crime, infection of all our family!
 O Oedipus, father and brother!
 Your marriage strikes from the grave to murder mine.
 I have been a stranger here in my own land:
 All my life
 The blasphemy of my birth has followed me.

CHORUS Reverence is a virtue, but strength
 Lives in established law: that must prevail.
 You have made your choice,
 Your death is the doing of your conscious hand.

ANTIGONE Then let me go, since all your words are bitter,   (EPODE)
 And the very light of the sun is cold to me.
 Lead me to my vigil, where I must have
 Neither love nor lamentation; no song, but silence.
 (CREON interrupts impatiently)

CREON If dirges and planned lamentations could put off death,
 Men would be singing for ever.
 (To the SERVANTS)   Take her, go!
 You know your orders: take her to the vault
 And leave her alone there. And if she lives or dies,
 That's her affair, not ours: our hands are clean.

ANTIGONE O tomb, vaulted bride-bed in eternal rock,
 Soon I shall be with my own again
 Where Persephone welcomes the thin ghosts underground:
 And I shall see my father again, and you, mother,

And dearest Polyneices—
                              dearest indeed
To me, since it was my hand
That washed him clean and poured the ritual wine:
And my reward is death before my time!

And yet, as men's hearts know, I have done no wrong,
I have not sinned before God. Or if I have,
I shall know the truth in death. But if the guilt
Lies upon Creon who judged me, then, I pray,
May his punishment equal my own.

CHORAGOS   O passionate heart,
Unyielding, tormented still by the same winds!

CREON   Her guards shall have good cause to regret their delaying.

ANTIGONE   Ah! That voice is like the voice of death!

CREON   I can give you no reason to think you are mistaken.

ANTIGONE   Thebes, and you my fathers' gods,
And rulers of Thebes, you see me now, the last
Unhappy daughter of a line of kings,
Your kings, led away to death. You will remember
What things I suffer, and at what men's hands,
Because I would not transgress the laws of heaven.
(*To the* GUARDS, *simply*)
Come: let us wait no longer.
(*Exit* ANTIGONE, *L., guarded*)

ODE IV

CHORUS   All Danae's beauty was locked away   (STROPHE 1)
In a brazen cell where the sunlight could not come:
A small room, still as any grave, enclosed her.
Yet she was a princess too,
And Zeus in a rain of gold poured love upon her.
O child, child,
No power in wealth or war
Or tough sea-blackened ships
Can prevail against untiring Destiny!

And Dryas' son also, that furious king,   (ANTISTROPHE 1)
Bore the god's prisoning anger for his pride:
Sealed up by Dionysos in deaf stone,
His madness died among echoes.
So at the last he learned what dreadful power
His tongue had mocked:
For he had profaned the revels,

And fired the wrath of the nine
Implacable Sisters that love the sound of the flute.

And old men tell a half-remembered tale   (STROPHE 2)
Of horror done where a dark ledge splits the sea
And a double surf beats on the gray shores:
How a king's new woman, sick
With hatred for the queen he had imprisoned,
Ripped out his two sons' eyes with her bloody hands
While grinning Ares watched the shuttle plunge
Four times: four blind wounds crying for revenge,

                       (ANTISTROPHE 2)
Crying, tears and blood mingled.—Piteously born,
Those sons whose mother was of heavenly birth!
Her father was the god of the North Wind
And she was cradled by gales,
She raced with young colts on the glittering hills
And walked untrammeled in the open light:
But in her marriage deathless Fate found means
To build a tomb like yours for all her joy.

SCENE V

(*Enter blind* TEIRESIAS, *led by a boy. The opening speeches of* TEIRESIAS *should be in singsong contrast to the realistic lines of* CREON.)

TEIRESIAS   This is the way the blind man comes, Princes, Princes,
                  Lock-step, two heads lit by the eyes of one.

CREON   What new thing have you to tell us, old Teiresias?

TEIRESIAS   I have much to tell you: listen to the prophet, Creon.

CREON   I am not aware that I have ever failed to listen.

TEIRESIAS   Then you have done wisely, King, and ruled well.

CREON   I admit my debt to you. But what have you to say?

TEIRESIAS   This, Creon: you stand once more on the edge of fate.

CREON   What do you mean? Your words are a kind of dread.

TEIRESIAS   Listen, Creon:
                  I was sitting in my chair of augury, at the place
                  Where the birds gather about me. They were all a-chatter,
                  As is their habit, when suddenly I heard
                  A strange note in their jangling, a scream, a
                  Whirring fury; I knew that they were fighting,
                  Tearing each other, dying
                  In a whirlwind of wings clashing. And I was afraid.

I began the rites of burnt-offering at the altar,
But Hephaistos failed me: instead of bright flame,
There was only the sputtering slime of the fat thigh-flesh
Melting: the entrails dissolved in gray smoke,
The bare bone burst from the welter. And no blaze!

This was a sign from heaven. My boy described it,
Seeing for me as I see for others.

I tell you, Creon, you yourself have brought
This new calamity upon us. Our hearths and altars
Are stained with the corruption of dogs and carrion birds
That glut themselves on the corpse of Oedipus' son.
The gods are deaf when we pray to them, their fire
Recoils from our offering, their birds of omen
Have no cry of comfort, for they are gorged
With the thick blood of the dead.
                                    O my son,
These are no trifles! Think: all men make mistakes,
But a good man yields when he knows his course is wrong,
And repairs the evil. The only crime is pride.

Give in to the dead man, then: do not fight with a corpse—
What glory is it to kill a man who is dead?
Think, I beg you:
It is for your own good that I speak as I do.
You should be able to yield for your own good.

CREON It seems that prophets have made me their especial province.
All my life long
I have been a kind of butt for the dull arrows
Of doddering fortune-tellers!
                                    No, Teiresias:
If your birds—if the great eagle of God himself
Should carry him stinking bit by bit to heaven,
I would not yield. I am not afraid of pollution:
No man can defile the gods.
                                    Do what you will,
Go into business, make money, speculate
In India gold or that synthetic gold from Sardis,
Get rich otherwise than by my consent to bury him.
Teiresias, it is a sorry thing when a wise man
Sells his wisdom, lets out his words for hire!

TEIRESIAS Ah Creon! Is there no man left in the world—

CREON To do what?—Come, let's have the aphorism!

TEIRESIAS No man who knows that wisdom outweighs any wealth?

CREON As surely as bribes are baser than any baseness.

TEIRESIAS	You are sick, Creon! You are deathly sick!
CREON	As you say: it is not my place to challenge a prophet.
TEIRESIAS	Yet you have said my prophecy is for sale.
CREON	The generation of prophets has always loved gold.
TEIRESIAS	The generation of kings has always loved brass.
CREON	You forget yourself! You are speaking to your King.
TEIRESIAS	I know it. You are a king because of me.
CREON	You have a certain skill; but you have sold out.
TEIRESIAS	King, you will drive me to words that—
CREON	Say them, say them! Only remember: I will not pay you for them.
TEIRESIAS	No, you will find them too costly.
CREON	No doubt. Speak: Whatever you say, you will not change my will.

TEIRESIAS Then take this, and take it to heart!
The time is not far off when you shall pay back
Corpse for corpse, flesh of your own flesh.
You have thrust the child of this world into living night,
You have kept from the gods below the child that is theirs:
The one in a grave before her death, the other,
Dead, denied the grave. This is your crime:
And the Furies and the dark gods of Hell
Are swift with terrible punishment for you.

Do you want to buy me now, Creon?

Not many days,
And your house will be full of men and women weeping,
And curses will be hurled at you from far
Cities grieving for sons unburied, left to rot
Before the walls of Thebes.

These are my arrows, Creon: they are all for you.

(To BOY) But come, child: lead me home.
Let him waste his anger upon younger men.
Maybe he will learn at last
To control a wiser tongue in a better head.
(Exit TEIRESIAS)

CHORAGOS The old man has gone, King, but his words
Remain to plague us. I am old, too,
But I cannot remember that he was ever false.

CREON	That is true. . . . It troubles me. Oh it is hard to give in! but it is worse To risk everything for stubborn pride.
CHORAGOS	Creon: take my advice.
CREON	What shall I do?
CHORAGOS	Go quickly: free Antigone from her vault And build a tomb for the body of Polyneices.
CREON	You would have me do this?
CHORAGOS	Creon, yes! And it must be done at once: God moves Swiftly to cancel the folly of stubborn men.
CREON	It is hard to deny the heart! But I Will do it: I will not fight with destiny.
CHORAGOS	You must go yourself, you cannot leave it to others.
CREON	I will go. 　　　　—Bring axes, servants: Come with me to the tomb. I buried her, I Will set her free. 　　　　　　Oh quickly! My mind misgives— The laws of the gods are mighty, and a man must serve them To the last day of his life!

(*Exit* CREON)

PAEAN

CHORAGOS	God of many names　　(STROPHE 1)
CHORUS	O Iacchos 　　　　　　son of Kadmeian Semele 　　　　O born of the Thunder! Guardian of the West 　　　　　Regent of Eleusis' plain 　　　　　O Prince of maenad Thebes and the Dragon Field by rippling Ismenos:
CHORAGOS	God of many names　　(ANTISTROPHE 1)
CHORUS	the flame of torches flares on our hills 　　　　the nymphs of Iacchos dance at the spring of Castalia:

from the vine-close mountain
                              come ah come in ivy:
Evohé evohé! sings through the streets of Thebes

CHORAGOS   God of many names   (STROPHE 2)

CHORUS   Iacchos of Thebes
heavenly Child
                              of Semele bride of the Thunderer!
The shadow of plague is upon us:
                                          come
with clement feet
                              oh come from Parnasos
down the long slopes
                              across the lamenting water

CHORAGOS   Io Fire! Chorister of the throbbing stars!   (ANTISTROPHE 2)
O purest among the voices of the night!
Thou son of God, blaze for us!

CHORUS   Come with choric rapture of circling Maenads
Who cry *Io Iacche!*
                              God of many names!

EXODOS

(*Enter* MESSENGER, *L.*)
MESSENGER   Men of the line of Kadmos, you who live
Near Amphion's citadel:
                              I cannot say
Of any condition of human life "This is fixed,
This is clearly good, or bad". Fate raises up,
And Fate casts down the happy and unhappy alike:
No man can foretell his Fate.
                              Take the case of Creon:
Creon was happy once, as I count happiness:
Victorious in battle, sole governor of the land,
Fortunate father of children nobly born.
And now it has all gone from him! Who can say
That a man is still alive when his life's joy fails?
He is a walking dead man. Grant him rich,
Let him live like a king in his great house:
If his pleasure is gone, I would not give
So much as the shadow of smoke for all he owns.

CHORAGOS   Your words hint at sorrow: what is your news for us?

MESSENGER   They are dead. The living are guilty of their death.

CHORAGOS   Who is guilty? Who is dead? Speak!

MESSENGER   Haimon.
        Haimon is dead; and the hand that killed him
        Is his own hand.

CHORAGOS   His father's? or his own?

MESSENGER   His own, driven mad by the murder his father had done.

CHORAGOS   Teiresias, Teiresias, how clearly you saw it all!

MESSENGER   This is my news: you must draw what conclusions you can
        from it.

CHORAGOS   But look: Eurydice, our Queen:
        Has she overheard us?

  (Enter EURYDICE from the Palace, C.)

EURYDICE   I have heard something, friends:
        As I was unlocking the gate of Pallas' shrine,
        For I needed her help today, I heard a voice
        Telling of some new sorrow. And I fainted
        There at the temple with all my maidens about me.
        But speak again: whatever it is, I can bear it:
        Grief and I are no strangers.

MESSENGER   Dearest Lady,
        I will tell you plainly all that I have seen.
        I shall not try to comfort you: what is the use,
        Since comfort could lie only in what is not true?
        The truth is always best.
                        I went with Creon
        To the outer plain where Polyneices was lying,
        No friend to pity him, his body shredded by dogs.
        We made our prayers in that place to Hecate
        And Pluto, that they would be merciful. And we bathed
        The corpse with holy water, and we brought
        Fresh-broken branches to burn what was left of it,
        And upon the urn we heaped up a towering barrow
        Of the earth of his own land.
                        When we were done, we ran
        To the vault where Antigone lay on her couch of stone.
        One of the servants had gone ahead,
        And while he was yet far off he heard a voice
        Grieving within the chamber, and he came back
        And told Creon. And as the King went closer,
        The air was full of wailing, the words lost,
        And he begged us to make all haste. "Am I a prophet?"
        He said, weeping, "And must I walk this road,
        The saddest of all that I have gone before?
        My son's voice calls me on. Oh quickly, quickly!

Look through the crevice there, and tell me
If it is Haimon, or some deception of the gods!"

We obeyed; and in the cavern's farthest corner
We saw her lying:
She had made a noose of her fine linen veil
And hanged herself. Haimon lay beside her,
His arms about her waist, lamenting her,
His love lost under ground, crying out
That his father had stolen her away from him.

When Creon saw him the tears rushed to his eyes
And he called to him: "What have you done, child? Speak
    to me.
What are you thinking that makes your eyes so strange?
O my son, my son, I come to you on my knees!"
But Haimon spat in his face. He said not a word,
Staring—
      And suddenly drew his sword
And lunged. Creon shrank back, the blade missed; and the boy,
Desperate against himself, drove it half its length
Into his own side, and fell. And as he died
He gathered Antigone close in his arms again,
Choking, his blood bright red on her white cheek.
And now he lies dead with the dead, and she is his
At last, his bride in the houses of the dead.

(*Exit* EURYDICE *into the Palace*)

CHORAGOS   She has left us without a word. What can this mean?

MESSENGER   It troubles me, too; yet she knows what is best,
    Her grief is too great for public lamentation,
    And doubtless she has gone to her chamber to weep
    For her dead son, leading her maidens in his dirge.

CHORAGOS   It may be so: but I fear this deep silence.
    (*Pause*)

MESSENGER   I will see what she is doing. I will go in.
    (*Exit* MESSENGER *into the Palace*)

(*Enter* CREON *with attendants, bearing* HAIMON's *body*)

CHORAGOS   But here is the King himself: oh look at him,
    Bearing his own damnation in his arms.

CREON   Nothing you say can touch me any more.
    My own blind heart has brought me
    From darkness to final darkness. Here you see
    The father murdering, the murdered son—
    And all my civic wisdom!

    Haimon my son, so young, so young to die,
    I was the fool, not you; and you died for me.

CHORAGOS	That is the truth; but you were late in learning it.
CREON	The truth is hard to bear. Surely a god Has crushed me beneath the hugest weight of heaven, And driven me headlong a barbaric way To trample out the thing I held most dear. The pains that men will take to come to pain!

(Enter MESSENGER *from the Palace)*

MESSENGER	The burden you carry in your hands is heavy, But it is not all: you will find more in your house.
CREON	What burden worse than this shall I find there?
MESSENGER	The Queen is dead.
CREON	O port of death, deaf world, Is there no pity for me? And you, Angel of evil, I was dead, and your words are death again. Is it true, boy? Can it be true? Is my wife dead? Has death bred death?
MESSENGER	You can see for yourself.

(The doors are opened, and the body of EURYDICE *is disclosed within.)*

CREON	Oh pity! All true, all true, and more than I can bear! O my wife, my son!
MESSENGER	She stood before the altar, and her heart Welcomed the knife her own hand guided, And a great cry burst from her lips for Megareus dead, And for Haimon dead, her sons; and her last breath Was a curse for their father, the murderer of her sons. And she fell, and the dark flowed in through her closing eyes.
CREON	O God, I am sick with fear. Are there no swords here? Has no one a blow for me?
MESSENGER	Her curse is upon you for the deaths of both.
CREON	It is right that it should be. I alone am guilty. I know it, and I say it. Lead me in, Quickly, friends. I have neither life nor substance. Lead me in.
CHORAGOS	You are right, if there can be right in so much wrong. The briefest way is best in a world of sorrow.
CREON	Let it come, Let death come quickly, and be kind to me. I would not ever see the sun again.
CHORAGOS	All that will come when it will; but we, meanwhile, Have much to do. Leave the future to itself.

CREON   All my heart was in that prayer!

CHORAGOS   Then do not pray any more: the sky is deaf.

CREON   Lead me away. I have been rash and foolish.
            I have killed my son and my wife.
            I look for comfort; my comfort lies here dead.
            Whatever my hands have touched has come to nothing.
            Fate has brought all my pride to a thought of dust.

(As CREON *is beong led into the house, the* CHORAGOS *advances and speaks directly to the audience.*)

CHORAGOS   There is no happiness where there is no wisdom;
            No wisdom but in submission to the gods.
            Big words are always punished,
            And proud men in old age learn to be wise.

First performed in 1604, Othello *is one of the succession of great tragedies Shakespeare wrote during the middle period of his career. It was written for and should when possible be produced in an Elizabethan theater (open-air in Shakespeare's time) with a large platform stage, no curtains in front but an enclosed space to the rear, and an acting space above, the whole making for a rapid, uninterrupted performance in which the audience is so close to the play as almost to be a part of it.*

Othello *is direct, straightforward, intense, uncomplicated by subplots. Although some of the characters are members of the nobility, the play is really a domestic tragedy of middle-class life. A friend persuades a husband that his wife has been unfaithful. The husband kills the wife and the friend is punished for his deception. Shakespeare has converted this sordid plot into a psychological drama that combines unrelenting horror with the most beautiful poetry.*

The story ought to be unbelievable, but when we see it in performance and even when we are reading the play the author induces us to accept it as possible truth. Among his dramatic devices are certain conventions of the theater of his time: the soliloquy, in which what a character tells the audience is supposed to be the truth; the testimony of other characters, also to be taken as true; and the fact that a villain of the type of Iago was (and still is) familiar— "out of stock" is the theater term. In the so-called "temptation scene," III.3, Iago so employs hints and innuendo, feigned reluctance to speak, and false evidence, and so effectively trades on his lifelong reputation for honesty, that Othello is persuaded.

We also believe in the secondary characters, who are prominent in the rest of the play. Desdemona, who is secondary because she is for the most part essentially passive, touches our emotions at every appearance. Roderigo is so completely a "snipe" (Iago's word for him) that we almost begin to feel for him the reluctant affection we reserve for someone else's bedraggled cur. Emilia, the realist, provides a deft contrast to the more ethereal Desdemona.

And through it all, Shakespeare carries us along on a stream of great poetry: blank verse filled with metaphor. From the opening to the final lines of the play we feel its spell.

*OTHELLO

THE MOOR OF VENICE

WILLIAM SHAKESPEARE

DRAMATIS PERSONAE

DUKE OF VENICE
BRABANTIO, a Senator
Other Senators
GRATIANO, brother to Brabantio
LODOVICO, kinsman to Brabantio
OTHELLO, a noble Moor in the service of the Venetian State
CASSIO, his lieutenant
IAGO, his ancient
RODERIGO, a Venetian gentleman

MONTANO, Othello's predecessor in the government of Cyprus
Clown, servant to Othello

DESDEMONA, daughter to Brabantio and wife of Othello

EMILIA, wife to Iago

BIANCA, mistress to Cassio

Sailor, Messengers, Herald, Officers, Gentlemen, Musicians, and Attendants

SCENE Venice: a sea-port in Cyprus.

ACT I

SCENE I. *Venice. A street.*

(*Enter* RODERIGO *and* IAGO.)

RODERIGO   Tush! never tell me; I take it much unkindly
            That thou, Iago, who hast had my purse
            As if the strings were thine, shouldst know of this.

IAGO   'Sblood, but you will not hear me:
If ever I did dream of such a matter
Abhor me.

RODERIGO   Thou told'st me thou didst hold him in thy hate.

IAGO   Despise me, if I do not. Three great ones of the city,
In personal suit to make me his lieutenant,
Off-capp'd to him: and, by the faith of man,
I know my price, I am worth no worse a place: 11
But he, as loving his own pride and purposes,
Evades them, with a bombast circumstance
Horribly stuff'd with epithets of war;
And, in conclusion,
Nonsuits my mediators: for, "Certes," says he,
"I have already chose my officer."
And what was he?
Forsooth, a great arithmetician,
One Michael Cassio, a Florentine,   20
A fellow almost damn'd in a fair wife;
That never set a squadron in the field,
Nor the division of a battle knows
More than a spinster; unless the bookish theoric,
Wherein the toged consuls can propose
As masterly as he: mere prattle, without practice,
Is all his soldiership. But he, sir, had the election:
And I, of whom his eyes had seen the proof
At Rhodes, at Cyprus and on other grounds
Christian and heathen, must be be-lee'd and calm'd   30
By debitor and creditor: this counter-caster,
He, in good time, must his lieutenant be,
And I—God bless the mark!—his Moorship's ancient.

RODERIGO   By heaven, I rather would have been his hangman.

IAGO   Why, there's no remedy; 't is the curse of service,
Preferment goes by letter and affection,
And not by old gradation, where each second
Stood heir to the first. Now, sir, be judge yourself,
Whether I in any just term am affined
To love the Moor.

RODERIGO   I would not follow him then.   40

IAGO   O, sir, content you;
I follow him to serve my turn upon him:
We cannot all be masters, nor all masters

---

l. 31 *counter-caster:* Bookkeeper, petty accountant.
l. 33 *ancient:* Ensign.

Cannot be truly follow'd. You shall mark
Many a duteous and knee-crooking knave,
That, doting on his own obsequious bondage,
Wears out his time, much like his master's ass,
For nought but provender, and when he's old, cashier'd:
Whip me such honest knaves. Others there are
Who, trimm'd in forms and visages of duty,   50
Keep yet their hearts attending on themselves,
And, throwing but shows of service on their lords,
Do well thrive by them, and when they have lined their
    coats
Do themselves homage: these fellows have some soul;
And such a one do I profess myself. For, sir,
It is as sure as you are Roderigo,
Were I the Moor, I would not be Iago:
In following him, I follow but myself;
But seeming so, for my peculiar end: 60
For when my outward action doth demonstrate
The native act and figure of my heart
In compliment extern, 't is not long after
But I will wear my heart upon my sleeve
For daws to peck at: I am not what I am.

RODERIGO   What a full fortune does the thicklips owe,
If he can carry 't thus!

IAGO   Call up her father,
Rouse him: make after him, poison his delight,
Proclaim him in the streets; incense her kinsmen,
And, though he in a fertile climate dwell,   70
Plague him with flies: though that his joy be joy,
Yet throw such changes of vexation on 't,
As it may lose some colour.

RODERIGO   Here is her father's house; I'll call aloud.

IAGO   Do; with like timorous accent and dire yell
As when, by night and negligence, the fire
Is spied in populous cities.

RODERIGO   What, ho, Brabantio! Signior Brabantio, ho!

IAGO   Awake! what, ho, Brabantio! thieves! thieves! thieves!
Look to your house, your daughter and your bags!   80
Thieves! thieves!

(BRABANTIO *appears above, at a window.*)

BRABANTIO   What is the reason of this terrible summons?
What is the matter there?

RODERIGO   Signior, is all your family within?

IAGO	Are your doors lock'd?
BRABANTIO	Why, wherefore ask you this?
IAGO	'Zounds, sir, you're robb'd; for shame, put on your gown;
	Your heart is burst, you have lost half your soul;
	Even now, very now, an old black ram
	Is tupping your white ewe. Arise, arise;
	Awake the snorting citizens with the bell, 90
	Or else the devil will make a grandsire of you:
	Arise, I say.
BRABANTIO	What, have you lost your wits?
RODERIGO	Most reverend signior, do you know my voice?
BRABANTIO	Not I: what are you?
RODERGIO	My name is Roderigo.
BRABANTIO	The worser welcome:
	I have charged thee not to haunt about my doors:
	In honest plainness thou hast heard me say
	My daughter is not for thee; and now, in madness,
	Being full of supper and distempering draughts,
	Upon malicious bravery, dost thou come 100
	To start my quiet.
RODERIGO	Sir, sir, sir,—
BRABANTIO	But thou must needs be sure
	My spirit and my place have in them power
	To make this bitter to thee.
RODERIGO	Patience, good sir.
BRABANTIO	What tell'st thou me of robbing? this is Venice;
	My house is not a grange.
RODERIGO	Most grave Brabantio,
	In simple and pure soul I come to you.
IAGO	'Zounds, sir, you are one of those that will not serve God, if the devil bid you. Because we come to do you service and you think we are ruffians, you'll have your daughter covered with a Barbary horse; you'll have your nephews neigh to you; you'll have coursers for cousins and gennets for germans.
BRABANTIO	What profane wretch are thou? 114

---

l. 106 *grange:* Farmhouse.
l. 113 *gennets:* Horses of a Spanish breed.
l. 113 *germans:* Relatives.

IAGO	I am one, sir, that comes to tell you your daughter and the Moor are now making the beast with two backs.
BRABANTIO	Thou art a villain.
IAGO	You are—a senator.
BRABANTIO	This thou shalt answer; I know thee, Roderigo.
RODERIGO	Sir, I will answer any thing. But I beseech you,
	If't be your pleasure and most wise consent,
	As partly I find it is, that your fair daughter, 120
	At this odd-even and dull watch o' the night,
	Transported, with no worse nor better guard
	But with a knave of common hire, a gondolier,
	To the gross clasps of a lascivious Moor,—
	If this be known to you and your allowance,
	We then have done you bold and saucy wrongs;
	But if you know not this, my manners tell me
	We have your wrong rebuke. Do not believe
	That, from the sense of all civility,
	I thus would play and trifle with your reverence: 130
	Your daughter, if you have not given her leave,
	I say again, hath made a gross revolt;
	Tying her duty, beauty, wit and fortunes
	In an extravagant and wheeling stranger
	Of here and every where. Straight satisfy yourself:
	If she be in her chamber or your house,
	Let loose on me the justice of the state
	For thus deluding you.
BRABANTIO	Strike on the tinder, ho!
	Give me a taper! call up all my people!
	This accident is not unlike my dream: 140
	Belief of it oppresses me already.
	Light, I say! light!
(Exit above.)	
IAGO	Farewell; for I must leave you:
	It seems not meet, nor wholesome to my place,
	To be produced—as, if I stay, I shall—
	Against the Moor: for, I do know, the state,
	However this may gall him with some check,
	Cannot with safety cast him, for he's embark'd
	With such loud reason to the Cyprus wars,
	Which even now stand in act, that, for their souls,
	Another of his fathom they have none, 150
	To lead their business: in which regard,
	Though I do hate him as I do hell-pains,
	Yet for necessity of present life,

I must show out a flag and sign of love,
Which is indeed but sign. That you shall surely find him,
Lead to the Sagittary the raised search;
And there will I be with him. So farewell.

(*Exit.*)

(*Enter below,* BRABANTIO, *and* SERVANTS *with torches.*)

BRABANTIO   It is too true an evil: gone she is;
And what's to come of my despised time
Is nought but bitterness. Now, Roderigo,   160
Where didst thou see her? O unhappy girl!
With the Moor, say'st thou? Who would be a father!
How didst thou know't was she? O, she deceives me
Past thought! What said she to you? Get more tapers;
Raise all my kindred. Are they married, think you?

RODERIGO   Truly, I think they are.

BRABANTIO   O heaven! How got she out? O treason of the blood!
Fathers, from hence trust not your daughters' minds
By what you see them act. Is there not charms
By which the property of youth and maidhood   170
May be abused? Have you not read, Roderigo,
Of some such thing?

RODERIGO   Yes, sir, I have indeed.

BRABANTIO   Call up my brother. O, would you had had her!
Some one way, some another. Do you know
Where we may apprehend her and the Moor?

RODERIGO   I think I can discover him, if you please
To get good guard and go along with me.

BRABANTIO   Pray you, lead on. At every house I'll call;
I may command at most. Get weapons, ho!
And raise some special officers of night.   180
On, good Roderigo: I'll deserve your pains.

(*Exeunt.*)

SCENE II. *Another street.*

(*Enter* OTHELLO, IAGO, *and* ATTENDANTS *with torches.*)

IAGO   Though in the trade of war I have slain men,
Yet do I hold it very stuff o' the conscience
To do no contrived murder: I lack iniquity
Sometimes to do me service: nine or ten times
I had thought to have yerk'd him here under the ribs.

---

l. 156 *Sagittary:* An inn.
l. 5 *yerk'd:* Stabbed.

OTHELLO	'T is better as it is.

IAGO
                      Nay, but he prated,
And spoke such scurvy and provoking terms
Against your honour
That, with the little godliness I have,
I did full hard forbear him. But, I pray you, sir,   10
Are you fast married? Be assured of this,
That the magnifico is much beloved,
And hath in his effect a voice potential
As double as the duke's: he will divorce you,
Or put upon you what restraint and grievance
The law, with all his might to enforce it on,
Will give him cable.

OTHELLO
                   Let him do his spite;
My services which I have done the signiory
Shall out-tongue his complaints. 'T is yet to know,—
Which, when I know that boasting is an honour,   20
I shall promulgate—I fetch my life and being
From men of royal siege, and my demerits
May speak unbonneted to as proud a fortune
As this that I have reach'd: for know, Iago,
But that I love the gentle Desdemona,
I would not my unhoused free condition
Put into circumscription and confine
For the sea's worth. But, look! what lights come yond?

IAGO
Those are the raised father and his friends:
You were best go in.

OTHELLO
                 Not I: I must be found   30
My parts, my title and my perfect soul
Shall manifest me rightly. Is it they?

IAGO   By Janus, I think no.

(Enter CASSIO, *and certain* OFFICERS *with torches*.)

OTHELLO   The servants of the duke, and my lieutenant.
The goodness of the night upon you, friends!
What is the news?

CASSIO
                The duke does greet you general,
And he requires your haste-post-haste appearance,
Even on the instant.

OTHELLO   What is the matter, think you?

CASSIO   Something from Cyprus, as I may divine:
It is a business of some heat: the galleys   40

---

l. 22 *siege:* Position, birth.

Have sent a dozen sequent messengers
This very night at one another's heels,
And many of the consuls, raised and met,
Are at the duke's already: you have been hotly call'd for;
When, being not at your lodging to be found,
The senate hath sent about three several quests
To search you out.

OTHELLO   'T is well I am found by you.
I will but spend a word here in the house,
And go with you.

(*Exit.*)

CASSIO   Ancient, what makes he here?

IAGO   'Faith, he to-night hath boarded a land carack: 50
If it prove lawful prize, he's made for ever.

CASSIO   I do not understand.

IAGO   He's married.

CASSIO   To who?

(*Re-enter* OTHELLO.)

IAGO   Marry, to—Come, captain, will you go?

OTHELLO   Have with you.

CASSIO   Here comes another troop to seek for you.

IAGO   It is Brabantio. General, be advised;
He comes to bad intent.

(*Enter* BRABANTIO, RODERIGO, *and* OFFICERS *with torches and weapons.*)

OTHELLO   Holla! stand there!

RODERIGO   Signior, it is the Moor.

BRABANTIO   Down with him, thief!

(*They draw on both sides.*)

IAGO   You, Roderigo! come, sir, I am for you.

OTHELLO   Keep up your bright swords, for the dew will rust them.
Good signior, you shall more command with years   60
Than with your weapons.

BRABANTIO   O thou foul thief, where hast thou stow'd my daughter?
Damn'd as thou art, thou hast enchanted her;
For I'll refer me to all things of sense,
If she in chains of magic were not bound,
Whether a maid so tender, fair and happy,
So opposite to marriage that she shunn'd

---
l. 50 *carack:* Merchant ship.
l. 55 *Marry:* By the Virgin Mary.

The wealthy curled darlings of our nation,
Would ever have, to incur a general mock,
Run from her guardage to the sooty bosom   70
Of such a thing as thou, to fear, not to delight.
Judge me the world, if 't is not gross in sense
That thou hast practised on her with foul charms,
Abused her delicate youth with drugs or minerals
That weaken motion: I'll have 't disputed on;
'T is probable and palpable to thinking.
I therefore apprehend and do attach thee
For an abuser of the world, a practiser
Of arts inhibited and out of warrant.
Lay hold upon him: if he do resist,   80
Subdue him at his peril.

OTHELLO   Hold your hands,
Both you of my inclining, and the rest:
Were it my cue to fight, I should have known it
Without a prompter. Where will you that I go
To answer this your charge?

BRABANTIO   To prison, till fit time
Of law and course of direct session
Call thee to answer.

OTHELLO   What if I do obey?
How may the duke be therewith satisfied,
Whose messengers are here about my side,
Upon some present business of the state   90
To bring me to him?

FIRST OFF.   'T is true, most worthy signior;
The duke's in council, and your noble self,
I am sure, is sent for.

BRABANTIO   How! the duke in council!
In this time of the night! Bring him away:
Mine's not an idle cause: the duke himself,
Or any of my brothers of the state,
Cannot but feel this wrong as 't were their own;
For if such actions may have passage free,
Bond-slaves and pagans shall our statesmen be.

    (*Exeunt.*)

SCENE III. *A council-chamber.*

(*The* DUKE *and* SENATORS *sitting at a table;* OFFICERS *attending.*)

DUKE   There is no composition in these news
That gives them credit.

---

l. 1 *composition:* Consistency.

FIRST SEN.	Indeed, they are disproportion'd; My letters say a hundred and seven galleys.
DUKE	And mine, a hundred and forty.
SECOND SEN.	And mine, two hundred: But though they jump not on a just account,— As in these cases, where the aim reports, 'T is oft with difference—yet do they all confirm A Turkish fleet, and bearing up to Cyprus.
DUKE	Nay, it is possible enough to judgment: I do not so secure me in the error, But the main article I do approve In fearful sense.
SAILOR	(*Within*) What, ho! what, ho! what, ho!
FIRST OFF.	A messenger from the galleys.

(*Enter a SAILOR.*)

DUKE	Now, what 's the business?
SAILOR	The Turkish preparation makes for Rhodes; So was I bid report here to the state By Signior Angelo.
DUKE	How say you by this change?
FIRST SEN.	This cannot be, By no assay of reason; 't is a pageant, To keep us in false gaze. When we consider The importancy of Cyprus to the Turk, And let ourselves again but understand, That as it more concerns the Turk than Rhodes, So may he with more facile question bear it, For that it stands not in such warlike brace, But altogether lacks the abilities That Rhodes is dress'd in: if we make thought of this, We must not think the Turk is so unskillful To leave that latest which concerns him first, Neglecting an attempt of ease and gain, To wake and wage a danger profitless.
DUKE	Nay, in all confidence, he's not for Rhodes.
FIRST OFF.	Here is more news.

10

20

30

---

l. 5 *jump:* Agree.
l. 6 *aim:* Guess.
l. 23 *So . . . it:* So may he (the Turk) capture it with less trouble.
l. 24 *brace:* State of defense.
l. 30 *wake and wage:* Arouse and risk.

(*Enter a* MESSENGER.)

MESSENGER	The Ottomites, reverend and gracious,
	Steering with due course towards the isle of Rhodes,
	Have there injointed them with an after fleet.

| FIRST SEN. | Ay, so I thought. How many, as you guess? |

MESSENGER	Of thirty sail: and now they do re-stem
	Their backward course, bearing with frank appearance
	Their purposes toward Cyprus. Signior Montano,
	Your trusty and most valiant servitor, 40
	With his free duty recommends you thus,
	And prays you to believe him.

| DUKE | 'T is certain, then, for Cyprus. |
| | Marcus Luccicos, is not he in town? |

| FIRST SEN. | He's now in Florence. |

| DUKE | Write from us to him; post-post-haste dispatch. |

| FIRST SEN. | Here comes Brabantio and the valiant Moor. |

(*Enter* BRABANTIO, OTHELLO, IAGO, RODERIGO, *and* OFFICERS.)

DUKE	Valiant Othello, we must straight employ you
	Against the general enemy Ottoman.
	(*To* BRABANTIO) I did not see you; welcome, gentle
	signior; 50
	We lack'd your counsel and your help tonight.

BRABANTIO	So did I yours. Good your grace, pardon me;
	Neither my place nor aught I heard of business
	Hath raised me from my bed, nor doth the general care
	Take hold on me, for my particular grief
	Is of so flood-gate and o'erbearing nature
	That it engluts and swallows other sorrows
	And it is still itself.

| DUKE | Why, what's the matter? |

| BRABANTIO | My daughter! O, my daughter! |

| DUKE AND SEN. | Dead? |

BRABANTIO	Ay, to me;
	She is abused, stol'n from me, and corrupted 60
	By spells and medicines bought of mountebanks;
	For nature so preposterously to err,
	Being not deficient, blind, or lame of sense,
	Sans witchcraft could not.

---

l. 35 *injointed:* Combined. *after:* Second.
l. 37 *re-stem:* Retrace.
l. 64 *Sans:* Without.

DUKE	Whoe'er he be that in this foul proceeding
	Hath thus beguiled your daughter of herself
	And you of her, the bloody book of law
	You shall yourself read in the bitter letter
	After your own sense, yea, though our proper son
	Stood in your action. 70
BRABANTIO	Humbly I thank your grace.
	Here is the man, this Moor, whom now, it seems,
	Your special mandate for the state-affairs
	Hath hither brought.
DUKE AND SEN.	We are very sorry for't.
DUKE	(*To* OTHELLO) What, in your own part, can you say
	to this?
BRABANTIO	Nothing, but this is so.
OTHELLO	Most potent, grave, and reverend signiors,
	My very noble and approved good masters,
	That I have ta'en away this old man's daughter,
	It is most true; true, I have married her:
	The very head and front of my offending 80
	Hath this extent, no more. Rude am I in my speech,
	And little bless'd with the soft phrase of peace;
	For since these arms of mine had seven years' pith,
	Till now some nine moons wasted, they have used
	Their dearest action in the tented field,
	And little of this great world can I speak,
	More than pertains to feats of broil and battle,
	And therefore little shall I grace my cause
	In speaking for myself. Yet, by your gracious patience,
	I will a round unvarnished tale deliver 90
	Of my whole course of love; what drugs, what charms,
	What conjuration and what mighty magic,
	For such proceeding I am charged withal,
	I won his daughter.
BRABANTIO	A maiden never bold;
	Of spirit so still and quiet, that her motion
	Blush'd at herself; and she, in spite of nature,
	Of years, of country, credit, every thing,
	To fall in love with what she fear'd to look on!
	It is a judgement maim'd and most imperfect
	That will confess perfection so could err 100
	Against all rules of nature and must be driven
	To find out practices of cunning hell,

_____

l. 69 *proper:* Own.

Why this should be. I therefore vouch again
That with some mixtures powerful o'er the blood,
Or with some dram conjured to this effect,
He wrought upon her.

DUKE   To vouch this, is no proof,
Without more wider and more overt test
Than these thin habits and poor likelihoods
Of modern seeming do prefer against him.

FIRST SEN.   But, Othello, speak: 110
Did you by indirect and forced courses
Subdue and poison this young maid's affections?
Or came it by request and such fair question
As soul to soul affordeth!

OTHELLO   I do beseech you,
Send for the lady to the Sagittary,
And let her speak of me before her father:
If you do find me foul in her report,
The trust, the office I do hold of you,
Not only take away, but let your sentence
Even fall upon my life.

DUKE   Fetch Desdemona hither.   120

OTHELLO   Ancient, conduct them; you best know the place.
(*Exeunt* IAGO *and* ATTENDANTS.)
And, till she come, as truly as to heavan
I do confess the vices of my blood,
So justly to your grave ears I'll present
How I did thrive in this fair lady's love,
And she in mine.

DUKE   Say it, Othello.

OTHELLO   Her father loved me; oft invited me;
Still question'd me the story of my life,
From year to year, the battles, sieges, fortunes,   130
That I have pass'd.
I ran it through, even from my boyish days,
To the very moment that he bade me tell it;
Wherein I spake of most disastrous chances,
Of moving accidents by flood and field,
Of hair-breadth scapes i' the imminent deadly breach,
Of being taken by the insolent foe
And sold to slavery, of my redemption thence
And portance in my travels' history:
Wherein of antres vast and deserts idle,   140

----

l. 140 *antres:* Caverns.

WILLIAM SHAKESPEARE / *Othello* **721**

Rough quarries, rocks and hills whose heads touch
    heaven,
It was my hint to speak,—such was the process;
And of the Cannibals that each other eat,
The Anthropophagi and men whose heads
Do grow beneath their shoulders. This to hear
Would Desdemona seriously incline:
But still the house-affairs would draw her thence:
Which ever as she could with haste dispatch,
She 'ld come again, and with a greedy ear
Devour up my discourse: which I observing,   150
Took once a pliant hour, and found good means
To draw from her a prayer of earnest heart
That I would all my pilgrimage dilate,
Whereof by parcels she had something heard,
But not intentively: I did consent,
And often did beguile her of her tears,
When I did speak of some distressful stroke
That my youth suffer'd. My story being done,
She gave me for my pains a world of sighs:
She swore, in faith, 't was strange, 't was passing
    strange   160
'T was pitiful, 't was wondrous pitiful:
She wish'd she had not heard it, yet she wish'd
That heaven had made her such a man: she thank'd
    me,
And bade me, if I had a friend that loved her,
I should but teach him how to tell my story,
And that would woo her. Upon this hint I spake:
She loved me for the dangers I had pass'd,
And I loved her that she did pity them.
This only is the witchcraft I have used:
Here comes the lady; let her witness it.   170

(*Enter* DESDEMONA, IAGO, *and* ATTENDANTS.)

DUKE   I think this tale would win my daughter too.
              Good Brabantio,
              Take up this mangled matter at the best:
              Men do their broken weapons rather use
              Than their bare hands.

BRABANTIO   I pray you, hear her speak:
              If she confess that she was half the wooer,
              Destruction on my head, if my bad blame
              Light on the man! Come hither, gentle mistress:

---

l. 144 *Anthropophagi:* Cannibals.
l. 163 *That . . . man:* That she had been a man like this.

Do you perceive in all this noble company
Where most you owe obedience?

DESDEMONA   My noble father,   180
I do perceive here a divided duty:
To you I am bound for life and education;
My life and education both do learn me
How to respect you; you are the lord of duty;
I am hitherto your daughter: but here's my husband,
And so much duty as my mother show'd
To you, preferring you before her father,
So much I challenge that I may profess
Due to the Moor my lord.

BRABANTIO   God be wi' you! I have done.
Please it your grace, on to the state-affairs: 190
I had rather to adopt a child than get it.
Come hither, Moor:
I here do give thee that with all my heart
Which, but thou hast already, with all my heart
I would keep from thee. For your sake, jewel,
I am glad at soul I have no other child;
For thy escape would teach me tyranny,
To hang clogs on them. I have done, my lord.

DUKE   Let me speak like yourself, and lay a sentence,
Which, as a grise or step, may help these lovers   200
Into your favour.
When remedies are past, the griefs are ended
By seeing the worst, which late on hopes depended.
To mourn a mischief that is past and gone
Is the next way to draw new mischief on.
What cannot be preserved when fortune takes,
Patience her injury a mockery makes.
The robb'd that smiles steals something from the thief;
He robs himself that spends a bootless grief.

BRABANTIO   So let the Turk of Cyprus us beguile;   210
We lose it not, so long as we can smile.
He bears the sentence well that nothing bears
But the free comfort which from thence he hears,
But he bears both the sentence and the sorrow
That, to pay grief, must of patience borrow.
These sentences, to sugar, or to gall,
Being strong on both sides, are equivocal:
But words are words: I never yet did hear

---

l. 198 *clogs:* Chains, hindrances.
l. 200 *grise:* Step.

| | That the bruised heart was pierced through the ear. | |
| | I humbly beseech you, proceed to the affairs of state. | 220 |

DUKE   The Turk with a most mighty preparation makes for
Cyprus. Othello, the fortitude of the place is best
known to you; and though we have there a substitute
of most allowed sufficiency, yet opinion, a sovereign
mistress of effects, throws a more safer voice on you:
you must therefore be content to slubber the gloss of
your new fortunes with this more stubborn and boisterous expedition.

OTHELLO The tyrant custom, most grave senators,
Hath made the flinty and steel couch of war   230
My thrice-driven bed of down: I do agnize
A natural and prompt alacrity
I find in hardness, and do undertake
These present wars against the Ottomites.
Most humbly therefore bending to your state,
I crave fit disposition for my wife,
Due reference of place and exhibition,
With such accommodation and besort
As levels with her breeding.

DUKE   If you please,
Be 't at her fathers.   240

BRABANTIO   I 'll not have it so.

OTHELLO Nor I.

DESDEMONA   Nor I; I would not there reside,
To put my father in impatient thoughts
By being in his eye. Most gracious duke,
To my unfolding lend your prosperous ear;
And let me find a charter in your voice,
To assist my simpleness.

DUKE   What would you, Desdemona?

DESDEMONA That I did love the Moor to live with him,
My downright violence and storm of fortunes
May trumpet to the world: my heart's subdued   250
Even to the very quality of my lord:
I saw Othello's visage in his mind,
And to his honours and his valiant parts

---

l. 222 *fortitude:* Strength.
l. 226 *slubber:* Soil.
l. 231 *agnize:* Acknowledge.
l. 237 *reference:* Assignment. *exhibition:* Allowance of money.
l. 238 *besort:* Fitness.

Did I my soul and fortunes consecrate.
So that, dear lords, if I be left behind,
A moth of peace, and he go to war,
The rites for which I love him are bereft me,
And I a heavy interim shall support
By his dear absence. Let me go with him.

OTHELLO   Let her have your voices.   260
Vouch with me, heaven, I therefore beg it it not,
To please the palate of my appetite,
Nor to comply with heat—the young affects
In me defunct—and proper satisfaction,
But to be free and bounteous to her mind:
And heaven defend your good souls, that you think
I will your serious and great business scant
For she is with me: no, when light-wing'd toys
Of feather'd Cupid seel with wanton dullness
My speculative and officed instruments,   270
That my disports corrupt and taint my business,
Let housewives make a skillet of my helm,
And all indign and base adversities
Make head against my estimation!

DUKE   Be it as you shall privately determine,
Either for her stay or going: the affair cries haste,
And speed must answer it.

FIRST SEN.   You must away to-night.

OTHELLO   With all my heart.

DUKE   At nine i' the morning here we 'll meet again.
Othello, leave some officer behind,   280
And he shall our commission bring to you;
With such things else of quality and respect
As doth import you.

OTHELLO   So please your grace, my ancient;
A man he is of honesty and trust:
To his conveyance I assign my wife,
With what else needful your good grace shall think
To be sent after me.

DUKE   Let it be so.
Good night to every one. (*To* BRABANTIO) And, noble
    signior,

---

l. 263 *affects:* Desires.
l. 269 *seel:* Close.
l. 270 *My . . . instruments:* My eyes.
l. 273 *indign:* Disgraceful.
l. 274 *estimation:* Reputation.

	If virtue no delighted beauty lack, Your son-in-law is far more fair than black.	290
FIRST SEN.	Adieu, brave Moor; use Desdemona well.	
BRABANTIO	Look to her, Moor; if thou hast eyes to see: She has deceived her father, and may thee.	

(Exeunt DUKE, SENATORS, OFFICERS, *&c.)*

OTHELLO	My life upon her faith! Honest Iago, My Desdemona must I leave to thee: I prithee, let thy wife attend on her; And bring them after in the best advantage. Come, Desdemona: I have but an hour Of love, of worldly matters and direction, To spend with thee: we must obey the time.	300

(Exeunt OTHELLO *and* DESDEMONA.)

RODERIGO	Iago—	
IAGO	What say'st thou, noble heart?	
RODERIGO	What will I do, thinkest thou?	
IAGO	Why, go to bed, and sleep.	
RODERIGO	I will incontinently drown myself.	
IAGO	If thou dost, I shall never love thee after. Why, thou silly gentleman!	
RODERIGO	It is silliness to live when to live is torment; and then have we a prescription to die when death is our physician.	310
IAGO	O villanous! I have looked upon the world for four times seven years; and since I could distinguish betwixt a benefit and an injury, I never found man that knew how to love himself. Ere I would say I would drown myself for the love of a guinea-hen, I would change my humanity with a baboon.	
RODERIGO	What should I do? I confess it is my shame to be so fond; but it is not in my virtue to amend it.	
IAGO	Virtue! a fig! 't is in ourselves that we are thus or thus. Our bodies are our gardens, to the which our wills are gardeners; so that if we will plant nettles or sow lettuce, set hyssop and weed up thyme, supply it with one gender of herbs or distract it with many, either to have it sterile with idleness or manured with industry, why, the power and corrigible authority of this lies in	319

---

l. 318 *fond:* Foolish.

our wills. If the balance of our lives had not one scale of reason to poise another of sensuality, the blood and baseness of our natures would conduct us to most preposterous conclusions: but we have reason to cool our raging motions, our carnal stings, our unbitted 330 lusts, whereof I take this that you call love to be a sect or scion.

RODERIGO   It cannot be.

IAGO   It is merely a lust of the blood and a permission of the will. Come, be a man. Drown thyself! drown cats and blind puppies. I have professed me thy friend, and I confess me knit to thy deserving with cables of perdurable toughness; I could never better stead thee 338 than now. Put money in thy purse; follow thou the wars; defeat thy favour with an usurped beard; I say, put money in thy purse. It cannot be that Desdemona should long continue her love to the Moor,—put money in thy purse,—nor he his to her; it was a violent commencement, and thou shalt see an answerable sequestration—put money in thy purse. These Moors are changeable in their wills:—fill thy purse with money:—the food that to him now is as luscious as locusts, shall be to him shortly as bitter as coloquintida. She must change for youth: when she is sated with his body, she will find the error of her choice: she must 350 have change, she must: therefore put money in thy purse. If thou wilt needs damn thyself, do it a more delicate way than drowning. Make all the money thou canst: If sanctimony and a frail vow betwixt an erring barbarian and a super-subtle Venetian be not too hard for my wits and all the tribe of hell, thou shalt enjoy her; therefore make money. A pox of drowning thyself! it is clean out of the way: seek thou rather to be hanged in compassing thy joy than to be drowned and go without her.

RODERIGO   Wilt thou be fast to my hopes, if I depend on the issue?

IAGO   Thou art sure of me:—go, make money:—I have told thee again and again, I hate the Moor: my cause is

---

l. 327 *poise:* Balance.
l. 330 *stings:* Desires. *unbitted:* Unbridled.
l. 331 *sect or scion:* Cutting or graft.
l. 338 *stead*: Assist.
l. 340 *defeat thy favour:* Spoil thy looks.
l. 345 *sequestration:* Estrangement.
l. 348 *coloquintida:* A medicine.

hearted thine hath no less reason. Let us be conjunctive in our revenge against him; if thou canst cuckold him, thou dost thyself a pleasure, me a sport. There are many events in the womb of time which will be delivered. Traverse! go, provide thy money. We will have more of this to-morrow. Adieu.   370

RODERIGO   Where shall we meet i' the morning?

IAGO   At my lodging.

RODERIGO   I 'll be with thee betimes.

IAGO   Go to; farewell. Do you hear, Roderigo?

RODERIGO   What say you?

IAGO   No more of drowning, do you hear?

RODERIGO   I am changed: I 'll go sell all my land.
(Exit.)

IAGO   Thus do I ever make my fool my purse;
For I mine own gain'd knowledge should profane,
If I would time expend with such a snipe,   380
But for my sport and profit. I hate the Moor;
And it is thought abroad, that 'twixt my sheets
He has done my office: I know not if 't be true;
But I, for mere suspicion in that kind,
Will do as if for surety. He holds me well;
The better shall my purpose work on him.
Cassio's a proper man: let me see now:
To get his place and to plume up my will
In double knavery—How, how?—Let's see:—
After some time, to abuse Othello's ear   390
That he is too familiar with his wife.
He hath a person and a smooth dispose
To be suspected, framed to make women false.
The Moor is of a free and open nature,
That thinks men honest that but seem to be so,
And will as tenderly be led by the nose
As asses are.
I have 't. It is engender'd. Hell and night
Must bring this monstrous birth to the world's light.
(Exit.)

---

l. 380 *snipe:* Fool.
l. 388 *plume up:* Gratify (by decorating).

ACT II

SCENE I. *A sea-port in Cyprus. An open place near the quay.*

(Enter MONTANO *and two* GENTLEMEN.)

MONTANO	What from the cape can you discern at sea?
FIRST GENT.	Nothing at all: it is a highwrought flood;
	I cannot, 'twixt the heaven and the main,
	Descry a sail.
MONTANO	Methinks the wind hath spoke aloud at land;
	A fuller blast ne'er shook our battlements:
	If it hath ruffian'd so upon the sea,
	What ribs of oak, when mountains melt on them,
	Can hold the mortise? What shall we hear of this?

SECOND GENT.   A segregation of the Turkish fleet: 10
For do but stand upon the foaming shore,
The chidden billow seems to pelt the clouds;
The wind-shaked surge, with high and monstrous mane,
Seems to cast water on the burning bear,
And quench the guards of the ever-fixed pole:
I never did like molestation view
On the enchafed flood.

MONTANO   If that the Turkish fleet
Be not enshelter'd and embay'd, they are drown'd;
It is impossible they bear it out.

(Enter a third GENTLEMAN.)

THIRD GENT.   News, lads! our wars are done.   20
The desperate tempest hath so bang'd the Turks,
That their designment halts: a noble ship of Venice
Hath seen a grievous wreck and sufferance
On most part of their fleet.

MONTANO   How! is this true?

THIRD GENT.   The ship is here put in,
A Veronesa; Michael Cassio,
Lieutenant to the warlike Moor Othello,
Is come on shore: the Moor himself at sea,
And is in full commission here for Cyprus.

MONTANO   I am glad on 't: 't is a worthy governor.   30

THIRD GENT.   But this same Cassio, though he speak of comfort
Touching the Turkish loss, yet he looks sadly,

---

l. 10 *segregation:* Scattering.
l. 16 *molestation:* Disturbance.

And prays the Moor be safe; for they were parted
With foul and violent tempest.

MONTANO   Pray heavens he be;
For I have served him, and the man commands
Like a full soldier. Let 's to the seaside, ho!
As well to see the vessel that's come in
As to throw out our eyes for brave Othello,
Even till we make the main and the aerial blue
An indistinct regard.

THIRD GENT.   Come, let 's do so;   40
For every minute is expectancy
Of more arrivance.

(Enter CASSIO.)
CASSIO   Thanks, you the valiant of this warlike isle,
That so approve the Moor! O, let the heavens
Give him defence against the elements,
For I have lost him on a dangerous sea.

MONTANO   Is he well shipp'd?

CASSIO   His bark is stoutly timber'd, and his pilot
Of very expert and approved allowance;
Therefore my hopes, not surfeited to death,   50
Stand in bold cure.
(A cry within "A sail, a sail, a sail!")

(Enter a fourth GENTLEMAN.)
CASSIO   What noise?

FOURTH GENT.   The town is empty; on the blow o' the sea
Stand ranks of people, and they cry "A sail!"

CASSIO   My hopes do shape him for the governor.
(Guns heard.)

SECOND GENT.   They do discharge their shot of courtesy:
Our friends at least.

CASSIO   I pray you, sir, go forth,
And give us truth who 't is that is arrived.

SECOND GENT.   I shall.
(Exit.)

MONTANO   But, good lieutenant, is your general wived?   60

---

l. 40 *An indistinct regard:* Indistinguishable.
l. 49 *allowance:* Reputation.
l. 51 *Stand in bold cure:* May be fulfilled.

CASSIO   Most fortunately: he hath achieved a maid
That paragons description and wild fame;
One that excels the quirks of blazoning pens,
And in the essential vesture of creation
Does tire the ingener.

(Re-enter second GENTLEMAN.)

How now! who has put in?

SECOND GENT.   'T is one Iago, ancient to the general.

CASSIO   Has had most favourable and happy speed:
Tempests themselves, high seas and howling winds,
The gutter'd rocks and congregated sands,—   70
Traitors ensteep'd to clog the guiltless keel,—
As having sense of beauty, do omit
Their mortal natures, letting go safely by
The divine Desdemona.

MONTANO   What is she?

CASSIO   She that I spake of, our great captain's captain,
Left in the conduct of the bold Iago,
Whose footing here anticipates our thoughts
A se'nnight's speed. Great Jove, Othello guard,
And swell his sail with thine own powerful breath,
That he may bless this bay with his tall ship,
Make love's quick pants in Desdemona's arms,   80
Give renew'd fire to our extincted spirits,
And bring all Cyprus comfort!

(Enter DESDEMONA, EMILIA, IAGO, RODERIGO, *and* ATTENDANTS.)

O, behold,
The riches of the ship is come on shore!
Ye men of Cyprus, let her have your knees.
Hail to thee, lady! and the grace of heaven.
Before, behind thee, and on every hand,
Enwheel thee round!

DESDEMONA   I thank you, valiant Cassio.
What tidings can you tell me of my lord?

CASSIO   He is not yet arrived: nor know I aught
But that he's well and will be shortly here.   90

DESDEMONA   O, but I fear—How lost you company?

---

l. 62 *paragons:* Surpasses. *fame:* Rumor.
l. 63 *quirks:* Extravagant phrases. *blazoning:* Praising.
l. 64–5 *And . . . ingener:* The genuine qualities with which she is endowed surpass the ability
of an inventor of phrases to praise her.
l. 70 *gutter'd:* Furrowed.
l. 71 *ensteep'd:* Submerged.
l. 72 *omit:* Give up.

CASSIO   The great contention of the sea and skies
                    Parted our fellowship—But, hark! a sail.

   (*Within* "A sail, a sail!" *Guns heard.*)

SECOND GENT.   They give their greeting to the citadel:
                    This likewise is a friend.

CASSIO   See for the news.

   (*Exit* GENTLEMAN.)

                    Good ancient, you are welcome.

   (*To Emilia*)

                                                Welcome, mistress:
                    Let it not gall your patience, good Iago,
                    That I extend my manners; 't is my breeding
                    That gives me this bold show of courtesy.   100

   (*Kissing her.*)

IAGO   Sir, would she give you so much of her lips
                    As of her tongue she oft bestows on me,
                    You 'ld have enough.

DESDEMONA   Alas, she has no speech.

IAGO   In faith, too much;
                    I find it still, when I have list to sleep:
                    Marry, before your ladyship, I grant,
                    She puts her tongue a little in her heart,
                    And chides with thinking.

EMILIA   You have little cause to say so.

IAGO   Come on, come on; you are pictures out of doors,   110
                    Bells in your parlours, wild-cats in your kitchens,
                    Saints in your injuries, devils being offended,
                    Players in your housewifery, and housewives in your
                        beds.

DESDEMONA   O, fie upon thee, slanderer!

IAGO   Nay, it is true, or else I am a Turk:
                    You rise to play and go to bed to work.

EMILIA   You shall not write my praise.

IAGO   No, let me not.

DESDEMONA   What wouldst thou write of me, if thou shouldst praise
                        me?

IAGO   O gentle lady, do not put me to 't;
                    For I am nothing, if not critical.   120

---

l. 106 *Marry:* By the Virgin Mary.
l. 113 *Players:* Triflers. *housewives:* Hussies.

DESDEMONA	Come on, assay. There's one gone to the harbour?
IAGO	Ay, madam.
DESDEMONA	I am not merry; but I do beguile The thing I am by seeming otherwise. Come, how wouldst thou praise me?
IAGO	I am about it; but indeed my invention Comes from my pate as birdlime does from frize; It plucks out brains and all: but my Muse labours, And thus she is deliver'd. If she be fair and wise, fairness and wit, 130 The one's for use, the other useth it.
DESDEMONA	Well praised; How if she be black and witty?
IAGO	If she be black, and thereto have a wit, She 'll find a white that shall her blackness fit.
DESDEMONA	Worse and worse.
EMILIA	How if fair and foolish?
IAGO	She never yet was foolish that was fair; For even her folly help'd her to an heir.
DESDEMONA	These are old fond paradoxes to make fools laugh i' the alehouse. What miserable praise hast thou for her that 's foul and foolish? 141
IAGO	There 's none so foul and foolish thereunto, But does foul pranks which fair and wise ones do.
DESDEMONA	O heavy ignorance! thou praisest the worst best. But what praise couldst thou bestow on a deserving woman indeed, one that, in the authority of her merit, did justly put on the vouch of very malice itself?
IAGO	She that was ever fair and never proud, Had tongue at will and yet was never loud, Never lack'd gold and yet went never gay, 150 Fled from her wish and yet said "Now I may," She that being anger'd, her revenge being nigh, Bade her wrong stay and her displeasure fly, She that in wisdom never was so frail To change the cod's head for the salmon's tail, She that could think and ne'er disclose her mind, See suitors following and not look behind, She was a wight, if ever such wight were,—

---

l. 127 *birdlime:* Sticky substance to catch birds. *frize:* Woolen cloth.
l. 139 *fond,* foolish.
l. 147 *vouch:* Approval.
l. 155 *To . . . tail:* Prefer the worst part of a good thing.
l. 158 *wight:* Person.

DESDEMONA	To do what?
IAGO	To suckle fools and chronicle small beer. 160
DESDEMONA	O most lame and impotent conclusion! Do not learn of him, Emilia, though he be thy husband. How say you, Cassio? is he not a most profane and liberal counsellor?
CASSIO	He speaks home, madam: you may relish him more in the soldier than in the scholar.
IAGO	(*Aside*) He takes her by the palm: ay, well said, whisper: with as little a web as this will I ensnare as great a fly as Cassio. Ay, smile upon her, do; I will gyve thee in thine own courtship. You say true; 't is so, indeed: if such tricks as these strip you out of your lieutenantry, it had been better you had not kissed your three fingers so oft, which now again you are most apt to play the sir in. Very good; well kissed! an excellent courtesy! 't is so, indeed. Yet again your fingers to your lips? would they were cylster-pipes for your sake! (*Trumpet within.*) The Moor! I know his trumpet.
CASSIO	'T is truly so.
DESDEMONA	Let 's meet him and receive him.
CASSIO	Lo, where he comes!

(*Enter* OTHELLO *and* ATTENDANTS.)

OTHELLO	O my fair warrior!
DESDEMONA	My dear Othello! 180
OTHELLO	It gives me wonder great as my content
	To see you here before me. O my soul's joy!
	If after every tempest come such calms,
	May the winds blow till they have waken'd death!
	And let the labouring bark climb hills of seas
	Olympus-high and duck again as low
	As hell 's from heaven! If it were now to die,
	'T were now to be most happy; for, I fear,
	My soul hath her content so absolute
	That not another comfort like to this 190
	Succeeds in unknown fate.
DESDEMONA	The heavens forbid
	But that our loves and comforts should increase,
	Even as our days do grow!

---

l. 160 *chronicle small beer:* Keep petty accounts.
l. 163 *liberal:* Licentious.
l. 173 *sir:* Gentleman.
l. 175 *clyster-pipes:* Syringes.

OTHELLO   Amen to that, sweet powers!
                    I cannot speak enough of this content;
                    It stops me here; it is too much of joy:
                    And this, and this, the greatest discords be
(Kissing her.)   That e'er our hearts shall make!

IAGO   (Aside) O, you are well tuned now!
                    But I'll set down the pegs that make this music,
                    As honest as I am.

OTHELLO   Come, let us to the castle.   200
                    News, friends; our wars are done, the Turks are
                        drown'd.
                    How does my old acquaintance of this isle?
                    Honey, you shall be well desired in Cyprus;
                    I have found great love amongst them. O my sweet,
                    I prattle out of fashion, and I dote
                    In mine own comforts. I prithee, good Iago,
                    Go to the bay and disembark my coffers:
                    Bring thou the master of the citadel;
                    He is a good one, and his worthiness
                    Does challenge much respect. Come, Desdemona,   210
                    Once more, well met at Cyprus.
(Exeunt OTHELLO, DESDEMONA, and ATTENDANTS.)

IAGO   Do thou meet me presently at the harbour. Come hither.
                    If thou be'st valiant,—as, they say, base men being in
                    love have then a nobility in their natures more than is
                    native to them,—list me. The lieutenant tonight watches
                    on the court of guard:—First, I must tell thee this—
                    Desdemona is directly in love with him.

RODERIGO   With him! why, 't is not possible.

IAGO   Lay thy finger thus, and let thy soul be instructed.
                    Mark me with what violence she first loved the Moor,   220
                    but for bragging and telling her fantastical lies: and
                    will she love him still for prating? let not thy discreet
                    heart think it. Her eye must be fed; and what delight
                    shall she have to look on the devil? When the blood is
                    made dull with the act of sport, there should be, again
                    to inflame it and to give satiety a fresh appetite, loveli-
                    ness in favour, sympathy in years, manners and
                    beauties; all which the Moor is defective in: now, for
                    want of these required conveniences, her delicate
                    tenderness will find itself abused, begin to heave the
                    gorge, disrelish and abhor the Moor; very nature will
                    instruct her in it and compel her to some second
                    choice. Now, sir, this granted,—as it is a most pregnant

and unforced position—who stands so eminent in the degree of this fortune as Cassio does? a knave very voluble; no further conscionable than in putting on the mere form of civil and humane seeming, for the better compassing of his salt and most hidden loose affection? why, none; why, none: a slipper and subtle knave, a finder of occasions, that has an eye can stamp and counterfeit advantages, though true advantage never present itself; a devilish knave. Besides, the knave is handsome, young, and hath all those requisites in him that folly and green minds look after: a pestilent complete knave; and the woman hath found him already. 236

RODERIGO I cannot believe that in her; she 's full of most blessed condition.

IAGO Blessed fig's-end! the wine she drinks is made of grapes: if she had been blessed, she would never have loved the Moor. Blessed pudding! Didst thou not see her paddle with the palm of his hand? didst not mark that?

RODERIGO Yes, that I did; but that was but courtesy.

IAGO Lechery, by this hand; an index and obscure prologue to the history of lust and foul thoughts. They met so near with their lips that their breaths embraced together. Villanous thoughts, Roderigo! when these mutualities so marshal the way, hard at hand comes the master and main exercise, the incorporate conclusion. Pish! But, sir, be you ruled by me: I have brought you from Venice. Watch you to-night; for the command, I 'll lay 't upon you. Cassio knows you not. I 'll not be far from you: do you find some occasion to anger Cassio, either by speaking too loud, or tainting his discipline; or from what other course you please, which the time shall more favourably minister. 253

261

RODERIGO Well.

IAGO Sir, he is rash and very sudden in choler, and haply may strike at you: provoke him, that he may; for even out of that will I cause these of Cyprus to mutiny; whose qualification shall come into no true taste again but by the displanting of Cassio. So shall you have a shorter journey to your desires by the means I shall then have to prefer them; and the impediment most profitably

l. 236 *conscionable:* Conscientious.
l. 238 *salt:* Licentious.

RODERIGO	removed, without the which there were no expectation of our prosperity.
RODERIGO	I will do this, if I can bring it to any opportunity.
IAGO	I warrant thee. Meet me by and by at the citadel: I 277 must fetch his necessaries ashore. Farewell.
RODERIGO (*Exit.*)	Adieu.

IAGO   That Cassio loves her, I do well believe it;
That she loves him, 't is apt and of great credit:
The Moor, howbeit that I endure him not,
Is of a constant, loving, noble nature,
And I dare think he 'll prove to Desdemona
A most dear husband. Now, I do love her too;
Not out of absolute lust, though peradventure
I stand accountant for as great a sin,
But partly led to diet my revenge,
For that I do suspect the lusty Moor
Hath leap'd into my seat; the thought whereof   290
Doth, like a poisonous mineral, gnaw my inwards;
And nothing can or shall content my soul
Till I am even'd with him, wife for wife,
Or failing so, yet that I put the Moor
At least into a jealousy so strong
That judgement cannot cure. Which thing to do,
If this poor trash of Venice, whom I trash
For his quick hunting, stand the putting on,
I 'll have our Michael Cassio on the hip,
Abuse him to the Moor in the rank garb—   300
For I fear Cassio with my night-cap too—
Make the Moor thank me, love me and reward me,
For making him egregiously an ass
And practising upon his peace and quiet
Even to madness. 'T is here, but yet confused.
Knavery's plain face is never seen till used.

(*Exit.*)

SCENE II. *A street.*

(*Enter a* HERALD *with a proclamation;* PEOPLE *following.*)

HERALD   It is Othello's pleasure, our noble and valiant general,
that, upon certain tidings now arrived, importing the
mere perdition of the Turkish fleet, every man put him-

---

ll. 297–98 *whom . . . hunting:* Whom I keep from acting too fast.
l. 299 *on the hip:* In my power.

self into triumph; some to dance, some to make bon-
fires, each man to what sport and revels his addiction
leads him: for, besides these beneficial news, it is the
celebration of his nuptial. So much was his pleasure
should be proclaimed. All offices are open, and there
is full liberty of feasting from this present hour of five
till the bell have told eleven. Heaven bless the isle of
Cyprus and our noble general Othello!

(*Exeunt.*)

SCENE III. *A hall in the castle.*

(*Enter* OTHELLO, DESDEMONA, CASSIO, *and* ATTENDANTS.)

OTHELLO   Good Michael, look you to the guard to-night:
             Let 's teach ourselves that honourable stop,
             Not to outsport discretion.

CASSIO   Iago hath direction what to do;
             But, notwithstanding, with my personal eye
             Will I look to 't.

OTHELLO   Iago is most honest.
             Michael, good night: to-morrow with your earliest
             Let me have speech with you.

(*To* DESDEMONA)

                             Come, my dear love,
             The purchase made, the fruits are to ensue;
             That profit's yet to come 'tween me and you.
             Good night.   11

(*Exeunt* OTHELLO, DESDEMONA, *and* ATTENDANTS.)

(*Enter* IAGO.)

CASSIO   Welcome, Iago; we must to the watch.

IAGO   Not this hour, lieutenant; 't is not yet ten o' the clock.
             Our general cast us thus early for the love of his Des-
             demona; who let us not therefore blame: he hath not
             yet made wanton the night with her; and she is sport
             for Jove.

CASSIO   She's a most exquisite lady.

IAGO   And, I'll warrant her, full of game.

CASSIO   Indeed, she's a most fresh and delicate creature.   21

IAGO   What an eye she had! methinks it sounds a parley
             to provocation.

CASSIO   An inviting eye; and yet methinks right modest.

IAGO   And when she speaks, is it not an alarum to love?

CASSIO	She is indeed perfection.
IAGO	Well, happiness to their sheets! Come lieutenant, I have a stoup of wine; and here without are a brace of Cyprus gallants that would fain have a measure to the health of black Othello.
CASSIO	Not to-night, good Iago: I have very poor and unhappy brains for drinking: I could well wish courtesy would invent some other custom of entertainment.
IAGO	O, they are our friends; but one cup: I 'll drink for you.
CASSIO	I have drunk but one cup to-night, and that was craftily qualified too, and behold, what innovation it makes here: I am unfortunate in the infirmity, and dare not task my weakness with any more.
IAGO	What, man! 't is a night of revels: the gallants desire it.
CASSIO	Where are they?

39

IAGO	Here at the door; I pray you, call them in.
CASSIO	I 'll do 't; but it dislikes me.
(Exit.)	

IAGO

If I can fasten but one cup upon him,
With that which he hath drunk to-night already,
He 'll be as full of quarrel and offence
As my young mistress' dog. Now, my sick fool Roderigo,
Whom love hath turn'd almost the wrong side out,
To Desdemona hath to-night caroused
Potations pottle-deep; and he 's to watch:
Three lads of Cyprus, noble swelling spirits,
That hold their honours in a wary distance,   50
The very elements of this warlike isle,
Have I to-night fluster'd with flowing cups,
And they watch too. Now, 'mongst this flock of
    drunkards,
Am I to put our Cassio in some action
That may offend the isle.—But here they come:
If consequence do but approve my dream,
My boat sails freely, both with wind and stream.

(Re-enter CASSIO; with him MONTANO and GENTLEMEN; SERVANTS following with wine.)

CASSIO	'Fore God, they have given me a rouse already.
MONTANO	Good faith, a little one; not past a pint, as I am a soldier. 59
IAGO	Some wine, ho!
(Sings)	And let me the canakin clink, clink;

	And let me the canakin clink:
	A soldier's a man;
	A life's but a span;
	Why, then, let a soldier drink.
	Some wine, boys!
CASSIO	'Fore God, an excellent song.
IAGO	I learned it in England, where, indeed, they are most potent in potting: your Dane, your German, and your swag-bellied Hollander—Drink, ho!—are nothing to 70 your English.
CASSIO	Is your Englishman so expert in his drinking?
IAGO	Why, he drinks you, with facility, your Dane dead drunk; he sweats not to overthrow your Almain; he gives your Hollander a vomit, ere the next pottle can be filled.
CASSIO	To the health of our general!
MONTANO	I am for it, lieutenant; and I 'll do you justice.
IAGO	O sweet England!
	King Stephen was a worthy peer, 80
	His breeches cost him but a crown;
	He held them sixpence all too dear,
	With that he call'd the tailor lown.
	He was a wight of high renown.
	And thou art but of low degree:
	'T is pride that pulls the country down;
	Then take thine auld cloak about thee.
	Some wine, ho!
CASSIO	Why, this is a more exquisite song than the other.
IAGO	Will you hear 't again? 90
CASSIO	No; for I hold him to be unworthy of his place that does those things. Well, God's above all; and there be souls must be saved, and there be souls must not be saved.
IAGO	It 's true, good lieutenant.
CASSIO	For mine own part,—no offence to the general, nor any man of quality,—I hope to be saved.
IAGO	And so do I too, lieutenant.

---

l. 83 *lown:* Lout, rascal.

CASSIO   Ay, but, by your leave, not before me; the lieutenant
            is to be saved before the ancient. Let 's have no more   100
            of this; let's to our affairs. God forgive us our sins!
            Gentlemen, let's look to our business. Do not think,
            gentlemen, I am drunk: this is my ancient; this is my
            right hand, and this is my left: I am not drunk now; I
            can stand well enough, and speak well enough.

ALL   Excellent well.

CASSIO   Why, very well then; you must not think that I am drunk.
  (Exit.)

MONTANO   To the platform, masters; come, let 's set the watch.

IAGO   You see this fellow that is gone before;
            He is a soldier fit to stand by Caesar
            And give direction: and do but see his vice;   111
            'T is to his virtue a just equinox,
            The one as long as the other: 't is pity of him.
            I fear the trust Othello puts him in,
            On some odd time of his infirmity,
            Will shake this island.

MONTANO   But is he often thus?

IAGO   'T is evermore the prologue to his sleep:

            He 'll watch the horologe a double set,
            If drink rock not his cradle.

MONTANO   It were well
            The general were put in mind of it.   120
            Perhaps he sees it not, or his good nature
            Prizes the virtue that appears in Cassio,
            And looks not on his evils: is not this true?

  (Enter RODERIGO.)
IAGO   (Aside to him) How now, Roderigo!
            I pray you, after the lieutenant; go.
  (Exit RODERIGO.)

MONTANO   And 't is great pity that the noble Moor
            Should hazard such a place as his own second
            With one of an ingraft infirmity:
            It were an honest action to say
            So to the Moor.

IAGO   Not I, for this fair island: 130
            I do love Cassio well; and would do much
            To cure him of this evil—But, hark! what noise?
  (Cry within: Help! Help!")

l. 112 a just equinox: Exactly equal.
l. 118 horologe: Clock. double set: Twenty-four hours.

(*Re-enter* CASSIO, *driving in* RODERIGO.)

CASSIO You rogue! you rascal!

MONTANO   What's the matter, lieutenant?

CASSIO A knave teach me my duty!
I'll beat the knave into a twiggen bottle.

RODERIGO Beat me!

CASSIO Dost thou prate, rogue?
(*Striking* RODERIGO.)

MONTANO Nay, good lieutenant; I pray you, sir, hold your hand.
(*Staying him.*)

CASSIO Let me go, sir, or I 'll knock you o'er the mazzard.   140

MONTANO Come, come, you 're drunk.

CASSIO Drunk!
(*They fight.*)

IAGO (*Aside to* RODERIGO) Away, I say; go out, and cry a
                   mutiny.
(*Exit* RODERIGO.)
Nay, good lieutenant!—alas, gentlemen;—
Help, ho! Lieutenant,—sir,—Montano,—sir;—
Help, masters!—Here 's a goodly watch indeed!
(*Bell rings.*)
Who 's that which rings the bell—Diablo, ho!
The town will rise: God 's will, lieutenant, hold!
You will be shamed for ever.

(*Re-enter* OTHELLO *and* ATTENDANTS.)

OTHELLO   What is the matter here?

MONTANO 'Zounds, I bleed still; I am hurt to the death.
(*Faints.*)

OTHELLO Hold, for your lives!

IAGO Hold, ho! Lieutenant,—sir,—Montano,—gentlemen,—
Have you forgot all sense of place and duty?
Hold! the general speaks to you; hold, hold, for shame!

OTHELLO Why, how now, ho! from whence ariseth this?
Are we turn'd Turks, and to ourselves do that
Which heaven hath forbid the Ottomites?
For Christian shame, put by this barbarous brawl:
He that stirs next to carve for his own rage
Holds his soul light; he dies upon his motion.   159
Silence that dreadful bell: it frights the isle

---

l. 136 *twiggen:* Covered with wicker.
l. 140 *mazzard:* Head.

From her propriety. What is the matter, masters?
Honest Iago, that look'st dead with grieving,
Speak, who began this? on thy love, I charge thee.

IAGO   I do not know; friends all but now, even now,
In quarter, and in terms like bride and groom
Devesting them for bed; and then, but now,
As if some planet had unwitted men,
Swords out, and tilting one at other's breast,
In opposition bloody. I cannot speak   169
Any beginning to this peevish odds;
And would in action glorious I had lost
Those legs that brought me to a part of it!

OTHELLO   How comes it, Michael, you are thus forgot?

CASSIO   I pray you, pardon me; I cannot speak.

OTHELLO   Worthy Montano, you were wont be civil;
The gravity and stillness of your youth
The world hath noted, and your name is great
In mouths of wisest censure: what 's the matter,
That you unlace your reputation thus
And spend your rich opinion for the name   180
Of a night-brawler? give me answer to it.

MONTANO   Worthy Othello, I am hurt to danger:
Your officer, Iago, can inform you,—
While I spare speech, which something now offends
   me,—
Of all that I do know: nor know I aught
By me that's said or done amiss this night;
Unless self-charity be sometimes a vice,
And to defend ourselves it be a sin
When violence assails us.

OTHELLO   Now, by heaven,
My blood begins my safer guides to rule;   190
And passion, having my best judgement collied,
Assays to lead the way: if I once stir,
Or do but lift this arm, the best of you
Shall sink in my rebuke. Give me to know
How this foul rout began, who set it on;
And he that is approved in this offence,
Though he had twinn'd with me, both at a birth,
Shall lose me. What! in a town of war,
Yet wild, the people's hearts brimful of fear,

---

l. 165 *quarter:* Friendship.
l. 191 *collied:* Darkened.

	To manage private and domestic quarrel,	200
	In night, and on the court and guard of safety!	
	'T is monstrous. Iago, who began 't?	

MONTANO   If partially affined, or leagued in office,
Thou dost deliver more or less than truth,
Thou art no soldier.

IAGO   Touch me not so near:
I had rather have this tongue cut from my mouth
Than it should do offence to Michael Cassio;
Yet, I persuade myself, to speak the truth
Shall nothing wrong him. Thus it is, general.
Montano and myself being in speech,   210
There comes a fellow crying out for help;
And Cassio following him with determined sword,
To execute upon him. Sir, this gentleman
Steps in to Cassio and entreats his pause:
Myself the crying fellow did pursue,
Lest by his clamour—as it so fell out—
The town might fall in fright: he, swift of foot,
Outran my purpose; and I return'd the rather
For that I heard the clink and fall of swords,
And Cassio high in oath; which till to-night
I ne'er might say before. When I came back—   221
For this was brief—I found them close together,
At blow and thrust; even as again they were
When you yourself did part them.
More of this matter cannot I report:
But men are men; the best sometimes forget:
Though Cassio did some little wrong to him,
As men in rage strike those that wish them best,
Yet surely Cassio, I believe, received
From him that fled some strange indignity,   230
Which patience could not pass.

OTHELLO   I know, Iago,
Thy honesty and love doth mince this matter,
Making it light to Cassio. Cassio, I love thee;
But never more be officer of mine.

(Re-enter DESDEMONA, attended.)
Look, if my gentle love be not raised up!
I'll make thee an example,

DESDEMONA   What's the matter?

---

l. 203 *If . . . office:* If prejudiced by friendship.

OTHELLO   All 's well now, sweeting; come away to bed.
    (To MONTANO, *who is led off.*)
                Sir, for your hurts, myself will be your surgeon:
                Lead him off.
                Iago, look with care about the town,   240
                And silence those whom this vile brawl distracted.
                Come, Desdemona: 't is the soldiers' life
                To have their balmy slumbers waked with strife.
    (*Exeunt all but* IAGO *and* CASSIO.)

IAGO   What, are you hurt, Lieutenant?

CASSIO   Ay, past all surgery.

IAGO   Marry, heaven forbid!

CASSIO   Reputation, reputation, reputation! O, I have lost my
            reputation! I have lost the immortal part of myself, and
            what remains is bestial. My reputation, Iago, my repu-
            tation!

IAGO   As I am an honest man, I thought you had received   250
            some bodily wound; there is more sense in that than
            in reputation. Reputation is an idle and most false
            imposition: oft got without merit, and lost without
            deserving: you have lost no reputation at all, unless you
            repute yourself such a loser. What, man! there are
            ways to recover the general again: you are but now
            cast in his mood, a punishment more in policy than in
            malice; even so as one would beat his offenceless dog
            to affright an imperious lion: sue to him again, and
            he 's yours.   260

CASSIO   I will rather sue to be despised than to deceive so
            good a commander with so slight, so drunken, and so
            indiscreet an officer. Drunk? and speak parrot? and
            squabble? swagger? swear? and discourse fustian
            with one's own shadow? O thou invisible spirit of wine,
            if thou hast no name to be known by, let us call thee
            devil!

IAGO   What was he that you followed with your sword? What
            had he done to you?

CASSIO   I know not.

IAGO   Is 't possible?

CASSIO   I remember a mass of things, but nothing distinctly; a
            quarrel, but nothing wherefore. O God, that men should

---

l. 257 *cast in his mood:* Dismissed in his anger.
l. 264 *fustian:* Nonsense.

put an enemy in their mouths to steal away their brains! that we should, with joy, pleasance, revel and applause, transform ourselves into beasts!

IAGO Why, but you are now well enough: how came you   277
thus recovered?

CASSIO It hath pleased the devil drunkenness to give place to the devil wrath: one unperfectness shows me another, to make me frankly despise myself.

IAGO Come, you are too severe a moraler: as the time, the place, and the condition of this country stands, I could heartily wish this had not befallen; but, since it is as it is, mend it for your own good.

CASSIO I will ask him for my place again; he shall tell me I am a drunkard! Had I as many mouths as Hydra, such an answer would stop them all. To be now a sensible   288
man, by and by a fool, and presently a beast! O strange! Every inordinate cup is unblessed and the ingredient is a devil.

IAGO Come, come, good wine is a good familiar creature, if it be well used: exclaim no more against it. And, good lieutenant, I think you think I love you.

CASSIO I have well approved it, sir. I drunk!

IAGO You or any man living may be drunk at some time, man. I 'll tell you what you shall do. Our general's wife is now the general: I may say so in this respect, for that he hath devoted and given up himself to the con-templation, mark, and denotement of her parts and   300
graces: confess yourself freely to her; importune her help to put you in your place again: she is of so free, so kind, so apt, so blessed a disposition, she holds it a vice in her goodness not to do more than she is requested: this broken joint between you and her husband entreat her to splinter; and, my fortunes against any lay worth naming, this crack of your love shall grow stronger than it was before.

CASSIO You advise me well.

IAGO I protest, in the sincerity of love and honest kindness.

CASSIO I think it freely; and betimes in the morning I will beseech the virtuous Desdemona to undertake for me: 312
I am desperate of my fortunes if they check me here.

---

l. 287 *Hydra:* Mythical monster with many heads.

IAGO	You are in the right. Good night, lieutenant; I must to the watch.

CASSIO	Good night, honest Iago.

(Exit.)

IAGO And what 's he then that says I play the villain?
When this advice is free I give and honest,
Probal to thinking and indeed the course
To win the Moor again? For 't is most easy
The inclining Desdemona to subdue
In any honest suit: she 's framed as fruitful
As the free elements. And then for her
To win the Moor—were 't to renounce his baptism,
All seals and symbols of redeemed sin,
His soul is so enfetter'd to her love,
That she may make, unmake, do what she list,
Even as her appetite shall play the god
With his weak function. How am I then a villain
To counsel Cassio to this parallel course,
Directly to his good? Divinity of hell!
When devils will the blackest sins put on,   332
They do suggest at first with heavenly shows,
As I do now: for whiles this honest fool
Plies Desdemona to repair his fortunes
And she for him pleads strongly to the Moor,
I 'll pour this pestilence into his ear,
That she repeals him for her body's lust;
And by how much she strives to do him good,
She shall undo her credit with the Moor.   340
So will I turn her virtue into pitch,
And out of her own goodness make the net
That shall enmesh them all.
(Re-enter RODERIGO.)   How now, Roderigo!

RODERIGO I do follow here in the chase, not like a hound that hunts, but one that fills up the cry. My money is almost spent; I have been to-night exceedingly well cudgelled; and I think the issue will be, I shall have so much experience for my pains, and so, with no money at all and a little more wit, return again to Venice.

IAGO How poor are they that have not patience!   350
What wound did ever heal but by degrees?
Thou know'st we work by wit, and not by witchcraft;
And wit depends on dilatory time.
Does 't not go well? Cassio hath beaten thee,

---

l. 338 *repeals:* Recalls; here, sues for his recall.

And thou by that small hurt hast cashier'd Cassio:
Though other things grow fair against the sun,
Yet fruits that blossom first will first be ripe:
Content thyself awhile. By the mass, 't is morning;
Pleasure and action make the hours seem short.
Retire thee; go where thou are billeted: 360
Away, I say; thou shalt know more hereafter:
Nay, get thee gone. (*Exit* RODERIGO.) Two things are
        to be done:
My wife must move for Cassio to her mistress;
I 'll set her on;
Myself the while to draw the Moor apart,
And bring him jump when he may Cassio find
Soliciting his wife: ay, that's the way:
Dull not device by coldness and delay

(*Exit.*)

ACT III

SCENE I. *Cyprus. Before the castle.*

(*Enter* CASSIO *and some* MUSICIANS.)

CASSIO   Masters, play here; I will content your pains;
Something that 's brief; and bid "Good morrow, general."

(*Music.*)

(*Enter* CLOWN.)

CLOWN   Why, masters, have your instruments been in Naples, that they speak i' the nose thus?

FIRST MUS.   How, sir, how!

CLOWN   Are these, I pray you, wind-instruments?

FIRST MUS.   Ay, marry, are they, sir.

CLOWN   O, thereby hangs a tail.

FIRST MUS.   Whereby hangs a tale, sir?   9

CLOWN   Marry, sir, by many a wind-instrument that I know. But, masters, here 's money for you: and the general so likes your music, that he desires you, for love's sake, to make no more noise with it.

FIRST MUS.   Well, sir, we will not.

CLOWN   If you have any music that may not be heard, to 't again: but, as they say, to hear music the general does not greatly care.

FIRST MUS.   We have none such, sir.

CLOWN	Then put up your pipes in your bag, for I 'll away: go; vanish into air; away!

(Exeunt MUSICIANS.)

CASSIO	Dost thou hear, my honest friend?	19
CLOWN	No, I hear not your honest friend; I hear you.	
CASSIO	Prithee, keep up thy quillets. There's a poor piece of gold for thee: if the gentlewoman that attends the general's wife be stirring, tell her there's one Cassio entreats her a little favour of speech: wilt thou do this?	
CLOWN	She is stirring, sir: if she will stir hither, I shall seem to notify unto her.	
CASSIO	Do, good my friend.	

(Exit CLOWN.)
(Enter IAGO.)

           In happy time, Iago.

IAGO	You have not been a-bed, then?	
CASSIO	Why, no; the day had broke	
	Before we parted. I have made bold, Iago,	
	To send in to your wife: my suit to her	31
	Is, that she will to virtuous Desdemona	
	Procure me some access.	
IAGO	I 'll send her to you presently;	
	And I 'll devise a mean to draw the Moor	
	Out of the way, that your converse and business	
	May be more free.	
CASSIO	I humbly thank you for 't.	

(Exit IAGO.)

        I never knew
A Florentine more kind and honest.

(Enter EMILIA.)

EMILIA	Good morrow, good lieutenant: I am sorry	
	For your displeasure; but all will sure be well.	40
	The general and his wife are talking of it;	
	And she speaks for you stoutly: the Moor replies,	
	That he you hurt is of great fame in Cyprus	
	And great affinity, and that in wholesome wisdom	
	He might not but refuse you; but he protests he loves	
	you	
	And needs no other suitor but his likings	
	To take the safest occasion by the front	
	To bring you in again.	

---

l. 21 *quillets:* Plays on words.
l. 44 *affinity:* Kindred.
l. 47 *front:* Forelock.

CASSIO
                                    Yet, I beseech you,
        If you think fit, or that it may be done,
        Give me advantage of some brief discourse   50
        With Desdemona alone.

EMILIA
                                    Pray you, come in:
        I will bestow you where you shall have time
        To speak your bosom freely.

CASSIO   I am much bound to you.
    (*Exeunt.*)

SCENE II. *A room in the castle.*

(*Enter* OTHELLO, IAGO, *and* GENTLEMEN.)

OTHELLO   These letters give, Iago, to the pilot;
        And by him do my duties to the senate:
        That done, I will be walking on the works;
        Repair there to me.

IAGO   Well, my good lord, I 'll do 't.

OTHELLO   This fortification, gentlemen, shall we see 't?

GENT.   We 'll wait upon your lordship.
    (*Exeunt.*)

SCENE III. *The garden of the castle.*

(*Enter* DESDEMONA, CASSIO, *and* EMILIA.)

DESDEMONA   Be thou assured, good Cassio, I will do
        All my abilities in thy behalf.

EMILIA   Good madam, do: I warrant it grieves my husband,
        As if the case were his.

DESDEMONA   O, that 's an honest fellow. Do not doubt, Cassio,
        But I will have my lord and you again
        As friendly as you were.

CASSIO
                                    Bounteous madam,
        Whatever shall become of Michael Cassio,
        He 's never any thing but your true servant.

DESDEMONA   I know 't; I thank you. You do love my lord: 10
        You have known him long; and be you well assured
        He shall in strangeness stand no further off
        Than in a politic distance.

CASSIO
                                    Ay, but, lady,

That policy may either last so long,
Or feed upon such nice and waterish diet,
Or breed itself so out of circumstance,
That, I being absent and my place supplied,
My general will forget my love and service.

DESDEMONA   Do not doubt that; before Emilia here   19
I give thee warrant of thy place: assure thee,
If I do vow a friendship, I 'll perform it
To the last article: my lord shall never rest;
I 'll watch him tame and talk him out of patience;
His bed shall seem a school, his board a shrift;
I 'll intermingle everything he does
With Cassio's suit: therefore be merry, Cassio;
For thy solicitor shall rather die
Than give thy cause away.

EMILIA   Madam, here comes my lord.

CASSIO   Madam, I 'll take my leave.   30

DESDEMONA   Nay, stay, and hear me speak.

CASSIO   Madam, not now: I am very ill at ease,
Unfit for mine own purposes.

DESDEMONA   Well, do your discretion.
   (Exit CASSIO.)

  (Enter OTHELLO and IAGO.)
IAGO   Ha! I like not that.

OTHELLO   What dost thou say?

IAGO   Nothing, my lord: or if—I know not what.

OTHELLO   Was not that Cassio parted from my wife?

IAGO   Cassio, my lord! No, sure, I cannot think it,
That he would steal away so guilty-like,
Seeing you coming.

OTHELLO   I do believe 't was he.

DESDEMONA   How now, my lord!   41
I have been talking with a suitor here,
A man that languishes in your displeasure.

OTHELLO   Who is 't you mean?

DESDEMONA   Why, your lieutenant, Cassio. Good my lord,
If I have any grace or power to move you,
His present reconciliation take;

---

l. 23 watch him tame: Keep him awake.

	For if he be not one that truly loves you,	
	That errs in ignorance and not in cunning,	
	I have no judgement in an honest face;	50
	I prithee, call him back.	

OTHELLO   Went he hence now?

DESDEMONA   Ay, sooth; so humbled
That he hath left part of his grief with me,
To suffer with him. Good love, call him back.

OTHELLO   Not now, sweet Desdemona; some other time.

DESDEMONA   But shall 't be shortly?

OTHELLO   The sooner, sweet, for you.

DESDEMONA   Shall 't be to-night at supper?

OTHELLO   No, not to-night.

DESDEMONA   To-morrow dinner, then?

OTHELLO   I shall not dine at home;
I meet the captains at the citadel.

DESDEMONA   Why then to-morrow night; or Tuesday morn;   60
On Tuesday noon, or night; on Wednesday morn:
I prithee, name the time; but let it not
Exceed three days: in faith he's penitent;
And yet his trespass, in our common reason—
Save that, they say, the wars must make examples
Out of their best—is not almost a fault
To incur a private check. When shall he come?
Tell me, Othello: I wonder in my soul,
What you would ask me, that I should deny,
Or stand so mammering on. What! Michael Cassio,   70
That came a-wooing with you, and so many a time,
When I have spoke of you dispraisingly,
Hath ta'en your part; to have so much to do
To bring him in! Trust me, I could do much,—

OTHELLO   Prithee, no more: let him come when he will;
I will deny thee nothing.

DESDEMONA   Why, this is not a boon;
'T is as I should entreat you wear your gloves,
Or feed on nourishing dishes, or keep you warm,
Or sue to you to do a peculiar profit   79
To your own person: nay, when I have a suit
Wherein I mean to touch your love indeed,

---

l. 70 *mammering:* Hesitating.

It shall be full of poise and difficult weight,
And fearful to be granted.

OTHELLO   I will deny thee nothing:
Whereon, I do beseech thee, grant me this,
To leave me but a little to myself.

DESDEMONA   Shall I deny you? no: farewell, my lord.

OTHELLO   Farewell, my Desdemona: I'll come to thee straight.

DESDEMONA   Emilia, come. Be as your fancies teach you;
Whate'er you be, I am obedient.
    (*Exeunt* DESDEMONA *and* EMILIA.)

OTHELLO   Excellent wretch! Perdition catch my soul,   90
But I do love thee! and when I love thee not,
Chaos is come again.

IAGO   My noble, lord,—

OTHELLO   What dost thou say, Iago?

IAGO   Did Michael Cassio, when you woo'd my lady,
Know of your love?

OTHELLO   He did, from first to last: why dost thou ask?

IAGO   But for a satisfaction of my thought;
No further harm.

OTHELLO   Why of thy thought, Iago?

IAGO   I did not think he had been acquainted with her.

OTHELLO   O, yes; and went between us very oft.   100

IAGO   Indeed!

OTHELLO   Indeed! ay, indeed: discern'st thou aught in that?
Is he not honest?

IAGO   Honest, my lord!

OTHELLO   Honest! ay, honest.

IAGO   My lord, for aught I know.

OTHELLO   What dost thou think?

IAGO   Think, my lord!

OTHELLO   Think, my lord!
        By heaven, he echoes me,
As if there were some monster in his thought
Too hideous to be shown. Thou dost mean something:

---

l. 82 *poise:* Weight.

I heard thee say even now, thou likedst not that,
When Cassio left my wife: what didst not like?   110
And when I told thee he was of my counsel
In my whole course of wooing, thou criedst "Indeed!"
And didst contract and purse thy brow together,
As if thou then hadst shut up in thy brain
Some horrible conceit: if thou dost love me,
Show me thy thought.

IAGO   My lord, you know I love you.

OTHELLO   I think thou dost;
And, for I know thou 'rt full of love and honesty,
And weigh'st thy words before thou givest them breath,
Therefore these stops of thine fright me the more: 120
For such things in a false disloyal knave
Are tricks of custom, but in a man that's just
They are close delations, working from the heart
That passion cannot rule.

IAGO   For Michael Cassio,
I dare be sworn I think that he is honest.

OTHELLO   I think so too.

IAGO   Men should be what they seem;
Or those that be not, would they might seem none!

OTHELLO   Certain, men should be what they seem.

IAGO   Why, then, I think Cassio's an honest man.

OTHELLO   Nay, yet there's more in this: 130
I prithee, speak to me as to thy thinkings,
As thou dost ruminate, and give thy worst of thoughts
The worst of words.

IAGO   Good my lord, pardon me:
Though I am bound to every act of duty,
I am not bound to that all slaves are free to.
Utter my thoughts? Why, say they are vile and false;
As where 's that palace whereinto foul things
Sometimes intrude not? who has a breast so pure,
But some uncleanly apprehensions   139
Keep leets and law-days and in session sit
With meditations lawful?

OTHELLO   Thou dost conspire against thy friend, Iago,

---

l. 115 *conceit:* Notion.
l. 123 *close delations:* Secret accusations.
l. 140 *Keep leets:* Hold court.

If thou but think'st him wrong'd and makest his ear
A stranger to thy thoughts.

IAGO   I do beseech you—
Though I perchance am vicious in my guess,
As, I confess, it is my nature's plague
To spy into abuses, and oft my jealousy
Shapes faults that are not—that your wisdom yet,
From one that so imperfectly conceits,
Would take no notice, nor build yourself a trouble   150
Out of his scattering and unsure observance.
It were not for your quiet nor your good,
Nor for my manhood, honesty, or wisdom,
To let you know my thoughts.

OTHELLO   What dost thou mean?

IAGO   Good name in man and woman, dear my lord,
Is the immediate jewel of their souls:
Who steals my purse steals trash; 't is something,
            nothing;
'T was mine, 't is his, and has been slave to thousands;
But he that filches from me my good name
Robs me of that which not enriches him,
And makes me poor indeed.   161

OTHELLO   By heaven, I 'll know thy thoughts.

IAGO   You cannot, if my heart were in your hand;
Nor shall not, whilst 't is in my custody.

OTHELLO   Ha!

IAGO   O, beware, my lord, of jealousy;
It is the green-eyed monster which doth mock
The meat it feeds on: that cuckold lives in bliss
Who, certain of his fate, loves not his wronger;
But, O, what damned minutes tells he o'er
Who dotes, yet doubts, suspects, yet strongly loves!   170

OTHELLO   O misery!

IAGO   Poor and content is rich and rich enough,
But riches fineless is as poor as winter
To him that ever fears he shall be poor.
Good heaven, the souls of all my tribe defend
From jealousy!

OTHELLO   Why, why is this?
Think'st thou I 'ld make a life of jealousy,

---

l. 173 *fineless:* Boundless.

To follow still the changes of the moon
With fresh suspicions? No; to be once in doubt
Is once to be resolved: exchange me for a goat,   180
When I shall turn the business of my soul
To such exsufflicate and blown surmises,
Matching thy inference. 'T is not to make me jealous
To say my wife is fair, feeds well, loves company,
Is free of speech, sings, plays and dances well;
Where virtue is, these are more virtuous:
Nor from mine own weak merits will I draw
The smallest fear or doubt of her revolt;
For she had eyes, and chose me. No, Iago;
I 'll see before I doubt; when I doubt, prove;
And on the proof, there is no more but this,
Away at once with love or jealousy!   192

IAGO   I am glad of it; for now I shall have reason
To show the love and duty that I bear you
With franker spirit: therefore, as I am bound,
Receive it from me. I speak not yet of proof.
Look to your wife; observe her well with Cassio;
Wear your eye thus, not jealous nor secure:
I would not have your free and noble nature,
Out of self-bounty, be abused; look to 't:
I know our country disposition well;   201
In Venice they do let heaven see the pranks
They dare not show their husbands; their best con-
      science
Is not to leave 't undone, but keep 't unknown.

OTHELLO   Dost thou say so?

IAGO   She did deceive her father, marrying you;
And when she seem'd to shake and fear your looks,
She loved them most.

OTHELLO   And so she did.

IAGO   Why, go to, then;
She that, so young, could give out such a seeming,
To seel her father's eyes up close as oak—
He thought 't was witchcraft—but I am much to blame;   211
I humbly do beseech you of your pardon
For too much loving you.

OTHELLO   I am bound to thee for ever.

IAGO   I see this hath a little dash'd your spirits.

l. 182 *exsufflicate and blown:* Exaggerated.
l. 188 *revolt:* Misconduct.
l. 210 *seel:* Close.

OTHELLO   Not a jot, not a jot.

IAGO   I' faith, I fear it has.
            I hope you will consider what is spoke
            Comes from my love. But I do see you 're moved;
            I am to pray you not to strain my speech
            To grosser issues nor to larger reach
            Than to suspicion.   220

OTHELLO   I will not.

IAGO   Should you do so, my lord,
            My speech should fall into such vile success
            As my thoughts aim not at. Cassio 's my worthy friend—
            My lord, I see you're moved.

OTHELLO   No, not much moved:
            I do not think but Desdemona's honest.

IAGO   Long live she so! and long live you to think so!

OTHELLO   And yet, how nature erring from itself,—

IAGO   Ay, there 's the point: as—to be bold with you—
            Not to affect many proposed matches   229
            Of her own clime, complexion, and degree,
            Whereto we see in all things nature tends—
            Foh! one may smell in such a will most rank,
            Foul disproportion, thoughts unnatural.
            But pardon me; I do not in position
            Distinctly speak of her; though I may fear
            Her will, recoiling to her better judgement,
            May fall to match you with her country forms
            And happily repent.

OTHELLO   Farewell, farewell:
            If more thou dost perceive, let me know more;   239
            Set on thy wife to observe: leave me, Iago.

IAGO   (Going) My lord, I take my leave.

OTHELLO   Why did I marry? This honest creature doubtless
            Sees and knows more, much more, than he unfolds.

IAGO   (Returning) My lord, I would I might entreat your honour
            To scan this thing no further; leave it to time:
            Though it be fit that Cassio have this place
            For, sure, he fills it up with great ability,
            Yet, if you please to hold him off awhile,
            You shall by that perceive him and his means: 249

---

l. 229 *affect:* Favor.

                    Note, if your lady strain his entertainment
                    With any strong or vehement importunity;
                    Much will be seen in that. In the mean time,
                    Let me be thought too busy in my fears—
                    As worthy cause I have to fear I am—
                    And hold her free, I do beseech your honour.

OTHELLO   Fear not my government.

IAGO   I once more take my leave.
    (*Exit.*)

OTHELLO   This fellow 's of exceeding honesty,
                    And knows all qualities, with a learned spirit,
                    Of human dealings. If I do prove her haggard,   260
                    Though that her jesses were my dear heartstrings,
                    I'ld whistle her off and let her down the wind,
                    To prey at fortune. Haply, for I am black
                    And have not those soft parts of conversation
                    That chamberers have, or for I am declined
                    Into the vale of years,—yet that's not much—
                    She 's gone. I am abused; and my relief
                    Must be to loathe her. O curse of marriage,
                    That we can call these delicate creatures ours,
                    And not their appetites! I had rather be a toad,   270
                    And live upon the vapour of a dungeon,
                    Than keep a corner in the thing I love
                    For others' uses. Yet, 't is the plague of great ones;
                    Prerogatived are they less than the base;
                    'T is destiny unshunnable, like death:
                    Even then this forked plague is fated to us
                    When we do quicken. Desdemona comes:
    (*Re-enter* DESDEMONA *and* EMILIA.)
                    If she be false, O, then heaven mocks itself!
                    I 'll not believe 't.

DESDEMONA   How now, my dear Othello!
                    Your dinner, and the generous islanders   280
                    By you invited, do attend your presence.

OTHELLO   I am to blame.

---

l. 250 *strain his entertainment:* Urge his reinstatement.
l. 255 *hold her free:* Consider her innocent.
l. 256 *government:* Self-control.
l. 260 *haggard:* Unfaithful (a wild hawk).
l. 261 *jesses:* Leg-straps.
ll. 262–3 *I'ld . . . fortune:* I would release her and let her shift for herself.
l. 263 *Haply:* Perhaps.
l. 265 *chamberers:* Gallants.
l. 276 *forked plague:* Cuckoldry (a cuckold is said to wear horns in his forehead).

DESDEMONA	Why do you speak so faintly?
	Are you not well?
OTHELLO	I have a pain upon my forehead here.
DESDEMONA	'Faith, that 's with watching; 't will away again:
	Let me but bind it hard, within this hour
	It will be well.
OTHELLO	Your napkin is too little:

(*He puts the handkerchief from him; and it drops.*)
          Let it alone. Come, I 'll go in with you.

DESDEMONA	I am very sorry that you are not well.

(*Exeunt* OTHELLO *and* DESDEMONA.)

EMILIA	I am glad I have found this napkin:	290
	This was her first remembrance from the Moor:	
	My wayward husband hath a hundred times	
	Woo'd me to steal it; but she so loves the token,	
	For he conjured her she should ever keep it,	
	That she reserves it evermore about her	
	To kiss and talk to. I 'll have the work ta'en out,	
	And give 't Iago: what he will do with it	
	Heaven knows, not I;	
	I nothing but to please his fantasy.	

(*Re-enter* IAGO.)

IAGO	How now! what do you here alone?	
EMILIA	Do not you chide; I have a thing for you.	301
IAGO	A thing for me? it is a common thing—	
EMILIA	Ha!	
IAGO	To have a foolish wife.	
EMILIA	O, is that all? What will you give me now	
	For that same handkerchief?	
IAGO	What handkerchief?	
EMILIA	What handkerchief!	
	Why, that the Moor first gave to Desdemona;	
	That which so often you did bid me steal.	
IAGO	Hast stol'n it from her?	310
EMILIA	No, 'faith; she let it drop by negligence,	
	And, to the advantage, I, being here, took 't up.	
	Look, here it is.	

---

l. 296 *the work ta'en out:* The embroidery copied.

IAGO	A good wench; give it me.
EMILIA	What will you do with 't, that you have been so earnest To have me filch it?
IAGO	(*Snatching it*) Why, what 's that to you?
EMILIA	If 't be not for some purpose of import Give 't me again: poor lady, she 'll run mad When she shall lack it.
IAGO	Be not acknown on 't; I have use for it. Go, leave me. 320

(*Exit* EMILIA.)

I will in Cassio's lodging lose this napkin,
And let him find it. Trifles light as air
Are to the jealous confirmations strong
As proofs of holy writ: this may do something.
The Moor already changes with my poison,
Dangerous conceits are in their natures poisons,
Which at the first are scarce found to distaste,
But with a little act upon the blood,
Burn like the mines of sulphur. I did say so:
Look, where he comes!

(*Re-enter* OTHELLO.)   Not poppy, nor mandragora,   330
Nor all the drowsy syrups of the world,
Shall ever medicine thee to that sweet sleep
Which thou owedst yesterday.

OTHELLO	Ha! ha! false to me?
IAGO	Why, how now, general! no more of that.
OTHELLO	Avaunt! be gone! thou hast set me on the rack: I swear 't is better to be much abused Than but to know 't a little.
IAGO	How now, my lord!
OTHELLO	What sense had I of her stol'n hours of lust? I saw 't not, thought it not, it harm'd not me: I slept the next night well, was free and merry; 340 I found not Cassio's kisses on her lips; He that is robb'd, not wanting what is stol'n, Let him not know 't, and he 's not robb'd at all.
IAGO	I am sorry to hear this.
OTHELLO	I had been happy, if the general camp, Pioners and all, had tasted her sweet body,

---

l. 330 *mandragora:* A soporific drug.
l. 346 *Pioners:* Sappers and miners, soldiers of a low type.

So I had nothing known. O, now for ever
Farewell the tranquil mind! farewell content!
Farewell the plumed troop and the big wars
That make ambition virtue! O, farewell!   350
Farewell the neighing steed and the shrill trump,
The spirit-stirring drum, the ear-piercing fife,
The royal banner, and all quality,
Pride, pomp and circumstance of glorious war!
And, O you mortal engines whose rude throats
The immortal Jove's dread clamours counterfeit,
Farewell! Othello's occupation 's gone!

IAGO   Is 't possible, my lord?

OTHELLO   Villain, be sure thou prove my love a whore,
          Be sure of it; give me the ocular proof;   360
          Or, by the worth of man's eternal soul,
          Thou hadst been better have been born a dog
          Than answer my waked wrath!

IAGO   Is 't come to this?

OTHELLO   Make me to see 't; at the least, so prove it,
          That the probation bear no hinge nor loop
          To hang a doubt on; or woe upon thy life!

IAGO   My noble lord,—

OTHELLO   If thou dost slander her and torture me,
          Never pray more; abandon all remorse;
          On horror's head horrors accumulate;   370
          Do deeds to make heaven weep, all earth amazed;
          For nothing canst thou to damnation add
          Greater than that.

IAGO   O grace! O heaven forgive me!
          Are you a man? have you a soul or sense?
          God be wi' you; take mine office. O wretched fool,
          That livest to make thine honesty a vice!
          O monstrous world! Take note, take note, O world,
          To be direct and honest is not safe.
          I thank you for this profit, and from hence
          I 'll love no friend, sith love breeds such offence.   380

OTHELLO   Nay, stay: thou shouldst be honest.

IAGO   I should be wise, for honesty 's a fool
          And loses that it works for.

---

l. 355 *mortal engines:* Deadly cannon.

OTHELLO	By the world, I think my wife be honest and think she is not; I think that thou art just and think thou art not. I'll have some proof. Her name, that was as fresh As Dian's visage, is now begrimed and black As mine own face. If there be cords, or knives, Poison, or fire, or suffocating streams, I 'll not endure it. Would I were satisfied!

389

IAGO	I see, sir, you are eaten up with passion: I do repent me that I put it to you. You would be satisfied?

OTHELLO	Would! nay, I will.

IAGO	And may: but, how? how satisfied, my lord? Would you, the supervisor, grossly gape on— Behold her topp'd?

OTHELLO	Death and damnation! O!

IAGO	It were a tedious difficulty I think, To bring them to that prospect: damn them then, If ever mortal eyes do see them bolster More than their own! What then? how then? What shall I say? Where 's satisfaction? It is impossible you should see this, Were they as prime as goats, as hot as monkeys, As salt as wolves in pride, and fools as gross As ignorance made drunk. But yet, I say, If imputation and strong circumstances, Which lead directly to the door of truth, Will give you satisfaction, you may have 't.

402

OTHELLO	Give me a living reason she's disloyal.

IAGO	I do not like the office: But, sith I am enter'd in this cause so far, Prick'd to 't by foolish honesty and love, I will go on. I lay with Cassio lately; And, being troubled with a raging tooth, I could not sleep. There are a kind of men so loose of soul, That in their sleeps will mutter their affairs: One of this kind is Cassio: In sleep I heard him say "Sweet Desdemona, Let us be wary, let us hide our loves";

410

420

---

l. 399 *bolster:* Lie together.
l. 403 *prime:* Lustful.
l. 404 *salt:* Wanton.

And then, sir, would he gripe and wring my hand,
Cry "O sweet creature!" and then kiss me hard,
As if he pluck'd up kisses by the roots
That grew upon my lips; then laid his leg
Over my thigh, and sigh'd, and kiss'd; and then
Cried "Cursed fate that gave thee to the Moor!"

OTHELLO   O monstrous! monstrous!

IAGO   Nay, this was but his dream.

OTHELLO   But this denoted a foregone conclusion:
'T is a shrewd doubt, though it be but a dream.

IAGO   And this may help to thicken other proofs   430
That do demonstrate thinly.

OTHELLO   I'll tear her all to pieces.

IAGO   Nay, but be wise: yet we see nothing done;
She may be honest yet. Tell me but this,
Have you not sometimes seen a handkerchief
Spotted with strawberries in your wife's hand?

OTHELLO   I gave her such a one; 't was my first gift.

IAGO   I know not that; but such a handkerchief—
I am sure it was your wife's—did I to-day
See Cassio wipe his beard with.

OTHELLO   If it be that,—

IAGO   If it be that, or any that was hers,
It speaks against her with the other proofs.

OTHELLO   O, that the slave had forty thousand lives!   442
One is too poor, too weak for my revenge.
Now do I see 't is true. Look here, Iago;
All my fond love thus do I blow to heaven.
'T is gone.
Arise, black vengeance, from thy hollow cell!
Yield up, O love, thy crown and hearted throne
To tyrannous hate! Swell, bosom, with thy fraught,
For 't is of aspics' tongues!

IAGO   Yet be content.   450

OTHELLO   O, blood, blood, blood!

IAGO   Patience, I say; your mind perhaps may change.

OTHELLO   Never, Iago. Like to the Pontic sea,

---

l. 449 *fraught:* Freight, burden.
l. 450 *aspics':* Asps'.

Whose icy current and compulsive course
Ne'er feels retiring ebb, but keeps due on
To the Propontic and the Hellespont,
Even so my bloody thoughts, with violent pace,
Shall ne'er look back, ne'er ebb to humble love,
Till that a capable and wide revenge
Swallow them up. Now, by yond marble heaven,   460
(*Kneels*) In the due reverence of a sacred vow
I here engage my words.

IAGO   Do not rise yet.
(*Kneels*) Witness, you ever-burning lights above,
You elements that clip us round about,
Witness that here Iago doth give up
The execution of his wit, hands, heart,
To wrong'd Othello's service! Let him command,
And to obey shall be in me remorse,
What bloody business ever.

(*They rise.*)

OTHELLO   I greet thy love,
Not with vain thanks, but with acceptance bounteous,   470
And will upon the instant put thee to 't:
Within these three days let me hear thee say
That Cassio's not alive.

IAGO   My friend is dead; 't is done at your request:
But let her live.

OTHELLO   Damn her, lewd minx! O, damn her!
Come, go with me apart; I will withdraw,
To furnish me with some swift means of death
For the fair devil. Now art thou my lieutenant.

IAGO   I am your own for ever.
(*Exeunt.*)

SCENE IV. *Before the castle.*

(*Enter* DESDEMONA, EMILIA, *and* CLOWN.)

DESDEMONA   Do you know, sirrah, where Lieutenant Cassio lies?

CLOWN   I dare not say he lies any where.

DESDEMONA   Why, man?

---

l. 459 *capable and wide:* Sufficient.
l. 464 *clip:* Embrace.
l. 468 *remorse:* Pity.

CLOWN	He is a soldier, and for one to say a soldier lies, is stabbing.
DESDEMONA	Go to: where lodges he?
CLOWN	To tell you where he lodges, is to tell you where I lie.
DESDEMONA	Can any thing be made of this?
CLOWN	I know not where he lodges, and for me to devise a lodging and say he lies here or he lies there, were to 10 lie in mine own throat.
DESDEMONA	Can you inquire him out, and be edified by report?
CLOWN	I will catechize the world for him; that is, make questions, and by them answer.
DESDEMONA	Seek him, bid him come hither: tell him I have moved my lord on his behalf, and hope all will be well.
CLOWN	To do this is within the compass of man's wit; and therefore I will attempt the doing it.
(Exit.)	
DESDEMONA	Where should I lose that handkerchief, Emilia?
EMILIA	I know not, madam. 20
DESDEMONA	Believe me, I had rather have lost my purse Full of crusadoes: and, but my noble Moor Is true of mind and made of no such baseness As jealous creatures are, it were enough To put him to ill thinking.
EMILIA	Is he not jealous?
DESDEMONA	Who, he? I think the sun where he was born Drew all such humours from him.
EMILIA	Look, where he comes.
DESDEMONA	I will not leave him now till Cassio Be call'd to him.
(Enter OTHELLO.)	How is 't with you, my lord?
OTHELLO	Well, my good lady. (*Aside*) O, hardness to dissemble!— 30 How do you, Desdemona?
DESDEMONA	Well, my good lord.
OTHELLO	Give me your hand: this hand is moist, my lady.

---

l. 12 *edified:* Instructed.
l. 22 *crusadoes:* Portuguese gold coins.
l. 27 *humours:* Notions.

DESDEMONA	It yet hath felt no age nor known no sorrow.
OTHELLO	This argues fruitfulness and liberal heart:
	Hot, hot, and moist: this hand of yours requires
	A sequester from liberty, fasting and prayer,
	Much castigation, exercise devout;
	For here 's a young and sweating devil here,
	That commonly rebels. 'T is a good hand, 39
	A frank one.
DESDEMONA	You may, indeed, say so;
	For 't was that hand that gave away my heart.
OTHELLO	A liberal hand: the hearts of old gave hands;
	But our new heraldry is hands, not hearts.
DESDEMONA	I cannot speak of this. Come now, your promise.
OTHELLO	What promise, chuck?
DESDEMONA	I have sent to bid Cassio come speak with you.
OTHELLO	I have a salt and sorry rheum offends me;
	Lend me thy handkerchief.
DESDEMONA	Here, my lord.
OTHELLO	That which I gave you.
DESDEMONA	I have it not about me.
OTHELLO	Not?
DESDEMONA	No, indeed, my lord. 50
OTHELLO	That is a fault. That handkerchief
	Did an Egyptian to my mother give;
	She was a charmer, and could almost read
	The thoughts of people: she told her, while she kept it,
	'T would make her amiable and subdue my father
	Entirely to her love, but if she lost it
	Or made a gift of it, my father's eye
	Should hold her loathed and his spirits should hunt
	After new fancies; she, dying, gave it me;
	And bid me, when my fate would have me wive, 60
	To give it her. I did so: and take heed on 't;
	Make it a darling like your precious eye;
	To lose 't or give 't away were such perdition
	As nothing else could match.
DESDEMONA	Is 't possible?

---

l. 36 *sequester:* Separation.
l. 42–3 *the . . . hearts:* Unlike the past, we now join hands but not hearts in marriage.
l. 47 *salt and sorry rheum:* Wretched cold.

OTHELLO	'T is true: there's magic in the web of it:
	A sibyl, that had number'd in the world
	The sun to course two hundred compasses,
	In her prophetic fury sew'd the work;
	The worms were hallow'd that did breed the silk;
	And it was dyed in mummy which the skillful 70
	Conserved of maidens' hearts.
DESDEMONA	Indeed! is 't true?
OTHELLO	Most veritable; therefore look to 't well.
DESDEMONA	Then would to God that I had never seen 't!
OTHELLO	Ha! wherefore?
DESDEMONA	Why do you speak so startingly and rash?
OTHELLO	It 't lost? is 't gone? speak, is it out o' the way?
DESDEMONA	Heaven bless us!
OTHELLO	Say you?
DESDEMONA	It is not lost; but what an if it were?
OTHELLO	How! 80
DESDEMONA	I say, it is not lost.
OTHELLO	Fetch 't, let me see 't.
DESDEMONA	Why, so I can, sir, but I will not now.
	This is a trick to put me from my suit:
	Pray you let Cassio be received again.
OTHELLO	Fetch me the handkerchief: my mind misgives.
DESDEMONA	Come, come;
	You 'll never meet a more sufficient man.
OTHELLO	The handkerchief!
DESDEMONA	I pray, talk me of Cassio.
OTHELLO	The handkerchief!
DESDEMONA	A man that all his time
	Hath founded his good fortunes on your love, 90
	Shared dangers with you,—
OTHELLO	The handkerchief!
DESDEMONA	In sooth, you are to blame.
OTHELLO	Away!
(*Exit.*)	
EMILIA	Is not this man jealous?

DESDEMONA   I ne'er saw this before.
Sure, there's some wonder in this handkerchief:
I am most unhappy in the loss of it.

EMILIA   'T is not a year or two shows us a man:
They are all but stomachs, and we all but food;   100
They eat us hungerly, and when they are full,
They belch us. Look you, Cassio and my husband!

(*Enter* CASSIO *and* IAGO.)

IAGO   There is no other way; 't is she must do 't:
And, lo, the happiness! go, and importune her.

DESDEMONA   How now, good Cassio! what 's the news with you?

CASSIO   Madam, my former suit: I do beseech you
That by your virtuous means I may again
Exist, and be a member of his love
Whom I with all the office of my heart
Entirely honour: I would not be delay'd.   110
If my offence be of such mortal kind
That nor my service past, nor present sorrows,
Nor purposed merit in futurity,
Can ransom me into his love again,
But to know so must be my benefit;
So shall I clothe me in a forced content,
And shut myself up in some other course,
To fortune's alms.

DESDEMONA   Alas, thrice-gentle Cassio!
My advocation is not now in tune;   119
My lord is not my lord; nor should I know him
Were he in favour as in humour alter'd.
So help me every spirit sanctified,
As I have spoken for you all my best
And stood within the blank of his displeasure
For my free speech! you must awhile be patient:
What I can do I will; and more I will
Than for myself I dare: let that suffice you.

IAGO   Is my lord angry?

EMILIA   He went hence but now,
And certainly in strange unquietness.

IAGO   Can he be angry? I have seen the cannon,   130
When it hath blown his ranks into the air,
And, like the devil, from his very arm

---

l. 121 *favour:* Features. *humour:* Mood.
l. 124 *blank:* Center of the target.

Puff'd his own brother:—and can he be angry?
Something of moment then: I will go meet him:
There's matter in 't indeed, if he be angry.

DESDEMONA   I prithee, do so.
  (*Exit* IAGO.)
                  Something, sure, of state,
Either from Venice or some unhatch'd practice
Made demonstrable here in Cyprus to him,
Hath puddled his clear spirit; and in such cases
Men's natures wrangle with inferior things,
Though great ones are their object. 'T is even so;   141
For let our fingers ache, and it indues
Our other healthful members even to that sense
Of pain: nay, we must think men are not gods,
Nor of them look for such observances
As fit the bridal. Beshrew me much, Emilia,
I was, unhandsome warrior as I am,
Arraigning his unkindness with my soul;
But now I find I had suborn'd the witness,
And he 's indicted falsely.

EMILIA   Pray heaven it be state-matters as you think,   151
And no conception nor no jealous toy
Concerning you.

DESDEMONA   Alas the day, I never gave him cause!

EMILIA   But jealous souls will not be answer'd so;
They are not ever jealous for the cause,
But jealous for they are jealous: 't is a monster
Begot upon itself, born on itself.

DESDEMONA   Heaven keep that monster from Othello's mind!

EMILIA   Lady, amen.   160

DESDEMONA   I will go seek him. Cassio, walk hereabout:
If I do find him fit, I 'll move your suit,
And seek to effect it to my uttermost.

CASSIO   I humbly thank your ladyship.
  (*Exeunt* DESDEMONA *and* EMILIA.)

  (*Enter* BIANCA.)
BIANCA   Save you, friend Cassio!

CASSIO   What make you from home?
How is it with you, my most fair Bianca?
I' faith, sweet love, I was coming to your house.

---

l. 137 *unhatch'd practice:* Unmatured plot.
l. 149 *suborn'd:* Induced to swear falsely.

BIANCA	And I was going to your lodging, Cassio.
	What, keep a week away? seven days and nights?
	Eight score eight hours? and lovers' absent hours,
	More tedious than the dial eight score times? 171
	O weary reckoning!
CASSIO	Pardon me, Bianca:
	I have this while with leaden thoughts been press'd;
	But I shall, in a more continuate time,
	Strike off this score of absence. Sweet Bianca,
	(Giving her DESDEMONA's *handkerchief.)*
	Take me this work out.
BIANCA	O Cassio, whence came this?
	This is some token from a newer friend:
	To the felt absence now I feel a cause: now
	Is 't come to this? Well, well.
CASSIO	Go to, woman!
	Throw your vile guesses in the devil's teeth, 180
	From whence you have them. You are jealous
	That this is from some mistress, some remembrance:
	No, in good troth, Bianca.
BIANCA	Why, whose is it?
CASSIO	I know not, sweet: I found it in my chamber.
	I like the work well: ere it be demanded—
	As like enough it will—I 'ld have it copied:
	Take it, and do 't; and leave me for this time.
BIANCA	Leave you! wherefore?
CASSIO	I do attend here on the general;
	And think it no addition, nor my wish,
	To have him see me woman'd.
BIANCA	Why, I pray you?
CASSIO	Not that I love you not.
BIANCA	But that you do not love me.
	I pray you, bring me on the way a little,
	And say if I shall see you soon at night.
CASSIO	'Tis but a little way that I can bring you;
	For I attend here: but I 'll see you soon.
BIANCA	'T is very good; I must be circumstanced.
(Exeunt.)	

---

l. 174 *more continuate:* Less interrupted.
l. 175 *strike off this score:* Erase this tally.
l. 176 *Take . . .out:* Copy this embroidery for me.
l. 190 *addition:* Credit.
l. 197 *be circumstanced:* Yield to necessity.

ACT IV

(*Enter* OTHELLO *and* IAGO.)

IAGO   Will you think so?

OTHELLO   Think so, Iago!

IAGO   What,
To kiss in private?

OTHELLO   An unauthorized kiss.

IAGO   Or to be naked with her friend in bed
An hour or more, not meaning any harm?

OTHELLO   Naked in bed, Iago, and not mean harm!
It is hypocrisy against the devil:
They that mean virtuously, and yet do so,
The devil their virtue tempts, and they tempt heaven.

IAGO   So they do nothing, 't is a venial slip;
But if I give my wife a handkerchief,—   10

OTHELLO   What then?

IAGO   Why, then, 't is hers, my lord; and, being hers,
She may, I think, bestow 't on any man.

OTHELLO   She is protectress of her honour too:
May she give that?

IAGO   Her honour is an essence that 's not seen;
They have it very often that have it not:
But, for the handkerchief,—

OTHELLO   By heaven, I would most gladly have forgot it.   19
Thou said'st—O, it comes o'er my memory
As doth the raven o'er the infected house,
Boding to all—he had my handkerchief.

IAGO   Ay, what of that?

OTHELLO   That's not so good now.

IAGO   What,
If I had said I had seen him do you wrong?
Or heard him say,—as knaves be such abroad,
Who having, by their own importunate suit,
Or voluntary dotage of some mistress,
Convinced or supplied them, cannot choose
But they must blab—

---

l. 22 *Boding:* Ominous.

OTHELLO	Hath he said any thing?
IAGO	He hath, my lord; but be you well assured, 30 No more than he 'll unswear.
OTHELLO	What hath he said?
IAGO	'Faith, that he did—I know not what he did.
OTHELLO	What? what?
IAGO	Lie—
OTHELLO	With her?
IAGO	With her, on her; what you will.
OTHELLO	Lie with her! lie on her! We say lie on her, when they belie her. Lie with her! that 's fulsome.—Handker- chief—confessions—handkerchief!—To confess, and be hanged for his labour;—first to be hanged, and then to confess.—I tremble at it. Nature would not invest herself in such shadowing passion without some instruction. It is not words that shake me thus. Pish! Noses, ears, and lips.—Is 't possible?—Confess—handkerchief!—O devil!

(Falls in a trance.)

IAGO	Work on, My medicine, work! Thus credulous fools are caught; And many worthy and chaste dames even thus, All guiltless, meet reproach. What, ho! my lord! My lord, I say! Othello!

(Enter CASSIO.)

           How now, Cassio!

CASSIO	What 's the matter?
IAGO	My lord is fall'n into an epilepsy: This is his second fit; he had one yesterday. 50
CASSIO	Rub him about the temples.
IAGO	No, forbear; The lethargy must have his quiet course: If not, he foams at mouth and by and by Breaks out to savage madness. Look, he stirs: Do you withdraw yourself a little while, He will recover straight: when he is gone, I would on great occasion speak with you.

(Exit CASSIO.)

  How is it, general? have you not hurt your head?

OTHELLO	Dost thou mock me?

---

l. 36 *fulsome:* Disgusting.

IAGO	I mock you! no, by heaven.
	Would you would bear your fortune like a man! 60
OTHELLO	A horned man 's a monster and a beast.
IAGO	There 's many a beast then in a populous city,
	And many a civil monster.
OTHELLO	Did he confess it?
IAGO	Good sir, be a man;
	Think every bearded fellow that's but yoked
	May draw with you: there 's millions now alive
	That nightly lie in those unproper beds
	Which they dare swear peculiar: your case is better.
	O, 't is the spite of hell, the fiend's archmock,
	To lip a wanton in a secure couch, 70
	And to suppose her chaste! No, let me know;
	And knowing what I am, I know what she shall be.
OTHELLO	O, thou art wise; 't is certain.
IAGO	Stand you awhile apart;
	Confine yourself but in a patient list.
	Whilst you were here o'erwhelmed with your grief—
	A passion most unsuiting such a man—
	Cassio came hither: I shifted him away,
	And laid good 'scuse upon your ecstasy,
	Bade him anon return and here speak with me;
	The which he promised. Do but encave yourself, 80
	And mark the fleers, the gibes, and notable scorns,
	That dwell in every region of his face;
	For I will make him tell the tale anew,
	Where, how, how oft, how long ago, and when
	He hath, and is again to cope your wife:
	I say, but mark his gesture. Marry, patience;
	Or I shall say you are all in all in spleen,
	And nothing of a man.
OTHELLO	Dost thou hear, Iago?
	I will be found most cunning in my patience;
	But—dost thou hear?—most bloody.
IAGO	That 's not amiss;
	But yet keep time in all. Will you withdraw?

(OTHELLO *retires.*)

---

l. 66 *draw with you:* Share your fate.
l. 67 *unproper:* Not their own.
l. 68 *peculiar:* Their own.
l. 74 *a patient list:* Within bounds.
l. 78 *ecstasy:* Trance.
l. 85 *cope:* Meet illicitly.
l. 91 *keep time:* Act prudently.

	Now will I question Cassio of Bianca,	92
	A housewife that by selling her desires	
	Buys herself bread and clothes: it is a creature	
	That dotes on Cassio; as 't is the strumpet's plague	
	To beguile many and be beguiled by one:	
	He, when he hears of her, cannot refrain	
	From the excess of laughter. Here he comes:	

(*Re-enter* CASSIO.)

	As he shall smile, Othello shall go mad;	99
	And his unbookish jealousy must construe	
	Poor Cassio's smiles, gestures and light behaviour,	
	Quite in the wrong. How do you now, lieutenant?	

CASSIO   The worser that you give me the addition
Whose want even kills me.

IAGO   Ply Desdemona well, and you are sure on 't.
(*Speaking lower*) Now, if this suit lay in Bianca's power,
How quickly should you speed!

CASSIO   Alas, poor caitiff!

OTHELLO   Look, how he laughs already!

IAGO   I never knew woman love man so.

CASSIO   Alas, poor rogue! I think, i' faith, she loves me.   110

OTHELLO   Now he denies it faintly, and laughs it out.

IAGO   Do you hear, Cassio?

OTHELLO   Now he importunes him
To tell it o'er: go to; well said, well said.

IAGO   She gives it out that you shall marry her:
Do you intend it?

CASSIO   Ha, ha, ha!

OTHELLO   Do you triumph, Roman? Do you triumph?

CASSIO   I marry her! what! a customer! Prithee, bear some
charity to my wit; do not think it so unwholesome.
Ha, ha, ha!   120

OTHELLO   So, so, so, so: they laugh that win.

IAGO   'Faith the cry goes that you shall marry her.

CASSIO   Prithee, say true.

---

l. 100 *unbookish:* Ignorant.
l. 103 *addition:* Title.
l. 107 *caitiff:* Wretch.
l. 118 *customer:* Prostitute.

IAGO	I am a very villain else.
OTHELLO	Have you scored me? Well.
CASSIO	This is the monkey's own giving out; she is persuaded I will marry her, out of her own love and flattery, not out of my promise.
OTHELLO	Iago beckons me; now he begins the story.
CASSIO	She was here even now; she haunts me in every place. I was the other day talking on the sea-bank with certain 130 Venetians; and thither comes the bauble, and, by this hand, she falls me thus about my neck—
OTHELLO	Crying "O dear Cassio!" as it were: his gesture imports it.
CASSIO	So hangs, and lolls, and weeps upon me; so hales, and pulls me: ha, ha, ha!
OTHELLO	Now he tells how she plucked him to my chamber. O, I see that nose of yours, but not that dog I shall throw it to.
CASSIO	Well, I must leave her company. 140
IAGO	Before me! look, where she comes.
CASSIO (*Enter* BIANCA.)	'T is such another fitchew! marry, a perfumed one. What do you mean by this haunting of me?
BIANCA	Let the devil and his dam haunt you! What did you mean by that same handkedchief you gave me even now? I was a fine fool to take it. I must take out the work?—A likely piece of work, that you should find it in your chamber, and not know who left it there! This is some minx's token, and I must take out the work? There; give it your hobby-horse: wheresoever you had it, I'll take out no work on 't. 151
CASSIO	How now, my sweet Bianca! how now! how now!
OTHELLO	By heaven, that should be my handkerchief!
BIANCA (*Exit.*)	An you 'll come to supper to-night, you may; an you will not, come when you are next prepared for.
IAGO	After her, after her.
CASSIO	'Faith, I must; she 'll rail in the street else.
IAGO	Will you sup there?

---

l. 142 *such another fitchew:* Such a polecat.
l. 150 *hobby-horse:* Harlot.

CASSIO	'Faith, I intend so.
IAGO	Well, I may chance to see you: for I would very fain speak with you. 161
CASSIO	Prithee, come; will you?
IAGO	Go to; say no more. (*Exit* CASSIO.)
OTHELLO	(*Advancing*) How shall I murder him, Iago?
IAGO	Did you perceive how he laughed at his vice?
OTHELLO	O Iago!
IAGO	And did you see the handkerchief?
OTHELLO	Was that mine?
IAGO	Yours, by this hand: and to see how he prizes the foolish woman your wife! she gave it him, and he hath given it 170 his whore.
OTHELLO	I would have him nine years a-killing. A fine woman! a fair woman! a sweet woman!
IAGO	Nay, you must forget that.
OTHELLO	Ay, let her rot, and perish, and be damned to-night; for she shall not live: no, my heart is turned to stone; I strike it, and it hurts my hand. O, the world hath not a sweeter creature: she might lie by an emperor's side and command him tasks.
IAGO	Nay, that 's not your way. 180
OTHELLO	Hang her! I do but say what she is: so delicate with her needle: an admirable musician: O! she will sing the savageness out of a bear: of so high and plenteous wit and invention:—
IAGO	She 's the worse for all this.
OTHELLO	O, a thousand thousand times: and then, of so gentle a condition!
IAGO	Ay, too gentle.
OTHELLO	Nay, that 's certain: but yet the pity of it, Iago! O Iago, the pity of it, Iago! 190
IAGO	If you are so fond over her iniquity, give her patent to offend; for, if it touch not you, it comes near nobody.
OTHELLO	I will chop her into messes: cuckold me!
IAGO	O, 't is foul in her.

OTHELLO	With mine officer!
IAGO	That 's fouler.
OTHELLO	Get me some poison, Iago; this night: I 'll not expostu-late with her, lest her body and beauty unprovide my mind again: this night, Iago.
IAGO	Do it not with poison, strangle her in her bed, even the bed she hath contaminated. 201
OTHELLO	Good, good: the justice of it pleases: very good.
IAGO	And for Cassio, let me be his undertaker: you shall hear more by midnight.
OTHELLO	Excellent good. (*A trumpet within.*) What trumpet is that same?
IAGO	Something from Venice, sure. 'T is Lodovico. Come from the duke: and, see, your wife is with him.

(*Enter* LODOVICO, DESDEMONA, *and* ATTENDANTS.)

LODOVICO	Save you, worthy general!
OTHELLO	With all my heart, sir.
LODOVICO	The duke and senators of Venice greet you. (*Gives him a letter.*)
OTHELLO	I kiss the instrument of their pleasures. 210 (*Opens the letter, and reads.*)
DESDEMONA	And what's the news, good cousin Lodovico?
IAGO	I am very glad to see you, signior; Welcome to Cyprus.
LODOVICO	I thank you. How does Lieutenant Cassio?
IAGO	Lives, sir.
DESDEMONA	Cousin, there 's fall'n between him and my lord An unkind breach: but you shall make all well.
OTHELLO	Are you sure of that?
DESDEMONA	My lord? 219
OTHELLO	(*Reads*) "This fail you not to do, as you will—"
LODOVICO	He did not call; he 's busy in the paper. Is there division 'twixt my lord and Cassio?
DESDEMONA	A most unhappy one: I would do much To atone them, for the love I bear to Cassio.

---

l. 203 *let . . . undertaker:* Leave him to me.

OTHELLO	Fire and brimstone!
DESDEMONA	My lord?
OTHELLO	Are you wise?
DESDEMONA	What, is he angry?
LODOVICO	May be the letter moved him; For, as I think, they do command him home, Deputing Cassio in his government.
DESDEMONA	Trust me, I am glad on 't.
OTHELLO	Indeed!
DESDEMONA	My lord?
OTHELLO	I am glad to see you mad.
DESDEMONA	Why, sweet Othello,—
OTHELLO	(*Striking her*) Devil!
DESDEMONA	I have not deserved this.
LODOVICO	My lord, this would not be believed in Venice, Though I should swear I saw 't: 't is very much: Make her amends; she weeps.
OTHELLO	O devil, devil! If that the earth could teem with woman's tears, Each drop she falls would prove a crocodile. Out of my sight!
DESDEMONA (*Going.*)	I will not stay to offend you.
LODOVICO	Truly, an obedient lady: I do beseech your lordship, call her back.
OTHELLO	Mistress!
DESDEMONA	My lord?
OTHELLO	What would you with her, sir?
LODOVICO	Who, I, my lord?
OTHELLO	Ay; you did wish that I would make her turn: Sir, she can turn, and turn, and yet go on, And turn again; and she can weep, sir, weep; And she 's obedient, as you say, obedient, Very obedient. Proceed you in your tears, Concerning this, sir,—O well-painted passion!—

231

240

---

l. 237 *crocodile:* Hypocrite.

I am commanded home. Get you away;
I 'll send for you anon. Sir, I obey the mandate, 251
And will return to Venice. Hence, avaunt!

(*Exit* DESDEMONA.)

Cassio shall have my place. And, sir, to-night,
I do entreat that we may sup together:
You are welcome, sir, to Cyprus.—Goats and monkeys!

(*Exit.*)

LODOVICO Is this the noble Moor whom our full senate
Call all in all sufficient? Is this the nature
Whom passion could not shake? whose solid virtue
The shot of accident, nor dart of chance, 259
Could neither graze nor pierce?

IAGO   He is much changed.

LODOVICO Are his wits safe? is he not light of brain?

IAGO He 's that he is: I may not breathe my censure
What he might be: if what he might he is not,
I would to heaven he were!

LODOVICO   What, strike his wife!

IAGO 'Faith, that was not so well; yet would I knew
That stroke would prove the worst!

LODOVICO   Is it his use?
Or did the letters work upon his blood,
And new-create his fault?

IAGO   Alas, alas!
It is not honesty in me to speak
What I have seen and known. You shall observe him, 270
And his own courses will denote him so
That I may save my speech: do but go after,
And mark how he continues.

LODOVICO I am sorry that I am deceived in him.
(*Exeunt.*)

SCENE II. *A room in the castle.*

(*Enter* OTHELLO *and* EMILIA.)

OTHELLO You have seen nothing then?

EMILIA Nor ever heard, nor ever did suspect.

OTHELLO Yes, you have seen Cassio and she together.

-----
l. 266 *use:* Custom.

| EMILIA | But then I saw no harm, and then I heard |
| | Each syllable that breath made up between them. |

| OTHELLO | What, did they never whisper? |

| EMILIA | Never, my lord. |

| OTHELLO | Nor send you out o' the way? |

| EMILIA | Never. |

| OTHELLO | To fetch her fan, her gloves, her mask, nor nothing? |

| EMILIA | Never, my lord. | 10 |

| OTHELLO | That 's strange. |

EMILIA	I durst, my lord, to wager she is honest,
	Lay down my soul at stake: if you think other,
	Remove your thought; it doth abuse your bosom.
	If any wretch have put this in your head,
	Let heaven requite it with the serpent's curse!
	For, if she be not honest, chaste, and true,
	There 's no man happy; the purest of their wives
	Is foul as slander.

OTHELLO	Bid her come hither: go.
(*Exit* EMILIA.)	
	She says enough; yet she 's a simple bawd
	That cannot say as much. This is a subtle whore,	21
	A closet lock and key of villainous secrets:
	And yet she 'll kneel and pray; I have seen her do 't.

(*Enter* DESDEMONA *with* EMILIA.)

| DESDEMONA | My lord, what is your will? |

| OTHELLO | Pray, chuck, come hither. |

| DESDEMONA | What is your pleasure? |

| OTHELLO | Let me see your eyes; |
| | Look in my face. |

| DESDEMONA | What horrible fancy 's this? |

OTHELLO	(*To Emilia*) Some of your function, mistress;
	Leave procreants alone and shut the door;
	Cough, or cry "hem," if any body come:
	Your mystery, your mystery: nay, dispatch.
(*Exit* EMILIA.)	

DESDEMONA	Upon my knees, what doth your speech import?	31
	I understand a fury in your words,
	But not the words.

---

l. 30 *mystery:* Trade, business.

OTHELLO	Why, what art thou?

DESDEMONA	Your wife, my lord; your true
	And loyal wife.

OTHELLO	Come, swear it, damn thyself;
	Lest, being like one of heaven, the devils themselves
	Should fear to seize thee: therefore be double damn'd;
	Swear thou art honest.

DESDEMONA	Heaven doth truly know it.

OTHELLO	Heaven truly knows that thou art false as hell.

DESDEMONA	To whom, my lord? with whom? how am I false?	40

OTHELLO	O Desdemona! Away! away! away!

DESDEMONA	Alas the heavy day! Why do you weep?
	Am I the motive of these tears, my lord?
	If haply you my father do suspect
	An instrument of this your calling back,
	Lay not your blame on me: if you have lost him,
	Why, I have lost him too.

OTHELLO	Had it pleased heaven
	To try me with affliction; had they rain'd
	All kinds of sores and shames on my bare head,
	Steep'd me in poverty to the very lips,
	Given to captivity me and my utmost hopes,
	I should have found in some place of my soul
	A drop of patience: but, alas, to make me
	A fixed figure for the time of scorn
	To point his slow unmoving finger at!
	Yet could I bear that too; well, very well:
	But there, where I have garner'd up my heart,
	Where either I must live, or bear no life;
	The fountain from the which my current runs,
	Or else dries up; to be discarded thence!
	Or keep it as a cistern for foul toads
	To knot and gender in! Turn thy complexion there,
	Patience, thou young and rose-lipp'd cherubin,—
	Ay, there, look grim as hell!

(50 at line "Steep'd me in poverty to the very lips,")
(60 at line "Or else dries up; to be discarded thence!")

DESDEMONA	I hope my noble lord esteems me honest.

OTHELLO	O, ay; as summer flies are in the shambles,
	That quicken even with blowing. O thou weed,
	Who art so lovely fair and smell'st so sweet

---

l. 61 *cistern:* Cesspool.
l. 62 *Turn . . . there:* Blush at that.
l. 66 *shambles:* Slaughterhouse.

	That the sense aches at thee, would thou hadst ne'er been born!	
DESDEMONA	Alas, what ignorant sin have I committed?	70
OTHELLO	Was this fair paper, this most goodly book, Made to write "whore" upon? What committed! Committed! O thou public commoner! I should make very forges of my cheeks, That would to cinders burn up modesty, Did I but speak thy deeds. What committed! Heaven stops the nose at it and the moon winks, The bawdy wind that kisses all it meets Is hush'd within the hollow mine of earth, And will not hear it. What committed! Impudent strumpet!	80
DESDEMONA	By heaven, you do me wrong.	
OTHELLO	Are you not a strumpet?	
DESDEMONA	No, as I am a Christian: If to preserve this vessel for my lord From any other foul unlawful touch Be not to be a strumpet, I am none.	
OTHELLO	What, not a whore?	
DESDEMONA	No, as I shall be saved.	
OTHELLO	Is 't possible?	
DESDEMONA	O, heaven forgive us!	
OTHELLO	I cry you mercy, then: I took you for that cunning whore of Venice That married with Othello.	

(Raising his voice.)   You mistress,   90
That have the office opposite to Saint Peter,
And keep the gate of hell!

(Re-enter EMILIA.)   You, you, ay, you!
We have done our course; there 's money for your pains:
I pray you, turn the key and keep our counsel.

(Exit.)

EMILIA	Alas, what does this gentleman conceive? How do you, madam? how do you, my good lady?
DESDEMONA	'Faith, half asleep.
EMILIA	Good madam, what 's the matter with my lord?

---

l. 73 *commoner:* Prostitute.

DESDEMONA	With who?
EMILIA	Why, with my lord, madam. 100
DESDEMONA	Who is thy lord?
EMILIA	He that is yours, sweet lady.
DESDEMONA	I have none: do not talk to me, Emilia;
	I cannot weep; nor answer have I none,
	But what should go by water. Prithee, to-night
	Lay on my bed my wedding sheets: remember;
	And call thy husband hither.
EMILIA	Here 's a change indeed!
(Exit.)	
DESDEMONA	'T is meet I should be used so, very meet.
	How have I been behaved, that he might stick
	The small'st opinion on my least misuse?

(Re-enter EMILIA and IAGO.)

IAGO	What is your pleasure, madam? How is 't with you! 110
DESDEMONA	I cannot tell. Those that do teach young babes
	Do it with gentle means and easy tasks:
	He might have chid me so; for, in good faith,
	I am a child to chiding.
IAGO	What 's the matter, lady?
EMILIA	Alas, Iago, my lord hath so bewhored her,
	Thrown such despite and heavy terms upon her,
	As true hearts cannot bear.
DESDEMONA	Am I that name, Iago?
IAGO	What name, fair lady?
DESDEMONA	Such as she says my lord did say I was.
EMILIA	He call'd her whore: a beggar in his drink 120
	Could not have laid such terms upon his callet.
IAGO	Why did he so?
DESDEMONA	I do not know; I am sure I am none such.
IAGO	Do not weep, do not weep. Alas the day!
EMILIA	Hath she forsook so many noble matches,
	Her father and her country and her friends,
	To be call'd whore? would it not make one weep?

---

l. 104 *go by water:* Be expressed in tears.
ll. 108–9 *that . . . misuse:* That he might consider me guilty of the slightest fault.
l. 121 *callet:* Prostitute.

DESDEMONA	It is my wretched fortune.
IAGO	Beshrew him for 't! How comes this trick upon him?
DESDEMONA	Nay, heaven doth know.
EMILIA	I will be hang'd, if some eternal villain, 130 Some busy and insinuating rogue, Some cogging, cozening slave, to get some office, Have not devised this slander; I'll be hang'd else.
IAGO	Fie, there is no such man; it is impossible.
DESDEMONA	If any such there be, heaven pardon him!
EMILIA	A halter pardon him! and hell gnaw his bones! Why should he call her whore? who keeps her com- pany? What place? what time? what form? what likelihood? The Moor abused by some most villainous knave, Some base notorious knave, some scurvy fellow. 140 O heaven, that such companions thou'ldst unfold, And put in every honest hand a whip To lash the rascals naked through the world Even from the east to the west!
IAGO	Speak within door.
EMILIA	O, fie upon them! Some such squire he was That turn'd your wit the seamy side without, And made you to suspect me with the Moor.
IAGO	You are a fool; go to.
DESDEMONA	O good Iago, What shall I do to win my lord again? Good friend, go to him; for, by this light of heaven, 150 I know not how I lost him. Here I kneel: If e'er my will did trespass 'gainst his love, Either in discourse of thought or actual deed, Or that mine eyes, mine ears, or any sense, Delighted them in any other form; Or that I do not yet, and ever did, And ever will—though he do shake me off To beggarly divorcement—love him dearly, Comfort forswear me! Unkindness may do much;

---

l. 129 *trick:* Delusion.
l. 132 *cogging:* Tricking. *cozening:* Cheating.
l. 141 *companions:* Knaves. *unfold:* Reveal.
l. 144 *within door:* Quietly.
l. 145 *squire:* Fellow.
l. 159 *Comfort forswear me:* May happiness abandon me.

And his unkindness may defeat my life,
But never taint my love. I cannot say "whore";   161
It doth abhor me now I speak the word;
To do the act that might the addition earn
Not the world's mass of vanity could make me.

IAGO   I pray you, be content; 't is but his humour:
The business of the state does him offence,
And he does chide with you.

DESDEMONA   If 't were not other—

IAGO   'T is but so, I warrant.
(*Trumpets within.*) Hark, how those instruments summon to supper!   169
The messengers of Venice stay the meat:
Go in, and weep not; all things shall be well.
(*Exeunt* DESDEMONA *and* EMILIA.)

(*Enter* RODERIGO.)
How now, Roderigo!

RODERIGO   I do not find that thou dealest justly with me.

IAGO   What in the contrary?

RODERIGO   Every day thou daffest me with some device, Iago; and
rather, as it seems to me now, keepest from me all
conveniency than suppliest me with the least advantage
of hope. I will indeed no longer endure it, nor am I yet
persuaded to put in peace what already I have foolishly
suffered.

IAGO   Will you hear me, Roderigo?

RODERIGO   'Faith, I have heard too much, for your words and per-   182
formances are no kin together.

IAGO   You charge me most unjustly.

RODERIGO   With nought but truth. I have wasted myself out of my
means. The jewels you have had from me to deliver to
Desdemona would half have corrupted a votarist: you
have told me she hath received them and returned me
expectations and comforts of sudden respect and
acquaintance, but I find none.

IAGO   Well; go to; very well.

RODERIGO   Very well! go to! I cannot go to, man; nor 't is not very
well: nay, I think it is scurvy, and begin to find myself   193
fopped in it.

---

l. 163 *addition:* title.
l. 165 *humour:* whim.
l. 187 *votarist:* A person who has sworn a religious vow; *e.g.,* a nun.
l. 194 *fopped:* Made a fool of.

IAGO Very well.

RODERIGO I tell you 't is not very well. I will make myself known to Desdemona: if she will return me my jewels, I will give over my suit and repent my unlawful solicitation; if not, assure yourself I will seek satisfaction of you.

IAGO You have said now.

RODERIGO Ay, and said nothing but what I protest intendment of doing.

IAGO Why, now I see there 's mettle in thee, and even from this instant do build on thee a better opinion than ever before. Give me thy hand, Roderigo: thou hast taken against me a most just exception; but yet, I protest, I have dealt most directly in thy affair.

RODERIGO It hath not appeared.

IAGO I grant indeed it hath not appeared, and your suspicion is not without wit and judgement. But, Roderigo, if thou hast that in thee indeed, which I have greater reason to believe now than ever, I mean purpose, courage and valour, this night show it: if thou the next night following enjoy not Desdemona, take me from this world with treachery and devise engines for my life.

RODERIGO Well, what is it? is it within reason and compass?

IAGO Sir, there is especial commission come from Venice to depute Cassio in Othello's place.

RODERIGO Is that true? why, then Othello and Desdemona return again to Venice.

IAGO O, no; he goes into Mauritania and takes away with him the fair Desdemona, unless his abode be lingered here by some accident: wherein none can be so determinate as the removing of Cassio.

RODERIGO How do you mean, removing of him?

IAGO Why, by making him uncapable of Othello's place; knocking out his brains.

RODERIGO And that you would have me to do?

IAGO Ay, if you dare do yourself a profit and a right. He sups to-night with a harlotry, and thither will I go to him: he knows not yet of his honourable fortune. If you will

l. 215 *engines:* Instruments of torture.
l. 216 *compass:* Possibility.

watch his going thence, which I will fashion to fall out between twelve and one, you may take him at your pleasure: I will be near to second your attempt, and he shall fall between us. Come, stand not amazed at it, but go along with me; I will show you such a necessity in his death that you shall think yourself bound to put it on him. It is now high supper-time, and the night grows to waste: about it. 233

RODERIGO I will hear further reason for this.

IAGO And you shall be satisfied.
(*Exeunt.*)

SCENE III. *Another room in the castle.*

(*Enter* OTHELLO, LODOVICO, DESDEMONA, EMILIA, *and* ATTENDANTS.)

LODOVICO I do beseech you, sir, trouble yourself no further.

OTHELLO O, pardon me; 't will do me good to walk.

LODOVICO Madam, good night; I humbly thank your ladyship.

DESDEMONA Your honour is most welcome.

OTHELLO Will you walk, sir?
O,—Desdemona,—

DESDEMONA My lord?

OTHELLO Get you to bed on the instant: I will be returned forthwith: dismiss your attendant there: look it be done.

DESDEMONA I will, my lord.
(*Exeunt* OTHELLO, LODOVICO, *and* ATTENDANTS.)

EMILIA How goes it now? he looks gentler than he did. 10

DESDEMONA He says he will return incontinent:
He hath commanded me to go to bed,
And bade me to dismiss you.

EMILIA Dismiss me!

DESDEMONA It was his bidding; therefore, good Emilia,
Give me my nightly wearing, and adieu:
We must not now displease him.

EMILIA I would you had never seen him!

DESDEMONA So would not I: my love doth so approve him,
That even his stubbornness, his checks, his frowns,—
Prithee, unpin me,—have grace and favour in them. 20

---

l. 11 *incontinent:* Immediately.

EMILIA	I have laid those sheets you bade me on the bed.
DESDEMONA	All 's one. Good faith, how foolish are our minds! If I do die before thee, prithee, shroud me In one of those same sheets.
EMILIA	Come, come, you talk.
DESDEMONA	My mother had a maid call'd Barbara: She was in love, and he she loved proved mad And did forsake her: she had a song of "willow"; An old thing 't was, but it express'd her fortune, And she died singing it: that song to-night Will not go from my mind; I have much to do But to go hang my head all at one side, 31 And sing it like poor Barbara. Prithee, dispatch.
EMILIA	Shall I go fetch your night-gown?
DESDEMONA	No, unpin me here. This Lodovico is a proper man.
EMILIA	A very handsome man.
DESDEMONA	He speaks well.
EMILIA	I know a lady in Venice would have walked barefoot to Palestine for a touch of his nether lip.

DESDEMONA	(*Singing*) The poor soul sat sighing by a sycamore
	    tree,
	      Sing all a green willow. 40
	    Her hand on her bosom, her head on her knee,
	      Sing willow, willow, willow:
	    The fresh streams ran by her, and murmur'd her
	      moans;
	      Sing willow, willow, willow;
	    Her salt tears fell from her, and soften'd the
	      stones;—
	Lay by these:—
	(*Singing*) Sing willow, willow, willow;
	Prithee, hie thee; he 'll come anon:—
	(*Singing*) Sing all a green willow must be my garland.
	    Let nobody blame him; his scorn I approve,— 50
	Nay, that 's not next—Hark! who is 't that knocks?

EMILIA	It 's the wind.
DESDEMONA	(*Singing*) I call'd my love false love; but what said he then?

---

l. 22 *All 's one:* No matter.

Sing willow, willow, willow:
If I court moe women, you 'll couch with moe
men.—
So, get thee gone; good night. Mine eyes do itch;
Doth that bode weeping?

EMILIA   'T is neither here nor there.

DESDEMONA   I have heard it said so. O, these men, these men!
Dost thou in conscience think,—tell me, Emilia,—
That there be women do abuse their husbands   60
In such gross kind?

EMILIA   There be some such, no question.

DESDEMONA   Wouldst thou do such a deed for all the world?

EMILIA   Why, would not you?

DESDEMONA   No, by this heavenly light!

EMILIA   Nor I neither by this heavenly light;
I might do 't as well i' the dark.

DESDEMONA   Wouldst thou do such a deed for all the world?

EMILIA   The world 's a huge thing: it is a great price
For a small vice.   69

DESDEMONA   In troth, I think thou wouldst not.

EMILIA   In troth, I think I should; and undo 't when I had done.
Marry, I would not do such a thing for a joint-ring, nor
for measures of lawn, nor for gowns, petticoats, nor
caps, nor any petty exhibition; but, for the whole
world,—why, who would not make her husband a cuckold to make him a monarch? I should venture purgatory
for 't.

DESDEMONA   Beshrew me, if I would do such a wrong
For the whole world.   79

EMILIA   Why, the wrong is but a wrong i' the world; and having
the world for your labour, 't is a wrong in your own
world, and you might quickly make it right.

DESDEMONA   I do not think there is any such woman.

EMILIA   Yes, a dozen; and as many to the vantage as would
store the world they played for.
But I do think it is their husbands' faults
If wives do fall: say that they slack their duties,
And pour our treasures into foreign laps,

---

l. 74 *exhibition:* Present.

Or else break out in peevish jealousies,
Throwing restraint upon us; or say they strike us, 90
Or scant our former having in despite;
Why, we have galls, and though we have some grace,
Yet have we some revenge. Let husbands know
Their wives have sense like them: they see and smell
And have their palates both for sweet and sour,
As husbands have. What is it that they do
When they change us for others? Is it sport?
I think it is: and doth affection breed it?
I think it doth: is 't frailty that thus errs?
It is so too: and have not we affections,
Desires for sport, and frailty, as men have?
Then let them use us well: else let them know,
The ills we do, their ills instruct us so. 103

DESDEMONA   Good night, good night: heaven me such uses send,
                Not to pick bad from bad, but by bad mend!

    (*Exeunt.*)

ACT V

SCENE I. *Cyprus A street.*

(*Enter* IAGO *and* RODERIGO.)

IAGO   Here, stand behind this bulk; straight will he come:
                Wear thy good rapier bare, and put it home:
                Quick, quick; fear nothing; I 'll be at thy elbow:
                It makes us, or it mars us; think on that,
                And fix most firm thy resolution.

RODERIGO   Be near at hand; I may miscarry in 't.

IAGO   Here, at thy hand: be bold, and take thy stand.
    (*Retires.*)

RODERIGO   I have no great devotion to the deed;
                And yet he hath given me satisfying reasons:
                'T is but a man gone. Forth, my sword: he dies. 10

IAGO   I have rubb'd this young quat almost to the sense,
                And he grows angry. Now, whether he kill Cassio,
                Or Cassio him, or each do kill the other,
                Every way makes my gain: live Roderigo,

---

l. 91 *scant . . . despite:* Spitefully deprive us of our customary allowance.
l. 92 *galls:* Capacity to resent.
l. 104 *uses:* Practices.
l. 1 *bulk:* Projection, wall.
l. 11 *quat:* Pimple. *sense:* Quick.

He calls me to a restitution large
Of gold and jewels that I bobb'd from him,
As gifts to Desdemona;
It must not be: if Cassio do remain,
He hath a daily beauty in his life   19
That makes me ugly; and, besides, the Moor
May unfold me to him; there stand I in much peril:
No, he must die. But so: I hear him coming.

(*Enter* CASSIO.)

RODERIGO   I know his gait, 't is he.—Villain, thou diest!

(*Makes a pass at* CASSIO.)

CASSIO   That thrust had been mine enemy indeed,
But that my coat is better than thou know'st:
I will make proof of thine.

(*Draws, and wounds* RODERIGO.)

RODERIGO   O, I am slain!

(IAGO *from behind wounds* CASSIO *in the leg, and exit.*)

CASSIO   I am maim'd for ever. Help, ho! murder! murder!

(*Falls.*)

(*Enter* OTHELLO.)

OTHELLO   The voice of Cassio: Iago keeps his word.

RODERIGO   O, villain that I am!

OTHELLO   It is even so.

CASSIO   O, help, ho! light! a surgeon!   30

OTHELLO   'T is he:—O brave Iago, honest and just,
That hast such noble sense of thy friend's wrong!
Thou teachest me. Minion, your dear lies dead,
And your unblest fate hies: strumpet, I come.
Forth of my heart those charms, thine eyes, are blotted;
Thy bed, lust-stain'd, shall with lust's blood be spotted.

(*Exit.*)

(*Enter* LODOVICO *and* GRATIANO.)

CASSIO   What ho! no watch? no passage? murder! murder!

GRATIANO   'T is some mischance; the cry is very direful.

CASSIO   O help!

LODOVICO   Hark!   40

RODERIGO   O wretched villain!

---

l. 16 *bobb'd:* cheated.
l. 33 *Minion:* Hussy.
l. 37 *no passage:* No one passing.

LODOVICO	Two or three groan: it is a heavy night:
	These may be counterfeits: let 's think 't unsafe
	To come in to the cry without more help.
RODERIGO	Nobody come? then shall I bleed to death.
LODOVICO	Hark!

(Re-enter IAGO, *with a light.)*

GRATIANO	Here 's one comes in his shirt, with light and weapons.
IAGO	Who's there? whose noise is this that cries on murder?
LODOVICO	We do not know.
IAGO	Did not you hear a cry?
CASSIO	Here, here! for heaven's sake, help me!
IAGO	What 's the matter?
GRATIANO	This is Othello's ancient, as I take it.
LODOVICO	The same indeed; a very valiant fellow. 52
IAGO	What are you here that cry so grievously?
CASSIO	Iago? O, I am spoil'd, undone by villains!
	Give me some help.
IAGO	O me, lieutenant! what villains have done this?
CASSIO	I think that one of them is hereabout,
	And cannot make away.
IAGO	O treacherous villains!

(To LODOVICO *and* GRATIANO.)

	What are you there? come in, and give some help.
RODERIGO	O, help me here! 60
CASSIO	That 's one of them.
IAGO	O murderous slave! O villain!

(Stabs RODERIGO.)

RODERIGO	O damn'd Iago! O inhuman dog!
IAGO	Kill men i' the dark!—Where be these bloody thieves?—
	How silent is this town!—Ho! murder! murder!—
	What may you be? are you of good or evil?
LODOVICO	As you shall prove us, praise us.
IAGO	Signior Lodovico?
LODOVICO	He, sir.
IAGO	I cry you mercy. Here's Cassio hurt by villains.

GRATIANO	Cassio!
IAGO	How is 't, brother!
CASSIO	My leg is cut in two.
IAGO	Marry, heaven forbid! Light, gentlemen: I'll bind it with my shirt.

(*Enter* BIANCA.)

BIANCA	What is the matter, ho? who is 't that cried?
IAGO	Who is 't that cried!
BIANCA	O my dear Cassio! my sweet Cassio! O Cassio, Cassio, Cassio!
IAGO	O notable strumpet! Cassio, may you suspect Who they should be that have thus mangled you?
CASSIO	No.

GRATIANO	I am sorry to find you thus: I have been to seek you.
IAGO	Lend me a garter. So. O, for a chair, To bear him easily hence!
BIANCA	Alas, he faints! O Cassio, Cassio, Cassio!
IAGO	Gentlemen all, I do suspect this trash To be a party to this injury. Patience awhile, good Cassio. Come, come; Lend me a light. Know we this face or no? Alas, my friend and my dear countryman Roderigo! no:—yes, sure:—O heaven! Roderigo.

GRATIANO	What, of Venice?
IAGO	Even he, sir: did you know him?
GRATIANO	Know him! ay.
IAGO	Signior Gratiano? I cry you gentle pardon; These bloody accidents must excuse my manners, That so neglected you.
GRATIANO	I am glad to see you.
IAGO	How do you, Cassio? O, a chair, a chair!
GRATIANO	Roderigo!
IAGO	He, he, 't is he.

(*A chair brought in.*) O, that 's well said; the chair.
Some good man bear him carefully from hence;
I 'll fetch the general's surgeon.

(*To* BIANCA) For you, mistress,

Save you your labour. He that lies slain here, Cassio,
Was my dear friend: what malice was between you?

CASSIO	None in the world; nor do I know the man.
IAGO	(*To* BIANCA) What, look you pale? O, bear him out o' the air.

(CASSIO *and* RODERIGO *are borne off.*)

Stay you, good gentlemen. Look you pale, mistress?
Do you perceive the gastness of her eye?
Nay, if you stare, we shall hear more anon.
Behold her well; I pray you, look upon her:
Do you see, gentlemen? nay, guiltiness will speak,
Though tongues were out of use.   110

(*Enter* EMILIA.)

EMILIA	'Las, what 's the matter? what 's the matter, husband?
IAGO	Cassio hath here been set on in the dark By Roderigo and fellows that are scaped: He 's almost slain, and Roderigo dead.
EMILIA	Alas, good gentleman! alas, good Cassio!
IAGO	This is the fruit of whoring. Prithee, Emilia, Go know of Cassio where he supp'd to-night. (*To* BIANCA) What, do you shake at that?
BIANCA	He supp'd at my house; but I therefore shake not.
IAGO	O, did he so? I charge you, go with me. 120
EMILIA	Fie, fie upon thee, strumpet!
BIANCA	I am no strumpet; but of life as honest As you that thus abuse me.
EMILIA	As I! foh! fie upon thee!
IAGO	Kind gentlemen, let 's go see poor Cassio dress'd. Come, mistress, you must tell 's another tale. Emilia, run you to the citadel, And tell my lord and lady what hath happ'd. Will you go on? I pray. (*Aside*) This is the night That either makes me or fordoes me quite.

(*Exeunt.*)

SCENE II. *A bedchamber in the castle:*
DESDEMONA *in bed asleep; a light burning.*

(*Enter* OTHELLO.)

OTHELLO	It is the cause, it is the cause, my soul,— Let me not name it to you, chaste stars!— It is the cause. Yet I'll not shed her blood; Nor scar that whiter skin of hers than snow,

---

l. 106 *gastness of:* Terror in.

And smooth as monumental alabaster.
Yet she must die, else she 'll betray more men.
Put out the light, and then put out the light:
If I quench thee, thou flaming minister,
I can again thy former light restore,
Should I repent me: but once put out thy light,   10
Thou cunning'st pattern of excelling nature,
I know not where is that Promethean heat
That can thy light relume. When I have pluck'd the rose,
I cannot give it vital growth again,

(Kissing her.) It must needs wither: I 'll smell it on the tree.
Ah, balmy breath, that dost almost persuade
Justice to break her sword! One more, one more,
Be thus when thou art dead, and I will kill thee,
And love thee after. One more, and this the last: 19
So sweet was ne'er so fatal. I must weep,
But they are cruel tears: this sorrow's heavenly;
It strikes where it doth love. She wakes.

DESDEMONA   Who 's there? Othello?

OTHELLO   Ay, Desdemona.

DESDEMONA   Will you come to bed, my lord?

OTHELLO   Have you pray'd to-night, Desdemona?

DESDEMONA   Ay, my lord.

OTHELLO   If you bethink yourself of any crime
Unreconciled as yet to heaven and grace,
Solicit for it straight.

DESDEMONA   Alas, my lord, what do you mean by that?

OTHELLO   Well, do it, and be brief; I will walk by: 30
I would not kill thy unprepared spirit;
No; heaven forfend! I would not kill thy soul.

DESDEMONA   Talk you of killing?

OTHELLO   Ay, I do.

DESDEMONA   Then heaven
Have mercy on me!

OTHELLO   Amen, with all my heart!

DESDEMONA   If you say so, I hope you will not kill me.

OTHELLO   Hum!

DESDEMONA   And yet I fear you; for you are fatal then
When your eyes roll so: why I should fear I know not,
Since guiltiness I know not; but yet I feel I fear.

OTHELLO	Think on thy sins.
DESDEMONA	They are loves I bear to you.
OTHELLO	Ay, and for that thou diest. 41
DESDEMONA	That death 's unnatural that kills for loving.
	Alas, why gnaw you so your nether lip?
	Some bloody passion shakes your very frame:
	There are portents; but yet I hope, I hope,
	They do not point on me.
OTHELLO	Peace, and be still!
DESDEMONA	I will so. What 's the matter?
OTHELLO	That handkerchief which I so love and gave thee
	Thou gavest to Cassio.
DESDEMONA	No, by my life and soul!
	Send for the man, and ask him.
OTHELLO	Sweet soul, take heed,
	Take heed of perjury; thou art on thy deathbed. 51
DESDEMONA	Ay, but not yet to die.
OTHELLO	Yes, presently:
	Therefore confess thee freely of thy sin;
	For to deny each article with oath
	Cannot remove nor choke the strong conception
	That I do groan withal. Thou art to die.
DESDEMONA	Then Lord have mercy on me!
OTHELLO	I say, amen.
DESDEMONA	And have you mercy too! I never did
	Offend you in my life; never loved Cassio
	But with such general warranty of heaven
	As I might love; I never gave him token.
OTHELLO	By heaven, I saw my handkerchief in's hand. 62
	O perjured woman! thou dost stone my heart,
	And makest me call what I intend to do
	A murder, which I thought a sacrifice:
	I saw the handkerchief.
DESDEMONA	He found it then;
	I never gave it him: send for him hither;
	Let him confess a truth.
OTHELLO	He hath confess'd.
DESDEMONA	What, my lord? 69

OTHELLO	That he hath used thee.
DESDEMONA	How? unlawfully?
OTHELLO	Ay.
DESDEMONA	He will not say so.
OTHELLO	No, his mouth is stopp'd; Honest Iago hath ta'en order for 't.
DESDEMONA	O! my fear interprets: what, is he dead?
OTHELLO	Had all his hairs been lives, my great revenge Had stomach for them all.
DESDEMONA	Alas! he is betray'd and I undone.
OTHELLO	Out, strumpet! weep'st thou for him to my face?
DESDEMONA	O, banish me, my lord, but kill me not!
OTHELLO	Down, strumpet!
DESDEMONA	Kill me to-morrow: let me live to-night! 80
OTHELLO	Nay, if you strive,—
DESDEMONA	But half an hour!
OTHELLO	Being done, there is no pause.
DESDEMONA	But while I say one prayer!
OTHELLO (*He stifles her.*)	It is too late.
EMILIA	(*Within*) My lord, my lord! what, ho! my lord, my lord!
OTHELLO	What noise is this? Not dead? not yet quite dead? I that am cruel am yet merciful; I would not have thee linger in thy pain: So, so.
EMILIA	(*Within*) What, ho! my lord, my lord!
OTHELLO	Who 's there?
EMILIA	(*Within*) O, good my lord, I would speak a word with you! 90
OTHELLO	Yes: 't is Emilia. By and by. She 's dead. 'T is like she comes to speak of Cassio's death.— The noise was here. Ha! no more moving? Still as the grave. Shall she come in? were 't good?— I think she stirs again:—no. What 's best to do? If she come in, she 'll sure speak to my wife: My wife! my wife! what wife! I have no wife.

O, insupportable! O heavy hour!
Methinks it should be now a huge eclipse
Of sun and moon, and that the affrighted globe 100
Should yawn at alteration.

EMILIA   (*Within*) I do beseech you
That I may speak with you, O, good my lord!

OTHELLO   I had forgot thee: O, come in, Emilia:
Soft; by and by. Let me the curtains draw.
Where art thou?

(*Unlocks the door.*)

(*Enter* EMILIA.)   What 's the matter with thee now?

EMILIA   O, my good lord, yonder 's foul murders done!

OTHELLO   What, now?

EMILIA   But now, my lord.

OTHELLO   It is the very error of the moon;
She comes more nearer earth than she was wont, 110
And makes men mad.

EMILIA   Cassio, my lord, hath kill'd a young Venetian
Call'd Roderigo.

OTHELLO   Roderigo kill'd
And Cassio kill'd!

EMILIA   No, Cassio is not kill'd.

OTHELLO   Not Cassio kill'd! then murder 's out of tune,
And sweet revenge grows harsh.

DESDEMONA O, falsely, falsely murder'd!

EMILIA   Alas, what cry is that?

OTHELLO   That! what?

EMILIA   Out, and alas! that was my lady's voice. 119
Help! help, ho! help! O lady, speak again!
Sweet Desdemona! O sweet mistress, speak!

DESDEMONA A guiltless death I die.

EMILIA   O, who hath done this deed?

DESDEMONA Nobody; I myself. Farewell:
Commend me to my kind lord: O farewell!

(*Dies.*)

——— ———
ll. 100–1 *affrighted . . . alteration:* That the terrified earth should open at the catastrophe (of the eclipse).
l. 109 *error:* Aberration.

OTHELLO	Why, how should she be murder'd?
EMILIA	Alas, who knows?
OTHELLO	You heard her say herself, it was not I.
EMILIA	She said so: I must needs report the truth.
OTHELLO	She 's like a liar gone to burning hell: 'T was I that kill'd her.
EMILIA	O, the more angel she, And you the blacker devil! 131
OTHELLO	She turn'd to folly, and she was a whore.
EMILIA	Thou dost belie her, and thou art a devil.
OTHELLO	She was false as water.
EMILIA	Thou art rash as fire, to say That she was false: O, she was heavenly true!
OTHELLO	Cassio did top her; ask thy husband else. O, I were damn'd beneath all depth in hell, But that I did proceed upon just grounds To this extremity. Thy husband knew it all.
EMILIA	My husband! 140
OTHELLO	Thy husband.
EMILIA	That she was false to wedlock?
OTHELLO	Ay, with Cassio. Nay, had she been true, If heaven would make me such another world Of one entire and perfect chrysolite, I 'ld not have sold her for it.
EMILIA	My husband!
OTHELLO	Ay, 't was he that told me first: An honest man he is, and hates the slime That sticks on filthy deeds.
EMILIA	My husband!
OTHELLO	What needs this iteration, woman? I say thy husband. 150
EMILIA	O mistress, villainy hath made mocks with love! My husband say that she was false!
OTHELLO	He, woman; I say thy husband: dost understand the word? My friend, thy husband, honest, honest Iago.

---

l. 145 *chrysolite:* A precious stone.

EMILIA	If he say so, may his pernicious soul Rot half a grain a day! he lies to the heart: She was too fond of her most filthy bargain.
OTHELLO	Ha!
EMILIA	Do thy worst: 159 This deed of thine is no more worthy heaven Than thou wast worthy her.
OTHELLO	Peace, you were best.
EMILIA	Thou hast not half that power to do me harm As I have to be hurt. O gull! O dolt! As ignorant as dirt! thou hast done a deed— I care not for thy sword; I 'll make thee known, Though I lost twenty lives.—Help! help, ho! help! The Moor hath kill'd my mistress! Murder! murder!

(Enter MONTANO, GRATIANO, IAGO, *and others.*)

MONTANO	What is the matter? How now, general!
EMILIA	O, are you come, Iago? you have done well, That men must lay their murders on your neck. 170
GRATIANO	What is the matter?
EMILIA	Disprove this villain, if thou be'st a man: He says thou told'st him that his wife was false: I know thou didst not, thou 'rt not such a villain: Speak, for my heart is full.
IAGO	I told him what I thought, and told no more Than what he found himself was apt and true.
EMILIA	But did you ever tell him she was false?
IAGO	I did.
EMILIA	You told a lie; an odious, damned lie; 180 Upon my soul, a lie, a wicked lie. She false with Cassio!—did you say with Cassio?
IAGO	With Cassio, mistress. Go to, charm your tongue.
EMILIA	I will not charm my tongue; I am bound to speak: My mistress here lies murder'd in her bed,—
ALL	O heavens forfend!
EMILIA	And your reports have set the murder on.
OTHELLO	Nay, stare not, masters: it is true, indeed.
GRATIANO	'T is a strange truth.
MONTANO	O monstrous act!

EMILIA	Villainy, villainy, villainy!

EMILIA   Villainy, villainy, villainy!
          I think upon 't: I think: I smell 't: O villainy—   191
          I thought so then:—I 'll kill myself for grief:—
          O villainy, villainy!

IAGO   What, are you mad? I charge you, get you home.

EMILIA   Good gentlemen, let me have leave to speak:
          'T is proper I obey him, but not now.
          Perchance, Iago, I will ne'er go home.

OTHELLO   O! O! O!
          (*He falls on the bed.*)

EMILIA   Nay, lay thee down and roar;
          For thou hast kill'd the sweetest innocent
          That e'er did lift up eye.

OTHELLO   (*Rising*) O, she was foul!
          I scarce did know you, uncle: there lies your niece,   201
          Whose breath, indeed, these hands have newly stopp'd:
          I know this act shows horrible and grim.

GRATIANO Poor Desdemona; I am glad thy father 's dead:
          Thy match was mortal to him, and pure grief
          Shore his old thread in twain: did he live now,
          This sight would make him do a desperate turn,
          Yea, curse his better angel from his side,
          And fall to reprobation.   209

OTHELLO   'T is pitiful; but yet Iago knows
          That she with Cassio hath the act of shame
          A thousand times committed; Cassio confess'd it:
          And she did gratify his amorous works
          With that recognizance and pledge of love
          Which I first gave her; I saw it in his hand:
          It was a handkerchief, an antique token
          My father gave my mother.

EMILIA   O heaven! O heavenly powers!

IAGO   Come, hold your peace.

EMILIA   'T will out, 't will out: I peace!
          No, I will speak as liberal as the north: 220
          Let heaven and men and devils, let them all,
          All, all, cry shame against me, yet I 'll speak.

IAGO   Be wise and get you home.

---

l. 207 *turn:* Act.
l. 209 *reprobation:* Damnation.
l. 220 *liberal as the north:* Freely as the north wind.

EMILIA   I will not.
   (IAGO *offers to stab* EMILIA.)

GRATIANO   Fie!
     Your sword upon a woman?

EMILIA   O thou dull Moor! that handkerchief thou speak'st of
     I found by fortune and did give my husband;
     For often with a solemn earnestness,
     More than indeed belong'd to such a trifle,
     He begg'd of me to steal it.

IAGO   Villainous whore!

EMILIA   She give it Cassio! no, alas! I found it,   230
     And I did give 't my husband.

IAGO   Filth, thou liest!

EMILIA   By heaven, I do not, I do not, gentlemen.
     O murderous coxcomb! what should such a fool
     Do with so good a wife?

OTHELLO   Are there no stones in heaven
     But what serve for the thunder?—Precious villain!
   (*He runs at* IAGO; IAGO, *from behind, stabs* EMILIA, *and exit.*)

GRATIANO   The woman falls; sure, he hath kill'd his wife.

EMILIA   Ay, ay: O, lay me by my mistress' side.

GRATIANO   He 's gone, but his wife 's kill'd.

MONTANO   'T is a notorious villain. Take you this weapon,   239
     Which I have here recover'd from the Moor:
     Come, guard the door without; let him not pass,
     But kill him rather. I 'll after that same villain,
     For 't is a damned slave.
   (*Exeunt* MONTANO *and* GRATIANO.)

OTHELLO   I am not valiant neither,
     But every puny whipster gets my sword:
     But why should honour outlive honesty?
     Let it go all.

EMILIA   What did thy song bode, lady?
     Hark, canst thou hear me? I will play the swan,
     And die in music. (*Singing*) Willow, willow, willow.—
     Moor, she was chaste; she loved thee, cruel Moor;   249
     So come my soul to bliss, as I speak true;
     So speaking as I think, I die, I die.
   (*Dies.*)

---

l. 233 *coxcomb: Fool.*
l. 234 *stones: Bolts of lightning.*

OTHELLO	I have another weapon in this chamber;
	It is a sword of Spain, the ice-brook's temper:—
	O, here it is. Uncle, I must come forth.

GRATIANO	(*Within*) If thou attempt it, it will cost thee dear:
	Thou hast no weapon, and perforce must suffer.

OTHELLO	Look in upon me then and speak with me,
	Or, naked as I am, I will assault thee.

(*Re-enter* GRATIANO.)

GRATIANO	What is the matter?

OTHELLO	Behold, I have a weapon;

A better never did itself sustain   260
Upon a soldier's thigh: I have seen the day
That, with this little arm and this good sword,
I have made my way through more impediments
Than twenty times your stop: but, O vain boast!
Who can control his fate? 't is not so now.
Be not afraid, though you do see me weapon'd;
Here is my journey's end, here is my butt,
And very sea-mark of my utmost sail.
Do you go back dismay'd? 't is a lost fear;
Man but a rush against Othello's breast,
And he retires. Where should Othello go?
Now, how dost thou look now? O ill-starr'd wench!   272
Pale as thy smock! when we shall meet at compt,
This look of thine will hurl my soul from heaven,
And fiends will snatch at it. Cold, cold, my girl!
Even like thy chastity. O cursed slave!
Whip me, ye devils,
From the possession of this heavenly sight!
Blow me about in winds! roast me in sulphur!   279
Wash me in steep-down gulfs of liquid fire!
O Desdemona! Desdemona! dead!
Oh! Oh! Oh!

(*Enter* LODOVICO, MONTANO, CASSIO *carried in a chair, and* OFFICERS *with* IAGO *prisoner.*)

LODOVICO	Where is this rash and most unfortunate man?

OTHELLO	That 's he that was Othello: here I am.

LODOVICO	Where is that viper? bring the villain forth.

---

l. 253 *the ice-brook's temper:* Tempered in an ice-cold brook.
l. 258 *naked:* Unarmed.
ll. 267–8 *here . . . sail:* Here is the end of my voyage.
l. 270 *man but a rush:* Take up only a reed.
l. 273 *compt:* Judgment day.

OTHELLO	I look down towards his feet; but that's a fable.
	If that thou be'st a devil, I cannot kill thee.
(*Wounds* IAGO.)	
LODOVICO	Wrench his sword from him.
IAGO	I bleed, sir; but not kill'd.
OTHELLO	I am not sorry neither: I 'ld have thee live;
	For, in my sense, 't is happiness to die.
LODOVICO	O thou Othello, that wert once so good,
	Fall'n in the practice of a damned slave,
	What shall be said to thee?
OTHELLO	Why, any thing:
	An honourable murderer, if you will;
	For nought I did in hate, but all in honour.
LODOVICO	This wretch hath part confess'd his villany:
	Did you and he consent in Cassio's death?
OTHELLO	Ay.
CASSIO	Dear general, I never gave you cause.
OTHELLO	I do believe it, and I ask your pardon.
	Will you, I pray, demand that demi-devil
	Why he hath thus ensnared my soul and body?
IAGO	Demand me nothing: what you know, you know:
	From this time forth I never will speak word.
LODOVICO	What, not to pray?
GRATIANO	Torments will ope your lips.
OTHELLO	Well, thou dost best.
LODOVICO	Sir, you shall understand what hath befall'n,
	Which, as I think, you know not. Here is a letter
	Found in the pocket of the slain Roderigo;
	And here another: the one of them imports
	The death of Cassio to be undertook
	By Roderigo.
OTHELLO	O villain!
CASSIO	Most heathenish and most gross!
LODOVICO	Now here 's another discontented paper,
	Found in his pocket too; and this, it seems,
	Roderigo meant to have sent this damned villain;
	But that belike Iago in the interim
	Came in and satisfied him.

291

300

311

---

l. 286 *I . . . feet:* I examine his feet to see whether they are cloven.

OTHELLO	O the pernicious caitiff!

OTHELLO   O the pernicious caitiff!
How came you, Cassio, by that handkerchief
That was my wife's?

CASSIO   I found it in my chamber:
And he himself confess'd but even now
That there he dropp'd it for a special purpose   322
Which wrought to his desire.

OTHELLO   O fool! fool! fool!

CASSIO   There is besides in Roderigo's letter,
How he upbraids Iago, that he made him
Brave me upon the watch; whereon it came
That I was cast: and even but now he spake,
After long seeming dead, Iago hurt him,
Iago set him on.

LODOVICO   You must forsake this room, and go with us: 330
Your power and your command is taken off,
And Cassio rules in Cyprus. For this slave,
If there be any cunning cruelty
That can torment him much and hold him long,
It shall be his. You shall close prisoner rest,
Till that the nature of your fault be known
To the Venetian state. Come, bring him away.

OTHELLO   Soft you; a word or two before you go.
I have done the state some service, and they know 't.
No more of that. I pray you, in your letters,
When you shall these unlucky deeds relate,
Speak of me as I am; nothing extenuate,
Nor set down aught in malice: then must you speak   343
Of one that loved not wisely but too well;
Of one not easily jealous, but, being wrought,
Perplex'd in the extreme; of one whose hand,
Like the base Indian, threw a pearl away
Richer than all his tribe; of one whose subdued eyes,
Albeit unused to the melting mood,
Drop tears as fast as the Arabian trees
Their medicinal gum. Set you down this;
And say besides, that in Aleppo once,   352
Where a malignant and a turban'd Turk
Beat a Venetian and traduced the state,
I took by the throat the circumcised dog,
And smote him, thus.

(*Stabs himself.*)

LODOVICO   O bloody period!

GRATIANO   All that 's spoke is marr'd.

OTHELLO   I kiss'd thee ere I kill'd thee: no way but this;
               Killing myself, to die upon a kiss.

(Falls on the bed, and dies.)

CASSIO   This did I fear, but thought he had no weapon;   360
               For he was great of heart.

LODOVICO   (*To* IAGO) O Spartan dog,
               More fell than anguish, hunger, or the sea!
               Look on the tragic loading of this bed;
               This is thy work: the object poisons sight;
               Let it be hid. Gratiano, keep the house,
               And seize upon the fortunes of the Moor,
               For they succeed on you. To you, lord governor,
               Remains the censure of this hellish villain;
               The time, the place, the torture: O, enforce it!   369
               Myself will straight aboard; and to the state
               This heavy act with heavy heart relate.

(Exeunt.)

---

l. 362 *fell:* Cruel.
l. 365 *keep:* Guard.

When, about 1879, Nora Helmer slammed the door at the end of the
first performance of A Doll's House, she caused a reverberation
whose echoes have not yet died down. The play was not the first plea
for the liberation of women, of course, but it is a notable skirmish in
that long struggle. In spite of certain old-fashioned traits found in any
play by Ibsen, this one has tremendous power for us a century later.

Until the first part of Act III the play seems to be about Nora's problem: how she will free herself from the consequences of the crime of
forgery she had committed a few years before. Then the play
changes direction. Because of her husband's reaction to the revelation of the threatening fact, Nora realizes something about herself,
her husband, and her marriage. It is a kind of recognition scene, an
ancient device in plays—but here the recognition is self-recognition.
Nora realizes that as a "squanderbird" she has lived a false life and
has built her marriage on false premises. The terms and circumstances are those of northern Europe in the nineteenth century, but
the idea that women need not be dependent on men is of permanent
value, to be restated again and again in our own time and our own
society.

Students of drama are interested in Ibsen's analytic technique. He
commonly withholds part of his story from the audience, only gradu-

ally revealing necessary facts about his characters. So in A Doll's House we learn about Nora's dereliction at the end of Act I, Dr. Rank's problem during Act II, and the previous relationship between Krogstad and Mrs. Linde in Act III. The truth comes out slowly but inexorably, detail by detail. Some of it is foreshadowed by "plants" (another ancient story-telling device). Facts supplied early in the play, such as the character of Nora's father and his death, turn out later to have a significance not understood when we learned about them. A Doll's House is a neatly constructed play, though its machinery may seem somewhat obvious to modern readers of drama.

The theater for which Ibsen wrote was the proscenium arch theater, the only kind in which plays were produced in Europe and the United States during the nineteenth and much of the twentieth century. The stage was a room with one wall missing so that the audience could look through at a set with realistic pictures, curtains, furniture, and at actors costumed like real people. All plays, even Shakespeare's, were produced in this fashion during this period. A Doll's House requires only one set: an artificial device, since the important events in our lives do not all take place in one room, but so effective a means of simplifying the staging of a play that modern playwrights are still using it.

*A Doll's House

HENRIK IBSEN

Translated by Michael Meyer

CHARACTERS

TORVALD HELMER, a lawyer
NORA, his wife
DR. RANK
MRS. LINDE
NILS KROGSTAD, also a lawyer

The HELMERS' three small children
ANNE-MARIE, their nurse
HELEN, the maid
A PORTER

The action takes place in the HELMERS' apartment.

ACT I

(A comfortably and tastefully, but not expensively furnished room. Backstage right a door leads out to the hall; backstage left, another door to HELMER's study. Between these two doors stands a piano. In the middle of the left-hand wall is a door, with a window downstage of it. Near the window, a round table with armchairs and a small sofa. In the right-hand wall, slightly upstage, is a door; downstage of this, against the same wall, a stove lined with porcelain tiles, with a couple of armchairs and a rocking-chair in front of it. Between the stove and the side door is a small table. Engravings on the wall. A what-not with china and other bric-a-brac; a small bookcase with leather-bound books. A carpet on the floor; a fire in the stove. A winter day.

(A bell rings in the hall outside. After a moment, we hear the front door being opened. NORA enters the room, humming contentedly to herself. She is wearing outdoor clothes and carrying a lot of parcels, which she puts down on the table right. She leaves the door to the hall open; through it, we can see a PORTER carrying a Christmas tree and a basket. He gives these to the MAID, who has opened the door for them.)

NORA Hide that Christmas tree away, Helen. The children mustn't see it before I've decorated it this evening. *(To the* PORTER, *taking out her purse.)* How much—?

PORTER A shilling.

NORA Here's half a crown. No, keep it.

(The PORTER touches his cap and goes. NORA closes the door. She continues to laugh happily to herself as she removes her coat, etc. She takes from her pocket a bag containing macaroons and eats a couple. Then she tiptoes across and listens at her husband's door.)

NORA Yes, he's here. *(Starts humming again as she goes over to the table, right.)*

HELMER *(from his room)* Is that my skylark twittering out there?

NORA *(opening some of the parcels)* It is!

HELMER Is that my squirrel rustling?

NORA Yes!

HELMER When did my squirrel come home?

NORA Just now. *(Pops the bag of macaroons in her pocket and wipes her mouth.)* Come out here, Torvald, and see what I've bought.

HELMER You mustn't disturb me! *(Short pause; then he opens the door and looks in, his pen in his hand.)* Bought, did you say? All that? Has my little squanderbird been overspending again?

NORA Oh, Torvald, surely we can let ourselves go a little this year! It's the first Christmas we don't have to scrape.

HELMER Well, you know, we can't afford to be extravagant.

NORA Oh yes, Torvald, we can be a little extravagant now. Can't we? Just a tiny bit? You've got a big salary now, and you're going to make lots and lots of money.

HELMER Next year, yes. But my new salary doesn't start till April.

NORA Pooh; we can borrow till then.

HELMER Nora! *(Goes over to her and takes her playfully by the ear.)* What a little spendthrift you are! Suppose I were to borrow fifty pounds today, and you spent it all over Christmas, and then on New Year's Eve a tile fell off a roof on to my head—

NORA (*puts her hand over his mouth*) Oh, Torvald! Don't say such dreadful things!

HELMER Yes, but suppose something like that did happen? What then?

NORA If anything as frightful as that happened, it wouldn't make much difference whether I was in debt or not.

HELMER But what about the people I'd borrow from?

NORA Them? Who cares about them? They're strangers.

HELMER Oh, Nora, Nora, how like a woman! No, but seriously, Nora, you know how I feel about this. No debts! Never borrow! A home that is founded on debts can never be a place of freedom and beauty. We two have stuck it out bravely up to now; and we shall continue to do so for the short time we still have to.

NORA (*goes over towards the stove*) Very well, Torvald. As you say.

HELMER (*follows her*) Now, now! My little songbird mustn't droop her wings. What's this? Is little squirrel sulking? (*Takes out his purse.*) Nora; guess what I've got here!

NORA (*turns quickly*) Money!

HELMER Look. (*Hands her some banknotes.*) I know how these small expenses crop up at Christmas.

NORA (*counts them*) One—two—three—four. Oh, thank you, Torvald, thank you! I should be able to manage with this.

HELMER You'll have to.

NORA Yes, yes, of course I will. But come over here, I want to show you everything I've bought. And so cheaply! Look, here are new clothes for Ivar—and a sword. And a horse and a trumpet for Bob. And a doll and a cradle for Emmy—they're nothing much, but she'll pull them apart in a few days. And some bits of material and handkerchiefs for the maids. Old Anne-Marie ought to have had something better, really.

HELMER And what's in that parcel?

NORA (*cries*) No, Torvald, you mustn't see that before this evening!

HELMER Very well. But now, tell me, you little spendthrift, what do you want for Christmas?

NORA Me? Oh, pooh, I don't want anything.

HELMER Oh, yes, you do. Now tell me, what, within reason, would you most like?

NORA No, I really don't know. Oh, yes—Torvald—!

HELMER Well?

NORA (*plays with his coat-buttons; not looking at him*) If you really want to give me something, you could—you could—

HELMER Come on, out with it.

NORA (*quickly*) You could give me money, Torvald. Only as much as you feel you can afford; then later I'll buy something with it.

HELMER But, Nora—

NORA Oh yes, Torvald dear, please! Please! Then I'll wrap up the notes in pretty gold paper and hang them on the Christmas tree. Wouldn't that be fun?

HELMER What's the name of that little bird that can never keep any money?

NORA Yes, yes, squanderbird; I know. But let's do as I say, Torvald; then I'll have time to think about what I need most. Isn't that the best way? Mm?

HELMER (*smiles*) To be sure it would be, if you could keep what I give you and really buy yourself something with it. But you'll spend it on all sorts of useless things for the house, and then I'll have to put my hand in my pocket again.

NORA Oh, but Torvald—

HELMER You can't deny it, Nora dear. (*Puts his arm around her waist.*) The squanderbird's a pretty little creature, but she gets through an awful lot of money. It's incredible what an expensive pet she is for a man to keep.

NORA For shame! How can you say such a thing? I save every penny I can.

HELMER (*laughs*) That's quite true. Every penny you can. But you can't.

NORA (*hums and smiles, quietly gleeful*) Hm. If you only knew how many expenses we larks and squirrels have, Torvald.

HELMER You're a funny little creature. Just like your father used to be. Always on the look-out for some way to get money, but as soon as you have any it just runs through your fingers, and you never know where it's gone. Well, I suppose I must take you as you are. It's in your blood. Yes, yes, yes, these things are hereditary, Nora.

NORA Oh, I wish I'd inherited more of Papa's qualities.

HELMER And I wouldn't wish my darling little songbird to be any different from what she is. By the way, that reminds me. You look awfully—how shall I put it?—awfully guilty today.

NORA Do I?

HELMER Yes, you do. Look me in the eyes.

NORA (*looks at him*) Well?

HELMER (*wags his finger*) Has my little sweet-tooth been indulging herself in town today, by any chance?

NORA No, how can you think such a thing?

HELMER Not a tiny little digression into a pastry shop?

NORA No, Torvald, I promise—

HELMER Not just a wee jam tart?

NORA Certainly not.

HELMER Not a little nibble at a macaroon?

NORA No, Torvald—I promise you, honestly—

HELMER There, there. I was only joking.

NORA (*goes over to the table, right*) You know I could never act against your wishes.

HELMER Of course not. And you've given me your word—(*Goes over to her.*) Well, my beloved Nora, you keep your little Christmas secrets to yourself. They'll be revealed this evening, I've no doubt, once the Christmas tree has been lit.

NORA Have you remembered to invite Dr. Rank?

HELMER No. But there's no need; he knows he'll be dining with us. Anyway,

I'll ask him when he comes this morning. I've ordered some good wine. Oh, Nora, you can't imagine how I'm looking forward to this evening.

NORA So am I. And, Torvald, how the children will love it!

HELMER Yes, it's a wonderful thing to know that one's position is assured and that one has an ample income. Don't you agree? It's good to know that, isn't it?

NORA Yes, it's almost like a miracle.

HELMER Do you remember last Christmas? For three whole weeks you shut yourself away every evening to make flowers for the Christmas tree, and all those other things you were going to surprise us with. Ugh, it was the most boring time I've ever had in my life.

NORA I didn't find it boring.

HELMER (*smiles*) But it all came to nothing in the end, didn't it?

NORA Oh, are you going to bring that up again? How could I help the cat getting in and tearing everything to bits?

HELMER No, my poor little Nora, of course you couldn't. You simply wanted to make us happy, and that's all that matters. But it's good that those hard times are past.

NORA Yes, it's wonderful.

HELMER I don't have to sit by myself and be bored. And you don't have to tire your pretty eyes and your delicate little hands—

NORA (*claps her hands*) No, Torvald, that's true, isn't it—I don't have to any longer? Oh, it's really all just like a miracle. (*Takes his arm.*) Now, I'm going to tell you what I thought we might do, Torvald. As soon as Christmas is over— (*A bell rings in the hall.*) Oh, there's the doorbell. (*Tidies up one or two things in the room.*) Someone's coming. What a bore.

HELMER I'm not at home to any visitors. Remember!

MAID (*in the doorway*) A lady's called, madam. A stranger.

NORA Well, ask her to come in.

MAID And the doctor's here too, sir.

HELMER Has he gone to my room?

MAID Yes, sir.

(HELMER *goes into his room. The* MAID *shows in* MRS. LINDE, *who is dressed in travelling clothes, and closes the door.*)

MRS. LINDE (*shyly and a little hesitantly*) Good evening, Nora.

NORA (*uncertainly*) Good evening—

MRS. LINDE I don't suppose you recognize me.

NORA No, I'm afraid I—Yes, wait a minute—surely—(*exclaims*) Why, Christine! Is it really you?

MRS. LINDE Yes, it's me.

NORA Christine! And I didn't recognize you! But how could I—? (*more quietly*) How you've changed, Christine!

MRS. LINDE Yes, I know. It's been nine years—nearly ten—

NORA Is it so long? Yes, it must be. Oh, these last eight years have been such a happy time for me! So you've come to town? All the way in winter! How brave of you!

MRS. LINDE I arrived by the steamer this morning.

NORA Yes, of course—to enjoy yourself over Christmas. Oh, how splendid! We'll have to celebrate! But take off your coat. You're not cold, are you? (*Helps her off with it.*) There! Now let's sit down here by the stove and be comfortable. No, you take the armchair. I'll sit here in the rocking-chair. (*Clasps* MRS. LINDE's *hands.*) Yes, now you look like your old self. It was just at first that—you've got a little paler, though, Christine. And perhaps a bit thinner.

MRS. LINDE And older, Nora. Much, much older.

NORA Yes, perhaps a little older. Just a tiny bit. Not much. *checks herself suddenly and says earnestly*) Oh, but how thoughtless of me to sit here and chatter away like this? Dear, sweet Christine, can you forgive me?

MRS. LINDE What do you mean, Nora?

NORA (*quietly*) Poor Christine, you've become a widow.

MRS. LINDE Yes. Three years ago.

NORA I know, I know—I read it in the papers. Oh, Christine, I meant to write to you so often, honestly. But I always put it off, and something else always cropped up.

MRS. LINDE I understand, Nora dear.

NORA No, Christine, it was beastly of me. Oh, my poor darling, what you've gone through! And he didn't leave you anything?

MRS. LINDE No.

NORA No children, either?

MRS. LINDE No.

NORA Nothing at all, then?

MRS. LINDE Not even a feeling of loss or sorrow.

NORA (*looks incredulously at her*) But, Christine, how is that possible?

MRS. LINDE (*smiles sadly and strokes* NORA's *hair*) Oh, these things happen, Nora.

NORA All alone. How dreadful that must be for you. I've three lovely children. I'm afraid you can't see them now, because they're out with nanny. But you must tell me everything—

MRS. LINDE No, no, no. I want to hear about you.

NORA No, you start. I'm not going to be selfish today. I'm just going to think

MRS. LINDE No, no, no. I want to hear about you.

NORA No, you start. I'm not going to be selfish today. I'm just going to think about you. Oh, but there's one thing I *must* tell you. Have you heard of the wonderful luck we've just had?

MRS. LINDE No. What?

NORA Would you believe it—my husband's just been made manager of the bank!

MRS. LINDE Your husband? Oh, how lucky—!

NORA Yes, isn't it? Being a lawyer is so uncertain, you know, especially if one isn't prepared to touch any case that isn't—well—quite nice. And of course Torvald's been very firm about that— and I'm absolutely with him. Oh, you can imagine how happy we are! He's joining the bank in the New Year, and he'll be getting a big salary, and lots of percentages too. From now on we'll be able to live quite differently—we'll be able to do whatever we want. Oh, Christine, it's such a relief! I feel so happy! Well, I mean, it's lovely to have heaps of money and not to have to worry about anything. Don't you think?

MRS. LINDE   It must be lovely to have enough to cover one's needs, anyway.

NORA   Not just our needs! We're going to have heaps and heaps of money!

MRS. LINDE   (*smiles*) Nora, Nora, haven't you grown up yet? When we were at school you were a terrible little spendthrift.

NORA   (*laughs quietly*) Yes, Torvald still says that. (*Wags her finger.*) But "Nora, Nora" isn't as silly as you think. Oh, we've been in no position for me to waste money. We've both had to work.

MRS. LINDE   You too?

NORA   Yes, little things—fancy work, crocheting, embroidery and so forth. (*casually*) And other things too. I suppose you know Torvald left the Ministry when we got married? There were no prospects of promotion in his department, and of course he needed more money. But the first year he overworked himself quite dreadfully. He had to take on all sorts of extra jobs, and worked day and night. But it was too much for him, and he became frightfully ill. The doctors said he'd have to go to a warmer climate.

MRS. LINDE   Yes, you spent a whole year in Italy, didn't you?

NORA   Yes. It wasn't easy for me to get away, you know. I'd just had Ivar. But of course we had to do it. Oh, it was a marvellous trip! And it saved Torvald's life. But it cost an awful lot of money, Christine.

MRS. LINDE   I can imagine.

NORA   Two hundred and fifty pounds. That's a lot of money, you know.

MRS. LINDE   How lucky you had it.

NORA   Well, actually, we got it from my father.

MRS. LINDE   Oh, I see. Didn't he die just about that time?

NORA   Yes, Christine, just about then. Wasn't it dreadful, I couldn't go and look after him. I was expecting little Ivar any day. And then I had my poor Torvald to care for—we really didn't think he'd live. Dear, kind Papa! I never saw him again, Christine. Oh, it's the saddest thing that's happened to me since I got married.

MRS. LINDE   I know you were very fond of him. But you went to Italy—?

NORA   Yes. Well, we had the money, you see, and the doctors said we mustn't delay. So we went the month after Papa died.

MRS. LINDE   And your husband came back completely cured?

NORA   Fit as a fiddle!

MRS. LINDE   But—the doctor?

NORA   How do you mean?

MRS. LINDE   I thought the maid said that the gentleman who arrived with me was the doctor.

NORA   Oh yes, that's Doctor Rank, but he doesn't come because anyone's ill. He's our best friend, and he looks us up at least once every day. No, Torvald hasn't had a moment's illness since we went away. And the children are fit and healthy and so am I. (*Jumps up and claps her hands.*) Oh God, oh God, Christine, isn't it a wonderful thing to be alive and happy! Oh, but how beastly of me! I'm only talking about myself. (*Sits on a footstool and rests her arms on* MRS. LINDE's *knee*.) Oh, please don't be angry with me! Tell me, is it really true you didn't love your husband? Why did you marry him, then?

MRS. LINDE Well, my mother was still alive; and she was helpless and bed-ridden. And I had my two little brothers to take care of. I didn't feel I could say no.

NORA Yes, well, perhaps you're right. He was rich then, was he?

MRS. LINDE Quiite comfortably off, I believe. But his business was unsound, you see, Nora. When he died it went bankrupt, and there was nothing left.

NORA What did you do?

MRS. LINDE Well, I had to try to make ends meet somehow, so I started a little shop, and a little school, and anything else I could turn my hand to. These last three years have been just one endless slog for me, without a moment's rest. But now it's over, Nora. My poor dear mother doesn't need me any more; she's passed away. And the boys don't need me either; they've got jobs now and can look after themselves.

NORA How relieved you must feel—

MRS. LINDE No, Nora. Just unspeakably empty. No one to live for any more. (*Gets up restlessly.*) That's why I couldn't bear to stay out there any longer, cut off from the world. I thought it'd be easier to find some work here that will exercise and occupy my mind. If only I could get a regular job—office work of some kind—

NORA Oh but, Christine, that's dreadfully exhausting; and you look practically finished already. It'd be much better for you if you could go away somewhere.

MRS. LINDE (*goes over to the window*) I have no Papa to pay for my holidays, Nora.

NORA (*gets up*) Oh, please don't be angry with me.

MRS. LINDE My dear Nora, it's I who should ask you not to be angry. That's the worst thing about this kind of situation—it makes one so bitter. One has no one to work for; and yet one has to be continually sponging for jobs. One has to live; and so one becomes completely egocentric. When you told me about this luck you've just had with Torvald's new job—can you imagine? —I was happy not so much on your account, as on my own.

NORA How do you mean? Oh, I understand. You mean Torvald might be able to do something for you?

MRS LINDE Yes, I was thinking that.

NORA He will too, Christine. Just you leave it to me. I'll lead up to it so delicately, so delicately; I'll get him in the right mood. Oh, Christine, I do so want to help you.

MRS. LINDE It's sweet of you to bother so much about me, Nora. Especially since you know so little of the worries and hardships of life.

NORA I? You say *I* know little of—?

MRS. LINDE (*smiles*) Well, good heavens—those bits of fancy work of yours— well, really—! You're a child, Nora.

NORA (*tosses her head and walks across the room*) You shouldn't say that so patronisingly.

MRS. LINDE   Oh?

NORA   You're like the rest. You all think I'm incapable of getting down to anything serious—

MRS. LINDE   My dear—

NORA   You think I've never had any worries like the rest of you.

MRS. LINDE   Nora dear, you've just told me all about your difficulties—

NORA   Pooh—that! (*quietly*) I haven't told you about the big thing.

MRS. LINDE   What big thing? What do you mean?

NORA   You patronise me, Christine; but you shouldn't. You're proud that you've worked so long and so hard for your mother.

MRS. LINDE   I don't patronise anyone, Nora. But you're right—I am both proud and happy that I was able to make my mother's last months on earth comparatively easy.

NORA   And you're also proud at what you've done for your brothers.

MRS. LINDE   I think I have a right to be.

NORA   I think so too. But let me tell you something, Christine. I too have done something to be proud and happy about.

MRS. LINDE   I don't doubt it. But—how do you mean?

NORA   Speak quietly! Suppose Torvald should hear! He mustn't, at any price—no one must know, Christine—no one but you.

MRS. LINDE   But what is this?

NORA   Come over here. (*Pulls her down on to the sofa beside her.*) Yes, Christine—I too have done something to be happy and proud about. It was I who saved Torvald's life.

MRS. LINDE   Saved his—? How did you save it?

NORA   I told you about our trip to Italy. Torvald couldn't have lived if he hadn't managed to get down there—

MRS. LINDE   Yes, well—your father provided the money—

NORA   (*smiles*) So Torvald and everyone else thinks. But—

MRS. LINDE   Yes?

NORA   Papa didn't give us a penny. It was I who found the money.

MRS. LINDE   You? All of it?

NORA   Two hundred and fifty pounds. What do you say to that?

MRS. LINDE   But Nora, how could you? Did you win a lottery or something?

NORA   (*scornfully*) Lottery? (*sniffs*) What would there be to be proud of in that?

MRS. LINDE   But where did you get it from, then?

NORA   (*hums and smiles secretively*) Hm; tra-la-la-la!

MRS. LINDE   You couldn't have borrowed it.

NORA   Oh? Why not?

MRS. LINDE   Well, a wife can't borrow money without her husband's consent.

NORA   (*tosses her head*) Ah, but when a wife has a little business sense, and knows how to be clever—

MRS. LINDE   But Nora, I simply don't understand—

NORA   You don't have to. No one has said I borrowed the money. I could have got it in some other way. (*Throws herself back on the sofa.*) I could have got it from an admirer. When a girl's as pretty as I am—

MRS. LINDE Nora, you're crazy!

NORA You're dying of curiosity now, aren't you, Christine?

MRS. LINDE Nora dear, you haven't done anything foolish?

NORA (*sits up again*) Is it foolish to save one's husband's life?

MRS. LINDE I think it's foolish if without his knowledge you—

NORA But the whole point was that he mustn't know! Great heavens, don't you see? He hadn't to know how dangerously ill he was. I was the one they told that his life was in danger and that only going to a warm climate could save him. Do you suppose I didn't try to think of other ways of getting him down there? I told him how wonderful it would be for me to go abroad like other young wives; I cried and prayed; I asked him to remember my condition, and said he ought to be nice and tender to me; and then I suggested he might quite easily borrow the money. But then he got almost angry with me, Christine. He said I was frivolous, and that it was his duty as a husband not to pander to my moods and caprices—I think that's what he called them. Well, well, I thought, you've got to be saved somehow. And then I thought of a way—

MRS. LINDE But didn't your husband find out from your father that the money hadn't come from him?

NORA No, never. Papa died just then. I'd thought of letting him into the plot and asking him not to tell. But since he was so ill—! And as things turned out, it didn't become necessary.

MRS. LINDE And you've never told your husband about this?

NORA For heaven's sake, no! What an idea! He's frightfully strict about such matters. And besides—he's so proud of being a *man*—it'd be so painful and humiliating for him to know that he owed anything to me. It'd completely wreck our relationship. This life we have built together would no longer exist.

MRS. LINDE Will you never tell him?

NORA (*thoughtfully, half-smiling*) Yes—some time, perhaps. Years from now, when I'm no longer pretty. You mustn't laugh! I mean of course, when Torvald no longer loves me as he does now; when it no longer amuses him to see me dance and dress up and play the fool for him. Then it might be useful to have something up my sleeve. (*breaks off*) Stupid, stupid, stupid! That time will never come. Well, what do you think of my big secret, Christine? I'm not completely useless, am I? Mind you, all this has caused me a frightful lot of worry. It hasn't been easy for me to meet my obligations punctually. In case you don't know, in the world of business there are things called quarterly instalments and interest, and they're a terrible problem to cope with. So I've had to scrape a little here and save a little there as best I can. I haven't been able to save much on the housekeeping money, because Torvald likes to live well; and I couldn't let the children go short of clothes— I couldn't take anything out of what he gives me for them. The poor little angels!

MRS. LINDE So you've had to stint yourself, my poor Nora?

NORA Of course. Well, after all, it was my problem. Whenever Torvald gave me money to buy myself new clothes, I never used more than half of it;

and I always bought what was cheapest and plainest. Thank heaven anything suits me, so that Torvald's never noticed. But it made me a bit sad sometimes, because it's lovely to wear pretty clothes. Don't you think?

MRS. LINDE   Indeed it is.

NORA   And then I've found one or two other sources of income. Last winter I managed to get a lot of copying to do. So I shut myself away and wrote every evening, late into the night. Oh, I often got so tired, so tired. But it was great fun, though, sitting there working and earning money. It was almost like being a man.

MRS. LINDE   But how much have you managed to pay off like this?

NORA   Well, I can't say exactly. It's awfully difficult to keep an exact check on these kinds of transactions. I only know I've paid everything I've managed to scrape together. Sometimes I really didn't know where to turn. (*Smiles.*) Then I'd sit here and imagine some rich old gentleman had fallen in love with me—

MRS. LINDE   What! What gentleman?

NORA   Silly! And that now he'd died and when they opened his will it said in big letters: "Everything I possess is to be paid forthwith to my beloved Mrs. Nora Helmer in cash."

MRS. LINDE   But, Nora dear, who was this gentleman?

NORA   Great heavens, don't you understand? There wasn't any old gentleman; he was just something I used to dream up as I sat here evening after evening wondering how on earth I could raise some money. But what does it matter? The old bore can stay imaginary as far as I'm concerned, because now I don't have to worry any longer! (*Jumps up.*) Oh, Christine, isn't it wonderful? I don't have to worry any more! No more troubles! I can play all day with the children, I can fill the house with pretty things, just the way Torvald likes. And, Christine, it'll soon be spring, and the air'll be fresh and the skies blue,—and then perhaps we'll be able to take a little trip somewhere. I shall be able to see the sea again. Oh, yes, yes, it's a wonderful thing to be alive and happy!

(*The bell rings in the hall.*)

MRS. LINDE   (*gets up*) You've a visitor. Perhaps I'd better go.

NORA   No, stay. It won't be for me. It's someone for Torvald—

MAID   (*in the doorway*) Excuse me, madam, a gentleman's called who says he wants to speak to the master. But I didn't know—seeing as the doctor's with him—

NORA   Who is this gentleman?

KROGSTAD   (*in the doorway*) It's me, Mrs. Helmer.

(MRS. LINDE *starts, composes herself and turns away to the window.*)

NORA   (*takes a step towards him and whispers tensely*) You? What is it? What do you want to talk to my husband about?

KROGSTAD   Business—you might call it. I hold a minor post in the bank, and I hear your husband is to become our new chief—

NORA   Oh—then it isn't—?

KROGSTAD   Pure business, Mrs. Helmer. Nothing more.

NORA   Well, you'll find him in his study.

(Nods indifferently as she closes the hall door behind him. Then she walks across the room and sees to the stove.)

MRS. LINDE   Nora, who was that man?

NORA   A lawyer called Krogstad.

MRS. LINDE   It was him, then.

NORA   Do you know that man?

MRS. LINDE   I used to know him—some years ago. He was a solicitor's clerk in our town, for a while.

NORA   Yes, of course, so he was.

MRS. LINDE   How he's changed!

NORA   He was very unhappily married, I believe.

MRS. LINDE   Is he a widower now?

NORA   Yes, with a lot of children. Ah, now it's alight.

(She closes the door of the stove and moves the rocking-chair a little to one side.)

MRS. LINDE   He does—various things now, I hear?

NORA   Does he? It's quite possible—I really don't know. But don't let's talk about business. It's so boring.

(DR. RANK enters from HELMER's study.)

RANK   *(still in the doorway)* No, no, my dear chap, don't see me out. I'll go and have a word with your wife. *(Closes the door and notices MRS. LINDE.)* Oh, I beg your pardon. I seem to be *de trop* here too.

NORA   Not in the least. *(introduces them)* Dr. Rank. Mrs. Linde.

RANK   Ah! A name I have often heard in this house. I believe I passed you on the stairs as I came up.

MRS. LINDE   Yes. Stairs tire me; I have to take them slowly.

RANK   Oh, have you hurt yourself?

MRS. LINDE   No, I'm just a little run down.

RANK   Ah, is that all? Then I take it you've come to town to cure yourself by a round of parties?

MRS. LINDE   I have come here to find work.

RANK   Is that an approved remedy for being run down?

MRS. LINDE   One has to live, Doctor.

RANK   Yes, people do seem to regard it as a necessity.

NORA   Oh, really, Dr. Rank. I bet you want to stay alive.

RANK   You bet I do. However miserable I sometimes feel, I still want to go on being tortured for as long as possible. It's the same with all my patients; and with people who are morally sick, too. There's a moral cripple in with Helmer at this very moment—

MRS. LINDE   *(softly)* Oh!

NORA   Whom do you mean?

RANK   Oh, a lawyer fellow called Krogstad—you wouldn't know him. He's crippled all right; morally twisted. But even he started off by announcing, as though it were a matter of enormous importance, that he had to live.

NORA   Oh? What did he want to talk to Torvald about?

RANK   I haven't the faintest idea. All I heard was something about the bank.

NORA   I didn't know that Krog—that this man Krogstad had any connection with the bank.

RANK   Yes, he's got some kind of job down there. (*to* MRS. LINDE) I wonder if in your part of the world you too have a species of human being that spends its time fussing around trying to smell out moral corruption? And when they find a case they give him some nice, comfortable position so that they can keep a good watch on him. The healthy ones just have to lump it.

MRS. LINDE   But surely it's the sick who need care most?

RANK   (*shrugs his shoulders*) Well, there we have it. It's that attitude that's turning human society into a hospital.

(NORA, *lost in her own thoughts, laughs half to herself and clasps her hands.*)

RANK   Why are you laughing? Do you really know what society is?

NORA   What do I care about society? I think it's a bore. I was laughing at something else—something frightfully funny. Tell me, Dr. Rank—will everyone who works at the bank come under Torvald now?

RANK   Do you find that particularly funny?

NORA   (*smiles and hums*) Never you mind! Never you mind! (*Walks around the room.*) Yes, I find it very amusing to think that we—I mean, Torvald—has obtained so much influence over so many people. (*Takes the paper bag from her pocket.*) Dr. Rank, would you like a small macaroon?

RANK   Macaroons! I say! I thought they were forbidden here.

NORA   Yes, well, these are some Christine gave me.

MRS. LINDE   What? I—?

NORA   All right, all right, don't get frightened. You weren't to know Torvald had forbidden them. He's afraid they'll ruin my teeth. But, dash it—for once—! Don't you agree, Dr. Rank? Here! (*Pops a macaroon into his mouth.*) You too, Christine. And I'll have one too. Just a little one. Two at the most. (*Begins to walk round again.*) Yes, now I feel really, really happy. Now there's just one thing in the world I'd really love to do.

RANK   Oh? And what is that?

NORA   Just something I'd love to say to Torvald.

RANK   Well, why don't you say it?

NORA   No, I daren't. It's too dreadful.

MRS. LINDE   Dreadful?

RANK   Well, then, you'd better not. But you can say it to us. What is it you'd so love to say to Torvald?

NORA   I've the most extraordinary longing to say: "Bloody hell!"

RANK   Are you mad?

MRS. LINDE   My dear Nora—!

RANK   Say it. Here he is.

NORA   (*hiding the bag of macaroons*) Ssh! Ssh!

(HELMER, *with his overcoat on his arm and his hat in his hand, enters from his study.*)

NORA   (*goes to meet him*) Well, Torvald dear, did you get rid of him?

HELMER   Yes, he's just gone.

NORA   May I introduce you—? This is Christine. She's just arrived in town.

HELMER Christine—? Forgive me, but I don't think—

NORA Mrs. Linde, Torvald dear. Christine Linde.

HELMER Ah. A childhood friend of my wife's, I presume?

MRS. LINDE Yes, we knew each other in earlier days.

NORA And imagine, now she's travelled all this way to talk to you.

HELMER Oh?

MRS. LINDE Well, I didn't really—

NORA You see, Christine's frightfully good at office work, and she's mad to come under some really clever man who can teach her even more than she knows already—

HELMER Very sensible, madam.

NORA So when she heard you'd become head of the bank—it was in her local paper—she came here as quickly as she could and—Torvald, you will, won't you? Do a little something to help Christine? For my sake?

HELMER Well, that shouldn't be impossible. You are a widow, I take it, Mrs. Linde?

MRS. LINDE Yes.

HELMER And you have experience of office work?

MRS. LINDE Yes, quite a bit.

HELMER Well then, it's quite likely I may be able to find some job for you—

NORA (claps her hands) You see, you see!

HELMER You've come at a lucky moment, Mrs. Linde.

MRS. LINDE Oh, how can I ever thank you—?

HELMER There's absolutely no need. (Puts on his overcoat.) But now I'm afraid I must ask you to excuse me—

RANK Wait. I'll come with you.

(He gets his fur coat from the hall and warms it at the stove.)

NORA Don't be long, Torvald dear.

HELMER I'll only be an hour.

NORA Are you going too, Christine?

MRS. LINDE (puts on her outdoor clothes) Yes, I must start to look round for a room.

HELMER Then perhaps we can walk part of the way together.

NORA (helps her) It's such a nuisance we're so cramped here—I'm afraid we can't offer to—

MRS. LINDE Oh, I wouldn't dream of it. Goodbye, Nora dear, and thanks for everything.

NORA Au revoir. You'll be coming back this evening, of course. And you too, Dr. Rank. What? If you're well enough? Of course you'll be well enough. Wrap up warmly, though.

(They go out, talking, into the hall. Children's voices are heard from the stairs.)

NORA Here they are! Here they are!

(She runs out and opens the door. ANNE-MARIE, the nurse, enters with the CHILDREN.)

NORA Come in, come in! (Stoops down and kisses them.) Oh, my sweet darlings—! Look at them, Christine! Aren't they beautiful?

RANK Don't stand here chattering in this draught!

HELMER Come, Mrs. Linde. This is for mothers only.

(DR. RANK, HELMER *and* MRS. LINDE *go down the stairs. The* NURSE *brings the* CHILDREN *into the room.* NORA *follows, and closes the door to the hall.*)

NORA How well you look! What red cheeks you've got! Like apples and roses! (*The* CHILDREN *answer her inaudibly as she talks to them.*) Have you had fun? That's splendid. You gave Emmy and Bob a ride on the sledge? What, both together? I say! What a clever boy you are, Ivar! Oh, let me hold her for a moment, Anne-Marie! My sweet little baby doll! (*Takes the smallest child from the* NURSE *and dances with her.*) Yes, yes, Mummy will dance with Bob too. What? Have you been throwing snowballs? Oh, I wish I'd been there! No, don't—I'll undress them myself, Anne-Marie. No, please let me; it's such fun. Go inside and warm yourself; you look frozen. There's some hot coffee on the stove. (*The* NURSE *goes into the room on the left.* NORA *takes off the children's outdoor clothes and throws them anywhere while they all chatter simultaneously.*) What? A big dog ran after you? But he didn't bite you? No, dogs don't bite lovely little baby dolls. Leave those parcels alone, Ivar. What's in them? Ah, wouldn't you like to know! No, no; it's nothing nice. Come on, let's play a game. What shall we play? Hide and seek. Bob shall hide first. You want me to? All right, let me hide first.

(NORA *and the* CHILDREN *play around the room, and in the adjacent room to the left, laughing and shouting. At length* NORA *hides under the table. The* CHILDREN *rush in, look, but cannot find her. Then they hear her half-stifled laughter, run to the table, lift up the cloth and see her. Great excitement. She crawls out as though to frighten them. Further excitement. Meanwhile, there has been a knock on the door leading from the hall, but no one has noticed it. Now the door is half-opened and* KROGSTAD *enters. He waits for a moment; the game continues.*)

KROGSTAD Excuse me, Mrs. Helmer—

NORA (*turns with a stifled cry and half jumps up*) Oh! What do you want?

KROGSTAD I beg your pardon; the front door was ajar. Someone must have forgotten to close it.

NORA (*gets up*) My husband is not at home, Mr. Krogstad.

KROGSTAD I know.

NORA Well, what do you want here, then?

KROGSTAD A word with you.

NORA With—? (*to the* CHILDREN, *quietly*) Go inside to Anne-Marie. What? No, the strange gentleman won't do anything to hurt Mummy. When he's gone we'll start playing again.

(*She takes the* CHILDREN *into the room on the left and closes the door behind them.*)

NORA (*uneasy, tense*) You want to speak to me?

KROGSTAD Yes.

NORA Today? But it's not the first of the month yet.

KROGSTAD No, it is Christmas Eve. Whether or not you have a merry Christmas depends on you.

NORA What do you want? I can't give you anything today—

KROGSTAD We won't talk about that for the present. There's something else. You have a moment to spare?

NORA Oh, yes. Yes, I suppose so; though—

KROGSTAD   Good. I was sitting in the café down below and I saw your husband cross the street—

NORA   Yes.

KROGSTAD   With a lady.

NORA   Well?

KROGSTAD   Might I be so bold as to ask: was not that lady a Mrs. Linde?

NORA   Yes.

KROGSTAD   Recently arrived in town?

NORA   Yes, today.

KROGSTAD   She is a good friend of yours, is she not?

NORA   Yes, she is. But I don't see—

KROGSTAD   I used to know her too once.

NORA   I know.

KROGSTAD   Oh? You've discovered that. Yes, I thought you would. Well, then, may I ask you a straight question: is Mrs. Linde to be employed at the bank?

NORA   How dare you presume to cross-examine me, Mr. Krogstad? You, one of my husband's employees? But since you ask, you shall have an answer. Yes, Mrs. Linde is to be employed by the bank. And I arranged it, Mr. Krogstad. Now you know.

KROGSTAD   I guessed right, then.

NORA   (*walks up and down the room*) Oh, one has a little influence, you know. Just because one's a woman it doesn't necessarily mean that— When one is in a humble position, Mr. Krogstad, one should think twice before offending someone who—hm—

KROGSTAD   —who has influence?

NORA   Precisely.

KROGSTAD   (*changes his tone*) Mrs. Helmer, will you have the kindness to use your influence on my behalf?

NORA   What? What do you mean?

KROGSTAD   Will you be so good as to see that I keep my humble position at the bank?

NORA   What do you mean? Who is thinking of removing you from your position?

KROGSTAD   Oh, you don't need to play the innocent with me. I realize it can't be very pleasant for your friend to risk bumping into me; and now I also realize whom I have to thank for being hounded out like this.

NORA   But I assure you—

KROGSTAD   Look, let's not beat about the bush. There's still time, and I'd advise you to use your influence to stop it.

NORA   But, Mr. Krogstad, I have no influence!

KROGSTAD   Oh? I thought you just said—

NORA   But I didn't mean it like that! I? How on earth could you imagine that I would have any influence over my husband?

KROGSTAD   Oh, I've known your husband since we were students together. I imagine he has his weaknesses like other married men.

NORA   If you speak impertinently of my husband, I shall show you the door.

KROGSTAD   You're a bold woman, Mrs. Helmer.

NORA   I'm not afraid of you any longer. Once the New Year is in, I'll soon be rid of you.

KROGSTAD   (*more controlled*) Now listen to me, Mrs. Helmer. If I'm forced to, I shall fight for my little job at the bank as I would fight for my life.

NORA   So it sounds.

KROGSTAD   It isn't just the money; that's the last thing I care about. There's something else—well, you might as well know. It's like this, you see. You know of course, as everyone else does, that some years ago I committed an indiscretion.

NORA   I think I did hear something—

KROGSTAD   It never came into court; but from that day, every opening was barred to me. So I turned my hand to the kind of business you know about. I had to do something; and I don't think I was one of the worst. But now I want to give up all that. My sons are growing up; for their sake, I must try to regain what respectability I can. This job in the bank was the first step on the ladder. And now your husband wants to kick me off that ladder back into the dirt.

NORA   But my dear Mr. Krogstad, it simply isn't in my power to help you.

KROGSTAD   You say that because you don't want to help me. But I have the means to make you.

NORA   You don't mean you'd tell my husband that I owe you money?

KROGSTAD   And if I did?

NORA   That'd be a filthy trick! (*almost in tears*) This secret that is my pride and my joy—that he should hear about it in such a filthy, beastly way— hear about it from you! It'd involve me in the most dreadful unpleasantness—

KROGSTAD   Only—unpleasantness?

NORA   (*vehemently*) All right, do it! You'll be the one who'll suffer. It'll show my husband the kind of man you are, and than you'll never keep your job.

KROGSTAD   I asked you whether it was merely domestic unpleasantness you were afraid of.

NORA   If my husband hears about it, he will of course immediately pay you whatever is owing. And then we shall have nothing more to do with you.

KROGSTAD   (*takes a step closer*) Listen, Mrs. Helmer. Either you've a bad memory or else you know very little about financial transactions. I had better enlighten you.

NORA   What do you mean?

KROGSTAD   When your husband was ill, you came to me to borrow two hundred and fifty pounds.

NORA   I didn't know anyone else.

KROGSTAD   I promised to find that sum for you—

NORA   And you did find it.

KROGSTAD   I promised to find that sum for you on certain conditions. You were so worried about your husband's illness and so keen to get the money to take him abroad that I don't think you bothered much about the details. So it won't be out of place if I refresh your memory. Well—I promised to get you the money in exchange for an I.O.U., which I drew up.

NORA   Yes, and which I signed.

KROGSTAD   Exactly. But then I added a few lines naming your father as security for the debt. This paragraph was to be signed by your father.

NORA   Was to be? He did sign it.

KROGSTAD   I left the date blank for your father to fill in when he signed this paper. You remember, Mrs. Helmer?

NORA   Yes, I think so—

KROGSTAD   Then I gave you back this I.O.U. for you to post to your father. Is that not correct?

NORA   Yes.

KROGSTAD   And of course you posted it at once; for within five or six days you brought it along to me with your father's signature on it. Whereupon I handed you the money.

NORA   Yes, well. Haven't I repaid the instalments as agreed?

KROGSTAD   Mm—yes, more or less. But to return to what we were speaking about—that was a difficult time for you just then, wasn't it, Mrs. Helmer?

NORA   Yes, it was.

KROGSTAD   Your father was very ill, if I am not mistaken.

NORA   He was dying.

KROGSTAD   He did in fact die shortly afterwards?

NORA   Yes.

KROGSTAD   Tell me, Mrs. Helmer, do you by any chance remember the date of your father's death? The day of the month, I mean.

NORA   Papa died on the twenty-ninth of September.

KROGSTAD   Quite correct; I took the trouble to confirm it. And that leaves me with a curious little problem—(*takes out a paper*)—which I simply cannot solve.

NORA   Problem? I don't see—

KROGSTAD   The problem, Mrs. Helmer, is that your father signed this paper three days after his death.

NORA   What? I don't understand—

KROGSTAD   Your father died on the twenty-ninth of September. But look at this. Here your father has dated his signature the second of October. Isn't that a curious little problem, Mrs. Helmer? (NORA *is silent*.) Can you suggest any explanation? (*She remains silent*.) And there's another curious thing. The words "second of October" and the year are written in a hand which is not your father's, but which I seem to know. Well, there's a simple explanation to that. Your father could have forgotten to write in the date when he signed, and someone else could have added it before the news came of his death. There's nothing criminal about that. It's the signature itself I'm wondering about. It *is* genuine, I suppose, Mrs. Helmer? It was your father who wrote his name here?

NORA   (*after a short silence, throws back her head and looks defiantly at him*) No, it was not. It was I who wrote Papa's name there.

KROGSTAD   Look, Mrs. Helmer, do you realize this is a dangerous admission?

NORA   Why? You'll get your money.

KROGSTAD   May I ask you a question? Why didn't you send this paper to your father?

NORA   I couldn't. Papa was very ill. If I'd asked him to sign this, I'd have to tell him what the money was for. But I couldn't have told him in his condition that my husband's life was in danger. I couldn't have done that!

KROGSTAD   Then you would have been wiser to have given up your idea of a holiday.

NORA   But I couldn't! It was to save my husband's life. I couldn't put it off.

KROGSTAD   But didn't it occur to you that you were being dishonest towards me?

NORA   I couldn't bother about that. I didn't care about you. I hated you because of all the beastly difficulties you'd put in my way when you knew how dangerously ill my husband was.

KROGSTAD   Mrs. Helmer, you evidently don't appreciate exactly what you have done. But I can assure you that it is no bigger nor worse a crime than the one I once committed, and thereby ruined my whole social position.

NORA   You? Do you expect me to believe that you would have taken a risk like that to save your wife's life?

KROGSTAD   The law does not concern itself with motives.

NORA   Then the law must be very stupid.

KROGSTAD   Stupid or not, if I show this paper to the police, you will be judged according to it.

NORA   I don't believe that. Hasn't a daughter the right to shield her father from worry and anxiety when he's old and dying? Hasn't a wife the right to save her husband's life? I don't know much about the law, but there must be something somewhere that says that such things are allowed. You ought to know about that, you're meant to be a lawyer, aren't you? You can't be a very good lawyer, Mr. Krogstad.

KROGSTAD   Possibly not. But business, the kind of business we two have been transacting—I think you'll admit I understand something about that? Good. Do as you please. But I tell you this. If I get thrown into the gutter for a second time, I shall take you with me.

(*He bows and goes out through the hall.*)

NORA   (*stands for a moment in thought, then tosses her head*) What nonsense! He's trying to frighten me! I'm not that stupid. (*Busies herself gathering together the children's clothes; then she suddenly stops.*) But—? No, it's impossible. I did it for love, didn't I?

THE CHILDREN   (*in the doorway, left*) Mummy, the strange gentleman's gone out into the street.

NORA   Yes, yes, I know. But don't talk to anyone about the strange gentleman. You hear? Not even to Daddy.

CHILDREN   No, Mummy. Will you play with us again now?

NORA   No, no. Not now.

CHILDREN   Oh but, Mummy, you promised!

NORA   I know, but I can't just now. Go back to the nursery. I've a lot to do. Go away, my darlings, go away. (*She pushes them gently into the other room, and closes the door behind them. She sits on the sofa, takes up her embroidery, stitches for a few moments, but soon stops.*) No! (*throws the embroidery aside, gets up, goes to the door leading to the hall and calls*)

Helen! Bring in the Christmas tree! (*She goes to the table on the left and opens the drawer in it; then pauses again.*) No, but it's utterly impossible!

MAID   (*enters with the tree*) Where shall I put it, madam?

NORA   There, in the middle of the room.

MAID   Will you be wanting anything else?

NORA   No, thank you. I have everything I need.

(*The* MAID *puts down the tree and goes out.*)

NORA   (*busy decorating the tree*) Now—candles here—and flowers here. That loathsome man! Nonsense, nonsense, there's nothing to be frightened about. The Christmas tree must be beautiful. I'll do everything that you like, Torvald. I'll sing for you, dance for you—

(HELMER, *with a bundle of papers under his arm, enters.*)

NORA   Oh—are you back already?

HELMER   Yes. Has anyone been here?

NORA   Here? No.

HELMER   That's strange. I saw Krogstad come out of the front door.

NORA   Did you? Oh yes, that's quite right—Krogstad was here for a few minutes.

HELMER   Nora, I can tell from your face, he's been here and asked you to put in a good word for him.

NORA   Yes.

HELMER   And you were to pretend you were doing it of your own accord? You weren't going to tell me he'd been here? He asked you to do that too, didn't he?

NORA   Yes, Torvald. But—

HELMER   Nora, Nora! And you were ready to enter into such a conspiracy? Talking to a man like that, and making him promises—and then, on top of it all, to tell me an untruth!

NORA   An untruth?

HELMER   Didn't you say no one had been here? (*Wags his finger.*) My little songbird must never do that again. A songbird must have a clean beak to sing with; otherwise she'll start twittering out of tune. (*Puts his arm round her waist.*) Isn't that the way we want things? Yes, of course it is. (*Lets go of her.*) So let's hear no more about that. (*Sits down in front of the stove.*) Ah, how cosy and peaceful it is here. (*Glances for a few moments at his papers.*)

NORA   (*busy with the tree; after a short silence*) Torvald.

HELMER   Yes.

NORA   I'm terribly looking forward to that fancy dress ball at the Stenborgs on Boxing Day.

HELMER   And I'm terribly curious to see what you're going to surprise me with.

NORA   Oh, it's so maddening.

HELMER   What is?

NORA   I can't think of anything to wear. It all seems so stupid and meaningless.

HELMER   So my little Nora's come to that conclusion, has she?

NORA   (*behind his chair, resting her arms on its back*) Are you very busy, Torvald?

HELMER Oh—

NORA What are those papers?

HELMER Just something to do with the bank.

NORA Already?

HELMER I persuaded the trustees to give me authority to make certain immediate changes in the staff and organization. I want to have everything straight by the New Year.

NORA Then that's why this poor man Krogstad—

HELMER Hm.

NORA (*still leaning over his chair, slowly strokes the back of his head*) If you hadn't been so busy, I was going to ask you an enormous favour, Torvald.

HELMER Well, tell me. What was it to be?

NORA You know I trust your taste more than anyone's. I'm so anxious to look really beautiful at the fancy dress ball. Torvald, couldn't you help me to decide what I shall go as, and what kind of costume I ought to wear?

HELMER Aha! So little Miss Independent's in trouble and needs a man to rescue her, does she?

NORA Yes, Torvald. I can't get anywhere without your help.

HELMER Well, well, I'll give the matter thought. We'll find something.

NORA Oh, how kind of you! (*Goes back to the tree. Pause.*) How pretty these red flowers look! But, tell me, is it so dreadful, this thing that Krogstad's done?

HELMER He forged someone else's name. Have you any idea what that means?

NORA Mightn't he have been forced to do it by some emergency?

HELMER He probably just didn't think—that's what usually happens. I'm not so heartless as to condemn a man for an isolated action.

NORA No, Torvald, of course not!

HELMER But Krogstad didn't do that. He chose to try and trick his way out of it; and that's what has morally destroyed him.

NORA You think that would—?

HELMER Just think how a man with that load on his conscience must always be lying and cheating and dissembling; how he must wear a mask even in the presence of those who are dearest to him, even his own wife and children! Yes, the children. That's the worst danger, Nora.

NORA Why?

HELMER Because an atmosphere of lies contaminates and poisons every corner of the home. Every breath that the children draw in such a house contains the germs of evil.

NORA (*comes closer behind him*) Do you really believe that?

HELMER Oh, my dear, I've come across it so often in my work at the bar. Nearly all young criminals are the children of mothers who are constitutional liars.

NORA Why do you say mothers?

HELMER It's usually the mother; though of course the father can have the same influence. Every lawyer knows that only too well. And yet this fellow Krogstad has been sitting at home all these years poisoning his children with his lies and pretences. That's why I say that, morally speaking, he is dead.

(*Stretches out his hands towards her.*) So my pretty little Nora must promise me not to plead his case. Your hand on it. Come, come, what's this? Give me your hand. There. That's settled, now. I assure you it'd be quite impossible for me to work in the same building as him. I literally feel physically ill in the presence of a man like that.

NORA   (*draws her hand from his and goes over to the other side of the Christmas tree*) How hot it is in here! And I've so much to do.

HELMER   (*gets up and gathers his papers*) Yes, and I must try to get some of this read before dinner. I'll think about your costume too. And I may even have something up my sleeve to hang in gold paper on the Christmas tree. (*Lays his hand on her head.*) My precious little songbird!

(*He goes into his study and closes the door.*)

NORA   (*softly, after a pause*) It's nonsense. It must be. It's impossible. It *must* be impossible!

NURSE   (*in the doorway, left*) The children are asking if they can come in to Mummy.

NORA   No, no, no; don't let them in! You stay with them, Anne-Marie.

NURSE   Very good, madam. (*Closes the door.*)

NORA   (*pale with fear*) Corrupt my little children—! Poison my home! (*Short pause. She throws back her head.*) It isn't true! It *couldn't* be true!

ACT II

(*The same room. In the corner by the piano the Christmas tree stands, stripped and dishevelled, its candles burned to their sockets. NORA's outdoor clothes lie on the sofa. She is alone in the room, walking restlessly to and fro. At length she stops by the sofa and picks up her coat.*)

NORA   (*drops the coat again*) There's someone coming! (*Goes to the door and listens.*) No, it's no one. Of course—no one'll come today, it's Christmas Day. Nor tomorrow. But perhaps—! (*Opens the door and looks out.*) No. Nothing in the letter-box. Quite empty. (*Walks across the room.*) Silly, silly. Of course he won't do anything. It couldn't happen. It isn't possible. Why, I've three small children.

(*The NURSE, carrying a large cardboard box, enters from the room on the left.*)

NURSE   I found those fancy dress clothes at last, madam.

NORA   Thank you. Put them on the table.

NURSE   (*does so*) They're all rumpled up.

NORA   Oh, I wish I could tear them into a million pieces!

NURSE   Why, madam! They'll be all right. Just a little patience.

NORA   Yes, of course. I'll go and get Mrs. Linde to help me.

NURSE   What, out again? In this dreadful weather? You'll catch a chill, madam.

NORA   Well, that wouldn't be the worst. How are the children?

NURSE   Playing with their Christmas presents, poor little dears. But—

NORA   Are they still asking to see me?

NURSE   They're so used to having their Mummy with them.

NORA   Yes, but, Anne-Marie, from now on I shan't be able to spend so much time with them.

NURSE   Well, children get used to anything in time.

NORA   Do you think so? Do you think they'd forget their mother if she went away from them—for ever?

NURSE   Mercy's sake, madam! For ever!

NORA   Tell me, Anne-Marie—I've so often wondered. How could you bear to give your child away—to strangers?

NURSE   But I had to when I came to nurse my little Miss Nora.

NORA   Do you mean you wanted to?

NURSE   When I had the chance of such a good job? A poor girl what's got into trouble can't afford to pick and choose. That good-for-nothing didn't lift a finger.

NORA   But your daughter must have completely forgotten you.

NURSE   Oh no, indeed she hasn't. She's written to me twice, once when she got confirmed and then again when she got married.

NORA   (hugs her) Dear old Anne-Marie, you were a good mother to me.

NURSE   Poor little Miss Nora, you never had any mother but me.

NORA   And if my little ones had no one else, I know you would—no, silly, silly, silly! (Opens the cardboard box.) Go back to them, Anne-Marie. Now I must—Tomorrow you'll see how pretty I shall look.

NURSE   Why, there'll be no one at the ball as beautiful as my Miss Nora.

(She goes into the room, left.)

NORA   (begins to unpack the clothes from the box, but soon throws them down again) Oh, if only I dared go out! If I could be sure no one would come, and nothing would happen while I was away! Stupid, stupid! No one will come. I just mustn't think about it. Brush this muff. Pretty gloves, pretty gloves! Don't think about it, don't think about it! One, two, three, four, five, six—(cries) Ah—they're coming—!

(She begins to run towards the door, but stops uncertainly. MRS. LINDE enters from the hall, where she has been taking off her outdoor clothes.)

NORA   Oh, it's you, Christine. There's no one else out there, is there? Oh, I'm so glad you've come.

MRS. LINDE   I hear you were at my room asking for me.

NORA   Yes, I just happened to be passing. I want to ask you to help me with something. Let's sit down here on the sofa. Look at this. There's going to be a fancy dress ball tomorrow night upstairs at Consul Stenborg's, and Torvald wants me to go as a Neapolitan fisher-girl and dance the tarantella. I learned it on Capri.

MRS. LINDE   I say, are you gong to give a performance?

NORA   Yes, Torvald says I should. Look, here's the dress. Torvald had it made for me in Italy; but now it's all so torn, I don't know—

MRS. LINDE   Oh, we'll soon put that right; the stitching's just come away. Needle and thread? Ah, here we are.

NORA   You're being awfully sweet.

MRS. LINDE   (sews) So you're going to dress up tomorrow, Nora? I must pop over for a moment to see how you look. Oh, but I've completely forgotten to thank you for that nice evening yesterday.

NORA (*gets up and walks across the room*) Oh, I didn't think it was as nice as usual. You ought to have come to town a little earlier, Christine. . . . Yes, Torvald understands how to make a home look attractive.

MRS. LINDE I'm sure you do, too. You're not your father's daughter for nothing. But, tell me. Is Dr. Rank always in such low spirits as he was yesterday?

NORA No, last night it was very noticeable. But he's got a terrible disease; he's got spinal tuberculosis, poor man. His father was a frightful creature who kept mistresses and so on. As a result Dr. Rank has been sickly ever since he was a child—you understand—

MRS. LINDE (*puts down her sewing*) But, my dear Nora, how on earth did you get to know about such things?

NORA (*walks about the room*) Oh, don't be silly, Christine—when one has three children, one comes into contact with women who—well, who know about medical matters, and they tell one a thing or two.

MRS. LINDE (*sews again; a short silence*) Does Dr. Rank visit you every day?

NORA Yes, every day. He's Torvald's oldest friend, and a good friend to me too. Dr. Rank's almost one of the family.

MRS. LINDE But, tell me—is he quite sincere? I mean, doesn't he rather say the sort of thing he thinks people want to hear?

NORA No, quite the contrary. What gave you that idea?

MRS. LINDE When you introduced me to him yesterday, he said he'd often heard my name mentioned here. But later I noticed your husband had no idea who I was. So how could Dr. Rank—?

NORA Yes, that's quite right, Christine. You see, Torvald's so hopelessly in love with me that he wants to have me all to himself—those were his very words. When we were first married, he got quite jealous if I as much as mentioned any of my old friends back home. So naturally, I stopped talking about them. But I often chat with Dr. Rank about that kind of thing. He enjoys it, you see.

MRS. LINDE Now listen, Nora. In many ways you're still a child; I'm a bit older than you and have a little more experience of the world. There's something I want to say to you. You ought to give up this business with Dr. Rank.

NORA What business?

MRS. LINDE Well, everything. Last night you were speaking about this rich admirer of yours who was going to give you money—

NORA Yes, and who doesn't exist—unfortunately. But what's that got to do with—?

MRS. LINDE Is Dr. Rank rich?

NORA Yes.

MRS. LINDE And he has no dependants?

NORA No, no one. But—

MRS. LINDE And he comes here to see you every day?

NORA Yes, I've told you.

MRS. LINDE But how dare a man of his education be so forward?

NORA What on earth are you talking about?

MRS. LINDE Oh, stop pretending, Nora. Do you think I haven't guessed who it was who lent you that two hundred pounds?

NORA Are you out of your mind? How could you imagine such a thing? A friend, someone who comes here every day! Why, that'd be an impossible situation!

MRS. LINDE Then it really wasn't him?

NORA No, of course not. I've never for a moment dreamed of—anyway, he hadn't any money to lend then. He didn't come into that till later.

MRS. LINDE Well, I think that was a lucky thing for you, Nora dear.

NORA No, I could never have dreamed of asking Dr. Rank—Though I'm sure that if I ever did ask him—

MRS. LINDE But of course you won't.

NORA Of course not. I can't imagine that it should ever become necessary. But I'm perfectly sure that if I did speak to Dr. Rank—

MRS. LINDE Behind your husband's back?

NORA I've got to get out of this other business; and *that's* been going on behind his back. I've *got* to get out of it.

MRS. LINDE Yes, well, that's what I told you yesterday. But—

NORA (*walking up and down*) It's much easier for a man to arrange these things than a woman—

MRS. LINDE One's own husband, yes.

NORA Oh, bosh. (*Stops walking.*) When you've completely repaid a debt, you get your I.O.U. back, don't you?

MRS. LINDE Yes, of course.

NORA And you can tear it into a thousand pieces and burn the filthy, beastly thing!

MRS. LINDE (*looks hard at her, puts down her sewing and gets up slowly*) Nora, you're hiding something from me.

NORA Can you see that?

MRS. LINDE Something has happened since yesterday morning. Nora, what is it?

NORA (*goes towards her*) Christine! (*listens*) Ssh! There's Torvald. Would you mind going into the nursery for a few minutes? Torvald can't bear to see sewing around. Anne-Marie'll help you.

MRS. LINDE (*gathers some of her things together*) Very well. But I shan't leave this house until we've talked this matter out.

(*She goes into the nursery, left. As she does so,* HELMER *enters from the hall.*)

NORA (*runs to meet him*) Oh, Torvald dear, I've been so longing for you to come back!

HELMER Was that the dressmaker?

NORA No, it was Christine. She's helping me mend my costume. I'm going to look rather splendid in that.

HELMER Yes, that was quite a bright idea of mine, wasn't it?

NORA Wonderful! But wasn't it nice of me to give in to you?

HELMER (*takes her chin in his hand*) Nice—to give in to your husband? All right, little silly, I know you didn't mean it like that. But I won't disturb you. I expect you'll be wanting to try it on.

NORA Are you going to work now?

HELMER Yes. (*shows her a bundle of papers*) Look at these. I've been down to the bank— (*Turns to go into his study.*)

NORA Torvald.

HELMER (*stops*) Yes.

NORA If little squirrel asked you really prettily to grant her a wish—

HELMER Well?

NORA Would you grant it to her?

HELMER First I should naturally have to know what it was.

NORA Squirrel would do lots of pretty tricks for you if you granted her wish.

HELMER Out with it, then.

NORA Your little skylark would sing in every room—

HELMER My little skylark does that already.

NORA I'd turn myself into a little fairy and dance for you in the moonlight, Torvald.

HELMER Nora, it isn't that business you were talking about this morning?

NORA (*comes closer*) Yes, Torvald—oh, please! I beg of you!

HELMER Have you really the nerve to bring that up again?

NORA Yes, Torvald, yes, you must do as I ask! You must let Krogstad keep his place at the bank!

HELMER My dear Nora, his is the job I'm giving to Mrs. Linde.

NORA Yes, that's terribly sweet of you. But you can get rid of one of the other clerks instead of Krogstad.

HELMER Really, you're being incredibly obstinate. Just because you thoughtlessly promised to put in a word for him, you expect me to—

NORA No, it isn't that, Torvald. It's for your own sake. That man writes for the most beastly newspapers—you said so yourself. He could do you tremendous harm. I'm so dreadfully frightened of him—

HELMER Oh, I understand. Memories of the past. That's what's frightening you.

NORA What do you mean?

HELMER You're thinking of your father, aren't you?

NORA Yes, yes. Of course. Just think what those dreadful men wrote in the papers about Papa! The most frightful slanders. I really believe it would have lost him his job if the Ministry hadn't sent you down to investigate, and you hadn't been so kind and helpful to him.

HELMER But my dear little Nora, there's a considerable difference between your father and me. Your father was not a man of unassailable reputation. But I am; and I hope to remain so all my life.

NORA But no one knows what spiteful people may not dig up. We could be so peaceful and happy now, Torvald—we could be free from every worry— you and I and the children. Oh, please, Torvald, please—!

HELMER The very fact of your pleading his cause makes it impossible for me to keep him. Everyone at the bank already knows that I intend to dismiss Krogstad. If the rumour got about that the new manager had allowed his wife to persuade him to change his mind—

NORA Well, what then?

HELMER Oh, nothing, nothing. As long as my little Miss Obstinate gets her way—! Do you expect me to make a laughing-stock of myself before my entire staff—give people the idea that I am open to outside influence? Believe me, I'd soon feel the consequences! Besides—there's something else that makes it impossible for Krogstad to remain in the bank while I am its manager.

NORA   What is that?

HELMER   I might conceivably have allowed myself to ignore his moral obloquies—

NORA   Yes, Torvald, surely?

HELMER   And I hear he's quite efficient at his job. But we—well, we were schoolfriends. It was one of those friendships that one enters into overhastily and so often comes to regret later in life. I might as well confess the truth. We—well, we're on Christian name terms. And the tactless idiot makes no attempt to conceal it when other people are present. On the contrary, he thinks it gives him the right to be familiar with me. He shows off the whole time, with "Torvald this," and "Torvald that." I can tell you, I find it damned annoying. If he stayed, he'd make my position intolerable.

NORA   Torvald, you can't mean this seriously.

HELMER   Oh? And why not?

NORA   But it's so petty.

HELMER   What did you say? Petty? You think *I* am petty?

NORA   No, Torvald dear, of course you're not. That's just why—

HELMER   Don't quibble! You call my motives petty. Then I must be petty too. Petty! I see. Well, I've had enough of this. (*goes to the door and calls into the hall*) Helen!

NORA   What are you going to do?

HELMER   (*searching among his papers*) I'm going to settle this matter once and for all. (*The* MAID *enters.*) Take this letter downstairs at once. Find a messenger and see that he delivers it. Immediately! The address is on the envelope. Here's the money.

MAID   Very good, sir. (*Goes out with the letter.*)

HELMER   (*putting his papers in order*) There now, little Miss Obstinate.

NORA   (*tensely*) Torvald—what was in that letter?

HELMER   Krogstad's dismissal.

NORA   Call her back, Torvald! There's still time. Oh, Torvald, call her back! Do it for my sake—for your own sake—for the children! Do you hear me, Torvald? Please do it! You don't realize what this may do to us all!

HELMER   Too late.

NORA   Yes. Too late.

HELMER   My dear Nora, I forgive you this anxiety. Though it is a bit of an insult to me. Oh, but it is! Isn't it an insult to imply that I should be frightened by the vindictiveness of a depraved hack journalist? But I forgive you, because it so charmingly testifies to the love you bear me. (*Takes her in his arms.*) Which is as it should be, my own dearest Nora. Let what will happen, happen. When the real crisis comes, you will not find me lacking in strength or courage. I am man enough to bear the burden for us both.

NORA   (*fearfully*) What do you mean?

HELMER   The whole burden, I say—

NORA   (*calmly*) I shall never let you do that.

HELMER   Very well. We shall share it, Nora—as man and wife. And that is as it should be. (*Caresses her.*) Are you happy now? There, there, there; don't look at me with those frightened little eyes. You're simply imagining things. You go ahead now and do your tarantella, and get some practice on that tambourine. I'll sit in my study and close the door. Then I won't hear anything, and you can make all the noise you want. (*turns in the doorway*) When Dr. Rank comes, tell him where to find me. (*He nods to her, goes into his room with his papers and closes the door.*)

NORA   (*desperate with anxiety, stands as though transfixed, and whispers*) He said he'd do it. He will do it. He will do it, and nothing'll stop him. No, never that. I'd rather anything. There must be some escape—! Some way out—! (*The bell rings in the hall.*) Dr. Rank—! Anything but that! Anything, I don't care—!

(*She passes her hand across her face, composes herself, walks across and opens the door to the hall. DR. RANK is standing there, hanging up his fur coat. During the following scene it begins to grow dark.*)

NORA   Good evening, Dr. Rank. I recognized your ring. But you mustn't go in to Torvald yet. I think he's busy.

RANK   And—you?

NORA   (*as he enters the room and she closes the door behind him*) Oh, you know very well I've always time to talk to you.

RANK   Thank you. I shall avail myself of that privilege as long as I can.

NORA   What do you mean by that? As long as you *can?*

RANK   Yes. Does that frighten you?

NORA   Well, it's rather a curious expression. Is something going to happen?

RANK   Something I've been expecting to happen for a long time. But I didn't think it would happen quite so soon.

NORA   (*seizes his arm*) What is it? Dr. Rank, you must tell me!

RANK   (*sits down by the stove*) I'm on the way out. And there's nothing to be done about it.

NORA   (*sighs with relief*) Oh, it's you—?

RANK   Who else? No, it's no good lying to oneself. I am the most wretched of all my patients, Mrs. Helmer. These last few days I've been going through the books of this poor body of mine, and I find I am bankrupt. Within a month I may be rotting up there in the churchyard.

NORA   Ugh, what a nasty way to talk!

RANK   The facts aren't exactly nice. But the worst is that there's so much else that's nasty to come first. I've only one more test to make. When that's done I'll have a pretty accurate idea of when the final disintegration is likely to begin. I want to ask you a favour. Helmer's a sensitive chap, and I know how he hates anything ugly. I don't want him to visit me when I'm in the hospital—

NORA   Oh but, Dr. Rank—

RANK   I don't want him there. On any pretext. I shan't have him allowed in. As soon as I know the worst, I'll send you my visiting card with a black cross on it, and then you'll know that the final filthy process has begun.

NORA   Really, you're being quite impossible this evening. And I did hope you'd be in a good mood.

RANK   With death on my hands? And all this to atone for someone else's sin? Is there justice in that? And in every single family, in one way or another, the same merciless law of retribution is at work—

NORA   (*holds her hands to her ears*) Nonsense! Cheer up! Laugh!

RANK   Yes, you're right. Laughter's all the damned thing's fit for. My poor innocent spine must pay for the fun my father had as a gay young lieutenant.

NORA   (*at the table, left*) You mean he was too fond of asparagus and *foie gras?*

RANK   Yes; and truffles too.

NORA   Yes, of course, truffles, yes. And oysters too, I suppose?

RANK   Yes, oysters, oysters. Of course.

NORA   And all that port and champagne to wash them down. It's too sad that all those lovely things should affect one's spine.

RANK   Especially a poor spine that never got any pleasure out of them.

NORA   Oh yes, that's the saddest thing of all.

RANK   (*looks searchingly at her*) Hm—

NORA   (*after a moment*) Why did you smile?

RANK   No, it was you who laughed.

NORA   No, it was you who smiled, Dr. Rank!

RANK   (*gets up*) You're a worse little rogue than I thought.

NORA   Oh, I'm full of stupid tricks today.

RANK   So it seems.

NORA   (*puts both her hands on his shoulders*) Dear, dear Dr. Rank, you mustn't die and leave Torvald and me.

RANK   Oh, you'll soon get over it. Once one is gone, one is soon forgotten.

NORA   (*looks at him anxiously*) Do you believe that?

RANK   One finds replacements, and then—

NORA   Who will find a replacement?

RANK   You and Helmer both will, when I am gone. You seem to have made a start already, haven't you? What was this Mrs. Linde doing here yesterday evening?

NORA   Aha! But surely you can't be jealous of poor Christine?

RANK   Indeed I am. She will be my successor in this house. When I have moved on, this lady will—

NORA   Ssh—don't speak so loud! She's in there!

RANK   Today again? You see!

NORA   She's only come to mend my dress. Good heavens, how unreasonable you are! (*Sits on the sofa.*) Be nice now, Dr. Rank. Tomorrow you'll see how beautifully I shall dance; and you must imagine that I'm doing it just for you. And for Torvald, of course; obviously. (*Takes some things out of the box.*) Dr. Rank, sit down here and I'll show you something.

RANK   (*sits*) What's this?

NORA   Look here! Look!

RANK   Silk stockings!

NORA   Flesh-coloured. Aren't they beautiful? It's very dark in here now, of course, but tomorrow—! No, no, no; only the soles. Oh well, I suppose you can look a bit higher if you want to.

RANK   Hm—

NORA   Why are you looking so critical? Don't you think they'll fit me?

RANK   I can't really give you a qualified opinion on that.

NORA   (*looks at him for a moment*) Shame on you! (*flicks him on the ear with the stockings*) Take that. (*Puts them back in the box.*)

RANK   What other wonders are to be revealed to me?

NORA   I shan't show you anything else. You're being naughty.

(*She hums a little and looks among the things in the box.*)

RANK   (*after a short silence*) When I sit here like this being so intimate with you, I can't think—I cannot imagine what would have become of me if I had never entered this house.

NORA   (*smiles*) Yes, I think you enjoy being with us, don't you?

RANK   (*more quietly, looking into the middle distance*) And now to have to leave it all—

NORA   Nonsense. You're not leaving us.

RANK   (*as before*) And not to be able to leave even the most wretched token of gratitude behind; hardly even a passing sense of loss; only an empty place, to be filled by the next comer.

NORA   Suppose I were to ask you to—? No—

RANK   To do what?

NORA   To give me proof of your friendship—

RANK   Yes, yes?

NORA   No, I mean—to do me a very great service—

RANK   Would you really for once grant me that happiness?

NORA   But you've no idea what it is.

RANK   Very well, tell me, then.

NORA   No, but, Dr. Rank, I can't. It's far too much—I want your help and advice, and I want you to do something for me.

RANK   The more the better. I've no idea what it can be. But tell me. You do trust me, don't you?

NORA   Oh, yes, more than anyone. You're my best and truest friend. Otherwise I couldn't tell you. Well then, Dr. Rank—there's something you must help me to prevent. You know how much Torvald loves me—he'd never hesitate for an instant to lay down his life for me—

RANK   (*leans over towards her*) Nora—do you think he is the only one—?

NORA   (*with a slight start*) What do you mean?

RANK   Who would gladly lay down his life for you?

NORA   (*sadly*) Oh, I see.

RANK   I swore to myself I would let you know that before I go. I shall never have a better opportunity. . . . Well, Nora, now you know that. And now you also know that you can trust me as you can trust nobody else.

NORA   (*rises; calmly and quietly*) Let me pass, please.

RANK   (*makes room for her but remains seated*) Nora—

NORA   (*in the doorway to the hall*) Helen, bring the lamp. (*Goes over to the stove.*) Oh, dear Dr. Rank, this was really horrid of you.

RANK   (*gets up*) That I have loved you as deeply as anyone else has? Was that horrid of me?

NORA   No—but that you should go and tell me. That was quite unnecessary—

RANK   What do you mean? Did you know, then—?

(*The* MAID *enters with the lamp, puts it on the table and goes out.*)

RANK   Nora—Mrs. Helmer—I am asking you, did you know this?

NORA   Oh, what do I know, what did I know, what didn't I know—I really can't say. How could you be so stupid, Dr. Rank? Everything was so nice.

RANK   Well, at any rate now you know that I am ready to serve you, body and soul. So—please continue.

NORA   (*looks at him*) After this?

RANK   Please tell me what it is.

NORA   I can't possibly tell you now.

RANK   Yes, yes! You mustn't punish me like this. Let me be allowed to do what I can for you.

NORA   You can't do anything for me now. Anyway, I don't need any help. It was only my imagination—you'll see. Yes, really. Honestly. (*Sits in the rocking chair, looks at him and smiles.*) Well, upon my word you *are* a fine gentleman, Dr. Rank. Aren't you ashamed of yourself, now that the lamp's been lit?

RANK   Frankly, no. But perhaps I ought to say—*adieu?*

NORA   Of course not. You will naturally continue to visit us as before. You know quite well how Torvald depends on your company.

RANK   Yes, but you?

NORA   Oh, I always think it's enormous fun having you here.

RANK   That was what misled me. You're a riddle to me, you know. I'd often felt you'd just as soon be with me as with Helmer.

NORA   Well, you see, there are some people whom one loves, and others whom it's almost more fun to be with.

RANK   Oh yes, there's some truth in that.

NORA   When I was at home, of course I loved Papa best. But I always used to think it was terribly amusing to go down and talk to the servants; because they never told me what I ought to do; and they were such fun to listen to.

RANK   I see. So I've taken their place?

NORA   (*jumps up and runs over to him*) Oh, dear, sweet Dr. Rank, I didn't mean that at all. But I'm sure you understand—I feel the same about Torvald as I did about Papa.

MAID   (*enters from the hall*) Excuse me, madam. (*Whispers to her and hands her a visiting card.*)

NORA   (*glances at the card*) Oh! (*Puts it quickly in her pocket.*)

RANK   Anything wrong?

NORA   No, no, nothing at all. It's just something that—it's my new dress.

RANK   What? But your costume is lying over there.

NORA   Oh—that, yes—but there's another—I ordered it specially—Torvald mustn't know—

RANK   Ah, so that's your big secret?

NORA   Yes, yes. Go in and talk to him—he's in his study—keep him talking for a bit—

RANK Don't worry. He won't get away from me. (*Goes into* HELMER's *study.*)

NORA (*to the* MAID) Is he waiting in the kitchen?

MAID Yes, madam, he came up the back way—

NORA But didn't you tell him I had a visitor?

MAID Yes, but he wouldn't go.

NORA Wouldn't go?

MAID No, madam, not until he'd spoken with you.

NORA Very well, show him in; but quietly. Helen, you mustn't tell anyone about this. It's a surprise for my husband.

MAID Very good, madam. I understand. (*Goes.*)

NORA It's happening. It's happening after all. No, no, no, it can't happen, it mustn't happen.

(*She walks across and bolts the door of* HELMER's *study. The* MAID *opens the door from the hall to admit* KROGSTAD, *and closes it behind him. He is wearing an overcoat, heavy boots and a fur cap.*)

NORA (*goes towards him*) Speak quietly. My husband's at home.

KROGSTAD Let him hear.

NORA What do you want from me?

KROGSTAD Information.

NORA Hurry up, then. What is it?

KROGSTAD I suppose you know I've been given the sack.

NORA I couldn't stop it, Mr. Krogstad. I did my best for you, but it didn't help.

KROGSTAD Does your husband love you so little? He knows what I can do to you, and yet he dares to—

NORA Surely you don't imagine I told him?

KROGSTAD No, I didn't really think you had. It wouldn't have been like my old friend Torvald Helmer to show that much courage—

NORA Mr. Krogstad, I'll trouble you to speak respectfully of my husband.

KROGSTAD Don't worry, I'll show him all the respect he deserves. But since you're so anxious to keep this matter hushed up, I presume you're better informed than you were yesterday of the gravity of what you've done?

NORA I've learned more than you could ever teach me.

KROGSTAD Yes, a bad lawyer like me—

NORA What do you want from me?

KROGSTAD I just wanted to see how things were with you, Mrs. Helmer. I've been thinking about you all day. Even duns and hack journalists have hearts, you know.

NORA Show some heart, then. Think of my little children.

KROGSTAD Have you and your husband thought of mine? Well, let's forget that. I just wanted to tell you, you don't need to take this business too seriously. I'm not going to take any action, for the present.

NORA Oh, no—you won't, will you? I knew it.

KROGSTAD It can all be settled quite amicably. There's no need for it to become public. We'll keep it among the three of us.

NORA My husband must never know about this.

KROGSTAD How can you stop him? Can you pay the balance of what you owe me?

NORA   Not immediately.

KROGSTAD   Have you any means of raising the money during the next few days?

NORA   None that I would care to use.

KROGSTAD   Well, it wouldn't have helped anyway. However much money you offered me now I wouldn't give you back that paper.

NORA   What are you going to do with it?

KROGSTAD   Just keep it. No one else need ever hear about it. So in case you were thinking of doing anything desperate—

NORA   I am.

KROGSTAD   Such as running away—

NORA   I am.

KROGSTAD   Or anything more desperate—

NORA   How did you know?

KROGSTAD   —just give up the idea.

NORA   How did you know?

KROGSTAD   Most of us think of that at first. I did. But I hadn't the courage—

NORA   (dully) Neither have I.

KROGSTAD   (relieved) It's true, isn't it? You haven't the courage either?

NORA   No. I haven't. I haven't.

KROGSTAD   It'd be a stupid thing to do anyway. Once the first little domestic explosion is over. . . . I've got a letter in my pocket here addressed to your husband—

NORA   Telling him everything?

KROGSTAD   As delicately as possibly.

NORA   (quickly) He must never see that letter. Tear it up. I'll find the money somehow—

KROGSTAD   I'm sorry, Mrs. Helmer, I thought I'd explained—

NORA   Oh, I don't mean the money I owe you. Let me know how much you want from my husband, and I'll find it for you.

KROGSTAD   I'm not asking your husband for money.

NORA   What do you want, then?

KROGSTAD   I'll tell you. I want to get on my feet again, Mrs. Helmer. I want to get to the top. And your husband's going to help me. For eighteen months now my record's been clean. I've been in hard straits all that time; I was content to fight my way back inch by inch. Now I've been chucked back into the mud, and I'm not going to be satisfied with just getting back my job. I'm going to get to the top, I tell you. I'm going to get back into the bank, and it's going to be higher up. Your husband's going to create a new job for me—

NORA   He'll never do that!

KROGSTAD   Oh, yes he will. I know him. He won't dare to risk a scandal. And once I'm in there with him, you'll see! Within a year I'll be his right-hand man. It'll be Nils Krogstad who'll be running that bank, not Torvald Helmer!

NORA   That will never happen.

KROGSTAD   Are you thinking of—?

NORA   Now I *have* the courage.

KROGSTAD   Oh, you can't frighten me. A pampered little pretty like you—

NORA   You'll see! You'll see!

KROGSTAD   Under the ice? Down in the cold, black water? And then, in the spring, to float up again, ugly, unrecognizable, hairless—?

NORA   You can't frighten me.

KROGSTAD   And you can't frighten me. People don't do such things, Mrs. Helmer. And anyway, what'd be the use? I've got him in my pocket.

NORA   But afterwards? When I'm no longer—?

KROGSTAD   Have you forgotten that then your reputation will be in my hands? (*She looks at him speechlessly.*) Well, I've warned you. Don't do anything silly. When Helmer's read my letter, he'll get in touch with me. And remember, it's your husband who's forced me to act like this. And for that I'll never forgive him. Goodbye, Mrs. Helmer. (*He goes out through the hall.*)

NORA   (*runs to the hall door, opens it a few inches and listens*) He's going. He's not going to give him the letter. Oh, no, no, it couldn't possibly happen. (*Opens the door a little wider.*) What's he doing? Standing outside the front door. He's not going downstairs. Is he changing his mind? Yes, he—!

(*A letter falls into the letter-box.* KROGSTAD's *footsteps die away down the stairs.*)

NORA   (*with a stifled cry, runs across the room towards the table by the sofa; a pause*) In the letter-box. (*Steals timidly over towards the hall door.*) There it is! Oh, Torvald, Torvald! Now we're lost!

MRS. LINDE   (*enters from the nursery with* NORA's *costume*) Well, I've done the best I can. Shall we see how it looks—?

NORA   (*whispers hoarsely*) Christine, come here.

MRS. LINDE   (*throws the dress on the sofa*) What's wrong with you? You look as though you'd seen a ghost!

NORA   Come here. Do you see that letter? There—look—through the glass of the letter-box.

MRS. LINDE   Yes, yes, I see it.

NORA   That letter's from Krogstad—

MRS. LINDE   Nora! It was Krogstad who lent you the money!

NORA   Yes. And now Torvald's going to discover everything.

MRS. LINDE   Oh, believe me, Nora, it'll be best for you both.

NORA   You don't know what's happened. I've committed a forgery—

MRS. LINDE   But, for heaven's sake—!

NORA   Christine, all I want is for you to be my witness.

MRS. LINDE   What do you mean? Witness what?

NORA   If I should go out of my mind—and it might easily happen—

MRS. LINDE   Nora!

NORA   Or if anything else should happen to me—so that I wasn't here any longer—

MRS. LINDE   Nora, Nora, you don't know what you're saying!

NORA   If anyone should try to take the blame, and say it was all his fault—you understand—?

MRS. LINDE   Yes, yes—but how can you think—?

NORA   Then you must testify that it isn't true, Christine. I'm not mad—I know exactly what I'm saying—and I'm telling you, no one else knows anything about this. I did it entirely on my own. Remember that.

MRS. LINDE All right. But I simply don't understand—

NORA Oh, how could you understand? A—miracle—is about to happen.

MRS. LINDE Miracle?

NORA Yes. A miracle. But it's so frightening, Christine. It *mustn't* happen, not for anything in the world.

MRS. LINDE I'll go over and talk to Krogstad.

NORA Don't go near him. He'll only do something to hurt you.

MRS. LINDE Once upon a time he'd have done anything for my sake.

NORA He?

MRS. LINDE Where does he live?

NORA Oh, how should I know—? Oh yes, wait a moment—! (*feels in her pocket*) Here's his card. But the letter, the letter—!

HELMER (*from his study, knocks on the door*) Nora!

NORA (*cries in alarm*) What is it?

HELMER Now, now, don't get alarmed. We're not coming in; you've closed the door. Are you trying on your costume?

NORA Yes, yes—I'm trying on my costume. I'm going to look so pretty for you, Torvald.

MRS. LINDE (*who has been reading the card*) Why, he lives just around the corner.

NORA Yes; but it's no use. There's nothing to be done now. The letter's lying there in the box.

MRS. LINDE And your husband has the key?

NORA Yes, he always keeps it.

MRS. LINDE Krogstad must ask him to send the letter back unread. He must find some excuse—

NORA But Torvald always opens the box at just about this time—

MRS. LINDE You must stop him. Go in and keep him talking. I'll be back as quickly as I can.

(*She hurries out through the hall.*)

NORA (*goes over to* HELMER's *door, opens it and peeps in*) Torvald!

HELMER (*offstage*) Well, may a man enter his own drawing-room again? Come on, Rank, now we'll see what— (*in the doorway*) But what's this?

NORA What, Torvald dear?

HELMER Rank's been preparing me for some great transformation scene.

RANK (*in the doorway*) So I understood. But I seem to have been mistaken.

NORA Yes, no one's to be allowed to see me before tomorrow night.

HELMER But, my dear Nora, you look quite worn out. Have you been practising too hard?

NORA No, I haven't practised at all yet.

HELMER Well, you must.

NORA Yes, Torvald, I must, I know. But I can't get anywhere without your help. I've completely forgotten everything.

HELMER Oh, we'll soon put that to rights.

NORA Yes, help me, Torvald. Promise me you will? Oh, I'm so nervous. All those people—! You must forget everything except me this evening. You mustn't think of business—I won't even let you touch a pen. Promise me, Torvald?

HELMER   I promise. This evening I shall think of nothing but you—my poor, helpless little darling. Oh, there's just one thing I must see to— (*Goes towards the hall door.*)

NORA   What do you want out there?

HELMER   I'm only going to see if any letters have come.

NORA   No, Torvald, no!

HELMER   Why, what's the matter?

NORA   Torvald, I beg you. There's nothing there.

HELMER   Well, I'll just make sure.

(*He moves towards the door.* NORA *runs to the piano and plays the first bars of the tarantella.*)

HELMER   (*at the door, turns*) Aha!

NORA   I can't dance tomorrow if I don't practise with you now.

HELMER   (*goes over to her*) Are you really so frightened, Nora dear?

NORA   Yes, terribly frightened. Let me start practising now, at once—we've still time before dinner. Oh, do sit down and play for me, Torvald dear. Correct me, lead me, the way you always do.

HELMER   Very well, my dear, if you wish it.

(*He sits down at the piano.* NORA *seizes the tambourine and a long multi-coloured shawl from the cardboard box, wraps the latter hastily around her, then takes a quick step into the centre of the room.*)

NORA   Play for me! I want to dance!

(HELMER *plays and* NORA *dances.* DR. RANK *stands behind* HELMER *at the piano and watches her.*)

HELMER   (*as he plays*) Slower, slower!

NORA   I can't!

HELMER   Not so violently, Nora.

NORA   I must!

HELMER   (*stops playing*) No, no, this won't do at all.

NORA   (*laughs and swings her tambourine*) Isn't that what I told you?

RANK   Let me play for her.

HELMER   (*gets up*) Yes, would you? Then it'll be easier for me to show her.

RANK *sits down at the piano and plays.* NORA *dances more and more wildly.* HELMER *has stationed himself by the stove and tries repeatedly to correct her, but she seems not to hear him. Her hair works loose and falls over her shoulders; she ignores it and continues to dance.* MRS. LINDE *enters.*)

MRS. LINDE   (*stands in the doorway as though tongue-tied*) Ah—!

NORA   (*as she dances*) Oh, Christine, we're having such fun!

HELMER   But, Nora darling, you're dancing as if your life depended on it.

NORA   It does.

HELMER   Rank, stop it! This is sheer lunacy. Stop it, I say!

(RANK *ceases playing.* NORA *suddenly stops dancing.*)

HELMER   (*goes over to her*) I'd never have believed it. You've forgotten everything I taught you.

NORA   (*throws away the tambourine*) You see!

HELMER I'll have to show you every step.

NORA You see how much I need you! You must show me every step of the way. Right to the end of the dance. Promise me you will, Torvald?

HELMER Never fear. I will.

NORA You mustn't think about anything but me—today or tomorrow. Don't open any letters—don't even open the letter-box—

HELMER Aha, you're still worried about that fellow—

NORA Oh, yes, yes, him too.

HELMER Nora, I can tell from the way you're behaving, there's a letter from him already lying there.

NORA I don't know. I think so. But you mustn't read it now. I don't want anything ugly to come between us till it's all over.

RANK (*quietly to* HELMER) Better give her her way.

HELMER (*puts his arm round her*) My child shall have her way. But tomorrow night, when your dance is over—

NORA Then you will be free.

MAID (*appears in the doorway, right*) Dinner is served, madam.

NORA Put out some champagne, Helen.

MAID Very good, madam. (*Goes.*)

HELMER I say! What's this, a banquet?

NORA We'll drink champagne until dawn! (*calls*) And, Helen! Put out some macaroons! Lots of macaroons—for once!

HELMER (*takes her hands in his*) Now, now, now. Don't get so excited. Where's my little songbird, the one I know?

NORA All right. Go and sit down—and you too, Dr. Rank. I'll be with you in a minute. Christine, you must help me put my hair up.

RANK (*quietly, as they go*) There's nothing wrong, is there? I mean, she isn't—er—expecting—?

HELMER Good heavens no, my dear chap. She just gets scared like a child sometimes—I told you before—

(*They go out, right.*)

NORA Well?

MRS. LINDE He's left town.

NORA I saw it from your face.

MRS. LINDE He'll be back tomorrow evening. I left a note for him.

NORA You needn't have bothered. You can't stop anything now. Anyway, it's wonderful really, in a way—sitting here and waiting for the miracle to happen.

MRS. LINDE Waiting for what?

NORA Oh, you wouldn't understand. Go in and join them. I'll be with you in a moment.

(MRS. LINDE *goes into the dining-room.*)

NORA (*stands for a moment as though collecting herself. Then she looks at her watch*) Five o'clock. Seven hours till midnight. Then another twenty-four hours till midnight tomorrow. And then the tarantella will be finished. Twenty-four and seven? Thirty-one hours to live.

HELMER (appears in the doorway, right) What's happened to my little songbird?

NORA (runs to him with her arms wide) Your songbird is here!

ACT III

(The same room. The table which was formerly by the sofa has been moved into the
centre of the room; the chairs surround it as before. The door to the hall stands open.
Dance music can be heard from the floor above. MRS. LINDE is seated at the table,
absent-mindedly glancing through a book. She is trying to read, but seems unable to
keep her mind on it. More than once she turns and listens anxiously towards the front
door.)

MRS. LINDE (looks at her watch) Not here yet. There not much time left.
Please God he hasn't—! (Listens again.) Ah, here he is. (Goes out into the
hall and cautiously opens the front door. Footsteps can be heard softly
ascending the stairs. She whispers.) Come in. There's no one here.

KROGSTAD (in the doorway) I found a note from you at my lodgings. What
does this mean?

MRS. LINDE I must speak with you.

KROGSTAD Oh? And must our conversation take place in this house?

MRS. LINDE We couldn't meet at my place; my room has no separate
entrance. Come in. We're quite alone. The maid's asleep, and the Helmers
are at the dance upstairs.

KROGSTAD (comes into the room) Well, well! So the Helmers are dancing
this evening? Are they indeed?

MRS. LINDE Yes, why not?

KROGSTAD True enough. Why not?

MRS. LINDE Well, Krogstad. You and I must have a talk together.

KROGSTAD Have we two anything further to discuss?

MRS. LINDE We have a great deal to discuss.

KROGSTAD I wasn't aware of it.

MRS. LINDE That's because you've never really understood me.

KROGSTAD Was there anything to understand? Its the old story, isn't it—
a woman chucking a man because something better turns up?

MRS. LINDE Do you really think I'm so utterly heartless? You think it was
easy for me to give you up?

KROGSTAD Wasn't it?

MRS. LINDE Oh, Nils, did you really believe that?

KROGSTAD Then why did you write to me the way you did?

MRS. LINDE I had to. Since I had to break with you, I thought it my duty
to destroy all the feelings you had for me.

KROGSTAD (clenches his fists) So that was it. And you did this for money!

MRS. LINDE You mustn't forget I had a helpless mother to take care of, and
two little brothers. We couldn't wait for you, Nils. It would have been so
long before you'd had enough to support us.

KROGSTAD Maybe. But you had no right to cast me off for someone else.

MRS. LINDE Perhaps not. I've often asked myself that.

KROGSTAD (*more quietly*) When I lost you, it was just as though all solid ground had been swept from under my feet. Look at me. Now I am a shipwrecked man, clinging to a spar.

MRS. LINDE Help may be near at hand.

KROGSTAD It was near. But then you came, and stood between it and me.

MRS. LINDE I didn't know, Nils. No one told me till today that this job I'd found was yours.

KROGSTAD I believe you, since you say so. But now you know, won't you give it up?

MRS. LINDE No—because it wouldn't help you even if I did.

KROGSTAD Wouldn't it? I'd do it all the same.

MRS. LINDE I've learned to look at things practically. Life and poverty have taught me that.

KROGSTAD And life has taught me to distrust fine words.

MRS. LINDE Then it's taught you a useful lesson. But surely you still believe in actions?

KROGSTAD What do you mean?

MRS. LINDE You said you were like a shipwrecked man clinging to a spar.

KROGSTAD I have good reason to say it.

MRS. LINDE I'm in the same position as you. No one to care about, no one to care for.

KROGSTAD You made your own choice.

MRS. LINDE I had no choice—then.

KROGSTAD Well?

MRS. LINDE Nils, suppose we two shipwrecked souls could join hands?

KROGSTAD What are you saying?

MRS. LINDE Castaways have a better chance of survival together than on their own.

KROGSTAD Christine!

MRS. LINDE Why do you suppose I came to this town?

KROGSTAD You mean—you came because of me?

MRS. LINDE I must work if I'm to find life worth living. I've always worked, for as long as I can remember; it's been the greatest joy of my life—my only joy. But now I'm alone in the world, and I feel so dreadfully lost and empty. There's no joy in working just for oneself. Oh, Nils, give me something—someone—to work for.

KROGSTAD I don't believe all that. You're just being hysterical and romantic. You want to find an excuse for self-sacrifice.

MRS. LINDE Have you ever known me to be hysterical?

KROGSTAD You mean you really—? Is it possible? Tell me—you know all about my past?

MRS. LINDE Yes.

KROGSTAD And you know what people think of me here?

MRS. LINDE You said just now that you might have become a different person.

KROGSTAD I know I could have.

MRS. LINDE   Couldn't it still happen?

KROGSTAD   Christine—do you really mean this? Yes—you do—I see it in your face. Have you really the courage—?

MRS. LINDE   I need someone to be a mother to; and your children need a mother. And you and I need each other. I believe in you, Nils. I am afraid of nothing—with you.

KROGSTAD   (*clasps her hands*) Thank you, Christine—thank you! Now I shall make the world believe in me as you do! Oh—but I'd forgotten—

MRS. LINDE   (*listens*) Ssh! The tarantella! Go quickly, go!

KROGSTAD   Why? What is it?

MRS. LINDE   You hear that dance? As soon as it's finished, they'll be coming down.

KROGSTAD   All right, I'll go. It's no good, Christine. I'd forgotten—you don't know what I've just done to the Helmers.

MRS. LINDE   Yes, Nils. I know.

KROGSTAD   And yet you'd still have the courage to—?

MRS. LINDE   I know what despair can drive a man like you to.

KSOGSTAD   Oh, if only I could undo this!

MRS. LINDE   You can. Your letter is still lying in the box.

KROGSTAD   Are you sure?

MRS. LINDE   Quite sure. But—

KROGSTAD   (*looks searching at her*) Is that why you're doing this? You want to save your friend at any price? Tell me the truth. Is that the reason?

MRS. LINDE   Nils, a woman who has sold herself once for the sake of others doesn't make the same mistake again.

KROGSTAD   I shall demand my letter back.

MRS. LINDE   No, no.

KROGSTAD   Of course I shall. I shall stay here till Helmer comes down. I'll tell him he must give me back my letter—I'll say it was only to do with my dismissal, and that I don't want him to read it—

MRS. LINDE   No, Nils, you mustn't ask for that letter back.

KROGSTAD   But—tell me—wasn't that the real reason you asked me to come here?

MRS. LINDE   Yes—at first, when I was frightened. But a day has passed since then, and in that time I've seen incredible things happen in this house. Helmer must know the truth. This unhappy secret of Nora's must be revealed. They must come to a full understanding; there must be an end of all these shiftings and evasions.

KROGSTAD   Very well. If you're prepared to risk it. But one thing I can do—and at once—

MRS. LINDE   (*listens*) Hurry! Go, go! The dance is over. We aren't safe here another moment.

KROGSTAD   I'll wait for you downstairs.

MRS. LINDE   Yes, do. You can see me home.

KROGSTAD   I've never been so happy in my life before!

(*He goes out through the front door. The door leading from the room into the hall remains open.*)

MRS. LINDE (*tidies the room a little and gets her hat and coat*) What a change! Oh, what a change! Someone to work for—to live for! A home to bring joy into! I won't let this chance of happiness slip through my fingers. Oh, why don't they come? (*Listens.*) Ah, here they are. I must get my coat on.

(*She takes her hat and coat. HELMER's and NORA's voices become audible outside. A key is turned in the lock and HELMER leads NORA almost forcibly into the hall. She is dressed in an Italian costume with a large black shawl. He is in evening dress, with a black cloak.*)

NORA (*still in the doorway, resisting him*) No, no, no—not in here! I don't want to leave so early.

HELMER But my dearest Nora—

NORA Oh, please, Torvald, please! Just another hour!

HELMER Not another minute, Nora, my sweet. You know what we agreed. Come along, now. Into the drawing-room. You'll catch cold if you stay out here.

(*He leads her, despite her efforts to resist him, gently into the room.*)

MRS. LINDE Good evening.

NORA Christine!

HELMER Oh, hullo, Mrs. Linde. You still here?

MRS. LINDE Please forgive me. I did so want to see Nora in her costume.

NORA Have you been sitting here waiting for me?

MRS. LINDE Yes. I got here too late, I'm afraid. You'd already gone up. And I felt I really couldn't go back home without seeing you.

HELMER (*takes off NORA's shawl*) Well, take a good look at her. She's worth looking at, don't you think? Isn't she beautiful, Mrs. Linde?

MRS. LINDE Oh, yes, indeed—

HELMER Isn't she unbelievably beautiful? Everyone at the party said so. But dreadfully stubborn she is, bless her pretty little heart. What's to be done about that? Would you believe it, I practically had to use force to get her away!

NORA Oh, Torvald, you're going to regret not letting me stay—just half an hour longer.

HELMER Hear that, Mrs. Linde? She dances her tarantella—makes a roaring success—and very well dressed—though possibly a trifle too realistic—more so than was aesthetically necessary, strictly speaking. But never mind that. Main thing is—she had a success—roaring success. Was I going to let her stay on after that and spoil the impression? No, thank you. I took my beautiful little Capri signorina—my capricious little Capricienne, what?—under my arm—a swift round of the ballroom, a curtsey to the company, and, as they say in the novels, the beautiful apparition disappeared! An exit should always be dramatic, Mrs. Linde. But unfortunately that's just what I can't get Nora to realize. I say, it's hot in here. (*Throws his cloak on a chair and opens to the door to his study.*) What's this? It's dark in here. Ah, yes, of course—excuse me. (*Goes in and lights a couple of candles.*)

NORA (*whispers swiftly, breathlessly*) Well?

MRS. LINDE (*quietly*) I've spoken to him.

NORA   Yes?

MRS. LINDE   Nora—you must tell your husband everything.

NORA   (dully) I knew it.

MRS. LINDE   You've nothing to fear from Krogstad. But you must tell him.

NORA   I shan't tell him anything.

MRS. LINDE   Then the letter will.

NORA   Thank you, Christine. Now I know what I must do. Ssh!

HELMER   (returns) Well, Mrs. Linde, finished admiring her?

MRS. LINDE   Yes. Now I must say good night.

HELMER   Oh, already? Does this knitting belong to you?

MRS. LINDE   (takes it) Thank you, yes. I nearly forgot it.

HELMER   You knit, then?

MRS. LINDE   Why, yes.

HELMER   Know what? You ought to take up embroidery.

MRS. LINDE   Oh? Why?

HELMER   It's much prettier. Watch me, now. You hold the embroidery in your left hand, like this, and then you take the needle in your right hand and go in and out in a slow, easy movement—like this. I am right, aren't I?

MRS. LINDE   Yes, I'm sure—

HELMER   But knitting, now—that's an ugly business—can't help it. Look— arms all huddled up—great clumsy needles going up and down—makes you look like a damned Chinaman. I say, that really was a magnificant champagne they served us.

MRS. LINDE   Well, good night, Nora. And stop being stubborn. Remember!

HELMER   Quite right, Mrs. Linde!

MRS. LINDE   Good night, Mr. Helmer.

HELMER   (accompanies her to the door) Good night, good night! I hope you'll manage to get home all right? I'd gladly—but you haven't far to go, have you? Good night, good night. (She goes. He closes the door behind her and returns.) Well, we've got rid of her at last. Dreadful bore that woman is!

NORA   Aren't you very tired, Torvald?

HELMER   No, not in the least.

NORA   Aren't you sleepy?

HELMER   Not a bit. On the contrary, I feel extraordinarily exhilarated. But what about you? Yes, you look very sleepy and tired.

NORA   Yes, I am very tired. Soon I shall sleep.

HELMER   You see, you see! How right I was not to let you stay longer!

NORA   Oh, you're always right, whatever you do.

HELMER   (kisses her on the forehead) Now my little songbird's talking just like a real big human being. I say, did you notice how cheerful Rank was this evening?

NORA   Oh? Was he? I didn't have a chance to speak with him.

HELMER   I hardly did. But I haven't seen him in such a jolly mood for ages. (Looks at her for a moment, then comes closer.) I say, it's nice to get back to one's home again, and be all alone with you. Upon my word, you're a distractingly beautiful young woman.

NORA   Don't look at me like that, Torvald!

HELMER What, not look at my most treasured possession? At all this wonderful beauty that's mine, mine alone, all mine.

NORA (*goes round to the other side of the table*) You mustn't talk to me like that tonight.

HELMER (*follows her*) You've still the tarantella in your blood, I see. And that makes you even more desirable. Listen! Now the other guests are beginning to go. (*more quietly*) Nora—soon the whole house will be absolutely quiet.

NORA Yes, I hope so.

HELMER Yes, my beloved Nora, of course you do! Do you know—when I'm out with you among other people like we were tonight, do you know why I say so little to you, why I keep so aloof from you, and just throw you an occasional glance? Do you know why I do that? It's because I pretend to myself that you're my secret mistress, my clandestine little sweetheart, and that nobody knows there's anything at all between us.

NORA Oh, yes, yes, yes—I know you never think of anything but me.

HELMER And then when we're about to go, and I wrap the shawl round your lovely young shoulders, over this wonderful curve of your neck—then I pretend to myself that you are my young bride, that we've just come from the wedding, that I'm taking you to my house for the first time—that, for the first time, I am alone with you—quite alone with you, as you stand there young and trembling and beautiful. All evening I've had no eyes for anyone but you. When I saw you dance the tarantella, like a huntress, a temptress, my blood grew hot, I couldn't stand it any longer! That was why I seized you and dragged you down here with me—

NORA Leave me, Torvald! Get away from me! I don't want all this.

HELMER What? Now, Nora, you're joking with me. Don't want, don't want—? Aren't I your husband—?

(*There is a knock on the front door.*)

NORA (*starts*) What was that?

HELMER (*goes towards the hall*) Who is it?

RANK (*outside*) It's me. May I come in for a moment?

HELMER (*quietly, annoyed*) Oh, what does he want now? (*calls*) Wait a moment. (*Walks over and opens the door.*) Well! Nice of you not to go by without looking in.

RANK I thought I heard your voice, so I felt I had to say goodbye. (*His eyes travel swiftly around the room.*) Ah, yes—these dear rooms, how well I know them. What a happy, peaceful home you two have.

HELMER You seemed to be having a pretty happy time yourself upstairs.

RANK Indeed I did. Why not? Why shouldn't one make the most of this world? As much as one can, and for as long as one can. The wine was excellent—

HELMER Especially the champagne.

RANK You noticed that too? It's almost incredible how much I managed to get down.

NORA Torvald drank a lot of champagne too, this evening.

RANK Oh?

NORA   Yes. It always makes him merry afterwards.

RANK   Well, why shouldn't a man have a merry evening after a well-spent day?

HELMER   Well-spent? Oh, I don't know that I can claim that.

RANK   (*slaps him across the back*) I can, though, my dear fellow!

NORA   Yes, of course, Dr. Rank—you've been carrying out a scientific experiment today, haven't you?

RANK   Exactly.

HELMER   Scientific experiment! Those are big words for my little Nora to use!

NORA   And may I congratulate you on the finding?

RANK   You may indeed.

NORA   It was good, then?

RANK   The best possible finding—both for the doctor and the patient. Certainty.

NORA   (*quickly*) Certainty?

RANK   Aboslute certainty. So aren't I entitled to have a merry evening after that?

NORA   Yes, Dr. Rank. You were quite right to.

HELMER   I agree. Provided you don't have to regret it tomorrow.

RANK   Well, you never get anything in this life without paying for it.

NORA   Dr. Rank—you like masquerades, don't you?

RANK   Yes, if the disguises are sufficiently amusing.

NORA   Tell me. What shall we two wear at the next masquerade?

HELMER   You little gadabout! Are you thinking about the next one already?

RANK   We two? Yes, I'll tell you. You must go as the Spirit of Happiness—

HELMER   You try to think of a costume that'll convey that.

RANK   You wife need only appear as her normal, everyday self—

HELMER   Quite right! Well said! But what are you going to be? Have you decided that?

RANK   Yes, my dear friend. I have decided that.

HELMER   Well?

RANK   At the next masquerade, I shall be invisible.

HELMER   Well, that's a funny idea.

RANK   There's a big, black hat—haven't you heard of the invisible hat? Once it's over your head, no one can see you any more.

HELMER   (*represses a smile*) Ah yes, of course.

RANK   But I'm forgetting what I came for. Helmer, give me a cigar. One of your black Havanas.

HELMER   With the greatest pleasure. (*Offers him the box.*)

RANK   (*takes one and cuts off the tip*) Thank you.

NORA   (*strikes a match*) Let me give you a light.

RANK   Thank you. (*She holds out the match for him. He lights his cigar.*) And now—goodbye.

HELMER   Goodbye, my dear chap, goodbye.

NORA   Sleep well, Dr. Rank.

RANK   Thank you for that kind wish.

NORA   Wish me the same.

RANK   You? Very well—since you ask. Sleep well. And thank you for the light. (*He nods to them both and goes.*)

HELMER   (*quietly*) He's been drinking too much.

NORA   (*abstractedly*) Perhaps.

(HELMER *takes his bunch of keys from his pocket and goes out into the hall.*)

NORA   Torvald, what do you want out there?

HELMER   I must empty the letter-box. It's absolutely full. There'll be no room for the newspapers in the morning.

NORA   Are you going to work tonight?

HELMER   You know very well I'm not. Hullo, what's this? Someone's been at the lock.

NORA   At the lock—?

HELMER   Yes, I'm sure of it. Who on earth—? Surely not one of the maids? Here's a broken hairpin. Nora, it's yours—

NORA   (*quickly*) Then it must have been the children.

HELMER   Well, you'll have to break them of that habit. Hm, hm. Ah, that's done it. (*Takes out the contents of the box and calls into the kitchen.*) Helen! Helen! Put out the light on the staircase. (*Comes back ino the drawing-room with the letters in his hand and closes the door to the hall.*) Look at this! You see how they've piled up? (*Glances through them.*) What on earth's this?

NORA   (*at the window*) The letter! Oh, no, Torvald, no!

HELMER   Two visiting cards—from Rank.

NORA   From Dr. Rank?

HELMER   (*looks at them*) Peter Rank, M.D. They were on top. He must have dropped them in as he left.

NORA   Has he written anything on them?

HELMER   There's a black cross above his name. Look. Rather gruesome, isn't it? It looks just as though he was announcing his death.

NORA   He is.

HELMER   What? Do you know something? Has he told you anything?

NORA   Yes. When these cards come, it means he's said goodbye to us. He wants to shut himself up in his house and die.

HELMER   Ah, poor fellow. I knew I wouldn't be seeing him for much longer. But so soon—! And now he's going to sink away and hide like a wounded beast.

NORA   When the time comes, it's best to go silently. Don't you think so, Torvald?

HELMER   (*walks up and down*) He was so much a part of our life. I can't realize that he's gone. His suffering and loneliness seemed to provide a kind of dark background to the happy sunlight of our marriage. Well, perhaps it's best this way. For him, anyway. (*Stops walking.*) And perhaps for us too, Nora. Now we have only each other. (*Embraces her.*) Oh, my beloved wife—I feel as though I could never hold you close enough. Do you know, Nora, often I wish some terrible danger might threaten you, so that I could offer my life and my blood, everything, for your sake.

NORA   (*tears herself loose and says in a clear, firm voice*) Read your letters now, Torvald.

HELMER   No, no. Not tonight. Tonight I want to be with you, my darling wife—

NORA   When your friend is about to die—?

HELMER You're right. This news has upset us both. An ugliness has come between us; thoughts of death and dissolution. We must try to forget them. Until then—you go to your room; I shall go to mine.

NORA (*throws her arms round his neck*) Good night, Torvald! Good night!

HELMER (*kisses her on the forehead*) Good night, my darling little songbird. Sleep well, Nora. I'll go and read my letters.

(*He goes into the study with the letters in his hand, and closes the door.*)

NORA (*wild-eyed fumbles around, seizes* HELMER's *cloak, throws it round herself and whispers quickly, hoarsely*) Never see him again. Never. Never. Never. (*Throws the shawl over her head.*) Never see the children again. Them too. Never. Never. Oh—the icy black water! Oh—that bottomless—that—! Oh, if only it were all over! Now he's got it—he's reading it. Oh, no, no! Not yet! Goodbye, Torvald! Goodbye, my darlings!

(*She turns to run into the hall. As she does so,* HELMER *throws open his door and stands there with an open letter in his hand.*)

HELMER Nora!

NORA (*shrieks*) Ah—!

HELMER What is this? Do you know what is in this letter?

NORA Yes, I know. Let me go! Let me go!

HELMER (*holds her back*) Go? Where?

NORA (*tries to tear herself loose*) You mustn't try to save me, Torvald!

HELMER (*staggers back*) Is it true? Is it true, what he writes? Oh, my God! No, no—it's impossible, it can't be true!

NORA It *is* true. I've loved you more than anything else in the world.

HELMER Oh, don't try to make silly excuses.

NORA (*takes a step towards him*) Torvald—

HELMER Wretched woman! What have you done?

NORA Let me go! You're not going to suffer for my sake. I won't let you!

HELMER Stop being theatrical. (*Locks the front door.*) You're going to stay here and explain yourself. Do you understand what you've done? Answer me! Do you understand?

NORA (*looks unflinchingly at him and, her expression growing colder, says*) Yes. Now I am beginning to understand.

HELMER (*walking round the room*) Oh, what a dreadful awakening! For eight whole years—she who was my joy and my pride—a hypocrite, a liar—worse, worse—a criminal! Oh, the hideousness of it! Shame on you, shame!

(NORA *is silent and stares unblinkingly at him.*)

HELMER (*stops in front of her*) I ought to have guessed that something of this sort would happen. I should have foreseen it. All your father's reckless-ness and instability—be quiet!—I repeat, all your father's recklessness and instability he has handed on to you. No religion, no morals, no sense of duty! Oh, how I have been punished for closing my eyes to his faults! I did it for your sake. And now you reward me like this.

NORA Yes. Like this.

HELMER Now you have destroyed all my happiness. You have ruined my whole future. Oh, it's too dreadful to contemplate! I am in the power of a man who is completely without scruples. He can do what he likes with me, demand what he pleases, order me to do anything—I dare not disobey him. I am condemned to humiliation and ruin simply for the weakness of a woman.

NORA   When I am gone from this world, you will be free.

HELMER   Oh, don't be melodramatic. Your father was always ready with that kind of remark. How would it help me if you were "gone from this world," as you put it? It wouldn't assist me in the slightest. He can still make all the facts public; and if he does, I may quite easily be suspected of having been an accomplice in your crime. People may think that I was behind it—that it was I who encouraged you! And for all this I have to thank you, you whom I have carried on my hands through all the years of our marriage! Now do you realize what you've done to me?

NORA   (coldly calm) Yes.

HELMER   It's so unbelievable I can hardly credit it. But we must try to find some way out. Take off that shawl. Take it off, I say! I must try to buy him off somehow. This thing must be hushed up at any price. As regards our relationship—we must appear to be living together just as before. Only appear, of course. You will therefore continue to reside here. That is understood. But the children shall be taken out of your hands. I dare no longer entrust them to you. Oh, to have to say this to the woman I once loved so dearly—and whom I still—! Well, all that must be finished. Henceforth there can be no question of happiness; we must merely strive to save what shreds and tatters— (The front door bell rings. HELMER starts.) What can that be? At this hour? Surely not—? He wouldn't—? Hide yourself, Nora. Say you're ill.

(NORA does not move. HELMER goes to the door of the room and opens it. The MAID is standing half-dressed in the hall.)

MAID   A letter for madam.

HELMER   Give it me. (Seizes the letter and shuts the door.) Yes, it's from him. You're not having it. I'll read this myself.

NORA   Read it.

HELMER   (by the lamp) I hardly dare to. This may mean the end for us both. No. I must know. (Tears open the letter hastily; reads a few lines; looks at a piece of paper which is enclosed with it; utters a cry of joy.) Nora! (She looks at him questioningly.) Nora! No—I must read it once more. Yes, yes, it's true! I am saved! Nora, I am saved!

NORA   What about me?

HELMER   You too, of course. We're both saved, you and I. Look! He's returning your I.O.U. He writes that he is sorry for what has happened—a happy accident has changed his life—oh, what does it matter what he writes? We are saved, Nora! No one can harm you now. Oh, Nora, Nora— no, first let me destroy this filthy thing. Let me see—! (Glances at the I.O.U.) No, I don't want to look at it. I shall merely regard the whole business as a dream. (He tears the I.O.U. and both letters into pieces, throws them into the stove and watches them burn.) There. Now they're destroyed. He wrote that ever since Christmas Eve you've been—oh, these must have been three dreadful days for you, Nora.

NORA Yes. It's been a hard fight.

HELMER It must have been terrible—seeing no way out except—no, we'll forget the whole sordid business. We'll just be happy and go on telling ourselves over and over again: "It's over! It's over!" Listen to me, Nora. You don't seem to realize. It's over! Why are you looking so pale? Ah, my poor little Nora, I understand. You can't believe that I have forgiven you. But I have, Nora. I swear it to you. I have forgiven you everything. I know that what you did you did for your love of me.

NORA That is true.

HELMER You have loved me as a wife should love her husband. It was simply that in your inexperience you chose the wrong means. But do you think I love you any the less because you don't know how to act on your own initiative? No, no. Just lean on me. I shall counsel you. I shall guide you. I would not be a true man if your feminine helplessness did not make you doubly attractive in my eyes. You mustn't mind the hard words I said to you in those first dreadful moments when my whole world seemed to be tumbling about my ears. I have forgiven you, Nora. I swear it to you; I have forgiven you.

NORA Thank you for your forgiveness.

(She goes out through the door, right.)

HELMER No, don't go— (*Looks in.*) What are you doing there?

NORA (*offstage*) Taking off my fancy dress.

HELMER (*by the open door*) Yes, do that. Try to calm yourself and get your balance again, my frightened little songbird. Don't be afraid. I have broad wings to shield you. (*Begins to walk around near the door.*) How lovely and peaceful this little home of our is, Nora. You are safe here; I shall watch over you like a hunted dove which I have snatched unharmed from the claws of the falcon. Your wildly beating little heart shall find peace with me. It will happen, Nora; it will take time, but it will happen, believe me. Tomorrow all this will seem quite different. Soon everything will be as it was before. I shall no longer need to remind you that I have forgiven you; your own heart will tell you that it is true. Do you really think I could ever bring myself to disown you, or even to reproach you? Ah, Nora, you don't understand what goes on in a husband's heart. There is something indescribably wonderful and satisfying for a husband in knowing that he has forgiven his wife—forgiven her unreservedly, from the bottom of his heart. It means that she has become his property in a double sense; he has, as it were, brought her into the world anew; she is now not only his wife but also his child. From now on that is what you shall be to me, my poor, helpless, bewildered little creature. Never be frightened of anything again, Nora. Just open your heart to me. I shall be both your will and your conscience. What's this? Not in bed? Have you changed?

NORA (*in her everyday dress*) Yes, Torvald. I've changed.

HELMER But why now—so late—?

NORA I shall not sleep tonight.

HELMER But, my dear Nora—

NORA (*looks at her watch*) It isn't that late. Sit down here, Torvald. You and I have a lot to talk about.

(She sits down on one side of the table.)

HELMER Nora, what does this mean? You look quite drawn—

NORA Sit down. It's going to take a long time. I've a lot to say to you.

HELMER *(sits down on the other side of the table)* You alarm me, Nora. I don't understand you.

NORA No, that's just it. You don't understand me. And I've never understood you—until this evening. No, don't interrupt me. Just listen to what I have to say. You and I have got to face facts, Torvald.

HELMER What do you mean by that?

NORA *(after a short silence)* Doesn't anything strike you about the way we're sitting here?

HELMER What?

NORA We've been married for eight years. Does it occur to you that this is the first time that we two, you and I, man and wife, have ever had a serious talk together?

HELMER Serious? What do you mean, serious?

NORA In eight whole years—no, longer—ever since we first met—we have never exchanged a serious word on a serious subject.

HELMER Did you expect me to drag you into all my worries—worries you couldn't possibly have helped me with?

NORA I'm not talking about worries. I'm simply saying that we have never sat down seriously to try to get to the bottom of anything.

HELMER But, my dear Nora, what on earth has that got to do with you?

NORA That's just the point. You have never understood me. A great wrong has been done to me, Torvald. First by Papa, and then by you.

HELMER What? But we two have loved you more than anyone in the world!

NORA *(shakes her head)* You have never loved me. You just thought it was fun to be in love with me.

HELMER Nora, what kind of a way is this to talk?

NORA It's the truth, Torvald. When I lived with Papa, he used to tell me what he thought about everything, so that I never had any opinions but his. And if I did have any of my own, I kept them quiet, because he wouldn't have liked them. He called me his little doll, and he played with me just the way I played with my dolls. Then I came here to live in your house—

HELMER What kind of a way is that to describe our marriage?

NORA *(undisturbed)* I mean, then I passed from Papa's hands into yours. You arranged everything the way you wanted it, so that I simply took over your taste in everything—or pretended I did—I don't really know—I think it was a little of both—first one and then the other. Now I look back on it, it's as if I've been living here like a pauper, from hand to mouth. I performed tricks for you and you gave me food and drink. But that was how you wanted it. You and Papa have done me a great wrong. It's your fault that I have done nothing with my life.

HELMER Nora, how can you be so unreasonable and ungrateful? Haven't you been happy here?

NORA No; never. I used to think I was; but I haven't ever been happy.

HELMER Not—not happy?

NORA   No. I've just had fun. You've always been very kind to me. But our home has never been anything but a playroom. I've been your doll-wife, just as I used to be Papa's doll-child. And the children have been my dolls. I used to think it was fun when you came in and played with me, just as they think it's fun when I go in and play games with them. That's all our marriage has been, Torvald.

HELMER   There may be a little truth in what you say, though you exaggerate and romanticize. But from now on it'll be different. Playtime is over. Now the time has come for education.

NORA   Whose education? Mine or the children's?

HELMER   Both yours and the children's, my dearest Nora.

NORA   Oh, Torvald, you're not the man to educate me into being the right wife for you.

HELMER   How can you say that?

NORA   And what about me? Am I fit to educate the children?

HELMER   Nora!

NORA   Didn't you say yourself a few minutes ago that you dare not leave them in my charge?

HELMER   In a moment of excitement. Surely you don't think I meant it seriously?

NORA   Yes. You were perfectly right. I'm not fitted to educate them. There's something else I must do first. I must educate myself. And you can't help me with that. It's something I must do by myself. That's why I'm leaving you.

HELMER   (jumps up) What did you say?

NORA   I must stand on my own feet if I am to find out the truth about myself and about life. So I can't go on living here with you any longer.

HELMER   Nora, Nora!

NORA   I'm leaving you now, at once. Christine will put me up for tonight—

HELMER   You're out of your mind! You can't do this; I forbid you!

NORA   It's no use your trying to forbid me any more. I shall take with me nothing but what is mine. I don't want anything from you, now or ever.

HELMER   What kind of madness is this?

NORA   Tomorrow I shall go home—I mean, to where I was born. It'll be easiest for me to find some kind of job there.

HELMER   But you're blind! You've no experience of the world—

NORA   I must try to get some, Torvald.

HELMER   But to leave your home, your husband, your children! Have you thought what people will say?

NORA   I can't help that. I only know that I must do this.

HELMER   But this is monstrous! Can you neglect sacred duties?

NORA   What do you call my most sacred duties?

HELMER   Do I have to tell you? Your duties towards your husband, and your children.

NORA   I have another duty which is equally sacred.

HELMER   You have not. What on earth could that be?

NORA   My duty towards myself.

HELMER   First and foremost you are a wife and a mother.

NORA   I don't believe that any longer. I believe that I am first and foremost a human being, like you—or anyway, that I must try to become one. I know most people think as you do, Torvald, and I know there's something of the sort to be found in books. But I'm no longer prepared to accept what people say and what's written in books. I must think things out for myself, and try to find my own answer.

HELMER   Do you need to ask where your duty lies in your own home? Haven't you an infallible guide in such matters—your religion?

NORA   Oh, Torvald, I don't really know what religion means.

HELMER   What are you saying?

NORA   I only know what Pastor Hansen told me when I went to confirmation. He explained that religion meant this and that. When I get away from all this and can think things out on my own, that's one of the questions I want to look into. I want to find out whether what Pastor Hansen said was right—or anyway, whether it is right for me.

HELMER   But it's unheard of for so young a woman to behave like this! If religion cannot guide you, let me at least appeal to your conscience. I presume you have some moral feelings left? Or—perhaps you haven't? Well, answer me.

NORA   Oh, Torvald, that isn't an easy question to answer. I simply don't know. I don't know where I am in these matters. I only know that these things mean something quite different to me from what they do to you. I've learned now that certain laws are different from what I'd imagined them to be; but I can't accept that such laws can be right. Has a woman really not the right to spare her dying father pain, or save her husband's life? I can't believe that.

HELMER   You're talking like a child. You don't understand how society works.

NORA   No, I don't. But now I intend to learn. I must try to satisfy myself which is right, society or I.

HELMER   Nora, you're ill; you're feverish. I almost believe you're out of your mind.

NORA   I've never felt so sane and sure in my life.

HELMER   You feel sure that it is right to leave your husband and your children?

NORA   Yes. I do.

HELMER   Then there is only one possible explanation.

NORA   What?

HELMER   That you don't love me any longer.

NORA   No, that's exactly it.

HELMER   Nora! How can you say this to me?

NORA   Oh, Torvald, it hurts me terribly to have to say it, because you've always been so kind to me. But I can't help it. I don't love you any longer.

HELMER   (controlling his emotions with difficulty) And you feel quite sure about this too?

NORA   Yes, absolutely sure. That's why I can't go on living here any longer.

HELMER   Can you also explain why I have lost your love?

NORA   Yes, I can. It happened this evening, when the miracle failed to happen. It was then that I realized you weren't the man I'd thought you to be.

HELMER   Explain more clearly. I don't understand you.

NORA   I've waited so patiently, for eight whole years—well, good heavens, I'm not such a fool as to suppose that miracles occur every day. Then this dreadful thing happened to me, and then I *knew:* "Now the miracle will take place!" When Krogstad's letter was lying out there, it never occurred to me for a moment that you would let that man trample over you. I *knew* that you would say to him: "Publish the facts to the world." And when he had done this—

HELMER   Yes, what then? When I'd exposed my wife's name to shame and scandal—

NORA   Then I was certain that you would step forward and take all the blame on yourself, and say: "I am the one who is guilty!"

HELMER   Nora!

NORA   You're thinking I wouldn't have accepted such a sacrifice from you? No, of course I wouldn't! But what would my word have counted for against yours? That was the miracle I was hoping for, and dreading. And it was to prevent it happening that I wanted to end my life.

HELMER   Nora, I would gladly work for you night and day, and endure sorrow and hardship for your sake. But no man can be expected to sacrifice his honour, even for the person he loves.

NORA   Millions of women have done it.

HELMER   Oh, you think and talk like a stupid child.

NORA   That may be. But you neither think nor talk like the man I could share my life with. Once you'd got over your fright—and you weren't frightened of what might threaten me, but only of what threatened you—once the danger was past, then as far as you were concerned it was exactly as though nothing had happened. I was your little songbird just as before—your doll whom henceforth you would take particular care to protect from the world because she was so weak and fragile. (*Gets up.*) Torvald, in that moment I realized that for eight years I had been living here with a complete stranger, and had borne him three children—! Oh, I can't bear to think of it! I could tear myself to pieces!

HELMER   (*sadly*) I see it, I see it. A gulf has indeed opened between us. Oh, but Nora—couldn't it be bridged?

NORA   As I am now, I am no wife for you.

HELMER   I have the strength to change.

NORA   Perhaps—if your doll is taken from you.

HELMER   But to be parted—to be parted from you! No, no, Nora, I can't conceive of it happening!

NORA   (*goes into the room, right*) All the more necessary that it should happen.

(*She comes back with her outdoor things and a small travelling-bag, which she puts down on a chair by the table.*)

HELMER   Nora, Nora, not now! Wait till tomorrow!

NORA   (*puts on her coat*) I can't spend the night in a strange man's house.

HELMER   But can't we live here as brother and sister, then—?

NORA   (*fastens her hat*) You know quite well it wouldn't last. (*Puts on her shawl.*) Goodbye, Torvald. I don't want to see the children. I know they're in better hands than mine. As I am now, I can be nothing to them.

HELMER   But some time, Nora—some time—?

NORA   How can I tell? I've no idea what will happen to me.

HELMER   But you are my wife, both as you are and as you will be.

NORA   Listen, Torvald. When a wife leaves her husband's house, as I'm doing now, I'm told that according to the law he is freed of any obligations towards her. In any case, I release you from any such obligations. You mustn't feel bound to me in any way, however small, just as I shall not feel bound to you. We must both be quite free. Here is your ring back. Give me mine.

HELMER   That too?

NORA   That too.

HELMER   Here it is.

NORA   Good. Well, now it's over. I'll leave the keys here. The servants know about everything to do with the house—much better than I do. Tomorrow, when I have left town. Christine will come to pack the things I brought here from home. I'll have them sent on after me.

HELMER   This is the end then! Nora, will you never think of me any more?

NORA   Yes, of course. I shall often think of you and the children and this house.

HELMER   May I write to you, Nora?

NORA   No. Never. You mustn't do that.

HELMER   But at least you must let me send you—

NORA   Nothing. Nothing.

HELMER   But if you should need help—?

NORA   I tell you, no. I don't accept things from strangers.

HELMER   Nora—can I never be anything but a stranger to you?

NORA   (*picks up her bag*) Oh, Torvald! Then the miracle of miracles would have to happen.

HELMER   The miracle of miracles?

NORA   You and I would both have to change so much that—oh, Torvald, I don't believe in miracles any longer.

HELMER   But I want to believe in them. Tell me. We should have to change so much that—?

NORA   That life between us two could become a marriage. Goodbye.

(*She goes out through the hall.*)

HELMER   (*sinks down on a chair by the door and buries his face in his hands*) Nora! Nora! (*Looks round and gets up.*) Empty! She's gone! (*A hope strikes him.*) The miracle of miracles—?

(*The street door is slammed shut downstairs.*)

George Bernard Shaw (or Bernard Shaw, or GBS), liked to compare himself with Shakespeare. His plays are unlike those of Shakespeare except in the respect of popularity. Probably at any moment someone somewhere in the world is performing a play by Shakespeare and someone else is performing a play by Shaw.

We know nothing about Shakespeare's opinions, but we know everything about Shaw's, and it is necessary to keep them in mind when we read such a play as Arms and the Man. Shaw was a Fabian Socialist, a vegetarian, a teetotaller, and a non-user of tobacco. He was also, for the most part, anti-science, opposing vivisection and the ideas contained in the theory of evolution as set forth by the Darwinian-Mendelian school of thought. In short, throughout the latter half of his long life Shaw seemed to conventional folk to be a perverse and crotchety opponent of most of the ideas that ordinary people take for granted.

Nevertheless Shaw said some things with which most people can agree. One such idea is the chief point of Arms and the Man. The play teaches us that war, "the dream of patriots and heroes," is a fraud. Shaw's protagonist, Captain Bluntschli, is a chocolate cream soldier instead of the traditional war hero of drama and fiction. (This play, incidentally, became the basis for one of the best known of all American musicals, The Chocolate Soldier.)

Shaw developed his anti-war ideas in 1894, twenty years before the beginning of World War I. Few would now disagree with him as to the hollow glories of war, not merely because of the distressing events we have experienced in the twentieth century but also because of the fact that, partly under Shaw's leadership, much of our literature has turned toward a denial of the false and naive idealism or romanticism enjoyed by the Rainas and Saranoffs of the world. Here, then, is one of the primary functions of literature: in the hands of a Shaw it can not only state for us but also sometimes anticipate an attitude toward life that is characteristic of a period.

Shaw used comic effects to bring out his ideas. One of these is ironic reversal or paradox. Another is the age-old boy-meets-girl formula that brings Bluntschli and Raina together. Others include the running gag, the threat of physical pain, stage properties such as the coat and the photograph, the hero turning out to be richer than he appears at first.

In many ways, Bernard Shaw rejuvenated drama in the English language. He used the old tricks, but he used them to make palatable the taste of his new ideas. Some of his ideas, new at the beginning of the century, are still just as alive as the old tricks. Arms and the Man, which is still being performed, is among the first modern plays to prove that one of the functions of the drama (as of all other literature) is that of calling attention to ideas, old and new.

*Arms and the Man

A PLEASANT PLAY

GEORGE BERNARD SHAW

CHARACTERS
in the order of their appearance

RAINA PETKOFF, a young Bulgarian lady
CATHERINE PETKOFF, her mother
LOUKA, Raina's maid
CAPTAIN BLUNTSCHLI, a Swiss in the Serbian army

A RUSSIAN OFFICER, in the Bulgarian army
NICOLA, the Petkoffs' manservant
MAJOR PETKOFF, Raina's father
MAJOR SERGIUS SARANOFF, Raina's fiancé

The action takes place at the home of MAJOR PETKOFF, in a small town in Bulgaria, in the years 1885 and 1886.

ACT I

(*Night: A ladys bedchamber in Bulgaria, in a small town near the Dragoman Pass, late in November in the year 1885. Through an open window with a little balcony a peak of the Balkans, wonderfully white and beautiful in the starlit snow, seems quite close at hand, though it is really miles away. The interior of the room is not like anything to be seen in the west of Europe. It is half rich Bulgarian, half cheap Viennese. Above the head of the bed, which stands against a little wall cutting off the left hand corner of the room, is a painted wooden shrine, blue and gold, with an ivory image of Christ, and a light hanging before it in a pierced metal ball suspended by three chains. The principal seat, placed towards the other side of the room and opposite the window, is a Turkish ottoman. The counterpane and hangings of the bed, the window curtains, the little carpet, and all the ornamental textile fabrics in the room are oriental and gorgeous; the paper on the walls is occidental and paltry. The washstand, against the wall on the side nearest the ottoman and window, consists of an enamelled iron basin with pail beneath it in a painted metal frame, and a single towel on the rail at the side. The dressing table, between the bed and the window, is a common pine table, covered with a cloth of many colours, with an expensive toilet mirror on it. The door is on the side nearest the bed; and there is a chest of drawers between. This chest of drawers is also covered by a variegated native cloth; and on it there is a pile of paper backed novels, a box of chocolate creams, and a miniature easel with a large photograph of an extremely handsome officer, whose lofty bearing and magnetic glance can be felt even from the portrait. The room is lighted by a candle on the chest of drawers, and another on the dressing table with a box of matches beside it*

(The window is hinged doorwise and stands wide open. Outside, a pair of wooden shutters, opening outwards, also stand open. On the balcony a young lady, intensely conscious of the romantic beauty of the night, and of the fact that her own youth and beauty are part of it, is gazing at the snowy Balkans. She is in her nightgown, well covered by a long mantle of furs, worth, on a moderate estimate, about three times the furniture of the room.

(Her reverie is interrupted by her mother, CATHERINE PETKOFF, a woman over forty, imperiously energetic, with magnificent black hair and eyes, who might be a very splendid specimen of the wife of a mountain farmer, but is determined to be a Viennese lady, and to that end wears a fashionable tea gown on all occasions.)

CATHERINE   *(entering hastily, full of good news)* Raina! *(She pronounces it Rah-eena, with the stress on the ee.)* Raina! *(She goes to the bed, expecting to find RAINA there.)* Why, where—? *(RAINA looks into the room.)* Heavens, child! are you out in the night air instead of in your bed? You'll catch your death. Louka told me you were asleep.

RAINA   *(dreamily)* I sent her away. I wanted to be alone. The stars are so beautiful! What is the matter?

CATHERINE   Such news! There has been a battle.

RAINA   *(her eyes dilating)* Ah! *(She comes eagerly to CATHERINE.)*

CATHERINE   A great battle at Slivnitza! A victory! And it was won by Sergius.

RAINA   *(with a cry of delight)* Ah! *(They embrace rapturously.)* Oh, mother! *(then, with sudden anxiety)* Is father safe?

CATHERINE   Of course! he sends me the news. Sergius is the hero of the hour, the idol of the regiment.

RAINA   Tell me, tell me. How was it? *(ecstatically)* Oh, mother! mother! mother! *(She pulls her mother down on the ottoman; and they kiss one another frantically.)*

CATHERINE   *(with surging enthusiasm)* You cant guess how splendid it is. A cavalry charge! think of that! He defied our Russian commanders—acted without orders—led a charge on his own responsibility—headed it himself— was the first man to sweep through their guns. Cant you see it, Raina: our gallant splendid Bulgarians with their swords and eyes flashing, thundering down like an avalanche and scattering the wretched Serbs and their dandified Austrian officers like chaff. And you! you kept Sergius waiting a year before you would be betrothed to him. Oh, if you have a drop of Bulgarian blood in your veins, you will worship him when he comes back.

RAINA   What will he care for my poor little worship after the acclamations of a whole army of heroes? But no matter: I am so happy! So proud! *(She rises and walks about excitedly.)* It proves that all our ideas were real after all.

CATHERINE   *(indignantly)* Our ideas real! What do you mean?

RAINA   Our ideas of what Sergius would do. Our patriotism. Our heroic ideals. I sometimes used to doubt whether they were anything but dreams. Oh, what faithless little creatures girls are! When I buckled on Sergius's sword he looked so noble: it was treason to think of disillusion or humiliation or failure. And yet—and yet—(*She sits down again suddenly.*) Promise me you'll never tell him.

CATHERINE Dont ask me for promises until I know what I'm promising.

RAINA Well, it came into my head just as he was holding me in his arms and looking into my eyes, that perhaps we only had our heroic ideas because we are so fond of reading Byron and Pushkin, and because we were so delighted with the opera that season at Bucharest. Real life is so seldom like that; indeed never, as far as I knew it then. (*remorsefully*) Only think, mother: I doubted him: I wondered whether all his heroic qualities and his soldiership might not prove mere imagination when he went into a real battle. I had an uneasy fear that he might cut a poor figure there beside all those clever officers from the Tsar's court.

CATHERINE A poor figure! Shame on you! The Serbs have Austrian officers who are just as clever as the Russians; but we have beaten them in every battle for all that.

RAINA (*laughing and snuggling against her mother*) Yes: I was only a prosaic little coward. Oh, to think that it was all true! that Sergius is just as splendid and noble as he looks! that the world is really a glorious world for women who can see its glory and men who can act its romance! What happiness! what unspeakable fulfilment!

(*They are interrupted by the entry of* LOUKA, *a handsome proud girl in a pretty Bulgarian peasant's dress with double apron, so defiant that her servility to* RAINA *is almost insolent. She is afraid of* CATHERINE, *but even with her goes as far as she dares.*)

LOUKA If you please, madam, all the windows are to be closed and the shutters made fast. They say there may be shooting in the streets. (RAINA *and* CATHERINE *rise together, alarmed.*) The Serbs are being chased right back through the pass; and they say they may run into the town. Our cavalry will be after them; and our people will be ready for them, you may be sure, now theyre running away. (*She goes out on the balcony, and pulls the outside shutters to; then steps back into the room.*)

CATHERINE (*businesslike, housekeeping instincts aroused*) I must see that everything is made safe downstairs.

RAINA I wish our people were not so cruel. What glory is there in killing wretched fugitives?

CATHERINE Cruel! Do you suppose they would hesitate to kill you, or worse?

RAINA (*to* LOUKA) Leave the shutters so that I can just close them if I hear any noise.

CATHERINE (*authoritatively, turning on her way to the door*) Oh no, dear: you must keep them fastened. You would be sure to drop off to sleep and leave them open. Make them fast, Louka.

LOUKA Yes, madam. (*She fastens them.*)

RAINA Dont be anxious about me. The moment I hear a shot, I shall blow out the candles and roll myself up in bed with my ears well covered.

CATHERINE Quite the wisest thing you can do, my love. Goodnight.

RAINA Goodnight. (*Her emotion comes back for a moment.*) Wish me joy. (*They kiss.*) This is the happiest night of my life—if only there are no fugitives.

CATHERINE   Go to bed, dear; and dont think of them. (*She goes out.*)

LOUKA   (*secretly to* RAINA) If you would like the shutters open, just give them a push like this (*she pushes them: they open: she pulls them to again.*) One of them ought to be bolted at the bottom; but the bolt's gone.

RAINA   (*with dignity, reproving her*) Thanks, Louka; but we must do what we are told. (LOUKA *makes a grimace.*) Goodnight.

LOUKA (*carelessly*) Goodnight. (*She goes out, swaggering.*)

(RAINA, *left alone, takes off her fur cloak and throws it on the ottoman. Then she goes to the chest of drawers, and adores the portrait there with feelings that are beyond all expression. She does not kiss it or press it to her breast, or shew it any mark of bodily affection; but she takes it in her hands and elevates it, like a priestess.*)

RAINA   (*looking up at the picture*) Oh, I shall never be unworthy of you any more, my soul's hero; never, never, never. (*She replaces it reverently. Then she selects a novel from the little pile of books. She turns over the leaves dreamily; finds her page; turns the book inside out at it; and, with a happy sigh, gets into bed and prepares to read herself to sleep. But before abandoning herself to fiction, she raises her eyes once more, thinking of the blessed reality, and murmurs*) My hero! my hero!

(*A distant shot breaks the quiet of the night. She starts listening; and two more shots, much nearer, follow, startling her so that she scrambles out of bed, and hastily blows out the candle on the chest of drawers. Then, putting her fingers in her ears, she runs to the dressing table, blows out the light there, and hurries back to bed in the dark, nothing being visible but the glimmer of the light in the pierced ball before the image, and the starlight seen through the slits at the top of the shutters. The firing breaks out again: there is a startling fusillade quite close at hand. Whilst it is still echoing, the shutters disappear, pulled open from without; and for an instant the rectangle of snowy starlight flashes out with the figure of a man silhouetted in black upon it. The shutters close immediately; and the room is dark again. But the silence is now broken by the sound of panting. Then there is a scratch; and the flame of a match is seen in the middle of the room.*)

RAINA   (*crouching on the bed*) Who's there? (*The match is out instantly.*) Who's there? Who is that?

A MAN'S VOICE   (*in the darkness, subduedly, but threateningly*) Sh—sh! Dont call out; or youll be shot. Be good; and no harm will happen to you. (*She is heard leaving her bed, and making for the door.*) Take care: it's no use trying to run away.

RAINA   But who—

THE VOICE   (*warning*) Remember: if you raise your voice my revolver will go off. (*commandingly*) Strike a light and let me see you. Do you hear. (*Another moment of silence and darkness as she retreats to the chest of drawers. Then she lights a candle; and the mystery is at an end. He is a man of about 35, in a deplorable plight, bespattered with mud and blood and snow, his belt and the strap of his revolver case keeping together the torn ruins of the blue tunic of a Serbian artillery officer. All that the candle-light and his unwashed unkempt condition make it possible to discern is that he is of middling stature and undistinguished appearance, with strong neck and shoulders, roundish obstinate looking head covered with short crisp bronze curls, clear quick eyes and good brows and mouth, hopelessly*

*prosaic nose like that of a strong minded baby, trim soldierlike carriage
and energetic manner, and with all his wits about him in spite of his desperate
predicament: even with a sense of the humor of it, without, however, the
least intention of trifling with it or throwing away a chance. Reckoning up
what he can guess about* RAINA: *her age, her social position, her character,
and the extent to which she is frightened, he continues, more politely but
still most determinedly.*) Excuse my disturbing you; but you recognize my
uniform? Serb! If I'm caught I shall be killed. (*menacingly*) Do you understand that?

RAINA Yes.

THE MAN Well, I dont intend to get killed if I can help it. (*still more formidably.*) Do you understand that? (*He locks the door quickly but quietly.*)

RAINA (*disdainfully*) I suppose not. (*She draws herself up superbly, and looks
him straight in the face, adding, with cutting emphasis*) Some soldiers, I
know, are afraid to die.

THE MAN (*with grim goodhumour*) All of them, dear lady, all of them, believe
me. It is our duty to live as long as we can. Now, if you raise an alarm—

RAINA (*cutting him short*) You will shoot me. How do you know that *I* am
afraid to die?

THE MAN (*cunningly*) Ah; but suppose I dont shoot you, what will happen
then? A lot of your cavalry will burst into this pretty room of yours and
slaughter me here like a pig; for I'll fight like a demon: they shant get me
into the street to amuse themselves with: I know what they are. Are you prepared to receive that sort of company in your present undress? (RAINA,
*suddenly conscious of her nightgown, instinctively shrinks and gathers it
more closely about her neck. He watches her and adds pitilessly*) Hardly
presentable, eh? (*She turns to the ottoman. He raises his pistol instantly,
and cries.*) Stop! (*She stops.*) Where are you going?

RAINA (*with dignified patience*) Only to get my cloak.

THE MAN (*passing swiftly to the ottoman and snatching the cloak*) A good
idea! I'll keep the cloak; and youll take care that nobody comes in and
sees you without it. This is a better weapon than the revolver: eh? (*He
throws the pistol down on the ottoman.*)

RAINA (*revolted*) It is not the weapon of a gentleman!

THE MAN It's good enough for a man with only you to stand between him
and death. (*As they look at one another for a moment,* RAINA *hardly able
to believe that even a Serbian officer can be so cynically and selfishly
unchivalrous, they are startled by a sharp fusillade in the street. The chill
of imminent death hushes the man's voice as he adds*) Do you hear? If you
are going to bring those blackguards in on me you shall receive them
as you are.

(*Clamor and disturbance. The pursuers in the street batter at the house door, shouting*
Open the door! Open the door! Wake up, will you! *A man servant's voice calls to them
angrily from within* This is Major Petkoff's house: you cant come in here; *but a renewal
of the clamor, and a torrent of blows on the door end with his letting a chain down with
a clank, followed by a rush of heavy footsteps and a din of triumphant yells, dominated
at last by the voice of* CATHERINE, *indignantly addressing an officer with* What does this
mean, sir? Do you know where you are? *The noise subsides suddenly.*)

GEORGE BERNARD SHAW / Arms and the Man   **865**

LOUKA (*outside, knocking at the bedroom door*) My lady! get up quick and open the door. If you dont they will break it down.

(*The fugitive throws up his head with the gesture of a man who sees that it is all over with him, and drops the manner he has been assuming to intimidate RAINA.*)

THE MAN *(sincerely and kindly) No use, dear:* I'm done for. (*flinging the cloak to her*) Quick! wrap yourself up: theyre coming.

RAINA Oh, thank you. (*She wraps herself up with intense relief.*)

THE MAN (*between his teeth*) Dont mention it.

RAINA (*anxiously*) What will you do?

THE MAN (*grimly*) The first man in will find out. Keep out of the way; and dont look. It wont last long; but it will not be nice. (*He draws his sabre and faces the door, waiting.*)

RAINA (*impulsively*) I'll help you. I'll save you.

THE MAN You cant.

RAINA I can. I'll hide you. (*She drags him towards the window.*) Here! behind the curtains.

THE MAN (*yielding to her*) Theres just half a chance, if you keep your head.

RAINA (*drawing the curtain before him*) S-sh! (*She makes for the ottoman.*)

THE MAN (*putting out his head*) Remember—

RAINA (*running back to him*) Yes?

THE MAN —nine soldiers out of ten are born fools.

RAINA Oh! (*She draws the curtain angrily before him.*)

THE MAN (*looking out at the other side*) If they find me, I promise you a fight: a devil of a fight.

(*She stamps at him. He disappears hastily. She takes off her cloak, and throws it across the foot of the bed. Then, with a sleepy, disturbed air, she opens the door. LOUKA enters excitedly.*)

LOUKA One of those beasts of Serbs has been seen climbing up the water-pipe to your balcony. Our men want to search for him; and they are so wild and drunk and furious. (*She makes for the other side of the room to get as far from the door as possible.*) My lady says you are to dress at once and to—(*She sees the revolver lying on the ottoman, and stops, petrified.*)

RAINA (*as if annoyed at being disturbed*) They shall not search here. Why have they been let in?

CATHERINE (*coming in hastily*) Raina, darling, are you safe? Have you seen anyone or heard anything?

RAINA I heard the shooting. Surely the soldiers will not dare come in here?

CATHERINE I have found a Russian officer, thank Heaven: he knows Sergius. (*speaking through the door to someone outside*) Sir: will you come in now. My daughter will receive you.

(*A Young Russian officer, in Bulgarian uniform, enters, sword in hand.*)

OFFICER (*with soft feline politeness and stiff military carriage*) Good evening, gracious lady. I am sorry to intrude; but there is a Serb hiding on the balcony. Will you and the gracious lady your mother please to withdraw whilst we search?

RAINA (*petulantly*) Nonsense, sir: you can see that there is no one on the balcony. (*She throws the shutters wide open and stands with her back to the curtain where the man is hidden, pointing to the moonlit balcony. A couple of shots are fired under the window; and a bullet shatters the glass opposite* RAINA, *who winks and gasps, but stands her ground; whilst* CATHERINE *screams, and the* OFFICER, *with a cry of* Take care! *rushes to the balcony.*)

THE OFFICER   (*on the balcony, shouting savagely down to the street*) Cease firing there, you fools: do you hear? Cease firing, damn you! (*He glares down for a moment; then turns to* RAINA, *trying to resume his polite manner.*) Could anyone have got in without your knowledge? Were you asleep?

RAINA   No: I have not been to bed.

THE OFFICER   (*impatiently, coming back into the room*) Your neighbors have their heads so full of runaway Serbs that they see them everywhere. (*politely*) Gracious lady: a thousand pardons. Goodnight. (*Military bow, which* RAINA *returns coldly. Another to* CATHERINE, *who follows him out.*)

(RAINA *closes the shutters. She turns and sees* LOUKA, *who has been watching the scene curiously.*)

RAINA   Dont leave my mother, Louka, until the soldiers go away.

(LOUKA *glances at* RAINA, *at the ottoman, at the curtain; then purses her lips secretively, laughs insolently, and goes out.* RAINA, *highly offended by this demonstration, follows her to the door, and shuts it behind her with a slam, locking it violently. The man immediately steps out from behind the curtain, sheathing his sabre. Then, dismissing the danger from his mind in a businesslike way, he comes affably to* RAINA.)

THE MAN   A narrow shave; but a miss is as good as a mile. Dear young lady: your servant to the death. I wish for your sake I had joined the Bulgarian army instead of the other one. I am not a native Serb.

RAINA   (*haughtily*) No: you are one of the Austrians who set the Serbs on to rob us of our national liberty, and who officer their army for them. We hate them!

THE MAN   Austrian! not I. Dont hate me, dear young lady. I am Swiss, fighting merely as a professional soldier. I joined the Serbs because they came first on the road from Switzerland. Be generous: you've beaten us hollow.

RAINA   Have I not been generous?

THE MAN   Noble! Heroic! But I'm not saved yet. This particular rush will soon pass through; but the pursuit will go on all night by fits and starts. I must take my chance to get off in a quiet interval. (*pleasantly*) You dont mind my waiting just a minute or two, do you?

RAINA   (*putting on her most genteel society manner*) Oh, not at all. Wont you sit down?

THE MAN   Thanks (*He sits on the foot of the bed.*)

(RAINA *walks with studied elegance to the ottoman and sits down. Unfortunately she sits on the pistol, and jumps up with a shriek. The man, all nerves, shies like a frightened horse to the other side of the room.*)

THE MAN   (*irritably*) Dont frighten me like that. What is it?

RAINA   Your revolver! It was staring that officer in the face all the time. What an escape!

THE MAN   (*vexed at being unnecessarily terrified*) Oh, is that all?

RAINA (*staring at him rather superciliously as she conceives a poorer and poorer opinion of him, and feels proportionately more and more at ease*) I am sorry I frightened you. (*She takes up the pistol and hands it to him.*) Pray take it to protect yourself against me.

THE MAN (*grinning wearily at the sarcasm as he takes the pistol*) No use, dear young lady: theres nothing in it. It's not loaded. (*He makes a grimace at it, and drops it disparagingly into his revolver case.*)

RAINA Load it by all means.

THE MAN Ive no ammunition. What use are cartridges in battle? I always carry chocolate instead; and I finished the last cake of that hours ago.

RAINA (*outraged in her most cherished ideals of manhood*) Chocolate! Do you stuff your pockets with sweets—like a schoolboy—even in the field?

THE MAN (*grinning*) Yes: isnt it contemptible? (*hungrily*) I wish I had some now.

RAINA Allow me. (*She sails away scornfully to the chest of drawers, and returns with the box of confectionery in her hand.*) I am sorry I have eaten them all except these. (*She offers him the box.*)

THE MAN (*ravenously*) Youre an angel! (*He gobbles the contents.*) Creams! Delicious! (*He looks anxiously to see whether there are any more. There are none: he can only scrape the box with his fingers and suck them. When that nourishment is exhausted he accepts the inevitable with pathetic good-humor, and says, with grateful emotion*) Bless you, dear lady! You can always tell an old soldier by the inside of his holsters and cartridge boxes. The young ones carry pistols and cartridges: the old ones, grub. Thank you. (*He hands back the box. She snatches it contemptuously from him and throws it away. He shies again, as if she had meant to strike him.*) Ugh! Dont do things so suddenly, gracious lady. It's mean to revenge yourself because I frightened you just now.

RAINA (*loftily*) Frighten me! Do you know, sir, that though I am only a woman, I think I am at heart as brave as you.

THE MAN I should think so. You havnt been under fire for three days as I have. I can stand two days without shewing it much; but no man can stand three days: I'm as nervous as a mouse. (*He sits down on the ottoman, and takes his head in his hands.*) Would you like to see me cry?

RAINA (*alarmed*) No.

THE MAN If you would, all you have to do is scold me just as if I were a little boy and you my nurse. If I were in camp now, theyd play all sorts of tricks on me.

RAINA (*a little moved*) I'm sorry. I wont scold you. (*Touched by the sympathy in her tone, he raises his head and looks gratefully at her: she immediately draws back and says stiffly*) You must excuse me: our soldiers are not like that. (*She moves away from the ottoman.*)

THE MAN Oh yes they are. There are only two sorts of soldiers: old ones and young ones. Ive served fourteen years: half of your fellows never smelt powder before. Why, how is it that youve beaten us? Sheer ignorance of the art of war, nothing else. (*indignantly*) I never saw anything so unprofessional.

RAINA (*ironically*) Oh! was it unprofessional to beat you?

THE MAN Well, come! is it professional to throw a regiment of cavalry on a battery of machine guns, with the dead certainty that if the guns go off not a horse or man will ever get within fifty yards of the fire? I couldnt believe my eyes when I saw it.

RAINA (*eagerly turning to him, as all her enthusiasm and her dreams of glory rush back on her*) Did you see the great cavalry charge? Oh, tell me about it. Describe it to me.

THE MAN You never saw a cavalry charge, did you?

RAINA How could I?

THE MAN Ah, perhaps not. No: of course not! Well, it's a funny sight. It's like slinging a handful of peas against a window pane: first one comes; then two or three close behind him; and then all the rest in a lump.

RAINA (*her eyes dilating as she raises her clasped hands ecstatically*) Yes, first One! the bravest of the brave!

THE MAN (*prosaically*) Hm! you should see the poor devil pulling at his horse.

RAINA Why should he pull at his horse?

THE MAN (*impatient of so stupid a question*) It's running away with him, of course: do you suppose the fellow wants to get there before the others and be killed? Then they all come. You can tell the young ones by their wildness and their slashing. The old ones come bunched up under the number one guard: they know that theyre mere projectiles, and that it's no use trying to fight. The wounds are mostly broken knees, from the horses cannoning together.

RAINA Ugh! But I dont believe the first man is a coward. I know he is a hero!

THE MAN (*goodhumoredly*) Thats what youd have said if youd seen the first man in the charge today.

RAINA (*breathless, forgiving him everything*) Ah, I knew it! Tell me. Tell me about him.

THE MAN He did it like an operatic tenor. A regular handsome fellow, with flashing eyes and lovely moustache, shouting his warcry and charging like Don Quixote at the windmills. We did laugh.

RAINA You dared to laugh!

THE MAN Yes; but when the sergeant ran up as white as a sheet, and told us theyd sent us the wrong ammunition, and that we couldnt fire a round for the next ten minutes, we laughed at the other side of our mouths. I never felt so sick in my life; though Ive been in one or two very tight places. And I hadnt even a revolver cartridge: only chocolate. We'd no bayonets: nothing. Of course, they just cut us to bits. And there was Don Quixote flourishing like a drum major, thinking he'd done the cleverest thing ever known, whereas he ought to be courtmartialled for it. Of all the fools ever let loose on a field of battle, that man must be the very maddest. He and his regiment simply committed suicide; only the pistol missed fire: thats all.

RAINA (*deeply wounded, but steadfastly loyal to her ideals*) Indeed! Would you know him again if you saw him?

THE MAN Shall I ever forget him!

(*She goes to the chest of drawers. He watches her with a vague hope that she may have something more for him to eat. She takes the portrait from its stand and brings it to him.*)

RAINA   That is a photograph of the gentleman—the patriot and hero—to whom I am betrothed.

THE MAN   (*recognizing it with a shock*) I'm really very sorry. (*Looking at her*) Was it fair to lead me on? (*He looks at the portrait again.*) Yes: thats Don Quixote: not a doubt of it. (*He stifles a laugh.*)

RAINA   (*quickly*) Why do you laugh?

THE MAN   (*apologetic, but still greatly tickled*) I didnt laugh, I assure you. At least I didnt mean to. But when I think of him charging the windmills and imagining he was doing the finest thing—(*He chokes with suppressed laughter.*)

RAINA   (*sternly*) Give me back the portrait, sir.

THE MAN   (*with sincere remorse*) Of course. Certainly. I'm really very sorry. (*He hands her the picture. She deliberately kisses it and looks him straight in the face before returning to the chest of drawers to replace it. He follows her, apologizing.*) Perhaps I'm quite wrong, you know: no doubt I am. Most likely he had got wind of the cartridge business somehow, and knew it was a safe job.

RAINA   That is to say, he was a pretender and a coward! You did not dare say that before.

THE MAN   (*with a comic gesture of despair*) It's no use, dear lady: I cant make you see it from the professional point of view. (*As he turns away to get back to the ottoman, a couple of distant shots threaten renewed trouble.*)

RAINA   (*sternly, as she sees him listening to the shots*) So much the better for you!

THE MAN   (*turning*) How?

RAINA   You are my enemy; and you are at my mercy. What would I do if I were a professional soldier?

THE MAN   Ah, true, dear young lady: youre always right. I know how good youve been to me: to my last hour I shall remember those three chocolate creams. It was unsoldierly; but it was angelic.

RAINA   (*coldly*) Thank you. And now I will do a soldierly thing. You cannot stay here after what you have just said about my future husband; but I will go out on the balcony and see whether it is safe for you to climb down into the street. (*She turns to the window.*)

THE MAN   (*changing countenance*) Down that waterpipe! Stop! Wait! I cant! I darent! The very thought of it makes me giddy. I came up it fast enough with death behind me. But to face it now in cold blood—! (*He sinks on the ottoman.*) It's no use: I give up: I'm beaten. Give the alarm. (*He drops his head on his hands in the deepest dejection.*)

RAINA   (*disarmed by pity*) Come: dont be disheartened. (*She stoops over him almost maternally: he shakes his head.*) Oh, you are a very poor soldier: a chocolate cream soldier! Come, cheer up! it takes less courage to climb down than to face capture: remember that.

THE MAN   (*dreamily, lulled by her voice*) No: capture only means death; and death is sleep: oh, sleep, sleep, sleep, undisturbed sleep! Climbing down the pipe means doing something—exerting myself—thinking! Death ten times over first.

RAINA (*softly and wonderingly, catching the rhythm of his weariness*) Are you as sleepy as that?

THE MAN Ive not had two hours undisturbed sleep since I joined. I havnt closed my eyes for forty-eight hours.

RAINA (*at her wit's end*) But what am I to do with you?

THE MAN (*staggering up, roused by her desperation*) Of course. I must do something. (*He shakes himself; pulls himself together; and speaks with rallied vigor and courage.*) You see, sleep or no sleep, hunger or no hunger, tired or not tired, you can always do a thing when you know it must be done. Well, that pipe must be got down: (*he hits himself on the chest*) do you hear that, you chocolate cream soldier? (*He turns to the window.*)

RAINA (*anxiously*) But if you fail?

THE MAN I shall sleep as if the stones were a feather bed. Goodbye. (*He makes boldly for the window; and his hand is on the shutter when there is a terrible burst of firing in the street beneath.*)

RAINA (*rushing to him*) Stop! (*She seizes him recklessly, and pulls him quite round.*) Theyll kill you.

THE MAN (*coolly, but attentively*) Never mind: this sort of thing is all in my day's work. I'm bound to take my chance. (*decisively*) Now do what I tell you. Put out the candle; so that they shant see the light when I open the shutters. And keep away from the window, whatever you do. If they see me theyre sure to have a shot at me.

RAINA (*clinging to him*) Theyre sure to see you: it's bright moonlight. I'll save you. Oh how can you be so indifferent! You want me to save you, don't you?

THE MAN I really dont want to be troublesome. (*She shakes him in her impatience.*) I am not indifferent, dear young lady, I assure you. But how is it to be done?

RAINA Come away from the window. (*She takes him firmly back to the middle of the room. The moment she releases him he turns mechanically towards the window again. She seizes him and turns him back, exclaiming.*) Please! (*He becomes motionless, like a hypnotized rabbit, his fatigue gaining fast on him. She releases him, and addresses him patronizingly.*) Now listen. You must trust to our hospitality. You do not yet know in whose house you are. I am a Petkoff.

THE MAN A pet what?

RAINA (*rather indignantly*) I mean that I belong to the family of the Petkoffs, the richest and best known in our country.

THE MAN Oh yes, of course. I beg your pardon. The Petkoffs, to be sure. How stupid of me!

RAINA You know you never heard of them until this moment. How can you stoop to pretend!

THE MAN Forgive me: I'm too tired to think; and the change of subject was too much for me. Dont scold me.

RAINA I forgot. It might make you cry. (*He nods, quite seriously. She pouts and then resumes her patronizing tone.*) I must tell you that my father holds the highest command of any Bulgarian in our army. He is (*proudly*) a Major.

THE MAN   (*pretending to be deeply impressed*) A Major! Bless me! Think of that!

RAINA   You shewed great ignorance in thinking it was necessary to climb up to the balcony because ours is the only private house that has two rows of windows. There is a flight of stairs inside to get up and down by.

THE MAN   Stairs! How grand! You live in great luxury indeed, dear young lady.

RAINA   Do you know what a library is?

THE MAN   A library? A roomful of books?

RAINA   Yes. We have one, the only one in Bulgaria.

THE MAN   Actually a real library! I should like to see that.

RAINA   (*affectedly*) I tell you these things to shew you that you are not in the house of ignorant country folk who would kill you the moment they saw your Serbian uniform, but among civilized people. We go to Bucharest every year for the opera season; and I have spent a whole month in Vienna.

THE MAN   I saw that, dear young lady. I saw at once that you knew the world.

RAINA   Have you ever seen the opera of Ernani?

THE MAN   Is that the one with the devil in it in red velvet, and a soldiers' chorus?

RAINA   (*contemptuously*) No!

THE MAN   (*stifling a heavy sigh of weariness*) Then I dont know it.

RAINA   I thought you might have remembered the great scene where Ernani, flying from his foes just as you are tonight, takes refuge in the castle of his bitterest enemy, an old Castilian noble. The noble refuses to give him up. His guest is sacred to him.

THE MAN   (*quickly, waking up a little*) Have you people got that notion?

RAINA   (*with dignity*) My mother and I can understand that notion, as you call it. And if instead of threatening me with your pistol as you did you had simply thrown yourself as a fugitive on our hospitality, you would have been as safe as in your father's house.

THE MAN   Quite sure?

RAINA   (*turning her back on him in disgust*) Oh, it is useless to try to make you understand.

THE MAN   Dont be angry: you see how awkward it would be for me if there was any mistake. My father is a very hospitable man: he keeps six hotels; but I couldnt trust him as far as that. What about your father?

RAINA   He is away at Slivnitza fighting for his country. I answer for your safety. There is my hand in pledge of it. Will that reassure you? (*She offers him her hand.*)

THE MAN   (*looking dubiously at his own hand*) Better not touch my hand, dear young lady. I must have a wash first.

RAINA   (*touched*) That is very nice of you. I see that you are a gentleman.

THE MAN   (*puzzled*) Eh?

RAINA   You must not think I am surprised. Bulgarians of really good standing —people in our position—wash their hands nearly every day. So you see I can appreciate your delicacy. You may take my hand. (*She offers it again.*)

THE MAN   (*kissing it with his hands behind his back*) Thanks, gracious young lady: I feel safe at last. And now would you mind breaking the news to your mother? I had better not stay here secretly longer than is necessary.

RAINA   If you will be so good as to keep perfectly still whilst I am away.

THE MAN   Certainly. (*He sits down on the ottoman.*)

(RAINA *goes to the bed and wraps herself in the fur cloak. His eyes close. She goes to the door. Turning for a fast look at him, she sees that he is dropping off to sleep.*)

RAINA   (*at the door*) You are not going asleep, are you? (*He murmurs inarticulately: she runs to him and shakes him.*) Do you hear? Wake up: you are falling asleep.

THE MAN   Eh? Falling aslee—? Oh no: not the least in the world: I was only thinking. It's all right: I'm wide awake.

RAINA   (*severely*) Will you please stand up while I am away. (*He rises reluctantly.*) All the time, mind.

THE MAN   (*standing unsteadily*) Certainly. Certainly: you may depend on me.

(RAINA *looks doubtfully at him. He smiles weakly. She goes reluctantly, turning again at the door, and almost catching him in the act of yawning. She goes out.*)

THE MAN   (*drowsily*) Sleep, sleep, sleep, sleep, slee—(*The words trail off into a murmur. He wakes again with a shock on the point of falling.*) Where am I? Thats what I want to know: where am I? Must keep awake. Nothing keeps me awake except danger: remember that: (*trailing off again: another shock*) Wheres danger? Mus' find it. (*He starts off vaguely round the room in search of it.*) What am I looking for? Sleep—danger—dont know. (*He stumbles against the bed.*) Ah yes: now I know. All right now. I'm to go to bed, but not to sleep. Be sure not to sleep, because of danger. Not to lie down either, only sit down. (*He sits on the bed. A blissful expression comes into his face.*) Ah! (*With a happy sigh he sinks back at full length; lifts his boots into the bed with a final effort; and falls fast asleep instantly.*)

(CATHERINE *comes in, followed by* RAINA.)

RAINA   (*looking at the ottoman*) He's gone! I left him here.

CATHERINE   Here! Then he must have climbed down from the—

RAINA   (*seeing him*) Oh! (*She points.*)

CATHERINE   (*scandalized*) Well! (*She strides to the bed, Raina following until she is opposite her on the other side.*) He's fast asleep. The brute!

RAINA   (*anxiously*) Sh!

CATHERINE   (*shaking him*) Sir! (*shaking him again, harder*) Sir! (*vehemently, shaking very hard*) Sir!!!

RAINA   (*catching her arm*) Dont, mamma; the poor darling is worn out. Let him sleep.

CATHERINE   (*letting him go, and turning amazed to* RAINA) The poor darling! Raina!!! (*She looks sternly at her daughter.*)

(*The man sleeps profoundly.*)

ACT II

(*The sixth of March, 1886. In the garden of Major Petkoff's house. It is a fine spring morning: the garden looks fresh and pretty. Beyond the paling the tops of a couple of minarets can be seen, shewing that there is a valley there, with the little town in it. A few miles further the Balkan mountains rise and shut in the landscape. Looking towards them from within the garden, the side of the house is seen on the left, with a garden door reached by a little flight of steps. On the right the stable yard, with its gateway, encroaches on the garden. There are fruit bushes along the paling and house, covered with washing spread out to dry. A path runs by the house, and rises by two steps at the corner, where it turns out of sight. In the middle, a small table, with two bent wood chairs at it, is laid for breakfast with Turkish coffee pot, cups, rolls, etc.; but the cups have been used and the bread broken. There is a wooden garden seat against the wall on the right.*)

LOUKA, *smoking a cigaret, is standing between the table and the house, turning her back with angry disdain on a man servant who is lecturing her. He is a middle-aged man of cool temperament and low but clear and keen intelligence, with the complacency of the servant who values himself on his rank in servitude, and the imperturbability of the accurate calculator who has no illusions. He wears a white Bulgarian costume: jacket with embroidered border, sash, wide knickerbockers, and decorated gaiters. His head is shaved up to the crown, giving him a high Japanese forehead. His name is NICOLA.*)

NICOLA   Be warned in time, Louka: mend your manners. I know the mistress. She is so grand that she never dreams that any servant could dare be disrespectful to her; but if she once suspects that you are defying her, out you go.

LOUKA   I do defy her. I will defy her. What do I care for her?

NICOLA   If you quarrel with the family, I never can marry you. It's the same as if you quarrelled with me!

LOUKA   You take her part against me, do you?

NICOLA   (*sedately*) I shall always be dependent on the good will of the family. When I leave their service and start a shop in Sofia, their custom will be half my capital: their bad word would ruin me.

LOUKA   You have no spirit. I should like to catch them saying a word against me!

NICOLA   (*pityingly*) I should have expected more sense from you, Louka. But youre young: youre young!

LOUKA   Yes; and you like me the better for it, dont you? But I know some family secrets they wouldnt care to have told, young as I am. Let them quarrel with me if they dare!

NICOLA   (*with compassionate superiority*) Do you know what they would do if they heard you talk like that?

LOUKA   What could they do?

NICOLA   Discharge you for untruthfulness. Who would believe any stories you told after that? Who would give you another situation? Who in this house would dare be seen speaking to you ever again? How long would your father be left on his little farm? (*She impatiently throws away the end of her cigaret, and stamps on it.*) Child: you dont know the power such high people have over the like of you and me when we try to rise out of our poverty against them. (*He goes close to her and lowers his voice.*) Look at me, ten years in their service. Do you think I know no secrets? I know things about the mistress that she wouldnt have the master know for a thousand levas. I know things about him that she wouldnt let him hear the last of for six months if I blabbed them to her. I know things about Raina that would break off her match with Sergius if—

LOUKA (*turning on him quickly*) How do you know? I never told you!

NICOLA (*opening his eyes cunningly*) So thats your little secret, is it? I thought it might be something like that. Well, you take my advice and be respectful; and make the mistress feel that no matter what you know or dont know, she can depend on you to hold your tongue and serve the family faithfully. Thats what they like; and thats how youll make most out of them.

LOUKA (*with searching scorn*) You have the soul of a servant, Nicola.

NICOLA (*complacently*) Yes: thats the secret of success in service.

(*A loud knocking with a whip handle on a wooden door is heard from the stable yard.*)

MALE VOICE OUTSIDE Hollo! Hollo there! Nicola!

LOUKA Master! back from the war!

NICOLA (*quickly*) My word for it, Louka, the war's over. Off with you and get some fresh coffee. (*He runs out into the stable yard.*)

LOUKA (*as she collects the coffee pot and cups on the tray, and carries it into the house*) Youll never put the soul of a servant into me.

(MAJOR PETKOFF *comes from the stable yard, followed by* NICOLA. *He is a cheerful, excitable, insignificant, unpolished man of about 50, naturally unambitious except as to his income and his importance in local society, but just now greatly pleased with the military rank which the war has thrust on him as a man of consequence in his town. The fever of plucky patriotism which the Serbian attack roused in all the Bulgarians has pulled him through the war; but he is obviously glad to be home again.*)

PETKOFF (*pointing to the table with his whip*) Breakfast out here, eh?

NICOLA Yes, sir. The mistress and Miss Raina have just gone in.

PETKOFF (*sitting down and taking a roll*) Go in and say Ive come; and get me some fresh coffee.

NICOLA It's coming, sir. (*He goes to the house door.* LOUKA, *with fresh coffee, a clean cup, and a brandy bottle on her tray, meets him.*) Have you told the mistress?

LOUKA Yes: she's coming.

(NICOLA *goes into the house.* LOUKA *brings the coffee to the table.*)

PETKOFF Well: the Serbs havnt run away with you, have they?

LOUKA No, sir.

PETKOFF Thats right. Have you brought me some cognac?

LOUKA (*putting the bottle on the table*) Here, sir.

PETKOFF Thats right. (*He pours some into his coffee.*)

(CATHERINE, *who, having at this early hour made only a very perfunctory toilet, wears a Bulgarian apron over a once brilliant but now half worn-out dressing gown, and a colored handkerchief tied over her thick black hair, comes from the house with Turkish slippers on her bare feet, looking astonishingly handsome and stately under all the circumstances.* LOUKA *goes into the house.*)

CATHERINE My dear Paul: what a surprise for us! (*She stoops over the back of his chair to kiss him.*) Have they brought you fresh coffee?

PETKOFF   Yes: Louka's been looking after me. The war's over. The treaty was signed three days ago at Bucharest; and the decree for our army to demobilize was issued yesterday.

CATHERINE   (*springing erect, with flashing eyes*) Paul: have you let the Austrians force you to make peace?

PETKOFF   (*submissively*) My dear: they didnt consult me. What could *I* do? (*She sits down and turns away from him.*) But of course we saw to it that the treaty was an honorable one. It declares peace—

CATHERINE   (*outraged*) Peace!

PETKOFF   (*appeasing her*)—but not friendly relations: remember that. They wanted to put that in; but I insisted on its being struck out. What more could I do?

CATHERINE   You could have annexed Serbia and made Prince Alexander Emperor of the Balkans. Thats what I would have done.

PETKOFF   I dont doubt it in the least, my dear. But I should have had to subdue the whole Austrian Empire first; and that would have kept me too long away from you. I missed you greatly.

CATHERINE   (*relenting*) Ah! (*She stretches her hand affectionately across the table to squeeze his.*)

PETKOFF   And how have you been, my dear?

CATHERINE   Oh, my usual sore throats: thats all.

PETKOFF   (*with conviction*) That comes from washing your neck every day. Ive often told you so.

CATHERINE   Nonsense, Paul!

PETKOFF   (*over his coffee and cigaret*) I dont believe in going too far with these modern customs. All this washing cant be good for the health: it's not natural. There was an Englishman at Philippopolis who used to wet himself all over with cold water every morning when he got up. Disgusting! It all comes from the English: their climate makes them so dirty that they have to be perpetually washing themselves. Look at my father! he never had a bath in his life; and he lived to be ninety-eight, the healthiest man in Bulgaria. I dont mind a good wash once a week to keep up my position; but once a day is carrying the thing to a ridiculous extreme.

CATHERINE   You are a barbarian at heart still, Paul. I hope you behaved yourself before all those Russian officers.

PETKOFF   I did my best. I took care to let them know that we have a library.

CATHERINE   Ah; but you didnt tell them that we have an electric bell in it? I have had one put up.

PETKOFF   Whats an electric bell?

CATHERINE   You touch a button; something tinkles in the kitchen; and then Nicola comes up.

PETKOFF   Why not shout for him?

CATHERINE   Civilized people never shout for their servants. Ive learnt that while you were away.

PETKOFF   Well I'll tell you something Ive learnt too. Civilized people dont hang out their washing to dry where visitors can see it; so youd better have all that (*indicating the clothes on the bushes*) put somewhere else.

CATHERINE   Oh, thats absurd, Paul: I dont believe really refined people notice such things.

SERGIUS   (*knocking at the stable gates*) Gate, Nicola!

PETKOFF   Theres Sergius. (*Shouting*) Hollo, Nicola!

CATHERINE   Oh, dont shout, Paul: it really isnt nice.

PETKOFF   Bosh! (*He shouts louder than before*) Nicola!

NICOLA   (*appearing at the house door*) Yes, sir.

PETKOFF   Are you deaf? Dont you hear Major Saranoff knocking? Bring him round this way. (*He pronounces the name with the stress on the second syllable: Sarahnoff.*)

NICOLA   Yes, Major. (*He goes into the stable yard.*)

PETKOFF   You must talk to him, my dear, until Raina takes him off our hands. He bores my life out about our not promoting him. Over my head, if you please.

CATHERINE   He certainly ought to be promoted when he marries Raina. Besides, the country should insist on having at least one native general.

PETKOFF   Yes; so that he could throw away whole brigades instead of regiments. It's no use, my dear: he hasnt the slightest chance of promotion until we're quite sure that the peace will be a lasting one.

NICOLA   (*at the gate, announcing*) Major Sergius Saranoff! (*He goes into the house and returns presently with a third chair, which he places at the table. He then withdraws.*)

(MAJOR SERGIUS SARANOFF, *the original of the portrait in* RAINA's *room, is a tall romantically handsome man, with the physical hardihood, the high spirit, and the susceptible imagination of an untamed mountaineer chieftain. But his remarkable personal distinction is of a characteristically civilized type. The ridges of his eyebrows, curving with an interrogative twist round the projections at the outer corners; his jealously observant eye; his nose, thin, keen, and apprehensive in spite of the pugnacious high bridge and large nostril; his assertive chin would not be out of place in a Parisian salon, shewing that the clever imaginative barbarian has an acute critical faculty which has been thrown into intense activity by the arrival of western civilization in the Balkans. The result is precisely what the advent of nineteenth century thought first produced in England: to wit, Byronism. By his brooding on the perpetual failure, not only of others, but of himself, to live up to his ideals; by his consequent cynical scorn for humanity; by his jejune credulity as to the absolute validity of his concepts and the unworthiness of the world in disregarding them; by his wincings and mockeries under the sting of the petty disillusions which every hour spent among men brings to his sensitive observation, he has acquired the half tragic, half ironic air, the mysterious moodiness, the suggestion of a strange and terrible history that has left nothing but undying remorse, by which Childe Harold fascinated the grandmothers of his English contemporaries. It is clear that here or nowhere is* RAINA's *ideal hero.* CATHERINE *is hardly less enthusiastic about him than her daughter, and much less reserved in shewing her enthusiasm. As he enters from the stable gate, she rises effusively to greet him.* PETKOFF *is distinctly less disposed to make a fuss about him.*)

PETKOFF   Here already, Sergius! Glad to see you.

CATHERINE   My dear Sergius! (*She holds out both her hands.*)

SERGIUS   (*kissing them with scrupulous gallantry*) My dear mother, if I may call you so.

PETKOFF   (*drily*) Mother-in-law, Sergius: mother-in-law! Sit down; and have some coffee.

SERGIUS   Thank you: none for me. (*He gets away from the table with a certain distaste for* PETKOFF's *enjoyment of it, and posts himself with conscious dignity against the rail of the steps leading to the house.*)

CATHERINE   You look superb. The campaign has improved you, Sergius. Everybody here is mad about you. We were all wild with enthusiasm about that magnificent cavalry charge.

SERGIUS   (*with grave irony*) Madam: it was the cradle and the grave of my military reputation.

CATHERINE   How so?

SERGIUS   I won the battle the wrong way when our worthy Russian generals were losing it the right way. In short, I upset their plans, and wounded their self-esteem. Two Cossack colonels had their regiments routed on the most correct principles of scientific warfare. Two major-generals got killed strictly according to military etiquette. The two colonels are now major-generals; and I am still a simple major.

CATHERINE   You shall not remain so, Sergius. The women are on your side; and they will see that justice is done you.

SERGIUS   It is too late. I have only waited for the peace to send in my resignation.

PETKOFF   (*dropping his cup in his amazement*) Your resignation!

CATHERINE   Oh, you must withdraw it!

SERGIUS   (*with resolute measured emphasis, folding his arms*) I never withdraw.

PETKOFF   (*vexed*) Now who could have supposed you were going to do such a thing?

SERGIUS   (*with fire*) Everyone that knew me. But enough of myself and my affairs. How is Raina; and where is Raina?

RAINA   (*suddenly coming round the corner of the house and standing at the top of the steps in the path*) Raina is here.

(*She makes a charming picture as they turn to look at her. She wears an underdress of pale green silk, draped with an overdress of thin ecru canvas embroidered with gold. She is crowned with a dainty eastern cap of gold tinsel.* SERGIUS *goes impulsively to meet her. Posing regally, she presents her hand; he drops chivalrously on one knee and kisses it.*)

PETKOFF   (*aside to* CATHERINE, *beaming with parental pride*) Pretty, isnt it? She always appears at the right moment.

CATHERINE   (*impatiently*) Yes; she listens for it. It is an abominable habit.

(SERGIUS *leads* RAINA *forward with splendid gallantry. When they arrive at the table, she turns to him with a bend of the head: he bows; and thus they separate, he coming to his place and she going behind her father's chair.*)

RAINA   (*stooping and kissing her father*) Dear father! Welcome home!

PETKOFF   (*patting her cheek*) My little pet girl. (*He kisses her. She goes to the chair left by* NICOLA *for* SERGIUS, *and sits down.*)

CATHERINE   And so youre no longer a soldier, Sergius.

SERGIUS   I am no longer a soldier. Soldiering, my dear madam, is the coward's art of attacking mercilessly when you are strong, and keeping out of harm's way when you are weak. That is the whole secret of successful fighting. Get your enemy at a disadvantage; and never, on any account, fight him on equal terms.

PETKOFF They wouldnt let us make a fair stand-up fight of it. However, I suppose soldiering has to be a trade like any other trade.

SERGIUS Precisely. But I have no ambition to shine as a tradesman; so I have taken the advice of that bagman of a captain that settled the exchange of prisoners with us at Pirot, and given it up.

PETKOFF What! that Swiss fellow? Sergius: Ive often thought of that exchange since. He over-reached us about those horses.

SERGIUS Of course he over-reached us. His father was a hotel and livery stable keeper; and he owed his first step to his knowledge of horse-dealing. (*with mock enthusiasm*) Ah, he was a soldier: every inch a soldier! If only I had bought the horses for my regiment instead of foolishly leading it into danger, I should have been a field-marshal now!

CATHERINE A Swiss? What was he doing in the Serbian army?

PETKOFF A volunteer, of course: keen on picking up his profession. (*chuckling*) We shouldnt have been able to begin fighting if these foreigners hadnt shewn us how to do it: we knew nothing about it; and neither did the Serbs. Egad, there'd have been no war without them!

RAINA Are there many Swiss officers in the Serbian Army?

PETKOFF No. All Austrians, just as our officers were all Russians. This was the only Swiss I came across. I'll never trust a Swiss again. He humbugged us into giving him fifty ablebodied men for two hundred worn out chargers. They werent even eatable!

SERGIUS We were two children in the hands of that consummate soldier, Major: simply two innocent little children.

RAINA What was he like?

CATHERINE Oh, Raina, what a silly question!

SERGIUS He was like a commercial traveller in uniform. Bourgeois to his boots!

PETKOFF (*grinning*) Sergius: tell Catherine that queer story his friend told us about how he escaped after Slivnitza. You remember. About his being hid by two women.

SERGIUS (*with bitter irony*) Oh yes: quite a romance! He was serving in the very battery I so unprofessionally charged. Being a thorough soldier, he ran away like the rest of them, with our cavalry at his heels. To escape their sabres he climbed a waterpipe and made his way into the bedroom of a young Bulgarian lady. The young lady was enchanted by his persuasive commercial traveller's manners. She very modestly entertained him for an hour or so, and then called in her mother lest her conduct should appear unmaidenly. The old lady was equally fascinated; and the fugitive was sent on his way in the morning, disguised in an old coat belonging to the master of the house, who was away at the war.

RAINA (*rising with marked stateliness*) Your life in the camp has made you coarse, Sergius. I did not think you would have repeated such a story before me. (*She turns away coldly.*)

CATHERINE (*also rising*) She is right, Sergius. If such women exist, we should be spared the knowledge of them.

PETKOFF   Pooh! nonsense! what does it matter?

SERGIUS   (*ashamed*) No, Petkoff: I was wrong. (*to* RAINA, *with earnest humility*) I beg your pardon. I have behaved abominably. Forgive me, Raina. (*She bows reservedly.*) And you too, madam. (CATHERINE *bows graciously and sits down. He proceeds solemnly, again addressing* RAINA.) The glimpses I have had of the seamy side of life during the last few months have made me cynical; but I should not have brought my cynicism here: least of all into your presence, Raina. I—(*Here, turning to the others, he is evidently going to begin a long speech when the Major interrupts him.*)

PETKOFF   Stuff and nonsense, Sergius! Thats quite enough fuss about nothing: a soldier's daughter should be able to stand up without flinching to a little strong conversation. (*He rises.*) Come: it's time for us to get to business. We have to make up our minds how those three regiments are to get back to Philippopolis: theres no forage for them on the Sofia route. (*He goes towards the house.*) Come along. (SERGIUS *is about to follow him when* CATHERINE *rises and intervenes.*)

CATHERINE   Oh, Paul, cant you spare Sergius for a few moments? Raina has hardly seen him yet. Perhaps I can help you to settle about the regiments.

SERGIUS   (*protesting*) My dear madam, impossible: you—

CATHERINE   (*stopping him playfully*) You stay here, my dear Sergius: theres no hurry. I have a word or two to say to Paul. (SERGIUS *instantly bows and steps back.*) Now, dear (*taking* PETKOFF's *arm*): come and see the electric bell.

PETKOFF   Oh, very well, very well.

(*They go into the house together affectionately.* SERGIUS, *left alone with* RAINA, *looks anxiously at her, fearing that she is still offended. She smiles, and stretches out her arms to him.*)

SERGIUS   (*hastening to her*) Am I forgiven?

RAINA   (*placing her hands on his shoulders as she looks up at him with admiration and worship*) My hero! My king!

SERGIUS   My queen! (*He kisses her on the forehead.*)

RAINA   How I have envied you, Sergius! You have been out in the world, on the field of battle, able to prove yourself there worthy of any woman in the world; whilst I have had to sit at home inactive—dreaming—useless—doing nothing that could give me the right to call myself worthy of any man.

SERGIUS   Dearest: all my deeds have been yours. You inspired me. I have gone through the war like a knight in a tournament with his lady looking down at him!

RAINA   And you have never been absent from my thoughts for a moment. (*very solemnly*) Sergius: I think we two have found the higher love. When I think of you, I feel that I could never do a base deed, or think an ignoble thought.

SERGIUS   My lady and my saint! (*He clasps her reverently.*)

RAINA   (*returning his embrace*) My lord and my—

SERGIUS   Sh—sh! Let me be the worshipper, dear. You little know how unworthy even the best man is of a girl's pure passion!

RAINA   I trust you. I love you. You will never disappoint me, Sergius. (LOUKA is heard singing within the house. They quickly release each other.) I cant pretend to talk indifferently before her: my heart is too full. (LOUKA comes from the house with her tray. She goes to the table, and begins to clear it, with her back turned to them.) I will get my hat; and then we can go out until lunch time. Wouldnt you like that?

SERGIUS Be quick. If you are away five minutes, it will seem five hours. (RAINA runs to the top of the steps, and turns there to exchange looks with him and wave him a kiss with both hands. He looks after her with emotion for a moment; then turns slowly away, his face radiant with the loftiest exaltation. The movement shifts his field of vision, into the corner of which there now comes the tail of LOUKA's double apron. His attention is arrested at once. He takes a stealthy look at her, and begins to twirl his moustache mischievously, with his left hand akimbo on his hip. Finally, striking the ground with his heels in something of a cavalry swagger, he strolls over to the other side of the table, opposite her, and says) Louka: do you know what the higher love is?

LOUKA (astonished) No, sir.

SERGIUS Very fatiguing thing to keep up for any length of time, Louka. One feels the need of some relief after it.

LOUKA (innocently) Perhaps you would like some coffee, sir? (She stretches her hand across the table for the coffee pot.)

SERGIUS (taking her hand) Thank you, Louka.

LOUKA (pretending to pull) Oh, sir, you know I didnt mean that. I'm surprised at you!

SERGIUS (coming clear of the table and drawing her with him) I am surprised at myself, Louka. What would Sergius, the hero of Slivnitza, say if he saw me now? What would Sergius, the apostle of the higher love, say if he saw me now? What would the half dozen Sergiuses who keep popping in and out of this handsome figure of mine say if they caught us here? (Letting go her hand and slipping his arm dexterously round her waist) Do you consider my figure handsome, Louka?

LOUKA Let me go, sir. I shall be disgraced. (She struggles: he holds her inexorably.) Oh, will you let go?

SERGIUS (looking straight into her eyes) No.

LOUKA Then stand back where we cant be seen. Have you no common sense?

SERGIUS Ah! thats reasonable. (He takes her into the stable yard gateway, where they are hidden from the house.)

LOUKA (plaintively) I may have been seen from the windows: Miss Raina is sure to be spying about after you.

SERGIUS (stung: letting her go) Take care, Louka. I may be worthless enough to betray the higher love; but do not you insult it.

LOUKA (demurely) Not for the world, sir, I'm sure. May I go on with my work, please, now?

SERGIUS (again putting his arm round her) You are a provoking little witch, Louka. If you were in love with me, would you spy out of windows on me?

LOUKA Well, you see, sir, since you say you are half a dozen different gentlemen all at once, I should have a great deal to look after.

SERGIUS (*charmed*) Witty as well as pretty. (*He tries to kiss her.*)

LOUKA (*avoiding him*) No: I dont want your kisses. Gentlefolk are all alike: you making love to me behind Miss Raina's back; and she doing the same behind yours.

SERGIUS (*recoiling a step*) Louka!

LOUKA It shews how little you really care.

SERGIUS (*dropping his familiarity, and speaking with freezing politeness*) If our conversation is to continue, Louka, you will please remember that a gentleman does not discuss the conduct of the lady he is engaged to with her maid.

LOUKA It's so hard to know what a gentleman considers right. I thought from your trying to kiss me that you had given up being so particular.

SERGIUS (*turning from her and striking his forehead as he comes back into the garden from the gateway*) Devil! devil!

LOUKA Ha! ha! I expect one of the six of you is very like me, sir; though I am only Miss Raina's maid. (*She goes back to her work at the table, taking no further notice of him.*)

SERGIUS (*speaking to himself*) Which of the six is the real man? thats the question that torments me. One of them is a hero, another a buffoon, another a humbug, another perhaps a bit of a blackguard. (*He pauses, and looks futively at* LOUKA *as he adds, with deep bitterness*) And one, at least, is a coward: jealous, like all cowards. (*He goes to the table.*) Louka.

LOUKA Yes?

SERGIUS Who is my rival?

LOUKA You shall never get that out of me, for love or money.

SERGIUS Why?

LOUKA Never mind why. Besides, you would tell that I told you; and I should lose my place.

SERGIUS (*holding out his right hand in affirmation*) No! on the honor of a— (*He checks himself; and his hand drops, nerveless, as he concludes sardonically*)—of a man capable of behaving as I have been behaving for the last five minutes. Who is he?

LOUKA I dont know. I never saw him. I only heard his voice through the door of her room.

SERGIUS Damnation! How dare you?

LOUKA (*retreating*) Oh, I mean no harm: youve no right to take up my words like that. The mistress knows all about it. And I tell you that if that gentleman ever comes here again, Miss Raina will marry him, whether he likes it or not. I know the difference between the sort of manner you and she put on before one another and the real manner.

(SERGIUS *shivers as if she had stabbed him. Then, setting his face like iron, he strides grimly to her, and grips her above the elbows with both hands.*)

SERGIUS Now listen to me.

LOUKA (*wincing*) Not so tight: youre hurting me.

SERGIUS That doesnt matter. You have stained my honor by making me a party to your eavesdropping. And you have betrayed your mistress.

LOUKA (*writhing*) Please—

SERGIUS That shews that you are an abominable little clod of common clay, with the soul of a servant. (*He lets her go as if she were an unclean thing, and turns away, dusting his hands of her, to the bench by the wall, where he sits down with averted head, meditating gloomily.*)

LOUKA (*whimpering angrily with her hands up her sleeves, feeling her bruised arms*) You know how to hurt with your tongue as well as with your hands. But I dont care, now Ive found out that whatever clay I'm made of, youre made of the same. As for her, she's a liar; and her fine airs are a cheat; and I'm worth six of her. (*She shakes the pain off hardily; tosses her head; and sets to work to put the things on the tray.*)

(*He looks doubtfully at her. She finishes packing the tray, and laps the cloth over the edges, so as to carry all out together. As she stoops to lift it, he rises.*)

SERGIUS Louka! (*She stops and looks defiantly at him.*) A gentleman has no right to hurt a woman under any circumstances. (*with profound humility, uncovering his head*) I beg your pardon.

LOUKA That sort of apology may satisfy a lady. Of what use is it to a servant?

SERGIUS (*rudely crossed in his chivalry, throws it off with a bitter laugh, and says slightingly*) Oh! you wish to be paid for the hurt! (*He puts on his shako, and takes some money from his pocket.*)

LOUKA (*her eyes filling with tears in spite of herself*) No: I want my hurt made well.

SERGIUS (*sobered by her tone*) How?

(*She rolls up her left sleeve; clasps her arm with the thumb and fingers of her right hand; and looks down at the bruise. Then she raises her head and looks straight at him. Finally, with a superb gesture, she presents her arm to be kissed. Amazed, he looks at her; at the arm; at her again; hesitates; and then, with shuddering intensity, exclaims* Never! *and gets away as far as possible from her.*

(*Her arm drops. Without a word, and with unaffected dignity, she takes her tray, and is approaching the house when* RAINA *returns, wearing a hat and jacket in the height of the Vienna fashion of the previous year, 1885.* LOUKA *makes way proudly for her, and then goes into the house.*)

RAINA I'm ready. What's the matter? (*gaily*) Have you been flirting with Louka?

SERGIUS (*hastily*) No, no. How can you think such a thing?

RAINA (*ashamed of herself*) Forgive me, dear: it was only a jest. I am so happy today.

(*He goes quickly to her, and kisses her hand remorsefully.* CATHERINE *comes out and calls to them from the top of the steps.*)

CATHERINE (*coming down to them*) I am sorry to disturb you, children; but Paul is distracted over those three regiments. He doesnt know how to send them to Philippopolis; and he objects to every suggestion of mine. You must go and help him, Sergius. He is in the library.

RAINA (*disappointed*) But we are just going out for a walk.

SERGIUS I shall not be long. Wait for me just five minutes. (*He runs up the steps to the door.*)

RAINA (*following him to the foot of the steps and looking up at him with timid coquetry*) I shall go round and wait in full view of the library windows. Be sure you draw father's attention to me. If you are a moment longer than five minutes, I shall go in and fetch you, regiments or no regiments.

SERGIUS (*laughing*) Very well. (*He goes in.*)

(RAINA *watches him until he is out of her sight. Then, with a perceptible relaxation of manner, she begins to pace up and down the garden in a brown study.*)

CATHERINE Imagine their meeting that Swiss and hearing the whole story! The very first thing your father asked for was the old coat we sent him off in. A nice mess you have got us into!

RAINA (*gazing thoughtfully at the gravel as she walks*) The little beast!

CATHERINE Little beast! What little beast?

RAINA To go and tell! Oh, if I had him here, I'd cram him with chocolate creams till he couldnt ever speak again!

CATHERINE Dont talk such stuff. Tell me the truth, Raina. How long was he in your room before you came to me?

RAINA (*whisking round and recommencing her march in the opposite direction*) Oh, I forget.

CATHERINE You cannot forget! Did he really climb up after the soldiers were gone; or was he there when that officer searched the room?

RAINA No. Yes: I think he must have been there then.

CATHERINE You think! Oh, Raina! Raina! Will anything ever make you straightforward? If Serguis finds out, it will be all over between you.

RAINA (*with cool impertinence*) Oh, I know Sergius is your pet. I sometimes wish you could marry him instead of me. You would just suit him. You would pet him, and spoil him, and mother him to perfection.

CATHERINE (*opening her eyes very widely indeed*) Well, upon my word!

RAINA (*capriciously: half to herself*) I always feel a longing to do or say something dreadful to him—to shock his propriety—to scandalize the five senses out of him. (*to* CATHERINE, *perversely*) I dont care whether he finds out about the chocolate cream soldier or not. I half hope he may. (*She again turns and strolls flippantly away up the path to the corner of the house.*)

CATHERINE And what should I be able to say to your father, pray?

RAINA (*over her shoulder, from the top of the two steps*) Oh, poor father! As if he could help himself! (*She turns the corner and passes out of sight.*)

CATHERINE (*looking after her, her fingers itching*) Oh, if you were only ten years younger! (LOUKA *comes from the house with a salver, which she carries hanging down by her side.*) Well?

LOUKA Theres a gentleman just called, madam. A Serbian officer.

CATHERINE (*flaming*) A Serb! And how dare he—(*checking herself bitterly*) Oh, I forgot. We are at peace now. I suppose we shall have them calling every day to pay their compliments. Well: if he is an officer why dont you tell your master? He is in the library with Major Saranoff. Why do you come to me?

LOUKA But he asks for you, madam. And I dont think he knows who you are: he said the lady of the house. He gave me this little ticket for you. (*She takes a card out of her bosom; puts it on the salver; and offers it to* CATHERINE.)

CATHERINE (*reading*) "Captain Bluntschli"? Thats a German name.

LOUKA Swiss, madam, I think.

CATHERINE (*with a bound that makes* LOUKA *jump back*) Swiss! What is he like?

LOUKA   (*timidly*) He has a big carpet bag, madam.

CATHERINE   Oh Heavens! he's come to return the coat. Send him away: say we're not at home: ask him to leave his address and I'll write to him. Oh stop: that will never do. Wait! (*She throws herself into a chair to think it out. LOUKA waits.*) The master and Major Saranoff are busy in the library, arnt they?

LOUKA   Yes, madam.

CATHERINE   (*decisively*) Bring the gentleman out here at once. (*peremptorily*) And be very polite to him. Dont delay. Here (*impatiently snatching the salver from her*): leave that here; and go straight back to him.

LOUKA   Yes, madam (*going*).

CATHERINE   Louka!

LOUKA   (*stopping*) Yes, madam.

CATHERINE   Is the library door shut?

LOUKA   I think so, madam.

CATHERINE   If not, shut it as you pass through.

LOUKA   Yes, madam (*going*).

CATHERINE   Stop. (LOUKA *stops.*) He will have to go that way (*indicating the gate of the stable yard*). Tell Nicola to bring his bag here after him. Dont forget.

LOUKA   (*surprised*) His bag?

CATHERINE   Yes: here: as soon as possible. (*vehemently*) Be quick! (LOUKA *runs into the house.* CATHERINE *snatches her apron off and throws it behind a bush. She then takes up the salver and uses it as a mirror, with the result that the handkerchief tied around her head follows the apron. A touch to her hair and a shake to her dressing gown make her presentable.*) Oh, how? how? how can a man be such a fool! Such a moment to select! (LOUKA *appears at the door of the house, announcing* Captain Bluntschli. *She stands aside at the top of the steps to let him pass before she goes in again. He is the man of the midnight adventure in* RAINA's *room, clean, well brushed, smartly uniformed, and out of trouble, but still unmistakably the same man. The moment* LOUKA's *back is turned,* CATHERINE *swoops on him with impetuous, urgent, coaxing appeal.*) Captain Bluntschli: I am very glad to see you; but you must leave this house at once. (*He raises his eyebrows.*) My husband has just returned with my future son-in-law; and they know nothing. If they did, the consequences would be terrible. You are a foreigner: you do not feel our national animosities as we do. We still hate the Serbs: the effect of the peace on my husband has been to make him feel like a lion baulked of his prey. If he discovers our secret, he will never forgive me; and my daughter's life will hardly be safe. Will you, like the chivalrous gentleman and soldier you are, leave at once before he finds you here?

BLUNTSCHLI   (*disappointed, but philosophical*) At once, gracious lady. I only came to thank you and return the coat you lent me. If you will allow me to take it out of my bag and leave it with your servant as I pass out, I need detain you no further. (*He turns to go into the house.*)

CATHERINE   (*catching him by the sleeve*) Oh, you must not think of going back that way. (*coaxing him across to the stable gates*) This is the shortest way out. Many thanks. So glad to have been of service to you. Goodbye.

BLUNTSCHLI   But my bag?

CATHERINE   It shall be sent on. You will leave me your address.

BLUNTSCHLI   True. Allow me. (*He takes out his cardcase, and stops to write his address, keeping* CATHERINE *in an agony of impatience. As he hands her the card,* PETKOFF, *hatless, rushes from the house in a fluster of hospitality, followed by* SERGIUS.)

PETKOFF   (*as he hurries down the steps*) My dear Captain Bluntschli—

CATHERINE   Oh heavens! (*She sinks on the seat against the wall.*)

PETKOFF   (*too preoccupied to notice her as he shakes* BLUNTSCHLI's *hand heartily*) Those stupid people of mine thought I was out here, instead of in the—haw!—library. (*He cannot mention the library without betraying how proud he is of it.*) I saw you through the window. I was wondering why you didnt come in. Saranoff is with me: you remember him, dont you?

SERGIUS   (*saluting humorously, and then offering his hand with great charm of manner*) Welcome, our friend the enemy!

PETKOFF   No longer the enemy, happily. (*rather anxiously*) I hope youve called as a friend, and not about horses or prisoners.

CATHERINE   Oh, quite as a friend, Paul. I was just asking Captain Bluntschli to stay to lunch; but he declares he must go at once.

SERGIUS   (*sardonically*) Impossible, Bluntschli. We want you here badly. We have to send on three cavalry regiments to Philippopolis; and we dont in the least know how to do it.

BLUNTSCHLI   (*suddenly attentive and businesslike*) Philippopolis? The forage is the trouble, I suppose.

PETKOFF   (*eagerly*) Yes: thats it. (*to* SERGIUS) He sees the whole thing at once.

BLUNTSCHLI   I think I can shew you how to manage that.

SERGIUS   Invaluable man! Come along! (*Towering over* BLUNTSCHLI, *he puts his hand on his shoulder and takes him to the steps,* PETKOFF *following.*)

(RAINA *comes from the house as* BLUNTSCHLI *puts his foot on the first step.*)

RAINA   Oh! the chocolate cream soldier!

(BLUNTSCHLI *stands rigid.* SERGIUS, *amazed, looks at* RAINA, *then at* PETKOFF, *who looks back at him and then at his wife.*)

CATHERINE   (*with commanding presence of mind*) My dear Raina, dont you see that we have a guest here? Captain Bluntschli: one of our new Serbian friends.

(RAINA *bows:* BLUNTSCHLI *bows.*)

RAINA   How silly of me! (*She comes down into the centre of the group, between* BLUNTSCHLI *and* PETKOFF.) I made a beautiful ornament this morning for the ice pudding; and that stupid Nicola has just put down a pile of plates on it and spoilt it. (*to* BLUNTSCHLI, *winningly*) I hope you didnt think that you were the chocolate cream soldier, Captain Bluntschli.

BLUNTSCHLI   (*laughing*) I assure you I did. (*stealing a whimsical glance at her*) Your explanation was a relief.

PETKOFF   (*suspiciously, to* RAINA) And since when, pray, have you taken to cooking?

CATHERINE   Oh, whilst you were away. It is her latest fancy.

PETKOFF   (*testily*) And has Nicola taken to drinking? He used to be careful enough. First he shews Captain Bluntschli out here when he knew quite well I was in the library; and then he goes downstairs and breaks Raina's chocolate soldier. He must—(NICOLA *appears at the top of the steps with the bag. He descends; places it respectfully before* BLUNTSCHLI; *and waits for further orders. General amazement.* NICOLA, *unconscious of the effect he is producing, looks perfectly satisfied with himself. When* PETKOFF *recovers his power of speech, he breaks out at him with*) Are you mad, Nicola?

NICOLA   (*taken aback*) Sir?

PETKOFF   What have you brought that for?

NICOLA   My lady's orders, major. Louka told me that—

CATHERINE   (*interrupting him*) My orders! Why should I order you to bring Captain Bluntschli's luggage out here? What are you thinking of, Nicola?

NICOLA   (*after a moment's bewilderment, picking up the bag as he addresses* BLUNTSCHLI *with the very perfection of servile discretion*) I beg your pardon, captain. I am sure. (*to* CATHERINE) My fault, madame: I hope youll overlook it. (*He bows, and is going to the steps with the bag, when* PETKOFF *addresses him angrily.*)

PETKOFF   Youd better go and slam that bag, too, down on Miss Raina's ice pudding! (*This is too much for* NICOLA. *The bag drops from his hand almost on his master's toes, eliciting a roar of*) Begone, you butter-fingered donkey.

NICOLA   (*snatching up the bag, and escaping into the house*) Yes, Major.

CATHERINE   Oh, never mind. Paul: dont be angry.

PETKOFF   (*blustering*) Scoundrel! He's got out of hand while I was away. I'll teach him. Infernal blackguard! The sack next Saturday! I'll clear out the whole establishment—(*He is stifled by the caresses of his wife and daughter, who hang round his neck, petting him.*)

CATHERINE   (*together*) ⎰Now, now, now, it mustnt be angry. He meant no
RAINA   ⎱Wow, wow, wow: not on your first day at home.
              ⎰harm. Be good to please me, dear. Sh-sh-sh-sh!
              ⎱I'll make another ice pudding. Tch-ch-ch!

PETKOFF   (*yielding*) Oh well, never mind. Come, Bluntschli: lets have no more nonsense about going away. You know very well youre not going back to Switzerland yet. Until you do go back youll stay with us.

RAINA   Oh, do, Captain Bluntschli.

PETKOFF   (*to* CATHERINE) Now, Catherine: it's of you he's afraid. Press him: and he'll stay.

CATHERINE   Of course I shall be only too delighted if (*appealingly*) Captain Bluntschli really wishes to stay. He knows my wishes.

BLUNTSCHLI   (*in his driest military manner*) I am at madam's orders.

SERGIUS   (*cordially*) That settles it!

PETKOFF   (*heartily*) Of course!

RAINA   You see you must stay.

BLUNTSCHLI   (*smiling*) Well, if I must, I must. (*Gesture of despair from* CATHERINE.)

ACT III

(*In the library after lunch. It is not much of a library. Its literary equipment consists of a single fixed shelf stocked with old paper covered novels, broken backed, coffee stained, torn and thumbed; and a couple of little hanging shelves with a few gift books on them: the rest of the wall space being occupied by trophies of war and the chase. But it is a most comfortable sitting room. A row of three large windows shews a mountain panorama, just now seen in one of its friendliest aspects in the mellowing afternoon light. In the corner next the right hand window a square earthenware stove, a perfect tower of glistening pottery, rises nearly to the ceiling and guarantees plenty of warmth. The ottoman is like that in RAINA's room, and similarly placed; and the window seats are luxurious with decorated cushions. There is one object, however, hopelessly out of keeping with its surroundings. This is a small kitchen table, much the worse for wear, fitted as a writing table with an old canister full of pens, an eggcup filled with ink, and a deplorable scrap of heavily used pink blotting paper.*)

(*At the end of this table, which stands to the left of anyone facing the window, BLUNT-SCHLI is hard at work with a couple of maps before him, writing orders. At the head of it sits SERGIUS, who is supposed to be also at work, but is actually gnawing the feather of a pen, and contemplating BLUNTSCHLI's quick, sure, business-like progress with a mixture of envious irritation at his own incapacity and awestruck wonder at an ability which seems to him almost miraculous, though its prosaic character forbids him to esteem it. The Major is comfortably established on the ottoman, with a newspaper in his hand and the tube of his hookah within easy reach. CATHERINE sits at the stove, with her back to them, embroidering. RAINA, reclining on the divan, is gazing in a daydream out at the Balkan landscape, with a neglected novel in her lap.*)

(*The door is on the same side as the stove, farther from the window. The button of the electric bell is at the opposite side, behind BLUNTSCHLI.*)

PETKOFF   (*looking up from his paper to watch how they are getting on at the table*) Are you sure I cant help in any way, Bluntschli?

BLUNTSCHLI   (*without interrupting his writing or looking up*) Quite sure, thank you. Saranoff and I will manage it.

SERGIUS   (*grimly*) Yes: we'll manage it. He finds out what to do; draws up the orders; and I sign em. Division of labor! (BLUNTSCHLI *passes him a paper.*) Another one? Thank you. (*He plants the paper squarely before him; sets his chair carefully parallel to it; and signs with his cheek on his elbow and his protruded tongue following the movements of his pen.*) This hand is more accustomed to the sword than to the pen.

PETKOFF   It's very good of you, Bluntschli: it is indeed, to let yourself be put upon in this way. Now are you quite sure I can do nothing?

CATHERINE   (*in a low warning tone*) You can stop interrupting, Paul.

PETKOFF   (*starting and looking round at her*) Eh? Oh! Quite right. (*He takes his newspaper up again, but presently lets it drop.*) Ah, you havnt been campaigning, Catherine: you dont know how pleasant it is for us to sit here, after a good lunch, with nothing to do but enjoy ourselves. Theres only one thing I want to make me thoroughly comfortable.

CATHERINE.   What is that?

PETKOFF   My old coat. I'm not at home in this one: I feel as if I were on parade.

CATHERINE   My dear Paul, how absurd you are about that old coat! It must be hanging in the blue closet where you left it.

PETKOFF   My dear Catherine, I tell you Ive looked there. Am I to believe my
   own eyes or not? (CATHERINE *rises and crosses the room to press the button
   of the electric bell.*) What are you shewing off that bell for? (*She looks at him
   majestically, and silently resumes her chair and her needlework.*) My dear:
   if you think the obstinacy of your sex can make a coat out of two old dressing gowns of Raina's, your waterproof, and my mackintosh, youre mistaken.
   Thats exactly what the blue closet contains at present.

(NICOLA *presents himself.*)

CATHERINE   Nicola: go to the blue closet and bring your master's old coat
   here: the braided one he wears in the house.

NICOLA   Yes, madame. (*He goes out.*)

PETKOFF   Catherine.

CATHERINE   Yes, Paul.

PETKOFF   I bet you any piece of jewellry you like to order from Sofia against
   a week's housekeeping money that the coat isnt there.

CATHERINE   Done, Paul.

PETKOFF   (*excited by the prospect of a gamble*) Come: here's an opportunity
   for some sport. Wholl bet on it? Bluntschli: I'll give you six to one.

BLUNTSCHLI   (*imperturbably*) It would be robbing you, Major. Madame is sure
   to be right. (*Without looking up, he passes another batch of papers to
   SERGIUS.*)

SERGIUS   (*also excited*) Bravo, Switzerland! Major: I bet my best charger
   against an Arab mare for Raina that Nicola finds the coat in the blue closet.

PETKOFF   (*eagerly*) Your best char—

CATHERINE   (*hastily interrupting him*) Dont be foolish, Paul. An Arabian mare
   will cost you 50,000 levas.

RAINA   (*suddenly coming out of her picturesque revery*) Really, mother, if you
   are going to take the jewellry, I dont see why you should grudge me my
   Arab.

(NICOLA *comes back with the coat, and brings it to* PETKOFF, *who can hardly believe
his eyes.*)

CATHERINE   Where was it, Nicola?

NICOLA   Hanging in the blue closet, madame.

PETKOFF   Well, I am d—

CATHERINE   (*stopping him*) Paul!

PETKOFF   I could have sworn it wasnt there. Age is beginning to tell on me.
   I'm getting hallucinations. (*to* NICOLA) Here: help me to change. Excuse me,
   Bluntschli. (*He begins changing coats,* NICOLA *acting as valet.*) Remember:
   I didnt take that bet of yours, Sergius. Youd better give Raina that Arab
   steed yourself, since youve roused her expectations. Eh, Raina? (*He looks
   round at her; but she is again rapt in the landscape. With a little gush of
   parental affection and pride, he points her out to them, and says*) She's
   dreaming, as usual.

SERGIUS   Assuredly she shall not be the loser.

PETKOFF   So much the better for her. *I* shant come off so cheaply, I expect.
   (*The change is now complete.* NICOLA *goes out with the discarded coat.*) Ah,

now I feel at home at last. (*He sits down and takes his newspaper with a grunt of relief.*)

BLUNTSCHLI   (*to* SERGIUS, *handing a paper*) Thats the last order.

PETKOFF   (*jumping up*) What! Finished?

BLUNTSCHLI   Finished.

PETKOFF   (*with childlike envy*) Havnt you anything for me to sign?

BUNTSCHLI   Not necessary. His signature will do.

PETKOFF   (*inflating his chest and thumping it*) Ah well, I think weve done a thundering good day's work. Can I do anything more?

BLUNTSCHLI   You had better both see the fellows that are to take these. (*Sergius rises.*) Pack them off at once; and shew them that Ive marked on the orders the time they should hand them in by. Tell them that if they stop to drink or tell stories—if theyre five minutes late, theyll have the skin taken off their backs.

SERGIUS   (*stiffening indignantly*) I'll say so. (*He strides to the door.*) And if one of them is man enough to spit in my face for insulting him, I'll buy his discharge and give him a pension. (*He goes out.*)

BLUNTSCHLI   (*confidentially*) Just see that he talks to them properly, Major, will you?

PETKOFF   (*officiously*) Quite right, Bluntschli, quite right. I'll see to it. (*He goes to the door importantly, but hesitates on the threshold.*) By the bye, Catherine, you may as well come too. Theyll be far more frightened of you than of me.

CATHERINE   (*putting down her embroidery*) I daresay I had better. You would only splutter at them. (*She goes out,* PETKOFF *holding the door for her and following her.*)

BLUNTSCHLI   What an army! They make cannons out of cherry trees; and the officers send for their wives to keep discipline! (*He begins to fold and docket the papers.*)

(RAINA, *who has risen from the divan, marches slowly down the room with her hands clasped behind her, and looks mischievously at him.*)

RAINA   You look ever so much nicer than when we last met. (*He looks up, surprised.*) What have you done to yourself?

BLUNTSCHLI   Washed; brushed; good night's sleep and breakfast. Thats all.

RAINA   Did you get back safely that morning?

BLUNTSCHLI   Quite, thanks.

RAINA   Were they angry with you for running away from Sergius's charge?

BLUNTSCHLI   (*grinning*) No: they were glad; because theyd all just run away themselves.

RAINA   (*going to the table, and leaning over it towards him*) It must have made a lovely story for all them: all that about me and my room.

BLUNTSCHLI   Capital story. But I only told it to one of them: a particular friend.

RAINA   On whose discretion you could absolutely rely?

BLUNTSCHLI   Absolutely.

RAINA   Hm! He told it all to my father and Sergius the day you exchanged the prisoners. (*She turns away and strolls carelessly across to the other side of the room.*)

BLUNTSCHLI (*deeply concerned, and half incredulous*) No! You dont mean that, do you?

RAINA (*turning, with sudden earnestness*) I do indeed. But they dont know that it was in this house you took refuge. If Sergius knew, he would challenge you and kill you in a duel.

BLUNTSCHLI Bless me! then dont tell him.

RAINA Please be serious, Captain Bluntschli. Can you not realize what it is to me to deceive him? I want to be quite perfect with Sergius: no meanness, no smallness, no deceit. My relation to him is the one really beautiful and noble part of my life. I hope you can understand that.

BLUNTSCHLI (*sceptically*) You mean that you wouldnt like him to find out that the story about the ice pudding was a—a—a—You know.

RAINA (*wincing*) Ah, dont talk of it in that flippant way. I lied: I know it. But I did it to save your life. He would have killed you. That was the second time I ever uttered a falsehood. (BLUNTSCHLI *rises quickly and looks doubtfully and somewhat severely at her.*) Do you remember the first time?

BLUNTSCHLI I! No. Was I present?

RAINA Yes; and I told the officer who was searching for you that you were not present.

BLUNTSCHLI True. I should have remembered it.

RAINA (*greatly encouraged*) Ah, it is natural that you should forget it first. It cost you nothing: it cost me a lie! A lie!

(*She sits down on the ottoman, looking straight before her with her hands clasped around her knee. BLUNTSCHLI, quite touched, goes to the ottoman with a particularly reassuring and considerate air, and sits down beside her.*)

BLUNTSCHLI My dear young lady, dont let this worry you. Remember: I'm a soldier. Now what are the two things that happen to a soldier so often that he comes to think nothing of them? One is hearing people tell lies (*Raina recoils.*): the other is getting his life saved in all sorts of ways by all sorts of people.

RAINA (*rising in indignant protest*) And so he becomes a creature incapable of faith and of gratitude.

BLUNTSCHLI (*making a wry face*) Do you like gratitude? I dont. If pity is akin to love, gratitude is akin to the other thing.

RAINA Gratitude! (*turning on him*) If you are incapable of gratitude you are incapable of any noble sentiment. Even animals are grateful. Oh, I see now exactly what you think of me! You were not surprised to hear me lie. To you it was something I probably did every day! every hour! That is how men think of women. (*She paces the room tragically.*)

BLUNTSCHLI (*dubiously*) Theres reason in everything. You said youd told only two lies in your whole life. Dear young lady: isnt that rather a short allowance? I'm quite a straight-forward man myself; but it wouldnt last me a whole morning.

RAINA (*staring haughtily at him*) Do you know, sir, that you are insulting me?

BLUNTSCHLI I cant help it. When you strike that noble attitude and speak in that thrilling voice, I admire you; but I find it impossible to believe a single word you say.

RAINA   (superbly) Captain Bluntschli!

BLUNTSCHLI   (unmoved) Yes?

RAINA   (standing over him, as if she could not believe her senses) Do you mean what you said just now? Do you know what you said just now?

BLUNTSCHLI   I do.

RAINA   (gasping) I! I!!! (She points to herself incredulously, meaning "I, Raina Petkoff tell lies!" He meets her gaze unflinchingly. She suddenly sits down beside him, and adds, with a complete change of manner from the heroic to a babyish familiarity) How did you find me out?

BLUNTSCHLI   (promptly) Instinct, dear young lady. Instinct, and experience of the world.

RAINA   (wonderingly) Do you know, you are the first man I ever met who did not take me seriously?

BLUNTSCHLI   You mean, dont you, that I am the first man that has ever taken you quite seriously?

RAINA   Yes: I suppose I do mean that. (cosily, quite at her ease with him) How strange it is to be talked to in such a way! You know, Ive always gone on like that.

BLUNTSCHLI   You mean the—?

RAINA   I mean the noble attitude and the thrilling voice. (They laugh together.) I did it when I was a tiny child to my nurse. She believed in it. I do it before my parents. They believe in it. I do it before Sergius. He believes in it.

BLUNTSCHLI   Yes: he's a little in that line himself, isnt he?

RAINA   (startled) Oh! Do you think so?

BLUNTSCHLI   You know him better than I do.

RAINA   I wonder—I wonder is he? If I thought that—! (discouraged) Ah, well; what does it matter? I suppose, now youve found me out, you despise me.

BLUNTSCHLI   (warmly, rising) No, my dear young lady, no, no, no a thousand times. It's part of your youth: part of your charm. I'm like all the rest of them: the nurse, your parents, Sergius: I'm your infatuated admirer.

RAINA   (pleased) Really?

BLUNTSCHLI   (slapping his breast smartly with his hand, German fashion) Hand aufs Herz! Really and truly.

RAINA   (very happy) But what did you think of me for giving you my portrait?

BLUNTSCHLI   (astonished) Your portrait! You never gave me your portrait.

RAINA   (quickly) Do you mean to say you never got it?

BLUNTSCHLI   No. (He sits down beside her, with renewed interest, and says, with some complacency) When did you send it to me?

RAINA   (indignantly) I did not send it to you. (She turns her head away, and adds, reluctantly) It was in the pocket of that coat.

BLUNTSCHLI   (pursing his lips and rounding his eyes) Oh-o-oh! I never found it. It must be there still.

RAINA   (springing up) There still! for my father to find the first time he puts his hand in his pocket! Oh, how could you be so stupid?

BLUNTSCHLI   (rising also) It doesnt matter: I suppose it's only a photograph: how can he tell who it was intended for? Tell him he put it there himself.

RAINA   (*bitterly*) Yes: that is so clever! isnt it? (*distractedly*) Oh! what shall I do?

BLUNTSCHLI   Ah, I see. You wrote something on it. That was rash.

RAINA   (*vexed almost to tears*) Oh, to have done such a thing for you, who care no more—except to laugh at me—oh! Are you sure nobody has touched it?

BLUNTSCHLI   Well, I cant be quite sure. You see, I couldnt carry it about with me all the time: one cant take much luggage on active service.

RAINA   What did you do with it?

BLUNTSCHLI   When I got through to Pirot I had to put it in safe keeping somehow. I thought of the railway cloak room; but thats the surest place to get looted in modern warfare. So I pawned it.

RAINA   Pawned it!!!

BLUNTSCHLI   I know it doesnt sound nice: but it was much the safest plan. I redeemed it the day before yesterday. Heaven only knows whether the pawnbroker cleared out the pockets or not.

RAINA   .(*furious: throwing the words right into his face*) You have a low shop-keeping mind. You think of things that would never come into a gentleman's head.

BLUNTSCHLI   (*phlegmatically*) Thats the Swiss national character, dear lady. (*He returns to the table.*)

RAINA   Oh, I wish I had never met you. (*She flounces away, and sits at the window fuming.*)

(*LOUKA comes in with a heap of letters and telegrams on her salver, and crosses, with her bold free gait, to the table. Her left sleeve is looped up to the shoulder with a brooch, shewing her naked arm, with a broad gilt bracelet covering the bruise.*)

LOUKA   (*to BLUNTSCHLI*) For you. (*She empties the salver with a fling on to the table.*) The messenger is waiting. (*She is determined not to be civil to an enemy, even if she must bring him his letters.*)

BLUNTSCHLI   (*to RAINA*) Will you excuse me: the last postal delivery that reached me was three weeks ago. These are the subsequent accumulations. Four telegrams: a week old. (*He opens one.*) Oho! Bad news!

RAINA   (*rising and advancing a little remorsefully*) Bad news!

BLUNTSCHLI   My father's dead. (*He looks at the telegram with his lips pursed, musing on the unexpected change in his arrangements. LOUKA crosses herself hastily.*)

RAINA   Oh, how very sad!

BLUNTSCHLI   Yes: I shall have to start for home in an hour. He has left a lot of big hotels behind him to be looked after. (*He takes up a fat letter in a long blue envelope.*) Here's a whacking letter from the family solicitor. (*He pulls out the enclosures and glances over them.*) Great Heavens! Seventy! Two hundred! (*in a crescendo of dismay*) Four hundred! Four thousand!! Nine thousand six hundred!!! What on earth am I to do with them all?

RAINA   (*timidly*) Nine thousand hotels?

BLUNTSCHLI   Hotels! Nonsense. If you only knew! Oh, it's too ridiculous! Excuse me: I must give my fellow orders about starting. (*He leaves the room hastily, with the documents in his hand.*)

LOUKA (*knowing instinctively that she can annoy* RAINA *by disparaging* BLUNTSCHLI) He has not much heart, that Swiss. He has not a word of grief for his poor father.

RAINA (*bitterly*) Grief! A man who has been doing nothing but killing people for years! What does he care? What does any soldier care? (*She goes to the door, restraining her tears with difficulty.*)

LOUKA Major Saranoff has been fighting too; and he has plenty of heart left. (RAINA, *at the door, draws herself up haughtily and goes out.*) Aha! I thought you wouldnt get much feeling out of your soldier. (*She is following* RAINA *when* NICOLA *enters with an armful of logs for the stove.*)

NICOLA (*grinning amorously at her*) Ive been trying all the afternoon to get a minute alone with you, my girl. (*His countenance changes as he notices her arm.*) Why, what fashion is that of wearing your sleeve, child?

LOUKA (*proudly*) My own fashion.

NICOLA Indeed! If the mistress catches you, she'll talk to you. (*He puts the logs down, and seats himself comfortably on the ottoman.*)

LOUKA Is that any reason why you should take it on yourself to talk to me?

NICOLA Come! dont be so contrary with me. Ive some good news for you. (*She sits down beside him. He takes out some paper money.* LOUKA, *with an eager gleam in her eyes, tries to snatch it; but he shifts it quickly to his left hand, out of her reach.*) See! a twenty leva bill. Sergius gave me that, out of pure swagger. A fool and his money are soon parted. Theres ten levas more. The Swiss gave me that for backing up the mistress's and RAINA's lies about him. He's no fool, he isnt. You should have heard old Catherine downstairs as polite as you please to me, telling me not to mind the Major being a little impatient; for they knew what a good servant I was—after making a fool and a liar of me before them all! The twenty will go to our savings; and you shall have the ten to spend if youll only talk to me so as to remind me I'm a human being. I get tired of being a servant occasionally.

LOUKA: Yes: sell your manhood for 30 levas, and buy me for 10! (*rising scornfully*) Keep your money. You were born to be a servant. I was not. When you set up your shop you will only be everybody's servant instead of somebody's servant. (*She goes moodily to the table and seats herself regally in* SERGIUS's *chair.*)

NICOLA (*picking up his logs, and going to the stove*) Ah, wait til you see. We shall have our evenings to ourselves; and I shall be master in my own house, I promise you. (*He throws the logs down and kneels at the stove.*)

LOUKA You shall never be master in mine.

NICOLA (*turning, still on his knees, and squatting down rather forlornly on his calves, daunted by her implacable disdain*) You have a great ambition in you, Louka. Remember: if any luck comes to you, it was I that made a woman of you.

LOUKA You!

NICOLA (*scrambling up and going to her*) Yes, me. Who was it made you give up wearing a couple of pounds of false black hair on your head and reddening your lips and cheeks like any other Bulgarian girl! I did. Who taught you to trim your nails, and keep your hands clean, and be dainty about yourself, like a fine Russian lady! Me: do you hear that? me! (*She tosses her head defiantly; and he turns away, adding more coolly*) Ive often thought that if Raina were out of the way, and you just a little less of a fool and Sergius just a little more of one, you might come to be one of my grandest customers, instead of only being my wife and costing me money.

LOUKA   I believe you would rather be my servant than my husband. You would make more out of me. Oh, I know that soul of yours.

NICOLA   (*going closer to her for greater emphasis*) Never you mind my soul; but just listen to my advice. If you want to be a lady, your present behaviour to me wont do at all, unless when we're alone. It's too sharp and impudent; and impudence is a sort of familiarity: it shews affection for me. And dont you try being high and mighty with me, either. Youre like all country girls: you think it's genteel to treat a servant the way I treat a stableboy. Thats only your ignorance; and dont you forget it. And dont be so ready to defy everybody. Act as if you expected to have your own way, not as if you expected to be ordered about. The way to get on as a lady is the same as the way to get on as a servant: youve got to know your place: thats the secret of it. And you may depend on me to know my place if you get promoted. Think over it, my girl. I'll stand by you: one servant should always stand by another.

LOUKA   (*rising impatiently*) Oh, I must behave in my own way. You take all the courage out of me with your cold-blooded wisdom. Go and put those logs in the fire: thats the sort of thing you understand.

(*Before* NICOLA *can retort,* SERGIUS *comes in. He checks himself a moment on seeing* LOUKA; *then goes to the stove.*)

SERGIUS   (*to* NICOLA) I am not in the way of your work, I hope.

NICOLA   (*in a smooth, elderly manner*) Oh no, sir: thank you kindly. I was only speaking to this foolish girl about her habit of running up here to the library whenever she gets a chance, to look at the books. Thats the worst of her education, sir: it gives her habits above her station. (*to* LOUKA) Make that table tidy, Louka, for the Major. (*He goes out sedately.*)

(LOUKA, *without looking at* SERGIUS, *pretends to arrange the papers on the table. He crosses slowly to her, and studies the arrangement of her sleeve reflectively.*)

SERGIUS   Let me see: is there a mark there? (*He turns up the bracelet and sees the bruise made by his grasp. She stands motionless, not looking at him: fascinated, but on her guard.*) Ffff! Does it hurt?

LOUKA   Yes.

SERGIUS   Shall I cure it?

LOUKA   (*instantly withdrawing herself proudly, but still not looking at him*) No. You cannot cure it now.

SERGIUS   (*masterfully*) Quite sure? (*He makes a movement as if to take her in his arms.*)

LOUKA   Dont trifle with me, please. An officer should not trifle with a servant.

SERGIUS   (*indicating the bruise with a merciless stroke of his forefinger*) That was no trifle, Louka.

LOUKA   (*flinching; then looking at him for the first time*) Are you sorry?

SERGIUS   (*with measured emphasis, folding his arms*) I am never sorry.

LOUKA   (*wistfully*) I wish I could believe a man could be as unlike a woman as that. I wonder are you really a brave man?

SERGIUS   (*unaffectedly, relaxing his attitude*) Yes: I am a brave man. My heart jumped like a woman's at the first shot; but in the charge I found that I was brave. Yes: that at least is real about me.

LOUKA   Did you find in the charge that the men whose fathers are poor like mine were any less brave than the men who are rich like you?

SERGIUS   (*with bitter levity*) Not a bit. They all slashed and cursed and yelled like heroes. Psha! the courage to rage and kill is cheap. I have an English bull terrier who has as much of that sort of courage as the whole Bulgarian nation, and the whole Russian nation at its back. But he lets my groom thrash him, all the same. Thats your soldier all over! No, Louka: your poor men can cut throats; but they are afraid of their officers; they put up with insults and blows; they stand by and see one another punished like children: aye, and help to do it when they are ordered. And the officers!!! Well (*with a short harsh laugh*) I am an officer. Oh, (*fervently*) give me the man who will defy to the death any power on earth or in heaven that sets itself up against his own will and conscience: he alone is the brave man.

LOUKA   How easy it is to talk! Men never seem to me to grow up: they all have schoolboy's ideas. You dont know what true courage is.

SERGIUS   (*ironically*) Indeed! I am willing to be instructed. (*He sits on the ottoman, sprawling magnificently.*)

LOUKA   Look at me! How much am I allowed to have my own will? I have to get your room ready for you: to sweep and dust, to fetch and carry. How could that degrade me if it did not degrade you to have it done for you? But (*with subdued passion*) if I were Empress of Russia, above everyone in the world, then!! Ah then, though according to you I could shew no courage at all, you should see, you should see.

SERGIUS   What would you do, most noble Empress?

LOUKA   I would marry the man I loved, which no other queen in Europe has the courage to do. If I loved you, though you would be as far beneath me as I am beneath you, I would dare to be the equal of my inferior. Would you dare as much if you loved me? No: if you felt the beginnings of love for me you would not let it grow. You would not dare: you would marry a rich man's daughter because you would be afraid of what other people would say to you.

SERGIUS   (*bounding up*) You lie: it is not so, by all the stars! If I loved you, and I were the Czar himself, I would set you on the throne by my side. You know that I love another woman, a woman as high above you as heaven is above earth. And you are jealous of her.

LOUKA   I have no reason to be. She will never marry you now. The man I told you of has come back. She will marry the Swiss.

SERGIUS   (*recoiling*) The Swiss!

LOUKA   A man worth ten of you. Then you can come to me; and I will refuse you. You are not good enough for me. (*She turns to the door.*)

SERGIUS   (*springing after her and catching her fiercely in his arms*) I will kill the Swiss; and afterwards I will do as I please with you.

LOUKA (*in his arms, passive and steadfast*) The Swiss will kill you, perhaps. He has beaten you in love. He may beat you in war.

SERGIUS (*tormentedly*) Do you think I believe that she—she! whose worst thoughts are higher than your best ones, is capable of trifling with another man behind my back?

LOUKA Do you think she would believe the Swiss if he told her now that I am in your arms?

SERGIUS (*releasing her in despair*) Damnation! Oh, damnation! Mockery! mockery everywhere! everything I think is mocked by everything I do. (*He strikes himself frantically on the breast.*) Coward! liar! fool! Shall I kill myself like a man, or live and pretend to laugh at myself? (*She again turns to go.*) Louka! (*She stops near the door.*) Remember: you belong to me.

LOUKA (*turning*) What does that mean? An insult?

SERGIUS (*commandingly*) It means that you love me, and that I have had you here in my arms, and will perhaps have you there again. Whether that is an insult I neither know nor care: take it as you please. But (*vehemently*) I will not be a coward and a trifler. If I choose to love you, I dare marry you, in spite of all Bulgaria. If these hands ever touch you again, they shall touch my affianced bride.

LOUKA We shall see whether you dare keep your word. And take care. I will not wait long.

SERGIUS (*again folding his arms and standing motionless in the middle of the room*) Yes: we shall see. And you shall wait my pleasure.

(BLUNTSCHLI, *much preoccupied, with his papers still in his hand, enters, leaving the door open for* LOUKA *to go out. He goes across to the table, glancing at her as he passes.* SERGIUS, *without altering his resolute attitude, watches him steadily.* LOUKA *goes out, leaving the door open.*)

BLUNTSCHLI (*absently, sitting at the table as before, and putting down his papers*) Thats a remarkable looking young woman.

SERGIUS (*gravely, without moving*) Captain Bluntschli.

BLUNTSCHLI Eh?

SERGIUS You have deceived me. You are my rival. I brook no rivals. At six o'clock I shall be in the drilling-ground on the Klissoura road, alone, on horseback, with my sabre. Do you understand?

BLUNTSCHLI (*staring, but sitting quite at his ease*) Oh, thank you: thats a cavalry man's proposal. I'm in the artillery; and I have the choice of weapons. If I go, I shall take a machine gun. And there shall be no mistake about the cartridges this time.

SERGIUS (*flushing, but with deadly coldness*) Take care, sir. It is not our custom in Bulgaria to allow invitations of that kind to be trifled with.

BLUNTSCHLI (*warmly*) Pooh! dont talk to me about Bulgaria. You dont know what fighting is. But have it your own way. Bring your sabre along. I'll meet you.

SERGIUS (*fiercely delighted to find his opponent a man of spirit*) Well said, Switzer. Shall I lend you my best horse?

BLUNTSCHLI No: damn your horse! thank you all the same, my dear fellow.

(RAINA *comes in, and hears the next sentence.*) I shall fight you on foot. Horseback's too dangerous; I dont want to kill you if I can help it.

RAINA (*hurrying forward anxiously*) I have heard what Captain Bluntschli said, Sergius. You are going to fight. Why? (SERGIUS *turns away in silence, and goes to the stove, where he stands watching her as she continues, to* BLUNTSCHLI) What about?

BLUNTSCHLI I dont know: he hasnt told me. Better not interfere, dear young lady. No harm will be done: Ive often acted as sword instructor. He wont be able to touch me; and I'll not hurt him. It will save explanations. In the morning I shall be off home; and youll never see me or hear of me again. You and he will then make it up and live happily ever after.

RAINA (*turning away deeply hurt, almost with a sob in her voice*) I never said I wanted to see you again.

SERGIUS (*striding forward*) Ha! That is a confession.

RAINA (*haughtily*) What do you mean?

SERGIUS You love that man!

RAINA (*scandalized*) Sergius!

SERGIUS You allow him to make love to you behind my back, just as you treat me as your affianced husband behind his. Bluntschli: you knew our relations; and you deceived me. It is for that that I call you to account, not for having received favors *I* never enjoyed.

BLUNTSCHLI (*jumping up indignantly*) Stuff! Rubbish! I have received no favors. Why, the young lady doesn't even know whether I'm married or not.

RAINA (*forgetting herself*) Oh! (*collapsing on the ottoman*) Are you?

SERGIUS You see the young lady's concern, Captain Bluntschli. Denial is useless. You have enjoyed the privilege of being received in her own room, late at night—

BLUNTSCHLI (*interrupting him pepperily*) Yes, you blockhead! she received me with a pistol at her head. Your cavalry were at my heels. I'd have blown out her brains if she'd uttered a cry.

SERGIUS (*taken aback*) Bluntschli! Raina: is this true?

RAINA (*rising in wrathful majesty*) Oh, how dare you, how dare you?

BLUNTSCHLI Apologize, man: apologize. (*He resumes his seat at the table.*)

SERGIUS (*with the old measured emphasis, folding his arms*) I never apologize!

RAINA (*passionately*) This is the doing of that friend of yours, Captain Bluntschli. It is he who is spreading this horrible story about me. (*She walks about excitedly.*)

BLUNTSCHLI No: he's dead. Burnt alive.

RAINA (*stopping, shocked*) Burnt alive!

BLUNTSCHLI Shot in the hip in a woodyard. Couldnt drag himself out. Your fellows' shells set the timber on fire and burnt him, with half a dozen other poor devils in the same predicament.

RAINA How horrible!

SERGIUS And how ridiculous! Oh, war! war! the dream of patriots and heroes! A fraud, Bluntschli. A hollow sham, like love.

RAINA (*outraged*) Like love! You say that before me!

BLUNTSCHLI   Come, Saranoff: that matter is explained.

SERGIUS   A hollow sham, I say. Would you have come back here if nothing had passed between you except the muzzle of your pistol? Raina is mistaken about your friend who was burnt. He was not my informant.

RAINA   Who then? (*suddenly guessing the truth*) Ah, Louka! my maid! my servant! You were with her this morning all that time after—after—Oh, what sort of god is this I have been worshipping! (*He meets her gaze with sardonic enjoyment of her disenchantment. Angered all the more, she goes closer to him, and says, in a lower, intenser tone*) Do you know that I looked out of the window as I went upstairs, to have another sight of my hero; and I saw something I did not understand then. I know now that you were making love to her.

SERGIUS   (*with grim humor*) You saw that?

RAINA   Only too well. (*She turns away, and throws herself on the divan under the centre window, quite overcome.*)

SERGIUS   (*cynically*) Raina: our romance is shattered. Life's a farce.

BLUNTSCHLI   (*to* RAINA, *whimsically*) You see: he's found himself out now.

SERGIUS   (*going to him*) Bluntschli: I have allowed you to call me a blockhead. You may now call me a coward as well. I refuse to fight you. Do you know why?

BLUNTSCHLI   No; but it doesnt matter. I didn't ask the reason when you cried on; and I dont ask the reason now that you cry off. I'm a professional soldier! I fight when I have to, and am very glad to get out of it when I havnt to. Youre only an amateur: you think fighting's an amusement.

SERGIUS   (*sitting down at the table, nose to nose with him*) You shall hear the reason all the same, my professional. The reason is that it takes two men—real men—men of heart, blood and honor—to make a genuine combat. I could no more fight with you than I could make love to an ugly woman. Youve no magnetism: youre not a man: youre a machine.

BLUNTSCHLI   (*apologetically*) Quite true, quite true. I always was that sort of chap. I'm very sorry.

SERGIUS   Psha!

BLUNTSCHLI   But now that youve found that life isnt a farce, but something quite sensible and serious, what further obstacle is there to your happiness?

RAINA   (*rising*) You are very solicitous about my happiness and his. Do you forget his new love—Louka? It is not you that he must fight now, but his rival, Nicola.

SERGIUS   Rival!! (*bounding half across the room*)

RAINA   Dont you know that theyre engaged?

SERGIUS   Nicola! Are fresh abysses opening? Nicola!

RAINA   (*sarcastically*) A shocking sacrifice, isnt it? Such beauty! such intellect! such modesty! wasted on a middle-aged servant man. Really, Sergius, you cannot stand by and allow such a thing. It would be unworthy of your chivalry.

SERGIUS   (*losing all self-control*) Viper! Viper! (*He rushes to and fro, raging.*)

BLUNTSCHLI   Look here, Saranoff: youre getting the worst of this.

RAINA   (*getting angrier*) Do you realize what he has done, Captain Bluntschli?

He has set this girl as a spy on us; and her reward is that he makes love to her.

SERGIUS False! Monstrous!

RAINA Monstrous! (*confronting him*) Do you deny that she told you about Captain Bluntschli being in my room?

SERGIUS No; but—

RAINA (*interrupting*) Do you deny that you were making love to her when she told you?

SERGIUS No; but I tell you—

RAINA (*cutting him short contemptuously*) It is unnecessary to tell us anything more. That is quite enough for us. (*She turns away from him and sweeps majestically back to the window.*)

BLUNTSCHLI (*quietly, as Sergius, in an agony of mortification, sinks on the ottoman, clutching his averted head between his fists*) I told you you were getting the worst of it, Saranoff.

SERGIUS Tiger cat!

RAINA (*running excitedly to Bluntschli*) You hear this man calling me names, Captain Bluntschli?

BLUNTSCHLI What else can he do, dear lady? He must defend himself somehow. Come: (*very persuasively*) dont quarrel. What good does it do?

(RAINA, *with a gasp, sits down on the ottoman, and after a vain effort to look vexedly at* BLUNTSCHLI, *falls a victim to her sense of humor, and actually leans back babyishly against the writhing shoulder of* SERGIUS.)

SERGIUS Engaged to Nicola! Ha! ha! Ah well, Bluntschli, you are right to take this huge imposture of a world coolly.

RAINA (*quaintly to Bluntschli, with an intuitive guess at his state of mind*) I daresay you think us a couple of grown-up babies, dont you?

SERGIUS (*grinning savagely*) He does: he does. Swiss civilization nursetending Bulgarian barbarism, eh?

BLUNTSCHLI (*blushing*) Not at all, I assure you. Im only very glad to get you two quieted. There! there! let's be pleasant and talk it over in a friendly way. Where is this other young lady?

RAINA Listening at the door, probably.

SERGIUS (*shivering as if a bullet had struck him, and speaking with quiet but deep indignation*) I will prove that that, at least, is a calumny. (*He goes with dignity to the door and opens it. A yell of fury bursts from him as he looks out. He darts into the passage, and returns dragging in* LOUKA, *whom he flings violently against the table, exclaiming*) Judge her, Bluntschli. You the cool impartial man: judge the eavesdropper.

(LOUKA *stands her ground, proud and silent.*)

BLUNTSCHLI (*shaking his head*) I mustnt judge her. I once listened myself outside a tent when there was a mutiny brewing. It's all a question of the degree of provocation. My life was at stake.

LOUKA My love was at stake. I am not ashamed.

RAINA (*contemptuously*) Your love! Your curiosity, you mean.

LOUKA (*facing her and returning her contempt with interest*) My love, stronger than anything you can feel, even for your chocolate cream soldier.

SERGIUS (*with quick suspicion, to* LOUKA) What does that mean?

LOUKA (*fiercely*) I mean—

SERGIUS (*interrupting her slightly*) Oh, I remember: the ice pudding. A paltry taunt, girl!

(MAJOR PETKOFF *enters, in his shirtsleeves.*)

PETKOFF Excuse my shirtsleeves, gentlemen. Raina: somebody has been wearing that coat of mine: I'll swear it. Somebody with a differently shaped back. It's all burst open at the sleeve. Your mother is mending it. I wish she'd make haste: I shall catch cold. (*He looks more attentively at them.*) Is anything the matter?

RAINA No. (*She sits down at the stove, with a tranquil air.*)

SERGIUS Oh no. (*He sits down at the end of the table, as at first.*)

BLUNTSCHLI (*who is already seated*) Nothing. Nothing.

PETKOFF (*sitting down on the ottoman in his old place*) Thats all right. (*He notices* LOUKA.) Anything the matter, Louka?

LOUKA No, sir.

PETKOFF (*genially*) Thats all right. (*He sneezes.*) Go and ask your mistress for my coat, like a good girl, will you?

(NICOLA *enters with the coat.* LOUKA *makes a pretence of having business in the room by taking the little table with the hookah away to the wall near the windows.*)

RAINA (*rising quickly as she sees the coat on* NICOLA'*s arm*) Here it is, papa. Give it to me, Nicola; and do you put some more wood on the fire. (*She takes the coat, and brings it to the Major, who stands up to put it on.* NICOLA *attends to the fire.*)

PETKOFF (*to* RAINA, *teasing her affectionately*) Aha! Going to be very good to poor old papa just for one day after his return from the wars, eh?

RAINA (*with solemn reproach*) Ah, how can you say that to me, father?

PETKOFF Well, well, only a joke, little one. Come: give me a kiss. (*She kisses him.*) Now give me the coat.

RAINA No: I am going to put it on for you. Turn your back. (*He turns his back and feels behind him with his arms for the sleeves. She dexterously takes the photograph from the pocket and throws it on the table before* BLUNTSCHLI, *who covers it with a sheet of paper under the very nose of* SERGIUS, *who looks on amazed, with his suspicions roused in the highest degree. She then helps* PETKOFF *on with his coat.*) There, dear! Now are you comfortable?

PETKOFF Quite, little love. Thanks. (*He sits down; and* RAINA *returns to her seat near the stove.*) Oh, by the bye, Ive found something funny. Whats the meaning of this? (*He puts his hand into the picked pocket.*) Eh? Hallo! (*He tries the other pocket.*) Well, I could have sworn—! (*Much, puzzled, he tries the breast pocket.*) I wonder—(*trying the original pocket*) Where can it—? (*He rises, exclaiming*) Your mother's taken it!

RAINA (*very red*) Taken what?

PETKOFF Your photograph, with the inscription: "Raina, to her Chocolate Cream Soldier: a Souvenir." Now you know theres something more in this than meets the eye; and I'm going to find it out. (*shouting*) Nicola!

NICOLA (*coming to him*) Sir!

PETKOFF Did you spoil any pastry of Miss Raina's this morning?

NICOLA You heard Miss Raina say that I did, sir.

PETKOFF I know that, you idiot. Was it true?

NICOLA I am sure Miss Raina is incapable of saying anything that is not true, sir.

PETKOFF Are you? Then I'm not. (*turning to the others*) Come: do you think I dont see it all? (*He goes to* SERGIUS, *and slaps him on the shoulder.*) Sergius: youre the chocolate cream soldier, arnt you?

SERGIUS (*starting up)* I! A chocolate cream soldier! Certainly not.

PETKOFF Not! (*He looks at them. They are all very serious and very conscious.*) Do you mean to tell me that Raina sends things like that to other men?

SERGIUS (*enigmatically)* The world is not such an innocent place as we used to think, Petkoff.

BLUNTSCHLI (*rising*) It's all right, Major. I'm the chocolate cream soldier. (PETKOFF *and* SERGIUS *are equally astonished.*) The gracious young lady saved my life by giving me chocolate creams when I was starving: shall I ever forget their flavour! My late friend Stolz told you the story at Pirot. I was the fugitive.

PETKOFF You! (*He gasps.*) Sergius: do you remember how those two woman went on this morning when we mentioned it? (SERGIUS *smiles cynically.* PETKOFF *confronts* RAINA *severely.*) Youre a nice young lady, arnt you?

RAINA (*bitterly*) Major Saranoff has changed his mind. And when I wrote that on the photograph, I did not know that Captain Bluntschli was married.

BLUNTSCHLI (*startled into vehement protest*) I'm not married.

RAINA (*with deep reproach*) You said you were.

BLUNTSCHLI I did not. I positively did not. I never was married in my life.

PETKOFF (*exasperated*) Raina: will you kindly inform me, if I am not asking too much, which of these gentlemen you are engaged to?

RAINA To neither of them. This young lady (*introducing* LOUKA, *who faces them all proudly*) is the object of Major Saranoff's affections at present.

PETKOFF Louka! Are you mad, Sergius? Why, this girl's engaged to Nicola.

NICOLA I beg your pardon, sir. There is a mistake. Louka is not engaged to me.

PETKOFF Not engaged to you, you scoundrel! Why, you had twenty-five levas from me on the day of your betrothal; and she had that gilt bracelet from Miss Raina.

NICOLA (*with cool unction*) We gave it out so, sir. But it was only to give Louka protection. She had a soul above her station; and I have been no more than her confidential servant. I intend, as you know, sir, to set up a shop later on in Sofia; and I look forward to her custom and recommendation should she marry into the nobility. (*He goes out with impressive discretion, leaving them all staring after him.*)

PETKOFF (*breaking the silence*) Well, I am—hm!

SERGIUS This is either the finest heroism or the most crawling baseness. Which is it, Bluntschli?

BLUNTSCHLI Never mind whether it's heroism or baseness. Nicola's the ablest man Ive met in Bulgaria. I'll make him manager of a hotel if he can speak French and German.

LOUKA (*suddenly breaking out at* SERGIUS) I have been insulted by everyone here. You set them the example. You owe me an apology.

(SERGIUS, *like a repeating clock of which the spring has been touched, immediately
begins to fold his arms.*)

BLUNTSCHLI (*before he can speak*) It's no use. He never apologizes.

LOUKA Not to you, his equal and his enemy. To me, his poor servant, he
will not refuse to apologize.

SERGIUS (*approvingly*) You are right. (*He bends his knee in his grandest
manner.*) Forgive me.

LOUKA I forgive you. (*She timidly gives him her hand, which he kisses.*) That
touch makes me your affianced wife.

SERGIUS (*springing up*) Ah! I forgot that.

LOUKA (*coldly*) You can withdraw if you like.

SERGIUS Withdraw! Never! You belong to me. (*He puts his arm about her.*)

(CATHERINE *comes in and finds* LOUKA *in* SERGIUS' *arms, with all the rest gazing at
them in bewildered astonishment.*)

CATHERINE What does this mean?

(SERGIUS *releases* LOUKA.)

PETKOFF Well, my dear, it appears that Sergius is going to marry Louka
instead of Raina. (*She is about to break out indignantly at him: he stops
her by exclaiming testily*) Dont blame me: I've nothing to do with it. (*He
retreats to the stove.*)

CATHERINE Marry Louka! Sergius: you are bound by your word to us!

SERGIUS (*folding his arms*) Nothing binds me.

BLUNTSCHLI (*much pleased by this piece of common sense*) Saranoff: your
hand. My congratulations. These heroics of yours have their practical side
after all. (*to* LOUKA) Gracious young lady: the best wishes of a good Repub-
lican! (*He kisses her hand, to* RAINA's *great disgust, and returns to his seat.*)

CATHERINE Louka: you have been telling stories.

LOUKA I have done Raina no harm.

CATHERINE (*haughtily*) Raina!

(RAINA, *equally indignant, almost snorts at the liberty.*)

LOUKA I have a right to call her Raina: she calls me Louka. I told Major
Saranoff she would never marry him if the Swiss gentleman came back.

BLUNTSCHLI (*rising, much surprised*) Hallo!

LOUKA (*turning to Raina*) I thought you were fonder of him than of Sergius.
You know best whether I was right.

BLUNTSCHLI What nonsense! I assure you, my dear Major, my dear Madame,
the gracious young lady simply saved my life, nothing else. She never
cared two straws for me. Why, bless my heart and soul, look at the young
lady and look at me. She, rich, young, beautiful, with her imagination full
of fairy princes and noble natures and cavalry charges and goodness knows
what! And I, a commonplace Swiss soldier who hardly knows what a decent
life is after fifteen years of barracks and battles: a vagabond, a man who
has spoiled all his chances in life through an incurably romantic disposition, a man—

SERGIUS (*starting as if a needle had pricked him and interrupting* BLUNT-SCHLI *in incredulous amazement*) Excuse me, Bluntschli: what did you say had spoiled your chances in life?

BLUNTSCHLI (*promptly*) An incurably romantic disposition. I ran away from home twice when I was a boy. I went into the army instead of into my father's business. I climbed the balcony of this house when a man of sense would have dived into the nearest cellar. I came sneaking back here to have another look at the young lady when any other man of my age would have sent the coat back—

PETKOFF My coat!

BLUNTSCHLI —yes: thats the coat I mean—would have sent it back and gone quietly home. Do you suppose I am the sort of fellow a young girl falls in love with? Why, look at our ages! I'm thirty-four: I dont suppose the young lady is much over seventeen. (*This estimate produces a marked sensation, all the rest turning and staring at one another. He proceeds innocently.*) All that adventure which was life or death to me, was only a schoolgirl's game to her—chocolate creams and hide and seek. Heres the proof! (*He takes the photograph from the table.*) Now, I ask you, would a woman who took the affair seriously have sent me this and written on it "Raina, to her Chocolate Cream Soldier: a Souvenir"? (*He exhibits the photograph triumphantly, as if it settled the matter beyond all possibility of refutations.*)

PETKOFF Thats what I was looking for. How the deuce did it get there? (*He comes from the stove to look at it, and sits down on the ottoman.*)

BLUNTSCHLI (*to* RAINA, *complacently*) I have put everything right, I hope, gracious young lady.

RAINA (*going to the table to face him*) I quite agree with your account of yourself. You are a romantic idiot. (*Bluntschli is unspeakably taken aback.*) Next time, I hope you will know the difference between a schoolgirl of seventeen and a woman of twenty-three.

BLUNTSCHLI (*stupefied*) Twenty-three?

(RAINA *snaps the photograph contemptuously from his hand; tears it up; throws the pieces in his face; and sweeps back to her former place.*)

SERGIUS (*with grim enjoyment of his rival's discomfiture*) Bluntschli: my last belief is gone. Your sagacity is a fraud, like everything else. You have less sense than even I!

BLUNTSCHLI (*overwhelmed*) Twenty-three! Twenty-three!! (*He considers.*) Hm! (*swiftly making up his mind and coming to his host*) In that case, Major Petkoff, I beg to propose formally to become a suitor for your daughter's hand, in place of Major Saranoff retired.

RAINA You dare!

BLUNTSCHLI If you were twenty-three when you said those things to me this afternoon, I shall take them seriously.

CATHERINE (*loftily polite*) I doubt sir, whether you quite realize either my daughter's position or that of Major Sergius Saranoff, whose place you propose to take. The Petkoffs and the Saranoffs are known as the richest and most important families in the country. Our position is almost historical: we can go back for twenty years.

PETKOFF   Oh, never mind that, Catherine. (*to* BLUNTSCHLI) We should be most happy, Bluntschli, if it were only a question of your position; but hang it, you know, Raina is accustomed to a very comfortable establishment. Sergius keeps twenty horses.

BLUNTSCHLI   But who wants twenty horses? We're not going to keep a circus.

CATHERINE   (*severely*) My daughter, sir, is accustomed to a first-rate stable.

RAINA   Hush, mother: youre making me ridiculous.

BLUNTSCHLI   Oh well, if it comes to a question of establishment, here goes! (*He darts impetuously to the table; seizes the papers in the blue envelope; and turns to* SERGIUS.) How many horses did you say?

SERGIUS   Twenty, noble Switzer.

BLUNTSCHLI   I have two hundred horses. (*They are amazed.*) How many carriages?

SERGIUS   Three.

BLUNTSCHLI   I have seventy. Twenty-four of them will hold twelve inside, beside two on the box, without counting the driver and conductor. How many tablecloths have you?

SERGIUS   How the deuce do I know?

BLUNTSCHLI   Have you four thousand?

SERGIUS   No.

BLUNTSCHLI   I have. I have nine thousand six hundred pairs of sheets and blankets, with two thousand four hundred eider-down quilts. I have ten thousand knives and forks, and the same quantity of dessert spoons. I have three hundred servants. I have six palatial establishments, besides two livery stables, a tea garden, and a private house. I have four medals for distinguished services; I have the rank of an officer and the standing of a gentleman; and I have three native languages. Shew me any man in Bulgaria that can offer as much!

PETKOFF   (*with childish awe*) Are you Emperor of Switzerland?

BLUNTSCHLI   My rank is the highest known in Switzerland: I am a free citizen.

CATHERINE   Then, Captain Bluntschli, since you are my daughter's choice—

RAINA   (*mutinously*) He's not.

CATHERINE   (*ignoring her*)—I shall not stand in the way of her happiness. (PETKOFF *is about to speak.*) That is Major Petkoff's feeling also.

PETKOFF   Oh, I shall be only too glad. Two hundred horses! Whew!

SERGIUS   What says the lady?

RAINA   (*pretending to sulk*) The lady says that he can keep his tablecloths and his omnibuses. I am not here to be sold to the highest bidder. (*She turns her back on him.*)

BLUNTSCHLI   I wont take that answer. I appealed to you as a fugitive, a beggar, and a starving man. You accepted me. You gave me your hand to kiss, your bed to sleep in, and your roof to shelter me.

RAINA   I did not give them to the Emperor of Switzerland.

BLUNTSCHLI   Thats just what I say. (*He catches her by the shoulders and turns her face-to-face with him.*) Now tell us whom you did give them to.

RAINA   (*succumbing with a shy smile*) To my chocolate cream soldier.

BLUNTSCHLI (*with a boyish laugh of delight*) Thatll do. Thank you. (*He looks at his watch and suddenly becomes businesslike.*) Time's up, Major. Youve managed those regiments so well that youre sure to be asked to get rid of some of the infantry of the Timok division. Send them home by way of Lom Palanka. Saranoff: dont get married until I come back: I shall be here punctually at five in the evening on Tuesday fortnight. Gracious ladies (*his heels click*), good evening. (*He makes them a military bow, and goes.*)

SERGIUS What a man! Is he a man?

When read for the first time, The Cherry Orchard *seems to contain difficulties of a sort not found in most plays. When reread, or when read for the second time and then seen in a good performance,* The Cherry Orchard *is likely to become one of the most realistic and sensible plays in the reader's experience.*

Perhaps we can account for this paradox in two ways. First, the play is Russian and is therefore foreign in a particular and peculiar sense. But second, and much more important, in The Cherry Orchard, *his last play, Chekhov brought to perfection his realistic technique.*

First produced in 1904, The Cherry Orchard *represents one phase of life in prerevolutionary Russia. The time seems longer ago than 1904, for the characters, who at first look and sound like us, are subtly different. They drink quantities of tea instead of quantities of coffee. They kiss each other's hands. They sit about and talk in a tone of melancholy reminiscence. So also the passing of the estate containing the once profitable cherry orchard is a symbol of the disappearance of the old Russia, and Trofimoff's speeches (for he may be taken as Chekhov's spokesman) contain both Chekhov's realization of the change and his prescription for health in the Russia to come. (Chekhov was by profession a physician.)*

Finally, certain language difficulties may make this seem like a foreign play. Russian is further removed from English than French and German, and in The Cherry Orchard *we are confronted with Russian proper names and nicknames of bewildering complexity.*

All these—Russian manners, the differences caused by the erosion of time, and the strange Russian names—are, after all, only superficialities. Far more important is an understanding of the reasons why this is a play of complete and delightful realism.

First, there is no violence in The Cherry Orchard— *not a single pistol shot, Chekhov boasted—because violence plays a small part in people's lives. Chekhov concentrates on the internal scene: what* happens inside us. According to Chekhov's theory, the highest aim of a playwright is to show character revealing itself subtly rather than "dramatically." So Chekhov brings out these internalities of character by skillful imitation of the mood and tone of conversations full of inconsequential and incoherent remarks.

Second, he converts part of the realism into comedy. Chekhov thought of The Cherry Orchard as a comic play, a hilarious affair tending to farce in some places. But he could not get his original actors to play for comedy. They persisted in seeing pathos and tragedy in these figures, and so have actors ever since. Probably the actors are right, for there is evidence that Chekhov also thought of his play as a means of discussing serious ideas. One example is the message spoken by Trofimoff: "all Russia is our orchard." Here Chekhov criticizes the irresponsibility and laziness of certain types of Russians.

Third, Chekhov uses symbols, and the symbols, with one exception, make for realism: the cherry orchard itself, the various sound effects, especially the chopping sounds offstage as the last curtain and the first cherry tree fall. Each sound underscores in a particular way the significance of what is happening on the stage. (The one exception is the twang of a breaking string in Act II and at the very end. It was for Chekhov a private, nonrealistic symbol, a note of romanticism.)

From all this the reader may well conclude that The Cherry Orchard is in its substance a play of intellectual sophistication and philosophical wisdom, in its technique an example of dramatic art of a high order. It does not discuss the really big questions, as do the tragedies in this volume, but on its own level it too enters into the essential complexities of life. It assumes that art must be a compendium and compost of tragedy, pathos, comedy, farce, and everyday living—just as life is.

*The Cherry Orchard

ANTON CHEKHOV

Translated by Jennie Covan

CHARACTERS

LIUBOFF ANDREIEVNA RANEVSKAYA, a landowner

ANYA, her daughter, aged seventeen

VARYA, her adopted daughter, aged twenty-seven

LEONID ANDREIEVITCH GAIEFF, Liuboff Andreievna's brother

YERMOLAI ALEXEIEVITCH LOPAKHIN, a merchant

PETER SERGEIEVEITCH TROFIMOFF, a student

BORIS BORISOVITCH SEMYONOFF-PISH-CHIK, a landowner

CHARLOTTA IVANOVNA, a governness

SEMYON PANTELEIEVITCH YEPIKHODOFF, a clerk

DUNYASHA (AVDOTYA FYODOROVNA), a maid-servant

FIRCE, an old footman, aged eighty-seven

YASHA, a young footman

A TRAMP

A STATION-MASTER

POST-OFFICE CLERK

GUESTS

A SERVANT

SCENE: Mme. Ranevskaya's estate.

ACT I

(*A room still called the nursery. One of the doors lead into* ANYA's *room. It is almost sunrise of a day in May. The cherry-trees are in bloom, but the chill of early morning is in the garden. The windows are shut.*)

(DUNYASHA *enters with a candle, and* LOPAKHIN *with a book in his hand.*)

LOPAKHIN   The train has arrived, thank God. What's the time?

DUNYASHA   It will soon be two. (*Blows out candle.*) It is already light.

LOPAKHIN   How late was the train? At least two hours. (*Yawns and stretches himself.*) I certainly made a fool of myself! I came here on purpose to meet them at the station and then overslept myself . . . in my chair. It's a pity. I wish you'd called me.

DUNYASHA   I thought you'd gone. (*Listening.*) I think I hear them coming.

LOPAKHIN   (*listens*) No . . . They have to collect their baggage and so on. . . . (*Pause.*) Liuboff Andreievna has been living abroad for five years; I don't know what she'll be like now . . . She's a good sort—an easy, simple person. I remember when I was a boy of fifteen, my father, who is dead—he used to keep a shop in the village here—hit me with his fist, and my nose bled . . . We had gone into the yard for something or other, and he was a little drunk. Liuboff Andreievna, as I remember her now, was still young, and very slight, and she took me to the wash-stand here in this very room, the nursery. She said, "Don't cry, my small peasant, all wounds heal at last." (*Pause.*) . . . Small peasant! My father was a peasant, true, but here I am in a white vest and brown shoes . . . like a pearl in an oyster shell. I'm rich now, with lots of money, but just think about it and examine me, and you'll find I'm still a peasant to the core. (*Turns over the pages of his book.*) Here I've been reading this book, but I understand nothing. I read and fell asleep. (*Pause.*)

DUNYASHA   The dogs didn't sleep all night; they feel that their masters are coming.

LOPAKHIN   What's the matter with you, Dunyasha. . . .

DUNYASHA   My hands are shaking. I am going to faint.

LOPAKHIN   You're too sensitive, Dunyasha. You dress just like a lady, and you do your hair like one, too. You shouldn't. You must remember your place in life.

YEPIKHODOFF   (*enters with a bouquet. He wears a short jacket and brilliantly polished boots which squeak audibly. He drops the bouquet as he enters, then picks it up.*) The gardener sent these; says they're to go into the dining-room. (*Gives the bouquet to* DUNYASHA.)

LOPAKHIN   And you'll bring me some kvass.

DUNYASHA   Yes, sir. (*Exit.*)

YEPIKHODOFF   There's a frost this morning—three degrees, and the cherry-trees are all in flower. I can't approve of our climate. (*Sighs.*) I can't. Our climate refuses to favor us even this once. And, Yermolai Alexeievitch, allow me to say to you, in addition, that I bought myself a pair of boots two days ago, and I beg to assure you that they squeak in a perfectly intolerable manner. What shall I put on them?

LOPAKHIN   Go away. You bore me.

YEPIKHODOFF   Some misfortune happens to me every day. But I don't complain; I'm used to it, and I even smile at it. (DUNYASHA *comes in and brings* LOPAKHIN *a glass of kvass.*) I am going. (*Knocks over a chair.*) There. . . . (*triumphantly*) There, you see, if I may use the word, what circumstances I am in, so to speak. It is simply extraordinary. (*Exit.*)

DUNYASHA   Let me confess to you, Yermolai Alexeievitch, that Yepikhodoff has proposed to me.

LOPAKHIN   Ah!

DUNYASHA   I don't know what to do about it. He's a nice young man, but every now and then, when he begins talking, you can't understand a word he says. It sounds sincere enough, only I can't understand it. I think I like him. He's madly in love with me. He's an unlucky man; every day something happens to him. We tease him about it. They call him "Two-and-twenty troubles."

LOPAKHIN   (*listens*) There they come, I think.

DUNYASHA   They're coming! What's the matter with me? I'm cold all over.

LOPAKHIN   There they are, really. Let's go and meet them. Will she know me? We haven't seen each other for five years.

DUNYASHA   (*excited*) I shall faint in a minute. . . . Oh, I'm fainting!

(*Two carriages are heard driving up to the house. LOPAKHIN and DUNYASHA quickly go out. The stage is empty. There are noises in the adjoining rooms. FIRCE, leaning on a stick, walks quickly across the stage; he has just been to meet LIUBOFF ANDREIEVNA. He wears an old-fashioned livery and a tall hat. He is saying something to himself, but not a word can be made out. The noise back stage grows louder and louder. A voice is heard: "Let's go in there." Enter LIUBOFF ANDREIEVNA, ANYA, and CHARLOTTA IVANOVNA leading a little dog on a chain, all dressed in traveling clothes, VARYA in a long coat and with a kerchief on her head. GAIEFF, SEMYONOFF-PISHCHIK, LOPAKHIN, DUNYASHA with a parcel and an umbrella, and a servant with suitcases—all cross the room.*)

ANYA   Let's go through here. Do you remember this room, mother?

LIUBOFF   (*joyfully, through her tears*) The nursery!

VARYA   How cold it is! My hands are quite numb. (*to LIUBOFF ANDREIEVNA*) Your rooms, the white one and the violet one, are just as they used to be, mother.

LIUBOFF   My dear, beautiful nursery . . . I used to sleep here when I was a baby. (*Kisses her brother, then VARYA, then her brother again.*) And Varya is just as she used to be, exactly like a nun. And I recognized Dunyasha. (*Kisses her.*)

GAIEFF   The train was two hours late. There now; how's that for punctuality?

CHARLOTTA   (*to PISHCHIK*) My dog eats nuts, too.

PISHCHIK   (*astonished*) Just imagine!

(*All leave except ANYA and DUNYASHA.*)

DUNYASHA   We did have to wait for you! (*Takes off ANYA's cloak and hat.*)

ANYA   For four nights on the journey I didn't sleep . . . I'm awfully cold.

DUNYASHA   You left during Lent, when it was snowing and frosty, but now? Darling? (*Laughs and kisses her.*) We did have to wait for you, my darling pet! . . . I must tell you at once, I can't wait a minute.

ANYA   (*listlessly*) Something else now . . . ?

DUNYASHA   The clerk, Yepikhodoff, proposed to me after Easter.

ANYA   Always the same . . . (*puts her hair straight.*) I've lost all my hairpins . . . (*She is very tired, and even staggers as she walks.*)

DUNYASHA   I don't know what to think about it. He loves me, he loves me so much!

ANYA   (*looks into her room; in a gentle voice*) My room, my windows, as if I'd never left! I'm at home! Tomorrow morning I'll get up and run out into the garden. . . . Oh, if I could only sleep! I didn't sleep the whole journey, I was so restless.

DUNYASHA   Peter Sergeievitch came two days ago.

ANYA   (*joyfully*) Peter!

DUNYASHA   He sleeps in the bath-house, he lives there. He said he was afraid he'd be in the way. (*Looks at her watch.*) I should call him, but Varvara Mihkailovna told me not to. "Don't wake him," she said.

(*Enter* VARYA, *a bunch of keys hanging from her belt.*)

VARYA Dunyasha, coffee, quick. Mother wishes some.

DUNYASHA In a moment. (*Exit.*)

VARYA Well, you've come, thank God. Home again. (*Caressing her.*) My darling is home again! My pretty one is back at last!

ANYA I had an awful time, I tell you.

VARYA I can just imagine it!

ANYA I went away in Holy Week; it was very cold then. Charlotta talked the whole way and would go on performing her tricks. Why did you force her on me?

VARYA You couldn't go alone, darling, at seventeen!

ANYA We went to Paris; it's cold there and snowing. I talk French perfectly dreadfully. My mother lives on the fifth floor. I go to her, and find her there with several Frenchmen, women, an old abbé with a book, and everything wreathed in tobacco smoke and the whole place so uninviting. I suddenly became very sorry for mother—so sorry that I took her head in my arms and hugged her and wouldn't let her go. Then mother started hugging me and crying. . . .

VARYA (*weeping*) Don't say any more, don't say any more . . .

ANYA She's already sold her villa near Mentone; she has nothing left, nothing. And I haven't a kopeck either; we only just managed to get here. And mother won't understand! We had dinner at a station; she asked for all the expensive things, and tipped the waiters one ruble each. And Charlotta too. Yasha demands a share, too— It is simply awful. Mother has a footman now, Yasha; we've brought him along.

VARYA I saw the fellow.

ANYA How's business? Has the interest been paid?

VARYA Not much chance of that.

ANYA Oh God, oh God . . .

VARYA The place will be sold in August.

ANYA Oh God . . .

LOPAKHIN (*looks in at the door and moos*) Moo! (*Exit.*)

VARYA (*through her tears*) I'd like to . . . (*Shakes her fist.*)

ANYA (*embraces* VARYA, *softly*) Varya, has he proposed to you? (VARYA *shakes her head.*) But he loves you. . . . Why don't you decide? Why do you keep on waiting?

VARYA I'm afraid it will all come to nothing. He's a busy man. I'm not his sort . . . he pays no attention to me. Bless the man, I don't wish to see him. . . . But everybody talks about our marriage, everybody congratulates me, and there's nothing in it at all, it's all like a dream. (*A different voice.*) You have a brooch that looks like a bee.

ANYA (*wistfully*) Mother bought it. (*Goes into her room, and talks lightly, like a child.*) In Paris I went up in a balloon!

VARYA My darling has come back, my pretty one is home again! (DUNYASHA *has already returnd with the coffee-pot and is making coffee.*) I go about all day, looking after the house, and I think all the time, if only you could marry a rich man, I'd be happy and would go away somewhere by myself, perhaps to Kieff . . . or to Moscow, and so on, from one holy place to another. I'd tramp and tramp. That would be splendid!

ANYA   The birds are singing in the garden. What time is it now?

VARYA   It must be getting on towards three. It's time you went to sleep, darling. (*Goes into* ANYA'S *room.*) Splendid!

(*Enter* YASHA *with a plaid shawl and a traveling bag.*)

YASHA   (*crossing the stage; politely*) May I go this way?

DUNYASHA   I hardly recognized you, Yasha. You have changed abroad.

YASHA   Hm . . . and who are you?

DUNYASHA   When you went away I was only so high. (*showing with her hand*) I'm Dunyasha, the daughter of Fyodor Kozoyedoff. You don't remember?

YASHA   Oh, you small cucumber! (*Looks round and embraces her. She screams and drops a saucer.* YASHA *goes out quickly.*)

VARYA   (*in the doorway in an angry voice*) What's that?

DUNYASHA   (*through her tears*) I've broken a saucer.

VARYA   It may bring luck.

ANYA   (*coming out of her room*) We must tell mother that Peter's here.

VARYA   I told them not to call him.

ANYA   (*thoughtfully*) Father died six years ago, and a month later my brother Grisha was drowned in the river—such a dear little boy of seven! Mother couldn't bear it; she went away, away, without looking round. . . . (*Shudders.*) Now I understand her; if only she knew! (*Pause.*) And Peter Trofimoff was Grisha's tutor, he might remind her. . . .

(*Enter* FIRCE *in a short jacket and white vest. Goes to the coffee-pot.*)

FIRCE   Madame is going to have a bite here. (*He is preoccupied, putting on white gloves.*) Is the coffee ready? (*to* DUNYASHA, *severely*) You!

DUNYASHA   Oh, dear me . . . ! (*leaving hurriedly*)

FIRCE   (*fussing round the coffee-pot*) Oh, you bungler . . . (*Murmurs to himself.*) Back from Paris . . . the master went to Paris once . . . in a carriage . . . (*Laughs.*)

VARYA   What are you mumbling, Firce?

FIRCE   I beg your pardon? (*joyfully*) The mistress is home again. I've lived to see her! I don't care if I die now . . . (*Weeps with joy.*)

(*Enter* LIUBOFF ANDREIEVNA, GAIEFF, LOPAKHIN, *and* SEMYONOFF-PISHCHIK, *the latter in a long jacket of thin cloth and loose trousers.* GAIEFF, *coming in, moves his arms and body about as if he were playing billiards.*)

LIUBOFF   Let me remember now. Red into the corner! Twice into the center!

GAIEFF   Right into the pocket! Once upon a time you and I, sister, both slept in this room, and now I'm fifty-one; it does seem strange.

LOPAKHIN   Yes, time does fly!

GAIEFF   What?

LOPAKHIN   I said that time does fly.

GAIEFF   It smells of patchouli here.

ANYA   I'm going to bed. Good-night, mother. (*Kisses her.*)

LIUBOFF My dear little child. (*Kisses her hand*.) Glad to be at home? I can't
get over it.

ANYA Good-night, uncle.

GAIEFF (*kisses her face and hands*) God be with you. How you do resemble
your mother! (*to his sister*) You were just like her at her age, Liuba.

(ANYA *gives her hand to* LOPAKHIN *and* PISHCHIK *and goes out shutting the door
behind her*.)

LIUBOFF She's awfully tired.

PISHCHIK It's a very long journey.

VARYA (*to* LOPAKHIN *and* PISHCHIK) Well, gentlemen, it's getting on toward
three. High time to retire.

LIUBOFF (*laughs*) You're just the same as ever, Varya. (*Draws her close and
kisses her*.) I'll have some coffee now; then we'll all go. (FIRCE *lays a
cushion under her feet*.) Thank you, dear. I'm used to coffee. I drink it day
and night. Thank you, dear old man. (*Kisses* FIRCE.)

VARYA I'll go and see whether they've brought in all the luggage. (*Exit*.)

LIUBOFF Is it really I who am sitting here? (*Laughs*.) I feel like jumping about
and waving my arms. (*Covers her face with her hands*.) But suppose I'm
dreaming! God knows I love my own country, I love it dearly; I couldn't look
out of the railway carriage, I cried so much. (*through her tears*) Still, I must
have my coffee. Thank you, Firce. Thank you, dear old man. I'm so glad
you're still with us.

FIRCE The day before yesterday.

GAIEFF He doesn't hear well.

LOPAKHIN I have to go to Kharkoff by the five o'clock train. I'm awfully sorry!
I should like to have a look at you, to gossip a little. You're as fine-looking
as ever.

PISHCHIK (*breathes heavily*) Even finer-looking . . . dressed in Paris fashion
. . . confound it all.

LOPAKHIN Your brother, Leonid Andreievitch, says I'm a snob, a usurer, but
that is absolutely nothing to me. Let him talk. Only I do wish you would
believe in me as you once did, that your wonderful, touching eyes would
look at me as they used to. Merciful God! My father was the serf of your
grandfather and your own father, but you—more than anybody else—did so
much for me once upon a time that I've forgotten everything and love you
as if you were one of my own family . . . and even more.

LIUBOFF I can't sit still, I can't! (*Jumps up and walks about in great excitement*.) I'll never survive this happiness. . . . You can laugh at me; I'm a silly
woman . . . My dear little cupboard. (*Kisses cupboard*.) My little table.

GAIEFF Nurse died during your absence.

LIUBOFF (*sits and drinks coffee*) Yes, God rest her soul. I heard by letter.

GAIEFF And Anastasia died, too. Peter Kosoy has left me and now lives in
town with the Commissioner of Police. (*Takes a box of candy out of his
pocket and sucks a piece*.)

PISHCHIK My daughter, Dashenka, sends her love.

LOPAKHIN I wish to say something very pleasant, very delightful, to you.
(*Looks at his watch*.) I'm going away at once, I haven't much time . . . but

I'll tell you all about it in two or three words. As you already know, your cherry orchard is to be sold to pay your debts, and the sale is arranged for August 22; but you needn't be alarmed, dear madam, you may sleep in peace; there's a way out. Here's my plan. Please listen carefully! Your estate is only thirteen miles from town, the railway runs past it and if the cherry orchard and the land by the river are broken up into building parcels and are then leased as villa sites, you'll have at least twenty-five thousand rubles a year income.

GAIEFF How utterly absurd!

LIUBOFF I don't understand you at all, Yermolai Alexeievitch.

LOPAKHIN You will get twenty-five rubles a year for each dessiatine from the leaseholders at the very least, and if you advertise now, I'm willing to bet that you won't have a vacant parcel left by the autumn; they'll all go. In a word, you're saved. I congratulate you. Only, of course, you'll have to straighten things out carefully . . . For instance, you'll have to pull down all the old buildings, this house, which is of no use to anybody now, and cut down the old cherry orchard. . . .

LIUBOFF Cut it down? My dear man, you must forgive me, but you don't understand anything at all. If there's anything interesting or remarkable in the whole province, it's this cherry orchard of ours.

LOPAKHIN The only remarkable thing about the orchard is its great size. It bears fruit only every other year, and even then you don't know what to do with the cherries; nobody buys any.

GAIEFF This orchard is mentioned in the "Encyclopaedia."

LOPAKHIN (looks at his watch) If we can't think of anything and don't make up our minds, then on August 22 both the cherry orchard and the whole estate will be sold at auction. Make up your mind! I swear there's no other way out. You may believe me!

FIRCE In the old days, forty or fifty years ago, they dried the cherries, soaked them and pickled them, and made jam, and it used to happen that . . .

GAIEFF Be quiet, Firce.

FIRCE And then we'd send the dried cherries in carts to Moscow and Kharkoff. And money! And the dried cherries were soft, juicy, sweet, and fragrant. They knew the way. . . .

LIUBOFF How was it done?

FIRCE They've forgotten. Nobody remembers.

PISHCHIK (to LIUBOFF ANDREIEVNA) What about Paris? Eh? Did you eat frogs?

LIUBOFF I ate crocodiles.

PISHCHIK Just imagine!

LOPAKHIN Formerly there were only the gentry and the laborers, in the villages, and now the people who live in villas have arrived. All towns now, even small ones, are surrounded by villas. And it's safe to say that in twenty years' time the villa residents will have increased tremendously. At present they sit on their balconies, and drink tea, but it may well happen that they'll commence to cultivate their patches of land, and then your cherry orchard will be happy, rich, glorious.

GAIEFF (*angry*) What nonsense!

(*Enter* VARYA *and* YASHA.)

VARYA There are two telegrams for you, mother dear. (*Picks out a key and noisily unlocks an antique cupboard.*) Here they are.

LIUBOFF They're from Paris . . . (*Tears them up without reading them.*) I'm through with Paris.

GAIEFF And do you know, Liuba, how old this cupboard is? A week ago I pulled out the bottom drawer; I looked and saw numbers carved in it. That cupboard was made exactly a hundred years ago. What do you think of that? What? We could celebrate its jubilee. It hasn't a soul of its own, but still, say what you will, it's a fine piece of furniture.

PISHCHIK (*astonished*) A hundred years . . . Just imagine!

GAIEFF Yes . . . it's a genuine thing. (*examining it*) My dear and honored cupboard! I congratulate you on your career, which has for more than a hundred years been devoted to the noble ideals of good and justice; your silent call to productive labor has not decreased in the hundred years (*weeping*) during which you have inspired in our generation virtue and courage and faith for a better future, holding before our eyes lofty ideals and the knowledge of a common consciousness. (*Pause.*)

LOPAKHIN Yes.

LIUBOFF You're just the same as ever, Leon.

GAIEFF (*a little confused*) Off the white on the right, into the corner pocket. Red ball goes into the center pocket!

LOPAKHIN (*looks at his watch*) It's time I went.

YASHA (*giving* LIUBOFF ANDREIEVNA *her medicine*) Will you take your pills now?

PISHICK You shouldn't take medicine, dearest; they do you neither harm nor good . . . Give them to me, dearest (*Takes the pills, turns them out into the palm of his hand, blows on them, puts them into his mouth, and drinks some kvass.*) There!

LIUBOFF (*frightened*) You're mad!

PISHCHIK I've swallowed all the pills.

LOPAKHIN You greedy man! (*All laugh.*)

FIRCE They were here in Easter week and ate half a pailful of cucumbers . . . (*Mumbles.*)

LIUBOFF What does he mean?

VARYA He's been mumbling away for three years. We're used to that.

YASHA Senile decay.

(CHARLOTTA IVANOVNA *crosses the stage, dressed in white; she is very thin and tightly laced; she has a lorgnette at her waist.*)

LOPAKHIN Excuse me, Charlotta Ivanovna, I haven't bidden you welcome yet. (*Tries to kiss her hand.*)

CHARLOTTA (*takes her hand away*) If you let people kiss your hand, then they'll want your elbow, then your shoulder, and then . . .

LOPAKHIN I'm out of luck today! (*All laugh.*) Show us a trick, Charlotta Ivanovna!

LIUBOFF Charlotta, do a trick for us!

CHARLOTTA It's not necessary. I must go to bed. (*Exit.*)

LOPAKHIN We shall see each other in three weeks. (*Kisses* LIUBOFF AN-DREIEVNA's *hand.*) Now, good-bye. It's time I went. (*to* GAIEFF) See you again. (*Kisses* PISHCHIK.) Au revoir. (*Gives his hand to* VARYA, *then to* FIRCE *and to* YASHA.) I don't want to go away. (*to* LIUBOFF ANDREIEVNA) If you think about the villas and come to a decision, just let me know, and I'll raise a loan of 50,000 rubles at once. Think about it seriously.

VARYA (*angrily*) Do go, now!

LOPAKHIN I'm going, I'm going. . . . (*Exit.*)

GAIEFF Snob. Still, I beg pardon . . . Varya's going to marry him, he's Varya's young man.

VARYA Don't talk too much, uncle.

LIUBOFF Why not, Varya? I should be glad of it. He's a good man.

PISHCHIK To speak the honest truth . . . he's a worthy man . . . And my Dashenka . . . also says that . . . she says lots of things. (*Snores, but wakes up again at once.*) But still, dear madam, if you could lend me . . . 240 rubles . . . to pay the interest on my mortgage tomorrow . . .

VARYA (*frightened*) We haven't it, we haven't it!

LIUBOFF It's quite true. I've nothing at all.

PISHCHIK You'll manage somehow. (*Laughs.*) I never lose hope. I used to think, "Everything's lost now. I'm a dead man," when, lo and behold, a railway was built across my land . . . and they paid me for it. And something else will happen today or tomorrow. Dashenka may win 20,000 rubles . . . she's got a lottery ticket.

LIUBOFF The coffee's all gone, we can go to bed.

FIRCE (*brushing* GAIEFF's *trousers; in an insistent tone*) You are wearing the wrong trousers again. What am I to do with you?

VARYA (*quietly*) Anya's asleep. (*Opens window quietly.*) The sun has risen already; it isn't cold. Look, mother, dear; what lovely trees! And the air! The starlings are singing!

GAIEFF (*opens the other window*) The whole garden is white. You haven't forgotten, Liuba? There's that long avenue going straight, straight, like an arrow; it shines on moonlight nights. Do you remember? You haven't forgotten?

LIUBOFF (*looks into the garden*) Oh, my childhood, days of my innocence! In this nursery I used to sleep; I used to look out from here into the orchard. Happiness used to wake with me every morning, and then it was just as it is now; nothing has changed. (*Laughs with joy.*) It's all, all white! Oh, my orchard! After the dreary autumns and the cold winters, you're young again, full of happiness, the angels of heaven haven't left you . . . If only I could take this strong burden from my breast and shoulders, if I could forget my past!

GAIEFF Yes, and they'll sell this orchard to pay off the debts. How strange it seems!

LIUBOFF Look, there's my dead mother walking in the orchard . . . dressed in white! (*Laughs with joy.*) That's she.

GAIEFF Where?

VARYA   God be with you, mother dear!

LIUBOFF   Nobody is there; I thought I saw somebody. On the right, at the turning by the summer-house, a little white tree bent down, resembling a woman. (*Enter TROFIMOFF in a worn student uniform and spectacles.*) What a marvelous garden! White masses of flowers, the blue sky. . . .

TROFIMOFF   Liuboff Andreievna! (*She looks round at him.*) I only wish to pay my respects to you, and I'll go away. (*Kisses her hand warmly.*) I was told to wait till the morning, but I didn't have the patience. (LIUBOFF ANDREIEVNA *looks surprised.*)

VARYA   (*crying*) It's Peter Trofimoff.

TROFIMOFF   Peter Trofimoff, once the tutor of your Grisha . . . Have I changed so much? (LIUBOFF ANDREIEVNA *embraces him and cries softly.*)

GAIEFF   (*confused*) That's enough, that's enough, Liuba.

VARYA   (*weeps*) But I told you, Peter, to wait till tomorrow.

LIUBOFF   My Grisha . . . my boy . . . Grisha . . . my son.

VARYA   What are we to do, dear mother? It's the will of God.

TROFIMOFF   (*softly, through his tears*) It's all right, it's all right.

LIUBOFF   (*still weeping*) My boy's dead; he was drowned. Why, my friend? (*softly*) Anya's asleep in there. I am speaking so loudly, making so much noise . . . Well, Peter? What's made you look so bad? Why have you grown so old?

TROFIMOFF   In the train an old woman called me a decayed gentleman.

LIUBOFF   You were quite a boy then, a jolly little student, and now your hair has grown thin and you wear spectacles. Are you really still a student? (*Goes to the door.*)

TROFIMOFF   I suppose I shall always be a student.

LIUBOFF   (*kisses her brother, then* VARYA) Well, let's go to bed . . . And you've grown older, Leonid.

PISHCHIK   (*follows her*) Yes, we must go to bed . . . Oh! my gout! I'll stay the night here. If only, Liuboff Andreievna, my dear, you could get me 240 rubles tomorrow morning—

GAIEFF   Still the same story.

PISHCHIK   Two hundred and forty rubles . . . to pay the interest on the mortgage.

LIUBOFF   I haven't any money, dear man.

PISHCHIK   I'll give it back . . . it's a small sum . . .

LIUBOFF   Well then, Leonid will give it to you . . . Let him have it, Leonid.

GAIEFF   By all means; hold out your hand.

LIUBOFF   Why not? He wants it; he'll give it back.

(LIUBOFF ANDREIEVNA, TROFIMOFF, PISHCHIK *and* FIRCE *go out.* GAIEFF, VARYA, *and* YASHA *remain.*)

GAIEFF   My sister hasn't lost the habit of throwing money away. (*to* YASHA) Don't come near me: you smell like a chickencoop!

YASHA   (*grins*) You are just the same as ever, Leonid Andreievitch.

GAIEFF   Really? (*to* VARYA) What's he saying?

VARYA   (*to* YASHA) Your mother has come from the village; she's been sitting in the servants' room since yesteday, and wishes to see you . . .

YASHA   Bless the woman!

VARYA   Shameless man.

YASHA   A lot of use there is in her coming. She might just as well have come tomorrow. (*Exit.*)

VARYA   Mother hasn't altered a bit, she's just as she always was. She'd give away everything, if the idea only entered her head.

GAIEFF   Yes . . . (*Pause.*) If there's any illness for which people have a remedy of remedies, you may be sure that particular illness is incurable. I work my brains as hard as I can. I've several remedies, very many, and that really means I've none at all. It would be nice to inherit a fortune from somebody, it would be nice to marry off our Anya to a rich man, it would be nice to go to Yaroslavl and try my luck with my aunt the Countess. My aunt is very, very rich.

VARYA   (*weeps*) If only God would help us.

GAIEFF   Don't cry. My aunt's very rich, but she doesn't like us. My sister, in the first place, married a lawyer, not an aristocrat . . . (ANYA *appears in the doorway.*) She not only married a man who was not an aristocrat, but she behaved in a way which cannot be described as proper. She's nice and kind and charming and I'm very fond of her, but say what you will in her favor and you still have to admit that she's bad; you can feel it in her slightest movements.

VARYA   (*whispers*) Anya's in the doorway.

GAIEFF   Really? (*Pause.*) It's curious, something's blown into my right eye . . . I can't see out of it properly. And on Thursday, when I was at the District Court . . .

(*Enter* ANYA.)

VARYA   Why aren't you in bed, Anya?

ANYA   I can't sleep. It's no use.

GAIEFF   By darling. (*Kisses* ANYA's *face and hands.*) My child. (*crying*) You're not my niece, you're my angel, you're my all . . . Believe in me, believe . . .

ANYA   I do believe you, uncle. Everybody loves and respects you . . . but, uncle dear, you should say nothing, no more than that. What were you saying just now about my mother, about your own sister! Why did you say such things?

GAIEFF   Yes, yes. (*Covers his face with her hand.*) Yes, really, it was terrible. Save me, my God! And only just now I made a speech before a cupboard . . . it's so silly! And only when I'd finished I knew how silly it was.

VARYA   Yes, uncle dear, you really should say less. Keep quiet, that's all.

ANYA   You'd be so much happier if you only kept quiet.

GAIEFF   All right, I'll be quiet. (*Kisses their hands.*) I'll be quiet. But let's talk business. On Thursday I was in the District Court, and a lot of us met there and we began to talk of this, that, and the other, and now I think I can arrange a loan to pay the interest to the bank.

VARYA   If only God would help us!

GAIEFF   I'll go on Tuesday. I'll talk to you about it again. (*to* VARYA) Don't cry. (*to* ANYA) Your mother will have a talk with Lopakhin; he, of course, won't refuse . . . And when you've rested you'll go to Yaroslavl to the Countess, your grandmother. So you see, we shall have three irons in the fire, and we shall be safe. We'll pay the interest. I'm certain. (*Puts some candy in his mouth.*) I swear on my honor, on anything you wish, that the estate will not be sold! (*excitedly*) I swear on my happiness! Here's my hand on it! You may call me a dishonorable sinner if I let it be sold at auction. I swear by all I am!

ANYA (*calm again and happy*) How good and clever you are, uncle. (*Embraces him.*) I'm happy now! I'm happy! All's well!

(*Enter* FIRCE.)

FIRCE (*reproachfully*) Leonid Andreievitch, don't you fear God? When are you going to bed?

GAIEFF Soon, soon. You go away, Firce! I'll undress myself. Well, children, au revoir . . . ! I'll tell you the details tomorrow, but let's go to bed now. (*Kisses* ANYA *and* VARYA.) I'm a man of the eighties . . . People don't praise those years much, but I can still say that I've suffered for my beliefs. The peasants don't love me for nothing, I assure you. We have to learn how to understand the peasants! We should learn how . . .

ANYA You're doing it again, uncle!

VARYA Be quiet, uncle!

FIRCE (*angrily*) Leonid Andreievitch!

GAIEFF I'm coming, I'm coming . . . Go to bed now. Off two cushions into the center! I turn over a new leaf . . . (*Exit.* FIRCE *goes out after him.*)

ANYA I'm more quiet now. I don't wish to go to Yaroslavl, I don't like grandmother; but I'm calm now, thanks to uncle. (*Sits down.*)

VARYA It's time to go to sleep. I'll go. There have been amazing things happening here during your absence. In the old servants' quarter of the house, as you know, only the old people live—little old Yefim and Polya and Yevstigny, and Karp as well. They commenced letting tramps or the like spend the night there—I said nothing. Then I heard that they were saying I had ordered them to be fed on peas and nothing else; from meanness, you see . . . And it was all Yevstigny's doing. Very well, I thought, if that's what the matter is, just you wait. So I call Yevstigny . . . (*Yawns.*) He comes. "What's this," I say. "Yevstigny, you old fool" . . . (*Looks at* ANYA.) Anya dear! (*Pause.*) She's dozed off . . . (*Takes* ANYA's *arm.*) Let's go to bed . . . Come along! . . . (*Leads her.*) My darling's gone to sleep! Come on . . . (*They go. In the distance, the other side of the orchard, a shepherd plays his pipe.* TROFIMOFF *crosses the stage and stops when he sees* VARYA *and* ANYA.) Sh! She's asleep, asleep. Come on, dear.

ANYA (*quietly, half-asleep*) I'm so tired . . . I hear bells . . . uncle, dear! Mother and uncle!

VARYA Come on, dear, come on! (*They go into* ANYA's *room.*)

TROFIMOFF (*deeply moved*). Sunshine! Springtime of my life!

ACT II

(*A field. An old, tumble-down shrine, which has been long abandoned; near it a well and large stones, which apparently are old tombstones, and an old garden seat. The road to GAIEFF's estate is seen. On one side dark poplars rise, behind them the cherry orchard begins. In the distance is a row of telegraph poles, and on the far horizon are the indistinct signs of a large town, which can be seen only on the finest and clearest days. It is near sunset.*)

(*CHARLOTTA, YASHA, and DUNYASHA are sitting on a bench. YEPIKHODOFF stands nearby playing on a guitar; all seem thoughtful. CHARLOTTA wears a man's old peaked cap; she has unslung a rifle from her shoulders and is straightening the strap-buckle.*)

CHARLOTTA (*thoughtfully*) I haven't a real passport. I don't know how old I am, but I think I'm young. When I was a little girl my father and mother used to travel from fair to fair and give very good performances, and I used to do the somersault and various little things. And when papa and mamma died, a German lady took me to her home and brought me up. I liked it. I grew up and became a governess. And where I came from and who I am, I don't know. . . . Who my parents were—perhaps they weren't married—I don't know. (*Takes a cucumber from her pockets and eats.*) I don't know anything. (*Pause.*) I do wish to talk, but I haven't anybody to talk to. . . . I haven't anybody at all.

YEPIKHODOFF (*plays on the guitar and sings*)

"What do I care for this noisy earth?
What do I care for friend and foe?"

I like playing on the mandolin!

DUNYASHA That's a guitar, not a mandolin. (*Looks at herself in a little pocket mirror and powders herself.*)

YEPIKHODOFF For a lovelorn lunatic, this constitutes a mandolin. (*Sings.*)

"Oh would the fire of love
Warm my pitiful heart!"

(*YASHA sings, too.*)

CHARLOTTA These people sing so badly. . . . Bah! like jackals.

DUNYASHA (*to YASHA*) Still it must be nice to live abroad.

YASHA Yes, it is. I can't differ from you there. (*Yawns and lights a cigar.*)

YEPIKHODOFF That is perfectly natural. Abroad everything is in such complete harmony.

YASHA That goes without saying.

YEPIKHODOFF I'm an educated man, I read various remarkable books, but I cannot understand where I want to go, myself—whether to keep on living or to shoot myself, as it were. So at any rate, I always carry a revolver about with me. Here it is. (*Shows a revolver.*)

CHARLOTTA I've finished. Now I'll go. (*Slings the rifle over her shoulder.*) You, Yepikohodoff, are a very clever man and very frightful; women must be madly in love with you. Brr! (*going*) These wise people are all so stupid. I've nobody to talk to. I'm always alone, alone; I've nobody at all . . . and I don't know who I am or why I live. (*Exit slowly.*)

YEPIKHODOFF As a matter of fact, independently of everything else, I must express my conviction, among other things, that fate has been as merciless in her dealings with me as a storm is to a small ship. Suppose, let us grant, I am wrong; then why did I wake up this morning, for example, and behold an enormous spider on my chest as big as this? (*Shows with both hands.*) And if I do drink kvass, why must I always find in the glass such an unsociable animal as a cockroach! (*Pause.*) Have you read Buckle? (*Pause.*) May I have a few words with you, Avdotya Fyodorovna?

DUNYASHA Go on!

YEPIKHODOFF I should prefer to be alone with you. (*Sighs.*)

DUNYASHA (*shy*) Very well only please bring me my cloak first. . . . It's by the cupboard. It's a little damp here.

YEPIKHODOFF Very well. . . . I'll bring it. . . . Now I know what to do with my revolver. (*Takes guitar and exits, strumming.*)

YASHA Two-and-twenty troubles! A foolish man, between you and me and the gatepost. (*Yawns.*)

DUNYASHA (*pause*) I hope to goodness he won't shoot himself. (*Pause.*) I'm so nervous, so worried. I entered service when I was quite a little girl, and now I'm not used to common life, and my hands are as white as a lady's. I'm so tender and so delicate now, respectable and afraid of everything. . . . I'm so frightened. And I don't know what will happen to my nerves if you deceive me, Yasha.

YASHA (*kisses her*) Tiny cucumber! Of course, every girl must respect herself; there's nothing I dislike more than a badly behaved girl.

DUNYASHA I'm so much in love with you; you're educated, you can talk about everything. (*Pause.*)

YASHA (*yawns*) Yes, I think that if a girl loves anybody, it means she's immoral. (*Pause.*) It's nice to smoke a cigar out in the open air. . . . (*Listens.*) Somebody's coming. It's the mistress, and people with her. (DUNYASHA *embraces him suddenly.*) Go to the house, as if you'd been bathing in the river; go by this path, or they'll run across you and will think I've been meeting you. I can't stand that sort of thing.

DUNYASHA (*coughs quietly*) Your cigar has given me a headache.

(*Exit.* YASHA *remains, sitting by the shrine. Enter* LIUBOFF ANDREIEVNA, GAIEFF, *and* LOPAKHIN.)

LOPAKHIN You must make up your mind definitely—there's no time to waste. The question is perfectly simple. Are you willing to let the land for villas or no? Just one word, yes or no? Just one word!

LIUBOFF Who's smoking bad cigars here? (*Sits.*)

GAIEFF They built that railway; that's made this place very convenient. (*Sits.*) Went to town and had lunch . . . red in the center! I'd like to go to the house now and have just one game.

LIUBOFF You'll have time.

LOPAKHIN Just one word! (*imploringly*) Give me an answer!

GAIEFF (*yawns*) Really!

LIUBOFF (*looks in her purse*) I had a lot of money yesterday, but there's very little left today. My poor Varya feeds everybody on milk soup to save money;

in the kitchen the old people get peas only; and I spend recklessly. (*Drops the purse, scattering gold coins.*) There, money all over the place.

YASHA   Permit me to pick them up. (*Collects the coins.*)

LIUBOFF   Please do, Yasha. And why did I go and lunch there? . . . A terrible restaurant with a band and tablecloths smelling of soap. . . . Why do you drink so much, Leon? Why do you eat so much? Why do you talk so much? You talked too much again today in the restaurant, and it wasn't at all to the point—about the seventies and about decadents. And to whom? Talking to the waiters about decadents! Imagine!

LOPAKHIN   Yes.

GAIEFF   (*waves his hand*) I can't be cured, that's obvious. . . . (*irritably to* YASHA) What's the matter? Why do you always manage to keep in front of me?

YASHA   (*laughs*) I can't listen to your voice without laughing.

GAIEFF   (*to his sister*) Either he or I . . .

LIUBOFF   Go away, Yasha! Go!

YASHA   (*gives her purse to* LIUBOFF ANDREIEVNA) I'll go at once. (*hardly able to keep from laughing*) This minute. . . . (*Exit.*)

LOPAKHIN   That rich man Deriganoff is preparing to buy your estate. They say he'll attend the sale in person.

LIUBOFF   Where did you hear that?

LOPAKHIN   They say so in town.

GAIEFF   Our aunt in Yaroslavl promised to send something, but I don't know when or how much.

LOPAKHIN   How much will she send? A hundred thousand rubles? Or two, perhaps?

LIUBOFF   I'd be glad if we get ten or fifteen thousand.

LOPAKHIN   You must excuse my saying so, but I've never met such frivolous people as you before, or anybody so unbusinesslike and peculiar. Here I am telling you in plain language that your estate will be sold, and you don't seem to understand.

LIUBOFF   What are we to do? Tell us, what?

LOPAKHIN   I tell you every day. Every day I say the same thing. Both the cherry orchard and the land must be leased for villas and at once,—the auction is staring you in the face: Understand! Once you definitely make up your minds to the villas, you'll have as much money as you wish and you'll be saved.

LIUBOFF   Villas and villa residents—it's so vulgar, pardon me.

GAIEFF   I agree with you entirely.

LOPAKHIN   I must cry or yell or faint. I can't! You're too much for me! (*to* GAIEFF) You old woman!

GAIEFF   Really!

LOPAKHIN   Old woman! (*going out*)

LIUBOFF   (*frightened*) No, don't go away, stop; be a dear. Please. Perhaps we'll find some way out!

LOPAKHIN   There is nothing to think about.

LIUBOFF   Please don't go. It's nicer when you're here. . . . (*Pause.*) I keep on waiting for something to happen, as if the house were going to collapse over our heads.

GAIEFF   (*thinking deeply*) Double in the corner . . . across the center.

LIUBOFF   We have been too sinful. . . .

LOPAKHIN   What sins have you been guilty of?

GAIEFF   (*puts candy in his mouth*) They say that I've wasted all my money in buying candy. (*Laughs.*)

LIUBOFF   Oh, my sins . . . I've always scattered money about without being able to control myself, like a madwoman, and I married a man who made nothing but debts. My husband died of champagne—he drank terribly—and to my misfortune, I fell in love with another man and went off with him, and just at that time—it was my first punishment, a blow that struck me squarely on the head—here, in the river . . . my boy was drowned, and I went away, abroad, never to return, never to see this river again. . . . I closed my eyes and ran without thinking, but he ran after me . . . without mercy, without respect. I bought a villa near Mentone because he fell ill there, and for three years I knew no rest, day or night; the sick man wore me out, and my soul dried up. And last year, when they had sold the villa to pay my debts, I went to Paris, and there he robbed me of all I had and threw me over and went off with another woman. I tried to poison myself. . . . It was so silly, so shameful . . . And suddenly I longed to go back to Russia, my own country, with my little daughter . . . (*Wipes her tears.*) Lord, Lord be merciful to me, forgive my sins! Punish me no more! (*Takes a telegram from her pocket.*) I had this today from Paris. . . . He begs my forgiveness, he implores me to return . . . (*Tears it up.*) Don't I hear music? (*Listens.*)

GAIEFF   That is our famous Jewish band. You remember—four violins, a flute, and a double-brass.

LIUBOFF   So it still exists? It would be nice if they came some evening.

LOPAKHIN   (*listens*) I can't hear. . . . (*Sings quietly.*) "For money will the Germans make a Frenchman of a Russian." (*Laughs.*) I saw such an awfully funny thing at the theatre last night.

LIUBOFF   I'm quite sure there wasn't anything funny at all. You shouldn't go and see plays, you ought to go and look at yourself. What a drab life you lead! What a lot of unnecessary things you say!

LOPAKHIN   It's true. To speak the honest truth, we live a silly life. (*Pause.*) My father was a peasant, an idiot, he understood nothing, he didn't teach me, he was always drunk, and always beat me. As a matter of fact, I'm a fool and an idiot, too. I've never learned anything, my handwriting is bad, I write so that I'm quite ashamed before people, like a pig!

LIUBOFF   You should marry, my friend.

LOPAKHIN   Yes . . . that's true.

LIUBOFF   Why not our Varya? She's a nice girl.

LOPAKHIN   Yes.

LIUBOFF   She's a simple, unaffected girl, works all day, and, what matters most, she's in love with you. And you've liked her for a long time.

LOPAKHIN   Well? I don't mind . . . She's a nice girl. (*Pause.*)

GAIEFF   I'm offered a place in a bank. Six thousand rubles a year . . . Did you hear?

LIUBOFF   What's the matter with you! Stay where you are . . .

(*Enter* FIRCE *with an overcoat.*)

FIRCE   (*to* GAIEFF) Please sir, put this on, it's damp.

GAIEFF   (*putting it on*) You're a nuisance, old man.

FIRCE   It's all very well. . . . You went away this morning without telling me. (*examining* GAIEFF)

LIUBOFF   How old you've grown, Firce!

FIRCE   I beg your pardon?

LOPAKHIN   She says you've grown very old!

FIRCE   I've lived a long time. They were getting ready to marry me before your father was born . . . (*Laughs.*) And when the Emancipation came I was already first valet. Only I didn't agree with the Emancipation and remained with my masters . . . (*Pause.*) I remember everybody was happy, but they didn't know why.

LOPAKHIN   It was very good for them in the old days. At any rate, they beat them formerly.

FIRCE   (*not hearing*) Rather. The peasants kept their distance from the masters and the masters kept their distance from the peasants, but now everything is in a muddle, and you can't make head or tail of anything.

GAIEFF   Be quiet, Firce. I have to go to town tomorrow. I have the promise of an introduction to a General who may lend me money on a note.

LOPAKHIN   Nothing will come of it. And you won't pay your interest, don't you worry.

LIUBOFF   He's out of his head. There's no General at all.

(*Enter* TROFIMOFF, ANYA, *and* VARYA.)

GAIEFF   Here, come on, folks!

ANYA   Mother's sitting down here.

LIUBOFF   (*tenderly*) Come, come, my dears . . . (*embracing* ANYA *and* VARYA) If you two only knew how much I love you. Sit down next to me, like that. (*All sit down.*)

LOPAKHIN   Our eternal student is always with the ladies.

TROFIMOFF   That's none of your business.

LOPAKHIN   He'll soon be fifty, and she's still a student.

TROFIMOFF   Stop your silly jokes!

LOPAKHIN   Getting angry, eh, silly?

TROFIMOFF   Shut up, can't you?

LOPAKHIN   (*laughs*) I wonder what you think of me?

TROFIMOFF   I think, Yermolai Alexeievitch, that you're rich, and you'll soon be a millionaire. Just as the wild beast which eats everything it finds is needed to make certain changes in cosmic matter, so you are needed too. (*All laugh.*)

VARYA   Better tell us something about the planets, Peter.

LIUBOFF   No, let's continue yesterday's discussion.

TROFIMOFF   What was it about?

GAIEFF   About the proud man.

TROFIMOFF   Yesterday we talked for a long time, but we arrived at no conclusion. In your opinion there's something mystic in pride. Perhaps you are right from your point of view, but if you look at the matter sanely, without complicating it, then what pride can there be, what logic in a man who is imperfectly made, physiologically speaking, and who in the vast majority of cases is coarse and stupid and profoundly unhappy? We must stop admiring one another. We must work, nothing more.

GAIEFF   You'll die, all the same.

TROFIMOFF   Who knows? And what does it mean—you'll die? Perhaps a man has a hundred senses, and when he dies only the five known to us are destroyed and the remaining ninety-five are left alive.

LIUBOFF   How clever of you Peter!

LOPAKHIN   (ironically) Oh, awfully!

TROFIMOFF   The human race progresses, perfecting its powers. Everything that is unattainable now will some day be near and intelligible, but we must work, we must help with all our energy, those who seek to know the truth. Meanwhile in Russia only a very few of us work. The vast majority of those intellectuals whom I know seek for nothing, do nothing, and are at present incapable of hard work. They call themselves intellectuals, but they use "thou" and "thee" to their servants, they treat the peasants like animals, they learn slowly, they read nothing with discernment, they do absolutely nothing, they gabble on about science, about art they understand little. They are all serious, they all have severe faces. They all talk about important things. They philosophize, and at the same time, the vast majority of us, ninety-nine out of a hundred, live like savages, fighting and cursing on the slightest excuse, have filthy table manners, sleep in the dirt, in stuffiness among fleas, stinks, smells, moral stench, and so on. . . . And it's obvious that all our nice talk is only carried on to delude ourselves and others. Tell me, where are those crèches we hear so much of? And where are those reading-rooms? People only write novels about them; they don't really exist. Only dirt, coarseness, and Asiatic barbarism really exist. . . . I'm afraid; and I don't like serious faces at all. I don't like serious conversation. Let's say no more about it.

LOPAKHIN   You know, I get up at five every morning, I work till evening, I am always dealing with money—my own and other people's—and I see what others are like. You have only to start doing anything at all, and you'll find out how few honest, honorable people there are. Sometimes, when I can't sleep, I think: "Oh Lord, you've given us huge forests, infinite fields, and endless horizons, and we, living here, ought really to be giants."

LIUBOFF   You want giants, do you? . . . They're only good in stories, and even there they frighten one. (YEPIKHODOFF enters at the back of the stage playing his guitar. LIUBOFF ANDREIEVNA speaks thoughtfully.) Yepikhodoff has come.

ANYA   (thoughtfully) Yepikhodoff has come.

GAIEFF   The sun's set.

TROFIMOFF Yes.

GAIEFF (*not loudly, as if declaiming*) Oh, Nature, thou art wonderful, thou shinest with eternal radiance! Oh, beautiful and lofty one, thou whom we call mother, thou containest in thyself life and death, thou livest and destroyest. . . .

VARYA (*entreatingly*) Uncle, dear!

ANYA Uncle, you're doing it again!

TROFIMOFF You'd better double the yellow into the center.

GAIEFF I'll be quiet, I'll be quiet.

(*They all sit thoughtfully. It is quiet. Only the mumbling of* FIRCE *is heard. Suddenly a distant sound comes as if from the sky, the sound of a breaking string, which dies away sadly.*)

LIUBOFF What's that?

LOPAKHIN I don't know. Perhaps a bucket fell, down a well somewhere. But it's a long way off.

GAIEFF Or perhaps it's some bird . . . like a heron.

TROFIMOFF Or an owl.

LIUBOFF (*shudders*) It's unpleasant, somehow. (*A pause.*)

FIRCE Before the catastrophe the same thing happened. An owl screamed and the samovar hummed without stopping.

GAIEFF Before what catastrophe?

FIRCE Before the Emancipation. (*A pause.*)

LIUBOFF You know, my friends, let's go in; it's evening now. (*to* ANYA) You've tears in your eyes. . . . What is it, little girl? (*Embraces her.*)

ANYA It's nothing, mother.

TROFIMOFF Someone's coming.

(*Enter a* TRAMP *in an old white peaked cap and overcoat. He is slightly drunk.*)

TRAMP Excuse me, may I go this way straight through to the station?

GAIEFF You may. Go along this path. . . .

TRAMP (I thank you with all my heart. (*Hiccoughs*). Lovely weather. . . . (*Declaims*) My brother, my suffering brother. . . . Come out on the Volga, you whose groans . . . (*to* VARYA) Mademoiselle, please give a hungry Russian thirty kopecks. . . . (VARYA *screams, frightened.*)

LOPAKHIN (*angrily*) Everybody should have some sort of manners!

LIUBOFF (*with a start*) Take this . . . here you are . . . (*Feels in her purse.*) There's no silver . . . It doesn't matter, here's gold.

TRAMP I am very grateful to you! (*Exit. Laughter.*)

VARYA (*frightened*) I'm going, I'm going. . . . Oh, mother dear, at home there's nothing for the servants to eat, and yet you gave him gold.

LIUBOFF What is to be done with such a fool as I am! At home, I'll give you everything I have. Yermolai Alexeievitch, lend me some more! . . .

LOPAKHIN Very well.

LIUBOFF Let's go, it's time. And Varya, we've settled your affairs; I congratulate you.

VARYA (*crying*) You shouldn't joke about this, mother.

LOPAKHIN Ophelia! Get thee to a nunnery.

GAIEFF   My hands are trembling; I haven't played billiards for a long time.

LOPAKHIN   Ophelia! Nymph! Remember me in thine orisons!

LIUBOFF   Come along; it'll soon be suppertime.

VARYA   He frightened me. My heart is beating fast.

LOPAKHIN   Let me remind you, ladies and gentlemen, on August 22nd, the cherry orchard will be sold. Think of that! . . . Think of that! . . . (*All go out except* TROFIMOFF *and* ANYA).

ANYA   (*laughs*) Thanks to the tramp who frightened Varya, we're alone now.

TROFIMOFF   Varya's afraid that we may fall in love with each other and won't leave us alone for days on end. Her narrow mind won't permit her to understand that we are above love. To escape all the petty and deceptive things which prevent our being happy and free, such is the aim and object of our lives. Forward! We go irresistibly on to that bright star which burns there, in the distance! Don't lag behind, friends!

ANYA   (*clapping her hands*) How beautifully you talk! (*Pause.*) It is glorious here today!

TROFIMOFF   Yes, the weather is wonderful.

ANYA   What have you done to me, Peter? I don't love the cherry orchard as I used to. I loved it so tenderly, I thought there was no better place in the world than our orchard.

TROFIMOFF   All Russia is our orchard. The land is great and beautiful, there are many glorious places in it. (*Pause.*) Think, Anya, your grandfather, your great-grandfather, and all your ancestors were serf-owners, they owned human beings; and now, doesn't something human look at you from every cherry in the orchard, every leaf and every branch? Don't you hear voices . . . ? Oh, it's awful, your orchard is frightful; and when in the evening or at night you walk through the orchard, then the old bark on the trees sheds a dim light and the old cherry-trees seem to dream of all that happened a hundred, two hundred years ago, and are burdened with their heavy visions. Still, we've left those two hundred years behind us. So far we've gained nothing at all—we don't yet know what the past will bring us—we only philosophize, we complain that we are dull, or we drink vodka. For it's so clear that to begin to live in the present we must first redeem the past, and that can be done only by suffering, by strenuous, uninterrupted work. Understand that, Anya.

ANYA   The house in which we live has long ceased to be our house; I shall go away, I give you my word.

TROFIMOFF   If you have the keys of the household, throw them down the well and go away. Be as free as the wind.

ANYA   (*enthusiastically*) How beautifully you said that!

TROFIMOFF   Believe me, Anya, believe me! I'm not thirty yet, I'm young, I'm still a student, but I have gone through so much already! I'm as hungry as the winter, I'm ill, I'm shaken. I'm as poor as a beggar, and where haven't I been—fate has tossed me everywhere! But my soul is always my own; every minute of the day and the night it is filled with glorious and dim visions. I feel that happiness is coming, Anya, I see it already. . . .

ANYA   (*thoughtfully*) The moon is rising.

(YEPIKHODOFF *is heard playing the same sad song on his guitar. The moon rises. Somewhere near the poplars* VARYA *is looking for* ANYA *and calling, "Anya, where are you?"*)

TROFIMOFF   Yes, the moon has risen. (*Pause.*) There is happiness, there it comes; it comes nearer and nearer; I hear its footsteps already. And if we do not see it, we shall not know it, but what does that matter? Others will see it!

VARYA'S VOICE   Anya! Where are you?

TROFIMOFF   That's Varya again! (*Angry.*) Disgraceful!

ANYA   Never mind. Let's go to the river. It's nice there.

TROFIMOFF   Let's go. (*They leave.*)

VARYA'S VOICE   Anya! Anya!

ACT III

(*A reception-room, separated by an arch from a drawing-room. Lighted chandelier. A Jewish band, the one referred to in Act II, is heard playing in another room. Evening. In the drawing-room the cotillion is being danced.*)

(*Voice of* SEMYONOFF PISHCHIK, *"Promenade à une paire!" Dancers come into the reception-room; the first pair are* PISHCHIK *and* CHARLOTTA IVANOVNA; *the second* TROFIMOFF *and* LIUBOFF ANDREIEVNA; *the third* ANYA *and the* POST OFFICE CLERK; *the fourth* VARYA *and the* STATION-MASTER, *and so on.* VARYA *is crying gently and dries her eyes as she dances.* DUNYASHA *is in the last pair. They go off into the drawing-room, shouting, "Grand rond, balancez:" and "Les cavaliers à genoux et remerciez vos dames!"* FIRCE, *in a dress-coat, carries a tray with seltzer-water across the stage. Enter* PISHCHIK *and* TROFIMOFF *from the drawing-room.*)

PISHCHIK   I'm full-blooded and already I've had two strokes; it's hard for me to dance, but, as they say, if you're in Rome, you must do as the Romans do. I've the constitution of a horse. My late father, who liked a joke, peace to his ashes, used to say, talking of our ancestors, that the ancient stock of the Semyonoff Pishchiks was descended from the identical horse that Caligula appointed senator. . . . (*Sits.*) But the trouble is, I've no money! A hungry dog believes only in meat. (*Drops off to sleep and wakes up again immediately.*) So I . . . believe only in money. . . .

TROFIMOFF   Yes. There is something horsy about your figure.

PISHCHIK   Well . . . a horse is a valuable animal . . . you can sell a horse.

(*The sound of billiard playing comes from the next room,* VARYA *appears under the arch.*)

TROFIMOFF   (*teasing*) Madame Lopakhin! Madame Lopakhin!

VARYA   (*angry*) Decayed gentleman!

TROFIMOFF   Yes, I am a decayed gentleman, and I'm proud of it!

VARYA   (*bitterly*) We've hired the musicians, but how are they to be paid? (*Exit.*)

TROFIMOFF   (*to* PISHCHIK) If you would put to better use the energy which you are wasting day by day, in looking for money to pay interest, I believe you'd finally succeed in moving heaven and earth.

PISHCHIK   Nietzsche . . . a philosopher . . . a very great and famous man . . . a man of enormous brain, says in his books that you can forge bank-notes.

TROFIMOFF   And have you read Nietzsche?

PISHCHIK   Well . . . Dashenka told me. Now I'm in such a position, I wouldn't mind making counterfeit money . . . I have to pay 310 rubles day after tomorrow . . . I've obtained 130 already . . . (*Feels his pockets, nervously.*) I've lost the money! The money's gone! (*crying*) Where's the money? (*joyfully*) Here it is in the lining. . . . Why I was in a cold sweat!

(*Enter* LIUBOFF ANDREIEVNA *and* CHARLOTTA IVANOVNA.)

LIUBOFF   (*humming a Caucasian dance song*) What is keeping Leonid so long? What's he doing in town? (*to* DUNYASHA) Dunyasha, give the musicians some tea.

TROFIMOFF   The business is off, I suppose.

LIUBOFF   And the musicians needn't have come, and we needn't have arranged this ball. . . . Well, never mind. . . . (*Sits and sings softly.*)

CHARLOTTA   (*gives a pack of cards to* PISHCHIK) Here's a deck of cards, think of any card you like.

PISHCHIK   I've thought of one.

CHARLOTTA   Now shuffle. All right, now. Pass them over, my dear Mr. Pishchik. Eins, zwei, drei! Now look and you'll find it in your hind pocket.

PISHCHIK   (*takes a card out of his hind pocket*) Eight of spades, quite right! (*surprised*) Just imagine!

CHARLOTTA   (*holds the deck of cards in the palm of her hand. To* TROFIMOFF) Now tell me quickly. What's the top card?

TROFIMOFF   Well, the queen of spades.

CHARLOTTA   Right! (*to* PISHCHIK) And now? What card's on top?

PISHCHIK   Ace of hearts.

CHARLOTTA   Right! (*Clasps her hands, the deck of cards vanishes.*) How lovely the weather is today. (*A mysterious woman's voice answers her, as if from under the floor, "Oh yes, it's lovely weather, Madam."*) You are so beautiful, you are my ideal. (*Voice, "You Madam, please me very much too."*)

STATION-MASTER   (*applauds*) Madame the ventriloquist, bravo!

PISHCHIK   (*surprised*) Just imagine! Delightful, Charlotta Ivanovna . . . I'm in love. . . .

CHARLOTTA   In love? (*shrugging her shoulders*) Can you love? Guter Mensch aber schlechter Musikant.

TROFIMOFF   (*slaps* PISHCHIK *on the shoulder*) Oh, you horse!

CHARLOTTA   Attention, please, here's another trick. (*Takes a shawl from a chair.*) Here's a very nice plaid shawl. I'm going to sell it. . . . (*Shakes it.*) Won't somebody buy it?

PISHCHIK   (*astonished*) Just imagine!

CHARLOTTA   Eins, zwei, drei. (*She quickly lifts up the shawl, which is hanging down.* ANYA *appears behind it; she bows and runs to her mother, hugs her and runs back to the drawing-room amid general applause.*)

LIUBOFF   (*applauds*) Bravo, bravo!

CHARLOTTA   Once again! *Eins, zwei, drei!* (*Lifts the shawl.* VARYA *appears behind it and bows.*)

PISHCHIK   (*astonished*) Just imagine!

CHARLOTTA   The end! (*Throws the shawl at* PISHCHIK, *curtseys and runs into the drawing-room.*)

PISHCHIK   (*runs after her*) Little witch! . . . What? Would you? (*Exit.*)

LIUBOFF   Leonid hasn't come yet. I don't understand what is keeping him so long in town! Everything must be over by now. The estate must be sold; or, if the sale never came off, then why does he stay away so long?

VARYA   (*tries to soothe her*) Uncle has bought it. I'm certain of it.

TROFIMOFF   (*sarcastically*) Oh, yes!

VARYA   Grandmother sent him her authority to buy it in her name and transfer the debt to her. She's doing it for Anya. And I'm certain that God will help us and that Uncle will buy it.

LIUBOFF   Grandmother sent fifteen thousand rubles from Yaroslavl to buy the property in her name—she won't trust us— and that wasn't even enough to pay the interest. (*Covers her face with her hands.*) My fate will be settled today, my fate. . . .

TROFIMOFF   (*teasing VARYA*) Madame Lopakhin!

VARYA   (*angry*) Eternal student? He's been expelled from the university, twice already.

LIUBOFF   Why are you growing angry, Varya? He's teasing you about Lopakhin. Well, what of it? You can marry Lopakhin if you wish. He's a good, interesting man. . . . You needn't if you don't wish to; nobody is going to force you against your will, my darling.

VARYA   I look at the matter seriously, mother dear, to be quite frank. He's a good man, and I like him.

LIUBOFF   Then marry him. I don't understand what you're waiting for.

VARYA   I can't propose to him myself, mother dear. People have been talking about him to me for two years now, but he either says nothing, or jokes about it. I understand. He's getting rich, he's busy, he can't bother about me. If I had some money, even a little, even only a hundred rubles, I'd throw up everything and go away. I'd go into a convent.

TROFIMOFF   What bliss!

VARYA   (*to TROFIMOFF*) A student should have common sense! (*gently, in tears*) How ugly you are now, Peter, how old you've grown! (*to LIUBOFF ANDREIEVNA, no longer crying*) But I can't go on without working, mother dear. I'm eager to be doing something every minute.

(*Enter YASHA.*)

YASHA   (*nearly laughing*) Yepikhodoff's broken a billiard cue! (*Exit.*)

VARYA   Why is Yepikhodoff here? Who said he could play billiards? I don't understand these people. (*Exit.*)

LIUBOFF   Don't tease her, Peter, you see that she's unhappy enough without it.

TROFIMOFF   She undertakes too much herself; she is continually interfering in other people's business. The whole summer she gave Anya and me not a moment's peace. She's afraid we'll have a romance all to ourselves. What concern of hers is it? As if I'd ever given her grounds to believe I'd stoop to such vulgarity! We are above love.

LIUBOFF   Then I suppose I must be beneath love. (*in agitation*) Why isn't Leonid here? If I only knew whether the estate is sold or not! The catastrophe seems to me so unbelievable that I don't know what to think, I'm all at sea

. . . I may scream . . . or do something foolish. Save me, Peter. Say something, say something.

TROFIMOFF Isn't it all the same whether the estate is sold today or not? For a long time it's been a foregone conclusion that it would be sold. There's no turning back, the path is obliterated. Be calm, dear, you shouldn't deceive yourself; for once in your life, at any rate, you must look the truth straight in the eyes.

LIUBOFF What truth? You see where truth is, and where falsehood is, but I seem to have lost my sight and see nothing. You settle all important questions boldly, but tell me, dear, isn't it because you're young, because you have not as yet had time to suffer in settling any one of these questions? You look forward boldly, but isn't it because you neither feel nor expect anything terrible, because so far life has been hidden from your young eyes? You are bolder, more honest, deeper than we are, but only think, be just a little magnanimous, and have pity on me. I was born here, my father and mother lived here, my grandfather, too. I love this house. I couldn't understand my life without that cherry orchard, and if it really must be sold, sell me with it! (*Embraces* TROFIMOFF, *kisses his forehead*) My son was drowned here . . . (*Weeps.*) Have pity on me, good, kind man.

TROFIMOFF You know that I sympathize with all my heart.

LIUBOFF Yes, but it should be said differently. . . . (*Takes another handkerchief, a telegram falls on the floor.*) I'm so sick at heart today, you can't imagine. Here it's so noisy, my soul trembles at every sound. I shake all over, and I can't go away by myself, I'm afraid of the silence. Don't judge me harshly, Peter. . . . I love you, as if you belonged to the family. I'd gladly let Anya marry you, I swear it, only, dear, you ought to work to finish our studies. You don't do anything, only fate tosses you about from place to place, it's so strange. . . . Isn't it true? Yes? And you ought to do something to your beard to make it grow better. (*Laughs.*) You are funny!

TROFIMOFF (*picking up telegram*) I don't wish to be a Beau Brummell.

LIUBOFF This telegram's from Paris. I receive one every day. Yesterday and today. That wild man is ill again, he's bad again. . . . He begs for forgiveness, and implores me to come, and I really should go to Paris to be near him. You look severe, Peter, but what can I do, my dear, what can I do? He's ill, he's alone, unhappy, and who's to look after him, who's to keep him out of harm's way, to give him his medicine punctually? And why should I conceal it and say nothing about it? I love him, that's plain, I love him, I love him. . . . That love is a stone round my neck; I shall sink with it to the bottom, but I love that stone and can't live without it. (*Squeezes* TROFIMOFF's *hand.*) Don't think harshly of me, Peter, don't say anything to me, don't say . . .

TROFIMOFF (*weeping*) For God's sake forgive my speaking candidly, but that man has robbed you!

LIUBOFF No, no, you should not say that! (*Stops her ears.*)

TROFIMOFF But he's a scoundrel, you alone don't know it! He's a petty thief, a nobody. . . .

LIUBOFF (*angry, but restrained*) You're twenty-six or twenty-seven, and still a school-boy of the second grade!

TROFIMOFF   Why not?

LIUBOFF   You should be a man, at your age you should be able to understand those who love. And you should be in love yourself, you must fall in love! (*Angry.*) Yes, yes! You aren't pure, you're just a freak, a queer fellow, a funny fungus.

TROFIMOFF   (*in horror*) What is she saying?

LIUBOFF   "I'm above love!" You're not above love, you're just what our Firce calls a bungler. Not to have a mistress at your age!

TROFIMOFF   (*in horror*) This is terrible! What is she saying? (*Goes quickly into the drawing-room, seizing his head with both his hands.*) It's awful . . . I can't stand it, I'll go away. (*Exit, but returns at once.*) All is over between us! (*Exit.*)

LIUBOFF   (*shouts after him*) Peter, wait! Silly boy, I was joking! Peter! (*Somebody is heard going out and falling downstairs noisily. ANYA and VARYA scream; laughter is heard immediately.*) What's that? (ANYA *comes running in, laughing.*)

ANYA   Peter's fallen downstairs. (*Runs out again.*)

LIUBOFF   This Peter's a funny creature!

(*The* STATION-MASTER *stands in the middle of the drawing-room and recites "The Magdalen" by Tolstoy. They listen to him, but he has delivered only a few lines when a waltz is heard from the front room, and the recitation is stopped. Everybody dances.* TROFIMOFF, ANYA, VARYA, *and* LIUBOFF ANDREIEVNA *come in from the front room.*)

LIUBOFF   Well, Peter . . . you pure soul . . . I beg your pardon. . . . Let's dance.

(*She dances with* PETER, ANYA *and* VARYA *dance.* FIRCE *enters and leans his stick against a side door.* YASHA *has also come in and watches the dance.*)

YASHA   Well, grandfather?

FIRCE   I'm not well. At our balls some time ago, generals and barons and admirals used to dance, and now we send for post office clerks and the station-master, and even they come reluctantly. I'm very weak. The dead master, the grandfather, used to give everybody sealing-wax when anything was wrong. I've taken sealing-wax every day for twenty years, and more; possibly that's why I am still alive.

YASHA   I'm tired of you, grandfather. (*Yawns.*) If you'd only hurry up and kick the bucket.

FIRCE   (*muttering*) Oh, you . . . bungler!

(TROFIMOFF *and* LIUBOFF ANDREIEVNA *dance in the reception-room, then into the sitting-room.*)

LIUBOFF   Merci. I'll sit down. (*Sits.*) I'm tired.

(*Enter* ANYA.)

ANYA   (*excited*) Somebody in the kitchen was saying just now that the cherry orchard was sold today.

LIUBOFF   Sold to whom?

ANYA   He didn't say to whom. He went away. (*Dances out into the reception-room with* TROFIMOFF.)

YASHA   Some old man was chattering about it a long time ago. A stranger!

FIRCE   And Leonid Andreievitch isn't here yet, he hasn't come. He's wearing a light autumn overcoat. He'll catch cold. Oh, these young fellows.

LIUBOFF   I'll die of this. Go and find out, Yasha, to whom it's sold.

YASHA   Oh, but he's been gone a long time, the old man. (*Laughs.*)

LIUBOFF   (*slightly vexed*) Why do you laugh? What are you so happy about?

YASHA   Yepikhodoff's too funny. He's a foolish man. Two-and-twenty troubles.

LIUBOFF   Firce, if the estate is sold, where will you go?

FIRCE   I'll go wherever you command me to go.

LIUBOFF   Why do you look like that? Are you ill? I think you should go to bed. . . .

FIRCE   Yes . . . (*with a smile*) I'll go to bed, and who'll hand things round and give orders without me? I've the whole house on my shoulders.

YASHA   (*to* LIUBOFF ANDREIEVNA) Liuboff Andreievna! I wish to ask a favor of you, if you'll be so kind! If you go to Paris again, take me along. I beg of you! It's absolutely impossible for me to remain here. (*looking round; in an undertone*) What's the good of talking about it? You see for yourself that this is an uncivilized country, with an immoral population, and it's so dull. The food in the kitchen is wretched, and here's this Firce walking about mumbling all kinds of inappropriate things. Take me with you. Please!

(*Enter* PISHCHIK.)

PISHCHIK   May I have the pleasure of a little waltz, dear lady . . . ? (LIUBOFF ANDREIEVNA *goes to him*.) But all the same, you wonderful woman, I must have 180 little rubles from you. . . . I must. . . . (*They dance.*) 180 little rubles. . . . (*They go through into the drawing-room.*)

YASHA   (*sings softly*)

> "Oh, will you understand
> My soul's deep restlessness?"

(*In the drawing-room a figure in a gray tophat and in baggy check trousers is waving its hands; and there are cries of "Bravo, Charlotta Ivanovna!"*)

DUNYASHA   (*stops to powder her face*) The young mistress tells me to dance —there are lots of gentlemen, but few ladies—and my head whirls when I dance, and my heart beats, Firce Nikolaievitch; the post office clerk told me something just now that almost took my breath away. (*The music grows faint.*)

FIRCE   What did he tell you?

DUNYASHA   He says, "You're like a little flower."

YASHA   (*yawns*) Impolite. . . . (*Exit.*)

DUNYASHA   Like a little flower. I'm such a delicate girl; I simply love tender words.

FIRCE   You'll lose your head.

(*Enter* YEKIKHODOFF.)

YEPIKHODOFF   You, Avdotya Fyodorovna, are about as anxious to see me as if I were some insect. (*Sighs.*) Oh, life!

DUNYASHA   What do you wish?

YEPIKHODOFF   Perhaps, doubtless, you may be right. (*Sighs.*) But, certainly, if you consider the matter in that light, then you, if I may say so, and you must excuse my candidness, have absolutely reduced me to the state of mind in which I find myself. I know my fate. Every day something unfortunate happens to me, and I've grown used to it a long time ago. I never look at my fate with a smile. You gave me your word, and though I. . . .

DUNYASHA Please, we'll talk later on, but leave me alone now. I'm thinking now. (*Fans herself.*)

YEPIKHODOFF Every day something unfortunate happens to me, and I, if I may so express myself, only smile, and even laugh.

(VARYA *enters from the drawing-room.*)

VARYA Haven't you gone yet, Semyon? You really have no respect for anybody. (*to* DUNYASHA) Go away, Dunyasha. (*to* YEPIKHODOFF) You play billiards and break a cue, and stroll about the drawing-room as if you were a visitor!

YEPIKHODOFF You cannot, if I may say so, call me to order.

VARYA I'm not calling you to order, I'm only telling you. You just walk about from place to place and never do your work. Goodness only knows why we keep a clerk.

YEPIKHODOFF (*offended*) Whether I work, or walk about, or eat, or play billiards, is only a matter to be settled by people of understanding and my elders.

VARYA You dare talk to me like that! (*Furious.*) You dare? You mean to insinuate that I know nothing? Go away! This minute!

YEPIKHODOFF (*nervous*) I must ask you to express yourself more delicately.

VARYA (*beside herself*) Get out this minute. Get out! (*He goes to the door, she follows.*) Two-and-twenty troubles! Not another sign of you here! I don't wish to set eyes on you again! (YEPIKHODOFF *has gone out; his voice can be heard outside: "I'll make a complaint against you."*) What, coming back? (*Snatches up the stick left by* FIRCE *near the door.*) Go . . . go . . . go. I'll show you . . . Are you going? Are you going? Well, then take that. (*She lashes out with the stick as* LOPAKHIN *enters.*)

LOPAKHIN Much obliged.

VARYA (*angry but amused*) I'm sorry.

LOPAKHIN Never mind. I thank you for the pleasant reception you gave me!

VARYA It isn't worthy of thanks. (*Walks away, then holds back and asks gently.*) I didn't hurt you, did I?

LOPAKHIN No, not at all. There'll be a huge bump, no more.

VOICES FROM THE DRAWING-ROOM Lopakhin's returned! Yermolai Alexeievitch!

PISHCHIK Now we'll see what there is to see and hear what there is to hear. . . . (*Kisses* LOPAKHIN.) You smell of brandy, my dashing soul. And we're all enjoying ourselves.

(*Enter* LIUBOFF ANDREIEVNA.)

LIUBOFF Is that you, Yermolai Alexeievitch? Why were you so long? Where's Leonid?

LOPAKHIN Leonid Andreievitch returned with me, he's coming. . . .

LIUBOFF (*excited*) Well, what? Is it sold? Tell me?

LOPAKHIN (*confused, afraid to show his pleasure*) The sale was over at four o'clock. . . . We missed the train, and had to wait till half-past nine. (*Sighs heavily.*) Ooh! My head's swimming a little.

(*Enter* GAIEFF; *in his right hand he carries things that he has bought, with his left he dries his eyes.*)

LIUBOFF Leon, what's happened? Leon, well? (*impatiently, in tears*) Quick, for the love of God. . . .

GAIEFF (*says nothing to her, only waves his hand; to* FIRCE *weeping*) Here, take this . . . Here are anchovies, herrings from Kertch. . . . I've had no food today. . . . I have had a time! (*The door from the billiard-room is open; the clicking of the balls is heard, and* YASHA's *voice, "Seven, eighteen!"* GAIEFF's *expression changes, he no longer cries.*) I'm awfully tired. Let me change my clothes, Firce. (*Goes out through the drawing-room;* FIRCE *following him.*)

PISHCHIK What happened? Come on, tell us!

LIUBOFF Is the cherry orchard sold?

LOPAKHIN It is sold.

LIUBOFF Who bought it?

LOPAKHIN I bought it. (*Pause.* LIUBOFF ANDREIEVNA *is overwhelmed; she would fall if she were not leaning against an armchair and a table.* VARYA *takes her keys off her belt, throws them on the floor into the middle of the room and goes out.*) I bought it! Wait, ladies and gentlemen, please, my head's going round, I can't talk. . . . (*Laughing.*) When we reached the sale, Deriganoff was there already. Leonid Andreievitch had only fifteen thousand rubles, and Deriganoff offered thirty thousand on top of the mortgage to begin with. I saw how matters stood, so I went right after him and bid forty. He raised his bid to forty-five, I offered fifty-five. That means he went up by fives and I went up by tens. . . . Well, it came to an end at last, I bid ninety more than the mortgage; and it stayed with me. The cherry orchard is mine now, mine! (*Roars with laughter.*) My God, my God, the cherry orchard's mine! Tell me I'm drunk, or crazy, or dreaming. . . . (*Stamps his feet.*) Don't laugh at me! If my father and grandfather rose from their graves and looked at the whole affair, and saw how their Yermolai, their whipped and illiterate Yermolai, who used to run barefoot in the winter, how that very Yermolai has bought an estate, the most beautiful spot in the world! I've bought the estate where my grandfather and my father were slaves, where they weren't even allowed to enter the kitchen. I'm asleep, it's only a dream, an illusion. . . . It's the fruit of imagination, wrapped in the fog of the unknown. . . . (*Picks up the keys, gaily smiling.*) She threw down the keys, she wished to show that she was no longer mistress here. . . . (*Jingles keys.*) Well, it's all one! (*Hears the band tuning up.*) Eh, musicians, play, I wish to hear you! Come and look at Yermolai Lopakhin swinging his ax against the cherry orchard, come and look at the trees falling! We'll build villas here, and our grandsons and great-grandsons will see a new life here. . . . Play on, music. (*The band plays.* LIUBOFF ANDREIEVNA *sinks into a chair and weeps bitterly.* LOPAKHIN *continues reproachfully.*) Why then, why didn't you take my advice? My poor, dear woman, you can't go back now. (*Weeps.*) Oh, if only the whole thing were finished, if only our uneven, unhappy lives were changed!

PISHCHIK (*takes his arm; in an undertone*) She's crying. Let's go into the drawing-room and leave her by herself . . . come on . . . (*Takes his arm and leads him out.*)

LOPAKHIN What's that? Bandsmen, play up! Go on, do just as I wish you to!

(*ironically*) The new owner, the owner of the cherry orchard is coming! (*He accidentally knocks up against a little table and nearly upsets the candelabra.*) I can pay for everything now! (*Exit with* PISHCHIK.)

(*In the reception-room and the drawing-room nobody remains except* LIUBOFF ANDREI-EVNA, *who sits huddled up and weeping bitterly. The band plays softly.* ANYA *and* TROFIMOFF *come in quickly.* ANYA *goes up to her mother and kneels in front of her.* TROFIMOFF *stands at the drawing-room entrance.*)

ACT IV

(*Same as Act I. There are no curtains on the windows, no pictures; only a few pieces of furniture are left piled up in a corner as if for sale. The emptiness is apparent. There are bags and suitcases by the door that leads out of the house and at the back of the stage.*

(*The door at the left is open; the voices of* VARYA *and* ANYA *can be heard through it.* LOPAKHIN *stands and waits.* YASHA *holds a tray with little glasses of champagne. Outside,* YEPIKHODOFF *is tying up a box. Voices are heard behind the stage. The peasants have come to say good-bye. The voice of* GAIEFF *is heard: "Thank you, brothers, thank you."*)

YASHA   The peasants have come to say good-bye. I am of the opinion, Yermolai Alexeievitch, that they're good people, but they don't understand very much.

(*The voices die away.* LIUBOFF ANDREIEVNA *and* GAIEFF *enter. She is not crying but is pale, and her face twitches; she can hardly speak.*)

GAIEFF   You gave them your purse, Liuba. You can't go on like that, you can't!

LIUBOFF   I couldn't help myself, I couldn't! (*They go out.*)

LOPAKHIN   (*in the doorway, looking after them*) Please, I ask you most humbly! Just a little glass for farewell. I didn't remember to bring any from town and I found only one bottle at the station. Please, do! (*Pause.*) Won't you really have any? (*Goes away from the door.*) If I only knew—I wouldn't have bought any. Well, I shan't drink any, either. (YASHA *carefully puts the tray on a chair.*) You have a drink, Yasha, at any rate.

YASHA   To those departing! And good luck to those who stay behind! (*Drinks.*) I can assure you that this isn't real champagne.

LOPAKHIN   Eight rubles a bottle. (*Pause.*) It's frightfully cold here.

YASHA   We made no fire today, since we're going away. (*Laughs.*)

LOPAKHIN   What's the matter with you?

YASHA   I'm happy—that's all!

LOPAKHIN   It's October, but it's as sunny and quiet as if it were summer. Good for building. (*looking at his watch and speaking through the door*) Ladies and gentlemen, please remember that it's only forty-seven minutes till train time! You must leave for the station in twenty minutes. Hurry up.

(TROFIMOFF, *in an overcoat, enters from the outside.*)

TROFIMOFF   I think it's time we went. The carriages are waiting. Where the devil are my rubbers? They're lost. (*through the door*) Anya, I can't find my rubbers! I can't!

LOPAKHIN   I have to go to Kharkoff. I'm going on the same train as you. I'm going to spend the whole winter in Kharkoff. I've been hanging around with you people. I am tired of doing nothing. I must have something to do with my hands; they seem to belong to a different person if I don't use them.

TROFIMOFF We'll go away now and then you'll start again on your useful occupations!

LOPAKHIN Have a glass?

TROFIMOFF No—thanks!

LOPAKHIN So you're off to Moscow now?

TROFIMOFF Yes. I'll see them into town and tomorrow I'm going to Moscow.

LOPAKHIN Yes . . . I suppose the professors aren't lecturing yet; they're waiting till you turn up!

TROFIMOFF That does not concern you.

LOPAKHIN How many years have you been going to the university?

TROFIMOFF Think of something new! This is old and trite! (*looking for his rubbers*) You know, we may not meet again, so just let me give you a parting bit of advice: Don't wave your hands about! Get rid of that habit of waving them about. And then, building villas and reckoning on their residents becoming freeholders in time—that's the same thing; it's all a matter of waving your hands . . . I like you in spite of everything . . . You've slender, delicate fingers, like those of an artist, and you've a gentle, refined soul. . . .

LOPAKHIN (*embraces him*) Good-bye, dear fellow. Thanks for all you've said. If you need money for the journey, let me give you some.

TROFIMOFF What for? I don't need any.

LOPAKHIN But you've nothing!

TROFIMOFF Yes, I have, thank you; I received some for a translation. Here it is in my pocket. (*nervously*) But I can't find my rubbers!

VARYA (*from the other room*) Take your rubbish away! (*Throws a pair of rubbers on stage.*)

TROFIMOFF Why are you angry, Varya? H'm! These aren't my rubbers!

LOPAKHIN In the spring I sowed three thousand acres of poppies, and now I've netted forty thousand rubles profit. Why turn up your nose at it? I'm just a simple peasant. . . . And when my poppies were in bloom, what a picture it was! So, as I was saying, I made forty thousand rubles, and I mean I'd like to lend you some, because I can afford it.

TROFIMOFF Your father was a peasant, mine was a druggist, and that means nothing at all. (LOPAKHIN *takes out his pocketbook*.) No, no . . . Even if you gave me twenty thousand I should refuse. I'm a free man. And everything that rich and poor alike value so highly carries no more weight with me than thistledown in a wind. I can do without you, I can pass you by. I'm strong and proud. Mankind goes on to the highest possible truths and happiness on earth, and I march in the front ranks!

LOPAKHIN Will you reach there?

TROFIMOFF I shall! (*Pause.*) I'll reach there and show the way to others. (*Axes cutting the trees are heard in the distance.*)

LOPAKHIN Well, good-bye, old man. It's time to go. Here we stand pulling one another's noses, but life goes its own way all the while. When I work for a long stretch tirelessly, my thoughts become clearer and it seems to me that I understand the reasons for existence. But think, brother, how many people live in Russia without knowing why—? But all this is beside the point. Leonid Andreievitch, they say, has accepted a post in a bank; he will get six thousand rubles a year . . . But he won't stand it; he's very lazy.

ANYA (*at the door*) Mother asks if you will stop them cutting down the orchard until she has gone away.

TROFIMOFF Yes, really, you ought to have enough tact not to do that. (*Exit.*)

LOPAKHIN All right, all right . . . What funny people! (*Exit.*)

ANYA Has Firce been sent to the hospital?

YASHA I gave the order this morning. I suppose they've sent him.

ANYA (*to* YEPIKHODOFF, *who crosses the room*) Semyon Panteleievitch, please make inquiries if Firce has been sent to the hospital.

YASHA (*offended*) I told Yegor this morning. What's the use of asking ten times?

YEPIKHODOFF That old Firce, in my conclusive opinion, isn't worth mending; he had better join his ancestors. I only envy him. (*Puts a trunk on a hat-box and squashes it.*) Well, of course. I thought so! (*Exit.*)

YASHA (*grinning*) Two-and-twenty troubles.

VARYA (*behind the door*) Has Firce been taken away to the hospital?

ANYA Yes.

VARYA Why didn't they take the letter to the doctor?

ANYA It'll have to be sent after him. (*Exit.*)

VARYA (*in the next room*) Where's Yasha? Tell him his mother has come and wishes to say good-bye to him.

YASHA (*waving his hand*) She'll make me lose all patience!

(DUNYASHA *meanwhile has been busying herself with the bags; now that* YASHA *is left alone, she goes to him.*)

DUNYASHA If you would only look at me once, Yasha. You're going away, leaving me behind . . . (*Weeps and hugs him.*)

YASHA What's the use of crying? (*Drinks champagne.*) In six days I'll be back again in Paris. Tomorrow we get into the express and off we go. I can hardly believe it. Vive la France! It doesn't suit me here, I can't live here . . . it's no good. Well, I've seen the uncivilized world; I have had enough of it. (*Drinks champagne.*) What are you crying for? Behave decently and then you'll have no cause for tears!

DUNYASHA (*powders herself, looking in the mirror*) Write me from Paris! I loved you so much, Yasha, so much! I am a delicate girl, Yasha.

YASHA Somebody's coming.

(*He bustles around the baggage, singing softly. Enter* LIUBOFF ANDREIEVNA, GAIEFF, ANYA, *and* CHARLOTTA IVANOVNA.)

GAIEFF We'd better be off. There's no time to lose. (*Looks at* YASHA.) Somebody smells of herring!

LIUBOFF We needn't get into our carriages for ten minutes. (*Looks round the room.*) Good-bye, dear house, old grandfather. The winter will pass, the spring will come, and then you'll be here no more. You'll be pulled down. How much these walls have seen! (*Passionately kisses her daughter.*) My treasure, you're radiant, your eyes flash like two jewels! Are you happy? Very?

ANYA   Very! A new life is beginning, mother!

GAIEFF   (*gaily*) Yes, really, everything's all right now. Before the cherry orchard was sold we all were excited and worried, and then, when the question was solved once and for all, we all calmed down, and even became cheerful. I'm a bank official now, and a financier . . . red in the center; and you, Liuba, look better for some reason or other, there's no doubt about it.

LIUBOFF   Yes. My nerves are better, it's true. (*She puts on her coat and hat.*) I sleep well. Take my baggage out, Yasha. It's time. (*to* ANYA) My little girl, we'll soon see each other again . . . I'm off to Paris. I'll live there on the money your grandmother from Yaroslavl sent to buy the estate—bless her!—though it won't last long.

ANYA   You'll come back soon, soon, mother, won't you? I'll get ready, and pass the examination at the High School, and then I'll work and help you. We'll read all sorts of books together, won't we? (*Kisses her mother's hands.*) We'll read in the autumn evenings; we'll read many books, and a beautiful new world will open up before us . . . (*thoughtfully*) You'll come, mother. . . .

LIUBOFF   I'll come, my darling. (*Embraces her.*)

(*Enter* LOPAKHIN. CHARLOTTA *is singing to herself.*)

GAIEFF   Charlotta is happy; she's singing!

CHARLOTTA   (*takes a bundle, looking like a wrapped-up baby*) My little baby, bye-bye. (*The baby seems to answer, "Oua, oua!"*) Hush, my little boy. (*"Oua! Oua!"*) I'm so sorry for you! (*Throws the bundle back.*) So please find me a new place. I can't go on like this.

LOPAKHIN   We'll find one, Charlotta Ivanovna, don't you be afraid.

GAIEFF   Everybody's leaving us. Varya's going away . . . we've suddenly become unnecessary.

CHARLOTTA   I've nowhere to live in town. I must go away. (*Hums.*) Never mind.

(*Enter* PISHCHIK.)

LOPAKHIN   The miracle of nature!

PISHCHIK   (*puffing*) Oh, let me get my breath again. I'm fagged . . . My honorable friends, give me some water . . .

GAIEFF   Come for money, did you? I'm your humble servant, and I'm going out of the way of temptation. (*Exit.*)

PISHCHIK   I haven't been here for ever so long . . . dear madam. (*to* LOPAKHIN) You here? Glad to see you . . . man of tremendous brain . . . take this . . . take it . . . (*Gives* LOPAKHIN *money.*) Four hundred rubles . . . that leaves 841—

LOPAKHIN   (*shrugs his shoulders in surprise*) It's like a dream. Where did you get this?

PISHCHIK   Stop . . . it's hot . . . A most unexpected thing happened. A group of Englishmen came along and found some white clay on my land. . . . (*to* LIUBOFF ANDREIEVNA) And here's four hundred for you . . . beautiful lady . . . (*Gives her money.*) Give you the rest later . . . (*Drinks water.*) Just now a young man in the train was saying that some great philosopher advises us all to jump from the roofs. "Jump!" he says, and that's all. (*astonished*) Just imagine! More water!

LOPAKHIN   Who were these Englishmen?

PISHCHIK   I've leased the land with the clay to them for twenty-four years . . . Now, excuse me, I've no time. I must hurry or—I'll go to Gnoikoff—to Kardamanoff—I owe everybody—(*Drinks.*) Good-bye—I'll drop in Thursday.

LIUBOFF   We're just starting off to town, and tomorrow I go abroad.

PISHCHIK   (*agitated*) What? Why to town? I see furniture . . . trunks . . . Well, never mind. (*crying*) Never mind. These Englishmen are men of tremendous intellect . . . Never mind . . . Be happy . . . God will help you . . . Never mind . . . Everything in this world comes to an end . . . (*Kisses* LIUBOFF ANDREI-EVNA's *hand.*) And if you should happen to hear that my end has come, just remember this old . . . horse and say: "There used to be a certain fellow called Semyonoff-Pishchik, God bless his soul. . . ." Wonderful weather . . . yes . . . (*exit deeply moved, but returns at once and says in the door*) Dash-enka sent her love! (*Exit.*)

LIUBOFF   Now we can go. I've two worries, though. The first is poor Firce. (*Looks at her watch.*) We've still five minutes . . .

ANYA   Mother, Firce has already been sent to the hospital. Yasha sent him off this morning.

LIUBOFF   The second is Varya. She's used to getting up early and to work, and now she has no work to do, she's like a fish out of water. She's grown thin and pale, and she cries, poor thing. . . . (*Pause.*) You know very well, Yermolai Alexeievitch, that I hoped formerly to marry her to you, and I suppose you are going to marry somebody? (*Whispers to* ANYA, *who nods to* CHARLOTTA, *and they both go out.*) She loves you, she's your sort, and I don't understand, I really don't, why you seem to be keeping away from each other. I don't understand!

LOPAKHIN   To tell the truth, I don't understand it myself. It's all so strange. . . . If there's still time, I'll be ready at once. Let's get it over, once and for all; I don't feel as if I could ever propose to her without you.

LIUBOFF   Excellent. It'll take only a minute. I'll call her.

LOPAKHIN   The champagne comes in very handy. (*looking at the glass*) They're empty, somebody's drunk them already. (YASHA *coughs.*) I call that licking it up. . . .

LIUBOFF   (*animated*) Excellent. We'll go out. Yasha, *allez.* I'll call her . . . (*at the door*) Varya, leave that and come here. Come! (*Exit with* YASHA.)

LOPAKHIN   (*looks at his watch*) Yes . . . (*Pause.*)

(*There is a restrained laugh behind the door, a whisper, then* VARYA *comes in. She examines the luggage at length.*)

VARYA   I can't seem to find it . . .

LOPAKHIN   What are you looking for?

VARYA   I packed it myself and I don't remember. (*Pause.*)

LOPAKHIN   Where are you going now, Varvara Mikhailovna?

VARYA   I? To the Ragulins . . . I've accepted a position, to look after their household . . . housekeeper or something.

LOPAKHIN   Is that at Yashnevo? It's about fifty miles. (*Pause.*) So life in this house is finished now. . . .

VARYA (*looking at the baggage*) Where is it? . . . perhaps I've put it away in the trunk . . . Yes, there'll be no more life in this house . . .

LOPAKHIN And I'm off to Kharkoff at once . . . by this train. I've a lot of business on hand. I'm leaving Yepikhodoff here . . . I've hired him.

VARYA Well, well!

LOPAKHIN Last year at this time the snow was nice and sunny. Only it's rather cold . . . There's three degrees of frost.

VARYA I didn't look. (*Pause.*) And our thermometer's broken. . . . (*Pause.*)

VOICE AT THE DOOR Yermolai Alexeievitch!

LOPAKHIN (*as if he has long been waiting to be called*) Just a minute. (*Exit quickly. VARYA, sitting on the floor, puts her face against a bundle of clothes and weeps gently. The door opens. LIUBOFF ANDREIEVNA enters carefully.*)

LIUBOFF Well? (*Pause.*) We must go.

VARYA (*not crying now, wipes her eyes*) Yes, it's quite time, dear mother. I'll get to the Ragulins today, if I don't miss the train. . . .

LIUBOFF (*at the door*) Anya, put on your things. (*Enter ANYA, then GAIEFF, and CHARLOTTA IVANOVNA. GAIEFF wears a warm overcoat with a cape. A servant and drivers come in. YEPIKHODOFF bustles around the baggage.*) Now we can go away.

ANYA (*joyfully*) Away!

GAIEFF My friends, my dear friends! Can I be silent, in leaving this house forever?—can I restrain myself, in saying farewell, from expressing those feelings which now fill all my soul?

ANYA (*imploringly*) Uncle!

VARYA Uncle, you shouldn't!

GAIEFF (*stupidly*) Double the red into the center . . . I'll be quiet.

(*Enter TROFIMOFF, then LOPAKHIN.*)

TROFIMOFF Well, it's time to go!

LOPAKHIN Yepikhodoff, my coat!

LIUBOFF I'll sit here one minute more. It's as if I'd never really noticed what the walls and ceilings of this house were like, and now I look at them greedily, with such tender love. . . .

GAIEFF I remember, when I was six years old, on Trinity Sunday, I sat at this window and looked and watched my father go to church. . . .

LIUBOFF Have all the things been taken away?

LOPAKHIN Yes, all, I think. (*to YEPIKHODOFF, putting on his coat*) You see that everything's quite straight. Yepikhodoff.

YEPIKHODOFF (*hoarsely*) You may depend upon me, Yermolai Alexeievitch!

LOPAKHIN What's the matter with your voice?

YEPIKHODOFF I swallowed something just now; I was taking a drink of water.

YASHA (*suspiciously*) What manners . . .

LIUBOFF We go away, and not a soul remains behind.

LOPAKHIN Till the spring.

VARYA (*drags an umbrella out of a bundle, and seems to be waving it about. LOPAKHIN appears to be frightened.*) What are you doing? . . . I never thought . . .

TROFIMOFF Come along, let's take our seats . . . it's time! The train will be in presently.

VARYA Peter, here they are, your rubbers, by that trunk. (*in tears*) And how old and dirty they are . . .

TROFIMOFF (*putting them on*) Come on!

GAIEFF (*deeply moved, nearly crying*) The train . . . the station . . . Cross in the center, a white double in the corner. . . .

LIUBOFF Let's go!

LOPAKHIN Are you all here? There's nobody else? (*Locks the side-door on the left.*) There's a lot of things in there. I must lock them up. Come!

ANYA Good-bye, home! Good-bye, old life!

TROFIMOFF Welcome, new life. (*Exit with* ANYA. VARYA *looks around the room and goes out slowly.* YASHA *and* CHARLOTTA, *with her little dog, go out.*)

LOPAKHIN Till the spring then! Come on . . . till we meet again!

(LIUBOFF ANDREIEVNA *and* GAIEFF *are left alone. They seem to have been waiting for this moment. They fall into each other's arms and sob restrainedly and quietly, fearing that somebody might hear them.*)

GAIEFF (*in despair*) My sister, my sister . . .

LIUBOFF My dear, my gentle, beautiful orchard! My life, my youth, my happiness, good-bye! Good-bye!

ANYA'S VOICE (*gaily*) Mother!

TROFIMOFF'S VOICE (*gaily, excited*) Coo-ee!

LIUBOFF To look at the walls and the windows for the last time . . . My late mother used to like to walk about this room . . .

GAIEFF My sister, my sister!

ANYA'S VOICE Mother!

TROFIMOFF'S VOICE (*gaily, excited*) Coo-ee!

LIUBOFF We're coming! (*They go out. The stage is empty. The sound of keys turned in the locks is heard, and then the noise of the carriages driving off. It is quiet. Then the sound of an ax against the trees is heard in the silence sadly and staccato. Footsteps are heard.* FIRCE *comes in from the door on the right. He is dressed as usual, in a short jacket and white vest, with slippers on his feet. He is ill. He goes to the door and tries the handle.*)

FIRCE It's locked. They've left. (*Sits on sofa.*) They've forgotten me. . . . Never mind, I'll sit here . . . And Leonid Andreievitch has probably gone in a light overcoat instead of putting on his fur coat . . . (*Sighs anxiously.*) I didn't see. . . . Oh, these young people! (*Mumbles something unintelligible.*) Life's gone on as if I'd never lived. (*lying down*) I'll lie down. . . . You've no strength left in you, nothing left at all. . . . Oh, you . . . bungler! (*He lies motionless. The distant sound is heard, as if from the sky, of a string breaking, dying away morosely. Silence follows it, and only the sound somewhere in the distance, of the ax falling on the trees, is audible.*)

Philosophers and theologians have always been concerned with what is known as "the problem of evil." The question is, in the words of a famous clergyman: "Why is God silent while evil rages?" Why does an omnipotent God plague man with so many afflictions: cancer, sudden earthquakes and tidal waves, war, destruction, and inevitable death? Many writers have addressed themselves to this question, notably a very ancient writer in The Book of Job, Shakespeare in King Lear, and, in a less direct way, Melville in Moby Dick. In our time the distinguished American man of letters, Archibald MacLeish, has given us a modern version of The Book of Job in the play J.B.

Religious people have found various answers to the problem of evil, none of them statisfactory to others who are not religiously inclined. One answer is found at the end of The Book of Job itself, where we are told simply that man has no power to understand the unfathomable ways of God:

> 38:4. Where wast thou when I laid the foundations of the earth? declare, if thou hast understanding?

God is great. Man is small and must accept.

MacLeish has cleverly transmuted the story of Job into modern terms. Job is J.B., a millionaire with a happy, loving family. He suffers a skin affliction, as did Job, but he loses his family and possessions in twentieth-century catastrophes: war, an automobile accident, rape-murder, atomic explosion. God is Mr. Zuss (Zeus), and Satan is Nickles (the old Nick). Job's comforters (the phrase is proverbial) are Zophar, a man of religion, who puts forward the Christian doctrine of Original Sin; Eliphaz, a psychiatrist, who says it is the mind that must be treated; and Bildad, a Marxist-materialist, who believes that the catastrophes are simply part of the inexorable procession of history. They are no more comforting to J.B. than Job's comforters were to Job.

The reader will perceive that at the end of the play MacLeish supplies an answer not found in The Book of Job. There is no justice. God exists, but only as the boiling point of water exists. If there is love in the universe, it is human love.

> J.B.   He does not love. He
>   Is.
> SARAH   But we do. That's the wonder . . .
>   Then blow on the coal of the heart, my darling.

It is essentially the answer of the modern humanist-liberal. There is a universe consisting of physical laws. Nowhere but in man is there a regard for fellow beings.

The methods and devices of the playwright are interesting. The words are arranged in a loose sort of free verse. The first interior scene, the Thanksgiving dinner, is mounted realistically. Thenceforth the scenes become progressively barer and more symbolic. God and Satan are two decrepit ham actors who comment on J.B.'s plight. They look down from a symbolic platform inside a symbolic circus tent. Perhaps the most important stage device is the use of lights, which continuously create flexibility by causing a change of scene. Technically, this play is an excellent example of the modern free use of the stage's various resources.

⁂J.B.

ARCHIBALD MACLEISH

(The scene throughout is a corner inside an enormous circus tent where a side show of some kind has been set up. There is a rough stage across the corner, on the left of which a wooden platform has been built at a height of six or seven feet. A wooden ladder leans against it. To the right is a deal table with seven straight chairs. There is a door-shaped opening in the canvas to the right rear. Above, a huge, slanted pole thrusts the canvas out and up to make the peak of the corner. Clothes that have the look of vestments of many churches and times have been left about at one side and the other of the stage and the light at the beginning—such light as there is—is provided by bulbs dangling from hanks of wire. The feel is of a public place at late night, the audience gone, no one about but maybe a stagehand somewhere cleaning up, fooling with the lights.)

THE PROLOGUE

(MR. ZUSS, followed by NICKLES, enters from the dimness off to the left. They stop at the edge of the side-show stage. Both wear the white caps and jackets of circus vendors. Both are old. MR. ZUSS, who has a bunch of balloons hitched to his belt, is large, florid, deep-voiced, dignified, imposing. NICKLES is gaunt and sardonic; he has a popcorn tray slung from straps across his shoulders. Both betray in carriage and speech the broken-down actor fallen on evil days but nevertheless and always actor. Throughout the Prologue, from the moment when they mount the side-show stage, they jockey for position, gesture, work themselves up into theatrical flights and rhetorical emotions, play to each other as though they had an actual audience before them in the empty dark.)

MR. ZUSS	This is it.
NICKLES	This is what?
MR. ZUSS	Where they play the play, Horatio!
NICKLES	Bare stage?
MR. ZUSS	Not in the least. Heaven and earth. That platform's Heaven.

(*They step up onto the stage together.*)

NICKLES	Looks like Heaven!
MR. ZUSS	As you remember it?
NICKLES	Somebody's got to. You weren't there. They never sold balloons in Heaven— Not in my time.
MR. ZUSS	Only popcorn.

(NICKLES *shrugs a shudder of disgust, heaving his tray.*)

NICKLES	The two best actors in America Selling breath in bags . . .
MR. ZUSS	and bags To butter breath with . . .
NICKLES	when they sell.
MR. ZUSS	Merchandise not moving, Nickles?
NICKLES	Moves wherever I do—all of it. No rush to buy your worlds, I notice.
MR. ZUSS	I could sell one to a . . .
NICKLES	. . . child! , You told me. Where's the earth?
MR. ZUSS	Earth? Earth is where that table is: That's where Job sits—at the table. God and Satan lean above.

(MR. ZUSS *peers anxiously up into the canvas sky.*)

	I wonder if we'd better?
NICKLES	What?
MR. ZUSS	Play it.
NICKLES	Why not? Who cares? *They* don't.
MR. ZUSS	At least we're actors. They're not actors. Never acted anything.
NICKLES	That's right. They only own the show.

MR. ZUSS	I wonder . . .
NICKLES	They won't care and they won't know.

(His eyes follow MR. ZUSS's *up to the dangling bulbs.)*

Those stars that stare their stares at me—
Are those the staring stars I see
Or only lights . . .

not meant for me?

MR. ZUSS	What's that got to do with anything?
NICKLES	Very little. Shall we start?
MR. ZUSS	You think we ought to?
NICKLES	They won't care.
MR. ZUSS	Let's start . . .

What staring stars?

NICKLES	They aren't.

They're only lights. Not meant.

MR. ZUSS	Why don't we

Start?

NICKLES	You'll play the part of . . .
MR. ZUSS	Naturally!
NICKLES	Naturally! And your mask?
MR. ZUSS	Mask!
NICKLES	Mask. Naturally. You wouldn't play God in your

Face would you?

MR. ZUSS	What's the matter with it?
NICKLES	God the Creator of the Universe?

God who hung the world in time?
You wouldn't hang the world in time
With a two-days' beard on your chin or a pinky!
Lay its measure! Stretch the line on it!

(MR. ZUSS stares coldly at NICKLES, unhitches his balloon belt with magnificent deliberation, drops it, steps forward to the front of the wooden stage, strikes an attitude.)

MR. ZUSS	*Whatsoever is under the whole*

Heaven is mine!

NICKLES	That's what I mean.

You need a mask.

MR. ZUSS (*heavy irony*)	Perhaps a more

Accomplished actor . . .

NICKLES	Kiss your accomplishments!

                    Nobody doubts your accomplishments—none of them—
                    The one man for God in the theater!
                    They'd all say that. Our ablest actor.
                    Nobody else for the part, they'd say.

MR. ZUSS   You make me humble.

NICKLES   No! I'm serious.
                    The part was written for you.

MR. ZUSS (*gesture of protest*)   Oh!

NICKLES   But this is God in *Job* you're playing:
                    God the Maker: God Himself!
                    Remember what He says?—the hawk
                    Flies by His wisdom! And the goats—
                    Remember the goats? He challenges Job with them:
                    Dost thou know the time of the wild goats?
                    What human face knows time like that time?
                    You'd need a face of fur to know it.
                    Human faces know too much too little.

MR. ZUSS (*suspiciously*)
                    What kind of mask?

NICKLES   You'll find one somewhere.
                    They never play without the masks.

MR. ZUSS   It's God the Father I play—not
                    God the boiling point of water!

NICKLES   Nevertheless the mask is imperative.
                    If God should laugh
                    The mare would calf
                    The cow would foal:
                    Diddle my soul . . .

MR. ZUSS (*shocked*)
                    God never laughs! In the whole Bible!

NICKLES   That's what I say. *We* do.

MR. ZUSS   *I* don't.

NICKLES   *Job* does. He covers his mouth with his hand.

MR. ZUSS   Job is abashed.

NICKLES   He says he's abashed.

MR. ZUSS   He should be abashed: it's rank irreverence—
                    Job there on the earth . . .

NICKLES   On his dung heap . . .

MR. ZUSS   Challenging God!

NICKLES	Crying to God.
MR. ZUSS	Demanding *justice* of *God!*

NICKLES
> Justice!
> No wonder he laughs. It's ridiculous. All of it.
> God has killed his sons, his daughters,
> Stolen his camels, oxen, sheep,
> Everything he has and left him
> Sick and stricken on a dung heap—
> Not even the consciousness of crime to comfort him—
> The rags of reasons.

MR. ZUSS
> God is reasons.

NICKLES
> For the hawks, yes. For the goats. They're grateful.
> Take their young away they'll sing
> Or purr or moo or splash—whatever.
> Not for Job though.

MR. ZUSS
> And that's why.

NICKLES
> Why what?

MR. ZUSS
> He suffers.

NICKLES
> Ah? Because he's . . .
> Not a bird you mean?

MR. ZUSS
> You're frivolous . . .

NICKLES
> That's precisely what you do mean!
> The one thing God can't stomach is a man,
> That scratcher at the cracked creation!
> That eyeball squinting through into His Eye,
> Blind with the sight of Sight!

(NICKLES *tugs himself free of his tray.*)   Blast this . . .

MR. ZUSS
> God created the whole world.
> Who is Job to . . .

NICKLES
> Agh! the world!
> The dirty whirler! The toy top!

MR. ZUSS (*kicking savagely at the popcorn tray and the balloon belt to shove them under the platform*)
> What's so wrong with the world?

NICKLES
> Wrong with it!
> Try to spin one on a dung heap!

(MR. ZUSS *does not answer. He goes on kicking at the tray.*)

(NICKLES *sits on a rung of the ladder. After a time he begins to sing to himself in a kind of tuneless tune.*)

NICKLES	I heard upon his dry dung heap
	That man cry out who cannot sleep:
	"If God is God He is not good,
	If God is good He is not God;
	Take the even, take the odd,
	I would not sleep here if I could
	Except for the little green leaves in the wood
	And the wind on the water."

(There is a long silence.)

| MR. ZUSS | You are a bitter man. |

NICKLES *(pompously)*	I taste of the world!
	I've licked the stick that beat my brains out:
	Stock that broke my father's bones!

MR. ZUSS	Our modern hero! Our Odysseus
	Sailing sidewalks toward the turd
	Of truth and touching it at last in triumph!
	The honest, disillusioned man!
	You sicken me.

NICKLES *(hurt)*	All right, I sicken you.
	No need to be offensive, is there?
	If you would rather someone else ...

| MR. ZUSS | Did what? |

| NICKLES | Played Job. |

| MR. ZUSS | What's Job to do with it? |

NICKLES	Job was honest. He saw God—
	Saw him by that icy moonlight,
	By that cold disclosing eye
	That stares the color out and strews
	Our lives ... with light ... for nothing.

| MR. ZUSS | Job! |
| | I never thought of you for Job. |

| NICKLES | You never thought of me for Job! |
| | What did you think of? |

| MR. ZUSS | Oh! there's always |
| | Someone playing Job. |

NICKLES	There must be
	Thousands! What's that got to do with it?
	Thousands—not with camels either:
	Millions and millions of mankind
	Burned, crushed, broken, mutilated,
	Slaughtered, and for what? For thinking!

For walking round the world in the wrong
Skin, the wrong-shaped noses, eyelids:
Sleeping the wrong night wrong city—
London, Dresden, Hiroshima.
There never could have been so many
Suffered more for less. But where do
I come in?

(MR. ZUSS *shuffles uncomfortably.*)
Play the dung heap?

MR. ZUSS   All we have to do is start.
Job will join us. Job will be there.

NICKLES   I know. I know. I know. I've seen him.
Job is everywhere we go,
His children dead, his work for nothing,
Counting his losses, scraping his boils,
Discussing himself with his friends and physicians,
Questioning everything—the times, the stars,
His own soul, God's providence.
What do *I* do?

MR. ZUSS   What do *you* do?

NICKLES   What do I do? You play God.

MR. ZUSS   I play God. I think I mentioned it.

NICKLES   You play God and I play . . .
(*He lets himself down heavily on the rung of the ladder.*)
Ah!

MR. Zuss (*embarrassed*)
I had assumed you knew.
(NICKLES *looks up at him, looks away.*)   You see,
I think of you and me as . . . opposites.

NICKLES   Nice of you.

MR. ZUSS   I didn't mean to be nasty.

NICKLES   Your opposite! A demanding role!

MR. ZUSS   I know.

NICKLES   But worthy of me? Worthy of me!

MR. ZUSS   I have offended you. I didn't mean to.

NICKLES   Did I say I was offended?

(*There is an awkward silence. NICKLES, his face in his hands, begins to hum the tune
to his little song. MR. ZUSS looks up and around into the corners of the sky, his head
moving cautiously. At length NICKLES begins to sing the words.*)

I heard upon his dry dung heap

That man cry out who cannot sleep:
"If God is God He is not good,
If God is good He is not God;
Take the even, take the odd,
I would not sleep here if I could . . ."

(*Silence.*)

So I play opposite to God!

(*Silence.*)

Father of Lies they call me, don't they?

(MR. ZUSS *does not answer. He is still searching the dark above. Silence.* NICKLES *goes back to the song.*)

"I would not sleep here if I could
Except for the little green leaves in the wood
And the wind on the water."

(*Silence. Then suddenly, theatrically,* NICKLES *is on his feet.*)

Who knows enough to know they're lies?
Show me the mask!

MR. ZUSS   What mask?

NICKLES (*attitude*)   My mask!

MR. ZUSS   Are you sure you wear a mask?

NICKLES   Meaning only God should wear one?

MR. ZUSS   Meaning are you sure it's there.

NICKLES   *They* never play without them.

MR. ZUSS   Yes but
Where?

NICKLES   Where? In Heaven probably:
Up on the platform there in Heaven!

MR. ZUSS   Yes . . . . You wouldn't care to . . .

NICKLES   What?

MR. ZUSS   Find it for yourself?

NICKLES   In Heaven?
Heaven is your department, Garrick.

MR. ZUSS   My department! I suppose it is.
Here! Hold this! Hold it! Steady . . .

(NICKLES *steadies the ladder.* MR. ZUSS *climbs warily, keeping his eye on the canvas darkness; heaves himself over the rail; rummages around on the platform; turns, holding out a huge white, blank, beautiful, expressionless mask with eyes lidded like the eyes of the mask in Michelangelo's* Night.)

NICKLES   That's not mine—not *his.* It's His.
I've known that face before. I've seen it.
They find it under bark of marble

Deep within the rinds of stone:
God the Creator . . . (*nastily*) of the animals!

MR. ZUSS (*outraged*)   God of
Everything that is or can!

NICKLES   Is or can—but cannot know.

MR. ZUSS   There is nothing those closed eyes
Have not known and seen.

NICKLES   Except
To know they see: to know they've seen it.
Lions and dolphins have such eyes.
They know the way the wild geese know—
Those pin-point travelers who go home
To Labradors they never meant to,
Unwinding the will of the world like string.
What would they make of a man, those eyelids?

MR. ZUSS   Make of him! They *made* him.

NICKLES   Made him
Animal like any other
Calculated for the boughs of
Trees and meant to chatter and be grateful!
But womb-worm wonders and grows wings—
(NICKLES *breaks off, struck by his own words, goes on:*)
It actually does! The cock-eyed things
Dream themselves into a buzz
And drown on windowpanes. He made them
Wingless but they learn to wish.
That's why He fumbles Job. Job wishes!—
Thinks there should be justice somewhere—
Beats his bones against the glass.
Justice! In this cesspool! Think of it!
Job knows better when it's over.

MR. ZUSS   Job knows justice when it's over.
Justice has a face like this.

NICKLES   Like blinded eyes?

MR. ZUSS   Like skies.

NICKLES   Of stone.
Show me the other.

(MR. ZUSS *ducks away, rummaging in the clutter on the platform; turns again.*)
MR. ZUSS   You won't find it
Beautiful, you understand.

NICKLES   I know that.
                    Beauty's the Creator's bait,
                    Not the Uncreator's: his
                    Is Nothing, the no-face of Nothing
                    Grinning with its not-there eyes.
                    Nothing at all! Nothing ever! . . .
                    Never to have been at all!

(MR. ZUSS *turns, lifts the second mask above* NICKLES' *gesturing. This is large as the first but dark to the other's white, and open-eyed where the other was lidded. The eyes, though wrinkled with laughter, seem to stare and the mouth is drawn down in agonized disgust.*)
MR. ZUSS   Well?
    (NICKLES *is silent.*)
              (*cheerfully*)   That's it.
    (*Silence.*)
                               You don't care for it?
                    It's not precisely the expression
                    Anyone would choose. I know that.
                    Evil is never very pretty:
                    Spitefulness either. Nevertheless it's
                    His—you'll grant that, won't you?—the traditional
                    Face we've always found for him anyway.
                    God knows where we go to find it:
                    Some subterranean memory probably.
    (NICKLES *has approached the ladder, staring. He does not reply.*)
                    Well, if you won't you won't. It's your
                    Option. I can't say I blame you.
                    I wouldn't do it. Fit my face to
                    That! I'd scrub the skin off afterward!
                    Eyes to those eyes!

NICKLES (*harshly*)   You needn't worry.
                    Your beaux yeux would never bear that
                    Look of . . .

MR. ZUSS (*smugly*)   No. I know.

NICKLES   . . . of pity!
                    Let me have it.
    (NICKLES *starts up the ladder, the mask in* MR. ZUSS's *hands above him.*)
                               Evil you call it!
                    Look at those lips: they've tasted something
                    Bitter as a broth of blood
                    And spat the sup out. Was that evil?
    (*He climbs another rung.*)
                    Was it?
    (*Another rung.*)
                         Spitefulness you say:
                    You call that grin of anguish spite?
    (*He pulls himself over the rail, takes the mask in his hands.*)

I'd rather wear this look of loathing
Night after night than wear that other
Once—that cold complacence . . .

(MR. ZUSS *has picked up the first mask again, lifts it.*)

Horrible!

Horrible as a star above
A burning, murdered, broken city!
I'll play the part! . . .

Put your mask on! . . .

Give me the lines! . . .

MR. ZUSS   What lines?

NICKLES   His!

Satan's!

MR. ZUSS   They're in the Bible aren't they?

NICKLES   We're supposed to speak the Bible?

MR. ZUSS   *They* do . . .

(*The light bulbs fade out, yellow to red to gone. A slow, strong glow spots the platform throwing gigantic shadows up across the canvas. Back to back the shadows of MR. ZUSS and* NICKLES *adjust their masks. The masked shadows turn to each other and gravely bow. Their gestures are the stiff formal gestures of pantomime. Their voices, when they speak, are so magnified and hollowed by the masks that they scarcely seem their own.*)

GODMASK   *Whence comest thou?*

SATANMASK   *From going to and fro in the earth*

(*There is a snicker of suppressed laughter.*)

And from walking up and down in it . . .

(*A great guffaw.* MR. ZUSS *tears off his mask.*)

MR. ZUSS (*shouting*)   Lights!

(*The spotlight fades out. The dangling bulbs come feebly on.*)

Nobody told you to laugh like that.
What's so funny? It's irreverent. It's impudent.
After all, you are talking to God.
That doesn't happen every Saturday
Even to kitchen kin like you.
Take that face off! It's indecent!
Makes me feel like scratching somewhere!

(NICKLES *painfully removes his mask.*)

NICKLES   Do I look as though I'd laughed?
If you had seen what I have seen
You'd never laugh again! . . .

(*He stares at his mask.*)

Weep either . . .

MR. ZUSS   You roared. I heard you.

NICKLES   Those eyes *see.*

MR. ZUSS	Of course they see—beneath the trousers
	Stalking up the pulpit stair:
	Under the skirts at tea—wherever
	Decent eyes would be ashamed to.
	Why should you laugh at that?

NICKLES   It isn't
That! It isn't that at all!
They see the *world*. They do. They see it.
From going to and fro in the earth,
From walking up and down, they see it.
I know what Hell is now—to *see*.
Consciousness of consciousness . . .

MR. ZUSS   Now
Listen! This is a simple scene.
I play God. You play Satan.
God is asking where you've been.
All you have to do is tell him:
Simple as that. "In the earth," you answer.

NICKLES   *Satan* answers.

MR. ZUSS   All right—Satan.
What's the difference?

NICKLES   Satan *sees*.
He sees the parked car by the plane tree.
He sees behind the fusty door,
Beneath the rug, those almost children
Struggling on the awkward seat—
Every impossible delighted dream
She's ever had of loveliness, of wonder,
Spilled with her garters to the filthy floor.
Absurd despair! Ridiculous agony!

(*He looks at the mask in his hands.*)
What has any man to laugh at!
The panting crow by the dry tree
Drags dusty wings. God's mercy brings
The rains—but not to such as he.

MR. ZUSS   You play your part, I'll say that for you.
In it or out of it, you play.

NICKLES   You really think I'm playing?

MR. ZUSS   Aren't you?
Somebody is. Satan maybe.
Maybe Satan's playing *you*.
Let's begin from the beginning.
Ready!

(They take their places back to back.)
                    Masks!
(They raise their masks to their faces.)
                         Lights!

(The bulbs go out. Darkness. Silence. In the silence:)

A DISTANT VOICE   *Whence comest thou?*

MR. ZUSS   That's my line.

NICKLES   I didn't speak it.

MR. ZUSS   You did. Stop your mischief, won't you?

NICKLES   Stop your own! Laughing. Shouting.

MR. ZUSS   Lights, I said!

(The spotlight throws the enormous shadows on the canvas sky.)
GODMASK   *Whence comest thou?*

SATANMASK   *From going to and fro in the earth . . .*
   (A choked silence.)
                    And from walking up and down in it.

GODMASK   *Hast thou considered my servant Job*
                  That there is none like him on the earth
                  A perfect and an upright man, one
                  That feareth God and escheweth evil?

(The platform lights sink, the masked shadows fading with them, as a strong light comes on below isolating the table where J.B. stands with his wife and children.)

SCENE ONE

(The Platform is in darkness, the Table in light. J.B., a big, vigorous man in his middle or late thirties, stands at one end. At the other stands his wife, SARAH, a few years younger than her husband, a fine woman with a laughing, pretty face but a firm mouth and careful eyes, all New England. She is looking reprovingly but proudly at her five blond sons and daughters, who shift from foot to foot behind their chairs, laughing and nudging each other: DAVID, 13; MARY, 12; JONATHAN 10; RUTH, 8; REBECCA, 6. Two buxom, middle-aged maids in frilly aprons stand behind with their hands folded. The children subside under their mother's eyes.)

SARAH   J.B. . . .
(The heads bow.)

J.B.   Our Father which art in Heaven
                  Give us this day our daily bread.

REBECCA AND RUTH *(pulling their chairs out, clattering into them)*
                  Amenamen.

THE OLDER CHILDREN *(less haste but no less eagerness)*
                         Amen!

THE MAIDS (*wheeling majestically but urgently to go out*)
Amen!

SARAH (*to J.B. over the rattle of dishes and the clatter of talk as she sits down*)
That was short and sweet, my darling.

J.B. (*sitting down*) What was?

SARAH   Grace was.

J.B. (*cheerfully*)   All the essentials.

SARAH   Give? Eat?

J.B.   Besides they're hungry.

SARAH   That's what grace is for—the hunger.
Mouth and meat by grace amazed,
God upon my lips is praised.

J.B.   You think they stand in need of it—grace?
Look at them!

SARAH (*beaming*)   Yes! Look! Oh look!
(*The maids parade in with a huge turkey on a silver platter, china serving dishes with domed, blue covers, a gravy boat, a bottle of wine in a napkin.*)

MARY   Papá! Papá! He heard! He heard!

DAVID   Who did?

RUTH   Ourfatherwhichartinheaven.

J.B. (*nudging the bird gently with his finger*)
He did indeed. What a bird He sent us!
Cooked to a turn!

RUTH   He heard! He heard!

JONATHAN   He heard! He heard! He sent a bird!

SARAH   That's enough now, children. Quiet!
Your father's counting.

J.B.   Not today.
Not this gobbler. Feed a regiment.
Know what I was thinking, Sally?

SARAH   What?

J.B.   How beautiful you are.

SARAH   With your eye on a turkey? I like that!

J.B.   Why not? It's an eye-filling bird. Just look at it.

SARAH   Someday you might look at *me*.

J.B.   I'm always looking at you, Sarah.
(*He rises, knife and steel in hand, clashing them against each other in a noble rhythm.*)
                             Everywhere I look I see you.

SARAH (*scornfully*)
                             You never even see my clothes.

J.B. (*a shout of laughter*)
                             It's true. I don't. But I see *you.*

SARAH (*mock indignation*)
                             J! B!

J.B.   And what's wrong with the turkey?
                             What's wrong with that bottle of wine, either—
                             Montrachet or I'll drink the whole of it!
                             What's wrong with the bird or the wine or with anything—
                             The day either—what's wrong with the day?
(*He begins carving expertly and rapidly.*)
                             Tell me what day it is.

JONATHAN   Turkey Day.

MARY   Cranberry Day.

RUTH   Succotash Day.

DAVID   When we all can have white.

JONATHAN   And giblets to bite.

RUTH   And two kinds of pie.

JONATHAN   And squash in your eye.

MARY   And mashed potatoes with puddles of butter.

JONATHAN   And gravy and such.

REBECCA   . . . and. . . and. . .
(*The children are screaming with laughter.*)

SARAH   Children!

JONATHAN (*gasping*)   And all eat too much.

SARAH   Children!
                             Quiet! Quiet every one of you or
                             Kate will take it all—everything—
                             Knives, forks, turkey, glasses . . .

J.B.   Not the wine though.

SARAH   Job, I'm serious.
                             Answer your father's question, Jonathan.
                             Tell him what day it is.

JONATHAN (*hushed*)   Thanksgiving.

SARAH	What day is that?
JONATHAN	Thanksgiving Day
DAVID	The Day we give thanks to God.
MARY	For His goodness.
SARAH	And did you, David? Did you, Mary?
	Has any one of you thanked God?
	Really thanked Him?

(There is an awkward silence.)

Thanked Him for everything?

(The children's heads are down. J. B. busies himself with his carving.)

SARAH *(gently)*   God doesn't give all this for nothing:
A good home, good food,
Father, mother, brothers, sisters.
We too have our part to play.
If we do our part He does His,
He always has. If we forget Him
He will forget. Forever. In everything.
David!

(DAVID raises his head reluctantly.)

Did you think of God?

(DAVID does not reply.)

Did you think, when you woke in your beds this morning,
Any one of you, of Him?

(Silence.)

J.B. *(uncomfortable)*

Of course they did. They couldn't have helped it . . .

Bit of the breast for you, Rebecca?

SARAH   Please, Job. I want them to answer me.

J.B.   How can they answer things like that?

Gravy? That's the girl . . .

They know though.
Gift of waking, grace of light,
You and the world brought back together,
You from sleep, the world from night,
By God's great goodness and mercy . . .

Wing for Mary? Wing for Mary! . . .

They know all that. It's hard to talk about.

SARAH *(flushed, an edge to her voice)*
Even if it's hard we have to.
We can't just take, just eat, just—relish!
Children aren't animals.

J.B. (*he goes on with his serving*)   Sweet Sal! Sweet Sal!
  Children know the grace of God
  Better than most of us. They see the world
  The way the morning brings it back to them,
  New and born and fresh and wonderful . . .

  Ruth? She's always ravenous . . .

        I remember . . .

  Jonathan? He never is . . .

       . . . when I was
  Ten I used to stand behind
  The window watching when the light began,
  Hidden and watching.

      That's for David—
  Dark and thin.

MARY   Why? Why hidden?

J.B.   Hidden from the trees of course.
  I must have thought the trees would see me
  Peeking at them and turn back.

REBECCA   Back where?

J.B.   Back where they came from, baby.
  That's for your mother: crisp and gold.

RUTH   Father, you'd be cold. You didn't.

SARAH (*the edge still there*)
      He still does. He lies there watching
  Long before I see the light—
  Can't bear to miss a minute of it:
  Sun at morning, moon at night,
  The last red apple, the first peas!
  I've never seen the dish he wouldn't
  Taste and relish and want more of:
  People either!

J.B. (*serving himself with heaping spoons*)
      Come on, Sal!
  Plenty of people I don't like.
(*He sits down. Pours himself a glass of wine.*)
    I like their being people though . . .
(*Sips his wine.*)
    Trying to be.

SARAH   You're hungry for them—
  Any kind. People and vegetables:
  Any vegetables so long as
  Leaves come out on them. He loves leaves!

J.B. You love them too. You love them better.
Just because you know their names
You think you choose among your flowers:
Well, you don't. You love the lot of them.

SARAH I can't take them as a gift though:
I owe for them. We do. We *owe*.

J.B. Owe for the greening of the leaves?

SARAH Please!
Please, Job. I want the children
Somehow to understand this day, this . . .
Feast . . .

(Her voice breaks.)

J.B. Forgive me, Sal. I'm sorry—but they
Do. They understand. A little.
Look at me, all of you

Ruth, you answer:
Why do we eat all this, these dishes,
All this food?

(RUTH twists her napkin.)
You say, Rebecca.
You're the littlest of us all.
Why?

REBECCA Because it's good?

SARAH Baby!
Ah, my poor baby!

J.B. Why your poor baby?
She's right, isn't she? It is. It's good.

SARAH Good—and God has sent it to us!

J.B. She knows that.

SARAH Does she?
(She raises her head sharply.)
Job! . . .

do *you*?

(Their eyes meet; hers drop.)
Oh, I think you do . . .

but sometimes—
Times like this when we're together—
I get frightened, Job . . .

we have so
Much!

J.B. (*dead serious*)   You ought to think I do.
Even if no one else should, you should.
Never since I learned to tell
My shadow from my shirt, not once,
Not for a watch-tick, have I doubted
God was on my side, was good to me.
Even young and poor I knew it.
People called it luck: it wasn't.
I never thought so from the first
Fine silver dollar to the last
Controlling interest in some company
I couldn't get—and got. It isn't
Luck.

MARY   That's in the story.

JONATHAN   Tell the
Story.

RUTH   Tell the lucky story.

REBECCA   Lucky, lucky, tell the lucky.

J.B. (*getting to his feet again to carve*)
Tell the story?

        Drumstick, David?
Man enough to eat a drumstick?
You too, Jonathan?

REBECCA   Story, story.

J.B.   Fellow came up to me once in a restaurant:
"J.B.," he says—I knew him . . .

Mary, want the other wing?

"Why do you get the best of the rest of us?"
Fellow named Foley, I think, or Sullivan:
New-come man he was in town.

MARY   Your turn, Mother.

SARAH   Patrick Sullivan.

J.B. AND THE CHILDREN (*together in a shouted chant*)
Patrick Sullivan, that's the man!

J.B.   "Why do you get the best of the rest of us?
I've got as many brains as you.
I work as hard. I keep the lamp lit.
Luck! That's what it is," says Sullivan.
"Look!" I said. "Look out the window!"
"What do you see?" "The street," he tells me.

J.B. AND THE CHILDREN (*as before*)

> "The street?" says I. "The street," says he.

J.B.

> "What do you want me to call it?" he asks me.
> "What do I want you to call it?" says I.
> "A road," says I. "It's going somewhere."
> "Where?" says he. "You say," I said to him.

J.B. AND THE CHILDREN

> "God knows!" says Mr. Sullivan.

J.B.

> "He does," says I. "That's where it's going.
> That's where I go too. That's why."
> "Why what?" says he. "I get the best of you:
> It's God's country, Mr. Sullivan."

J.B. AND THE CHILDREN

> "God forbid!" says Mr. Sullivan.

J.B.

> I laughed till I choked. He only looked at me.
> "Lucky so-and-so," he yells.

SARAH

> Poor Mr. Sullivan.

J.B. (*soberly*)

> He was wrong.
> It isn't luck when God is good to you.
> It's something more. It's like those dizzy
> Daft old lads who dowse for water.
> They feel the alder twig twist down
> And know they've got it and they have:
> They've got it. Blast the ledge and water
> Gushes at you. And they knew.
> It wasn't luck. They knew. They felt the
> Gush go shuddering through their shoulders, huge
> As some mysterious certainty of opulence.
> They couldn't hold it. I can't hold it.

(*He looks at* SARAH.)

> I've always known that God was with me.
> I've tried to show I knew it—not
> Only in words.

SARAH (*touched*)

> Oh, you have,
> I know you have. And it's ridiculous,
> Childish, and I shouldn't be afraid . . .
> Not even now when suddenly everything
> Fills to overflowing in me
> Brimming the fulness till I feel
> My happiness impending like a danger.
> If ever anyone deserved it, you do.

J.B.

> That's not true. I don't deserve it.
> It's not a question of deserving.

SARAH   Oh, it is. That's all the question.
                 However could we sleep at night . . .

J.B.   Nobody *deserves* it, Sarah:
                 Not the world that God has given us.
(There is a moment's strained silence, then J.B. is laughing.)
J.B.   But I believe in it, Sal. I trust in it.
                 I trust my luck—my life—our life—
                 God's goodness to me.

SARAH (*trying to control her voice*)   Yes! You do!
                 I know you do! And that's what frightens me!
                 It's not so simple as all that. It's not.
                 They mustn't think it is. God punishes.
                 God rewards and God can punish.
                 God is just.

J.B. (*easy again*)   Of course He's just.
                 He'll never change. A man can count on Him.
                 Look at the world, the order of it,
                 The certainty of day's return
                 And spring's and summer's: the leaves' green—
                 That never cheated expectation.

SARAH (*vehemently*)
                 God can reward and God can punish.
                 Us He has rewarded. Wonderfully.
                 Given us everything. Preserved us.
                 Kept us from harm, each one—each one.
                 And why? Because of you . . .
(J.B. raises his head sharply.)
                                               No!
                 Let me say it! Let me say it!
                 I need to speak the words that say it—
                 I need to hear them spoken. Nobody,
                 Nobody knows of it but me.
                 You never let them know: not anyone—
                 Even your children. They don't know.

(J.B. heaves himself out of his chair, swings round the table, leans over SARAH, his arms around her.)
J.B.   Eat your dinner, Sal my darling.
                 We love our life because it's good:
                 It isn't good because we love it—
                 Pay for it—in thanks or prayers. The thanks are
                 Part of love and paid like love:
                 Free gift or not worth having.
                 You know that, Sal . . .
(He kisses her.)
                                   better than anyone.

Eat your dinner, girl! There's not a
Harpy on the roof for miles.

(She reaches up to touch his cheek with her hand.)

SARAH   Nevertheless it's true, Job. You
Can trust your luck because you've earned the
Right to trust it: earned the right
For all of us to trust it.

J.B. *(back at his own place, filling his glass again)*
Nonsense!
We get the earth for nothing, don't we?
It's given to us, gift on gift:
Sun on the floor, airs in the curtain.
We lie a whole day long and look at it
Crowing or crying in our cribs:
It doesn't matter—crow or cry
The sun shines, the wind blows . . .

Rebecca! Back for more already?

REBECCA   I want the wishbone please.

J.B.   Whatever
For?

REBECCA   To wish.

SARAH   For what, my baby?

REBECCA   For the wishbone.

SARAH *(pulling REBECCA into her lap)*
Little pig!
Wishing for wishes!

J.B. *(forking the wishbone onto REBECCA's plate)*
That's my girl!

SARAH   She is! The spit and image of you!
Thinking she can eat the world
With luck and wishes and no thanks!

J.B.   That isn't fair. We're thankful, both of us.

SARAH *(cuddling REBECCA)*
Both! And both the same! Just look at you!
A child shows gratitude the way a woman
Shows she likes a pretty dress—
Puts it on and takes it off again—
That's the way a child gives thanks:
She tries the world on. So do you.

J.B.   God understands that language, doesn't He?
He should. He made the colts.

SARAH   But you're not
                   Colts! You talk. With tongues. Or ought to.

J.B.   And we use them, don't we, baby?
                   We love Monday, Tuesday, Wednesday . . .

SARAH (*rocking* REBECCA *on her knees*)
                   We love Monday, Tuesday, Wednesday.
                   Where have Monday, Tuesday, gone?
                   Under the grass tree,
                   Under the green tree,
                   One by one.

JONATHAN   Say it again Mother . . . Mother!

SARAH   I never said it before. I don't
                   Know . . .

                                      How would you think it would go?
                   How does it go, Job? You said it.

J.B.   I didn't. I said we loved the world:
                   Monday, Tuesday, Wednesday, all of it.

SARAH   How would you think it would go, Jonathan?
       (*The words fall into a little tune as she repeats them.*)
                   I love Monday, Tuesday, Wednesday.
                   Where have Monday, Tuesday, gone?
                   Under the grass tree,
                   Under the green tree,
                   One by one.

                   Caught as we are in Heaven's quandary,
                   Is it they or we are gone
                   Under the grass tree,
                   Under the green tree?

                   I love Monday, Tuesday, Wednesday.
                   One by one.

REBECCA (*drowsily*)   Say it again.

SARAH   Say it again?

JONATHAN   You say it, Father.

J.B.   To be, become, and end are beautiful.

REBECCA   That's not what she said at all.

J.B.   Isn't it? Isn't it?

SARAH (*kissing her*)   Not at all.

       (*The light fades, leaving the two shadows on the canvas sky.*)

SCENE TWO

(The Platform. As the platform lights come on, the figures fade from the canvas sky and MR. ZUSS *and* NICKLES *straighten up, lifting their masks off, stretching, yawning.)*

MR. ZUSS   Well, that's our pigeon.

NICKLES   Lousy actor.

MR. ZUSS   Doesn't really act at all.

NICKLES   Just eats.

MR. ZUSS   And talks.

NICKLES   The love of life!
Poisoning their little minds
With love of life! At that age!

MR. ZUSS   No!
Some of that, I thought, was beautiful.

NICKLES   Best thing you can teach your children
Next to never drawing breath
Is choking on it.

MR. ZUSS   Who said that?
Someone's spoiled philosophy, it sounds like:
Intellectual butter a long war
And too much talking have turned rancid.
I thought he made that small familiar
Feast a true thanksgiving . . . only . . .

NICKLES   Only what?

MR. ZUSS   Something went wrong.

NICKLES   That's what I've been telling you.

MR. ZUSS   He didn't
Act.

NICKLES   He can't. He's not an actor.

MR. ZUSS   I wonder if he knows?

NICKLES   Knows what?

MR. ZUSS   Knows that he's in it?

NICKLES   Is he?

MR. ZUSS   Certainly.

NICKLES   How can you tell?

MR. ZUSS   That's him. That's Job.
He has the wealth, the wife, the children,
Position in the world.

NICKLES	The piety!
MR. ZUSS	He loves God, if that's what you're saying.
	A perfect and an upright man.
NICKLES	Piety's hard enough to take
	Among the poor who *have* to practice it.
	A rich man's piety stinks. It's insufferable.
MR. ZUSS	You're full of fatuous aphorisms, aren't you!
	A poor man's piety is hope of having:
	A rich man *has* his—and he's grateful.
NICKLES	Bought and paid for like a waiter's smirk!
	You know what talks when that man's talking?
	All that gravy on his plate—
	His cash—his pretty wife—his children!
	Lift the lot of them, he'd sing
	Another canticle to different music.
MR. ZUSS	That's what Satan says—but better.
NICKLES	It's obvious. No one needs to say it.
MR. ZUSS	You don't like him.
NICKLES	I don't have to.
	You're the one who has to like him.
MR. ZUSS	I thought you spoke of Job with sympathy.
NICKLES	Job on his dung hill, yes. That's human.
	That makes sense. But this world-master,
	This pious, flatulent, successful man
	Who feasts on turkey and thanks God!—
	He sickens me!
MR. ZUSS	Of course he sickens you,
	He trusts the will of God and loves—

(MR. ZUSS *is swollen with indignation and rhetoric. He swoops his mask up from the rail with a magnificent gesture, holds it.*)

Loves a woman who must sometime, somewhere,
Later, sooner, leave him; fixes
All his hopes on little children
One night's fever or a running dog
Could kill between the dark and day;
Plants his work, his enterprise, his labor,
Here where every planted thing
Fails in its time but still he plants it . . .

NICKLES (*nastily*) God will teach him better won't He?
God will show him what the world is like—
What man's like—the ignoble creature,
Victim of the spinning joke!

MR. ZUSS   Teach him better than he knows!
                  God will show him God!

NICKLES (*shrugging*)   It's the same
                  Thing. It hurts.

MR. ZUSS (*gathering momentum*) God will teach him!
                  God will show him what God *is*—
                  Enormous pattern of the steep of stars,
                  Minute perfection of the frozen crystal,
                  Inimitable architecture of the slow,
                  Cold, silent, ignorant sea-snail:
                  The unimaginable will of stone:
                  Infinite mind in midge of matter!

NICKLES   Infinite mush! Wait till your pigeon
                  Pecks at the world the way the rest do—
                  Eager beak to naked bum!

MR. ZUSS   You ought to have your tongue torn out!

NICKLES   All men should: to suffer silently.

MR. ZUSS   Get your mask back on! I tell you
                  Nothing this good man might suffer,
                  Nothing at all, would make him yelp
                  As you do. He'd praise God no matter.

NICKLES (*whispering*)
                  Why must he suffer then?

(*The question catches* MR. ZUSS *with his mask halfway to his face. He lowers it slowly staring into it as though the answer might be written inside.*)
MR. ZUSS (*too loud*)   To praise!

NICKLES (*softly*)   He praises now. Like a canary.

(MR. ZUSS *lifts his mask again.*)
MR. ZUSS   Well, will you put it on or won't you?

NICKLES (violently)
                  Shall I tell you why?
                            To learn!
                  Every human creature born
                  Is born into the bright delusion
                  Beauty and loving-kindness care for him.
                  Suffering teaches! Suffering's good for us!
                  Imagine men and women dying
                  Still believing that the cuddling arms
                  Enclosed them! They would find the worms
                  Peculiar nurses, wouldn't they? Wouldn't they?
(*He breaks off; picks his mask up; goes on in a kind of jiggling chant half to himself.*)
                  What once was cuddled must learn to kiss

	The cold worm's mouth. That's all the mystery.
	That's the whole muddle. Well, we learn it.
	God is merciful and we learn it . . .
	We learn to wish we'd never lived!
MR. ZUSS	This man will not.
NICKLES	Won't he? Won't he?
	Shall I tell you how it ends?
	Shall I prophesy? I see our
	Smug world-master on his dung heap,
	Naked, miserable, and alone,
	Pissing the stars. Ridiculous gesture!—
	Nevertheless a gesture—meaning
	All there is on earth to mean:
	Man's last word . . . and worthy of him!
MR. ZUSS	This man will not. He trusts God.
	No matter how it ends, he trusts Him.
NICKLES	Even when God tests him?—tortures him?
MR. ZUSS	Would God permit the test unless
	He knew the outcome of the testing?
NICKLES	Then why test him if God knows?
MR. ZUSS	So Job can see.
NICKLES	See what?
MR. ZUSS	See God.
NICKLES	A fine sight from an ash heap, certainly!
MR. ZUSS	Isn't there anything you understand?
	It's from the ash heap God is seen
	Always! Always from the ashes.
	Every saint and martyr knew that.
NICKLES	And so he suffers to see God:
	Sees God because he suffers. Beautiful!
MR. ZUSS	Put on your mask. I'd rather look at . . .
NICKLES	I should think you would! A human
	Face would shame the mouth that said that!

(*They put their masks on fiercely, standing face to face. The platform light fades out. The spotlight catches them, throwing the two masked shadows out and up. The voices are magnified and hollow, the gestures formal, as at the end of the Prologue.*)

GODMASK	*Hast thou considered my servant Job*
	That there is none like him on the earth,
	A perfect and an upright man, one
	That feareth God and escheweth evil?

SATANMASK (*sardonic*)
>
> Doth Job fear God for naught?

(*The God-shadow turns away in a gesture of anger.*)
>
> (*deprecatingly*)
>
> Hast thou not made an hedge about him
> And about his house
> And about all that he hath on every side?
> Thou hast blessed the work of his hands
> And his substance is increased.

(*The voice drops.*)
>
> But put forth thine hand now and touch
> All that he hath . . .

(*The voice becomes a hissing whisper.*)
>
> and he will
> Curse thee to thy face!

GODMASK (*in a furious great voice, arm thrown out in a gesture of contemptuous commitment*)
>
> Behold!
> All that he hath is in thy power!

(*The Satan-shadow bows mockingly; raises its two arms, advancing until the shadows become one shadow. The light fades. Suddenly, out of the darkness the Distant Voice of the Prologue.*)

THE DISTANT VOICE
>
> Only . . .

(*Silence.*)

GODMASK
>
> Only
> Upon himself
> Put not forth thy hand!

(*Darkness. The crash of a drum; a single stroke. Silence.*)

Note *The play is conceived and written without breaks, but if recesses in the action are desired one might well be made at this point.*

SCENE THREE

(*The Table. As the lights come on the two leaning shadows, one thrown upon the other, are visible on the canvas sky. They fade as the scene brightens. The table has been pushed to one side as though against a window in a living room. SARAH stands before it arranging flowers in a bowl. J.B. is straddling a chair, watching.*)

SARAH
>
> Look, Job! Look! Across the street.
> Two soldiers.

J.B.
>
> What about them?

SARAH
>
> Only they
> Stare so.

J.B.	Stare at what?
SARAH	The house.

I think they're drunk . . . A little.

(J.B. rises, stands beside her, his arm around her waist.)

J.B.	Plastered!
SARAH	One of them anyway. He wobbles.
J.B.	That's no wobble. That's a waltz step.
SARAH	They're crossing over.
J.B.	They sure are.
SARAH	What do you think they . . .
J.B.	Listen!
SARAH	Yes . . .

What do you think they want, two soldiers?

J.B.	No idea. Johnson will tend to them.
SARAH	I've never seen such staring eyes.
J.B.	Glazed. Just glazed.
SARAH	They keep on ringing.

I know what it is, J.B.,
They have some kind of message for us.
David has sent them with a message—
Something about his regiment. They're coming
Every day now, ship by ship.
I hear them in the harbor coming.
He couldn't write and so he sent them.

J.B.	Pretty drunk for messengers, those soldiers.
SARAH	What does it matter. They're just boys.

They've just got home. It doesn't matter.

J.B.	Johnson's a judge of drunks. He'll handle them.
SARAH	He mustn't send them off. Don't let him!

(There is a commotion outside the canvas door. A voice, off.)

VOICE	Two young . . . gentlemen to see you.

Friends, they say, of Mr. David.

SARAH	Oh, I knew! I knew! I knew!
VOICE (OFF)	That's telling him, Puss-foot!
VOICE (OFF)	Puss-face!

(The two MESSENGERS enter, dressed as soldiers. The FIRST is flushed and loud; the SECOND, very drunk, pale as bone.)

J.B.   Come in, gentlemen. Come in. Come in.
                        David's friends are always welcome.
                        This is David's mother.

SARAH   Won't you sit
                        Down?

FIRST MESSENGER   What did I tell you, Punk!
                        Any friends of David's.

SECOND MESSENGER   Any at
                        All . . .

FIRST M.   I told you that boy meant it.
                        What did I say when I see the joint?
                        That's the number, Punk, I told you.
                        Old Ten Twenty: that's the number.
        (He turns to SARAH.)
                        Twenty if you're men, he told us—
                        Ten for horses' whatses. What the
                        Hell, he always said: we're friends.

SECOND M.   Any at all he always . . .

FIRST M.   Pardon the
                        Language, lady.

SECOND M.   Any a' . . .

SARAH   There!
                        Sit down.

FIRST M.   It's just, we saw the number.

SARAH   And David asked you to drop in.

FIRST M.   Any friend of his, he told us.
                        Any time.

SECOND M.   And we were cold:
                        A cold, hard match . . .

FIRST M.   What the
                        Hell's the matter with *you!* You drunk?

SARAH   Sit by the fire, both of you. Where was he?

FIRST M.   Where was who?

SARAH   David.

FIRST M.   When?

J.B.   When he told you.

FIRST M.	In the mess.
	Any friend of his, he told us.
	Any time at all. Why?
	You think we're lying to you?

| J.B. | Certainly |
| | Not. |

| FIRST M. | You think we never knew him? |

| SARAH | Of course. Of course you do. |

| FIRST M. | We knew him. |

| SECOND M. | Fumbling among the faces . . . knew him . . . |
| | Night . . . our fingers numb . . . |

FIRST M.	Will you shut
	Up or will I clout you, Big Mouth!
(To SARAH.)	That's why we come: because we knew him.
	To tell you how we knew him.

| SARAH | Thank you. |
| (Silence.) | |

| SECOND M. | How it was with him . . . |

| FIRST M. | Listen, Punk! |

| SECOND M. | How, by night, by chance, darkling . . . |
| | By the dark of chance . . . |

| FIRST M. | He's drunk. |

| SECOND M. | How, the war done, the guns silent . . . |
| | No one knows who gave the order. |

FIRST M. (raising his voice)	
	Like I say, because he said to.
	Any friend of his he said to.
	Just to tell you we knew David:
	Maybe drink to David maybe . . .

| SARAH | Yes! Oh yes! Let's drink to David! |
| | J.B.! |

| J.B. | Bourbon? Scotch? |

FIRST M.	Now you're
	Cooking! Take your pants off, Punk:
	We're in.

SARAH	That's right. Put your feet up.
	Oh, they're not too dirty. David's are
	Dirtier. I'm sure of that.

FIRST M.   David's feet! I'll say they are.
Look! What's going on here! David's
Feet!

SARAH   I meant—with all that marching.

FIRST M.   I don't get it. Look, it's true
They didn't have the right length lumber:
We did the best we could . . .

(J.B. starts to his feet.)
J.B.   What in
God's name are you saying, soldier?

SARAH (*rising*)   What does he mean, the lumber?
(Silence.)

FIRST M.   You don't
Know? Ain't that the army for you!
(To the SECOND MESSENGER.*)*
They don't know. They never told them.

SARAH   Told us what?

FIRST M.   We better go.

SARAH   No! Please! Please! No!

FIRST M.   Come on, we're getting out, you lunkhead.

J.B.   Not until you've told me. Sarah!
Perhaps you'd better, Sarah . . .

SARAH   Please,
I want to hear it.

FIRST M.   Jesus! . . . Jesus! . . .

(There is a long silence. The SECOND MESSENGER *turns slowly to J.B., his face drunken white, his eyes blank.)*
SECOND M.   *I only am escaped alone to tell thee . . .*

(The focus of light opens to include the platform where MR. ZUSS *and* NICKLES *stand staring down, their masks in their hands.* MR. ZUSS's *face is expressionless.* NICKLES *wears a twisted grin. The* SECOND MESSENGER's *head falls forward onto his knees.)*
. . . My tongue loosened by drink . . .

my thought
Darkened as by wind the water . . .

That day is lost where it befell . . .

SARAH (*she is holding herself by the straining of her clenched hands*)
What is it we were never told?

J.B.   It isn't
True you little drunken liar!
it can't be true! It isn't possible!

(Silence. The passion ebbs from J.B.'s voice.)
We had a letter from him.
(Silence. Then, uncertainly)
After the
End of it we had a letter. . . .

(NICKLES jerks a crooked leg over the rail, starts awkwardly down the ladder, watching intently, peering back up at MR. ZUSS, watching.)

SECOND M.   What shall I say to you . . . ?

What I saw . . . ?

What I believe I saw . . . ?

Or what

I must have seen . . .

and have forgotten?

SARAH *(a cry)*   David is our son, our son, our son.

NICKLES *(prompting her from his ladder in a harsh half-whisper)*
That's the tune. He's *ours.* Go on with it:
Can't be happening to *us!* Can't be!
God won't let it happen, not to
Our kind, God won't!
(He leers up at MR. ZUSS.)

J.B. *(turning Sarah away from the SECOND MESSENGER into his arms)*
Sarah! Sarah!
David's all right. He has to be. He is.
I know he is. The war is over.
It never could have happened—never—
Never in this world.

NICKLES *(the whisper harsher)*   Couldn't it?
Ask him! Couldn't it? Suppose it did though:
What would the world be made of then?

SECOND M.   I only am escaped alone, companions
Fallen, fallen, fallen . . .

the earth
Smell remembers that there was a man.

SARAH   Job! He's dead! God has taken him!

(The focus of light narrows, is extinguished.)

SCENE FOUR

(Darkness. Silence. Then the crash of a drum. Silence again. Then two cigarettes are lighted, one high above the stage, one lower. Then gradually the lights come on, making four circles across the front of the stage like the circles of sidewalk brightness under

street lamps. Where the cigarettes were lighted MR. ZUSS and NICKLES are now visible on the platform rail and the ladder, squatting there like two tramps on the stairs of a stoop, turning their heads together one way and then the other, watching, not speaking. After a time the FIRST MESSENGER comes strolling in from their right, a news camera slung from his neck. The SECOND follows with a notebook. They wear battered felt hats with their khaki shirts and trousers. They are followed at a little distance by a stylishly dressed girl.)

GIRL   I don't like it.

FIRST MESSENGER   You'll do fine.

GIRL   I wish I was home in bed with a good
         Boy or something. I don't like it.

FIRST M.   You'll do fine.

GIRL   I won't do fine:
         I'm frightened.

FIRST M.   All you do, you go up to them,
         Get them talking, keep them looking.

GIRL   Go up to them yourselves, why don't you?

FIRST M.   Sure, and get the brush-off. Girl like
         You can keep them talking; keep them
         Looking, that is. Pretty girl.

GIRL   I don't like it.

SECOND MESSENGER   You'll get used to it.

GIRL   Not where I work. Not Society.
         Society page they never die.
         Girl gets asked. Girl gets married.
         Girl gets photographed in night club.
         Girl gets older. Girl gets off.
         Never catch them dead on Society.

SECOND M.   Like the robins.

FIRST M.   Yeah, like robins.

GIRL   Why the robins?

SECOND M.   Never see one
       Dead.

FIRST M.   Nor sparrows neither.

SECOND M.   Either.

FIRST M.   Never hardly. Must be millions.

SECOND M.   Hardly ever see one dead.

GIRL   What happens to them?

SECOND M.	They get over it.
GIRL	Over what?
SECOND M.	Over being there.
GIRL	All I know is I don't like it. Keep them talking till a flash bulb Smacks them naked in the face— It's horrible!
FIRST M.	It's genius! Listen, lady! How do I get the photograph without? Answer me that. How do I get the Look a mother's face has maybe Once in a lifetime: just before Her mouth knows, when her eyes are knowing?
GIRL	I can't do it.
FIRST M.	*She* can't do it! All you got to do is walk. Wiggle your can. Keep them looking. Then he tells them. Then I take them. Then you beat it. Then that's that. Except the drink we're going to buy you Payday evening if you're good— And if you're not there's lots of liars.
SECOND M.	You don't have to tell them: I do.
GIRL	Why do *you?*
SECOND M.	Because I have to. I'm the one that has to tell them.
GIRL	Why?
SECOND M. (*shrugging*) Oh . . .
GIRL	Why?
SECOND M.	There's always Someone has to tell them, isn't there?
GIRL	Someone else can.
SECOND M.	No. There's always . . .

(*He is groping from word to word.*)

           Someone chosen by the chance of seeing,
           By the accident of sight,
           By stumbling on the moment of it,
           Unprepared, unwarned, unready,
           Thinking of nothing, of his drink, his bed,

His belly, and it happens, and he sees it . . .

(*He winces his eyes shut.*)
          Caught in that inextricable net
          Of having witnessed, having seen . . .

          He alone!

GIRL (*gently*)   But you don't have to.
  (*To the* FIRST MESSENGER.)
          Why does he have to?

SECOND M.   It was I.
          I only. I alone. The moment
          Closed us together in its gaping grin
          Of horrible incredulity. I saw their
          Eyes see mine! We *saw* each other!

FIRST M.   He has to. He was there. He saw it.
          Route Two. Under the viaduct.
          Traveling seventy—seventy-five—
          Kid was driving them was drunk,
          Had to be drunk, just drove into it.
          He was walking home. He saw it.
          Saw it start to, saw it had to,
          Saw it. J.B.'s son. His daughter.
          Four in all and all just kids.
          They shrieked like kids he said.

SECOND M.   Then silent.
          Blond in all that blood that daughter.

GIRL (*her voice rising*)
          He can't tell them *that!*

FIRST M.   He has to.
          Someone has to. They don't know.
          They been out all evening somewhere.

GIRL (*hysterically*) They don't have to know!

FIRST M.   They have to.

(NICKLES *and* MR. ZUSS *on their perches have seen something off to their right. They turn their heads together.*)
GIRL   No!

FIRST M. (*looking right, pulling his camera around*)
          That's them. They're coming. Quiet!

GIRL   I can't do it.

FIRST M. (*brutally*)   You can do it.

(J.B. *and* SARAH, *arm in arm, walk slowly into the first circle of light.* NICKLES *and* MR. ZUSS *lean forward, their masks dangling from their hands.*)

SECOND M. (*under his breath, staring at them as they come*)
>> I only, I alone, to tell thee . . .
>> I who have understood nothing, have known
>> Nothing, have been answered nothing . . .

GIRL (*crossing to meet them with an affected walk, the* FIRST MESSENGER *screening himself behind her, the* SECOND *following*) Good
>> Evening! What a pleasant evening!

>> Back from the theatre so soon?
>> We're neighbors, don't you know? You've met my
>> Miffklin walking me each morning:
>> You know Muff, my purple poodle . . .

>> Isn't it a pleasant evening!

SECOND M.   I'm from the press. There's been an accident . . .
(*He falters.*)

FIRST M.   Four kids in a car. They're dead.
>> Two were yours. Your son. Your daughter.
>> Cops have got them in a cab.
>> Any minute now they'll be here.
(*He raises his camera over the girl's shoulder.*)

GIRL (*in her own voice, screaming*)
>> Don't look! Cover your face!

SARAH (*with scarcely the breath to say it*)
>> Mary . . . Jonathan . . .

(*The flash. J.B. throws his elbow up as if to ward off a blow.* SARAH *does not move.*)
J.B.   You bastards!
>> I'll beat your god damned brains out . . .
(*He lunges after them blinded by the flash as they scatter.*)
>>   Where have you
>> Gone?
(SARAH *moves like a sleepwalker through the circles of light, one after the other, touches a chair, goes down on her knees beside it, clinging to it.*)
>>   Answer me!
(*Silence.*)
>>   Answer me!
(*Silence.*)

SARAH (*her voice dead*)   It wasn't
>> *They* that did it . . .
(*J.B. comes slowly back out of the darkness, sees her, crosses to her. There is a long silence, J.B. looking right and left along the street.*)

>>   Why did He do it to them?
>> What had they done to Him—those children . . .
>> What had they done to Him

>>   and we—

What had *we* done? . . .

What had *we* done?

J.B.   Don't, Sarah. Don't!
(NICKLES *lights a cigarette, grins back over his shoulder to* MR. ZUSS *in the handful of yellow glare.*)

It doesn't
Help to think that.

Nothing helps! . . .

SARAH   Nothing helps! . . .
Nothing can help them now.

J.B. (*a clumsy gesture*)   It . . . happened . . .

SARAH (*fiercely*)
Yes, and Who let it happen?

J.B. (*awkwardly*)   Shall we . . .
Take the good and not the evil?
We have to take the chances, Sarah:
Evil with good.
(*then, in a desperate candor*)
It doesn't mean there
Is no good!

NICKLES (*in his cracked whisper*)
Doesn't it? Doesn't it?

MR. ZUSS (*silencing* NICKLES *with his hand, his whisper hardly heard*)
Go on! Go on! That path will lead you.

SARAH (*bitterly*)
When you were lucky it was God!

J.B.   Sticks and stones and steel are chances.
There's no will in stone and steel . . .
(*His voice breaks.*)
It happens to us . . .
(*He drops on his knees beside her.*)

SARAH   No! . . .

Don't touch me!
(*She clings to the chair, motionless, not weeping.*)

(*The circles of light fade out.*)

SCENE FIVE

(*The dark diminishes until the white coats of* MR. ZUSS *and* NICKLES *are visible on the platform.* MR. ZUSS *lifts a padded drumstick.* NICKLES *balances on the rail and starts cautiously down the ladder.*)

MR. ZUSS   Ready?

NICKLES (*cheerfully*)   Got to be, don't they?

MR. ZUSS   I meant
                          You.

NICKLES   They've got no choice. Disaster—
                          Death—mankind are always ready—
                          Ready for anything that hurts.

MR. ZUSS   And you?

NICKLES   I too! I too!

MR. ZUSS   Provided
                          Someone else will bleed the blood
                          And wipe the blinded eye?

NICKLES   I watch
                          Your world go round!

MR. ZUSS   It must be wearing.

NICKLES   Oh, it has its compensations.
                          Even a perfect and an upright man
                          Learns if you keep turning long enough.
                          First he thought it wasn't happening—
                          Couldn't be happening—not to him—
                          Not with you in the stratosphere tooting the
                          Blue trombone for the moon to dance.
                          Then he thought it chanced by chance!
          (*a dry hiccup of laughter*)
                          Childish hypothesis of course
                          But still hypothesis—a start—
                          A pair of tongs to take the toad by—
                          Recognition that it *is* a toad:
                          Not quite comfort but still comfortable,
                          Eases the hook in the gills a little:
                          He'll learn.

MR. ZUSS (*preoccupied*)   Learn what?

NICKLES   Your—purpose for him!

MR. ZUSS   Keep your tongue in your teeth, will you?
          (*He notices* NICKLES' *descent on the ladder for the first time.*)
                          Here! Wait a minute! Wait a
                          Minute! Where are you off to?

NICKLES   Bit of a
                          Walk in the earth for my health—or somebody's.
          (*bitterly*)   Up and down in the earth, you know—
                          Back and forth in it . . .

MR. ZUSS   Leave him alone!

NICKLES   He needs a helping hand: you've seen that—
           A nudge from an old professional.

MR. ZUSS   Leave him a'
           Lone! He can't act and you know it.

NICKLES   He doesn't have to act. He suffers.
           It's an old role—played like a mouth-organ.
           Any idiot on earth
           Given breath enough can breathe it—
           Given tears enough can weep.
           All he needs is help to see.

MR. ZUSS   See what?

NICKLES   That bloody drum-stick-striking;
           See Who lets it strike the drum!

(MR. ZUSS, whose *lifted arm has been slowly falling, raises it abruptly.*)
MR. ZUSS   Wait!
(*He starts to strike the drum, stops the stroke in mid-air.*)
                    Wait for me. I'm coming.
                Down!
                    Wait!
                    Wait I tell you!
(*The stroke of the drum. The light fades out.*

(*Out of the dark two circles of light, one on the platform, one on the table. Behind the table are the two MESSENGERS. The FIRST, wearing a police sergeant's cap, sits on a chair. The SECOND, wearing a patrolman's cap, stands beside him. J.B., a raincoat over rumpled clothes, stands facing them. Above, on the platform, as on the landing of a stair, SARAH stands pulling a dressing gown around her shoulders. NICKLES and MR. ZUSS, their masks in their hands, straddle a couple of chairs beyond the circle of light which centers on the table.*)
FIRST MESSENGER
                Sorry to question you like this.
                We got to get the story.

J.B. (*impatiently*)   Go on.

FIRST M.   Turning your house into a . . .

J.B.   No. Go on.
                It doesn't matter.

SARAH (*toneless*)   Nothing matters but to
           Know.

FIRST M.   How many children?
       (*Silence.*)

J.B.   Two.

FIRST M. (*writing*)   Girls?

SARAH   We had two boys.

FIRST M. (*writing*)   Girls.
                    Names?

J.B.   Ruth. Rebecca.

SARAH   Ruth is the
                    Oldest . . . now.

FIRST M.   And you last saw her?

J.B.   Ruth?

SARAH (*her voice rising*) It's Rebecca is missing!

J.B. (*silencing her*)   He
                    Knows!

SARAH (*harshly*)   No, it's God that knows!
          (*There is an awkward silence. When SARAH speaks again her voice is dead.*)
                    She's the littlest one. She's gone.

FIRST M.   How long ago?

SARAH   Oh . . . hours!

FIRST M.   It's three in the morning now.

J.B.   Since seven.

FIRST M. (*writing*) And you reported it?

J.B.   Yes.

FIRST M.   When?

J.B.   One o'clock. A quarter after.
                    We looked for her everywhere, of course.
                    Then we thought—I thought—if somebody . . .

                    Maybe the telephone would ring.

FIRST M.   And you'd do better on your own?

J.B. (*reluctantly*)   Yes.

SARAH (*with rising violence*)
                        Yes! Yes! Yes!
                    We believe in our luck in this house!
                    We've earned the right to! We believe in it . . .
          (*bitterly*)   All but the bad!

NICKLES (*rocking back on his chair*)
                            That's playing it!
                    That's playing it!
          (*He begins to sing in his cracked whisper, beating a jazzed rhythm on the back of his mask as though it were a banjo.*)

If God is Will
And Will is well
Then what is ill?
God still?
Dew tell!

(MR. ZUSS *does not seem to hear. He is listening intently to the scene at the table.*)

FIRST M.   And nobody telephoned?

J.B.   Nobody telephoned.

FIRST M. (*writing*)   Dressed? How was she
            Dressed?

J.B. (*turning for the first time to look up at Sarah*)
                       White?

SARAH   White! You saw her
            Glimmering in the twilight.

FIRST M. (*writing*)   White.

SARAH   All but her
            Shoes.

(*The* FIRST MESSENGER *looks up at the* SECOND.)
FIRST M.   Her shoes were what?

SARAH   Red.

(*The* FIRST MESSENGER *looks up again. The* SECOND *turns his face away.*)
FIRST M.   Rebecca have a red umbrella?

SARAH   Parasol.

FIRST M.   Little toy umbrella.

SARAH (*startled*)   Parasol. Yes, she might have had one.

FIRST M.   You mean she owned one?

SARAH   Yes. It belonged to a
            Big doll we bought her once.
            Scarlet silk. It opens and closes.
            She kept it when the doll gave out.
            She used to take it to bed with her even—
            Open and close it.

(*The* FIRST MESSENGER *looks up for the third time at the* SECOND, *whose face, still turned away, is like stone.*)

J.B. (*a step forward*)   You've found the parasol!

SECOND M. (*not looking at him; a voice without expression or tone*)
            What will it tell you? Will it tell you why?

J.B. (*to* FIRST M.)   I asked you: have you found the parasol?

FIRST M.   He's the one. Ask him. He'll tell you.

SECOND M. (*with difficulty, like a man speaking out of physical pain*)
Can the tooth among the stones make answer? . . .

Can the seven bones reply? . . .

Out in the desert in the tombs
Are potter's figures: two of warriors,
Two of worthies, two of camels,
Two of monsters, two of horses.
Ask them why. They will not answer you . . .
(*He brushes his hand heavily across his face.*)
Death is a bone that stammers . . .

                                                  a tooth
Among the flints that has forgotten.

J.B. (*violently*)   Ask him! Has he found the parasol!

FIRST M.   We don't know. He found an umbrella—
Doll's umbrella—red.

SARAH   Oh, where?

J.B.   Nothing else? Just the umbrella?

FIRST M. (*to* SECOND)
Tell them, will you!
(*The* SECOND MESSENGER *does not move or speak. The* FIRST *shrugs, looks down at his pencil, rattles it off in a matter-of-fact monotone.*)
                                Just past midnight
Pounding his beat by the back of the lumberyard
Somebody runs and he yells and they stumble—
Big kid—nineteen maybe—
Hopped to the eyes and scared—scared
Bloodless he could barely breathe.
Constable yanks him up by the britches:
"All right! Take me to it!"
Just a shot in the dark, he was so
Goddam scared there had to be something . . .

Well . . .

He took him to it . . .

                                        back of the
Lumber trucks beside the track.

J.B.   Go on.

FIRST M.   She had a toy umbrella.
That was all she had—but shoes:
Red shoes and a toy umbrella:
It was tight in her fist when he found her—still.

J.B.   Let me see it! The umbrella!

FIRST M.   Constable will show it to you.

(*The* SECOND MESSENGER *takes something wound in newspaper out of his pocket. He does not look at it or them. The* FIRST MESSENGER *half opens it, lays it on the table.*)

SARAH   Oh, my baby! Oh, my baby!

(*The* FIRST MESSENGER *gets out of his chair, stands a moment awkwardly, goes out. The* SECOND *follows.* J.B. *stands motionless over the table.* SARAH *hugs her dressing gown around her, rocking herself slowly, her head bowed.*)

NICKLES (*leaning forward toward* J.B., *a wheedling whisper*)
                 Now's the time to say it, mister.

MR. ZUSS   Leave him alone!

J.B. (*touching the parasol*)   The Lord giveth . . .
(*His voice breaks.*)
                                                        the
                 Lord taketh away!

MR. ZUSS (*rising, whispering*)   Go on!
                 Go on! Finish it! Finish it!

NICKLES   What should he
                 Finish when he's said it all?

MR. ZUSS   Go on!

NICKLES   To what? To where? He's got there, hasn't he?
                 Now he's said it, now he knows.
                 He knows Who gives, he knows Who takes now.

(J.B. *stands silent over the parasol.*)
MR. ZUSS   Why won't he play the part he's playing?

NICKLES   Because he isn't.

MR. ZUSS   Isn't what?

NICKLES   Isn't playing. He's not playing.
                 He isn't in the play at all.
                 He's where we all are—in our suffering.
                 Only . . .
(NICKLES *turns savagely on* MR. ZUSS.)
                      . . . Now he knows its Name!

(NICKLES *points dramatically toward the canvas sky.* MR. ZUSS's *head tilts back following the gesture. He freezes into immobility.*)
MR. ZUSS   Look! Look up!

NICKLES   That's your direction.

MR. ZUSS   Look, I say! The staring stars!

NICKLES   Or only lights not meant . . .
(NICKLES *twists his crooked neck, looks sidewise upward. The canvas sky has disappeared into a profound darkness. There seem to be stars beyond it.*)
                                 You're mad.

You've lost your mind. You're maundering . . .

(*They rise together, their heads back, peering into the darkness overhead.*)

. . . maundering.

MR. ZUSS   Let's get back where we belong.

NICKLES   Go on!

MR. ZUSS   No; you.

NICKLES   All right . . . together.

(*They take each other's arm as the light fades.*)

SCENE SIX

(*Darkness and silence as before. The drum—a great crash and a long roll fading out. A gray light which has no visible source drifts across the stage where tables and chairs are scattered and overturned. MR. ZUSS and NICKLES are huddled together on their platform peering down. J.B., his clothes torn and white with dust, faces what was once the door. The two MESSENGERS, wearing steel helmets and brassards, stand there, carrying SARAH between them.*)

FIRST MESSENGER
          She said she lived around here somewhere.
          This is all there is.

J.B.   Sarah!

FIRST M.   Where do you want her?

J.B.   Sarah! Sarah!

FIRST M.   On the floor? You got a floor.
          You're lucky if you got a floor.

(*They lay her carefully down. J.B. takes his torn coat off, rolls it into a pillow, kneels to put it under her head.*)

J.B.   Where was she?

FIRST M.   Underneath a wall.
     (*indicating SECOND MESSENGER*)
          He heard her underneath a wall
          Calling.
     (*to SECOND MESSENGER*)
              Tell him what you heard her . . .

SECOND M. (*imitating*)
          Ruth! . . . Ruth!

FIRST M.   Nobody answered:
          Nobody could have.

(*J.B. does not look up or speak. The FIRST MESSENGER starts toward the door, kicking a fallen chair out of his way.*)

              You been down there?

Whole block's gone. Bank block. All of it.
J.B.'s bank. You know. Just gone.
Nothing left to show it ever.
Just the hole.

(SARAH *stirs, opens her eyes.* J.B. *leans over her. She turns away.*)

J.B.'s millions!
That's a laugh now—J.B.'s millions!
All he's got is just the hole.
Plant went too—all of it—everything.
Ask him! Just the hole. He'll tell you.

SARAH (*faintly, her voice following the rhythm of the* SECOND MESSENGER)
Ruth! . . . Ruth!

FIRST M.   He can tell you.
He can tell you what he saw.

SARAH (*tonelessly like a voice counting*)
David . . . Jonathan . . . Mary . . . Ruth . . .
I cannot say the last.

J.B. (*his hands on hers*)   Rebecca.

SARAH   David . . . Jonathan . . . Mary . . . Ruth . . .

J.B. (*looking up over his shoulder, to the* SECOND MESSENGER)
You didn't find . . . there wasn't . . .

FIRST M.   Tell him.
Tell him what you heard.

SECOND M.   I heard
Two words. I don't know what they mean.
I have brought them to you like a pair of pebbles
Picked up in a path or a pair of
Beads that might belong to somebody.

J.B.   There wasn't . . . anyone beside?

SECOND M. (*almost a whisper*)
I only am escaped alone to tell thee.

SARAH   David . . . Jonathan . . . Mary . . . Ruth . . .

J.B.   Sarah!
(*Silence.*)
                    Listen to me!
(*Silence.*)
                          Sarah!
Even desperate we can't despair—
Let go each other's fingers—sink
Numb in that dumb silence—drown there
Sole in our cold selves . . .

We cannot! ...

God is there too, in the desperation.
I do not know why God should strike
But God is what is stricken also:
Life is what despairs in death
And, desperate, is life still ...

Sarah!
Do not let my hand go, Sarah!

Say it after me:

The Lord
Giveth ... Say it.

SARAH (*mechanically*)　　　　　　　The Lord giveth.

J.B.　　　　　　　The Lord taketh away ...

SARAH (*flinging his hand from hers, shrieking*)

Takes!
Kills! Kills! Kills! Kills!

(*Silence.*)

J.B.　　　　　　　Blessed be the name of the Lord.

(*The light fades.*)

SCENE SEVEN

(*Darkness. Silence. Then, out of the dark,* MR. ZUSS's *voice. It has recovered its confidence and timbre.*)

MR. ZUSS　　　　　　　Well, my friend ...

(*The platform comes into light,* MR. ZUSS *and* NICKLES *are still where they were, leaning over, elbows on the rail. They straighten up, stretching.*)

... you see the position.
You see how it all comes out in the end.
Your fears were quite unfounded, weren't they?

NICKLES (*sourly*)　　My fears for you?

MR. ZUSS　　　　　　　For me? ... For me!
Why should you fear for me?

NICKLES　　　　　　　I can't
Think!

MR. ZUSS　　　　　No, for him.

NICKLES　　　　　　　That ham!

MR. ZUSS　　　　Ham?

NICKLES   Ham!

MR. ZUSS (pleasantly)   And you've been telling me
Over and over that he isn't in it—
Isn't acting even: only
Living—breathing . . .

NICKLES   Man can muff his
Life as badly as his lines and louder.
In it or out of it he's ham.
He wouldn't understand if twenty
Thousand suffocating creatures
Shrieked and tore their tongues out at him
Choking in a bombed-out-town. He'd be
Thankful!

MR. ZUSS (*stiffly*)   I think he understands it
Perfectly! I think that great
Yea-saying to the world was wonderful—
That wounded and deliberate Amen—
That—affirmation!

NICKLES   Affirmation!
Ever watch the worms affirming?
Ever hear a hog's Amen
Just when the knife first hurt? Death is
Good for you! It makes you glisten!
Get the large economy container,
Five for the price of one!

                        You think it's
Wonderful . . .
(*He wheels on* MR. ZUSS *in a sudden fury.*)
                        I think it stinks!
One daughter raped and murdered by an idiot,
Another crushed by stones, a son
Destroyed by some fool officer's stupidity,
Two children smeared across a road
At midnight by a drunken child—
And all with God's consent!—foreknowledge!—
And he blesses God!
(NICKLES *points dramatically at the white, calm, unconcerned mask in* MR. ZUSS's
hands.)
                        It isn't decent!
It isn't moral even! It's disgusting!
His weeping wife in her despair
And he beside her on his trembling ham-bones
Praising God! . . . It's nauseating!

MR. ZUSS   You don't lose gracefully, do you?

NICKLES (*snarling*)	I don't
	Lose.
MR. ZUSS	You have.
NICKLES	That's not the end of it.
MR. ZUSS	No, but that's the *way* it ends.
NICKLES	Could have ended.
MR. ZUSS	What do you mean?
NICKLES	Would have, if God had been content With this poor crawling victory. He isn't. Still He must pursue, still follow— Hunt His creature through his branching veins With agony until no peace is left him— All one blazing day of pain: Corner him, compel the answer. He cannot rest until He wrings The proof of pain, the ultimate certainty. God always asks the proof of pain.
MR. ZUSS	And Job, in his affliction, gives it.
NICKLES	No! God overreaches at the end— Pursues too far—follows too fearfully. He seals him in his sack of skin And scalds his skin to crust to squeeze The answer out, but Job evades Him.
MR. ZUSS	Who can evade the will of God! It waits at every door we open. What does Dante say? His will . . .
NICKLES	Don't chant that chill equation at me!
MR. ZUSS	His will: our peace.
NICKLES	Will was never peace, no matter Whose will, whose peace. Will is rule: surrender is surrender. You *make* your peace: you don't give in to it. Job will make his own cold peace When God pursues him in the web too far— Implacable, eternal Spider. A man can always cease: it's something— A judgment anyway: reject The whole creation with a stale pink pill.
MR. ZUSS	World is Will. Job can't reject it.
NICKLES	God has forgotten what a man can do

Once his body hurts him—once
Pain has penned him in where only
Pain has room to breathe. He learns!
He learns to spit his broken teeth out—
Spit the dirty world out—spit!

MR. ZUSS   And that's the end of everything—to *spit?*

NICKLES   Better than that other end
Of pain, of physical agony, of suffering
God prepares for all His creatures.

MR. ZUSS   *Is* it better? *Is* it better?
Job has suffered and praised God.
Would Job be better off asleep
Among the clods of earth in ignorance?

NICKLES   Yes, when he suffers in his body:
Yes, when his suffering is *him.*

MR. ZUSS   His suffering will praise.

NICKLES   It will not.

MR. ZUSS   Well,
We still have time to see.

NICKLES   Put on your
Mask! You'll see!

(*The light has faded but the faces of the actors are still visible.*)
MR. ZUSS (*raising his mask*)   Put on your own!

(NICKLES *leans over to find it, searching the floor of the platform with his hands. A long silence. From the silence at length:*)
THE DISTANT VOICE
                    Hast thou considered my servant Job
                    That there is none like him on the earth,
                    A perfect and an upright man, one
                    That feareth God and escheweth evil?

NICKLES   Wait a minute! I can't find . . .

THE DISTANT VOICE (*louder*)
                    And still he holdeth fast his integrity . . .

NICKLES   Wait a minute, can't you? What the . . .

THE DISTANT VOICE (*almost a whisper*)
                    Although thou movedst me against him
                    To destroy him . . .

(NICKLES *rises, his mask in his two hands. He wheels on* MR. ZUSS *only to see that* MR. ZUSS *also has his mask in his hands and stands staring up into the canvas sky.*)

(*The* DISTANT VOICE *is barely audible.*)
                    without cause . . .

(Silence. The two old actors stand side by side, holding their masks, their heads moving slowly together as they search the dark.)

NICKLES   Who said that?

   (Silence.)

MR. ZUSS   They want us to go on.

NICKLES   Why don't you?

MR. ZUSS   He was asking *you.*

NICKLES   Who was?

MR. ZUSS   He was.

NICKLES   Prompter probably. Prompter somewhere.
               Your lines he was reading weren't they?

MR. ZUSS   Yes but . . .

NICKLES *(shouting)*   Anybody there?

   (Silence.)

MR. ZUSS   They want us to go on. I told you.

NICKLES   Yes. They want us to go on . . .
               I don't like it.

MR. ZUSS   We began it.

(They put their masks on slowly. The lights fade out. The huge shadows appear on the canvas sky, facing each other.)

GODMASK   *. . . And still he holdeth fast his integrity*
               Although thou movedst me against him
               To destroy him . . .

(His voice breaks.)

                      without cause.

SATANMASK   *Skin for skin, yea, all that a man*
               Hath will he give for his life.
               But put forth thine hand now and touch
               His bone and his flesh
               And he will curse thee to thy face.

(The God-shadow raises its arm again in the formal gesture of contemptuous commitment.)

GODMASK   *Behold he is in thine hand . . .*

(The God-shadow turns away. Silence.)

                    but . . .

      Save his life!

(The two shadows lean together over the earth.)

Note *A second break in the action may be made here if it is thought desirable.*

SCENE EIGHT

(There is no light but the glow on the canvas sky, which holds the looming, leaning shadows. They fade as a match is struck. It flares in SARAH's hand, showing her face, and glimmers out against the wick of a dirty lantern. As the light of the lantern rises, J.B., is seen lying on the broken propped-up table, naked but for a few rags of clothing. SARAH looks at him in the new light, shudders, lets her head drop into her hands. There is a long silence and then a movement in the darkness of the open door where four women and a young girl stand, their arms filled with blankets and newspapers. They come forward slowly into the light.)

NICKLES *(unseen, his cracked, cackling voice drifting down from the darkness of the platform overhead)*

> Never fails! Never fails!
> Count on you to make a mess of it!
> Every blessed blundering time
> You hit at one man you blast thousands.
> Think of that Flood of yours—a massacre!
> Now you've fumbled it again:
> Tumbled a whole city down
> To blister one man's skin with agony.

(NICKLES' white coat appears at the foot of the ladder. The women, in the circle of the lantern, are walking slowly around J.B. and SARAH, staring at them as though they were figures in a show window.)

NICKLES
> Look at your works! Those shivering women
> Sheltering under any crumbling
> Heap to keep the sky out! Weeping!

MRS. ADAMS   That's him.

JOLLY ADAMS   Who's him?

MRS. ADAMS   Grammar, Jolly.

MRS. LESURE   Who did she say it was?

MRS. MURPHY   Him she said it was.
> Poor soul!

MRS. LESURE   Look at them sores on him!

MRS. ADAMS   Don't look, child. You'll remember them.

JOLLY ADAMS *(proudly)*
> Every sore I seen I remember.

MRS. BOTTICELLI   Who did she say she said it was?

MRS. MURPHY   Him.

MRS. ADAMS   That's his wife.

MRS. LESURE   She's pretty.

MRS. BOTTICELLI   Ain't she.
> Looks like somebody we've seen.

MRS. ADAMS (*snooting her*)
>
> I don't believe you would have seen her:
> Picture possibly—her picture
> Posed in the penthouse.

MRS. BOTTICELLI   Puce with pants?

MRS. ADAMS   No, the negligee.

MRS. BOTTICELLI   The net?

MRS. ADAMS   The simple silk.

MRS. BOTTICELLI   Oh la! With sequins?

MRS. MURPHY   Here's a place to park your poodle—
>
> Nice cool floor.

MRS. LESURE   Shove over, dearie.
>
> (*The women settle themselves on their newspapers off at the edge of the circle of light. NICKLES has perched himself on a chair at the side. Silence.*)

J.B. (*a whisper*)   God, let me die!
>
> (*NICKLES leers up into the dark toward the unseen platform.*)

SARAH (*her voice dead*)   You think He'd help you
>
> Even to that?
>
> (*Silence. SARAH looks up, turning her face away from J.B. She speaks without passion, almost mechanically.*)
>
> God is our enemy

J.B.   No . . . No . . . No . . . Don't
>
> Say that Sarah!
>
> (*SARAH's head turns toward him slowly as though dragged against her will. She stares and cannot look away.*)
>
> God has something
> Hidden from our hearts to show.

NICKLES   She knows! She's looking at it!

J.B.   Try to
>
> Sleep.

SARAH (*bitterly*)   He should have kept it hidden.

J.B.   Sleep now.

SARAH   You don't have to see it:
>
> I do.

J.B.   Yes, I know.

NICKLES (*a cackle*)   He knows!
>
> He's back behind it and he knows!
> If he could see what she can see
> There's something else he might be knowing.

J.B.   Once I knew a charm for sleeping—

      Not as forgetfulness but gift,
      Not as sleep but second sight,
      Come and from my eyelids lift
      The dead of night.

SARAH   The dead . . .
             of night . . .

(*She drops her head to her knees, whispering.*)
      Come and from my eyelids lift
      The dead of night.

(*Silence.*)
J.B.   Out of sleep
      Something of our own comes back to us:
      A drowned man's garment from the sea.

(SARAH *turns the lantern down. Silence. Then the voices of the women, low.*)
MRS. BOTTICELLI Poor thing!

MRS. MURPHY   Poor thing!
      Not a chick nor a child between them.

MRS. ADAMS   First their daughters. Then their sons.

MRS. MURPHY   First son first. Blew him to pieces.
      More mischance it was than war.
      Asleep on their feet in the frost they walked into it.

MRS. ADAMS   Two at the viaduct: that makes three.

JOLLY ADAMS (*a child's chant*)
      Jolly saw the picture! the picture!

MRS. ADAMS   Jolly Adams, you keep quiet.

JOLLY ADAMS   Wanna know? The whole of the viaduct . . .

MRS. ADAMS   Never again will you look at them! Never!

MRS. LESURE   Them magazines! They're awful! Which?

MRS. MURPHY   And after that the little one.

MRS. BOTTICELLI   Who in the
      World are they talking about, the little one?
      What are they talking?

MRS. LESURE   I don't know.
      Somebody dogged by death it must be.

MRS. BOTTICELLI Him it must be.

MRS. LESURE   Who's him?

MRS. ADAMS   You know who.

MRS. MURPHY	You remember the . . .
MRS. ADAMS	Hush! The child!
MRS. MURPHY	Back of the lumberyard.
MRS. LESURE	Oh! Him!
MRS. MURPHY	Who did you think it was— Penthouse and negligees, daughters and dying?
MRS. BOTTICELLI	Him? That's him? That millionaire?
MRS. LESURE	Millionaires he buys like cabbages.
MRS. MURPHY	He couldn't buy cabbages now by the look of him: The rags he's got on.
MRS. BOTTICELLI	Look at them sores!
MRS. MURPHY	All that's left him now is her.
MRS. BOTTICELLI	Still that's something—a good woman.
MRS. MURPHY	What good is a woman to him with that side on him?— Or he to her if you think of it.
MRS. ADAMS	Don't!
MRS. LESURE	Can you blame her?
MRS. MURPHY	I don't blame her. All I say is she's no comfort. She won't cuddle.
MRS. ADAMS	Really, Mrs. . . .
MRS. MURPHY	Murphy call me. What's got into you? . . . Nothing recently I'd hazard.
MRS. ADAMS	You're not so young yourself, my woman.
MRS. MURPHY	Who's your woman? I was Murphy's.
MRS. LESURE	None of us are maids entirely.
MRS. MURPHY	Maids in mothballs some might be.
MRS. ADAMS	Who might?
MRS. MURPHY	You might.
MRS. ADAMS	You! you're . . . historical!
MRS. MURPHY	I never slept a night in history!
MRS. BOTTICELLI	*I* have. Oh, my mind goes back.
MRS. ADAMS (*Silence.*)	None of that! We have a child here! How far back?

MRS. BOTTICELLI   I often wonder.
                   Farther than the first but . . . where?

MRS. MURPHY   What do you care? It's lovely country.
  (*Silence.*)

                   Roll a little nearer, dearie,
                   Me back side's froze.

MRS. LESURE   You smell of roses.

MRS. MURPHY   Neither do you but you're warm.

MRS. BOTTICELLI   Well,
                   Good night, ladies. Good night, ladies . . .

(*Silence. Out of the silence, felt rather than heard at first, a sound of sobbing, a muffled
monotonous sound like the heavy beat of a heart.*)
J.B.   If you could only sleep a little
                   Now they're quiet, now they're still.

SARAH (*her voice broken*)
                   I try. But oh I close my eyes and . . .
                   Eyes are open there to meet me!
(*Silence. Then* SARAH's *voice in an agony of bitterness.*)
                   My poor babies! Oh, my babies!

(J.B. *pulls himself painfully up, sits huddled on his table in the feeble light of the lamp,
his rags about him.*)

J.B. (*gently*) Go to sleep.

SARAH   Go! Go where?
                   If there were darkness I'd go there.
                   If there were night I'd lay me down in it.
                   God has shut the night against me.
                   God has set the dark alight
                   With horror blazing blind as day
                   When I go toward it . . .
                                    close my eyes.

J.B.   I know. I know those waking eyes.
                   His will is everywhere against us—
                   Even in our sleep, our dreams . . .

NICKLES (*a snort of laughter up toward the dark of the platform*)
                   Your will, *his* peace!
                   Doesn't seem to grasp that, does he?
                   Give him another needling twinge
                   Between the withers and the works—
                   He'll understand you better.

J.B.   If I
                   Knew . . . If I knew why!

NICKLES   If he knew
            Why he wouldn't be there. He'd be
            Strangling, drowning, suffocating,
            Diving for a sidewalk somewhere . . .

J.B.   What I *can't* bear is the blindness—
            Meaninglessness—the numb blow
            Fallen in the stumbling night.

SARAH (*starting violently to her feet*)
            Has death no meaning? Pain no meaning?
    (*She points at his body.*)
            Even these suppurating sores—
            Have they no meaning for you?

NICKLES   Ah!

J.B. (*from his heart's pain*)
            God will not punish without cause.
    (NICKLES *doubles up in a spasm of soundless laughter.*)
            God is just.

SARAH (*hysterically*)   God is just!
            If God is just our slaughtered children
            Stank with sin, were rotten with it!
    (*She controls herself with difficulty, turns toward him, reaches her arms out, lets them fall.*)
            Oh, my dear! my dear! my dear!
            Does God demand deception of us?—
            Purchase His innocence by ours?
            Must we be guilty for Him?—bear
            The burden of the world's malevolence
            For Him who made the world?

J.B.   He
            Knows the guilt is mine. He must know:
            Has He not punished it? He knows its
            Name, its time, its face, its circumstance,
            The figure of its day, the door,
            The opening of the door, the room, the moment . . .

SARAH (*fiercely*)   And you? Do you? You do not know it.
            Your punishment is all you know.
    (*She moves toward the door, stops, turns.*)
            I will not stay here if you lie—
            Connive in your destruction, cringe to it:
            Not if you betray my children . . .

            I will not stay to listen . . .

                                    They are
            Dead and they were innocent: I will not

Let you sacrifice their deaths
To make injustice justice and God good!

J.B. (*covering his face with his hands*)
My heart beats. I cannot answer it.

SARAH
If you buy quiet with their innocence—
Theirs or yours . . .

(*softly*)
I will not love you.

J.B.
I have no choice but to be guilty.

SARAH (*her voice rising*)
We have the choice to live or die,
All of us . . .
curse God and die . . .

(*Silence.*)
J.B.
God is God or we are nothing—
Mayflies that leave their husks behind—
Our tiny lives ridiculous—a suffering
Not even sad that Someone Somewhere
Laughs at as we laugh at apes.
We have no choice but to be guilty.
God is unthinkable if we are innocent.

(SARAH *turns, runs soundlessly out of the circle of light, out of the door. The women stir.* MRS. MURPHY *comes up on her elbow.*)

MRS. MURPHY   What did I say? I said she'd walk out on him.

MRS. LESURE   She did.

MRS. BOTTICELLI   Did she?

MRS. MURPHY   His hide was too much for her.

MRS. BOTTICELLI   His hide or his heart.

MRS. MURPHY   The hide comes between.

MRS. BOTTICELLI   The heart is the stranger.

MRS. MURPHY   Oh, strange!
It's always strange the heart is: only
It's the skin we ever know.

J.B. (*raising his head*)
Sarah, why do you not speak to me? . . .
Sarah!

(*Silence.*)
MRS. ADAMS   Now he knows.

MRS. MURPHY   And he's alone now.

J.B.'s *head falls forward onto his knees. Silence. Out of the silence his voice in an agony of prayer.*)

J.B.   *Show me my guilt, O God!*

NICKLES   *His*

               Guilt! His! You heard that didn't you?
               He wants to feel the feel of guilt—
               That putrid poultice of the soul
               That draws the poison in, not out—
               Inverted catheter! You going to show him?

(Silence. NICKLES rises, moves toward the ladder.)
               Well? You going to show him . . . Jahveh?

(Silence. He crosses to the ladder's foot.)
               Where are those cold comforters of yours
               Who justify the ways of God to
               Job by making Job responsible?—
               Those three upholders of the world—
               Defenders of the universe—where are they?

(Silence. He starts up the ladder. Stops. The jeering tone is gone. His voice is bitter.)
               Must be almost time for comfort! . . .

(NICKLES vanishes into the darkness above. The light fades.)

SCENE NINE

(Darkness.)

J.B.'S VOICE   *If I had perished from the womb, not having Been . . .*

(A light without source rises slowly like the light at evening which enlarges everything. The canvas walls dissolve into distance, the canvas sky into endlessness. The platform has been pushed away to the side until only the ladder is visible. The women and the child are huddled together like sleeping figures on a vast plain. J.B. is alone in an enormous loneliness. Out of that seeming distance the THREE COMFORTERS come shuffling forward in worn-out clothing. ZOPHAR, a fat, red-faced man, wears the wreck of a clerical collar. ELIPHAZ, lean and dark, wears an intern's jacket which once was white. BILDAD is a squat, thick man in a ragged wind-breaker. The women do not see them, but JOLLY ADAMS, sits suddenly up clapping her hands to her mouth. J.B., his head on his arms, sees nothing.)

J.B.   Death cannot heal me . . .

                           Death
               Will leave my having been behind it
               Like a bear's foot festering in a trap . . .

JOLLY ADAMS *(her voice rising word by word to a scream)*
               Look! Look! Look! Look!
               Mother! Mother!

(The women pull themselves up. The THREE COMFORTERS shuffle on, squat in the rubbish around J.B.: ZOPHAR lighting the stub of a fat, ragged cigar; ELIPHAZ lighting a broken pipe; BILDAD lighting a crumpled cigarette.)

MRS. MURPHY   Agh, the scavengers!

MRS. BOTTICELLI Three old pokey crows they look like.

MRS. MURPHY	They are, too. It's the smell of the suffering.
	See that leather-backed old bucket?—
	Kind of character you hear from
	Sundays in a public park
	Pounding the hell out of everything . . . *you* know.

MRS. BOTTICELLI *I* know. Wall Street. Bakers. Bankers.

MRS. LESURE   All the answers in a book.

MRS. BOTTICELLI Russkys got them all—the answers.

MRS. MURPHY	Characters like that, they smell the
	Human smell of heartsick misery
	Farther than a kite smells carrion.

MRS. LESURE   Who's the collar?

MRS. MURPHY   Some spoiled priest.

MRS. BOTTICELLI They can smell it farther even.

MRS. LESURE	Not as far as dead-beat doctors:
	They're the nosies.

MRS. MURPHY   Let them nose!
   (*A tremendous yawn.*)
            Ohhh, I'm halfway over . . .
                              drownding
            Down and down . . .
                     I hear the seagulls
            Singing soundings in the sea . . .
(*She lets herself fall back on her newspapers. The others follow one by one.*)

JOLLY ADAMS   I don't hear them.

MRS. BOTTICELLI   Pound your ears.

MRS. LESURE   Slip your moorings . . . Oh, I'm numb.

MRS. MURPHY   Come alongside, dear.

MRS. LESURE   I'm coming.

MRS. BOTTICELLI That doctor one, he makes me creep.

MRS. MURPHY   Keep your thumb on your thoughts or he'll diddle them.

MRS. BOTTICELLI Let him pry: he'll lose an eyeball.

MRS. LESURE   He's a peeper. Watch your sleep.

MRS. MURPHY	Who was she, all gore, all story,
	Dabbed in a deep blood sea,
	And what she washed in, that was she?

MRS. LESURE (*from her dream*)
           Some queen of Scotland . . .

MRS. MURPHY   Queen of Scones . . .

(A long silence. The THREE COMFORTERS *squat smoking and waiting. At length J.B. pulls himself painfully up to kneel on his table, his face raised.)*

J.B. (*a whisper*)   God! My God! My God! What have I
Done?

(Silence.)

BILDAD (*removing his cigarette*)
                              Fair question, Big Boy.
                    Anyone answer you yet? No answer?

ZOPHAR (*removing his cigar*)
                    That was answered long ago—
                    Long ago.

ELIPHAZ (*knocking out his pipe*)
                              In dreams are answers.
                    How do your dreams go, Big Boy? Tell!

J.B. (*peering*)   Is someone there? Where? I cannot
                    See you in this little light
                    My eyes too fail me . . .

(Silence.)

                                        Who is there?

(Silence.)

                    I know how ludicrous I must look,
                    Covered with rags, my skin pustulant . . .

(Silence.)

                    I know . . .

(Silence.)

                              I know how others see me.

(A long silence.)

                    Why have you come?

BILDAD (*a coarse laugh*)   For comfort, Big Boy.
                    Didn't you ring?

ZOPHAR (*a fat laugh*)   That's it: for comfort!

ELIPHAZ (*a thin laugh*)
                    All the comfort you can find.

BILDAD   All the kinds of.

ELIPHAZ   *All* the comforts.

ZOPHAR   You called us and we came.

J.B.   I called
                God.

BILDAD   Didn't you!

ELIPHAZ   Didn't you just!

| ZOPHAR | Why should God reply to *you* |
| | From the blue depths of His Eternity? |

| ELIPHAZ | Blind depths of His Unconsciousness? |

| BILDAD | Blank depths of His Necessity? |

| ZOPHAR | God is far above in Mystery. |

| ELIPHAZ | God is far below in Mindlessness. |

| BILDAD | God is far within in History— |
| | Why should God have time for you? |

J.B.   The hand of God has touched me. Look at me!
Every hope I ever had,
Every task I put my mind to,
Every work I've ever done
Annulled as though I had not done it.
My trace extinguished in the land,
My children, my father's name
Obliterated in the sunlight everywhere . . .

Love too has left me.

BILDAD   Love!
(a great guffaw)
         What's love to Him? One man's misery!

J.B. *(hardly daring)*
         If I am innocent . . . ?

BILDAD *(snort of jeering laughter)*   Innocent! Innocent!
Nations shall perish in their innocence.
Classes shall perish in their innocence.
Young men in slaughtered cities
Offering their silly throats
Against the tanks in innocence shall perish.
What's your innocence to theirs?
God is History. If you offend Him
Will not History dispense with you?
History has no time for innocence.

J.B.   God is just. We are not squeezed
Naked through a ridiculous orifice
Like bulls into a blazing ring
To blunder there by blindfold laws
We never learn or can, deceived by
Stratagems and fooled by feints,
For sport, for nothing, till we fall
We're pricked so badly.

BILDAD (*all park-bench orator*)   Screw your justice!
                        History is justice!—time
                        Inexorably turned to truth!—
                        Not for one man. For humanity.
                        One man's life won't measure on it..
                        One man's suffering won't count, no matter
                        What his suffering; but All will.
                        At the end there will be justice!—
                        Justice for All! Justice for everyone!
      (*subsiding*)
                        On the way—it doesn't matter.

J.B.
                        Guilt matters. Guilt must always matter.
                        Unless guilt matters the whole world is
                        Meaningless. God too is nothing.

BILDAD (*losing interest*)
                        You may be guiltier than Hell
                        As History counts guilt and not
                        One smudging thumbprint on your conscience.
                        Guilt is a sociological accident:
                        Wrong class—wrong century—
                        You pay for your luck with your licks, that's all.

(ELIPHAZ *has been fidgeting. Now he breaks in like a professor in a seminar, poking a forefinger at the air.*)
ELIPHAZ
                        Come! Come! Come! Guilt is a
                        Psychophenomenal situation—
                        An illusion, a disease, a sickness:
                        That filthy feeling at the fingers,
                        Scent of dung beneath the nails . . .

ZOPHAR (*outraged, flushed, head thrown back*)
                        Guilt is illusion? Guilt is reality!—
                        The one reality there is!
                        All mankind are guilty always!

BILDAD (*jeering*)   The Fall of Man it felled us all!

(J.B.'s *voice breaks through the squabbling with something of its old authority.*)
J.B.
                        No doubt ye are the people
                        And wisdom shall die with you! I am
                        Bereaved, in pain, desperate, and you mock me?
                        There was a time when men found pity
                        Finding each other in the night:
                        Misery to walk with misery—
                        Brother in whose brother-guilt
                        Guilt could be conceived and recognized.
                        We have forgotten pity.

ELIPHAZ
                              No.
              We have surmounted guilt. It's quite,
              Quite different, isn't it? You see the difference.
              Science knows now that the sentient spirit
              Floats like the chambered nautilus on a sea
              That drifts it under skies that drive:
              Beneath, the sea of the subconscious;
              Above, the winds that wind the world.
              Caught between that sky, that sea,
              Self has no will, cannot be guilty.
              The sea drifts. The sky drives.
              The tiny, shining bladder of the soul
              Washes with wind and wave or shudders
              Shattered between them.

ZOPHAR   Blasphemy!

BILDAD   Bullshit!

ELIPHAZ (*oblivious*)
              There is no guilt, my man. We all are
              Victims of our guilt, not guilty.
              We kill the king in ignorance: the voice
              Reveals: we blind ourselves. At our
              Beginning, in the inmost room,
              Each one of us, disgusting monster
              Changed by the chilling moon to child,
              Violates his mother. Are we guilty?
              Our guilt is underneath the Sybil's
              Stone: not known.

J.B. (*violently*)   I'd rather suffer
              Every unspeakable suffering God sends,
              Knowing it was I that suffered,
              I that earned the need to suffer,
              I that acted, I that chose,
              Than wash my hands with yours in that
              Defiling innocence. Can we be men
              And make an irresponsible ignorance
              Responsible for everything? I will not
              Listen to you!
(J.B. *pulls his rags over his head.*)

ELIPHAZ (*shrugging*)   But you will. You will.

ZOPHAR   Ah, my son, how well you said that!
              How well you said it! Without guilt
              What is a man? An animal, isn't he?
              A wolf forgiven at his meat,
              A beetle innocent in his copulation.

What divides us from the universe
Of blood and seed, conceives the soul in us,
Brings us to God, but guilt? The lion
Dies of death: we die of suffering.
The lion vanishes: our souls accept
Eternities of reparation.
But for our guilt we too would vanish,
Bundles of corrupting bones
Bagged in a hairless hide and rotting.
Happy the man whom God correcteth!
He tastes his guilt. His hope begins.
He is in league with the stones in certainty.

(J.B. *pulls his rags from his head, drags himself around toward the voice.*)

J.B.   *Teach me and I will hold my tongue.*
                                     Show me my transgression.

ZOPHAR (*gently*)   No.
                            No, my son. You show *me*.
(*He hunches forward dropping his voice.*)
                            Search your inmost heart! Question it!
                            Guilt is a deceptive secret,
                            The labor often of years, a work
                            Conceived in infancy, brought to birth
                            In unpredictable forms years after:
                            At twelve the palpable elder brother;
                            At seventeen, perhaps, the servant
                            Seen by the lamp by accident . . .

J.B. (*urgently, the words forced from him*)   My
                            Sin! Teach me my sin! My wickedness!
                            Surely iniquity that suffers
                            Judgment like mine cannot be secret.
                            Mine is no childish fault, no nastiness
                            Concealed behind a bathroom door,
                            No sin a prurient virtue practices
                            Licking the silence from its lips
                            Like sugar afterwards. Mine is flagrant,
                            Worthy of death, of many deaths,
                            Of shame, loss, hurt, indignities
                            Such as these! Such as these!
                            Speak of the sin I must have sinned
                            To suffer what you see me suffer.

ZOPHAR   Do we need to name our sins
                            To know the need to be forgiven?
                            Repent, my son! Repent!

J.B. (*an agony of earnestness*)   I sit here
                            Such as you see me. In my soul

I suffer what you guess I suffer.
Tell me the wickedness that justifies it.
Shall I repent of sins I have not
Sinned to understand it? Till I
Die I will not violate my integrity.

ZOPHAR (*a fat chuckle*)
Your integrity! Your integrity!
What integrity have you?—
A man, a miserable, mortal, sinful,
Venal man like any other.
You squat there challenging the universe
To tell you what your crime is called,
Thinking, because your life was virtuous,
It can't be called. It can. Your sin is
Simple. You were born a man!

J.B.
What is my fault? What have I done?

ZOPHAR (*thundering*)
What is your fault? Man's heart is evil!
What have you done? Man's will is evil.
Your fault, your sin, are heart and will:
The worm at heart, the wilful will
Corrupted with its foul imagining.

(J.B. *crouches lower in his rags. Silence.*)

J.B.
Yours is the cruelest comfort of them all,
Making the Creator of the Universe
The miscreator of mankind—
A party to the crimes He punishes . . .

Making my sin . . .
a horror . . .
a deformity . . .

ZOPHAR (*collapsing into his own voice*)
If it were otherwise we could not bear it . . .
Without the fault, without the Fall,
We're madmen: all of us are madmen . . .

(*He sits staring at his hands, then repeats the phrase:*)
Without the Fall
We're madmen all.
We watch the stars
That creep and crawl . . .

BILDAD
Like dying flies
Across the wall
Of night . . .

ELIPHAZ
and shriek . . .
And that is all.

ZOPHAR   Without the Fall . . .

(A long silence. Out of the silence at last J.B.'s voice, barely audible.)
J.B.   *God, my God, my God, answer me!*
(Silence.

(His voice rises.)   *I cry out of wrong but I am not heard . . .*
                       I cry aloud but there is no judgment.
(Silence.

(Violently)   *Though He slay me, yet will I trust in Him . . .*
(Silence.

(His voice drops.)   *But I will maintain my own ways before Him . . .*
(Silence.
(The ancient human cry.)
                       Oh, that I knew where I might find Him!—
                       That I might come even to His seat!
                       I would order my cause before Him
                       And fill my mouth with arguments.
(There is a rushing sound in the air.)

                                              Behold,
                       I go forward but He is not there,
                       Backward, but I cannot perceive Him . . .

(Out of the rushing sound, the DISTANT VOICE; *J.B. cowers as he hears it, his rags over his head.)*
THE DISTANT VOICE
                       Who is this that darkeneth counsel
                       By words without knowledge? . . .

                                              Where wast thou
                       When I laid the foundations of the earth . . .

                       When the morning stars sang together
                       And all the sons of God shouted for
                       Joy?
                                Hast thou commanded the morning?

                       Hast thou entered into the springs of the sea
                       Or hast thou walked in the search of the depth?

                       Have the gates of death been opened unto thee?

                       Where is the way where light dwelleth?
                       And as for darkness, where is the place thereof?

                       Hast thou entered into the treasures of the snow?

                       By what way is the light parted
                       Which scattereth the east wind upon the earth?

                       Can'st thou bind the sweet influences of the Pleiades?

                       Hast thou given the horse strength?
                       Hast thou clothed his neck with thunder?

He saith among the trumpets, Ha, ha;
He smelleth the battle afar off,
The thunder of the captains and the shouting.

Doth the eagle mount up at thy command?

Her eyes behold afar off.
Her young ones also suck up blood:
And where the slain are, there is she . . .

(*The rushing sound dies away. The* THREE COMFORTERS *stir uneasily, peering up into the darkness. One by one they rise.*)

BILDAD   The wind's gone round.

ZOPHAR   It's cold.

BILDAD   I told you.

ELIPHAZ   I hear the silence like a sound.

ZOPHAR   Wait for me!

BILDAD   The wind's gone round.

(*They go out as they came. Silence.* J.B. *sits motionless, his head covered. The rushing sound returns like the second, stronger gust of a great storm. The* VOICE *rises above it.*)

THE DISTANT VOICE
                Shall he that contendeth with the Almighty instruct
                Him? . . .

(*The rushing sound dies away again. The women sit up, huddle together.*)

JOLLY ADAMS (*screaming*)
                        Mother! Mother! what was
        That?

MRS. ADAMS   The wind, child. Only the wind.
        Only the wind.

JOLLY ADAMS   I heard a word.

MRS. ADAMS   You heard the thunder in the wind.

JOLLY ADAMS (*drowsy*)
        Under the wind there was a word . . .

(MRS. ADAMS *picks her up. The women gather their newspapers and blankets and stumble out into the darkness through the door. For the third time the rushing sound returns.*)

THE DISTANT VOICE
        He that reproveth God, let him answer it!

J.B.   *Behold, I am vile; what shall I answer thee?*
                I will lay mine hand upon my mouth.

THE DISTANT VOICE
                Gird up thy loins like a man:
                I will demand of thee, and declare thou unto me.

(J.B. *pulls himself painfully to his knees.*)

          Wilt thou disannul my judgment?

(J.B. *does not answer.*)

          Wilt thou condemn
          Me that thou mayest be righteous?

          Hast thou an arm like God? Or canst thou
          Thunder with a voice like Him?

          Deck thyself now with majesty and excellency
          And array thyself with glory and beauty . . .

          Then will I also confess unto thee
          That thine own right hand can save thee.

(J.B. *raises his bowed head.*)

J.B. (*gently*)   *I know that thou canst do everything . . .*

(*The rushing sound dies away.*)

          And that no thought can be withholden from thee.
          Who is he that hideth counsel without knowledge?
          Therefore have I uttered that I understood not:
          Things too wonderful for me, which I knew not.

          Hear, I beseech thee, and I will speak: . . .

(*Silence.*)

          I have heard of thee by the hearing of the ear . . .
          But now . . .

(*His face is drawn in agony.*)

                mine eye seeth thee!

(*He bows his head. His hands wring each other.*)

                     Wherefore
          I abhor myself . . . and repent . . .

(*The light fades.*)

SCENE TEN

(*The Platform. As the lights come on the two actors turn violently away from each other, tearing their masks off.* NICKLES, *with a gesture of disgust, skims his into a corner.*)

NICKLES   Well, that's that!

MR. ZUSS   That's . . . that!

(*Silence. After a time* NICKLES *looks cautiously around at* MR. ZUSS.)

NICKLES   What's the matter with you?

MR. ZUSS   Nothing.

NICKLES   You don't look pleased.

MR. ZUSS   Should I?

NICKLES   Well,
      You were right weren't you?

MR. ZUSS (*too loud*)   Of course I was right.

NICKLES (*too soft*)
                     Anyway, you were magnificent.

MR. ZUSS   Thank you.

(*He looks at the mask in his hands: puts it down as though it had stung him. Silence.*
MR. ZUSS *pretends to be busy with a shoelace.*)
MR. ZUSS   Why did you say that?

NICKLES   What did I say?

MR. ZUSS   Why did you say it like that?

NICKLES   Like what?

MR. ZUSS (*imitating*)
                  "Anyway!" . . .
                           "*Anyway,* you were magnificent!"

NICKLES   You know. "Anyway." Regardless.

MR. ZUSS   Regardless of
            What?

NICKLES   Now, wait a minute! Wait a
            Minute! You were magnificent. I said so.

MR. ZUSS   Go on. Finish it.

NICKLES   Finish what?

MR. ZUSS   Regardless of . . . ?

NICKLES   . . . being right, of course.
            What's got into you, my friend? What's eating you?
            Being magnificent and being right
            Don't go together in this universe.
            It's being wrong—a desperate stubbornness
            Fighting the inextinguishable stars—
            Excites imagination. You were
            Right. And knew it. And were admirable.
            Notwithstanding!
        (*snickering*)   anyway!
        (*a snarl*)   regardless!

MR. ZUSS   I knew you noticed.

NICKLES   Of course I noticed.
            What lover of the art could fail to!
(*Something in* MR. ZUSS's *expression stops him.*)
                                    Noticed
            What?

MR. ZUSS	That tone! That look he gave me!
NICKLES	He misconceived the part entirely.
MR. ZUSS	Misconceived the world! Buggered it!
NICKLES	Giving in like that! Whimpering!
MR. ZUSS	Giving in! You call that arrogant, Smiling, supercilious humility Giving in to God?

NICKLES

        Arrogant!
His suppurating flesh—his children—
Let's not talk about those children—
Everything he ever had!
And all he asks is answers of the universe:
All he asks is reasons why—
Why? Why? And God replies to him:
God comes whirling in the wind replying—
What? That God knows more than he does.
That God's more powerful than he!—
Throwing the whole creation at him!
Throwing the Glory and the Power!
What's the Power to a broken man
Trampled beneath it like a toad already?
What's the Glory to a skin that stinks!
And this ham actor!—what does *he* do?
How does he play Job to that?

    (*attitude*)

      "Thank you!" "I'm a worm!" "Take two!"

Plays the way a sheep would play it—
Pious, contemptible, goddam sheep
Without the spunk to spit on Christmas!

(MR. ZUSS *has watched* NICKLES' *mounting rage in silence, staring at him.* NICKLES *breaks off, shuffles, looks at* MR. ZUSS, *crosses to the ladder, swings a leg across the rail.*)

    Well . . .

(*He swings the other over.*)

      you said he would . . .

(*He starts down.*)

               You're right.

(*Another rung.*)

    I'm wrong.

(*Another.*)

      You win.

(*Another.*)

        God always wins.

(*He peers down into the dark under the platform.*)

    Where did I put that . . . popcorn?

MR. ZUSS

                                                Win!
                Planets and Pleiades and eagles—
                Screaming horses—scales of light—
                The wonder and the mystery of the universe—
                The unimaginable might of things—
                Immeasurable knowledge in the waters somewhere
                Wandering their ways—the searchless power
                Burning on the hearth of stars—
                Beauty beyond the feel of fingers—
                Marvel beyond the maze of mind—
                The whole creation! And God showed him!
                God stood stooping there to show him!
                Last Orion! Least sea shell! . . .
                And what did Job do?
(MR. ZUSS *has worked himself up into a dramatic fury equaling* NICKLES'.)
                                Job . . . just . . . sat!

(*Silence.*)
                Sat there!

(*Silence.*)
                                Dumb!

(*Silence.*)
                                        Until it ended!
                Then! . . . you heard him!
(MR. ZUSS *chokes.*)
                                        Then, he *calmed* me!
                Gentled me the way a farmhand
                Gentles a bulging, bugling bull!
                Forgave me! . . .
                                for the world! . . .
                                        for everything!

NICKLES (*poking around in the shadow under the platform*)
                Nonsense! He repented, didn't he—
                The perfect and the upright man!
                He repented!

MR. ZUSS
                                That's just it!
                He repented. It was *him*—
                Not the fear of God but *him!*

NICKLES   Fear? Of course he feared. Why wouldn't he?
                God with all those stars and stallions!
                He with little children's bones!

MR. ZUSS (*pursuing his mounting indignation*)
                . . . As though Job's suffering were justified
                Not by the Will of God but Job's
                Acceptance of God's Will . . .

NICKLES   Well,
                What did you hope for? Hallelujahs?

MR. ZUSS (*not hearing*)

> . . . In spite of everything he'd suffered!
> In spite of all he'd lost and loved
> *He* understood and he forgave it! . . .

NICKLES (*a contemptuous snort as he straightens to face* MR. ZUSS *on the plat-*
    form)   What other victory could God win?

> The choice is swallowing this swill of world
> Or vomiting in the trough. Job swallowed it,
> That's your triumph!—that he swallowed it.

MR. ZUSS

> . . . He'd heard of God and now he saw Him!
> Who's the judge in judgment there?
> Who plays the hero, God or him?
> Is God to be *forgiven?*

NICKLES

> Isn't he?
> Job was innocent, you may remember . . .

(*Silence.*)

    (*a nasty singsong*)

> The perfect and the upright man!

MR. ZUSS (*deflated*)

> Don't start that again! I'm sick of it.

NICKLES

> *You* are!

MR. ZUSS

> *I* am. Sick to death.

    (*swinging his leg over the rail and starting down the ladder*)

> I'd rather sell balloons to children . . .
> Lights! . . .

(*He shouts.*)

> Turn those lights on, can't you?
> Want to see me break my neck?

(*The platform lights go out. Total darkness.*)

    (*Louder.*)   Lights! Lights! That's not the end of it.

NICKLES (*in the darkness*)

> Why isn't that the end? It's over.
> Job has chosen how to choose.
> You've made your bow? You want another?

(*The dangling light bulbs come feebly on. By their light J.B. can still be seen kneeling on his broken table.* MR. ZUSS *and* NICKLES *crawl under the platform after their traps. Their voices come from the shadow, punctuated by grunts and wheezes.*)

MR. ZUSS   You know as well as I there's more . . .

> There's always one more scene no matter
> Who plays Job or how he plays it . . .

> God restores him at the end.

NICKLES (*a snort*)
> God restores us all. That's normal.
> That's God's mercy to mankind . . .
>
> We never asked Him to be born . . .
>
> We never chose the lives we die of . . .
>
> They beat our rumps to make us breathe . . .
>
> But God, if we have suffered patiently,
> Borne it in silence, stood the stench,
> Rewards us . . .
>
> > gives our dirty selves back.

(MR. ZUSS *emerges in his white jacket, adjusting his cap.*)
MR. ZUSS   Souls back!

NICKLES   Selves back! Dirty selves
We've known too well and never wanted.

MR. ZUSS   That's not this play.

(NICKLES *backs out with his jacket and cap and tray; puts them on.*)
NICKLES   Hell it isn't.

(MR. ZUSS *tightens his balloon belt.*)
MR. ZUSS   God restores him *here.* On earth.

NICKLES (*balancing his tray*)
> So Job gets his in cash. That's generous.
> What percentage off for cash?

MR. ZUSS   Gets all he ever had and more—
Much more.

NICKLES (*cheerfully ironic*)   Sure. His wife. His children!

MR. ZUSS (*embarrassed*)
> He gets his wife back, and the children . . .
> Follow in nature's course.

(NICKLES, *who has stooped to pick up a bag of popcorn, straightens slowly, stares at* MR. ZUSS.)
NICKLES (*harshly*)   You're lying.

MR. ZUSS   I'm not lying.

NICKLES   I say you're lying.

MR. ZUSS   Why should I lie. It's in the Book.

NICKLES (*jeering*) Wife back! Balls! He wouldn't touch her.
> He wouldn't take her with a glove!
> After all that filth and blood and
> Fury to begin again! . . .

This fetid earth! That frightened Heaven
Terrified to trust the soul
It made with Its own hands, but testing it,
Tasting it, by trial, by torture,
Over and over till the last, least town
On all this reeling, reeking earth
Stinks with a spiritual agony
That stains the stones with excrement and shows
In shadow on each greasy curtain!
After life like his to take
The seed up of the sad creation
Planting the hopeful world again—
He can't! . . . he won't! . . . he wouldn't touch her!

MR. ZUSS   He does though.

NICKLES (*raging*)   Live his life again?—
Not even the most ignorant, obstinate,
Stupid or degraded man
This filthy planet ever farrowed,
Offered the opportunity to live
His bodily life twice over, would accept it—
Least of all Job, poor, trampled bastard!

(MR. ZUSS *has finished fooling with his balloons. He straightens up and marches off without a glance at* NICKLES.)
It can't be borne twice over! Can't be!

MR. ZUSS   It is though. Time and again it is—
Every blessed generation . . .

(*His voice drifts back as he disappears.*)
Time and again . . .

                      Time and again . . .

(NICKLES *starts to follow, looks back, sees J.B. kneeling in his rubble, hesitates, crosses, squats behind him, his vendor's cap pushed back on his head, his tray on his knees.*)
NICKLES   J.B.!

J.B.   Let me alone.

NICKLES   It's me.

((J.B. *shrugs.*)
I'm not the Father. I'm the—Friend.

J.B.   I have no friend.

NICKLES   Oh come off it.
You don't have to act with me.

(J.B. *is silent.*)
O.K. Carry on.
All I wanted was to help.
Professional counsel you might call it . . .

(J.B. *is silent.*)

Of course you know how all this ends? . . .

(J.B. *is silent.*)

I wondered how you'd play the end.

J.B.   Who knows what the end is, ever?

NICKLES   I do. You do.

J.B.   Then don't tell me.

NICKLES   What's the worst thing you can think of?

J.B.   I have asked for death. Begged for it. Prayed for it.

NICKLES   Then the worst thing can't be death.

J.B.   Ah!

NICKLES   You know now.

J.B.   No. You tell me.

NICKLES   Why should I tell you when you know?

J.B.   Then don't. I'm sick of mysteries. Sick of them.

NICKLES   He gives it back to you.

J.B.   What back?

NICKLES   All of it.
Everything He ever took:
Wife, health, children, everything.

J.B.   I have no wife.

NICKLES   She comes back to you.

J.B.   I have no children.

NICKLES (*a nasty laugh*)   You'll have better ones.

J.B.   My skin is . . .
(*He breaks off, staring at the skin of his naked arms.*)

NICKLES   Oh come on! I know the
Look of grease paint!

J.B.   . . . whole! It's healed!

NICKLES (*heavily ironic*)
            You see? You see what I mean? What He plans for you?
(J.B., *staring at his arms, is silent.*)

NICKLES (*leaning forward, urgently*)

Tell me how you play the end.
Any man was screwed as Job was! . . .

(J.B. *does not answer.*)

I'll tell you how you play it. Listen!
Think of all the mucked-up millions
Since this buggered world began
Said, No!, said, Thank you!, took a rope's end,
Took a window for a door,
Swallowed something, gagged on something . . .

(J.B. *lifts his head: he is listening but not to* NICKLES.)

None of them knew the truth as Job does.
None of them had his cause to know.

J.B.   Listen! Do you hear? There's someone . . .

NICKLES (*violently*)

Job won't take it! Job won't touch it!
Job will fling it in God's face
With half his guts to make it spatter!
He'd rather suffocate in dung—
Choke in ordure—

J.B. (*rising*)   There is someone—
Someone waiting at the door.

NICKLES (*pulling his cap down, rising slowly*)   I know.

(*The dangling lights dim out.*)

SCENE ELEVEN

(*A light comes from the canvas door. It increases as though day were beginning somewhere.* NICKLES *has gone.*)

J.B.   Who is it?

(*He crosses toward the door walking with his old ease. Stops.*)

Is there someone there?

(*There is no answer. He goes on. Reaches the door.*)

Sarah!

(*The light increases. She is sitting on the sill, a broken twig in her hand.*)

SARAH   Look, Job: the forsythia,
The first few leaves . . .

not leaves though . . .

petals . . .

J.B. (*roughly*)   Get up!

SARAH   Where shall I go?

J.B.   Where you went!
Wherever!

(*She does not answer.*)

(*More gently.*)   Where?

SARAH   Among the ashes.
                         All there is now of the town is ashes.
                         Mountains of ashes. Shattered glass.
                         Glittering cliffs of glass all shattered
                         Steeper than a cat could climb
                         If there were cats still . . .
                                           And the pigeons—
                         They wheel and settle and whirl off
                         Wheeling and almost settling . . .
                                           And the silence—
                         There is no sound there now—no wind sound—
                         Nothing that could sound the wind—
                         Could make it sing—no door—no doorway . . .

                         Only this.
(She looks at the twig in her hands.)
                                   Among the ashes!
                         I found it growing in the ashes,
                         Gold as though it did not know . . .
(Her voice rises hysterically.)
                         I broke the branch to strip the leaves off—
                         Petals again! . . .
(She cradles it in her arms.)   But they so clung to it!

J.B.   Curse God and die, you said to me.

SARAH   Yes.
(She looks up at him for the first time, then down again.)
                         You wanted justice, didn't you?
                         There isn't any. There's the world . . .
(She begins to rock on the doorsill, the little branch in her arms.)
                         Cry for justice and the stars
                         Will stare until your eyes sting. Weep,
                         Enormous winds will thrash the water.
                         Cry in sleep for your lost children,
                         Snow will fall . . .
                                           snow will fall . . .

J.B.   Why did you leave me alone?

SARAH   I loved you.
                         I couldn't help you any more.
                         You wanted justice and there was none—
                         Only love.

J.B.   He does not love. He
                 Is.

SARAH   But we do. That's the wonder.

J.B.   Yet you left me.

SARAH   Yes, I left you.
I thought there was a way away . . .

Water under bridges opens
Closing and the companion stars
Still float there afterwards. I thought the door
Opened into closing water.

J.B.   Sarah!

(He drops on his knees beside her in the doorway, his arms around her.)

SARAH   Oh, I never could!
I never could! Even the forsythia . . .

(She is half laughing, half crying.)
Even the forsythia beside the
Stair could stop me.

(They cling to each other. Then she rises, drawing him up, peering at the darkness inside the door.)

J.B.   It's too dark to see.

(She turns, pulls his head down between her hands and kisses him.)

SARAH   Then blow on the coal of the heart, my darling.

J.B.   The coal of the heart . . .

SARAH   It's all the light now.

(SARAH comes forward into the dim room, J.B. behind her. She lifts a fallen chair, sets it straight.)
Blow on the coal of the heart.
The candles in churches are out.
The lights have gone out in the sky.
Blow on the coal of the heart
And we'll see by and by . . .

(J.B. has joined her, lifting and straigtening the chairs.)
                                We'll see where we are.
The wit won't burn and the wet soul smoulders.
Blow on the coal of the heart and we'll know . . .
We'll know . . .

(The light increases, plain white daylight from the door, as they work.)

Curtain

We have seen that a play, like other forms of literature, usually reflects the concerns and preoccupations of its time. Some plays go a step further: the playwright uses the play as a partisan document in the endless struggle between opposing social and economic forces. During the second half of the twentieth century social conflict in the United States has intensified and broadened. One specific example is the revolt of black Americans against suppression and oppression. Consequently black writers have used their talents both to reflect and describe the revolt and also to convince others of the justice of their cause.

One such play is A Raisin in the Sun. Not a militant play, it supports the cause by means of quiet statement. The Younger family is typical of black Americans confined to menial jobs, inferior housing, semi-respectable squalor. Both Walter and Ruth Younger make a precarious living as domestic servants. The sister, Beneatha, has learned at her University something about what life could be for her, but she is prevented by poverty from training for a profession. The really convincing figure is the matriarch, Lena Younger. In her the author has created a character who typifies the transition from agricultural poverty in the American South to the frustrations of life on the Southside of Chicago. She is also an admirable and lovable woman. Sociologists have written millions of words about the social phenomena reflected in this play, but perhaps the life described here, especially in the figure of Mama Younger, is more moving and more inciting to remedial action than sociological prose or even militant plays and stories.

Just as part of the appeal of the play comes from the fact that it is a quiet statement, so the play is in no way innovative in technique. All the action takes place on one set. The furniture and properties are precisely those that would be found in the home of a real family named Younger. The commonplace stage setting matches and adds to the feeling of sympathy the playgoer or reader has for this family and, through them, for the oppressed everywhere.

*A RAISIN IN THE SUN

LORRAINE HANSBERRY

The action of the play is set in Chicago's Southside, sometime between World War II and the present.

ACT I Scene One: Friday morning.
    Scene Two: The following morning.
ACT II Scene One: Later, the same day.
    Scene Two: Friday night, a few weeks later.
    Scene Three: Moving day, one week later.
ACT III An hour later.

ACT 1

SCENE ONE

(*The* YOUNGER *living room would be a comfortable and well-ordered room if it were not for a number of indestructible contradictions to this state of being. Its furnishings are typical and undistinguished and their primary feature now is that they have clearly had to accommodate the living of too many people for too many years—and they are tired. Still, we can see that at some time, a time probably no longer remembered by the family except perhaps for* MAMA) *the furnishings of this room were actually selected with care and love and even hope—and brought to this apartment and arranged with taste and pride.*

(*That was a long time ago. Now the once loved pattern of the couch upholstery has to fight to show itself from under acres of crocheted doilies and couch covers which have themselves finally come to be more important than the upholstery. And here a table or a chair has been moved to disguise the worn places in the carpet; but the carpet has fought back by showing its weariness, with depressing uniformity, elsewhere on its surface.*

(*Weariness has, in fact, won in this room. Everything has been polished, washed, sat on, used, scrubbed too often. All pretenses but living itself have long since vanished from the very atmosphere of this room.*

(*Moreover, a section of this room, for it is not really a room unto itself, though the land-lord's lease would make it seem so, slopes backward to provide a small kitchen area, where the family prepares the meals that are eaten in the living room proper, which must also serve as dining room. The single window that has been provided for these "two" rooms is located in this kitchen area. The sole natural light the family may enjoy in the course of a day is only that which fights its way through this little window.*

(*At left, a door leads to a bedroom which is shared by* MAMA *and her daughter,* BE-NEATHA. *At right, opposite, is a second room [which in the beginning of the life of this apartment was probably a breakfast room] which serves as a bedroom for* WALTER *and his wife,* RUTH.)

TIME
Somewhere between World War II and the present.

PLACE
Chicago's Southside.

AT RISE
It is morning dark in the living room. TRAVIS *is asleep on the make-down bed at center. An alarm clock sounds from within the bedroom at right, and presently* RUTH *enters from that room and closes the door behind her. She crosses sleepily toward the window. As she passes her sleeping son she reaches down and shakes him a little. At the window she raises the shade and a dusky Southside morning light comes in feebly. She fills a pot with water and puts it on to boil. She calls to the boy, between yawns, in a slightly muffled voice.*

RUTH *is about thirty. We can see that she was a pretty girl, even exceptionally so, but now it is apparent that life has been little that she expected, and disappointment has already begun to hang in her face. In a few years, before thirty-five even, she will be known among her people as a "settled woman."*

She crosses to her son and gives him a good, final, rousing shake.

RUTH   Come on now, boy, it's seven thirty! (*Her son sits up at last, in a stupor of sleepiness.*) I say hurry up, Travis! You ain't the only person in the world got to use a bathroom! (*The child, a sturdy, handsome little boy of ten or eleven, drags himself out of the bed and almost blindly takes his towels and "today's clothes" from drawers and a closet and goes out to the bathroom, which is in an outside hall and which is shared by another family or families on the same floor.* RUTH *crosses to the bedroom door at right and opens it and calls in to her husband*) Walter Lee! . . . It's after seven thirty! Lemme see you do some waking up in there! (*She waits*) You better get up from there, man! It's after seven thirty I tell you. (*She waits again*) All right, you just go ahead and lay there and next thing you know Travis be finished and Mr. Johnson'll be in there and you'll be fussing and cussing round here like a mad man! And be late too! (*She waits, at the end of patience*) Walter Lee—it's time for you to get up!

(*She waits another second and then starts to go into the bedroom, but is apparently satisfied that her husband has begun to get up. She stops, pulls the door to, and returns to the kitchen area. She wipes her face with a moist cloth and runs her fingers through her sleep-disheveled hair in a vain effort and ties an apron around her housecoat. The bedroom door at right opens and her husband stands in the doorway in his pajamas, which are rumpled and mismated. He is a lean, intense young man in his middle thirties, inclined to quick nervous movements and erratic speech habits—and always in his voice there is a quality of indictment.*)

WALTER Is he out yet?

RUTH What you mean *out*? He ain't hardly got in there good yet.

WALTER (*Wandering in, still more oriented to sleep than to a new day*) Well, what was you doing all that yelling for if I can't even get in there yet? (*Stopping and thinking*) Check coming today?

RUTH They *said* Saturday and this is just Friday and I hopes to God you ain't going to get up here first thing this morning and start talking to me 'bout no money—'cause I 'bout don't want to hear it.

WALTER Something the matter with you this morning?

RUTH No—I'm just sleepy as the devil. What kind of eggs you want?

WALTER Not scrambled. (RUTH *starts to scramble eggs*) Paper come? (RUTH *points impatiently to the rolled up* Tribune *on the table, and he gets it and spreads it out and vaguely reads the front page*) Set off another bomb yesterday.

RUTH (*Maximum indifference*) Did they?

WALTER (*Looking up*) What's the matter with you?

RUTH Ain't nothing the matter with me. And don't keep asking me that this morning.

WALTER Ain't nobody bothering you. (*Reading the news of the day absently again*) Say Colonel McCormick is sick.

RUTH (*Affecting tea-party interest*) Is he now? Poor thing.

WALTER (*Sighing and looking at his watch*) Oh, me. (*He waits*) Now what is that boy doing in that bathroom all this time? He just going to have to start getting up earlier. I can't be being late to work on account of him fooling around in there.

RUTH (*Turning on him*) Oh, no he ain't going to be getting up no earlier no such thing! It ain't his fault that he can't get to bed no earlier nights 'cause he got a bunch of crazy good-for-nothing clowns sitting up running their mouths in what is supposed to be his bedroom after ten o'clock at night . . .

WALTER That's what you mad about, ain't it? The things I want to talk about with my friends just couldn't be important in your mind, could they?

(*He rises and finds a cigarette in her handbag on the table and crosses to the little window and looks out, smoking and deeply enjoying this first one.*)

RUTH (*Almost matter of factly, a complaint too automatic to deserve emphasis*) Why you always got to smoke before you eat in the morning?

WALTER (*At the window*) Just look at 'em down there . . . Running and racing to work . . . (*He turns and faces his wife and watches her a moment at the stove, and then, suddenly*) You look young this morning, baby.

RUTH (*Indifferently*) Yeah?

WALTER Just for a second—stirring them eggs. It's gone now—just for a second it was—you looked real young again. (*Then, drily*) It's gone now—you look like yourself again.

RUTH Man, if you don't shut up and leave me alone.

WALTER (*Looking out to the street again*) First thing a man ought to learn in life is not to make love to no colored woman first thing in the morning. You all some evil people at eight o'clock in the morning.

(TRAVIS *appears in the hall doorway, almost fully dressed and quite wide awake now, his towels and pajamas across his shoulders. He opens the door and signals for his father to make the bathroom in a hurry*)

TRAVIS (*Watching the bathroom*) Daddy, come on!

(WALTER *gets his bathroom utensils and flies out to the bathroom.*)

RUTH Sit down and have your breakfast, Travis.

TRAVIS Mama, this is Fiday. (*Gleefully*) Check coming tomorrow, huh?

RUTH You get your mind off money and eat your breakfast.

TRAVIS (*Eating*) This is the morning we supposed to bring the fifty cents to school.

RUTH Well, I ain't got no fifty cents this morning.

TRAVIS Teacher say we have to.

RUTH I don't care what teacher say. I ain't got it. Eat your breakfast, Travis.

TRAVIS I *am* eating.

RUTH Hush up now and just eat!

(*The boy gives her an exasperated look for her lack of understanding, and eats grudgingly.*)

TRAVIS You think Grandmama would have it?

RUTH No! And I want you to stop asking your grandmother for money, you hear me?

TRAVIS (*Outraged*) Gaaaleee! I don't ask her, she just gimmie it sometimes!

RUTH Travis Willard Younger—I got too much on me this morning to be—

TRAVIS Maybe Daddy—

RUTH *Travis!*

(*The boy hushes abruptly. They are both quiet and tense for several seconds.*)

TRAVIS (*Presently*) Could I maybe go carry some groceries in front of the supermarket for a little while after school then?

RUTH   Just hush, I said. (*Travis jabs his spoon into his cereal bowl viciously, and rests his head in anger upon his fists*) If you through eating, you can get over there and make up your bed.

(*The boy obeys stiffly and crosses the room, almost mechanically, to the bed and more or less carefully folds the covering. He carries the bedding into his mother's room and returns with his books and cap.*)

TRAVIS   (*Sulking and standing apart from her unnaturally*) I'm gone.

RUTH   (*Looking up from the stove to inspect him automatically*) Come here. (*He crosses to her and she studies his head*) If you don't take this comb and fix this here head, you better! (TRAVIS *puts down his books with a great sigh of oppression, and crosses to the mirror. His mother mutters under her breath about his "slubbornness"*) 'Bout to march out of here with that head looking just like chickens slept in it! I just don't know where you get your slubborn ways . . . And get your jacket, too. Looks chilly out this morning.

TRAVIS   (*With conspicuously brushed hair and jacket*) I'm gone.

RUTH   Get carfare and milk money—(*Waving one finger*)—and not a single penny for no caps, your hear me?

TRAVIS   (*With sullen politeness*) Yes'm.

(*He turns in outrage to leave. His mother watches after him as in his frustration he approaches the door almost comically. When she speaks to him, her voice has become a very gentle tease*)

RUTH   (*Mocking; as she thinks he would say it*) Oh, Mama makes me so mad sometimes, I don't know what to do! (*She waits and continues to his back as he stands stock-still in front of the door*) I wouldn't kiss that woman good-bye for nothing in this world this morning! (*The boy finally turns around and rolls his eyes at her, knowing the mood has changed and he is vindicated; he does not, however, move toward her yet*) Not for nothing in this world! (*She finally laughs aloud at him and holds her arms to him and we see that it is a way between them, very old and practiced. He crosses to her and allows her to embrace him warmly but keeps his face fixed with masculine rigidity. She holds him back from her presently and looks at him and runs her fingers over the features of his face. With utter gentleness—*) Now—whose little old angry man are you?

TRAVIS   (*The masculinity and gruffness start to fade at last*) Aw gaalee—Mama . . .

RUTH   (*Mimicking*) Aw—gaaaaalleeeee, Mama! (*She pushes him, with rough playfulness and finality, toward the door*) Get out of here or you going to be late.

TRAVIS   (*In the face of love, new aggressiveness*) Mama, could I *please* go carry groceries?

RUTH   Honey, it's starting to get so cold evenings.

WALTER   (*Coming in from the bathroom and drawing a make-believe gun from a make-believe holster and shooting at his son*) What is it he wants to do?

RUTH   Go carry groceries after school at the supermarket.

WALTER   Well, let him go . . .

TRAVIS   (*Quickly, to the ally*) I *have* to—she won't gimme the fifty cents . . .

WALTER   (*To his wife only*) Why not?

RUTH   (*Simply, and with flavor*) 'Cause we don't have it.

WALTER   (*To* RUTH *only*) What you tell the boy things like that for? (*Reaching down into his pants with a rather important gesture*) Here, son—

(*He hands the boy the coin, but his eyes are directed to his wife's.* TRAVIS *takes the money happily.*)

TRAVIS   Thanks, Daddy.

(*He starts out.* RUTH *watches both of them with murder in her eyes.* WALTER *stands and stares back at her with defiance, and suddenly reaches into his pocket again on an afterthought.*)

WALTER   (*Without even looking at his son, still staring hard at his wife*) In fact, here's another fifty cents . . . Buy yourself some fruit today—or take a taxicab to school or something!

TRAVIS   Whoopee—

(*He leaps up and clasps his father around the middle with his legs, and they face each other in mutual appreciation; slowly* WALTER LEE *peeks around the boy to catch the violet rays from his wife's eyes and draws his head back as if shot.*)

WALTER   You better get down now—and get to school, man.

TRAVIS   (*At the door*) O.K. Good-bye.

(*He exits.*)

WALTER   (*After him, pointing with pride*) That's *my* boy. (*She looks at him in disgust and turns back to her work*) You know what I was thinking 'bout in the bathroom this morning?

RUTH   No.

WALTER   How come you always try to be so pleasant!

RUTH   What is there to be pleasant 'bout!

WALTER   You want to know what I was thinking 'bout in the bathroom or not!

RUTH   I know what you thinking 'bout.

WALTER   (*Ignoring her*) 'Bout what me and Willy Harris was talking about last night.

RUTH   (*Immediately—a refrain*) Willy Harris is a good-for-nothing loud mouth.

WALTER   Anybody who talks to me has got to be a good-for-nothing loud mouth, ain't he? And what you know about who is just a good-for-nothing loud mouth? Charlie Atkins was just a "good-for-nothing loud mouth" too, wasn't he! When he wanted me to go in the dry-cleaning business with him. And now—he's grossing a hundred thousand a year. A hundred thousand dollars a year! You still call *him* a loud mouth!

RUTH   (*Bitterly*) Oh, Walter Lee . . .

(*She folds her head on her arms over the table.*)

WALTER   (*Rising and coming to her and standing over her*) You tired, ain't you? Tired of everything. Me, the boy, the way we live—this beat-up hole—everything. Ain't you? (*She doesn't look up, doesn't answer*) So tired—moaning and groaning all the time, but you wouldn't do nothing to help, would you? You couldn't be on my side that long for nothing, could you?

RUTH   Walter, please leave me alone.

WALTER   A man needs for a woman to back him up . . .

RUTH Walter—

WALTER Mama would listen to you. You know she listen to you more than she do me and Bennie. She think more of you. All you have to do is just sit down with her when you drinking your coffee one morning and talking 'bout things like you do and—(*He sits down beside her and demonstrates graphically what he thinks her methods and tone should be*)—you just sip your coffee, see, and say easy like that you been thinking 'bout that deal Walter Lee is so interested in, 'bout the store and all, and sip some more coffee, like what you saying ain't really that important to you—And the next thing you know, she be listening good and asking you questions and when I come home—I can tell her the details. This ain't no fly-by-night proposition, baby. I mean we figured it out, me and Willy and Bobo.

RUTH (*With a frown*) Bobo?

WALTER Yeah. You see, this little liquor store we got in mind cost seventy-five thousand and we figured the initial investment on the place to be 'bout thirty thousand, see. That be ten thousand each. Course, there's a couple of hundred you got to pay so's you don't spend your life just waiting for them clowns to let your license get approved.

RUTH You mean graft?

WALTER (*Frowning impatiently*) Don't call it that. See there, that just goes to show you what women understand about the world. Baby, don't *nothing* happen for you in this world 'less you pay *somebody* off!

RUTH Walter, leave me alone! (*She raises her head and stares at him vigorously—then says, more quietly*) Eat your eggs, they gonna be cold.

WALTER (*Straightening up from her and looking off*) That's it. There you are. Man say to his woman: I got me a dream. His woman say: Eat your eggs. (*Sadly, but gaining in power*) Man say: I got to take hold of this here world, baby! And a woman will say: Eat your eggs and go to work. (*Passionately now*) Man say: I got to change my life, I'm choking to death, baby! And his woman say—(*In utter anguish as he brings his fists down on his thighs*)—Your eggs is getting cold!

RUTH (*Softly*) Walter, that ain't none of our money.

WALTER (*Not listening at all or even looking at her*) This morning, I was lookin' in the mirror and thinking about it . . . I'm thirty-five years old; I been married eleven years and I got a boy who sleeps in the living room—(*Very, very quietly*)—and all I got to give him is stories about how rich white people live . . .

RUTH Eat your eggs, Walter.

WALTER *Damn my eggs . . . damn all the eggs that ever was!*

RUTH Then go to work.

WALTER (*Looking up at her*) See—I'm trying to talk to you 'bout myself—(*Shaking his head with the repetition*)—and all you can say is eat them eggs and go to work.

RUTH (*Wearily*) Honey, you never say nothing new. I listen to you every day, every night and every morning, and you never say nothing new. (*Shrugging*) So you would rather *be* Mr. Arnold than his chauffeur. So— I would *rather* be living in Buckingham Palace.

WALTER   That is just what is wrong with the colored woman in this world . . . Don't understand about building their men up and making 'em feel like they somebody. Like they can do something.

RUTH   (*Drily, but to hurt*) There *are* colored men who do things.

WALTER   No thanks to the colored woman.

RUTH   Well, being a colored woman, I guess I can't help myself none.

(*She rises and gets the ironing board and sets it up and attacks a huge pile of rough-dried clothes, sprinkling them in preparation for the ironing and then rolling them into tight fat balls.*)

WALTER   (*Mumbling*) We one group of men tied to a race of woman with small minds.

(*His sister BENEATHA enters. She is about twenty, as slim and intense as her brother. She is not as pretty as her sister-in-law, but her lean, almost intellectual face has a hand-someness of its own. She wears a bright-red flannel nightie, and her thick hair stands wildly about her head. Her speech is a mixture of many things; it is different from the rest of the family's insofar as education has permeated her sense of English—and per-haps the Midwest rather than the South has finally—at last—won out in her inflection; but not altogether, because over all of it is a soft slurring and transformed use of vowels which is the decided influence of the Southside. She passes through the room without looking at either RUTH or WALTER and goes to the outside door and looks, a little blindly, out to the bathroom. She sees that it has been lost to the Johnsons. She closes the door with a sleepy vengeance and crosses to the table and sits down a little defeated.*)

BENEATHA   I am going to start timing those people.

WALTER   You should get up earlier.

BENEATHA   (*Her face in her hands. She is still fighting the urge to go back to bed*) Really—would you suggest dawn? Where's the paper?

WALTER   (*Pushing the paper across the table to her as he studies her almost clinically, as though he has never seen her before*) You a horrible-looking chick at this hour.

BENEATHA   (*Drily*) Good morning, everybody.

WALTER   (*Senselessly*) How is school coming?

BENEATHA   (*In the same spirit*) Lovely. Lovely. And you know, biology is the greatest. (*Looking up at him*) I dissected something that looked just like you yesterday.

WALTER   I just wondered if you've made up your mind and everything.

BENEATHA   (*Gaining in sharpness and impatience*) And what did I answer yesterday morning—and the day before that?

RUTH   (*From the ironing board, like someone disinterested and old*) Don't be so nasty, Bennie.

BENEATHA   (*Still to her brother*) And the day before that and the day before that!

WALTER   (*Defensively*) I'm interested in you. Something wrong with that? Ain't many girls who decide—

WALTER AND BENEATHA (*In unison*)—"to be a doctor."

(*Silence.*)

WALTER   Have we figured out yet just exactly how much medical school is going to cost?

RUTH Walter Lee, why don't you leave that girl alone and get out of here to work?

BENEATHA (*Exits to the bathroom and bangs on the door*) Come on out of there, please!

(*She comes back into the room.*)

WALTER (*Looking at his sister intently*) You know the check is coming tomorrow.

BENEATHA (*Turning on him with a sharpness all her own*) That money belongs to Mama, Walter, and it's for her to decide how she wants to use it. I don't care if she wants to buy a house or a rocket ship or just nail it up somewhere and look at it. It's hers. Not ours—*hers.*

WALTER (*Bitterly*) Now ain't that fine! You just got your mother's interest at heart, ain't you, girl? You such a nice girl—but if Mama got that money she can always take a few thousand and help you through school too—can't she?

BENEATHA I have never asked anyone around here to do anything for me!

WALTER No! And the line between asking and just accepting when the time comes is big and wide—ain't it!

BENEATHA (*With fury*) What do you want from me, Brother—that I quit school or just drop dead, which!

WALTER I don't want nothing but for you to stop acting holy 'round here. Me and Ruth done made some sacrifices for you—why can't you do something for the family?

RUTH Walter, don't be dragging me in it.

WALTER You are in it—Don't you get up and go work in somebody's kitchen for the last three years to help put clothes on her back?

RUTH Oh, Walter—that's not fair . . .

WALTER It ain't that nobody expects you to get on your knees and say thank you, Brother; thank you, Ruth; thank you, Mama—and thank you, Travis, for wearing the same pair of shoes for two semesters—

BENEATHA (*Dropping to her knees*) Well—I *do*—all right?—thank everybody . . . and forgive me for ever wanting to be anything at all . . . forgive me, forgive me!

RUTH Please stop it! Your mama'll hear you.

WALTER Who the hell told you you had to be a doctor? If you so crazy 'bout messing 'round with sick people—then go be a nurse like other women—or just get married and be quiet . . .

BENEATHA Well—you finally got it said . . . It took you three years but you finally got it said. Walter, give up; leave me alone—it's Mama's money.

WALTER *He was my father, too!*

BENEATHA So what? He was mine, too—and Travis' grandfather—but the insurance money belongs to Mama. Picking on me is not going to make her give it to you to invest in any liquor stores—(*Underbreath, dropping into a chair*)—and I for one say, God bless Mama for that!

WALTER (*To* RUTH) See—did you hear? Did you hear!

RUTH Honey, please go to work.

WALTER Nobody in this house is ever going to understand me.

BENEATHA Because you're a nut.

WALTER Who's a nut?

BENEATHA You—you are a nut. Thee is mad, boy.

WALTER (*Looking at his wife and his sister from the door, very sadly*) The world's most backward race of people, and that's a fact.

BENEATHA (*Turning slowly in her chair*) And then there are those prophets who would lead us out of the wilderness—(WALTER *slams out of the house*)—into the swamps!

RUTH Bennie, why you always gotta be pickin' on your brother? Can't you be a little sweeter sometimes? (*Door opens. WALTER walks in*)

WALTER (*To* RUTH) I need some money for carfare.

RUTH (*Looks at him, then warms; teasing, but tenderly*) Fifty cents? (*She goes to her bag and gets money*) Here, take a taxi.

(WALTER *exits.* MAMA *enters. She is a woman in her early sixties, full-bodied and strong. She is one of those women of a certain grace and beauty who wear it so unobtrusively that it takes a while to notice. Her dark-brown face is surrounded by the total whiteness of her hair, and, being a woman who has adjusted to many things in life and overcome many more, her face is full of strength. She has, we can see, wit and faith of a kind that keep her eyes lit and full of interest and expectancy. She is, in a word, a beautiful woman. Her bearing is perhaps most like the noble bearing of the women of the Hereros of Southwest Africa—rather as if she imagines that as she walks she still bears a basket or a vessel upon her head. Her speech, on the other hand, is as careless as her carriage is precise—she is inclined to slur everything—but her voice is perhaps not so much quiet as simply soft.*)

MAMA Who that 'round here slamming doors at this hour?

(*She crosses through the room, goes to the windnw, opens it, and brings in a feeble little plant growing doggedly in a small pot on the window sill. She feels the dirt and puts it back out.*)

RUTH That was Walter Lee. He and Bennie was at it again.

MAMA My children and they tempers. Lord, if this little old plant don't get more sun than it's been getting it ain't never going to see spring again. (*She turns from the window*) What's the matter with you this morning, Ruth? You looks right peaked. You aiming to iron all them things? Leave some for me. I'll get to 'em this afternoon. Bennie honey, it's too drafty for you to be sitting 'round half dressed. Where's your robe?

BENEATHA In the cleaners.

MAMA Well, go get mine and put it on.

BENEATHA I'm not cold, Mama, honest.

MAMA I know—but you so thin . . .

BENEATHA (*Irritably*) Mama, I'm not cold.

MAMA (*Seeing the make-down bed as* TRAVIS *has left it*) Lord have mercy look at that poor bed. Bless his heart—he tries, don't he?

(*She moves to the bed* TRAVIS *has sloppily made up.*)

RUTH No—he don't half try at all 'cause he knows you going to come along behind him and fix everything. That's just how come he don't know how to do nothing right now—you done spoiled that boy so.

MAMA Well—he's a litle boy. Aint supposed to know 'bout housekeeping. My baby, that's what he is. What you fix for his breakfast this morning?

RUTH (*Angrily*) I feed my son, Lena!

MAMA I ain't meddling—(*Underbreath; busy-bodyish*) I just noticed all last week he had cold cereal, and when it starts getting this chilly in the fall a child ought to have some hot grits or something when he goes out in the cold—

RUTH (*Furious*) I gave him hot oats—is that all right!

MAMA I ain't meddling. (*Pause*) Put a lot of nice butter on it? (RUTH *shoots her an angry look and does not reply*) He likes lots of butter.

RUTH (*Exasperated*) Lena—

MAMA (*To* BENEATHA. MAMA *is inclined to wander conversationally sometimes*) What was you and your brother fussing 'bout this morning?

BENEATHA It's not important, Mama.

(*She gets up and goes to look out at the bathroom, which is apparently free, and she picks up her towels and rushes out.*)

MAMA What was they fighting about?

RUTH Now you know as well as I do.

MAMA (*Shaking her head*) Brother still worrying hisself sick about that money?

RUTH You know he is.

MAMA You had breakfast?

RUTH Some coffee.

MAMA Girl, you better start eating and looking after yourself better. You almost thin as Travis.

RUTH Lena—

MAMA Un-hunh?

RUTH What are you going to do with it?

MAMA Now don't you start, child. It's too early in the morning to be talking about money. It ain't Christian.

RUTH It's just that he got his heart set on that store—

MAMA You mean that liquor store that Willy Harris want him to invest in?

RUTH Yes—

MAMA We ain't no business people, Ruth. We just plain working folks.

RUTH Ain't nobody business people till they go into business. Walter Lee say colored people ain't never going to start getting ahead till they start gambling on some different kinds of things in the world—investments and things.

MAMA What done got into you, girl? Walter Lee done finally sold you on investing.

RUTH No. Mama, something is happening between Walter and me. I don't know what it is—but he needs something—something I can't give him any more. He needs this chance, Lena.

MAMA (*Frowning deeply*) But liquor, honey—

RUTH Well—like Walter say—I spec people going to always be drinking themselves some liquor.

MAMA Well—whether they drinks it or not ain't none of my business. But whether I go into business selling it to 'em *is,* and I don't want that on my ledger this late in life. (*Stopping suddenly and studying her daughter-in-law*) Ruth Younger, what's the matter with you today? You look like you could fall over right there.

RUTH   I'm tired.

MAMA   Then you better stay home from work today.

RUTH   I can't stay home. She'd be calling up the agency and screaming at them, "My girl didn't come in today—send me somebody! My girl didn't come in!" Oh, she just have a fit . . .

MAMA   Well, let her have it. I'll just call her up and say you got the flu—

RUTH   (*Laughing*) Why the flu?

MAMA   'Cause it sounds respectable to 'em. Something white people get, too. They know 'bout the flu. Otherwise they think you been cut up or something when you tell 'em you sick.

RUTH   I got to go in. We need the money.

MAMA   Somebody would of thought my children done all but starved to death the way they talk about money here late. Child, we got a great big old check coming tomorrow.

RUTH   (*Sincerely, but also self-righteously*) Now that's your money. It ain't got nothing to do with me. We all feel like that—Walter and Bennie and me—even Travis.

MAMA   (*Thoughtfully, and suddenly very far away*) Ten thousand dollars—

RUTH   Sure is wonderful.

MAMA   Ten thousand dollars.

RUTH   You know what you should do, Miss Lena? You should take yourself a trip somewhere. To Europe or South America or someplace—

MAMA   (*Throwing up her hands at the thought*) Oh, child!

RUTH   I'm serious. Just pack up and leave! Go on away and enjoy yourself some. Forget about the family and have yourself a ball for once in your life—

MAMA   (*Drily*) You sound like I'm just about ready to die. Who'd go with me? What I look like wandering 'round Europe by myself?

RUTH   Shoot—these here rich white women do it all the time. They don't think nothing of packing up they suitcases and piling on one of them big steamships and—swoosh!—they gone, child.

MAMA   Something always told me I wasn't no rich white woman.

RUTH   Well—what are you going to do with it then?

MAMA   I ain't rightly decided. (*Thinking. She speaks now with emphasis.*) Some of it got to be put away for Beneatha and her schoolin'—and ain't nothing going to touch that part of it. Nothing. (*She waits several seconds, trying to make up her mind about something, and looks at RUTH a little tentatively before going on*) Been thinking that we maybe could meet the notes on a little old two-story somewhere, with a yard where Travis could play in the summertime, if we use part of the insurance for a down payment and everybody kind of pitch in. I could maybe take on a little day work again, few days a week—

RUTH   (*Studying her mother-in-law furtively and concentrating on her ironing, anxious to encourage without seeming to*) Well, Lord knows, we've put enough rent into this here rat trap to pay for four houses by now . . .

MAMA   (*Looking up at the words "rat trap" and then looking around and leaning back and sighing—in a suddenly reflective mood—*) "Rat trap"—yes, that's all it is. (*Smiling*) I remember just as well the day me and Big Walter moved in here. Hadn't been married but two weeks and wasn't planning on living here no more than a year. (*She shakes her head at the dissolved dream*) We was going to set away, little by little, don't you know, and buy a little place out in Morgan Park. We had even picked out the house. (*Chuckling a little*) Looks right dumpy today. But Lord, child, you should know all the dreams I had 'bout buying that house and fixing it up and making me a little garden in the back—(*She waits and stops smiling*) And didn't none of it happen.

(*Dropping her hands in a futile gesture.*)

RUTH (*Keeps her head down, ironing*) Yes, life can be a barrel of disappointments, sometimes.

MAMA Honey. Big Walter would come in here some nights back then and slump down on that couch there and just look at the rug, and look at me and look at the rug and then back at me—and I'd know he was down then . . . really down. (*After a second very long and thoughtful pause; she is seeing back to times that only she can see*) And then, Lord, when I lost that baby—little Claude—I almost thought I was going to lose Big Walter too. Oh, that man grieved hisself! He was one man to love his children.

RUTH Ain't nothin' can tear at you like losin' your baby.

MAMA I guess that's how come that man finally worked hisself to death like he done. Like he was fighting his own war with this here world that took his baby from him.

RUTH He sure was a fine man, all right. I always liked Mr. Younger.

MAMA Crazy 'bout his children! God knows there was plenty wrong with Walter Younger—hard-headed, mean, kind of wild with women—plenty wrong with him. But he sure loved his children. Always wanted them to have something—be something. That's where Brother gets all these notions, I reckon. Big Walter used to say, he'd get right wet in the eyes sometimes, lean his head back with the water standing in his eyes and say, "Seem like God didn't see fit to give the black man nothing but dreams—but He did give us children to make them dreams seem worth while." (*She smiles.*) He could talk like that, don't you know.

RUTH Yes, he sure could. He was a good man, Mr. Younger.

MAMA Yes, a fine man—just couldn't never catch up with his dreams, that's all.

(BENEATHA *comes in, brushing her hair and looking up to the ceiling, where the sound of a vacuum cleaner has started up.*)

BENEATHA What could be so dirty on that woman's rugs that she has to vacuum them every single day?

RUTH I wish certain young women 'round here who I could name would take inspiration about certain rugs in a certain apartment I could also mention.

BENEATHA (*Shrugging*) How much cleaning can a house need, for Christ's sakes.

MAMA (*Not liking the Lord's name used thus*) Bennie!

RUTH Just listen to her—just listen!

BENEATHA Oh, God!

MAMA   If you use the Lord's name just one more time—

BENEATHA   (*A bit of a whine*) Oh, Mama—

RUTH   Fresh—just fresh as salt, this girl!

BENEATHA   (*Drily*) Well—if the salt loses its savor—

MAMA   Now that will do. I just ain't going to have you 'round here reciting the scriptures in vain—you hear me?

BENEATHA   How did I manage to get on everybody's wrong side by just walking into a room?

RUTH   If you weren't so fresh—

BENEATHA   Ruth, I'm twenty years old.

MAMA   What time you be home from school today?

BENEATHA   Kind of late. (*With enthusiasm*) Madeline is going to start my guitar lessons today.

(MAMA *and* RUTH *look up with the same expression.*)

MAMA   Your *what* kind of lessons?

BENEATHA   Guitar.

RUTH   Oh, Father!

MAMA   How come you done taken it in your mind to learn to play the guitar?

BENEATHA   I just want to, that's all.

MAMA   (*Smiling*) Lord, child, don't you know what to do with yourself? How long it going to be before you get tired of this now—like you got tired of that little play-acting group you joined last year? (*Looking at Ruth*) And what was it the year before that?

RUTH   The horseback-riding club for which she bought that fifty-five-dollar riding habit that's been hanging in the closet ever since!

MAMA   (*To* BENEATHA) Why you got to flit so from one thing to another, baby?

BENEATHA   (*Sharply*) I just want to learn to play the guitar. Is there anything wrong with that?

MAMA   Ain't nobody trying to stop you. I just wonders sometimes why you has to flit so from one thing to another all the time. You ain't never done nothing with all that camera equipment you brought home—

BENEATHA   I don't flit! I—I experiment with different forms of expression—

RUTH   Like riding a horse?

BENEATHA   —People have to express themselves one way or another.

MAMA   What is it you want to express?

BENEATHA   (*Angrily*) Me! (MAMA *and* RUTH *look at each other and burst into raucous laughter*) Don't worry—I don't expect you to understand.

MAMA   (*To change the subject*) Who you going out with tomorrow night?

BENEATHA   (*With displeasure*) George Murchison again.

MAMA   (*Pleased*) Oh—you getting a little sweet on him?

RUTH   You ask me, this child ain't sweet on nobody but herself—(*Under-breath*) Express herself!

(*They laugh.*)

BENEATHA   Oh—I like George all right, Mama. I mean I like him enough to go out with him and stuff, but—

RUTH (*for devilment*) What does *and stuff* mean?

BENEATHA   Mind your own business.

MAMA   Stop picking at her now, Ruth. (*A thoughtful pause, and then a suspicious sudden look at her daughter as she turns in her chair for emphasis*) What *does* it mean?

BENEATHA   (*Wearily*) Oh, I just mean I couldn't ever really be serious about George. He's—he's so shallow.

RUTH   Shallow—what do you mean he's shallow? He's *rich!*

MAMA   Hush, Ruth.

BENEATHA   I know he's rich. He knows he's rich, too.

RUTH   Well—what other qualities a man got to have to satisfy you, little girl?

BENEATHA   You wouldn't even begin to understand. Anybody who married Walter could not possibly understand.

MAMA   (*Outraged*) What kind of way is that to talk about your brother?

BENEATHA   Brother is a flip—let's face it.

MAMA   (*To* RUTH, *helplessly*) What's a flip?

RUTH   (*Glad to add kindling*) She's saying he's crazy.

BENEATHA   Not crazy. Brother isn't really crazy yet—he—he's an elaborate neurotic.

MAMA   Hush your mouth!

BENEATHA   As for George. Well. George looks good—he's got a beautiful car and he takes me to nice places and as my sister-in-law says, he is probably the richest boy I will ever get to know and I even like him sometimes—but if the Youngers are sitting around waiting to see if their little Bennie is going to tie up the family with the Murchisons, they are wasting their time.

RUTH   You mean you wouldn't marry George Murchison if he asked you someday? That pretty, rich thing? Honey, I knew you was odd—

BENEATHA   No I would not marry him if all I felt for him was what I feel now. Besides, George's family wouldn't really like it.

MAMA   Why not?

BENEATHA   Oh, Mama—The Murchisons are honest-to-God-real-*live*-rich colored people, and the only people in the world who are more snobbish than rich white people are rich colored people. I thought everybody knew that. I've met Mrs. Murchison. She's a scene!

MAMA   You must not dislike people 'cause they well off, honey.

BENEATHA   Why not? It makes just as much sense as disliking people 'cause they are poor, and lots of people do that.

RUTH   (*A wisdom-of-the-ages manner. To* MAMA) Well, she'll get over some of this—

BENEATHA   Get over it? What are you talking about, Ruth? Listen, I'm going to be a doctor. I'm not worried about who I'm going to marry yet—if I ever get married.

MAMA AND RUTH   *If!*

MAMA   Now, Bennie—

BENEATHA   Oh, I probably will . . . but first I'm going to be a doctor, and George, for one, still thinks that's pretty funny. I couldn't be bothered with that. I am going to be a doctor and everybody around here better understand that!

MAMA (*Kindly*) 'Course you going to be a doctor, honey, God willing.

BENEATHA (*Drily*) God hasn't got a thing to do with it.

MAMA Beneatha—that just wasn't necessary.

BENEATHA Well—neither is God. I get sick of hearing about God.

MAMA Beneatha!

BENEATHA I mean it! I'm just tired of hearing about God all the time. What has He got to do with anything? Does he pay tuition?

MAMA You 'bout to get your fresh little jaw slapped!

RUTH That's just what she needs, all right!

BENEATHA Why? Why can't I say what I want to around here, like anybody else?

MAMA It don't sound nice for a young girl to say things like that—you wasn't brought up that way. Me and your father went to trouble to get you and Brother to church every Sunday.

BENEATHA Mama, you don't understand. It's all a matter of ideas, and God is just one idea I don't accept. It's not important. I am not going out and be immoral or commit crimes because I don't believe in God. I don't even think about it. It's just that I get tired of Him getting credit for all the things the human race achieves through its own stubborn effort. There simply is no blasted God—there is only man and it is he who makes miracles!

(MAMA *absorbs this speech, studies her daughter and rises slowly and crosses to* BENEATHA *and slaps her powerfully across the face. After, there is only silence and the daughter drops her eyes from her mother's face, and* MAMA *is very tall before her.*)

MAMA Now—you say after me, in my mother's house there is still God. (*There is a long pause and* BENEATHA *stares at the floor wordlessly.* MAMA *repeats the phrase with precision and cool emotion*) In my mother's house there is still God.

BENEATHA In my mother's house there is still God.

(*A long pause.*)

MAMA (*Walking away from* BENEATHA, *too disturbed for triumphant posture. Stopping and turning back to her daughter*) There are some ideas we ain't going to have in this house. Not long as I am at the head of this family.

BENEATHA Yes, ma'am.

(MAMA *walks out of the room.*)

RUTH (*Almost gently, with profound understanding*) You think you a woman, Bennie—but you still a little girl. What you did was childish—so you got treated like a child.

BENEATHA I see. (*Quietly*) I also see that everybody thinks it's all right for Mama to be a tyrant. But all the tyranny in the world will never put a God in the heavens!

(*She picks up her books and goes out.*)

RUTH (*Goes to* MAMA's *door*) She said she was sorry.

MAMA (*Coming out, going to her plant*) They frightens me, Ruth. My children.

RUTH You got good children, Lena. They just a little off sometimes—but they're good.

MAMA No—there's something come down between me and them that don't
  let us understand each other and I don't know what it is. One done almost
  lost his mind thinking 'bout money all the time and the other done commence
  to talk about things I can't seem to understand in no form or fashion. What
  is it that's changing, Ruth?
RUTH (*Soothingly, older than her years*) Now . . . you taking it all too seriously. You just got strong-willed children and it takes a strong woman like
  you to keep 'em in hand.
MAMA (*Looking at her plant and sprinkling a little water on it*) They spirited
  all right, my children. Got to admit they got spirit—Bennie and Walter. Like
  this old plant that ain't never had enough sunshine or nothing—and look at
  it . . .

(*She has her back to* RUTH, *who has had to stop ironing and lean against something
and put the back of her hand to her forehead.*)
RUTH (*Trying to keep* MAMA *from noticing*) You . . . sure . . . loves that little
  old thing, don't you? . . .
MAMA Well, I always wanted me a garden like I used to see sometimes at the
  back of the houses down home. This plant is close as I ever got to having
  one. (*She looks out of the window as she replaces the plant*) Lord, ain't
  nothing as dreary as the view from this window on a dreary day, is there?
  Why ain't you singing this morning, Ruth? Sing that "No Ways Tired." That
  song always lifts me up so—(*She turns at last to see that* RUTH *has slipped
  quietly into a chair, in a state of semiconsciousness*) Ruth! Ruth honey—
  what's the matter with you . . . Ruth!

Curtain

SCENE TWO

(*It is the following morning; a Saturday morning, and house cleaning is in progress at
the* YOUNGERS. *Furniture has been shoved hither and yon and* MAMA *is giving the
kitchen-area walls a washing down.* BENEATHA, *in dungarees, with a handkerchief tied
around her face, is spraying insecticide into the cracks in the walls. As they work, the
radio is on and a Southside disk-jockey program is inappropriately filling the house with
a rather exotic saxophone blues.* TRAVIS, *the sole idle one, is leaning on his arms, looking out of the window.*)

TRAVIS Grandmama, that stuff Bennie is using smells awful. Can I go down-
  stairs, please?
MAMA Did you get all them chores done already? I ain't seen you doing
  much.
TRAVIS Yes'm—finished early. Where did Mama go this morning?
MAMA (*Looking at* BENEATHA) She had to go on a little errand.
TRAVIS Where?
MAMA Tend to her business.
TRAVIS Can I go outside then?
MAMA Oh, I guess so. You better stay right in front of the house, though . . .
  and keep a good lookout for the postman.

TRAVIS   Yes'm. (*He starts out and decides to give his* AUNT BENEATHA *a good swat on the legs as he passes her*) Leave them poor little old cock-roaches alone, they ain't bothering you none.

(*He runs as she swings the spray gun at him both viciously and playfully.* WALTER *enters from the bedroom and goes to the phone.*)

MAMA   Look out there, girl, before you be spilling some of that stuff on that child!

TRAVIS   (*Teasing*) That's right—look out now!

(*He exits.*)

BENEATHA   (*Drily*) I can't imagine that it would hurt him—it has never hurt the roaches.

MAMA   Well, little boys' hides ain't as tough as Southside roaches.

WALTER   (*Into phone*) Hello—let me talk to Willy Harris.

MAMA   You better get over there behind the bureau. I seen one marching out of there like Napoleon yesterday.

WALTER   Hello, Willy? It ain't come yet. It'll be here in a few minutes. Did the lawyer give you the papers?

BENEATHA   There's really only one way to get rid of them, Mama—

MAMA   How?

BENEATHA   Set fire to this building.

WALTER   Good. Good. I'll be right over.

BENEATHA   Where did Ruth go, Walter?

WALTER   I don't know.

(*He exits abruptly.*)

BENEATHA   Mama, where did Ruth go?

MAMA   (*looking at her with meaning*) To the doctor, I think.

BENEATHA   The doctor? What's the matter? (*They exchange glances*) You don't think—

MAMA   (*With her sense of drama*) Now I ain't saying what I think. But I ain't never been wrong 'bout a woman neither.

(*The phone rings.*)

BENEATHA   (*At the phone*) Hay-lo . . . (*Pause, and a moment of recognition.*) Well—when did you get back! . . . And how was it? . . . Of course I missed you—in my way . . . This morning? No . . . house cleaning and all that and Mama hates it if I let people come over when the house is like this . . . You *have?* Well, that's different . . . What is it—Oh, what the hell, come on over . . . Right, see you then.

(*She hangs up.*)

MAMA   (*Who has listened vigorously, as is her habit*) Who is that you inviting over here with this house looking like this? You ain't got the pride you was born with!

BENEATHA   Asagai doesn't care how houses look, Mama—he's an intellectual.

MAMA   *Who?*

BENEATHA   Asagai—Joseph Asagai. He's an African boy I met on campus. He's been studying in Canada all summer.

MAMA   What's his name?

BENEATHA Asagai, Joseph. Ah-sah-guy . . . He's from Nigeria.

MAMA Oh, that's the little country that was founded by slaves way back . . .

BENEATHA No, Mama—that's Liberia.

MAMA I don't think I never met no African before.

BENEATHA Well, do me a favor and don't ask him a whole lot of ignorant questions about Africans. I mean, do they wear clothes and all that—

MAMA Well, now, I guess if you think we so ignorant 'round here maybe you shouldn't bring your friends here—

BENEATHA It's just that people ask such crazy things. All anyone seems to know about when it comes to Africa is Tarzan—

MAMA (Indignantly) Why should I know anything about Africa?

BENEATHA Why do you give money at church for the missionary work?

MAMA Well, that's to help save people.

BENEATHA You mean save them from heathenism—

MAMA (Innocently) Yes.

BENEATHA I'm afraid they need more salvation from the British and the French.

(RUTH comes in forlornly and pulls off her coat with dejection. They both turn to look at her.)

RUTH (Dispiritedly) Well, I guess from all the happy faces—everybody knows.

BENEATHA You pregnant?

MAMA Lord have mercy, I sure hope it's a little old girl. Travis ought to have a sister.

(BENEATHA and RUTH give her a hopeless look for this grandmotherly enthusiasm.)

BENEATHA How far along are you?

RUTH Two months.

BENEATHA Did you mean to? I mean did you plan it or was it an accident?

MAMA What do you know about planning or not planning?

BENEATHA Oh, Mama.

RUTH (Wearily) She's twenty years old, Lena.

BENEATHA Did you plan it, Ruth?

RUTH Mind your own business.

BENEATHA It is my business—where is he going to live, on the roof? (There is silence following the remark as the three women react to the sense of it) Gee—I didn't mean that, Ruth, honest. Gee, I don't feel like that at all. I—I think it is wonderful.

RUTH (Dully) Wonderful.

BENEATHA Yes—really.

MAMA (Looking at RUTH, worried) Doctor say everything going to be all right?

RUTH (Far away) Yes—she says everything is going to be fine . . .

MAMA (Immediately suspicious) "She"—What doctor you went to?

(RUTH folds over, near hysteria.)

     (Worriedly hovering over RUTH) Ruth honey—what's the matter with you—you sick?

(RUTH has her fists clenched on her thighs and is fighting hard to suppress a scream that seems to be rising in her.)

BENEATHA   What's the matter with her, Mama?

MAMA   (*Working her fingers in* RUTH's *shoulder to relax her*) She be all right. Women gets right depressed sometimes when they get her way. (*Speaking softly, expertly, rapidly*) Now you just relax. That's right . . . just lean back, don't think 'bout nothing at all . . . nothing at all—

RUTH   I'm all right . . .

(*The glassy-eyed look melts and then she collapses into a fit of heavy sobbing. The bell rings.*)

BENEATHA   Oh, my God—that must be Asagai.

MAMA   (*To* RUTH) Come on now, honey. You need to lie down and rest awhile . . . then have some nice hot food.

(*They exit,* RUTH's *weight on her mother-in-law.* BENEATHA, *herself profoundly disturbed, opens the door to admit a rather dramatic-looking young man with a large package.*)

ASAGAI   Hello, Alaiyo—

BENEATHA   (*Holding the door open and regarding him with pleasure*) Hello . . . (*Long pause*) Well—come in. And please excuse everything. My mother was very upset about my letting anyone come here with the place like this.

ASAGAI   (*Coming into the room*) You look disturbed too . . . Is something wrong?

BENEATHA   (*Still at the door, absently*) Yes . . . we've all got acute ghetto-itus. (*She smiles and comes toward him, finding a cigarette and sitting*) So—sit down! How was Canada?

ASAGAI   (*A sophisticate*) Canadian.

BENEATHA   (*Looking at him*) I'm very glad you are back.

ASAGAI   (*Looking back at her in turn*) Are you really?

BENEATHA   Yes—very.

ASAGAI   Why—you were quite glad when I went away. What happened?

BENEATHA   You went away.

ASAGAI   Ahhhhhhhh.

BENEATHA   Before—you wanted to be so serious before there was time.

ASAGAI   How much time must there be before one knows what one feels?

BENEATHA   (*Stalling this particular conversation. Her hands pressed together, in a deliberately childish gesture*) What did you bring me?

ASAGAI   (*Handing her the package*) Open it and see.

BENEATHA   (*Eagerly opening the package and drawing out some records and the colorful robes of a Nigerian woman*) Oh, Asagai! You got them for me! . . . How beautiful . . . and the records too! (*She lifts out the robes and runs to the mirror with them and holds the drapery up in front of herself*)

ASAGAI   (*Coming to her at the mirror*) I shall have to teach you how to drape it properly. (*He flings the material about her for the moment and stands back to look at her*) Ah—Oh-pay-gay-day, oh-gbah-mu-shay. (*A Yoruba exclamation for admiration*) You wear it well . . . very well . . . mutilated hair and all.

BENEATHA   (*Turning suddenly*) My hair—what's wrong with my hair?

ASAGAI   (*Shrugging*) Were you born with it like that?

BENEATHA   (*Reaching up to touch it*) No . . . of course not.

(*She looks back to the mirror, disturbed.*)

ASAGAI   (*Smiling*) How then?

BENEATHA   You know perfectly well how . . . as crinkly as yours . . . that's how.

ASAGAI   And it is ugly to you that way?

BENEATHA   (*Quickly*) Oh, no—not ugly . . . (*More slowly, apologetically*) But it's so hard to manage when it's, well—raw.

ASAGAI   And so to accommodate that—you mutilate it every week?

BENEATHA   It's not mutilation!

ASAGAI   (*Laughing aloud at her seriousness*) Oh . . . please! I am only teasing you because you are so very serious about these things. (*He stands back from her and folds his arms across his chest as he watches her pulling at her hair and frowning in the mirror*) Do you remember the first time you met me at school? . . . (*He laughs*) You came up to me and said—and I thought you were the most serious little thing I had ever seen—you said: (*He imitates her*) "Mr. Asagai—I want very much to talk with you. About Africa. You see, Mr. Asagai, I am looking for my *identity!*"
(*He laughs.*)

BENEATHA   (*Turning to him, not laughing*) Yes—
(*Her face is quizzical, profoundly disturbed.*)

ASAGAI   (*Still teasing and reaching out and taking her face in his hands and turning her profile to him*) Well . . . it is true that this is not so much a pro-file of a Hollywood queen as perhaps a queen of the Nile—(*A mock dis-missal of the importance of the question*) But what does it matter? Assimila-tionism is so popular in your country.

BENEATHA   (*Wheeling, passionately, sharply*) I am not an assimilationist!

ASAGAI   (*The protest hangs in the room for a moment and* ASAGAI *studies her, his laughter fading.*) Such a serious one. (*There is a pause*) So—you like the robes? You must take excellent care of them—they are from my sister's personal wardrobe.

BENEATHA   (*With incredulity*) You—you sent all the way home—for me?

ASAGAI   (*With charm*) For you—I would do much more . . . Well, that is what I came for. I must go.

BENEATHA   Will you call me Monday?

ASAGAI   Yes . . . We have a great deal to talk about. I mean about identity and time and all that.

BENEATHA   Time?

ASAGAI   Yes. About how much time one needs to know what one feels.

BENEATHA   You never understood that there is more than one kind of feeling which can exist between a man and a woman—or, at least, there should be.

ASAGAI   (*Shaking his head negatively but gently*) No. Between a man and a woman there need be only one kind of feeling. I have that for you . . . Now even . . . right this moment . . .

BENEATHA   I know—and by itself—it won't do. I can find that anywhere.

ASAGAI   For a woman it should be enough.

BENEATHA   I know—because that's what it says in all the novels that men write. But it isn't. Go ahead and laugh—but I'm not interested in being someone's little episode in America or—(*With feminine vengeance*)—one of them! (ASAGAI *has burst into laughter again*) That's funny as hell, huh!

ASAGAI It's just that every American girl I have known has said that to me. White—black—in this you are all the same. And the same speech, too!

BENEATHA (*Angrily*) Yuk, yuk, yuk!

ASAGAI It's how you can be sure that the world's most liberated women are not liberated at all. You all talk about it too much!

(MAMA *enters and is immediately all social charm because of the presence of a guest.*)

BENEATHA Oh—Mama—this is Mr. Asagai.

MAMA How do you do?

ASAGAI (*Total politeness to an elder*) How do you do, Mrs. Younger. Please forgive me for coming at such an outrageous hour on a Saturday.

MAMA Well, you are quite welcome. I just hope you understand that our house don't always look like this. (*Chatterish*) You must come again. I would love to hear all about—(*Not sure of the name*)—your country. I think it's so sad the way our American Negroes don't know nothing about Africa 'cept Tarzan and all that. And all that money they pour into these churches when they ought to be helping you people over there drive out them French and Englishmen done taken away your land.

(*The mother flashes a slightly superior look at her daughter upon completion of the recitation.*)

ASAGAI (*Taken aback by this sudden and acutely unrelated expression of sympathy*) Yes . . . yes . . .

MAMA (*Smiling at him suddenly and relaxing and looking him over*) How many miles is it from here to where you come from?

ASAGAI Many thousands.

MAMA (*Looking at him as she would* WALTER) I bet you don't half look after yourself, being away from your mama either. I spec you better come 'round here from time to time and get yourself some decent homecooked meals.

ASAGAI (*Moved*) Thank you. Thank you very much. (*They are all quiet, then—*) Well . . . I must go. I will call you Monday, Alaiyo.

MAMA What's that he call you?

ASAGAI Oh—"Alaiyo." I hope you don't mind. It is what you would call a nickname, I think. It is a Yoruba word. I am a Yoruba.

MAMA (*Looking at* BENEATHA) I—I thought he was from—

ASAGAI (*Understanding*) Nigeria is my country. Yoruba is my tribal origin—

BENEATHA You didn't tell us what Alaiyo means . . . for all I know, you might be calling me Little Idiot or something . . .

ASAGAI Well . . . let me see . . . I do not know how just to explain it . . . The sense of a thing can be so different when it changes languages.

BENEATHA You're evading.

ASAGAI No—really it is difficult . . . (*Thinking*) It means . . . it means One for Whom Bread—Food—Is Not Enough (*He looks at her*) Is that all right?

BENEATHA (*Understanding, softly*) Thank you.

MAMA (*Looking from one to the other and not understanding any of it*) Well . . . that's nice . . . You must come see us again—Mr.—

ASAGAI Ah-sah-guy . . .

MAMA Yes . . . Do come again.

ASAGAI Good-bye.

(He exits.)

MAMA (After him) Lord, that's a pretty thing just went out here! (insinuatingly, to her daughter) Yes, I guess I see why we done commence to get so interested in Africa 'round here. Missionaries my aunt Jenny!

(She exits.)

BENEATHA Oh, Mama! . . .

(She picks up the Nigerian dress and holds it up to her in front of the mirror again. She sets the headdress on haphazardly and then notices her hair again and clutches at it and then replaces the headdress and frowns at herself. Then she starts to wriggle in front of the mirror as she thinks a Nigerian woman might. TRAVIS enters and regards her.)

TRAVIS You cracking up?

BENEATHA Shut up.

(She pulls the headdress off and looks at herself in the mirror and clutches at her hair again and squinches her eyes as if trying to imagine something. Then, suddenly, she gets her raincoat and kerchief and hurriedly prepares for going out.)

MAMA (Coming back into the room) She's resting now. Travis, baby, run next door and ask Miss Johnson to please let me have a little kitchen cleanser. This here can is empty as Jacob's kettle.

TRAVIS I just came in.

MAMA Do as you told. (He exits and she looks at her daughter.) Where are you going?

BENEATHA (Halting at the door) To become a queen of the Nile!

(She exits in a breathless blaze of glory. RUTH appears in the bedroom doorway.)

MAMA Who told you to get up?

RUTH Ain't nothing wrong with me to be lying in no bed for. Where did Bennie go?

MAMA (Drumming her fingers) Far as I could make out—to Egypt. (RUTH just looks at her) What time is it getting to?

RUTH Ten twenty. And the mailman going to ring that bell this morning like he done every morning for the last umpteen years.

(TRAVIS comes in with the cleanser can.)

TRAVIS She say to tell you that she don't have much.

MAMA (Angrily) Lord, some people I could name sure is tight-fisted! (Directing her grandson) Mark two cans of cleanser down on the list there. If she that hard up for kitchen cleanser, I sure don't want to forget to get her none!

RUTH Lena—maybe the woman is just short on cleanser—

MAMA (Not listening) —Much baking powder as she done borrowed from me all these years, she could of done gone into the baking business!

(The bell sounds suddenly and sharply and all three are stunned—serious and silent—mid-speech. In spite of all the other conversations and distractions of the morning, this is what they have been waiting for, even TRAVIS, who looks helplessly from his mother to his grandmother. RUTH is the first to come to life again.)

RUTH (To TRAVIS) *Get down them steps, boy!*

(TRAVIS snaps to life and flies out to get the mail.)

MAMA (Her eyes wide, her hand to her breast) You mean it done really come?

RUTH   (*Excited*) Oh, Miss Lena!

MAMA   (*Collecting herself*) Well . . . I don't know what we all so excited about 'round here for. We known it was coming for months.

RUTH   That's a whole lot different from having it come and being able to hold it in your hands . . . a piece of paper worth ten thousand dollars . . . (TRAVIS *bursts back into the room. He holds the envelope high above his head, like a little dancer, his face is radiant and he is breathless. He moves to his grandmother with sudden slow ceremony and puts the envelope into her hands. She accepts it, and then merely holds it and looks at it*) Come on! Open it . . . Lord have mercy, I wish Walter Lee was here!

TRAVIS   Open it, Grandmama!

MAMA   (*Staring at it*) Now you all be quiet. It's just a check.

RUTH   Open it . . .

MAMA   (*Still staring at it*) Now don't act silly . . . We ain't never been no people to act silly 'bout no money—

RUTH (*Swiftly*) We ain't never had none before—*open it!*

(MAMA *finally makes a good strong tear and pulls out the thin blue slice of paper and inspects it closely. The boy and his mother study it raptly over* MAMA's *shoulders.*)

MAMA   *Travis!* (*She is counting off with doubt*) Is that the right number of zeros?

TRAVIS   Yes'm . . . ten thousand dollars. Gaalee, Grandmama, you rich.

MAMA   (*She holds the check away from her, still looking at it. Slowly her face sobers into a mask of unhappiness*) Ten thousand dollars. (*She hands it to* RUTH) Put it away somewhere, Ruth. (*She does not look at* RUTH; *her eyes seem to be seeing something somewhere very far off*) Ten thousand dollars they give you. Ten thousand dollars.

TRAVIS   (*To his mother, sincerely*) What's the matter with Grandmama—don't she want to be rich?

RUTH   (*Distractedly*) You go on out and play now, baby. (TRAVIS *exits.* MAMA *starts wiping dishes absently, humming intently to herself.* RUTH *turns to her, with kind exasperation*) You've gone and got yourself upset.

MAMA   (*Not looking at her*) I spec if it wasn't for you all . . . I would just put that money away or give it to the church or something.

RUTH   Now what kind of talk is that. Mr. Younger would just be plain mad if he could hear you talking foolish like that.

MAMA   (*Stopping and starting off*) Yes . . . he sure would. (*Sighing*) We got enough to do with that money, all right. (*She halts then, and turns and looks at her daughter-in-law hard;* RUTH *avoids her eyes and* MAMA *wipes her hands with finality and starts to speak firmly to* RUTH) Where did you go today, girl?

RUTH   To the doctor.

MAMA   (*Impatiently*) Now, Ruth . . . you know better than that. Old Doctor Jones is strange enough in his way but there ain't nothing 'bout him make somebody slip and call him "she"—like you done this morning.

RUTH   Well, that's what happened—my tongue slipped.

MAMA   You went to see that woman, didn't you?

RUTH   (*Defensively, giving herself away*) What woman you talking about?

MAMA (*Angrily*) That woman who—

(WALTER *enters in great excitement.*)

WALTER Did it come?

MAMA (*Quietly*) Can't you give people a Christian greeting before you start asking about money?

WALTER (*To* RUTH) Did it come? (RUTH *unfolds the check and lays it quietly before him, watching him intently with thoughts of her own.* WALTER *sits down and grasps it close and counts off the zeroes.*) Ten thousand dollars—(*He turns suddenly, frantically to his mother and draws some papers out of his breast pocket*) Mama—look. Old Willy Harris put everything on paper—

MAMA Son—I think you ought to talk to your wife . . . I'll go on out and leave you alone if you want—

WALTER I can talk to her later—Mama, look—

MAMA Son—

WALTER WILL SOMEBODY PLEASE LISTEN TO ME TODAY!

MAMA (*Quietly*) I don't 'low no yellin' in this house, Walter Lee, and you know it—(WALTER *stares at them in frustration and starts to speak several times*) And there ain't going to be no investing in no liquor stores. I don't aim to have to speak on that again.

(*A long pause.*)

WALTER Oh—so you don't aim to have to speak on that again? So *you* have decided . . . (*Crumpling his papers*) Well, *you* tell that to my boy tonight when you put him to sleep on the living-room couch . . . (*Turning to* MAMA *and speaking directly to her*) Yeah—and tell it to my wife, Mama, when she has to go out of here to look after somebody else's kids. And tell it to *me*, Mama, every time we need a new pair of curtains and I have to watch *you* go out and work in somebody's kitchen. Yeah, you tell me then!

(WALTER *starts out.*)

RUTH Where you going?

WALTER I'm going out!

RUTH Where?

WALTER Just out of this house somewhere—

RUTH (*Getting her coat*) I'll come too.

WALTER I don't want you to come!

RUTH I got something to talk to you about, Walter.

WALTER That's too bad.

MAMA (*Still quietly*) Walter Lee—(*She waits and he finally turns and looks at her*) Sit down.

WALTER I'm a grown man, Mama.

MAMA Ain't nobody said you wasn't grown. But you still in my house and my presence. And as long as you are—you'll talk to your wife civil. Now sit down.

RUTH (*Suddenly*) Oh, let him go on out and drink himself to death! He makes me sick to my stomach! (*She flings her coat against him.*)

WALTER (*Violently*) And you turn mine too, baby! (RUTH *goes into their bedroom and slams the door behind her.*) That was my greatest mistake—

MAMA   (*Still quietly*) Walter, what is the matter with you?

WALTER   Matter with me? Ain't nothing the matter with *me!*

MAMA   Yes there is. Something eating you up like a crazy man. Something more than me not giving you this money. The past few years I been watching it happen to you. You get all nervous acting and kind of wild in the eyes— (WALTER *jumps up impatiently at her words*) I said sit there now, I'm talking to you!

WALTER   Mama—I don't need no nagging at me today.

MAMA   Seem like you getting to a place where you always tied up in some kind of knot about something. But if anybody ask you 'bout it you just yell at 'em and bust out the house and go out and drink somewheres. Walter Lee, people can't live with that. Ruth's a good, patient girl in her way—but you getting to be too much. Boy, don't make the mistake of driving that girl away from you.

WALTER   Why—what she do for me?

MAMA   She loves you.

WALTER   Mama—I'm going out. I want to go off somewhere and be by myself for a while.

MAMA   I'm sorry 'bout your liquor store, son. It just wasn't the thing for us to do. That's what I want to tell you about—

WALTER   I got to go out, Mama—

(*He rises.*)

MAMA   It's dangerous, son.

WALTER   What's dangerous?

MAMA   When a man goes outside his home to look fo peace.

WALTER   (*Beseechingly*) Then why can't there never be no peace in this house then?

MAMA   You done found it in some other house?

WALTER   No—there ain't no woman! Why do women always think there's a woman somewhere when a man gets restless. (*Coming to her*) Mama—Mama—I want so many things . . .

MAMA   Yes, son—

WALTER   I want so many things that they are driving me kind of crazy . . . Mama—look at me.

MAMA   I'm looking at you. You a good-looking boy. You got a job, a nice wife, a fine boy and—

WALTER   A job. (*Looks at her*) Mama, a job? I open and close car doors all day long. I drive a man around in his limousine and I say, "Yes, sir; no, sir; very good, sir; shall I take the Drive, sir?" Mama, that ain't no kind of job . . . that ain't nothing at all. (*Very quietly*) Mama, I don't know if I can make you understand.

MAMA   Understand what, baby?

WALTER   (*Quietly*) Sometimes it's like I can see the future stretched out in front of me—just plain as day. The future, Mama. Hanging over there at the edge of my days. Just waiting for me—a big, looming blank space—full of *nothing.* Just waiting for *me.* (*Pause*) Mama—sometimes when I'm downtown and I pass them cool, quiet-looking restaurants where them white boys are sitting back and talking 'bout things . . . sitting there turning deals worth millions of dollars . . . sometimes I see guys don't look much older than me—

MAMA Son— how come you talk so much 'bout money?

WALTER (*With immense passion*) Because it is life, Mama!

MAMA (*Quietly*) Oh—(*Very quietly*) So now it's life. Money is life. Once upon a time freedom used to be life—now it's money. I guess the world really do change . . .

WALTER No—it was always money, Mama. We just didn't know about it.

MAMA No . . . something has changed. (*She looks at him*) You something new, boy. In my time we was worried about not being lynched and getting to the North if we could and how to stay alive and still have a pinch of dignity too . . . Now here come you and Beneatha—talking 'bout things we ain't never even thought about hardly, me and your daddy. You ain't satisfied or proud of nothing we done. I mean that you had a home; that we kept you out of trouble till you was grown; that you don't have to ride to work on the back of nobody's streetcar— You my children—but how different we done become.

WALTER You just don't understand, Mama, you just don't understand.

MAMA Son—do you know your wife is expecting another baby? (WALTER *stands, stunned, and absorbs what his mother has said*) That's what she wanted to talk to you about. (WALTER *sinks down into a chair*) This ain't for me to be telling—but you ought to know. (*She waits*) I think Ruth is thinking 'bout getting rid of that child.

WALTER (*Slowly understanding*) No — no — Ruth wouldn't do that.

MAMA When the world gets ugly enough—a woman will do anything for her family. *The part that's already living.*

WALTER You don't know Ruth, Mama, if you think she would do that.

(RUTH *opens the bedroom door and stands there a little limp.*)

RUTH (*Beaten*) Yes I would too, Walter. (*Pause*) I gave her a five-dollar down payment.

(*There is total silence as the man stares at his wife and the mother stares at her son.*)

MAMA (*Presently*) Well — (*Tightly*) Well — son, I'm waiting to hear you say something . . . I'm waiting to hear how you be your father's son. Be the man he was . . . (*Pause*) Your wife say she going to destroy your child. And I'm waiting to hear you talk like him and say we a people who give children life, not who destroys them—(*She rises.*) I'm waiting to see you stand up and look like your daddy and say we done give up one baby to poverty and that we ain't going to give up nary another one . . . I'm waiting.

WALTER Ruth—

MAMA If you a son of mine, tell her! (WALTER *turns, looks at her and can say nothing. She continues, bitterly*) You . . . you are a disgrace to your father's memory. Somebody get me my hat.

Curtain

ACT II

SCENE ONE

TIME
Later the same day.

AT RISE
RUTH *is ironing again. She has the radio going. Presently* BENEATHA's *bedroom door opens and* RUTH's *mouth falls and she puts down the iron in fascination.*

RUTH What have we got on tonight!

BENEATHA (*Emerging grandly from the doorway so that we can see her thoroughly robed in the costume Asagai brought*) You are looking at what a well-dressed Nigerian woman wears—(*She parades for* RUTH, *her hair completely hidden by the headdress; she is coquettishly fanning herself with an ornate oriental fan, mistakenly more like Butterfly than any Nigerian that ever was*) Isn't it beautiful? (*She promenades to the radio and, with an arrogant flourish, turns off the good loud blues that is playing*) Enough of this assimilationist junk! (RUTH *follows her with her eyes as she goes to the phonograph and puts on a record and turns and waits ceremoniously for the music to come up. Then, with a shout—*) OCOMOGOSIAY!

(RUTH *jumps. The music comes up, a lovely Nigerian melody.* BENEATHA *listens enraptured, her eyes far away—"back to the past." She begins to dance.* RUTH *is dumbfounded.*)

RUTH What kind of dance is that?

BENEATHA A folk dance.

RUTH (*Pearl Bailey*) What kind of folks do that, honey?

BENEATHA It's from Nigeria. It's a dance of welcome.

RUTH Who you welcoming?

BENEATHA The men back to the village.

RUTH Where they been?

BENEATHA How should I know—out hunting or something. Anyway, they are coming back now . . .

RUTH Well, that's good.

BENEATHA (*With the record*)

Alundi, alundi
Alundi alunya
Jop pu a jeepua
Ang gu sooooooooooo

Ai yai yae . . .
Ayehaye—alundi . . .

(WALTER *comes in during this performance; he has obviously been drinking. He leans against the door heavily and watches his sister, at first with distaste. Then his eyes look off—"back to the past"—as he lifts both his fists to the roof screaming.*)

WALTER YEAH . . . AND ETHIOPIA STRETCH FORTH HER HANDS AGAIN!. . .

RUTH (*Drily, looking at him*) Yes—and Africa sure is claiming her own tonight. (*She gives them both up and starts ironing again*)

WALTER (*All in a drunken, dramatic shout*) Shut up! . . . I'm digging them drums . . . them drums move me! . . . (*He makes his weaving way to his wife's face and leans in close to her*) In my *heart of hearts*—(*He thumps his chest*)—I am much warrior!

RUTH (*Without even looking up*) In your heart of hearts you are much drunkard.

WALTER (*Coming away from her and starting to wander around the room, shouting*) Me and Jomo . . . (*Intently, in his sister's face. She has stopped dancing to watch him in this unknown mood*) That's my man, Kenyatta. (*Shouting and thumping his chest*) FLAMING SPEAR! HOT DAMN! (*He is suddenly in posession of an imaginary spear and actively spearing enemies all over the room*) OCOMOGOSIAY . . . THE LION IS WAKING . . .OWIMO-WEH! (*He pulls his shirt open and leaps up on a table and gestures with his spear. The bell rings. RUTH goes to answer*)

BENEATHA (*To encourage WALTER, thoroughly caught up with this side of him*) OCOMOGOSIAY, FLAMING SPEAR!

WALTER (*On the table, very far gone, his eyes pure glass sheets. He sees what we cannot, that he is a leader of his people, a great chief, a descendant of Chaka, and that the hour to march has come*) Listen, my black brothers—

BENEATHA OCOMOGOSIAY!

WALTER —Do you hear the waters rushing against the shores of the coast-lands—

BENEATHA OCOMOGOSIAY!

WALTER —Do you hear the screeching of the cocks in yonder hills beyond where the chiefs meet in council for the coming of the mighty war—

BENEATHA OCOMOGOSIAY!

WALTER —Do you hear the beating of the wings of the birds flying low over the mountains and the low places of our land—

(RUTH *opens the door.* GEORGE MURCHISON *enters.*)

BENEATHA OCOMOGOSIAY!

WALTER —Do you hear the singing of the women, singing the war songs of our fathers to the babies in the great houses . . . singing the sweet war songs? OH, DO YOU HEAR, MY BLACK BROTHERS!

BENEATHA (*Completely gone*) We hear you, Flaming Spear—

WALTER Telling us to prepare for the greatness of the time—(*To* GEORGE) Black Brother!

(*He extends his hand for the fraternal clasp.*)

GEORGE Black Brother, hell!

RUTH (*Having had enough, and embarrassed for the family*) Beneatha, you got company—what's the matter with you? Walter Lee Younger, get down off that table and stop acting like a fool . . .

(WALTER *comes down off the table suddenly and makes a quick exit to the bathroom.*)

RUTH He's had a little to drink . . . I don't know what her excuse is.

GEORGE (*To* BENEATHA) Look honey, we're going *to* the theatre—we're not going to be *in* it . . . so go change, huh?

RUTH You expect this boy to go out with you looking like that?

BENEATHA (*Looking at* GEORGE) That's up to George. If he's ashamed of his heritage—

GEORGE Oh, don't be so proud of yourself, Bennie—just because you look eccentric.

BENEATHA How can something that's natural be eccentric?

GEORGE That's what being eccentric means—being natural. Get dressed.

BENEATHA I don't like that, George.

RUTH Why must you and your brother make an argument out of everything people say?

BENEATHA Because I hate assimilationist Negroes!

RUTH Will somebody please tell me what assimila-who-ever means!

GEORGE Oh, it's just a college girl's way of calling people Uncle Toms—but that isn't what it means at all.

RUTH Well, what does it mean?

BENEATHA (*Cutting* GEORGE *off and staring at him as she replies to* RUTH) It means someone who is willing to give up his own culture and submerge himself completely in the dominant, and in this case, *oppressive* culture!

GEORGE Oh, dear, dear, dear! Here we go! A lecture on the African past! On our Great West African Heritage! In one second we will hear all about the great Ashanti empires; the great Songhay civilizations; and the great sculpture of Bénin—and then some poetry in the Bantu—and the whole monologue will end with the word *heritage!* (*Nastily*) Let's face it, baby, your heritage is nothing but a bunch of raggedy-assed spirituals and some grass huts!

BENEATHA *Grass huts!* (RUTH *crosses to her and forcibly pushes her toward the bedroom*) See there . . . you are standing there in your splendid ignorance talking about people who were the first to smelt iron on the face of the earth! (RUTH *is pushing her through the door*) The Ashanti were performing surgical operations when the English—(RUTH *pulls the door to, with* BENEATHA *on the other side, and smiles graciously at* GEORGE. BENEATHA *opens the door and shouts the end of the sentence defiantly at* GEORGE)— were still tatooing themselves with blue dragons . . . (*She goes back inside*)

RUTH Have a seat, George. (*They both sit.* RUTH *folds her hands rather primly on her lap, determined to demonstrate the civilization of the family*) Warm, ain't it? I mean for September. (*Pause*) Just like they always say about Chicago weather: If it's too hot or cold for you, just wait a minute and it'll change. (*She smiles happily at this cliché of clichés*) Everybody say it's got to do with them bombs and things they keep setting off. (*Pause*) Would you like a nice cold beer?

GEORGE No, thank you. I don't care for beer. (*He looks at his watch*) I hope she hurries up.

RUTH What time is the show?

GEORGE It's an eight-thirty curtain. That's just Chicago, though. In New York standard curtain time is eight forty.

(*He is rather proud of this knowledge.*)

RUTH (*Properly appreciating it*) You get to New York a lot?

GEORGE (*Offhand*) Few times a year.

RUTH   Oh—that's nice. I've never been to New York.

(WALTER *enters. We feel he has relieved himself, but the edge of unreality is still with him.*)

WALTER   New York ain't got nothing Chicago ain't. Just a bunch of hustling people all squeezed up together—being "Eastern."

(*He turns his face into a screw of displeasure.*)

GEORGE   Oh—you've been?

WALTER   *Plenty* of times.

RUTH   (*Shocked at the lie*) Walter Lee Younger!

WALTER   (*Staring her down*) Plenty! (*Pause*) What we got to drink in this house? Why don't you offer this man some refreshment. (*To* GEORGE) They don't know how to entertain people in this house, man.

GEORGE   Thank you—I don't really care for anything.

WALTER   (*Feeling his head; sobriety coming*) Where's Mama?

RUTH   She ain't come back yet.

WALTER   (*Looking* MURCHISON *over from head to toe, scrutinizing his carefully casual tweed sports jacket over cashmere V-neck sweater over soft eyelet shirt and tie, and soft slacks, finished off with white buckskin shoes*) Why all you college boys wear them fairyish-looking white shoes?

RUTH   Walter Lee!

(GEORGE MURCHISON *ignores the remark.*)

WALTER   (*To* RUTH) Well, they look crazy as hell—white shoes, cold as it is.

RUTH   (*Crushed*) You have to excuse him—

WALTER   No he don't! Excuse me for what? What you always excusing me for! I'll excuse myself when I needs to be excused! (*A pause*) They look as funny as them black knee socks Beneatha wears out of here all the time.

RUTH   It's the college *style,* Walter.

WALTER   Style, hell. She looks like she got burnt legs or something!

RUTH   Oh, Walter—

WALTER   (*An irritable mimic*) Oh, Walter! Oh, Walter! (*To* MURCHISON) How's your old man making out? I understand you'll be going to buy that big hotel on the Drive? (*He finds a beer in the refrigerator, wanders over to* MURCHISON, *sipping and wiping his lips with the back of his hand, and straddling a chair backwards to talk to the other man*) Shrewd move. Your old man is all right, man. (*Tapping his head and half winking for emphasis*) I mean he knows how to operate. I mean he thinks *big,* you know what I mean, I mean for a *home,* you know? But I think he's kind of running out of ideas now. I'd like to talk to him. Listen, man, I got some plans that could turn this city upside down. I mean I think like he does. *Big.* Invest big, gamble big, hell, lose *big* if you have to, you know what I mean. It's hard to find a man on this whole Southside who understands my kind of thinking—you dig? (*He scrutinizes* MURCHISON *again, drinks his beer, squints his eyes and leans in close, confidential, man to man*) Me and you ought to sit down and talk sometimes, man. Man, I got me some ideas . . .

MURCHISON   (*With boredom*) Yeah—sometimes we'll have to do that, Walter.

WALTER   (*Understanding the indifference, and offended*) Yeah—well, when you got the time, man. I know you a busy little boy.

RUTH Walter, please—

WALTER (*Bitterly, hurt*) I know ain't nothing in this world as busy as you colored college boys with your fraternity pins and white shoes . . .

RUTH (*Covering her face with humiliation*) Oh, Walter Lee—

WALTER I see you all all the time—with the books tucked under your arms—going to your (*British A—a mimic*) "clahsses." And for what! What the hell you learning over there? Filling up your heads— (*Counting off on his fingers*) —with the sociology and the psychology—but they teaching you how to be a man? How to take over and run the world? They teaching you how to run a rubber plantation or a steel mill? Naw—just to talk proper and read books and wear white shoes . . .

GEORGE (*Looking at him with distaste, a little above it all*) You're all wacked up with bitterness, man.

WALTER (*Intently, almost quietly, between the teeth, glaring at the boy*) And you—ain't you bitter, man? Ain't you just about had it yet? Don't you see no stars gleaming that you can't reach out and grab? You happy?—You contented son-of-a-bitch—you happy? You got it made? Bitter? Man, I'm a volcano. Bitter? Here I am a giant—surrounded by ants! Ants who can't even understand what it is the giant is talking about.

RUTH (*Passionately and suddenly*) Oh, Walter—ain't you with nobody!

WALTER (*Violently*) No! 'Cause ain't nobody with me! Not even my own mother!

RUTH Walter, that's a terrible thing to say!

(BENEATHA *enters, dressed for the evening in a cocktail dress and earrings.*)

GEORGE Well—hey, you look great.

BENEATHA Let's go, George. See you all later.

RUTH Have a nice time.

GEORGE Thanks. Good night. (*To* WALTER, *sarcastically*) Good night, *Prometheus.*

(BENEATHA *and* GEORGE *exit.*)

WALTER (*To* RUTH) Who is Prometheus?

RUTH I don't know. Don't worry about it.

WALTER (*In fury, pointing after* GEORGE) See there—they get to a point where they can't insult you man to man—they got to go talk about something ain't nobody never heard of!

RUTH How do you know it was an insult? (*To humor him*) Maybe Prometheus is a nice fellow.

WALTER Prometheus! I bet there ain't even no such thing! I bet that simple-minded clown—

RUTH Walter—

(*She stops what she is doing and looks at him.*)

WALTER (*Yelling*) Don't start!

RUTH Start what?

WALTER Your nagging! Where was I? Who was I with? How much money did I spend?

RUTH (*Plaintively*) Walter Lee—why don't we just try to talk about it . . .

WALTER (*Not listening*) I been out talking with people who understand me. People who care about the things I got on my mind.

RUTH (*Wearily*) I guess that means people like Willy Harris.

WALTER Yes, people like Willy Harris.

RUTH (*With a sudden flash of impatience*) Why don't you all just hurry up and go into the banking business and stop talking about it!

WALTER Why? You want to know why? 'Cause we all tied up in a race of people that don't know how to do nothing but moan, pray and have babies!

(*The line is too bitter even for him and he looks at her and sits down.*)

RUTH Oh, Walter . . . (*Softly*) Honey, why can't you stop fighting me?

WALTER (*Without thinking*) Who's fighting you? Who even cares about you?

(*This line begins the retardation of his mood.*)

RUTH Well—(*She waits a long time, and then with resignation starts to put away her things*) I guess I might as well go on to bed . . . (*More or less to herself*) I don't know where we lost it . . . but we have . . . (*Then to him*) I—I'm sorry about this new baby, Walter. I guess maybe I better go on and do what I started . . . I guess I just didn't realize how bad things was with us . . . I guess I just didn't really realize—(*She starts out to the bedroom and stops*) You want some hot milk?

WALTER Hot milk?

RUTH Yes—hot milk.

WALTER Why hot milk?

RUTH 'Cause after all that liquor you come home with you ought to have something hot in your stomach.

WALTER I don't want no milk.

RUTH You want some coffee then?

WALTER No, I don't want no coffee. I don't want nothing hot to drink. (*Almost plaintively*) Why you always trying to give me something to eat?

RUTH (*Standing and looking at him helplessly*) What else can I give you, Walter Lee Younger?

(*She stands and looks at him and presently turns to go out again. He lifts his head and watches her going away from him in a new mood which began to emerge when he asked her "Who cares about you?"*)

WALTER It's been rough, ain't it, baby? (*She hears and stops but does not turn around and he continues to her back*) I guess between two people there ain't never as much understood as folks generally thinks there is. I mean like between you and me—(*She turns to face him*) How we gets to the place where we scared to talk softness to each other. (*He waits, thinking hard himself*) Why you think it got to be like that? (*He is thoughtful, almost as a child would be*) Ruth, what is it gets into people ought to be close?

RUTH I don't know, honey. I think about it a lot.

WALTER On account of you and me, you mean? The way things are with us. The way something done come between us.

RUTH There ain't so much between us, Walter . . . Not when you come to me and try to talk to me. Try to be with me . . . a little even.

WALTER (*Total honesty*) Sometimes . . . sometimes . . . I don't even know how to try.

RUTH Walter—

WALTER Yes?

RUTH (*Coming to him, gently and with misgiving, but coming to him*) Honey . . . life don't have to be like this. I mean sometimes people can do things so that things are better . . . You remember how we used to talk when Travis was born . . . about the way we were going to live . . . the kind of house . . . (*She is stroking his head*) Well, it's all starting to slip away from us . . .

(MAMA *enters, and* WALTER *jumps up and shouts at her.*)

WALTER Mama, where have you been?

MAMA My—them steps is longer than they used to be. Whew! (*She sits down and ignores him*) How you feeling this evening, Ruth?

(RUTH *shrugs, disturbed some at having been prematurely interrupted and watching her husband knowingly.*)

WALTER Mama, where have you been all day?

MAMA (*Still ignoring him and leaning on the table and changing to more comfortable shoes*) Where's Travis?

RUTH I let him go out earlier and he ain't come back yet. Boy, is he going to get it!

WALTER Mama!

MAMA (*As if she has heard him for the first time*) Yes, son?

WALTER Where did you go this afternoon?

MAMA I went downtown to tend to some business that I had to tend to.

WALTER What kind of business?

MAMA You know better than to question me like a child, Brother.

WALTER (*Rising and bending over the table*) Where were you, Mama? (*Bringing his fists down and shouting*) Mama, you didn't go do something with that insurance money, something crazy?

(*The front door opens slowly, interrupting him, and* TRAVIS *peeks his head in, less than hopefully.*)

TRAVIS (*To his mother*) Mama, I—

RUTH "Mama I" nothing! You're going to get it, boy! Get on in that bedroom and get yourself ready!

TRAVIS But I—

MAMA Why don't you all never let the child explain hisself.

RUTH Keep out of it now, Lena.

(MAMA *clamps her lips together, and* RUTH *advances toward her son menacingly.*)

RUTH A thousand times I have told you not to go off like that—

MAMA (*Holding out her arms to her grandson*) Well—at least let me tell him something. I want him to be the first one to hear . . . Come here, Travis. (*The boy obeys, gladly*) Travis—(*She takes him by the shoulder and looks into his face*)—you know that money we got in the mail this morning?

TRAVIS Yes'm—

MAMA Well—what you think your grandmama gone and done with that money?

TRAVIS   I don't know, Grandmama.

MAMA   (*Putting her finger on his nose for emphasis*) She went out and she bought you a house! (*The explosion comes from* WALTER *at the end of the revelation and he jumps up and turns away from all of them in a fury.* MAMA *continues, to* TRAVIS) You glad about the house? It's going to be yours when you get to be a man.

TRAVIS   Yeah—I always wanted to live in a house.

MAMA   All right, gimme some sugar then—(TRAVIS *puts his arms around her neck as she watches her son over the boy's shoulder. Then, to* TRAVIS, *after the embrace*) Now when you say your prayers tonight, you thank God and your grandfather—'cause it was him who give you the house—in his way.

RUTH   (*Taking the boy from* MAMA *and pushing him toward the bedroom*) Now you get out of here and get ready for your beating.

TRAVIS   Aw, Mama—

RUTH   Get on in there—(*Closing the door behind him and turning radiantly to her mother-in-law*) So you went and did it!

MAMA   (*Quietly, looking at her son with pain*) Yes, I did.

RUTH   (*Raising both arms classically*) Praise God! (*Looks at* WALTER *a moment, who says nothing. She crosses rapidly to her husband*) Please, honey—let me be glad . . . you be glad too. (*She has laid her hands on his shoulders, but he shakes himself free of her roughly, without turning to face her*) Oh, Walter . . . a home . . . a home. (*She comes back to* MAMA) Well—where is it? How big is it? How much it going to cost?

MAMA   Well—

RUTH   When we moving?

MAMA   (*Smiling at her*) First of the month.

RUTH   (*Throwing back her head with jubilance*) Praise God!

MAMA   (*Tentatively, still looking at her son's back turned against her and* RUTH) It's—it's a nice house too . . . (*She cannot help speaking directly to him. An imploring quality in her voice, her manner, makes her almost like a girl now*) Three bedrooms—nice big one for you and Ruth. . . . Me and Beneatha still have to share our room, but Travis have one of his own—and (*With difficulty*) I figure if the—new baby—is a boy, we could get one of them double-decker outfits . . . And there's a yard with a little patch of dirt where I could maybe get to grow me a few flowers . . . And a nice big basement . . .

RUTH   Walter honey, be glad—

MAMA   (*Still to his back, fingering things on the table*) 'Course I don't want to make it sound fancier than it is . . . It's just a plain little old house—but it's made good and solid—and it will be *ours*. Walter Lee—it makes a difference in a man when he can walk on floors that belong to *him* . . .

RUTH   Where is it?

MAMA   (*Frightened at this telling*) Well—well—it's out there in Clybourne Park—

(RUTH's *radiance fades abruptly, and* WALTER *finally turns slowly to face his mother with incredulity and hostility.*)

RUTH   Where?

MAMA   (*Matter-of-factly*) Four o six Clybourne Street, Clybourne Park.

RUTH Clybourne Park? Mama, there ain't no colored people living in Clybourne Park.
MAMA (*Almost idiotically*) Well, I guess there's going to be some now.
WALTER (*Bitterly*) So that's the peace and comfort you went out and brought
for us today!
MAMA (*Raising her eyes to meet his finally*) Son—I just tried to find the nicest
place for the least amount of money for my family.
RUTH (*Trying to recover from the shock*) Well—well—'course I ain't one never
been 'fraid of no crackers, mind you—but—well, wasn't there no other
houses nowhere?
MAMA Them houses they put up for colored in them areas way out all seem
to cost twice as much as other houses. I did the best I could.
RUTH (*Struck senseless with the news, in its various degrees of goodness
and trouble, she sits a moment, her fists propping her chin in thought, and
then she starts to rise, bringing her fists down with vigor, the radiance spreading from cheek to cheek again*) Well—well!—All I can say is—if this is my time
in life—my time—to say good-bye—(*And she builds with momentum as she
starts to circle the room with an exuberant, almost tearfully happy release*)—
to these Goddamned cracking walls!—(*She pounds the walls*)—and these
marching roaches!—(*She wipes at an imaginary army of marching roaches*)
—and this cramped little closet which ain't now or never was no kitchen! . . .
then I say it loud and good, Hallelujah! and good-bye misery . . . I don't
never want to see your ugly face again! (*She laughs joyously, having practically destroyed the apartment, and flings her arms up and lets them come
down happily, slowly, reflectively, over her abdomen, aware for the first time
perhaps that the life therein pulses with happiness and not despair*) Lena?
MAMA (*Moved, watching her happiness*) Yes, honey?
RUTH (*Looking off*) Is there—is there a whole lot of sunlight?
MAMA (*Understanding*) Yes, child, there's a whole lot of sunlight.
(*Long pause.*)

RUTH (*Collecting herself and going to the door of the room* TRAVIS *is in*)
Well—I guess I better see 'bout Travis. (*To* MAMA) Lord, I sure don't feel like
whipping nobody today!
(*She exits.*)

MAMA (*The mother and son are left alone now and the mother waits a long
time, considering deeply, before she speaks*) Son—you—you understand
what I done, don't you? (WALTER *is silent and sullen*) I—I just seen my family
falling apart today . . . just falling to pieces in front of my eyes . . . We
couldn't of gone on like we was today. We was going backwards 'stead of
forwards—talking 'bout killing babies and wishing each other was dead . . .
When it gets like that in life—you just got to do something different, push on
out and do something bigger . . . (*She waits*) I wish you say something, son
. . . I wish you'd say how deep inside you you think I done the right thing—
WALTER (*Crossing slowly to his bedroom door and finally turning there and
speaking measuredly*) What you need me to say you done right for? *You* the
head of this family. You run our lives like you want to. It was your money

and you did what you wanted with it. So what you need for me to say it was all right for? (*Bitterly, to hurt her as deeply as he knows is possible*) So you butchered up a dream of mine—you—who always talking 'bout your children's dreams . . .

MAMA Walter Lee—

(*He just closes the door behind him. MAMA sits alone, thinking heavily.*)

Curtain

SCENE TWO

TIME
Friday night. A few weeks later.

AT RISE
Packing crates mark the intention of the family to move. BENEATHA and GEORGE come in, presumably from an evening out again.

GEORGE O.K. . . . O.K., whatever you say . . . (*They both sit on the couch. He tries to kiss her She moves away*) Look, we've had a nice evening; let's not spoil it, huh? . . .

(*He again turns her head and tries to nuzzle in and she turns away from him, not with distaste but with momentary lack of interest; in a mood to pursue what they were talking about.*)

BENEATHA I'm *trying* to talk to you.

GEORGE We always talk.

BENEATHA Yes—and I love to talk.

GEORGE (*Exasperated; rising*) I know it and I don't mind it sometimes . . . I want you to cut it out, see—The moody stuff, I mean. I don't like it. You're a nice-looking girl . . . all over. That's all you need, honey, forget the atmosphere. Guys aren't going to go for the atmosphere—they're going to go for what they see. Be glad for that. Drop the Garbo routine. It doesn't go with you. As for myself, I want a nice—(*Groping*)—simple (*Thoughtfully*)—sophisticated girl . . . not a poet—O.K.?

(*She rebuffs him again and he starts to leave.*)

BENEATHA Why are you angry?

GEORGE Because this is stupid! I don't go out with you to discuss the nature of "quiet desperation" or to hear all about your thoughts—because the world will go on thinking what it thinks regardless—

BENEATHA Then why read books? Why go to school?

GEORGE (*With artificial patience, counting on his fingers*) It's simple. You read books—to learn facts—to get grades—to pass the course—to get a degree. That's all—it has nothing to do with thoughts.

(*A long pause.*)

BENEATHA I see. (*A longer pause as she looks at him*) Good night, George.

(*GEORGE looks at her a little oddly, and starts to exit. He meets MAMA coming in.*)

GEORGE Oh—hello, Mrs. Younger.

MAMA   Hello, George, how you feeling?

GEORGE   Fine—fine, how are you?

MAMA   Oh, a little tired. You know them steps can get you after a day's work. You all have a nice time tonight?

GEORGE   Yes—a fine time. Well, good night.

MAMA   Good night. (*He exits.* MAMA *closes the door behind her*) Hello, honey. What you sitting like that for?

BENEATHA   I'm just sitting.

MAMA   Didn't you have a nice time?

BENEATHA   No.

MAMA   No? What's the matter?

BENEATHA   Mama, George is a fool—honest. (*She rises*)

MAMA   (*Hustling around unloading the packages she has entered with. She stops*) Is he, baby?

BENEATHA   Yes.

(BENEATHA *makes up* TRAVIS' *bed as she talks.*)

MAMA   You sure?

BENEATHA   Yes.

MAMA   Well—I guess you better not waste your time with no fools.

(BENEATHA *looks up at her mother, watching her put groceries in the refrigerator. Finally she gathers up her things and starts into the bedroom. At the door she stops and looks back at her mother.*)

BENEATHA   Mama—

MAMA   Yes, baby—

BENEATHA   Thank you.

MAMA   For what?

BENEATHA   For understanding me this time.

(*She exits quickly and the mother stands, smiling a little, looking at the place where* BENEATHA *just stood.* RUTH *enters.*)

RUTH   Now don't you fool with any of this stuff, Lena—

MAMA   Oh, I just thought I'd sort a few things out.

(*The phone rings.* RUTH *answers.*)

RUTH   (*At the phone*) Hello—Just a minute. (*Goes to door*) Walter, it's Mrs. Arnold. (*Waits. Goes back to the phone. Tense*) Hello. Yes, this is his wife speaking . . . He's lying down now. Yes . . . well, he'll be in tomorrow. He's been very sick. Yes—I know we should have called, but we were so sure he'd be able to come in today. Yes—yes, I'm very sorry. Yes . . . Thank you very much. (*She hangs up.* WALTER *is standing in the doorway of the bedroom behind her*) That was Mrs. Arnold.

WALTER   (*Indifferently*) Was it?

RUTH   She said if you don't come in tomorrow that they are getting a new man . . .

WALTER   Ain't that sad—ain't that crying sad.

RUTH   She said Mr. Arnold has had to take a cab for three days . . . Walter, you ain't been to work for three days! (*This is a revelation to her*) Where you been, Walter Lee Younger? (WALTER *looks at her and starts to laugh*) You're going to lose your job.

WALTER   That's right . . .

RUTH   Oh, Walter, and with your mother working like a dog every day—

WALTER   That's sad too— Everything is sad.

MAMA   What you been doing for these three days, son?

WALTER   Mama—you don't know all the things a man what got leisure can find to do in this city . . . What's this—Friday night? Well—Wednesday I borrowed Willy Harris' car and I went for a drive . . . just me and myself and I drove and drove . . . Way out . . . way past South Chicago, and I parked the car and I sat and looked at the steel mills all day long. I just sat in the car and looked at them big black chimneys for hours. Then I drove back and I went to the Green Hat. (*Pause*) And Thursday—Thursday I borrowed the car again and I got in it and I pointed it the other way and I drove the other way—for hours—way, way up to Wisconsin, and I looked at the farms. I just drove and looked at the farms. Then I drove back and I went to the Green Hat. (*Pause*) And today—today I didn't get the car. Today I just walked. All over the Southside. And I looked at the Negroes and they looked at me and finally I just sat down on the curb at Thirty-ninth and South Parkway and I just sat there and watched the Negroes go by. And then I went to the Green Hat. You all sad? You all depressed? And you know where I am going right now—

(RUTH *goes out quietly.*)

MAMA   Oh, Big Walter, is this the harvest of our days?

WALTER   You know what I like about the Green Hat? (*He turns the radio on and a steamy, deep blues pours into the room*) I like this little cat they got there who blows a sax . . . He blows. He talks to me. He ain't but 'bout five feet tall and he's got a conked head and his eyes is always closed and he's all music—

MAMA   (*Rising and getting some papers out of her handbag*) Walter—

WALTER   And there's this other guy who plays the piano . . . and they got a sound. I mean they can work on some music . . . They got the best little combo in the world in the Green Hat . . . You can just sit there and drink and listen to them three men play and you realize that don't nothing matter worth a damn, but just being there—

MAMA   I've helped do it to you, haven't I, son? Walter, I been wrong.

WALTER   Naw—you ain't never been wrong about nothing, Mama.

MAMA   Listen to me, now. I say I been wrong, son. That I been doing to you what the rest of the world been doing to you. (*She stops and he looks up slowly at her and she meets his eyes pleadingly*) Walter—what you ain't never understood is that I ain't got nothing, don't own nothing, ain't never really wanted nothing that wasn't for you. There ain't nothing as precious to me . . . There ain't nothing worth holding on to, money, dreams, nothing else —if it means—if it means it's going to destroy my boy. (*She puts her papers in front of him and he watches her without speaking or moving*) I paid the man thirty-five hundred dollars down on the house. That leaves sixty-five hundred dollars. Monday morning I want you to take this money and take three thousand dollars and put it in a savings account for Beneatha's medical schooling. The rest you put in a checking account—with your name on it.

And from now on any penny that come out of it or that go in it is for you to look after. For you to decide. (*She drops her hands a little helplessly*) It ain't much, but it's all I got in the world and I'm putting it in your hands. I'm telling you to be the head of this family from now on like you supposed to be.

WALTER   (*Stares at the money*) You trust me like that, Mama?

MAMA   I ain't never stop trusting you. Like I ain't never stop loving you.

(*She goes out, and* WALTER *sits looking at the money on the table as the music continues in its idiom, pulsing in the room. Finally, in a decisive gesture, he gets up, and, in mingled joy and desperation, picks up the money. At the same moment,* TRAVIS *enters for bed.*)

TRAVIS   What's the matter, Daddy? You drunk?

WALTER   (*Sweetly, more sweetly than we have ever known him*) No, Daddy ain't drunk. Daddy ain't going to never be drunk again. . . .

TRAVIS   Well, good night, Daddy.

(*The* FATHER *has come from behind the couch and leans over, embracing his son.*)

WALTER   Son, I feel like talking to you tonight.

TRAVIS   About what?

WALTER   Oh, about a lot of things. About you and what kind of man you going to be when you grow up. . . . Son—son, what do you want to be when you grow up?

TRAVIS   A bus driver.

WALTER   (*Laughing a little*) A what? Man, that ain't nothing to want to be!

TRAVIS   Why not?

WALTER   'Cause, man—it ain't big enough—you know what I mean.

TRAVIS   I don't know then. I can't make up my mind. Sometimes Mama asks me that too. And sometimes when I tell you I just want to be like you—she says she don't want me to be like that and sometimes she says she does. . . .

WALTER   (*Gathering him up in his arms*) You know what, Travis? In seven years you gong to be seventeen years old. And things is going to be very different with us in seven years, Travis. . . . One day when you are seventeen I'll come home—home from my office downtown somewhere—

TRAVIS   You don't work in no office, Daddy.

WALTER   No—but after tonight. After what your daddy gonna do tonight, there's going to be offices—a whole lot of offices. . . .

TRAVIS   What you gonna do tonight, Daddy?

WALTER   You wouldn't understand yet, son, but your daddy's gonna make a transaction . . . a business transaction that's going to change our lives. . . . That's how come one day when you 'bout seventeen years old I'll come home and I'll be pretty tired, you know what I mean, after a day of conferences and secretaries gettings things wrong the way they do . . . 'cause an executive's life is hell, man—(*The more he talks the farther away he gets*) And I'll pull the car up on the driveway . . . just a plain black Chrysler, I think, with white walls—no—black tires. More elegant. Rich people don't have to be flashy . . . though I'll have to get something a little sportier for Ruth—maybe a Cadillac convertible to do her shopping in. . . . And I'll come up the steps to the house and the gardener will be clipping away at the hedges and he'll say, "Good evening, Mr. Younger." And I'll say, "Hello, Jefferson, how are you this evening?" And I'll go inside and Ruth will come downstairs and meet me at the door and we'll kiss each other and she'll take my arm and we'll go up to your room to see you sitting on the floor with the catalogues of all the great schools in America around you. . . . All the great schools in the world! And—and I'll say, all right son—it's your seventeenth birthday, what is it you've decided? . . . Just tell me, what it is you want to be—and you'll *be* it. . . . Whatever you want to be—Yessir! (*He holds his arms open for* TRAVIS) You just name it, son . . . (TRAVIS *leaps into them*) and I hand you the world!

(WALTER's *voice has risen in pitch and hysterical promise and on the last line he lifts* TRAVIS *high.*)

(*Blackout*)

SCENE THREE

TIME
Saturday, moving day, one week later.

(*Before the curtain rises,* RUTH's *voice, a strident, dramatic church alto, cuts through the silence.*

(*It is, in the darkness, a triumphant surge, a penetrating statement of expectation: "Oh, Lord, I don't feel no ways tired! Children, oh, glory hallelujah!"*

(*As the curtain rises we see that* RUTH *is alone in the living room, finishing up the family's packing. It is moving day. She is nailing crates and tying cartons.* BENEATHA *enters, carrying a guitar case, and watches her exuberant sister-in-law.*)

RUTH Hey!

BENEATHA (*Putting away the case*) Hi.

RUTH (*Pointing at a package*) Honey—look in that package there and see what I found on sale this morning at the South Center. (RUTH *gets up and moves to the package and draws out some curtains*) Lookahere—hand-turned hems!

BENEATHA How do you know the window size out there?

RUTH (*Who hadn't thought of that*) Oh— Well, they bound to fit something in the whole house. Anyhow, they was too good a bargain to pass up. (RUTH *slaps her head, suddenly remembering something*) Oh, Bennie—I meant to put a special note on that carton over there. That's your mama's good china and she wants 'em to be very careful with it.

BENEATHA I'll do it.

(BENEATHA *finds a piece of paper and starts to draw large letters on it.*)

RUTH You know what I'm going to do soon as I get in that new house?

BENEATHA What?

RUTH Honey—I'm going to run me a tub of water up to here . . . (*With her fingers practically up to her nostrils*) And I'm going to get in it—and I am going to sit . . . and sit . . . and sit in that hot water and the first person who knocks to tell *me* to hurry up and come out—

BENEATHA   Gets shot at sunrise.

RUTH   (*Laughing happily*) You said it, sister! (*Noticing how large* BENEATHA *is absent-mindedly making the note*) Honey, they ain't going to read that from no airplane.

BENEATHA   (*Laughing herself*) I guess I always think things have more emphasis if they are big, somehow.

RUTH   (*Looking up at her and smiling*) You and your brother seem to have that as a philosophy of life. Lord, that man—done changed so 'round here. You know—you know what we did last night? Me and Walter Lee?

BENEATHA   What?

RUTH   (*Smiling to herself*) We went to the movies. (*Looking at* BENEATHA *to see if she understands*) We went to the movies. You know the last time me and Walter went to the movies together?

BENEATHA   No.

RUTH   Me neither. That's how long it been. (*Smiling again*) But we went last night. The picture wasn't much good, but that didn't seem to matter. We went —and we held hands.

BENEATHA   Oh, Lord!

RUTH   We held hands—and you know what?

BENEATHA   What?

RUTH   When we come out of the show it was late and dark and all the stores and things was closed up . . . and it was kind of chilly and there wasn't many people on the streets . . . and we was still holding hands, me and Walter.

BENEATHA   You're killing me.

(WALTER *enters with a large package. His happiness is deep in him; he cannot keep still with his new-found exuberance. He is singing and wiggling and snapping his fingers. He puts his package in a corner and puts a phonograph record, which he has brought in with him, on the record player. As the music comes up he dances over to* RUTH *and tries to get her to dance with him. She gives in at last to his raunchiness and in a fit of giggling allows herself to be drawn into his mood and together they deliberately burlesque an old social dance of their youth.*)

BENEATHA   (*Regarding them a long time as they dance, then drawing in her breath for a deeply exaggerated comment which she does not particularly mean*) Talk about—olddddddddddd-fashioneddddddd—Negroes!

WALTER   (*Stopping momentarily*) What kind of Negroes?

(*He says this in fun. He is not angry with her today, nor with anyone. He starts to dance with his wife again.*)

BENEATHA   Old-fashioned.

WALTER   (*As he dances with* RUTH) You know, when these *New Negroes* have their convention—(*Pointing at his sister*)—that is going to be the chairman of the Committee on Unending Agitation. (*He goes on dancing, then stops*) Race, race, race! . . . Girl, I do believe you are the first person in the history of the entire human race to successfully brainwash yourself. (BENEATHA *breaks up and he goes on dancing. He stops again, enjoying his tease*) Damn, even the N double A C P takes a holiday sometimes! (BENEATHA *and* RUTH *laugh. He dances with* RUTH *some more and starts to laugh and stops and pantomines someone over an operating table*) I can just see that chick someday looking down at some poor cat on an operating table before she starts to slice him, saying . . . (*Pulling his sleeves back maliciously*) "By the way, what are your views on civil rights down there? . . ."

(*He laughs at her again and starts to dance happily. The bell sounds.*)

BENEATHA   Sticks and stones may break my bones but . . . words will never hurt me!

(BENEATHA *goes to the door and opens it as* WALTER *and* RUTH *go on with the clowning.* BENEATHA *is somewhat surprised to see a quiet-looking middle-aged white man in a business suit holding his hat and a briefcase in his hand and consulting a small piece of paper.*)

MAN   Uh—how do you do, miss. I am looking for a Mrs.—(*He looks at the slip of paper*) Mrs. Lena Younger?

BENEATHA   (*Smoothing her hair with slight embarrassment*) Oh—yes, that's my mother. Excuse me (*She closes the door and turns to quiet the other two*) Ruth! Brother! Somebody's here. (*Then she opens the door. The man casts a curious quick glance at all of them*) Uh—come in please.

MAN   (*Coming in*) Thank you.

BENEATHA   My mother isn't here just now. Is it business?

MAN   Yes . . . well, of a sort.

WALTER   (*Freely, the Man of the House*) Have a seat. I'm Mrs. Younger's son. I look after most of her business matters.

(RUTH *and* BENEATHA *exchange amused glances.*)

MAN   (*Regarding* WALTER, *and sitting*) Well— My name is Karl Lindner . . .

WALTER   (*Stretching out his hand*) Walter Younger. This is my wife—(RUTH *nods politely*)—and my sister.

LINDNER   How do you do.

WALTER   (*Amiably, as he sits himself easily on a chair, leaning with interest forward on his knees and looking expectantly into the newcomer's face*) What can we do for you, Mr. Lindner!

LINDNER   (*Some minor shuffling of the hat and briefcase on his knees*) Well— I am a representative of the Clybourne Park Improvement Association—

WALTER   (*Pointing*) Why don't you sit your things on the floor?

LINDNER   Oh—yes. Thank you. (*He slides the briefcase and hat under the chair*) And as I was saying—I am from the Clybourne Park Improvement Association and we have had it brought to our attention at the last meeting that you people—or at least your mother—has bought a piece of residential property at—(*He digs for the slip of paper again*)—four o six Clybourne Street . . .

WALTER   That's right. Care for something to drink? Ruth, get Mr. Lindner a beer.

LINDNER   (*Upset for some reason*) Oh—no, really. I mean thank you very much, but no thank you.

RUTH   (*Innocently*) Some coffee?

LINDNER   Thank you, nothing at all.

(BENEATHA *is watching the man carefully.*)

LINDNER   Well, I don't know how much you folks know about our organization. (*He is a gentle man; thoughtful and somewhat labored in his manner*) It is one of these community organizations set up to look after—oh, you know, things like block upkeep and special projects and we also have what we call our New Neighbors Orientation Committee . . .

BENEATHA   (*Drily*) Yes—and what do they do?

LINDNER   (*Turning a little to her and then returning the main force to* WAL-TER) Well—it's what you might call a sort of welcoming committee, I guess. I mean they, we, I'm the chairman of the committee—go around and see the new people who move into the neighborhood and sort of give them the low-down on the way we do things out in Clybourne Park.

BENEATHA   (*With appreciation of the two meanings, which escape* RUTH *and* WALTER) Un-huh.

LINDNER   And we also have the category of what the association calls—(*He looks elsewhere*)—uh—special community problems . . .

BENEATHA   Yes—and what are some of those?

WALTER   Girl, let the man talk.

LINDNER   (*With understated relief*) Thank you. I would sort of like to explain this thing in my own way. I mean I want to explain to you in a certain way.

WALTER   Go ahead.

LINDNER   Yes. Well. I'm going to try to get right to the point. I'm sure we'll all appreciate that in the long run.

BENEATHA   Yes.

WALTER   Be still now!

LINDNER   Well—

RUTH   (*Still innocently*) Would you like another chair—you don't look comfortable.

LINDNER   (*More frustrated than annoyed*) No, thank you very much. Please. Well—to get right to the point I—(*A great breath, and he is off at last*) I am sure you people must be aware of some of the incidents which have happened in various parts of the city when colored people have moved into certain areas—(BENEATHA *exhales heavily and starts tossing a piece of fruit up and down in the air*) Well—because we have what I think is going to be a unique type of organization in American community life—not only do we deplore that kind of thing—but we are trying to do something about it. (BENEATHA *stops tossing and turns with a new and quizzical interest to the man*) We feel—(*gaining confidence in his mission because of the interest in the faces of the people he is talking to*)—we feel that most of the trouble in this world, when you come right down to it—(*He hits his knee for emphasis*)—most of the trouble exists because people just don't sit down and talk to each other.

RUTH   (*Nodding as she might in church, pleased with the remark*) You can say that again, mister.

LINDNER   (*More encouraged by such affirmation*) That we don't try hard enough in this world to understand the other fellow's problem. The other guy's point of view.

RUTH   Now that's right.

(BENEATHA *and* WALTER *merely watch and listen with genuine interest.*)

LINDNER   Yes—that's the way we feel out in Clybourne Park. And that's why I was elected to come here this afternoon and talk to you people. Friendly like, you know, the way people should talk to each other and see if we couldn't find some way to work this thing out. As I say, the whole business is a matter of *caring* about the other fellow. Anybody can see that you are a nice family of folks, hard working and honest I'm sure. (BENEATHA *frowns slightly, quizzically, her head tilted regarding him*) Today everybody knows what it means to be on the outside of *something.* And of course, there is always somebody who is out to take the advantage of people who don't always understand.

WALTER   What do you mean?

LINDNER   Well—you see our community is made up of people who've worked hard as the dickens for years to build up that little community. They're not rich and fancy people; just hard-working, honest people who don't really have much but those little homes and a dream of the kind of community they want to raise their children in. Now, I don't say we are perfect and there is a lot wrong in some of the things they want. But you've got to admit that a man, right or wrong, has the right to want to have the neighborhood he lives in a certain kind of way. And at the moment the overwhelming majority of our people out there feel that people get along better, take more of a common interest in the life of the community, when they share a common background. I want you to believe me when I tell you that race prejudice simply doesn't enter into it. It is a matter of the people of Clybourne Park believing, rightly or wrongly, as I say, that for the happiness of all concerned that our Negro families are happier when they live in their *own* communities.

BENEATHA   (*With a grand and bitter gesture*) This, friends, is the Welcoming Committee!

WALTER   (*Dumbfounded, looking at* LINDNER) is this what you came marching all the way over here to tell us?

LINDNER   Well, now we've been having a fine conversation. I hope you'll hear me all the way through.

WALTER   (*Tightly*) Go ahead, man.

LINDNER   You see —in the face of all things I have said, we are prepared to make your family a very generous offer . . .

BENEATHA   Thirty pieces and not a coin less!

WALTER   Yeah?

LINDNER   (*Putting on his glasses and drawing a form out of the briefcase*) Our association is prepared, through the collective effort of our people, to buy the house from you at a financial gain to your family.

RUTH   Lord have mercy, ain't this the living gall!

WALTER   All right, you through?

LINDNER   Well, I want to give you the exact terms of the financial arrangement—

WALTER   We don't want to hear no exact terms of no arrangements. I want to know if you got any more to tell us 'bout getting together?

LINDNER   (*Taking off his glasses*) Well—I don't suppose that you feel . . .

WALTER   Never mind how I feel—you got any more to say 'bout how people ought to sit down and talk to each other? . . . Get out of my house, man.

(He turns his back and walks to the door.)

LINDNER   *(Looking around at the hostile faces and reaching and assembling his hat and briefcase)* Well—I don't understand why you people are reacting this way. What do you think you are going to gain by moving into a neighborhood where you just aren't wanted and where some elements—well—people can get awful worked up when they feel that their whole way of life and everything they've ever worked for is threatened.

WALTER   Get out.

LINDNER   *(At the door, holding a small card)* Well—I'm sorry it went like this.

WALTER   Get out.

LINDNER   *(Almost sadly regarding WALTER)* You just can't force people to change their hearts, son.

(He turns and put his card on a table and exits. WALTER pushes the door to with stinging hatred, and stands looking at it. RUTH just sits and BENEATHA just stands. They say nothing. MAMA and TRAVIS enter.)

MAMA   Well—this all the packing got done since I left out of here this morning. I testify before God that my children got all the energy of the dead. What time the moving men due?

BENEATHA   Four o'clock. You had a caller, Mama.

(She is smiling, teasingly.)

MAMA   Sure enough—who?

BENEATHA   *(Her arms folded saucily)* The Welcoming Committee.

(WALTER and RUTH giggle.)

MAMA   *(Innocently)* Who?

BENEATHA   The Welcoming Committee. They said they're sure going to be glad to see you when you get there.

WALTER   *(Devilishly)* Yeah, they said they can't hardly wait to see your face.

(Laughter.)

MAMA   *(Sensing their facetiousness)* What's the matter with you all?

WALTER   Ain't nothing the matter with us. We just telling you 'bout the gentleman who came to see you this afternoon. From the Clybourne Park Improvement Association.

MAMA   What he want?

RUTH   *(In the same mood as BENEATHA and WALTER)* To welcome you, honey.

WALTER   He said they can't hardly wait. He said the one thing they don't have, that they just *dying* to have out there is a fine family of colored people! *(To RUTH and BENEATHA)* Ain't that right!

RUTH AND BENEATHA *(Mockingly)* Yeah! He left his card in case—

(They indicate the card, and MAMA picks it up and throws it on the floor—understanding and looking off as she draws her chair up to the table on which she has put her plant and some sticks and some cord.)

MAMA   Father, give us strength. *(Knowingly—and without fun)* Did he threaten us?

BENEATHA   Oh—Mama—they don't do it like that any more. He talked

Brotherhood. He said everybody ought to learn how to sit down and hate each other with good Christian fellowship.

(*She and* WALTER *shake hands to ridicule the remark.*)

MAMA   (*Sadly*) Lord, protect us . . .

RUTH   You should hear the money those folks raised to buy the house from us. All we paid and then some.

BENEATHA   What they think we going to do—eat 'em?

RUTH   No, honey, marry 'em.

MAMA   (*Shaking her head*) Lord, Lord, Lord . . .

RUTH   Well—that's the way the crackers crumble. Joke.

BENEATHA   (*Laughingly noticing what her mother is doing*) Mama, what are you doing?

MAMA   Fixing my plant so it won't get hurt none on the way . . .

BENEATHA   Mama, you going to take *that* to the new house?

MAMA   Un-huh—

BENEATHA   That raggedly-looking old thing?

MAMA   (*Stopping and looking at her*) It expresses *me.*

RUTH   (*With delight, to* BENEATHA) So there, Miss Thing!

(WALTER *comes to* MAMA *suddenly and bends down behind her and squeezes her in his arms with all his strength. She is overwhelmed by the suddenness of it and, though delighted, her manner is like that of* RUTH *with* TRAVIS.)

MAMA   Look out now, boy! You make me mess up my thing here!

WALTER   (*His face lit, he slips down on his knees beside her, his arms still about her*) Mama . . . you know what it means to climb up in the chariot?

MAMA   (*Gruffly, very happy*) Get on away from me now . . .

RUTH   (*Near the gift-wrapped package, trying to catch* WALTER's *eye*) Psst—

WALTER   What the old song say, Mama . . .

RUTH   Walter— Now?

(*She is pointing at the package.*)

WALTER   (*Speaking the lines, sweetly, playfully, in his mother's face*)

> *I got wings . . . you got wings . . .*
> *All God's Children got wings . . .*

MAMA   Boy—get out of my face and do some work . . .

WALTER

> *When I get to heaven gonna put on my wings,*
> *Gonna fly all over God's heaven . . .*

BENEATHA   (*Teasingly, from across the room*) Everybody talking 'bout heaven ain't going there!

WALTER   (*To* RUTH, *who is carrying the box across to them*) I don't know, you think we ought to give her that . . . Seems to me she ain't been very appreciative around here.

MAMA   (*Eying the box, which is obviously a gift*) What is that?

WALTER   (*Taking it from* RUTH *and putting it on the table in front of* MAMA) Well—what you all think? Should we give it to her?

RUTH   Oh—she was pretty good today.

MAMA   I'll good you—

(*She turns her eyes to the box again.*)

BENEATHA   Open it, Mama.

(*She stands up, looks at it, turns and looks at all of them, and then presses her hands together and does not open the package.*)

WALTER   (*Sweetly*) Open it, Mama. It's for you. (MAMA *looks in his eyes. It is the first present in her life without its being Christmas. Slowly she opens her package and lifts out, one by one, a brand-new sparkling set of gardening tools.* WALTER *continues, prodding*) Ruth made up the note—read it . . .

MAMA   (*Picking up the card and adjusting her glasses*) "To our own Mrs. Miniver—Love from Brother, Ruth and Beneatha." Ain't that lovely . . .

TRAVIS   (*Tugging at his father's sleeve*) Daddy, can I give her mine now?

WALTER   All right, son. (TRAVIS *flies to get his gift*) Travis didn't want to go in with the rest of us, Mama. He got his own. (*Somewhat amused*) We don't know what it is . . .

TRAVIS   (*Racing back in the room with a large hatbox and putting it in front of his grandmother*) Here!

MAMA   Lord have mercy, baby. You done gone and bought your grandmother a hat?

TRAVIS   (*Very proud*) Open it!

(*She does and lifts out an elaborate, but very elaborate, wide gardening hat, and all the adults break up at the sight of it.*)

RUTH   Travis, honey, what is that?

TRAVIS   (*Who thinks it is beautiful and appropriate*) It's a gardening hat! Like the ladies always have on in the magazines when they work in their gardens.

BENEATHA   (*Giggling fiercely*) Travis—we were trying to make Mama Mrs. Miniver—not Scarlett O'Hara!

MAMA   (*Indignantly*) What's the matter with you all! This here is a beautiful hat! (*Absurdly*) I always wanted me one just like it!

(*She pops it on her head to prove it to her grandson, and the hat is ludicrous and considerably oversized.*)

RUTH   Hot dog! Go, Mama!

WALTER   (*Doubled over with laughter*) I'm sorry, Mama—but you look like you ready to go out and chop you some cotton sure enough!

(*They all laugh except* MAMA, *out of deference to* TRAVIS' *feelings.*)

MAMA   (*Gathering the boy up to her*) Bless your heart—this is the prettiest hat I ever owned— (WALTER, RUTH *and* BENEATHA *chime in—noisily, festively and insincerely congratulating* TRAVIS *on his gift*) What are we all standing around here for? We ain't finished packin' yet. Bennie, you ain't packed one book.

(*The bell rings.*)

BENEATHA   That couldn't be the movers . . . it's not hardly two good yet—

(BENEATHA *goes into her room,* MAMA *starts for door.*)

WALTER   (*Turning, stiffening*) Wait—wait—I'll get it.

(*He stands and looks at the door.*)

MAMA   You expecting company, son?

WALTER   (*Just looking at the door*) Yeah—yeah . . .

(MAMA *looks at* RUTH,, *and they exchange innocent and unfrightened glances.*)

MAMA   (*Not understanding*) Well, let them in, son.

BENEATHA   (*From her room*) We need some more string.

MAMA   Travis—you run to the hardware and get me some string cord.

(MAMA *goes out and* WALTER *turns and looks at* RUTH. TRAVIS *goes to a dish for money.*)

RUTH   Why don't you answer the door, man?

WALTER   (*Suddenly bounding across the floor to her*) 'Cause sometimes it hard to let the future begin!

(*Stooping down in her face.*)

> I got wings! You got wings!
> All God's children got wings!

(*He crosses to the door and throws it open. Standing there is a very slight little man in a not too prosperous business suit and with haunted frightened eyes and a hat pulled down tightly, brim up, around his forehead.* TRAVIS *passes between the men and exits.* WALTER *leans deep in the man's face, still in his jubilance.*)

> When I get to heaven gonna put on my wings,
> Gonna fly all over God's heaven . . .

(*The little man just stares at him.*)

> Heaven—

(*Suddenly he stops and looks past the little man into the empty hallway.*)

> Where's Willy, man?

BOBO   He ain't with me.

WALTER   (*Not disturbed*) Oh—come on in. You know my wife.

BOBO   (*Dumbly, taking off his hat*) Yes—h'you, Miss Ruth.

RUTH   (*Quietly, a mood apart from her husband already, seeing* BOBO) Hello, Bobo.

WALTER   You right on time today . . . Right on time. That's the way! (*He slaps* BOBO *on his back*) Sit down . . . lemme hear.

(RUTH *stands stiffly and quietly in back of them, as though somehow she senses death, her eyes fixed on her husband.*)

BOBO   (*His frightened eyes on the floor, his hat in his hands*) Could I please get a drink of water, before I tell you about it, Walter Lee?

(WALTER *does not take his eyes off the man.* RUTH *goes blindly to the tap and gets a glass of water and brings it to* BOBO.)

WALTER   There ain't nothing wrong, is there?

BOBO   Lemme tell you—

WALTER   Man—didn't nothing go wrong?

BOBO   Lemme tell you—Walter Lee. (*Looking at* RUTH *and talking to her more than to* WALTER) You know how it was. I got to tell you how it was. I mean first I got to tell you how it was all the way . . . I mean about the money I put in, Walter Lee . . .

WALTER   (*With taut agitation now*) What about the money you put in?

BOBO   Well—it wasn't much as we told you—me and Willy—(*He stops*) I'm sorry, Walter. I got a bad feeling about it. I got a real bad feeling about it . . .

WALTER   Man, what you telling me about all this for? . . . Tell me what happened in Springfield . . .

BOBO   Springfield.

RUTH   (*Like a dead woman*) What was supposed to happen in Springfield?

BOBO   (*To her*) This deal that me and Walter went into with Willy— Me and Willy was going to go down to Springfield and spread some money 'round so's we wouldn't have to wait so long for the liquor license . . . That's what we were going to do. Everybody said that was the way you had to do, you understand, Miss Ruth?

WALTER   Man—what happened down there?

BOBO   (*A pitiful man, near tears*) I'm trying to tell you, Walter.

WALTER   (*Screaming at him suddenly*) THEN TELL ME, GODDAMMIT . . . WHAT'S THE MATTER WITH YOU?

BOBO   Man . . . I didn't go to no Springfield, yesterday.

WALTER   (*Halted, life hanging in the moment*) Why not?

BOBO   (*The long way, the hard way to tell*) 'Cause I didn't have no reasons to . . .

WALTER   Man, what are you talking about!

BOBO   I'm talking about the fact that when I got to the train station yesterday morning—eight o'clock like we planned . . . Man—*Willy didn't never show up.*

WALTER   Why . . . where was he . . . where is he?

BOBO   That's what I'm trying to tell you . . . I don't know . . . I waited six hours . . . I called his house . . . and I waited . . . six hours . . . I waited in that train station six hours . . . (*Breaking into tears*) That was all the extra money I had in the world . . . (*Looking up at* WALTER *with the tears running down his face*) Man, *Willy is gone.*

WALTER   Gone, what you mean Willy is gone? Gone where? You mean he went by himself. You mean he went off to Springfield by himself—to take care of getting the license—(*Turns and looks anxiously at* RUTH) You mean maybe he didn't want too many people in on the business down there? (*Looks to* RUTH *again, as before*) You know Willy got his own ways. (*Looks back to* BOBO) Maybe you was late yesterday and he just went on down there without you. Maybe—maybe—he's been callin' you at home tryin' to tell you what happened or something. Maybe—maybe—he just got sick. He's somewhere—he's got to be somewhere. We just got to find him—me and you got to find him. (*Grabs* BOBO *senselessly by the collar and starts to shake him*) We got to!

BOBO   (*In sudden angry, frightened agony*) What's the matter with you, Walter! *When a cat take off with your money he don't leave you no maps!*

WALTER   (*Turning madly, as though he is looking for* WILLY *in the very room*) Willy! . . . Willy . . . don't do it . . . Please don't do it . . . Man, not with that money . . . Oh, God . . . Don't let it be true . . . (*He is wandering around, crying out for* WILLY *and looking for him or perhaps for help from God*) Man . . . I trusted you . . . Man, I put my life in your hands . . . (*He starts to crumple down on the floor as* RUTH *just covers her face in horror.* MAMA *opens the door and comes into the room, with* BENEATHA *behind her*) Man

. . . (*He starts to pound the floor with his fists, sobbing wildly*) *That money is made out of my father's flesh . . .*

BOBO (*standing over him helplessly*) I'm sorry, Walter . . . (*Only* WALTER's *sobs reply.* BOBO *puts on his hat*) I had my life staked on this deal, too . . .
(*He exits.*)

MAMA (*To* WALTER) Son—(*She goes to him, bends down to him, talks to his bent head*) Son . . . Is it gone? Son, I gave you sixty-five hundred dollars. Is it gone? All of it? Beneatha's money too?

WALTER (*Lifting his head slowly*) Mama . . . I never . . . went to the bank at all . . .

MAMA (*Not wanting to believe him*) You mean . . . your sister's school money . . . you used that too . . . Walter? . . .

WALTER Yessss! . . All of it . . . It's all gone . . .

(*There is total silence.* RUTH *stands with her face covered with her hands;* BENEATHA *leans forlornly against a wall, fingering a piece of red ribbon from the mother's gift.* MAMA *stops and looks at her son without recognition and then, quite without thinking about it, starts to beat him senselessly in the face.* BENEATHA *goes to them and stops it.*)

BENEATHA Mama!

(MAMA *stops and looks at both of her children and rises slowly and wanders vaguely, aimlessly away from them.*)

MAMA I seen . . . him . . . night after night . . . come in . . . and look at that rug . . . and then look at me . . . the red showing in his eyes . . . the veins moving in his head . . . I seen him grow thin and old before he was forty . . . working and working and working like somebody's old horse . . . killing himself . . . and you—you give it all away in a day . . .

BENEATHA Mama—

MAMA Oh, God . . . (*She looks up to Him*) Look down here—and show me the strength.

BENEATHA Mama—

MAMA (*Folding over*) Strength . . .

BENEATHA (*Plaintively*) Mama . . .

MAMA Strength!

Curtain

ACT III

(*An hour later.*

(*At curtain, there is a sullen light of gloom in the living room, gray light not unlike that which began the first scene of Act One. At left we can see* WALTER *within his room, alone with himself. He is stretched out on the bed, his shirt out and open, his arms under his head. He does not smoke, he does not cry out, he merely lies there, looking up at the ceiling, much as if he were alone in the world.*

(*In the living room* BENEATHA *sits at the table, still surrounded by the now almost ominous packing crates. She sits looking off. We feel that this is a mood struck perhaps an hour before, and it lingers now, full of the empty sound of profound disappointment. We see on a line from her brother's bedroom the sameness of their attitudes. Presently the bell rings and BENEATHA rises without ambition or interest in answering. It is ASAGAI, smiling broadly, striding into the room with energy and happy expectation and conversation.)*

ASAGAI   I came over . . . I had some free time. I thought I might help with the packing. Ah, I like the look of packing crates! A household in preparation for a journey! It depresses some people . . . but for me . . . it is another feeling. Something full of the flow of life, do you understand? Movement, progress . . . It makes me think of Africa.

BENEATHA   Africa!

ASAGAI   What kind of a mood is this? Have I told you how deeply you move me?

BENEATHA   He gave away the money, Asagai . . .

ASAGAI   Who gave away what money?

BENEATHA   The insurance money. My brother gave it away.

ASAGAI   Gave it away?

BENEATHA   He made an investment! With a man even Travis wouldn't have trusted.

ASAGAI   And it's gone?

BENEATHA   Gone!

ASAGAI   I'm very sorry . . . And you, now?

BENEATHA   Me? . . . Me? . . . Me I'm nothing . . . Me. When I was very small . . . we used to take our sleds out in the wintertime and the only hills we had were the ice-covered stone steps of some houses down the street. And we used to fill them in with snow and make them smooth and slide down them all day . . . and it was very dangerous you know . . . far too steep . . . and sure enough one day a kid named Rufus came down too fast and hit the sidewalk . . . and we saw his face just split open right there in front of us . . . And I remember standing there looking at his bloody open face thinking that was the end of Rufus. But the ambulance came and they took him to the hospital and they fixed the broken bones and they sewed it all up . . . and the next time I saw Rufus he just had a little line down the middle of his face . . . I never got over that . . .

(WALTER sits up, listening on the bed. Throughout this scene it is important that we feel his reaction at all times, that he visibly respond to the words of his sister and ASAGAI.)

ASAGAI   What?

BENEATHA   That that was what one person could do for another, fix him up— sew up the problem, make him all right again. That was the most marvelous thing in the world . . . I wanted to do that. I always thought it was the one concrete thing in the world that a human being could do. Fix up the sick, you know—and make them whole again. This was truly being God . . .

ASAGAI   You wanted to be God?

BENEATHA   No—I wanted to cure. It used to be so important to me. I wanted to cure. It used to matter. I used to care. I mean about people and how their bodies hurt . . .

ASAGAI   And you've stopped caring?

BENEATHA   Yes—I think so.

ASAGAI   Why?

(WALTER *rises, goes to the door of his room and is about to open it, then stops and stands listening, leaning on the door jamb.*)

BENEATHA   Because it doesn't seem deep enough, close enough to what ails mankind—I mean this thing of sewing up bodies or administering drugs. Don't you understand? It was a child's reaction to the world. I thought that doctors had the secret to all the hurts. . . . That's the way a child sees things—or an idealist.

ASAGAI   Children see things very well sometimes—and idealists even better.

BENEATHA   I know that's what you think. Because you are still where I left off—you still care. This is what you see for the world, for Africa. You with the dreams of the future will patch up all Africa—you are going to cure the Great Sore of colonialism with Independence—

ASAGAI   Yes!

BENEATHA   Yes—and you think that one word is the penicillin of the human spirit: "Independence!" But then what?

ASAGAI   That will be the problem for another time. First we must get there.

BENEATHA   And where does it end?

ASAGAI   End? Who even spoke of an end? To life? To living?

BENEATHA   An end to misery!

ASAGAI   (*Smiling*) You sound like a French intellectual.

BENEATHA   No! I sound like a human being who just had her future taken right out of her hands! While I was sleeping in my bed in there, things were happening in this world that directly concerned me—and nobody asked me, consulted me—they just went out and did things—and changed my life. Don't you see there isn't any real progress, Asagai, there is only one large circle that we march in, around and around, each of us with our own little picture—in front of us—our own little mirage that we think is the future.

ASAGAI   That is the mistake.

BENEATHA   What?

ASAGAI   What you just said—about the circle. It isn't a circle—it is simply a long line—as in geometry, you know, one that reaches into infinity. And because we cannot see the end—we also cannot see how it changes. And it is very odd but those who see the changes are called "idealists"—and those who cannot, or refuse to think, they are the "realists." It is very strange, and amusing too, I think.

BENEATHA   You—you are almost religious.

ASAGAI   Yes . . . I think I have the religion of doing what is necessary in the world—and of worshipping man—because he is so marvelous, you see.

BENEATHA   Man is foul! And the human race deserves its misery!

ASAGAI   You see: *you* have become the religious one in the old sense. Already, and after such a small defeat, you are worshipping despair.

BENEATHA   From now on, I worship the truth—and the truth is that people are puny, small and selfish. . . .

ASAGAI   Truth? Why is it that you despairing ones always think that only you have the truth? I never thought to see *you* like that. You! Your brother made a stupid, childish mistake—and you are grateful to him. So that now you can give up the ailing human race on account of it. You talk about what good is struggle; what good is anything? Where are we all going? And why are we bothering?

BENEATHA *And you cannot answer it!* All your talk and dreams about Africa and Independence. Independence and then what? What about all the crooks and petty thiefs and just plain idiots who will come into power to steal and plunder the same as before—only now they will be black and do it in the name of the new Independence— You cannot answer that.

ASAGAI (*Shouting over her*) *I live the answer!* (*Pause*) In my village at home it is the exceptional man who can even read a newspaper . . . or who ever *sees* a book at all. I will go home and much of what I will have to say will seem strange to the people of my village . . . But I will teach and work and things will happen, slowly and swiftly. At times it will seem that nothing changes at all . . . and then again . . . the sudden dramatic events which make history leap into the future. And then quiet again. Retrogression even. Guns, murder, revolution. And I even will have moments when I wonder if the quiet was not better than all that death and hatred. But I will look about my village at the illiteracy and disease and ignorance and I will not wonder long. And perhaps . . . perhaps I will be a great man . . . I mean perhaps I will hold on to the substance of truth and find my way always with the right course . . . and perhaps for it I will be butchered in my bed some night by the servants of empire . . .

BENEATHA *The martyr!*

ASAGAI . . . or perhaps I shall live to be a very old man, respected and esteemed in my new nation . . . And perhaps I shall hold office and this is what I'm trying to tell you, Alaiyo; perhaps the things I believe now for my country will be wrong and outmoded, and I will not understand and do terrible things to have things my way or merely to keep my power. Don't you see that there will be young men and women, not British soldiers then, but my own black countrymen . . . to step out of the shadows some evening and slit my then useless throat? Don't you see they have always been there . . . that they always will be. And that such a thing as my own death will be an advance? They who might kill me even . . . actually replenish me!

BENEATHA Oh, Asagai, I know all that.

ASAGAI Good! Then stop moaning and groaning and tell me what you plan to do.

BENEATHA Do?

ASAGAI I have a bit of a suggestion.

BENEATHA What?

ASAGAI (*Rather quietly for him*) That when it is all over that you come home with me—

BENEATHA (*Slapping herself on the forehead with exasperation born of mis-understanding*) Oh—Asagai—at this moment you decide to be romantic!

ASAGAI (*Quickly understanding the misunderstanding*) My dear, young creature of the New World—I do not mean across the city—I mean across the ocean; home—to Africa.

BENEATHA (*Slowly understanding and turning to him with murmured amazement*) To—to Nigeria?

ASAGAI Yes! . . . (*Smiling and lifting his arms playfully*) Three hundred years later the African Prince rose up out of the seas and swept the maiden back across the middle passage over which her ancestors had come—

BENEATHA (*Unable to play*) Nigeria?

ASAGAI Nigeria. Home. (*Coming to her with genuine romantic flippancy*) I will show you our mountains and our stars; and give you cool drinks from gourds and teach you the old songs and the ways of our people—and, in time, we will pretend that—(*Very softly*)—you have only been away for a day—

(*She turns her back to him, thinking. He swings her around and takes her full in his arms in a long embrace which proceeds to passion.*)

BENEATHA (*Pulling away*) You're getting me all mixed up—

ASAGAI Why?

BENEATHA Too many things—too many things have happened today. I must sit down and think. I don't know what I feel about anything right this minute.
(*She promptly sits down and props her chin on her fist.*)

ASAGAI (*Charmed*) All right, I shall leave you. No—don't get up. (*Touching her, gently, sweetly*) Just sit awhile and think . . . Never be afraid to sit awhile and think. (*He goes to door and looks at her*) How often I have looked at you and said, "Ah—so this is what the New World hath finally wrought . . ."
(*He exits. BENEATHA sits on alone. Presently WALTER enters from his room and starts to rummage through things, feverishly looking for something. She looks up and turns in her seat.*)

BENEATHA (*Hissingly*) Yes—just look at what the New World hath wrought . . . Just look! (*She gestures with bitter disgust*) There he is! *Monsieur le petit bourgeois noir*—himself! There he is—Symbol of a Rising Class! Entrepreneur! Titan of the system! (WALTER *ignores her completely and continues frantically and destructively looking for something and hurling things to floor and tearing things out of their place in his search.* BENEATHA *ignores the eccentricity of his actions and goes on with the monologue of insult*) Did you dream of yachts on Lake Michigan, Brother? Did you see yourself on that Great Day sitting down at the Conference Table, surrounded by all the mighty bald-headed men in America? All halted, waiting, breathless, waiting for your pronouncements on industry? Waiting for you—Chairman of the Board? (WALTER *finds what he is looking for—a small piece of white paper—and pushes it in his pocket and puts on his coat and rushes out without ever having looked at her. She shouts after him*) I look at you and I see the final triumph of stupidity in the world!

(*The door slams and she returns to just sitting again. RUTH comes quickly out of MAMA's room.*)

RUTH Who was that?

BENEATHA Your husband.

RUTH   Where did he go?

BENEATHA   Who knows—maybe he has an appointment at U.S. Steel.

RUTH   (*Anxiously, with frightened eyes*) You didn't say nothing bad to him, did you?

BENEATHA   Bad? Say anything bad to him? No—I told him he was a sweet boy and full of dreams and everything is strictly peachy keen, as the ofay kids say!

(MAMA *enters from her bedroom. She is lost, vague, trying to catch hold, to make some sense of her former command of the world, but it still eludes her. A sense of waste overwhelms her gait; a measure of apology rides on her shoulders. She goes to her plant, which has remained on the table, looks at it, picks it up and takes it to the window sill and sits it outside, and she stands and looks at it a long moment. Then she closes the window, straightens her body with effort and turns around to her children.*)

MAMA   Well—ain't it a mess in here, though? (*A false cheerfulness, a beginning of something*) I guess we all better stop moping around and get some work done. All this unpacking and everything we got to do. (RUTH *raises her head slowly in response to the sense of the line; and* BENEATHA *in similar manner turns very slowly to look at her mother*) One of you all better call the moving people and tell 'em not to come.

RUTH   Tell 'em not to come?

MAMA   Of course, baby. Ain't no need in 'em coming all the way here and having to go back. They charges for that too. (*She sits down, fingers to her brow, thinking*) Lord, ever since I was a little girl, I always remembers people saying, "Lena—Lena Eggleston, you aims too high all the time. You needs to slow down and see life a little more like it is. Just slow down some." That's what they always used to say down home—"Lord, that Lena Eggleston is a high-minded thing. She'll get her due one day!"

RUTH   No, Lena . . .

MAMA   Me and Big Walter just didn't never learn right.

RUTH   Lena, no! We gotta go. Bennie—tell her . . . (*She rises and crosses to* BENEATHA *with her arms outstretched.* BENEATHA *doesn't respond*) Tell her we can still move . . . the notes ain't but a hundred and twenty-five a month. We got four grown people in this house—we can work . . .

MAMA   (*To herself*) Just aimed too high all the time—

RUTH   (*Turning and going to* MAMA *fast—the words pouring out with urgency and desperation*) Lena—I'll work . . . I'll work twenty hours a day in all the kitchens in Chicago . . . I'll strap my baby on my back if I have to and scrub all the floors in America and wash all the sheets in America if I have to—but we got to move . . . We got to get out of here . . .

(MAMA *reaches out absently and pats* RUTH's *hand.*)

MAMA   No—I sees things differently now. Been thinking 'bout some of the things we could do to fix this place up some. I seen a second-hand bureau over on Maxwell Street just the other day that could fit right there. (*She points to where the new furniture might go.* RUTH *wanders away from her*) Would need some new handles on it and then a little varnish and then it look like something brand-new. And—we can put up them new curtains in the kitchen . . . Why this place be looking fine. Cheer us all up so that we forget trouble ever came . . . (*To* RUTH) And you could get some nice screens to put up in your room round the baby's bassinet . . . (*She looks at both of them, pleadingly*) Sometimes you just got to know when to give up some things . . . and hold on to what you got.

(WALTER *enters from the outside, looking spent and leaning against the door, his coat hanging from him.*)

MAMA   Where you been, son?

WALTER   (*Breathing hard*) Made a call.

MAMA   To who, son?

WALTER   To The Man.

MAMA   What man, baby?

WALTER   The Man, Mama. Don't you know who The Man is?

RUTH   Walter Lee?

WALTER   *The Man.* Like the guys in the streets say—The Man. Captain Boss— Mistuh Charley . . . Old Captain Please Mr. Bossman . . .

BENEATHA   (*Suddenly*) Lindner!

WALTER   That's right! That's good. I told him to come right over.

BENEATHA   (*Fiercely, understanding*) For what? What do you want to see him for!

WALTER   (*Looking at his sister*) We going to do business with him.

MAMA   What you talking 'bout, son?

WALTER   Talking 'bout life, Mama. You all always telling me to see life like it is. Well—I laid in there on my back today . . . and I figured it out. Life just like it is. Who gets and who don't get. (*He sits down with his coat on and laughs.*) Mama, you know it's all divided up. Life is. Sure enough. Between the takers and the "tooken." (*He laughs*) I've figured it out finally. (*He looks around at them*) Yeah. Some of us always getting "tooken" (*He laughs*) People like Willy Harris, they don't never get "tooken." And you know why the rest of us do? 'Cause we all mixed up. Mixed up bad. We get to looking 'round for the right and the wrong; and we worry about it and cry about it and stay up nights trying to figure out 'bout the wrong and the right of things all the time . . . And all the time, man, them takers is out there operating, just taking and taking. Willy Harris? Shoot—Willy Harris don't even count. He don't even count in the big scheme of things. But I'll say one thing for old Willy Harris . . . he's taught me something. He's taught me to keep my eye on what counts in this world. Yeah—(*Shouting out a little*) Thanks, Willy!

RUTH   What did you call that man for, Walter Lee?

WALTER   Called him to tell him to come on over to the show. Gonna put on a show for the man. Just what he wants to see. You see, Mama, the man came here today and he told us that them people out there where you want us to move—well they so upset they willing to pay us not to move out there. (*He laughs again*) And—and oh, Mama—you would of been proud of the way me and Ruth and Bennie acted. We told him to get out . . . Lord have mercy! We told the man to get out. Oh, we was some proud folks this afternoon, yeah. (*He lights a cigarette*) We were still full of that old-time stuff . . .

RUTH (*Coming toward him slowly*) You talking 'bout taking them people's money to keep us from moving in that house?

WALTER I ain't just talking 'bout it, baby—I'm telling you that's what's going to happen.

BENEATHA Oh, God! Where is the bottom! Where is the real honest-to-God bottom so he can't go any farther!

WALTER See—that's the old stuff. You and that boy that was here today. You all want everybody to carry a flag and a spear and sing some marching songs, huh? You wanna spend your life looking into things and trying to find the right and the wrong part, huh? Yeah. You know what's going to happen to that boy someday—he'll find himself sitting in a dungeon, locked in forever—and the takers will have the key! Forget it, baby! There ain't no causes—there ain't nothing but taking in this world, and he who takes most is smartest—and it don't make a damn bit of difference *how*.

MAMA You making something inside me cry, son. Some awful pain inside me.

WALTER Don't cry, Mama. Understand. That white man is going to walk in that door able to write checks for more money than we ever had. It's important to him and I'm going to help him . . . I'm going to put on the show, Mama.

MAMA Son—I come from five generations of people who was slaves and sharecroppers—but ain't nobody in my family never let nobody pay 'em money that was a way of telling us we wasn't fit to walk the earth. We ain't never been that poor. (*Raising her eyes and looking at him*) We ain't never been that dead inside.

BENEATHA Well—we are dead now. All the talk about dreams and sunlight that goes on in this house. All dead.

WALTER What's the matter with you all! I didn't make this world! It was give to me this way! Hell, yes, I want me some yachts someday! Yes, I want to hang some real pearls 'round my wife's neck. Ain't she supposed to wear no pearls? Somebody tell me—tell me, who decides which women is suppose to wear pearls in this world. I tell you I am a *man*—and I think my wife should wear some pearls in this world!

(*This last line hangs a good while and* WALTER *begins to move about the room. The word "Man" has penetrated his consciousness; he mumbles it to himself repeatedly between strange agitated pauses as he moves about.*)

MAMA Baby, how you going to feel on the inside?

WALTER Fine! . . . Going to feel fine . . . a man . . .

MAMA You won't have nothing left then, Walter Lee.

WALTER (*Coming to her*) I'm going to feel fine, Mama, I'm going to look that son-of-a-bitch in the eyes and say—(*He falters*)—and say, "All right, Mr. Lindner—(*He falters even more*)—that's your neighborhood out there. You got the right to keep it like you want. You got the right to have it like you want. Just write the check and—the house is yours." And, and I am going to say—(*His voice almost breaks*) And you—you people just put the money in my hand and you won't have to live next to this bunch of stinking niggers! . . . (*He straightens up and moves away from his mother, walking around the room*) Maybe—maybe I'll just get down on my black knees . . . (*He does so;* RUTH *and* BENNIE *and* MAMA *watch him in frozen horror*) Captain, Mistuh,

Bossman. (*He starts crying*) A-hee-hee-hee! (*Wringing his hands in profoundly anguished imitation*) Yassssuh! Great White Father, just gi' ussen de money, fo' God's sake, and we's ain't gwine come out deh and dirty up yo' white folks neighborhood . . .

(*He breaks down completely, then gets up and goes into the bedroom.*)

BENEATHA That is not a man. That is nothing but a toothless rat.

MAMA Yes—death done come in this here house. (*She is nodding, slowly, reflectively*) Done come walking in my house. On the lips of my children. You what supposed to be my beginning again. You—you what supposed to be my harvest. (*To* BENEATHA) You—you mourning your brother?

BENEATHA He's no brother of mine.

MAMA What you say?

BENEATHA I said that that individual in that room is no brother of mine.

MAMA That's what I thought you said. You feeling like you better than he is today? (BENEATHA *does not answer*) Yes? What you tell him a minute ago? That he wasn't a man? Yes? You give him up for me? You done wrote his epitaph too—like the rest of the world? Well, who give you the privilege?

BENEATHA Be on my side for once! You saw what he just did, Mama! You saw him—down on his knees. Wasn't it you who taught me—to despise any man who would do that. Do what he's going to do.

MAMA Yes—I taught you that. Me and your daddy. But I thought I taught you something else too . . . I thought I taught you to love him.

BENEATHA Love him? There is nothing left to love.

MAMA There is always something left to love. And if you ain't learned that, you ain't learned nothing. (*Looking at her*) Have you cried for that boy today? I don't mean for yourself and for the family 'cause we lost the money. I mean for him; what he been through and what it done to him. Child, when do you think is the time to love somebody the most; when they done good and made things easy for everybody? Well, then, you ain't through learning—because that ain't the time at all. It's when he's at his lowest and can't believe in hisself 'cause the world done whipped him so. When you starts measuring somebody, measure him right, child, measure him right. Make sure you done taken into account what hills and valleys he come through before he got to wherever he is.

(TRAVIS *bursts into the room at the end of the speech, leaving the door open.*)

TRAVIS Grandmama—the moving men are downstairs! The truck just pulled up.

MAMA (*Turning and looking at him*) Are they, baby? They downstairs?

(*She sighs and sits.* LINDNER *appears in the doorway. He peers in and knocks lightly, to gain attention, and comes in. All turn to look at him.*)

LINDNER (*Hat and briefcase in hand*) Uh—hello . . .

(RUTH *crosses mechanically to the bedroom door and opens it and lets it swing open freely and slowly as the lights come up on* WALTER *within, still in his coat, sitting at the far corner of the room. He looks up and out through the room to* LINDNER.)

RUTH He's here.

(A long minute passes and WALTER *slowly gets up.)*

LINDNER *(Coming to the table with efficiency, putting his briefcase on the table and starting to unfold papers and unscrew fountain pens)* Well, I certainly was glad to hear from you people. (WALTER *has begun the trek out of the room, slowly and awkardly, rather like a small boy, passing the back of his sleeve across his mouth from time to time)* Life can really be so much simpler than people let it be most of the time. Well—with whom do I negotiate? You, Mrs. Younger, or your son here? (MAMA *sits with her hands folded on her lap and her eyes closed as* WALTER *advances.* TRAVIS *goes close to* LINDNER *and looks at the papers curiously)* Just some official papers, sonny.

RUTH Travis, you go downstairs.

MAMA *(Opening her eyes and looking into* WALTER's) No. Travis, you stay right here. And you make him understand what you doing, Walter Lee. You teach him good. Like Willy Harris taught you. You show where our five generations done come to. Go ahead, son—

WALTER *(Looks down into his boy's eyes.* TRAVIS *grins at him merrily and* WALTER *draws him beside him with his arm lightly around his shoulders)* Well, Mr. Lindner. (BENEATHA *turns away)* We called you—(*There is a profound, simple groping quality in his speech)*—because, well, me and my family (*He looks around and shifts from one foot to the other)* Well—we are very plain people . . .

LINDNER Yes—

WALTER I mean—I have worked as a chauffeur most of my life—and my wife here, she does domestic work in people's kitchens. So does my mother. I mean—we are plain people . . .

LINDNER Yes, Mr. Younger—

WALTER *(Really like a small boy, looking down at his shoes and then up at the man)* And—uh—well, my father, well, he was a laborer most of his life.

LINDNER *(Absolutely confused)* Uh, yes—

WALTER *(Looking down at his toes once again)* My father almost beat a man to death once because this man called him a bad name or something, you know what I mean?

LINDNER No, I'm afraid I don't.

WALTER *(Finally straightening up)* Well, what I mean is that we come from people who had a lot of pride. I mean—we are very proud people. And that's my sister over there and she's going to be a doctor—and we are very proud—

LINDNER Well—I am sure that is very nice, but—

WALTER *(Starting to cry and facing the man eye to eye)* What I am telling you is that we called you over here to tell you that we are very proud and that this is—this is my son, who makes the sixth generation of our family in this country, and that we have all thought about your offer and we have decided to move into our house because my father—my father—he earned it. (MAMA *has her eyes closed and is rocking back and forth as though she were in church, with her head nodding the amen yes)* We don't want to make no trouble for nobody or fight no causes—but we will try to be good neighbors. That's all we got to say. (*He looks the man absolutely in the eyes*) We don't want your money.

(*He turns and walks away from the man.*)

LINDNER   (*Looking around at all of them*) I take it then that you have decided to occupy.

BENEATHA   That's what the man said.

LINDNER   (*To MAMA in her reverie*) Then I would like to appeal to you, Mrs. Younger. You are older and wiser and understand things better I am sure . . .

MAMA   (*Rising*) I am afraid you don't understand. My son said we was going to move and there ain't nothing left for me to say. (*Shaking her head with double meaning*) You know how these young folks is nowadays, mister. Can't do a thing with 'em. Good-bye.

LINDNER   (*Folding up his materials*) Well—if you are that final about it . . . There is nothing left for me to say. (*He finishes. He is almost ignored by the family who are concentrating on WALTER LEE. At the door LINDNER halts and looks around*) I sure hope you people know what you're doing.

(*He shakes his head and exits.*)

RUTH   (*Looking around and coming to life*) Well, for God's sake—if the moving men are here—LET'S GET THE HELL OUT OF HERE!

MAMA   (*Into action*) Ain't it the truth! Look at all this here mess. Ruth, put TRAVIS' good jacket on him . . . Walter Lee, fix your tie and tuck your shirt in, you look just like somebody's hoodlum. Lord have mercy, where is my plant? (*She flies to get it amid the general bustling of the family, who are deliberately trying to ignore the nobility of the past moment*) You all start on down . . . Travis child, don't go empty-handed . . . Ruth, where did I put that box with my skillets in it? I want to be in charge of it myself . . . I'm going to make us the biggest dinner we ever ate tonight . . . Beneatha, what's the matter with them stockings? Pull them things up, girl . . .

(*The family starts to file out as two moving men appear and begin to carry out the heavier pieces of furniture, bumping into the family as they move about.*)

BENEATHA   Mama, Asagai—asked me to marry him today and go to Africa—

MAMA   (*In the middle of her getting-ready activity*) He did? You ain't old enough to marry nobody—(*Seeing the moving men lifting one of her chairs precariously*) Darling, that ain't no bale of cotton, please handle it so we can sit in it again. I had that chair twenty-five years . . .

(*The movers sigh with exasperation and go on with their work.*)

BENEATHA   (*Girlishly and unreasonably trying to pursue the conversation*) To go to Africa, Mama—be a doctor in Africa . . .

MAMA   (*Distracted*) Yes, baby—

WALTER   Africa! What he want you to go to Africa for?

BENEATHA   To practice there . . .

WALTER   Girl, if you don't get all them silly ideas out your head! You better marry yourself a man with some loot . . .

BENEATHA   (*Angrily, precisely as in the first scene of the play*) What have you got to do with who I marry!

WALTER   Plenty. Now I think George Murchison—

(He and BENEATHA *go out yelling at each other vigorously;* BENEATHA *is heard saying that she would not marry* GEORGE MURCHISON *if he were Adam and she were Eve, etc. The anger is loud and real till their voices diminish.* RUTH *stands at the door and turns to* MAMA *and smiles knowingly.)*

MAMA   *(Fixing her hat at last)* Yeah—they something all right, my children . . .

RUTH   Yeah—they're something. Let's go, Lena.

MAMA   *(Stalling, starting to look around at the house)* Yes—I'm coming. Ruth—

RUTH   Yes?

MAMA   *(Quietly, woman to woman)* He finally come into his manhood today, didn't he? Kind of like a rainbow after the rain . . .

RUTH   *(Biting her lip lest her own pride explode in front of* MAMA) Yes, Lena.

*(*WALTER's *voice calls for them raucously.)*

MAMA   *(Waving* RUTH *out vaguely)* All right, honey—go on down. I be down directly.

*(*RUTH *hesitates, then exits.* MAMA *stands, at last alone in the living room, her plant on the table before her as the lights start to come down. She looks around at all the walls and ceilings and suddenly, despite herself, while the children call below, a great heaving thing rises in her and she puts her fist to her mouth, takes a final desperate look, pulls her coat about her, pats her hat and goes out. The lights dim down. The door opens and she comes back in, grabs her plant, and goes out for the last time.)*

Curtain

Although we know that drama, like other forms of fiction, reflects its own time, we can also say that, when a play originates behind the iron curtain or any barrier to free expression, it often reflects by seeming to distort. So Mrozek's The Police, written in Poland during the 1960's, is ostensibly a humorous play that satirizes a police state of the Western type. We in the West see it as a humorous play that satirizes a police state of the Communist type, and we wonder how it could be performed in Poland.

Perhaps the answer is that, although the play is a work of political satire, it is first of all comedy. How could officials in a "people's democratic republic" take seriously a farce in which at the end every character has been placed under arrest by some other character?

No commissar should be concerned about such nonsense! Or should he?

*THE POLICE

SLAWOMIR MROZEK

Translated by Nicholas Bethell

CHARACTERS

THE CHIEF OF POLICE
THE PRISONER, a former revolutionary, later
  the general's aide-de-camp
THE POLICE SERGEANT, an agent-provocateur

THE WIFE of the Sergeant-Provocateur
THE GENERAL
A POLICEMAN

Acts I and III take place in the CHIEF OF POLICE's *office. Act II takes place in the house of the* SERGEANT-PROVOCATEUR.

ACT I

(In the CHIEF OF POLICE's *office, which has a desk, two chairs and all other essential props. The office door is in a prominent position and there are two pictures on the wall. One is of the Infant King (a baby in an old-fashioned pram or a child dressed in the style of the nineteenth-century bourgeoisie), and the other of the Regent (a frightening-looking old man with a moustache). All those in any way connected with the police have big moustaches. The* PRISONER-REVOLUTIONARY *has a pointed beard like those of nineteenth-century progressives. All the policemen have jackboots, swords and high stiff collars. The interrogator has a civilian jacket, short and close fitting. The uniforms, which are all navy blue, have very shiny metal buttons.)*

CHIEF OF POLICE *(standing up and reading the end of some document)* . . . and so with feelings of shame and disgust I renounce my crimes, and the only desire I have is to serve our government with all my strength and with the deepest veneration and love for the rest of my life. *(Sits down, folds up the document.)*

PRISONER Don't put it away. I'll sign it.

CHIEF You'll sign it! What?

PRISONER I'll sign it and that's that.

CHIEF But why?

PRISONER What do you mean, why? For ten years you examine me, interrogate me, keep me in prison. Every day for ten years you give me that form to sign. When I refuse you threaten me with dreadful punishments and try to talk me round. Finally I agree to sign so that I can get out of prison and serve the government, and you look surprised and ask me why.

CHIEF   But it's so sudden, and without warning.

PRISONER   Colonel, I am undergoing a drastic change.

CHIEF   What change?

PRISONER   A drastic change of heart. I don't want to fight the government any more.

CHIEF   Why not?

PRISONER   I'm fed up with it. If anyone wants to fight the government, let them. I don't know who's going to do it. Spies for a foreign power, perhaps? Secret agents? But not me any more. I've done my bit.

CHIEF   (*sadly*) I'd never have expected this of you. Stop fighting the government? Become a conformist? You're a fine one to talk like that. The oldest prisoner in the country.

PRISONER   Exactly, Colonel. Is it true that I am the last man still in prison?

CHIEF   (*hesitatingly*) Yes . . .

PRISONER   You see? Some time ago it became obvious to everyone that we have the best political system in the world. My former colleagues confessed their guilt, received their pardon and went home. Now there's nobody left to arrest. I am the last remaining revolutionary; but what sort of a revolutionary? In my heart of hearts I'm a stamp collector.

CHIEF   That's what you say now, but who threw the bomb at the general?

PRISONER   Ancient history, Colonel. And the bomb didn't even explode. It's not worth raking that up.

CHIEF   Honestly, I can't believe my ears. For ten years you've refused to make a statement. You've held out splendidly. Time and time again you've been ordered to sign, but you never broke down. Instead you would stand up in disgust and spit at the picture (*gets up from his chair and stands to attention*) of our Infant King and his Uncle the Regent. (*Sits down.*) We've got used to living here together. Everything's nicely settled and now suddenly you want to destroy it all.

PRISONER   I tell you, there's just no point. If only I hadn't been so ideologically abandoned perhaps I could have gone on longer. But to think that the whole population of our beautiful, peaceful and fertile country has for so long been singing the praises (*gets up and stands to attention*) of our Infant King and his Uncle the Regent, that all the prisons are empty and that I alone, just me . . . No, Colonel, I promise you. I've given up my former beliefs. If the whole people supports the government and is against me, then there must be something in it. In fact, we've got a very good government, and that's that.

CHIEF   Hmmm . . . hmmm . . .

PRISONER   I beg your pardon?

CHIEF   (*gets up and adopts an official tone of voice*) While accepting with sincere joy and satisfaction the prisoner's confession, bearing witness to a change of heart which has come about under the corrective influence of imprisonment, I nevertheless consider it my duty to ascertain to what extent his new, favourable and entirely rational opinions are deep-rooted and lasting. (*Sits down. In a different tone.*) Why then, if I may ask, do you consider that our government is good?

PRISONER   You've got eyes, Colonel. Never before in history has our country reached such a high stage of development. You know, sometimes I move my plank bed against the window of my cell and put my latrine bucket on top of it upside down; then I can stand on the bucket on tiptoe and gaze out at a most beautiful meadow. Every spring it bursts into flower with different coloured blossoms. Then at haymaking time the farm workers come to the meadow and cut the grass. During the last ten years I have watched their faces light up with a happiness and satisfaction which grows in strength every year.

CHIEF   Do you realize that it is against the prison rules to look out of the window?

PRISONER   But for ideological purposes, Colonel, in the cause of corrective education. And that is not all. On the other side of the meadow there's a small hill, and on the other side of the hill during the last seven years an industrial building has been constructed. I can see a chimney, and sometimes there's smoke coming out of it.

CHIEF   To be strictly accurate I think I should tell you that that is a crematorium.

PRISONER   Why should they always bury dead people in the ground, like they've been doing for centuries and centuries? Don't atheists have the same right as believers to dispose of their bodies in the way they wish, with the sort of funeral they like. What you say only confirms what I've always felt, that this country of ours is a land of the broadest tolerance, even in religious matters.

CHIEF   Yeees . . .

PRISONER   Take culture and art. The hours I've spent walking up and down my cell—down the length of it, that is, because it's rectangular—all the time getting more and more excited.

CHIEF   Well yes. You've got to admit it.

PRISONER   You see, I'm right.

CHIEF   I am a civil servant and I can't settle this matter myself. That is to say I can't accept your change of heart too readily. I must first of all investigate that there are no doubts or hesitations left in your mind. It may be you are looking at things through rose-tinted spectacles. Take the economic situation, for example, are you not overlooking certain specialized matters like, say, the railway?

PRISONER   Even the most fanatical enemy of our state system could not deny that the railway, as a phenomenon, exists in this country.

(Pause. The CHIEF OF POLICE and the PRISONER look at each other. The CHIEF OF POLICE gets up, walks out from behind his desk and marches up and down the room in silence. Then he stops. For a moment he gazes at the pictures of the Infant King and his Uncle the Regent. The PRISONER watches him the whole time.)

CHIEF   Yes, and what about them? (Points to pictures.) I suppose you never had the slightest intention of . . . (impatiently) No, really! It's impossible!

PRISONER   I don't understand, Colonel.

CHIEF   Honestly, talking to you anyone would think you threw a tomato at the general, not a bomb, and that it never entered your head that (stands to *attention*) our Regent, the Uncle of our Infant King, is an idiot. (*Stands at ease.*)

PRISONER (*leaping to his feet in indignation*) Colonel!

CHIEF No, all right, that's enough, obviously he isn't. (*Goes on walking up and down.*) That is to say, as far as his intellect is concerned. But you must admit that even the most powerful brains have their little weaknesses; lower down, that is, among their habits, tastes.

(*He gets up, stares at the* PRISONER, *and winks at him. The* PRISONER *does not react. The* CHIEF OF POLICE *comes nearer, winks again very meaningfully and emphatically, moving his whole head and even his neck, as if he wanted to throw his eye at the* PRISONER. *The* PRISONER *turns round as if the wink were directed not at him, but at someone behind him. Pause.*)

PRISONER Why are you winking at me, Colonel?

CHIEF (*violently unbuttoning his tunic collar*) You ought to be ashamed of yourself! You, an old revolutionary, asking such a question.

PRISONER It's all this educational effect of prison life that you were talking about. I give you my word, I've simply forgotten what that wink might mean. Is it some sort of an allusion? Is it something unpleasant connected with the persons of our Infant King and of his Uncle the Regent?

CHIEF You don't think, then, that our Regent is—an old pervert?

PRISONER Him? That pure old man?

CHIEF (*again starts walking round the room*) All right, very good . . . As representative of the High Command I congratulate you on your progress. (*Offers his hand which the* PRISONER *takes.*) But this does not mean that we can give ourselves up to a sudden burst of rejoicing. It is a matter of great concern both to you, since you have undergone what we hope is a genuine change of heart, and to me, who must not accept your story too trustingly. You say that you do not believe that our Regent is a—a you know what. But psychologists tell us that often a man gives the impression that he is not thinking something, while in fact he is thinking it all the time. What have you got to say to that?

PRISONER You're right, Colonel. That's exactly the point. Sometimes it seems to us that we think we're not thinking, but we are thinking—while all the time we're not thinking at all. Thought is a powerful weapon, Colonel.

CHIEF (*pompously, sternly, suspiciously and testingly*) But only in the service of mankind!

PRISONER That is true.

CHIEF (*unwillingly*) Very well. Now please take a look at this picture of our Infant King. Small, isn't he?

PRISONER Like all children.

CHIEF You mean he's a shortarse, eh?

PRISONER You know, Colonel, if it wasn't for your uniform and high rank I might begin to think that you were right. But if the Chief of Police himself says that our Infant leader is a shortarse, then obviously such an opinion could never, never be the right one. If a shopkeeper had told me that, or a bricklayer out in the street, perhaps I'd have had my doubts. But the Chief of Police! No, this only confirms me in my great admiration and reverence for the person of our Infant King and—as a natural consequence—of his Uncle the Regent.

(*The* CHIEF OF POLICE *sits down again. Then the* PRISONER *gets up, walks towards the desk and takes up the initiative.*)

Please believe me. I've finished with my former mistaken anti-government point of view. The reasons for my change of heart fall into two categories: there are the external ones and the internal ones, and it is this double conviction which is the guarantee of the depth and permanence of my evolution—a thing which you, Colonel, for my own good are naturally concerned about. The external reasons are those we've already mentioned: the universal progress that our country has made. You only have to pick up a newspaper to be convinced of it. Look around you, Colonel. Don't hide your head in the sand in the face of these achievements. Is there anything wrong with the country? You've only got to look at your salary, Colonel, that in itself is enough to show how groundless are complaints of this sort. Anyway, I've become a keen government supporter, and I don't mind admitting it.

(*The* PRISONER *sits down and pulls his chair up nearer the desk. His tone is more confidential.*)

However, if you have any doubt that the emotions of nature are strong enough to make sure that I won't go back on my conversion, I'll show you that there are other emotions, internal emotions, which I feel more personally. You see, when I was a child I had no idea about law and order, about discipline and having an aim in life. All the time it was freedom and freedom. This—sort of—monotony in my spiritual diet could only satisfy part of my personality. Feelings of revolt against the established order, a desire to oppose all restrictions and authority—I had plenty of those. But in the course of time I began to feel a certain dissatisfaction. I came to the conclusion that I was in some way handicapped. I, a free rebel, a model revolutionary, began to feel a curious nostalgia. How is this? I asked myself. Why has Fate tormented me, deprived me of the joyful sensation of agreement, subservience and loyalty, the delightful feeling of unity with authority, the blissful capacity to carry out political inevitabilities, as well as the added delight of, without needing to be summoned by these inevitabilities, yielding myself up to them voluntarily, and having at the same time a complete, self-elevating confidence in myself as a man of action? I was a man unfulfilled, Colonel, but at last I understood that it was not too late. And it was then that the time came when my first me, rebellious and always complaining, perished as a result of over-indulgence, and a second me awoke, with a loud voice demanding the nourishment that was its due—a joyful and calm conformity, an eager hope in the future, and the peace which flows from full submission to authority. The joyful knowledge that the government of our Infant King and his Uncle the Regent (*both stand, then sit*) is just as good, wise and virtuous as we ourselves, arouses within us feelings of sheer delight unknown to those poor individuals, so imprisoned in their own negative outlook and so unfulfilled in their relationship with mankind. Only now, Colonel, have I achieved real fullness. So here I am—the last political prisoner in a country that is now flourishing and entirely loyal; the last dark cloud in the blue sky of the rule of our Infant King and his Uncle the Regent; one single crow, with the blackness of his wings marring the pure rainbow of our statedom. It is only on my account they still keep the police force going. If it wasn't for me they could send all the judges and guards off home. The prison would stand empty and could be turned into a preparatory school. Because of me, Colonel, you've got to hang around in this stuffy office. Otherwise you could get out far into the fields and meadows with a gun or fishing rod and throw off your suffocating uniform. I tell you, Colonel, you've won at last. The police have brought their mission to a close. The last man to oppose the government lays down his arms and his only desire is to join the chorus of citizens singing hosanna to our Infant King and his Uncle the Regent. For the first time in the world's history the ideal of law and order in a state has been achieved. When I leave here the last obstacle will be gone. Today should be a great occasion in your life, Colonel. It is the day of final victory. The task at which you have laboured your whole life and for which you were ordained has been crowned by success. Today I sign the paper that you have been trying to persuade me to sign for ten years. I will then go out into the free world and support the government. What is more, I will send an open letter to our Infant King and his Uncle the Regent —the most humble letter that has ever been written, filled with the deepest devotion and love.

CHIEF   You remember that stamp collection you were so proud of?

PRISONER   (*startled*) Yes, what's that got to do with it?

CHIEF   Just reflect for a moment whether you really want to leave us. Perhaps you could think it over once more and strengthen your convictions. Look before you leap, as they say. Meanwhile we could give you a hand in your stamp collecting. We've got secret agents in many interesting foreign countries who send us reports. We could soak the stamps off and give them to you for your album. Outside it's not so easy to get good stamps.

(*Enter a* POLICEMAN.)

POLICEMAN   Sir, the sergeant's back.

CHIEF   Tell him to come in.

(*Enter the* SERGEANT. *He is broad and red-faced, with moustaches twice as long as the others. He has one black eye and is limping. He comes to attention before the pictures of the Infant King and his Uncle the Regent and then flops into a chair. He is wearing a raincoat and a green hat with a narrow brim.*)

Well, Sergeant, how did you get on? My God! You look a sight! What happened?

(*The* SERGEANT *groans.*)

Does it hurt?

(*The* SERGEANT *nods his head, takes out a handkerchief and applies it to his eye. The* CHIEF OF POLICE *motions to the* POLICEMAN *to leave the room.*)

You can tell me now.

SERGEANT   Sir, as part of my duties as agent-provocateur I was trying to shout anti-government slogans—and they beat me up.

CHIEF   Who beat you up? No, you don't really mean that they . . . you were beaten up by . . .

SERGEANT   Unfortunately, yes. I was beaten up by the loyal population.

CHIEF   (*mutters gloomily to himself*) I expected as much.

PRISONER   You see, Colonel. It bears out my theory.

CHIEF   (*sharply*) Please don't interfere. Give me the details, Sergeant.

SERGEANT   Sir, immediately upon receiving your instructions I proceeded to carry them out. First of all I acquired a civilian suit, although if there's one thing I hate it's civilian clothes. To improve my disguise I obtained a green hat with a narrow brim, and a raincoat. I then went out into the street. For a short time I conducted myself defiantly opposite the government office of weights and measures, but nobody paid any attention. So I went to the square and made faces in front of the statue of our Infant King and his Uncle the Regent. (*Gets up, sits down.*) Again nobody saw me because, as you know, Colonel, everybody's in a hurry there. Then I went off and stood in a queue at a kiosk where they were selling beer. I looked around and saw that in front of the kiosk and all around me there was a collection of simple, ordinary citizens, in the thirtieth or thirty-eighth wage bracket, I should say. "This is fine," I thought to myself. The queque moved forward and all the time I was wondering what to do about it. At last I had an idea, and when my turn came I said to the man in my normal voice, "Two half pints, please, in quick succession." You see, Colonel, as if it was the royal succession that had brewed the beer, or something, and they were giving short measure, etc., etc. Well, either he didn't understand—he looked pretty stupid—or else he didn't want to understand—anyway he just asked me: "Mild or bitter, sir?" So then I let him have it straight. I said to him: "Our whole farming system's down the drain, and anyone who doesn't steal will die of starvation." Then the people who were standing in the queque with me came in closer and one of them asked if I was making any allusion to life in the present day, because he was an employee of the state, and he would not tolerate the state being insulted. So then I gave them the lot: the agricultural situation, foreign trade, then a few words about the police, especially the secret police. Then a young man in a cloth cap came out of the group and walked towards me. "You leave our police alone," he says. "I suppose next thing you'll start on the army; you'll want to cut down national service or get rid of it altogether, and next autumn I'm due to go before the recruiting board." And then some old bag who was standing a bit farther off yelled out: "Oh, so he doesn't like the police, eh? Why only last week they sent me a summons to arrange to have my house searched, and this so-and-so's going to get in the way, I suppose. After a search you always feel more comfortable and loyal, and if you don't have your house searched you get an uneasy feeling." I realized things were hotting up. But you know me, Colonel, I've been in the police since I was a child, and this job as agent-provocateur, it's something sacred to me, although it's hard work and, as I say, I'm sick of wearing these civilian clothes. Anyway, I didn't pay any attention and went on with all the usual things—the income tax, the health service and then a lot of stuff about our Infant King (*stands up*) and his Uncle the Regent (*sits down*). "So!" they all shouted, "you're one of those, are you? You're going to stand here and slander our beloved rulers." And then they all got together and beat me up.

PRISONER   Bravo, what a fine set of men.

SERGEANT   And you know, Colonel, when they were beating me up there were two conflicting feelings in my mind: a feeling of sadness and a feeling of joy. I was sad that I had not carried out your order, that I could not provoke anybody to be disloyal and that once more there's nobody we can arrest. But I was glad that love and reverence for the government and for the persons (*stands up*) of our Infant King and his Uncle the Regent (*sits down*) are so widespread and strongly felt by the population, as you can tell by my black eye.

PRISONER   (*half to himself, enthusiastically*) What a wonderful country! Wonderful people!

CHIEF   What you need is some steak on that eye.

PRISONER   Colonel! What the sergeant has said makes me even more convinced. I desire this instant to renounce my former ideals. They disgust me whenever I think of them. I will now sign the declaration of loyalty. Can I have a copy of it please, and pen and ink?

CHIEF   (*sadly*) Is your mind made up, then?

PRISONER   Nothing can alter my decision now. When I leave this building, with all its memories and recollections, I shall straight away apply to work for the state. Give me the paper, please.

CHIEF   You don't mind about the stamps?

PRISONER   Why should I think about postage stamps when I can join the service of our Infant King (*stands up*) and his Uncle the Regent? The passion of a collector is nothing compared to the spirit of service. Of what use are my stamp albums when I can give myself up to the delights of loyalty, which I have discovered for the first time in my life after such a long phase as an anarchist?

CHIEF   All right, then. I won't press you any more. Here is a pen, ink and paper. If that's what you want, you can have it. (*Angrily puts the paper in front of the* PRISONER.)

PRISONER   At last! (*Signs it.*)

(*The* CHIEF OF POLICE *takes the paper from him, blows on it and dries it. He rings the bell. Enter the* POLICEMAN.)

CHIEF   Bring his things in here. (*Exit the* POLICEMAN. *To the* PRISONER) You have disappointed me. I thought you'd hold out longer. It was so impressive the way you never broke down . . .

(*The* POLICEMAN *brings in the* PRISONER's *things: a cape, a mask and a bomb.*)

CHIEF   It is my duty to return you the things that were found on your person at the moment of your arrest.

PRISONER   Ghosts of the past!

(*Takes the conspirator's cloak from the* POLICEMAN, *throws it over his arm, and puts the mask in his pocket. The* POLICEMAN *then hands him the bomb.*)

Oh no! I don't want that. I've finished with that for ever. Colonel, I would be so pleased if you would accept this bomb as a present from me and as a souvenir of our happy times together. It can be a mark of the fatherly triumph that you have achieved over me. It is all that remains of the last revolutionary. You can have the mask too. (*takes the mask from his pocket*)

CHIEF   Just as you like.

Unconcernedly takes the bomb and mask from the PRISONER's *hand and puts them in drawer.*)

PRISONER   Allow me to congratulate you, Colonel. The last revolutionary is dead. A new citizen has been born. In your place I would order the rockets to be sent up and give my staff three days' holiday. And why only three days? From now on there will be nothing left for them to do. Goodbye all and thank you for everything.

CHIEF   Don't mention it.

(*The* PRISONER *kisses the hand of the* CHIEF OF POLICE, *then of the* SERGEANT *and of the* POLICEMAN. *He walks out of the door. The* POLICEMAN *makes a regulation about turn and also walks out. The* CHIEF OF POLICE *and the* SERGEANT *are left in silence. Suddenly a piercing shout is heard through the window from the* PRISONER *who is now in the street.*)

PRISONER   (*offstage*) Long live our Infant King and his Uncle the Regent!

CHIEF   (*hides his face in his hands and breaks down completely*). My God! My God!

SERGEANT   (*dreamily*) I wonder if I could provoke him to be disloyal . . . ?

ACT II

(*The action takes place in the home of the* AGENT-PROVOCATEUR. *On the wall are the well-known pictures of the Infant King and his Uncle the Regent. There is a wedding photograph of the* AGENT-PROVOCATEUR SERGEANT *and his* WIFE. *A door and a window are in clear view, and there are two chairs, a table and a tailor's dummy dressed in a very elaborate uniform of a police sergeant with a large number of medals. Near by is a small screen, under which a pair of jackboots can be seen. There is a fig plant, or possibly a palm, and a small table carrying a pair of dumb-bells. The* AGENT-PROVO-CATEUR's WIFE *is on stage, as is the* CHIEF OF POLICE, *who is dressed as in Act I, but disguised with a coat and hood thrown over his uniform. He is wearing his sword.*)

CHIEF OF POLICE   (*his hood pulled over his eyes*) Good morning. Is your husband at home?

WIFE   No, I'm afraid he's not back from work yet.

CHIEF   Not back from work? Today's his day off, isn't it?

WIFE   He doesn't like days off. What do you want to see him about?

(*The* CHIEF OF POLICE *moves into the centre of the room and throws off his hood.*)

Colonel! I didn't recognize you.

CHIEF   Shhh . . . Not so loud! Did your husband say when he'd be back?

WIFE   No. He went into town to do some voluntary provoking. I don't know when he'll be here.

CHIEF   Please don't let me interrupt you. You're sewing, I see.

WIFE   (*ashamedly putting down her work*) Er . . . yes. It's just some gold braid for my husband's underpants. He feels so terrible in civilian clothes these days and always likes to wear some tiny piece of military dress, even if it's underneath everything. (*suddenly changing her tones, imploringly*) Colonel!

CHIEF   Yes. What is it?

WIFE   I wish you'd take him off this job. Don't make him do any more provoking in civilian clothes.

CHIEF   Why not?

WIFE   You've no idea how thin and pale he's got since he's had to go about in civvies. He can't exist out of uniform. He's withering away.

CHIEF   I'm afraid that's just too bad, madam. Provoking is always done in civilian dress.

WIFE   Couldn't he just wear his helmet? He always used to feel much better then.

CHIEF   No, madam. A helmet would attract attention.

WIFE   (*in a confidential tone*) Oh yes, of course. It's such a long time since he's had anyone to arrest. He probably doesn't show it in front of you, Colonel, but at home he's become moody and quite intolerable. One new arrest would put him right again.

CHIEF   (*pompously*) You can't make arrests without an agent-provocateur.

WIFE   (*dully and sadly*) I'm afraid I've just given up hope.

CHIEF   *You* don't know anyone that we could arrest?

WIFE   No! All the people I know are as loyal as hell. And if there was anyone, my husband would be the first person I'd tell, just to give him a bit of peace of mind. He's always asking me.

CHIEF   Any neighbours, then? Any distant relatives?

WIFE   No. They're all law-abiding citizens. There was an old man on our street who used to complain, but with him it was the gout, not the government. He's just died, probably of being too careful.

CHIEF   Yes, nowadays it's all so peaceful, all so quiet. Tell me, how did you first meet your husband?

WIFE   Oh, that was ages ago, Colonel. He reported me to the secret police and I reported him. That's how we got to know each other.

CHIEF   Have you got any children?

WIFE   Two. But they're locked up now. Shall I get them down?

CHIEF   No, please. I don't want to inconvenience anyone. I just dropped in to have a word with your husband.

WIFE   He may be back by now. He always listens at the doors on the way upstairs. I'll go and have a look.

(*Exit. Light footsteps are heard on the stairs. The window opens and through it enters the SERGEANT in civilian clothes. He is carrying a raincoat and a small green hat.*)

SERGEANT   Colonel! Fancy seeing you in my house. How wonderful!

CHIEF   Psst! I'm here unofficially. I'll tell you why later. Why didn't you come in through the door?

SERGEANT   I was walking on the tops of the houses. When it was time to come home I thought I'd come back across the roofs. It's one way of getting here and there could have been something going on. Anyway down in the street it couldn't be quieter.

CHIEF   What did you find?

SERGEANT   Nothing at all, Colonel. Just a few birds. Is my wife here?

CHIEF   She went out on to the staircase. She thought you were there.

SERGEANT   She always listens at the doors when she goes down those stairs. You don't mind if I change now, do you, Colonel? I feel naked without my uniform on.

CHIEF   No, do change if you like. You're in your own home, and it's your day off anyway.

SERGEANT   (*going behind the screen*) Yes, I know. But you see, I thought maybe today would be my lucky day, and I went out. I did a bit of provoking before lunch, but as usual it was no good. They just said hello and walked on.

CHIEF   Sergeant, if it hadn't been for you perhaps we'd never have lived to see this alarming drop in the crime figures. That is to say, I meant, thanks to you we now have this perfect state of law and order. I must recommend you for promotion.

SERGEANT   (*all this time changing into uniform behind the screen*) It's nothing, Colonel. I just felt I had to go and try once more. I like doing it, really. (*Pause. The* SERGEANT *finishes changing.*)

(*He comes out in full uniform with sword and medals. He stretches himself luxuriously.*) Ah, what a relief. At last I feel I can relax. Coming home from work, changing into uniform, you've no idea how marvellous it is. Oh . . . er, excuse me, Colonel. (*realizes he has been behaving a little too informally. Comes to attention*) This is what comes of working in civvies. Civilian clothes are very bad for morale. You see, sir, I've got to take a grip on myself.

CHIEF   Oh, don't worry about that. I've got an important matter to discuss with you. Find some excuse to send your wife off; she mustn't come in here. I'm sure she's quite reliable, but what I have to talk to you about is most secret.

(*The* SERGEANT *exits. His footsteps die away on the stairs. The* CHIEF OF POLICE *takes off his coat and sits down. More footsteps. Enter the* SERGEANT.)

SERGEANT   I sent her off to get some waterproof glue.

CHIEF   Couldn't you think up a better pretext than that?

SERGEANT   It wasn't a pretext, Colonel. I really need it. My raincoat got torn when they beat me up last time.

CHIEF   Oh, all right. Has she gone far?

SERGEANT   She won't be back for three-quarters of an hour.

CHIEF   I suppose you're surprised by my visit.

SERGEANT   Just as you say, sir.

CHIEF   You're surprised, then?

SERGEANT   Yes, sir. The Chief of Police here in my house! I'd sooner have expected a revolution.

CHIEF   No wishful thinking now, Sergeant. And a keen sergeant must always be prepared for a revolution. No, I didn't really mean that. Your service record is irreproachable.

SERGEANT   But of course, Colonel.

CHIEF   Still, in your exemplary conduct there is something more than ordinary conscientiousness and sense of duty. (*The* SERGEANT *comes to attention.*) No, don't bother about that. Sit down.

SERGEANT   With your permission, sir, I'd rather do my exercises for a bit— that is if you don't mind, Colonel.

CHIEF   Your exercises?

SERGEANT   Always at this time, as soon as I get home, I do a little weight lifting or spring exercises. I must be able to cope with any situation that crops up. They're good for my muscles. (*Bends his biceps.*) You want to try them?

CHIEF   No thank you. I can see from here. If you want to do your exercises, do them.

(*The* SERGEANT *tucks up his sleeve, takes the dumb-bell from the table and returns to his place in front of the* CHIEF OF POLICE. *All the while listening to his boss he performs a few rhythmical lifts of the dumb-bell every now and again. Every now and then he checks his biceps to see if they have hardened. He then tries the other arm. All this time he is engaged in conversation with the* CHIEF OF POLICE.)

As I said, you are not only an excellent policeman. I have found that you are something more than that.

SERGEANT   (*in a very disciplined manner*) Sir!

CHIEF   I find that you have given me an idea.

SERGEANT   (*as before*) Sir! Yessir!

CHIEF   You put on civilian clothes, do you not, when your job requires it, even though you can't stand wearing them?

SERGEANT   Yessir! Anything for my job, sir.

CHIEF   Exactly, in other words you sacrifice your personal likes and dislikes on the altar of service to the state. But that's not important. In examining your case I have come to the conclusion that your keenness, readiness and devotion to duty are quite out of proportion to the tasks you fulfil so admirably, even though these tasks are certainly not easy.

SERGEANT   Yessir!

CHIEF   You give me the impression of a Hercules who spends his time cutting wood and carrying water. Of course, this sort of work is difficult and useful, but it is not the work of a Hercules. In you there is a strength, Sergeant, a strength which is only partly finding its outlet in ordinary work. For you are something more than a civil servant. You are inspired by the idea of order and general discipline. You are the mystic of the police force, the saint of the police. Why have you got so thin lately, Sergeant?

SERGEANT   It's my insomnia, Colonel.

CHIEF   Oh, I see. Tell me, do you have dreams?

SERGEANT   Well, I do sometimes, but they're silly.

CHIEF   Tell me about them.

SERGEANT   Often, I don't know why it is, but I dream that there are two of me.

CHIEF   Bravo! Bravo!

SERGEANT   One in uniform and another in civilian clothes. We are walking across a big field; the birds are singing, it's warm—and then I, that is both of us, or both of me, feel in my soul that I am being carried far, far away . . . and somewhere out there . . . and there's a smell of fresh grass, you know, like in the spring—and then I feel such a desire, such a longing to arrest someone, to arrest someone even if it's just a hare sitting under a ridge, or a little bird. Then I look, or rather we look, all round the field; we strain our eyes and there's nobody there, nobody to arrest, and then I throw myself on the soft earth, beat my head and the tears pour out. And it's then that the stupidest part of my dream comes.

CHIEF   (*in great suspense*) Tell me! Tell me!

SERGEANT   Then I dream that I arrest myself. That is to say—the I that's in uniform arrests the me that's in civilian clothes. Then I wake up covered in sweat.

(*Th recounting of the dream has been a severe effort for the* SERGEANT. *While he is telling it he stops doing his gymnastics.*)

CHIEF   This is very interesting, what you say, very interesting. Now, Sergeant, when was the last time that you made an arrest?

SERGEANT   (*heavily, despondently*) Oh, Colonel. I'm ashamed to tell you.

CHIEF   Well listen carefully to what I say.

SERGEANT   Yessir.

CHIEF   Do you realize that we shall never have the chance to arrest anyone again?

SERGEANT   (*letting the weight fall from his hand*) What did you say, sir?

CHIEF   (*gets up from his chair and begins to walk about the room*) I'll tell you something else. Not only will we never arrest anyone ever again, but your son, your grandson and your great-grandson—they won't arrest anyone either. The whole police force is standing on the edge of a precipice, on the eve of a catastrophe. What is the function of a policeman? It is to arrest those who offend against the existing order. But suppose there aren't any people like that left. Suppose that as a result of the operations of our improved and reconstituted police force the last trace of rebelliousness in our people has disappeared and that they have become universally enthusiastic for the regime. Suppose that they have formed once and for all a permanent love for our (*stands to attention*) Infant King and his Uncle the Regent. What is there for the police to do then? I did my best to improve matters and that is why I advised you to carry on provoking people to criticize the government but, as you see, even this last resort has come to nothing. Not only were you unable to provoke anyone, but when you started on your anti-government slogans they beat you up.

SERGEANT   That's nothing. It's healed up already.

CHIEF   That is not the point. We are dealing here with more general matters. For a long time I have been expecting and dreading the moment which has now arrived. Our last political prisoner has just signed the act of allegiance, has been released from prison and has begun to serve our Infant King and his Uncle the Regent. I tried to keep him back; I promised him stamps for his collection; it was no good. Do you know what this means? It means that we have beautiful prisons constructed at great expense; we have a highly trained, devoted staff; we have courtrooms, offices and card indexes—and we now have not one single prisoner, not one single suspect, not one single clue to follow up. The people have become wildly, cruelly, bestially loyal.

SERGEANT   That's true, Colonel. That's a fact. I'd . . .

CHIEF   Soon the time will come when we'll have to take off our uniforms; and then you'll toss and turn in bed at nights, longing hopelessly for one little interrogation. Your gold braid sewn on to your underpants won't be much good to you then. Already you're suffering from insomnia, and for the moment you've still got your job. Think what it'll be like soon, eh?

SERGEANT   No, no!

CHIEF   But yes, yes! They'll take away your uniform; they'll give you some sort of sports jacket, walking shoes and a pair of flannels. You'll be able to go out into the fields or on to the water, with a fishing rod or a shotgun if you like, and enjoy your spare time exactly as you wish. You'll be able to arrest hares and sparrows, so long as it isn't the mating season.

SERGEANT   Is there nothing we can do, Colonel?

CHIEF   (*putting his arm round his shoulder, warmly*) I have come to you not only in my capacity as Chief of Police, not only as your superior officer. At this dreadful time we are both of us just simple constables. In the face of the ruin which is facing our life's work we must give each other our hands and offer brotherly advice for its solution.

(*Gives the* SERGEANT *his hand. He is very much moved and squeezes it, at the same time wiping away a tear with his left hand.*)

And now listen to me. The man who can even now save the situation—is you.

SERGEANT   Me?

CHIEF   Yes, you. Pay attention to what I'm saying. What do we need? What we need is one person who we could lock up, whom we could arrest for something which could in some very slight degree be described as anti-government activity. Having several times attempted to find this man, it has become apparent that we shall not find him in the ordinary course of events, or in what we might call a natural manner. We must, so to speak, compose this man ourselves. My choice has fallen on you.

SERGEANT   I don't understand, sir.

CHIEF   What don't you understand?

SERGEANT   What I have to do.

CHIEF   Exactly the same as you've been doing all along: shout something against the government, but with this difference—this time we won't let you off; we'll lock you up.

SERGEANT   Me?

CHIEF   I assure you that the fulfilment of the task I have set you is far more admirable from the point of view of police morality than simply provoking any old citizen to criticize the government and arresting him. That would simply be carrying out your ordinary daily work. Here it is a question of fulfilling an act which is not without a certain poetry of its own, an act which belongs only to a policeman who is specially selected, inspired, pierced right to the marrow of his bones with the spirit of the police force. This is what I was thinking of when I said that I saw in you the fire of a policeman's vocation, something that is rare even among the best of us. I said that there was something in you that had not found its proper outlet, that had been eagerly awaiting the assignment that I can only now reveal to you. You are going to be our sergeant redeemer.

SERGEANT   Colonel, I'll always—anything I can do, sir—sir, I've got a headache.

CHIEF   Don't worry about that. Now change back into civilian clothes.

SERGEANT   What, again? What for?

CHIEF   You can't act as your own provocateur wearing uniform.

SERGEANT   All right, shall I change now? This minute?

CHIEF   Yes, of course, we've no time to waste. When you've changed we'll open the window so they can hear you better from the street. Then you can stand by the window and shout out something as loud as you can against our Infant King and his Uncle the Regent. (*Both stand to attention.*) Then I'll draw my sword, arrest you, and that's that.

SERGEANT   My God, but I'm supposed to be a policeman!

CHIEF   You are more a policeman than anyone else in the world. To be a member of the police and to pretend to others that you're not a policeman—that makes you a double policeman; but to be a policeman and to pretend to *yourself* that you're not a policeman—that makes you a policeman deep down, luxuriously, in the depths of your heart. We might say that you're a super-policeman, unlike any other policeman, even a double-police policeman.

(*The* SERGEANT *goes behind the screen. There, groaning and sobbing, he changes into civilian clothes. The screen is low so that his head is visible and, at the bottom, his calves too.*)

CHIEF   Before today is out I shall send a report to the general. Tomorrow morning our Infant King and his Uncle the Regent will be informed that we have discovered and arrested a revolutionary. We shall be saved.

SERGEANT   (*doing up his buttons*) What do I have to shout?

CHIEF   Haven't you got anything prepared from your previous experience?

SERGEANT   Shall I say that our Regent, the Uncle of our Infant (*stands to attention*) King, is a swine?

CHIEF   That's not direct enough. It must be something strong and forceful, with no understatement, so that I can arrest you one hundred per cent.

SERGEANT   Well then, what about—dirty swine?

CHIEF   That's much better. We'll open the window. (*They open the window.*) Now—one . . . two . . .

SERGEANT   Just a minute!

(*Runs away from the window and takes out a brush from behind the screen. With one careful movement he removes a speck of dust from the uniform which is now hanging again on the tailor's dummy. Puts down the brush and returns to the window.*)

All right, now! (*Fills his lungs with air.*)

CHIEF   One . . . two . . . three . . .

SERGEANT   (*shouts*) Our Regent, the Uncle of our Infant King, is a dirty swine.

CHIEF   (*drawing his sword, loudly*). I arrest you in the name of our Infant King and his Uncle the Regent.

SERGEANT'S WIFE   (*enters the room suddenly*). Good heavens! Still trying to provoke people. Can't you ever take a rest?

CHIEF   Silence, woman! At last he's made a success of it!

ACT III

(*The* CHIEF OF POLICE's *office, as in Act I. A* POLICEMAN *is nailing up some garlands made of leaves or something. He is preparing the decorations for the visit of the* GENERAL. *The* CHIEF OF POLICE *and the* SERGEANT *are sitting opposite each other; the* CHIEF *behind the desk and the* SERGEANT *where the* PRISONER *sat in the first act.*)

CHIEF   So—you've been trying to saw through the bars of your cell window. And you kicked one of the warders. This is the second time it's happened.

SERGEANT   I don't know what's come over me, really, Colonel.

CHIEF   Is there anything you need?

SERGEANT   (*sadly*) No, thank you.

CHIEF   Still, you look as if there's plenty you need. You're so pale, silent.

SERGEANT   Maybe that's because I'm locked up in prison, sir.

CHIEF   Every day I send reports about you to the general. Thanks to you we've been granted funds for rebuilding the prison, recruiting new personnel and strengthening the patrols. The general has become personally interested in your case. He says you're a very dangerous man and that it's extremely fortunate I got you in time. (*The* SERGEANT *shrugs his shoulders.*) Don't look so glum. If I didn't know you better I might think you were displeased with all this. The general says that today he will attend your interrogation in person.

SERGEANT   He—he—he . . .

CHIEF   Are you ill? Aren't you sleeping properly?

SERGEANT   Not very well.

CHIEF   Are you having dreams?

SERGEANT   Now and again.

CHIEF   What dreams?

SERGEANT   I dream I'm walking through a great big field . . .

CHIEF   The birds are singing, eh?

SERGEANT   How do you know?

CHIEF   Are you wearing uniform or civilian dress?

SERGEANT   Civilian dress! an overcoat and plus fours.

CHIEF   And what else?

SERGEANT   I walk on and I look upwards. There's a tree. And you, sir, are sitting on one of the branches and eating cheese.

CHIEF   I am sitting and eating cheese?

SERGEANT   Yes. I am standing under the tree and you open your mouth to arrest me, sir, and the cheese falls out of your mouth on to the ground.

CHIEF   And you pick it up?

SERGEANT   No. I don't like Gorgonzola.

CHIEF   (*displeased*) A very stupid dream.

SERGEANT   Yes, Colonel.

CHIEF   Would you like a drink?

(*Without waiting for an answer, wishing to improve an unpleasant situation, he reaches towards the desk, takes out a bottle of beer and glasses, pours.*)

SERGEANT   Thank you. (*Drinks. Suddenly he puts down the glass.*) No, really, Colonel, I mustn't drink with you.

CHIEF   Why not?

SERGEANT   Because I'm just an ordinary . . . Colonel, can you tell me, what am I?

CHIEF   What a question! You're yourself.

SERGEANT   But what I am now, a policeman or a prisoner. And another thing, if I'm a policeman, am I myself, or if I'm a prisoner, am I myself, and since I must be myself, am I a policeman or a prisoner?

CHIEF I explained all this to you at the time of your arrest. Why start all over again?

SERGEANT It was all quite clear then, sir, because that was just the beginning and I still knew what I was—an ordinary police sergeant in the secret service. But things really started to go wrong earlier, when I was working as an agent-provocateur. Please don't be angry, sir, but I see now that it was then that it all started, and if I'd known at that time I'd have asked you to put someone else on this provoking job. It wasn't just an idle whim that I was so upset at having to wear civvies. A policeman should never take off his uniform, under any circumstances.

CHIEF Still, it never entered your head to make a complaint. And when it was your day off you went out to work of your own free will.

SERGEANT But, sir. It wasn't anything like as bad as it is now. I didn't have the remotest idea, sir. Even when you came to my house yourself and talked about my golden future and said I reminded you of Hercules, even then it was pretty awful, but at least I knew that I was a first-class policeman and, as you said, Colonel, far better than all the others. It only really began to get bad when you arrested me and I started my time in prison. Prison has a terrible effect on a man, sir. From the moment I was arrested everything started getting more and more confused.

CHIEF What do you mean?

SERGEANT Well, sir, to start with I remembered everything just as you explained it to me. Then I began to have attacks and black-outs. I got frightened and started repeating to myself over and over again: 'I am a sergeant in the secret service. I am a sergeant in the secret service', or rather in the top-secret service. But then . . .

CHIEF What happened 'then'?

SERGEANT Then I stopped repeating it. I didn't see the sense. And it reached the point, Colonel, that . . . Oh, anyway, what I meant was that I am just an ordinary . . .

CHIEF An ordinary what, damn it?

SERGEANT Either an ordinary policeman or an ordinary prisoner, and whichever I am . . .

CHIEF Why do you have to bring out these stupid, childish arguments. This is what comes of giving responsible jobs to people with no higher education. In your place a man with any intelligence . . .

SERGEANT What I was going to say was that whichever of the two I am I do not think I should drink with you, sir. If I am to be a policeman, then I cannot condone your drinking with a prisoner—that is to say with me, because I am in fact under arrest. And if I am a prisoner, a revolutionary feared by the general himself and by the government of the country, there again I should not drink with you.

CHIEF Why not?

SERGEANT Because if I am a prisoner I must conduct myself according to the moral code of an imprisoned revolutionary, and I cannot drink with the chief of police, a representative of authority.

CHIEF Have you gone mad?

SERGEANT No, Colonel, this is something stronger than me. Are you in a position to release me from prison? No, you are not. So I've got to stay here. And if I have to stay in prison the effect of that environment upon me becomes stronger and stronger. I've tried to fight it, but I feel that every day I spend in prison does something horrible to me—something I don't quite understand.

CHIEF Maybe you *are* ill. Have you ever had trouble with your lungs?

SERGEANT No, it's not that, Colonel. I couldn't be more healthy. You saw me yourself doing my dumb-bell exercises, and I only wish you could have seen me doing my press-ups. This is something quite different. Do you know that since the time that you arrested me I have started to develop certain new ideas?

CHIEF Be careful what you say.

SERGEANT No, sir, I want you to know about it. For example, before this I used to travel quite often by train, and I've never thought about it particularly. But when a man's in prison he becomes, I think, much more critical, and you know what I've decided?

CHIEF How should I know? Tell me at once.

SERGEANT That our railway system is atrocious.

CHIEF Do you realize what you're saying? I warn you, I shall have to report this.

SERGEANT Do make a report, sir, please. This sort of thing gets a hold on a man and he just can't stay silent any longer. Take art and culture, for example. Will you tell me, Colonel, why did we have to torment and persecute those poor artists . . . ?

CHIEF (*writing quickly*) A little slower, please. What were those last two words?

SERGEANT I said "those poor artists."

CHIEF . . . tists. Right. (*taking his eyes from the paper and stopping writing*) No, I don't believe it. You, with your record of loyal service, do you really hold these opinions? We've worked together for so many years; everything's always gone smoothly, and all the time you were . . . Do you really think that things are so bad in this country? Think it over.

SERGEANT What is there to think over? Listen: if I move my plank bed against the wall, put the bucket on it upside down and stand on it, I can see out of the window of my cell. There's a field there and just now it's full of farmers because it's harvest time. When I examine them closely I can't help thinking—and I wish you could see it, sir—what sour expressions they've got on their faces, the general dissatisfaction that's painted on them.

CHIEF This is an entirely subjective outlook on your part. Quite apart from the conclusion to which it leads, whether they're loyal or disloyal, subjectivism as a method is entirely opposed to our party programme. I would have had to punish you even if you hadn't mentioned this so-called dissatisfaction. And besides, it's against the rules to look out of the window.

SERGEANT But not for someone who's fighting against the government, Colonel. Someone like that would not deprive himself even of the most trivial act of rebellion. On the contrary, he would consider it part of his duty, to bring his mission to fulfilment, not to mention the satisfaction it would give him. And another thing, when I look out of the window, I can see a newly-built crematorium on the other side of the field, and that also gives me food for thought. It is a non-productive investment.

CHIEF   Would you deny atheists the right to dispose of their bodies as they like, with their own sort of funeral? If you are against religious tolerance how can you have the nerve to criticize the government's record in that respect?

SERGEANT   Those people are dead, and your argument is not valid. And even if I hadn't looked out of the window there are writings scratched on the walls in my cell. A man sits there with nothing to do, so he reads. Some of them make you think. They aren't so stupid.

CHIEF   What, for instance?

SERGEANT   "Down with tyranny," Colonel.

CHIEF   So! That's the way it is! It's reached that stage. And I suppose our Regent (*comes to attention*), the Uncle of our Infant King (*the* SERGEANT *however remains seated*), is an idiot.

SERGEANT   (*sadly*) I'm afraid so, Colonel.

CHIEF   And I suppose our Infant King is a shortarse.

SERGEANT   I'm afraid so, Colonel.

CHIEF   (*choking with anger*) Umph!

(*The* POLICEMAN *is walking round the room all this time, but not in such a way as to interrupt the dialogue. He carries in a Christmas tree, hangs garlands on it, leaves the room and returns. Everything is done most discreetly. At this moment he enters the room.*)

POLICEMAN   Sir! The general's arrived, sir.

(*The* CHIEF OF POLICE *runs to put away the bottle and straightens his uniform. Shortly afterwards the former* PRISONER *and revolutionary enters the room in the uniform of an aide-de-camp. He has no beard but has policeman's moustaches. He stands at attention in front of the door, facing the audience, with his side towards the door where the* GENERAL *is going to enter. The* CHIEF OF POLICE *and the* POLICEMAN *are also at attention. The* SERGEANT *stands up reluctantly. Enter the* GENERAL *in suitable regalia, with a moustache, of course. He walks up to the* SERGEANT *and stands in front of him, inspecting him.*)

GENERAL   So! This is the man . . .

CHIEF   Yessir, that's him.

GENERAL   He looks to me like the ringleader. Have you managed to find the rest of his gang?

CHIEF   Not yet, but we're interrogating him systematically.

GENERAL   A dangerous bird. Did you find any explosive materials on him?

CHIEF   Not so far. But we haven't given up hope.

GENERAL   (*gives a whistle*) Hmmm. He's more dangerous than I thought. He's dishonest. Good, straightforward revolutionaries always have a couple of pounds of dynamite on them. It looks to me as if we've caught their key man. What do you think, Lieutenant?

AIDE   I agree, sir. If he's been searched and nothing's been found on him it means there's more to this than meets the eye.

GENERAL   Oh, Colonel, allow me to present to you my aide-de-camp. I've just chosen him as my special adviser on revolutionary affairs and anti-government activity. He's an expert on that subject.

CHIEF   Sir! No, it's impossible, sir.

GENERAL   What's the matter with you?

CHIEF   Your Excellency, you must allow me to speak, sir. You have become the victim of a mistake, sir, or of a deliberate trick. This man . . .

GENERAL   Speak up, man.

CHIEF   He was the one who threw the bomb at you, sir.

GENERAL   Who?

CHIEF   Your present assistant and my former prisoner.

GENERAL   Yes, Colonel, please continue.

CHIEF   I swear to you, sir, I am not mistaken. I know him well. For ten years I used to interrogate him here in my office—on this chair, sir. It is impossible that Your Excellency should have such an assistant.

GENERAL   What have you got to say, Lieutenant?

AIDE   The colonel's right, of course. I am his former prisoner. The fact that he recognized me in this uniform and with a different hair style is a great tribute to his keenness and professional skill.

CHIEF   Why, you impertinent . . .

AIDE   I am your former prisoner, Colonel, naturally. But you seem to have forgotten that I signed the act of allegiance and was released. His Excellency is perfectly well aware of all this.

GENERAL   Calm yourself, Colonel. I knew it all along, really. And you can see that if I introduce the lieutenant as an expert in matters concerning the fight against subversive activity, it is not without justification.

CHIEF   But the bomb . . . the bomb . . . I've still got it in my drawer.

GENERAL   My dear Colonel, everybody some time has to throw some bomb at some general or other. The organism of the body demands it. The sooner you get it over the better. As for me, I have complete confidence in my new assistant precisely because he has all this behind him. There are so many people who have still not satisfied this natural urge. You mustn't be angry if I ask you, Colonel, but have you ever thrown a bomb at a general?

CHIEF   Your Excellency!

GENERAL   You see. Neither have I. And therefore, if you'll forgive my saying so, I have more confidence in my assistant than I have in you, or even in myself. I promise you, Colonel, that if you want to be thought of as the ideal chief of police, part of your job should consist of taking precautions in case I throw a bomb at myself. Have you thought about that?

CHIEF   No, sir.

GENERAL   You see. You should think about it. The person of a general is the property of the state and the government, not of the individual who holds the rank. So any attempt of this sort, even on my part, must be considered an attack against the uniform of an officer and, so, indirectly, against the state. And if ever you should have to arrest me on this account, I trust you will remember that it was I who reported myself to you and brought this vital information to the notice of the Chief of Police, and in my trial this will be considered as an extenuating circumstance. That is the situation.

(*The* CHIEF OF POLICE *comes to attention.*)
To revert to our discussion about the lieutenant I will tell you something else. He entered the service not long ago and came to us from a situation that was, I need hardly tell you, extremely different from our own. Already he has achieved the rank of an officer. This requires some effort, as you can imagine. We must congratulate him on his keenness and hard work. We, Colonel, are the old guard, and have acquired our qualities of loyalty little by little. In him a love for the government has exploded suddenly, fresh and pure, and concentrated by his long years of anti-government activities. And as regards his qualifications for this present job, I can assure you that he is second to none in combating these same activities. Therefore in expressing your dislike of him you lay yourself open to the charge—groundless, I am sure—of being jealous of him because of his lightning success.

CHIEF   I can promise you, sir . . .

GENERAL   All right. Don't worry. I brought him here specially because I knew we had a tricky case on our hands with this enemy of (*stands to attention*) our Infant King and his Uncle the Regent. It'll be quite a business, you can be sure. Shall we begin?

(*They take their places and sit down ready for the interrogation. There is an air of expectation, as before a stage performance.*)
Proceed, Lieutenant, if you please.

CHIEF   Allow me to suggest . . .

GENERAL   What, you again? You ought to be ashamed of yourself. This aversion of yours towards our young people is beginning to look suspicious.

AIDE   I'm afraid you're going to be disappointed, Your Excellency, both you and the Chief of Police. The matter will be quite short and simple.

CHIEF   Oh, you think so do you, young man?

GENERAL   I agree with the Colonel; you are over-estimating the simplicity of the case. We know that as a result of the accused's incredible treachery and low cunning we have no evidence of any substance against him. The extent of his subversive activity is borne out by his outburst concerning our Regent (*They stand, then sit.*) the Uncle of our Infant King, the outburst which immediately unmasked the criminal and became the grounds for his summary arrest. And if the criminal shouted out things like that at the top of his voice, how much more terrible must be the things that he has been carrying on in silence. Still, we do not possess the materials that would enable us to discover what the criminal has done. I need only mention the fact that no explosives were found on him. On what ground, then, do you consider that the case is short and simple?

AIDE   I do not intend at this time to point to any hostile acts which the prisoner has committed openly. But I can state quite categorically that such acts are to be found lurking in their full baseness in the personality of the accused, and that even if they have not yet been carried out, they exist with the same reality as if they had been carried out. For we know, do we not, that time is one, and that it is not to be divided into time past and time present? And from the point of view of the investigation it is the most clear and damning truth.

CHIEF   If you will allow me, General, two words . . .

GENERAL   But of course! Please!

CHIEF   I do not deny that we have to deal with an exceptionally dangerous criminal, and that those who have been claiming that the police have nothing to do deserve simply to be pitied, if not actually arrested. It seems to me, though, that the method employed by my colleague the lieutenant is the sign of an engaging though, perhaps, over-rash belief in his own abilities—typical of the inexperienced.

GENERAL   Colonel, I thought I asked you . . .

AIDE   As far as I know the criminal began his unusually intensive enemy activity after a long period of loyalty, and even of cooperation with the government.

CHIEF   That is so, my young friend.

AIDE   We have then to deal with an exceptionally dangerous individual. It is a process analogical with the one which you, General, were so kind as to outline a moment ago when you were evaluating my career—that is to say a process of contrary direction. This man, at a comparatively late age—which leads to a sharpening of the symptoms—achieved his first sensual pleasures with the feeling that he was being persecuted. As you know, this feeling gives one an illusion of one's own importance and dignity, the same, in fact, in intensity as the feeling of God-fearing loyalty and agreement with the prevailing viewpoints, although entirely different from it in its detail of course, and this is why it is so extraordinarily attractive to people who have not yet experienced it.

CHIEF   I do not agree. This man is an abominable sort of criminal, that is obvious, but I do not see in what way he is worse than other such people who . . . who throw bombs at generals.

GENERAL   That damn bomb again!

(*Consternation, muttering.* CHIEF OF POLICE *puffs through his moustache.*)

AIDE   I can assure you, Colonel, that this man is capable of throwing a bomb at three generals without batting an eyelid.

CHIEF   (*impulsively, to the* SERGEANT, *in his old superior-officer tone of voice*) Attention!

(*The* SERGEANT *instinctively draws himself up to attention.*)

Speak up now! Would you throw a bomb at the general?

GENERAL   Answer frankly and truthfully, Sergeant. Don't take any notice of us.

SERGEANT   Well—er—no, sir. Of course I might have a few strange ideas, I admit, about the railways and the agriculture and things like that; but to throw a bomb at the general . . .

CHIEF   (*triumphantly*) You see, gentlemen.

AIDE   (*to the* SERGEANT, *pressingly*) Imagine that you are taking a stroll on Sunday afternoon and it so happens that you have a bomb with you. You've taken it from your house, though you don't quite know why. All around you there are people, beautiful women—and suddenly you see a general . . .

SERGEANT   A real one?

CHIEF (*sharply*) Behave yourself, Sergeant.

AIDE Right! The general is walking straight towards you. He doesn't turn aside, just keeps on walking straight ahead. His medals are sparkling, his jackboots are shining. You feel that now you can pay him back for everything; that such a beautiful general won't come your way a second time.

SERGEANT The bastard!

CHIEF For the last time . . .

AIDE Well? Well? (*Silence.*)

SERGEANT (*struggling with himself. At last, with a heavy sigh of resignation*) No, I can't. (*Everyone relaxes.*)

CHIEF I hope you're satisfied, General.

GENERAL To be quite frank I am beginning to wonder why you are obstructing the investigation.

CHIEF Me? Obstructing the investigation? Me?

GENERAL That's how it looks to me. How important is it to you that nothing be proved against this man?

CHIEF I protest . . .

GENERAL It seems clear to me that you are trying to hinder my assistant in his final unmasking of the criminal, in his laying bare of the full baseness of the man. I warn you that I may feel it my duty to discuss your position with the Regent, the Uncle of our Infant King. (*They stand, then sit.*)

CHIEF And for my part I should like to inform His Excellency that I possess adequate means to demonstrate to His Excellency the unprofitability of this sort of interference.

GENERAL Are you threatening me?

CHIEF I would not presume to do so, sir. I merely state that I am washing my hands of the whole affair and that I will accept no responsibility for the further development of the matter in hand.

GENERAL Very well. We shall return to our interrogation.

AIDE May I ask that the prisoner be removed for a moment?

GENERAL Certainly. Colonel, will you . . . ?

CHIEF (*rings a bell. Enter the* POLICEMAN.) Take him out into the corridor. Bring him back when I ring. (*The* POLICEMAN *takes the* SERGEANT *out.*)

AIDE I still maintain that basically the accused is guilty of a bomb attack on the general. The problem is simply that he is a man of low intelligence and has too little imagination. But I have a plan.

GENERAL We are listening.

AIDE In the colonel's desk there is a bomb—the same one that at a certain time in the past I threw at the general. The bomb does not work, the best proof of which is the fact that the general is still here among us. I propose that we call the suspect in and give him this bomb. We will open the door, the general will go out into the corridor, and then I guarantee that when he has the bomb in his hands and sees the general standing opposite him, all his libertarian and anarchist instincts will be aroused. Unable to resist them any longer, he throws the bomb. In this way we will acquire a dazzlingly clear proof of his extreme evil intentions and crimes in conditions as closely as possible approaching the natural.

GENERAL But this is madness. What do you think about it, Colonel?

CHIEF I think, sir, that your assistant, your chosen expert on these questions and an officer of great promise in spite of his short record of service, is quite right. You should not lightly reject the idea of this experiment, General, and obstruct the investigations.

AIDE I repeat, the bomb is harmless. The detonator didn't make contact. At least, last time it didn't.

GENERAL So, Lieutenant, you think that . . .

AIDE I am carrying out my duty and suggesting what I consider to be the most effective means of unearthing anti-government activities. I am an officer in the service of (*They all stand, they all sit.*) our Infant King and his Uncle the Regent.

GENERAL I think you may be a little bit too smart, young man.

CHIEF As a friend of yours, General, I would not advise any slackness in your conduct of this investigation. I may tell you in confidence that in the reports which I send *direct* to (*They stand, then sit.*) the Regent, the Uncle of our Infant King, I shall be forced to describe in detail your relationship with and attitude towards the police service, and in particular your enthusiasm for unmasking the enemies of our (*They all stand, they all sit.*) Infant King and his Uncle the Regent.

GENERAL (*dejectedly*) Show me the bomb. I must think.

(*The* CHIEF OF POLICE *goes to the desk and brings the bomb over to the* GENERAL. *He hands it to the* AIDE-DE-CAMP *who returns it to the* CHIEF OF POLICE.)

AIDE Yes, it's the same bomb.

GENERAL Definitely?

AIDE Quite definitely.

CHIEF Well then, General, do you agree?

GENERAL Are you suggesting, Colonel, that I'm being uncooperative? Please explain the situation to the prisoner.

(*The* CHIEF OF POLICE *rings the bell. The* POLICEMAN *brings in the* SERGEANT.)

CHIEF You can go, Constable. (*Exit* POLICEMAN.) You are going to throw this bomb at the general.

SERGEANT What, just like that?

CHIEF The general will stand in the corridor and you will be in here.

GENERAL Can't we put it off until tomorrow?

CHIEF Just as you like, General. Shall we consult the opinion of the government on this matter?

GENERAL Oh, no, no. I'm going.

(*Closes the door behind him. The* CHIEF OF POLICE *positions the* SERGEANT, *gives him a demonstration of how to throw and hands him the bomb. The idiocy of the situation grows clearer.*)

AIDE Just a moment, General.

GENERAL (*opens the door slightly*) What?

AIDE Leave the door open, please. Otherwise he can't throw the bomb at you.

GENERAL Oh, of course. (*Leaves the door open.*)

AIDE Give him my mask. It should be there in the drawer with the bomb. The illusion must be complete. (*Gives the mask to the* SERGEANT.)

CHIEF (*stepping back*) Ready. Right, Lieutenant, over to you.

AIDE O.K. Now, you are strolling along . . . There are beautiful women . . . Over here where the colonel is standing the sun is blazing in the sky, and there (*points to the corridor*), there is the general. His medals are sparkling, his jackboots are shining, and now you think to yourself, at last you'll pay him back for everything. You can see the general . . .

(*The* SERGEANT *throws the bomb. The lights are extinguished for a second. A flash and an explosion. For a second it stays dark and then normal light. The* CHIEF OF POLICE *and the* AIDE-DE-CAMP *stand opposite one another in silence.*)

CHIEF I suppose you liked the general. As your superior officer he always treated you with great courtesy.

AIDE Quite the opposite from the way in which he treated you. He seemed to ignore the fact that you have been the chief of police for years and years.

CHIEF What would you say if I were to place you under arrest. You must admit that that little matter of the bomb is, to say the least, doubtful.

AIDE Yes, I have to admit that. Doubtful to the extent that your part in it is extremely obscure. In that case we would find ourselves in the curious situation of mutual arrest.

CHIEF Young man, you will go far, but not so far as you think, and not towards my position, that of chief of police, but in precisely the opposite direction. I arrest you. (*Draws his sword and arrests the* AIDE-DE-CAMP.)

AIDE Fine. I'm afraid, though, that by acting in this way you have brought your career to a very sharp close. I must point out, sir, that your laughable attempts to charge me with the bomb attack can only turn themselves automatically to your disfavour.

CHIEF And why should that be, my friend?

AIDE Very simply, old boy. You are accusing me of opposing the government and of attempted murder. They will ask you where you were when that certain lieutenant signed the act of allegiance and was released from prison. What sort of a chief of police would you be if the meanest convicted prisoner was able to pull the wool over your eyes? What sort of a security officer were you if you failed to spot his little game and simply released him from custody. And if you argue that you were right to release me, because my repentance was genuine, you would be quite correct since I really was and am sincere in my loyalty and entirely devoted to the government. However, in this way you would bring to nothing your accusation against me of attempted murder, and would place yourself in the ludicrous situation of a squalid intriguer. But to return to the point. What would you say if I were to arrest you?

CHIEF Please do not think that the police are above arrest. On the contrary, arrest is above us. It is above everything. I am a policeman with a long record of service. So, if you think that you can establish a case . . .

AIDE Of course I can. This is how I see the situation: one of the most elementary duties of the head of the police is to protect generals against attacks by bombs. And what did you do? You personally pressed the bomb into the hands of the arrested revolutionary; you personally showed him how to throw it. It's frightful.

CHIEF Have you gone mad? The whole thing was your suggestion.

AIDE . . . Which you adopted with suspicious eagerness.

CHIEF But only under pressure from you. It was you who wanted to do it. It was you who were so keen on that experiment with the bomb.

AIDE But I am not the head of the police. I repeat: what is the most elementary duty of the chief of police? Any fool will tell you: to protect generals against bomb attacks.

CHIEF But the bomb ought never to have gone off. You told me yourself it was useless.

AIDE I've got nothing to do with it. You had no right to believe me.

CHIEF And you assured me a moment ago that you were speaking the truth, and that you are loyal to the government.

AIDE That is correct. I am loyal to the government. But you as the chief of police ought to know that the fact that something is correct does not necessarily have any special meaning. It can eventually have, or perhaps does have, an opposite meaning, depending on certain circumstances. You see, in spite of your record of long service you can still only understand the most primitive arguments.

CHIEF (*resigned*) All right. We will remain under mutual arrest until the situation is cleared up.

(*The* AIDE-DE-CAMP *draws his sword and arrests the* CHIEF OF POLICE. *Enter the* GENERAL.)

CHIEF General! You're alive!

GENERAL I'm not such a fool. I went and hid in the lavatory.

AIDE I must point out that the Chief of Police's outburst a moment ago must be considered as extremely incriminating. The astonishment expressed in the sentence "General! You're alive!" shows that the Chief of Police was expecting, if not actually counting on something else.

GENERAL I'm afraid that I am forced to arrest both of you. There are two possibilities: either it was an accident or else one of you three wound up the detonator. Unfortunately, even we are not yet able to arrest accidents, so we are left with the second possibility. The prisoner doesn't count because he is already under arrest, and so I am left with you two gentlemen.

CHIEF Precisely. The lieutenant's past record will doubtless give the tribunal plenty to think about.

AIDE The members of the court of inquiry will doubtless see the chief of police's motives as a classic example of their type. Leaving aside for the moment the real, more serious charges that he must face, I imagine that he intends to compromise the general's assistant. It is an understandable desire, but it arises from feelings that are purely personal and have nothing in common with the service of our government.

CHIEF I regret to inform you, General, that in the name of this government of yours I must place you under arrest.

GENERAL Me? What for?

CHIEF For irresponsibly exposing the uniform of a general to attacks by bombs. You are under suspicion of condoning subversive conduct. It was you who aroused my sense of duty in this matter, and that will be regarded as a mitigating circumstance at your trial.

AIDE   We still haven't sorted out the question of whether a policeman who has arrested an individual with whom he finds himself in a state of mutual arrest, like the chief of police is with me, is able to arrest a third individual, by whom he has at some time previously been arrested together with the first individual to whom he is united by the first double action of arrest.

CHIEF   Persons under arrest are not permitted to express an opinion.

AIDE   The same to you, Colonel.

GENERAL   It looks, gentlemen, as if the police now have plenty of work on their hands.

(*The* SERGEANT *has up to now been standing modestly apart from the others. He now utters a high-pitched cry and raises one arm in the air. The rebel in him has come completely to the fore.*)

SERGEANT   LONG LIVE FREEDOM!

*NOTES AND PROBLEMS ON DRAMA

The Playwright

Sophocles wrote more than one hundred plays for the Theater of Dionysos at Athens, but only eight have survived. Antigone, produced in 442 or 441 BC, is one of three plays concerning King Oedipus and his family, of which the others are Oedipus Rex and Oedipus at Colonus.

Antigone

Problems

(1) The introductory remarks preceding Antigone suggested that in all but the circumstances and customs of performance it is a modern play. Test this statement. Antigone does not hesitate to oppose the wicked decree of Creon even though she must forfeit her life. Some modern citizens agonize over such a decision, the alleged wickedness of a law often being a matter of debate. Others have no hesitation. Through most of the play Creon is convinced that his decree is right and reasonable. Do you see modern parallels to Creon and Antigone?

(2) At least two of the choruses deserve study as having special relevance for modern readers. Ode I describes the wonderful achievements of man. Ode II treats the topic that pervades the ancient plays: how the gods punish the man guilty of hubris, pride or excessive pride. Can you cite modern instances which support or contradict each Ode?

(3) Excluding Chorus and Choragos, how many speaking characters are on stage most of the time? What does the answer tell you about the size of the acting company that performed the plays in Athens? Remember that the actors wore masks that were effective disguises.

(4) Sophocles is concerned about the flaw (hamartia) of hubris and about the "reversal of intention" or peripateia. (In the play Oedipus Rex, for example, the protagonist is Oedipus himself, Antigone's father. His hubris is the center of the play.) Whose is the flaw in Antigone? Whose actions bring about deaths that he never intended? In short, who is the protagonist here?

(5) Antigone is one of a trilogy of plays by Sophocles about Thebes, the others being Oedipus Rex and Oedipus at Colo-

nus. *Reading the other two will add to your understanding of Antigone.*

Othello

The Playwright *William Shakespeare was born and reared in Stratford-upon-Avon, in the English countryside, but moved to London at an unknown date. There he became an actor and co-owner of a theater, for which he also wrote plays. In addition to Othello, the great Shakespearean tragedies include Hamlet, Macbeth, and King Lear. Shakespeare's poetry includes a sequence of sonnets. At the end of his career, he retired to Stratford as a well-to-do gentleman.*

The text and line numbering of this reprinting are from the Globe text. The vocabulary glosses are by the editors of this volume.

Problems *(1) The introductory remarks preceding Othello suggested reasons for Iago's villainy that are borne out by the play itself. As further study of Iago's character, consider his speech, 1, 3, 319–332, in which he states a philosophical attitude toward life. What is that attitude? (Where necessary, translate his words into modern English.) Iago apparently believes that the human will is free and that we can make ourselves into any sorts of persons we wish. Does this belief necessarily lead to evil, as in Iago? Consider the teachings on this point of any religion with which you may be familiar.*

(2) Elsewhere in Shakespeare's work, a tragic ending is at least partly caused by an accident—the delay of a messenger, for example, in Romeo and Juliet. To what extent does the tragedy in Othello derive from merely trivial circumstances and to what extent from the basic qualities of Othello's character? To answer, you need to investigate the importance of the handkerchief.

(3) The character Emilia is interesting. She is a realist; is she also a cynic? Consider in this connection her behavior and her fate in the final scene. Study carefully her speeches, III, 4, 99–102, and IV, 3.

(4) Introductory remarks preceding this play mentioned passages of superlative poetry for which the play is famous. Another example is IV, 2, 47–64, especially the basic metaphor and sound of:

> A fixed figure for the time of scorn
> To point his slow unmoving finger at!

Choose a passage in the play that attracted you and analyze its metaphor, sound, and other technical poetic devices.

(5) Though it is subordinate in importance, there is comedy in at least three scenes in Othello, perhaps in more. Which scenes? What sort of comedy is in each? Does any of it affect the action of the play?

(6) This is a play to be acted in a theater. A study of Othello would be incomplete without an attempt to visualize the play on the stage and to hear it spoken by actors. Assuming that you are the director, work out your method of directing the final scene, V, 2, as it would be performed in a modern theater. For example, where would you place your actors as they group and regroup themselves on the stage? Prepare to help your actors read certain of the difficult speeches—for instance, Othello's in lines 91–101. Careful study of this scene will reveal numerous other decisions that would be

forced on its director. Where, for example, does Othello find his second sword? With what implement does he stab himself?

A Doll's House

The Playwright *Henrik Ibsen was a Norwegian poet and playwright, author of a score of plays, of which* An Enemy of the People, The Wild Duck, Hedda Gabler, Ghosts, *and* A Doll's House *are most often performed on the modern stage. Sometimes called the father of modern drama, Ibsen is famous as one of the first playwrights to use political, social, and psychological problems as realistic material for plays.*

Problem *In our century, many wives use the family checkbook and know what the penalties for forgery are. Nevertheless many modern American women feel the same frustration as Nora Helmer. To them the world seems made for men, with women only delightful but inferior creatures who are excluded from important affairs. Even such a new and competent translation as that of Michael Meyer cannot disguise the fact that the specific terms and circumstances of Nora's problem are inevitably out of date. And yet* A Doll's House *remains the classic statement of the problem. It enjoys periodic revival on both the professional and the amateur stage, signifying that modern men and women on both sides of the Atlantic respond to it with sympathy and understanding. It should be easy, then, to bring the play forward a century and hypothesize Nora's present-day situation. What might make her slam the door on Torvald today?*

Arms and the Man

The Playwright *George Bernard Shaw was a well-known Irish-born dramatist, critic, and social reformer. Perhaps best known for his advocacy of Fabian Socialism (expounded in his play,* Major Barbara*), he believed in a form of "creative evolution" that he called the Life Force (developed in another of his plays,* Man and Superman*). Shaw wrote many plays and many thousands of words of social comment throughout a long and active life.*

Problems *(1) Most older plays, such as* Oedipus Rex *and* Othello, *have come down to us without the stage directions of their authors. Shaw believed that he should fully inform the reader as to the appearance of the stage and the characters and as to the successive emotions the actors are to portray. Examine the first pages of the play up to the entrance of Louka. Just what sorts of details are included in the directions? What would we know if these were not given? Do these directions run contrary to the modern custom of keeping a work af literature impersonal?*

(2) To what extent do you suppose Shaw relied on elements not visible in print: for example, the physical attractiveness of the actresses who play Raina and Louka?

(3) What details about the way of life of upperclass Bulgarians of the 1880's does Shaw use and exaggerate for comic effect?

(4) Good comedy moves rapidly. Seeing it on the stage is like watching the score while a Mozart opera is being performed: the voices traverse the page in an unbelievably short time. Although it is probably impossible for anyone but a practicing playwright to grasp fully the smoothness and rapidity of Shaw's dialogue, you will find it rewarding to try to read

some of it aloud, or at least hear it in your mind's ear, noting that it is dialogue cut and patterned for the stage. It illustrates the statement which one frequently hears that a great artist makes his art seem easy to the amateur—until the amateur tries it.

The Cherry Orchard

The Playwright Anton Chekov was noted during his relatively short career for the realism and humor of his short stories and plays. Starting out as a journalist, he achieved prominence also as a physician. Chekhov's best-known plays are Uncle Vanya and The Three Sisters, as well as The Cherry Orchard, which was produced for the first time shortly before the author's death from tuberculosis.

Problems (1) By what details does Chekhov indicate that the cherry orchard is a symbol of the passing of the old Russia?

(2) Although this play is not primarily a document in sociology and economics, Chekhov, as so often happens in literature, may have made a more vivid sociological study than the sociologists could give us. What details about Lopakhin's life could be used in a study of the rise of the Russian middle class in about 1900?

(3) Why do Lopakhin and Varya not marry? What is the real attitude of each toward the other?

(4) Semyonoff-Pishchik's essential qualities are shown in his name, which is deliberately comic. What details show him to be a kind of comic parody of, or parallel to, Liuboff and Gaieff?

(5) Each of the other minor characters is a fully described individual. What are the particular characteristics of Charlotta? Of Dunyasha? Of Yasha? Of Yepikodoff?

(6) Study the sound effects mentioned in the introductory remarks preceding this play. What do you think each symbolizes?

(7) We are not to believe that Firce is left in the house to die; he is merely left. How is the final incident symbolic of all that has gone on in the previous parts of the play?

J. B.

The Playwright Archibald MacLeish is a distinguished American playwright, poet, teacher, and man of affairs. In addition to winning many honors in literature, he has been a successful attorney, Librarian of Congress, Assistant Secretary of State, and a professor at Harvard. Important titles include his Conquistador, a narrative poem, and a radio play entitled The Fall of the City.

Problems (1) Effective study of this play should include a reading of The Book of Job or at least of its essential parts. Chapters 1 through 3 establish the situation: Job's afflictions and his complaints. Chapter 4 begins the debate between Job and his comforters. God's answer to Job out of the whirlwind takes up Chapters 38 through 41, and what happened to Job thereafter is told in Chapter 42.

Comparison of the two works can be on two levels. The first and easier is an analysis of the stories so as to identify the changes MacLeish has made. For instance, note the role of J.B.'s wife. The more complex question is how the two works treat the problem of evil. God says, "Hearken unto this, O Job: stand still, and consider the wondrous works of God." (37:14.) Nickles says, "God comes whirling in the wind replying—/What? That God knows more than he does./ That God is mores powerful than he!" Do you agree with Nickles' mockery here? Do you find comfort in either J.B. or The Book of Job?

(2) The introductory remarks preceding this play suggested that J.B. presents what is essentially the non-religious human-ist's attitude toward the problem of evil. God may be the boiling point of water, or the value of pi, but the only love found in the universe is human love. The classic statement of this point of view is Bertrand Russell's essay, "A Free Man's Worship" (published in Mysticism and Logic and in various collections). Reading that essay will illuminate what is apparently the point of view of MacLeish. Study also his short poem, "The End of the World."

(3) The introductory remarks preceding the play stated the attitude of each of the three comforters of Job. What evidence in the play tells us what they believe?

(4) Consider the circus tent and the side-show trappings in J.B., Mr. Zuss and Nickles as circus vendors, and the platform as representing heaven (It may be that MacLeish took the idea of the circus tent and sideshow trappings from the circus used in his poem "The End of the World," cited in Problem 2 above.) Note that Mr. Zuss and Nickles are in the play and yet not in it. Do you see any resemblance to the function of Choragos and the Chorus in Antigone? If so, what?

(5) What characteristics can you identify in the verse in which this play is written.

A Raisin in the Sun

The Playwright Lorraine Hansberry is known chiefly for the play reprinted in this volume and for a second play, The Sign in Sidney Bru-stein's Window. A Raisin in the Sun was perhaps the first distinguished play about American black people. Miss Hans-berry's career was cut short by cancer.

Problems (1) The title of this play comes from a line by the poet Langston Hughes, who wrote that a deferred dream perhaps dries up "like a raisin in the sun." What are the deferred dreams in the play?

(2) A Raisin in the Sun is unlike much modern drama written by black authors in that it is non-violent and its language does not contain obscenities. As a play about a specific sociological situation, does it satisfy those who desire immediate remedies? Is it an accurate description of the way of life of certain urban types of people? Or is the situation in some of our cities so much worse that some readers would be justified in rejecting the play as in-sufficiently sharp propaganda? These are questions about the play as sociology, not as literature, but they are inevitable when an author tries to base his work directly on a socio-logical problem.

(3) Similarly, the individual problems of Ruth, Walter, and Beneatha deserve critical judgment. Are the characters real? Are their problems real?

(4) We can compare the play as a drama, a work of literature, with other plays in matters of technique. How is it conven-

tional and traditional in method? Use J.B. as your base point for comparison.

(5) How is the character Joseph Asagai a contrast with the Youngers?

The Police
The Playwright
Slawomir Mrozek lives and works in postwar Communist Poland. Trained in architecture and painting, he has also worked as a journalist as well as a playwright. Among his other plays translated into English are The Martyrdom of Peter Ohey *and* Out at Sea.

Problems
(1) The satire begins with the basic idea: if the last subversive criminal has repented and confessed, what further use is there for a police force? List other sources of satire in the play.

(2) The play makes use of what is known in the theater as the "running gag," a recurrent bit of action or joke. It is, of course, the constant coming to attention whenever someone says "our Infant King and his Uncle the Regent." But mere repetition of the action would soon lose its humor. Consider the problem of the director of the play. How could he change the gag to keep it fresh? Perhaps by causing parts of the body to come to attention at various times? A leg now, an arm next? How else?

(3) What are other sources of satirical humor in the play? Consider the mustaches, for instance.

The Playwrights:

Anton Chekhov	*(1860–1904)*
Lorraine Hansberry	*(1930–1965)*
Henrik Ibsen	*(1828–1906)*
Archibald MacLeish	*(b. 1892)*
Slawomir Mrozek	*(b. 1930)*
William Shakespeare	*(1564–1616)*
George Bernard Shaw	*(1856–1950)*
Sophocles	*(500–494—406–405 BC)*

Thematic Potentials
in Fiction, Poetry, and Drama

The following suggestions, of convenient groupings by which to approach selections in this volume from a thematic perspective, are useful, we hope, but not exhaustive. Certainly no analysis in terms of theme can be complete for all writers or readers. Everyone familiar with imaginative art knows that literary themes can be stated in many ways, and that most statements of themes come from readers rather than explicitly from the author. The author is more likely to suggest a theme (or complex of themes) than to state it "in so many words," for his method is usually to deliver meanings by implication rather than by direct statement.

The thematic potentials suggested here, therefore, are both arbitrary and incomplete. They should, however, provide some useful guides toward alternative ways to organize one's reading of works in this volume.

	Fiction	Poetry	Drama
YOUNG PEOPLE	Two Soldiers Tell Me How Long the Train's Been Gone Hodel To Hell with Dying Going Away Debbie Go Home The Eagles of the Valle Grande Everything That Rises Must Converge	Ode: Intimations of Immortality The Chimney Sweeper Fern Hill Boy at the Window The Pennycandy-store Beyond the El A City Child's Day a pretty a day To the Virgins, To Make Much of Time Reasons for Attendance The Ballad of Late Annie	Antigone _____ The House To an Athlete Dying Young The Flight in the Desert Rebellion The Party The Colossus

Fiction	Poetry	Drama
LITERATURE BY AND ABOUT WOMEN Flowering Judas Everything That Rises Must Converge Becky The Boarding House To Hell with Dying Delta Autumn Hodel Going Away Please Don't Kill Anything Debbie Go Home	Lucinda Matlock My Last Duchess Her Praise The Ballad of Late Annie The Old-Marrieds Question To a Lady to Answer Directly with Yea or Nay Upon Julia's Clothes Bonny Barbara Allan Brown is my Love The Nymph's Reply to the Shepherd The Soul selects her own Society La Belle Dame sans Merci The Lovepet What shall I do when the Summer troubles The River-Merchant's Wife: A Letter Bredon Hill Still to be neat Guitar Recitativos, No. III To the Virgins, To Make Much of Time To His Coy Mistress The Bait Song (Donne) The Indifferent The Colossus Frog Autumn Lethe Colonel Fantock Under Cover Euroclydon A loss of something ever felt I	Antigone A Doll's House The Cherry Orchard A Raisin in the Sun ——————— Finding is the first Act No Swan So Fine Sojourn in the Whale To a Steam Roller

	Fiction	**Poetry**	**Drama**
MEN AND WOMEN	The Lift That Went Down into Hell This Morning, This Evening, So Soon The Boarding House A Sick Call Hodel The Magic Barrel	*Poems under "Love" (pages 441-453) are pertinent here, as are:* The Bait The Good-Morrow The Anniversary The Canonization Peter Quince at the Clavier The Happy Three Her Praise No Second Troy Sonnet 23 from *The Growth of Love* Triolet (Bridges) The Funeral Bonny Barbara Allan La Belle Dame sans Merci Since there's no help, come let us kiss and part I said to Love In Tenebris He Abjures Love The Cold Heaven Among School Children The Twa Corbies The Host of the Air A slumber did my spirit seal Bredon Hill The Ghost Spring (Shakespeare) To the Virgins, To Make Much of Time To His Coy Mistress A Renouncing of Love Song (Donne) The Love Song of	Othello A Doll's House Arms and the Man The Cherry Orchard A Raisin in the Sun ————————— J. Alfred Prufrock Reasons for Attendance

THEMATIC POTENTIALS IN FICTION, POETRY, AND DRAMA

	Fiction	Poetry	Drama
FAMILIES	Hodel Going Away Debbie Go Home Everything That Rises Must Converge Tell Me How Long the Train's Been Gone Relatives Out West Two Soldiers This Morning, This Evening, So Soon Delta Autumn Harrison Bergeron The New Villa	The Flight in the Desert The Death of the Hired Man The River-Merchant's Wife: A Letter The Old-Marrieds The Ghost The Happy Three The Colossus The Party Rebellion Sonnet to My Mother Lucinda Matlock	The Cherry Orchard A Raisin in the Sun A Doll's House J.B.
MAN AND HIS ENVIRONMENT	Relatives Out West The Eagles of the Valle Grande Please Don't Kill Anything Going Away The Blue Hotel Heart of Darkness Two Soldiers	*Poems under "Man and Nature" (pages 473-488) are pertinent here, as are:* The world is too much with us London *from* Milton Composed Upon Westminster Bridge, September 3, 1802 To a Locomotive in Winter Limited To a Steam Roller Unidentified Flying Object The Unknown Citizen Bagpipe Music Sunday Morning (MacNeice) The Lotos-Eaters As a Plane Tree by the Water On the Move Rhapsody on a Windy Night A Supermarket in California	The Cherry Orchard _____ A Race of Sound Persecuted, Betrayal, Volkswagen Blues The Runaway Dust of Snow After Apple-Picking Nothing Gold Can Stay The Inquisitors

Fiction	Poetry	Drama
	Ode to the West Wind	
	Spring and Fall: To a Young Child	_____
	The Darkling Thrush	Birds at Winter Nightfall
	The Windhover	Dejection: An Ode
	Desert Places	A Side-Gallery for Some Insects
	The Snow Man	A Plague of Starlings
	A Rabbit as King of the Ghosts	Pot-Luck Among the Casuals
	Autumn	The force that through the green fuse drives
	Mr. Edwards and the Spider	
	Samantha Is My Negro Cat	Fern Hill
	You Tell Me	What I Will Think Of As the White Dog Truth
	Frog Autumn	
	Ode to a Nightingale	
THE PERSON WITHIN	Heart of Darkness	Poems under "On the Meaning of Life" (pages 496-510) are pertinent here, as are:	Antigone
	Flying Home		Othello
	Delta Autumn		A Doll's House
	The Guest		The Cherry Orchard
	The Eagles of the Valle Grande	Dust of Snow	J.B.
	Flowering Judas	Sunday Morning (Stevens)	A Raisin in the Sun
	The Magic Barrel	Fear no more	
	A Country Doctor	The Clod and the Pebble	
	To Hell with Dying	from Auguries of Innocence	
	Harrison Bergeron	Peter Quince at the Clavier	
		Don't Let That Horse	
		Lapis Lazuli	
		Ode on a Grecian Urn	
		Shakespearean Sonnets 18, 65, 106	
		The Love Song of J. Alfred Prufrock	
		Museums	

	Fiction	**Poetry**	**Drama**
RELIGIOUS CONCERNS	A Sick Call The Lift That Went Down into Hell Relatives Out West Heart of Darkness A Country Doctor Flowering Judas The Magic Barrel The Eagles of the Valle Grande Guests of the Nation	*Poems under "Religion" (pages 511-516) are pertinent here, as are:* The Human Abstract The Tyger Dover Beach By the Earth's Corpse Soliloquy of the Spanish Cloister The Oxen The Magi Heaven-Haven Pied Beauty Sunday Morning (Stevens) The Garden of Love Still, Citizen Sparrow Peter Quince at the Clavier Journey of the Magi Middle Passage When I consider how my light is spent The Windhover The Castaway A Lyke-Wake Dirge On the Late Massacre in Piedmont Spring and Fall: To a Young Child No worst, there is none Thou art indeed just, Lord As a Plane Tree by the Water Mr. Edwards and the Spider Slim in Hell	J.B.

	Fiction	Poetry	Drama
PEOPLE AT WORK	A Sick Call (priest) The Magic Barrel (marriage broker) Jean Beicke (doctor) A Country Doctor (doctor) File and Forget (writer) Heart of Darkness (colonial entrepreneur) This Morning, This Evening, So Soon (actor)	*The following poems treat the artist or poet at work:* Kubla Khan When I have fears that I may cease to be Dejection: An Ode Ode to the West Wind Lapis Lazuli The Idea of Order at Key West Constantly Risking Absurdity Museums My Last Duchess Musée des Beaux Arts Shakespearean Sonnets 18, 65, 106 Ode on a Grecian Urn Among School Children Lapis Lazuli Peter Quince at the Clavier No Swan So Fine Don't Let That Horse On First Looking into Chapman's Homer In Memory of W. B. Yeats A Supermarket in California	A Doll's House (banker) Arms and the Man (soldier) The Police (police chief)
THE INDIVIDUAL AND SOCIETY	Becky Debbie Go Home The New Villa This Morning, This Evening, So Soon Tell Me How Long the Train's Been Gone	*Poems under "Man, Machine, and Society" (pages 461-472) are pertinent here, as are:* nobody loses all the time The Death of the Hired Man	Antigone The Police A Raisin in the Sun

	Fiction	Poetry	Drama
	The Guest	The Three Beggars	
	Relatives Out West	Museums	
	Heart of Darkness	You Tell Me	
	File and Forget	Miniver Cheevy	
	The Magic Barrel	The Love Song of	
	Two Soldiers	J. Alfred Prufrock	
		Middle Passage	
		The Embankment	
		Mr. Flood's Party	
		The Old Men	
		England in 1819	
		Sojourn in the Whale	
		Samantha Is My Negro Cat	
		Constantly Risking Absurdity	
		Frederick Douglass	
		Slim in Hell	
WAR AND VIOLENCE	In Another Country	O What Is That Sound	Arms and the Man
	Guests of the Nation	To Lucasta, On Going to the Wars	Antigone
	The Guest	The Death of a Soldier	Othello
	Two Soldiers	The Inquisitors	The Police
	The Blue Hotel	Channel Firing	
	Flowering Judas	On the Late Massacre in Piedmont	
	Flying Home	Lament of the Frontier Guard	
		Rebellion	
		Fire and Ice	
		Lapis Lazuli	
		Meru	
		A Poison Tree	
		Johnie Armstrong	
DEATH AND LIFE	Jean Beicke	*Poems under "Death" (pages 453-461) are pertinent here, as are:*	Antigone
	To Hell with Dying		J.B.
	Please Don't Kill Anything		
	In Another Country	Channel Firing	
		The Listeners	

Fiction

A Country Doctor
A Sick Call
Becky
The Blue Hotel
Heart of Darkness

Poetry

Middle Passage
A Plague of Starlings
Lament of the Frontier Guard
My Last Duchess
Marie Hamilton
The Twa Corbies
Johnie Armstrong
Richard Cory
On the Suicide of a Friend
That the Night Come
Bonny Barbara Allan
On the Late Massacre in Piedmont
To an Athlete Dying Young
When smoke stood up from Ludlow
Heaven-Haven
Ode to a Nightingale
Waiting Both
To Daffodils
Proud Maisie
Colonel Fantock
The Death of the Hired Man
Sir Patrick Spence
A Lyke-Wake Dirge
Lethe
Without Benefit of Declaration
Question
The force that through the green fuse drives
When I have fears that I may cease to be
Shakespearean Sonnet 71
Ulysses
Socrates Entranced

Drama

Next, Please
The Life of Man
At the round earth's imagined corners
Death, be not proud
The Host of the Air
The Castaway
A Poison Tree
Slim in Hell
Lycidas
Elegy Written in a Country Churchyard
The Chimney Sweeper
In Memory of W. B. Yeats
After the Funeral
Elegy

Fiction	Poetry	Drama
HUMOR File and Forget	Constantly Risking	The Police
SATIRE, AND The Lift That Went	Absurdity	J.B.
IRONY* Down into Hell	Don't Let That	Arms and the Man
Harrison Bergeron	Horse	
A Country Doctor	A Supermarket in	
Flying Home	California	
Heart of Darkness	The Magi	
	Soliloquy of the	
	Spanish Cloister	
	Slim in Hell	
	Middle Passage	
	The Passionate	
	Shepherd to his	
	Love	
	The Nymph's Reply	
	to the Shepherd	
	Still to be neat	
	Guitar Recitativos,	
	No. III	
	Why so pale and	
	wan, fond lover	
	Spring	
	(Shakespeare)	
	Winter	
	To His Coy	
	Mistress	
	The Indifferent	
	The Bait	
	Song (Donne)	
	Unidentified Flying	
	Objects	
	You Tell Me	
	The Canonization	
	I Said to Love	
	The Love Song of	
	J. Alfred	
	Prufrock	
	Peter Quince at	
	the Clavier	
	Reasons for	
	Attendance	
	Ancient Music	
	Bagpipe Music	

*This heading is not "thematic" in the same sense as others. Yet we include it as an aid to readers. So many themes in literature are conveyed or at least colored by humor, satire, or irony as to make recognition of such tones essential to perceptive reading.

To the Virgins, To
  Make Much of
  Time
Miniver Cheevy
nobody loses all
  the time

Without Benefit of
  Declaration
The wayfarer
A Man said to the
  Universe
Geranium
The Party

Index of Literary Terms

General statement, 40
Grammatical expressiveness, 645, 648, 650, 652, 661, 665–6
Greek theater, 676
Greek tragedy, 677

Hamartia (tragic flaw), 1111
Happy endings, 17, 49
Heroic couplet, 640
Hexameter, 638, 640
Hubris, 1111
Humor, uses of, 17, 61, 64, 130, 131, 194

Iambic foot, 638
Ideas and beliefs,
   in fiction, 3–4, 40, 49, 57
   in poetry, 58
Imagery, 388–90, 429, 644–45, 646, 647, 650, 655, 665–67, 668
Immediate and delayed responses, 47–48
Implied meanings, in fiction, 4, 49–51, 78, 80, 194
Irony, 80, 81–82, 131, 375, 387, 391, 649, 662, 670
Italian sonnet, 518

Lyric, 517, 640

Masculine rhyme, 641
Meaning, 386–87, 390–91
Metaphor, 388–91, 640–41, 644, 1112
"Metaphysical" poetry, 656
Meter, 638–42
Modes, in fiction, 78, 84
Music, of verse, 385–86, 645

Narrative, 403
Narrative questions, 375
Narrator, 4, 38, 40, 94, 131
Nonrealism, 73, 78, 84; see also Symbolism

Objective point of view, 54, 130, 377
Ode, 526, 641, 653
One-time/one-place narrative, 39
Onomatopoeia, 641
Ottava rima, 641

Paradox, 860
Pattern, 384–86, 429–30, 646
Pentameter, 638, 641
Peripateia (reversal of intention), 1111
Pleasure in reading, 51, 55, 63
Plot, 5, 62
Poetic language, 387–88
Poetry as a source of ideas and beliefs, 58
Point of view or focus, 38–40, 52–54, 109
Problem of evil, 943, 1115
Problem plays, 676
Properties (stage), 860
Proscenium arch theater, 807
Prose, 383–84, 388
Public and private fact, 16
Pyrrhic foot, 638

Quality, in fiction, 16–17, 18, 51–52, 59, 64, 93, 194, 297
Quatrain, 641

Realism, 906
Recognition scene, 806
Reflective tone, 39–40, 131
Rhyme, 386, 641, 645–46
Rhythm, 384–86, 429–30
Running gag, 860, 1116
Run-on-line, 641

Satire, 72, 85, 1116
Satiric humor, 64, 73, 82, 131
Science fiction, 84
Sentimentality, 55–56, 93
Setting or environment, 18, 57, 60, 62, 94, 109, 378
Shift of focus, 53, 93, 108
Simile, 642
"Slice-of-life" stories, 62
Social conflict in drama, 1023
Sonnet, 517–18, 652–53
Spenserian stanza, 642, 651
Spondee, 638
Stage directions, 1113
Stereotyping, 55–56, 109
Story elements, 4, 47, 50, 60–61, 63
Strategies for reading fiction, 38, 41, 47–65;
   see also Fictional techniques; Implied meanings; Satire; Symbolism
Stream-of-consciousness, 53
Stress (metrical), 538–39
Style and meaning, 4, 40, 59, 73, 83, 108
Subjective events, 4, 16, 57, 62, 378
Summary narrative 38–39, 53, 93, 108, 130, 378
Syllabic verse, 613
Symbolic reality in fiction, 57–58, 73, 78, 79, 82, 94, 192, 377, 378
Symbolism, 78, 79, 84, 386–87, 388–90, 644, 645, 647–48, 649, 657, 660, 663–64, 669, 907
Symbols, 63, 81, 109, 194
   concrete, 79, 80, 93, 378–379
   special uses of, 82–84, 379
   traditional, 79–80, 82, 83, 375, 377
   verbal, 51, 79, 83

Tactics for readers, 38
Terza rima, 642, 654
Tetrameter, 638, 642
Theme, 62, 383, 386–87, 392, 440, 496, 510, 613, 650, 668
Third-person narrative, 52, 93, 130
Tone, 392
Tragedy, 675
Tragic accident, 1112
Tragicomedy, 676
Transferred epithet, 651

Index of Titles and Authors